Twentieth-Century Literary Criticism

Guide to Gale Literary Criticism Series

For criticism on	Consult these Gale series
Authors now living or who died after December 31, 1959	*CONTEMPORARY LITERARY CRITICISM (CLC)*
Authors who died between 1900 and 1959	*TWENTIETH-CENTURY LITERARY CRITICISM (TCLC)*
Authors who died between 1800 and 1899	*NINETEENTH-CENTURY LITERATURE CRITICISM (NCLC)*
Authors who died between 1400 and 1799	*LITERATURE CRITICISM FROM 1400 TO 1800 (LC)* *SHAKESPEAREAN CRITICISM (SC)*
Authors who died before 1400	*CLASSICAL AND MEDIEVAL LITERATURE CRITICISM (CMLC)*
Black writers of the past two hundred years	*BLACK LITERATURE CRITICISM (BLC)*
Authors of books for children and young adults	*CHILDREN'S LITERATURE REVIEW (CLR)*
Dramatists	*DRAMA CRITICISM (DC)*
Hispanic writers of the late nineteenth and twentieth centuries	*HISPANIC LITERATURE CRITICISM (HLC)*
Native North American writers and orators of the eighteenth, nineteenth, and twentieth centuries	*NATIVE NORTH AMERICAN LITERATURE (NNAL)*
Poets	*POETRY CRITICISM (PC)*
Short story writers	*SHORT STORY CRITICISM (SSC)*
Major authors from the Renaissance to the present	*WORLD LITERATURE CRITICISM, 1500 TO THE PRESENT (WLC)*

ISSN 0276-8178

Volume 56

Twentieth-Century Literary Criticism

**Excerpts from Criticism of the
Works of Novelists, Poets, Playwrights,
Short Story Writers, and Other Creative Writers
Who Lived between 1900 and 1960,
from the First Published Critical
Appraisals to Current Evaluations**

Joann Cerrito
Editor

**Pamela Willwerth Aue
Jeffery Chapman
Laurie Di Mauro
Nancy Dziedzic
Jennifer Gariepy
Christopher Giroux
Margaret A. Haerens
Kelly Hill
Thomas Ligotti
Brigham Narins
Sean René Pollock
Lynn M. Spampinato
Janet Witalec**
Associate Editors

Gale Research Inc.

An International Thomson Publishing Company

 I T P

NEW YORK • LONDON • BONN • BOSTON • DETROIT • MADRID
MELBOURNE • MEXICO CITY • PARIS • SINGAPORE • TOKYO
TORONTO • WASHINGTON • ALBANY NY • BELMONT CA • CINCINNATI OH

STAFF

Joann Cerrito, *Editor*

Pamela Willwerth Aue, Jeffery Chapman, Laurie Di Mauro, Nancy Dziedzic, Jennifer Gariepy, Christopher Giroux, Margaret A. Haerens, Kelly Hill, Thomas Ligotti, Brigham Narins, Sean René Pollock, Lynn M. Spampinato, Janet Witalec, *Associate Editors*

Christine M. Bichler, Martha Bommarito, Matthew McDonough, *Assistant Editors*

Marlene H. Lasky, *Permissions Manager*
Margaret A. Chamberlain, Linda M. Pugliese, *Permissions Specialists*
Susan Brohman, Diane Cooper, Maria Franklin, Pamela A. Hayes, Arlene Johnson, Josephine M. Keene, Michele Lonoconus, Maureen Puhl, Shalice Shah, Kimberly F. Smilay, Barbara A. Wallace, *Permissions Associates*
Brandy C. Merritt, Tyra Y. Phillips, *Permissions Assistants*

Victoria B. Cariappa, *Research Manager*
Eva M. Felts, Mary Beth McElmeel, Donna Melnychenko, Tamara C. Nott, Tracie A. Richardson, *Research Associates*
Maria E. Bryson, Michele McRobert, Michele P. Pica, Amy Beth Wieczorek, *Research Assistants*

Mary Beth Trimper, *Production Director*
Catherine Kemp, *Production Assistant*

Cynthia Baldwin, *Product Design Manager*
Barbara J. Yarrow, *Graphic Services Supervisor*
Sherrell Hobbs, *Macintosh Artist*
Willie F. Mathis, *Camera Operator*

Library of Congress Catalog Card Number 76-46132
ISBN 0-8103-2438-5
ISSN 0276-8178

Printed in the United States of America
Published simultaneously in the United Kingdom
by Gale Research International Limited
(An affiliated company of Gale Research Inc.)
10 9 8 7 6 5 4 3 2 1

I(T)P™ Gale Research Inc., an International Thomson Publishing Company.
ITP logo is a trademark under license.

Contents

Preface vii

Acknowledgments xi

Preface

Since its inception more than fifteen years ago, *Twentieth-Century Literary Criticism* has been purchased and used by nearly 10,000 school, public, and college or university libraries. *TCLC* has covered more than 500 authors, representing 58 nationalities, and over 25,000 titles. No other reference source has surveyed the critical response to twentieth-century authors and literature as thoroughly as *TCLC*. In the words of one reviewer, "there is nothing comparable available." *TCLC* "is a gold mine of information—dates, pseudonyms, biographical information, and criticism from books and periodicals—which many libraries would have difficulty assembling on their own."

Scope of the Series

TCLC is designed to serve as an introduction to authors who died between 1900 and 1960 and to the most significant interpretations of these author's works. The great poets, novelists, short story writers, playwrights, and philosophers of this period are frequently studied in high school and college literature courses. In organizing and excerpting the vast amount of critical material written on these authors, *TCLC* helps students develop valuable insight into literary history, promotes a better understanding of the texts, and sparks ideas for papers and assignments. Each entry in *TCLC* presents a comprehensive survey of an author's career or an individual work of literature and provides the user with a multiplicity of interpretations and assessments. Such variety allows students to pursue their own interests; furthermore, it fosters an awareness that literature is dynamic and responsive to many different opinions.

Every fourth volume of *TCLC* is devoted to literary topics that cannot be covered under the author approach used in the rest of the series. Such topics include literary movements, prominent themes in twentieth-century literature, literary reaction to political and historical events, significant eras in literary history, prominent literary anniversaries, and the literatures of cultures that are often overlooked by English-speaking readers.

TCLC is designed as a companion series to Gale's *Contemporary Literary Criticism,* which reprints commentary on authors now living or who have died since 1960. Because of the different periods under consideration, there is no duplication of material between *CLC* and *TCLC*. For additional information about *CLC* and Gale's other criticism titles, users should consult the Guide to Gale Literary Criticism Series preceding the title page in this volume.

Coverage

Each volume of *TCLC* is carefully compiled to present:

- criticism of authors, or literary topics, representing a variety of genres and nationalities

- both major and lesser-known writers and literary works of the period

- 8-15 authors or 4-6 topics per volume

- individual entries that survey critical response to each author's work or each topic in literary history, including early criticism to reflect initial reactions; later criticism to represent any rise or decline in reputation; and current retrospective analyses.

Organization of This Book

An author entry consists of the following elements: author heading, biographical and critical introduction, list of principal works, excerpts of criticism (each preceded by an annotation and followed by a bibliographic citation), and a bibliography of further reading.

- The **Author Heading** consists of the name under which the author most commonly wrote, followed by birth and death dates. If an author wrote consistently under a pseudonym, the pseudonym will be listed in the author heading and the real name given in parentheses on the first line of the biographical and critical introduction. Also located at the beginning of the introduction to the author entry are any name variations under which an author wrote, including transliterated forms for authors whose languages use nonroman alphabets.

- The **Biographical and Critical Introduction** outlines the author's life and career, as well as the critical issues surrounding his or her work. References to past volumes of *TCLC* are provided at the beginning of the introduction. Additional sources of information in other biographical and critical reference series published by Gale, including *Short Story Criticism, Children's Literature Review, Contemporary Authors, Dictionary of Literary Biography,* and *Something about the Author,* are listed in a box at the end of the entry.

- Most *TCLC* entries include **Portraits** of the author. Many entries also contain reproductions of materials pertinent to an author's career, including manuscript pages, title pages, dust jackets, letters, and drawings, as well as photographs of important people, places, and events in an author's life.

- The **List of Principal Works** is chronological by date of first book publication and identifies the genre of each work. In the case of foreign authors with both foreign-language publications and English translations, the title and date of the first English-language edition are given in brackets. Unless otherwise indicated, dramas are dated by first performance, not first publication.

- Critical excerpts are prefaced by **Annotations** providing the reader with information about both the critic and the criticism that follows. Included are the critic's reputation, individual approach to literary criticism, and particular expertise in an author's works. Also noted are the relative importance of a work of criticism, the scope of the excerpt, and the growth of critical controversy or changes in critical trends regarding an author. In some cases, these annotations cross-reference excerpts by critics who discuss each other's commentary.

- **Criticism** is arranged chronologically in each author entry to provide a perspective on changes in critical evaluation over the years. All titles of works by the author featured in the entry are printed in boldface type to enable the user to easily locate discussion of particular works. Also for purposes of easier identification, the critic's name and the publication date of the essay are given at the beginning of each piece of criticism. Unsigned criticism is preceded by the title of the journal in which it appeared. Some of the excerpts in *TCLC* also contain translated material. Unless otherwise noted, translations in brackets are by the editors; translations in parentheses or continuous with the text are by the critic. Publication information (such as footnotes or page and line references to specific editions of works) have been deleted at the editor's discretion to provide smoother reading of the text.

- A complete **Bibliographic Citation** designed to facilitate location of the original essay or book follows each piece of criticism.

- An annotated list of **Further Reading** appearing at the end of each author entry suggests secondary sources on the author. In some cases it includes essays for which the editors could not obtain reprint rights.

Cumulative Indexes

- Each volume of *TCLC* contains a cumulative **Author Index** listing all authors who have appeared in Gale's Literary Criticism Series, along with cross references to such biographical series as *Contemporary Authors* and *Dictionary of Literary Biography*. For readers' convenience, a complete list of Gale titles included appears on the first page of the author index. Useful for locating authors within the various series, this index is particularly valuable for those authors who are identified by a certain period but who, because of their death dates, are placed in another, or for those authors whose careers span two periods. For example, F. Scott Fitzgerald is found in *TCLC*, yet a writer often associated with him, Ernest Hemingway, is found in *CLC*.

- Each *TCLC* volume includes a cumulative **Nationality Index** which lists all authors who have appeared in *TCLC* volumes, arranged alphabetically under their respective nationalities, as well as Topics volume entries devoted to particular national literatures.

- Each new volume in Gale's Literary Criticism Series includes a cumulative **Topic Index,** which lists all literary topics treated in *NCLC, TCLC, LC 1400-1800,* and the *CLC* yearbook.

- Each new volume of *TCLC,* with the exception of the Topics volumes, includes a **Title Index** listing the titles of all literary works discussed in the volume. In response to numerous suggestions from librarians, Gale has also produced a **Special Paperbound Edition** of the *TCLC* title index. This annual cumulation lists all titles discussed in the series since its inception and is issued with the first volume of *TCLC* published each year. Additional copies of the index are available on request. Librarians and patrons will welcome this separate index; it saves shelf space, is easy to use, and is recyclable upon receipt of the following year's cumulation. Titles discussed in the Topics volume entries are not included *TCLC* cumulative index.

Citing *Twentieth-Century Literary Criticism*

When writing papers, students who quote directly from any volume in Gale's literary Criticism Series may use the following general forms to footnote reprinted criticism. The first example pertains to materials drawn from periodicals, the second to material reprinted from books.

[1]T. S. Eliot, "John Donne," *The Nation and the Athenaeum,* 33 (9 June 1923), 321-32; excerpted and reprinted in *Literature Criticism from 1400 to 1800,* Vol. 10, ed. James E. Person, Jr. (Detroit: Gale Research, 1989), pp. 28-9.

[2]Clara G. Stillman, *Samuel Butler: A Mid-Victorian Modern* (Viking Press, 1932); excerpted and reprinted in *Twentieth-Century Literary Criticism,* Vol. 33, ed. Paula Kepos (Detroit: Gale Research, 1989), pp. 43-5.

Suggestions Are Welcome

In response to suggestions, several features have been added to *TCLC* since the series began, including annotations to excerpted criticism, a cumulative index to authors in all Gale literary criticism series, entries devoted to criticism on a single work by a major author, more extensive illustrations, and a title index listing all literary works discussed in the series since its inception.

Readers who wish to suggest authors or topics to appear in future volumes, or who have other suggestions, are cordially invited to write the editors.

Acknowledgments

The editors wish to thank the copyright holders of the excerpted criticism included in this volume, the permissions managers of many book and magazine publishing companies for assisting us in securing reprint rights. We are also grateful to the staffs of the Detroit Public Library, the Library of Congress, the University of Detroit Mercy Library, Wayne State University Purdy/Kresge Library Complex, and the University of Michigan Libraries for making their resources available to us. Following is a list of the copyright holders who have granted us permission to reprint material in this volume of *TCLC*. Every effort has been made to trace copyright, but if omissions have been made, please let us know.

COPYRIGHTED EXCERPTS IN *TCLC*, VOLUME 56 , WERE REPRINTED FROM THE FOLLOWING PERIODICALS:

The Atlantic Monthly, v. 259, June, 1987 for "A Major Discovery" by Irving Howe. Copyright 1987 by The Atlantic Monthly Company, Boston, MA. Reprinted by permission of the Literary Estate of Irving Howe.—*Bulletin of Hispanic Studies,* v. XLIII, January, 1965; v. LXII, April, 1985. © copyright 1965, 1985 Liverpool University Press. Both reprinted by permission of the publisher.—*Canadian Forum,* v. LVII, June-July, 1977. Reprinted by permission of James Lorimer and Company Limited.—*Commonweal,* v. LXXXV, March 10, 1967. Copyright © 1967 Commonweal Publishing Co., Inc. Reprinted by permission of Commonweal Foundation.—*The Comparatist,* v. VIII, May, 1984. Reprinted by permission of the publisher.—*English Literature in Transition: 1880-1920,* v. 17, 1974. Copyright © 1974 *English Literature in Transition: 1880-1920.* Reprinted by permission of the publisher.—*The Horn Book Magazine,* v. XIX, May-June, 1943. Copyright 1943, renewed 1970, by The Horn Book, Inc., 11 Beacon St., Suite 1000, Boston, MA 02108. All rights reserved. Reprinted by permission of the publisher.—*Jewish Social Studies,* v. XXX, October, 1968. © 1968 by the Editors of *Jewish Social Studies.* Reprinted by permission of the publisher.—*Journal of Canadian Fiction,* v. IV, 1975./ v. IV, 1975 for "Raymond Knister: A Biographical Note" by Marcus Waddington. Reprinted by permission of the author.—*The Midwest Quarterly,* v. XXX, Autumn, 1988. Copyright, 1988, by *The Midwest Quarterly,* Pittsburg State University. Reprinted by permission of the publisher.—*The New Republic,* v. LXV, November 19, 1930. Copyright 1930, renewed 1958 The New Republic, Inc. Reprinted by permission of *The New Republic.*—*The New York Review of Books,* v. XXXIV, September 24, 1987. Copyright © 1987 Nyrev, Inc. Reprinted with permission from *The New York Review of Books.*—*The New York Times,* June 21, 1932. Copyright 1932, renewed 1960 by The New York Times Company. Reprinted by permission of the publisher.—*The New York Times Book Review,* January 3, 1965; July 12, 1987. Copyright © 1965, 1987 by The New York Times Company. Both reprinted by permission of the publisher./ October 3, 1920; August 25, 1925; October 13, 1935. Copyright 1920, renewed 1948; copyright 1925, renewed 1953; copyright 1935, renewed 1963 by The New York Times Company. All reprinted by permission of the publisher.—*The New Yorker,* v. 19, May 29, 1943. Copyright 1943, renewed 1970 by The New Yorker Magazine, Inc. Reprinted by permission of the publisher.—*Proceedings: Pacific Northwest Conference on Foreign Language,* v. XIX, April 19-20, 1968. Reprinted by permission of the publisher.—*Romance Notes,* v. XXV, Winter, 1984. Reprinted by permission of the publisher.—*The Roundup,* v. XII, June, 1964. Renewed 1992. Reprinted by permission of the publisher.—*The Russian Review,* v. 26, July, 1967 for "Lev Shestov: A Russian Existentialist" by Louis J. Shein. Copyright 1967 by The Russian Review, Inc. Reprinted by permission of the Literary Estate of Louis J. Shein./ v. 30, July, 1971. Copyright 1971 by The Russian Review, Inc. Reprinted by permission of the publisher.—*Slavic and East-European Journal,* v. 22, Summer, 1978, n.s. v. 25, Summer, 1981, n.s. v. 30, Summer, 1986. © 1978, 1981, 1986 by AATSEEL of the U.S., Inc. All reprinted by permission of the publisher.—*Slavic Review,* v. 35, December, 1976 for a review "In Job's Business: On the Sources of the Eternal Truths" by James P. Scanlan. Copyright © 1976 by the American Association for the Advancement of Slavic Studies, Inc. Reprinted by permission of the publisher and the author.—*Studies in Canadian Literature,* v. 3, 1978 for "Beyond Realism: Raymond Knister's 'White Narcissus' " by Paul Denham; v. 3, 1978 for "Point of View in 'White Narcissus' " by Glenn Clever. Copyright by the respective authors. Both reprinted by permission of the editors.—*Studies in Twentieth Century Literature,* v. 14, Winter, 1990. Copyright © 1990 by *Studies in Twentieth Century Literature.* Reprinted by permission of the publisher.—*Symposium,* v. XXI, Fall, 1967. Copyright © 1967 Helen Dwight Reid Educational Foundation. Reprinted with permission of the Helen Dwight Reid Educational Foundation, published by Heldref Publications, 1319 18th Street, N.W., Washington, D.C. 20036-1802.—*Texas Studies in Literature and Language,* v. XVII, 1975 for "Shestov's Use of Nietzsche in His Interpretation of Tolstoy and Dostoevsky" by James M. Curtis. Copyright © 1975 by the University of Texas Press. Reprinted by permission of the publisher and the author.—*The Times Literary Supplement,* n. 3526, September 25, 1969. © The Times Supplements Limited 1969. Reproduced from *The Times Literary Supplement* by permission.—*The Victorian Newsletter,* n. 67, Spring, 1985 for " 'Love in a Life': The Case of Nietzsche and Lou Salomé" by William Beatty Warner. Reprinted by permission of *The Victorian Newsletter* and the author.—*The Virginia Quarterly Review,* v. 56, Winter, 1980. Copyright, 1980, by *The Virginia Quarterly Review,* The University of Virginia. Reprinted by permission of the publisher.—*Western American Literature,* v. VII, Fall, 1972. Copyright, 1972, by the Western Literature Association. Reprinted by permission of the publisher.—*Wide Angle,* v. 5, 1982. Reprinted by permission of the publisher.—*World Literature Today,* v. 64, Summer, 1990. Copyright 1990 by the University of Oklahoma Press. Reprinted by permission of the publisher.—*Women's Studies: An Interdisciplinary Journal,* v. 12, 1986. © Gordon and Breach Science Publishers. Reprinted by permission of the publisher.—*The Yale Law Journal,* v. XXXVIII, March, 1929. Reprinted by permission of The Yale Law Journal Company and Fred B. Rothman & Company.

COPYRIGHTED EXCERPTS IN *TCLC,* VOLUME 56, WERE REPRINTED FROM THE FOLLOWING BOOKS:

Banjanin, Milica. From "Looking Out, Looking in: Elena Guro's Windows," in *Festschrift für Nikola R. Pribić.* Edited by Josip Matešić and Erwin Wedel. Hieronymus Verlag Neuried, 1983. © 1983 by Hieronymus Verlag GmbH. All rights reserved. Reprinted by permission of the publisher.—Binion, Rudolph. From *Frau Lou: Nietzsche's Wayward Disciple.* Princeton University Press, 1968. Copyright © 1968 by Princeton University Press. All rights reserved. Reprinted by permission of the publisher.—Bowen, Elizabeth. From a preface to "Orlando". *Seven Winters: Memories of a Dublin Childhood and Afterthoughts.* Alfred A. Knopf, 1962. Copyright © 1960, 1962 by Elizabeth Bowen. Renewed 1990 by Curtis Brown. Reprinted by permission of Curtis Brown Limited, London, as Literary Executors of Elizabeth Bowen.—Budd, Mike. From " 'The Cabinet of Doctor Caligari': Production, Reception, History," in *Close Viewings: An Anthology of New Film Criticism.* Edited by Peter Lehman. The Florida State University Press, 1990. Copyright 1990 by the Board of Regents of the State of Florida. Reprinted by permission of the publisher.—Casper, Joseph Andrew. From "I Never Met a Rose: Stanley Donen and 'The Little Prince'," in *Children's Novels and the Movies.* Edited by Douglas Street. Frederick Ungar Publishing Co., 1983. Copyright © 1983 by Frederick Ungar Publishing Co., Inc. Reprinted by permission of the publisher.—Caughie, Pamela L. From "Virginia Woolf's Double Discourse," in *Discontented Discourses: Feminism/Textual Intervention/Psychoanalysis.* Edited by Marleen S. Barr and Richard Feldstein. University of Illinois Press, 1989. © 1989 by the Board of Trustees of the University of Illinois. Reprinted by permission of the publisher and the author.—Close, Lorna. From "Vallejo, Heidegger and Language," in *Words of Power: Essays in Honour of Alison Fairlie.* Edited by Dorothy Gabe Coleman and Gillian Jondorf. University of Glasgow Publications in Language and Literature, 1987. Copyright © of papers by individual authors. All rights reserved. Reprinted by permission of the publisher and the author.—Daiches, David. From *Virginia Woolf.* New Directions Books, 1942. Renewed 1969 by David Daiches. Copyright 1942 by New Directions Publishing Corporation. Reprinted by permission of David Higham Associates.—Eisner, Lotte H. From *The Haunted Screen: Expressionism in the German Cinema and the Influence of Max Reinhardt.* Translated by Roger Greaves. University of California Press, 1969, Martin Secker & Warburg, 1973. Translation and new material © Thames & Hudson 1969. Reprinted by permission of Reed International Books. In North America by University of California Press.—Erhard, Thomas. From *Lynn Riggs: Southwest Playwright.* Steck-Vaughn, 1970. Copyright © 1970 by Steck-Vaughn Company. All rights reserved. Reprinted by permission of the publisher.—Gallagher, D.P. From *Modern Latin American Literature.* Oxford University Press, London, 1973. Copyright © Oxford University Press 1973. Reprinted by permission of the publisher.—Guiguet, Jean. From *Virginia Woolf and Her Works.* Translated by Jean

PHOTOGRAPHS AND ILLUSTRATIONS APPEARING IN *TCLC*, VOLUME 56, WERE RECEIVED FROM THE FOLLOWING SOURCES:

Andy Adams

1859-1935

American novelist, short story writer, and playwright.

INTRODUCTION

Adams is best known for his novel *The Log of a Cowboy: A Narrative of the Old Trail Days*, which is widely acknowledged as one of the most realistic and well-written accounts of cowboy life.

Biographical Information

Born in Whitley County, Indiana, Adams was raised on a cattle farm. He had little formal education and left home at the age of fifteen. After briefly working in a lumber camp near Newport, Arkansas, Adams worked as a cowboy in San Antonio, Texas, and in 1890 he moved to Rockport, Texas, where he started a feed and seed business. Four years later he followed the mining boom to Cripple Creek, Colorado, and later to Goldfield, Nevada, before settling in Colorado Springs. Adams began writing in 1898 after viewing what he considered to be an inaccurate portrayal of cattlemen in Harry O. Hoyt's play *Texas Steer*. Although his own first play was unsuccessful, he soon sold his first story, "The Passing of Peg-Leg," to *Frank Leslie's Popular Monthly*. Following the publication of his first novel, *The Log of a Cowboy,* in 1903, he published several more novels and short story collections. Adams died in 1935.

Major Works

The Log of a Cowboy is a first-person account of a cattle drive north from Texas to the Blackfoot Reservation in Northern Montana. In this work Adams provided an accurate picture of the hardships and rewards of cowboy life. Adams's later novels similarly deal with aspects of the cattle business. *The Outlet*, for example, depicts the world of railway companies, contractors, and congressional lobbyists and their interests in the cattle business, while *Reed Anthony, Cowman: An Autobiography* is the story of a Confederate Army veteran who becomes a cattle rancher in Texas.

Critical Reception

None of Adams's later novels are considered as successful as *The Log of a Cowboy*. Critics note that Adams's ability to portray realistic scenes and his leisurely narrative style were best utilized in the episodic form of his first novel. Nevertheless, all of Adams works have been widely praised for their accuracy and realism, and Levette J. Davidson has written: "In spite of his many failures, Andy Adams remains the champion in one significant field; he put into seven books of fiction more of the life of the open range, the ranch, and the cattle trail than any other writer has been able to capture."

PRINCIPAL WORKS

The Log of a Cowboy: A Narrative of the Old Trail Days (novel) 1903
A Texas Matchmaker (novel) 1904
The Outlet (novel) 1905
Cattle-Brands: A Collection of Western Camp-Fire Stories (short stories) 1906
Reed Anthony, Cowman: An Autobiography (novel) 1907
Wells Brothers: The Young Cattle Kings (novel) 1911
The Ranch on the Beaver (novel) 1927
Why the Chisholm Trail Forks, and Other Tales of the Cattle Country (short stories) 1956

CRITICISM

The Athenaeum   (essay date 1903)

SOURCE: A review of *The Log of a Cowboy* in *The Athenaeum*, No. 3972, December 12, 1903, p. 790.

[*In the following review, the critic praises* The Log of a Cowboy *for its realism.*]

[*The Log of a Cowboy*] bears about it all the marks of being what is called a document—a record of actual experience, rather than a work of imagination. A good deal of work of this sort has recently been published in the form associated with fiction, and is welcomed, one fancies, as a relief from the broad stream of ineffective, mediocre stuff which appears under that name. *The Log of a Cowboy* tells the story day by day of a trip with cattle, several thousand strong, from Texas, through Arkansas and Wyoming, to the Blackfoot Agency in Montana in the year 1882. The long journey was full of adventure, which is set forth in crisp, straightforward style, and forms very interesting reading. But the book is more than interesting and amusing; it is a compact and truthful picture of an important phase of American life, which can no longer be watched, for the reason that all the essential conditions have changed during the last twenty years. The reviewer has known many cowboys of the period dealt with in this book, and can vouch for the fidelity of their presentation here. The book is not burdened—as is nearly all the fiction of the Far West—with exaggerated accounts of cowboys' dissipation. We get incidental glimpses of this incidental feature of their lives, but are mainly concerned with the strenuous workaday life of the saddle and the camp, of sudden difficulties ably surmounted, of swift dangers bravely and coolly overcome. There are some amusing camp-fire stories. The chapter called 'The Republican' is the best account of a prairie racing swindle that has been published for some time, and there is hardly a chapter in the book which does not contain at least one good story.

The Dial   (essay date 1904)

SOURCE: A review of *A Texas Matchmaker*, in *The Dial*, Vol. XXXVII, No. 434, July 16, 1904, pp. 40-3.

[*In the following review of* A Texas Matchmaker, *the critic praises Adams's realistic treatment of life on a Texas cattle range.*]

[*A Texas Matchmaker*] is a 'human document' rather than a work exhibiting literary art, and possesses a certain historical interest in its portrayals of life on a Texas cattle-range thirty years ago, before the days of fences and railways. The ranch-owner, an early settler and veteran of the struggle for Texan independence, is the central figure of the story and gives the book its name through his persistent endeavors to make matches between every maid and bachelor whom he views with favor. Accounts of these love affairs, none of which run smooth, combined with interpolated tales of frontier life, make up the long volume, certain to bring conviction of the author's knowledge and sincerity.

The Nation   (essay date 1905)

SOURCE: A review of *The Outlet*, in *The Nation*, Vol. LXXX, No. 2082, May 25, 1905, p. 422.

[*Below, the reviewer commends Adams's treatment of Western life in the 1800s in* The Outlet.]

To take a big herd of cattle from the southwestern corner of Texas up through the Indian Territory, and so on to Fort Buford, at the mouth of the Yellowstone, in Dakota, and have them there in prime order after six months' travel, is no ordinary feat. [*The Outlet*] is an account of such a trip made from March to September, 1884, told with animation, and embellished here and there with bits of cowboy literature in the shape of stories that go the rounds of an evening after the cattle are "bedded" and the men group together to while away a social hour.

Dan Lovell, a train drover, holds a subcontract to deliver ten million pounds of beef on the hoof, *i. e.,* ten thousand cattle, to the Government officer at Fort Buford. He collects the herds in Texas, and he has unscrupulous rivals to deal with, so there is some uncertainty whether his cattle will be accepted. We are taken at once into Dan Lovell's confidence, and, before we know it, we are on his side and are ready to stand to it that no finer cattle than his ever came out of Texas. Once fairly started in this narrative, a reader will be loth to lay it down until he has gone straight through to the end. It is an out-of-door book, with no pretence to style or philosophy—a plain story that takes you right into the herd and its daily happenings. If you feel you are on shipboard while reading *Two Years before the Mast,* you are fully as conscious of being in the saddle and breathing fresh, invigorating air when you have taken *The Outlet* in hand. A smattering of Spanish will help the reader; otherwise, it is some time before he understands what a "remuda" is; and he may close the book without any clear apprehension of what it means to "wrangle a remuda." At page 152 a story is entertaining "the boys," and the narrator remarks, "You all know how locoed a bunch of dogies can get." Some of us might not feel at home should we meet the proposition in the course of a civil-service examination. There is more or less of the unconventionality of speech to be found here, but it always seems to be in its proper place. We might speak of it as "the refinement of slang."

When legal proceedings threaten to destroy the chance of "our" cattle being accepted, you are indignant. There was trouble at Ogalalla, and quick work had to be done:

> The lawyer was back within twenty minutes, bringing a draft, covering every item, and urged me to have it accepted by wire. The bank was closed, but I found the cashier in a poker game, and played his hand while he went over to the depot and sent the message.

The cattle arrived in the best condition, but the rival party secured the contract. The reader is taken through the scenes of the exciting events at the fort. The immediate prize is lost; but, by great good fortune, everything comes around right by the next spring, for the cattle, having been well wintered, brought a handsome profit to their owner.

We are glad to know it, as glad as one is to welcome the happy marriage at the close of a novel.

The story of the hospitable woman of the "sod shack" at Bull Foot Stage—told by John Officer "throwing himself down among us, and using Sponsilier for a pillow and myself for footstool"—and how (when she would take no pay) Bibleback Hunt got even with her at Christmas by "beefing" the "Wyoming stray" and hanging up 800 pounds of beef at her place, couldn't have been told better by Bret Harte himself:

> Old Bibleback was what you might call shy of women, and steered clear of the house until she sent her little boy out and asked us to come in. Well, we sat around in the room, owly-like, and to save my soul from the wrath to come I couldn't think of a word that was proper to say to the little woman, busy getting supper. Bibleback was worse off than I was; he couldn't do anything but look at the pictures on the wall.

The book is admirable of its kind. The illustrations are spirited and cleverly conceived.

The Nation   (essay date 1907)

SOURCE: A review of *Reed Anthony, Cowman: An Autobiography*, in *The Nation*, Vol. LXXXV, No. 2192, July 4, 1907, p. 16.

[*In the following excerpt, the reviewer faults* Reed Anthony, Cowman *for its lack of compelling action but praises Adams's ingenuousness.*]

Taking "Reed Anthony" to be Andy Adams himself, we suppose [*Reed Anthony, Cowman: An Autobiography*] to be simply a further chapter in autobiography. His earlier books about the life of the cowboy and the cattleman have been widely read, not, we suppose, because they are particularly good books, but because they have to do with a picturesque and passing type of American experience. The cowboy and the miner, with the old Southern gentlemen, very nearly exhaust our slender romantic treasure, and we naturally make the most of every direct manifestation of them in literature. But Mr. Adams hardly does for the plains what Mr. Bullen and Mr. Conrad have done for the sea. The present reviewer finds his latest book pretty dull; a mass of detail which it is a marvel that any one should have remembered or cared to remember. A great many drives and dickers are described to the last steer and the last dollar for all whom such things may concern. Being Southern-born, the writer has a turn for eloquence as well as for business, and once or twice he gets fairly into the senatorial stride. He looks from a hilltop upon a wide prospect: "It was like a rush of fern-scents, the breath of pine forests, the music of the stars, the first lovelight in a mother's eyes." The pleasant thing about the narrative is its ingenuousness. He has, he remarks, lived in the pit of despair for the want of money, and again, with the use of it, has bent a Legislature to his will and wish. What else, to be sure, is money for? It is a disappointment that there should be so little shooting and gambling, but now and then comes a reassuring anecdote like that in which the cattleman gets even with an enemy who has slandered him.

> I located my traducer in a well-known saloon. I invited him to a seat at a table, determined to bring matters to an issue. He reluctantly complied, when I branded him with every vile epithet that my tongue could command, concluding by arraigning him as a coward. I was hungering for him to show some resistance, expecting to kill him, and when he refused to notice my insults, I called for the barkeeper and asked for two glasses of whiskey and a pair of six-shooters. Not a word passed between us till the bartender brought the drinks and guns on a tray. "Now, take your choice," said, I. He replied, "I believe a little whiskey will do me good."

The Nation (essay date 1911)

SOURCE: A review of *Wells Brothers: The Young Cattle Kings* in *The Nation*, Vol. XCII, No. 2392, May 4, 1911, p. 448.

[*The following anonymous review characterizes* Wells Brothers: The Young Cattle Kings *as stilted and unconvincing in tone compared to Adams's earlier novels.*]

The writer of [*Wells Brothers, the Young Cattle Kings*] began his writing a few years ago with *The Log of a Cowboy*, a book which, since he himself had been a cowboy for a long time, had a certain stamp of freshness and force. His later books, as his consciousness of "literary" activity has steadily increased, have declined in naturalness. The case is something like that of A. H. Bullen, whose *Cruise of the Cachalot* gave him a public which has not been increased by his subsequent books. We suppose even Othello might have turned out a bore in print after he had exhausted the record of his personal adventures. It is to be feared that Mr. Adams has abandoned the range for authorship. From the internal evidence of this book it may be supposed that he deliberately set out to write a "boy's story." His style closely resembles that of Messrs. Castlemon, Alger & Co. His cowmen and boys speak a lingo compounded of plains slang and stilted bookish speech.

> "What is the reason," inquired Joel, "that so many cattle are leaving your State for the upper country?"
>
> "The reasons are numerous and valid," replied the elder cowman. "It's the natural outgrowth or expansion of the pastoral interests of our State."
>
> "There is also an economic reason for the present exodus of cattle," added the young man.. ..

Perhaps we ought to go back to the Rollo books, and the conversation of the inspired Jonas, for our sources here. The Wells Brothers are left alone, at sixteen and fourteen, on a poor farm in good cattle country; and in three years become wealthy cattlemen.

J. Frank Dobie (essay date 1926)

SOURCE: "Andy Adams, Cowboy Chronicler," in *Southwest Review,* Vol. XI, No. 2, January, 1926, pp. 92-101.

[*J. Frank Dobie was an American educator and author who often wrote about the American southwest and southwestern literature. In the following essay, Dobie discusses critical neglect of Adams's works during the 1920s and provides an overview of the author's career.*]

Five or six years ago I hunted all over San Antonio for some books by Andy Adams, and I found just one. That was one more than the Austin bookstores then had. A year ago the proprietor of the largest book-shop in Houston assured me that Andy Adams was out of print. Bookstores of Oklahoma, Kansas, and Boston have proved as indifferent. Happily, however, the apathy of some of the book dealers in Texas, particularly in Austin and Dallas, has been overcome. Now, thanks to Mr. W. P. Webb of the University of Texas, the present writer, and perhaps one or two other individuals who have insisted on the extraordinary merit of Andy Adams as a writer and as a historian of the old-time cow people, thousands of his books are being sold over the Southwest and his delayed fame is gaining over the entire country. Katharine Fullerton Gerould and Carl Van Doren have during the past year alluded to him. But the neglect is significant.

The histories of American literature have been singularly silent on him. A contributor to the *Cambridge History of American Literature* mentions him only to show that he has not read him. Boynton and Haney in their recent surveys of the field are silent; that considerate snapper-up of trifles, Fred Lewis Pattee, is silent. Several late authorities, however, mention in one way or another Harold Bell Wright and Zane Grey. Mr. Pattee quotes approvingly somebody's saying that Owen Wister's *The Virginian* is "our last glimpse of the pioneer plainsman and cowboy types, then passing and now gone." By "then" is, I suppose, meant the time at which *The Virginian* appeared; that was 1902. *The Log of a Cowboy* by Andy Adams, his first and perhaps best work, came out in 1903. Following it appeared *A Texas Matchmaker* (1904), *The Outlet* (1905), *Cattle Brands* (1906), *Reed Anthony, Cowman* (1907), and *Wells Brothers*—a book for "boys"—(1911).

The first four books are the best perhaps, and I should rank them first, second, third, and fourth just as they appeared. Other readers disagree. *The Log of a Cowboy* is the best book that has ever been written of cowboy life, and it is the best book that ever can be written of cowboy life. With its complement, *The Outlet,* it gives a complete picture of trail cattle and trail drivers. Why has it been so overlooked by critics and historians?

In the first place, twenty years ago literary magazines and literary gentlemen were not concerning themselves with the cowboy. Occasionally an article on that subject got into polite print, but honest matter like Charlie Siringo's *A Texas Cowboy* was bound in paper and sold by butcher-boys—a far cry from this day when the Yale University Press publishes James H. Cook's *Fifty Years on the Old Frontier* and then—with a Ph. D. preface—reprints Cap-

A portrait of Adams painted in 1904.

tain James B. Gillett's *Six Years with the Texas Rangers.* It is true that Owen Wister was at once accepted, but he went west as an Easterner and wrote of the cattle people not as one to the manner born but as a literary connoisseur. Even before him Frederic Remington with *Pony Tracks* and *Crooked Trails* had been accepted into a well deserved position that he has never lost, but Remington was an artist to whom literature was secondary and to whom the cowboy was tertiary in comparison with Indians and army men. Remington also came into the West looking for local color.

Andy Adams did not come into the cow country looking for "copy." Like Sam Bass, he "was born in Indiana," and again like Sam Bass, "he first came out to Texas a cowboy for to be." He drove the trail as one of the hands. He followed it very much as Conrad and Masfield followed the sea, not as a writer but as a man of the element. The miracle is that when he did write he found such respectable publishers as the Houghton Mifflin Company. He now lives in Colorado Springs, Colorado, aged sixty-six.

Of course, critics not only arouse interest but they follow it, and Mr. Adams, in a letter, attributes neglect of his books to the fact that he "could never make water run uphill or use a fifth wheel," namely, a girl. But there is another reason more paradoxical. Generally the development of a particular field by one writer creates a demand for the works of other writers in the same milieu. Unfortunately, however, the demand for cowboy material was first aroused by the "Alkali Bill" type of writers; once aroused, that demand has never been satiated, and an avalanche of shoddy has literally buried meritorious writing. Could Andy Adams have led the van, he might have become as well known in his own field as Parkman became known in his. Only just now are responsible readers coming to wonder what the truth about the cowboy is. It is true that twenty years ago *The Log of a Cowboy* was having something of a run and that the newspapers were recording the usual indiscriminating banalities that they record concerning any Western book, but the present attempt at a serious review is just twenty-three years late.

The great virtue of Andy Adams is fidelity, and *The Log of a Cowboy* is a masterpiece for the same reason that *Two Years Before the Mast, Moby Dick,* and *Life on the Mississippi* are master pieces. All three of these chronicle-records are of the water, and it is "symbolic of something," as Hawthorne would say, that the themes of three of the most faithful expository narratives of America should be off-shore.

Now the one part of America that has approached the sea in its length and breadth and dramatic solitude and its elemental power to overwhelm puny man has been the great plains. The one phase of American life that has approached the life of a ship's crew alone on the great deep battling the elements has been that of a cow outfit alone on the great trail that stretched across open ranges from Brownsville at the toe of the nation to north-western Montana and on into Canada. All of Andy Adams' books treat of trail life, except one, *A Texas Matchmaker,* and it treats of ranch life in Southwest Texas during the trail driving days. I have no hesitancy in saying that Mr. Adams has as truthfully and fully expressed the life of a trail outfit as Dana expressed the life of a crew that sailed around the Horn; that he is as warm in his sympathy for cowmen and horses and cattle as Mark Twain is in his feeling for pilots and the Mississippi River; and that he has treated of cattle as intimately and definitely, though not so scientifically or dramatically, as Melville treated of whales. Certainly, I have no idea of ranking Andy Adams as the equal of Mark Twain; I do not believe that he can be ranged alongside Herman Melville; but I should put him on an easy level with Richard Henry Dana, Jr. The immense importance of his subject to the western half of the United States makes him in a way more important historically than either Melville or Dana.

Andy Adams has a racy sympathy for the land and for the cattle and horses and men of the land. He savors them deep, but he savors them quietly. Sometimes there are storms and stampedes, but generally the herds just "mosey along." Cattle bog in the quicksands and there is desperate work to pull them out, but oftener they graze in the sunshine and chew their cuds by still waters while the owner rides among them from sheer love of seeing their contentment and thirstiness. One old Texas steer took so much pleasure in hearing the Confederate boys sing "Rock of Ages" that they could not bear to slaughter him. One trail outfit made a great pet of a calf, and for hundreds of miles it followed the chuck-wagon, much to the exasperation of its mother. On another trip there was a certain muley steer that the horned cattle hooked, and at night the boys used to let him wander out of the herd to lie down in a private

bed. One spring Reed Anthony, the great cowman, could not find it in his heart to order a round-up because "chousing" the cattle would disturb the little calves "playing in groups" and "lying like fawns in the tall grass." **"The Story of a Poker Steer"** in *Cattle Brands* is a classic; its delineation of the life of a "line-backed calf" is as quiet and easy as Kipling's portrayal of the life of a seal in one of his best-known stories. Tom Quirk, boarding a train in Montana, thousands of miles away from his Texas home, was sad indeed to part from his saddle horse forever.

No matter whether the theme is a pet calf or a terrible "die-up" in "the Territory," there is absolutely no strain in Andy Adams. This quality of reserve distinguishes him from all other Western writers that I know of. One can but contrast him with the Zane Grey school so ubiquitously exploited by nearly every American institution ranging from a two-bit drugstore to Harper and Brothers. In Zane Grey's *U. P. Trail,* for instance, which has often been hailed as a piece of real history, the men "were grim; they were indomitable;" and the heroine "clutched Neal with fingers of steel, in a grip that he could not have loosened without breaking her bones."

Not long ago a friend was telling me of an incident so expressive that I must repeat it. This friend was camping in a canyon out in Arizona, where he was excavating some Indian ruins. One night he was awakened by unearthly yeowling and shooting and the clatter of horses' hoofs. Rushing out of his tent, he met a cowboy whom he knew. "What, what is the matter?" he asked. "Oh," replied the cowboy, "there's a feller coming back yonder who hired us to give him some local color, as he calls it. His name's Zane Grey, and we're doing our damnedest to give him all the hell he calls for."

Now, in Andy Adams always "there is ample time," as he makes "a true Texan" say. To quote the words of Gilbert Chesterton on Sir Walter heroes, "the men linger long at their meals." Indeed, I think that the best things in the books of Mr. Adams are the tales that the men tell around the chuck-wagon and the jokes and the chaff that they indulge in there.

An easy intimacy with the life shows on every page. The man writes of the only life he knows, in the only language he knows. "Now, Miller, the foreman, hadn't any use for a man that wasn't dead tough under any condition. I've known him to camp his outfit on alkali water, so the men would get out in the morning, and every rascal beg leave to ride outside circle on the morning round-up." "Cattle will not graze freely in a heavy dew or too early in the morning." When Don Lovell's outfit received a herd of cattle on the Rio Grande, the Texas boss tallied the hundreds with a tally string and the Mexican *caporal* tallied them by dropping pebbles from one hand to the other. When June Deweese, *segundo,* showed off his boss's horses to a buyer below San Antonio, he had them grazing on a hillside and drove the buyer along on the lower slope so that they would appear larger.

The language that the Andy Adams cowboys use is as natural and honest as the exposition; it is often picturesque, too, as all language of the soil is. I quote sentences almost at random from various of the books. "I'll build a fire in your face that you can read the San Francisco *Examiner* by at midnight." "We had the outfits and the horses, and our men were plainsmen and were at home as long as they could see the north star." "The old lady was bogged to the saddle skirts in her story." "Blankets? Never use them; sleep on your belly and cover with your back, and get up with the birds in the morning." "Every good cowman takes his saddle wherever he goes, though he may not have clothes enough to dust a fiddle."

When I began reading Andy Adams a number of years ago, the humor of his books did not impress me. Lately I have found it to be one of their highest virtues. Folk yarns salt page after page, and many a good-natured drawl sets me laughing. The humor is as unconscious as the green of grass, but I do not know of anything in Mark Twain funnier than the long story of the "chuckline rider" who blew into a cow camp in **"The Strip"** about Christmas time and proceeded to earn his board by cooking "bear sign" (the name for doughnuts). The cowboys often play like colts: one of them gets down off his horse and butts his head into a muddy bank, imitative of the cattle; some of them dress up one of their number like a wild Indian and take him to the hotel for dinner. This is horseplay, to be sure, but as it is told it generates health in a healthy reader like a good feed of roast beef and plum pudding.

There are, of course, many shortcomings in Mr. Adams. His books have no plots, but lack of plot sometimes allows of an easier fidelity to facts. He lacks great dramatic power, unless the quiet truth be dramatic. However, there is plenty of action on occasion. "The men of that day," says the author of **Reed Anthony, Cowman,** which like all the other novels but one is written in the autobiographic style, "were willing to back their opinions, even on trivial matters, with their lives. 'I'm the quickest man on the trigger that ever came over the trail,' said a cowpuncher to me one night in a saloon in Abilene. 'You're a blankety blank liar,' said a quiet little man, a perfect stranger to both of us, not even casting a glance our way. I wrested a six-shooter from the hands of my acquaintance, and hustled him out of the house, getting roundly cursed for my interference, though no doubt I saved human life."

The greatest shortcoming, perhaps, is too much love of prosperity. Andy Adams loves cowmen and cattle and horses so that he can hardly suffer any of them to undergo ruin. The trail has hardships, but it is delightful. The path of the owner and his cowboys is sometimes rocky, but it generally leads down into pleasant pastures. As they travel it, they never go into heroics about their "grim sacrifices," etc.; they take great gusto in the traveling. When I read **Reed Anthony, Cowman,** or **Wells Brothers,** I think of old Daniel Defoe's love for goods of the earth, and I would no more think of holding their prosperity against the actuality of Reed Anthony, Don Lovell, and other prosperous cattle people of Andy Adams' creation than I would think of impeaching the life-likeness of Mulberry Sellers on account of his optimism.

There are no women in Andy Adams, excepting those in the melancholy **Matchmaker.** Well, there were no women

in the action that he treats of. Why should he lug them in? Nor has Andy Adams any thesis to advance. He has no absorbing philosophy of life that mingles with the dark elements of earth as in Joseph Conrad. "To those who love them, cattle and horses are good company." Perhaps that is his philosophy.

It is easy to let one's enthusiasm run away with one's judgment. I have waited a long time to write these words on Andy Adams. Perhaps sympathy for his subject has biased me. Perhaps the memory of how a dear uncle of mine used to "run" with him at the end of the trail in Caldwell, Kansas, has affected me. I try to rule those elements out. It is my firm conviction that one hundred, three hundred years from now people will read Andy Adams to see what the life of those men who went up the trail from Texas was like, just as now we read the diary of Pepys to see what life in London was like following the Restoration, or as we read the *Spectator* papers to see what it was like in the Augustan Age. Those readers of other centuries will miss in Andy Adams the fine art of Addison, though they will find something of the same serenity; they will miss the complex character and debonair judgements of Pepys; but they will find the honesty and fidelity of a man who rode his horses straight without giving them the sore-back and then who traced his trail so plainly that even a tenderfoot may follow it without getting lost.

Levette J. Davidson   (essay date 1951)

SOURCE: "The Unpublished Manuscripts of Andy Adams," *Colorado Magazine,* Vol. XXVIII, No. 2, April, 1951, pp. 97-107.

[*In the essay below, Davidson evaluates Adams's unpublished novels, plays, and short stories.*]

At his death in 1935, at the age of seventy-six, Andy Adams left a considerable number of manuscripts which, a few years later, were given to the State Historical Society of Colorado by his nephew Andrew T. Adams, of Denver. An examination of these unpublished writings of the author of the acknowledged masterpiece of the literature of the cattle industry, **The Log of a Cowboy,** reveals much concerning his range of interests, his literary ambitions, and his strengths and weaknesses as a writer.

The published works of Andy Adams include seven books, all issued by Houghton Mifflin Company of Boston, and a few stories and articles scattered through newspapers and magazines. **The Log of a Cowboy** (1903), Andy's first appearance in print although he was already forty-four, was followed by **The Texas Matchmaker** (1904), a novel depicting Texas ranch life. The next year another novel of the cattle trails appeared, **The Outlet** (1905). It supplements **The Log of a Cowboy,** emphasizing the business and financial aspects of the long drives to the northern markets, rather than the life of the cowboys along the way. Andy's fourth book, **Cattle Brands** (1906), was made up of short stories. All fifteen of these stories deal one way or another with cowboys and cattle. **Reed Anthony, Cowman** (1907), is told in the form of an autobiography. The Texas cattle baron in this novel resembles Charles Goodnight, but Andy explained that Reed Anthony was a composite of a number of old cattlemen. The hero makes a fortune by good management and shrewd marketing. Andy was not so lucky. His publishers accepted no more manuscripts until 1911; then they brought out a juvenile novel, *Wells Brothers, The Young Cattle Kings.* In a sequel, Andy's last book, *The Ranch on the Beaver,* the Wells boys continued their rapid development into successful cattlemen, but it did not appear until 1927.

Anyone who reads through Andy's seven published volumes will have learned in detail the essential facts concerning one of America's most historically significant and spectacular occupations. Although his storytelling technique resembles the leisurely reminiscing of an old-timer rather than the plot-ridden, speedy, stereotyped, and slick narrative methods of so-called Western fiction today, his style fits his materials perfectly. Andy's writings lack highly contrived, exciting plots, and they contain practically no love interest; but they do have authentic, humanly significant descriptions of cowboys and cattlemen, of cattle, of ranches, of trails, of cattle towns, of storytelling around the chuckwagon, of honest and dishonest cattle dealers, and of the great plains extending from the Mexican border to Canada. No better record exists of the life of the cattle kingdom during the seventies and eighties than the account that Andy Adams wove into his fiction. Modern critics have declared his *Log of a Cowboy* worthy of a place beside *Moby Dick,* the classic of the whaling industry, and alongside *Two Years Before the Mast,* the classic of the sailing ship era and of freighting around the Horn; they have praised his Defoe-like realism. [Robert Spiller, et al. Literary History of the United States, 1948]. But Andy Adams wrote a vast amount of material that no one wanted to publish. Did the fault lie in the manuscripts themselves or in contemporary reading taste?

The Andy Adams manuscripts in the library of the State Historical Society of Colorado contain the following: two novels, one of 264 typescript pages and one of 298 pages, a carbon copy; two articles, one of 23 pages, printed a few years ago in the *Colorado Magazine,* and one of two pages; five dramas, containing 69 pages, 88 pages, 125 pages, 122 pages, and 128 pages; and fourteen short stories, with the following number of pages: 7, 13, 14, 15 (2), 16 (2), 17 (3), 18, 20, and 26, with another beginning for one of the stories on 4 pages and the complete story in duplicate, but with a different title, 14 pages,—a total of 230 pages of short fiction.

In addition to these 1349 pages of manuscript several other unpublished works are known to exist or to have existed. Mrs. Jean Henry, in her unpublished thesis, lists a novel in manuscript, entitled *Army Beef,* now in the possession of Eugene Cunningham; *Barb Wire,* a novel in manuscript, in the possession of Mrs. Walter Ferguson, Tulsa Oklahoma, in 1938, which had been written first in dramatic form, according to statements in Andy Adams' letters; a novel entitled *Cohen, the Outcast,* known only through a mention in a letter from Andy to J. Evetts Haley, October 27, 1931; and a dramatization of Andy's second published novel, *A Texas Matchmaker.* Mrs. Henry was able to borrow a manuscript copy of one of the stories included in the Colorado collection, **"Judgment Hour,"** from a Colorado Springs resident. She also reported that, according to Dr. Newton Gaines, Andy Adams had told Dr. Gaines in 1934 that he had sent several scenario manuscripts to Hollywood, but that all had been rejected.

In a letter to J. Frank Dobie, February 9, 1927, according to Mrs. Henry, Andy stated that he had sold two articles to the *Breeder's Gazette:* **"Westward Ho!"** and **"The Cow Coroner."** One of his short stories, entitled **"The First Christmas at the 4D Ranch,"** appeared in the *Denver Post,* Sunday, December 18, 1904. It is probable that other stories were published, but it seems that their location is unknown today. Many of his letters to friends have appeared in articles about him; many more, no doubt, remain unpublished. It is probable that little more from the pen of Andy Adams will be discovered, and that the materials are now available for a definitive study of his writing career. The remainder of this article will, however, attempt only a description and an evaluation of the manuscripts in the Colorado collection.

Probably the most interesting and readable of the manuscripts is *Dividends,* "Dedicated to the Memory of Winfield Scott Stratton, Founder of the Myron Stratton Home. (A Miner's Home located at Colorado Springs, Colorado.)" The first of twenty-four chapters of the 264 page novel opens as follows: "It was pay-day in camp. O'Keefe's ore haulers stood in a row on the foot-rail of the Alamo bar." Tom Bragdon, the shift boss of the graveyard relief, entered the Alamo bar, looking for the drunken but essential blacksmith Jack Moss, to get him to go back to work in the Revenue mine, operated by Billy Owens, on a lease that would expire within a month. The blacksmith must sharpen and temper the drills or the work could not go forward and precious ore would be lost by the operator. But Jack Moss is on a spree. He is finally won over by Bragdon, who promises to go partners with him, rent a cabin, take in the blacksmith's young daughter, Susie, and hire a house-keeper to look after the girl so that the county officers will not take her away from Moss. The blacksmith is discouraged and bitter, but not hopeless. " 'If I had someone to believe in me,' he muttered to himself, 'one who would hold out a hand to a sinking man, I believe I could brace up and pay dividends.' " The chapter ends as follows: "The invitation to drink was forgotten, and the two men passed out of the place. The whirl of the roulette ball mingled with scraps of vulgar songs from the wine rooms; without end, the din arose and fell, for night and day were one at the Alamo bar."

As might be expected, the rest of the story depicts the struggle of Moss to regain respectability, to gain a fortune on Bull Mountain in Cripple Creek, to educate his daughter, to build a hospital and home for miners in Colorado Springs, and to encourage the courtship of his daughter by the young doctor who becomes superintendent of the hospital. The plot and the romantic episodes are not remarkable, but there are many scenes and episodes in the work that testify to Andy Adams' skill in observing and recording the details of an occupation in which men fight against nature and, at times, against each other in order to win a livelihood and a fortune if possible.

It may be recalled that Andy left Texas and came to Colorado at the time of the Cripple Creek gold rush, about 1891. In one of his few autobiographical sketches he told that he had spent some little time and his accumulated savings on Cripple Creek mining ventures. These investments did not pay off in cash dividends, but they did yield authentic materials for a mining novel. Accidents in the mine, crooked deals in mining claims, the dreary work of the toilers underground, their sordid amusements, the periods of enforced idleness and poverty, the feverish prospecting for new veins of rich ore, and the big deals when a real discovery had been made, all are here presented realistically. The Stratton story and the Cripple Creek setting are sound foundations for a novel; but Andy's fictional treatment seems a bit old-fashioned and sentimental. Although the work is dated, it is better than many a novel that was popular in America between 1900 and 1914. Since stories of Western mining are none too numerous, it is to be regretted that *Dividends* was never published.

The novel *Lo, The Poor Indian* was designed to show Indian life on the plains as it centered in horses. It does reflect Adams' extensive knowledge of horses, but its Indians are mere stereotypes. Quite conventional also are the episodes, such as Lone Horse being adopted by "an old Ogalalla Brule squaw" after his tribe had been "surprised at daybreak one morning in the early '40's of the last century, and murdered in merciless, savage cruelty," and Lone Horse establishing his manhood by stealing a horse herd from an enemy tribe. The story ends when Lone Horse wins White Feather, in spite of the opposition of her father, Strike-Ax. Our hero is chosen to be chief of the fall hunt and the father is then powerless to prevent the marriage. This work is of little value.

A third novel in manuscript, entitled *Army Beef,* was turned over in 1926 to Eugene Cunningham, a Western writer, now living in California, for reworking with a view to possible publication. This work is unavailable for examination; Mr. Cunningham, on October 20, 1950, wrote that he still hopes to do something with the story. According to an earlier letter from Mr. Cunningham, quoted in Mrs. Henry's thesis, "the novel is epic in scope, dealing with the delivery of Strip cattle to northern army posts—hence the title. A girl accompanies the herd belonging to her widowed mother and herself. . . . This is in the original script as great as *The Log of a Cowboy,* considering *The Log* in any way. It is in many respects a much better book and one potentially of interest to a far wider audience." Until more evidence is available one may question Mr. Cunningham's enthusiasm for *Army Beef.* Andy Adams never did very well with "the girl interest." He criticized Emerson Hough for sending a girl along with a trail outfit, in *North of 36;* one wonders if he succeeded any better when he attempted it.

Among the fourteen short stories in the Colorado manuscript collection is a thirty-page tale entitled **"A Romance in Oil."** About 1920 Andy went back to Kentucky for two years and worked as a paymaster in the oil fields, in response to an old friend's offer at a time when Andy's finances were running low. Again he accumulated vocational lore that could be used fictionally. His story is, however, too romantic, too stilted, and too leisurely in style for modern taste. The narrator saves a widow from being victimized by oil lease speculators in the Sequatchie oil field in Texas. The charming widow falls into her rescuer's arms, on the last page. Again one wishes that the story were better, for the information about wildcatting, gushers, and unscrupulous oil promoters all seems authentic. There is, even today, a dearth of good fiction concerning this occupation.

Six of the stories concern a fox-hunting social group living on the Kentucky-Virginia border. No doubt Andy studied the customs of the hunt while he was back in Kentucky, and he did love horses; but his heroines and his love plots are the wish fulfillments of a lonely and aging bachelor, not plausible likenesses of reality. The titles are **"A Chicken or a Horse," "End of the Chase," "An Interrupted Fox Hunt," "Out-foxed," "All in the Day's Hunt,"** and **"The Girl, the Horse, and the Hounds."** In rejecting the last of these, the associate editor of *McCall's Magazine* wrote to "Dear Mr. Adams," on October 20, 1933, "Thank you so much for letting us see your story,'**The Girl, the Horse, and the Hounds.'** We are only sorry that it does not fit our needs at present, and we must therefore return it." Again Andy had discovered a promising field for fiction and had accumulated realistic background data, but he had failed to create convincing characters and adequate plot.

The remaining eight short stories can be described briefly. **"A Forthcoming Book"** tells how the narrator is signalled to by a prisoner in a jail, who reveals that he is writing a book, a mystery story of the ax-murder of a prospector by the man he had sheltered. The situation is not very convincing. *Mixed Brands* is a delightful collection of half-a-dozen campfire cowboy yarns such as those included in Andy's published books. They are held together only by the setting or story-telling framework. **"Transplanting a Texan"** is another bachelor's dream, recounting how the cowboy, Allen Quick, gave a cow won at poker to the young daughter of a stage station keeper. Six years later the girl is grown and the returning cowboy makes love to her, marrying her a few years afterwards, when he is ready to leave the trail. **"Benefit Day"** tells of a Colorado Springs father who loves baseball, but opposes the courtship of his daughter by a professional ball player. When our hero saves the game for the home town team by knocking out a home run, all ends well. Needless to say, this story does not even faintly suggest the popular and the literary appeals to be found later in the baseball fiction created by Ring Lardner. **"The Residue Under the Will"** is all about the money left by the proprietor of the Northwest Printing Company, but the reader does not get interested. **"Judgment Hour"** is somewhat better, although this story of a newspaper reporter in Colorado Springs has nothing more subtle about it than the O'Henry-like ending in which it is revealed that the reporter is himself the mysterious husband of the romantic heiress who had eloped and from whom, the editor thought, the reporter had failed to get an interview.

One other story remains, **"Nature in the Raw,"** which is repeated in another typescript under the title **"The Barren Mare,"** and for which there is another four-page beginning, entitled, "The Quality of Mercy." Attached to the first manuscript is a newspaper clipping of an old Lucky Strike cigarette advertisement, showing two horses battling, "as portrayed by the famous animal painter, Paul Bransom," with the caption "Nature in the Raw is seldom Mild." The story opens with the trial in a Texas court of "the case of Ann Helm, spinster, charged with abducting a child." She pleads "guilty;" but the judge, a friend of her family, tries to find out why she still refuses to give up the child. It appears that she had early observed that barren mares are unwelcome in the manada of a stallion. A pet colt that Ann had reared was thus driven out to wander alone; when wolves chased her, she rushed back into the manada only to be killed by the hooves of the hostile mares. Having been denied motherhood, Ann kidnapped the neglected child of the man to whom she was once "betrothed." She tells the judge that her betrothed, "after galloping away with a company of Texas cavalry confederates, and with never a word of explanation, returned years afterward with a wife and five children. At his death recently, the tenth one, the youngest, fell to me. At least, I have it safely in hiding." It is assumed that the sympathetic judge will see to it that the barren mare is allowed to adopt the tenth colt of another. Perhaps Jack London could have made something of the idea that inspired this story, but again Andy's efforts were unsuccessful.

In an early interview Andy said that he had no thought of becoming an author until he saw in Colorado Springs, about 1900, a performance of the unrealistic but popular cowboy play *A Texas Steer,* by Charles H. Hoyt. If people would pay for such a false picture, surely they would welcome stories from one who had lived the life of the cowboy himself and would endeavor to give them the truth. Although Andy tried his hand at many plays and even attempted to dramatize one or two of his novels, his dramatic efforts never reached the stage nor print. The five complete play manuscripts in the Colorado collection provide ample evidence to justify the conclusion that Andy just did not know how to write a play.

Graybeal's Guest is a four-act, romantic play with scenes in the camp of some Texas rangers sent out to catch border criminals, and on a Texas ranch where a mysterious young female from the East is visiting while trying to locate the grave of her brother. When it is discovered that she is not a spy on the side of the criminals, the drama can be concluded with her marriage to a young officer in the Texas rangers. Augustus Thomas did make successful melodramas out of such materials; not being a man of the theatre, Andy Adams could only try. His *Dr. Clinksales,* however, has a plot that would require even more expert handling. Dr. Clinksales had been expelled from the Maryland Medical Association after a patient of his had died as the result of an accident following surgery. The Doctor rises from his degradation as a professional gambler in the Turf gambling house at Pecos City, Texas, when he falls in love with a visiting girl from the East. He begins by practicing medicine in Cheyenne, without a license, and is so successful that he moves on to New York. Professional jealousy leads to the unearthing of his past. He fights against what he considers the unethical code of the association's "profes-

Adams (left) with his father and a nephew in 1905.

sional ethics." The heroine realizes that he is right, and rushes into his arms.

The Saving Salt, another four-act drama, presents life on a Texas ranch where the second wife of Marion Reeves, cattleman, is so discontented with the monotony of ranch life that she wants Reeves to sell out. She encourages two fast-talking, slick promoters who wish to buy the ranch and cut it up into small homesteads, in spite of the lack of water. She also tries to marry off Reeves' daughter to one of the slickers, because she considers Julia's cowboy lover, Mason, to be too crude. Of course the villains are outwitted by Reeves and Mason just in time to save the ranch and to prevent Julia's wedding to the wrong man. In spite of the melodramatic plot and some stereotyped situations, the play is readable. Some of the dialogue contains realistic cowboy language. But one could not expect *The Saving Salt* to satisfy a modern theatre audience unless it were transformed into a sort of Texas version of *Oklahoma.*

Rio Grande is a four-act drama based upon the Garza Revolution in 1893. A raiding band from Mexico has kidnapped Mary Ringgold's father and is holding him for ransom. His sister Margaret has the money, but only Mary knows the way to Padre Guiteriz's old hermitage, where the prisoner is dying. She leads the men to the meeting place. Fortunately the Texas rangers help out, recover the ransom money, and provide a husband for Mary.

The remaining drama, *Agua Dulce,* is prefaced with the following statement by the author:

> Theme: The first law of nature—self defense and the protection of one's property.
>
> Story of Proposition: Two half brothers, John and Marion Blair comprise the firm of Blair Brothers, ranchmen and trail drivers. The latter was a high roller, the former a conservative, shrewd business man. John, the elder one, has married late in life, and had an only daughter. In Marion's family were three girls. Marion died and his two oldest daughters married adventures, who believed that the holdings of Blair Brothers was an equal partnership. Shielding themselves behind the widow, a suit, in behalf of the heirs of Marion Blair, was instituted by these two fortune hunters, claiming a half interest in the Agua Dulce land and cattle. The trial resulted in a non-suit and the two son-in-laws and their attorneys attack John Blair at a cow camp and are killed in the fight that follows. The fall of the action is a reconciliation between John Blair and Marion's widow, and the working out of the necessary love threads. Pronounced, Ah-wa Doolce. (Sweet water.)

At the end of the fourth and last act of *Agua Dulce* is the notation "Copyrighted, March 16th, '06." It is evident from this dating and from evidence in his letters that Andy Adams worked at playwriting throughout his literary career, but that he had no success in this field. His plays are little more than amateur attempts at sentimental romance and at melodrama. In them we miss the realistic characters, the detailed pictures of everyday life on ranch and trail, and the leisurely—but pleasant—storytelling style usually found in Andy's cowboy fiction.

Andy's own attitude towards his limited success in getting his manuscripts published is indicated in the following letter, the original of which was donated, together with several others, to the Pioneer Museum in Colorado Springs, by Houghton Mifflin and Company.

Columbia, Nevada, Aug. 15, '07.

Andy Adams,
Western Correspondent,
Syndicate Work A Specialty,
Colorado Springs, Colorado.

Houghton Mifflin & Co.,
Boston, Mass.

Dear Sirs:-

I was glad to have your favor of the 7th instant. My experience of getting anything out of stories serially is not encouraging. In the first place I am a poor peddler, and further the eastern viewpoint of the West is a hard one to meet. Eastern writers, with little or no knowledge of their subject, can satisfy the short story market better than Western ones. Seemingly the standard is set, lurid and distorted, and unless one can drop into that vein, he or she will find their wares a drug on the market.

However, I am thankful for your inquiry to look at my proposed group of stories, and later I may give them a revision and send them on for a reading. In the meantime, I will await the September statement on *Reed Anthony, Cowman.* If a valid book like it is not wanted, there is surely a lesson in it to me, and to further inflict a public with stuff for which there is no demand, would be inexcusable.

Very truly yours,
(Signed) ANDY ADAMS

The non-fiction prose of Andy Adams is slight in quantity and in significance. It was a by-product of his fame as the author of *The Log of a Cowboy* and similar works. A two-page article, **"Barb Wire,"** describing the conditions at the time when fencing the range caused cattlemen to cut the wires to permit their cattle to get to the old watering places, and a twenty-three-page address entitled **"The Cattle on a Thousand Hills"** are in the Colorado collection. The former probably contains the germ of the idea developed into Andy's drama *Barb Wire* and the novelized version of it, both now lost. The latter was printed in *The Colorado Magazine,* XV, 5 (September, 1938), pp. 168-180, soon after Andy T. Adams gave his late uncle's manuscripts to the State Historical Society (acknowledged on page 37 of the January, 1938, issue of the same magazine). It is a sympathetic sketch of the history of cattle from ancient times and a glowing tribute to the pastoral way of life, ending with a dozen lines of verse, including these: "And cattle gathered from a thousand hills / Have kept the trail with men." It is probable that a few other sketches by Andy appeared in the *Breeder's Gazette* and other periodicals, but none has been tracked down except his evaluation of cowboy writings by other authors, published under the title **"Western Interpreters,"** in the *Southwest Review,* X, 1 (October, 1924, pp. 70-74.)

From the preceding description of Andy's unpublished manuscripts his limitation as a writer should be evident. He was unable to contrive an original plot, he did not understand feminine character, he rarely penetrated below the surface in depicting motivation and emotion, and he lacked interest in all philosophy except practical rules for material success in life and a simple code for ethical behavior in personal relationships. His keen eye for the details of occupational lore, his ear for the strong and vivid language of men at work, his joy in outdoor activity, and his skill in telling a plotless narrative at a leisurely and effortless pace characterize many of the pages of his manuscripts, as they do his printed books. But the self-taught fiction writer, Andy Adams, ventured into too many fields for which his limited personal experience, his limited reading, and his limited writing skills proved inadequate.

In spite of his many failures Andy Adams remains the champion in one significant field; he put into seven books of fiction more of the life of the open range, the ranch, and the cattle trail than any other writer has been able to capture. His *The Log of a Cowboy* is, in fact, the best book yet written about the West's most popular folk character.

Kenneth Porter (essay date 1957)

SOURCE: A review of *Why the Chisholm Trail Forks, and Other Tales of the Cattle Country* in *Midwest Folklore,* Vol. VII, No. 4, Winter, 1957, pp. 245-46.

[*In the following excerpt Porter characterizes the stories in Adams's collection* Why the Chisholm Trail Forks *as simple but convincing narratives.*]

Andy Adams (1859-1935) was, like Sam Bass, a Hoosier who became a Texas cowboy. When over forty, he began writing out of his first-hand knowledge of the range and the trail and ultimately produced seven books. His first, *The Log of a Cowboy* (1903), is generally recognized as one of the best portrayals of trail-driving days ever published, despite the fact that, although often taken for auto-biography, it is actually a novel.

Andy Adams's volumes have long been out of print, except for a truncated version of the *Log,* and, since one of their most important and characteristic features is their camp-fire tales, Prof. Wilson M. Hudson, of the University of Texas English department and the Texas Folklore Society, has collected fifty-one such tales, four of them unpublished, into *Why the Chisholm Trail Forks.*

Prof. Hudson suggests that a "case might be made for the camp-fire tale as a form of folk literature comparable to the ballad." Certainly these tales are as far as possible from the ingenious stories with their "surprise endings" which that other adopted Texan, O. Henry, drew from the same environment. And, except for such a stray example as **"The Cat in the Jacal,"** they are almost equally remote from the ordinary folktale. They are simply and unassumingly narratives of experiences which almost any man of that time and environment might have undergone (interesting sometimes because exciting but more often because they exemplify human—or sometimes animal—behavior). Although they involve perhaps half a dozen brushes with Indians and outlaws, they include not a single gunfight of the Hickok-Earp type or romantic love episode.

The first two tales are reasonably representative. The first tells of how a green boy escapes unscathed from his innocent involvement in a Regulator-Moderator feud, the second of a schoolteacher who nearly becomes engaged to the principal local belle, only to have his hopes dashed when the mother of his inamorata is informed that instead of his being "the son of that big farmer who raises so many cattles and horses," he is a member of a poor family with the same surname. It is easy to imagine what a member of the O. Henry school would do with such material; the results, perhaps, would be more immediately and superficially appetizing, but the Adams tales will stick to your ribs better and certainly leave the reader with a more authentic understanding of cow-country society.

The content of these stories is rather more memorable and important than the style, which, without being either pedestrian or cliché-ridden, is still not particularly distinguished for vivid descriptions or picturesque phrases. Such colorful expressions as, of a pretty waitress, "She can ride a string of my horses until they all have sore backs," do occur, but are comparatively infrequent. An exception both to this statement and to the author's usual lack of interest in distinguishing individual "Cattle-trail Pilgrims" by their narrative styles is the case of Ace Gee, who in a dozen pages . . . is credited with more colorful phraseology than appears in any other hundred, e. g.: "I can tell you more about that country [Montana] than you want to know"; "I sometimes think that I will burn my saddle and never . . . look a cow in the face again, nor ride anything but a plow mule and that bareback"; etc., etc. Was Ace Gee, like so many of the Adams narrators, a real person? Perhaps Prof. Hudson will tell us in the "full-length biography and critical study" on which he is working and of which his introductory essay is such a delightful and tantalizing sample.

Mody C. Boatright (essay date 1957)

SOURCE: "Cow Camp Trails," in *Southwest Review,* Vol. XLII, No. 3, Summer, 1957, pp. 254-55.

[*Boatright was an American educator who edited many histories and studies of the American Southwest during his thirty-year career. In the following excerpt, Boatright offers a favorable review of* Why the Chisholm Trail Forks, and Other Tales of the Cattle Country.]

Andy Adams published *The Log of a Cowboy* one year after Owen Wister had published *The Virginian.* Adams remained poor the rest of his life. *The Virginian* made Wister a wealthy man, and unfortunately the most influential of the "Western" writers; for although he had had predecessors in some of the dime novelists, he as a respectable writer publishing in a respectable magazine, and issued by a respectable publisher, largely established the traditions of the synthetic Western fiction as now exemplified by the mass media.

Wister was a class-conscious easterner taken in by the easy manners of the Chegem Club. Adams was a working man before he was a writer. He came to Texas at the age of twenty-three. For some ten years he traded horses and drove them up the trail from South Texas. So accurate is his portrayal of trail driving that J. Frank Dobie has said, "If all the other books on trail driving were destroyed, a reader could still get a just and authentic conception of trail men, trail work, range cattle, cow horses, and the cow country in general from *The Log.*"

Adams' bent was toward a realism that stopped short of naturalism. His raw material was his own experience—what he had seen and done—the people he had known, their recollections and their tales. He knew that an authentic portrayal of cowboys' life must include their relaxations as well as their work—what they did around the campfire at night as well as what they did during the day.

> The campfire [he noted in *The Log of a Cowboy*] is to all outdoor life what the evening fireside is to domestic life. After the labors of the day are over, the men gather around the fire, and the social hour of the day is spent in yarning. The stories told may run from the sublime to the ridiculous, from a true incident to a base fabrication, or from a touching bit of pathos to the most vulgar vulgarity.

The stories however, serve other purposes than verisimilitude. They embrace a wide variety of subjects and moods, and reveal the attitudes of the tellers and listeners toward a great many subjects, including women, Negroes, Indians, and the mores of the older states.

Integral parts of the novels in which they occur, the tales are yet interesting and significant when read by themselves. Wilson Hudson has done a service both to Adams and to the public by going through the Adams books and manuscripts, taking out the campfire tales, and placing them in a single volume—particularly since all the Adams books except *The Log of a Cowboy* are out of print, and it is available only in a shortened edition. . . .

Benjamin Capps   (essay date 1964)

SOURCE: "A Critical Look at a Classic Western Novel," in *The Roundup,* Vol. XII, No. 6, June, 1964, pp. 2, 4.

[*Capps is an American novelist whose works are often set in New Mexico, Texas, Oklahoma, and Colorado. In the following explication of* Log of a Cowboy, *he affirms the book's primary value as a work of social history.*]

In his history *The Great Plains,* published in 1936, Walter Prescott Webb makes a definite and all-inclusive statement about cowboy novels published before that time: "Hitherto there has been written but one novel of the cattle country that is destined to become a classic—*The Log of a Cowboy,* by Andy Adams." Many critics might quarrel with the narrow limits of Webb's definition of a classic. Another statement might be more acceptable, but it is still a strong statement and it is true in 1964: any list of classic western novels, no matter how long or short the list, is incomplete without *The Log of a Cowboy.*

The book was published in 1902 and was immediately acclaimed. It made Adams as a writer. Today, in the public domain, it is still making money for publishers and can be found in any complete library of western Americana. Surely it has stood the test of time.

The novel's unique value was defined by WWA writer Stephen Payne in these pages in 1962 with these words: ". . . genuine cow-country stuff . . . Simple, homespun, *authentic* . . ." He might have added that it is rich and direct and artless and full of good humor. Like Mark Twain and Will Rogers and a few other rare Americans, Andy Adams had the natural ability to interest people.

Perhaps a close look at the book will show something about the relationship between fiction and history; indeed, it may indicate that *The Log of a Cowboy* is not essentially fiction at all, by which statement I do not mean to quibble over definitions, but only to get at the nature of the book. Note this fact: that the question is not whether Adams' characters and events actually existed in 1882, for the writer of fiction often uses actual fact, and the writer of non-fiction uses hypothetical people and events to illustrate ideas. Let us look at three aspects of *The Log of a Cowboy:* the characters, the story, and the relationship between character and story.

Probably no writer has given us a better picture of the real old-time cowboy. He shows us a fun-loving, sentimental, easy-going, hard-working, skilled laborer—no myth. But the question Adams answers about the nature of the American cowboy is a non-fiction question. What was the cowboy really like? Adams tells you. Pick any of his characters there's the answer. They are all alike. You can remember the names: Flood, Priest, McCann, Rountree, Wheat, Stray-horn, but if you haven't read the book in the past month, you will find it hard to remember any difference between them, except, perhaps, that Flood was the boss. A reader who is weary of cheap stereotypes and the heroic cowboy myth finds Adams' people delightful. But Adams fails to show us the deeper truth that people are individuals, each different. And the difference lies at the heart of all good fiction. Authenticity is not the crucial criterion of good fiction. Shakespeare, for example, was an atrocious historian.

Look at Adams' story. An editor would say it is episodic. One event after another happens, separate events, almost unrelated. Each is interesting in itself, colorful, superbly descriptive. They capture some rustlers. They stop a stampede. They get cows out of the quicksand. They repair a broken wagon. They build a bridge. If one made a list of the events and found thirty, then he would find that he could exchange the order of numbers three and twenty-seven, numbers nine and sixteen, etc. —this with little re-writing and little damage to the story. The incidents do not have fictional organization.

A look at the relation between character and event is even more revealing. The relationship hardly exists in Adams' narrative. Which particular man did what? One does not remember. A good piece of fiction has in it people that can hardly be separated from the things that happen to them. A fictional character is moulded by events and he causes events; to a great extent, he is defined by events. Try to write an interesting character sketch of Hamlet without using any of Shakespeare's story. The reverse is also true: fictional events take their very nature from the nature of the people involved.

Adams' lack as a conscious artist in fiction is shown by the fact that he wrote only this one really successful book, though he kept trying. He could not repeat himself. In this book he had unconsciously hit upon an organizing principle, a sort of automatic story framework: a cattle drive. If one tells the truth about a cattle drive, he has sense of movement, a progression. He has a beginning, a middle, and an end. So Adams' narrative hangs together. He was never able to hit upon such unity again.

This evaluation is not intended to disparage *The Log of a Cowboy.* It is not only interesting reading still today. It is valuable primary source material. Adams knew what he was talking about. But his book belongs more with *The Oregon Trail,* by Parkman, and *Roughing It,* by Mark Twain, than it does with classic fiction.

Wilson M. Hudson   (essay date 1964)

SOURCE: *Andy Adams: His Life and Writings,* Southern Methodist University Press, 1964, 274 p.

[*In the following excerpt from his* Andy Adams: His Life and Writings, *Hudson describes the publication history of* Log of a Cowboy *and evaluates the novel.*]

In July, 1901, J. O'H. Cosgrove rejected some stories that Andy had sent to Doubleday, Page and Company and took occasion to give some literary advice. Instead of a number of stories about prospectors, he said, it would be better to write a novel about one successful prospector and turn the stories into incidents in his career. The sketch of Mexican outlaws he found confused, with too many details and no tense dramatic effect. As a model he recommended Emerson Hough and suggested that Andy send him two or three sketches and ask his opinion. Andy had already begun to exchange letters with Hough; after reading **"The Passing of Peg-Leg"** in January, 1901, Hough had written to compliment Andy and inquire what else he had on hand.

Andy's manuscript went on to Houghton Mifflin Company and was rejected by W. B. Parker in August. He said he had found "these sketches of cowboy life" interesting, but would prefer to have "a Log of a Cowboy—a closely woven connected treatment of the cowboy's life, equipment, activity, hardships, amusements and the conditions under which he lives." He and Andy had previously mentioned this project in their letters to each other. Parker was calling for a book that had already been written, *The Story of the Cowboy,* which Emerson Hough had published with D. Appleton and Company in 1897.

Andy sent his stories next to Hough's publisher, Appleton. Again he received a rejection and some advice. In October Ripley Hitchcock wrote that he had read, with "interest and delight," Andy's "short stories of cowboy life"—really sketches rather than stories, he thought—but could not publish them because of the public's reluctance to buy collections. He advised Andy to send his sketches to periodicals; if the weeklies or monthlies would not take them, then perhaps the *New York Sun* could use them in the Sunday edition. Hitchcock's second piece of advice was that Andy should try his hand at a novel of the trail and ranch. "It is necessary to have a plot which will serve as a scaffolding or skeleton and it is necessary to also give considerable care to the simple construction as well as the decoration and finish of the house." This letter was much more than a polite rejection; Hitchcock was showing sincere interest in Andy's work and was taking pains to give him good advice.

Andy replied immediately that he was at work on a novel to be called *The Log of a Cow Herd,* which would deal with a trail drive from Texas to Montana. Evidently he was already writing his novel when Hitchcock's letter came; he was developing a narrative instead of the general exposition suggested by Parker, a narrative that would involve only one phase of the cowboy's life. Hitchcock replied that the title would not do and that Andy's plan would produce "a very different thing from a novel." When Andy finished his manuscript it was accepted by Houghton Mifflin; on October 13, 1902, a contract was signed for the publication of *The Log of a Cowherd.* The title was wisely changed before the day of publication, May 23, 1903.

The publishers sent Hough a copy of the *Log* before its release and elicited a comment from him which they used in a paragraph in the *Boston Evening Transcript* on May 27: "Andy Adams is the real thing, and the first time the real thing has appeared in print." In a personal letter Hough generously wrote Andy, "I want to thank you very much for writing **The Log of a Cowboy.** It is really *The Story of the Cowboy* as it ought to have been written, and I can't tell you how glad I am to see this subject assigned to a Western man who could do it thoroughly." He welcomed Andy enthusiastically as a writer for whom he had been looking and whom the West needed, the opposite of the easterner in search of local color who saw only the superficial and understood nothing.

The Log of a Cowboy has a simple and clear-cut plot: in 1882 a trail outfit take a herd of cattle from the Rio Grande to the Blackfoot reservation in northwestern Montana, encountering and overcoming various obstacles along the way. The general pattern to which this plot belongs is the performance of a group task. Unlike the archetypal tasks, this one falls within the realm of the natural and possible. The task consists in doing a special kind of work, not in securing a golden fleece or slaying a dragon and taking his treasure, and the obstacles are dry drives, stampedes, quicksand, flooded streams, and rustlers and Indians who would like to take their toll, not clashing rocks, man-eating monsters, or enamored goddesses. Two shooting scrapes that occur in trail towns have a limited potentiality as obstacles; they can cause the loss of one or more members of the group but cannot thwart the completion of the task. They are not necessarily connected with driving cattle, but they are probable occurrences in the lives of men whose brief and vigorous periods of play may lead to trouble. The telling of campfire tales is not a necessary phase of the work either, but it is almost as much to be expected as the eating of the evening meal. Andy's scheme permits the inclusion of many incidents and sequences bearing on the main plot and also additional tales that do not influence the working out of the plot but are blended in harmoniously.

The action progresses through space and time; the cattle have to be moved more than two thousand miles by a certain date, September 10. The narrative question is, are these men going to move the cattle without loss to the point of delivery on time? The action proper begins with the receiving of the cattle on the Rio Grande and concludes with the delivery on Two Medicine Creek. Every good day's travel brings the action nearer a successful conclusion, and every obstacle has the effect of retardation. There are some delays, some moments when it seems that the herd may be lost or seriously diminished, but there is no single great crisis. The plot proceeds steadily to its solution. It is fully worked out and well rounded; the initial data are clearly given and no loose ends are left over. What comes before the receiving of the cattle is prologue and what comes after the delivery is epilogue. The plot coincides with the task set at the beginning; it is enacted by cowboys at work.

The task is performed by a group of men without an individual hero. Jim Flood is the foreman representing Don

Lovell, the owner, but once he has assigned the men to their particular duties he does not have to watch over them. They know what is to be done and how to do it; they are faithful to the work and the well-being of the herd. With the exception of the foreman, cook, and horse wrangler, every man rides guard along with two other men at the same time every night, there being four watches. During the day each man has his place beside the herd when it is grazing along, at the point, swing, or drag. There are fifteen men in all, and they work together in a joint effort. They form a group whose function is work; but when threatened from the outside they are immediately transformed into a band that can fight for the protection of the cattle or themselves, all being armed. This work band is analogous to the ancient armed band or comitatus with which many stories and tales deal, but it is not dominated by a heroic leader who has more prowess or cleverness than the others, such as Jason, Ulysses, Beowulf, Finn McCumhail, or Robin Hood. Different degrees of complexity in such armed bands can be distinguished, all the way from a handful of warriors in the primeval forests of Germany or a boatful of Viking raiders to King Arthur and his knights. The cowboy band is another instance of an ancient and simple social organization of males in which the male virtues are prized—loyalty, courage, strength, and skill with the appropriate weapons or tools. Stories involving an armed band usually turn on the attainment of some important group goal, often the overcoming of a rival band, in the course of which outstanding men emerge as heroes; when the conflict is internal it obstructs the securing of the group goal or perhaps even leads to the dissolution of the group.

The *Log* contains no love story; it seldom makes mention of women, though one night Fox Quarternight and Billy Honeyman tell about attractions of theirs that came to nothing. Several times in letters written twenty-five years after the appearance of the *Log* Andy said he did not know what a woman would be doing in a story of the trail; as he expressed it, she would be like a fifth wheel. In stories about male bands a woman can be present in a limited number of ways. If she is a direct participant in the action along with the men, she has to play a man's part and may disguise herself as a man; she is then a kind of maiden warrior like Camilla or Harpalyce. She can be the prize, the object of contention between warring groups, like Helen of Troy. Or she can be a special helper who imparts secrets to the hero and enables him to obtain the treasure, as Medea helps Jason obtain the Golden Fleece and make his escape with his men, at the price of accompanying him. She can delay and deflect the hero and his band from their purpose, as Circe keeps Odysseus and his men on her isle for a year. She can be a comforter not involved in the action and serving as a love object, in which case she is a consort (Andromache) or concubine (Chryseis). She may be an object of contention within the band and act as a disruptive element, as Briseis causes Achilles and Agamemnon to quarrel and stirs dissension among the Argives. For the sake of completeness it should be said that the last and most remote possibility is that she can be a member of an opposing war band made up of women, like Penthesilea of the Amazons, who is killed by Achilles.

Of course Andy did not consider and reject these possibilities in turn; the only women that come into the lives of his trail drivers are the dance hall girls in the cow towns. After visiting Dodge City, John Officer slips an embroidered handkerchief and a silver-mounted garter into the coat pocket of the cook, Barney McCann, who throws them into the fire when he discovers them, saying, "Good whiskey and bad women will be the ruin of you varmints yet." At the Dew-Drop-In dance hall in Ogallala the boys see "the frailty of women in every grade and condition" from girls in their teens to wornout beauties ready for the last dose of opium.

No one of Andy's boys is a hero and no one of them is in love, but it does not follow that they are inhuman creations without substance. On the contrary, most of them are very substantial and lifelike. They are men of action and their problems are not internal. Their thoughts are left unstated and their characters do not undergo change in the course of the book. Nevertheless, Jim Flood, Quince Forrest, and Paul Priest (nicknamed the Rebel) are individual and distinct. Jim is a good foreman, thoughtful of his men and relying on them to do the right thing at the right time. Once when "a self-appointed guardian" took him aside and told him that he had hired a drunkard, he replied, "Just so the herd don't count out shy on the day of delivery, I don't mind how many drinks the outfit takes." Though he has not placed himself on the night watch, he rides more than anybody else, circling the moving herd and scouting ahead for water and good bed ground. He shows canniness and courage in outmaneuvering the dishonest men who want to cut the herd on the Colorado and claim for themselves all the range cattle that have joined it along the way.

Quince Forrest is a playful fellow who will sometimes try to "get the goat" of the other boys. He interrupts a tale of Bull Durham's when he hears a technical law term, pretending to make note of it for future use. The boys draw him on to tell a tale and then pretend to fall asleep. For revenge he later works off a sell on them, a story about an ox that steals a ride in a freight wagon. The boys should not have been taken in, because they knew that "where he thought they would pass muster he was inclined to overcolor his statements." They think of Quince as "a cheerful, harmless liar," and when he gets into trouble in Dodge City they stand by him.

The Rebel is an older man; he fought on the southern side in the Civil War and reveres the cause of the South, hence his nickname. He is rather moody and is capable of severe anger. He is the bunkie of Tom Quirk (this means they shared their blankets) and gives Tom, who is going up the trail for the first time, a few pointers. He does not mingle too freely with the others, but he often tells Tom an amusing anecdote as they are waking up or falling asleep. He will not gamble until he feels he is in luck; when the right time comes in Ogallala he has Tom and John Officer play monte with his money to get around the house limit. In Frenchman's Ford the Rebel is insulted by a bad man of the long-haired variety and is forced to shoot him in self-defense.

Don Lovell, the owner of the herd, fought on the side of

the North, but he and the Rebel are good friends—in fact, it was Lovell who coined the nickname. The boys are all southerners with the memory of fathers and brothers who died in the Civil War, but they like old Don Lovell, who knows enough to turn over the cattle to Jim Flood with only the statement that they have to be delivered by September 10 in Montana. Lovell takes special interest in Tom Quirk as the brother of Bob Quirk, who is foreman of another herd of his headed north. He says goodbye to Tom and calls him "son." Tom, the narrator of the *Log,* says, "And as he gave me a hearty, wringing grip of the hand, I couldn't help feeling friendly toward him, Yankee that he was." Lovell meets the boys in Dodge City and entertains them, and he plies them with drinks in Silver Bow, Montana, while they are waiting to take the train back to Texas, and speeds them with a bottle apiece for the journey. Old Don Lovell is a hearty and generous man with a fatherly attitude to his boys. His last name, incidentally, is the same as that of a man who had a cattle camp sixty-five miles southeast of Dodge City.

Other characters stand out less distinctly, though none is artificial or stereotyped. They take part in the action, join in the conversation, and tell tales around the campfire. In addition to those already mentioned—Jim Flood, Quince Forrest, Paul Priest, John Officer, Bull Durham, Fox Quarternight, Billy Honeyman, Barney McCann, and Tom Quirk—the others driving Lovell's herd are Wyatt Roundtree, Joe Stallings, Bob Blades, "Rod" Wheat, Ash Borrowstone, and "Moss" Strayhorn. It is evident from this list that Andy liked to make use of proper names corresponding to common nouns; but it would be a mistake to suppose, because of its strangeness, that he must have invented a name. Strayhorn in particular sounds so appropriate for a cowboy that it seems to have been made up, but as a matter of fact it is a name existing in Texas. Quirk is a real name too. A search might turn up Quarternight, Borrowstone, and Honeyman, to complete the list.

Nat Straw is the name of the foreman of another herd going up the trail at the same time as Lovell's. Andy had known a real Nat Straw, whose name he liked and used for a character in the *Log.* There seems to be little resemblance between the two Straws, beyond the name. Once when asked about the origin of his characters Andy replied, "My characters generally are composites rather than faithful pictures of individuals." Some composites are recognizable. The Rebel owes something but not everything to Tom Worsham, and Tom Quirk has some features and biographical details that make him kin to Red Earnest and Andy himself. Thomas Moore Quirk was the youngest of three brothers whose parents had moved from Georgia to Texas after the war; their mother was Scotch and their father was from the north of Ireland. In the naming and creation of characters Andy was free to use his imagination, and there is no reason to suppose he did not do so.

Mixed in with the seemingly invented names there are many real ones. Andy used Nat Straw's name because it sounded good to him, though the part played by Straw in the *Log* is fictitious. Straw is foreman of an Ellison herd from Goliad County. He passes the Circle Dots while they are recuperating at the Indian Lakes from their almost disastrous dry drive, and is passed below the Colorado while he reshapes his herd after a stampede. Straw visits Flood's wagon several times and he is with the boys in Ogallala, where he arranges a fiddling match between a Negro cook and a locoed white man. He is very breezy and sociable. He and Flood trick the Rebel into leaving a monte game while still a big winner; in the street Straw throws his arm around the Rebel and says, "My dear sir, the secret of successful gambling is to quit when you're a winner, and before luck turns. You may think this is a low down trick, but we're your friends. . . ."

Straw is said to be foreman of a herd for Ellison, one of the great names in the trailing business. Colonel J. F. Ellison of Caldwell County bought and had cattle trailed north from 1869 to 1882; he was in a partnership with Colonel John O. Dewees from 1870 to 1877. It is said that Ellison and Dewees sent from twenty thousand to forty thousand cattle over the trail a year. (In the *Matchmaker* Andy will use the Dewees name.) In Dodge City, Tom Quirk sees Jesse Ellison in the Wright House dining at the same table with other well-known Texas cowmen waiting for their herds to arrive—"Uncle" Henry Stevens, "Lum" Slaughter, John Blocker, Ike Pryor, "Dun" Houston, and "Shanghai" Pierce. In his voluminous voice Shanghai says to a cattle solicitor,

> No, I'll not ship any more cattle to your town until you adjust your yardage charges. Listen! I can go right up into the heart of your city and get a room for myself, with a nice clean bed in it, plenty of soap, water, and towels, and I can occupy that room for twenty-four hours for two bits. And your stockyards, away out in the suburbs, want to charge me twenty cents a head and let my steer stand out in the weather.

Andy himself had heard Shanghai Pierce make this complaint in Dodge City. The result of Andy's mingling the names of real people with his own names is that the fiction takes credibility from the reality. Andy mentions two other famous Texas cowmen, Richard King and Mifflin Kenedy, who have a representative at Dodge waiting for Billy Mann to arrive with a herd of Running W cattle.

Two other real people, Bat Masterson and Ben Thompson, come into the narrative in Dodge. Some of the boys are present when Bat takes part in one of the famous practical jokes of Dodge City; in Andy's version, which coincides rather closely with the story told around Dodge, Bat pretends to keep order at a lecture on the occult which ends in a gun battle with blanks when someone in the audience calls the "professor" a liar the second time. Andy changed the professor's specialty from "private diseases" to the occult. Bat was never marshal of Dodge, as Andy says, but he was deputy marshal and later sheriff of Ford County. In 1882, when Andy's Circle Dot boys were supposed to have been in Dodge, Bat was no longer living there. Ben Thompson, whom the Rebel looks up at a gambling house and with whom he spends an hour pledging friendship and talking about the days when they were in the Confederate cavalry together, was not living in Dodge then either. Ben had served in the Texas cavalry and had gambled professionally in Dodge, but from the middle of

July, 1882, until the following January he was in a San Antonio jail awaiting trial for the shooting of Jack Harris—mean-while continuing officially as marshal of Austin.

Geographical names also lend reality to the *Log*. Never having been over the Western Trail, Andy worked with a map. He was very scrupulous and accurate, but he did not hesitate to create four geographical fictions so that he could include four interesting sequences that otherwise might have been hard to introduce. These fictions are the Indian Lakes northwest of San Antonio, Big Boggy Creek in Kansas, Forty Islands Ford on the North Platte below Fort Laramie, and Frenchman's Ford on the Yellowstone, a raw frontier town. Andy divides the *Log* into chapters according to the phases of the drive (receiving, start, delivery) and the water-courses and towns passed on the way; all but a few of the twenty-four chapter headings contain geographical references. Unified sequences tend to form around streams crossed or towns briefly visited. There are parallel situations in different chapters, but incidents and sequences show considerable variety. Twelve campfire tales, which are interesting in themselves and also contribute to variety, are judiciously spaced throughout the book.

When Lovell's herd, purchased in Mexico and already bearing the Circle Dot road brand, are swum across the Rio Grande six miles below Brownsville, the horse of one of the Mexican vaqueros goes under and never comes up again. The vaquero is saved. This incident foreshadows the drowning of Wade Scholar at Forty Islands Ford, which Andy places on the North Platte below Fort Laramie. Foreman of an outfit waiting to cross the swollen

Adams in the early 1920's.

river, Wade is reluctant to cross, and is thought by Flood's men to be lacking in courage. Flood crosses and urges Wade to follow. Wade and his horse go down together, and his body is not found until the next day. It is learned after Wade's death that two of his brothers had drowned and his mother had pleaded with him to beware of flooded rivers. There was no Forty Islands Ford such as Andy describes. When on a big rise the water was deep enough to swim a horse, but there never was as much swimming water in this stretch of the river as Andy said there was. For literary purposes he invented, legitimately, the geography and the story of the crossing.

The first stream that causes the Circle Dots trouble is the Arroyo Colorado, some thirty-five miles north of Brownsville. The problem is solved by crossing over a sandbar thrown up by the stream as it flows into the salt water of the Laguna Madre. Flood stage on the Brazos forces the herd to seek a crossing ten miles below the regular ford, but quicksand in the Canadian is worse than high water. It causes a delay of three days. Two crossings are attempted, but cattle bog down and have to be dragged out by a tedious and difficult process. Each foot has to be dug out, doubled back, and tied, and so does the tail, so that the animal can be pulled out by a heavy rope looped around the horns, with lighter ropes attached to the heavy one and leading to five or six saddle pommels. The gripping power of the sand is so great that the hind leg of one heavy steer which comes untied is twisted off at the knee. After reading the *Log* a young doctor told Andy he doubted that such a thing could happen; Andy replied, "I was foreman of the herd, on the trail, where this incident occurred, and felt justified in using it. He also told the doctor that he had tried more than once to pull the brush of a cow's tail out of quicksand and failed. Only a few cattle were bogged on the third attempt, but a large number got stuck when they came back to the river farther up to drink.

Between the Arkansas and the Solomon River Andy locates Big Boggy Creek, which is presented as being even worse than the Canadian for miring cattle. (In that locality there is no Big Boggy.) It is shallow and not more than fifty or sixty feet wide, but the June rains have turned it into a soupy slough. Jim Flood brings back this news after scouting ahead; a herd of Millet's has lost a number of cattle in trying to cross and is stopped on the south side. (Captain Eugene B. Millet of Seguin was another well-known Texas cattleman.) No one knows what to do. A young man rides up and introduces himself as Pete Slaughter. He is driving for his brother Lum, whom the boys have seen in Dodge. Pete cheerfully proposes that they build a bridge as he did on Rush Creek on the Chisholm Trail; they are doubtful, but when Pete comes up the next day with his men they begin cutting cottonwoods. Horsemen drag brush and branches to the stream by ropes and make a pile in the shallow water. Logs go on the brush and dirt on the logs. Slaughter even has guardrails placed along the sides. He gets his herd across by leading a team of oxen ahead, and Flood gets his across the same way, but Millet's herd will not follow the oxen. The foremen try every method they can think of but all fail; finally a "one-eyed, pox-marked fellow" who has noticed a calf in the herd suggests roping it and pulling it across. The calf bellows, the mother follows, and so do some steers; the excitement passes back through the cattle like a wave, and all are put across the bridge.

Pete Slaughter built such a bridge, but not on the Western Trail. Dobie asked Pete's brother, W. B. Slaughter, about this bridge and wrote Andy what he had learned. Andy replied in a letter of February 9, 1927, that W. B. was right about the location of the bridge.

> As I have it from his brother [Pete], it occurred on Big Boggy Creek, which is not on the Western trail which crossed Red River at Doan's. A little thing like that need never worry one when writing fiction. That bridge had to find a place, even if there were no boggy crossings within a hundred miles.

Slaughter's bridge probably crossed the Clear Boggy on the Shawnee Trail in the southeastern part of the Indian Territory. Nat Straw told Dobie in New Mexico that he had heard Pete Slaughter tell Andy the story of his bridge very much as it was related in the *Log*, an inscribed copy of which Andy sent Nat. Pete's story was too good to leave out and so Andy moved the creek and the bridge.

The Indian Lakes which Andy places about eighty miles north northwest of San Antonio are a geographical feature that did not exist. He says they are seven in number, spaced about a mile apart. There has been a local drought and it is sixty miles to the next water, but Jim Flood is determined to follow the old trail instead of taking what seems to be a new one to the west. For three days the cattle have no water and on reaching the watercourse ahead they find it dry. Flood gives orders to drive on, but in spite of the boys' efforts the cattle turn back to their last watering place. Some go blind from heat and thirst and a few die; the leaders reach the Indian Lakes and stragglers keep coming in for twelve hours. The Circle Dots remain by the lakes for three days to recover. It is at this point that Nat Straw passes Flood's herd, taking the new trail that strikes off to the west. The chapter called "A Dry Drive" has been the most frequently reprinted and anthologized part of the *Log*, and no one so far has questioned Andy's geography in print. George W. Saunders, prime mover in the establishment of the Old Time Trail Drivers' Association, once remarked to Dobie that no stretch of the trail in Texas fitted Andy's geography in this chapter, but he did not question the behavior attributed to the thirst-crazed cattle. In *The Trail Drivers of Texas,* which was compiled and edited by J. Marvin Hunter under Saunders' direction, Andy's story of the dry drive is rewritten and ascribed to Joseph A. Spaugh of Hope, Indiana. The dry drive is said to start in "the alkali country in Central Texas" from a "small chain of lakes"—which is vaguer than Andy's geography but just as faulty. It seems that J. Marvin slipped his little joke by George.

After the Circle Dots quit the North Platte in Wyoming there is another dry drive over more plausible terrain. Flood has profited by his experience at the Indian Lakes and plans to have the herd sleep in the middle of the day and travel at night. In the high country the days are cool, and luckily there is a full moon. The eighty-mile dry stretch is traversed without mishap.

On the way to the Blackfoot Agency the Circle Dots go near or through three towns, Dodge City, Ogallala, and Frenchman's Ford, and Andy devotes a chapter to what happens in each one. A few men at a time hold the herd, and the others are permitted to go into town. They visit barber shops, clothing stores, saloons, gambling houses, and dance halls. Perhaps visits to these towns should be considered part of the hazards of trail driving, for the cowboy had to have his holiday, which carried with it the possibility of conflict and shooting scrapes. When the boys are ready to go in to Dodge, old McNulta, a friend of Lovell's who is waiting for two of his herds, advises them to leave their six-shooters at the first place they stop, whether hotel, livery stable, or store. (In the late 1870's a rancher named McNulty owned the Turkey Track outfit in the Texas Panhandle and visited Dodge on business.) He tells them that the peace officers will not permit them to ride into a saloon or shoot out the lights. They take his advice, but when Quince Forrest lets out a Comanche yell while dancing and the bouncer, wearing an officer's star, threatens to throw him out, it does not take them long to repossess their guns and return to the dance hall. They go in a few at a time. Quince confronts the bouncer and they fire without wasting words; the bouncer goes down and the boys shoot out the lights. They rush to their horses, held by Honeyman at the rear; they ride through the town and exchange shots with the officers, no one being hit. The work band has become a war band.

Ogallala has the same amusements to offer as Dodge, and it is more lenient with cowboys at play. "The officers of Ogallala were a different crowd from what we had encountered at Dodge, and everything went." They make no objection when a horse race is run through the main street with Nat Straw and Jim Flood as judges. It is in Ogallala that Straw arranges the fiddling match and the Rebel has his streak of luck at monte. John Officer, playing the Rebel's luck with the Rebel's money, lays his six-shooter across the bet when he suspects the dealer of cheating, but the dealer declines to show the remaining cards and Officer takes the money. In Ogallala the boys visit the Dew-Drop-In dance hall while making the rounds. Ogallala has treated them pretty well, though they agree when leaving that it is a tough place.

Three chapters later they are in Frenchman's Ford on the Yellowstone, a frontier town of Andy's invention. There are two tents for every building. Bull trains are bringing in freight from navigable points on the Missouri and hauling out bales of buffalo hides. "The men were fine types of the pioneer—buffalo hunters, freighters, and other plainsmen, though hardly as picturesque in figure and costume as a modern artist would paint them." Northern Indians in gaudy blankets walk about, and many tongues can be heard in the streets. This is different from the cow towns of Kansas and Nebraska. On the wall of a saloon where the boys are having a drink Jim Flood sees a picture of Grant and jokingly proposes to the Rebel that they drink to him. The Rebel declines with good humor, but when a stranger wearing his hair long and dressed in beaded buckskin proposes the same toast to the Rebel, who has accepted his invitation to have a drink, the Rebel responds by throwing his whiskey in the face of the "picturesque gentleman." Nothing more happens at this time. In another saloon the long-haired man mounts the bar theatrically and fires at the Texans with two guns, but is coolly shot off his stage by the Rebel. Only one of the long-haired man's three friends gets off a shot before being disarmed by John Officer. After it is all over Billy Honeyman says, "If that horse thief had not relied on pot shooting, and had been modest and only used one gun, he might have hurt some of you fellows." This story shows Andy's contempt for the kind of man who makes himself picturesque and fancies himself as a bad man. The Rebel disappears and rejoins the outfit a few days later. Quince Forrest used the same tactics after his shooting scrape in Dodge.

The Circle Dots stampede three times, first on the Atascosa, next below the Wichita, and last on the North Platte. A stampede is one of the most exciting and dangerous events that can happen on the trail. Before the first stampede Andy explains that if cattle are watered and bedded down properly they are not likely to run, but any unexpected or unfamiliar sound or scent is capable of spreading fear instantly in the herd and bringing them to their feet. One night on the Atascosa Officer's horse steps into a hole and falls—the cattle are off. They split into groups and scatter; this happens at about one or two in the morning and it takes the men until sundown the next day to put the herd back together. Below the Wichita a herd ahead of the Circle Dots, stampeded one night by a few curious buffalo, doubles back on the trail and frightens the Circle Dots, who in turn run into another herd. Three herds are mixed and have to be separated. On the North Platte the cattle are uneasy because they have not been well watered and are reluctant to bed down. Something sets them off, but the leaders are turned to the right by the time they have run a mile and the herd is thrown into a mill, that is, made to run in an unbroken circle. Riders force their way through the mill and break it up after an hour of effort. It begins to rain. Bob Blades vows in disgust, "If I ever get home again, you all can go up the trail that want to, but here's one chicken that won't. There isn't a cowman in Texas who has money enough to hire me again."

Most of the obstacles to the success of the drive arise from natural causes such as dry stretches, flooded streams, miry crossings, and stampedes, but there is some delaying or opposing action on the part of human beings. As the herd approaches the Colorado River, four men ride up from the west and represent themselves as trail cutters, men authorized by local cowmen to cut out range cattle that have joined through herds. Jim Flood has been warned by Nat Straw, who suspects that rustlers have stampeded his cattle the night before. Flood meets the pretended cutters courteously and tells them he would like to go ahead and put his herd across the Colorado in the warmest part of the day. On the other side he asks to see their inspection papers; they can show none, and so he will not let them ride into the cattle and cut out every animal not bearing the Circle Dot. He offers to cut out their own brand, which they tell him is the Window Sash, a suspicious brand because it can be readily produced by altering other brands. After some blustering the four leave with three Window Sash cattle, the leader threatening to return later with more men. Not far up the trail Flood is approached by two

riders, who turn out to be Rangers scouting out of a camp north of the Colorado crossing. It has already been reported to Austin from Abilene that rustlers are preying on through herds in the vicinity. The rustlers return twenty-two strong and are taken by the detachment of Rangers under Corporal Joe Hames, who produces and consults the Black Book of men wanted. He and his boys are well pleased with their catch, which will mean a distribution of reward money.

Indians cause some delay in the Territory. A few days above Doan's Crossing on the Red River the herd is stopped by a Comanche chief and a band of mounted bucks. He demands ten beeves as a fee for passing through his land. After a parley of several hours Flood gives the Indians three, a lame steer and two stray cows. It is learned from two Spanish-speaking Apaches who have acted as interpreters that ahead on the trail there is a big summer encampment of Comanches and Kiowas. Flood decides to strike west and leave the trail, which here runs between the Salt and the North Forks of the Red River. Falling weather dampens the boy's spirits and they begin to think they are as good as lost. The horses scatter badly one night and have to be trailed and recovered the next day. Frightened by some buffalo bulls at another time, they stampede and cause the cattle to run a short mile. For a week afterward the horses are skittish, and more rain falls. The boys are gloomy and almost lose confidence in their foreman, and one even asks him if he knows where he is. On the next afternoon Flood gives orders to point a little east of north, and the gloom begins to lessen. They come back into the trail and meet Nat Straw, scouting ahead of his herd. He tells them he gave the Indians at the big encampment ten strays but won them all back on a horse race, with four ponies besides.

On the Republican River near the Kansas-Nebraska line the operators of a deadfall win the boys' money, their watches and pistols, and two saddles in a crooked horse race. An old man, who pretends to be looking for a homestead, lets Joe Stallings, who is acting as foreman in Flood's absence, talk him into a match between a mare that he is driving in harness and the fastest horse in the remuda. Stallings has secretly matched the two while the old man was spending the night with the outfit, and the boys think they have a sure thing. With a publicly made loan from the generous keeper of a canvas saloon and gambling joint on the Republican, the old man covers the boys' money, and then they put up their watches and pistols. Stallings and Quarternight bet their saddles, and others are getting ready to, but they are prevented by Flood, who has returned to the herd with a man who has just agreed to buy the remuda after delivery of the cattle. At dusk the race is run and the mare wins easily. McCann and the Rebel, who have stayed with the herd, have a good laugh when they see Stallings and Quarternight returning bareback. Men without saddles and pistols, which are used for turning stampeding cattle and also signaling, would be seriously hampered in their work. To redeem the tools of their trade the humbled losers have to borrow from McCann, Priest, Flood, and the buyer of the horses. When Nat Straw overtakes Flood's outfit below Ogallala, he tells them of seeing old "Says I" Littlefield and hearing how he has skinned them by substituting an identical but fast mare.

The *Log*'s twelve campfire tales are fitted perfectly into place. They are divided among eight chapters spread from III to XXII and no more than two are told in the same chapter. "The campfire is to all outdoor life what the evening fireside is to domestic life," says Andy. "After the labors of the day are over, the men gather around the fire, and the social hour of the day is spent in yarning." Not every campfire brings forth tales; the mood has to be right and some happening of the day or something just said has to serve as a prompter. A letter that Billy Honeyman picks up in Mason mentions that a girl some of the boys have sparked has recently married; this sets off a conversation about love, and Fox Quarternight and Billy Honeyman each tell stories in which they are romantically involved. One night when the boys are gloomy John Officer tells about a similar time in the J. H. camp in the Cherokee Strip (referred to as the "J+H" camp in *Cattle Brands*). It is Christmas, but everyone is glum. Along comes a man "riding the chuck line" who admits that he knows how to make bear sign—doughnuts. Miller, the foreman, welcomes the bear sign artist and keeps him at work for three days until he finally fills a tub, which has been kept low by men from other outfits as well as the J. H. boys. Joe Stallings tells a very amusing story in which a horse that he and his brothers have secretly taught to race runs away with his father at a funeral. He tells also about how queer his relatives in Tennessee seem to him when he goes there for a visit. This story Andy revised slightly from one told by Ace in "Corporal Segundo," his first piece of writing. While the campfire tales do not advance the plot of the *Log*, they enrich the book and their omission would be a serious loss.

Expression in the *Log* is familiar and natural, in both the parts where Tom Quirk or Andy is writing and the parts where the boys are talking. Dialogue and campfire tales have the genuine ring of spoken language without the disregard for grammar and the love of the outlandish that has come to be thought of as typical of Western fiction. There are some grammatical errors and some doubtful constructions, as always when people speak, but they are not unduly prominent. The boys sometimes use syntactically incomplete or unusual sentences—perhaps it would be better to say sentences not often seen in print but frequently heard. They like slang and colorful idioms and also figures and comparisons drawn from what is near them, particularly their occupation. The flavor of their talk can be shown in a few examples. When Quince Forrest interrupts John Officer's story about the bear sign artist, Officer says, "Will you kindly hobble your lip; I have the floor at present." Fox Quarternight is telling about being taken into the parlor of a well-to-do family that has invited him to supper: "Say, fellows, it was a little the nicest thing that ever I went against. Carpet that made you think you were going to bog down every step, springy like marsh land, and I was glad I came." Nat Straw is expressing his thanks to Flood's outfit for holding some of his stampeded cattle, lending him and two men fresh horses, and feeding them at the wagon: "But you see there's nothing like being lucky and having good neighbors—cattle caught, fresh horses,

and a warm breakfast all waiting for you." Joe Stallings passes judgment on a promising racing filly made much of in Tennessee: "And that same colt, you couldn't cut a lame cow out of the shade of a tree on her."

In the parts where Andy (or Tom Quirk) is the narrator the prose belongs to the tradition of the English plain style deriving from the King James Bible and *Pilgrim's Progress* and associated with Defoe. It is straightforward, unhurried, and circumstantial; well-formed, rhythmical sentences advance the story in a steady and orderly way. Never losing the main thread, Andy skilfully introduces needful exposition and provides the reader with relevant or amusing sidelights.

In *The Log of a Cowboy* Andy succeeded in writing fiction "as convincingly as fact." He had driven cattle only once, most of his experience having been with horses. He never traveled the old Western Trail, though he must have gone over at least part of the cutoff leading from the Chisholm Trail to Dodge City, and he was never farther north than Dodge on the trail, never in Nebraska, Wyoming, or Montana in trail driving days; but the *Log* was thought to be autobiography by Charlie Russell, who had punched cattle in the Judith Basin, which the Circle Dots crossed, and later lived in Great Falls, near the end of the Circle Dot's route. "Andy Adams, who wrote *The Log of a Cowboy* (the best trail story I ever read), came with a herd from Texas to Badger Creek Agency, Montana, which is not far from the Canadian line—70 miles to be exact," Charlie said in 1924.

Again and again the *Log* has been read as autobiography or chronicle, but it is actually fiction. Andy got most of his geography from maps and invented some himself; his incidents and sequences came from his own experiences and those of cowmen whose talk he had heard or whom he had drawn out, and also from his imagination. No historical narrative of the trail contains such a variety or number of events. Andy gave his material "fictional treatment," selecting, arranging, and heightening. The form and expression of the book are his. The *Log* is no mere day-to-day recording of events as they happen to fall out; progression through time and space is an important formative determinant, but this is contributory to the carrying out of the set task, which constitutes the plot. From beginning to end the *Log* is an artistically controlled whole; its organization, grounded on the reality of the life represented, permits the inclusion of collateral tales which add to the book's richness.

The *Log* owes its position as the classic of the cattle country not only to its fidelity of representation but to its foundation on the working of cattle, specifically, a drive. Without the drive there would be no plot and no book. This contrasts strongly with *The Virginian,* which preceded the *Log* by a year and which does not significantly involve cattle or ranching. The plot turns on the relationship between the Virginian, who has become a westerner, and Molly Wood, an easterner who comes to Wyoming to teach school. Before her appearance he is emphatically established as a hero possessing handsomeness, strength, and cleverness. The obstructions to their union are their differences in education and social status and their sense of values, one typical of the East and the other of the West. Before they can be united the Virginian has to read a series of books selected by Molly and rise from cowhand to foreman with promise of further improvement in status, and she has to understand and accept the western attitude toward lynching rustlers and defending oneself in a man-to-man gunfight. A hero-villain relationship which exists from the outset between the Virginian and Trampas gradually develops into a potential divisive force between the Virginian and Molly. She nurses him back to health from wounds inflicted by Indians and becomes engaged to him, but she is greatly troubled when the Virginian takes part in the lynching of two cattle rustlers under the leadership of Trampas, one of them (Steve) having been the Virginian's closest friend. She is quieted by Judge Henry, the Virginian's employer, who has sent him on this mission and who explains why lynching is right and necessary at this time in Wyoming. When the Virginian takes Molly into town to marry her, Trampas turns up and gives him until sundown to get out; Molly urges him to go and when he refuses tells him all is over between them. Now comes the "walkdown"—the approach of the duelists and the blaze of guns on the main street. The Virginian returns to Molly and tells her he has killed Trampas, whereupon she exclaims, "Oh, thank God!" and throws herself into his arms. Thus the Virginian's principal relationship with Molly and his secondary one with Trampas have both achieved finality through gunfire; he has won his beloved and killed his enemy in the same violent action.

Charlie Russell illustrated *The Virginian* (not the first edi-

Adams with the daughter of a friend, in 1934.

tion) and presumably read it, but there was no danger of his mistaking it for a true narrative. In 1924 Andy said, "In a popular book like *The Virginian* the reader never catches a glimpse of the cattle. It is like a lord without lands or a master without slaves." Other and more damaging criticism can be lodged against this novel, which has set the pattern for a long line of imitators.

The first reviewer of the *Log,* Stephenson Browne of Boston, did not interpret it as a novel. In the *New York Times Saturday Review* for May 16, 1903, he said, "The book contains the raw material of a narrative which in Mr. Kipling's hands would be the land complement of *Captains Courageous,* and even as it stands need fear comparison with no other record of labor requiring combined skill and bravery." According to this view, the material of the Log might have been given form as a novel but was not; as it is, the book is a record of labor which compares well with other books of its kind. After commending the campfire tales and narrative style—"often many consecutive pages are written with perfect art"—Browne concluded, "Merely as a record of an extinct phase of Western life the book is valuable, but as a means of amusement it should become a classic such as *Two Years Before the Mast.*" This statement placed the *Log* in the same literary class as *Two Years Before the Mast,* that is, autobiographical-historical narrative which performs the double function of recording reality and amusing its readers. Besides assigning Andy's book to the same genre as Dana's, Browne anticipated that the *Log* might attain an equally high rank.

The *Log* was generally received and praised as a faithful depiction of the life of cowboys on the trail and of trail driving days instead of as a work of fiction. An anonymous reviewer in the *Boston Evening Transcript* for May 20, 1903, thought that the book was "evidently an accurately kept record of the daily doings" of Texas cowboys on the trail. The campfire tales and other incidental stories, he said, "do not belong in a properly written log," though he welcomed them as the best part of the narrative. He seemed to enjoy the gunfighting, which he exaggerated, but he did not fail to praise Andy's fidelity to the times: "Mr. Adams . . . took a prominent part in all the doings of his party and it is clear that he has written a picture of cowboy life that is as faithful as it is thrilling."

Andy seemed to be a kind of historian of a recently passed epoch, and he awakened nostalgic reminiscence. A westerner who had become a leading member of the Massachusetts bar was thus quoted in the *Boston Evening Transcript* for May 27, 1903:

> The book deals with a period of history with which I was intimately associated, having spent twenty years of my life on the plains amidst the scenes and circumstances so faithfully described by the author. Most of the places mentioned by him I know well, and many of them I visited during the year mentioned by him. The book is well written, has the true flavor, and on the whole is the best description of that portion of the West I have seen. It is the product of a "thoroughbred" and carries me back to scenes and circumstances I am glad to have thus recalled.

An English reviewer who had been in the American West said, "This book bears about it all the marks of being what is called a document—a record of actual experience, rather than a work of imagination." After a brief summary of the story he continued:

> The long journey was full of adventure, which is set forth in crisp, straightforward style, and forms very interesting reading. But the book is more than interesting and amusing; it is a compact and truthful picture of an important phase of American life, which can no longer be watched, for the reason that all the essential conditions have changed during the last twenty years. The reviewer has known many cowboys of the period dealt with in this book, and can vouch for the fidelity of their presentation here.

The reviewer for the *Denver Republican,* which devoted most of a whole page to the *Log,* declared that Andy

> has gone back to the early days of the cattle trail, and in his *The Log of a Cowboy* has given a picture of the old Western life that makes *The Virginian* seem colorless in comparison. There isn't any fiction in *The Log of a Cowboy.* There is no "love interest" and one will look in vain for any smart talk of the *Dolly Dialogue* order. The author didn't set out to write a "best selling novel," but simply to set down some of his own experiences in the days when herds of thousands of head of cattle were driven across country, and when every cowpuncher who went with such a herd did not know whether the day was to end in a comedy or a tragedy.

Andy succeeded so well in writing fiction "as convincingly as fact" that he caused his novel to be placed outside its proper literary category. Like the contemporary reviewers, most later commentators on the *Log* have seen it as a species of history and have dealt with it accordingly. Andy was proud of his reputation for having been true to the West, but he took offense when Emerson Hough referred to his work in 1923 as "quasi fiction of the trail days." He protested to Walter Prescott Webb that he had tried to make his books "fiction, pure and simple.""

Barbara Quissel   (essay date 1972)

SOURCE: "Andy Adams and the Real West," in *Western American Literature,* Vol. VII, No. 3, Fall 1972, pp. 211-19.

[*In the following essay, Quissel comments on Adams's treatment of the American West in* Log of a Cowboy.]

Andy Adams' *The Log of a Cowboy* ranks as an established classic of Western American literature because it is a chronicle of the cattle drive days. Indeed Adams' fictional realism is more often praised for its authenticity than its plausibility. The adjectives of praise for the *Log* emphasize its historical recording of events: the book is "genuine," "truthful," "accurate," "authentic." This is the usual assessment of Adams' writing from 1903 when the *Log* was published. Emerson Hough, who read the novel in manuscript, stated that "Andy Adams is the real thing, and the first time the real thing has appeared in print."

Forty years later in *Guide to the Life and Literature of the Old Southwest,* J. Frank Dobie asserted,

> If all other books on trail-driving were destroyed, a reader could still get a just and authentic conception of trail men, trail work, range cattle, cow horses, and the cow country in general from the *Log of a Cowboy.*

On the back cover of the recent paperback edition of the *Log,* Dobie's statement is printed with others which advertise the novel as "the work of a realist."

In the few statements of literary tenets that Adams made, he emphasized the same idea of accuracy and authenticity. Adams was particularly concerned with describing the real Western life of cowboys rather than the romanticized view of popular fiction. In his 1905 essay **"The American Cowboy"** Adams tries to correct the view of the cowboy's life which pictured him roping cattle whenever he was not romancing the dark-eyed heroines. Adams asserts that the cowboy did not spend his entire life herding cattle but instead worked at a variety of tasks: treating cattle for blowflies, building corrals, repairing pumps, fighting forest fires, and only occasionally rounding up and separating different herds of cattle. Adams concludes:

> I dare say my boy readers have been disappointed in this all too brief article concerning the life and work of the American cowboy. Whence came the old, old stories of the cowboy's romance, I know not . . . no harder life is lived by any working man. And that I know whereof I speak, rest assured, for I have been myself a cowboy.

To Adams a first-hand, accurate knowledge of Western life was the most important qualification for the writer. In another essay **"Western Interpreters"** Adams emphasizes that it is an authoritative knowledge of the West which separates the pulp fiction from the true works of art. As an example of a great artist of the West, Adams describes the paintings of Charles Russell, praising him for his accurate knowledge of Montana scenes. Here Adams also specifies the proper techniques for the western artist: recording an infinity of details as vividly and honestly as possible. For Adams the novelist is primarily a chronicler or historian who closely details the facts, what he terms "transcripts of life."

However, a literary theory that claims to transcribe life by putting down as many accurate details as possible neglects the ordering or structuring of those details. Unlike the historians, the novelist creates the events; and therefore, all details must justify themselves within the fictional context, proving their validity in relation to the characters and conflicts of the work. The real thing in Jamesian terms is the plausible. When Adams defines his brand of realism in terms of authenticity and first-hand knowledge, he restricts his fiction to an unimaginative, "tell it like it is" formula. With such an approach to a novelist's materials, the successive tellings become tedious.

Adams' writing career dramatically illustrates the failure of his kind of restricted realism. The only successful work, *The Log of a Cowboy* (1903), was the first novel Adams wrote. He retold the trail drive experiences in the subsequent novels, **The Outlet** (1905), **Reed Anthony, Cowman** (1907), and **Wells Brothers** (1911), but these novels are boring and now unread. Adams' novels and especially his unpublished manuscripts indicate that after the publication of the *Log,* he was modifying his techniques and studying the important contemporary models for writing about the West. He was aware of the popularity and success of Wister's *The Virginian* and London's *Call of the Wild.* But in trying to adapt the pattern of the sentimental and then the naturalistic novel to his view of the West, Adams showed himself to be a greenhorn novelist.

In the essay **"Western Interpreters"** Adams discusses *The Virginian.* Although Adams condemns most other Western romances for their inaccurate view of a cowboy's life, he moderates his view of Wister's novel. He calls it a "readable book" and describes it as

> originally a series of short stories, it was finally unified with a love thread; and a number of incidents, delightfully in their way, complete the picture. Still, the story might have been more convincing to some readers if the author had given one glimpse of his hero in connection with his occupation.

Here Adams acknowledges the appeal that the love story has for the reader and modifies the formula by adding scenes of the cowboy at work. Adams tried this combination of sentimental romance and wild-eyed Texas cows in his second novel, *A Texas Matchmaker* (1904). The result is a divided novel with some romantic intrigues and some mundane ranch work. Yet Adams does change the formula somewhat: there is no heroine, no Molly Wood or Tasie Lockhart, as a main character but instead the two main characters are men, the matchmaker Uncle Lovelace and the young cowhand Tom Quirk. Furthermore, the novel does not end with a happy marriage but with Tom's being jilted.

After Adams' uneasy compromise with the demands of popular fiction in this novel, he left out the love story in the other three novels that he published. The opinion of Reed Anthony at the beginning of his fictional autobiography certainly speaks for Adams' views:

> At my time of life, now nearing my allotted span, I have little sympathy with the mass of fiction which exploits the world-old passion. In no sense of the word am I a well-read man, yet I am conscious of the fact that during my younger days the love story interested me; but when compared with the real thing, the transcript is usually a poor one.

Although in these novels Adams rejects the sentimental romance as unreal, that is, untrue to human experience, he never abandoned the love interest.

Many of the stories in his unpublished manuscripts indicate that he was trying to write a saleable Western fiction by exploiting *The Virginian* formula. In his unpublished plays about the Texas Rangers, **Barb Wire** (1907), **Graybeal's Guest** (1914), and **The Ransom of John Ringgold** (1921?), there is a beautiful young heroine who is engaged to or marries one of the Rangers by the end of the play.

Each of these plays deals with the fencing of the open range in Texas and the range war conflicts; yet the focus is not on an authentic drama of Rangers establishing justice but on the sentimental love drama. The important question is "Will the heroine marry her true love?" That Adams was writing a typical sentimental story can be illustrated by the stage instructions for the final scene of one of the plays: "The dominant idea should be that above the ashes of conflict, love endures, triumphant even over the grave."

Perhaps these sentimental plays as well as the number of manuscript short stories that are copies of the popular cliches can be dismissed as hack work to earn money from the audience that made *The Virginian* and its magazine copies so successful. However, the unpublished manuscripts indicate that Adams was searching for new subject matter to replace the cattle drive experiences as well as new writing techniques. The impulse to accurately relate the cowboy's life that Adams began writing with became an increasingly ambiguous, unsuccessful literary tenet. In the novels after the *Log* Adams added more details about the cattle business: including the trail drive in accounts which traced the beginning of the open range era through its prosperous years and eventual decline; detailing the buying and selling of cattle, cattle lands, and stocks; describing the accumulation of large herds of cattle and the maintenance of large ranches. And yet this infinity of detail did not produce another novel as successful as the *Log.*

Many of the manuscripts written after 1910 indicate that Adams was studying naturalistic novels. Certainly this brand of realism would be interesting to Adams in his desire to escape from the sentimental novel and yet write a realistic account of the West that readers would accept.

Adams adopts the themes of naturalism: one brief preface, for example, states that the story illustrates the first law of nature—self-defense and the protection of one's property. Another story is entitled **"Nature in the Raw."** Noticeable, too, is the vocabulary of naturalism—"instinct," "savagery of animal life," "call of kind to kind," "survival of the fittest." The longest of the unpublished manuscripts is **Barb Wire,** the same story first written as a play and then rewritten as a novel. In the preface to the novel Adams applies the theme survival of the fittest to the conflict between the independent cowman and the cattle companies: ". . . and in the outcome the little cowman awoke to the fact that during the dark days of his struggle for existence conditions, Fate, or what not, had stacked the cards on him." The title refers to the age of barb wire which is replacing the days of the open range. However, in the final outcome of events, the small cowman wins; the Ranger, not the wealthy and powerful supervisor of the cattle company, marries the young heroine; and in the final scene the sun is shining over the Sweetwater River. The cattle company with its legal and financial strength should be victorious in a naturalistic struggle, but Adams insists on a moral victory. It is the old-time rancher who wins; he is the good man who condemns the cattle companies with this philosophy:

> I never saw human greed before. Human hatred, as it exists today, in range affairs, staggers belief.

Ask me about pioneer days and I'll give a correct answer. . . . We were a peaceful pastoral people until this invasion of outside capital. Our herds sustained us, supplied our few wants, and we lived at peace with our neighbors.

The old rancher represents the days of the open range, the 1880's, and in Adams' mind these were the days of an innocent, intrinsically good age when everyone was at peace. Greed and with it the disruptive conflicts of the range wars has been introduced by the encroaching civilization, in this instance, the organized cattle companies primarily financed by Easterners. Throughout the novel Adams describes the struggle with naturalistic language: "Pastoral interests had clashed in a grapple, the outcome of which was in solution." "Primal instincts had forged to the front." And yet in this struggle Adams does not follow the historical facts which could be interpreted with a survival of the fittest theme. He does not show the decline of the rancher who owned little land and grazed his herds on free, open range. In both the novel and play versions of **Barb Wire** the old pioneer rancher is rescued from the new and more powerful age by the Texas Rangers.

The same contrast between naturalistic rhetoric and primitivistic assumptions is evident in Adams' essay **"The Cattle on a Thousand Hills."** A combination of mythology, anecdote, and commentary, this essay is the only statement by Adams in which he discusses the cattle industry from a philosophical rather than an historical point of view. This essay is important for evaluating all of Adams' fiction because here he states his assumptions about the West, primitivistic assumptions that contradict the basic theories of naturalism and modify any theories of realism which value authenticity.

In the essay Adams asks one of the recurring questions in Western American literature: "Why should the cowboy appeal to and interest those outside his sphere in life?" Adams' answer, though stated in naturalistic phrases, describes the cowboy as a man of primitive goodness and natural strength and virtue:

> The cowboy is our nearest approach to the primal man, the incarnation of the herdsman of old, or the shepherd on the plains of Bethlehem. . . . the range man of the West, rough, barbarous and strong, will figure in our literature, and his life will awaken many heartthrobs, for by heredity, we are all barbarians.

Adams defines the "primal man" and the "barbarian" as possessing innate goodness and innocence, not innate savagery. Adams defines the nature of the cowboy and the characteristics of his life on the open range in primitivistic not naturalistic terms. Thus the pastoral life, the life close to nature, develops a simple, virtuous character:

> Cattle are the embodiment of innocence and strength. Man is a creature of environment, absorbing into his nature alike from the earth, air, the animals and objects that surround his daily life. The effect of pastoral life on a people, grounding them in simple ways and strengthening the moral fibers of their natures, if given expression, would fill a volume.

Adams thinks that along with the developing cattle industry in Texas there has been a development in the innate character of the men: the simple life on the range has produced moral and physical giants. For the beginnings of this evolutionary development, Adams refers to the Old Testament, not to the *Origin of Species* or the *Descent of Man*. The cattlemen of Texas are children of Abraham; the cattle drives the most recent form of the ancient occupation of herding cattle. The West to Adams is "the climax of all pastoral days from 'In the beginning' to the present hours."

With such primitivistic assumptions Adams' definition of the real west, the West as he knew it in the 1880's, is a Golden Age. It is not an age of conflict, struggle, or competition but rather an age of peace, happiness, and plenty. In the novel **Reed Anthony** the old rancher who has narrated his life as a cattleman concludes: "My lot was cast with the palmy days of the golden West, with its indefinable charm, now past and gone and never to return." It is the days of the free and uncomplicated life of a cowhand that Adams celebrates.

In **The Log of a Cowboy** Adams most successfully recreates these days, for in the **Log** Adams has chosen the literary form consistent with his philosophical view of the West. The **Log** is an American pastoral. The young narrator of the novel lives the happy, carefree life of the cattle drive, wandering across the open range unrestricted by the rules and regulations or frustrations of the established culture of the East. Adams conveys his feeling of the unspoiled newness of the West through the point of view of young Tom Quirk who is experiencing the trail drive for the first time. Tom leaves behind the monotonous life on the farm for the new lands in the West. In the European pastoral tradition the writer escapes from a world that is too civilized and complex to an imaginary Arcadia, but often in American thought that land was an actuality in the Western frontier. In the **Log** Tom Quirk travels West to escape the drudgery of the farm and family life, but more important, he leaves behind the complex problems of his era: the recent agonies of the Civil War and the difficulties of reconstructing the established society. Tom fulfills that important desire to avoid the press of civilization that has always made pastoral literature so satisfying. Tom acts on that desire as voiced by Huck Finn—to light out for the Territory.

The life that Tom finds on the open range is a simpler, happier, more peaceful one. I am not denying the hardships of the cattle drive that Adams describes—the stampedes, cattle thieves, floods, lack of water, threat of Indians—but these problems do not overwhelm or long frustrate the cowboys. Indeed the dominant impression is of the carefree, joking, yarn-spinning camaraderie of the drive. At least one-third of the chapters end with the peaceful and entertaining campfires. There is a playfulness in the practical jokes, poker games, and horse races. This playfulness is echoed by the humorous vernacular speech, remarks such as the cook's statement: "Good whiskey and bad women will be the ruin of you varmits yet."

Adams maintains the pastoral atmosphere throughout the **Log** because the young Tom never becomes disillusioned.

He responds to the hard work with enthusiasm and to the joking and yarn-spinning with delight. Potentially the most perplexing encounter is the confrontation with death in the drowning of a cowhand. The death, sight of the body, and the funeral depress Tom, but he travels on, indeed travels away from the crisis. He remains the anxiety-free, young innocent whose simple character responds to the harmonies of nature:

> The unfortunate accident at the ford had depressed our feelings to such an extent that there was an entire absence of hilarity. . . . The herd trailed out like an immense serpent, and was guided and controlled by our men as if by mutes. Long before the noon hour, we passed out of sight of Forty Islands, and in the next few days, with the change of scene, the gloom gradually lifted. We were bearing almost due north, and passing through a delightful country.

Nor do questions of justice cause Tom any troublesome introspection. In the shooting incident between the Rebel and the frontier gambler, both men act quite belligerently. Yet after the killing when Rebel returns to camp, Tom along with the other men welcomes him as a hero. To Tom, the gambler and his friends acted as typical representatives of the decidedly evil cowtowns; whereas Rebel was simply defending his honor. Implicit in Tom's reactions is the contrast between the virtuous country life and the perfidious city life.

Adams concludes the novel with the celebration after the cattle have been delivered. As in the usual pastoral, song and happiness prevail: in this case, it is piano music in the bar and free drinks and cigars.

In the *Log* nothing intrudes on this Golden Age. The experience as presented through Tom's narration is immediate and vivid. In Adams' other novels, however, the simple life of the cowboy is complicated by the intrusion of the larger world of economics and politics. The bankers, lawyers, stock brokers and Washington politicians have invaded the Western garden, destroying the peaceful, self-sustaining way of life. The tone of the novels changes noticeably, as do the narrators—from the zestful anticipation of Tom to the nostalgic reminiscences of the old-timers. Having once created the days when the West was unspoiled and the man was young and free, Adams searched for other approaches to his Western materials. Introducing the same character Tom Quirk to the world of women and romance, in the novel *A Texas Matchmaker,* only exposed the wanderer to one of the primary restraints of civilization. The sentimental heroine, for all her frailty, certainly was demanding and tenacious—she usually got her man. Whereas in the *Log,* the campfire anecdotes about sweethearts are told by men who escaped. When Adams adapted the popular literary models of his day, the sentimental and the naturalistic novels, he contradicted his primitivistic view of the West. The result is badly flawed writing.

The *Log* remains Adams' best work and continues to interest readers with its description of a pastoral West, for it presents the reader with an imaginative retreat to an age unlike his own. This interpretation of the West has often been successful as escape literature, providing the reader with idealized memories. Thus in the *Log,* all the specific and vivid facts of the cattle drive days meet literary not historical demands because they provide the illusion that life in the West was once meaningful, free, exciting and uncomplicated. The appeal of that illusion is concisely expressed by a physician in one of Adams' novels:

> A life in the open, an evening by a camp-fire, a saddle for a pillow—well, I wish I had my life to live over.

The "real West" that Adams recorded in *The Log of a Cowboy* is an ideal life, a golden age.

FURTHER READING

Bibliography

Hudson, Wilson M. "Andy Adams: A Bibliography." In his *Andy Adams: His Life and Writings,* pp. 259-65. Dallas: Southern Methodist University Press, 1964.

> Detailed primary bibliography of Adams's fiction, stories, and dramas.

Criticism

Branch, Douglas. "Andy Adams." In his *The Cowboy and His Interpreters*, pp. 254-70. New York: D. Appleton and Co., 1926.

> Applauds the realism of Adams's works.

Graham, Don. "Old and New Cowboy Classics." *Southwest Review* 65, No. 3 (Summer 1980): 293-303.

> Asserts that Benjamin Capp's novel *The Trail to Oglalla* is superior to Adams's *The Log of a Cowboy.*

Additional information on Adams's life and works can be found in the following source published by Gale Research: *Yesterday's Authors of Books for Children,* Vol. 1.

Lou Andreas-Salomé

1861-1937

(Born Louisa von Salomé) Russian-born German novelist, novella writer, critic, autobiographer, and psychotherapist.

INTRODUCTION

Known primarily for her associations with several prominent figures in European culture, including Friedrich Nietzsche, Rainer Maria Rilke, and Sigmund Freud, Andreas-Salomé produced a diverse body of writings that includes fiction, literary criticism, religious and philosophical works, and psychoanalytic studies. While her works are not often accorded an intrinsic literary value, they nevertheless reflect the growth of a profoundly charismatic, spiritual and independent woman whose sexually liberated, peripatetic life served as a model for subsequent generations of feminists.

Biographical Information

Born in St. Petersburg, Andreas-Salomé was the fourth child of a German general in the service of Russian army. As a child she displayed a precocious capacity as an autodidact, mastering German and French. When she was seventeen Andreas-Salomé began studies with a Dutch preacher named Hendrik Gillot, who tutored her in theology and philosophy. She abruptly severed the relationship in 1880 after becoming apprehensive about sexual tensions between her and Gillot. Unwilling to capitulate her independence, Andreas-Salomé resisted her mother's entreaties to marry and adopted a severe study regimen. After becoming ill from the strain of her endeavors, she began a period of convalescence in Italy, where in 1882 she met Nietzsche and the French philosopher Paul Rée. The two men and Andreas-Salomé decided to live and work together for the purpose of mutually supporting one another's intellectual development. Despite the idealistic pretensions of this arrangement, Nietzsche soon fell in love with Andreas-Salomé, who broke off their relationship after rejecting his proposal of marriage. In 1887, Andreas-Salomé married Friedrich Carl Andreas, a philologist. For reasons unknown to her biographers, Andreas-Salomé's marriage remained unconsummated, and she found sexual fulfillment in relationships with several other men, including Rilke, whom she met in 1897. Fourteen years his senior, Andreas-Salomé became the exalted subject of many of Rilke's poems, and he credited her with his reawakened sensitivity to simple and concrete expression. In 1911 Andreas-Salomé met Freud at the Weimar Congress of the International Psychoanalytic Association. After attending seminars and lectures, and initiating a correspondence and friendship with Freud, Andreas-Salomé began her own psychoanalytic practice. She died in 1937.

Major Works

Andreas-Salomé's first published book, *Im Kampf um Gott* (*A Struggle for God*), is a thinly disguised roman à clef depicting her experiences with Rée and Nietzsche. Andreas-Salomé produced several other novels during her career which drew general praise for their psychological insight, though none are highly regarded by contemporary standards. More notable are her achievements in her essays and monographs, which range from religious and philosophical meditations to theater reviews and literary criticism. Her third book, *Friedrich Nietzsche in seinen Werken*, is a study of Nietzsche's life and work that interprets his philosophical activity as symptomatic of his mental illness. Andreas-Salomé's propensity for psychological analysis is also apparent in her study *Rainer Maria Rilke*, which presents a censorious view of the poet as hysterical and unbalanced. Andreas-Salomé's journal from her years as a student of Freud, *In der Schule bei Freud: Tagebuch eines Jahres* (*The Freud Journal of Lou Andreas-Salomé*), sheds an intriguing light on her contributions to psychoanalysis at a critical stage in its development. In her essays on religion, dependent to a large degree upon Nietzsche's philosophy, Andreas-Salomé argued that God is a human invention, a projection of our need for paternalistic love and protection.

Critical Reception

Most criticism on Andreas-Salomé is largely biographical, focusing in particular on her relationships with Nietzsche, Rilke, and Freud. This fascination with Andreas-Salomé's life, which some critics maintain unjustly neglects her fictional and dramatic works, is sanctioned by the view that her writings are of minor value and that her real genius lay in her ability to enter the world of male intellectual privilege and influence the development of great ideas on her own terms. More recently, some feminist studies have suggested that this approach perpetuates sexist assumptions about intellectual and artistic creativity, and consequently they have focused more substantially on her works.

PRINCIPAL WORKS

Im Kampf um Gott (novel) 1885
Hendrik Ibsens Frauengestalten nach seinen sechs Familien-Dramen (criticism) 1892
  [*Ibsen's Heroines*, 1985]
Friedrich Nietzsche in seinen Werken (criticism) 1894
  [*Nietzsche*, 1988]
Menschenkinder (novellas) 1899
Ma: Ein Portrait (novel) 1901
Die Erotik (essay) 1910
Der Teufel und seine Großmutter (drama) 1922
Rodinka: Russische Erinnerung (novel) 1923
Rainer Maria Rilke (criticism) 1928
Lebensrückblick: Grundriß einiger Lebenser innerungen
  (memoirs) 1951
In der Schule bei Freud: Tagebuch eines Jahres, 1912-1913
  (journal) 1958
  [*The Freud Journal of Lou Andreas-Salomé*, 1964]

CRITICISM

D. L. Hobman (essay date 1960)

SOURCE: "Lou Andreas-Salomé," in *The Hibbert Journal,* Vol. 58, January, 1960, pp. 149-56.

[*In the following essay, Hobman offers an overview of Andreas-Salomé's life.*]

Lou Andreas-Salomé wanted love—the love of man and the love of God—and she took what she wanted. Throughout her whole being and throughout her whole life she was filled with an awareness of God. This Russo-German woman writer, famous on the Continent but scarcely known in England, divided her autobiography [***Lebensrückblick: Grundrißeiniger Lebenser innerungen,***

1951] into separate parts, not in chronological order but according to her experiences; one of the last sections, about Sigmund Freud, is an account of her close friendship with him. She was his disciple, and her intuitive understanding of men and women was further enlarged by his discoveries concerning the psyche, but although she learned much from him, she never learned to explain away religious faith as an illusion. The title of the first and most important chapter in the story of her life is *Experience of God.*

She recalls that as a very small and naughty child, if she was occasionally whipped by her adoring parents, she complained of this treatment to God who invariably agreed heartily with her resentment; indeed it made him so angry that, for the sake of the father and mother whom she dearly loved, she then persuaded him to ignore the whole affair. In a postscript to this book the editor, Ernst Pfeiffer relates that as an old woman shortly before her death in 1937 she said: "No matter what happens to me, I never lose the certainty that in the background there are arms open to receive me."

Her mysticism was bound up with a strongly erotic temperament and a passionate zest for life. She would not accept any form of orthodoxy and already in adolescence gave up the Protestant creed in which she had been brought up. "He who loves God does not need a Church," was a Russian saying which she quoted with approval. She felt that this explained a peculiarity of Russianized Christianity, which gave devotion less to the clerical hierarchy than to individual pilgrims, "in whose footsteps anyone could walk, so that this reverence included something of which each man in secret felt himself capable. Conversely, it could happen to any man to find himself in the position of one condemned—a criminal." This attitude accounted for a lack of discrimination in values, a kind of fatalism, since all things for good or evil lay ultimately in the hands of God.

Lou Andreas-Salomé believed that, in spite of all their superstition, the Russian masses provided a basis of profound primitive strength for the educated classes as well, and that in this passionate inner life the tensions of sexual love were somehow lessened, so that love was accepted with greater natural simplicity in Russia than in more civilized nations. She analyses the Slav attitude as though it were also her own, as no doubt to some extent it was. Although she was of mixed, partly German origin, and spent the greater part of her adult life in Germany, she seems to embody a point of view which belongs to Eastern rather than to Western Europe, where goodness and morality are not necessarily equated. Educated Russian women of the nineteenth century might have been puzzled by the idea of subordinating personal emotion to a generalized code. Famous English-women, on the other hand, were usually moral, not in the accepted sense only, but in their efforts at improving their social surroundings. Their faith in public opinion, and therefore in Parliament, to redress social evils was the result of living in a country with democratic institutions, however imperfect. In Russia any faith in reform was almost inevitably bound up with the desire for revolution, and Lou Andreas-Salomé was neither a political rebel, nor indeed was she politically minded at all. In her life and work she was first and foremost an artist, and her concern was with the individual and not with society. The edifice of religion seemed to her a dreary ruin, cumbering ground which was urgently needed for a more rational development, yet she was no rationalist. She was a primitive impulsive creature, avid for life, awed by its mystery. As a child she comforted herself by talking to God as a friend, and in old age she still depended upon his love.

She sought the reflection of her own feelings in the hearts of her friends. Many years after she had refused Nietzsche's offer of marriage, she published a long book about him, an analysis of his nature through his works, and she was convinced that religious genius permeated all that he had written. According to her, his entire development sprang from his own loss of faith, from his "emotion over the loss of God." He was a split individual who had "achieved health through disease, genuine adoration through illusion, genuine affirmation and enhancement of the self through self-wounding." In the same way, in the poet Rilke, it was the mystic to whom she responded out of the depth of her own nature. She gave him an understanding which bound them together during a passionate friendship of nearly thirty years. He left the manuscript of his *Book of Hours* in her keeping until in 1905 his publisher persuaded him to let it be brought out. After she had sent it back to him, he wrote to her of his longing for her presence, and said that the old prayers were re-echoing within him, "vibrating inwardly down to the very foundations, and echoing outwardly far beyond myself. Echoing to you . . ."

Louisa (Ljola) von Salomé, later always known as Lou, was born in St. Petersburg on February 6th, 1861. Her father, General von Salomé, was of Huguenot descent, whose ancestors had emigrated from Avignon, and after the French Revolution had wandered across Germany to the Baltic Provinces, where he was born. He had been brought to St. Petersburg as a little boy and had there received a military education. He was given a patent of hereditary Russian nobility after he had taken part in putting down the Polish insurrection of 1830. His wife was of mixed Danish and German origin, and at home the family spoke German or sometimes French. This was by no means unusual in the cosmopolitan society of the Russian capital, where foreign languages were much in fashion. The fact that they were Protestant made the General's wife feel herself an emigrant in a Greek-Orthodox land, and she passed on something of this feeling to her children. Her husband, on the other hand, felt deep love for the *narod,* the common people, which found an echo in Lou.

As the sixth child and only girl, she was cherished by her family, so that in after life she said that her instinct led her to seek a brother in every man whom she met. To judge by an early picture she was a beautiful little girl, with boyishly short curly hair, a high forehead, full sensuous lips, and eyes which seemed to be asking a question of the world.

In spite of all the affection by which she was surrounded she seems to have been a curiously lonely child, and some-

thing of a rebel against authority from her earliest years. Like all imaginative children she was much given to making up stories, and in bed at night, with two dolls beside her pillow, she told these stories to God, beginning with an invariable formula: "As thou knowest." Sometimes she told them to her family, but was to discover with a shock that not every audience was favourably impressed. One day, on her return from a walk with a little cousin, she related a dramatic adventure which was supposed to have befallen them both on the way, when to her consternation she saw the other child staring at her, not in admiration, and heard her exclaim: "But you're telling lies!" Her father once brought home for her from a Court ball a fine large cracker, which was said to contain a dress. Lou at once pictured to herself a golden robe, and when it was explained that the gown could only be made of tissue-paper, with perhaps a little tinsel trimming, she refused to pull the cracker at all. As long as it remained intact she could keep her illusion, and that mattered more to the child than reality.

She was devoted to her parents, especially to her father, who liked to fondle her, but their caresses always ceased as soon as her mother—Muschka—came into the room. Sometimes in the summer the latter, who enjoyed seabathing, took her for a drive to the coast. On one such occasion, when she was still very young, she watched her mother in the water through a little window in the bathing-hut, and suddenly cried out eagerly: "Oh, dear Muschka, do drown!"

Laughing, her mother called back: "Why, child, then I should die."

Lou's response to this was a shout of *"Nitschevo!"* (No matter.)

She was once bitten by a favourite dog who, to her great grief, had to be destroyed, because hydrophobia was rampant in the town. Told that a mad dog usually attacked his beloved master before anybody else, she was in anguish lest—having gone mad herself—she might bite him whom she loved above all else on earth. It was only in later life that she realized the full implication of this fear of injuring her father; in childhood she seemed to herself to love both parents equally.

One winter's day, when she was eight years old, walking down the frozen stone steps in front of the house she slipped and fell. An adjutant of the Czar who happened to be passing at the moment rushed to her aid, but himself fell down, and there they both sat on the ice, opposite one another, the handsome young officer laughing, and the little girl gazing at him in silent ecstasy: she was for the first time in love.

Her father died when she was eighteen, and soon afterwards she took the unusual step of leaving the Church officially. He had originally obtained permission from the Czar to found a German Reformed Church in St. Petersburg, yet in spite of this she felt inwardly certain that, unlike her mother, he would have approved the honesty of her action, no matter how much her lack of faith might have grieved him. Her adolescence was unduly tormented and prolonged, until an event occurred which ended her youthful loneliness and changed the future course of her life.

Somebody persuaded her to hear a sermon by a Dutchman, chaplain to the Dutch Embassy and the most famous Protestant preacher in St. Petersburg. He was a man of liberal and unorthodox views, and she immediately recognized in him a kindred spirit, who saw the world as she saw it, and to whom she was linked by invisible bonds. She felt this so strongly that she wrote and asked for an interview; her request was granted and she appears to have been received literally with open arms. Soon she was visiting him regularly, and was being instructed by him in religious history and philosophy. She worked hard under his severe tuition, perhaps too hard, for on one occasion, either because she was over-tired or else because she was emotionally overwrought, he took her on his knee and she lost consciousness in his arms. He was a widower with two children, one of them near her own age, but that did not prevent the adoration which filled her whole being. On the contrary, the very fact that he was so much older and wiser than herself, pastor and teacher, only inflamed her heart the more, as though the profound capacity for love, which had once been devoted to God, was now blended with love for a God-like human being.

The girl was living in a romantic fairy-tale, but the man's affection for her was realistic and practical, and he intended to make her his second wife. He understood the child-like nature of her feelings, and in order not to startle her he did not reveal his intentions at first, no doubt hoping that in time the master-pupil relationship would be transmuted into the more perfect one which he desired. He did not guess that, in an attempt to raise a young girl's dream to the plane of reality, the whole thing would be completely shattered. Lou had adored him as though he were a God, but at the moment when he asked her to marry him the cloak of divinity fell from his shoulders, and he became almost a stranger. The magic cracker was opened, revealing tinsel instead of the golden robe of glory which she had imagined. Much later she made the whole affair the theme of a novel, *Ruth,* in which she recorded this episode in her own life.

The middle-aged man must have suffered a disillusion as great as her own, but he loved her well enough to continue to help her. He persuaded her to study at the University of Zurich, and prepared her for her entrance. She studied there during the winter of 1881-82, and then, on account of her ill-health, her mother came and took her away to Rome. Here, through mutual acquaintances, she met Friedrich Nietzsche, who already had an international reputation. A friend was with him, a young graduate of philosophy, a half-Jew called Paul Rée, and soon the three were inseparable, referring to themselves as the Trinity. Such triangular relationships are proverbially untenable: Nietzsche fell in love with the brilliant girl, but Lou preferred Paul Rée.

She tried to make Nietzsche understand that marriage was against her principles, and sent Rée to him as the bearer of her refusal of his offer. In spite of this he seems to have considered himself engaged to her, and after she had left Rome he strove in his letters to put her against his former

friend. She went to Bayreuth on a short visit to hear Wagner's operas, and there met Nietzsche's sister, Elizabeth, who was insanely jealous of her and made a scandal out of Lou's friendship with a Russian artist who was there at the same time. There were quarrels and recriminations, not improved by the fact that she declared her intention of setting up house together with Rée, as a pair of friends. Madame von Salomé sent for one of her sons to try and dissuade his sister from such a compromising step, but she had made up her mind, and it was not until many years later that she came to understand how deeply she had made her mother suffer by her unconventional behaviour.

Lou and Paul Rée settled in Berlin and remained together for several years, travelling a good deal, and everywhere meeting famous writers and artists. She began to write herself, novels and short stories (her first book was called **The Struggle for God**), and Rée finally decided to take up the study of medicine. For the sake of his work they thought it best to live apart for a time, although she had actually suggested sharing his studies; such a step was unnecessary, he declared, for two people who would never part. While she was living alone in a pension she met a man who came to teach German to some Turkish officers living there. Karl Friedrich Andreas, later Professor of Oriental Languages, was a reserved and melancholy man with an admixture of Malayan and Armenian blood. She does not give any account of his wooing, but merely states that she became engaged to him in May 1887. She insisted that it was to make no difference to her relationship with Paul Rée, and at first both he and Andreas agreed. However, the former soon realized that the situation was impossible, and one evening he came to say goodbye and stayed until it was almost dawn. After he had gone, Lou found a little photograph of her as a child, which he had left behind, wrapped in a piece of paper on which he had written: "Be merciful. Do not try to find me."

Paul Rée subsequently settled in the Engadine as a doctor and devoted himself to the poverty-stricken population. He was killed in a mountain accident.

A month after she became engaged, in June 1887, Lou von Salomé was married to Karl Friedrich Andreas.

They lived at first in Berlin and later in Göttingen, where Professor Andreas taught at the University. They had a literary and artistic circle, and entertained their friends with tea and cake or sandwiches and a glass of wine. Their tastes were simple and they shared a great love of nature and of animals. Lou visited her mother in Russia at intervals, and wrote books and essays and reviews, and in later life, after she had taken up psycho-analysis, she accepted patients for treatment. On the whole, both she and Andreas seem to have found contentment in their marriage, which lasted for many years, although towards the end they became inwardly estranged. Her account of her husband, written after his death, is full of affection.

In 1897, when Lou was thirty-six, a young man of twenty-two was introduced to her at the theatre, whose name was Rainer Maria Rilke. An essay of hers, **"Jesus the Jew,"** had recently appeared in a literary review, and after their meeting he wrote to thank her for having written it. He sent her a poem, and bought roses which, however, he was too shy to present to her, although he wrote that for her all the roses in the world were blossoming. It was the beginning of a relationship and a correspondence which lasted until the end of his life. The letters of this excessively neurotic poet, full of lush outpouring and sentimental yearning, read strangely to English eyes. Lou was his burning bush, he was her slave or her king, but actually he seems in some ways to have been more like her son. He hated his mother, who during his early childhood had dressed him like a little girl and treated him as one. At the age of ten he had been plunged from this hothouse environment into the icy atmosphere of an Austrian military academy, and the gross bullying to which he had there been subjected had caused him inner torment for the rest of his life.

Lou gave him what he most needed—understanding of his morbid and his mystic moods, and a sense of protection and stability, and he came to depend on her more than he ever depended on any of the many other women of whom he was enamoured. E. M. Butler says in her biography, *Rainer Maria Rilke,* that he and Lou were lovers, and that she became pregnant by him; if so, the child must have been stillborn, for she does not refer to it in her own book. Professor Andreas accepted the relationship between his wife and the poet, whatever it may have been. Rilke stayed with them in Berlin, wandering barefoot with Lou in the pinewoods round the town, helping her to chop wood, to cook and wash up. They studied Russian together, and at one time they translated *The Seagull* into German. In 1899 they all three went on a journey to Russia, and the following year the two friends went again, this time without the Professor. They spent several weeks in Moscow, then travelled about the country and ended up in St Petersburg. They visited Tolstoy, but do not appear to have been very warmly welcomed by the sage or his wife.

In 1901 Rilke married the sculptress Klara Westhoff, a pupil of Rodin, but he never took any responsibility, either as husband or later as father of their child. In due course they were separated, and on that occasion Lou took Klara's part, recognizing the cause in the poet's intense egoism. She believed in Rilke's redemptive mission, and thought that God was the object of his art: "in the fulfilment of the task 'God' his humanity and his poetic faculty met: the human being in living and immediate receptivity, the poet in action, to create that which he had received."

At the outbreak of the 1914 War he at first shared the general exaltation, but the frenzy did not last, and Lou thought that he had already "anticipated the suffering of the war by the agonies he had undergone in the realization of what we human beings are" (E. M. Butler). She was not a Pacifist herself, although she felt a general sense of guilt which all must share for the War. Her friendship with Rilke lasted through all the subsequent vicissitudes of his life, and when he lay dying in Switzerland in 1926, by his own wish accounts of his illness were sent to her alone.

Rilke's neurosis was the chief cause of Lou's intense interest in psychology. She attended a psycho-analytic Congress in Weimar in the autumn of 1911, and asked Freud to teach her his technique. He was amused by her request,

for at that time there was not yet any institution for disseminating his principles; nevertheless she persisted, and six months later arrived in Vienna, to work under him, and also to learn from his former colleague, who had broken away from him, Alfred Adler. She very soon gave up attending the latter's lectures, and concentrated entirely on the teachings of Freud. Lou began as his disciple—she ended as his friend. She, who had been a mother-figure to Rilke, found in Freud a father-figure to herself, and in this reversal of rôles she was given a hitherto unknown sense of peace. She rejoiced in his scientific dedication, and the stark honesty of his rationalism, and she loved the man. The last time she was with him, in 1928, when he had already become the victim of a terrible disease, she began to weep bitterly at his sufferings. "Freud did not reply," she wrote, "I only felt his arm around me."

She sent him an essay for his seventy-fifth birthday in the form of an open letter, called **"My Thanks to Freud."** In reply he wrote that hers was the true synthesis of an artist, in which she had transformed the body dissected by the analyst's knife once more into a living organism, and he asked her to have the letter published as a pamphlet under the title, "My Thanks to Psycho-Analysis." She always cherished this letter from him, and had it read aloud to her a few days before her death.

Here in outline is a brief sketch of a remarkable woman. She was a modern intellectual, but she was also gifted with the artist's sensibility to a realm outside the perception of the intellect. As a child she had refused to open a cracker lest its contents should prove a disillusion; as a woman she had no such apprehensions—fearlessly she explored life, and discovered that it held a golden robe.

H. F. Peters (essay date 1962)

SOURCE: *My Sister, My Spouse: A Biography of Lou Andreas-Salomé,* W. W. Norton & Company, Inc., 1962, 320 p.

[*Peters is a German-born American educator and critic. In the following excerpt from his biography of Andreas-Salomé, he offers an account of her love affair with the Austrian poet Rainer Maria Rilke, which left a profound stamp on Rilke's poetry.*]

At the end of April, 1897, Lou went to Munich where she was joined by her friend Frieda von Bülow, who was to give a public lecture on her exploits in Africa. The Bavarian capital was one of the cities Lou liked to visit, although she did not particularly care for what she called the "Munich atmosphere," that peculiar blend of Bavarian patriotism, incense and beer. Most of her Munich friends were non-Bavarians like herself and congregated in Schwabing, the Munich Latin Quarter. Some of them, like Max Halbe and Frank Wedekind, she had met before in Berlin or Paris. In Munich she got to know Count Edward Keyserling, the architect August Endell, who remained a close friend the rest of her life, and the writers Michael Georg Conrad, Ernst von Wolzogen and Jakob Wassermann. The last, a promising writer whose novel *The Jews of Zirndorf* had attracted much attention, introduced Lou to the young and unknown Austrian poet Rainer Maria Rilke.

Rilke, then twenty-two years old, had recently moved to Munich from Prague, where he was born and brought up, ostensibly to carry on his studies at the University. Actually, he was far more interested in his literary career. He wrote poetry, plays, prose tales, book reviews, edited a literary journal and proposed the formation of a "League of truly modern writers." Although shy and retiring by nature he threw himself into a hectic literary activity because he wanted to prove to his skeptical family that he could make a living as a writer. He was a slender youth, gentle rather than robust, and with the chivalrous bearing characteristic of the young Austrian man-about-town. His small, pale face, dominated by deeply set eyes that looked at the world with anxious wonder, was framed by a thin straggling beard and a drooping mustache. In contrast to his full sensuous mouth was his slight, receding chin that sprouted a fuzzy goatee as soft and downy as the feathers on a young duck's head.

This was the young Austrian *littérateur* on the make, still known by his rather effeminate first name of René; and when Lou met him in Wassermann's apartment on May 12, 1897, he was a far cry from the great poet he was to become. A less likely contender for her feminine favors it would be hard to imagine. But Rilke's appearance was misleading. He was by no means the weak-willed youth he seemed. And what he lacked in physical prowess he made up for in an inner intensity that took Lou by surprise. Like most men Rilke was bent on her conquest the moment he met her. He applied himself to that objective with great skill and resourcefulness.

The day following their meeting he wrote her a letter in which he told her that it had not been the first time he had been privileged to spend a "twilight hour" in her company. Several months previously he had come across her essay **"Jesus the Jew"** in the April number of the *Neue Deutsche Rundschau*. It had been a revelation to him, for she had expressed with "the gigantic force of a sacred conviction" what he had been trying to say in a cycle of poems entitled "Visions of Christ." "I felt like one whose great dreams had come true," he told her, for she had said what he had merely dreamed. Her essay and his poetry were as mysteriously related as dreams are to reality. He had wanted to thank her for it but was incapable of doing so in the presence of others. Hence his letter. "For if one owes something very precious to another his gratitude should remain a secret between them." He added that it would give him great pleasure if he could read her some of these poems and closed with the hope that he would meet her the following night in the theatre.

Lou's reaction to the youthful fervor of Rilke's letter was mixed. On the one hand, she could not help feeling flattered by it. It reminded her of her own youthful impetuosity. And although she had long since learned to eschew romantic sentiments, she was still responsive to any spontaneous expression of feeling. The unbashful sentimentality of Rilke's letter made her smile. As she scrutinized his handwriting it dawned on her that he was the author of some mystifying anonymous letters she had received previously with poems enclosed. So Rilke was the young poet who had worshiped her from afar.

Lou would have been even more amused if she had known that Rilke had sent her poems because he was desperately eager to establish connections with prominent people. Having just embarked on a literary career he was anxious to be accepted by those who had made a success of it. He needed their encouragement both for reasons of self-assurance and because he wanted to impress his family with the illustrious names of his friends. Thus soon afterward he proudly informed his mother—herself an eager reader of the *Almanach de Gotha*—that he had made the acquaintance of the "famous Lou Andreas-Salomé" and her friend the African explorer Frieda von Bülow, "two magnificent women."

Whatever reservations Lou had when she met Rilke, she could not long resist his passionate pursuit. He sought her out with a single-minded zeal that surpassed anything she had encountered before. Wherever she went he tried to be there too. When he missed her in the theatre he looked for her all over Munich.

> With a few roses in my hand I have been walking about the town and the entrance of the English Garden because I wanted to give you these roses. But instead of leaving them at your door with the golden key, I have been carrying them around, trembling with eagerness to meet you somewhere.

After every meeting he rushed home and poured out his heart in poetry. He knew instinctively that the spontaneity of his lyrical adoration was his strongest weapon. It disarmed her intellectual resistance by appealing to her own emotional spontaneity. The long and severe training to which she had subjected her mind had made her wary of uncontrolled emotions, but she could not long resist the intensity of Rilke's lyrical assault. When she succumbed to him a few weeks after they had met, he rushed into her arms like a child who has finally found his long-lost mother. But once she received him, she discovered to her surprise that the child was really a passionate young man, well versed in the arts of love. Suddenly their roles were reversed; it was now Rilke who played the dominant role. Mounted on Pegasus like another Bellerophon, he slew the Chimera that guarded the entrance to Lou's privacy and made her his wife. It happened so suddenly that even in retrospect Lou shuddered when she thought of it. In her memoirs she writes:

> I was your wife for years because you were the first reality, body and man undistinguishably one, the incontestable fact of life itself. I could have said literally the same you said when you confessed your love: "You alone are real." In this we became husband and wife even before we had become friends, not from choice but from this unfathomable marriage. It was not that two halves were seeking one another: shudderingly, our surprised unity recognized a preordained unity. We were brother and sister, but as in the remote past, before marriage between brother and sister had become sacrilegious.

On the face of it the whole affair was, of course, ridiculous. Here she was, a mature woman and almost old enough to be Rilke's mother—a woman, moreover, who was passionately desired by many men, some of them far more virile than Rilke. She had resisted most of them and now, in her thirty-sixth year, she succumbed to a boy. Why? Rilke's friends and admirers cast Lou in the role of a wily seductress who took advantage of an innocent youth and lured him into her nets. But it was more complex than that. Rilke was by no means an innocent youth when he met Lou. He had had his fair share of erotic adventures and knew that the surest way to win a woman's love was by appealing both to her motherly instincts and her feminine ardor. This he did with consummate skill. He penetrated Lou's intellectual armor and aroused her passion, but soon after their first embrace her critical faculties reasserted themselves and she began to look upon her young lover with increasing suspicion. His tremulous state worried her. She wondered whether his lyrical exultations, alternating with fierce moods of depression, were not the danger sign of mental sickness. There seemed to be two Rilkes, one confident and self-assured, the other morbidly introspective. In her letters and memoirs she writes that it was a frightening spectacle to see "the other" suddenly emerge, trembling with fear and giving vent to bitter self-reproaches and self-pity. She hoped at first that her love would cure him, but gradually her fears increased and she decided to end the affair. However, between its sudden beginning and its equally sudden end lay almost three years of love and poetry.

When Rilke met Lou he had already published a great deal of poetry. Under the signature of René Maria Rilke there had appeared in quick succession the slender volumes of *Life and Songs* (1894), *Wild Chicory: Songs Given to the People* (1896), *An Offering to the Lares* (1896), and *Crowned with Dreams* (1897). It was pure poetry of mood, vaguely yearning for something to come, vaguely nostalgic for something that has been; perfect of its kind; sentimental, sensitive and subtle. Its recurrent theme was the strangeness and mystery of life—life not lived or observed but felt, intuitively felt, as oneness:

> Dreams seem to me like orchids
> Rich and gay.
> They draw their strength from life's
> Gigantic tree.
> Proud of their borrowed blood
> They boast and flee
> A minute later: pale and dead.
> And as the worlds above
> Move silently
> Do you not feel a fragrance overhead?
> Dreams seem to me like orchids. . . .

Although Lou was struck emotionally by Rilke's verbal virtuosity, by the melodious rhythms, evocative alliterations and ornate assonances of his poems, they did not appeal to her intellect. She did not deny that many of them were beautiful, some even beguilingly so, but if you tried to grasp them they dissolved, like dreams just beyond recall. She complained that she could not understand them and Rilke made a conscious effort to write more simply and about simple things.

Helped and encouraged by Lou, the young poet entered upon a long period of severe self-discipline which came to fruition many years later in the plastic splendor of *New*

Poems. One sign of Lou's influence can be seen in the striking change in his handwriting. Before he met Lou, Rilke wrote sloppily and often illegibly. Now his writing became as neat and precise as hers. When she scorned the somewhat effeminate French form of his name, René, he changed it to Rainer. Even after their break, when Lou told him that she could help him no longer, his letters bear moving testimony to the great debt he owed her.

> I felt it then and I know it today, that the infinite reality that surrounded you was the most important event of that extremely good, great and productive time. The transforming experience which then seized me at a hundred places at once emanated from the great reality of your being. I had never before in my groping hesitancy felt life so much, believed in the present and recognized the future so much. You were the opposite of all doubt and witness to the fact that everything you touch, reach and see, *exists.* The world lost its clouded aspect, the flowing together and dissolving, so typical of my first poor verses. Things arose. I learned to distinguish animals and flowers. Slowly and with difficulty I learned how simple everything is and I matured and learned to say simple things. All this happened because I was fortunate enough to meet you at a time when I was in danger of losing myself in formlessness.

Lou's failure to respond to his poetry as wholeheartedly as he wished made Rilke concentrate on that theme which he knew occupied her deeply, religion. Here they were on common ground. They were both extremely fond of the Bible, especially of the Old Testament. And when they were alone together in the privacy of Lou's rooms, Rilke sometimes read to her. He selected those passages that corresponded most closely to his feeling for the beloved woman. "Thou hast ravished my heart, my sister, my spouse; thou hast ravished my heart with one of thine eyes, with one chain of thy neck. How fair is thy love, my sister, my spouse! how much better is thy love than wine!" On and on, Rilke read and he could feel the current of sympathy that his words aroused in Lou's heart.

Sometimes their discussions touched on the significance of the Christ figure which Lou had pondered in her essay **"Jesus the Jew,"** and Rilke in his poetry. It is possible, indeed likely, that Rilke received further stimulus for his poems "Visions of Christ" from Lou's essay. He read it about the time he started the cycle, and certainly there are striking similarities in the treatment of the theme. Both saw in Christ, not the son of God but of man, a religious genius infinitely moving in the solitary agony of his passion.

Starting from the premise that all gods are manmade, Lou's concern was with the retroaction, as she called it, of these manmade gods on those who believe in them. The intensification of man's emotional response to figures originally created to assuage his fear of death and the unknown seemed to her to be the heart of the religious phenomenon. It propelled men to become saints. The classic example of that process was Jesus. Here was a young Jew brought up in the stern tradition of Judaism and taught to believe in the messianic promises of Jehovah, the God of Wrath. But he had concentrated the rays of his fervent heart on this forbidding deity, transforming Him into a God of Love. His childlike, unwavering faith, his absolute trust in Him whom he called his heavenly Father, had resolved the contradiction that lies at the root of all religions: men kneeling in front of a manmade God. For it is the human heart in which the mystery of the religious experience takes place, causing a manmade God to give birth to a godlike man. This happened to Jesus and made him the Christ, the begetter of a new religion.

But Lou insisted that in order to understand the real tragedy of the historic Jesus it must be remembered that he grew up in the Judaic tradition of an essentially just, if stern, God. It was this God whom he loved and to whom he cried out in the hour of his greatest need. Who knows what terrible doubts assailed him on the road to martyrdom from Gethsemane to Golgotha, and what despair filled his heart when he finally realized that his heavenly Father had forsaken him.

> Even at the last moment, when he was already hanging on the cross, he must have forgiven his God, for a miracle was still possible and it *had* to happen: a just man could not be made to perish miserably, handed over to his enemies, least of all could he be forced to suffer that form of death most dreaded and most shameful to Jewish eyes—death on the cross, even if he was not the Messiah but merely another just Jew. God's firm and sacred promise preserved him from such a fate.

And yet it happened. Hence Christ's agonized outcry: "My God, my God, why has thou forsaken me?"

These anguished words, spoken by a martyr of his faith, sum up the suffering of all religious men. They pose the problem of God's very existence. But while Jesus may have died with this doubt in his heart, his disciples succeeded in transforming his moment of deepest despair into his greatest triumph by the grandiose paradox of asserting that God punishes those He loves. Christ's death on the cross became the prologue of his ascent to heaven, his solitary agony the symbol of a new religion. However, "amidst the triumphant shouts of a solid faith, useful to all, there echoes very gently and painfully the ultimate word of religion to which only now and again a poor solitary genius can rise who has experienced it deeply: *Eli, Eli! lama sabachthani.*"

Christ's anguished cry on the cross is also the theme of Rilke's poem "Annual Fair," written six months after Lou's essay. In his first letter to her Rilke told Lou that he had read her essay at the suggestion of a Dr. Conrad, one of the editors of the journal *Die Gesellschaft* who, having seen a few poems of his "Visions of Christ," thought that her essay would interest him. Rilke added that Conrad was going to publish five of these poems, a claim which he had made earlier in a letter to Ludwig Ganghofer. But he was mistaken. They never appeared in *Die Gesellschaft,* nor anywhere else until they were published more than sixty years later in the third volume of his collected works. What caused this long delay? One thing is certain: Rilke had no doubts about their poetic merits. At a time when he was very critical of his early verses he referred to them as "these great poems." The mystery heightens if we ponder the significance of Rilke's reply to Wilhelm von Scholz who, in 1899, wanted to publish them. "I have many reasons," Rilke told Scholz, "to conceal the Christ figures for a long, long time. They are the future which accompanies me all my life."

Between these two dates—1897 when he seemed eager to publish them, and 1899 when he rejected any thought of publication—falls Rilke's encounter with Lou. How intimately these poems are linked to Lou is further evidenced by the fact that it was Lou to whom he turned when in 1912 his publisher, Kippenberg, urged again that they be published:

> Unfortunately, I have once hinted that the *Visions of Christ* exist and since Kippenberg now attaches great importance to offering unpublished work in this new edition, he urges me to include these great poems (which I myself have not seen for many years) in this new publication. Under no circumstances will I do this without knowing what you think of it. Do you think that there is something else from that time which might rather be published, or has the time really come for these things?

Lou's answer to this request appears to be lost. But whatever she said, Rilke decided against publication. He mentioned them once more to Lou eighteen months later in the postscript of a letter written in the home of his publisher in Leipzig.

> Perhaps the *Visions of Christ* in a yellow folder have remained with you? In this case, please read them.

This time Lou replied at once telling him that he was right, his poems were in her bank safe. She had reread them and, for the first time, had been struck by amazing relationships, difficult to explain in writing.

> In tone they [*Visions of Christ*] are very different from the two recent ones [a reference to the first two *Duino Elegies*] and yet everything you have written moves with an inner unity between these old *Visions of Christ* and the coming visions of the angel.

Rilke felt comforted by these words. Once again he was torn by self-doubts and needed reassurance. If Lou still believed in him, could he not believe in himself? Perhaps he recalled those intimate hours in Munich, now long ago, when he had first read his poems to Lou. It had been an unforgettable experience. She had listened with a quiet intensity that forged an invisible bond between them. Imperceptibly she had become involved in his poetry and, through it, in him. He could feel that it was more than sympathy he aroused in her. It was an upsurge of wonder, admiration and love. Her whole being responded; her heart to his music, her head to his words. They sounded so familiar to her that she might have written them herself and perhaps she had, perhaps she was listening to an echo of her own voice? It was certainly the voice of her brother in spirit.

In his poem "Annual Fair" Rilke treated the Christ theme in the context of a visit to the Munich Oktoberfest. In colorful images he describes the gay and noisy life at the fair, the huge beer tents, merry-go-rounds, ferris wheels, and the multitudinous attractions from all over the world that assail the eyes and ears of the visiting throng. He strolls among them until he comes to a booth at the end of the fair where a sign says that here one can see the life and death of Christ. Without knowing why, he pays ten pfennigs, gets a ticket and enters. He finds himself in the presence of waxen figures representing various scenes from the life of Christ: his birth at Bethlehem, his visit to the Temple, his entrance into Jerusalem, his solitary vigil in the Garden of Gethsemane and finally his crucifixion. As he watches the figure of Christ on the Cross his heart suddenly stops, for:

> The waxen God opened and closed his eyes,
> his glance concealed by thin and bluish lids,
> his narrow, wounded chest heaved and sighed,
> his sponge-drenched lips in deadly pallor tried
> to grasp a word and force it through his teeth:
> My God, my God—hast thou forsaken me?
> And as I, horrified and at a loss
> to understand these martyred words, remain
> fixed to the spot and stare and stare
> at him, his hands let go the cross.
> He groans and says: "It is I."
> I listen speechless to his anguished cry,
> look at the walls covered with glaring cloth
> and feel the cheap deception of the fair,
> the smell of oil and wax. But there
> it starts again and says: "This is my curse;
> Since my disciples stole me from the grave,
> deluded by their vain and boastful faith,
> there is no pit that holds me—none.
> As long as rushing brooks reflect the stars
> and life bursts forth under a spring sun,
> I must go on and on across the earth,
> I must pay penance now from Cross to
>   Cross . . .
>
> Do you know the legend of the Wandering Jew?
> I am myself that ancient Ahasver
> Who daily dies and daily lives anew."

This was language that Lou understood and with it Rilke gained her love. Two weeks after their first meeting his letters already sound ardent and intimate. He sent her poems, songs of longing, that were different from his former songs because "I have looked into the eyes of longing beside me." The only clouds on the bright horizon of their love were Lou's husband in Berlin and, more immediately, a call from Rilke's Austrian draft board ordering him to appear before them. He was disconsolate and grasped every second to be with Lou. At the end of May they spent two days together in search of solitude and mountain air in the little Upper Bavarian village of Wolfratshausen. When the dreaded day of departure came Rilke was heartbroken. Fortunately, his draft board decided, after examining him, that he was not needed after all. He communicated this good news to Lou in a joyous telegram from Prague and a few days later he rejoined her in Munich. From then on they were inseparable.

The growing ardor of Rilke's letters and poems shows how quickly his love found fulfillment. On June 6, Whitsunday, he sent her greetings, told her that this spring had a particular significance for him and submitted himself humbly to her "sweet slavery." Two days later he vowed that it would be many years before she understood how much he loved her. What a mountain spring means to a man dying of thirst, her love meant to him. He said he wanted to see the world through her for "then I do not see the world but only you, you, you." In a poem three days later he called her his "Empress." She had made him rich, and even though he tried to hide his riches, everybody could see his happiness shining in his eyes. He wanted to "lose his separate identity and dissolve completely" into her. "I want to be you. I don't want to have any dreams that do not know you, nor any wishes that you cannot grant. I do not want to do anything that does not praise you. . . . I want to be you. And my heart burns before your grace like the eternal lamp before the picture of Mary."

Lou's answers to these rapturous effusions are unfortunately lost, because of their joint decision to destroy all documents of their love. In her memoirs she says that "the prevailing and unalterable condition of their lives"—an allusion to her marriage—made this action necessary. And there is no doubt that Andreas' fierce pride made it imperative that they be discreet and avoid an open display of their affection. For this reason Lou was not altogether happy with the lyrical adoration in prose and verse with which the young poet pursued her and she hints at black-inked corrections that resulted in the mutilation and destruction of many of Rilke's love poems. She then quotes a fragment that had somehow survived, still in the original and by now faded envelope in which Rilke had sent it to her:

> With gentle blessing did your letter greet me;
> I knew that distance cannot stop our love.
> From all that's beautiful you come to meet me,
> My spring wind you, my summer rain above.
> You my June night on thousand pathways lead
>   me,
> Upon which no initiated walked before:
> I am in you.

It is easy to imagine what Andreas' reaction to this poem would have been if he had seen it. For it describes, although veiled in poetic language, the course of his wife's love affair. It was obviously a reply to a letter she had written Rilke, and obviously, too, he had been waiting impatiently for it. When it came his pent-up emotions burst into song. In rhapsodic language he recalls the passionate hours they had spent together. They had met in May, hence the allusion to spring wind, had become lovers in June—"my June night"—and had spent the summer months in close proximity in a small peasant house in Wolfratshausen. All these events are faithfully recorded in the poem. But most revealing, and from Andreas' point of view, most painful, is the penultimate line with its oblique reference to Rilke being Lou's first lover—or so he thought. It is understandable that Lou felt embarrassed by his lyrical indiscretions and tried to suppress them. She was not altogether successful, for many of the poems she eliminated from a manuscript collection of love poems, *In*

Your Honor, which Rilke gave her were preserved in Rilke's notebooks.

However, the occasional displeasure Rilke's lyrical exuberance caused Lou was far outweighed by the pleasure she derived from his company. They had left Munich in the middle of June and had retired to Wolfratshausen accompanied, one suspects mainly for the sake of appearances, by Frieda von Bülow and August Endell. Wolfratshausen, a typical small Upper Bavarian town with a charming old market square, baroque churches with onion-shaped steeples, and a fair number of the traditional Bavarian inns, is situated in the broad valley of the Inn at the foot of the Kalvarienberg. Pleasant walks lead up to the top of the hill and offer magnificent views of the Alpine range to the south. They had rented a small peasant house with a garden and a shady arbor in the back—an idyllic setting for a love tryst. Lou recalls that her room was on the ground floor facing the street, and that Rilke always closed the shutters when he visited her, to prevent passersby from looking in. In the semi-darkness of these summer days they celebrated their honeymoon.

It was a passionate affair, with Lou always, at first, being overawed by Rilke's male aggressiveness before her greater maturity asserted itself. Then she would take her young lover into the garden behind the house and teach him to walk barefoot over the dewy grass. She would tell him the names of her favorite flowers, make him listen to the wind in the trees and the rushing water of the brook. Her husband had taught her to observe the animals at daybreak and now she passed this knowledge on to her young lover. For the first time in his life Rilke entered into a real relationship with nature, a simple, direct and non-literary relationship. Lou communicated to him her sense of wonder at the oneness of the world, her joy of living, and her vitality. The healthy vigor of her sensuous enjoyment made him feel ashamed of the mawkish sentimentality of his adolescent dreams. A new world opened before his eyes, less tortured than the one he had known. He felt as if reborn. His whole life, he now realized, had been influenced by the false piety and the artificial values of his mother. She was responsible for the unhealthy exaltations which alienated him from reality. He had met Lou just in time. She would help him find himself. Inspired by his love for her, and with her guidance, he tried to express his feelings more simply and directly. This was not easy and many poems he wrote during this extremely productive time reflect his "pre-Wolfratshausen mood," as he called it, that floating between day and dream which is so typical of his first verses. But with others one feels the effort toward greater concreteness:

> The land is bright and darkly glows the arbor.
> You speak in whispers while I watch with awe.
> And every word you say is like an altar
> Built by my faith upon my quiet shore.
> I love you. You're sitting in a chair, your cool
> white hands asleep as in a bed.
> My life is lying like a silver spool
> within your hands. Release my thread.

Boldly this poem comes to grips with the love theme, first by setting the scene—land and arbor: an allusion to the arbor in Wolfratshausen, where they spent so much of their time. Lou is talking. We get an idea of how intently Rilke listened from the image "altar" to which he likens her words, thereby elevating his love to the level of religious adoration. But this feeling is immediately brought down to earth again by the simple statement, particularly moving in this context: "I love you." With it the poem returns to a concrete image. Lou is sitting in a garden chair, her hands folded in her lap. As he watches her the poet realizes that he is completely in her power. She holds the thread of his life in her hands. The image is completed with the gentle request, stated with the utmost verbal economy, that she untangle his life and set him free: "Release my thread."

It is in poems such as these that one can see how much Rilke was under Lou's influence. He clung to her with an almost desperate helplessness, and could not bear the thought of being separated from her. Periods of separation were, however, unavoidable. Lou could not subordinate her life completely to his as he wanted her to. This would have been against her nature. She had to interrupt even their Wolfratshausen honeymoon to keep a prearranged appointment in Hallein with her friend Broncia Koller. But no sooner was she gone than Rilke's passionate letters with their pale-blue seals followed her. He wrote her daily, protesting his love and imploring her to return to him. Perhaps he sensed the danger of another man in the background, although Lou had not told him much about Zemek. To her dismay she noted that he indulged once again in the most extravagant language, and once again she felt uneasy and disturbed.

To make matters worse her official husband, Andreas, who had been in Berlin all this time, announced his arrival and said he would spend a month in Wolfratshausen with her. It was therefore particularly important that her young lover learn to control his emotions. Since there is no record of discord, Lou and Rilke seem to have succeeded in keeping Andreas in the dark. To be sure, cynics have said that so far from trying to conceal her affection for Rilke, Lou confessed it to her husband and that he acquiesced in it. But in view of Andreas' well-known temper this is hardly likely. The fact that he did not notice anything is a tribute to Lou's expert handling of the affair. She had always been surrounded by adoring males and Andreas may have thought that of all his wife's numerous admirers Rilke was the least dangerous. He seems to have grown quite fond of the young poet and raised no objections when Rilke proposed to return to Berlin with them. Thus ended the first chapter of Lou's affair with Rilke. Henceforth she would become more and more his friend, his teacher and his mother-confessor. Their honeymoon was over.

Michael Hamburger   (review date 1965)

SOURCE: A review of *The Freud Journal of Lou Andreas-Salomé,* in *The New York Times Book Review,* January 3, 1965, p. 5.

[*A German-born English poet, translator and critic, Hamburger has been widely praised for his translations of such poets as Friedrich Hoelderlin and Georg Trakl. In the fol-*

Rilke (left) and Andreas-Salomé on their second trip to Russia in 1900, at the home of the poet Spiridon Drozhzhin in the village of Nizovka.

lowing mixed review of The Freud Journal of Lou Andreas-Salomé, *he asserts that Andreas-Salomé incisively confronts the central issues in Freud's psychology.*]

Of the many kinds of readers who will be interested in [**The Freud Journal of Lou Andreas-Salomé**], my kind may well be the most peripheral, since I am not a psychologist or even a literary Freudian. It is to such as these that Lou Andreas-Salomé's record of the psychoanalytic inner circle's transactions in 1912 and 1913 will prove indispensable for what is revealed, not only about Freud's personality and opinions, but also about the schisms of those years, the secession of men like Adler, Jung and Stekel.

Lou Andreas-Salomé, novelist, poet, essayist, and great friend of the poet, Rainer Maria Rilke, and of Nietzsche, took an active interest in psychoanalysis at the age of 50 and was a practicing analyst in her later years. In the beginning, as a privileged member of the inner circle—Freud would address his remarks to her and twice commented on the disturbing effect upon him of her empty chair—she was allowed to attend the lectures and discussions in Adler's group, and indeed she testifies repeatedly to Freud's tolerance and openness to correction even in these critical years. Her summaries of the papers read and discussed in both groups are crucial to the history of psychoanalysis; but as Stanley A. Leavy observes in his introduction, they lack the lucidity of Freud's own writings, and this will limit their appeal to non-specialists.

Lou came to psychology from literature and philosophy, not from clinical research or medical practice; it is ideas that continued to fascinate her, for all her interest in spe-

cific cases and her skepticism towards the "premature synthesis" of which she accuses revisionists like Jung. Her fervent admiration for Freud—whom she calls "heroic" and contrasts with Jung, whose "earnestness is composed of pure aggression, ambition, and intellectual brutality"— owes much not only to Freud's fitness as a father-figure, but to the attraction of opposites. It is in almost mystical terms that Lou sums up her debt to Freud and psychoanalysis in the brief Conclusion to her journal; her tone and style are the very opposite of Freud's.

Yet it is the continuity and consistency of Lou's preoccupations that strike and interest a non-Freudian reader like myself. As Lou makes quite clear, Freud's "heroism" lay in his honesty, in an intellectual radicalism that braved every kind of opposition; that same honesty in Nietzsche had attracted her some 30 years earlier, even if Nietzsche's honesty came to grief through insufficient self-knowledge. Only Freud made this self-knowledge possible, though Nietzsche's intuitions and insights had come close to it at times. Freud, therefore, held the key both to Lou's self-knowledge and to her understanding of a whole succession of personal relationships, including that with Nietzsche, as well as then current relationships with Rilke, her husband and other men. That is why she could write in the Conclusion that, thanks to psychoanalysis, "all the vanished persons of the past arise anew, whom one has sinned against by letting them go; they are there as from all eternity, marked by eternity—peaceful, monumental, and [at] one with being itself . . ."

It is the non-Freudian in me, however, that feels uncomfortable when Nietzsche is described as "that sadomasochist unto himself "—as though Nietzsche's internal quarrel could be explained by that neat and stereotyped label—or when Rilke, who is still Lou's friend, if not her lover, is described as "a typical hysteric" and compared with another of her lovers, "a no less typical obsessional neurotic bound up in a thousand reproaches and fixations." This kind of "detachment" points not so much to her self-knowledge—she is somewhat more discreet about her own neuroses—as to her narcissistic exploitation of men from the very beginning, whether for intellectual stimulus, physical satisfaction, or psychological investigation, as in these instances.

Lou's interest in narcissism comes out not in self-analyses, but in general and theoretical speculations scattered through the journal. Somehow it seems to me that the same delicacy or discretion might have been extended to such a man as Rilke, who has suffered more than enough from the posthumous disclosures of his friends. She adds details about his physical ailments, as well as a sympathetic and valuable account of his state of mind in 1913, when "his production has become fragmentary."

Yet Lou was well aware that "in his case the only index of these things is to be found in his creative work." Like Freud himself, she was prepared to make every sort of allowance for the exceptional problems of exceptional men and women. She records this very important admission by Freud: "It appeared that the world is indeed less in need of improvement and less capable of it than one might think. One finds types whose socially harmful instincts have developed in such intimate union with their most valuable ones, that one might at best strive only for a better distribution of the forces than that which took place in their childhood. Or conversely, those types in which one sees not so much the neurotic patient as a neurotic world; they would need only courage to attain their natural development within their unnatural milieu, but with it they would destroy this milieu too."

To Lou, this was an instance of Freud's weariness and pessimism; to me, it's an instance of his wisdom, his continuous awareness that many things are beyond the reach of psychoanalysis. She herself was always ready to admit that certain Freudian concepts were still too crude and undifferentiated to be generally effective in diagnosis or treatment; but she was less ready than Freud to dispense with the consolations of dogmatism. As Nietzsche knew, it takes strength to doubt, as well as to believe.

Lou is at her best—and at her least turgid—when she does speak from personal experience, as in her analysis and justification of infidelity in erotic relationships, or her frequent disquisitions on the psychology of women. Mr. Leavy rightly points out that her feminism was quite different from the more widespread sort that stresses the equality of the sexes. Her experience of Nietzsche and other intellectually outstanding men—not including Freud—had rather tended to confirm her belief in the emotional superiority of women, if not in the superiority of the emotions over the intellect.

This is one reason why she was attracted to Nietzsche's irrationalism and Rilke's "bisexual" inwardness before her discovery of the Freudian unconscious. She comments on the concept of the libido in Freud, Jung and Ferenczi: "We must realize that man can never have suffered more fundamentally than in becoming a conscious being, seeing the abyss plunging between himself and the rest, between his race and the world, the beginning of the inner-outer division."

This division was Lou's, as it was Nietzsche's and Rilke's, and this is where her philosophical and literary concerns link up with the psychological, and psychoanalysis itself links up with philosophical and literary developments going back the best part of three centuries. Even Lou's passing remark on schizophrenia, which she sees as the "wish to be the whole, to be All," touches in the most illuminating way on this central dilemma of modern Western man. One does not need to be a Freudian to appreciate Freud's heroic confrontation of it, or to find much that is relevant and engrossing in the present book.

Rudolph Binion (essay date 1968)

SOURCE: "The Wayward Disciple," *Frau Lou: Nietzsche's Wayward Disciple,* Princeton University Press, 1968, pp. 141-71.

[*Binion is an American educator and critic. In the following excerpt from his highly praised biography of Andreas-Salomé, he discusses her 1894 study of Friedrich Nietzsche's life and work.*]

[After Nietzsche's breakdown in 1889] Lou could develop no farther as authoress, feminist, or female except as Nietzsche's ex-disciple. In **"Der Realismus in der Religion"** of late 1891, she implicitly declared herself loyal to Nietzsche's sometime Réealism. Her professed purpose was to pin down "the religious affect," as Nietzsche had prompted her to—and she did identify its two edifying components quite nicely: a feeling of deepest personal insufficiency and the very opposite. Her final purpose was what she took Nietzsche's to have been: religious prophecy. She contended that the "science of religion" must henceforth attend to the religious affect, presumably an all-human affect given a huge recent crop of books arguing from man's "inner need" for religion to its "pragmatic value." And she went on to present worship as the supreme manifestation of man, which rises with him from crude wishing through god-making to a longing for holy communion. She saw nothing to hamper piety in the recognition that gods are man-made; on the contrary, she declared that the only true gods were those knowingly devised by a worshipper to suit himself. Her hints at how gods are devised were strictly rhetorical: once the religious affect is self-avowed, "human strength and majesty . . . create a god owing to no inconsequence of thought, but to the religious productivity of the entire self aspiring aloft"; religious mystification will soonest cease "if modern man gains the force not only to turn away from whatever his reason exposes as deception, but also to turn toward whatever conduces to his uninhibited inner development"; to become religiously productive as of old despite the new "frightful unbridgeable gap" between "thinking and believing," we must face up to "our need and loneliness in our god-abandonment" and not "try to fool our-selves with any philosophical sham-god"; the "one thing needful" is the courage to look within ourselves to where "the saving god has every time emerged." These prescrip-tions resemble nothing so much as Lou's Tautenburg for-mula for Nietzsche's idealizing, the more since now as then she treated ideals as equivalent to gods for devotional purposes. Thus she set up as Nietzschean god-maker—while tacitly asserting that she had created her childhood god knowingly and that he had been true nonetheless.

Following Nietzsche's breakdown, Lou filled in her old sketch of him and brought it up-to-date as she pored over his life's work. The result was the first significant treat-ment of him in print: ten precursory articles of 1891-1893, elaborated into *Friedrich Nietzsche in seinen Werken* of 1894. This final product was intended as a case study of a freethinker religiously creating and miscreating ideals and as an object lesson in reducing a philosophy to a per-sonal dossier on its author. Nietzsche's writings emerged as symptomatic expressions of a self-induced nervous de-rangement at distinct stages of its development toward in-sanity. This thesis, startling for its time, was damning for Nietzsche in effect and in aftereffect, confused as were Lou's intent and argument respectively.

According to *Friedrich Nietzsche in seinen Werken,* Nietzsche's life was dominated successively by his boy-hood religious faith, his philological studies, his devotion to Schopenhauer and Wagner, his positivism, and finally a prophetic-mystical exaltation of the will. The transi-tions, abrupt, were marked by acute pathological crises. Each was a deliberate *"falling ill through thoughts and get-ting well through thoughts."* For "whenever he began to feel at ease within one outlook" he would repudiate it, un-loosing instinctual turmoil within himself; then he would engage in a new intellectual enterprise entailing a new in-stinctual harmony. This "psychic process . . . is his ever-recurrent typical experience, through which he ever again straightened himself out, raised himself up over himself—and finally fell head over heels to his ruin." He took his power of recovery for a sign of health; just as surely as he ever cured himself, however, "just as necessarily did he, after long convalescence, require suffering and struggle, fever and wounds" again. "Over every goal reached, every convalescence completed, stand the same words: 'He who attains his ideal thereby goes beyond it.' "

This pattern was possible because of what Nietzsche him-self called his "decadent" emotional constitution. Even just before a crisis, when he was at his healthiest, his drives were at variance, only directed to a common goal—as if vying for honors in the same heroic campaign. And yet even then his drive to knowledge actually lorded it over the others, since it was as knower that he set his drives their new goal of knowledge in the first place, then watched them rally. The "power of knowledge" was in fact so "divisive" as to "make it *look*" as though the goal lay *"outside"* of the drives, which consequently only pressed the harder toward it "as if to elude themselves and their conflict." Nietzsche could draw bliss "from such a transparent self-deception" through all his suffering be-cause his religious affect, stirred by this sacrifice of one

part of himself to another, fixed upon his own person for want of a more credible object—wherewith the "cleavage" turned into a "dividuum." [Binion adds in a footnote: "Choice rhetoric follows: 'Health was attained, to be sure, but by means of illness; real worship, but by means of self-deception; real self-affirmation and self-elevation, but by means of self-injury. Whence in the potent religious affect, from which alone in Nietzsche's case all knowledge pro-ceeds, lie inextricably interwined: self-sacrifice and self-apotheosis, cruel self-destruction and voluptuous self-divinization, woeful languishing and triumphant conva-lescing, glowing ecstasy and cool self-awareness,' each 'ceaselessly' conditioning its opposite—'a chaos that would, that *must* bear a god.' "]

Indeed, his mental peregrinations began when in his boy-hood he forsook the paternal faith, dear as it was to his heart, because "his mind needed emotional battles, pains, and convulsions so as to attain to itself in potent develop-ment." Thereafter he "longed for the lost paradise, while his mental development compelled him to depart from it in a straight line," so that he sought God *"in the most di-verse forms of self-divinization:* that is the story of his mind, his works, his illness." In his positivist period, he exalted rationality over against affectivity as if to spite himself. The result was "that religiously motivated *self-split* required by Nietzsche by dint of which the knower can look down upon his own being with its stirrings and drives as upon a *second* being"; thereby "he so to say sacri-ficed himself to the truth as to an ideal power" in "an at-tempt to intoxicate himself through this self-coercion," even while regarding his new ideal as cool balm for his overheated soul. Even at that the new unity set in, where-upon he sang and sighed again with his whole heart. Only the next time round did he (with "secret ruse") "finally solve the tragic conflict of his life—the conflict of needing God and yet having to deny him. First, drunk with long-ing, he fashioned the mystical overman-ideal in dreams and raptures, seer-like; then, to escape from himself, he strove to identify himself with his creature by a frightful leap. Thus at the last he turned into a double personage: half sick, suffering man and half redeemed, laughing over-man." This was madness already—and through his mind's "highest sacrifice, the sacrifice of itself," he had come full circle, "like a weary child returning to its first home."

Nietzsche's memory grew offensive to Lou over the years—although she was always pleased to be known socially as his sometime girl friend. She decried his late philosophizing: in 1900 she noted that "sick Nietzsche fashioned the vision of a super-Nietzsche only so as to make the lack of a healthy, normal Nietzsche bearable to himself."

—Rudolph Binion

In point of fact Nietzsche's insanity was due to a brain ailment of physical origin, hence was not mentally self-induced, and there is no correlation whatever between the onsets of his malady, his intellectual self-renewals, and his alternations between felt instinctual harmony and felt instinctual chaos. He does seem to have induced and relished many a crisis, only not knowingly. Lou, however, lacked a conception of unconscious purpose, for all her strong sense of it: thus she was attempting a psychoanalysis without the theoretic means. Nietzsche did somehow, from childhood on, prepare for a psychic split "into sacrificial god and sacrificial animal." Lou, though, despite her reductive intent, respected his own intellectualizations of his instinctual trouble—beginning with the "religious affect" and the "knowledge-drive." Besides, if his knowledge-drive did set the direction for all his other drives, there was no "inner cleavage." And anyhow, this whole problematical scheme loosely adapted from Nietzsche cannot accommodate his transition of 1882 from exalting the dispassionate quest for knowledge to denigrating it on the instincts' behalf. As to the why of his successive self-renewals, her referring them back to an original repudiation of Christianity merely displaced the question. What "drove him" from his "warm 'home' " in the first place (along that straight circular course)? A "dark instinct."

Were his new departures so very abrupt? The one treated as prototypical—his abandonment of Christianity—appears to have been gradual, and Lou's own detailed account gradualized those to and away from positivism. Again, were they so very radical? Possibly he said so in Tautenburg. But later he boasted lifelong philosophic constancy for all his Wagnerite and positivist posturing—and, at the other extreme, perpetual philosophic experimentation. There was certainly more continuity, even fixity, to his constructions and valuations than Lou's thesis allowed. His self-imposed orientations remain: philologic scholarship, discipleship to Schopenhauer and Wagner, positivism. But after 1882 did he not simply come into his own? And was his output all of a piece from the visionary *Zarathustra* through the reflective, argumentative *Beyond Good and Evil* and *The Genealogy of Morals* to the frantic Nietzscheana of 1888? Her characterization of his final personality split, lurid as it may be, is quite apposite to these last (except for the laughing) and premonitorily to *Zarathustra*—only in that case he took his "frightful leap" right over those two sturdy, searching works in between.

Actually Lou had more than she could do to schematize Nietzsche's last six years' work, let alone schematize it under the sign of self-imposition, especially as she rightly denied that it came to any "system." On one of her pages Nietzsche, dreading a final solution to his beloved problems, "plunges definitively into the eternal riddles of mysticism"—which just won't do. On another he is a "Columbus in reverse" in that, striking out from positivism, he alights unknowingly on his prepositivist shores of "metaphysics"—only these same old shores turn antipodal when the late as against the early "metaphysics" is called an affirmation as against a negation of life: "sansara" as against "nirvana." Into her extensive definition of "Nietzsche's final philosophy" went a "repudiation of his former purely logical ideal of knowledge" together with a "displacement

of the foundation for truth into the world of emotional impulses, source for a new appraisal of all things," a "mystical philosophy of the will" informed by a conception of "everything highest" as "a kind of atavism," a preoccupation with dreams and madness, a "glorification of artistry" as alone imparting final meaning to existence, and, overriding even this last, a cult of genius amounting to "the mystery of a prodigious self-apotheosis" and issuing in "a religious mysticism in which God, world, and man fuse into a single prodigious superbeing."

Lou's aptest point was of no real use to her argument: that then as before, only more so, Nietzsche "generalized his soul into a world soul" and voiced his "inner inspiration" as "a commandment for all mankind." Accordingly, his own instincts being anarchic, he called all mankind decadent, and hailed the overman for the sake of his own self-redemption. Only she added that his late hypotheses—and "most particularly" those about Jesus as "bait"—were consequently not to be taken seriously "on their scientific side," for "exact scientific inquiry now played no further role with him": that he was merely "out to elicit from and project into human history something the significance of which lay for him within a hidden emotional problem. . . . The basic question for him was not what the emotional history of mankind had been, but how to construe his own emotional history as that of all mankind." This is inexact and unjust enough for Lou to have "most particularly" *sensed* what "hidden emotional problem" he was construing. For, properly stated, his purpose was to study his own *moral pre*history introspectively while knowing the external facts of it. And the resultant hypotheses were scientific inasmuch as they cut straight through a whole mass of historical data, cutting out none. Hypotheses drawn from introspection are, if anything, less liable to be vitiated by unwitting projection than others. The "slave nature," Lou contended, was Nietzsche's own ego, the "master nature" his self-ideal, "whence his conception of the historical battle between the two is in its entire import nothing but a coarsened illustration of what goes on in the highest human individual." But of course! Except for that sly "entire," Lou's reduction was here no less valid than Nietzsche's introspection—only to reduce is still not to refute. At the same time, it was her good right—and better—to reject his oracular valuation of historic values. For whereas it took introspective genius to date the human soul from when bullied weaklings first made a virtue of bullying themselves in retaliation, and even granted that self-bullying is self-defeating in the long run, Nietzsche's prescription for speeding delivery of the overman (through intensifying humanity's nihilistic birth-pangs) was no more binding on others than were his incessant dictates concerning good taste. Yet again, through nothing did he show up our ethic as ascetical and other-worldly (hence superannuated) so neatly as through the demonic question of whether, if we knew that we should be bound to relive our lives *ad infinitum,* we would not live them differently. Lou, however, saw in this "eternal repetition of that which is of itself senseless" only a fearsome *idée fixe* of his late period from which he looked to himself as philosopher-savior for deliverance.

Lou's animus against Nietzsche's postpositivism is

plain—and was plainly affectionate at the source, for the sense of it is that Nietzsche had taken a bad turn in quitting the Trinity. Yet she was also insisting that, as his disinherited daughter-bride, she had missed out on only desultory ravings. Through her thesis about his self-induced transitional crises, meanwhile, she was declaring herself the merest innocent occasion for his pain and fury after Leipzig. Representing his ailments as psychogenic, she was returning the compliment of his last letters to her. Representing his madness as psychogenic, she was denying the hereditary factor—anxiously, given her felt kinship with him. For all that, she did not vent her spleen on post-Leipzig Nietzsche alone. His religious genius, which had enticed her in Tautenburg, was morbific in her book. Further, her drift was that his philosophizing was false from the first inasmuch as it was from the first directed and redirected according to his neuropathic needs, with his impulse to know straining over against his other impulses as he investigated these on the wild assumption that his was the European psyche. She refuted him piecemeal here and there besides, begging off for the rest on the ground that what mattered to him was not whether his ideas were right or wrong, but only what it felt like to have them. And not even *his* ideas at that, for, she affirmed, he took up others' continually. He was fertilized intellectually the way women were physically, she added: thus she claimed masculinity for herself. The "original form" of his positivism, she maintained in particular, was Réealism. He made a passionate experience out of Rée's radical segregation of thought from sentiment, she pursued; over all their years of "constant association and intellectual exchange" Rée, "the sharper mind," had the theoretic initiative, while Nietzsche "drew the practical consequences from the theories and sought out their inner significance for culture and life"; Rée, "acutely onesided," despised himself as a sentient being, his cold head taking no hint from his warm heart, so that Nietzsche, being prone to the opposite excess, "valued and overvalued in Rée what came hardest to him himself"; and so on—from one plausible misrepresentation to the next.

But Lou's anti-Nietzschean drift was stemmed all along the surface of her book. What with his "genial manysidedness," ran her text on his Réealism, Nietzsche filled in the gaps left by Rée's logic and made Rée's very mistakes exciting, so that Rée "saw with astonishment how his tight and clean-spun threads of thought were transformed into living, fresh-blooming tendrils at Nietzsche's magic hands." Again, that Nietzsche "trimmed others' theories" was "a fact absolutely immaterial to Nietzsche's true significance," which lay not in any "theoretic originality, not in what can be substantiated or refuted by argument, but in the intimate power with which a personality here speaks to the personality." A supreme master of language, "he so to say created a *new style* in philosophy," one "which expresses the thought not only as such, but along with the entire tonal wealth of its emotive resonance and with all its subtle, secret connotations," and which exceeds the confines of language "in enunciating through the mood what otherwise remains mute in the word. But in no other mind could mere thinking turn so completely into true experiencing, for no other life was ever so completely devoted to turning the whole inner man to account in thinking.

His thoughts did not arise out of real life and its happenings [!] as thoughts ordinarily do; rather, they *constituted* the only real happening of that solitary life." Here was mere considerate compensation. There was also discrepancy, however, as again and again Lou lauded Nietzsche's strict, methodical thinking along with its ever so novel and significant results. But even short of such discrepancy, ambivalence sounded through every tribute that rang true in that depreciative context. And Lou conveyed true admiration through her words on "his talent for subtleties, his genius in the handling of finest things," and the like— indeed, true awe through her depiction of his self-renewals themselves as a "heroism of readiness to sacrifice convictions." As in Tautenburg, she still deemed him most heroic in his "apotheosis of life," since it only intensified his misery; once she called "this emotional struggle" in its turn "the true [!] source of his whole final philosophy" and final ruination—perhaps, though, only as pretext for an apocryphal anecdote about his interrupting musical labors on her "Hymn to Life" in Tautenburg to pen the message: "I despise life." No one has more movingly evoked his need for masks (masks of formality and of foolishness, of cruelty and of godly laughter) or the impress of suffering and solitude on his works. Her descriptions of his person, finally, were loving and lovely both, as well as scrupulously exact—which last entitled her to fable about her relations with him.

Nearly all of Lou's fables in *Friedrich Nietzsche in seinen Werken* come under a double head: heiress pose and Nietzsche romance. She later claimed to have authored the work "exclusively" out of "a sort of obligation toward Nietzsche" to set his philosophic purposes straight. It does manifest a will to expound along with the will to reduce, refute, reject. For the bulk of it she sorted out Nietzschean thematic threads and tied them together expertly— authoritatively. At the very start she claimed special investiture in that she quoted his letter hailing both her "thought from the 'sister brain' " and her prospective sketch of his character. Similarly, she told of his initiating her into the "eternal recurrence" as if into a holy mystery, citing an imaginary "series of letters on the subject" for good measure. By sleight of hand, meanwhile, she contrived to imply a lifelong intimacy about which she was seemingly being discreet for reasons easy to supply. She told of his youth as if from direct personal acquaintance, then drew on his old letters to Rée as if they were to herself. From his actual letters to herself she quite gratuitously quoted insinuative-tender passages followed up by suggestive suspension dots . . . . which in fact suspended only innocuous matter. In contrast to her fanciful retrospect of New Year's Day 1883, she now presented her trip northward from Rome as an idyll with Nietzsche alone. Or rather, she did this only by deftest intimation: " . . . as he visited the Tribschen estate near Lucerne with me during a trip together from Italy . . ." Indeed, she registered all her encounters with Nietzsche only incidentally and as if ever so sparingly, on the order of " . . . while he was staying with me in Thuringia, near Dornburg, in the summer of 1882." She reduced the Trinitarian study plan to a lone resolve of Nietzsche's to which she was privy—one abandoned because of "his headache," or again for "inner and outer reasons." This last was her closest allusion to the aftermath of Leipzig. For the rest her Nietzsche, on closing accounts with positivism, took his leave of Rée through "the beautiful words" in *The Gay Science* about friends whose ways part—his relations with *her* persisting uncontradicted. Beyond the material particulars, the mood of these relations was transformed: what had been tempestuous emerged as serene. It was probably during this emergence that she removed all traces of his nastiness toward her from the papers in her possession. Her first large-scale autobiographic hoax was, then, an approximation to that great coveted but forbidden spiritual and carnal union between them, rendered celestial and eternal by being depicted only dimly and solemnly and without temporal beginning or end.

Lou romanced the more intensely with Nietzsche throughout in that she was concurrently identifying him with herself following the precedent of her novel. Her explanation for his going mad—that he had created a deity, then taken its place—was doubly autobiographic. In the first place, she had once done just that herself. Indeed, his "tragic conflict" commenced, by her account, with his mind's declaration of war upon a beloved childhood god—a traditional god, to be sure, but one to whom, she insisted, his divine creature of the final hour threw back. Thus his starting point was identified with hers, as it had been in *Im Kampf um Gott.* Only what in her case had been a progression toward sanity came out the reverse in his: evidently *she* was homesick for Kuno's childhood god. According to her Tautenburg diary, moreover, *she* had driven her childhood faith from her heart on her mind's account, whereas Nietzsche's heart had felt nothing more for his childhood faith one day and his mind had followed suit; now according to her Nietzsche book, Nietzsche (as he "again and again emphasized," she having "discussed the matter with him in especial detail") did just as, by the earlier account, she had done in pointed contrast to him. "With Nietzsche," she had noted further in Tautenburg, "pain has always been the *cause* of a new development; with me it was always a calculated *means* to grasp at my new goal looming higher"—as now it became for Nietzsche instead. Again, she had taken Nietzsche at his word in Tautenburg that his goals were external as hers were not, whereas now she exposed the difference as a fatal self-deception on his part. And again, her Tautenburg Nietzsche had felt himself to be passively bearing up under his goals, whereas the Nietzsche of her Nietzsche book felt his goals to be invigorating as he robustly struggled toward them—just like her Tautenburg Lou. Thus her self-version as of Tautenburg supplied the mental mechanism now ascribed to Nietzsche to explain away his post-Leipzig crisis. Besides, Tautenburg apart, whose psyche was she probing when she discovered a regressive aspiration toward God at the pit of his? And if now she called him "the philosopher of our times" because he suffered "in his flesh the whole frightful fire and fury of a religiously inclined freethinker," just what was she calling herself? But her chronicle of his folly was autobiographic in the second place in that she had identified herself unawares with an exalted Nietzsche by fits and starts beginning in 1882, then in late 1891 through a leap back to her childhood religion, the ground for her parallel identification of Nietzsche with herself—through her "Gottesschöpfung"

(God-Creation), which, published along with her first articles on Nietzsche, told of how already in earliest childhood she on her side had divinized herself unawares in a prototypical "fusion and confusion of what is most intimate, most personal, with what is highest." By her telling, her "fusion and confusion" was of course so neat and naïve and wholesome that it put any more rationalized religious construction to shame. But the payoff was that, blissfully unsophisticated, it had yielded altogether to her very first rational doubt, with no struggle of mind against heart—and accordingly "no secret hope of reconstructing along the path of knowledge what has been lost to religious ardor." This "no secret hope" was illicit gain from the pious exchange with Nietzsche. She overcompensated the loser: in "Gottesschöpfung" she designated the earliest religious experiences the healthiest upon backdating her loss of faith, whereupon she issued Nietzsche a tacit bill of health in her Nietzsche book by backdating his correspondingly. Moreover, if her reduction of his high mental purposes was perhaps only retaliatory, she was surely identifying herself with him when, at the very start of her book, she reclaimed the "thought from the 'sister brain' " only to adopt the thought from the brother brain in turn and insist that, though his philosophy could be refuted, he could not—or when she asserted in the same context that his three philosophical periods, which he had delineated for her in 1882 as of that date, "were distinguished and distinctly characterized for the first time" in one of her articles. There was room in her book for no further self-identification with him than this. And there was need for none: after her "Gottesschöpfung" leap of 1891, her need was rather for her diabolization of him to catch up, proceeding as it did haltingly from article to article to book. It proceeded autonomously too: at the time of her book she was still devoted to him in her uppermost as well as her innermost thoughts—in rating him as well as in romancing and identifying with him—despite her reductive thesis in between. Her readers were bound to notice the conflict at the surface and sense the one in the depths. And of Nietzsche's intimates, one at all odds, galled by her thesis, was bound to attack her on it *ad feminam,* exposing the romance as fraud while dismissing the eulogies as deceit. This she expected: it was the built-in penalty.

The book was grandly launched by Lou's literary set, which took her to have surmounted Nietzsche's influence by refuting his philosophy after having been his confidante and disciple until his breakdown. Most neutral reviewers "were quick to hail it as a psychological masterpiece," noted one big exception, Josef Hofmiller. Within Nietzsche's old circle Erwin Rohde, after deeming Lou's first articles on Nietzsche incomparably fine and deep, now told Overbeck that she was "above all a literary parasite who would just like to live off Nietzsche a while as off a suitable substratum while also putting her own person to advantage, and this not so tactfully or nicely." Overbeck in 1894 called Lou's "the best and most qualified word ever publicly sounded on Nietzsche"; subsequently, though, he shook his head at her fakery and pronounced her "reflexions and constructions" about Nietzsche's illness "sufficient in themselves to rule out any really intimate association or communication." In July 1893 Peter Gast, in his introduction to a reedition of Nietzsche's

Human, All Too Human, upbraided Lou for her latest articles: he threw back her charge against Nietzsche of mystical madness, refuted her on point after point beginning with Nietzsche's having come to positivism through Rée, and denounced her trickery about how long she knew Nietzsche—all this too late, however, to affect her book. In July 1894 Gast discerned in the book itself "only rejection: Nietzsche rejected by the ink-stained hand of a Russian general's daughter: so long as there are such spectacles, life is a heartening thing." Two months later Gast nonetheless considered that "Lou's culture is simply too extraordinary; she may even be 'right' about much, as abnormal high tension in feeling and thinking is nothing for the masses, who dismiss it as 'pathological,' 'crazy,' and the like, then go about their business. It was clever of Lou to prove the point with great psychological to-do and win the assent of all the 'healthy.' Yet for all that, her book remains an astonishing achievement. I know of no woman's work that could come near hers (for intellectual schooling)." Gast eventually wrote off these concessions to Lou on "my animosity toward Mrs. Förster [Nietzsche's sister] at the time."

Mr. and Mrs. Förster had founded their colony—"New Germania"—in Paraguay early in 1886. In 1889, facing financial ruin, Bernhard took his life; Lisbeth carried on alone, slowly retrieving the deficit. She returned to Germany in the fall of 1890 for eighteen months to boost subscriptions, then definitively in September 1893 to cash in on her brother's growing fame. She wrested his literary estate from Gast's hands, then from her mother's proprietorship. In February 1894 she founded the Nietzsche Archiv in Naumburg with Gast's help—only to turn Gast out that very spring. For she intended using the Archiv to represent Nietzsche's life and thought in the way of her neo-Germanic propaganda, anti-Semitism and all. Her very own first project was known in Archiv parlance as "the biography."

Lou's quasi-biography incensed her for every reason beginning with its success—and perhaps most for its allusion, however skeptical, to the paternal brain ailment. Of her old motives for rancor toward Lou, one was more valid than ever: Lou was the cause of her latterly warped relations with her brother, which she now had to smooth out for the record. The scholar's fee for the use of Archiv material was set at a poke or two at Lou in a preface. . . .

In 1904 the volume of the Archiv biography covering 1882 appeared. By this account, Lou approached Nietzsche as a would-be disciple, but fast showed herself to be intellectually unfit and only out for an amour, so Nietzsche, who really just wanted a secretary anyhow, sent her packing. Lou's book, "utterly false and untrue," contained "conversations never held, excerpts from imaginary letters, and events that never took place." It was "an act of revenge upon sick Nietzsche due to wounded feminine vanity"—and was "perhaps meant to win back Paul Rée's alienated affections" to boot. . . .

Due largely to the Archiv forgeries, Nietzsche's memory grew offensive to Lou over the years—although she was always pleased to be known socially as his sometime girl friend. For the rest, her diverse motives toward him per-sisted. She paid him occasional huge tributes, more often than not in a negative context. She decried his late philosophizing in new terms: in 1900 she noted that "sick Nietzsche fashioned the vision of a super-Nietzsche only so as to make the lack of a healthy, normal Nietzsche bearable to himself," and again in 1911 that "he foundered on a certain philosophic-theoretical shallowness" when instead of inverting his positivist maxim, "Even the though-drive is a life-drive," he exalted its second term at the expense of the first. She romanced with him with the full latent force of her pseudoreminiscences about propositions and proposals. She heaped scorn upon her "sort of memoirs and seminovel," ***Im Kampf um Gott.*** Indeed, only insofar as her Nietzsche experience was repetitive did it show on the surface of her later fiction—though one reader caught it anyway in the recurrent theme of a young girl's free discipleship to a self-willed master turning of a sudden into a frenzied temptation to mental and erotic thralldom defended against "with a sure instinct."

Meanwhile Nietzsche grew on her. She contracted personal habits of his, such as alternately working long weeks or months in solitude, then living socially awhile. She took up physical attitudes of his once lovingly noted by her, such as his cautious, pensive gait and his air of "hearkening to all things"; likewise, her voice softened to a hush, and stopped for any but intimate company, even as her youthful forwardness gave way to a discretion and reserve far too marked to have been a mere matter of age or marriage. She also drew a dispensation from "second-rank scruples," meaning all scruples, from Nietzsche's "sacred self-seeking, or instinctive obedience to what is highest"—to which Nietzsche had denied her title. But what she took from Nietzsche was chiefly intellectual, from pet expressions (such as going out "among men" and returning "to myself") to historical theses (about justice, Christianity, and the like), by way of his new psychological approach according to which the psyche is an archive, culture denotes inhibition, memory is weaker than forgetfulness, perception works to prevent seeing too much and intellection to prevent understanding too much, a manifest virtue is the obverse of a latent vice, and one's sexuality informs the highest reaches of one's mind. She was to work through many a Tautenburg topic—including notably woman as such—on these terms to his own conclusions and beyond, even as in her expository prose the sentence gradually yielded to the paragraph, didactics to imagery and incantation: Lou as positivist to Lou as Nietzsche. And in her case in turn, the ideal of cold-blooded cognition yielded to awe before the instincts. In fact she filled her own bill for Nietzsche's late thought in due course—all the way from a "repudiation of [her] former purely logical ideal of knowledge" to "a religious mysticism in which God, world, and man fuse into a single prodigious superbeing." Thus she took up his succession after all—which shows that she had never really said no to it in her heart. Just so, she now denied the postpositivist Nietzsche in terms pointedly (and poorly) calculated to dissociate her own postpositivist course from his. . . .

In one vital respect Lou's postpositivism did differ from Nietzsche's—the one to be expected from her having had not only an enforced asceticism of the spirit to surmount, but also an inveterate asceticism of the flesh.

Stuart Hampshire   (essay date 1969)

SOURCE: "Freud and Lou Andreas-Salomé," translated by Stanley A. Leavy, in his *Modern Writers and Other Essays,* Chatto & Windus, 1969, pp. 88-95.

[*Hampshire is an English philosopher, critic, and educator. In the following excerpt he discusses Andreas-Salomé's personal and intellectual influence on Sigmund Freud during the years 1912-13.*]

Lou Andreas-Salomé was the intimate friend of Nietzsche and of Rilke, and a pupil, friend, and confidante of Freud. She was a sentimental tourist. She can be seen as one of the 'free spirits' of late romanticism, a voracious adorer, Ibsen's Rebecca West, a woman who urged men of intellect to assert their powers, and particularly their powers of intellectual destruction. Shaw, converting the heroines of Ibsen into figures of high comedy, would have been delighted by her. Her writings on the then fashionable topics of femininity and narcissism are often murky and tiresome, as romanticized biology is apt to be; they fall into a half-world of new thought, which is neither literature nor science. But the evidence of her *Freud Journal* shows that the picture of her we have had so far has been incomplete.

There is an easy explanation of the interest that she aroused in such diverse men of genius: simply that she was an extraordinarily intelligent woman. She could grasp new ideas with a quite unfeigned clarity; she could immediately see connections which others could not yet see. She was therefore able to relieve the loneliness of men who had long taken it for granted that they would always be misunderstood, and therefore feared, even if the fear was masked by reverence. Freud was wholly at ease with her. She was quite free from the envy that any extravagance of imagination, or of intellectual power, arouses in most people. Her biographers, and biographers of Nietzsche, may speculate that her envy was of the other, the sexual kind. This cannot be known.

The *Journal,* written during her association with Freud in the years 1912-1913, when Lou Andreas-Salomé was fifty years old, shows a precocious understanding of his purposes and methods which naturally amazed him. He directed his lectures at her, solicited her comments afterwards, and was disappointed whenever she could not attend. Though the story of her relations with Nietzsche is well known, the story of Freud's lectures in Vienna, of the discussions of the disciples, walking home in the snow after the lectures, of the formation of groups and selection of favourites, of the crossing of the lines of loyalty involved in knowing Jung and Stekel—all this is not so well known. The atmosphere of the middle years of the founding of psychoanalysis in Vienna—something that is largely missing from Ernest Jones's biography, and even from Freud's published letters—is alive in this *Journal.*

Behind the gossip and anecdotes, often in themselves delightful, some of Freud's own uncertainties are revealed.

One sees more clearly why his tentative speculation was so often converted into hard doctrine: why he found it necessary to be so absolute in insisting on his theoretical distinctions, even when the clinical evidence, still minute in quantity, evidently left many alternatives open. He was frightened of being welcomed as a philosopher. It has already been remarked that Freud both disliked and distrusted philosophy, or anything that resembled it. One reason for his distrust is more than once suggested in this book. Psychoanalysis could in those years, and in that city, very easily have become one more variety of new thought, an eclectic philosophy of life, or a key to a new *Weltanschauung.*]

In the period of the *Last Days of Mankind,* as Kraus recorded them, or of the decline of the west as Lou Andreas-Salomé believed, new doctrines of regeneration were springing up all across Europe, as they had in the late Hellenistic Period and in other periods of anticipated disaster; and nowhere more feverishly than in the Vienna of Mahler, Schönberg, Wittgenstein, Schnitzler, and Kraus. In his association with Fliess, Freud had come close to the abyss that separates medical science from a regenerative philosophy of the soul. When the pull was constant towards a higher synthesis of philosophy and biology, towards a California-style doctrine of salvation, Freud had to over-compensate in the opposite direction, if psychoanalysis was to survive at all as a branch of clinical psychology. The over-precise mechanical metaphors, the doctrine of psychological forces, the pseudo-quantitative explanations of conflict, amounted to a kind of promissory note; this note might perhaps be redeemed later when a more adequate physiology was available. In the meantime, the appearance of scientific precision, even if it was sometimes illusory, might serve its purpose of keeping philosophers of the soul at bay.

As Lou Andreas-Salomé noted, this was part of the significance of the battle with Jung. The concept of libido, with its unique expression in sexuality, prevented psychology from being satisfied with explanations in purely mental terms. The danger that Freud saw in Jung's hypotheses, as in all the heresies which rejected his concept of sexuality, was that they suggested explanations in terms of the concept of the mind alone. They thereby cut the cord that might at some time re-unite clinical psychology with physiology. Freud contrasted philosophy with science, not only as seeking syntheses rather than a more minute analysis of the data, but also as explaining behaviour in terms of ideas only, whether conscious or unconscious ideas.

Although he mocked, he could tolerate Lou Andreas-Salomé's philosophizing, because from the beginning she understood his strategy of driving neo-Freudianism, as an eclectic doctrine of mental healing, outside the movement. She might wilfully speculate on the relation of mind and body, and on Freud's resemblance to Spinoza; but she agreed that sexual drives and feelings must be the centre of psychology, if only because they are already the accepted point of contact between the physical and the psychical realms. Freud himself always turned away from general speculation of the kind that engaged Lou Andreas-Salomé, just because her speculations could not suggest specific and testable solutions to specific problems. He sometimes can be seen to be wearily hoping that problems, when stated in his terms, would allow specific tests and solutions; in those early stages it was essential to keep up the appearance of tentative advance rather than to fall into the surrounding morass of philosophical generalities. In the last twenty years one has seen how empty, and how consoling, neo-Freudian generalities can be, particularly in sociology. Freud loathed consolation; for him the first condition of science was the suppression of wish and the postponement of total solutions.

There are pictures of Freud in Lou Andreas-Salomé's *Journal* that deserve to be remembered. 'He enters the class with the appearance of moving to the side. There is in this gesture a will to solitude, a concealment of himself within his own purposes.' One encounters again his wilful melancholy, his tired and persistent pessimism about human beings and their opportunities of happiness. It is as if he had abandoned all spontaneity in an earlier existence, and was now, in some attenuated form of life, looking back upon the unavoidable errors of normal experience. His disillusion seems to have been so radical as to cause him, after his marriage, to deny, like Spinoza's free man, that any mere passive emotions, unmodified by irony, could be imputed to him. He often speaks here as if he were only reflecting on experience, which for him was in the past and complete, as a man in mourning might speak. Ten hours of analysis during the day would be followed by the delivery, or preparation, of lectures in the evening. His living was working; and only in his emotional demands upon his followers does his temperament appear in this *Journal.* The reader of the *Journal* must, therefore, be warned of frustrations: upon introducing Rilke to Freud, Lou Andreas-Salomé writes: 'I was delighted to bring Rainer to Freud, they liked each other, and we stayed together that evening until late at night.' That is all. The *Journal* is both fragmentary and egotistical in this way.

Coming to psychoanalysis from literature and philosophy, Lou Andreas-Salomé did not seriously question its scientific credentials: in this she was typical of her time. Vienna in 1912 was the decaying centre of Europe in which the beginnings of the new music, of the new architecture, of the new philosophy, the new psychology, were being sketched and formed, as parts of a general revolution of ideas. We cannot now deny that the revolutionary ideas of this century have been mainly scientific ideas—in physics, biology, and in the mathematics of probability, logic and information theory. But in a longer perspective this might turn out not to be the whole truth. For the dividing line between the empirical sciences, as previously defined, and other human inquiries may now be less clearly marked; those inquiries which lie on the margin of science may still prove surprisingly fruitful. Freud's hypotheses, judged by existing criteria, were at many points improbable guesses, elaborated in the terminology of an exact science. In the process of analysis itself, he had invented a variant of scientific observation; for the fantasies that he detected in free association and in dreams were to be detected through interpretation. And interpretation was a procedure of literary and aesthetic inquiry and of literary and aesthetic explanation. In his own life, as he is partially revealed in reminiscences of him and in his letters, he alternated between two poles: at one extreme was the requirement that he should be a pure scientist, and that his theory of repression and of neurosis should be precise, and should be spelled out as a scientific hypothesis; at the other extreme there was the requirement that he should be a kind of artist, who needed extraordinary sensitiveness, and a suspension of disbelief, in uncovering the fantasies concealed in most forms of human expression and behavior. The hybrid that results is unintelligible without the same aesthetic and scientific culture which he inherited and preserved. An empiricist philosopher will be repelled by a hybrid claim to knowledge, which substitutes interpretation for mere observation of the data as its base. How can there be theory worthy of respect which does not rest on unchallengeable fact, independent of interpretive insight? This principle of exclusion, as applied to claims to systematic knowledge, may be unanswerable. But at least a similar hybridness can be suspected in other tentative inquiries which are characteristic of our time. For example, he who studies as scientifically as he can, the forms of language and the process by which a child learns language, might find that he cannot isolate the unchallengeable phenomena which his theories are required to cover. The isolation of distinct phenomena in this field may not be independent of interpretations, which in turn are to some degree guided by the theory. If this were the situation, and if therefore theories of language were less than scientific judged by established standards, it would not follow that the inquiry was uninformative and useless. It would follow only that alternative reconstructions were possible, and that certainty had not been achieved. One cannot always know in advance whether a given complex subject matter—e. g., the forms of language or the content of dreams—is susceptible to a scheme of explanation that has proved adequate in the natural sciences. The material that is of interest may be just too complex, and we may need to be satisfied, at least for a time, with a hybrid understanding of it.

In these early years Freud was not in a position even to guess what limitations upon precise knowledge he would encounter. He could only go ahead, and Lou Andreas Salomé's *Journal* shows at least some of his strategies: above all, his two-sided attachment to an idea of himself as an empirical scientist and also as an imaginative interpreter of the language of the passions. The interpretations are made to fit the theory, and the theory is adjusted to fit the interpretations. The argument is therefore circular, and we have no detachable conclusion, which so far constitutes systematic knowledge. We are left with a method of inquiry, indefinitely extendable, which shows the mechanism of repression at work, and which may always be used to retrieve some of the ideas and wishes that are repressed, and to recover some of the energies that are lost.

Angela Livingstone   (essay date 1984)

SOURCE: *Lou Andreas-Salomé,* Gordon Fraser, 1984, pp. 74-86.

[*Livingstone is an English educator and critic. In the fol-*

lowing excerpt she assesses Andreas-Salomé's theories on the historical origins and development of religion.]

When Nietzsche encouraged Lou von Salomé to philosophise about religion, he was recognising an inclination she showed long before she met him. Faith and loss of faith had been her main childhood experience, history of religion had been her main study with both [Hendrik] Gillot and [Alois] Biedermann. She went on thinking about religion all her life. Her theories about art, love, femaleness and Russia are all closely related to her religious views. More specifically, though, during the years 1891-8, and still under Nietzsche's influence, she devoted eleven long essays to this subject.

Some of the essays are more scholarly, some more personal. All suffer from looseness of expression and structure; one would like to rewrite them concisely, put in paragraphing, and request some references and facts. She often talks of history, of developments and changes, without mentioning time or place, and sums up literatures without naming a book; she seems carried away by ideas too pressing to allow time for detail or proof. None the less, all are worth reading: in addition to their interest as part of a contemporary debate, there is in these writings a forthrightness and vitality which greatly commend them. Forthrightness is not a quality of Nietzsche's; if what Lou Andreas-Salomé took from Nietzsche was the confident glorification of the individual mind, the habit of thinking evolutionarily, and the assumption of a responsibility for 'culture', what eluded her in him was the whole of his irony and paradox. Nietzsche could praise intelligence while showing the ambiguity of all its achievements, but Lou was uncomplexly enthusiastic, and the uncritical confidence of her style gives, to put it mildly, a tolerant restfulness to ideas that in Nietzsche are utterly demanding.

Lou Andreas-Salomé's study of religion amounts to a study of religious feeling. The 'death of God' is central, for her argument usually starts from the conviction (still novel in her time) that 'God' has a history: he was born, he lived and he died. The big divergence from Nietzsche is that, in her theory, God also has an after-life. The object of faith has indeed disappeared (ceased to be believed in), but while it was there it caused the growth of feelings which would otherwise never have come into being, and these are the most valuable feelings we are capable of. Her concern is to describe and promote these feelings.

Like Nietzsche, she is dismayed at the banality with which some Bible critics and 'free-thinking' writers approach matters so serious as the shattering of a great tradition, and scornful of their inability to *feel* what they were doing. She would have shared the attitude of George Eliot, who had translated both Strauss and Feuerbach into English and been in the forefront of debates in England about Darwin, yet still said that to her 'the Development Theory and all other explanations of processes by which things came to be, produce a feeble impression compared with the mystery that lies under the processes', and also that she cared 'only to know, if possible, the lasting meaning that lies in all religious doctrine from the beginning till now'. Lou, though, spoke less of a 'lasting meaning' than of an ever-changing meaning, itself the product of change.

Lou's central ideas are set out in her first long article, **'Realism in Religion'** (1891). The divine has a history, and its history has two stages: in the first the gods were created and were worshipped, though without the inner devotion that appears only in the second. First of all, man made God. Then the man-made God made plain man into god-made man—that is, into man with a need for God, a need not merely to explain the mysteries of nature but to satisfy the idealism that had developed in him through his evolving relationship with the God he had made.

This is not a concern with ethics; it is not a matter of people having changed through *behaviour* resulting from their faith, nor of evolution of feelings towards other people; it is solely a concern with the feelings that are addressed to the Deity and that survive its demise. This idea is elaborated repeatedly in Lou's essays on religion, as if she is forever engaging with something she can never finally express. Man creates gods. Then the gods influence man. Whereby it is most characteristic that she does not say 'the idea of the gods', or 'the idea of God', influences man.

The formulation is perhaps most succinct in her essay **'Jesus the Jew'** a few years later:

> If one starts from **the** human being instead of—as one used to—from the God, then one realises almost involuntarily that the actual religious phenomenon first comes to be present in the *back-effect* of a godhead—no matter how it arose—upon the person who believes in that godhead.

She was to become known as the propounder of the theory of the 'back-effect' (*Rückwirkung*). As late as 1955, Karl Kerényi quotes this sentence (on which he bases a large part of his inquiry into the history of religion) and comments: 'Here that precise borderpoint is identified at which a science of religion becomes possible; at which the religious already exists . . . The science of religion begins with the concern with what Lou Salomé calls the "back-effect".'

This first article started with the need for a new approach to religion. No naive belief, nor positivist denial, nor the current matter-of-fact efforts to rescue something of Christianity for 'modern man': instead an approach which would start from the fact of religious *experience*—a 'psychology of religion', an exploration of the obscure areas of religious mood and impulse which are not (*pace* Paul Rée) explained away by their origination in error.

Lou discusses here a recent book about religious experience and dwells on two affective moments in the unnamed author's account of this: humility and pride. She has a lot to say about pride in this context. Christian writers usually stress humility—Rudolf Otto, for instance, speaks of 'creature-consciousness', the sense of one's own abasement, of being overpowered by something other than oneself, the feeling 'I am nought', and calls the feeling of identification of the personal self with the transcendent reality not 'pride' but 'bliss'. Lou Andreas-Salomé, by contrast, dwells on the exhilaration of the very swing from 'I am nought' to 'I am all'. Seeing it another way, from 'I am all' to 'I *have* all'; or again, in another image, of the friction between these opposite attitudes:

> Neither the sincerest humility and self-prostration before an ideal conceived as divine, nor the most full and satisfying enjoyment of all self-assertive powers for themselves alone, is able to produce the religious affect. Only the two together in enigmatic self-contradiction yield that friction from which suddenly, hot and vivid, the flame leaps out.

She often uses pairs of words, like *'Demut'* and *'Hochmut'* ('humility' and 'pride') and claims there is in all of us this inebriant seesawing between 'the awareness of weakness and helplessness in the face of all reality and the pride of being, as a human, in a certain sense superior to it all'. These combined, she says, make up our highest feeling, which is also described as 'the knowledge of our limit, and at that limit the exaltation that grows beyond it'.

This is not equally available to everyone. Fascinated with the idea that evolution means ever greater individuation, she sees the desire for God as an increasingly individual desire, leading to ever more individual God-creating. I make a God for *me*. So, as well as collective God-making, followed historically by the back-effect of the shared God upon people in general, there is also an individual God-making, with consequent lasting effect upon 'Me'. Indeed, the 'greater' the individual personality, the greater its capacity to pray to what is conceived as the holiest. Echoing her Tautenburg diary notes, she states:

> The religious affect is thus also the characteristic sign of all *great egoists*—taking greatness here in the sense of a *force,* not as a mere selfish *direction* of the being.

This is what religion always is, she says, for it aims at 'egoism' and the individual, its chief and reckless question being 'What must I do to be blessed?' (In German, as in Russian, 'blessed' and 'blissful' are the same word.)

Lou sounds like Nietzsche when she upbraids her author for becoming too theoretical and adapting his own experience to the existing theology. One would like to take each thing he says he values and ask 'How do *you* stand in relation to this: was it the ladder for *you* to climb up by toward yourself . . . ?' and she quotes Zarathustra: 'Let yourself be in the deed, as the mother is in the child: let this be *your* word about virtue!' The conclusion of the essay is Nietzschean, too—a vehement page or so on most people's inability to care about what is going on. Religion is increasingly enfeebled, God is vanishing behind abstractions, and yet

> Nothing is more amazing than the ease, even the pleasure, with which nearly every cultivated person of today is capable of swallowing down the vastest helping of doubts—so long as they're 'modern' ones—without getting the slightest spiritual discomfort from it; they are like conjurors who swallow swords.

And she adds:

> *May* it tear us to bits! If only we *were* less conju-

rors and more real people who feel in their innermost life the things that they think and do.

One has to keep in mind that what she laments is the disappearance not of faith, but of feeling. The courage to *feel* the loss of God is more creative than any clinging to His image, and only from courage will great personalities be born. By implication, the purpose of our existence is the production of great personalities; this is a part of Nietzsche's thought that she has made her own.

Between **'Realism in Religion'** and the important **'Jesus the Jew'** of 1896, Lou published five other articles on religion. Two were in 1892, the polemic **'Harnack and the Apostolic Creed'** and the self-indulgent **'God-creation'**. The latter is an autobiographical piece, less well argued than most. It could have been entitled 'self-creation', for it seems that the projecting of the self into an invisible being, wholly believed in as existing 'out there in the real', is what the 'religious' means; and the article is written in a spirit of somewhat complacent gratitude for having had, in infancy, the naive and sober certainty of the existence of—such a—God. It is hard to grasp that she is *not* saying that God is only a projection of the self. But the essay is anything but a coolly reductive exercise. When she says 'This involuntary blending and exchanging of the most intimate . . . with the most lofty—this conception of the intimate *as* the lofty, already contains the characteristic basic element of the religious', she is conceiving of that 'loftiest' as somehow really existent. If it slides out of the categories of subjective and objective, without clarity as to whether a third category is intended, or a transcending of these two, then this appears to be a non-definition essential to the experience.

'Harnack and the Apostolic Creed' is much more interesting and Nietzsche's influence is palpable in it. It praises the courageous, godless life and distinguishes between the few who can live such a life and the many who cannot. Un-Nietzschean, though, is the way Lou Andreas-Salomé does not scorn the 'many'; in fact the article is written in their defence, and for their protection. It is her response to a tract [*Das Apostolische Glaubensbekemntnis,* 1892] by the Protestant theologian, Adolf Harnack, just published in its fifteenth edition, widely on sale and a talking-point in many circles. As an inquiry into the origin and varied history of the apostolic creed, it angered the orthodox and delighted the free-thinkers. Andreas-Salomé, while approving of its historical approach, curiously enough argues for orthodoxy, and asserts that not only are Harnack's revelations unlikely to shake the rigours of orthodoxy, but they *ought* not to shake them.

Her argument is ingenious. Precisely because religious forms sprang up in consequence of human wishes and needs—because, that is, they are not about something objectively there (here she appears to say straight out that there is no God), they are vulnerable and might disappear; but religion is good for us, we evolve and deepen through it. Rigid, even petrified dogma, and all the firm traditional forms, far from being a deathly element, have been—and for some still are—essential to the preserving of religious life. Even Protestantism needs some orthodoxy. Those who talk of individual assent, moral uplift and spiritual transport, rather than of doctrine and formality, are confused about the way religion arises: need creates God, then God creates in His believers specific religious feelings, but those feelings are not felt by all to the same extent and at the same time. For instance, not by certain simple people, or by people in despair and suffering. What these people may need in addition to our efforts to do what we can to improve the conditions of their lives (and this is one of the few places where she says anything of this order) is the consolation and support of firm doctrine. So while the stronger and luckier no longer need it, it must be kept for the weaker and less fortunate. This may sound a little like the view of Dostoyevsky's Grand Inquisitor, the benevolent dictator who, himself an atheist, spends his life promoting belief in God for the multitude who cannot do without it, only where he is burdened with anguish and the strain of keeping it all going, Lou's more developed and prosperous non-believer, who is to protect the belief for the others, is thought of as purely happy, the only true enjoyer of religion's natural and wonderful fruits. (Also, of course, she does not envisage either tyranny or Utopia.)

These true enjoyers should leave the church, she says, while (presumably) continuing to present church-protective arguments. Free-thinking has no business to be going on *in* the church. It damages the interests of the simple and the poor, and also dissuades stronger minds from leaving. Full of the enthusiasm they have gained from religion, these people should leave all beaten tracks and take their light into pathlessness (*'das Weglose'*)—all the dark places the church knows nothing of. Again we hear Nietzsche: the highest daring is that which explores places never yet made habitable by any kind of meaning. Lou's paradoxical and optimistic variant of this is that the most valuable thing religion gives us is the courage to explore the dark places without its help. Truth, she says, is a more jealous God than the Judaeo-Christian one, and you have to be ready to be destroyed by it.

The early 'history of God' is developed in two subsequent studies: **'From the Beast to the God'** (1893) outlines, among the early Semites, an evolution from tribal gods through animal totems to 'God' as 'king of the land'. **'The Problems of Islam'**, a year later, is an enthusiastic piece of scholarship (perhaps inspired by Andreas) arguing that the ancient Arabs, the very type of the original uncultivated human being, not yet religious, but lordly, proud and full of splendid virtues, were weakened by the humbling and levelling effects of the later Islamic culture; clearly with Nietzsche in mind, she writes of 'an original master morality and its destruction through the slave morality of religious culture.' Then, in **'On the Origin of Christianity'** (1895), Lou is concerned with how the few plain facts of Jesus's life were transformed into legend and glory. But her main study of Jesus is the essay of 1896, which was to impress and influence Rilke.

'Jesus the Jew' re-states Lou Andreas-Salomé's main ideas and develops them to a new conclusion. The conclusion—which we are largely left to draw—is that Jesus belongs among the great unbelievers, the geniuses of unbelief.

Rehearsing her two stages in the life of God, she points out that while the first one is amazing enough, even more amazing is the second, when the idea of God may so drench someone's inner life that he grows into something greater than he could otherwise ever have been. By stressing Jesus's Jewishness—he was not the overcomer of Judaism but its sharpest expression—she is able to make him a forerunner of her great religious unbelievers. For, as a Jew, he believed God would manifest himself upon earth at the right time and believed this quite simply and practically—'The Jew did not brood over his God, he suffered and lived and felt', and trusted not in breath but in blood, that is not in a hereafter but in the keeping of divine promises on earth. Like some other martyrs, then, Jesus expected God's manifestation at the last moment: and at the last moment he found that it was not going to happen. He thus faced something far more terrible than did later Christian martyrs, for they were to die expecting Heaven, while he died expecting nothing. In this way she interprets the cry 'My God, why have you forsaken me?' as his *really* taking upon himself in that moment, just as we say he did, 'the suffering of all mankind'. For he suffered the suffering that lies in wait for us all when, having trusted in a personal God, we find out that there is none.

Although she does not explicitly connect Jesus with the ideal of the free-thinking genius, the conjunction of very great love with complete and sharply felt unbelief, and the fortitude in enduring the two together, suggest the connection. Jesus was essentially and solely the lonely genius, capable of the highest human feeling and so deep in it that nothing else mattered to him; he was not the founder of a new religion, although a new religion was, paradoxically, born of the events connected with him.

> Religion in its whole truth and its whole illusion, embodied in a human being, bled away to death here on the cross, which, since then, strangely enough, has become the symbol of religion.

The Cross (she ends the essay), whatever it may mean in Christianity, should really remind us

> that it is always only the individual, the great individual who attains the peaks of religion, its genuine blissfulness and its full tragedy. What he experiences up there, the crowd below does not learn.

After **'Jesus the Jew'** Lou published four more long essays on religion. **'Egoism in Religion'** (1899) is largely a replay of former themes, but three essays of 1897-8 offer interesting developments of them.

According to **'Religion and Culture'** (1898), all cultural activities originated in religion like children from one mother; and each, as it grew up and away, ceased to need parental guidance, so that the lonely mother was thrown back on her own resources: that is, religion became specialised, concerned only with the belief in God and visibly separated off from the rest of life. But the 'children' carried an invisible aspect of religion further and further along with them, and this emerges at peak points in the lives of individuals. For:

> Innumerable people have innumerable times applied the name God to something other than

God; innumerable souls have let their most ardent pieties and enthusiasms overflow away from faith and into life . . . God is not God but only a symbol for all that in human life that is too intimate, intense and dear to be called by a human name.

Rather mysteriously, she says that religion's dream of salvation, the dream of God as the life of life, is perhaps only true and 'blessed-making' at the two extremes: deep below in the dark places where man was born as man, believing he derived from God; and high above on the summits of culture where he feels he is at last truly man—and gives birth to God.

Then, in part of **'From the History of God'** (1897) and in most of **'On the Religious Affect'** (1898), Lou Andreas-Salomé sets out what I will call her theory of sublime moods. Both these essays are written with an excitement that shows she is describing her own experiences. She is deeply convinced of the possibility of joy. Her tone is that of urging people to stop being dry-as-dust, to look upwards and to realise how intensely happy they could be. They should stop both protesting against old articles of faith and rehearsing old habits of belief, and should instead take a fresh look and see the whole phenomenon of religion anew, as someone might look again at his wintry old home in the spring.

'From the History of God' starts with another attack on the accommodations of the modern church to rationalism and science, and quotes Nietzsche's 'madman' [in *The Gay Science*] who cried out that 'we have killed God' and 'who will wipe this blood from us?'

It is followed by a weird account of the history of religion in five stages, unsupported by evidence. These she says go from intoxicated freedom in interpretation, through the demand for orthodoxy (not ossification but a necessary harness), then a stage of asceticism and self-humbling (which produces for the first time the 'objective godhead', or rather conceals for the first time its actually human origin), to another of mysticism, and finally to one of rationalism, in which the mysteries are put to the test of reason. After this nothing much is left but a dubious brew of allegory. Thus is the contemporary church—feeble and droughted. It is this rationalistic dreariness that is now contrasted with her account of what, in an age after the death of God, the religiously-inclined person could be having. Her own theory of sublime feelings is now presented as a contrast to the pettiness of those who couldn't care less about the death of God. The sublime feeling (a chief part of which is actually 'devotion') comes when external events, no longer speaking in their everyday voice, appear to reveal themselves as symbols, 'as if they were uttering something divine to us'. The man of a particular faith was able to give clear expression to this state; we cannot. None the less, at such moments of self-communion [*'Einkehr und Sammlung'*] we are totally concerned and participant; everything becomes unified, peaceful, profound. (Although Lou does not derive this mood from childhood or countryside, nor connect it with impulses to perform acts of kindness, there is an obvious similarity to many other accounts of an experienced quasi-religious

peace, for example to Wordsworth's 'serene and blessed mood' in which 'with an eye made quiet by the power / Of harmony, and the deep power of joy, / we see into the life of things'.) Now this mood, she declares, is not a sentimental reminiscence of faith, but a new growth from the soil from which all religion grows. And non-believers can in fact have intenser religious experience than believers, for the latter may be hindered by the weight of their fixed faith from daring 'to enter into all the hidden blisses where the faithless person frequently feels and experiences something'.

'On the Religious Affect' then proceeds to distinguish two basic states of mind. One kind is shared with people in general, the other is not. Above the stable, indubitable and universally shared everyday moments of our existences there tower, like mountain peaks over a great plain, our lofty moments of beauty and ecstasy, which are *not* shared, and which we don't feel any need to share, so confident are we of their reality:

> Plains flow effortlessly into one another, but that which rises above the flat ground is separated— to the extent that it reaches upward—from neighbours and comrades; certainly the summits may be similar to each other in kind and in height, yet you will only get from the one to the other by a detour over the common ground and by climbing painfully up.

Despite their tremendous separateness, we feel in those moments that we are breathing 'the air of home'; what's more, we feel certain that others have their own such experiences, and without needing even to think about it (whether they do or not) we quite naturally seek to express that experience in words or deeds. Not, she stresses, for the *sake* of others, although it will turn out to have *been* expressed for them.

Mountain peaks are Nietzsche's frequent image, and when Lou writes here—

> then come the individuals once again to one another and they recognise and greet one another, and there goes a laughter from summit to summit . . .

she echoes Nietzsche's 'republic of geniuses', in which 'one giant calls to another across the arid intervals of the ages, and, undisturbed by wanton noisy dwarfs creeping about beneath them, the lofty intercourse of spirits continues.'

Unlike Nietzsche, she also conceives of the most extreme individuality as a moving away into the experience of something no longer to be called *self.* 'At these heights of our self we are released from ourselves.'

The essay culminates in prophecy. An epoch is to come in which all fragmentation and isolation will be overcome. A time of harmony and of blossoming when, instead of endlessly collecting pieces of new scientific knowledge like gathering gold coins into an enormous heap, we shall join together and begin to *spend* our wealth. All will come together 'and close into a whole, in art, science, ethics and life' and there goes a laughter from summit to summit, as if what had seemed, not long past, to be shapeless mountain-ranges rising up meaninglessly here and there, and just as meaninglessly plunging down to the flat plain, were being quietly shaped and arranged into a gigantic human building, like a temple, with the immeasurable sky above it.

An impracticable vision, yet not a vision of Heaven or the end of time. It is conceived evolutionarily and relatively; for it, too, she says, will pass away, and we must not mind that this will happen. Just as she put it in *Struggling for God,* she says here:

> What does it matter if late-following generations look back upon this as upon collapsed ruins and see in them only what we ourselves see in the highest dreams of past epochs: a mere symbol of our own highest dream?

Is this Lou Andreas-Salomé's equivalent of Nietzsche's 'eternal recurrence of all things'? She endures, and makes a part of her scheme, the thought of the inevitable disappearance of all things. Since she is certain that happiness and perfection are not only definitely coming in the future in all their fullness, but are already intimated, already being enjoyed; since she herself already enjoyed their intimations with a peace and security such as Nietzsche never knew; the thought of Disappearance must be a far more desolating one than that of Recurrence would be. It is impressive to see how she accepts temporality and transience with a wave of the hand, with a light gesture, an almost aesthetic flourish, at the end of this solemn, ecstatic essay.

On the central question Lou is never quite clear. She will build a complex argument leading to it but, reaching it, behaves as if it were not there: instead of the peak of a hill with a view all round, there is a cloud, into which she walks. I mean the question: given that we 'make' God, what can be meant by 'God's existence'? Does God exist or not? Repeatedly she argues that God came into being in the course of history, as the product of human wishing, willing, believing. Does it not follow that He is a figment, a fiction?

We postulate God, learn this *was* only a postulate, abandon it, but not before we have developed a whole range of valuable feelings in relation to it. That is, we have become religious beings, enriched and enabled. These feelings now need fresh objects, so we set up new ideals, something else to revere, love and work for—hence the best in our culture—and in our finest achievements we recreate God. For those who have not learnt that God was merely our postulate, the church with its dogma and mysteries should continue, but we luckier and cleverer ones already overflow with the best it was able to give us, and can now bear to know it was a beneficial error. But when she comes to the point of saying God was an error, and there is no God without us, she doesn't say it. Instead it appears, without scrutiny, that there is no difference between emotion about God, and God. It seems that God *is,* wherever He is needed, and He is needed not only by the weak as a prop, but also by the strong as recipient of their gratitude.

It would be unendurable, indeed quite simply

impossible . . . to be without him in those highest moments in which one does not wish to be consoled and raised up by someone else's help but only to relieve one's heart of a gratitude such as only a God can receive . . . However, at that point there never is such a lack, for there God is always.

It is true that in **'Religion and Culture'** she does say God is not God but 'only a symbol' for everything that is 'too intimate, intense and dear to be called by a human name'; but thereupon the question is begged again: *what* is too dear, etc.? What *are* we aware of in those moments? If no human name, then surely no human thing? And what does the end of that essay mean, saying religion is 'true' at the two historical human extremes? *True?* If only she would say something like: reverence proves there must be something to be reverent *to*; or even that when we create God through feeling, this makes Him really *be* there. But though these things are what she seems to mean, she prefers to keep the matter just turbid enough to make the reader feel he is forever floundering.

In many other writings, Lou talked quite unproblematically of 'God' or—often—of 'der Gott' (the God: easier in German because of the normality of the phrase 'der liebe Gott' which English would have to render 'the good Lord' or 'the dear Lord'). She found it easy to say of the Russian peasants not merely that they were very religious but that they were 'filled with God' and to say 'I love this land because God is in it,' despite having spent the preceding eight years showing that God had died out. Sometimes she seemed to mean as pantheistic a concept as that God is 'everything': sunshine and meadows . . . Sometimes, that God is happiness, or is the renewal of our sense of self, or is the certainty of meaning, or even that necessary trust in the world's meaningfulness which accompanies moral goodness. All this ought to introduce confusion into her theory, since if the religious feelings can themselves be called God, then God does not die, but survives whole. Perhaps this *is* the explanation of the confusion. Or perhaps there are always, to our imperfect understanding, these two meanings of 'God'; depending on us, and not depending on us. If she meant this, then she was close to experiences related by Tolstoy, as when Levin (in *Anna Karenina*) suddenly understands what 'God' *means* when he hears someone described as 'living for God' because he lives unselfishly; or as when, at the end of *Confession,* tormented by the question of whether God exists, Tolstoy alternately thinks 'he does, he doesn't', till he notices that each 'he does' coincides with a sense of life and joy, each 'he doesn't' with despair and senselessness.

The difference for Lou is that she did not have corresponding moments of despair and loss of meaning—or at least did not utter them. Much of her writing about religion prompts us to place her in the category William James had in mind when he wrote [in *The Varieties of Religious Experience,* 1902]:

> In many persons, happiness is congenital and irreclaimable. 'Cosmic emotion' inevitably takes in them the form of enthusiasm and freedom. I speak not of those who are animally happy. I mean those who, when unhappiness is offered or

proposed to them, positively refuse to feel it, as if it were something mean and wrong. We find such persons in every age, passionately flinging themselves upon their sense of the goodness of life, in spite of the hardships of their own condition, and in spite of the sinister theologies into which they may be born. From the outset their religion is one of union with the divine.

But we should also bear in mind that the philosopher she most admired in her youth was Spinoza, and what she later came to see herself as doing was emulating Spinoza's attempt to think the Absolute, to unite—in thought—God and Nature 'without supernaturalising the natural nor dragging the name of his God down to the level of things'.

Although it is true to say she does not discuss Spinoza in the essays on religion, he must have been a philosophical model no less than—and perhaps only reactivated by—Nietzsche (with his comparable attempt to 'think *totally*' and his greater contempt for those who did not do so). This must suggest more of an effort towards enthusiasm, a more conscious refusal to 'feel unhappiness' than would fit the healthy-minded worshipper described by William James. In her Journal of 1912, Lou writes of our coming to rediscover what 'more primitive people' always knew, namely that Joy is Perfection and she adds the name Spinoza in brackets. In fact what Spinoza wrote—in the passage she apparently has in mind—is not that joy is perfection, but that joy is 'the affect by which the mind crosses over to a greater perfection'. It is most telling that Lou, forgetting this, set up an equation between happiness and sublimity, while behind it lay, as she also really knew, something else: the long transition to happiness, the effort of aspiration to the sublime, which she had made so earnestly in her youth and which remains tacitly present in all her writings on religion.

Andreas-Salomé and Nietzsche on Christianity:

[Andreas-Salomé's] review of the history of interpretations of Jesus converges with Nietzsche's attacks on Christianity in the Antichrist. Both attack the distortions, the flattening out, of the significance of the figure of the son of God. For Nietzsche and for Salomé, Jesus represents precisely that which cannot be adequately represented, namely, the unconscious roots of the construction of gods.

Biddy Martin, in her Woman and Modernity: The (Life) Styles of Lou Andreas-Salomé, *1991.*

William Beatty Warner   (essay date 1985)

SOURCE: " 'Love in a Life': The Case of Nietzsche and Lou Salomé," in *The Victorian Newsletter*, No. 67, Spring 1985, pp. 14-17.

[*In the following essay, Warner speculates that the idealistic "holy trinity" formed between Andreas-Salomé, Friedrich Nietzsche, and Paul Rée was fraught with sexual tension and conflicting intentions from the outset, leading to*

an emotional rupture which significantly altered the course of Nietzsche's philosophy.]

In reading the lives and writing of the men and women of the Victorian period, I think we have been too ready to divine that society into those Victorians whose idea of love carries the purity of its idealism to an abstract and impossible extreme, and those "Other Victorians" who simply reduce love to forbidden sex. The first group appear as great believers in the most metaphysically-charged versions of love, the second as the failed idealists-become-skeptics, who leave the marriage bed for adultery or the brothel. To the observer of this century, the first are simply too complete in their demands upon love; the second group, being perhaps too cynical for love, is hardly less "uptight" for all that. Such a polarization on the question of love seems to be *part* of Victorian reality. It helps explain why the same novel can contain a Becky Sharp and an Amelia Sedley, why the same period can accommodate *The Secret Life* and *The Sonnets from the Portuguese.* But this polarization fails to see the Victorians as experimenters in love, who, in both their writing and life, were engaged in a dialogue about the nature and possibilities of love. I will give an example of what I mean. If one reads the essays Henry James wrote in criticism of George Eliot's representation of love in *Middlemarch,* one can see that *The Portrait of a Lady* is partly a rewriting of *Middlemarch,* so that the reader gets a more "modern" and realistic interpretation of love. Now marriage is no longer the "solution" to the love problem, but the beginning and ground of its most urgent problems. But since the question of love passes so readily between art and life, this debate is hardly abstract. It needs to be read in relation to the idealisms and compromises of George Eliot's love for George Henry Lewes, James's own complex decision not to marry, and the way James's early rivalry in love for his cousin Minny Temple offers the biographical point of departure for both Isabel Archer and the Milly Teale of *The Wings of the Dove.* James's art, no less than Eliot's, is part of a lover's discourse; but both are also part of a cultural dialogue about love.

All of this is a way of saying that artistic and philosophic investigations of love are not at an abstract remove from, they are always coextensive with, attempts at love within life. To show how this is so, I would like to sketch a love story of this period as it told itself through the lives and writing of two who contested and recomposed the Victorian conventions they lived, not in England but on the continent: the love between Nietzsche and Lou Salomé. I will pass over most of the details of this relationship as it unfolded in eight months between April and December of 1882: their meeting, their falling in love, the rivalry for Lou's love that opens between Paul Rée and Nietzsche, the idyllic three weeks Lou spends at Nietzsche's summer retreat in Tautenberg chaperoned by Nietzsche's sister Elizabeth, and the breakup of the relationship. Since most of this love affair is quite conventional, I will focus upon two salient moments of this relationship, two actions and two events which allow me to gauge its distinctive and experimental character: the arrangement Salomé, Rée, and Nietzsche make to live together and Lou Salomé's indiscretion.

In Lucerne, on May 13, 1882, after a good many weeks of negotiations, Lou Salomé, Paul Rée, and Fredrich Nietzsche agreed to form a "holy trinity" to live and study together the following winter in Vienna. To commemorate the moment, Salomé prevailed upon Nietzsche and Rée to be photographed pulling a small cart, with her in the driver's seat wielding a small whip. At the moment they assumed this playful pose, did the parties to this plan and this picture have an intuition of the pleasure and suffering this act would entail? The forging of this arrangement is an act which is opaque and symptomatic for the way it exceeds conscious intentions and projects these three into unforeseen relations. A collaborative act, it nonetheless expresses contradictory purposes and interpretations. Though Nietzsche and Rée had often projected forming a social and intellectual community outside marriage that would protect a personal independence Lou Salomé was no less determined to guard, none of the triad anticipated the bitter rivalry for her this photo predicts. The triangular arrangement for living is at once a parody of the marriage convention and a substitute for it. By blocking the need to think of marriage it seems to foreclose the very intimacy it also promotes.

Why did two mature men in their thirties and a young woman of twenty-one embark on this arrangement? For Lou Salomé the projected living arrangement expresses the tension between two currents of her life. On the one hand, it allows her to pursue a new more equal relationship with men by sharing a co-equal intellectual quest for Truth. On the other, it forges this independent relationship with men within a sexually and romantically charged scene of rivalry, where two men will vie for her attentions. I can demonstrate these conflicting currents of her motivation by describing how Salomé defends the living plan in a letter written to Gillot, her first love. Gillot was a married Lutheran minister and her confirmation teacher. When Salomé developed a strong passion for Gillot and he fell in love with her, Salomé's mother devised a protracted tour of the continent to remove her from this awkward situation. When Salomé begins to urge the idea of what she called "the holy trinity" upon Rée, even before Nietzsche arrives in Rome to meet her, her mother has Gillot write her to discourage the idea. Gillot writes that he had conceived her travel and education as part of a "transition" to some more permanent condition (perhaps marriage? marriage to him?).

Salomé's response is a kind of manifesto of her intention to win her own freedom by challenging Victorian convention: "Just what do you mean by 'transition'? If some new ends for which one must surrender that which is most glorious on earth and hardest won, namely freedom, then may I stay stuck in transition forever, for that I will not give up. Surely no one could be happier than I am now, for the gay fresh holy war likely about to break out does not frighten me: quite the contrary, let it break. We shall see whether the so-called 'inviolable bounds' drawn by the world do not just about all prove to be innocuous chalk-lines." There is a youthful zest and exuberance in the way Salomé here endorses an idea of life as a condition of ongoing transition, and joins a "gay fresh holy war" against convention. To the Germans with whom she is now waging this war, this convention weighs much more heavily. Thus in this same letter to Gillot, there is a note of condescension in the way she describes her efforts to persuade Rée to embrace the idea of a trinity. She describes her assault on the "inviolable" bounds of convention as a scene of seduction: "[Rée] too is not completely won over yet, he is still somewhat perplexed, but in our walks by night between 12 and 2 in the Roman moonlight, when we emerge from the gatherings at Malwida von Meysenbug's, I put it to him with increasing success." These walks shocked Malwida, and she cautioned against them. They cannot but help remind the modern reader of the scandal caused by Daisy Miller's indiscreet nighttime rendezvous under a moonlit sky at the Colosseum, or the much more thoughtful way Isabel Archer contemplated Gilbert Osmond's proposals in an Italian setting. Lou and Daisy and Isabel are all women who come from a less inhibited place, in possession of a beauty which is coimplicated with their independence of spirit; all three trigger a rivalry for their affections; and each is intent on finding a risky new way of living in a European world too much defined by strict convention.

Salomé sought to insure her independence of any one man, not by removing to a distance from all men, but by stationing herself between two men that loved her equally. Thus this very description of moonlit walks could not but have caused Gillot some difficult moments, at the same time that it challenged him to be clear about the proposal he may have hinted at. When Salomé visited Rée at his Prussian family estate in Stibbe, she kept a portrait of Gillot in "an ivory picture frame." When Salomé visits Nietzsche at Tautenberg in August, "the ivory picture frame" was again placed on her dressing table, but the image to be found within was of Rée. One should not be in too much of a rush to accuse Salomé of confusion or duplicity in her use of male rivalry. It is one way she works within Victorian constraints to win the freedom and equality she seeks. The arrangement allows her to fight a system which left her largely powerless to shape her own life. At one moment when her mother seemed a particularly intractable problem, Salomé writes to Rée, "It is unpleasant to be able to do nothing but plead in a matter so close to one's heart."

In letters to his closest friends in June and July of 1882, Nietzsche expresses his joy with his new "find" Salomé, and justifies the projected living arrangement, in a particular way: living with her promises to bring about a new concordance between his life and thought, and this, in turn, will make possible the writing of *Zarathustra*. He expresses much the same idea, in a more indirect fashion, in a letter to her at the same period. This letter helps us to understand the meaning Nietzsche is giving to this new love. Nietzsche's letter to Salomé of July 3rd is organized around a series of explicit messages. He begins by expressing his joy and gratitude at the way an excess of gifts has coincided in their arrival this day: "Now the sky above me is bright! Yesterday at noon I felt as if it was my birthday. *You* sent your acceptance, the most lovely present that anyone could give me now; my sister sent cherries; Teubner sent the first three page proofs of *The Gay Science*." Then Nietzsche salutes himself for the completion of an arduous phase of his philosophic project: "I had just finished the very last part of the manuscript and therewith the work of six years [1876-82], my entire *Freigeisterei,* O what years! What tortures of every kind, what solitudes and weariness with life! and against all that as it were against death *and* life, I have brewed this medicine of mine, these thoughts with their small strip of *unclouded* sky overhead. O dear friend, whenever I think of it, I am thrilled and touched and do not know how I could have *succeeded* in doing it—I am filled with self-compassion and the sense of victory." This victory is so "complete," that even his "physical health has reappeared, I do not know where from and everyone tells me that I am looking younger than ever." Finally he assures Salomé that his commitment to the living arrangement is complete, and he has no consideration for either his sister's plans or going South alone. After explicitly projecting his future toward her, he closes the letter expressing a blend of caution, trust, and confidence: "Heaven preserve me from doing foolish things—but from now on! —whenever you advise me, I shall be *well* advised and do not need to be afraid. . . . I want to be lonely no longer, but to learn again to be a human being. Ah, here I have practically everything to learn! Accept my thanks, dear friend. Everything will be well, as you have said. Very best wishes to our Rée!"

Behind its more explicit messages, Nietzsche's letter to Salomé carries a fictive design of more covert meaning which express the scope of Nietzsche's demands on her. In sending her "acceptance" of the proposal that she stay with Nietzsche in Tautenberg, she has given a gift (of herself) which has brought back his health, youth and vigor. In the long heroical self-description of his "triumph" in finishing his writings of the free spirit, Nietzsche transforms himself into the intrepid hero of romance: he has overcome "tortures," "solitudes," "weariness," and finally even "death." In this way, her gift is no longer freely given; it is a reward for Nietzsche's bravery. Lou Salomé is put in the position of the maiden who has offered herself to the conquering knight who has returned in triumph with the holy grail. Quite ironically, the letter's grandest compliment to her sagacity and independence subordinates her to Nietzsche's work: she is not to be Nietzsche's "student" but his "teacher." For though it had been an understood assumption of their relationship that Nietzsche was to function as her teacher, by giving her the role of the teacher, Nietzsche not only implies that he can be as receptive and compliant as a pupil; he invites her to subordinate her itinerary and interests to his needs for companionship and socialization. In this role, she is not to show the narcissism of the student, but the selfless generosity of a teacher (and woman).

Nietzsche's exuberant letters following the arrangement of the living plan all demonstrate the same idea: what can happen now between him and Salomé may be important personally, but it also is somehow fundamentally secondary. It is research, background work, a time but for pleasure, eating cherries, and learning to be "human"—all this on the way to the more important work that lies ahead, writing *Zarathustra.* But there is something problematic about the very degree of confidence Nietzsche here ex-

Andreas-Salomé with Paul Rée and Friedrich Nietzsche, posing as her cart-horses.

presses in the living arrangement. In separating himself from the accustomed support of his sister, and the blue skies of the south, Nietzsche strikes a note of caution. He is "united to Lou," "by a bond of firm friendship," "so far as anything of the sort can be firm on this earth"; and he surmounts his own self-caution—"heaven preserve me from doing foolish things"—with an enunciation of his faith that when she advises him he will "be *well* advised." This expression of trust in her implies what he does not quite acknowledge: that by beginning this love, and this experiment with convention, Nietzsche is embarking upon dangerously uncharted seas.

The only serious threat to Nietzsche's relationship with Salomé, and their projected living plan, comes with the action/event which can be grouped under the rubric of "the quarrel." While at the Bayreuth festival, according to Elizabeth, Salomé criticized Nietzsche to his Wagnerite enemies and, flaunting the Lucerne photo, "told whoever would or wouldn't listen that Nietzsche and Rée wanted to study with her and would go with her anywhere *she* wanted." Elizabeth's report of these events to Nietzsche, and the heated arguments between Elizabeth and Lou Salomé that follow, almost prevent Salomé's visit to Tautenberg, and lead Nietzsche to cancel the whole living arrangement more than once. The indiscretion and the quarrels show how a relationship aglow with convergent intentions becomes complex. They are the most telling index of her refusal to be coopted, in a passive and compliant manner, into the writing plans Nietzsche's letter of July 3rd has given such grandiose expression. The living arrangement has always been vulnerable to this kind of crisis. To develop a daring anti-traditional relationship like the trinity, it is essential to put out of play the prior claims of the society one inhabits, with its interests, laws, and morality. But, how does one exclude—one never can exclude—this social law from intruding into a privately contrived society imagined as a place where a select few can live freely, apart from convention's constraints? In this instance the social law comes to Nietzsche and Salomé in the form of a jealous sister. On the journey to Tautenberg, Salomé counters Elizabeth's comprehensive disapproval of her, by venting her anger at Nietzsche's vacillations. She seeks to disabuse Elizabeth of her ideal notions of Nietzsche's purity. Here is a small part of the exchange Elizabeth records in a letter to a friend. "Of the arrangement Lou says: 'Besides, were they to pursue any aims together, two weeks wouldn't go by before they were sleeping together, men all wanted only that, pooh to mental friendship! . . . ' As I, now naturally beside myself, said that might well be the case with her Russians only she didn't know my pure-minded brother, she retorted full of scorn (word for word) 'Who first soiled our study plan with his low designs, who started up with mental friendship when he couldn't get me for something else, who first thought of concubinage—your brother! . . . Yes indeed your noble pure-minded brother first had the dirty design of a concubinage!' "

What does the quarrel evidence? First, and most blatantly, Salomé's desire for a sense of control. Thus the Lucerne photograph is now given a new meaning. Taken as a jest on a lark two months before, when shown at Bayreuth, coupled with a disclosure of the projected living scheme, it becomes a warrant of Salomé's mastery. By insisting, quite accurately, that the men would follow her choice as to the site of their winter residence, Salomé found a way to make her mastery seem quite complete. But Salomé's casual disrespect for Nietzsche also indicates something else. Like the graduate student who seems ready to say almost any scathing thing about their professor, at Bayreuth and Jena, Salomé is protecting herself against an intellectual engulfment by Nietzsche at the very moment when she is opening herself up to his influence as part of her own intellectual project. When Nietzsche simply cancels their plans, she must have felt her actual powerlessness most acutely. How pleasant it must have been to have found in these vituperative scenes a way to express her anger with Nietzsche by making his devoted sister squirm.

Salomé's tirade brings to the fore what is contradictory and symptomatic about the whole living scheme, and subsists as a problem in Salomé's relationship with Nietzsche. When the plan for a trinity is formed, sex is quite explicitly left to one side. To conceive the "holy trinity" is for Salomé and Nietzsche and Rée a critique of the way marriage had turned relations between men and women into a crude material and sexual transaction. It is also an assertion of faith in a particular ideal: that men and women can know each other in and through a shared intellectual quest. This idealism is implicit in Salomé's judgment of Nietzsche for "soiling" the study plan with "low designs." But the "trinity" was from its beginning always flirting with becoming a "melange a trois"—and a pretty kinky one at that. Thus,

even before Nietzsche meets Lou Salomé, a letter to Rée about the living plan assumes the arch and cavalier style of men sharing talk of the women they intend to share: "Greet the Russian girl for me, if that makes any sense: I am greedy for souls of that species. In fact, in view of what I mean to do these next ten years, I need them! Matrimony is quite another story. I could consent at most to a two-year marriage, and then only in view of what I mean to do these next ten years." Here superiority to marriage is not ideal, but an effect of masculine license and licentiousness. Of course, Nietzsche's words strike a pose much more aesthetically controlled than the ardent passion he ends feeling for Salomé. Nonetheless, when Nietzsche's and Rée's feelings for her intensify, the term whose exclusion made the trinity thinkable—sex—returns. At Stibbe, Rée describes to Salomé this letter in which Nietzsche limits interest in her to a "two year marriage," and this becomes the "concubinage" with which Salomé shocks Elizabeth. From the beginning the unity was fascinating—whether to the eager principals or the skeptical observers—for the way it triggered curiosity and suppositions. But when the officially-excluded term returns, sex appears as the ulterior motive which threatens to make the plans for study, and the whole intellectual life, a pretext and charade.

Space does not allow me a full description of the way this love becomes a crucial moment of collaboration in the separate intellectual careers of Lou Salomé and Nietzsche. For Salomé knowing Nietzsche helped advance her study of two subjects upon which she would write books: religion and Nietzsche's philosophy. The arrangement is also a first attempt at a compromise formation that seeks ways of living which the Victorian definition of women's place made appear incompatible: a social relationship with men that would include intellectual equality, emotional intimacy, and personal independence. For Nietzsche, the experiences of 1882 compel a decisive shift in his thought. In *The Gay Science* Nietzsche's narrator overcomes obstacles by practicing a kind of aesthetic finesse of the negative. But the breakup of his relationship with Salomé, and the nasty mutual recriminations that follow, bring an unforeseen kind of negativity. It is an acute challenge to Nietzsche's brightly affirmed ethos for saying "yes" to life. As the locus of unexpected passion and conflict, Salomé becomes a figure in Nietzsche's life for the resistant "other," the contingent which traverses life, displacing it out of its intended directions. Nietzsche is shoved, quite rudely, toward a confrontation with the problem of the will. He wills to have Salomé, but she will not have him. He wants the self-composure which accompanies an affirming and unified will; instead, Nietzsche must try to swallow conflicting passions, many of which are quite galling. The experiences of the year, as they unfold around the axis of the passion for Lou Salomé, test, confound, and displace the philosophic postulates of *The Gay Science* which first seemed to give this love so much support. In the task which he takes up in the midst of his blackest feelings of loss—writing *Zarathustra*—Nietzsche fulfills, short-circuits and sometimes even reverses the themes and positions of *The Gay Science,* as they are refracted and realigned around a quite new, and much more conflictal, concept of the will operating within interpretation. This way of placing love in relation to Nietzsche's intellectual work means that Salomé and the Salomé episode can be *neither* something uncalled for, completely exterior, and radically contingent in its happening, *nor* something choreographed by Nietzsche, a simple repetition of his desire. She is not even an "aporia" implied by Nietzsche's text. Rather this episode is *both* something which unfolds in a space invented for Lou Salomé by the text of *The Gay Science, and,* in this happening, something that exceeds or violates that place and space. And this helps explain why the Salomé episode must be thought of, not as a measured application of philosophical "theory," to living "practice," but as that which comes between *The Gay Science* and *Zarathustra,* not as a bridge, but as a fissure, a violent displacing, a challenge, a mockery and—even a joke. The fact of love, as traumatic experience, has interrupted the writing of philosophy, and then collaborated in its revision.

Biddy Martin   (essay date 1989)

SOURCE: "Woman and Modernity: The [Life]Styles of Lou Andreas-Salomé," in *Modernity and the Text: Revisions of German Modernism,* edited by Andreas Huyssen and David Bathrick, Columbia University Press, 1989, pp. 183-99.

[*In the following essay, Martin discusses Andreas-Salomé's polemical engagement with Freud on the issues of narcissism and gender difference, noting her resistance to the rigid categories of orthodox psychoanalysis.*]

Alice Jardine begins her study of the "Configurations of Woman and Modernity," or *Gynesis,* by staging an encounter between American feminism and contemporary French thought. Cognizant of the inevitable risks of homogenizing both actors in her standoff, Jardine outlines the tension between the two in terms that have an uncanny familiarity—in terms of a conflict between feminism, "a concept inherited from the humanist and rationalist eighteenth century about a group of human beings in history whose identity is defined by that history's representation of sexual decidability, *and* contemporary French thought which has put every term of that definition into question." It is, of course, a profound reduction to imagine that feminist theory and politics are so neatly caught between a political feminism that seems to assume and hence reproduce the very representations of difference it wants to subvert, and a theoretical modernity that has itself been accused of subordinating the discontinuities of the social to the totalizing self-referentiality of philosophical deconstruction. However, for the sake of argument, let us acknowledge that the tensions in feminist practices between empiricism and its philosophical/theoretical critique not only exist but could operate productively. It was my own interest in those tensions and reciprocal interruptions that led to my preoccupation with Lou Andreas-Salomé, whose figurations of self and woman refuse the alternatives masculine/feminine, rational/irrational, life/style, who cannot be turned into an advocate for one or the other side of those hierarchical divides.

Salomé has survived the exclusionary practices of conventional literary historiography on the basis of her liaison with famous male modernists, her appeal for, and her putative power over, such master stylists of the feminine as Nietzsche, Rilke, and Freud, in short, on the basis of what is both fetishized and trivialized as her "lifestyle." We are alert to the ways in which women and "deviance" are made safe by being turned into issues of lifestyle that demand no more of those upholding the norm than fascination and tolerance. What fascinates biographers and critics most in the case of Salomé's lack of conventionality is the marriage she refused to consummate with the Orientalist Friedrich Carl Andreas and the friendships and/or affairs with such masters of the modern as Rée, Nietzsche, Rilke, Beer-Hofmann, Ledebour, Wedekind, Hauptmann, Tausk, and Freud. What fascinates them less are the scores of women she is said to have "unsettled." The sustained fascination is in large part a consequence of her failure, as the biographers see it, to have left a clear record of those relations and of herself, the failure to demarcate clearly the line among friendship, intellectual exchange, and sexual liaison; she continues to fascinate because of the difficulties she creates in all attempts to separate out the intellectual from the erotic, scenes of pedagogy from scenes of seduction, norms from their transgression.

One response to the bases of her fame would be to suppress the fascination with what is called lifestyle and elevate her as male moderns have most recently been elevated, on the basis of her texts and the isolation of those texts from biographical, not to mention biological, contingency. But to suppress biographical contingency in favor of textuality has done little to undo the traditional biographical monumentalization of male heroes, or anti-heroes, and tends in any case simply to perpetuate a reduction of modernism to a question of language and form. The alternative is not to reprivilege the biographical but to renegotiate the relations between empirical and textual, without falling back on naive referentiality, or onto claims to an unspecific politics of language. It seems to me crucial that discussions of the modernist project address that which was and continues to be central to its provocations and its limits, its participation in what might be called a politics of subjectivity, of sexuality and gender, which is inextricably linked to questions of language and literary form, but involves different forms of social practice and institutional supports. It is in this context that I address the significance of Salomé as figure, and the importance of her own work. What has made her both object and fetish is precisely that which makes her important for us to take seriously, her resistance to various forms of institutional legitimacy, her refusal to occupy the positions held out for her within a number of discursive orders, that is to say, to occupy any one position in those orders, from the family, religion, and moral convention, to philosophical, literary, or psychiatric schools. It is, of course, a question not simply of exclusion from these institutions but of the tension between forms of legitimacy and illegitimacy, between the privileges that underwrote her access to male cultural elites and the strategies with which she negotiated her relations to them. It is within a context of shared privilege that her stated differences from her male colleagues/lovers/friends must be considered; the difference that will be most pertinent here is her insistence on the negotiation of social constraints and boundaries, as opposed to their emphasis on transgression and negativity.

Let me proceed with Salomé's performative defiance of the split between life and writing, on the one hand, and their reduction to one another, on the other. Salomé claimed over and over that all of her writing was autobiographical. She wrote fiction, "scholarly" studies of Ibsen, Nietzsche, Rilke, and Freud, numerous reviews, theoretical essays on the psychology of religion, eroticism, and femininity, and psychoanalytic treatments of all of the above; she also kept journals, and corresponded widely. What gives her writing its autobiographical quality and appeal is not self-representation but the continual repetition and recasting of certain themes and questions that invite but also frustrate attempts to get at the real Lou Andreas-Salomé. Salomé's fiction is inevitably read as thinly veiled autobiography in part because her novels and stories are expositions of questions that are posed by way of biographical anecdote in her theoretical work. Certainly, the most explicitly autobiographical of all her publications, her memoirs, works to turn her into her own figuration of the narcissistic woman, a Nietzschean *Freigeist* ["free spirit"], free from the prejudices of habit and moral convention, absolutely at home in exile, autotelic and impregnable, but without anxiety or the compulsion to self-overcoming. Salomé seems to have endlessly displayed but never represented herself, to have always been her own object of analysis without ever having made an object of herself even in explicitly autobiographical writings—writings that have a strangely anonymous and universal quality. Salomé revised and rewrote not only manuscripts meant for immediate publication but her diaries and journals as well. This constant remaking of herself in writing, that which she and Nietzsche celebrated as the importance of style, has confounded her biographers who cannot get at the origin, the truth behind what comes to be seen as deceptive mask or masquerades. Certainly, Salomé refused to subject herself to the kinds of truth in representation required of the complicit confessor. It would seem that she saw the relation between her life and her writing in terms of the attempt to produce cultural forms in spite of convention, not for the sake of transgression, but in the service of style, of life/style. Nietzsche once remarked that he had never known anyone who could match Salomé's brilliance in turning her experience, her psychic life, into speculation and analysis. I would like to take a brief look at how that compulsion, if not that brilliance, is borne out in Salomé's memoirs.

Certainly, her memoirs, ***Lebensrückblick,*** written in the twenties and early thirties, demonstrate an interesting relation between self-display and anonymity. The memoirs conceive her life as an enactment of the epistemological and experiential challenges of modernity. The first chapter of her memoirs, entitled "My Experience of God," begins with her conception of her own birth as a disappearance, a coercion into *human* being, and it continues with the narration of her, as any subject's, difficulties with the sacrifices demanded of every human subject. The result of her own resistance to those sacrifices was what she called her *Zurückrutsch,* a sliding back, and the regressive narcissistic production of a God of infinite generosity, one who au-

thorized her desire to have and be all. The death of this god, as well as the confrontation with the incommensurability of life and its forms, of desire and its representatives, of fantasy and its marriage to reality, had as a consequence, according to Salomé, both a profound demystification of a moral and social order robbed of self-evidence and a profound reverence for, and gratitude toward, the life that lived through but was not encompassed, mastered, or exhausted by the conscious self. According to Salomé, her childhood *Zurückrutsch* left her with an at least fantasized relation to an original indeterminate unity, without God, but equally without danger of falling out of the world. Precisely because of her relation to a presubject/pre-object indeterminate All, she, that is, woman, was more susceptible to the loss of self, to transferences of her desire onto god substitutes, or god-men as she called them. The task for woman in a godless universe, then, was conceived as continual disengagement from transferential relations without falling out of love, a negotiation of the feminine capacity for receptivity and submission to desire, and the human need for self-assertion. Her own relation to the modern world, one whose structures and forms of authority were no longer under-written by God, was not to leave the world but to be in it differently, to resist subjection to the social without defying her implication in it. The memoirs are conceived as her attempts to engage in the world without succumbing to its fraudulent claims to authority/inevitability. Her god-men were, as she wrote over and over, the occasion for the coming into being of her desire and her thought, not the source or the ends of them. Hence the increasing importance to her of the symbolic significance of the Father/God, and of the principle of infidelity.

Salomé's memoirs related her development from her God, through her teacher/god-man Hendrik Gillot, by way of Nietzsche to Freud, as an increasing effort to disengage from the desire of/for others without denying the inevitability of mediation itself. It is significant, I think, that she told her own story, in her early fiction as well as in her memoirs (in which the conflicts are tempered, if not erased), in terms of encounters in which she narrowly escapes the death of consciousness, or of desire. She developed those encounters as sites of intra- and intersubjective struggle, indeed as sites of seduction. And she made quite clear that the most significant of all those encounters was her relation to the Dutch reform preacher Hendrik Gillot, whose teaching/preachings of German idealism she claimed to have chosen over religious orthodoxy, on the one hand, and arid rationalism, on the other. It was with Gillot that the adolescent Salomé began her study of the history of Western thought, and she describes his own conception of his project as that of bringing her out of the world of fantasy, childhood, romance, the East, and orthodoxy into the world of rationality, logic, the West. She describes her own deification of Gillot, the erotics of that deification, and the necessity of overcoming it as the paradigm of all subsequent idealizations. It is no surprise that her early fiction, described by many commentators as teeming with desire and youthful passion, without form, plot, or resolution, employs the figure of incest for her expositions of the confrontation of daughter-figures with those fathers in whom she comes to recognize herself.

"Woman," she once wrote, "runs a zigzag path between the feminine and the human." This was not a problem to be solved once and for all, but a conflict at the heart of culture and subjectivity, a conflict that bourgeois feminism, according to Salomé, attempted to solve in two equally unsatisfactory ways. Salomé situated herself in relation to Germany's bourgeois feminisms by insisting on a double-edged polemic against the rationalist/humanist efforts to eradicate difference, and the romantic/metaphysical efforts to elevate femininity by way of its equation with motherhood and (hetero)sexuality. What makes women's lives in all their only apparent banalities significant, according to Salomé, are the ways in which they negotiate the double directionality at the heart of subjectivity from "Fall zu Fall."

At issue were not simply the rationalizations, normalizations, the iron cage of society, but the exclusion of women from the sphere of the social, from the possibility of the elaboration of their desire in the social. The emphasis on the impossibility of a solution, of resolution, is what interests me here, for it suggests that the modern crisis of the incommensurability of desire and language, desire and social positionality, desire and marriage in all of its metaphoric and analogical potential, opens up the very possibility for what Salomé calls woman and her strategic negotiations between resolution and dissolution. Hence, the lack of appeal for her of discourses of apocalypse and heroism that totalized domination in order to totalize liberation in an outside, often known as or conflated with woman, those false alternatives offered by the master narratives of modernism. It is in this context that her objection to what she saw as Nietzsche's totalizations becomes most interesting and clear.

Salomé's study of Nietzsche [*Friedrich Nietzsche in seinen Werken*], published in 1894, was the first major study of his work; it identified three major periods in his thought and identified the middle or realist period as his greatest achievement, that period in which Nietzsche most successfully disciplined his attempts to give life to the idea. Salomé's objections to the late period had to do with what she read as his paradoxical return to metaphysics, a return made inevitable by his totalizing critique of Reason and culture and his privileging of unmediated, instinctual, and autotelic will. The "Übermensch," she wrote, is "pure, timeless conscious power." And Salomé describes this conception as the postulation of the motherless child, identifying this will to knowledge with a will to be god, with a desire to escape the constraints of the social, indeed of the human condition as such, as a paradoxical effect of Nietzsche's profound antimetaphysical claim to life. Despite what she would continue throughout her life to call their fundamental similarity, their religious natures, their *Freigeisterei,* Salomé also continued to claim that to have followed Nietzsche in his totalizing critique of Reason, his contempt for the *Mensch des Geistes,* and in his appeal to unmediated instinctual life would have meant going back in the direction from which she had been moving, back into an exclusion from the social, an isolation, and a masochistic containment in desire. For woman was threatened not only by the mediation and the containment *of* her desire but by a necessarily masochistic containment *in* it, a

containment that has the mark not of unbridled nature but of a hopeless and, in the case of Nietzsche's metaphysical turn, willful blindness to one's inevitable mediation through the Other. In an 1899 essay ["**Die in Sich ruhende Frau**"] on "woman," Salomé had written that the demise of religion had left woman without a language for articulating the double directionality of the feminine. It is not uninteresting that she should have identified psychoanalysis as providing that language. And perhaps even more interesting that she refused to use its terms consistently, that is, that she insisted, in the words of François Roustang [in *Dire Mastery,* 1982], on turning psychoanalysis into a Russian novel.

Salomé approached Freud and psychoanalysis in 1911-12 at a critical moment in the history of the psychoanalytic movement. Alfred Adler had left Freud's circle to found an independent psychoanalytic association, Carl Jung's departure was imminent, and internal conflict was at a height. It was also a moment of expansion, of the increasing interest in psychoanalysis outside of the narrow circles to which it had been confined. There is no doubt that Salomé was perceived to be an important because prestigious outsider, and Ernest Jones's perception of her as outsider contrasts significantly with her own conception of herself as part of the brotherhood, albeit with a difference, with the freedom to move in and out of their circles. Salomé would write her memoirs as a lifelong search for the exchange she found in her relation to Freud, the only pedagogical relation that displaced that hierarchical gender divide and inevitable appropriation characterizing other pedagogical exchanges, other all-too-conventional scenes of seduction and tragedy. It is, of course, impossible to explore all of the factors that contributed to that possibility. However, it is significant that Salomé's allegiance to Freud was not her only allegiance at the age of fifty, that their relation was sustained through correspondence, that is, at a distance, and that the position of student was not the only position available to her in relation to the person Freud, or to psychoanalysis. Indeed, it is on the basis of that association that Salomé takes up her own position as analyst and teacher. What concerns me here are the ways in which Salomé negotiated her relationship to psychoanalysis and Freud, and the significance of gender in those negotiations.

Both their unity and their differences were played out on the field of narcissism. From the beginnings of her stay in Vienna in 1912, Salomé used her own difference with Alfred Adler over his conception of the unconscious to support her unity with Freud. "I am absorbed in *Beyond the Pleasure Principle,*" she writes to Freud in December 1920, "and you can imagine what pleasure this book has given me, since I was plagued by the worry that you were not in agreement with me on the matter of the passive instinct; and yet it is only from this standpoint that Adler can be conclusively disproved, as I told him in Vienna" [*Sigmund Freud and Lou Andreas-Salomé: Letters,* 1972]. Salomé understood the conception of passive instincts to be an advocacy for the unconscious in the face of Adler's overvaluation of the ego. Passivity meant an openness and receptivity to the life that lives through but is neither encompassed by, nor accessible to, the conscious subject—a yielding to that which exceeds and, from a certain point of view, may seem to threaten the ego and its demands for control and coherence. For her, what distinguished Freud's concept of the unconscious from Adler's was its bases in an inarticulable but material narcissism, from within which the ego sets itself apart, but from which it never fully departs. Given this narrative of the development of the ego, sharp distinctions between conscious and unconscious, ego and sexuality, masculine and feminine, active and passive are problematic, and it was this problematic that was at stake for Salomé.

Salomé explains the epistemological importance of Freud's narcissism concept in the following terms [in *The Freud Journal of Lou Andreas-Salomé,* 1964]:

> To hold fast to Freud's present concept of narcissism means to hold fast to psychology's right to its own media and methods no matter what. And that means to be allowed to write, with appropriate obscurity, its personal mark of X, even there where the psychic organization eludes it, instead of defecting into the alien clarity belonging to another side of existence called the physical.

In her critiques of Adler's recourse to simple determinism, Salomé emphasizes the connection between his overvaluation of the ego and his devaluation of femininity and passivity; she rejects his conception of masculine protest as the key to psychic development for reducing sexuality, the unconscious, the feminine to the status of fictions and tools.

Often it is in the very same letters in which she takes up her critique of Adler that Salomé introduces her objections to Freud's own tendency to conceive of the unconscious as contingent upon, even derived from, the ego and its repressions; and she opposes those tendencies for their erasure of the positivity of desire. Her differences with Freud over questions of religion, artistic creation, homosexuality, and ethics always turn on his derivation of those phenomena from inhibitions in development, his conception of them as compensations or compromises. Salomé stood by her conception of the specificity of the development of a presymbolic narcissism and its expression in creative and intellectual as well as "symptomatic" behavior. Far from simply representing compensatory formations in the negative sense, "primitive" religion, infantile preoccupations, artistic production, even neuroses manifested for her the positivity of a desire that has its bases in narcissism. In notes written to Freud about the relation between phantasy and reality, Salomé addresses Freud's explanation of the relationship between artistic expression and repression by arguing that pleasure and creativity are derived not only from the pleasurable opening up of the repressed, but "still more perhaps on account of the objective element in the primal experiences that is regained in this way: precisely those experiences that were not even indirectly reanimated through object-libido, but that are made accessible only under the powerful touch of phantasy to all reaches of the conscious intellect—and in this way extend our personality, hemmed in as it is by object-libido, to spheres that were once its province and that it now regains" [*Sigmund Freud and Lou Andreas-*

Salomé: Letters]. Again, a concept of the unconscious that is not subordinated to the demands or the strategies of the ego is fundamental to Salomé's project. And she blames developmental theory for the suppression of that creative, if regressive, direction of narcissism. What was at stake for Salomé was not obscurity or undecidability for its own sake but a challenge to the hypostasization of oppositions that set up rigid and antagonistic boundaries between the primitive and the civilized, between nature and culture, and perhaps most significantly, between sexuality and ego.

In response to what she saw as Freud's tendency to overemphasize the threat posed by sexuality to the ego, Salomé reminded Freud of what she took to be his own argument, that the relation between sexuality and ego has to do with the orientation of the boundary drawn between them. It is because of the rigid line drawn between them in "man" that narcissism's double directionality is clearer in "women." In an essay of 1928 entitled **"The Consequences of the Fact That It Was Not Woman Who Killed the Father,"** Salomé does what Sarah Kofman was to do somewhat differently fifty years later, namely, she uses Freud's work on narcissism against him [in *The Enigma of Woman: Woman in Freud's Writings,* 1985]. Salomé's 1928 essay is emblematic of her rhetorical/interpersonal strategy of setting herself apart from the terms that she claims unite her with Freud. She and Freud agree that, in the words of Kofman, "woman's enigmatic quality has to do with her affirmative self-sufficiency and indifference, not with the veiling of an inadequacy or lack." "It is no accident," Kofman writes, "that Freud's essay On Narcissism was written in 1914, a time when he was particularly taken with Lou Andreas-Salomé." What Salomé and Kofman emphasize is the difficulty Freud has in sustaining the division he sets up in that essay between masculine anaclitic (ethical) and feminine narcissistic object choices, since the masculine object choice and the male's overvaluation of the object develop by way of the prior narcissistic cathexis of the self, by way of the feminine. Even more problematic are Freud's ultimate ethical condemnation of woman's narcissism and his claim that motherhood provides the appropriate ethical redemption. "The theorist is subject to the same forms of forgetfulness as the little boy," the same fraud, the forgetting which draws too sharp and self-evident a line between unconscious and conscious, desire and autonomy, pleasure and ethics. "All ethical autonomy," writes Salomé in **"Narcissism as Double Directionality,"** "doubtless constitutes a compromise between command and desire . . . while it renders what is desired unattainable—given the ideal strictness of the value demanded—it draws what is commanded from the depths of the dream of all-encompassing, all sustaining Being." Freud cannot escape narcissism as the ground of ethics or of love, nor can he sustain what Salomé sees as the unnecessarily rigid dichotomy between narcissism and sociality, between self-sufficiency and ethics.

Salomé's essay on the consequences of the fact that it was not the daughter who killed the father begins by explaining her title. The title refers, Salomé reminds her readers, to Freud's proposition that the first human crime (and the advent of culture) was the murder of the father. With this beginning Salomé acknowledges her indebtedness to

Freud and her intention to work on woman's difference from within his narrative. The freedom she assumes in order to work both within and against Freud's terms characterizes both the method and the content of the essay. Indeed, the beginning of the second paragraph ventures the suggestion that if Freud's speculation is valid, is "so," then it cannot have been without consequence that the daughter remained free of the son's primal guilt. The "ist es so" (if it is true) marks the hypothetical nature of his and, by implication, her arguments, that which she would have called their symbolic as opposed to their truth value. Our myths, she once wrote to Freud, are that to which we resort when we reach the limit of what we can observe empirically and follow rationally. Following Freud's lead here, Salomé sets out to explain the process through which the son's murder of the father is transformed into a remorseful, deferential deification of the father on the part of the then conformist and obedient son. Salomé appeals to what she sees as the only instance of such deification/idealization accessible in our lived experience, namely, the idealization of the object in erotic love. Again, she takes up Freud's own work on masculine object choice, the aggressive as opposed to the passive type, characterized by an over-valuation of the love object and a dependence for one's sense of self on the reciprocation of that love. Her next move is to suggest that there is no natural basis for such object choice or for such idealization. Nothing prepares us for it in advance, she suggests, since what is prior is that lack of differentiation that Freud, she reminds us, called narcissism. She goes on to explain the lasting effects of narcissism in the relation between psyche and the body. As a consequence of the development of the ego and the separation between subject and object, the body becomes the material limit of our narcissism, in that it comes to mark the boundary between self and other, and is therefore experienced as if it were external to us; it is also the point of contact and connection through which the narcissistic remains at play—the body, then, as *Grenz* and *Bindestrich*, that to which we can have no unmediated relation, but can also not escape. Hence, by analogy, the inescapability of narcissism.

The masculine overvaluation of the object, its ethics, which has no natural basis, according to Salomé, can be said to involve a social intervention into a previously narcissistic state. The renunciation and the forgetting of narcissism require the threat and guilt over incestuous wishes and murderous fantasies. The son's fantasy of murdering the father involves a deep narcissistic wound, since the father is, after all, the son's future. The son, with his murderous omnipotence wishes, is transformed into a remorseful and obedient subject who overvalues the love object even as he misrecognizes what is actually his suppressed desire for a reunion in what he takes to be ethical ideals. The daughter, Salomé argues, need not suppress incestuous wishes so violently, need not fall out of love, at least if we take Freud's mythical narrative seriously; she is not forced, then, to internalize a prohibitive and punitive Law. Here Salomé subtly insists on the often forgotten distinction in Freud's own 1914 "On Narcissism" essay between ego ideal and superego or conscience, making conscience the fate of the male, and an unpunitive ego ideal, the daughter's difference. Salomé's woman is less likely to confuse desire with ethics, and hence her greater sobriety in relation to the Law. The daughter, Salomé writes, resolves her own tendency to idealize the Father through a series of ever more subtle, more refined sublimations without having to murder the father or repress her narcissistic sense of connectedness; hence the more peaceful coexistence of desire and self-assertion. Woman remains more "at home" in her materiality, no matter how sublimated, how spiritualized her relation to it. The sublimations required of her are articulated in terms of a rounding out, a growing and expanding that is horizontal, spatial, that does not depart for a point above or beyond, but reabsorbs the traces of a history that is never renounced. The man who has forgotten the desire at the basis of his ethics and his aspirations reacts more sensitively to external Law, vacillating between guilt and desire, between "natural rebelliousness that would destroy anything in its way" and the impulse to achieve his own worth in the approval of that punitive Other. For Salomé, the conflict between the desire for total independence from the Father and an equally strong desire to submit to Him explains the ambivalent relations of Freud's sons to their father. And the failure to work through this conflict, which has its basis in an only apparently paradoxical narcissistic desire for unity, makes men blind to their own desires, obliging them to separate mind and body, intellect and erotics, rational and irrational.

If there is lack, then, it is that of the son whose trajectory involves a linear, teleological, sacrificial verticality, the imperative to aspire and achieve with the illusory promise that identification with, and obedience to, the Father will reconstitute the lost whole. "It is no wonder," Salomé wrote elsewhere [in *The Freud Journal of Lou Andreas-Salomé*], "that the male neurotic's desire to be happy is often expressed as a desire to be a woman," to be what she called that "regressive without a neurosis." In **"Woman as Type,"** Salomé draws out the paradox that constitutes the daughter's difference and her advantage:

> Woman is able to experience what is most vital as most sublimated. This mentalizing, idealizing draws its spontaneity from the fact that, in the transferences of love, their point of departure remains more palpably present for the feminine-unitary nature throughout life. . . . The individual beloved person in all his factuality becomes for her transparent in all directions, a diaphane with human contour through which the fullness of the whole gleams, unbroken and unforgotten.

Salomé concludes her essay on the consequences of the differences between the sexes, an essay that consistently avoids anatomical determinations, by folding those differences back on themselves. For at the point of furthest development of his masculinity, the man exhibits submission, a giving of himself to his ideal that exposes the feminine-passive, the narcissistic moment that is always at work even in the most apparently total separations. Masculine and feminine approach the border of their difference and tend to become one another. If the masculine opens out onto the feminine in the drive to achieve, to become the father, motherhood constitutes at least the metaphorical point at which woman can be said to have opened onto the masculine; it combines the feminine capacity for giving with the masculine capacity to create, to protect, and to lead. In motherhood, Salomé argues, woman realizes her sublimated homosexuality. Indeed, motherhood has always elicited the fascination and envy of man both because it transgresses the conventional boundaries of femininity, reaching over into the masculine, and because it is an experience of the body that is denied him. For that reason, Salomé argues, the mother becomes the essence of that which is inaccessible, and figures for man as a symbol more than a real human being, a symbol of the inseparability, indeed, the ultimate undecidability of all human differentiations, that undecidability, that narcissism that must be repressed if masculine identity is to be secured. Woman exists for man somewhere between the *Kreatürlichem* and the *Überpersonellem,* a position of indeterminacy and a commonplace. This, of course, is not Freud's ethical mother, not the redemption of woman's narcissism, but its realization, the source of man's fascination and his horror.

Woman's position between the animal and the transcendental, this undecidability, became oppressive, Salomé continues, when the worship of god became the worship of man, and that undecidable figure, that *Mittelding,* was domesticated into the respectable wife. Whereas woman once belonged directly to the *Vater-Gott,* the worship of man and the domestication of woman cut her off from that world of possibility signified by the Father and unfulfillable by any human relation. Penis envy, writes Salomé, a form of desire for equality based in "ressentiment," emerged along with the possibility of the enslavement of woman by man. It is at this point, she suggests, that woman must struggle against the human male for access to that which is as naturally hers as it is his in its inaccessibility. Salomé's critique here of humanist glorifications of the hu*man* subject is directed at what she takes to be the assumption of a fraudulent complementarity that makes woman his lack and his completion. As soon as woman's access to her own desire is mediated through the human male, as soon as competition with him is her only hope of escape from domestication, the daughter begins to kill the father herself and, with "him," precious parts of herself.

The essay ends with a discussion of the implications of differences for the relations between the sexes. The only viable relation to the other, according to Salomé, is that based on the furthest possible development of the sexual differences within each one, rather than the projection of difference onto a supposedly complementary and ideal other half. Hence, the significance to her of Freud's notion of bisexuality, understood as a sexual indeterminacy that "can be awakened by the opposite sex, as a consequence of the other's profound approach, his understanding, and his embrace." So it is, Salomé wrote elsewhere, "that only slightly homosexual men see the universally human qualities in woman and are erotically disposed toward them" as opposed to the more exclusively heterosexual, self-repressive man who prefers the feminine woman in the most circumscribed sense of the word.

Salomé's 1928 essay is typical of her excavations of the internal differences of psychoanalysis, excavations formulated as reminders to Freud of the implications of his own work, perhaps of his own slight "homosexuality." Clearly, Salomé made use of what she characterized as the daughter's good fortune in her relation to Freud, maintaining the privilege and pleasure of speaking in his name without giving herself over to his terms. Salomé avoided war with Freud just as she avoided submission to him by sustaining a relation that she described as one beyond fidelity and infidelity, enabled by her concomitant acknowledgment and destabilization of gender and genre lines—the fact that she refused the exclusive positions of insider and out, that she insisted (in the words of François Roustang) on turning psychoanalysis into a Russian novel, that she contaminated science with the philosophical and aesthetic, even as she credited Freud and psychoanalysis with correcting her tendency toward romantic mystification and hallucinated syntheses.

FURTHER READING

Biography

Binion, Rudolph. *Frau Lou: Nietzsche's Wayward Disciple.* Princeton, N. J.: Princeton University Press, 1968, 587 p.
    Comprehensive biography.

Martin, Biddy. *Woman and Modernity: The (Life)Styles of Lou Andreas-Salomé.* Ithaca, N. Y.: Cornell University Press, 1991, 250 p.
    Critical biography with a feminist orientation.

Sorell, Walter. "Lou Andreas-Salomé: Mind and Body." In his *Three Women: Lives of Sex and Genius,* pp. 131-213. New York: Bobbs-Merrill Company, 1975.
    Offers a portrait of Andreas-Salomé as the mesmerizing and seductive muse of Nietzsche, Rilke, and Freud.

Criticism

Livingstone, Angela. *Lou Andreas-Salomé.* London: Gordon Fraser Gallery, 1984, 255 p.
    Biographical and critical study.

Matarasso, Michel. "Anthropoanalysis and the Biographical Approach: Lou Andreas-Salomé." *Diogenes,* No. 139 (Fall 1987): 127-166.
    Analyzes the complex public persona of Andreas-Salomé, whose life "incarnates for many the image of modern woman."

Pfeiffer, Ernst, ed. *Sigmund Freud and Lou Andreas-Salomé: Letters.* Translated by William and Elaine Robson-Scott. New York: Harcourt Brace Jovanovich, 1972, 244 p.
    Correspondence between Andreas-Salomé and Sigmund Freud that highlights their extensive debate on the fundamental concepts of psychoanalysis.

Additional coverage of Andreas-Salomé's life and career is contained in the following source published by Gale Research: *Dictionary of Literary Biography*, Vol. 66.

Franz Boas

1858-1942

German-born American anthropologist.

INTRODUCTION

Boas is widely acknowledged as the father of modern anthropology. In addition to bringing scientific techniques to the discipline, he was instrumental in developing the modern anthropology curriculum and, through his teaching, inspired the work of such notable figures as Margaret Mead and Ruth Benedict. Boas also did extensive fieldwork among native tribes of the Pacific Northwest, and his writings on that subject remain an important source of anthropological data.

Biographical Information

Boas was born in Westphalia, the son of a successful businessman. After attending local schools, he studied mathematics and the natural sciences at universities in Heidelberg, Bonn, and Kiel, receiving a doctorate in 1881. Two years later, he traveled to Baffin Island to do geographic research, and biographers believe it was his contact with and great admiration for the native people there that first interested him in the study of human cultures. After working in Berlin as a museum curator and lecturer, he returned to North America in 1886 to study the natives of the Pacific Northwest, the first of thirteen field trips he made to the area. Boas permanently relocated to the United States in 1887, accepting a position as an assistant editor for the journal *Science*. In 1888 he published his first book-length anthropological study, *The Central Eskimo*.

During the early 1890s Boas assisted in the creation of anthropological exhibits for the Columbian Exposition in Chicago and afterward stayed on to help develop the Field Museum, which occupies one of the pavilions originally erected for the exposition. In 1896 he became an assistant curator at the American Museum of Natural History in New York, and in that same year he began teaching at Columbia University, a position he retained until his retirement in 1937. During the last years of his life, Boas remained active, opposing the policies of Nazi Germany, working to end racial discrimination in the United States, and collecting his earlier writings for publication. He died in December 1942, during a meeting he had convened to discuss the problems of totalitarianism and racism.

Major Works

From the beginning of his career, Boas was dissatisfied with the basic assumptions of social science, many of them based on Western ideological biases. One of the central tenets of anthropology at the time was the evolutionary concept: the idea that human societies develop according to a single pattern from the primitive state to what was then regarded as civilization, with variations caused largely by environmental factors. Boas's early research among native tribes convinced him that environment played only a minor role in differentiating one group from another, and that societies formerly dismissed as primitive sometimes possessed highly developed social and linguistic features. Boas suggested that the development of societies was the result of a complex interaction of human psychology and unique historical factors, which he termed the "culture" of the group, and that there was in fact no single pattern for all human societies. Boas further proposed that only through exhaustive research and comparison could the universal principles governing the development of culture be discovered, and in his own studies of the tribes of the Pacific Northwest he attempted to exhaustively document the beliefs, customs, institutions, and language of the people he studied. In addition to his ethnographical and linguistic studies, Boas conducted research in physical anthropology, and through this research he was able to expose various racial fallacies, which were being used to justify discrimination against blacks as well as the extermination of various groups by the Nazis.

Critical Reception

Boas created controversy during his lifetime by adopting strident, sometimes unpopular, positions on many of the issues of the day. However, his contributions to the field of anthropology earned him wide respect, and he was revered by his many students, who expanded upon his ideas and dominated the field throughout the first half of the twentieth century. Some anthropologists have argued that while Boas clearly identified the importance of culture in the development of human societies, he failed to propose any viable theories concerning the properties of culture. However, his defenders argue that it was precisely in his reluctance to draw conclusions based on what might be incomplete evidence that constituted Boas's primary contribution to modern anthropology, elevating it from a speculative, elitist endeavor to one of the primary branches of the natural sciences.

PRINCIPAL WORKS

The Central Eskimo   (nonfiction)   1888
The Kwakiutl of Vancouver Island   (nonfiction)   1909
Changes in Bodily Form of Descendants of Immigrants (nonfiction)   1911
Handbook of American Indian Languages [editor]   (nonfiction)   1911
The Mind of Primitive Man   (nonfiction)   1911
Tsimshian Mythology   (nonfiction)   1916
Primitive Art   (nonfiction)   1927
Anthropology and Modern Life   (nonfiction)   1928
Race, Language, and Culture   (essays)   1940
Race and Democratic Society   (essays)   1945
Kwakiutl Grammar   (nonfiction)   1947
Kwakiutl Ethnography   (nonfiction)   1966

CRITICISM

Donald Slesinger   (essay date 1929)

SOURCE: A review of *Anthropology and Modern Life,* in *The Yale Law Journal,* Vol. XXXVIII, No. 5, March 1929, pp. 694-96.

[*In the following review of* Anthropology and Modern Life, *Slesinger commends Boas's scientific methods and applauds his major conclusions concerning the roots of human behavior.*]

Anthropology and psychoanalysis became popular in certain circles at about the same time, and for more or less the same reason. They both tended to discredit present day institutions and modes of thought by pointing to lowly origins in the infantile racial and individual past. It was fashionable a dozen years ago to be scornful of adult habits

because their origins might be traced to a feeling of guilt, or an attachment to one's mother during the first four or five years of life. It was an equally popular pastime to suggest the ridiculousness of wearing a wedding ring, which was only an ancient symbol of marriage by capture; or of believing in the virgin birth, because it was a direct cultural descendant of primitive tribal myths. This use of some of the spectacular results of scientific inquiry tended to obscure the real value of both psychoanalysis and anthropology, and to make social scientists in related fields skeptical of co-operative enterprises. As late as 1928 a distinguished sociologist expressed the belief that the use of anthropology was purely historical and had no light to throw on contemporary problems.

Boas, in *Anthropology and Modern Life,* with no special theological axe to grind, makes clear the worth not only of some of the results, but of the methods of anthropological research. With an understanding of the use and limitations of his field of investigation he discusses the light it throws on certain important contemporary problems, and the possible future use of the methodology elaborated in the past quarter of a century. A glance at the chapter headings and the references in the back of the book show a preoccupation on the part of some investigators at least with modern situations, and indicate that Boas is not merely translating his material in order to make it available to the general public or to technicians in other fields; the studies mentioned and the discussion that follows are immediately illuminating, not illuminating by analogy.

> The group, not the individual, is always the primary concern of the anthropologist. . . . The individual interests us only as a member of the group. We inquire into determinate factors and the manner of their action in the group. The relation between the composition of the social group and the distribution of individual statures interests us. The physiologist may study the effect of strenuous exercise upon the functions of the heart. The anthropologist will investigate the interrelation between social conditions that make for strenuous exercise in a group and the physiological behavior of its members. The psychologist may study the intellectual or emotional behavior of the individual. The anthropologist will investigate the social or racial conditions that determine the behavior as distributed in the group. . . . We cannot treat the individual as an isolated unit. He must be studied in his social setting, and the *question is relevant whether any valid laws exist that govern the life of society.* (Italics ours).

That statement is surely temperate and sceptical enough to satisfy the most exacting.

The application of this attitude and technique to the problem of race, for instance, leads to the conclusion that sharply defined racial traits do not exist. There is not only a type to be considered, but a distribution of traits. Thus an examination of family lines of Swedes reveals not only many "typical" blondes, but some with dark hair and brown eyes. A similar examination of southern Italians shows a distribution including some blondes. Stature is also variable, short people being found in tall races, and vice versa. From studies of distribution Boas concludes that:

> The vague impression of 'types' abstracted from our everyday experience does not prove that these are biologically distinct races. . . . It is . . . not admissible to identify types apparently identical that occur in populations of different composition. Each individual can only be considered as a member of his group.

Thus, a blonde may be an Italian variant instead of a true Swede. This distribution tends to throw some doubt on the existence of a racial purity.

When we come to study culture it seems to have little relation to race, or heredity. Children readily pick up the language spoken about them, even though it be an alien one. Various races studied in a city environment responded more quickly to certain simple tests than did members of the same racial group when studied in remote country districts. Negroes from Chicago did very much better on the army tests than negroes from Louisiana. We even find a tendency on the part of the children of immigrants to conform anatomically to the native group among whom they live.

The importance of culture and environment in determining human behavior, together with the wide distribution found in family lines make Boas doubt the value of eugenics. A further reason against accepting the eugenic program lies in the instability of culture, and the consequent change in the ideal to be eugenically created. One tribe would work toward warlike, another toward acquisitive, a third toward conforming individuals. There is no reason to suppose that the American ideal of today is so absolutely good that it will not be supplanted tomorrow. Animal husbandry, from which eugenics derives its theory and aim is confounded by no such problem. The type of cow desired today is not only fairly well agreed upon but less likely to change than are human ideals.

Again in the field of crime we find anthropological studies illuminating. In the first place comparative studies of different civilizations and historical studies of our own indicate that there can be no definition of "crime" stable enough to warrant calling it instinctive or hereditary. Yesterday the man who drank moderately was no criminal; today he is. The man who denied God yesterday was punished by the forfeit of his life; today he may shout his heresy freely even in the sacred halls of science. It is not always criminal to kill or steal even in our own society.

> The infinite complexity of conditions that bring an individual into the class of convicted criminals does not make such a conclusion (that the tendency to criminality is inherited in a simple Mendelian ratio) likely . . . The actual statistical data indicate only that in the population family lines differ in their degree of criminality.

Although anthropology may be of great assistance in predicting the average behavior of a group Boas limits its application by stating that "these results are not significant for the individual." "A prediction of the future development of a normal individual cannot be made with any degree of assurance." That should be obvious enough, but

it is too often overlooked by many investigators, who make use of statistical methods.

We see then that anthropology is not a collection of ancient implements and amusing anecdotes about primitive tribes; neither is it a social psychoanalysis. It is a social science with a methodology and data that are applicable to the study of contemporary problems. Some one is certain to rise at this point and object that when anthropology attempts to study modern civilization it is encroaching on the domain of sociology. To which the present reviewer at least says God speed. Nothing is more futile than airtight divisions of fields of knowledge. Nothing is more hopeful than the sudden discovery that chemistry is physics, or that most social sciences are anthropology. Like M. Jourdain in *The Bourgeois Gentilhomme* we approach a recondite subject only to learn that we have been talking "prose" all our lives. It becomes possible immediately to apply all the known laws of prose to conversation. The discovery that sociology is anthropology surely brings us one step nearer to a scientific understanding of ourselves.

Ruth Benedict   (essay date 1943)

SOURCE: An obituary in *Science*, Vol. 97, No. 2507, January 15, 1943, pp. 60-2.

[*Benedict was a renowned American cultural anthropologist who studied with Boas. The following excerpt is taken from her obituary tribute to her former teacher.*]

[Franz Boas] was born in Minden, Westphalia, and was educated at the universities of Heidelberg, Bonn and Kiel, where his particular fields of study were physics, geography and mathematics. The subject of his doctoral dissertation presented to the University of Kiel was "The Nature of the Color of Sea Water," and his first act after receiving his degree was typical of the man. He had already arrived at his life-long conviction that for most scientific problems mere examination of the existing data or cunningly devised laboratory experiments are not enough; he saw the necessity of gathering new first-hand material on conditions as they actually exist in human experience. He wanted, in fact, to investigate sea water and ice under winter conditions in the Arctic. There were no scientific funds to send a young man to winter among the Eskimos with his scientific instruments, so he financed himself by arranging with Berlin papers to act as a newspaper correspondent from the Arctic. He set out as a young philosophic materialist accustomed to seek "causes" in the natural environment; as he said much later, he went to the Arctic with "an exaggerated belief in the importance of geographical determinants." He returned with an abiding conviction that if we are ever to understand human behavior we must know as much about the eye that sees as about the object seen. And he had understood once and for all that the eye that sees is not a mere physical organ but a means of perception conditioned by the tradition in which its possessor has been reared.

He turned therefore to the study of culture. After a few years in Germany he returned to America under the auspices of the British Association for the Advancement of Science to study the tribes of the Pacific Coast of Canada.

For fifty years he was to continue his intensive work among these tribes, especially among the Kwakiutl. Every detail—linguistic, physical, archeological and cultural—was, it seemed to him, grist for his mill. No student of culture has ever been more tireless. On his first trip he interested himself in the languages, recorded texts in hitherto unwritten tongues, investigated complex forms of social organization and of economics, observed ceremonies and financial exchanges in minute detail. But this seemed to him only a beginning, and in 1897 he interested Morris K. Jesup, then president of the Museum of Natural History, to finance the Jesup North Pacific Expedition in order that archeological, linguistic and cultural investigation might be carried on by a number of investigators both in the New World and in Siberia. Boas directed the work and the resulting publications which he edited are a landmark in the history of the investigation of cultures historically unrelated to Western civilization. Even as late as 1930 he returned to the Kwakiutl for more fieldwork, and in 1937, no longer able to go to them, he brought a Kwakiutl to his home for the winter.

Boas' emphasis on obtaining accurate, detailed knowledge, both intensive and extensive, not only raised the standards of anthropology; it changed its methodology and problems. In phrasing these problems and in insisting that relevant data be used in answering them systematically, he was a great pioneer who led the way into new fields of investigation. He found anthropology a collection of wild guesses and a happy hunting ground for the romantic lover of primitive things; he left it a discipline in which theories could be tested and in which he had delimited possibilities from impossibilities.

The first general theoretical problem on which he worked was that of the importance of the diffusion of traits in human culture. It was necessary to show how each culture, however individual, is in reality one local variant of a far more wide-spread form. Ratzel, his teacher, had believed that this was due to direct influence of the geographic environment; orthodox scientific opinion more generally held that this was due to inevitable operations of the human psyche. He had to prove how constant and pervasive cultural borrowing was, not merely of useful inventions but of curious and even hampering ideas. The growth of human cultures, he demonstrated, had to be understood through a knowledge of the spread of inventions and institutions, whether they appear to us rational or irrational. It was the assembled documentation of this truth that led him to oppose the rational reconstructions of cultural evolutionists.

Historical reconstruction, with all its emphasis on diffusion of traits, never seemed to him separable from social processes which had to be studied in the flesh. He wanted to know as much about the revamping of a trait in a borrowing tribe as about the mere fact of borrowing. In his interest in this aspect of culture he wrote, as early as 1896 and 1904, discussions emphasizing the importance of cultural patterning; in his own words, how a tribe "in its setting among neighbouring cultures builds up its own fabric." This problem was closely allied to those concerning the working of the culture, "by which I mean the life of the individual as controlled by culture and the effect of the individual upon culture." Though he had spent many years of his life on historical reconstruction, he recognized clearly that even if we could obtain complete knowledge of how a trait or an institution came into being, that knowledge would not help in the solution of these functional problems. Institutions "affect the individual and he affects them only as they exist today." In 1923 he said that "diffusion was won" and that as he saw it, anthropology should spend its energies answering these questions of the interplay of the individual and culture. He sent a generation of students to Samoa, to New Guinea, to Melanesia, to Africa, to South America and to the North American Indian to study the conditions brought to bear upon individuals by the cultural forms under which they lived.

His insistence on phrasing questions so that they could be answered by investigation and upon gathering first-hand material to answer them was of equal importance in his two other chosen fields of research: linguistics and physical anthropology. He is identified in the public mind with his research in race problems. He came to these problems from researches in the influence of environment upon growth, researches which he began while at Clark University, 1888-1892, and which were stimulated by G. Stanley Hall. "When I turned to the consideration of racial problems I was shocked by the formalism of the work." He set himself against the whole methodology of a "racial" heredity. "Heredity acts only in lines of direct descent. There is no unity of descent in any of the existing races." Especially during the last twenty years Boas constantly had on hand researches in race and in problems of growth, for he recognized the seeds of social catastrophe in the doctrines of the racialists and hoped that if their contentions were disproved it would lessen the danger. As late as 1937 he made the journey to Paris to the Congrès International de la Population to emphasize before a gathering largely dominated by Nazi racialists that social conditions are determinative even for those aspects of behavior usually assigned to "race."

His scientific writings were voluminous and are well represented in the volume of selected papers he edited in 1940, *Race, Language and Culture.* His least technical volumes are *The Mind of Primitive Man,* 1911; *Primitive Art,* 1927; *Anthropology and Modern Life,* 1928; and his contributions in *General Anthropology,* 1938, which he planned and edited.

Boas' own personal researches are inextricably interwoven with work for which he supplied the inspiration, often arranged the financing and contributed counsel and editorial assistance. His work as editor alone would have been sufficient to fill the lifetime of an industrious man. To his classroom teaching also he gave his best. Until recent years most American anthropologists sat under him. As early as 1896 he began teaching physical anthropology and linguistics at Columbia University and in 1899 was made professor of anthropology there. He retired in 1936. Since then he has devoted himself to his researches and to his championing of social and political sanity. He was a great humanitarian and he believed in the social efficacy of the Golden Rule not merely in individual relations but between groups and between nations. He believed in civil liberties. For a man of Boas' integrity these convictions could not end in lip service; they meant to him taking strong positions about national and international affairs, about the conduct of education and the organization of schools. During the last decade the fact that his motherland was being allowed to run amok in the civilized world touched him nearly and he feared that the democratic nations would never unite against the Nazi plan of world domination. But he saw always that anything that could be done to stop this menace, even war when the world had let slip all other methods, should be a means to the end of Germany's salvation as well as ours.

Boas received many honors. He was made a member of the National Academy of Sciences in 1900. In 1931 he was president of the American Association for the Advancement of Science. He received the Sc.D. from Oxford University and from Columbia and the LL.D. from Clark University. His alma mater, the University of Kiel, solved its dilemma by awarding an honorary M.D. because that at least he did not have. They were fitting honors to a man of Boas' tirelessness, of his integrity, of his sanity. It was not the honors, however, but these special qualities, so pervaded by his great intellectual powers, which made him one of the noblest representatives of his generation.

Murray Wax   (essay date 1956)

SOURCE: "The Limits of Boas' Anthropology," in *American Anthropologist,* Vol. 58, No. 1, 1956, pp. 63-74.

[*In the following essay, Wax argues that while Boas was successful in introducing a spirit of critical inquiry and empiricism into modern anthropology, he failed to develop viable theories of his own.*]

This paper will examine the dominant convictions of Franz Boas on a variety of subjects. We will show that, whatever their individual merits, they formed, when linked together, a chain that constricted creative research in cultural anthropology. By their combined standards, scarcely any research was judged satisfactory. The great talents of Boas himself were so restricted that he could not produce any positive, integrated work of significance, and his function became that of critic.

The form of a typical ethnological study by Franz Boas was as follows: A general hypothesis about culture or about cultural processes had been advanced by some scholar. Boas would then collect a considerable mass of data of the most objective kind—material objects or texts. He would describe these succinctly and with little or no interpretation. The data, so presented, would speak for themselves: they were an exception to the general hypothesis and it was therefore refuted. Then Boas would present his own point of view: the situation was a complex one; the refuted hypothesis had ignored the complexities; a full analysis, if humanly possible, would reveal many factors in operation.

The logic of his argument was simple and potent. The hypothesis advanced could be framed in the form, "All A is B." Boas would present an entity that was clearly an A

and yet equally clearly not a B. Accordingly, the hypothesis was false.

This logic was and is frequently utilized by natural scientists. But the aim there is usually not to discredit completely but to test the limits, to discover the region where the hypothesis applies and that where it fails. Then the scientist attempts to reformulate the hypothesis so that in its revised form it fits both regions. But Boas was not interested in the partial truth that might be implicit in the refuted generalization; as a generalization it was wholly false and should no longer receive any respect whatsoever from the scientist. He would, therefore, attack it over and over again in his publications and in his classes. Lowie has reported on Boas as a pedagogue:

> Other men's views he often treated in a way likely to mislead the immature, for by concentrating on controversial issues he sometimes conveyed the impression of total condemnation where there was partial dissent. . . . His critique of environmentalism, for instance, was urged so forcibly that for years I failed to grasp how carefully he took cognizance of geographical factors.

Boas had been trained in Germany when the radical empiricist movement in the natural sciences was flourishing and was invading psychology via psychophysics. Men such as Rudolph Virchow, Gustav Fechner, and Ernst Mach, as well no doubt as Hermann Helmholtz, influenced Boas greatly by their research, writing, or teaching. Of Virchow, he wrote in 1902:

> There are but few students who possess that cold enthusiasm for truth that enables them to be always clearly conscious of the sharp line between an attractive theory and the observation that has been secured by hard and earnest work.

It is likely that the young Boas already saw himself as the introducer of strict empirical methods into ethnology.

At Columbia Boas preached empiricism to his students almost as a crusade. Science was a holy vocation, and the young men who entered it would be subjected to many temptations: Speculation, Theory, (traditional) Philosophy. The intelligence of the scientist would desire to generalize on the basis of inadequate data or would be attracted by the seductive phrases of an armchair theorist. He must train himself to resist such impulses and not to stray from the path of strictest empiricism. Boas' preaching, reinforced by his tremendous abilities and his sincere dedication to science, converted his students and decisively influenced the character of American anthropology. Even when his students, as mature scholars, could perceive that Boas' empiricism was so extreme as to be hurtful to the progress of the discipline, they still defended their teacher in emotionally and morally toned words. In the section from which the passage below is excerpted, Lowie noted quite clearly how Boas' reluctance to generalize had handicapped further research, and characterized his motives as "puritanical." But even Lowie, "That eminently sane man," could not permit this criticism to stand unmodified; he immediately turned to the defense and labeled the appreciation of generalization as a craving.

His critics suggest an incapacity for synthesis; his intimates know that he forms opinions on all anthropological questions but refrains from utterance when the evidence seems indecisive. That even the provisional syntheses of this independent and erudite thinker would shed floods of light is unquestionable; it is not, however, Boas' method of procedure. . . .

The craver of systems cannot understand a scientist's progress from problem to problem without at once generalizing a particular solution achieved. . . . [His] attitude is the scientist's as opposed to the philosopher's.

In replying publicly to the foreign scholars whose works he had so often attacked and who had responded with criticism of his antitheoretical position, Boas emphasized in 1920 a more positive attitude toward "ultimate problems":

It may seem to the distant observer that American students are engaged in a mass of detailed investigations without much bearing upon the solution of the ultimate problems of a philosophic history of human civilization. I think this interpretation of the American attitude would be unjust because the ultimate questions are as near to our hearts as they are to those of other scholars, only we do not hope to be able to solve an intricate historical problem by a formula.

Feeling, perhaps, that more than this verbal statement was necessary, he listed some of the "general conclusions" deriving from the American studies. Among them we note the following (the alphabetical labeling is my own):

(a) . . . a surplus of food supply is liable to bring about an increase of population and an increase of leisure, which gives opportunity for occupations that are not absolutely necessary for the needs of every day life. In turn the increase of population and of leisure, which may be applied to new inventions, gives rise to a greater food supply and to a further increase in the amount of leisure, so that a cumulative effect results.

(b) . . . the sequence of industrial inventions in the Old World and in America, which I consider as independent. A period of food gathering and of the use of stone was followed by the invention of agriculture, of pottery and finally of the use of metals. Obviously, this order is based on the increased amount of time given by mankind to the use of natural products, of tools and utensils, and to the variations that developed with it. Although in this case parallelism seems to exist on the two continents, it would be futile to follow out the order in detail.

(c) A similar consideration may be made in regard to the development of rationalism. It seems to be one of the fundamental characteristics of the development of mankind that activities which have developed unconsciously are gradually made the subject of reasoning. We may observe this process everywhere.

The excerpts demonstrate that Boas could not only refute significant hypotheses, he could advance them. Taken to-

gether and integrated, they constitute a good part of the basis for a neo-evolutionary or developmental schema in the style of V. Gordon Childe or of Robert Redfield. But Boas was unwilling to direct his own and his students' attention toward such a positive goal. As a matter of fact, he had no real warrant for describing (a) and (c) as general conclusions deriving from the American studies; the American students made no systematic studies of these phenomena. Boas preferred attacking the simple-minded, rigid, and ethnocentric evolutionary schemes to framing an accurate, flexible, and humanistic one.

To illustrate the kind of confusion this could precipitate: In 1945 and again in 1947 White accused the Boas school of hampering the development of anthropology as a science by its hostility to theory and, in particular, to evolutionary theory. In calm reply, Lowie denied the antievolutionary charge. Boas, he declared, had only attacked the unscientific speculations of the early evolutionists, but Boas himself and anthropologists today were really all evolutionists!

How, then, shall we classify and understand the labors of Boas in cultural anthropology? In 1935 Kroeber proposed an ideal typical dichotomy between *history* and *science,* which he evidently modeled after the German distinction between *Geisteswissenschaft* and *Naturwissenschaft.* In these terms he classified Boas as a scientist. Is this correct?

Both history and science seek the truth, but their typical methods of investigation are different and their typical end-products are different. The methods we shall discuss in a later section; here we confine ourselves to end-products. Science seeks the general statement, the universal proposition true of every situation yet not truly descriptive of any single situation. History seeks to understand the particular events of a past with their human ("historical") significances, and to convey this understanding to others. Thus conceived, science is epitomized by a treatise in mathematical physics; history (to use Kroeber's epitome) by Burckhardt's *The Renaissance.* On the one hand, the highest abstraction and greatest universality; on the other hand, the depiction of a particular epoch with its particular, and yet general, human significances and values. (Kroeber emphasized the depictive integration. I believe Weber was equally correct in emphasizing that history was oriented about unique events of human significance and value. But this is of little relevance here.)

Many disciplines have, limitedly, the goals of both history and science. Thus, astronomy seeks to generalize about the behaviour of galactic systems and also to describe the history of our solar system. Cultural anthropology seeks to generalize about human culture and society and also to describe particular human groups and their human significances. In such cases, the differently directed activities within the discipline may fruitfully assist each other, and a joint store of particular facts, generalizations about process, and insightful interpretations and understandings come to be accepted as valid. In its happier intervals, cultural anthropology has this appearance.

In terms of his history/science dichotomy Kroeber asserted that Boas was not a historian. Boas agreed that he did not write history, as Kroeber defined the term (but he contended that Kroeber's usage was "abnormal" and that his approach was historical in any legitimate sense).

By default, then, Boas appeared as a scientist. Yet, as he, himself, stated:

> Redfield's criticism of my work is summed up in the words: "he does not write histories, and he does not prepare scientific systems." The latter point agrees fully with my views.

Boas not only did not prepare scientific systems, he did not seek generalizations. As we have observed, he gave verbal allegiance to the pursuit of generalizations, but in fact his interest in them was confined to demonstrating their invalidity. At times, he contended that he was interested in a limited type of generalization about cultural processes, and it was on this basis, apparently, that Kroeber labeled him a scientist. But, again, no systematic pursuit of cultural processes is evident in his research; rather, he seemed to use the term "process" as an *ad hoc* slogan in his attack upon the rash proposers of scientific laws.

Thus, the history/science dichotomy seems to fail to classify Boas. This is not surprising, since the two concepts are not logical contradictories but only contraries; they are not mutually inclusive of the field. A moment's reflection reminds that there are many researchers, although few of the stature of Boas, who are neither historians nor scientists as Kroeber and we have defined them.

At first, Boas did not understand his former student, as his 1936 retort to Kroeber indicated. However, later, he did understand, and he gave a subtle answer by including in his volume of essays, *Race, Language and Culture,* "two very early general papers . . . because they indicate the general attitude underlying my later work."

Let us examine one of these papers, **"The Study of Geography,"** written in 1887: "The origin of every science we find in two different desires of the human mind,—its aesthetic wants, and its interest in the individual phenomenon." The aesthetic wants are satisfied by the elimination of confusion and chaos and the institution of order. "The more clearly all phenomena are arranged, the better will the aesthetic desire be satisfied, and for that reason the most general laws and ideas are considered the most valuable results of science."

Complementary to the aesthetic wants are the affective ones, which focus on the individual phenomenon as such. Where the physicist, governed by aesthetic desires, views the phenomenon as a specimen of a class, the cosmographer, as Boas termed him, takes the attitude of Goethe:

> It seems to me that every phenomenon, every fact, itself is the really interesting object. Whoever explains it, or connects it with other events, usually only amuses himself or makes sport of us, as, for instance, the naturalist or historian. But a single action or event is interesting, not because it is explainable, but because it is true.

Naturalists and physicists are dissatisfied with the study of geography on two grounds: first, because such study cannot lead to scientific laws; second, because the phenomena studied have no objective unity but only a subjective connection in the mind of the student. Phenomena which have an objective unity may be studied historically, and historical study leads to an objective arrangement which is as pleasing to the aesthetic sense as is the formulation of laws. In contrast, the cosmographer values geography as a study of individual phenomena for their own sake, much as does the artist. Boas insisted that no objective decision between these two positions was possible. The choice of the scholar merely revealed the strength of one set of his desires against the other. In himself, Boas at that time saw the affective desires as strongest.

If, now, we were to establish a typology of investigators on the basis jointly of Kroeber's and Boas' analyses, we would have three archetypes: scientist, historian, and (let us call him) phenomenalist. The chief function of the last would be, à la Boas, to concentrate on individual phenomena and to criticize scientists and historians for careless and rash generalizations and interpretations. Taken together, the three types of investigators would be complementary; each would be essential to the progress of a discipline such as cultural anthropology; and the sole danger would be the imbalance caused when one type dominated the field for too long a time.

However, it is difficult to know how much importance to give this early declaration by Boas. As an anthropologist, he was, it is true, intensely loyal to the individual phenomenon, whether by temperament (affective desires) or by epistemological conviction (radical empiricism), and this devotion gave his studies their scientific rigor. Yet, despite the 1887 article, his work displayed much of the temper of the scientist, particularly in its method. Also, as we have indicated, his attacks on other scholars did not have the tolerant character of one who feels merely that his temperament or desires are different from the others'. Consequently, it will be useful to postpone judgment until we have discussed other aspects of Boas' work—his conception of cultural anthropology and his methods.

If one knew of Franz Boas only that he had been trained in the natural sciences, one might have expected his to be a generalizing, abstracting method like that of Durkheim, in which society is considered a reality *sui generis* and purely social, superindividual laws are sought. But only occasionally, and especially in opposition to racist and environmentalist doctrines, did Boas stress the autonomy of culture and the passivity of the individual.

> The influence of an individual upon culture depends not only upon his strength but also upon the readiness of society to accept changes. During the unstable conditions of cultural life produced by contact between European and primitive civilizations many native prophets have arisen who have with more or less success modified the religious beliefs of the people. Their revelations, however, were reflexes of the mixed culture. The new ideas created in society are not free, but are determined by the culture in which they arise. The artist is hemmed in by the peculiar style of the art and the techniques of his environment; the religious mind by current belief;

the political leader by established political forms.

Strikingly enough, four years later, in the revised edition of the same work, this passage was omitted, and instead there were several pages of examples of cultural changes and the roles played by individuals in the changes.

It fitted with his adherence to radical empiricism that Boas emphasized the reality of the individual and warned against reifying culture. Thus, in both the first and revised editions of *Anthropology and Modern Life* he declared:

> It seems hardly necessary to consider culture a mystic entity that exists outside the society of its individual carriers, and that moves by its own force. The life of a society is carried on by individuals who act singly and jointly under the stress of the tradition in which they have grown up and surrounded by the products of their own activities and those of their forebears. . . .
>
> The forces that bring about the changes are active in the individuals composing the social groups, not in the abstract culture.

Even in his earliest essays on anthropological theory Boas was oriented social-psychologically. In 1888, when he was still a believer in evolutionary theory, he thought of ethnology as discovering the laws of folk psychology, the laws governing the development of the human mind. And this approach remained when he rejected evolutionary theory. Benedict is in agreement:

> It has never been sufficiently realized how consistently throughout his life Boas defined the task of ethnology as the study of "man's mental life," "fundamental psychic attitudes of cultural groups," man's "subjective worlds."

And Lowie recalls: "I remember his suddenly electrifying a seminar with the statement that he was concerned with detail only as a way to understanding human mentality."

Finally, we have, as an illustration from his own writings, a criticism by Boas of the search for sociological laws:

> The problems of the relation of the individual to his culture, to the society in which he lives have received too little attention. The standardized anthropological data that inform us of customary behavior, give no clue to the reaction of the individual to his culture, nor to an understanding of his influence upon it. Still, here lies the source of a true interpretation of human behavior. It seems a vain effort to search for sociological laws disregarding what should be called social psychology, namely, the reaction of the individual to culture.

Such citations could be multiplied greatly and selected from all periods of his work. Boas' theoretical orientation to cultural anthropology was social psychological rather than sociological or culture historical.

The same emphasis upon the individual appeared in Boas' political liberalism. His book, *Anthropology and Modern Life,* was written "to show that some of the most firmly rooted opinions of our times appear from a wider point of view as prejudices," and the opinions he singled out all bore the stamp of illiberalism. Six of the nine chapters are largely criticisms of the various forms of belief in the overwhelming social importance of heredity. They attacked the belief in the superiority of one race over others; the belief that race and nationality are one; the belief in eugenics; and the belief in the inheritance of criminal traits. In opposition to the belief in the social importance of heredity, Boas urged the importance of social environment, culture. But, cultures could be better or worse, confining to the individual or liberating him. He advocated such (early twentieth-century) liberal notions as: the desirability and inevitability of a world federation of nations; the desirability of individual freedom and the importance of designing education so that it liberates the mind of the child rather than confines it; the lack of tradition and therefore greater wisdom of the urban masses as against the classes; and the unnecessary harshness of contemporary sexual conventions.

Freedom of the individual is the central theme running throughout the book, and it places Boas' liberalism in the tradition of John Stuart Mill. From this perspective we can better appreciate the attacks in the book, and elsewhere, upon certain kinds of anthropological generalizations. Racist theories, evolutionary theories, geographical, economic, or cultural determinisms, all these minimize the importance, power, and value of the individual. In opposition, Boas felt that the individual was the actor in the adventure of mankind and that, accordingly, each individual should be judged by his actions, not by his nonvoluntary membership in some group or placement in some physical or historical situation.

Thus, when Boas studied, say, North American art, he focused on the individual craftsman and how he, or she, worked within the givens of tradition, tools, and raw material. For example:

> I have noticed that here, where in a fine imbricated technique color bands are produced, the basket weavers tend to use with great regularity certain groupings of the number of stitches belonging to each color, although, owing to the irregularity of the size of these stitches, these modifications can hardly be observed. If these facts have a wider application, it would seem that on the whole the pleasure given by much of the decorative work of primitive people must not be looked for in the beauty of the finished product, but rather in the enjoyment which the maker feels at his own cleverness in playing with the technical elements he is using.

From this focus on the social psychology of the individual craftsman Boas was able to attack sociological generalizations such as the assertion that in the decorative arts conventional designs develop from the degeneration of representational designs.

Clearly, the power of a social psychological approach, like that of Boas, depends directly upon the adequacy of the social psychology that is employed and elaborated in the course of research. If the anthropologist wishes to study "man's subjective worlds," or "fundamental psychic attitudes of cultural groups," he must have both excellent data and a rich psychological conceptual scheme or theory for handling and interpreting the data. Boas had access to the data. But the tragic flaw in his approach to cultural anthropology was that he operated with a simple-minded, mechanical psychology.

The influence of that psychology was expressed in many areas of his work, but one of the few places where he explicitly sketched it was in the chapter on "Stability of Culture" in *Anthropology and Modern Life*: Men act largely according to habit. The earlier in life the habit is inculcated, the more difficult is it to alter, the more automatic is its action, and the stronger are the emotions associated with it. Habit is fundamentally activity, not thought; and thought about habitual activity is usually rationalization.

This psychology was not the product of the research of Boas or of his students; it was never tested explicitly in the field or elaborated in consequence. It was one of the psychologies popular in the first quarter of this century, but it was far from being the best social psychology he might have selected. The great contribution of the American interactionist psychologists, Charles H. Cooley and George H. Mead, the conception of human interaction as mediated by symbols and as internalized in the form of the self, had escaped him. He was aware of psychoanalysis and accepted the notion that the first few years of life are critical for personality formation, but otherwise he was skeptical of its findings and methods. With such an impoverished view of human nature and human interaction as schematized by his habit psychology, Boas was unable to cope with social phenomena. The result was such a simplistic analysis as the following:

> Intolerance of sharply divided social sets is often based on the strength of automatic reactions and upon the feeling of intense displeasure felt in acts opposed to our own automatism. The apparent fanaticism exhibited in the persecution of heretics must be explained in this manner. At a time when the dogma taught by the Church was imposed upon each individual so intensely that it became an automatic part of his thought and action, it was accompanied by a strong feeling of hostility to any one who did not participate in this feeling. The term fanaticism does not quite correctly express the attitude of the Inquisition. Its psychological basis was rather the impossibility of changing a habit of thought that had become automatic and the consequent impossibility of new lines of thought, which, for this very reason, seemed antisocial; that is, criminal.

Clearly, Boas lacked the understanding and the conceptual scheme to handle phenomena such as religious beliefs, individual and group interests, bureaucratic organization, etc., that were an integral part of a complex such as the Inquisition.

Since, on the whole, h was dealing with simpler situations than that, and since he was so reluctant to advance a hypothesis publicly, Boas made no glaring errors in his handlings of ethnological materials. But, equally, he contributed no dazzling insights. When he dealt with the fascinating creations of primitive art, he confined himself to the most pedestrian description and analysis. His book on *Primitive Art* evoked, according to Kroeber, more respect than warmth of appreciation, for he did not deal with cultural or aesthetic values or with style as such. The reason for this deficiency Kroeber traces to "deliberate restraint," "the ice in his enthusiasm"; he felt that Boas the man was keenly aware of the aesthetic values which as a scientist he could not analyze and so refused to discuss. This was true, but there was more to it than that. As we shall see in the next section, the book was based on the habit psychology we have outlined, and the inadequacies of the psychology are clearly reflected in those of the book.

Kroeber typified history and science as seeking contrary *goals,* and in the first section of this paper we followed his lead. We saw history as seeking to understand the events of a past with their human significances and to convey this understanding to others; science as seeking to describe abstractly and with economy and elegance the processes of any situation of a certain class. But history and science differ not only in goals, they differ typically also in *methods.*

Since science seeks to generalize about the members of an indefinitely large class, its method emphasizes the notion of replicability. In theory, a scientist can duplicate the manipulations and observations of any other scientist in his discipline and, allowing for the vagaries of chance, emerge with identical findings. If two sets of observations are not in agreement, then the two observers were not really studying events belonging to the same class. Thus, it is a typical problem of science to discover, by criticism of observational techniques, by more refined observation, and by theoretical analysis, why the observations of a class of apparently identical events are at variance with each other.

The historian wishes to understand particular events of human significance (and then to convey this understanding to his audience). This means that his is primarily a task of insightful interpretation of whatever evidence has come to him from the particular past. Since it is a past, and since the events were not conceived of as especially significant until the passage of a long period of time, the evidence desired is usually meager, and the historian must develop his ability to wring the last drop of information from the documents at his disposal. He relies upon his knowledge of human nature generally and of the character of the particular people being studied to aid him in his interpretation. Historians frequently disagree as to the meanings of particular facts and, accordingly, as to the character of the events that occurred. A disagreement between historians is often attributed to the differences in their basic conceptions of man and society, and such disagreements are not simply resolvable by appeals to the facts.

While much of the data of cultural anthropology is essentially historical in character, the methods by which they are and can be handled are both scientific and historical. A study of the diffusion of, say, pottery styles leans toward the scientific pole. Here the ethnographer is dealing with objects which can be arranged into large classes and considered within each class as substantially identical. The proportions and design of any one pot in a class are the same as those of any other. In contrast, a study of the function and emotional meaning of pottery in the traditional culture based on interviews with a few aged women is essentially historical. The ethnographer, ideally, weighs each informant's testimony against her character, the interview situation, and the testimony of the others.

Boas thought of his task in scientific terms even when it was clearly historical. For example: He realized the value of collecting as much information as possible from living informants about the vanished or vanishing customs of American Indian groups. Furthermore, as a scientist, he realized that the best data were those which were independent of the observer; this meant exact texts in the language of the native. But, as Radin pointed out, he did not realize that the value of these texts was greatly reduced by the lack of historical method, the lack of background data as to who was the informant, what sort of individual was he, what was the nature of the interview situation, etc. Boas the scientist presented his readers with hundreds of pages of texts—the product of the most intensive labor—without the commentary that would have increased their (historical) value and reliability manyfold. Moreover, he did not, nor did he encourage his students to, draw the texts and field observations together into carefully wrought descriptions of the way of life of a people.

If we now link these various convictions of Boas together, we will find that they form a chain of conditions so divergent and opposing and so rigid that they make systematic, positive research in cultural anthropology all but impossible. Boas was a scientist in method and temper but not in his goals. He was interested in the individual phenomenon and the individual person, but he rejected historical method, which is adapted to such studies (e. g., the open interview, the biography), in favor of scientific method, and he attempted to work with an impoverished, "scientific" social psychology. His radical empiricism and scientific bent made him comfortable with only the "hardest" of data: skeletal proportions, material objects, texts. But his political liberalism was antagonistic to positive hereditary findings, and he was always seeking to demonstrate that differences apparently due to heredity had actually other causes. Pure distribution studies of designs and of folktales smacked of the superorganic and of reifying cultural processes; he insisted that we needed to find the individuals active behind the cultural process and the reasons for their behavior. Style and folktales are evidences about man's subjective worlds and the life of the individual but only when interpreted with the aid of historical insight and a rich social psychology. Thus, his divergent, conflicting, iron convictions added up to a set of limiting preconditions for ethnological work that might have broken the spirit of a lesser man.

We can illustrate by a consideration of one of the few works in which his positive, rather than critical, efforts are predominant, *Primitive Art* (1927). Boas' drive for knowledge of man's subjective worlds led him to investigate the decorative aspects of primitive art. His habit psychology and his refusal to make insightful interpretations handicapped him severely, but he doubtless feared that better vehicles would prove less governable and would propel him willy-nilly into the morass of aesthetic criticism or the quicksands of culture history.

Let us trace the principal argument of the chapter on "Style": Boas began by considering the influence of tradi-

tional or habitual motor habits on the design of various artifacts. Weapons, household furniture, clothes, and tools are designed in consonance with the habitual acts of which they are an element. When an act has been habitual since childhood, there is an emotional attachment to it and resistance to change; so, too, there will be an emotional attachment to the design of the artifacts customarily utilized, even when the design of the artifacts is not critical to the execution of the action. When the raw material from which the artifact has been made is changed, there will be an attempt to impose the old designs upon the new material. Boas then recalled an argument of the preceding chapters: as a craftsman works upon an object, he modifies or produces a surface; if he is highly skilled, a virtuoso, the surface produced is so regular as to be aesthetically pleasing. Moreover, the virtuoso will often play with his material, thus producing an intricate pattern. Such patterns may then, later, be transferred to a new medium, e. g., from cloth to pottery.

Here the principal argument of the chapter ended. Boas admitted that he had not explained the variation in style from group to group, technical conditions being otherwise similar. But, in his usual fashion, he concluded that the subject was complex and that it was doubtful whether all the factors would be fully elucidated.

We note how his analysis mirrored his social psychology in its emphasis upon ingrained habit, upon the dominance of motor habits over intellectual processes, and upon the emotional attachment to tradition. Boas' approach was adequate, perhaps, to a discussion of the craftsman who amuses himself with his own dexterity, but it fails completely in interpreting styles or genuine artistry. The artist, in contrast to Boas' craftsman, is aware of himself and of an audience for his creation. He looks at his work from the point of view of his audience, and he directs his virtuosity toward the creation of forms that, he anticipates, will have certain kinds of impact upon the audience. (Of course, many craftsmen will possess artistic self-consciousness although in weaker degree than the true artist.) But Boas could not perceive or discuss this essential ingredient of art: in his psychology the individual is dominated by habit; the individual has no self and cannot interact with himself in order to so control his actions as to produce forms whose impact he can anticipate.

Since he would not interpret historically, with insight, Boas could not cope with the richness of emotional and intellectual meanings in a cultural style. Even in the case of the Indians of the Northwest Coast, whom he had studied for so many years, he could not discuss the significances, values, meanings, and functions of their dramatic carvings. Viewed objectively, as the product of great labor by a distinguished anthropologist, *Primitive Art* was a failure. But when we understand the self-imposed restraints, it was a triumph that he produced anything at all on the subject.

Given these restraints, Boas' *forte* was criticism. He was a master at exposing the generalization that was false to the phenomena, or that explained away a serious problem by reifying culture, or that was constructed in violation of the canons of scientific method. In so far as his targets were would-be scientists relying upon inadequate data and slipshod methods, his criticism was healthful for the growing discipline. But cultural anthropology also required positive leadership, and here Boas failed.

Margaret Mead   (essay date 1959)

SOURCE: "Apprenticeship Under Boas," in *American Anthropologist,* Vol. 61, No. 5, 1959, pp. 29-45.

[*A respected American anthropologist, Mead is noted for her psychological and cultural studies of primitive societies, most notably* Coming of Age in Samoa. *Mead also studied with Boas, and in the following essay, which incorporates letters, conversations, and lecture notes, Mead discusses Boas's influence on her work as well as his impact on the field of anthropology.*]

The myths that obscure the personality of an intellectual leader gather thickest in the years immediately following his death, when there are many people alive who speak with varyingly authoritative voices, and the next younger generation listens. As one of Boas' students, and a student of his later, mellower years, I feel that it will be useful to include in this memoir something of the effects, as I see them, of the way he taught and the way he appeared to those who were learning from him in day-to-day contact. Melville Herskovits has written of Boas [in his *Franz Boas: The Science of Man in the Making,* 1953], using extensive documentation from his published work and fusing his account with his own long-time association with Boas, as a student and a research worker. I shall not attempt to duplicate this, but shall confine myself to some aspects of Boas' relationships to his students and to his role in anthropology as it appeared to me as a student—a subject to which Herskovits devoted only a couple of pages.

At the period (1922-1929) during which I was successively an undergraduate student, a graduate student, a research student, and a student assistant, Boas was playing several different roles in American anthropology. He saw the whole of the study of man—as he had once seen the life of the Central Eskimo—spread out in a great panorama, stretching back to the infrahuman world and forward as man gained greater control over those aspects of culture which he saw as cumulative—technological and scientific development. We were never permitted to forget man's oneness with the rest of the living world, or the problems that arose when man became the first domesticated animal. Within this great panorama Boas saw the scientific task as one of progressive probing into a problem now of language, now of physical type, now of art style—each a deep, sudden, intensive stab at some strategic point into an enormous untapped and unknown mass of information which we would some day master. No probe must go too far lest it lead to premature generalization—a development which he feared like the plague and against which he continually warned us.

Secondly, he himself, as a curious and wondering human being (and he never lost that quality of wonder which seems to be one of the essentials of greatness), was enormously preoccupied with what we today would call microcultural problems—problems of cultural change and development where individual differences and slight historical circumstances are magnified into long-term, significant effects. So, in seminars in which students reported on current pieces of fieldwork, he drew our attention again and again to the small, vivid detail and its possible relevance within the larger framework.

Thirdly, he had cast himself in the role of one of the responsible leaders of a giant rescue operation to preserve the vanishing fragments of primitive languages and cultures. This had to be done with almost no money, very few trained people, and no time to spare. His letters are filled with discussions of how some small sum—two or three hundred dollars—was somehow to be raised to keep someone writing up material or to keep someone a couple of months longer in the field. While he was extraordinarily exacting in the standards which he set for himself and his students, he also welcomed—because this was necessary for the sake of salvage—any concrete reliable work from anywhere. Once welcomed, and then almost immediately used, the data had also to be rigorously criticized. So, in addition to the criticism which he meted out to those who made premature and inadequately documented generalizations, there was criticism of the methods that lay back of the fragments with which he, and we, had to work.

Fourth, he thought of himself as morally responsible for the uses made of anthropology, for the provision of research materials relevant to human freedom, and also for keeping the subject itself open-ended. This sense of moral responsibility manifested itself in his reviews, his criticisms of Museum policy, his plans for great, inclusive expeditions and institutions, and what often seemed his high-handed interference in other people's plans. As he was not working for personal power but for the good of mankind, he had the moral freedom that goes with self-elected, complete dedication. It is true that he did not found a school, because he did not believe in schools. Yet he was in fact a prophet of an open-ended, continually revised scientific enterprise, and for this very reason he stood in opposition to all prophets, to all exclusive and final solutions of any problem, and had little compunction in attempting to stop others from becoming prophets. So he wrote to [Alfred Tozzer, December 2, 1932], objecting to the possibility of a large research grant for anthropological research being put under the direction of Radcliffe-Brown, since that would mean only one approach to a question that required many. Dillydallying, low-level politics, academic redtape—all threw him into a rage. I remember his description of a dream he had after a research council planning meeting—a dream in which he was trying to hang a curtain on a curtain rod that was made of rats biting each others' backs.

This sense of moral responsibility made us all feel that we were caught in an obligation to do more and better work, or we would "betray Dr. Boas." A mandate as vague as this carried with it its own heavy sense of responsibility. The extent to which Boas left us on our own was appropriate in a period when letters to and from the field might take several months, but it also produced that peculiar sense of obligation that accompanies the ill-defined task. I remember walking the floor of my office in the American

Museum the day I was to appear to have my manuscript of *Coming of Age in Samoa* criticized, saying over and over again, "I suppose I have betrayed him like all the rest"—in the sense of having failed to make the most of a unique chance, of funds to do fieldwork when funds were so few, and of my "field" when fields were every day being spoiled for ever.

The form that these very preoccupations took when he taught us was a curious amalgam, with consequences which have outlived him. He never talked about science or scientific method as such, except as he discussed mathematical methods in his formidable Anthropometry course which all of us had to take. He would take a theoretical finding and destroy its validity by citing chapter and verse around the world that showed it wasn't so. When it came to the study of culture, there was no discussion of the law of parsimony or of controls or of sampling, no invocation of models, none of the paraphernalia of the natural sciences with which students of human behavior who were more interested in being "scientists" than in understanding human behavior were beginning to surround themselves. We did not doubt that we were doing scientific work, that we had to live up to scientific standards and use all the methods, qualitative or quantitative, that were or would become available. But we did not talk about methods; instead, we talked about problems, the problems that should be tackled next.

Characteristically, there are no methods named after Boas, just as there is no Boas school, and when we went into the field, we made such methodological innovations as seemed called for by the problem and the local setting. We made these innovations almost unconsciously, or, as Boas would have said, "automatically." In Samoa I decided to include three complete communities so that I would have a total sample, and I set up cross-cutting age groups for study, chose special intelligence tests, and used the deviant individuals to delineate the pattern—without any sense that these were "methods," which would later be named and dignified with italics and capital letters, e. g., the study of the community in vivo, the cross-sectional as opposed to the longitudinal study of child development, the attempt to provide "culture-free tests," and so forth. With our attention focused on problems and with standards of work built in, we exemplified the kind of extension of the teacher's skill which is characteristic of apprenticeship learning, where the learning is inexplicit, rather than more formal kinds of teaching where learning is acquired through textbooks and formal demonstrations. It is significant that Boas disliked textbooks and seldom sent us to his own written work. He gave us the gist of it in his lectures and assumed that we would resort to it only when we needed the actual material.

It is probably also important that he did not teach us by laying out a systematic plan for future research, such as is possible in an experimental science. The outcome, in terms of science, would still depend upon what was actually found in ethnography, in archeology, in paleontology, in natural history. Some problems would never be solved, but the next field trip might shed unhoped-for light on some problem that no one had yet glimpsed. This recogni-

tion of the continuous possibilities of illumination from the material became as conscious as the idea of methods as such remained unconscious. Ruth Benedict defined her approach to the contrast between Plains and Pueblo cultures not as a method of analysis but as resulting from a sudden insight; and even such an obvious point as my recognition that it was nonsense to study adolescents without also studying preadolescents, I felt as an insight, not as methodology.

This inarticulateness about method has perhaps been a disadvantage. Students trained in other universities have learned only to recognize a method if it is labelled as such, and a good many of the innovations we made went unrecognized and had to be reinvented. In an article about Ruth Benedict [in the *University of Toronto Quarterly* XVIII, No. 3, 1949] Victor Barnouw remarked about Boas:

> When Franz Boas published page after page of blueberry-pie recipes in Kwakiutl, the old man probably knew what he was after; but when his students did the same kind of thing, they often lacked the driving central purpose which animated Boas.

It was not until I puzzled irritably about the meaning of this comment that I verbalized to myself just what Boas had been doing: that is, building an exhaustive corpus of materials which could be analyzed for negative as well as for positive points. And the materials which he chose—tales, recipes, technologies, art objects—were all of a kind that permitted the collection of an exhaustive corpus relatively independent of the idiosyncrasies of the individual collector.

Similarly, I realized the implications of sampling in anthropological field method only when I had to discuss problems of sampling with social psychologists and sociologists, as for example, where the sociologists argued that the 100 families included in the sample for a family study should have no contact with one another, while the anthropologist argued in favor of going from one family to another. What became clear was that, in a closed and well-studied community, every item of information on one individual is also an item of information on every other individual in the group. So, too, Boas' dicta in his letter to Mason [discussed in *American Anthropologist* 59, 1957]—but stated less definitely in the classroom—lay back of our development of the appropriate unit for the study of food habits. But in 1945 I saw our way of working in this study as a consequence of ethnological field responsibilities rather than as a formal, methodological point. Not until I tried to formulate an appropriate unit for the study of cultural evolution for the Simpson and Roe symposium, did I realize that this unit was in fact the one that I had been using in the field for thirty years, i.e., the small, interacting human group in which each individual member is specified.

This lack of self-consciousness about method could even lead to the making of a kind of somnambulistic choice. In 1953, we realized that one of the crucial changes which had taken place in Manus culture since the first study in 1928 was in the attitude toward boundaries in time and space. This showed up clearly in the way children filled a piece of drawing paper, and I complained, "If only I'd tested them on paper of different shapes in 1928!" But later, when I again went over the sets of drawings collected in 1928, I found that I had done this, and so could demonstrate the change that had taken place by 1953. Automatic methodological behavior of this kind is only transmissible from person to person. So, for example, it is striking that even with the degree of explicitness that has been introduced into the use of still photography as a research tool in anthropology, our method has been used only by those who have had research contact with Gregory Bateson or myself, and discussions of the method turn into attacks on the approach.

Boas called his course on theory "Methods." The distinction between covert and overt culture is now treated as a theoretical point, but when I first discussed this problem in 1933, I included it—together with a discussion of event-triggered as compared with calendrically-triggered cultures—in an article called "More Comprehensive Field Methods" [in *American Anthropologist* 35, No. 1, 1933], so continuing the tradition.

Here I have drawn on my own experience; elsewhere I have documented the development of Ruth Benedict's anthropological approach. Another student of Boas after whom no methods have been named is Melville Herskovits, although he has pioneered a whole field of Afro-American research. Likewise, an examination of the methods used by Ruth Bunzel in her study, *The Pueblo Potter* (1929), would provide another set of innovations: the use of papier maché models, the introduction of pots from other areas which the artist was asked to copy, a self-apprenticeship with analysis of Zuni teaching methods. Here method was so merged with problem that the methodological—and so to a degree the scientific and generalizable as opposed to the unique and historical contribution to the study of art—was blurred.

Ruth Bunzel described the circumstances in this way:

> You want to know how I came to write *The Pueblo Potter* and became an anthropologist. It is really a story about Boas and the things he believed in. It began in the spring of 1924. I had been working for Professor Boas for two years as secretary and editorial assistant and was becoming increasingly involved with anthropology, but without any formal training whatsoever. That summer Boas was going to Europe and Ruth Benedict was going to Zuni to collect mythology. I thought that if I could see an anthropologist at work at the most crucial and mysterious part of his study, and perhaps try a bit on my own, I would know whether or not I wanted to be and could be an anthropologist. So I thought that I would take my vacation time and a few dollars I had saved for a trip to Europe and instead meet Ruth Benedict in Zuni. My plan was not too ambitious—I was a good stenographer and I would take down folk tales and interviews in shorthand, and do all our typing. Ruth Benedict seemed pleased with the suggestion so I took it to Boas.
>
> Boas heard me out, snorted in his inimitable fashion and said, "Why do you want to waste your time typing?" (He always thought typing a "waste of time," though Heaven knows he wasted enough of his own precious time on similar donkey work to know that the gremlins didn't do it after funds were spent on informants.) "Why don't you work on a problem of your own?" I said that I didn't think I was equipped to do a "problem of my own," but he paid me no mind and went on. "You are interested in art. Why don't you do a problem in art? I have always wanted someone to work on the relation of the artist to his work." (Boas always had a long list of problems that he hoped someone would work on, things that he had started and hadn't had time to go on with, or things that had just occurred to him.) I asked how one would go about investigating such a problem; he recommended that I look at a big manuscript on Salish basketry by Teit and Haeberlin [*Coiled Basketry of British Colombia and Surrounding Areas,* 1925]; I might get suggestions from that.
>
> This plan raised something of a tempest in our little teapot. Elsie Parsons was outraged; sending an untrained person into the field, and to a pueblo at that! She threatened to withdraw her support of the mythology project were I permitted to go. Boas stuck to his point. Intelligence and will were what counted. Granted enough of these one would find the necessary tools. (You know how he always refused to give reading lists, hated examinations, scorned erudition for its own sake. One learned what one needed when one needed it. It was the sense of problem that was important. He always advised students to spend less time reading and more time thinking.) Elsie Parsons capitulated; I was permitted to go.
>
> It was the end of the academic year. Boas went off to Europe; Elsie Parsons went to the Caribbean; Ruth Benedict went to New Hampshire. I stayed in New York with my "problem"—and the basketry paper. The basketry paper proved to be a study of variation. It had nothing to do with what I conceived my problem to be although it contained many points on such matters as the influence of technique on design and analysis of style that stood me in good stead later. I was really alone in a big sea and I had to swim. I assumed that Zuni artists were not going to be any more articulate about what they were trying to do than the poets and painters I had met in Greenwich Village, and that direct questioning would get me nowhere. I had to approach the problem indirectly. I decided on three lines of approach—criticism, instruction, and problem solving. I gathered together as much relevant photographic material from the American Museum of Natural History and the National Museum as I could lay my hands on. I got together a lot of drawing materials. But one thing that I had learned from the Salish basketry paper was that painting a design on paper was not the same problem as putting it on a pot. So I made *papier maché* pots to take along for my informants to paint designs on. Three weeks later I was on the train to Zuni. After five weeks in Zuni I had found out what I wanted to know there, and moved on to other pueblos—this was

not part of the original plan, but it was what made the Zuni material tell.

I was too ignorant at the time to know that I was pioneering; that I was on the frontier of a whole new field of anthropology; that this was the first tentative approach to the study of the individual in culture; the first attempt at a systematic study of behavior. I didn't know that I was employing "participant observation" and "projective techniques" because I had never heard of these things. *The Pueblo Potter* does not have a chapter on methodology.

The Pueblo Potter was written the following winter, on weekends between my job. When I showed the first draft to Boas he said, "It seems to cover everything," and I was satisfied. I decided to become an anthropologist, and I learned about "methods." The following summer I went back to Zuni to learn the language and prepare to find out what it felt like to be a Zuni; I saw this as an extension of the study of the artist. Elsie Parsons sponsored this trip. A gallant lady, she acknowledged in her own gracious fashion that Boas had been right.

A consideration of the advantages and disadvantages of this kind of dependence upon face-to-face contact between teacher and student who are working at the growing edge of a science is too extensive a topic for discussion here. But when accusations of antiscientism are hurled at the man who made anthropology into a science, some knowledge of just how deeply and inexplicitly Boas ground his methodological approach into our bones should help students to understand him.

As further illustrations of some of the points made in this article, I have included a few selected materials from my own notes, from Ruth Benedict's notes, and from Boas' own letters. These are designed not to prove but to exemplify the points I have tried to make.

My notes on Boas' first lecture on Methods, for the spring term in 1925, read:

Development of civilization may:

1. Follow general laws

or

2. Unique historical developments which have to be studied where they occur. Most fundamental question is whether there is anything common to mankind the world over and at all times.

1. Man everywhere has articulate language—language with grammatical organization

2. Everywhere uses tools (not meant any kind of artificial object) but use of things shaped intentionally for particular purpose

3. (Fire)

4. We always find a certain kind of aesthetic principle—a certain valuation of form—

1. in ethics

2. in aesthetics

Idea of valuation is one which is common to all groups of mankind.

5. Actions adapted to ends become the subject of rationalization giving a reason why things are done.

The development of these [first two] characteristics is essentially a pre-human development and none of these features is exclusively human.

He then went on to discuss those categories among birds and animals, the rare cases of tool using, and the "strictly analogous" building of "shelter," the presence of "articulate communication among animals but no grammatically organized system," the decoration of nests, "but we have no clear indication that any idea of values really occurs to animals," and mentioned that "reason is often read into mechanical reproduction of learned adaptive activities." He then suggested that a point for the beginning of the study of man would be where all four of these behaviors were present.

In Boas' discussions of method, his comments would be like these:

In a lecture on parallelisms (February 17, 1925) in which he discussed polyandry among the Todas and the Eskimo, he said, according to my notes:

In reality the two ethnic phenomena with which we are dealing are not the same. So our task is not to emphasize the similarities but to go into detail with the dissimilarities.

In lecturing on Graebner the following week (February 24, 1925), he discussed the area of diffusion covered by the "Earthdiver" tale and the parallel diffusion, at a much later date, of bead embroidery, and commented:

So we find various elements of cultural life are gradually being distributed over the continent, but in entirely different ways. Psychological-socio conditions which bring about the distribution of a tale and a technique are quite different.

Later, in a seminar in which Ruth Benedict reported on "folklore" (April 23, 1925), Boas mused at the back of the room and to no one in particular:

So many of the widely distributed stories enter into the most sacred tales of the people. This is difficult to understand. *There must be a particular reason why they should be selected.* Earthdiver story for example (emphasis supplied).

And the student registered again, but quite inarticulately, an expectation that one day the diverse cultural phenomena would be ordered.

In a lecture on Cassirer (March 17, 1925), he said:

If we had enough information, I believe we would find the relation of time is clearer than space—that the idea of sacred time as against secular time does occur over and over again. . . . *But the proof that could be given is not easy. It would be necessary to have all the material the world over.* Justifiable query to ask: Are these three relations [space, time, and number, as Cassirer gives them] borne out the world over? If they are we might say with Cassirer: We do have these fundamental characteristics of human thought.

We have to be very critical and skeptical. Have these universal ideas developed historically or are they determined psychologically? *And if these ideas are not universal but scattered, unhistorically,* there might be psychological determinism under certain given conditions (emphasis supplied).

The teaching in the Department of Anthropology, all of which Boas did himself—for this was a period when anthropology at Columbia was still suffering from the effects of Boas' unpopularity during World War I—consisted of the series of lectures on anthropological theory (which he called "Methods"), a seminar in which he participated as a member and occasionally reported on a piece of work in which he was interested, a series of fast-moving, condensed lectures on anthropometry, and very detailed exercises in and explorations of the grammar of various languages—sometimes using texts which he had collected, sometimes using a native informant. The whole structure was held together by undertones and cross-references which still remain strangely vivid. When I was editing *An Anthropologist at Work,* I made a list of the points in Methods which I believed had had the most influence on Ruth Benedict and then resigned myself to the task of finding the lectures in question, either in Ruth Benedict's notes or in my own. However, I found that she herself had selected and put together in an envelope the very set of lectures for which I was searching.

I am reproducing selections from her notes here. For purposes of clarity the words which she had abbreviated have been spelled out in full. I have preserved the pattern of words on the page, the punctuation, and her own additions in parentheses as she made them, in order to give a more vivid picture of how the points Boas made appeared to her as she heard them for the first time. This is of course also the form to which she returned in later years, where someone who had not been Boas' student would have turned instead to *The Mind of Primitive Man*, to Boas' words unmediated by the form, handwriting, and personal selection. Not all pages were dated and new pages are indicated by asterisks.

Ruth Benedict's Notes on Boas' "Methods" Lectures

Spring 1922

She had chosen the February 7 lecture on the study of similarities within dissimilarities.

February 7 1922

. . . Fundamental thing we want to understand is their imaginative treatment of their everyday experiences. What are their everyday experiences? e.g. Imaginings in regard to wish fulfillments—overcoming nature etc. True in *all* material, i.e. different *psychological* sources for same developments? in behavior-moieties. Botanical analogy—very far-reaching morphological similarities, *but* in different families (Old &

New World). If I stress this point, it is not because similarities are not important. Quite the contrary. Just as it is important to know the morphological similarities in Old & New World plants. But two problems: 1. the fact of similarity (to be established & the similarities especially within the dissimilarities). Then follow both back psychologically. (Caution for actual material.)

How can we go about it when we want to study the basis of the similarities—

(Keep in mind: may be different)

2. How far can historical depth be determined?

One constant consideration: Transmission *never* a self-contained cultural life—even Bushmen and Esquimo who are intensely hostile to neighbors.

The next selection, five weeks later, dealt with the mechanisms of transmission within a culture.

March 16 1922?

What makes for cultural stability or change?

Conservative Elements—Example

Does not need elaboration, for are ever present.

Example: Pagan elements in European Christianity

Vierkandt—stetigkeit

G. Tarde—Les Lois de l'imitation

As long as we ask "Why does society repeat last generation's—?" —obscurity. Rather "the individual"—"why repeat actions of preceding generation?"

His upbringing in the family—

Unconscious and unintentional imitation plays very large part

People assuming dialects of people they are among—even contrary to will

Pace of people in N. Y., and small city

Imitation *very* deep seated—

basis of personality—begins before child speaks, etc. "Open the door" doesn't know what *door* means. Imitated as a whole, because has certain kind of effect.

Ought to lay great stress on this tendency toward imitation in life of child. Habits (become) are by their nature dogmatic, very hard to break.

Use of knife by African (=gravers tool, *toward* him)

and Indian

Mexican Indian and SW Indian, trot with carrying head-band

China over shoulder, very different

Arrow release—Morse

Arrow between 1 & 2nd finger China

Arrow between thumb & doubled fingers Europe

Yes & no gestures—cultural

South American raise circle of nose for no—wrinkle forehead by raising "eyebrow"

All these imitations of such a character as become automatic. Are not voluntary.

Disgust ordinarily accompanies divergence from own habits.

Smacking the lips in table manners Kwakiutl

Accompanied by very intense emotional resistance, but seems to my mind only a secondary consequence of the automatic character of these actions.

Literal meanings not necessarily present to speakers.

a *technical* analysis. English—"understand" (penknife)

Algonkian—fall down = movement, to come to an end, on the ground(?)

Kwakiutl—steamboat = moving in the water with fire on its back.

Do the metaphors shape the thought of speakers? (N.B. Note that total number of stems limited, in every language. Yet number of expressions *are* built metaphorically.) Can't say. Sometimes mechanical, sometimes not. Not easy to determine. Can see it (perhaps only) in poetry—and see that their imagery is determined by linguistic form.

2 questions: Relation of grammatical form to thought form. Has been attempted in European languages. Would be important too in primitive languages. Relation of metaphorical expression to thought form. No material collected. Would lead to important results.

Diffusion—

"In attempting to reconstruct general cultural history, the tendency to consider each feature due to inner forces. The realization of transmission leads us to entirely different results."

Stringed instruments (not discovered by each experimenter).

Wheat

Tales (. . . can take place only where conditions are such that one person would tell tale to *amuse* person of other language and other people.) Note also: the original much greater diversity of languages. Cannot see that linguistic barriers in any way hinder the distribution of tales. . . .

The March 20 lecture contains the only reference which I ever heard Boas make to Freud, in lecturing, and also foreshadows contemporary studies of nativistic cults.

March 20 1922

Break of automatic habit very difficult when . . . conflict develops.

Freudian unjustifiable to my mind to extend causality to this extent. Action actually depends on number of causes logically unrelated. No inner relation to stimulus to which he is exposed.

To exclude accident from mental life does not seem admissible.

Example—*some* forgetting due to causes he describes; but *all*?

?? especially weather—is determined but subject to accident for can't see nexus.

Vitiates whole Freudian introduction: that the full explanation of behavior is to be found in these preceding experiences.

The artificial behavior of children determined socially

The imposed and the imitative behavior of the young are fundamental sources of conservative tendencies of society

Formal education imposes definite ideals

Taboos in primitive society

Technique, chipping stone, basketry, trade groups

Behavior of the crowd

Of course we know that individual does not react in same way alone or with others, as he reacts one way when excited—Parade—peculiar kind of emotional disturbance in bystanders as well as— . . .

Different influences of crowd phase—

1. To *repeat* cultural pattern—North West Coast ceremonial

2. To *disrupt* cultural pattern—Shakers of Washington, Salvation Army . . . —not by any means always conservative.

The March 23 and 25 lectures which she had selected also deal with problems of internal change.

March 23, 1922

Observations of influence of group upon behavior of child in primitive tribes almost impossible to get. Must be observations among ourselves—much more (on individual behavior) investigations than commonly—

Local developments without any sort of external influence

Polynesia—example: Samoa, Hawaii, Easter Island

Eskimo—certain regions where any differences *must* be due to inner development.

cv Africa

Labrador and Greenland Eskimo—700 years no external influences. Examples following small, but doesn't matter if characteristic.

Kayak—not Smith Sound—might be geographical for so much ice, dangerous

Clothes—Baffinland, long tail for women, Arctic

Greenland, short tail . . . Distinct also for N & W Coast of Hudson Bay

Mythology—interest shifts

Easter Island, Gilbert Islands, Marquesas

In favorable areas may determine what occurs from inner forces without external influence

Also study of local details in any area (cf. zoological study of endemic forms) making due allowance for outer influences.

Also archaeological means.

Summary: Hard to obtain material to prove inner development but what we do know sufficient to show that it is always to be reckoned with.

Linguistic—Phonetic shifts—pervading whole language

Similar in all parts of world

Similar to biological changes which may also parallel each other in isolated communities in different parts of the world.

Assume too often—Example: where inner structure (inanimate things) unaffected by history, i.e. stone in one place or another, Example: where iron magnetized

History will determine its structure

History cannot be undone; certain effects will always remain which will influence future activities.

Actions of society depend on accumulated experience of individuals . . .

March 25 1922

Inner Changes

Drift in certain definite directions

Orthogenetic idea present in much theoretic discussion—Tylor's animism,

Haddon's Art, Ehrenreich's Mythology— Have to examine critically in how far such a steady drift is actually present in ethnic phenomena:

Example: linguistic, i.e. phonetic drift.

Counting

Terms of relationship

Ours: generation; sex of person spoken of. . . .

Indian: Relative age, Reciprocals, Opposite and like sex

What does this show in regard to Levy-Brühl's position

1. Primitive classifications do not agree with ours. Example: Constellations—Picture of Dipper and knowledge that are six stars exist side by side in civilized mind

Others have picture of whole starry universe as a whole—but may also have concept of individual stars

Daylight and whole aspect of early morning world separated from sun

Dream image and living man "identified?" But, from certain point of view, belong to same category.

Modern also

According to **Preuss**—primitive man's always wrong, **ours** always right.

Modern Fictions treatment of fever, etc.

Difference is that because of organized experience more of ours falls into realm of causality cf. Modern personification—How much reality given to it?—to creative mind, much at time of creation.

Differs.

So primitive

Poetic view of world ever so much more powerful—and leads to action. Each individual participates to very much greater extent in artistic life of people than in modern—based on certain unbounded (to us) sorts of classifications. But does not prove that primitive man cannot think logically and clearly.

Cf. modern, same 2 sorts of thinking.

Durkheim on primitive man. Crowd psychology

Opportunities for crowd action in primitive life very numerous. Anything that is established will have a chance to make itself felt very strongly.

The last lecture chosen emphasized the importance of both kinds of thought, the poetic and mystical as well as the rational and scientific.

May 10 1922

Human mind operates to very large extent with traditional experience, and importance of mystic element in mental make-up varies with individual. World may be viewed from teleological or causal point of view, and this mysticism may enter in both, more likely in former. No society where both not present. In *both* cases the logical and the a-logical. When do not understand the causal relations, *both* act a-logically. Accident is so irregular ordinary mind does not conceive it as belonging to causal realm, and consequently, amulets, etc. As scientific knowledge grows the chance for accident lessens.

> Example: tested tree for canoe on North West Coast proves rotted at core. We ("best educated") still say "Just my luck." Scientist recognizes working of the law of probabilities. Is a question of *knowledge,* not mental attitude.

In the seminars, Boas moved back and forth in the discussions, now considering large general principles and now wondering, with the delighted fresh curiosity of a child, about some small point. In a seminar in which Thelma Adamson reported on Secret Societies in North America and West Africa (December 10, 1924), my notes record his comment:

> It's interesting to follow out the question of principles of social grouping and function—kinship, age class, election—I think we'd get similar distribution of function—there may be certain elements that predominate—most interesting problem to compare the principles of organization and function.

Or in a seminar in a series in which the effects of density of population were being considered and in which Eleanor Phelps (Hunt) reported on Aztec and East African societies (February 4, 1925), he said:

> Next question is historical development of these types. Material so meagre, so defective, still—area like Europe—definite tendencies develop with complexity—like increase in size of unit. In America, Mexico and Peru—against whole American background. I presume we'd recognize certain peculiar lines of development due to complexity. Types a reference back to an earlier statement that "we can speak of a number of different types which develop in historical areas" must be taken as descriptive types—inductive—not total number of possibilities.

In the seminar (February 25, 1925) in which Ruth Bunzel reported on her work later published in *The Pueblo Potter,* she had put a series of examples on the blackboard. My notes record the following interchange:

> Boas: In all the cases on the blackboard difference in number of units on band and body.
>
> Bunzel: No relation. The Zuni will always tell you 4 or 5 is best, 3 and 6 good, 5 and more than 6 never used, predominantly arrangement is 3.
>
> MM: Wouldn't tendency not to have mirror design militate against optimum 4? (No answer)
>
> Boas: This independence of bands is also true in Tlingit basketry. (Draws a basket design on the board.) Two of these independent of the rest. In the basketry of the Chilkat three independent bands. *How far is this true of banded designs in the world?* In Mexican pottery painting becomes the background. This is true of designs in prehistoric Europe.

Here, in this discussion, the scientist is speaking—the interest in detail wholly within a context of possible generalization and ultimately of abstraction and law. Later in the same seminar, and only nine months after Ruth Bunzel had entered anthropology, Boas addressed her as a colleague:

> What is your idea of the theory that geometrical forms must go back to basketry? The step design, particularly in combination with the curvilinear is hard otherwise to account for. A relationship between the conditioned design and free paint design doesn't seem unlikely.

The minimum direction that Boas gave his students has been described trenchantly by Herskovits:

> Dissertation topics were brought to Boas for his approval, not suggested by him. Methods employed in obtaining and handling data, and the determination of the manner in which they were to be cast in final form, were the business of the student, to be worked out independently by him; only results were presented for appraisal.

From the wealth of wonder and speculation buried in the on-going process of the seminar and the lectures on Methods, we selected our topics. My experience was typical. I decided that I would like to work on the relative stability of different elements of culture, a topic to which Boas' comments periodically returned. I asked for an appointment and stated briefly—there was every encouragement to be brief in talking to someone who never seemed to have any time for dalliance with living—what I wanted to do. His advice took perhaps three minutes:

> You could do this in Siberia, but that would mean knowing Russian and Chinese. The Low Countries might be a good place but that would mean a lot of work with old Flemish, medieval Latin, etc. There is not good enough material to use the Algonkian-speaking peoples. You might try Polynesia where you would only need French and German.

The interview was over. I presented one seminar report and had one conference after [*Coming of Age in Samoa,* 1928] had been completed, in which Boas suggested that I expand my comments on Graebner in the introduction.

When the time came for my first fieldwork, the discussions again followed a characteristic course. I wanted to go to Polynesia, an area in the literature of which I was now at home; Boas disapproved of my going so far away into the unhealthful tropics. I wanted to study the relative affective strength of new and old elements in culture; Boas, always tailoring a particular piece of research to the exigencies of theoretical priorities, time, place, and personal ability, wanted me to study adolescence. In the end we compromised. I took his problem and he consented to my choice of Polynesia, providing I would work on an island to which a boat made regular visits. This accounted for the fortunate choice (as it turned out) of Samoa rather than one of the other Polynesian islands. In the single interview which we had, he cautioned me against being drawn into conventional ethnological enquiries and warned me that I must be prepared to waste a great deal of time just sitting about getting to know the adolescents. Later, just before I left, he wrote me a letter (July 14, 1925) in which he gave me the only other explicit advice I received. It begins characteristically:

> I am sure you have thought over the question very carefully, but there are one or two points which I have in mind and to which I would like to call your attention, even if you have thought of them before.
>
> One question that interests me very much is how the young girls react to the restraints of custom. We find very often among ourselves during the period of adolescence a strong rebellious spirit that may be expressed in sullenness or in sudden outbursts. In other individuals there is a weak submission which is accompanied, however, by a suppressed rebellion that may make itself felt in peculiar ways, perhaps in a desire for solitude which is really an expression of desire for freedom, or otherwise in forced participation in social affairs in order to drown mental troubles. I am not at all clear in my mind in how far similar conditions may occur in primitive society and in how far the desire for independence may be simply due to our modern conditions and to a more strongly developed individualism.
>
> Another point in which I am interested is the excessive bashfulness of girls in primitive society. I do not know whether you will find it there. It is characteristic of Indian girls of most tribes, and often not only in their relations to outsiders, but frequently within the narrow circle of the family. They are often afraid to talk and are very retiring before older people.
>
> Another interesting problem is that of crushes among girls. For the older ones you might give special attention to the occurrence of romantic love, which is not by any means absent as far as I have been able to observe, and which, of course, appears most strongly where the parents or society impose marriages which the girls may not want . . .
>
> . . . Stick to individual and pattern, problems like Ruth Bunzel on art in Pueblos and Haeberlin on Northwest Coast. I believe you have read Malinowski's paper in Psyche on the behavior of individuals in the family in New Guinea. I think he is much too influenced by Freudianism, but the problem he had in mind is one of those which I have in mind. . . .

The urgency of the disappearing primitive cultures and of the cruel inequalities in the world on which research was grievously needed was communicated to us not by preachments but by tempo, tone, and gesture, and this urgency remained with us.

Nor did Boas ever lose it himself. In 1930, at the age of 72, he made a return trip to the Kwakiutl to try out a new method—the use of film—on problems of style. From Fort Rupert, on November 9, 1930, he wrote to Ruth Benedict:

> I talk with difficulty and understand after I write

it. I follow conversation only partly. It goes too rapidly but I am getting into it again.

From Beaver Harbor, on November 13, he wrote:

> The dance problem is difficult. I hope the films will give us adequate material for making a real study. In music there are a number of quite distinct styles: summer songs, morning songs, love songs, but I shall not unravel that problem while here. The language also has baffling problems. There is no *good* informant because all are satisfied with a variety of forms. I rather think this is due to a merging of several dialects into one which is not equal in all individuals. I am mindful that this is an acculturation problem and I hope we shall get enough on that point.

And later, on November 26, he wrote again:

> I am worrying now about the style of oratory because I do not yet know how to get it down. Anyway I have my troubles with ordinary conversation. Narrative I can understand quite well, if they talk distinctly, but many have the Indian habit of slurring over the ends of their words— whispering—and that makes it difficult.

These letters I showed to an especially skillful handwriting analyst, and her first impression was that it was the writing of a quite young man, uncertain of himself!

Leslie Spier (essay date 1959)

SOURCE: "Some Central Elements in the Legacy," in *American Anthropologist,* Vol. 61, No. 5, 1959, pp. 146-55.

[*In the following essay, Spier provides an overview of Boas's contributions to the field of anthropology.*]

Boas left no body of dogma as a legacy. What he established, as a foundation to modern anthropology, was a series of guiding principles for action. These were expressed in concrete contributions, with little phrasing of theoretical points in extended form. Hence our survey of central elements here must stay close to the specific as he presented it.

The life of Boas coincided with the establishment of anthropology as a discipline of definite scope and method. He, more than any other individual, can be credited with determining the nature of its field and giving it the scientific approaches of objective empiricism, carefully controlled analysis, firmness of aims, and scrupulous self-discipline in defining the axioms of one's thoughts. For all he maintained that he was merely analyzing the fundamental views of his predecessors, so far as anthropology is a science he made it one.

Boas was perhaps the last man who can be said to have embraced the whole field of anthropology. Since his earlier days the field has become so ramified, and demands so intimate a knowledge of some segment, that no one can encompass it again in so masterly a fashion. Yet a fundamental of our heritage from him is that the wholeness of culture and the unity of problems of physical types must be borne in mind while dealing with particulars.

To appreciate the extent of his contribution, we must bear in mind that at the time he came into anthropology in the 1880's and for some decades after, it was given over largely to speculation and generalization—and this is not to deny that early writers had given it direction, some formulation of problems, and had tried to create a methodology. Now that its premises have been established for us, we tend to assume that the points were obvious and needed no demonstration, forgetting that at the opening of Boas' career quite other views were held as equally obvious with unshakable conviction. What he did, in contrast to his predecessors, was to formulate our problems in specific form and provide basic valid methodology. That there are now many more problems and approaches does not absolve us from remembering the circumstances in which the axioms were laid down.

His first field experience (1883-84), among the Baffinland Eskimo, set the pattern of his thinking. He confessed that he went with a crass belief in environmental compulsions of Eskimo life and thought, but his stay among them revolutionized his viewpoint. He then became convinced, he said, that while there was an adjustment of life to external physical conditions, social tradition—the result of a multiplicity of historical factors—was by far the more potent determinant of a man's thought and behavior. This was the compelling idea of his life's work: the complete molding of every human expression—inner thought and external behavior—by social conditioning.

What then are the relations between the bodily constitution and endowment and the cultural matrix in which it exists? Boas' career turned fundamentally on the relations between the two. Much that is basic is summed up in his *The Mind of Primitive Man*, a book which has had a profound influence on the thought of our generation—not narrowly on anthropologists, but on all social-minded thoughtful individuals. It has become part of the heritage of all educated persons. Perhaps its import is better understood by noting the title of the German edition, *Kultur und Rasse*. Where Boas would seem by the English title to have concerned himself with savage mentality alone, actually the book's aim so far transcended that as to make it a Magna Carta of race equality—or better, of the equivalence of hereditary endowment among races and the independence of cultural achievement from race. It is quite true that for decades a more enlightened attitude had been emerging in the Western world, but it was Boas who wrote quietus to any "scientific" pronunciamentos on "higher" and "lower" races.

Several main themes in the book are now axiomatic for us. (1) No racial group today can lay substantial claim to hereditary purity. (2) Races are not stable entities, immutably fixed in early times, but show evidences of change due to domestication, environmental influences, selection, and perhaps mutation. (3) The average differences in physical characteristics between races is small in contrast to the great overlapping of range and duplication of types among them. (4) There is no fixed relation between function and anatomy, between mind and brain for example, such as to warrant the view that any race is incapable of participating in any culture or even in creating it. On the side of cultural analysis Boas demonstrated (5) that there is no identity of race, language, and culture such that physical heredity can be credited with the formulation of languages and the achievements of civilizations. (6) On the contrary, there is overwhelming evidence that these aspects of human behavior are the products of involved historical growth, though they rest on fundamental traits of mind and body, traits probably uniformly distributed among all races.

This emphasis on historical determinants is the keynote to Boas' thinking about culture, and it is our legacy. Applied specifically to primitive men, he concluded that such groups are not primitive by reason of hereditary inferiority but because the circumstances of their life were more static than those of civilized men, the differences being products of their variant history and traditional equipment. Such a formulation disposed of the belief of an older generation in cultural evolution (or parallelism): that each race is primarily responsible for its own development; that cultural evolution (perhaps racial and cultural evolution going hand in hand) passes through the same sequences everywhere, with savages left behind on an inferior level (perhaps because of incomplete biological development).

It should be clear that by "historical" Boas meant only that each cultural trait and configuration must have had a specific antecedent form. This did not involve the need to provide a sweeping picture-in-time (though that appeals to some anthropologists of different temperament) or knowledge of which individuals brought about innovations. It sufficed for his purpose to envisage a "before and after" picture at a particular place and time. Cultures, obviously, are continually in a state of flux, whether slow or rapid; hence cultural forms evolve endlessly out of antecedent cultural forms. In this sense—and in this sense only—would one say that Boas was a cultural evolutionist—as we all are.

But such historical unravelling was not an end in itself. Boas was primarily interested in the processes of culture growth revealed in this historical panorama. Whether universals could be phrased with respect to processes, forms, and interrelations (functions) was a matter he approached with caution—and to the extent that we are like-minded, that caution, too, is a heritage. He wrote:

> . . . Certain laws exist which govern the growth of culture, and it is our endeavor to discover these laws. The object of our investigation is to find the *processes* [italics his] by which certain stages of culture have developed. The customs and beliefs themselves are not the ultimate objects of research. We desire to learn the reasons why such customs and beliefs exist—in other words, we wish to discover the history of their development. The method which is at present [1896] most frequently applied in investigations of this character compares the variations under which the customs or beliefs occur and endeavors to find the common psychological cause that underlies all of them. I have stated that this method is open to a very fundamental objection.
>
> We have another method, which in many respects is safer. A detailed study of customs in

their bearing to the total culture of the tribe practicing them, and in connection with an investigation of their geographical distribution among neighboring tribes, affords us almost always a means of determining with considerable accuracy the historical causes that led to the formation of the customs in question and to the psychological processes that were at work in their development.

An explanation is in order here—which is by no means a digression but significant for understanding this and comparable statements. Normally today the word "psychological" will evoke thought of the findings of modern experimental psychology (which hardly existed in 1896 and for many years after). Boas used the word in its older and more general sense alternatively with "mental." He had in mind always the inner states and mental content which are the realities of cultural habits and give meaning to their adherents—an aspect of the cultural whole which was either ignored or guessed at by his contemporaries.

Boas did not conceive his task as narrowly historical: he was concerned fundamentally with culture constructs as mental products. But where his predecessors sought general laws of psychic action by illusively simple analysis, he redefined the problem as that of the extent and character of mental operations at each specific point in their historically ascertained sequences. It has sometimes been said, without warrant, that Boas denied the possibility of deriving laws of culture and of mental action. He never phrased so drastic a statement: indeed, his firm belief in the essential similarity of minds in all races at all periods, and in the essentially equivalent nature of cultures the world over, presumed regularities of mental operation and of culture growth. Where he sought laws, if it were possible to formulate them, is indicated in a number of statements.

> While on the whole the unique historical character of cultural growth in each area stands out as a salient element in the history of cultural development, we may recognize at the same time that certain typical parallelisms do occur. We are, however, not so much inclined to look for these similarities in detailed customs but rather in certain dynamic conditions which are due to social or psychological causes that are liable to lead to similar results. . . . In short, if we look for laws, the laws relate to the effects of psychological, and social conditions, not to sequences of cultural achievement.

He held firmly to the principle that such regularities must be explicitly demonstrated and could or should be phrased only within their limiting circumstances. This tenet is that of an ever-rigorous and cautious thinker: he feared a recrudescence of premature formulations. These features of the nature of laws as known to the natural scientist (of which Boas, as a physicist by training, was undoubtedly more fully aware than his sociologist critics) are far from those of the facile generalizations offered by early writers.

The need for a substantial factual basis for such demonstration led him to a carefully conceived series of studies of primitive life: ethnographies monumental in scope and in detail; texts and grammatical analyses of many American Indian languages; vast collections of folktales—not as trivia, but for their variant forms which could provide materials for historical and psychological analysis. Primary in these efforts is the conviction that for a true picture of native action and thought the records must be made through the native tongue, or, if command of the native language is not feasible, in the form of dictated texts.

Boas' methodology and aims are well exemplified in his study of tales, a life-long interest. To understand these aims and the different temper of his approach to the subject, we must recall that at the close of the last century there were ardent advocates of the view that the essential unity of men's minds and fancies inevitably produced like tales the world over, and equally ardent proponents that such tales could only have spread from some early centers. From the beginning he insisted that "in order to investigate the physical laws of the human mind . . . we must treat the culture of primitive people [here the tales] by strict historical methods. We must understand the process by which the individual culture grew before we can undertake to lay down laws by which the culture of all mankind grew." In *Dissemination of Tales among the Natives of North America* (1891), he laid down a test for historical unity: namely, that the tales compared must contain the same arbitrary elements and be part of a continuous area of distribution. In his *Growth of Indian Mythologies* (1896), he demonstrated that the myths and tales on the Northwest Coast were reintegrated forms of unit tales which crossed and recrossed in the course of their diffusion; in short, that the tales were intricate historic constructs, not simple immediate products of minds at play with fancy. On a very much larger scale, he provided in the comparative notes to *Kutenai Tales* (1918)—an encyclopedic index of North American tales to the date of its publication—materials for a much broader approach to the same problem. Again, in reaction to the old rationalistic view that mythological tales arose from the anthropomorphizing of nature, he showed that, by a transfer of characters, the same tale was told of human, animal, and nature actors in adjacent areas. So too, that the explanatory (etiological) elements were in many cases not primary but later accretions to existing tales. These concepts of historically secondary connection and the reassembling and reintegration of existing elements played a significant part, not only in his view of the growth of mythologies but in Boas' whole conception of the history of culture processes.

Something of these discriminations between the historically determined and the universally human appears further in his folktale analyses. In *Stylistic Aspects of Primitive Literature* he pointed out that certain features must have been historically determined: the moralizing fable, proverb, and riddle of Old World folk literature in contrast to their rare occurrence in the New, the tendency to cluster unit tales in long narratives or cycles in some areas against its absence in others, the specific motivations given locally to tales in conformity with cultural interests, and so on. On the other hand, general mental traits could account for such things as rhythmic repetition as a literary device to heighten interest, the tendency to make use of formal elements at the expense of free narrative, and, indeed, the impulses to associate and coordinate tales of diverse historical origin and to rephrase them in terms of local culture, its motivations, and stylistic norms. Such norms for large areas were presented in *Mythology and Folk-Tales of the North American Indians.* He attacked the same problems on an extensive scale in his *Tsimshian Mythology* and again in *Kwakiutl Culture as Reflected in Mythology,* where by a very thorough inspection of a vast body of material, he gave answers to the questions how far—and in what ways—the culture of narrators determined content and form of the tales, what emotions and motives were expressed and how, and what formal elements or literary devices were utilized. His thought was that a series of such studies would enable us to discriminate the culturally determined and that residual part which could be ascribed to the free play of fancy. Parallel analyses have since been made, but it must be confessed that present-day anthropologists show little interest in the marked possibilities of this approach—or in anything else pertaining to tales.

Coupled with this was Boas' interest in the interplay of imagination and convention in the graphic arts and song: indeed, they are all treated as aspects of the same fundamental activity in his *Primitive Art.* He developed the thesis that some esthetic elements resulted from technical control, which with developing skill resulted in play with technique; that virtuosity itself became a source of esthetic gratification; that rhythmic repetition and balance of design resulted frequently from regularity of the craftsman's movements. In an analysis of *The Decorative Art of the Indians of the North Pacific Coast* (1897), Boas had shown that the pseudo-realistic carvings of that area were strictly limited in their execution by fixed conventions of art derived from historical developments in their past. These treatments were by no means the purely formal, atomistic dissection they may seem, for he understood full well that in each art there is a set of values—values of emotional concern to artist and beholder. But he attempted to unravel that with which most students of art are less concerned—the nature of such cultural constructs, the inventive or assimilative character of men's minds, and hence, the processes of culture growth. Here again are a set of leads waiting for some scholar.

Nor should it be thought that this emphasis on history and process left unregarded the individual in culture. What else was his basic concern with the attempt to discover the manner in which an individual's thought and activities become molded? Too great an emphasis on the historical might end in neglect of the carriers of culture. He wrote: ". . . the dynamics of social life can be understood only on the basis of the reaction of the individual to the culture in which he lives and of his influence upon society. . . . An error of modern anthropology, as I see it, lies in the overemphasis on historical reconstruction, the importance of which should not be minimized, as against a penetrating study of the individual under the stress of the culture in which he lives." Unquestionably the overwhelming mass of an individual's overt activities are culture-channeled, but how far does this hold for states in which affect is uppermost—emotions, temperamental biases, sentiments. What, he asked, are the nascent physiological bases and what forms do these affective states take? Although at no point did Boas make the culture-moulding of the individu-

al the sole objective of a study, there is material for it embedded in his ethnographies and in observations expressed in some more general papers; and, quite as significantly, he stimulated such studies among his students—for example, the study of adolescent behavior in differing cultural settings. Yet he was wary of "personality studies."

Some of our most familiar working concepts are a heritage from Boas, though commonly not recognized as such. The concept of the culture area first took form in his arrangement on a geographic basis of the exhibits at the World's Fair, Chicago, in 1893. When called to the American Museum of Natural History in 1895 he again embodied the idea in exhibits, where by display and label the concepts of areas of characterization, of typical and marginally variant cultures, were elaborated (and later developed and publicized by Wissler). Boas made no fetish of it: for him it served largely as a classificatory device for handling large bodies of data, but its utility for the analysis of the historical interrelations implied in such classifying has long been taken as a matter of course.

The legacy of Boas' long-time interest in language is not alone the great body of texts and grammatical analyses of previously unrecorded native tongues made by himself, his students, and their successors, but some general principles. What is axiomatic today—that each language must be viewed in terms of its own structure and operations—was a revolutionary proposition in the days when exotic languages were strained on the Procrustean frame of Old World "literary" languages. Boas was not concerned with linguistic analysis as an end in itself, that is, as a sort of mathematical play—as it is (quite properly) for some linguists. For him language is a cultural form, the components of which are to be investigated as is any other culture manifestation. One novelty of his presentations are the sections devoted to "Ideas Expressed by Grammatical Processes," an attempt to understand the weighting of grammatical forms for classifying experience. These observations are of inestimable value to the cultural anthropologist, and we can only wish that linguists of today would give us further insights of this nature.

His general viewpoint is expressed in the introduction to the *Handbook of American Indian Languages* and the inaugural article in the *International Journal of American Linguistics.* There he stressed the need of language study for an understanding of the more subtle aspects of a culture, its verbal forms and nuances of social behavior, and the analysis of grammatical categories for an appreciation of the formal verbal framework circumscribing expressions of thought. At the same time he discriminated carefully lest the logic of language structure be mistaken for the logic of thinking. Grammatical categories, he held, are not the categories of thought, but they constrain the logic of thinking in certain channels.

In his introductory article for the *Journal* he made perhaps his strongest and most unique methodological point: he insisted that the first historical problem with respect to languages was to discover how far lexical, morphological, and syntactic features had been incorporated in a language from diverse sources before assuming genetic connection. Pointing out that "In America we can discern various areas that have common phonetic characteristics . . . [which] do not coincide with any morphological groupings, and are apparently geographically well defined . . . , [while] certain morphological types have a wide continuous distribution," caution is necessary before positing the similarities as the consequence of genetic relationship. "It is quite inconceivable that similarities such as exist between Quilleyute, Kwakiutl, and Salish, should be due to mere accident, or that the morphological similarities of Californian languages, which Kroeber and Dixon have pointed out, should not be due to a definite cause. The experience of Aryan studies might induce us to agree that these must be members of single linguistic stocks; but this assumption leaves fundamental differences unaccounted for, and neglects the possibility of morphological assimilation, so that at the present time the conclusion does not seem convincing. . . . It is not safe to disregard the possibility of a complex origin of linguistic groups." Boas' insistence on rigor of demonstration—in contrast to the quick apperception by persons with a somewhat intuitive grasp of far-reaching similarities not easily conceptualized—may not have been wholly advantageous but did inevitably flow from his scientific habits of thought. If this was a somewhat negative attitude—but a healthy one—a more positive suggestion followed: "It seems probable that a safer basis will be reached by following out dialectic studies" which promise "rich returns in the field of the mechanical processes of linguistic development and of the psychological problems presented by languages of different types." Some dialectic studies have since been made, but rarely brought to any head with general statements of the processes involved in dialect differentiation.

Quite as fundamentally a part of our heritage were Boas' contributions to understanding the nature and composition of bodily types. His concern throughout was with questions of racial strains, their homogeneity and hereditary characteristics; how, in the course of growth, physical characteristics are established; and by inference, the bearing of similarity or difference of physical forms on hereditary mental endowment, and what its consequences for cultural behavior might be. Year after year he picked up these problems, systematically moving them toward definite conclusions.

Methodology here centered in the analysis of mass data by statistical measures. He was not only a master of statistical analysis but an originator of new forms (see inter alia his mathematical treatise *The Measurement of Variable Quantities* [1906]). It is patent that many of his contemporaries in physical anthropology, unused to mathematical thinking, were bewildered, and something of this unawareness of the utility of statistical devices persists.

A basic contribution was his demonstration of the plasticity of bodily types. Growth, commonly studied only as that of childhood and adolescence, was seen as a process continuing through adult life to death, a continuum of change. "The life span is the result of physiological processes that go on throughout life and that have been observed from the time of birth until death. When we study the distribution of moments of occurrence of definite phys-

iological changes, it appears that the variability in time of occurrence increases with great rapidity during life." The genesis of this view lay in the prior observation that mentally precocious children had better physical development than their age-mates, dull children the reverse. As mathematician Boas saw in the seriations of physical measurements for a given age the distributions characteristic of scattering of a group caused by a multiplicity of factors (the product of chance as portrayed in the probability curve). His interpretation was that this systematic scattering resulted from varying degrees of retardation and acceleration; that there was a close correlation between the several physical measurements and between these and mental status; and that this correlation varied systematically during the years of growth.

He saw another corollary. If the course of the child's physical development was determined by the exigencies of growth, it should be clear that the final adult form is not fixed by heredity alone but by somatic factors as well; and should such circumstances affect a local population as a whole, there should be not only evidence of the instability of racial types as we find them, but the whole set of assumptions of anthropometrists—that in measuring adults they were describing hereditary forms alone—would be subject to fundamental revision. Confirmation of the hypothesis came with the study of *Changes in Bodily Form of Descendants of Immigrants* wherein were found characteristic differences between immigrant parents and their children born in the United States, differences which were substantial, correlated with the length of residence of the mother, and persistent throughout life. An inspection of earlier studies showed parallel changes in local racial types of Europe and elsewhere to have been established but their significance overlooked. Further studies, e.g. on Italians and Puerto Ricans (1913: summed up in *New Evidence in Regard to the Instability of Human Types,*) confirmed the conclusion, as did the less extended studies of others prompted by these findings. It is important to note that Boas held that these observations implied only a limited plasticity of human types. But however limited, he did demonstrate that we cannot assume that measurements of a local group immediately reveal fixed hereditary characteristics.

Equally important for understanding the nature of racial types were his analyses of component strains in local populations. His analysis turned *On the Variety of Lines of Descent Represented in a Population.* He established that homogeneity within a racial group is not identical with purity of descent; that in such a group variability of families may well be small because each family represents all ancestral strains, while within families a high degree of variation may be predicted. This is a methodological point of importance for the study of local races, the consequences of in- or out-breeding, and genetic stability.

On these bases he could logically have little interest in the classification of races. The local intrabreeding group was his unit of analysis, and the emphasis was on discriminating hereditary contribution and environmental influences. Only when the biological histories of such groups became known would it be reasonable to arrange them in taxonomic order. This is obviously parallel to the basic principles of his treatment of the problems of culture and language.

In many ways the most fundamental of Boas' contributions was the rigor of scientific method: careful analysis, caution, and convincing demonstration.

Fashions change in anthropology; it is always more pleasant to graze in new pastures; it is far simpler to narrow to a specialty than to harass oneself with concern for the whole. Often enough we become absorbed in some minor segment, yet scientific rigor should obligate us, like Boas, to give consideration to interrelations with other aspects of culture and bodily form.

Much of Boas' legacy is now central in the corpus of beliefs of present-day anthropology, but some elements lie neglected awaiting the day when they will be the subject of renewed appreciation.

Ronald P. Rohner and Evelyn C. Rohner (essay date 1969)

SOURCE: An Introduction to *The Ethnography of Franz Boas,* edited by Ronald P. Rohner, translated by Hedy Parker, The University of Chicago Press, 1969, pp. xiii-xxx.

[*In the following excerpt, the critics describe Boas's approach to the study of human societies and place him in the context of nineteenth-century ethnographic theories.*]

Even today, a quarter of a century after his death, Franz Uri Boas remains one of the most controversial figures in the history of anthropology. Anthropologists have tended to take a categorical stance approaching adulation or condemnation regarding the value of his work. In 1943, for example, Benedict rhapsodized, "He found anthropology a collection of wild guesses and a happy hunting ground for the romantic lover of primitive things; he left it a discipline in which theories could be tested." [Leslie] White on the other hand, recently charged that "Boas came fairly close to leaving the 'chaos of beliefs and customs' [in the ethnological enterprise] just about where he found it."

Part of the controversy raging over the value of Boas' work centers in his field research and especially in his ethnographic publications. But until recently, scholars have known almost nothing about his field research. Consequently, they could do little more than speculate about Boas' field techniques or his attitudes toward field work. These and other questions such as how often he went to the field, why he did the kind of work he did, where he worked when he was on the Northwest Coast, and how he financed his field trips were unanswerable until a short time ago. Answers to these questions are essential, of course, in order to appraise the nature of this ethnographic research, and ultimately, to evaluate the overall significance of his monumental ethnographic and ethnological output. Now that the intensity of opinion has mellowed regarding his place in American anthropology, a more impartial assessment of these questions can be made. . . .

In this [essay] we also attempt to place Boas' field activi-

ties and his conceptual orientation toward ethnological and ethnographic research within the broader context of the work of his nineteenth-century North American predecessors and contemporaries. Several questions guide us in this aim: What was the climate of scholarly thought among Boas' predecessors and contemporaries when he came to this country in 1886? How did Boas react to this? What were the general characteristics of nineteenth-century American field work, and what contributions did Boas himself make to the development of field research?

A dominant but by no means the only late nineteenth-century ethnological perspective in North America and Europe was that of unilinear cultural evolution—the belief that all cultural systems, or specified parts of culture, progress slowly and unalterably through the same invariable stages of development. Students of early man and comparative customs formulated grand laws of cultural development in an effort to explain human progress over time. After placing educated, industrialized, nineteenth-century Europe and America (representing civilization) at the top of the structure, evolutionist scholars sequentially scaled the customs and societies of other people around the world into hypothetically earlier stages of development. Nonliterates such as the Australian aborigines were usually firmly secured to the bottom of the structure. Primitive peoples such as these were assumed to represent the earliest stages of civilized man's development. But as Daniel Brinton observed, present-day savages are not as rude or brutish as the hypothetical primeval man; they merely stand nearest to his condition.

These early scholars did not mean to imply that living nonliterates are in any way biologically inferior. To the contrary, most of them explicitly disavowed this. In fact one of their cardinal principles of cultural evolution, the psychic unity of man, clearly postulates the common humanity of man—the idea that all men share the same basic potential at birth for action, thought, and belief. This concept assumed the uniform working of men's minds as a basic explanation for the recurrence of similar institutions in widely separated areas. Without this assumption there could be no science of man. The presumed validity of psychic unity, then, not only supplied one of the necessary minimal assumptions for the study of man, but it was also a critical conceptual device for explaining the repetition of similar traits in noncontiguous and noncontemporaneous societies. Moreover, psychic unity was part of the evolutionists' conceptual apparatus used to fight church doctrine regarding man's fall from Grace.

Comparison of specific aspects of custom among tribal groups around the world—the comparative method—was the technique most frequently used to help evolutionists formulate laws of cultural development. Scholars believed that, because human nature is constant, nonliterates today live the same kind of life as their forefathers. By comparing societies and arranging them in order of complexity it became possible to reconstruct the history of our own society as well as of man in general. Once an evolutionary sequence was established, the comparative method became essentially a procedure for classifying new information.

In their attempt to give comprehensive answers evolutionist scholars often documented their theories through the arbitrary selection of evidence without regard to historical or geographic context. Features of a society which seemed out of place or inconsistent with what evolutionists thought should be there were often viewed as remnants of an earlier period surviving into the present. These survivals were interpreted as both examples and proof that society had evolved from an earlier stage of development.

Some societies, however, patently had customs that could not be reasonably explained in any way other than through cultural borrowing, or culture contact. Evolutionists—especially American scholars such as John W. Powell—recognized, for example, that some American Indians had learned to use metal through culture contact but that the Indians had not accordingly risen to the level of civilization. In general, these exceptions to their theories presented only minor problems for evolutionists because they minimized or discounted cultural borrowing as an important explanation of progress whenever any standard conceptions such as psychic unity or survivals could be used. Cultural borrowing implied to these early scholars that man is a passive, uninventive accepter of existing ideas, and this notion was incompatible with their assumption that all men are rational, creatively inventive beings striving for self-improvement.

By no means, however, were nineteenth-century ethnologists concerned only with total cultural systems. Indeed, the major interest of a number of students was in the origin and development of what we today call aspects of culture, such as art, folklore and mythology, and social organization. In their investigation of aspects of culture we see an emergent interest in historical explanations and an increasing interest in inductive, empirically based theory construction rather than speculative or deductive theory and evolutionary interpretation. Some nineteenth-century scholars were interested in other issues as well, including linguistic studies, the influence of environmental factors on culture growth and stability, culture contact (acculturation) and diffusion, the migration of Indian groups, and the origin of race—especially of the American Indian.

These interests represent some of the principal areas of concern among North American ethnologists when Boas moved to this country in 1886. What was Boas' position in relation to these issues? To begin with, he was the only nineteenth-century scholar in America who consistently attacked the deficiencies of unilinear evolution, as well as some of the other ethnological perspectives of that time. As described more fully below, he published a number of articles between 1886 and 1896 questioning the deductive reasoning behind theories of cultural evolution; he attacked the use of the concept psychic unity as an explanation for the appearance of cultural similarities among distant societies; he argued against using the comparative method for arranging societies into hierarchical sequences; he attempted to demonstrate that the notion of geographical determinism is invalid; and he pointed out that much of nineteenth-century ethnology was ethnocentric. In addition, he acutely felt the need for more fact and less speculative theory. Thus hc emphasized both an empirical and an inductive approach to data collection and

analysis. This need, however, was also recognized by a few other scholars before Boas moved to the United States. Samuel Haven, for example, had already denied that all cultural similarities could be explained by psychic unity; Horatio Hale warned against the danger of believing one's own cultural system to be superior to others; Daniel Wilson pointed out the need for more fact to test theories.

As suggested above, the concepts of diffusion, culture contact, borrowing, and acculturation were present in American ethnology before Boas' arrival, but he stimulated a shift of interest from the fact that diffusion occurs to an interest in the *process* of diffusion—even though he himself did not study process as such. He took the position that the widespread occurrence of diffusion invalidates theories of cultural evolution, but that, in turn, a study of diffusion itself is incomplete. More importantly, Boas asked, how do cultural systems change? Why do people accept some elements and not others under the conditions of culture contact and diffusion? One must look at real people, he urged, to understand such dynamic processes. Thus, the study of culture contact and diffusion must be psychological, and above all it must be empirical and inductive. Simply employing the assumption of psychic unity to explain the presence of cultural parallels among different tribal societies is insufficient.

Furthermore, he warned, the study of diffusion must work from the particular to the general. Investigators who are seriously concerned with problems of diffusion should plot the distribution of traits in small, delimited areas before mapping their distribution on a continental or worldwide basis. Attempts at what he called historical reconstruction, or the study of the actual historical contact of nonliterate peoples, should begin at a modest, empirically defensible level and not become involved in grand, sweeping schemes of universal reconstruction. Boas recognized that a catalogue of similar culture traits across diverse societies can never itself offer sufficient evidence of historical contact. Rather, the similarities must include traits that are interrelated in similar ways to offer adequate proof of diffusion. In addition, he concluded, we can reasonably assume contact only among geographically proximate societies. He reiterated these points many years later in an exchange of letters with A. L. Kroeber: "I call it an attempt at historical reconstruction when I assemble the available data that throw light upon the agents that have shaped a culture. I think you have to acknowledge that my analysis of Northwest Coast culture is based on that attempt" (1935).

Boas also challenged the evolutionists' use of comparison for arranging societies into unilinear sequences. He accused his evolutionist colleagues of attempting to establish, without the proper research tools, the existence of grand laws guiding the progressive development of man's culture from simple to complex. The then current use of the comparative method, he pointed out, was based on the investigator's assumptions that Western society is superior to Indian society and that primitive peoples necessarily move toward the same technological level as Western peoples. Boas accused most nineteenth-century scholars of approaching the data with the preconccived notion "that ethnological phenomena developed everywhere in the same manner" and then forcing these data into prefabricated theories—instead of going inductively from fact to theory as he felt they should.

Boas used a book by his first student, A. F. Chamberlain, to illustrate the nineteenth-century abuse of the comparative method. In his review of the volume Boas criticized ethnologists and ethnographers of merely collecting samples of similar culture elements in different societies in the hope of advancing science, rather than assuring comparability of the material and using the more defensible concept of diffusion. Concluding his review, he suggested that ethnological investigations should examine the history of a particular society and should search for general psychological laws governing the growth of society. Only after discovering these laws can one know if societies are comparable, because only phenomena coming from common psychological or historical causes can be compared. He does not make it clear what he means by psychological laws, however.

Continuing with this approach, in another article he reproached anthropologists who spent all their time searching for laws governing the development of man. He suggested that the fault with their search for a grand system of progressive development as well as for the existence of great universal laws was based on their circular reasoning that the similarity of customs or inventions among societies serves as proof of the existence of these laws. That is, Boas did not object to a belief in the existence of developmental laws, but he did object to this belief being based on what he considered to be an utterly tautological argument. Boas also disagreed with the assumption that primitive tribes are living examples of earlier stages of culture through which more advanced societies have passed. Cultural improvement is relative, he explained; it is not an absolute, with Western man representing the apogee.

Ethnologists in the 1880's and 1890's arranged museum specimens according to a sequence of types to demonstrate the evolutionary development of man's culture from simple to complex or from homogeneous to heterogeneous. The displayed items were often ordered without regard to time or geographic area. Boas pointed out that this approach to museum arrangements does nothing more than perpetuate nineteenth-century theories of cultural evolution. He and O. T. Mason, an outstanding representative of nineteenth-century museum work, engaged in a dispute over the proper organization of museums. Mason arranged museum items in a progressive sequence to portray the historical development of material traits, although he did recognize that museum exhibits cannot entirely disregard geography. Mason was aware that societies within a given region share more traits among themselves than they do with groups outside that region. But he insisted that these commonalities are the result of psychic unity, and he accordingly arranged his specimens in a simple-to-complex sequence—based on the deductive rationale of unilinear development.

Boas disagreed with Mason's approach. As an alternative he proposed that museum collections should be arranged to demonstrate principles of diffusion operating within geographic provinces, or what we today call culture areas. According to Boas, museums should function to display the cultural items of societies and show how these diffuse to neighboring societies. Powell, representing the traditional, conservative position, became involved in this controversy. He argued that Boas' idea of revealing diffusion by arranging artifacts according to tribe and geographic area was impossible because of the vast number of specimens that would be required. Furthermore, he dismissed Boas' notion that similarities in widely separated areas are due to diffusion, and he concluded his argument by stating his belief that Mason's classifications were much more reasonable than Boas' suggestions based on diffusion.

Many nineteenth-century ethnologists explained cultural similarities and differences through the mechanism of geographic determinism. That is, they believed that climate and other environmental conditions affect the cultural development of a people and in this way determine their rate of progress. Lewis Henry Morgan, for example, explained cultural diversity and the lack of progress in many human societies as the result of historical accident, borrowing, or geographic isolation. Daniel Brinton maintained a comparable position. He wrote that cultural parallels should be explained through borrowing or derivation from a common source only when there are special reasons to indicate this to be the case. When these reasons are absent, the explanation should be either that the two groups were at the same cultural level, or that their physical surroundings were similar. Frank Cushing also used geographic location as an explanatory device. The Indians of the Southwest developed toward civilization, he wrote, because of their need to overcome the difficulties of living in an arid waste. He also employed the concept of "adaptation to a wasteland" to explain the development of the Key Marco (Florida) Indians, who, he said, lived in a desert of water. The geographical environment (wasteland) of both areas, he continued, fostered rapid and high development of the people. The necessity of close and intimate living helped them develop their agriculture, which in turn required well-developed forms of social organization and government.

Boas, on the other hand, argued that ethnologists should not try to discover cultural origins or search for geographic or environmental determinants of culture. He maintained that geographical determinist philosophies are vacuous for theory construction, but he did concede that environment may play a part in influencing technological or economic development. If two groups live beside a body of water and both have developed a fishing economy, they probably have done so not because of psychic unity or even because of diffusion but simply because this was one real possibility open to them, given that kind of environment.

Boas was a major contributor to the nineteenth-century study of linguistics. He urged, for example, that languages should be studied from the point of view of their own structural characteristics and that they should not be cast into an Indo-European mould. This principle, however, was not a novel contribution, because it had already been well enunciated by Hermann Steinthal, a German philologist whom Boas knew as a student. Leading pioneers in language studies such as Albert Gallatin and J. W. Powell were already familiar with the inductive approach. Powell, for example, credited Gallatin with founding the inductive study of philology. Later, through his own efforts (having been stimulated by Joseph Henry), and by directing the work of others as head of the Bureau of American Ethnology (BAE), Powell systematized the inductive linguistic classification of western North American Indian tribes. Both of these men, however, classified languages according to the number and complexity of words used by a people to describe certain concepts. Gallatin's classifications were based primarily on similarities of words used to describe edible foods. Following this tradition, Powell too based his language taxonomies on vocabulary, despite the fact that he was primarily interested in the structure of grammar.

Boas took a significantly contrasting position. He argued that linguistic classifications should be established by morphological criteria. Moreover, regarding other linguistic issues he said that ethnocentric taxonomies based on the presumed superiority of Indo-European languages would not withstand the test of scientific analysis, and in 1893 he flatly rejected the notion of Hale and Brinton that race can be defined by linguistic criteria. Furthermore, he maintained that as important as linguistic classifications are for the scientific study of man, they should not be an end in themselves. He encouraged investigators to study language change because he believed the resulting knowledge would illuminate the history of a language, which in turn would reflect the history of that society. Later he advocated tracing the distribution of languages to facilitate the study of historical changes.

Boas' conceptual position on a number of ethnological and ethnographic issues in the late nineteenth century is often at variance with the scholarly and scientific research he himself actually did. His position regarding the collection of texts—verbatim ethnographic reports in the informant's own language—is one illustration of this fact. He pointed to the potential bias of using texts collected from a single informant. The idiosyncratic style of an informant can obscure the real grammatical form and phonetic elements of the language, and to avoid this pitfall he recommended training several informants to write texts in a given language. As revealed in his letters and diaries . . . , however, he did this infrequently in his own field work.

At a more general level it is apparent from Boas' publications between 1886 and 1896 that he favored a three-stage plan to determine man's place in the universe. The first step was to explore in detail the customs and traits of a single tribe. He recommended that field investigators collect and minutely describe every detail, every aspect, of culture including such disparate activities as canoe building and food preparation. A field worker's most valuable skill, according to Boas, is a knowledge of the language. He emphasized the importance of learning the language of a group well enough to keep notes and collect texts in it. In this way the almost inevitable descriptive distortions of customs and beliefs occurring through translations can be

minimized, and safeguards are provided against describing Indian culture in terms of one's own. In addition to studying the cultural history of a group, the scholar should study the physical environment and the group's relation to it, including man's relationship to man. And field workers should utilize archaeological methods to investigate prehistoric remains.

The second step was to investigate a number of neighboring tribes in a small, geographically limited area. A comparison of what Boas calls tribal histories, or the geographical distribution of culture traits or customs, leads to information regarding historical causes of the formation of these customs. This in turn leads to knowledge concerning the influence of environment on cultural development as well as to an understanding of the psychological factors creating the common customs among neighboring tribes. Investigators should look for origins of similar traits in a carefully delimited geographic area, and they should describe how these traits develop in each of the societies within that area. This method of comparison avoids the evolutionist pitfall of interpreting slight similarities of culture as proof of psychic unity, and instead it provides a means of tracing the history of the growth of ideas.

Boas recommended collecting museum specimens, collecting folktales, and investigating native languages to facilitate tracing the distribution of cultural elements in a small area. The study of comparative linguistics and comparative mythology was important to him because here one can find a clear expression of primitive thought. Furthermore, myths furnish clues to the religious ideas of a people, and Boas believed that a careful investigation of mythological elements in tales reveals customs missed by other methods of observation.

Finally, after the first two stages have been adequately treated, one can begin the careful search for general laws of cultural development. The final goal of anthropological investigations should be to discover the psychic laws governing the growth of ideas. Boas believed that the existence of these laws would be evident when the social life of different peoples was compared. To find these laws one must be aware of the way in which they are expressed among different tribes. That is, one must know the processes by which individual societies grow before one can lay down universal laws. Boas' own research, however, never really went beyond the first two stages. In fact the greatest part of his ethnographic production is inextricably embedded in the first stage. But what are some of the broader characteristics of his ethnographic output, and what is his position within the development of nineteenth-century field work in North America?

Boas worked with Northwest Coast materials for almost sixty years, but he also worked among the Eskimo of Baffinland as well as in New Mexico, Puerto Rico, and Mexico. The Indians of the North Pacific Coast, however, were his first love, particularly the Kwakiutl Indians, about whom he wrote well over five thousand pages. About one-quarter of his total publications deal wholly or in part with the Kwakiutl, but almost half of what he wrote during his life deals with the Indians of the Northwest Coast in general. George Hunt, Boas' principal Kwakiutl informant for over forty years, contributed the data for something more than two-third of Boas' major Kwakiutl reports. These facts reflect Boas' extensive involvement with the Kwakiutl.

Anthropologists have remarked many times that despite Boas' vast ethnographic output he never produced a complete, integrated ethnography of any Northwest Coast group. Part of the reason for this, no doubt, lies in his philosophy of field work: he insisted that ethnographers should collect all the facts about a people and only then allow themselves some cautious generalizations. Boas was never satisfied that he had all the facts about the Kwakiutl, and indeed he did not, because . . . he gave his major attention to the more symbolic, or expressive, aspects of culture such as language, mythology and folklore, art, and religion. He was less concerned with, and as a result collected less information on, the structural features of Northwest Coast social systems such as economic organization (including the precise nature of the potlatch) and social organization (including problems of class-rank stratification and social structure).

Also . . . Boas was less concerned with what people do than with what they say they do or say they should do. He took this position because he felt the most important task in ethnography is to present the culture of a people from their own point of view, as perceived by the people themselves. His repeatedly avowed purpose in ethnography was to study man's mental life, his subjective world. For this reason the greatest part of his North Pacific Coast publications are in the form of texts. These texts include interlinear translations but no explanation, interpretation, or analysis to make them more comprehensible to the reader. Resulting from his belief in the importance of texts are several thousand pages of ethnographic description that are exceedingly difficult to use. Moreover, Boas' texts and other ethnographic materials over time contain many inaccuracies and inconsistencies. He was aware of these difficulties, but he never corrected them in print.

Boas' field methods were essentially the same as those used by his nineteenth-century predecessors and contemporaries, except that he covered a broader range of issues than most of them. He did standard nineteenth-century ethnological research during his Northwest Coast field trips, such as collecting museum specimens and studying folk-lore; graphic arts; techniques of collecting, preparing, and using plants; and other aspects of customary behavior. He also collected texts and vocabularies, analyzed the grammatical structure of different languages, and worked on problems of physical anthropology. His research in physical anthropology was largely in the form of anthropometry—making bodily measurements and plaster casts of faces, collecting skeletal material, and photographing body types. Archaeology was the only area of anthropological inquiry that he missed in his research on the North Pacific Coast, and this he did during his trips to Mexico from 1910 to 1912.

The principal difference between Boas' ethnographic research and that of many of his peers is a matter of perspective. He did not approach field work with the same naïve ethnocentrism that some other enthnographers did, nor

did he arbitrarily select facts to fit some predesigned theory. Furthermore, whereas his associates only infrequently learned the language of the people they were studying, Boas argued for the necessity of learning the native tongue well. This injunction to learn the language constitutes another minor inconsistency, however, between what Boas wrote should be done and what he himself did. He learned the Chinook Jargon and used this lingua franca in his research along the coast, but he did not become fluent in any indigenous Northwest Coast language, including Kwakwala, the native language of the Kwakiutl.

But what are some of the other central characteristics, aims, and content of nineteenth-century North American ethnographic research? Who were some of these early ethnographers? How did they become involved in field work? What did they do in the field? And what comparability and differences are there between Boas as an ethnographer and his predecessors and peers?

In the first place almost all field workers in America until the closing years of the nineteenth century were involved in some nonanthropological profession such as geology, law, the military, medicine, or government administration. Boas was no exception. He came into anthropology from a German background in geography, mathematics, and physics. Ethnographers were recruited from outside anthropology because formal disciplinary training was nonexistent in this country until the turn of the century. Despite this, a cadre of dedicated scholars emerged before Boas' arrival in North America who believed that their obligation to humanity was to record as much as possible about the American Indians before their customs disap-

Boas (second from left) during his year of compulsory military service in Germany.

peared. Thus, North American field work developed, for the most part, out of a tradition of diffuse, nondirected, unsystematic, individualized, and often ethnocentric descriptions of Indian life by enthusiastic but untrained observers. By the end of the century field research was more systematic, organized, and focused, and professional training became a reality.

Washington Matthews, an army surgeon during the Civil War, serves as an illustration of one whose field investigations were secondary to his major professional involvement. He devoted much of his spare time to collecting information on Navaho language and culture, and he produced poetic translations of their chants. George Dawson, a geologist, collected field data between 1877 and 1890 while on geological surveys in the interior of southern British Columbia. And in the process of doing his own work among the coastal Kwakiutl in the summer of 1885 he collected information on their "traditions, myths and way of life."

Some of the people who began observing and recording Indian customs on a part-time basis later became full-time ethnographers and ethnologists. Henry R. Schoolcraft was an Indian agent when he became involved in ethnology and ethnography. Unlike Matthews and Dawson, Schoolcraft (by the 1830's) eventually became totally immersed in ethnology, perhaps because of his intense field experience. He became increasingly involved with the Ojibwa as he gathered data on their magic, taboos, social organization, and folk-lore. Powell provides yet another illustration of a convert to ethnology and ethnography, in this case from geology, in the 1870's. In the 1860's he began taking his students on summer field trips to give them firsthand experience with the geological world around them. He developed an interest in native customs from his Indian pack guides. While traveling through the West on a geological expedition in the winter of 1868, for example, he interviewed his Ute guides on their language, social organization, customs, and myths. He also collected vocabularies and grammars and recorded their songs. His interest in American Indians continually broadened throughout the decade. From 1870 to 1873 he studied the Paiute and other Indian tribes, including the Hopi who adopted him into their tribe. By the time he became director of the BAE in 1879 his geological career was greatly overshadowed by his interest in ethnology.

Morgan was a professional lawyer who became deeply committed to ethnology. He, among others, appreciated the fundamental value of field work, and he believed in the importance of firsthand contact with nonliterates as an antecedent to drawing theoretical generalizations. As a result of his personal involvement with the Iroquois he wrote the *League of the Iroquois,* in which he carefully distinguished between direct observations and verbal reports of others. He went into the field every summer between 1859 and 1862 to gather additional data. During this time he was adopted into the Seneca tribe and he became a close personal friend of several Iroquois. Morgan also pointed out the necessity of using a nomenclature consistent with the life of the Indians. He believed that as long as the terms of Westerners are used to describe primitive social

organization the result will be a caricature of the Indian and a self-deception. Morgan himself, however, was later criticized by Powell for using the culture-bound terms "nation" and "national" to describe Iroquois institutions.

As more people became involved in field work, scholars became increasingly aware that aboriginal Indian customs and languages were disappearing. The desperate cry could be heard that soon no unacculturated Indians would be left to study. This realization created an urgently felt need to record everything about the Indian as rapidly as possible. In 1849, for example, Joseph Henry, secretary of the Smithsonian Institution, asked the American government to continue supporting the research of Schoolcraft. "The learned world looks to our country for a full account of the race that we have dispossessed," Henry declared, "and as every year renders the task more difficult, it is hoped that the investigations on the subject now going on under the government will not only be continued, but that means may be afforded for their active prosecution." He emphasized the need for haste again in the Smithsonian report of 1857. It is the sacred duty of the country, he said, to relate the manners and customs of Indians to the civilized world.

This agitated concern to study the American Indian before it was too late prompted government support of ethnographic research in the second half of the nineteenth century. The BAE was the greatest government organization in America for promoting the science of man in the last century. Its original purpose was to aid in grouping Indians reservations, but its scope later expanded to include the investigation of tribal relations more generally. Attempts were also made under Powell's direction to systematize the spelling of tribal names and, most notably, to coordinate the field work being done by different investigators. The major contribution of the BAE, according to Boas, however, was to put an end to the dilettantism that had previously existed in American ethnology. Boas attributed the appearance of the first sound ethnographic and ethnological publications based on continued research in American ethnology to the BAE's broad and systematic plan for research. In short, government support contributed to the development of professionalism in American ethnology.

The survey approach to field work intensified both because of the increased field research opportunities through government aid and because museums such as the American Museum of Natural History and the United States National Museum wanted to expand their collections. Investigators spent two days to a few weeks at a given location collecting museum pieces, recording myths, eliciting texts, and describing Indian customs—usually without knowledge of the language. They then moved on to a new site and began the procedure again. This pattern continued until they returned to their homes, sold their artifacts to the organization under whose auspices they had conducted their research, and wrote up their field data. The resulting monographs consisted of a compilation of observations often heavily colored by value judgments; little attempt was made to do other than describe the strange customs of diverse Indian tribes.

Men who engaged in this type of survey research include John Powers, who traveled among groups of Indians in order to study their customs during the summers of 1871 and 1872. Jeffries Wyman traveled to Labrador, Florida, Surinam, Chili, and Peru to gather museum specimens. W J McGee worked among the Seri. Anita McGee, wife of W J McGee, visited several non-Indian American communities such as the Amana. She later gathered additional information from informants through correspondence with former community leaders. While he was still a graduate student, George Dorsey went to South America on a collecting expedition for the World Columbian Exposition at Chicago in 1893. And in 1895 Walter Fewkes was doing reconnaissance work in heretofore unexplored areas of Arizona.

The survey approach was also a significant feature of Boas' field work on the North Pacific Coast. Even though he acknowledged the need to intensively study a single people in the field, he did this infrequently in his own work. As revealed in his letters and diaries, he usually traveled from location to location for brief visits working on specialized problems and then moved on. Part of the reason for his extensive use of the survey approach was outside his immediate control. Relatively little was known about the area when he went to the Northwest Coast for the first time in 1886. Consequently the emphasis of his first trip was largely on general ethnogeographic reconnaissance—mapping the distribution of languages and cultural systems along the southern coast of British Columbia. This emphasis, however, also reflects his university training as a cultural geographer. His next seven field trips to the coast were guided by the aims of the British Association for the Advancement of Science (1888-94) and by the Jesup Expedition (1897-1901). In none of these was he completely free to engage in the type of intensive research of a single people that he might have liked to do. Oddly, however, he continued to do the same type of research during the last five trips, when he was free to do what he wanted independently of any sponsoring organization. In fact Boas' field procedures remained essentially unchanged throughout the half century that he worked with Northwest Coast materials.

A second factor that could account for his lack of extensive field involvement with any single people was the fact that nine of his thirteen trips to the coast were during the summer. Summer months were (and are today) poor times to do intensive research in villages along the coast because the Indians were heavily involved in different aspects of the fishing industry. Many of the men and women were away from their villages; consequently community life was truncated from late spring to early fall. With minor exceptions, however, even during his four winter trips he did not become personally involved in tribal affairs.

With some outstanding exceptions such as Frank Cushing, nineteenth-century field workers seldom actually lived with the Indians, participated in their daily routines, or learned their language. This was most notably true before the time of intensified government support. Boas is illustrative of this trend, even during the 1900's. . . . [He] rarely participated in the daily lives of the Indians (al-though he spent a considerable amount of time on different occasions observing and recording significant aspects of customary behavior), and he seldom lived in Indian households or communities unless circumstances required that he do so. He typically stayed at a boarding house, hotel, or other public accommodation within walking distance of the community where he was working. After he came to know George Hunt well, however, he usually lived with or near Hunt and his kinsmen in Fort Rupert and Alert Bay.

Most nineteenth-century ethnographers obtained information regarding Indian customs through the employment of selected Indian informants who spoke both English and their native language. Informants were often recruited by the resident missionary or government official with whom the investigator lived. Typically, the informant arrived at the field worker's residence and was interviewed. After the interview had been duly recorded, the informant returned to his village and the investigator moved on. As an alternative to this procedure, informants were sometimes brought out of the field to the ethnographer's home. When Mathilda Stevenson, for example, accompanied her husband, James, on his collecting expeditions, she became interested in the activities of women and children. After her husband's death her field work among the Indians of the Southwest became more extensive. In 1895 she brought a Zuni woman, Wai Weh, out of the field into her home. The woman taught Stevenson Zuni art, language, and myths, and when the appropriate season arrived for certain religious rites, Wai Weh performed them for Stevenson, Mason, and other interested ethnologists.

Boas, too, tended to work with single informants, but he made no attempt to select only Indians who were bilingual in English and their native tongue. Indeed the majority of his informants knew little or no English. Boas also occasionally brought Indians out of the field to his home. After his last trip to the Northwest Coast at the age of seventy-two, for example—when he thought he was too old for more field work—he brought several informants to New York. When he did not have direct access to informants in the field or in his home, he worked with them (especially George Hunt) by mail. In fact Boas' ethnographic research cannot be adequately appraised until his massive correspondence with George Hunt from 1894 until Hunt's death in 1933 has been analyzed. It seems probable that one of the reasons why Boas had such difficulty understanding aspects of Kwakiutl social organization, for example, is that he devoted little time to studying it himself *in situ*. Consequently he had no overall perspective in which to contextualize the minute details supplied in writing by Hunt and Boas' other informants.

Despite the apparent deficiencies in Boas' own ethnographic research he did make positive contributions regarding field methods in his writings. These contributions are largely in the form of recommendations, many of which are central to contemporary ethnography. In the first place, as we have already noted, he stressed the fundamental importance of empirical, inductive field work. He also insisted that the ethnographer learn the language of his people; he stressed the importance of collecting and interpreting field data from the viewpoint of the Indians themselves; and he acknowledged the value of intensively studying a single people over an extended period of time—although he did not mean participant observation type of research. Moreover, he was among the first to emphasize the value of training informants to record field data in their own language. And he was the first person to systematically identify the language and tribal groupings on the Northwest Coast as well as something about their historical relationships.

To conclude, Boas' work must be assessed, at least in part, from the perspective of the formative context in which it developed—not simply from the perspective of today's anthropology. One conclusion starkly emerges from this point of view. Boas did not *create* an intellectual tradition in either North American ethnology or ethnography, as some scholars have claimed. Rather, as Gruber suggests, he *joined* a well-established, ongoing but changing enterprise when he came to this country in 1886—although he did reshape a large part of American ethnology and, to a much lesser extent, ethnography, through his own personal influence. In other words, he clearly played an instrumental role in reorganizing American anthropology as a distinctive intellectual discipline, not so much by creating new concepts and approaches, but by effectively challenging and reformulating old ones. This appraisal does not reduce Boas' role in anthropology to that of a bland rethinker of old ideas, but it does indicate that many of his principal contributions are really the reformulation and espousal of preexisting ideas rather than the introduction of new ones.

George W. Stocking, Jr. (essay date 1979)

SOURCE: "Anthropology as *Kulturkampf*: Science and Politics in the Career of Franz Boas," in *The Ethnographer's Magic, and Other Essays in the History of Anthropology,* University of Wisconsin Press, 1992, pp. 92-113.

[*A distinguished American anthropologist, Stocking is the editor of numerous volumes of writings on the subject. In the following excerpt, which was originally published in the 1979 collection* The Uses of Anthropology, *he discusses the political dimension of Boas's thought.*]

Although it would be presumptuous in the space available to attempt systematic evaluation, one can scarcely avoid a few general comments on Boas' career as a scientific activist. Let us take as reference point certain limitations to Boas' activist role. Even after his move toward socialism, he was not much concerned with the redistribution of economic resources and political power. Nor was he ever much involved in the problems of the American Indian—though he was quite active privately in opposing John Collier's appointment as Indian Commissioner, regarding him as an "agitator" who would "make more acute the difficulties of the Indians which are inherent in their economic relations to their White neighbors." Although various reasons might be advanced for these neglects, one common factor underlying them would seem to be a certain fatalistic attitude toward technologically based historical processes—on the one hand, the movement toward more collectively oriented economic systems within Western European civilization, and on the other, its overpowering of more technologically primitive cultures in areas where the two were in direct confrontation.

If this seems paradoxical, in view of Boas' well-known opposition to economic determinism, it is not inconsistent with his general historical outlook. Boas never abandoned entirely a nineteenth-century liberal belief in a singular human progress in "civilization" that was based ultimately on the cumulation of rational knowledge—of which technology was the single most clearcut manifestation. Certain values deeply embedded in his own enculturative experience—scientific knowledge, human fellowship, and individual freedom—had in fact been cumulatively realized in human history, not merely in a generalized sense, but in the specific form of "modern" civilization, which Boas' language often made clear was "our own." Boas was far from satisfied with that civilization, and his alienation was ultimately expressed in his contribution to the modern pluralistic concept of "culture," which was founded on the legitimacy of alternative value systems. But anthropology, for Boas, did not lead to a "general relativistic attitude." Quite the contrary. Not only were there general values that were cumulatively realized in the history of human civilization, there were also general values that were variously realized in different human cultures—"fundamental truths" that, notwithstanding their form in "particular societies," were "common to mankind." Boas did not himself undertake the systematic comparison that might have revealed these values empirically, however, and his occasional specific references to them suggest that they, too, were rooted in his own enculturative experience. Thus the common moral ideas he saw underlying the varied ethical behavior of mankind turn out to be respect for "life, well-being, and property" within the range of the recognized social group.

Despite this deeply rooted optimistic and universalistic rationalism, there was a repressed emotional-aesthetic undercurrent in Boas' personality, and his life experience had made him painfully aware of the role of irrational factors in human life. Positively, these tendencies were realized in the variety of human cultural forms; negatively, in the way emotionally rooted customs within particular groups were retrospectively rationalized and given pseudo-universalistic valuation. This opposition—and the broader one underlying it, which resonates of the traditional Germanic opposition between "civilization" and "culture"—runs throughout Boas' career, expressing itself during certain extended historical moments in a rather deep pessimism.

Within these attitudinal parameters, Boas confronted the problems of the modern world. Although science had a hand in these—generating both technological progress and value conflict—they were essentially the product of emotion rather than reason and had primarily to do with the ways that men delimited the groups within which general human values were applied or the fruits of technological progress were distributed. Appropriately, Boas' scientific life was devoted to studying two phenomena in terms of which such exclusivity was defined—race and culture—and the gist of his scientific message was that groupings defined in these terms were profoundly conditioned by history. If he was willing to grant a certain contingent value to such particularistic groupings, which in the present phase of history might long endure, they could have no permanent place in the noncontingent realm of scientific truth.

Although there are moments in Boas' writings when scientific rationality itself is viewed in relativistic terms, in general he retained all his life a rather idealized and absolutistic conception of science. At the very end, he rejected the idea that scientists must lay aside their studies to devote themselves full-time to the anti-Nazi struggle: "the ice-cold flame of the passion for seeking the truth for truth's sake must be kept burning." And despite the frequently utilitarian tone of his appeals for research funds, he had—or came to have as he grew older—a rather limited conception of the practical utility of anthropological research. The "usefulness of the knowledge gained" by "pure science" was an "entirely irrelevant" question. True, anthropology might "illuminate the social processes of our own times"—might show us "what to do and what to avoid." But given Boas' increasingly pessimistic view of the possibility of finding general social laws and his feeling that the variation of socially based ideals would make the application of social scientific knowledge always problematic, the practical utility of anthropology was somewhat limited. It told us much more what to avoid than what to do. Its posture vis-à-vis society was defensive rather than constructive. However, in fighting prejudice and intolerance, and in defending cultural variety, it sought also to defend the cultural conditions of scientific activity itself. And by these means, it sought also to provide the basis for systematic criticism of the particularistic cultural assumptions and the pseudo-universals that still pervaded "modern civilization." Its ultimate application was to "see to it that the hard task of subordinating the love of traditional lore to clear thinking be shared with us [scientists] by larger and larger masses of our people."

On the bottom line, the tension in Boas' thought between emotional particularism and universalistic rationality was thus resolved in favor of the latter. But particularism nonetheless played a critical role in its achievement. The fundamental Eurocentrism of Boas' attitude toward "the mind of primitive man" may best be understood in this context. On the one hand, in defending the mental capacity of non-European peoples, he was defending their capacity to participate fully in "modern civilization"; on the other, in defending their cultural values, he was establishing a kind of Archimedian leverage point for the criticism of that civilization. The need for such an external reference point was one of the leitmotifs of Boas' career, and it tended to carry with it a double standard of cultural evaluation: a universalistic one in terms of which he criticized the society in which he lived and a relativistic one in terms of which he defended the cultural alternative. Whatever the emotional roots of this need, the external cultural alternative was for Boas an essential precondition for the achievement both of scientific knowledge in the so-

cial sphere and of the freedom of the individual in society. Just as the "scientific study of generalized social forms" required that the student "free himself from all valuations based on our [own] culture," so also did true freedom require that we be "able to rise above the fetters that the past imposes upon us." Without an external cultural reference point by which to bring these valuations and fetters to the level of consciousness, both scientific knowledge and true freedom would be impossible. This then was the ultimate meaning of Boas' lifelong fight for culture.

From the perspective of today, one may well question just how far Boas was able to bring the shackles of his own tradition fully to consciousness. Many of the values that late-nineteenth-century liberals assumed were universal seem now to be anchored in a particular cultural historical context. To many present anthropologists, Boas' outlook must surely seem naively idealist, in both an ethical and an epistemological sense. Its tacit Eurocentrism cannot help but offend many in a postcolonial world. Its limited and defensive conception of the anthropologist's political role—which by World War II was already undergoing modification—must seem quite inadequate to many of those who have come of age in the 1960s and 1970s. Questioning the assumptions underlying Boas' activism, one may question its achievements as well. Forty years of education in tolerance seem neither to have eliminated prejudice nor greatly to have strengthened "the power of clear thought"—nor to have fundamentally modified the social order of the United States.

But if he never transcended them, Boas nonetheless represents nineteenth-century liberal values at their most generically human, and we may still today appreciate his contribution to our cultural life. There is a sense in which he transmuted personal history into scientific paradigm: the experience of Jews in Germany provided him the archetype of an ostensibly racial group that was in fact biologically heterogeneous, which had assimilated itself almost completely to German national culture and which in multitudinous ways had enriched the general cultural life of modern civilization. Transported to the United States, the scientific viewpoint founded on that archetype offered strong support for certain fundamental American values that in the early twentieth century were much in need of reinforcement. By the time of his death, Boas' critique of traditional racial assumption and his contribution to the modern concept of culture had contributed not a little to that end. And if today his critical perspective and his anthropological activism may seem somewhat limited in scope, the standpoint from which he approached the issues of anthropology and public life is surely as sound as ever: "the whole basis of the anthropological viewpoint is the willingness to take the position of the non-conformist, not to take anything in our social structure for granted, and to be particularly ready to examine critically all those attitudes that are accompanied by strong outbursts of emotion, the more so the stronger the accompanying emotion."

Alexander Lesser   (essay date 1981)

SOURCE: "Franz Boas," in *Totems and Teachers: Per-*

spectives on the History of Anthropology, edited by Sydel Silverman, Columbia University Press, 1981, pp. 1-33.

[*Lesser was a distinguished American anthropologist who, like Boas, specialized in the study of Native American cultures. In the following excerpt, he summarizes Boas's achievements.*]

In retrospect, Franz Boas was the builder and architect of modern anthropology. This has come to be a general consensus, despite certain controversies. I propose to focus on four themes in his life and work:

1. The way in which Boas filled the role of architect of modern anthropology.

2. What Boas brought with him into anthropology that was the effective factor of factors in modernizing it.

3. How Boas, anthropologist and scientist, was a *citizen-scientist* all his life, whose ethics and ideals for the study of man were far-reaching, humane, and still hold true in our own day.

4. How Boas, far from being antitheory, was himself *the* great theorist of modern anthropology, who established the core of anthropological theory on which the science is based.

Modern anthropology begins with Franz Boas. It begins in the scientific skepticism with which he examined the traditional orthodoxies of the study of man, exposing and rejecting the false and unproven, calling for a return to empirical observation, establishing the truth of elementary fundamentals, opening new pathways and creating new methods. It begins in Boas' ways of thinking about man and his history, in his use of rigorous scientific requirements for data and for proof, in his rejection of old myths, old stereotypes, old emotionally charged assumptions.

Boas' contribution to the transformation of anthropology was therefore not a simple, single event, a formal statement of principles, or a generalized theory at a certain point of time. Boas worked from problem to problem, consolidating the truth gained and asking the next question. The framework and principles of the modern subject matter are emergents from this ongoing process, in part the residue of truth left after traditional materials and ideas were reevaluated, in part the positive discovery of empirical principles by fresh and original observation.

Boas was aware of this critical character of his method from his early professional years. In 1907, responding at Columbia to a Festschrift which was given him on the twenty-fifth anniversary of his Ph. D., he described himself as "one whose work rests essentially in an unfeeling criticism of his own work and that of others." He wrote a defense of the cephalic index (head form) and its traditional importance as a hereditary trait only a few years before his own research proved it was not strictly genetically determined but was affected significantly by environmental change. He condemned his early Kwakiutl and other Northwest Coast research as questionable, superseded by later work. He came to "disparage his early work on the Kwakiutl language," pointing out its shortcomings. He

was continually self-critical. "Flawless perfection, then, must not be sought in Boas," as Lowie has put it.

But in the end he restructured anthropology and its branches, leading physical anthropology from taxonomical race classification into human biology, breaking through the limitations of traditional philology into the problems of modern linguistics and cognitive anthropology, establishing the modern anthropological meaning and study of human culture.

Along his way, as Boas worked at problems in all fields of anthropology, he came to discoveries and understandings which, through his writing and teaching, became the convictions and effected the consensus from which the modern science of anthropology was born. Many of his writings were summations of plateaus of understanding he had reached in one area of anthropology or another. *The Mind of Primitive Man* in 1911 was his first great general consolidation in book form, a seminal book in modern social thought for technical readers and the lay public alike. In it, Boas reorganized and integrated studies of 1894 to 1911 into closely argued theses which became baselines of anthropology thereafter and fundamental conceptions in social science and social philosophy.

The book provided general anthropology and its separable branches—physical anthropology, linguistics, ethnology—with a structural framework. Establishing the relative autonomy of cultural phenomena, it gave to the concept of culture its modern meaning and usage. Boas proved that cultures are diverse historical developments, each the outcome of a prior history in which many factors and events, cultural and noncultural, have played a part. He made the plurality of cultures fundamental to the study of man. He showed how languages, both semantically and morphologically, are each a context of perception that affects human thought and action. Analogously, he showed how cultural environments, especially as contexts of traditional materials, shape and structure human behavior—actions and reactions—in each generation. In so doing he ended the traditional ambiguity in the term culture understood interchangeably as both humanistic and behavioral—an ambiguity perpetuated by endless quoting of Tylor's "culture or civilization"—and started the modern era of the concept of cultures, viewed as contexts of learned human behavior.

A much earlier paper shows that the same essential conception was in his mind more than twenty years before. In **"The Aims of Ethnology"** (written in 1888), Boas stated, "The data of ethnology prove that not only our language, but also our emotions are the result of the form of our social life and of the history of the people to whom we belong." The concept of social heritage was basic to Boas' thinking all his life.

Several of the theses of the book *The Mind of Primitive Man,* taken together, establish the relative autonomy of cultural phenomena, showing that there are no independent variables on which the cultural is dependent. First, establishing that race (physical type), language, and culture have relatively independent histories and are not interchangeable terms in classifying man, Boas showed that inner inborn traits ("race" or heredity) are not causal determinants of similarities or differences of cultures. Second, showing that geographical or natural environments are not neatly correlated with cultures as adaptations but always involve preexisting cultures, Boas proved that outer environmental conditions are not the causal determinants of similarities or differences of cultures. Finally, establishing that ideas of *orthogenetic* cultural evolution do not fit the facts of actual cultural sequences and history, Boas showed that no necessary predetermining process of change makes similarities or differences of cultures expressions of unfolding stages of development. These theses became principles of modern anthropology.

It is, I think, important to understand what it was in Boas' training and point of view that led him into the critical reconstruction of anthropology that he accomplished. This is especially important because of further implications for the understanding of Boas' thinking on theory and scientific method. It has been widely held that it was Boas' training in physics and mathematics that was responsible for his scientific reconstruction of the field of anthropology, which was largely preprofessional and somewhat amateurish at the time. Actually, I am convinced that it was an entirely different phase of his education and scientific experience that led to his future work, and I believe he tried to make that clear in his own statements.

Central to Boas' education in science and scientific thinking was the study of natural history, in which he indulged that "intense interest in nature" that he later recalled as characteristic of his youth. Boas attended the Froebel kindergarten in Minden founded and taught by his mother, which provided special nature studies. This experience was unusual for Boas' time, for kindergartens were rare then. Periods of recuperation after illness, spent in the countryside of Clus or at the seaside at Helgoland, acquainted him with the plant life of the woods and the wealth of animals and plants of the sea. He collected his own herbarium and for years "treasured"—his own word—the sea life specimens he gathered at Helgoland. He had a mineral collection and began to study mineralogy early in his Gymnasium years. In mid-Gymnasium he studied some zoology (including study on his own of the comparative bone structure of geese, ducks, and hares); astronomy and geology; more botany—physiology, plant anatomy, and the geographical distribution of plants. His interest in this last subject almost stifled other hobbies, but the study of cryptogams (plants such as ferns, moss, and algae, which reproduce by spores), begun in his own early herbarium collecting, became with a special teacher a subject which fascinated him ever after.

In his later Gymnasium years, drawn to all the natural sciences, he studied plant anatomy and physiology, used microscopes in plant study and in work on crystal forms and systems in mineralogy, and made his own map of the distribution of plants in the Minden region. In the universities, the special professors he sought included two biologists (one also a marine biologist), a botanist, and two mineralogists (one also a geologist). He found his studies of plant distributions among his most exciting work, and was elated when, by mid-Gymnasium years—for the most part

through study on his own—he could follow fairly well "the evolution of the animal and plant world" and "its transient geographical distribution."

Natural history with its empirical approach involved Boas in observation, description, comparison and classification, inductive generalization, and *an acceptance of the external world* which became a habit of thinking for Boas. In attempting to understand Boas and what he contributed to modern thought, his statements about his "intellectual interest" in physics and mathematics have been overemphasized, while other statements about his "intensive emotional interest in the phenomena of the world"—along with his long concentration on natural history studies—have been given too little attention. Boas' background before he became an anthropologist included physics and mathematics as well as geography as part of his intellectual training. But to understand what he made of anthropology it is far more important to know that he came to the study of man as a naturalist, as a student of natural history, and tried to understand man and peoples as part of the natural phenomena of the world.

Among anthropologists, Marian W. Smith is virtually alone in emphasizing this mode of understanding Boas. In a paper on Boas' approach to field method, Smith draws a sharp contrast between Boas' "natural history approach to the social sciences" and the "social philosophy approach of British social anthropology," and she shows that the contrast affected both the methods and content of fieldwork done by the two schools. The American approach includes all of culture, considers data inviolable, and seeks in data only generalizations or theories that can be reached inductively. The British school, in contrast, begins with assumptions and theories and uses field data and the field situation to test hypotheses that have been deductively derived.

Marian Smith's paper limits the scope of her interpretation, but one suspects from some of her comments that she would have gone on to a conception of Boas and his thinking similar to my own. For example, she says:

> Boas, more than any other person, first brought the very mind of man into the natural world. . . . Conceptualization and philosophy no longer breathed a finer air. They could be studied by the same techniques and approaches, by the same attitudes as other human characteristics and consequently lost much of their aura of revealed truth.

Smith's paper had a singular impact on some anthropologists. For example, Kroeber, in his discussion of "Boas as a Man," had emphasized the mathematical and physical character of Boas' education, training, and lifelong modes of thought. Even earlier, in 1935, in a famous exchange with Boas on history, Kroeber had written:

> To begin with, it is of indubitable significance that Boas' educational training was in the physical laboratory sciences, in physics in fact. This led him into psychophysics and physical geography. His doctoral dissertation was on the color of sea water. This in turn led to a one-man, two-year geographical expedition to Baffinland,

which brought with it intimate contacts with natives. The result was *The Central Eskimo* and a career of anthropology since. From physics Boas brought into anthropology a sense of definiteness of problem, of exact rigor of method, and of highly critical objectivity. These qualities have remained with him unimpaired, and his imparting them to anthropology remains his fundamental and unshakeable contribution to our discipline.

This attitude of Kroeber's is completely contrary to Boas' own explanation of his manner of thinking. In a paper called **"The Study of Geography,"** in 1887, Boas specifically contrasts the methods of physics with the methods of history. He uses "physics" and "history" as conceptual terms for two general types of approaches, the former seeking laws and subordinating particular events to abstract generalizations, the latter seeking the thorough understanding of phenomena—even individual events—and making laws or generalizations merely instrumental to that end. Boas identifies himself with the historical approach, temperamentally, in interests, and in methods, and he is unsympathetic to that of physics.

In contrast to his earlier statements, Kroeber wrote in his 1959 preface to *The Anthropology of Franz Boas,* the volume which contains Marian Smith's paper, that "natural scientists have never questioned the status of Boas and the importance of his massive contribution," that Boas' anthropological activity at first stemmed largely from both natural history and humanist interests, and that Boas dealt so extensively with non-European and nonclassical languages because they are a part of the total world of nature. "Given the combination of Boas' natural science adhesion and his predilection for human materials, it was almost inevitable that he should concern himself with culture, for culture, including its semiautonomous province of language, is precisely the phenomenal regularities of human behavior." This is fundamentally different from Kroeber's statements of a few years earlier.

Solon Kimball has made a special point of relating the "natural history" approach to anthropology itself. In a paper presented at an American Anthropological Association meeting some years ago, he offered the thesis that anthropology had developed historically from the approach of natural history, while sociology had developed from the approach of physics and the formal deductive sciences. Kimball has consistently taken the position—especially in studies of the relation of anthropology to methods and principles of modern education—that anthropology is rooted in the method of natural history (as exemplified by Darwin) and involves "inductive empiricism based upon methods of classification and interdependencies of components."

Empirical methods to Boas meant firsthand experience where data were lacking. It meant an end to brilliantly constructed speculations as a substitute for observation. In ethnology, of course, this meant fieldwork, and Boas' own work on the Eskimos is generally recognized as one early example which stimulated the development of fieldwork as the basis of ethnology and cultural anthropology. In discussions of the historical development of ethnology, attention is often drawn (as by Evans-Pritchard) to the Torres Straits Expedition of the English, in which W. H. R. Rivers and A. C. Haddon participated. Yet much of the work of that expedition was peripheral to ethnology, as, for example, the effort of Rivers to settle psychological questions of the sensibilities of indigenous peoples. Somewhat overlooked in this historical view are the monumental field researches of the Jesup North Pacific Expedition, which was mounted under Boas' inspiration, direction, and editorship while he was at the American Museum of Natural History and at Columbia. This project, which was contemporary with the Torres Straits Expedition, resulted in seventeen massive volumes on Siberia and Northwest Coast North America by various people (with an eighteenth still to be published) and far outweighs Torres Straits in its significance for the development of modern ethnological research.

There is another side to Boas as a scientist—the fact that he was a *citizen*-scientist. His careers as citizen and scientist are interwoven. He accepted a moral obligation to spread scientific knowledge as widely as possible, and he himself applied anthropological findings to human problems in education, race relations, nationalism and internationalism, war and peace, and the struggle for democracy and intellectual freedom.

In his first general book, *The Mind of Primitive Man,* the first words of the 1911 first edition are: "Proud of his wonderful achievements, civilized man looks down upon the humbler members of mankind." The last words on the last page read:

> I hope the discussions outlined in these pages have shown that the data of anthropology teach us a greater tolerance of forms of civilization different from our own, that we should learn to look on foreign races with greater sympathy and with a conviction that, as all races have contributed in the past to cultural progress in one way or another, so they will be capable of advancing the interests of mankind if we are only willing to give them a fair opportunity.

Later, in *Anthropology and Modern Life* (1928), he applied anthropological knowledge to racism, nationalism, eugenics, crime, and education. Still later, in *Race and Democratic Society,* published posthumously by his son in 1945, some of his hundreds of contributions to widely read magazines and newspapers were brought together.

Boas' commitment to active citizenship and social, liberal ideals began in his childhood home, enriched by the liberalism and free thought of his father and mother. Both had given up all formal religious activity and affiliation, and as Boas later recalled, he and his sisters were "spared the struggle against religious dogma that besets the lives of so many young people." With "an intense interest in nature," Boas was able to approach the world around him with an open mind, without religious preconceptions or inhibitions.

Politically, Boas found "the ideals of the revolution of 1848 a living force in [his] home." Relatives and friends of the family had been in the 1848 struggle in Germany and had left for the United States after its failure, some after getting out of jail. Drawn to the liberalism of his time, Boas was deeply troubled about Bismarck's Germany and the limitations and restrictions it could place upon his scientific career.

At twenty-five, while on his expedition to Baffinland, he wrote in a diary of letters that he sent to his fiancée, "Science alone is not the greatest good" (June 27, 1883). "I believe one can be really happy only as a member of humanity as a whole, if one works with all one's energy together with the masses toward high goals" (December 13, 1883). "And what I want, for what I want to live and die, is equal rights for all, equal possibilities to learn and work for rich and poor alike. Don't you believe that to have done even the smallest bit for this is more than all science taken together?" (January 22, 1884). And he added, "I do not think I would be allowed to do this in Germany" and "I do not wish for a German professorship because I would be restricted to my science and to teaching, for which I have no inclination. I should much prefer to live in American and to further these ideas."

It was in 1887 that circumstances combined to make it possible for him to remain in the United States when he returned to New York after a Northwest Coast trip—to marry, to apply for American citizenship (which he obtained five years later), and to begin his American career with the same "American dream" he shared with so many other immigrants to the United States.

Boas' active citizenship did not end with his effort to make his scientific work relevant to human affairs. He was active in matters of principles and in specific situations involving injustice and violations of academic freedom. He resigned from his first teaching position—at Clark University—in a joint protest with other faculty members against continuing infringement of academic freedom by the president, G. Stanley Hall. In his view, a college or university consisted of its faculty and students; trustees and nonacademic administrators were not inherent in it.

A first major test of his principles came in 1914, with the outbreak of World War I. Boas, a pacifist, opposed the war from the beginning. He saw it as fundamentally an imperialist war. In a series of letters to newspapers, he urged that the United States and Woodrow Wilson take the lead in forming a coalition of neutral countries to bring about a cease-fire, and he argued against actions by President Wilson that he charged were leading the United States into the war. In 1917, after the United States declared war, he denounced the action and Wilson in the press.

Boas was not pro-German, as of course was charged. I will support this with a single letter, a letter he wrote to his son Ernst from the field in British Columbia, a few days after the outbreak of war. It is a personal letter, from father to son; it was handwritten and clearly was never intended to get the public hearing I am giving it now.

> August 6, 1914
> Dear Ernst:
>
> . . . You can imagine that I can think of nothing else than the unfortunate war and the danger to which our aunts and grandmother are exposed. To me it seems like a terrible dream. I cannot visualize how reasonable people and nations which are "leaders of civilization" can conjure up such a terrible war. If Germany loses, such hatred will be created that it will stir up her nationalism for years to come; if she is victorious, such arrogance, that it will lead to the same consequence. If people would only realize what a source of hatred and misfortune the highly praised patriotism represents! That one cherishes one's own way of life is a natural thing. But does one need to nourish the thought that it is the best of all, that everything that is different is not good but useless, that it is right to despise the people of other nations? In our private lives we would not follow such an unethical rule. Why should it prevail in our national life? If one could only exclude this "patriotismus" from our schools and teach our children the good in our culture, and appreciation of the good in other cultures. Instead they artificially cultivate envy and rivalry.

During the war, Boas took public leadership of an effort to counteract wartime hysteria against German culture. Officially, all things German were condemned. The German language ceased to be taught in American schools. Orchestras eliminated German music from their programs. Boas once made a particular request of a conductor to include a certain Beethoven opus in his next concert; the conductor replied that he felt as Boas did about the quality of that opus, but regretted that it was impossible for him to perform it. Boas took the position that as an anthropologist he could not accept the identification of the art and literature of a people with its political administration at a particular time. Heine, Schiller, Bach, and other German artists represented cultural achievements and values that had nothing to do with the Kaiser. It was this position that he took with his students. When Columbia's president Nicholas Murray Butler, ardently prowar and anti-German, instituted student spying on what professors did and said, Boas responded by writing a full statement of his views and distributing it in mimeograph to all who came to his classes or requested it.

Boas was not alone at Columbia in his pacifism and anti-war ideas. After the 1917 U.S. declaration of war, when a draft to mobilize an army was being readied, J. McKeen Cattell, a professor of psychology, sent copies of a letter he had written to every member of the U.S. House and Senate. The letter urged that a military draft act provide exemption for those who objected to military service outside the continental borders of the United States. The letter was written on Columbia University stationery. President Butler terminated Cattell on twenty-four hours notice, making forfeit his right to tenure and his accumulations toward retirement. Faculty support for Cattell was immediate. Boas and John Dewey were members of a Cattell Committee, which worked in his support for years. Two other faculty members, James Harvey Robinson and Charles Beard, resigned and joined in the establishment of the New School for Social Research. In the end, Cattell took his case against Columbia to court and won a complete victory, Columbia settling out of court to avoid publicity. It was so quiet an ending to the case that many did not know and do not know that Columbia had lost its first case on academic rights.

Perhaps the most critical controversy involving Boas and World War I came in 1919, after the war, when he published the following letter in *The Nation*.

Scientists as Spies

To the Editor of *The Nation*

Sir: In his war address to Congress, President Wilson dwelt at great length on the theory that only autocracies maintain spies, that these are not needed in democracies. At the time that the President made this statement, the government of the United States had in its employ spies of unknown number. I am not concerned here with the familiar discrepancies between the President's words and the actual facts, although we may perhaps have to accept his statement as meaning correctly that we live under an autocracy, that our democracy is a fiction. The point against which I wish to enter a vigorous protest is that a number of men who follow science as their profession, men whom I refuse to designate any longer as scientists, have prostituted science by using it as a cover for their activities as spies.

A soldier whose business is murder as a fine art, a diplomat whose calling is based on deception and secretiveness, a politician whose very life consists in compromises with his conscience, a business man whose aim is personal profit within the limits allowed by a lenient law—such may be excused if they set patriotic devotion above common everyday decency and perform services as spies. They merely accept the code of morality to which modern society still conforms. Not so the scientist. The very essence of his life is the service of truth. We all know scientists who in private life do not come up to the standard of truthfulness, but who nevertheless would not consciously falsify the results of their researches. It is bad enough if we have to put up with these, because they reveal a lack of strength of character that is liable to distort the results of their work. A person, however, who uses science as a cover for political spying, who demeans himself to pose before a foreign government as an investigator and asks for assistance in his alleged researches in order to carry on, under this cloak, his political machinations, prostitutes science in an unpardonable way and forfeits the right to be classed as a scientist.

By accident, incontrovertible proof has come to my hands that at least four men who carry on anthropological work, while employed as government agents, introduced themselves to foreign governments as representatives of scientific researches. They have not only shaken the belief in the truthfulness of science, but they have also done the greatest possible disservice to scientific inquiry. In consequence of their acts, every nation will look with distrust upon the visiting foreign investigator who wants to do honest work, suspecting sinister designs. Such action has raised a new barrier against the development of international friendly cooperation.

New York, October 16 Franz Boas

In the light of controversies over ethics within the American Anthropological Association in recent years, this letter seems a direct and simple plea for scientific integrity. Its anti-Wilson innuendos were not new. Boas had opposed World War I openly and had criticized Wilson's policies in letter after letter in the *New York Times*.

However, Boas' letter in *The Nation* was denounced by the Anthropological Society of Washington in a lengthy statement to the American Anthropological Association at its meeting in December, 1919. The Harvard-Cambridge anthropology group sided with the Washington society. The statement of the Washington group read as follows:

Resolutions of the Anthropological Society of Washington

The attention of the Anthropological Society of Washington having been called to an open letter published in *The Nation* of December 20th by Dr. Franz Boas under the title, "Scientists as Spies," and after said article was read and duly considered, the following resolution was adopted and ordered to be submitted to the American Anthropological Association at its meeting in Boston; to Section H of the American Association for the Advancement of Science meeting in St. Louis; and to the Archeological Institute of America meeting in Pittsburgh, with the request that suitable action be taken by these associations. Also that a copy of this resolution be sent to *The Nation* and *Science* with a request for its publication.

Resolved: That the article in question unjustly criticizes the President of the United States and attacks the fundamental principles of American democracy; that the reflections contained in the article fall on all American anthropologists who have been anywhere outside the limits of the United States during the last five years; that the information thus given is liable to have future serious effects on the work of all anthropologists outside the boundaries of the United States; and that the accusation, given such prominent publicity and issuing from such a source, will doubtless receive wide attention and is liable to prejudice foreign governments against all scientific men coming from this country to their respective territories, particularly if under government auspices; therefore *Be it resolved,* that in the opinion of the Council of the Anthropological Society of Washington, the publication of the article in question was unwarranted and will prove decidedly injurious to the interests of American scientists in general; that the author has shown himself inconsiderate to the best interests of his American colleagues who may be obliged to carry on research in foreign countries, and that his action therefore deserves our emphatic disapproval.

At the meeting, after a great deal of discussion, the following resolution was moved instead of the long statement from the Washington Anthropological Society.

Resolved: That the expression of opinion by Dr. Franz Boas contained in an open letter to the editor of *The Nation* on the date of October 16, 1919, and published in the issue of that weekly for December 20, 1919, is unjustified and does not represent the opinion of the American Anthropological Association. *Be it further resolved:* That a copy of this resolution be forwarded to the Executive Board of the National Research Council and such other scientific associations as may have taken action on this matter.

I have presented the text of Boas' letter and if anyone can find a word in it that says it represents anybody's views but his own, I would like to know it. It was a personal statement of his convictions, and it involved no one else. He did not name the persons he was referring to. Nevertheless, Boas was censured, by a vote of about two to one.

The Washington Anthropological Society distributed its original statement widely, in spite of the fact that it had not been passed by the AAA. A great deal of the rancor aroused was allegedly due to Boas' publication of a professional statement in a public, nonprofessional magazine. Yet Boas had sent it earlier to *Science,* which was then edited by J. McKeen Cattell, the same Cattell who had been kicked out of Columbia for his pacifist letter to Congress on Columbia stationery. Cattell replied:

> I fear I must decide that it would not be advisable to print the letter entitled "Scientists as Spies" in *Science.* I of course concur in all that you say, but it seems to me desirable for *Science* to avoid, especially at the present time, all questions of a political character, even though they do relate to scientific matters.
>
> Sincerely yours,
>
> J. McKeen Cattell

I don't know how Boas felt about that letter, but he sent his statement right off to Henry Raymond Mussey, a friend who was editor of *The Nation.* Mussey immediately accepted it for publication and wrote to Boas:

> Thank you very much for your disturbing letter on "Scientists as Spies" sent us for publication. It is indeed a distressing thing that scientific men should stoop to such dishonorable practices, and I am very glad indeed to have the opportunity of giving publicity to your protest.

That is how Boas' letter happened to appear in *The Nation* rather than in *Science.*

There is a final note to this early controversy over professional ethics. The next month (on January 9, 1920), Cattell published in *Science* the full text of the communication from the Washington Anthropological Society, in the form that had been *rejected* by the AAA meeting.

I close this page of history by noting that one scientist wrote the Washington Anthropological Society to ask, in view of the statement it had circulated and had asked everybody to act upon, whether Boas' charges in the *Nation* letter were true. He noted that the Washington group had made no reference to that question at all.

Following his censure, Boas resigned as representative of the American Anthropological Association to the Nation-

al Research Council, who accepted the resignation regretfully. Apart from this, I have no evidence that his participation in the AAA was ever terminated, even transiently. Annual reports of the Association in succeeding years show him still to be a member of various committees that he had been on previously.

Stocking has treated this incident in the context of "The Scientific Reaction Against Cultural Anthropology, 1917-1920," the title of a paper in his book *Race, Culture, and Evolution.* He focuses on the manner in which opposition to the development of Boas' cultural anthropology, fortified by jealousy of his achievements, caused the *Nation* letter to be used as an excuse for violent anti-Boas action. I think the letter also stands as an example of Boas in action on issues of scientific ethics.

Over the years, as Boas became known through his work and public statements as a strong liberal on academic and political issues and on race relations, he accepted board memberships on and allowed the use of his name by many public-service citizens' organizations and ad hoc committees. He also organized some of his own. His main means of action was to make public statements to the press or through letters to the press, or to form a committee which then took public or private action as the matter required. It was in this way that Boas initiated two large-scale national actions in relation to the rise of Hitler and Nazism. The first followed a Nazi denunciation of Jewish science. Boas responded with a public statement signed by over 8,000 American scientists, affirming that there was only one science, to which religion and race were irrelevant. Later, after Hitler came to power in 1933 and Boas' books (among others) were burned, Boas organized a group at Columbia called the Committee for Democracy and Intellectual Freedom. The idea spread rapidly to other universities, where chapters were formed, until the committee had more than 11,000 members.

Boas also joined other American scientists in organizing committees to help scientific refugees from Hitler's Germany and other countries overrun by the Nazis. The primary effort was to find refugee scientists positions in the United States or elsewhere in the free world. Boas was engaged in this activity at the moment he died in December 1942. Along with Lévi-Strauss, Boas had arranged a luncheon at Columbia in honor of Paul Rivet, refugee linguist from Vichy France. Boas suddenly collapsed, in Lévi-Strauss' arms, and died even as he was in the middle of a sentence about a new idea on race.

A major part of Boas' scientific work and its application concerned race and race relations, especially the problems of the American Negro. He was probably the first scientist to publish that Negro and White were fundamentally equal, as were all so-called races. He embodied this view in the title of one paper, "The Genetic Basis for Democracy." American Negro leaders, organizations, and universities were quick to recognize in Boas a source of strength. For W. E. B. DuBois, a founder of the NAACP and editor of its publication *Crisis,* Boas wrote a paper for the first issue of that magazine, on the Negro and the race problem in America (1910). He gave a commencement address at Atlanta University in 1906. He participated in the organization and work of the Association for the Study of Negro Life and History and its publication *The Journal of Negro History,* and later of the Council on African Affairs, of which Paul Robeson was chairman and Max Yergan director.

As an indication of what such Afro-American leaders thought of Boas, I have a message Max Yergan sent to Helene Boas after Boas died.

> Mrs. Helene Yampolsky,
>
> Grantwood, N.J.
>
> On behalf of the Council on African Affairs, I express deepest regrets over the death of your father. He was a guide and inspiration to us in our deliberation and activities for the welfare of African peoples. The work of organizations like ours is possible because Franz Boas has lived.

I began this discussion by selecting four principal points for emphasis. I have touched on three: (1) that Boas was the architect of modern anthropology; (2) that the element in his training and experience that made him the modernizer of the study of man was the empirical way of thinking of natural history; and (3) that Boas was a *citizen*-scientist who applied the work of anthropology to problems of society, and was an activist on academic and political issues— in both ways serving as a model for anthropology as a humanitarian science.

I come now to my final theme, Boas as theorist. Far from being antitheory, Boas was himself, I would argue, *the* great theorist of modern anthropology, who established the core of anthropological theory on which the science is based.

Inescapably, discussions of Boas on theory must begin with his handling of the theory of evolution. Here are his words on that subject in 1888:

> The development of ethnology is largely due to the general recognition of the principle of biological evolution. It is a common feature of all forms of evolutionary theory that every living being is considered as the result of an historical development. The fate of an individual does not influence himself alone, but also all succeeding generations. . . . This point of view introduced an historical perspective into the natural sciences and revolutionized their methods. The development of ethnology is largely due to the adoption of the evolutionary standpoint, because it impressed the conviction upon us that no event in the life of a people passes without leaving its effect upon later generations. The myths told by our ancestors and in which they believed have left their impress upon the ways of thinking of their descendants.

Clearly, in his early anthropological thinking Boas (1) accepted biological evolution as scientifically valid, (2) understood evolution in *historical* terms, not as orthogenetic, and (3) affirmed evolution as a *first principle* of ethnology and anthropology.

These statements must be emphasized in view of oftrepeated assertions that Boas was antievolutionary. No statement could show more clearly that he not only accepted evolution but accepted it as *basic.* Yet he did reject the so-called evolutionary ideas of some anthropologists. What did he reject, as distinct from the evolution that he affirmed?

In *Primitive Art* he wrote,

> Evolution, meaning the continuous change of thought and action, or historic continuity, cannot be accepted unreservedly. It is otherwise when it is conceived as meaning the universally valid continuous development of one cultural form out of a preceding type.

Essentially he was opposing orthogenesis, which is defined as follows by Webster's dictionary:

> In biology, variations which in successive generations of an organism, follow some particular line, evolving some new type irrespective of natural selection or other external factor. Determinate variation or evolution. Sociologically, the theory that social evolution always follows the same direction and passes through the same stages in each culture despite differing external conditions.

Orthogenesis, by its very definition, is a contradiction of Darwin's theory of evolution. Darwin based evolutionary change on the principle of natural selection; among the vast number of variations occurring in each new generation, some were "selected" to survive and reproduce, others were not. Natural selection in turn must be understood as historical in character. Forms or species are subject to variation and change. So, too, is the environment in which they occur. The interaction between variations of form and the changing environment is an event of a particular time, not predetermined by either system. In modern biology, orthogenesis is not a fundamental evolutionary process. The point is made in Simpson's *Meaning of Evolution* and in various other treatments.

It was this distinction between orthogenesis and evolution in its historical, Darwinian sense that Boas had in mind, as has been noted by some. Washburn has written about this, referring to "evolution" as the term was used by Tylor, Spencer, Morgan, and their contemporary throwbacks. "There is no evolution in the traditional anthropological sense. What Boas referred to as evolution was orthogenesis, which receives no support from modern genetic theory. What the geneticist sees as evolution is far closer to what Boas called history than to what he called evolution." In an article on Boas I wrote, "Boas' critique was directed not against the principle of evolution as historical development, which he accepted, but against the orthogenesis of dominant English and American theory of the time. He opposed history to orthogenesis."

Boas himself made the distinction in clear terms in several places. In 1920, he wrote in **"The Methods of Ethnology"**:

> . . . the hypothesis [of evolution in traditional anthropology] implies the thought that our modern Western European civilization represents the highest cultural development toward which all other more primitive cultural types tend, and that therefore retrospectively we con-

struct an *orthogenetic* development towards our modern civilization.

In 1919, in a discussion at an American Ethnological Society meeting, Boas is reported by the Secretary, Robert H. Lowie, to have spoken as follows:

> Professor Boas pointed out that in comparing the doctrines of unilinear evolutionists to those of biologists we are not quite fair to the biologists, since they do not postulate a single line of evolution without any divergences; what the cultural theorists of the earlier period did was to stress the *orthogenetic* character of cultural evolution.

In 1938, discussing problems of the laws of historic development, Boas wrote:

> When these data are assembled, the question arises whether they present an orderly picture or whether history proceeds haphazardly; in other words, whether an *orthogenetic* development of human forms may be discovered, and whether a regular sequence of stages of historical development may be recognized. (italics mine)

Several aspects of this view of evolution help explain Boas' view of theory and his work as a scientific theorist. First, he uses the fact of evolution as proof "that every living being is the result of an historical development." He understands evolution as history and as evidence of the historicity of living things. In effect, Boas' view is a major theory, both of culture and of man. It states that every culture is the result of a long history, and that every such history involves a great complexity of events, accidents of history, and interrelation of factors.

In relation to Boas' view of evolution as basic to anthropology, note that he is speaking empirically. The empiricism he brought from natural history studies called for generalizations or scientific theories that are *inductive*— that come out of the data and that serve to bind them together.

As Darwin's theory of evolution expressed in a generalization both the continuity and change of living forms— *descent with modification*—so a similar theory of the historical evolution of cultures served to express their continuity through time and their diversification and change— the idea of *continuity with change.*

Additionally, Boas established the modern *theory* of culture. Stocking has shown that it was Boas who established the modern use and meaning of the term. But more than that, in doing so he established the central theory of modern anthropology.

When Boas showed that cultures and their diversities could not be explained by differences in outer environment, natural environment, or geography; when he showed that cultural diversity could not be explained by differences in inner makeup of human groups (the racial argument); and finally, when he showed that cultural diversity was not a matter of stages of predetermined development or orthogenetic evolution, he made cultures and their histories the primary determinants of diversities or similarities at any time. Cultures became the basic factor

in the understanding of cultural man. In anthropological thinking and explanation, the concept *cultural* replaced the concept *natural.* The culture concept did away at one blow with efforts to explain human nature biologically and physiologically (as with concepts of instinct or of inherent drives).

I would suggest, then, that two great theories in anthropology were contributed by Boas: the idea that in culture history, culture is the primary determinant, rather than some noncultural independent variable; and the theory of culture in its modern sense, as learned behavior. Both of these are inductive theories, based on the comparison and contrast of human cultures.

The immense influence of this anthropological discovery and development is indicated, for example, by John Dewey in his article, "Human Nature":

> Anthropology, on the other hand, has made it clear that the varieties of cultural and institutional forms which have existed are not to be traced to anything which can be called unmodified human nature, but are the products of interaction with the social environment. They are functions, in the mathematical sense, of institutional organization and cultural traditions, as these operate to shape raw biological material into definitively human shape.
>
> If we accept the extreme partisan stand, it may be regarded as now generally accepted that the immense diversities of culture which have existed and which still exist cannot possibly be derived directly from any stock of original powers and impulses, that the problem is one of explaining in its own terms the diversification of the cultural milieus which act upon original nature.
>
> As this fact gains recognition, the problem of modifiability is being placed upon the same level as the persistence of custom or tradition. It is wholly a matter of empirical determination, not of *a priori* theorizing.

Dewey adds further on:

> The present controversies between those who assert the essential fixity of human nature and those who believe in a great measure of modifiability center chiefly around the future of war and the future of a competitive economic system motivated by private profit. It is justifiable to say without dogmatism that both anthropology and history give support to those who wish to change these institutions. It is demonstrable that many of the obstacles to change which have been attributed to human nature are in fact due to the inertia of institutions and to the voluntary desire of powerful classes to maintain the existing status.

In Boas' own view of theory (in the sense of scientific generalizations or laws), as he outlined it in his early paper **"The Study of Geography"** (1887), he made the historical character of human phenomena basic. The goal in such a field of study is "the thorough understanding of phenomena"; in other places he speaks of "complex phenomena." Regularities or generalizations which are discoverable are viewed pragmatically, not as an end in themselves, but as an additional tool in analysis. This, I suggest, is not an antitheory or antigeneralization position, but a reversal of emphasis. He suggests that in the complex field of human cultural history, theory—read laws or generalizations—is not the end, but, where discoverable, one means among others to be used in scientific analysis and for the understanding of phenomena.

As a generalizer in his own right, Boas is the most generalizing anthropologist I have read. I once wrote a paper called "Research Procedure and Laws of Culture," in which I tried to show the nature of laws as working assumptions. I limited myself to selected illustrations from Boas, because he was supposed to be nontheoretical. I found most of the illustrations in the lengthy article he wrote years ago for the *Encyclopedia of the Social Sciences* on "Anthropology." In that article, on every phase of the subject, he tries to generalize as much as possible what the import of the data is. The article is full of generalizations, some of which even take the specific form of attempts to state laws. I think it is important to realize that a generalization for him was arrived at inductively and was an attempt to sum up, to pull together, the meanings of the many facts so far known. In practice, it was always subject to further questions, further inquiries, further verification.

Boas moved onward from problem to problem throughout his active scientific life. He taught his students to attempt to do the same. He left anthropology an open field of inquiry, its methods rooted in empirical observation and experience, its goal an ever wider and deeper knowledge of man, its ideal—contributions toward a better world for all men.

Marshall Hyatt   (essay date 1990)

SOURCE: *Franz Boas, Social Activist: The Dynamics of Ethnicity*, pp. ix-xii Greenwood Press, 1990.

[*In the following excerpt, Hyatt applauds Boas's efforts to effect social change.*]

The life and thought of Franz Boas has had a profound impact on many diverse elements of American society. In a sense this German-born anthropologist can be viewed as a symbol of the age in which the United States responded to its rapid modernization at the onset of the twentieth century. Finding himself caught up in the whirlwind that resulted from such wholesale disequilibrium, Boas did his part to ease the national process of readaptation. During his long career in the United States, he responded not only to the shifting nature of American values but also to two world wars fought against his land of birth and a massive economic depression. Far from confining himself solely to science, he tackled problems fundamental to his new society. He fused science with political and social activism to ensure that his ideological contributions to anthropological thought also had practical relevance to issues facing the world.

In the second half of the nineteenth century, the nation experienced a major transformation of values, aims and perceptions. After emerging from a bloody civil war, which altered America's agrarian face irrevocably, the country encountered traumatic dislocations. In what has been variously termed "a response to industrialism" or "a search for order," Americans grappled with the assorted dilemmas caused by frenzied industrialization, mass immigration from Europe and chaotic urbanization. In reacting to these new forces, the Progressive movement collectively hoped to bring order out of the chaos on all fronts by addressing the ramifications of such intense change.

Although Boas himself did not arrive in the United States until the late 1880s, he soon became enmeshed in many of the problems that faced the general society. His reaction to the vast transformation of the country's political, social and intellectual landscape had significant influence on that very metamorphosis. Addressing a variety of concerns during the course of his career, Boas attempted to help solve some of the weighty dilemmas facing the nation as it sought to adjust to the forces that had caused that full-scale deracination.

As an intellectual, Boas attacked the misusers of science who promulgated theories of racial inferiority based on alleged mental differences between ethnic groups. As a scientist, he directed the professionalization of the field of anthropology, overseeing its evolution from an amateur hobby to its maturity as a rigorous academic discipline. As a social activist, he strove to eradicate prejudice and bigotry from American society, in an effort to ensure that the promise of American democracy was articulated in reality and practice.

The motivation behind Boas's actions and ideology was not monocausal. Certainly his devotion to a liberal creed significantly influenced his weltanschauung. Raised in a progressive German household that supported the revolution of 1848, Boas adopted political views similar to those of his parents. His education reinforced those sentiments. Accordingly, this liberalism lay at the root of his activity.

Combined with this, and every bit as influential, was his commitment to scientific accuracy and purity. This persistent dedication figured importantly in Boas's research and publication, and also accounted for his desire to rid anthropology of amateur control. It was this attribute that led inevitably to the personal battles Boas frequently fought with other individuals who did not share his passion.

The third major factor that determined his course was more defensive and personal in nature. It placed Boas in the position of reacting to insult and forced him into frequent confrontation. From early on in his university days in Germany, and throughout his life, Boas experienced anti-Semitism firsthand. These incidents left a lasting impression and molded his behavior and consciousness. The way in which these feelings were intertwined with both his liberal bent and scientific orthodoxy is a revealing aspect of the story of his life, because it accounts for many of his actions and beliefs.

It is imperative to understand Boas's life experiences in order to analyze his intellectual contributions. He merged science with politics because his upbringing was consistent with such a path. Moreover, his early years were most relevant in forming his philosophy; they help explain both the direction in which he embarked and his orientation as a thinker.

Boas left an indelible mark on anthropology. His work was not confined to one branch of the discipline; his research, thought, and teaching penetrated all facets of the field, including linguistics, archaeology and physical and cultural anthropology. In each component he infused scientific rigor, intent on questioning existing hypotheses. Among his numerous major contributions were challenges to evolutionary theory and arguments about race, mental ability and hierarchical ranking; major linguistic studies concerning the nexus between race, language and culture; insight into mental-cognitive paradigms; and explication of the plasticity of the human form and the primacy of environment in shaping both physique and mental behavior.

In constructing this thought, Boas overturned many of the existing theories under which amateur anthropologists had labored. As a result, he successfully reoriented the field itself along more precise methodological lines. He was, perhaps, the last major figure who cast so large a shadow on the discipline as a whole. Boas's impact so enhanced and expanded the field that specialization became the norm rather than the exception. Following him, anthropologists, including many of his own students, found sufficient scope to work within the subdivisions of the discipline.

The symbolic quality of Boas's life is an equally important facet of his legacy. Beyond his personal response to America's industrialization, he met head-on the various dilemmas of twentieth-century United States history. His pacifist sentiments during World War I embroiled him in controversy. His experiences during the war years brought into sharp relief the issue of personal liberty versus patriotism and underscored the hysteria extant in America during those turbulent times.

In a marked transition, the second world war offered Boas the opportunity to show his allegiance to the United States. Although arguing for American neutrality once again, his forceful, outspoken condemnation of Hitler led inevitably to support for the Allied effort against the forces of Fascism. Boas had understood sooner and more precisely than most American intellectuals how World War II would illuminate the paradoxical aspects of American racial attitudes. Although the United States commenced its assault against Nazi race theory by late 1941, the contradictory condoning of racism at home continued to detract from America's professed democratic ideals. Squaring the nation's attack on racism abroad with its maintenance at home remained a task for postwar activists.

That Boas recognized this discrepancy so early points to another crucial aspect of his legacy. His role in forging a new consensus on race theory and his efforts to eradicate bigotry characterized his entire adult life. His thought in this area had substantial impact on the Afro-American civil rights movements, particularly during the depression decade, when a heightened concern for racial equality compelled various groups and individuals to challenge segregation and racism. The forceful restatement of his many pronouncements on the equipotential of the races and his condemnation of pseudoscientists who honed their craft in the service of continuing the myth of racial inferiority paved the way for change.

In combination with the interracialism espoused by the National Association for the Advancement of Colored People (NAACP), the Communist Party of the United States (CPUSA), and organized labor, and with W. E. B. Du Bois's articulation of the need for black economic self-determination and his concern for the masses, Boas's argument helped bring a multidirectional civil rights movement to national attention. His forceful and repetitive attacks on racial injustice led inevitably to more research, and to the gradual invalidation over time of the racists' claim to scientific legitimacy. Once science had abandoned bigotry, the struggle for equality began to chip away at the legal and political hegemony of Jim Crow society. Boas's legacy in this regard was significant and enduring.

Racism, of course, outlived Boas. What he left to America were the intellectual weapons to combat it and recognition of the urgency of the task. What he left to anthropology was a cadre of well-trained scientists who collectively continued his approach. Not only did they argue against prejudice and any misuse of science as its justification, they also conducted individual research into various cultures, languages, customs and beliefs. Taken as a whole, their studies informed Americans about the way in which different societies contributed to civilization's advance, thus reinforcing Boas's belief in cultural relativism.

Certainly not all of Boas's students appreciated his domineering, professional style or his paternalistic concern for them. Many chafed under his tutelage, frustrated by his demands that they master all facets of their discipline. Nevertheless, out of Boas's classroom marched many of the new generation of professional American anthropologists. As they themselves rose to prominence in the academy, they carried forward Boas's desire to make anthropology useful in the service of society. Ruth Benedict, Ruth Bunzel, Melville Herskovits, Zora Neale Hurston, Alfred Kroeber, Robert Lowie, Margaret Mead, Edward Sapir, Leslie Spier and John Swanton were among those fortunate to work under Boas. Their combined efforts are yet another part of Boas's legacy.

Boas the scientist and Boas the social activist were dynamically intertwined. The story of his life explains why he fashioned his ideology, while conversely his thought and activity illustrate much about his own background. . . . An assessment of his thoughts, actions and their motivations; his scientific acumen and academic discipline; and his concern for human freedom, provides a microcosmic view of twentieth-century American society and its history through the medium of one intellectual's voice in that process.

Arnold Krupat   (essay date 1990)

SOURCE: "Irony in Anthropology: The Work of Franz Boas," in *Modernist Anthropology: From Fieldwork to Text,* edited by Marc Manganaro, Princeton University Press, 1990, pp. 133-45.

Boas near the end of his life.

[*Krupat is an American critic and scholar who has written extensively on Native American cultures. In the following excerpt, he discusses elements of modernism in Boas's thought, noting the varieties and degrees of irony present in his writings.*]

Born in Minden, Westphalia, in 1858, Franz Boas was clearly an extraordinary figure, not only a teacher, but a maître in the grand sense, whose students often became disciples, and, in several cases (Kroeber, Mead, Sapir, Benedict, Radin), virtual masters themselves. Boas published extensively on linguistics, on folklore, art, race, and, of course, ethnography, a fabled "five foot shelf," of materials on the Kwakiutl. Yet Boas did not, like his contemporaries Sigmund Freud and Ferdinand de Saussure, found what Foucault refers to as a field of discursivity, a written discourse that gives rise to the endless possibility of further discourse, or a discipline, like psychoanalysis or structural linguistics. The exact nature of Boas's achievement yet remains to be specified.

In 1888, Boas went to Clark University where he taught anthropology until 1892. He held positions with the World's Columbian exposition in Chicago and at the American Museum of Natural History in New York be-

fore moving, in 1896, to Columbia University as a lecturer in physical anthropology. He received promotion to a professorship in 1899, a position that he held until his retirement in 1936. Boas died—in the arms of Lévi-Strauss—in 1942. From his academic base at Columbia, Boas's influence was enormous. By 1926, for example, as George Stocking has noted, every academic department of anthropology in the United States was headed by one of Boas's students. That the Winnebago were studied by Paul Radin or the Pawnee much later by Gene Weltfish, that Edward Sapir, and, after, Melville Jacobs gathered Native texts is largely due to Boas.

Both Boas's admirers—who are many—and his detractors—who have been fewer—have agreed only on the issue central to their disagreement, the question of Boas's contribution to a science of culture. No one can doubt that Boas did much of worth. But can what he did properly be summed up as serving to found anthropology as a scientific discipline—moving it, as it were, from impressionism to realism, as Alfred Kroeber, Margaret Mead, Ruth Bunzel, and others have insisted? Or is it, rather, as Leslie White and Marvin Harris foremost have claimed, that Boas's practice was, finally, no more "scientific" or "realistic" than that of his predecessors, the accidental "men on the spot," and the so-called "armchair anthropologists," no more "scientific" than his contemporaries, the "museum men," and the fieldworkers of the government bureaus. Moreover, to consider Boas in the context of this volume requires as well that we interrogate his relationship to that curious cultural development broadly called "modernism," as it may or may not be consistent with that "realism" generally taken as consistent with claims to scienticity.

I read Boas, as I do literary modernists, against the backdrop provided by what has been called the epistemological crisis of the later nineteenth century, the shift away from apparently absolute certainties—in religion, linguistics, mathematics, physics, and so on—in the direction of relativity. "In the twenty years between 1895 and 1915 the whole picture of the physical universe, which had appeared not only the most impressive but also the most secure achievement of scientific thought," as Alan Bullock has observed, "was brought into question." To recall some well-known contextual markers, I note that these are the years of work in the direction of Gödel's proof that certain mathematical problems cannot be solved; of the Heisenberg Uncertainty Principle, and finally, of Einstein's relativity equations. These are the years when more than once Freud would speak of psychoanalysis as the third wound to human narcissism, for it demonstrates—after the Copernican and Darwinian wounds—that we are not only not the center of the universe nor descended from the angels, but equally, not masters of our own minds. No wonder that de Saussure could look back upon the nineteenth century's solid accumulation of philological data and conclude only that in language there are no positive quantities but simply differences. This is the period in which Thomas Hardy's sense of the haphazardness of fate would be most fully developed (the last novel dates from 1896, but what is ostensibly Hardy's masterwork, *The Dynasts* was issued from 1903 to 1908). It is the time when Nietzsche's scorn for the unfounded pretenses of religion, logic, or history is felt; the time of fictional experiments with point of view in Conrad, James, and Ford Madox Ford. Consider as a telling image Stephen Crane's "open boat," in his work by the same name (1898), bobbing precariously on an infinity of ocean, its weary passengers trying to survive and to be good, as all the past had told them to do, but as the present made most difficult.

Now, the anglophone writers named were almost surely not direct influences on Boas (if they were at all), as, indeed, Nietszche was probably not. Marvin Harris has traced the German writers, neo-Kantian for the most part, who were directly influential on Boas. *Mutatis mutandis,* it looks as though the epistemological and discursive climate in which Boas's work took shape was one with a strong sense of the relative rather than the absolute; of an absence of fixity, of all in flux; of certainty nowhere, uncertainty everywhere. What attitude other than one of skepticism could claim to be appropriate to such a worldview? Irony is the trope identified by the West for the expression of skepticism as a response to uncertainty, and one may imagine either that Boas (1) somehow founded a science entirely against the grain of the ironic temper of his time, (2) that he founded a science in the ironic mode, or (3) that

he operated according to an ironic paradigm of a sort that was inconsistent with the establishment of any kind of science whatsoever. These latter two possibilities (I reject the first of these as theoretically improbable and in practice untrue) are what I shall explore in the remainder of this paper.

I take irony to be the central trope of modernism. But just as modernism is no monolith—as Marc Manganaro properly notes . . . , there are "many Modernisms to consider"—neither is irony; there are many ironies to consider, as well. Among ironic figures, let me name four: *antiphrasis* or negation, *aporia* or doubt, *oxymoron* or paradox, and *catachresis* or misuse. The figure of aporia (it was not invented by Jacques Derrida, Paul de Man, or J. Hillis Miller, but was well known to classical and Renaissance rhetoricians) is, as I have said, the ironic figure of doubt; the aporitical text, then, is one filled with "doubts and objection." Antiphrasis is the ironic trope of negation, the central trope, for example, of satirical writing in which prior assertions are denied in the interest of promoting opposite or alternative assertions. The figure of the oxymoron presents apparently absurd or incongruous linkages, but oxymoronic figures may be distinguished from catachrestical figures in that the absurdity or incongruity of the oxymoron is only apparent, not real; however paradoxical the statement on the face of it may be, a fully coherent, rational point may be extracted—e. g., in such phrases as "coarse gentleman," or "noble savage." The figure of catachresis is one whose force is particularly difficult to convey. The *OED* defines it as "misuse with a sense of perversion." According to Henry Peacham in his 1593 *Garden of Eloquence,* "Catachresis in Latine is called Abusio," and Peacham gives as one of his examples of catachresis, the "water runnes," the abuse consisting in attributing animate capacity to something that does not have life. For us this figure seems, I believe, purely metaphorical, however. Curiously, the *OED* describes, but does not provide examples of catachresis. Would Milton's "blind mouths," or Dylan Thomas's "the long friends" resonate as indicating perverse or abusive misuse? Or perhaps we need turn to something from popular culture, a phrase such as "jumbo shrimp"—which to me has more catachrestical than oxymoronic force.

The first three of these figures, I suggest, are tropes for the sort of skepticism that founds the modernist work of writers such as Hardy and Crane, of the early Pound and Eliot, of Joyce at least through some of *Ulysses.* And these tropes may also found nonfictional writing of a sort that may generally be considered scientific. The fourth one of these figures I see as the central trope of modernist work of a more radical nature, work such as Nietszche's, perhaps of Henry Adams's *Education,* of Henry James's *The Sacred Fount,* probably of *Finnegans Wake,* and of Virginia Woolf's *The Waves.* The catachrestical text cannot be considered scientific according to any of the usual understandings of the term. Merely to note what I shall not have space to develop, it is catachrestical modernism that postmodernism may be taken to continue or extend, while it is aporitic (to choose one of the terms possible here to stand for all others) modernism that postmodernism rejects and rebels against, constituting itself by means of a break.

It is my contention that Boas's work is ironic through and through—but it remains unclear which type of irony, the doubtful, paradoxical, and negational, consistent with some sense of realism and of science, or the perverse-absurd, subversive of any sense of science, dominates in it. On the one hand, essay after essay may be cited as instantiating just the sort of hearty skepticism that clears the field for more securely founded hypotheses; on the other hand, the work as a whole either perversely insists upon conditions for scienticity that are in no way attainable, or asserts positions that so thoroughly contradict one another as abusively to cancel each other out, moving beyond the oxymoronic to the catachrestic, and thus subverting the conditions of possibility for any scientific hypotheses whatsoever.

The case for Boasian anthropology, as constituted by the kind of aporitic irony that founds what I will call a modernist realism consistent with science, might focus on the meaning and function of the new relativism in Boas's work. Unlike the nineteenth-century historians who, in Hayden White's account, saw the specter of relativism as serving to "undermine confidence in history's claim to 'objectivity,' 'scienticity,' and 'realism'," Boas and his students seemed to find the new relativity not the foreclosure but the promise of objectivity, scienticity, and realism. Relativism, for Boas, was understood primarily to mean cultural relativism, and a stance of cultural relativism (which was not taken as implying a general epistemological relativism) as enabling a satiric method by which to expose the abundant undocumented generalizations indulged in by practitioners of "the comparative method in anthropology." In page after page of his writing both early and late, Boas shows a real delight in his ability to expose or deconstruct, as we might now say, generalizations that could not stand up to his aggressive ironic skepticism. In its historical moment, this aspect of Boas's intervention most certainly seems to have advanced the project of a scientific anthropology.

But then there is the famous Boasian hostility to theory and to laws. And there are, indeed, many passages in Boas's writing where he warns against the dangers of interposing aprioristic theory between the putatively innocent eye of the observer and the facts or data in themselves (his view of these matters seems positivist in a rather demodé manner). Boas also seems to have given many of his students and readers a strong impression that he was implacably opposed not only to theory but to all statements of phenomenal lawfulness, that for him anthropology was the sort of inquiry that best limits its view to the singularity or particularity of cultural phenomena. Nonetheless, as I shall try to show in only a moment more, one can also cite essays in which Boas asserts the statement of general laws as indeed the ultimate aim of anthropology as of any science. Besides the issue of deep self-contradiction, there is the further issue that even in his remarks approving the possibility of scientific generalization, Boas insists again and again on impossible conditions for such generaliza-

tion, noting that laws will legitimately be discovered only when all the facts are in.

The trajectory of a scientific anthropology, then, was to be the collection of facts in the interest of the discovery of laws. Facts, for Boas, are not conceptual constructs or even choices on the part of the researcher, but simply out there. And laws, for Boas, in the generalization of his understanding of facts, do not either have to be formulated or constructed; rather, once all the facts are in, laws will simply announce or dis-cover themselves to the assiduous observer. Boas would not abandon the goal of stating laws because that would be to abandon the project of a scientific anthropology, but he also would not abandon his adherence to impossible conditions for the actual achievement of a scientific anthropology. Insofar as it is obvious that all the facts will never be in, it is not possible ever to satisfy Boas's ironic skepticism, not possible ever to achieve exactly the science he is after. Such a position, I suggest, is not aporitic, but is best figured by the trope of catachresis. But it is surely time for us to do some reading.

In an 1887 text called **"The Study of Geography,"** Boas distinguishes between sciences as they derive from one or the other of two apparently invariant tendencies in the mind—or at least the Western mind. The natural sciences, such as physics, Boas claims, spring from what he calls the "aesthetic impulse," while those such as "cosmography," or history, what we would term the social sciences, are the expression of what he calls the "affective impulse." The first, a sort of "rage for order," is concerned with stating the general laws governing the phenomena under consideration, while the second is more particularistically concerned with the individual phenomenon itself. For the cosmographer, the historian, or, as Boas spent most of his life insisting, the anthropologist, the "mere occurrence of an event claims the full attention of our mind, because we are affected by it, and it is studied without any regard to its place in a system." As opposed to the physicist, who seeks to generalize from "mere occurrences," the cosmographer, Boas writes, "holds to the phenomenon which is the object of his study . . . and lovingly tries to penetrate into its secrets until every feature is plain and clear. This occupation with the object of his affection affords him a delight not inferior to that which the physicist enjoys in his systematical arrangement of the world." It is hard to resist noticing the erotic dimension of Boas's description of the cosmographical romance. But can such a conception be compatible with an anthropological science? Boas characteristically answers yes—and no. "Physicists," he writes, "will acknowledge that the study of the history of many phenomena is a work of scientific value," and, near the end of his essay, Boas pronounces both cosmographical and physical inquiry to be—and it would seem equivalently— "two branches of science."

What Boas says here of history and cosmography he would say again and again of anthropology: that it was to study its object of affection "without any regard to its place in a system." But he would also say again and again that anthropology, in this regard now quite like physical science ("aesthetic" as distinguished from "affective" science), must indeed search out systematic laws. Only a year after the publication of **"The Study of Geography,"** in an 1888 text called **"The Aims of Ethnology,"** we find Boas writing that "the human mind develops everywhere according to the same laws," and that the "discovery of these [laws] is the greatest aim of our science." As I have noted, to the end of his life, **Boas** continued to insist upon the necessity of reducing the multitudinous phenomenal data of culture to some kind of lawfulness—of finding its "place in a system"—while appending the condition that more and ever more data would first have to be examined before the formulation of explanatory generalizations might legitimately begin. Anthropology must ultimately discover some kind of laws, just as any proper science must, but such laws cannot be discovered until all the evidence is in. Since all the evidence will never be in, the anthropologist, now a kind of "connoisseur of chaos," had best stick to particularities and defer concern for pattern or general lawfulness—although the discovery of laws is, indeed, the goal of ethnology. It is a simple matter to quote Boas on both sides of what seem to me antithetical and—in the form in which they are stated—irreconcilable positions. But further quotation would not be especially helpful, nor, indeed, is it necessary, once we note that Boas himself chose just these two essays—**"The Aims of Ethnology"** and **"The Study of Geography"**—with their conflicting positions, to conclude the last major book of his lifetime, *Race, Language, and Culture* published in 1940.

Writing when he was more than eighty years old, Boas announces that these two papers, composed some fifty years earlier, were chosen to conclude his book "because they indicate the general attitude underlying [his] later work." Boas's attitude is such as to offer firm support for both sides of a great many questions, and such an attitude goes beyond the aporitic ironic skepticism compatible with science to the catachrestical irony that would subvert any pretense to science.

Now, *Race, Language, and Culture* is a volume of six hundred forty-seven pages, comprising sixty-three essays written over a period of forty-nine years. It is a wartime book, and Boas's Preface states his intention that the essays to come may show anthropology's bearing "upon problems that confront us." A section called "Race," consisting of twenty essays, is the first in the book; "Language," with five, is the second; the third section, "Culture," the category of Boas's most substantial contribution, has thirty-five essays.

One might well expect that Boas chose these divisions, representing the three main areas of his work over a long lifetime, and arranged the essays in them in some kind of ascending or progressive order; one might expect, that is, that this large book is organized in such a way as to permit some sort of climatic or at least clear statement of his position. But any such expectation is undercut by the presence of a fourth section, one that, in its structural and thematic effect, is decidedly anticlimactic. For Boas does not end this book, called *Race, Language and Culture,* with the section on "Culture" (or, for that matter, with an Afterword or Conclusion), but instead follows it with something called simply, "Miscellaneous." And it is in "Miscellaneous," that Boas places the texts indicative, as he states

in his Preface, of his final position on matters central to his understanding of anthropology. The texts in this final section are not recent work but three nineteenth-century essays that work backward, from 1898 with **"Advances in Methods of Teaching,"** to 1888 and **"The Aims of Ethnology"** (in which there was a call for the discovery of laws), to **"The Study of Geography"** of 1887 (a piece that announced that the discovery of laws was not the aim of social science at all).

To conclude his final book this way is to reveal a deeply ironic sense of structure (*which* irony, again, remains to be seen). For what is true of irony thematically, as an "attitude," is true of irony structurally, as a form, as well: ironic structures achieve their effects by frustrating traditional expectations for climax and closure. Ironic texts may seem to work according to the familiar Western patterns of tragedy, comedy, and romance, but in the end they always subvert them. Rather than the revelation and resignation of tragedy, the reconciliation and reintegration of comedy, or the idealistic transcendence of romance, the ironic ending suggests that things just happen as they happen, to no special point, or at least to no clear one. Think of a play such as Samuel Beckett's *Waiting for Godot,* with its last lines, "Well? Shall we go?" "Yes, let's go," and its final stage direction, "They don't move." Nothing moves for the ironist; *plus ça change, plus c'est la même chose.* Even more radically, moving again from aporitic to catachrestic irony, there is the suggestion that the very idea of an ending is an absurdity or paradox; no text can ever *end.* Think of Kafka's *Castle,* or of *Finnegans Wake,* whose final words lead back to its first words. Does the *apparently* contradictory juxtaposition of **"The Aims . . ."** and **"The Study . . ."** really have its oxymoronic point? Or is it Boas's ultimate instantiation of perverse misuse, *abusio* having the last word?

For all of this, the scientist reader, if not so hotly the literary reader, may well be asking what, after all, do the essays themselves have to *say*? Speaking from outside the disciplinary borders of anthropology, I would repeat that the essays on race seem ironic only so far as they are skeptical of entirely undocumented, unscientific, and self-serving statements about race. Throughout his long career, Boas insisted on the cultural explanation of cultural differences and profoundly intervened against German racist theories directed against Jews and American racist theories directed against blacks, and these essays lend themselves more readily than usual in his work to focused use and development.

I am not sure what to make of the few (five) essays on language, although it seems difficult to read them without the double sense of, first, Boas's clear insistence on the importance for the ethnographer of learning native languages, and, second, of the uncertainty surrounding his own knowledge of Kwa'kwala, the language of the Kwakiutl: of Helen Codere's statements, for example, that Kwakiutl people she interviewed in 1951 remembered Boas speaking their language, and Ronald Rohner's conclusion in 1969 that Boas had learned Chinook jargon but not Kwa'kwala, nor any other "indigenous Northwest Coast language."

The many essays on culture divide into more nearly general, theoretical pieces and specific ethnographic pieces. I will look briefly at the major theoretical piece shortly. As for the ethnographic work, it seems mostly an immense, even celebratory record of randomness: Boas was there when he was there, he saw what he saw, he left us whatever he happened to leave us. Even Helen Codere, for all her enormous respect for Boas, acknowledged that "it is not possible to present a synthesized account of Kwakiutl culture based upon Boas' works." Whether Boas purposely worked in such a way as to forestall what he would have considered an inevitably *premature* synthesis, or, rather, worked in such a way as to obstruct any synthesis whatsoever remains, I believe, undecidable.

Ronald Rohner, who found his own attempt to work in the field with Boas's Kwakiutl materials beset with difficulties, has noted that even when Boas was aware that some of his texts and ethnographic "materials over time contain[ed] many inaccuracies and inconsistencies . . . he never corrected them in print," an observation that reaffirms Alfred Kroeber's statement that Boas knew he was wrong in his account of how the Kwakiutl potlatch functioned "but that he never took the time to re-explain the system." Here, too, it might be that he just "never took the time"; but it also might be that this lack of concern to reconcile conflicting views was a consequence of a radically ironic, catachrestical commitment to sustaining contradiction.

I turn now to the essay Boas placed first in the section on culture, his 1932 presidential address to the American Association for the Advancement of Science, called **"The Aims of Anthropological Research."** Both the occasion of its original delivery and its placement in this book are such as to suggest that it may fairly be taken as representative of Boas's mature thought. What we find all through this text is irony's ability to doubt and deny; the question for science is whether the doubt and denial are, once again, in the interest of alternative affirmations or go so far as to deny affirmative statements of any kind.

Boas begins with a sketch of anthropology's beginnings from a variety of sources; next, he defines "our objective as the attempt to understand the steps by which man has come to be what he is, biologically, psychologically and culturally." It appears, Boas says, that "our material must necessarily be historical material, historical in the widest sense of the term." Having announced the need for historical data, however, Boas then goes on to show how unlikely it is that sufficient data will ever be forthcoming, and then lists the errors and dangers of a variety of positions. He next passes from considerations of race and psychology to those of "cultural anthropology." I will catalog some of his negational figures, without, to be sure, providing sufficient context to understand each of his remarks in itself. My claim is that the sheer number of these figures does the work of establishing Boas's commitment to ironic skepticism. Boas writes: "The material needed for the reconstruction of the biological history of mankind is insufficient on account of the paucity of remains . . ."; "Even this information is insufficient . . ."; "For these reasons it is well nigh impossible . . ."; "This method cannot be generalized . . ."; "It may be admitted that it is exceedingly

difficult to give absolutely indisputable proof . . ."; it "hardly admits of the argument that . . ."; "this view is not admissible without proof that . . ."; "It is not a safe method to assume that . . ."; "Even the fullest knowledge of the history of language does not help us to understand . . ."; "The phenomena of our science are so individualized, so exposed to outer accident that no set of laws could explain them . . .": and so on.

For all that aporia and antiphrasis structure Boas's text, still, the doubts and negations may yet imply some positive recommendations. Nonetheless, even if this first essay on culture is useful for the project of an anthropological science, *Race, Language, and Culture* will still present us, as its conclusion, the "miscellaneously" juxtaposed, contradictory final essays of the book.

And it does indeed seem to me that Boas's writing, taken as a whole, has a kind of abusive perversity that, as with Nietzsche, undermines the foundations for any claims to scienticity. At the furthest horizon, I believe Boas saw and perhaps rather anxiously was fascinated by cultural and epistemological chaos—that he temperamentally enjoyed an old-fashioned variant of postmodernist free play. If I am at all correct, he partook, therefore, of a kind of abysmal ironic vision, which I have tried to link to the figure of catachresis. In this regard, to the extent that he may have become "unreadable" in the present moment, Boas might be recuperated as a sort of precursor of postmodernism. But if I seem here to have conducted Boas to exactly the place Marilyn Strathern brought Frazer, yet I would want to warn even more strongly than she against any attempt actually to reread Boas as postmodernist. No one coming from (say) Stephen Tyler's work will very long be happy with Frazer *or* Boas as a postmodernist *writer.*

Short of the furthest horizon, however, I think Boas was regularly fascinated by the study of phenomena that he probably felt to be more orderly (whatever their order) than chaotic, phenomena that, looked at particularly and carefully, at least were probably coherent in themselves. This sense of cultural things was tropologically figured in varieties of what I have called aporitic irony, the central trope, to repeat, of a sort of realist/scientist modernism: distanced and distancing, skeptical, tough-minded, sensitive to paradox, self-conscious, and so on.

Like a number of writers of the modernist period—and I think this is particularly true of writers of the modernist period and not just of writers in general—Boas's work is difficult to characterize as a whole, the whole not at all comprehensible as the strict sum of its parts. In somewhat similar fashion, the Eliot of the "Preludes" or "Prufrock" is not consistent with the Eliot of the "Four Quartets," or, to cite an author not much considered . . . as a modernist, the D. H. Lawrence of *The Rainbow* is not fully consistent with the D. H. Lawrence of *Aaron's Rod, The Plumed Serpent,* or even the *Studies in Classic American Literature.* The same, as I have noted, is true of Henry James, whose *Sacred Fount* of 1901 cannot be understood as simply the "mature" work of the author of the *Portrait of a Lady* (1881). In all these authors, as in Boas, any estimate of the whole could not be arrived at simply by adding up the parts.

Yet, I will say that, for all the deep contradictions of his work, Boas today, in our moment as indeed in his own, is much more useful for the residual (in Raymond Williams's sense) project of a scientific anthropology (however modest and circumscribed current claims for scienticity must be) than for either Geertzian semiotic anthropologies or Tylerian postmodern anthropologies. I, at any rate, would like to see him recuperated for such a project, for all that we must allow to his work its catachrestical component.

FURTHER READING

Biography

Herskovits, Melville J. *Franz Boas: The Science of Man in the Making.* New York: Charles Scribner's Sons, 1953, 131 p.
> Appreciative biography.

Hyatt, Marshall. *Franz Boas: Social Activist.* New York: Greenwood Press, 1990, 174 p.
> Critical biography that traces the development of Boas's thought.

Criticism

Beardsley, Edward H. "The American Scientist as Social Activist." *ISIS* 64, No. 221 (March 1973): 50-66.
> Examines Boas's role in furthering racial justice in the United States.

Goldschmidt, Walter. *The Anthropology of Franz Boas: Essays on the Centennial of His Birth.* Washington, D.C.: American Anthropological Society, 1959, 165 p.
> Collection of essays discussing various aspects of Boas's career and legacy.

Hatch, Elvin. "The Rise of the Anti-Intellectual: E. B. Tylor and Franz Boas." In his *Theories of Man and Culture*, pp. 13-73. New York: Columbia University Press, 1973.
> Discusses Boas as a "representative of anti-intellectualism and of the modern view of behavior."

Helm, June, ed. *Pioneers of American Anthropology: The Uses of Biography.* Seattle: University of Washington Press, 1966, 247 p.
> Contains three essays on Boas: "Glimpses of a Friendship: Zelia Nuttall and Franz Boas," by Ross Parmenter; "Franz Boas: Ethnographer on the Northwest Coast," by Ronald P. Rohner; and "Franz Boas among the Kwakiutl," an interview with the daughter of one of Boas's colleagues.

Hinsley, Curtis M., Jr., and Holm, Bill. "A Cannibal in the National Museum: The Early Career of Franz Boas in America." *American Anthropologist* 78, No. 2 (June 1976): 306-16.
> Discusses Boas's experiences as a young immigrant struggling to establish himself in his profession.

Kroeber, A. L. "The Place of Boas in Anthropology." *American Anthropologist* 58, No. 1 (February 1956): 151-59.
> Responds to criticism of Boas's fieldwork and theories, noting that while Boas did not develop a unified theory of culture, he nevertheless contributed much pertinent discussion and data to the field of anthropology.

Sampson, Geoffrey. "The Descriptivists." In his *Schools of Linguistics: Competition and Evolution*, pp. 57-80. London: Hutchison, 1980.
> Discusses Boas as the founder of a school of linguists Sampson terms the "Descriptivists." Sampson explains: "The descriptivists tended to think of abstract linguistic theorizing as a means to the end of successful practical description of languages, rather than . . . thinking of individual languages as sources of data for the construction of a general theory of language."

Speth, William W. "The Anthropogeographic Theory of Franz Boas." *Anthropos* 73, Nos. 1-2 (1978): 1-31.
> Detailed analysis of the development and content of Boas's theories concerning the role of environment in human cultures.

Spier, Leslie. "Franz Boas and Some of His Views." *Acta Americana* 1 (1943): 108-27.
> Summarizes Boas's contributions to the development of modern anthropology.

Stocking, George W., Jr. "Franz Boas and the Culture Concept in Historical Perspective." *American Anthropologist* 68 (1966): 867-82.
> Examines the scientific and philosophical presumptions inherent in Boas's concept of culture.

Der Nister

1884-1950

(Pseudonym of Pinkhes Kahanovitsh; also transliterated as Pinchas Kahanovitch) Ukrainian novelist, short story writer, and essayist.

INTRODUCTION

Der Nister is considered by many critics to be one of the most accomplished Yiddish writers of his time. Noted for a distinctive style that incorporates elements of Jewish mysticism, Russian Symbolism, folklore, and mythology, his novels and stories opposed the strict realism once demanded of Soviet writers by the communist regime. Der Nister's best known work is *Di mishpokhe Mashber* (vol. 1, 1939; vol. 2, 1947; *The Family Mashber*), an epic saga of two Jewish brothers set in the Ukraine during the late nineteenth century.

Biographical Information

Born in Berditshev, Ukraine, Der Nister was influenced early in his life by Rabbi Nachman Bratslaver, a man known to his contemporaries as a gifted storyteller in the Hasidic tradition. Der Nister's older brother was a follower of Bratslaver, and from early childhood to adulthood Der Nister was exposed to Hebrew studies and literature. The name Der Nister, which, translated from the Hebrew, means "the hidden one," or "the concealer," was adopted by the author to avoid being drafted into the Russian army. In 1908 Der Nister left Berditshev and settled in Kiev. Following the overthrow of the czarist government during the Russian revolution, only Der Nister and a few other Yiddish writers continued to compose works that were not politically oriented, and to escape the ensuing isolation Der Nister left Kiev for Berlin, where he was free to publish his stories without censure. Der Nister returned to the Soviet Union in 1926 and settled in Kharkov. During World War II he wrote about the horrors occurring in Nazi-occupied Poland, and in 1947 he was sent to report on life in Birobidjan, a region designated by the Soviet government as an autonomous Jewish settlement. In 1949 Der Nister was arrested by Soviet forces following an order calling for the extermination of Yiddish writers during the suppression of Jewish culture that began in the Soviet Union in 1948. Der Nister died in a Soviet prison hospital in 1950.

Major Works

Der Nister's works treat such themes as the individual's moral choice between good and evil, idealism versus realism, and the nature of human emotion. His earliest works, such as *Gedanken un motiven* (1907), *Hekher fun der erd* (1910), and *Gezang un gebet* (1912), express reverence and sympathy for followers of the Hasidic way of life. Der Nister's short story "Unter a ployt" (1929; "Under a Fence") was fiercely condemned by Soviet critics who found Der Nister's departure from the prescribed realistic formula reactionary and subversive. To preserve his artistic conscience as well as his status as a Soviet writer, Der Nister devised an approach to his writing that appeared to follow the principles of realism, but incorporated his own distinctive brand of symbolic expression and endorsement of the Jewish community. In *Di mishpokhe Mashber*, Der Nister demonstrated this approach to writing by providing a realistic treatment of Jewish life, but setting his narrative in the city of Berditshev during the 1870s, a milieu that had ceased to exist. The first volume of *Di mishpokhe Mashber* delineates the experiences of Moshe and Luzi Mashber, and Luzi's friend Sruli Gol, a somewhat unorthodox Hasid. Moshe is a wealthy and arrogant merchant, while Luzi and Sruli are self-abasing, non-materialistic, and devoutly religious. When Moshe refuses to help the ailing mother of one of his clerks, Luzi and Sruli object, and Moshe throws them out of his home. Following this incident, Moshe must declare bankruptcy and is imprisoned for failing to pay his debts. While Moshe is in prison, his daughter dies and his wife becomes paralyzed, and shortly after his release from prison both Moshe and his wife die. In volume two, Sruli rescues Luzi from exile after the city leaders express disapproval of Luzi's associations with the poor and his utter lack of regard for social status.

Critical Reception

Critics have praised Der Nister's ability to encompass both fabulous, mystical circumstances and vivid, lifelike characters in his works. Commenting on *Di mishpokhe Mashber*, Charles A. Madison has asserted: "[Der Nister's] canvas is broad, rich, colorful. The major characters are portrayed with striking suggestiveness and sympathetic understanding; life spurts from them even though they become overshadowed by the veil of mysticism." Der Nister's lengthy and often deliberately cryptic sentences have been considered representative of Hasidic narratives, and many critics have noted that his blending of these literary styles with mythological and realistic elements is unique. Sol Liptzin has stated: "[Der Nister] was expected to revile a people and a tradition which he loved so fervently in his heart of hearts and he had no way of knowing whether this love . . . would ever penetrate to readers in later years or be intelligible to them. In the morass in which he was forced to move in his last years, he remained a hidden saint, the noblest personality among the Soviet Yiddish writers."

PRINCIPAL WORKS

Gedanken un motiven   (prose poems)   1907
Hekher fun der erd   (short stories)   1910
Gezang un gebet   (short stories)   1912
Mayselakh in ferzn   (short stories)   1919
Gedakht 2 vols.   (short stories)   1922-23
Geyendik   (short stories)   1923
Fun meine giter   (short stories)   1929
Tseykhenungen   (essays)   1931
Hoyptshtet   (short stories)   1934
Di mishpokhe Mashber 2 vols.   (novel)   1939-1947
    [*The Family Mashber*, 1987]
Der zeide mitn einikl   (short stories)   1943
Heshl Ansheles   (short stories)   1943
Korbones   (short stories)   1943

CRITICISM

Khone H. Shmeruk   (essay date 1965)

SOURCE: "Der Nister's 'Under a Fence': Tribulations of a Soviet Yiddish Symbolist," in *The Field of Yiddish: Studies in Language, Folklore, and Literature,* edited by Uriel Weinreich, Mouton & Co., 1965, pp. 263-87.

[*In the following essay, Shmeruk examines "Under a Fence" in light of the restrictions placed upon Yiddish writers by the Soviet government in the 1920s.*]

Literary analysis of works produced under a totalitarian regime must depend, even more than any other critical enterprise, on reading between the lines. For the historian, the very existence of "lines" written in Yiddish, like the mere fact of social organization on a Jewish basis, signify—in the light of the grudging toleration of Jewish group aspirations by the Soviet regime—an assertion of Jewish identity and loyalty comparable to more explicit and ambitious manifestations of Jewish nationhood under freer regimes. When a work has literary merit in addition—and a great deal of meritorious prose and poetry was produced by Yiddish writers in the Soviet Union until the liquidation of Yiddish literature in 1949—the interplay of intrinsic literary factors with external political considerations raises fascinating problems familiar to students of Soviet literature in all languages. In the tribulations of **"Unter a ployt"** ("Under a Fence"), a story by a master of the caliber of Der Nister, we can see reflected the struggle of a great literary artist with the solidifying political system in the 1920's, a period which from the vantage of the 1960's is not without its idyllic aspects.

In 1929, there appeared in Kiev a collection of Der Nister's stories under the title *Gedakht* (roughly, 'In Mind'). The book contained some of the author's tales and "visions" which had previously been collected in a two-volume edition published, under the same title, in Berlin in 1922-1923. Like the Berlin collection, the Kiev volume begins with **"A mayse mit a nozir un mit a tsigele"** ("A Tale of a Hermit and a Goat"), in which Der Nister, after

initial gropings, found his particular stylistic manner. In this story, the hermit sets out in search of the Seed of Truth, which he finds after overcoming many obstacles and temptations. The fantastic events, grotesquely recounted in a fairytale-like frame, end on an optimistic note. The Berlin edition of *Gedakht* ends with **"A bobe-mayse oder di mayse mit di melokhim"** ("An Old Wives' Tale, or the Story of the Kings"), which also closes on the happy note traditional in folktales, as the hero weds his intended. The Kiev collection, on the other hand, concludes with a new story, **"Unter a ployt"** ("Under a Fence"), subtitled "Revyu" ('Revue'), which had appeared shortly before in *Di royte velt* (Kharkov, 1929, no. 7). Here, too, is the story of a hermit, but this time he is put on trial and is convicted for having betrayed the principles of hermithood. While the conviction is depicted as just, the visionary sequence of confessions in **"Unter a ployt"** bears a distinctly pessimistic character. Thus the Kiev *Gedakht* collection, although it presumes to be a representative, retrospective summing-up of the writer's output up to 1929, also clearly expresses a certain direction in development of Der Nister's world view.

The summing-up of 1929 acquires special meaning and value if we consider the fact that **"Unter a ployt"** marks the end of a period in Der Nister's writing, one which we might concisely label as the visionary, fairytale-like phase. Until 1929 Der Nister's individual path in Yiddish literature was apparent in his special stylistic manner, in the artistic devices and the choice of themes expressed in a unique narrative form. For almost two years after the appearance of the Kiev volume, Der Nister kept his silence. It was not until 1931 that he reappeared in print with *Tseykhenungen (Drawings)*. This title corresponds to the Russian *očerki*, a genre of timely "feature"-type reportage which underwent lively discussion in the Soviet Union in the twenties and which later became well established in Soviet literature of all languages. Two groups of writers turned to the *očerk:* fledgling worker and peasant correspondents used it for their first steps in literature, while more mature writers, who under Soviet conditions had to renounce their previous non-"proletarian" artistic accomplishments and ideological inconsistencies, employed the *očerk* in an attempt to justify their existence in literature. The latter group included, among others, the Russian symbolist Andrej Belyj and the Yiddish symbolist, Der Nister. Despite a series of characteristic "relapses and deviations" in his *Drawings,* it is apparent that Der Nister's turn to a completely unfamiliar genre, after two years of silence, constituted an abrupt turning point in his writing. We hope to show in the present study that **"Under a Fence"**, dating from 1929, already anticipated this turn and revealed the most intimate sufferings which its author was going through.

Der Nister's work of any period has not yet had the privilege of being subjected to detailed analysis and evaluation by Yiddish literary criticism. Hardly a beginning has been made in the interpretation of his tales and visions of the pre-Soviet period or of his "Drawings." The complex problems connected with Der Nister's place in Yiddish literature have been disposed of with generalities that do little to help us understand his manner and the complicated formal and content structure of his work. It is all the more curious, therefore, that it was precisely **"Under a Fence"** that evoked a sharp discussion among Soviet Yiddish critics.

[In 1929, the] editors of *Di royte velt* announced the forthcoming publication of Der Nister's story in a preceding issue (no. 5-6) and gave it the following introduction:

> Der Nister is one of our most original artists; although, because of his themes and the manner of his writings, he requires interpretation, and is accessible only to selected individuals, he is unfailingly interesting. His new work, **"Under a Fence,"** is marked by all the features of Der Nister's work. It is a ring of allegoric and symbolic tales, mutually intertwined, expressed in a rich, rhythmic language. According to the problem which it treats, it is a kind of confession, a renunciation of the idealistic view of the world, and it marks a certain break in Der Nister's writing. The matter invites reflection and profound consideration. This may be the beginning of a search by Der Nister of a new path that would link him with reality and give him access to broader circles. [—Shakhne Epshteyn]

The publication of the story subjected the editors of the journal to vigorous attack. *Di royte velt* was a fellow-travelling journal, officially unconnected with the Jewish Section of the Organization of Proletarian Writers in the Ukraine. But in printing **"Under a Fence,"** the editors had gone too far, even for a forum of this type. Their compliments for Der Nister, although coupled with a forecast of a "new path" in his writing, evoked sharp protest. A. Vevyorke attacked not only Der Nister, but symbolism in general, as well as any other literature intended for select individuals. In the Kharkov daily *Der shtern,* there appeared an open letter from a "comrade in Odessa" inquiring why Der Nister was published at all.

The editors of the journal, forced to defend themselves, declared that "there had been times, and not so long ago, when such persons as are now disparaging Der Nister considered him one of the greatest phenomena in our modern literature." The tendency of the disputed story, they continued, was clear: "A renunciation of idealism and transition to materialism." Finally, the editors referred to the Party's policy toward fellow-travelling writers which justified the publication of Der Nister's work.

While this discussion was in progress, there appeared in Kiev the volume *Gedakht.* In an introduction, Y. Nusinov dwelt on the story in question. In this "edifying fable," he saw a reflection of the intellectual's fate. "All his life the intellectual boasted of his nationalism, his individualism, his search of God, his socialist-Menshevist revolutionary nature; in the light of the great revolutionary effort, this turned out to be historical mildew. Der Nister expresses the present mood of such a 'saint' of yesteryear in his most recent story, 'Under a Fence'."

As far as we have been able to ascertain, the controversy over the story was concluded with a clear judgement by Y. Bronshteyn: *" 'Under a Fence' is one of the most reactionary tales written by Der Nister. I declare this with full*

responsibility, even if this will cause me to be excluded from the circle of select individuals."

This discussion reveals quite vividly the situation of a writer like Der Nister at the end of the 1920's in the Soviet Union. It was the situation of a hunted man who had to "renounce" something and "make a transition" to something else if he intended to remain a writer. For someone who was considered an unreserved symbolist, there was no other way out whatever. But the discussion is also characterized by the diametrically opposed views which were voiced in it. Some saw in **"Under a Fence"** the desired break, while others found the same tale to be "the most reactionary" ever produced by this writer. While these opposite views may reflect a difference in the ideological and emotional attitudes to Der Nister's work, the great distance between them nevertheless remains a mystery, even if we take into account the fact that it is a symbolist work that is involved. None of the critics so much as tries to justify his opinion by a concrete analysis of the text. Is it indeed impossible to discover the meaning of Der Nister's **"Under a Fence"** from the tale itself ? Could it be that Der Nister himself intended a possibility of opposite conclusions?

The place of **"Under a Fence"** in the creative development of Der Nister makes it particularly important that a detailed analysis of the story be attempted. In a broader perspective, such an analysis can also help to throw light on a specific stage in the history of Soviet Yiddish literature.

> "My sorrow is deadly . . .
>
> "And only you, my daughter can feel and understand me." [**"Under a Fence"**]

Thus begins **"Under a Fence"**, a confession of a respected middle-aged scholar addressed to his own daughter. With profound regret, tinged with sarcasm, he tells her about his amorous failure with a circus equestrienne, Lili. The circus environment in which the scholar found himself "with a bouquet of last flowers from his garden" and "with whatever he had left of love" is described in detail. The equestrienne accepts his gifts, without, however, disguising her contempt for the strange suitor. During the scholar's visit in Lili's dressing room, a conflict develops with the circus athlete. The athlete ridicules the scholar and throws him out of the dressing room.

This episode, which does not occupy more than two pages out of forty, is depicted by fully "realistic" means and gives the impression of an "actual" occurrence.

After the scholar's departure from the circus "through labyrinthine-dark little corridors" there begins a kaleidoscopic vision of intoxication and dream, which again concludes with a "realistic" closing of the frame. The scholar awakens in dirt under a fence and "recalls" that "not far from the circus he had come upon a bar and probably drank and after drinking probably set out for home and did not reach it . . . fell asleep and dreamt the preceding." A policeman takes him home, where his daughter attends to the sick, humiliated father after his strange confession to her. Thus closes the frame which is supposed "realistically" to justify everything that will appear in the "revue."

The revue itself consists of dramatized, personified visions portraying the inner struggles and debates of the principal character with himself.

The device of a confession, or a revue, for presenting the inner contradictions and conflicts of a hero had been used by Der Nister before. We find it in earlier stories (for example, **"Muser"** and **"Gekept"**) and in his novel, *Di mishpokhe Mashber.* In **"Shiker"** (**"Drunk"**) the entire story is little but a conversation recounting events that had befallen a drunken man, his metamorphosis, and his double. In *Di mishpokhe Mashber,* Srole Gol is several times 'led into' intoxication, in order to have him disclose his inner turmoil in conversations with his bottle. Der Nister's method thus prepares the reader, by means of a "realistic" portrayal of a special physiological state of a character (drunkenness or sleep) for an internal, intimate debate of the character with himself. As a rule, the contradictory principles within a character are presented in personified form. This device is hardly new in literature. The figure of "double" which is never brought to the point of physical separation from the character, is represented as a real, live character. It is a temporary, pathological splitting of ego called into being by the liberated consciousness of the character while intoxicated or dreaming. Famous examples of this method appear in Dostoevski's *Brothers Karamazov* (in the chapter about Ivan's argument with the devil) and in Hermann Hesse's *Der Steppenwolf.*

Although in Der Nister's story, **"Under a Fence"**, the explicit reference to intoxication and dreaming does not come until the end, one can trace the succession of gradually increasing stages of intoxication, which frees the scholar's inhibition in increasing measure, until his imagination is liberated in a self-disparaging confession. The feeling of guilt, the driving force of the confession, seeks redemption in punitive visions. The three-stage process of guilt-confession-punishment which we find in **"Under a Fence"** was a favorite with the Nister:

1. In the frame of the revue, at the inception of inebriation, the motivation is provided by the guilt feelings which a father, turning to a strange woman, bears toward his daughter. This is the point of departure for the confession, which is resolved at the end of the frame and of the revue by the punishment of "actually" wallowing under a fence.

2. The scholar's guilt feelings are particularized further by a twofold self-revelation before one of his pupils. The vision of an accident involving the daughter and caused by the father is resolved in a vision of death by stoning. All of this takes place in a state of inebriation.

3. At a dream trial, the accused confesses to the court and is punished by burning.

As was said earlier, the revue begins after the scholar leaves the circus. The scenery (to use a term appropriate to the notion of revue) changes suddenly. The scholar, at home, is visited by a disciple. His appearance on the "stage" begins with a characteristic knock at the door and the exchange: "May I?" "Come in." This is also the way the scene in Lili's dressing-room had begun. The scholar is at this point in an initial stage of intoxication. He engages his pupil in a theoretical discussion about love, but

does not tell him of the incident with the equestrienne; the brakes of consciousness are still too powerful. However, this episode is, without doubt, already beyond the "realistic" tone of the initial scene and is the first level of the ensuing visions. The dialogue is couched in the form of an ordinary conversation between a teacher and his pupil. The scholar still speaks sensibly, but the true nature of the scene is determined by the oddity of the topic for such a conversation, even if the discussion does not go beyond general principles.

In the following episode the scholar loses his awareness of "his place and status" and sees himself as "a comedian and in leotards," as a circus equestrian. Together with Lili, he does a turn on horseback before a full circus. What had separated the scholar from the equestrian is overcome by means of a dream transformation. The differences of "place and status" are blurred. His daughter, too, is to enter the same status and to achieve intimacy with Lili. The transformed equestrian now performs an act with both, Lili and his daughter riding the same horse. Lili slips and causes an accident: the daughter falls and fractures her skull.

The scenery changes once more: the scholar returns home with his bandaged daughter. Once more there is a knock on the door and the question, "May I?" Again the pupil comes to visit. After the preceding episode, which was already free of the censorship of the conscious, the pupil's second visit takes place in a new situation. The entire city has heard of the accident. The pupil finds no explanation for his teacher's circus performance. "What were you doing on a horse, and how come you were riding, and no one can understand. . . ." No one believes in the transformation of the scholar. "They say that the circus director must have disguised one of his servants to look like you . . . " And, above all, the question: "What does all this mean and what shall I tell my friends, your pupils?" The scholar can only offer confirmation: "It is true; and here is proof, and here is my daughter lying in bed."

The scene changes again. A wall of the room opens. A hail of rocks pours on the scholar and there is shouting: "You old fornicator, and sold your daughter as a circus whore . . . " This episode is the climax of the second stage of the guilt-punishment sequence and serves as a transition to the next vision. Up to now the drunken man had been reacting to auditory stimuli, he had "heard" the knocking at the door. It does not matter that in "reality" this led to his feeling of being stoned during the vision. One can, however, here trace the transition to sleep and dream.

> . . . And one of the stones, a very pointed one, hit my head, and wounded me and stunned me, and I fell unconscious and I sensed nothing except that my head was bleeding, and that as the blood oozed I felt easier, and I felt emptyish and lighter.
>
> And suddenly, and I was no longer in our room, but as if a stranger in a court-room. . . .

The visionary sees himself as an accused man, completely losing his bond with his "real" self. He is now an ex-hermit in circus leotards. He is tried by the senior judge, his former teacher Medardus, of the school for hermits, along with his own pupils. The courtroom scene consists of several parts: the speech by the accused, the judgment, and the accused's justification of the verdict.

During the proceedings, the hermit tells about his transformation. Once, while alone in his hermit's tower chamber, when "one by one, one by one, the servants had begun to leave us, and after the servants also the weaker students, and those remaining were unable to criticize those who were leaving or to accuse them of anything," there appeared before his eyes "a wall-and-dust person." This apparition shows the hermit a father, a mother and a child, all made of straw. All three of them lie swooning on a bed, the father nursing the child. In the father the hermit recognizes himself. To the question, "What am I doing here?" he receives the following answer from the dust apparition: "You, it is your straw and your straw workings, yours and of all the brethren's of your ilk, and your straw life produced this type of children, and you nurse them but you have nothing to nurse them with, and you toss and you turn . . ."

The man of dust once more shows him his teacher, Medardus, who turns into a bird with a face resembling the man of dust. The bird crows and laughs dust.

Stunned by his visions, the hermit, obeying the man of dust, sets fire to the straw wife and the tower, and leaves the hermitage together with the man of dust and the straw child. On the street the man of dust performs new tricks. Elegantly clothed, he is now wearing a top hat and carrying a baton "like a conductor's or a magician's." To the surprised street audience the dust man recounts the hermit's deed—his burning of the woman and the house. He justifies him and reads from a "prophecy and clairvoyance manual" that he had taken along from the tower:

> First, it says [the prophecy], and he will be poor and no longer fit for anything, and he will draw his livelihood from a basket of ridicule which he will carry about—ridicule of himself "and his teachings and teachers of yesterday, a basket of blasphemies for sale." "Secondly, it says, and with all his paths tried and with his errands run, only one action will be left to him—to go to the circus and the tightrope . . . " "Thirdly, says the prophecy, and let him take this up in time, and let him associate with rope dancers and magicians and learn their trades from them, because only from them will he be able to improve his last bit of luck . . . "

> "And fourthly, says the clairvoyant, and let him be prepared to pay for this with everything, with the shirt off his back, with the hair of his head, eyes and with all that he holds dearest and whatever he possesses because otherwise he might as well immediately and upon his doorstep and before he departs from his house, dig himself a grave.

> "Who? The last hermit! . . . "

The dust man's next trick consists of transforming the straw child into the scholar's daughter, dressed as a danc-

er. He leads them into the circus and the circus owner hires them; it will make good publicity: "if the billboards announce that so and so . . . the famous hermit . . . of that well known hermitage . . . will perform today, the circus will certainly be full."

On the dust man's advice, the hermit is given the equestrienne, Lili, as a partner, in order to attach him to the circus. And he counsels further, as if to materialize the prophecy, that a trial of the hermits be enacted in the circus, with Medardus in charge. In the enacted trial, which ends with the burning of the hermits and of their teacher, the ex-hermit plays the chief judge and Lili the hangman.

Lili, however, cannot stand the hermit-scholar's daughter, who displays great equestrian talent. Her jealousy leads to the accident which befalls the daughter, which was already described in an earlier episode of the revue. This time the father knows that Lili failed to extend her hand to his daughter at the proper instant.

After a concluding statement, in which the ex-hermit admits to treachery, comes the verdict and the earlier scene is repeated, except that this time the ex-hermit is himself burned. Lili lights a cigarette from his ashes. Medardus and his pupils, as his mourners, remove their shoes. And the last hermit speaks from the ashes:

> Arise, my teacher and my pupils, for I have received what I have deserved and I have brought you shame, and you have made ashes of me and our score is even, and all are as *nothing* . . . and the circus, too, must not mourn, because what kind of circus man am I anyway, and if you had not cleared me away *now*, the circus-owner would himself have thrown me out, for he kept me, after all, only on account of my daughter, and if not for my daughter (because injured), what does he need me for, and what damned good am I? . . . and Lili, too, will certainly shed no tears over me, because I never meant anything to her, and especially now that she has freed herself from my daughter, of what value am I to her and why fuss over me. . . . Arise, teacher and pupils!

After this justification of the verdict the scholar awakens in dirt under a fence.

In summarizing the content of **"Under a Fence,"** we have laid special stress on the construction scheme in which one of Der Nister's principal characteristics is displayed. The descriptive portions were omitted and the quotations were selected mainly for the sake of the attempted interpretation, which follows.

The wall-and-dust-man is one of the central figures in the speech delivered by the last hermit in the trial portion of the revue. He is the actual cause of his guilt. It is he who brought him to the circus and led him to Lili. He is a constant unmasker; knowing exactly what the hermit is thinking and what ails him, he can take advantage of his weaknesses and lead him according to his whim. He is capable of subjecting the hermit's values to public ridicule. Omniscient and omnipotent, he is able to change his appearance instantly. At the same time, however, he is highly intimate with the last hermit and solicitous about him. "He was faithful to me and he really wanted to see me well adjusted to life." This is undoubtedly a personification of that part of the hermit's self which embodies a number of satanic, Mephistophelian attributes. Certain features suggest a resemblance between the dust man and figures in other "visions" of Der Nister.

In **"Shiker"** (**"Drunk"**), the vision is the reincarnated soul. There, too, the problem concerns values that have lost their power and meaning. In that story their transformation is brought about by the drunken man reincarnated.

> "What do you have there in the sacks?" The drunken man smiles and blushes and hesitates, as it were, to give any response; however, when the reincarnation asks again, the drunken man does answer, still embarrassed: "I have saved and gathered good deeds in the sacks . . ." "Is that so?" says the reincarnation, "and what, for example?" "Quietness, humility, and more and etc.," answers the drunken man. "I see," says the reincarnation. "Can you demonstrate these things?"

> And he can, and he goes ahead and unties one sack after another, and does not himself look into the sacks while untying them. But behind him the reincarnation watches and he does look in, and after he has seen one sack, another and a third, he cries out and says:

> "But look, it is only mold that I see in your sacks . . ."

Here we have the personification of Doubt, which is capable, in moments of weakness, of transforming all of the most cherished and intimately acquired values into straw and mold. This is a cynical denial of everything, an ability to demonstrate and prove that good deeds of the accumulated kind, or attachment to wife and child, have no foundations. From this point it is only a short road to betrayal of everything.

The comedian in **"Gekept"** (**"Beheaded"**) has exactly the same functions. In the course of the story the clown and the shadow are introduced as counterparts of the comedian. The clown is in the head of the central figure, Adam; he is his headache, who can tell him much about "his possessions." He, too, can transform himself into a traveling dervish or into a magician with his wand. Before the arrival of Adam's master, a figure parallel to Medardus in **"Under a Fence"**, the comedian says to Adam:

> I am speaking of your master . . . and soon midnight will be upon us, and he will appear before you here, in this room, along with his companions, and your great respect for him can already be sensed, and your fear and deference are already apparent on your face and as for me, you will drive me back into your head, and I shall watch the occurrence here through a crack in your eyes, and I shall have to observe and keep silent, and listen and not utter a word and be a mute witness, and not interrupt the entire deception, and be forbidden to interfere . . .

> "Comedian!"

The negating function of the comedian is apparent. Even when Adam's contrary principle prevails, the comedian can plague him with doubt and expose the "deception." But Adam, at least, was still able to denounce his dust man as a comedian and to learn, from his master, how to answer him. The last hermit in **"Under a Fence"** has lost this ability, although he does appreciate his comedian's essence. It is his submission to the dust man that constitutes his guilt feeling in the trial portion, the chief motif of the revue.

Until **"Under a Fence"** Der Nister's characters generally were without proper names. They are hermits, itinerants, saints, wanderers, old men, a green man, "a" man, Adam, Der Nister himself, the master, King of Aces and Queen of Myth, a drunkard, clowns, ghosts, a witch, demons, and the like. In **"Under a Fence"**, however, there appear two figures who have proper names: the equestrienne, Lili, and Medardus, the teacher of the hermits. This is an innovation for the Nister. It is safe to assume that these names have a special meaning and function beyond that of identifying the *dramatis personae*. Their function is to broaden the characters of their bearers through associations.

The name, Lili, is similar in sound, and hence associated with, Lilith—the traditional female demon who makes men stray from the path of righteousness. The seductive role played by Lili in **"Under a Fence"**, and her attitude as a whole, fit well into the traditional conception of Lilith. The coupling of the dust man with Lili in the plot of the revue suggests the couple of the Devil (Sam) and Lilith. Here a comparison with Y.-L. Peretz' poem *Monish* suggests itself. In both cases the goal of the demons' efforts is similar. In the one instance we find a student, in the other, a scholar. Both in Peretz' poem and in Der Nister's story the hero is tempted to blasphemy and is punished for it. The male and female devils embody materiality and carnal passion, which "in reality" are empty and whose function is merely to set up temptations which should be resisted. This characteristic of the dust man is revealed in **"Under a Fence"** in Medardus' statement at the end of the trial: ". . . that men of dust and similar creatures are neither men nor creatures, and merely visions, and are only born in the sick minds of hermits, and to allow oneself to be led by them is shameful, and to follow them in their paths—disgraceful."

The association Lili-Lilith is especially significant in conjunction with the figure of a hermit, whose task and profession it is to withdraw from wordly passions and pleasures. In the circus atmosphere, Lili(th) exerts her fascination even—or perhaps particularly—on such people as scholars and hermits. The powers wielded by a circus woman have interested Franz Kafka, Thomas Mann and Marc Chagall. Like all of them, Der Nister seems inhibited in his acceptance of her impact, and channels it into the grotesque.

More complex is the essence of the second bearer of a proper name in **"Under a Fence"**. Medardus was a Christian saint of the sixth century. There is no direct motivation for his appearance in Der Nister's revue. On the other hand, Medardus is also the hero of E. T. A. Hoffmann's *Die Elixiere des Teufels, Nachgelassene Papiere d. Bruder*

Medardus, eines Kapuziners. Hoffmann's Medardus is one of the most complicated alter ego figures in the works of this German romanticist. Two opposing natures vie with one another in Hoffmann's Medardus—the anchoritic with the worldly and sinful. Medardus leaves the monastery and casts himself into the vortex of pleasure, passion, sin, and crime. He returns to the Church but, pursued by his alter ego, finds no peace, no matter where he turns. Medardus and his doubles embody the demonic dualism in man's soul.

The conception of such a dualism is quite close to Der Nister's view of the world and of man, to which we have alluded in passing. But in Der Nister's works, a clear apotheosis of the dualistic world-view is elevated to the level of a peculiar cosmic eschatological myth.

In **"Gekept"** the master tells Adam the story of the creation. The "all-bridge" (*al-brik*) which leads from "the deepest abyss to the highest temples" was created along with other things on that famous Friday at twilight. The "all-bridge" at its creation "had its feet in the abyss and its head in a brightly lit temple." Satan stimulates the bridge to doubts and complaints against the Lord God because of the level of his lower part. "Evil thought" is enough to produce a catastrophe in the world order: that portion of the all-bridge located in the abyss falls away. And "at that very moment the light in its temple darkened." "And because of the sins of the head of the all-bridge and because of the diminution of its light many heads must fall, in order to replenish that temple-light with the light of their own heads. . . . "

One finds in Der Nister's myth definite echoes of the catastrophe and restoration motifs of Kabbalistic eschatology as well as a Christian sacrifice motif. In Der Nister's treatment, the myth is, however, paradoxical compared with the traditional striving toward the restoration of a destroyed state of harmony. It is not to harmony that one looks forward, since there never was any harmony, but rather a return to a joining of temple and abyss. Only then will the world be restored to its original state. Thus the myth of **"Gekept"** offers an apotheosis of dualism, an eternal clashing of opposites. A tragic state, which does not want harmonious repose, is set up as the ideal. This myth could be used to characterize in a nutshell the main problem of Der Nister's tales. Its heroes are in constant motion; they are eternally seeking and overcoming temptations and obstacles.

We could then, perhaps, conclude that the last hermit's act of betrayal consists in rejecting the dualistic Hoffmannian Medardus principle and in submitting to a single principle—and the negative one, at that. In **"Under a Fence"** this idea is symbolized by the act of arson of the hermit's tower and by the trial of Medardus and the hermits. This, however, is merely one possible aspect of the Hoffmannian Medardus-figure in the revue. It is another aspect that can serve as a key to the main problem of **"Under a Fence."**

Der Nister was well acquainted with classical and modern Russian literature. His symbols, despite their roots in tradition and their Jewish stylistic manner, also show clear traces of Russian symbolism. Hoffmann's influences on Russian literature in general, and particularly on Russian symbolism, are a topic in its own right. We should like to dwell here on an explicitly Soviet aspect of the relations between the German romanticist E. T. A. Hoffmann and a Russian literary school.

Among the various Russian literary groups of the twenties, the Petrograd "Serapion Brethren" (1921-1922) stood out with particular prominence. This group borrowed the name and the motto of their literary credo from another hermit figure of Hoffmann's, named Serapion. Into the frame of his stories, Hoffmann introduced a figure of a worldly man, who convinces himself that he is the martyr, Serapion, and lives a hermit's life in a forest, convincingly denying the reality of his "true" biographical personality and past. In Hoffmann's work this figure represents the Serapion principle of literary creativity—a principle that accepts every kind of fantasy and sees in it the true higher reality. In adopting this principle of Hoffmann's, the Petrograd group proclaimed that their patron was "the creator of the impossible and the unbelievable, was equal to Tolstoy and Balzac." This group, among others, was an expression of protest against the beginnings of the Party's ideological meddling in literature. The Serapion Brethren ran into vigorous attacks from official proletarian criticism and to this day are considered in the Soviet Union to have been one of the most negative manifestations in the Russian literature of the twenties.

Y. Dobrushin, a critic associated with the literary circles to which Der Nister also belonged, mentioned Hoffmann repeatedly in a book published in 1922 and expressed his dismay at the fact that Yiddish literature had not yet witnessed the appearance of a Hoffmann-tale of its own. It is certainly no mere coincidence that at the very same time, in 1922, Hoffmann's story "Nutcracker and Mouse Emperor" was published in Yiddish by the Kiev "Culture League." The translation was due to the Soviet Yiddish writer, Lipe Reznik, who is considered to have been a symbolist and a disciple of Der Nister. This story is also found in Hoffmann's collection "Serapion Brethren," and is one of the clearest and most typical examples of the Serapion principle in literature.

Der Nister undoubtedly was acquainted with the credo of the Petrograd group which was close to him, inasmuch as his entire production clearly shows his proximity to the Serapion principle. We may therefore view the Medardus-figure in **"Under a Fence"** as being closely related to the contemporary set of literary problems symbolized in Russia by another hermit of E. T. A. Hoffmann's. Since Serapion's name was by 1929 out of favor, Der Nister replaced it with the name of a different hermit in the works of the same writer.

We feel that Medardus in **"Under a Fence"** is a materialization and symbol of a literary credo, and that the ties between this figure and others create a scheme for the entire revue, a scheme of mutually connected associations and sometimes quite transparent allusions. Let us see how, on this assumption, the interrelations of themselves fit into a scheme.

The scholar, the last hermit, represents an intelligent man, an artist or perhaps even a writer, who grew out of the creative principles of the Hoffmannian Medardus-Serapion. External pressures and internal doubts pursue him ceaselessly. His daughter—his one creation up to now, his very own—is betrayed and harmed because of his attraction for Lili—an opposite creative principle, whose place is in the circus, and whose essence is tricks. External pressures are expressed by the loneliness of the last hermit, which inclines him and readies him to accept his own doubts, symbolized by the dust man. He begins to believe in the strawness of his former path. If we re-read the cited passages about the dust man's prophecy and about the hermit's justification of the verdict; and if we keep in mind the status of a fellow-traveling writer, who has not yet managed to adjust to the demands of "proletarian" criticism, the revue acquires a very special significance.

Der Nister had in advance put on trial the possible or the already achieved transformation of a symbolist writer working under Soviet conditions. The feeling of guilt seems to dominate and accompany this transformation. The threefold punishment seems to be justified and at the end the hero finds himself in dirt by a fence. Only his daughter, his creation, remains loyal to him; it is only to her that he can confess, and only she can understand him.

It is superfluous to develop the scheme any further. It will be even more convincing, however, if we dwell for a moment on the specific metaphors through which the opposing principles are presented in **"Under a Fence"**.

The circus is characterized by skin-colored leotards, by disrobement and nudity. Lili is dressed in this fashion; the athlete is half-nude. The transformed hermit, again, stands before the court in skin-colored leotards. The subject of bareness oppressed Der Nister in earlier works as well. In **"A Tale of a Clown and a Mouse and Der Nister Himself "**, the glass people are an expression of the beastly and vital bases in man. "In this land there is bare flesh and nakedness, and all are undressed, and to dress is shameful, and human clothing disgraceful and man is *not* wanted there while a donkey, on the other hand, is welcome." The people of this land learn their philosophy of life from the donkey. This is a clearly negative attitude to the principle represented by nudity. And again in **"Shiker"** (Drunk), the drunken man and his double, after shedding the superfluous ballast of the past, assume a very different countenance: "Like two magicians . . . their attire and their clothes acquired a trick color, and it is easy and suited to the skin and nothing unnecessary shall impede them, and nothing shall trail after them." Here the trick color is tied in with renunciation of encumbrances, and with a liberation from them—the shedding of the burden of heritage.

And another interesting case of combining comedians with nudity occurs in **"Tsum shnit" (To the Harvest")**, one of Der Nister's first *očerki*. This is a report of a visit among Jewish peasants in the Crimea during the height of collectivization and the struggle against the kulaks in 1931. No feature story could at that time be written without referring to the burning rural issues. Der Nister managed to fulfill this requirement, too. On the way to a village, he meets a group of young actors from Moscow, who have come to bring "the directives of the Party, the message of the workers through play and movement." It is they who put on a play in the village about "The Kulak's Secret Agency." Der Nister finds no other name for these actors than *komedyantlekh ('little comedians')*. And these, too, are half-nude when he meets them. It is apparent that disrobement is coupled by Der Nister with comedians, circuses, and magicians; it symbolizes vitality, freedom from burdens, and primitiveness—all concepts foreign to Der Nister and full of negative connotations for him.

Nudity is a concept that occurred in Der Nister's environment in connection with literature. Der Nister and the impressionist, Dovid Bergelson, had been the pillars of the Kiev *Eygns* ('One's Own') group, which published its collections in 1918 and 1920. In response to a review of the first issue of *Eygns* by M. Litvakov, Bergelson, in a programmatic article, formulated his literary credo. He sharply criticized the primitive *lubok* ('cheap literary print') and the "naked lines" in then accepted futuristic and expressionistic revolutionary poetry. As an example of true art he cited the Nister's story **"Tsum barg" ("To the Mountain")** in *Eygns*.

In Yiddish proletarian criticism, the struggle against the theories of the *Eygns* writers stretched on for many years. As early as 1929 Bronshteyn, at great length, settled his accounts with Bergelson for his negation of (Party-)Line Nudity (*lineyishe naketkeyt*). In his article, 'The Struggle of Styles During the Period of Military Communism', he asks solemnly: "Is not this 'naked' line-hewing style the only one possible for the flaming revolutionary streetsong, for the stormy poster, for the noisy revolutionary concert stage?" Let us recall how the last hermit begins his speech before the court in **"Under a Fence"**:

> You have allowed me to speak in self-defense, and I have nothing to defend myself with. And I stand now before you and feel like a turtle that has stepped out of its portable tower: bare-skinned and naked. . . . And yes, Master Medardus and I came out of my tower and our hermitage . . . and I felt cold . . . and when cold, one cuddles up to any kind of warmth, be it dirt, be it filth, as long as it is a cover . . . and let it be a rag, as long as it is clothing, and let it be leotards, as long as it is a garment. . . . And when hungry and jobless, even clowning is an occupation, and when homeless and roofless even a circus is home, and when things begin to go as they do in a circus, and your life is cheap and serves only to sate the visual lust of strangers, and your soul hangs on a wire and your life is of no importance, is it surprising then that the child, too, is of no importance, and that for a *nothing* and for a snack you can sell it to the tightrope. . . .

The relationship between the skin-colored leotards of the circus and the concrete situation of an artist in the Soviet Union seems to be clear, although Der Nister could equally well have intended either the proletarian placard art, or the futuristic-expressionistic school, or the naturalistic-realistic tendencies in the Soviet literature of the late twenties. All were essentially foreign to the symbolist.

With regard to the period when the Medardus house flourished, the last hermit says: "In your time our tower game shone over neighborhoods and distances." Tower game and hermit's tower are sufficiently transparent allusions from the treasury of the symbolist metaphors. It thus appears that a confrontation of two diametrically opposed literary schools is at the heart of **"Under a Fence"**.

Even so the issue is not too simple for Der Nister. One cannot ignore the opposition between the lonely tower of a last solitary hermit, filled with doubts, and the security of a seasoned circus actor in a packed hall. There remains the gnawing question: Is this, then, the way? Is it, after all, only for select individuals? There is no definite answer to this question. Insecurity coupled with hopelessness and with the necessity to submit, out of "hunger and joblessness," to the transformation, increase the depth and horror of the tragedy of the man undergoing the test.

Despite all of the doubts, Der Nister's judgment is, nevertheless, unequivocal. The feeling of guilt is stronger than the doubts, and the threefold punishment appears justified.

"The torment lasts until death. . . ."

The interpretation of **"Under a Fence"** attempted in this paper may leave open other alternatives. Our concentration on specific incidents and on a schematic interpretation of the revue may have distorted other possibilities and occasionally overshadowed some other meanings of the story. On the other hand, it seems that our analysis of a number of incidents in **"Under a Fence"** does bring to light a unique and original protest, powerless though it was, of a fellow-traveling Soviet writer of the late twenties. And it may be superfluous to add that Y. Bronshteyn's evaluation of **"Under a Fence"** is the only correct one from his point of view.

The fact that **"Under a Fence"** represents a turning point in Der Nister's writings now becomes perfectly clear. Der Nister himself had predicted that he would abandon the symbolist's tower. Not all of his prophecies, however, came to pass. The changes in Party policy in the thirties enabled him to find a new writing pattern by which to remain true to himself. *Di mishpokhe Mashber,* although considered a "realistic" piece, hardly fits any straightforward definition of realism. The true values of Der Nister's unfinished epic can be unlocked only with the key of his heritage from the visionary, fairy-tale period in his writings.

We know of no other case other than the vision in **"Under a Fence"** in which Der Nister denounced his own values. One horrible prophecy was, however, fulfilled: "The owner of the circus showed the door" and disposed not only of Der Nister but, along with his opponents and friends, of the entire Yiddish literature in the Soviet Union. This exceeded the imagination even of Der Nister's drunken visionary.

POSTSCRIPT

Since the preceding paper was written, in 1960, a number of important materials have come to light which are di-

rectly relevant to the problems of Der Nister as a Soviet writer and to our interpretation of **"Under a Fence"**.

(1) In a letter written in 1934 or so, Der Nister told his brother in Paris:

> What I have written so far is now deeply discredited here. It is an unwanted (*geshlogn*) article. Symbolism has no place in the Soviet Union. And I, as you know, have been a symbolist all my life. To pass from symbolism to realism is very difficult for someone like me, who has labored much to perfect his method and his manner of writing. This is not a matter of technique; in this case one must be born anew, as it were, one must turn one's soul inside out.
>
> I have made many attempts. At first nothing succeeded. Now, I think, I am on the right road. I have begun to write a book—in my opinion, and in the opinion of close acquaintances, an important one. I want to devote to this book all the strength in my possession. My whole generation is involved—what I have seen, heard, experienced, and fancied. Up to now I had found it hard to write altogether, because all my time was spent and wasted in earning enough for expenses. From my older things I was not able to realize one kopeck. But now, in connection with the transfer of the publishing houses from Kharkov to Kiev, I am even out of technical work. And yet the writing of my book is a necessity; otherwise I am nothing (*oys mentsh*), otherwise I am erased from literature and from living life. For what it means to be a writer who does *not* write I need not tell you. It means that he does not exist, he is missing from the world. . . .

This candid, shattering statement is one of the rarest documents of this kind which we possess for any Soviet writer. The letter explains Der Nister's struggles from the forced rupture with symbolism (after **"Under a Fence"**) until the time he found his new path in *The Mashber Family,* the book to which he alludes in the letter to his brother. Insofar as the light cast by the letter on the interpretation of **"Under a Fence"** is concerned, comments seem superfluous. (Regarding the letter, its background, and its dating, see my introduction to Der Nister's *Hanazir vehagdiyah.*

(2) The journal *Sovetish heymland* (Moscow), 1964, no. 1, presented . . . a work by Der Nister entitled *Fun finftn yor (From the Fifth Year,* i.e. 1905). It is characterized by the editors as a novel, found among Der Nister's unpublished manuscripts. The editor, L. Podryatshik, states in his concluding comments that the manuscript was a very difficult one; a great deal had been erased and revised, and "several pages were struck out by Der Nister," presumably with the intent "to rewrite them later on." But in printing the novel, the editor declares, he "attempted to reconstruct at least a small paragraph [out of the deleted pages!] in order to yield an organic transition to the sequel." The printed text does not indicate the reconstructed passages and does not reveal the principles which governed the posthumous edition of this complicated manuscript.

Although *From 1905* was printed as a finished piece, the manuscript clearly testifies that Der Nister had interrupted his work on this novel. To determine the time when he worked on this book is of major importance for Der Nister's creative biography and, indirectly, for the interpretation of **"Under a Fence"**. According to the testimony of the writer's second wife, cited in Podryatshik's comments, Der Nister "had begun to write this novel at the end of the 1930's." The editorial comments are marked by a clearcut tendency to set the date of the work as late as possible. By this means the discovery of a novel which is realistically consistent and "revolutionary" in an ideological sense helps to "destroy the legend that Der Nister's way of grasping reality remained the way of symbolic interpretation." But several specific peculiarities of the text seem to suggest that its date must be earlier:

(a) Der Nister had intended to bring his unfortunately unfinished work, *The Mashber Family,* at least up to the revolution of 1905 (according to the first chapter of Book I). It therefore seems impossible that while working on his major book he should have undertaken another novel depicting the same period and having no relation to *The Mashber Family.* It was in 1934 that Der Nister had begun to work on the major novel, a chapter of which was published in 1935. Accordingly, the novel *From 1905* appears to be a draft begun by Der Nister prior to 1934 and abandoned when he decided instead to treat this period in his Mashber novel.

(b) The novel *From 1905* as it appears in the *Sovetish heymland* edition is unambiguously realistic and is marked by an almost hackneyed ideological and artistic conception. This conception fits well the principles of the ruling Soviet "proletarian" criticism of the period 1928-1932. Apart from his *očerki* of the early 1930's, we do not find any signs in Der Nister's later works of his adjustment to the demands of criticism of those years. It therefore seems to us that *From 1905* is another piece of evidence regarding Der Nister's struggle for his existence as a writer.

The manuscript may be a remnant of Der Nister's "silent" years, 1929-1931 (before he wrote his *očerki*), or it may be a draft made after his disappointment with the *očerki* but before he began *The Mashber Family.* It is quite possible that in working on *From 1905* Der Nister came upon the idea of the Mashber novel. But we cannot exclude the possibility that *From 1905* represents a draft written before **"Under a Fence",** and that its history is reflected in the conversion and betrayal of the writer-scholar-hermit. One thing is certain: Der Nister did *not* complete and did *not* finish the novel *From 1905* during his lifetime. It follows that he looked upon the work as one of the unsuccessful attempts about which he wrote in the quoted letter to his brother. For the novel is free of any ideological deviations which might have forced the author to keep it in his "drawer." It could have been freely published at any time after Der Nister's return to the Soviet Union, and every Soviet publishing house would have been delighted to accept it.

The quotation from Der Nister's letter to his brother and our attempted dating of the novel *From 1905* cast fresh light on his story **"Under a Fence"** and confirm the direction of our interpretation of this key work.

Charles A. Madison   (essay date 1968)

SOURCE: "Yiddish in Soviet Russia," in his *Yiddish Literature: Its Scope and Major Writers,* Frederick Ungar Publishing Co., 1968, pp. 382-425.

[*Madison was a Russian-born American editor, nonfiction writer, and critic. In the following excerpt, he traces Der Nister's career.*]

Der Nister (Pinchas Kahanovitch) was *sui generis* among the Yiddish writers in the Soviet Union. Born in Berditchev, he was early influenced by his older brother, who had become a Braslaver Hasid, and was until adulthood steeped in the study of Hebrew and cabalistic literature. To avoid the draft he lived under an assumed name and earned his bread as a teacher of Hebrew. Unlike other young writers of his day, who saw only the ugly and musty side of Hasidism, he approached it sympathetically and appreciated the simple goodness and pure piety of the dedicated devout. This attitude he manifested in his first volume, [*Gedanken un motiven*] *Thoughts and Motives* (1907). His next two books, [*Hekher fun der erd*] *Higher than the Earth* (1910) and [*Gezang un gebet*] *Song and Prayer* (1912), concerned themselves with cabalistic themes and mystical attitudes. He sought to dig even deeper than Peretz, and more subjectively, into the sources of pietistic treasure, and wrote about it in the spirit of Nahman Braslaver: symbolically, secretively, concealingly. It was thus that he came upon his pseudonym, Der Nister, the Hebrew for concealer.

He came to Kiev in 1908, a gentle, modest, reticent young man, rather mysterious in behavior, obviously groping, searching for the hidden path to spiritual essence, sometimes losing himself in the byways of his own labyrinth, now and then emerging into a world completely unrelated to the one around him. In 1910 he went to visit Peretz and was elated by the older man's encouragement, yet he refused to remain in Warsaw because he felt the city was too large for him.

During World War I he exempted himself from the army by doing war work. When the revolution overthrew the Czarist government, he was one of very few Yiddish writers to remain apolitical. In 1919 he published [*Mayselakh in ferzn*] *Tales in Verse,* stories charged with mystical groping. Finding himself out of tune with the revolutionary exhilaration around him, he in 1921 left for Berlin, where he issued a new collection of his visionary fantasies. Neither was life in Germany to his liking, and he returned to the Soviet Union in 1926, settling in Kharkov. Unchanged in attitude, unwilling to become harnessed to political agitation, although acquiescing in the tenets of the revolution, he lived in relative seclusion and penury, without the perquisites reserved for accepted writers.

Orderly and punctual of habit, reticent and taciturn, though eager to see people and observe them closely, he worked steadily at his desk, revising and polishing his sentences as if he were performing a holy task. He lived with his characters and suffered with them. In some of his stories he would begin realistically, only to have his protagonists become drunk or fall asleep and be subject to fantastic visions or symbolical allegories. In one of his best-known stories, an elderly scholar becomes mystically enamored of a circus rider and recalls a prophecy that "he will be poor and without ability, and will earn his living from a basket of mockery which he will carry attached to himself . . . "; that he himself will act as a circus rider. The entire narrative is thus woven out of dreams and visions which he relates to his daughter. Most writers, while finding his stories irrelevant to the temper of the revolution, respected his moral integrity and persistence. It was easier for them to praise his stories for children, which were written with folklike simplicity, with an allegorical yet winsome content.

In 1929 he managed to publish [*Fun Meine giter*] *Of My Possessions,* a volume of mercurial fantasies, replete with magic and mystery and an underlying arcane symbolism. Critics demanding "socialist realism" derided the work as reactionary, thereby depriving him of his stipend as a creative writer. To support himself and his small family he now had no choice but to resort to reportage and write more realistically. This was for him a very complicated process, as he indicated in a letter to his brother in 1934: "I, as is known to you, have always been a symbolist. To change from symbolism to realism for one like myself, who had labored strenuously to perfect his method and manner of writing, is very hard. This is no question of technique. One must be born to it. It means turning one's soul inside out. . . . " The first result of this transmutation was [*Hoyptshtet*] *Capital Cities* (1934), a series of relatively realistic descriptions of the socialist changes in Kharkov, Leningrad, and Moscow.

Der Nister's canvas is broad, rich, colorful. The major characters are portrayed with striking suggestiveness and sympathetic understanding; life spurts from them even though they become overshadowed by the veil of mysticism.

—*Charles A. Madison*

Even earlier Nister had begun to write [*Di Mishpokhe Mashber*] *The Mashber Family* (1939, 1948), his chief work. Set in his native Berditchev of the 1870's, when it was still a commercially busy and teeming city, he depicts the rich and variegated life of the Jews with extraordinary vividness and insight. His general theme is social: the boorishness of the rich, the suffering and soundness of the poor, and the deep, simple faith of the Braslaver Hasidim. His canvas is broad, rich, colorful. The major characters are portrayed with striking suggestiveness and sympathetic understanding; life spurts from them even though they become overshadowed by the veil of mysticism.

To give the novel the required "socialist realism" for purposes of publication, Nister wrote an introduction in which he makes clear that his particular subject matter cannot well be narrated without a description of medieval mysticism:

> I have done it, however, for the sake of historical awareness, to acquaint the young generation with the extraordinary distance which we have traveled during a relatively short time, which separates our reality from that one. . . . Depicting these characters, already completed physically and spiritually, I have tried not to "fight" them but to let them go, quietly and slowly, to their distinct fate, to their last historically necessary way—to perdition. . . . The main purpose of my work was not to put an end to the old generation sunk up to its neck in medieval ways of life, but to show those secret powers, which lay deep in the "third estate" [the Jewish slum] and which were so tragically destroyed under the weight of life's yoke.

The novel teems with numerous characters but concerns primarily the brothers Luzi and Moshe Mashber and Sruli Gol, a thoroughly unconventional young Hasid and lout who becomes Luzi's disciple and protector. In the first part of the narrative, Moshe is the wealthy merchant and banker, doing business on a grand scale, living lavishly, arrogant as befits a moneyed man, but pious and respectful of his older brother Luzi, who disdains worldly goods and devotes himself solely to his spiritual salvation. In this Luzi follows their father who, in seeking absolution for his father's sin of having been a follower of Shabbati Zevi, had died young from fasting and self-abnegation. After visiting the courts of various Hasidic rabbis, Luzi gravitated to the dwindling group of Braslaver disciples. Now firm in his faith, he changes from reticence and seclusion to an attitude of embracing friendliness. He settles in Berditchev, "N" in the novel, and associates with the small sect of Braslaver followers, the poorest and most despised Jews in the city. Although he is on good terms with his brother and often visits him, Luzi prefers the bare table of the poor Braslavers to the rich food in Moshe's home.

Sruli Gol is an enigmatic character, careless in appearance, intimate with none, brazen in behavior, bold in action, uncurbed in his cursing, ready to intimidate the richest men in town if necessary for his mysterious purposes. In general he favors the poor at the expense of men of wealth. Highly articulate, ready to shout his anger at those he dislikes or who cross him in any way, he shows no outward love even to those he favors. He would attend the wedding of a poor couple "to make them happy," and he enters the homes of the rich uninvited and behaves as one of their intimates.

When one of Moshe's clerks becomes seriously ill and his mother comes to Moshe's home for help and is refused, Sruli, who happens to be present, commands Moshe to give the needed assistance. Angered at such brazenness, Moshe orders Sruli out of his house. Whereupon Luzi, who had sat quietly up to that moment, tells his brother to ask Sruli's pardon. All the angrier, Moshe tells Luzi that he too can leave. This the two ejected men do without delay.

Sruli had sometime back inherited a large bequest from a grandfather, but had made little use of it for himself. Like a fairy godmother he now provides the clerk's family with every possible assistance without revealing the source. He does the same for other poor families that seem worthy to him. From that day he makes Luzi his confidant, provides him with his meager needs, and watches over him with devoted solicitude.

At this juncture in the narrative Nister gives a masterly description of the behavior of Polish nobles and squires at the annual fair: their orgies and gambling proclivities, their financial decline, and their haughty behavior toward the Jews who finance them with loans and the purchase of chattels. The year being one of economic austerity, Moshe is unable to collect the large loans made to Polish squires and cannot meet payments due to his clients. When this becomes known, he is driven to bankruptcy and prison by the callousness of his fellow bankers. The events leading up to this financial and personal deterioration are related in vivid detail and with psychological acuteness. Without stating it, Nister implies that Moshe's arrogance toward Sruli and Luzi cursed him with Job's afflictions. A daughter sickens and dies, he himself—forsaken by his associates—is imprisoned for debt, his wife becomes stricken with paralysis, and both die shortly after he is released from prison. Moshe loses his arrogance in the process, achieves genuine meekness, becomes reconciled with Luzi, and dies purified of common dross. This gradual transformation is narrated with such insight and felicity that one accepts it as a matter of course. This is the more remarkable in view of Nister's old-fashioned personal intrusions, so common in 19th-century fiction.

When he could not publish the second volume in Russia, Nister managed to send it to the United States, where it was brought out in 1948. The dedication to his daughter, who had died of starvation during the siege of Leningrad, reads: "May thy father's broken heart be a monument on your lost grave, may this book be dedicated to your eternal memory—your father, the author."

The narrative proceeds with Mikhel, a poor teacher, a Braslaver Hasid and Luzi's friend, struggling with his religious doubts until he finally rejects his traditional piety. When this becomes known, his pupils are withdrawn by outraged parents and he and his family become destitute. Sruli secretly comes to their assistance, but in his anger at the respectable community becomes drunk and is robbed and abused. When Mikhel dies of a stroke and the city fathers refuse to give his body proper burial, Sruli creates a scene and succeeds in having his way by paying the required fee. Again and again he acts like a *deus ex machina* in seeing justice done and succoring the poor. He is most solicitous about Luzi's well-being, knowing that the conventional community looks askance at Luzi's consorting with the poor and dejected. Luzi has reached the spiritual condition which tolerates all human behavior and befriends all who have need of his word of comfort. No longer to be countenanced by the city fathers, a plan is made to drive him out of the city. But Sruli learns of the plot and manages to leave with Luzi in safety some hours before the planned expulsion. The peculiar personal relationship between the Nazarite Luzi and the irrepressible and loutish Sruli is made a beautiful manifestation of man's inner goodness and insight.

The long narrative provides a richly vivid panorama of traditional Jewish life and lore. With a wealth of intimate detail and illuminating description it expounds hoary customs and conventional piety as well as the various ways in which Jews carried on their businesses and trades. The mystical modesty and humble self-abasement of the destitute Braslaver Hasidim are depicted with singular and fascinating simplicity—Nister being the only one in the Soviet Union to have written about them with such sympathetic understanding. Of the dozens of characters in the book, nearly all come alive with a few deft strokes, as may be seen from the description of Itsikel, a cemetery official, who is very homely: "Not so much his body as his bit of a face, shrunken like a dried fig, with a few hairs on it and with two narrow eyes like slits, and with the voice of a newborn kitten." And if Luzi dominates with his saintly passivity, Moshe with his arrogance turned to sorrowful acquiescence by repentance, and Sruli with his mysterious and boisterous behavior, the story as a whole centers in the absorbing and unforgettable portrayal of traditional Jewish life in the 1870's.

During World War II Nister, like other Yiddish writers, could only write about the catastrophe in Nazi-occupied Poland. These stories were published in New York in 1957. One of the longest and best of these narratives, **"The Grandfather and the Grandson,"** tells of an old and very pious rabbi who ate little and prayed much, and of his grandson Itsik, the only remaining member of the family, who became a radical and atheist when he grew up. When the Nazis enter the town on Yom Kipper, the rabbi advises his parishioners to remain at prayer. With the aid of an informer, Itsik is the first to be arrested. Soon the rabbi and those at prayer are driven to the town square, where grandfather and grandson are ordered to spit at each other. They refuse and shout defiance in unison as they are led to the scaffold to be hanged. Other narratives have a similar intent and impact. Flora, for instance, the daughter of a highly respected and conscientious doctor who commits suicide in a Nazi prison, is plucky enough to outwit the German officers and become a successful partisan.

In 1947 Nister was sent to Birobidjan on a journalistic mission. He wrote with enthusiasm about his warm reception and the active life of the Jewish inhabitants. On his return he was delighted to learn that the first volume of [*Di Mishpokhe Mashber*] *The Mashber Family* was being brought out in Hebrew. Very early in 1949 he was arrested. By then a sick man, he was operated on in a prison hospital and died in 1950.

In January, 1964, *Sovietish Heymland* published Nister's last novel, [*Fun Finftn Yor*] *Of the Fifth Year,* on which he had worked on and off for nearly a decade. It concerns Label, an only son brought up by a hard-headed and domineering mother to be the pride of her life. When he is 17 she begins to ask matchmakers to find him a bride worthy of her wealth and position. Label, however, in possession of his own drive and determination, is caught up in the political turmoil agitating Russia in 1905, and in his association with underground radicals meets Millie "with the young light deer feet," and both love each other at first sight. His mother learns of it and insists that he give up his friends and do her bidding. When he refuses and leaves home, her anger and frustration are extreme. In her fury she informs the police and the group is arrested. Soon conscious-stricken and partly deranged from rankling aggravation, the mother hangs herself. At about the same time the abortive 1905 constitution is announced, political prisoners are released, and Label and Millie are reunited in freedom.

It is quite conceivable that another writer would have confined the narrative within the limits of a short story. Nister, however, did not write concisely. His interest here was not so much in the action as in the background, motivation, and individuality of his characters. Indeed, the most significant fact about this book is its realistic style. Even in [*Di Mishpokhe Mashber*] *The Mashber Family* he had not yet freed himself from the allegorical mysticism and fantasy which characterizes his earlier writing. In [*Fun Finftn Yor*] *Of the Fifth Year* he achieved the directness and psychological perception of the fictional realist. Writing with the old-fashioned leisure of 19th-century prose masters, he adds word to word and phrase to phrase with sculptural concreteness in building up the vivid uniqueness of his characters. In his description of the political turmoil of 1905 he is graphic, factual, and suggestive: police oppression, economic exploitation, and underground revolutionary agitation are shown in clear and comprehensive focus. At the same time he writes about idyllic young love with poetic beauty and remarkable freshness.

Sol Liptzin (essay date 1972)

SOURCE: "Soviet Yiddish Literature," in his *A History of Yiddish Literature,* Jonathan David Publishers, 1972, pp. 194-236

[*Liptzin is an accomplished Russian-born American editor, translator, critic, and noted scholar of German and Yiddish literature. In the following excerpt, he offers a survey of Der Nister's career, focusing particularly on* The Family Mashber.]

The Yiddish-Hebrew pseudonym, Der Nister, which may be translated as the Hidden One or the Occult Person, is an apt characterization of the outstanding representative of Neo-romanticism among the Yiddish writers of the Ukraine.

Der Nister began in 1907 with prose poems, dream images, in which Jewish, Christian and Olympian supernatural creatures were intermingled. He continued in 1912 and 1918 with songs, odes, versified prayers, allegories of God and Satan, mystic visions that spanned heaven and earth and dissolved in nebulous melancholy, ballads which were meant to delight children but which also hinted at meanings beyond their grasp. Thus, the tree that resists the peasant's axe and is as reluctant to die as the horse pursued by the bear, the white goat that lulls the infant to sleep, the sprites that dwell in abandoned ruins, the gnome that bestows wealth, the cat that feeds its playmate the mouse, the rooster that is the sole companion and nurse of the sick grandmother—all have traits and feelings not unlike those of human beings and yet they are at the same time symbols of abstractions and qualities. What Marc Chagall sought to express in color, Der Nister attempted in verse and poetic prose.

As the translator into Yiddish of Hans Christian Andersen's fairy tales and as a student of cabalistic lore, Der Nister succeeded in combining European and Hebraic elements in his tales. He also felt strongly the influence of Rabbi Nachman Bratslaver, the most talented of the Hassidic weavers of stories. Forests alternate with deserts, enchanters and witches with angels, demons and Nazarites, bears of the north with lions of the South. Amidst the whirl of events that traverse earth and moon and starry constellations, the loneliness of the individual peers through as he roams far and wide in search of holiness and ultimate wisdom. Unhappy with his own age and powerless to change it, such a person attempts to break out of it. He wanders on and on beyond any specific time or clearly defined realm. Now and then he encounters a hermit or a graybeard who is even further removed from normal pleasures and mundane pursuits and therefore closer to the source of essential insight. They help him to overcome demonic temptations. They find for him a track through seemingly trackless wastes. They accompany him for a while through the darkest mazes of forests. They weave their tales into his tales.

Der Nister's reputation as a leading member of the Kiev Group was already well established when the Russian Revolution broke out. As a non-political writer, he felt ever more and more isolated amidst the contending ideological coteries and left for Berlin. There he published two volumes of *Contemplations* (*Gedakht,* 1922), stories that followed the model of Nachman Bratslaver. In one story, he made a beggar the savior of kings. In others, he introduced magic stones, a healing mirror, a wolf that travelled faster than the wind. Transported on the back of the wolf, the hero of the *Bovo-Maisse* could quickly reach the remote land where his betrothed, a paralyzed princess, was awaiting his coming to bring about her recovery from a baneful spell.

After returning to the Ukraine, Der Nister was silent for several years and, when he resumed publishing in 1929, his volume *From My Treasures* (*Fun Meine Giter*) betrayed a pessimism not evident earlier. The opening narrative was put in the mouth of a madman in a madhouse. This madman related his experiences in converting mud to gold until he became the supreme lord of the land and arrogant beyond all mortals. Then Der Nister sketched the downfall and degradation of this plutocrat, who, in his final extremity, after exhausting all other means of feeding ten hungry bears, had to offer them his own ten fingers and his heart to gnaw at. Beyond the apparent meaning of these changes of fortune, the reader senses the author's hints of intense anguish and spiritual distress but hints so deeply veiled that their true import still defies clarification. Perhaps such labyrinthean mystification was necessary if the romantic writer wished to remain true to his inner self and yet to survive at a time when anti-

Romanticism and Socialist Realism were the prescribed slogans for literature.

A decade later, however, the pressure upon Der Nister was too great to be successfully resisted. In his major work *Family Mashber,* the first volume of which appeared in 1939, he adopted the realistic style of writing demanded of all Soviet novelists. However, he applied it not to contemporary life, but to an era which was already historic and to a social order of which only vestiges remained: Berdichev of the 1870's.

Caught between his sympathy for his tradition-rooted characters and the necessity of following the anti-religious Communist party line, he added an apologetic preface. In it, he explained that he deemed it artistically more desirable not to pronounce the doom of his characters in advance but rather to portray them proceeding slowly and inevitably to their historic destiny, the abyss. He wanted to let them unfold their glamorous traits no less than their ugly ones and then to show how the logic of their further inner development would drive them unalterably to decay and damnation. He promised that, together with the still uncompleted later volumes, his work would put the finishing touches to an old generation which was steeped in medievalism and would also trace the tragic beginning of a more enlightened way of life which would gradually ripen into revolutionary activities and sweep away the accumulated rot of centuries.

The city depicted by Der Nister developed in the form of three concentric circles. The innermost circle, the market district, was the heart of all business activities. The second circle embraced the residential area, in which were concentrated the religious and cultural activities of the Jewish community. The third circle, suburbia, was inhabited by the poorest of the poor, criminals, cranks, prostitutes, the subversive and revolutionary elements that would later topple the entire social edifice.

The Mashbers belong to the patricians of the city. Luzi, the oldest brother, faces a spiritual crisis when the Hassidic rabbi in whom he found sustenance and guidance passes away. Ultimately he discovers the genuineness he seeks; he joins the despised, poor, ardent Bratslaver Hassidim. Among them, he comes to understand and to appreciate the true humanity in the town's third circle.

Moshe Mashber, the second brother, puts his faith solely in business and lives primarily in order to accumulate wealth. By experiencing a business crisis and a decline of fortune, he is humbled in his pride and is saved from despair by a saintly pseudo-beggar, a *Lamedvovnik.*

Alter Mashber, the youngest brother, has to overcome pain and illness. When his clouded mind recovers, he accepts the equality of all human beings and is happy to marry the maid of the Mashber household. The stratified social structure, as exemplified by this well-to-do family, begins to show fissures and its ultimate collapse can be predicted.

This collapse occurs in the second volume, which was published in 1948 in the United States but not in Russia: in that year all Yiddish publications ceased in the Soviet Union, not to be resumed until after Stalin's death. Moshe Mashber's wealth disintegrates, he is forced into bankruptcy, he is imprisoned for fraud, and on his release he dies a broken man. Meanwhile, Luzi Mashber continues his quiet acts of kindness and love in behalf of the despised and oppressed members of the Jewish community, as befits an adherent of Bratslav Hassidism. He is joined by Sruli, a saint in tatters, and by Michael Bukier, whose eternal questioning leads to excessive skepticism and, as a result, to unmerited persecution on the part of the town's religious fanatics. In these three characters, but especially in Luzi Mashber, the author depicts himself and his kind, silent, self-effacing approach.

Only once does Luzi break out in eloquence. Then he expresses his undying hope and unshakable faith in his Jewish people. His words spring from the heart of the author, who otherwise had to masquerade his feelings:

> "Israel is beloved. Neither the pains of Galut nor his expulsion from his father's table stops him from feeling himself to be God's child, chosen to reign in the future. Let not the nations of the earth rejoice in the rich portion allotted to them now and let them not look down upon Israel, which is now black as are the tents of Kedar. Israel is indeed divided and left at the mercy of many swords which hang above his head and compel him to beg for life's sustenance of all the cruel murderers in this world. Let not the nations rejoice and mock Israel, who appears strange, disunited, an outcast stepchild among them. The curse upon Israel is only temporary, no matter how long it lasts. His lot, to be an unhappy beggar on accursed roads, will ultimately end. He will be the light and salvation predicted and promised by the Prophets. Yet even now and in all generations when catastrophes overwhelm Israel, saints arise who fathom the meaning of Israel's destiny, who accompany him on his thorny road with love and compassion, and who gladly receive the arrows meant for him. They and their followers are fortunate enough to feel Israel's sublime pain, the pain of the insulted, injured and tortured heart of the world. Israel is God's beloved, an example to mankind of the fortitude and dignity with which one bears suffering even when the knife is at one's throat. Beloved is Israel, who even in darkest moments still retains a shimmer of hope in salvation, salvation not alone for himself but for all mankind, for whom he is the blessed victim and also herald of the Messianic promise of a time when all tears will be wiped away from all faces. Yes, a time will come when to the Holy Mountain there will troop, as to a wedding, sages and crowned light-bearing saints with the Anointed One in their midst and the whole world following them— man, woman and child, not only of the human species but also of beasts and cattle and birds, all of whom will be lifted up and filled with knowledge of that day of universal rejoicing, every sage with his admirers, every prophet with his followers, every saint with his disciples, everyone who guarded the Holy Flame amidst storms and prevented its extinction. My brothers, guard this Flame bequeathed to you, guard it until the Messianic era when all knees will bend before

the Savior and all heads of all living creatures in which there is a living soul will ask His blessing. Guard the Flame, my brothers!"

Luzi's ardent words of hope and comfort were rudely interrupted by a stone hurled at him through a window. Even so was this valedictory of Der Nister, upon which he worked for more than a decade, rudely interrupted by the Soviet secret police who came to arrest him. His first words on that occasion are reported to have been: "Thank God, you came at last. I have waited for you so long." Thereafter silence engulfed him and he died in prison on June 4, 1950.

Premonitions of his end filled the second volume of Der Nister's masterpiece, upon which he continued to work while one after another of his friends, colleagues and followers were vanishing from the public eye and terror stalked the survivors. The final chapters, therefore, over-emphasized scenes of dying and bared the long hidden suffering of a tortured soul.

The author was expected to revile a people and a tradition which he loved so fervently in his heart of hearts and he had no way of knowing whether this love, concealed beneath an outer veneer of apparent dislike and locked up in not easily decipherable symbolic language, would ever penetrate to readers in later years or be intelligible to them. In the morass in which he was forced to move in his last years, he remained a hidden saint, the noblest personality among the Soviet Yiddish writers.

Irving Howe and Eliezer Greenberg (essay date 1977)

SOURCE: Introductory note to "Under a Fence: A Revue," in *Ashes Out of Hope: Fiction by Soviet-Yiddish Writers,* edited by Irving Howe and Eliezer Greenberg, Schocken Books, 1977, pp. 193-95.

[*One of America's most highly respected literary critics and social historians, Howe was a longtime editor of the leftist magazine* Dissent *and a regular contributor to the* New Republic. *Greenberg was a Russian-born American poet, essayist, translator, and critic who dedicated himself to bringing Yiddish literature to English readers. In the following introduction to "Under a Fence," the critics provide an outline of the story.*]

When **"Under a Fence"** first appeared in the Soviet Yiddish periodical, *Di royte velt,* in 1929, its editor, perhaps anticipating that it would evoke a storm of attack from the more orthodox party-line critics, wrote: "It is a ring of allegorical and symbolic tales, mutually intertwined, expressed in a rich, rhythmic language . . . It is a kind of confession, a renunciation of the idealistic view of the world . . ." Except for the last phrase, obviously mistaken though intended, no doubt, as a protective device, the editor's description was a helpful one. For it leads us into the labyrinth of the story, into the actual experience of it rather than a misconceived attempt to reduce it to an intellectual jigsaw puzzle. The important thing, we believe, is not to look for detailed one-to-one equivalents of meaning for the rendered events, but to yield oneself to its phantasmagoria and thereby gain a general sense of its implica-

tions. So we offer here not a worked-out interpretation, but a few notes that may be helpful.

The story begins with a confession by a middle-aged scholar. Obviously a man of some achievement and stature, he tells his daughter about his debasing involvement with Lili, a circus rider, and his seeming drunkenness after being rudely thrown out of the circus. As the daughter attends her sick father, he confesses to having been unworthy of his calling, and this ends the initial episode, or narrative frame, of the story.

Then comes the substance of the confession, staged (hence the subtitle) as a "revue." What follows apparently has to do, in various grotesque forms and through the imagery of dream symbolism, with an experience of guilt—the scholar's guilt before his pupils (his literary disciples?), the trial where he is punished by burning, etcetera.

The scholar, writes the Yiddish critic Khone Shmeruk [in *The Field of Yiddish,* 1965], "sees himself as an accused man, completely losing his bond with his 'real' self. He is now an ex-hermit in circus leotards. He is tried by the senior judge, his former teacher Medardus, of the school of hermits, along with his own pupils . . . During the trial, the hermit tells about his transformation."

A phantasmagorical figure, the "dustman," appears. This figure tells the scholar-hermit that all of his creatures—father, mother, child—are made of "straw." They are, that is, useless, obsolete, ready for destruction.

The dustman, writes Shmeruk, "is the actual cause" of the scholar's guilt. "It is he who brought him to the circus and led him to Lili . . . He is capable of subjecting the hermit's values to public ridicule . . . At the same time, however, he is highly intimate with the hermit and solicitous about him . . . This is undoubtedly a personification of that part of the hermit's self which embodies a number of satanic, Mephistophelian attributes."

The name of Lili "is similar in sound to and hence associated with Lilith—the traditional female demon who makes men stray from the path of righteousness." As for Medardus, the scholar-hermit's teacher or master, Shmeruk traces a complicated genealogy from a story by the German writer, E.T.A. Hoffmann, where the figure represents a literary tradition of seriousness and autonomy—the very tradition the circus denies.

"The scholar, the last hermit, represents an intelligent man, an artist or perhaps even a writer. . . . External pressures and internal doubts pursue him ceaselessly. His daughter—his one creation up to now, his very own—is betrayed and harmed because of his attraction for Lili—an opposite creative principle, whose place is in the circus, and whose essence is tricks. External pressures are expressed by the loneliness of the hermit, which inclines him and readies him to accept his own doubts, symbolized by the dustman. He begins to believe in the strawness of his former path."

This story is a complicated but extremely powerful and moving revelation—a kind of symbolist outcry—of the agonies experienced by a gifted writer who has been forced,

'Under a Fence: A Revue' is a complicated but extremely powerful and moving revelation—a kind of symbolist outcry—of the agonies experienced by a gifted writer who has been forced, in part, to submit to the demands of a repressive external authority. Obliquely, it tells us a great deal about the feelings of Soviet Yiddish writers as the inquisitors grew more demanding.

—Irving Howe and Eliezer Greenberg

in part, to submit to the demands of a repressive external authority. Obliquely, it tells us a great deal about the feelings of Soviet Yiddish writers as the inquisitors grew more demanding. And in a way, the party-line critics were "right" in denouncing the story.

"Even so," concludes Shmeruk, "the issue is not too simple for Der Nister. One cannot ignore the opposition between the lonely tower of a last solitary hermit, filled with doubts, and the security of a seasoned circus actor in a packed hall. There remains the gnawing questions: Is this, then, the way? Is it, after all, only for select individuals? There is no definite answer to this question. Insecurity coupled with hopelessness and with the necessity to submit, out of 'hunger and joblessness,' to the transformation, increase the depth and horror of the tragedy of the man undergoing the test.

"Despite all of the doubts, Der Nister's judgment is, nevertheless, unequivocal. The feeling of guilt is stronger than the doubts, and the threefold punishment appears justified."

Der Nister closes the story's frame on a poignant note: the scholar-hermit, "drunkard and ashamed," is wept over by his daughter while he had "nothing to comfort her with and couldn't lift my head up to her."

Irving Howe   (essay date 1987)

SOURCE: "A Major Discovery," in *The Atlantic Monthly,* Vol. 259, No. 6, June, 1987, pp. 80-2.

[*In the following essay, Howe assesses Leonard Wolf's English translation of* The Family Mashber, *likening Der Nister's difficulty with narrative in the novel form to that of Boris Pasternak in* Doctor Zhivago, *and praising Der Nister's realistic characterizations.*]

"Here one has to turn one's soul upside down"—so, in 1935, wrote a Yiddish writer in the Soviet Union to his brother in Paris. The writer, who went by the pen name of Der Nister (Yiddish for "The Hidden One"), had long been drawn to the mysteries and nuances of literary symbolism, making forays into esoteric knowledge that derived in part from cabalistic and Hasidic sources. But, as he told his brother, "what I have written until now

aroused strong opposition [from the Communist literary bureaucrats]. . . . Symbolism has no place in Soviet Russia." Nor, in the years of Stalin's terror, did any other free-spirited literary approach.

Der Nister, whose real name was Pinhas Kahanovitch (1884-1950), had come to be recognized in Yiddish cultural circles as part of a lively gathering of modern novelists and poets centered in Kiev a few years before the First World War. He was a man with an austere, if not always accessible, spiritual life, the kind of writer who could never make large noises or reach large audiences. He kept a skeptical distance from both the ideological debates within the Jewish milieu and, later on, the politics of the young Soviet regime. But by the mid-thirties—when all writers in Russia, no matter what their language or style, felt the heavy hand of the commissars—Der Nister had decided to abandon (or perhaps hide?) his literary symbolism, if only to protect himself and his family. He started to compose a large-scale, seemingly traditional family chronicle, the sort of spacious and transparent novel that had been popular in Europe during the early years of this century.

The first volume of *The Family Mashber* appeared in Soviet Russia in 1939; the second could be published, nine years later, only in New York. Word filtered out from Soviet Russia that Der Nister left a third, concluding volume, but if so, it has disappeared. Perhaps it lies buried in the vaults of the Soviet secret police, together with a good many other works proscribed during the Stalin years. . . .

Over the years a few attempts have been made to bring Der Nister's novel to an audience beyond the shrinking and aging Yiddish readership; the book has been translated into Hebrew and French, and now, because of the devoted skill of Leonard Wolf, we have a very readable English version, one that captures much of the range and color of the original text.

The Family Mashber hasn't a word directly referring to the situation of Yiddish writers in the Soviet Union, but for anyone familiar with the circumstances of its origin, it seems stained with the bloody marks of history. The book deals with Eastern European Jewish life in the 1870s, but as I read, images of the 1930s crossed my line of vision: censors brutalizing, writers suffering, prisoners shot. Critics, I suppose, must try to be dispassionate, and so I will offer a straight literary judgment: this is a work of major interest, gripping in its frequent pictorial brilliance, deeply serious in thought, yet finally elusive. It's a book to engage with and ponder over, even if it's not quite the masterpiece its translator takes it to be.

Der Nister locates the action of his novel in a moment when Eastern European Jewish life, no longer unified by a firm religious world view, is simultaneously falling apart and renewing itself. For the novelist, such a moment seems made to order. "The perfect literary situation," the poet-critic Allen Tate once wrote, is when "a spiritual community is breaking up." Such situations are rich in drama and consciousness: the interplay between tradition and rebellion, the crumbling old and the unshaped new.

In the earlier years of this century novelists often grappled with this theme by focusing on a single family, making it the central field of tension, while behind it the larger community provided a shifting, precarious background. In turning to this kind of novel, Der Nister was following the lead of Yiddish writers who had begun edging their way into European literature by imitating those sprawling family chronicles through which European writers both mirrored and assaulted bourgeois values.

The Family Mashber is set in the western Ukrainian town of Berditchev, once under Polish rule and now with a growing Jewish population. Cultures meet and clash. In the distance is the Russian autocracy, powerful and feared; nearby, the Polish nobility, sulking after its defeat in the 1863 rebellion against czarism and, at least as Der Nister portrays it, slipping into paths of decadence. And in the foreground is the thickly populated Jewish community, now fragmented into an enfeebled orthodoxy, an ambitious commercial class, a seething underclass of laborers and toughs, and the germ of what will soon become the powerful movement of Jewish secularism. Writing with a curious detachment, as if this world were not the very source of his being, Der Nister shows neither partisanship nor enmity. The calm, mildly ironic voice we hear throughout the book is that of a man surfeited with, perhaps nauseated by, historical experience.

Now, if we read *The Family Mashber* in a spirit of acquiescence, as we might read Thomas Mann's *Buddenbrooks* or I. J. Singer's *The Brothers Ashkenazi*—that is, as a socio-historical panorama reflecting the crisis of a culture—the novel can be extremely satisfying. More so, probably, than if it is read in the way I propose. Plot, setting, characters, all seem to signal that this is essentially another family chronicle—all except the writer's voice as it keeps emerging in self-reflexive casuistries and ironies.

But let's turn to the story itself, following it along the path of the family chronicle. Moshe Mashber, an intelligent if rather limited merchant, finances the Polish nobles in their escapades, and when, through sheer fecklessness, they sink into hopeless debt, he sinks with them, into bankruptcy and then imprisonment. Moshe is a decent bourgeois, still somewhat attached to the old pieties but increasingly absorbed in the pursuit of gain.

Set off against Moshe is his brother, Luzi, "a man of interior disturbances," an imperious and aristocratic searcher for spiritual transcendence who becomes the local head of an extremist Hasidic sect, one that follows the call to ecstasy, contemplation, and otherworldliness of Nakhman of Bratslav, a great Hasidic teacher. Luzi's house becomes "a gathering point to which young people, whispering stealthily, came." I find myself wondering whether Der Nister's description of this religious sect is meant, however faintly, to invoke another sect, the kind that a few decades later would draw young people, "whispering stealthily," to the Luzis of Marxism. And there's the further note, gently struck by Der Nister, that in this sect of fundamentalist pietism there may be echoes of the false messianism of Sabbatai Zevi, which two centuries earlier had created havoc among European Jews.

Surrounding the Mashber brothers are the toughs and thugs, "enforcers" and arm-breakers, at the base of Jewish life, shown here sharply etched in their heaving brawn and mindless loyalty to rabbinic authority. These figures lend the novel a grittiness of texture that helps save it from sentimentalism, a besetting weakness of Yiddish fiction.

One other character demands notice, a surly and enigmatic fellow named Sruli, at odds with every segment of the Jewish community yet also serving as a connective link between the segments. Sruli is the most interesting kind of fictional character, indisputably "there" but never fully accessible to our rational understanding. Sometimes he does good deeds, sometimes he sinks into moral degradation, and at the end, a self-appointed Sancho Panza, he joins Luzi on a journey of spiritual wandering. One follows this Sruli with puzzled fascination, and as far as I can make out, he represents the current of anarchic energy coursing through a community too long pent up by repressive rituals.

So, if we wish, we can certainly read with pleasure and absorption, contenting ourselves with the familiar patterns of the family chronicle and even concluding, with the inexpensive piety of the worldly, that Moshe Mashber's grubby materialism is trumped by Luzi's elevated spirituality. But it will not do: Der Nister is too serious, perhaps too sly, for this sort of stock response. When Moshe, on the edge of disaster, asks Luzi to help save his firm, Luzi turns coldly away, declaring a superior disdain for "mere" material concerns. Quester of spirit Luzi may be, but his brother's keeper he is not.

Something of the keenest literary interest is happening here: a mature writer who is not by nature or training a realistic novelist is writing a realistic novel, yet as it proceeds, the book turns and twists into something else, as if the writer's deeper, "better" nature cannot fully be suppressed. The book breaks into a number of panels of representation: the clashes between the brothers Mashber, the journeys of Sruli into the town's lower depths, the frenetic rituals of the Hasidic sect. There occurs a tensing of rhythms, with Der Nister's calm giving way to prose that approaches the vibrations of expressionism and scenes that take on a grotesque cast. Especially vivid are those scenes devoted to Luzi's sect (with the stately Luzi dancing himself into abandonment, as if he were "a winged creature waking at sunrise who, in sheer joy . . . , flung himself off into space").

Der Nister's struggle with the novel as a form has a certain similarity to Boris Pasternak's struggle in *Doctor Zhivago*. Gifted writers inclined by training and temperament to nonrealistic genres can find themselves driven by historical pressures to undertake straight realism. The risks are large, and surely, as they enter the treacherous precincts of the novel, they know it. Neither Pasternak nor Der Nister quite mastered the art of narrative movement, that blessing of craft by which a novelist creates the illusion that depicted events are progressing through time. These writers are masters of the "still," the grotesque episode and lyrical moment; yet the paradox of their creativity is that it's precisely through their "inexpertness" with the novel that, in *Doctor Zhivago* and *The Family Mashber,* they best realize their talents.

What, finally, can one say about the implied significance, the thematic intentions, of Der Nister's book? Nothing with any certainty, for we don't have the third volume, which might bring everything into a coherent scheme of symbolism. But as I read the book, it does bear the marks of the historical moment in which it was written. Listening to this writer from a lost time, a wretched place, I hear a weary skepticism about all claims to a unified grasp of the world, all modes of moral or ideological single-mindedness.

The Mashber brothers go their separate ways, and no doubt there's something to be said for each of them: the decency of ordinary aims, the exaltation of spiritual quest. But each also has major flaws: the moral carelessness of the worldly, the zealot's ruthlessness in imposing joy. And there seems no way of blending or linking these two ways of life. The disunities of our age are beyond repair, and they cannot be removed by either will or program. Or so I tentatively conclude, as one Mashber brother is lowered into the earth and the other grasps for ways to rise above it.

Ruth R. Wisse   (essay date 1987)

SOURCE: "Lured by the Messiah," in *The New York Times Book Review,* July 12, 1987, pp. 15-16.

[*Wisse is a Romanian-born Canadian educator, translator, essayist, novella writer, and critic. In the following laudatory review of* The Family Mashber, *she notes Der Nister's tendency to obscure his own opinion of characters and messianic ideas in the novel by providing several justifications for every action and introducing "objective" characters to view the events.*]

In 1928, shortly after his return from western Europe to the Soviet Union, and before the campaign of public denunciation forced artists into line, the Yiddish writer Pinhas Kahanovitch, who wrote under the pseudonym Der Nister, published a characteristically opaque story called **"In My Estates."** In it an impoverished student comes upon a story book by Der Nister ("the hidden man"), who is portrayed on the book jacket as an institutionalized madman. The story within the story is about a keeper of 10 bears who, discovering that he has nothing left to feed his animals, offers them each one of his fingers to stave off their hunger. One by one the bears take their meal, but the ninth bear, made ravenous by the smell of blood, snaps up the two remaining fingers leaving none for the tenth. To keep the last and largest beast from making a meal of him the author promises to reveal secret sources of nourishment. Spared for the moment, he begins to tell his story.

Several years later, Der Nister began writing *The Family Mashber* as just such an attempt to keep the Russian bear at bay. A large, sprawling historical novel reminiscent of Dostoyevsky in its concentration on the human soul, it was unlike anything the author had attempted before. Kahanovitch had made his debut under his concealing pseudonym in 1907 with a timeless, mysterious kind of short fiction. Combining elements of Russian symbolism and strains of Jewish mysticism, Hassidism and folklore, his writing challenged the populist spirit of most contemporary Yiddish fiction by advertising its difficulty. Der Nister's spare narrative style hinted at ultimate sources of meaning, and his abstract plots introduced alien pagan and Christian motifs. When Der Nister showed his early work to the Yiddish literary master I. L. Peretz he was urged to use more substantive and familiar materials.

But following World War I and the Russian Revolution Der Nister's symbolist stories only grew more layered and complex. As a member of the émigré community in Germany from 1922 to 1926, he was exposed to the atmosphere of intense, almost manic experimentation in the Weimar era. The stories he wrote during this period and in the first years after his return to Russia seemed at once a new gloss on the cabalistic mysteries and an expression of anxious adjustment to the new social order. In 1929 Der Nister was accused of decadence and individualism and he was forced, if he wanted to publish at all, to become a social realist. He settled down to translate and "observe," and he wrote lackluster reportage.

With the idea for *The Family Mashber* Der Nister felt he had found a way to satisfy both his own artistic needs and the demands of Soviet cultural policy. The choice of a historical setting—the bustling Ukrainian Jewish city of Berdichev (called N in the novel) in the 1870's—would allow him to describe his native ground without fear of political deviation. He could introduce Jewish mystics and their visionary quest as a legitimate part of the historical canvas. Indeed, from 1935 onward, as installments of the novel appeared in Soviet Yiddish journals, the work was hailed as one of the finest achievements in Soviet Yiddish literature.

What we finally have, however, is a truncated work. Part one of the novel appeared in Moscow in 1939; parts one and two—the basis of the [1987] translation—in New York in 1948; part three was confiscated and lost when Der Nister was arrested in 1948 along with all the other major Soviet Yiddish writers. He escaped their mass execution in 1952 only by dying in 1950 in a prison hospital. Yet he could not have blamed his death on a political lapse or artistic "failure." Even those of his colleagues who had gone much further than he in appeasing the bear were consumed in the purge.

The Family Mashber—"mashber" means crisis—betrays the urgent circumstance of its composition. Ostensibly patterned on the great social epics of 19th-century Russian literature, it traces the decline of the three Mashber brothers: the successful, respectable merchant, Moshe; his younger brother, Alter, an apparent simpleton with unpredictable flashes of high intelligence; and the oldest brother, Luzi, who carries the spiritual burden of the family. This burden derives from their grandfather, a Jew who believed in the Messianic pretender Shabtai Tsvi, and as one of his followers committed many sins in anticipation of the Messianic kingdom. Luzi, through a lifelong moral quest, takes over from his father in trying to atone for his ancestor's heretical lapse.

> **Der Nister's every hint of the radiant future reminds the reader that the entire world of the novel must be destroyed to bring it about. Writing of its destruction was Der Nister's dangerous way of rekindling the sparks of its life. The Messianic cinders at the heart of the Bratslaver faith glow through *The Family Mashber*. It reads like the testimony of a man who knew he was playing with fire.**
>
> **— *Ruth R. Wisse***

Luzi's pilgrimage brings him to the Bratslaver sect of Hasidim, and it is this unlikely affiliation that constitutes the major turning point in the plot. Of all the groups that arose since the Hasidic revivalist movement took hold among East European Jews in the 18th century, the followers of Rabbi Nakhman of Bratslav in the Ukraine alone resisted rabbinic succession, and upon his death in 1811, instead of rallying around a new authority, continued to visit his grave in Uman. The resulting anarchy made their communion as suspect as its religious intent did. Rabbi Nakhman had hinted at his Messianic role in the *tikkun,* the restoration of harmony in the world order; and by testifying to his exclusive leadership his followers, the "dead" Hasidim, kept that dangerous promise alive. Luzi's adherence to this semi-outcast sect undermines the prestige of the family, and the group's behavior arouses among ordinary Jews a distrust that eventually erupts in violence.

If Der Nister set out confidently to write about a reactionary religious sect at the height of Stalin's campaign for proletarian art, he obviously sensed an essential connection between the Bratslaver's faith in an imminent redemption and the pure revolutionary temper. The radical asceticism of the Bratslavers offended the bourgeois spirit, as much as the revolutionary idealists challenged the bourgeois policy. Here, for example, is Moshe Mashber's reaction when his brother joins the Bratslav sect:

> The heart of the matter was, and Moshe felt this keenly, that his brother had taken a stand against an essential principle that animated and was accepted by all the world: that one had a right to struggle for acquisitions, to work for wealth, and to become wealthy without feeling ashamed. Luzi, who had heretofore been indifferent to all questions of wealth, who had never thought much about whether anyone was rich or poor, seemed now on such matters to have had a change of heart. It seemed to Moshe that Luzi now looked down at wealth, that he despised it, as if it was sinful merely to look at it—how much more sinful to take pleasure from it.

The guilt and fear that Luzi engenders precipitate Moshe's moral collapse long before a blackmail scheme involving the Polish nobility, and the consequences of a disastrous harvest, force him into bankruptcy.

Alongside Luzi—who is always associated with light—is Sruli Gol, the kind of practical facilitator so often attached to a holy man. A vivid, bitter character, Sruli rejects his inherited wealth, but uses the power it gives him to punish the rich and reward the poor. Sruli orchestrates the fatal quarrel between the Mashber brothers and derives malicious pleasure from his success; but, once Moshe is ruined, Sruli also cushions his family from ultimate humiliation. His coarse effort to force an egalitarian justice on the Jewish town cannot fail to suggest the Communist movement that would soon set about equalizing society.

But what does Der Nister think of this Messianic venture? His wariness in answering that question constitutes the hidden quality of this novel, which is ambiguous in a way that his earlier veiled fiction never was. Despite his obvious sympathies for the oppressed, the author does not link good and bad actions to their consequences, leaving a curious moral vacuum where one would expect some moral resolution. To further disclaim responsibility for his characters he develops several strategies, such as offering a number of plausible reasons for a given action, or introducing a hypothetical "someone" to witness a scene in his stead. The translator's fidelity to the original Yiddish keeps all these features before us—even though it might have been tempting to make the book smoother or give it more variety by changing some of them.

Crisis overtakes the main characters so early in the plot that we are spared the normal suspense over what will happen next. The real tension derives from the narrator. He promises in his introduction to give us the economic underpinnings of Jewish Berdichev from which all social and cultural consequences flow, but we soon see him lost in the visions and dreams of his characters and then struggling back to his duty. He assures us that "anyone with a keen eye might even then [in the 1870's] have been able to see the seeds of the future floating in the air," leaving us to wonder whether the image suggests a hidden reservation about the future or is only accidentally sloppy.

By drawing our attention to what Soviet historiography expects of the writer, Der Nister repeatedly exposes his deviation from it, and his every hint of the radiant future reminds the reader that the entire world of the novel must be destroyed to bring it about. Writing of its destruction was Der Nister's dangerous way of rekindling the sparks of its life. The Messianic cinders at the heart of the Bratslaver faith glow through this work. It reads like the testimony of a man who knew he was playing with fire.

David Malouf   (essay date 1987)

SOURCE: "Moshe and His Brothers," in *The New York Review of Books,* Vol. XXXIV, No. 14, September 24, 1987, pp. 38-40.

[Malouf is an Australian poet, short story writer, novelist, memoirist, editor, and critic. In the following review of The Family Mashber, *he praises Der Nister's capacity for creat-*

ing a starkly realistic and intriguing portrait of Russia in the 1870s.]

There are points on the earth, some of them disconcertingly close, that seem forever blank. We cannot imagine that life goes on there in the ordinary way; we cannot imagine good weather there or any of the settled existence in time that belongs to London or Paris or even to newer places like Boston or Sydney. This is partly a matter of ignorance—who would have guessed that there is a city in the Ukraine, called Berdichev, that even in 1865 had two hundred thousand inhabitants? It is also a matter of chauvinism: a view of the world that attributes all mainstream events to Western Europe and its satellites and sees life elsewhere as so denuded of history that it seems entirely dark; until, that is, in the case of eastern Poland, Belorussia, the Ukraine, it is illuminated by events of such horror (I am thinking of the sweep through those areas by the SS in 1941) that we tell ourselves, yes, these things do happen, but only in dim out-of-the-way places we know nothing of. The events then seem appropriate to the darkness of a place we have never thought of as real.

One of the achievements of **The Family Mashber,** a book that comes to us out of the blue—written in the late Thirties and only now translated from Yiddish—is that it makes this part of the world, and all its rich, exotic life, the center of things, the norm. So much so that when, in the midst of it all, a Palm Sunday frond appears, or Aristotle is mentioned, we are genuinely startled; a chink has been opened into a strange and incomprehensible world—the familiar classical, Christian, post-enlightenment one from which most of us have come. Which is to say that, like all great fictions, Der Nister's vast two-volume account of the city of N. (Berdichev) in the 1870s seizes the imagination, commands interest (even in subjects we know nothing about), imposes belief, and creates in the reading a life so deeply rooted in experience, in our sense of the way the world feels and moves, that it becomes immediately our own.

Der Nister (a pen name that in Yiddish means "The Hidden One") has been fortunate in his translator, but also in the moment Leonard Wolf has chosen to reveal him to us. A decade ago he might have presented an insoluble difficulty, but we have easier views now of what we might mean by "realism." The way to that has been prepared by Marquez and other South American writers and in English by Salman Rushdie, and we will do better to welcome **The Family Mashber** as a work of magic realism than to evoke (*pace* Wolf) *The Brothers Karamazov* or *Buddenbrooks*. We might be warned against such a reading by the style of the narration itself.

The plot of the novel, all that part of it that has to do with realistic events, can be dealt with quickly. The main line of it follows the fall from prosperity of the moneylender Moshe Mashber, which comes partly from his involvement with a group of Polish nobles who have got into trouble with the authorities, and cannot pay their debts, partly because the district is having a bad year, but mostly through the machinations of his fellow money-lenders in the community. His fall is paralleled by the move of his brother Luzi from leader of the persecuted Bratslav sect

of Hasidim to a life as pilgrim wanderer, and by the withdrawal of another, younger brother, Alter, a retarded idiot-saint, into isolation.

The difficulties of Moshe and his brothers serve as plot, just enough to keep us reading but more than enough to involve a large number of subsidiary characters: Reb Dudi, the representative of an ossified Jewish orthodoxy that finds itself dependent, in the end, on violence; Schmulikl Fist and Yone the tavern keeper, two very different kinds of thug; beggars like Ten Groschen Pushke; usurers like the Kitten; ruthless merchants like the effete Yakov-Yossi; scholars and freethinkers like Mikhl Bukyer (one of the most attractive figures in the book) and Yossele Plague the enlightenment man; Polish nobles of a grotesque decadence and silliness; Perele the bawd and baby killer; and several wives and mothers of heroic fortitude of whom the most memorable are Esther-Rokhl, Malke-Rive, and the Mashber's maid Gnessye. But the development of the plot is negligible. Everything of real significance here happens either too deep inside the characters to be touched by it or outside the plot altogether, and the center of the book is not one of the major characters but a marginal one, Sruli Gol, who works both with the plot and against it. He is the agent of another force than the one that is on the move in the *social* world. Everything that is most original, and most disruptive of received values in **The Family Mashber,** is in Sruli Gol. If we are to discover what the book is finally about, we can do it only through him. He is a marvelous creation.

Sruli is the least pious character in a book where everyone, even the thugs, is pious, to a point where piety itself seems suspect. He is clown, drunk, sinner, and blasphemer; a parasite at rich men's tables but also their scourge; a protector of the poor, the weak, the insulted and injured; a guide to the erring. And he intervenes at crucial points in almost everyone's life. He has an odd facility (emphasized in the text each time as a prepared joke) for appearing on the threshold the moment anything new is about to occur. As a marginal figure the threshold is his proper place. He is a natural crosser of boundaries, as much at home with Yossele Plague, the secularist, and Schmulikl Fist, whom he has the knack of putting immediately to sleep, as with the saintly Luzi. He even crosses the line into the Christian world, and not only when in his youth he becomes a waiter in poor taverns. At the Prechistaya Fair (in honor of the Virgin's birthday) he stops to hear the *bandura* players sing an old song of Cossack prisoners among the Turks:

> There, in the midst of the racket of the town and the fair, in the tumult of buying and selling, and the shouting of thieves, a small island of people has been formed around the musicians, an island of people who have taken time to feel compassion for ancient captivities—national or individual. . . .

> Yes. And the peasants in the crowd are amazed at this strange fellow, this curiously dressed Jew; where does he come from; why, like themselves, does he have tears in his eyes; why is he taking this tale of Christian suffering so much to heart,

what is it that makes him give the bandura players such a large tip?

It is the insult to Sruli, a guest at his table, that creates the first rift in the Mashber family (a quarrel with Luzi) and reveals the slackening grip on family affairs that will lead to Moshe's fall. Yet it is Sruli who later saves the family from ruin. He talks about this when he sits alone drinking and addresses a wine glass as if it were Moshe himself. "It may be . . . that I have been designated from on high to be your incarnate punishment," Sruli says, "and that against my own will I am the whip wielded by your fate. And if that's the case, I swear by this brandy, I think you've been whipped enough." He is, one suspects, a subversive figure here; not just in himself but of the action as well, and most of all of that pious version of the world that Der Nister's narrative is meant to challenge. "If you want to know why I did it," Sruli goes on, speaking now of his attempts to save Moshe, "it's all because I wanted to frustrate fate for once—to pluck the rod from the wielder's hand—from fate's. That's something I have wanted to do ever since I came to the age of reason." It is part of the joke in this great scene that the tavern keeper Yone, suspecting Sruli of plotting a financial coup, has set eavesdroppers on him. They can make nothing of this "confession to the second glass." The reader too is left to puzzle out the odd relationship between Sruli as whip and that other Sruli who plucks the rod from the wielder's hand.

However contradictory he may be, however unruly or blasphemous, Sruli is the one character in the book who seems to have the author's clear approval. In one of his craziest moments he appears, in a burlesque of Hasidic practices, at the grave of a famous rabbi and enters into his own form of communion with it:

> The sun's heat beat down on his head. Sruli sat in a partly cooled space among tall grasses sharing his liquor with the rabbi whose name was inscribed on the headstone. A sip for him, a sip for the rabbi poured over the stone. Until finally the bottles were empty and his head—full. It felt heavy, things around him began to whirl: the cemetery, the gravestones. The tree above him seemed to rise up, roots and all; heaven and earth changed places; and everything he had seen that day at the fair—Layb the barber-surgeon and Menashe his apprentice, cutting into abscesses on the breasts or under the armpits of peasant women, the teeth extracted with pincers, veins opened or blood drawn by leeches, and what he had seen of the blind beggars, their eyelids open or closed; and what he had seen later in Malke-Rive's home—the sick Zisye, with sunken and yellow cheeks of a man who was more than half dead, and who bore the sign of death on his forehead; all of that, and the liquor he had drunk or poured out on the ground, mingled in his head making the world turn. He felt a spasm of nausea. Leaning his head against the gravestone he rested there awhile, then the nausea overwhelmed him and he threw up, covering the headstone from top to bottom with his vomit.

That is one side of the man. The other occurs when Sruli,

in the most solemn and elevated passage in the book, plays his flute at Luzi's house:

> Then Sruli played. And now he surpassed himself. His tone was so pure, the notes he struck so remarkable, that his hearers immediately forgot the poverty of their lives and who they were. Sruli seemed to have led them to a lofty palace, a spacious structure built on an appropriately elevated site amid splendid surroundings. A palace with a gate closed against intruders and against those who were unworthy to enter.

> And it seemed that Sruli stood before that gate-Sruli and his listeners whom he had brought with him. And as he played he seemed to be persuading the gates to open for them because they were worthy of that honor.

> "It is what they deserve," his flute seemed to say. "Now, they are the poor and the disappointed. But who can say what tomorrow will bring or who will inherit the earth on the day after tomorrow?"

> With that the gate opened. Sruli and those who were with him went in. At first those who followed him felt constrained and embarrassed, because they were not sure that they had been admitted because of their own merits. But Sruli walked before them, encouraging them with the sort of music one plays to welcome guests into a palace.

> And then they entered halls that were richly decorated and where there were tables with beautiful place settings. And there were people sitting there, like those whom Sruli had just brought in. They, too, were poorly clad, they, too, were sorry-looking, but they were relaxed and happy and hospitably made place for the newcomers and encouraged them to feel at ease.

> Then the owners of the palace came in. They were beautifully dressed and gave the impression that they had never before had anything to do with the sorts of people Sruli had brought there, and yet they were proud of their guests. They sat with them and shared food and drink with them. Later, when they had eaten and drunk, and the newcomers started to dance, the owners of the palace danced feverishly with them all until, for sheer joy, the palace roof began to rise and all who were there cried, "Let the world be free. Let all who will come share our celebration. Everyone, from the highest to the lowest, the wise as well as those who have but a penny's worth of it. All. All. And not only people, but the creatures of the forest and the cattle in the fields are welcome too."

Two other passages appear to offer hints of how we are to fit Sruli into the novel as a whole and how we are, therefore, to read it.

Money is at the center of Moshe's story and we might gather from this part of the book that Der Nister's attitude to it is conventional. But Sruli's use of it calls that in doubt. Sruli's reaction to money is visceral:

> He remembered that one day, hearing the word

"money," he was suddenly assailed by a head-ache and a profound pain deep in his bowels, and from that time on the word always produced nearly the same effect on him—a ghastly sense of revulsion, not only against the word "money" itself but even against those who owned it.

But Sruli too has money and he too puts it to use—though not in the commercial sense. It is the active agent of his good will. In drunken communion with Rabbi Liber's tombstone he confesses:

> And it's not just his notes that I have. Not just Moshe Mashber's. I have them from others greater than he is. From the richest of the rich. I tell you I have them from Him who can say, "The silver is mine, and mine is the gold." I have them from the Creator of the World Himself, and I beg you, dear Rabbi Liber, to tell Him up there that he, so and so, son of so and so, Sruli Gol has claims and complaints against Him. One day I'll come and stand before His throne and make them myself, but meanwhile, Reb Liber, be good enough to make them for me.

Money here, and promissory notes, have acquired a mystical quality—they are part of what gives Sruli his power among men to challenge fate and reverse it—or is it to challenge the punishing figure of man and the rabbi's "God"?

Der Nister was born Pinhas Kahanovitch in Berdichev in 1885. When he began writing it was as a mystical fabulist, creating tales that derived for the most part from the Hasidic teacher Nakhman of Bratslav (for those of us who know nothing of these things Leonard Wolf provides a useful introduction)—tales about angels, ghosts, doppelgängers, miracle workers, and dancing rabbis in which the "other world," the world of visions and dreams, is as real as the workaday one of marketplaces and household happenings.

The sect founded by "the Bratslaver," with Luzi at its head, is still active in *The Family Mashber;* the move to destroy it is a vivid part of the book. But more importantly Der Nister, in creating his documentary epic of Yiddish society, has kept faith with his origins as a writer by keeping the style and the narrative formulas, but also the freedoms, of the "tale." The action of his novel is grounded in shady deals and intrigue of every sort—a world of moneybags great and small, tavern keepers, porters, peddlers, thugs, beggars, whores, and rabbis of rival sects—but the book is shot through with the light of another order of being. Actuality may transform itself, at any moment, into a state in which dreams are a more significant clue to what is happening, or to motive or character, than either social background or psychology. This is true both of the large number of characters here who are god-obsessed and of those who are not, since it derives from the mind of the narrator; it is part of his mode of perception.

Der Nister as narrator is at hand in every paragraph of the work: as intermediary, picture maker, stage manager, commentator, speculator, and guide to his lost world. This form of narration, at once sophisticated and traditional, has little to do with the nineteenth-century novel but a great deal to do with a tradition of village storytelling that both engages the listener and plays with his engagement. It is full of formulations like "an observer might have noticed" or "should a stranger have approached he would have seen"; or plain statements followed by "Why?" and two or three plausible answers, then "No, that was not the principal cause, not *the* reason"; or Der Nister will stop the narrative altogether to create a tableau, saying, "It is necessary to see this scene clearly." Much of the ease we feel in entering this odd and unfamiliar world comes from the way the narration prepares a place for us as listeners. We are included, even before the narrator makes his world, in the voice he finds to breathe it forth.

The old-fashioned, formal mode of address—setting the reader close to the narrator but at a distance from the action—accounts, I think, for the odd sense we get of the novel's being grounded in actualities of place but of floating free in time. (Thomas Mann uses a similar method, but more knowingly, in *Joseph and his Brothers,* and **The Family Mashber** seems to me to be closer to that book than to *Buddenbrooks.*) Despite a reference here and there to telegraph wires or trains, we get no sense here that we are in the nineteenth-century fictional world of Zola or Tolstoy or Balzac. In its strict hierarchies, its definition of people according to their trade, its market fairs and taverns, its grotesqueries and gothic superstitions, **The Family Mashber** has the feel of the Middle Ages, a world not yet grounded in the secular and material, in which everything—every object, every gesture—is emblematic. This especially affects all that side of the novel that has to do with Moshe Mashber's financial ruin, which seems more like *Volpone* than *César Birotteau,* and will trouble only those who want to read the book as another nineteenth-century social documentary. For Der Nister, writing in the shadow of Stalinism in the Thirties, it must have been a conscious and necessary choice. For one thing it saved him from being too precise about the social forces that were to lead, in his own lifetime, to the revolution. More importantly, it allowed his writing to function at its richest and most original: in just that surviving medieval world of dual levels and double images that the bourgeois novel (not to speak of the social realist one) has no place for.

The third volume of **The Family Mashber** (which would have carried the tale forward into Der Nister's own lifetime) was completed but is lost. Der Nister himself was arrested with other Yiddish writers in 1950 and soon died in a prison hospital. Without it we cannot judge the novel's final shape. The opening, however, is full of foreboding, and not just for the family Mashber. Der Nister ends his evocation of the rich life of the city, its market, its synagogues of every kind, by suggesting that "anyone with a keen eye might even then have been able to see the seeds of the future floating in the air."

That future, as Der Nister knew, was dissolution: through secularization during the revolution, extermination by the Nazis, and official persecution under Stalin:

> Should a stranger come to the market, and should he stay for a while, he would very soon get a whiff of dissolution, the first hint that very soon the full stink of death would arise from the

whole shebang: the buying and selling, the hulla-
baloo of wheeling and dealing, the entire giddi-
ness of all those whirling there. . . . If a stranger did show up, we say . . . if he were a man
with somewhat refined sensibilities, he would
feel grief at his heart, he would sense that the
thresholds on which the night watchmen sat
were already mourning thresholds, that the
sealed doors, chain and locks would never be replaced, and that to enlarge the picture, to frame
it truly, one would need to hang a death lamp to
burn quietly here in the middle of the market to
be a memorial to the place itself.

What is remarkable, given the elegiac note, is that the picture "truly framed," the world of the book itself, is so un-
sentimental. The life it resurrects, a whole culture in fact,
for all its obsession with God and the Law, is neither better nor worse than any other: the seeds of corruption, of
dissolution, are within it. Whatever Der Nister may have
felt about the historical forces, this society as he paints it
has all it needs of fanaticism, intolerance, injustice, and
crude violence to destroy it from within. Over and over
again we see Moshe Mashber's household, the image of security and stable middle-class prosperity, savagely disrupted: by the screams of the "idiot" brother Alter, by the
arrival at Moshe's table of the hired bully Schmulikl Fist,
at last by the mob of looters. Outside this household, the
religious leader, Reb Dudi, in a rigid and inhuman adherence to the Laws, rejects the freethinking scholar Mikhl
Bukyer, condones his destruction, and in the persecution
of the Bratslav sect the rabbi allows town thugs to become
the effective arm of his authority. At the end the whole
community reverts to a state of blind superstition, haunted
by

> miracle workers, all sorts of fortune-tellers, Jew-
> ish and non-Jewish, . . . seekers after easy
> money, magicians, mezuzah examiners, squint-
> eyed cabalists who wore sheepskin and woolen
> socks in summer and in winter and who pulled
> their magic remedies and philters out of their
> filthy breast pockets, . . . famous *real* miracle
> rabbis from abroad, . . . exotic pilgrims . . .
> from Jerusalem and Safed, from Turkey and
> Yemen.

This is a world, to take a phrase from earlier in the book,
that is "giddily whirling," and not in ecstasy.

In all this moral and spiritual disintegration, the figures
who stand out are the apostates: Sruli, Mikhl Bukyer,
Yossele Plague, the rationalist with his schemes for social
improvement (though we know where some of those lead),
and the saintly Luzi, whom we respect mostly because
Sruli does. One of Sruli's great moments toward the end
is a dream in which he sees Mikhl Bukyer, who has rejected Judaism, as one of the true liberators:

> He dreamed:
>
> That Luzi was somehow the owner of a large
> garden fenced in on all sides and kept closed and
> locked. And Mikhl was the watchman there. But
> then he noticed that the garden fence was not a
> normal one. Rather it was like a prison wall. It
> was too tall to climb over and there was no crack
> or opening in it anywhere that would have per-
> mitted anyone to look in. Then Sruli saw that
> Luzi no longer had the look of an owner, but
> rather of a prisoner of this garden. Sruli was very
> distressed by this but there was no way to get in
> to help him. Then suddenly he saw that the wall
> was warping, groaning, and the deeply rooted
> pillars holding it up heaved and toppled, bring-
> ing the entire wall crashing down with them.
> And then when the wall had fallen, Mikhl, with
> a pleased smile on his face, appeared in the gar-
> den as if he alone, all by himself, had demolished
> the wall . . . or in any event as if he had been
> made very happy by its fall. And then the look
> of joy on his face was changed to the look of deep
> woe on the face of one who has labored with
> might and main to destroy something only to
> feel himself destroyed in the process. Sruli,
> grateful to him for his work of liberation, hur-
> ried over to thank him and to express his sympa-
> thy.

In the event, fifty years after it was written, the great
achievement of *The Family Mashber* is to have re-created
with such passionate objectivity, in all its complexity and
breadth, a world that exists now only in this enduring memorial to it—which is one of the things that literature, of
all the arts, can most grandly do. *The Family Mashber* is,
finally, a book that leads us, like Sruli, to cross thresholds,
most of all the threshold of our own experience; to enter
in and be moved like him by the "spirit of celebration."

Elena Guro

1877-1913

(Pseudonym of Eleonora Genrikhovna von Notenberg)
Russian poet, short story writer, and playwright.

INTRODUCTION

Guro was among the first representatives of the Russian
Futurist movement of the early 1900s. Influenced by the
visual art of the French Impressionist and Dada movements, the Futurists attempted to dispel the Symbolist notion of the mystical essence of poetry by focusing on form
and craft rather than on ideal beauty and romantic language. Guro, the only woman among the early Futurists,
often used single-word sentences in her prose and nonsense words in her poetry to illuminate the minute details
of specific moments and to capture a childlike perspective.
While she received little critical attention during her lifetime, she is now recognized as a unique voice in Russian
literature.

Biographical Information

Born in St. Petersburg, Guro grew up in a cultured household. She studied painting at the Society for the Encouragement of the Arts, and became respected as a professional artist after she was commissioned to illustrate the
1904 edition of George Sand's *Grandmother's Tales*. In
1909, Guro and her husband Mikhail Matyushin, an artist, composer, and musician, helped found the avant-garde
art group Venok ("Wealth"), the members of which eventually formed the core of Russian Futurism. Guro published her first short story, "Ranyaya vesna" ("Early
Spring"), in *Sbornik molodykh poetov* ("The Almanac of
Young Poets") in 1905. Her collection of poetry, short stories, and plays, *Sharmanka* (*The Hurdy-Gurdy*), appeared
in 1909. In 1910, with fellow Futurists David Burliuk, V.
Kamensky, and Viktor Khlebnikov, she published a miscellany entitled *Sadok sudei* (*A Trap for Judges*). Suffering
from leukemia, Guro died at her summer house in Finland
in 1913.

Major Works

Guro's dream-like imagery, attempts to capture fleeting
instants of perception, and reverence for nature and childhood are hallmarks of her work. Guro's books, including
The Hurdy Gurdy, Osennii son (*The Autumn Dream*), and
Nebesnye verblyuzhata (*The Baby Camels of the Sky*), are
collections of short pieces in a variety of forms. Like other
Futurists, she often interwove poetry and prose, experimenting with sparse language and unconventional prosody. Her child-like voice and use of lyrical nonsense words
and phrases coincides with the Futurists' emphasis on the
purely aesthetic aspect of language. Often her works evidence the strong influence of the plastic arts on Futurism

by abandoning plot to describe a setting or a moment rather than tell a story, particularly in her pieces that juxta-
pose images of rural and urban experience.

PRINCIPAL WORKS

Sharmanka [*The Hurdy Gurdy*] (poetry, prose, and
    drama) 1909
Osennii son [*The Autumn Dream*] (poetry, prose, and
    drama) 1912
Nebesnye verblyuzhata [*The Baby Camels of the Sky*]
    (poetry and prose) 1914

CRITICISM

Vladimir Markov (essay date 1968)

SOURCE: *Russian Futurism: A History*, University of
California Press, 1968, 467 p.

[*In the following excerpt, Markov provides an overview of Guro's major works.*]

Elena Guro was the pen name of Eleonora Genrikhovna von Notenberg, who seems in many respects to be a stranger among the early futurists. The only woman among the men, most of whom tried to be as masculine, loud, and colorful as possible both in their verse and in their lives, she was a quiet, introverted person who shunned people and was preoccupied with soft nuances in her work. Even the fact that she was born in St. Petersburg into a general's family (some say that she was an illegitimate daughter of the Emperor) sets her apart from her fellow futurists with their provincial and often plebeian backgrounds. Guro was a professional painter who, after graduating from the School of the Society for the Encouragement of the Arts, worked under such famous artists as Tsionglinsky, Bakst, and Dobuzhinsky, but she also had her own studio. She lived on a government pension and had an estate in Finland, where she died of tuberculosis after suffering for many years from pernicious anemia and neuritis of the heart. She knew French poetry well, and her work betrays an interest in German and Scandinavian literature. Among her favorite authors were Verhaeren, Vielé-Griffin, Alexander Blok, Ivan Konevskoi, Andrei Biely (with emphasis on his "symphonies"), and Remizov.

Guro is probably the most neglected among the early Russian futurists, a fate that is undeserved because she is one of the very original and talented Russian writers. She made her literary debut with a story, **"Rannyaya vesna"** (**"Early Spring"**), printed in 1905 in the inconspicuous *Sbornik molodykh pisatelei* (*An Anthology of New Writers*). She published some of her work in five of the futurist miscellanies. That published in *Troe* (*The Three*) appeared posthumously, as did the last of her three published books. The announced *Bednyi rytsar* (*The Poor Knight*) never materialized, although as late as 1917 Mayakovsky tried to persuade Maxim Gorky to publish it.

When *Sadok sudei* was being prepared, Guro was already the author of *Sharmanka* (*The Hurdy-Gurdy*), which appeared in February of 1909 and attracted no attention at all, though Guro showed herself in it as a mature and interesting writer. Most illustrations in the book are by Guro herself. Although the influence of symbolism is unmistakable in the prose, poetry, and especially the dramas printed in the book, Guro stands here on her own two feet as probably the most representative of all Russian impressionists. Guro's impressionism is particularly noticeable in the first part of the book, which contains eight examples of her prose. **"Pered vesnoi"** (**"Before Spring"**), for instance, is an impressionistic description of St. Petersburg first during the day, then at dusk, by a person who is drawn outside, unable to stay inside four walls, and who, at the end of the story, comes back home and falls asleep on the bed in street clothes, exhausted. Nothing happens in the story. There are hurried descriptions of passersby and memories of Nice; the narrator gives alms to a beggar, enters a florist's shop, imagines the ideal life of the shop owners (here Guro is on the verge of the stream-of-consciousness technique). The real content of the story is those "light thoughts, which touch everything lightly," brief, ephemeral states of mind the narrator experiences while walking around the city. Guro frequently resorts to short or single-word sentences to suggest those "light touches," as in the following brief excerpt: "Chisto umytaya. Syro. Veterok . . . —I svetlaya" ("Am washed clean. It's damp. A breeze . . . —And transfigured"). There are two more pieces that can be termed urbanistic, fragments of impressions of the same city, mostly at night, often disconnected and intermingled with passages in which the author tries to imagine what is going on in the minds of the people she meets or in the rooms behind the lighted windows, or what is going to happen to some of the passersby. Sometimes there are suggestions of a plot (as in **"Tak zhizn idet"** [**"Thus Life Goes"**] where the impressions of the city and the feelings of pain are those of Nelka, a man-crazy teenager, mistreated by her stepfather), but the story never materializes. Occasionally there is outright symbolism, as in the appearance of a mysterious king amidst the city crowds in **"Pesni goroda"** (**"Songs of the City"**).

Guro not only poeticizes the city, but she worships nature, as can be seen in her stories with a country background (it is invariably the Finnish *dacha* areas with pine trees and coastal landscapes). She almost equates nature with poetry: "Take a lump of black earth, dilute it with water from a rain barrel or from a ditch, and you will get excellent poetry." Nature is often anthropomorphic, as in the creative efforts of trees and stones in **"Da budet"** (**"Fiat"**); but, on the other hand, mankind is sometimes decivilized as in the same story, where modern life is presented as the eternal life of prehistoric people. In her attempt to animate the whole universe, Guro frequently makes inanimate things alive. In her prose, "chairbacks smile," "the dark day stoops and almost hides its head in its shoulders," armchairs and chests not only "gaily . . . look into your eyes," but are intimately tied with Fate. In her efforts to achieve freshness and closeness to nature, Guro is particularly attracted to the theme of childhood. Often things are presented as perceived or imagined by a child. In the prose miniature, **"Domashnie"** (**"Home Creatures"**), when there is rain outside, a child receives visits from all kinds of vague, fantastic creatures. Children are able not only to see things as if for the first time, but to hear words in their original freshness. In one story, the girls, having arrived at a newly bought estate, listen to the adults' conversations about a brick factory and about the delivery of the coal tar, and "both the novelty and the uplift from those new, fresh, raw, and hard words not worn by usage were communicated to them." One could see here futurism with its efforts to renovate words, but that would be an anachronism in a book published at the very beginning of 1909. Impressionism would be the correct word here, too, and any reader of Russian literature would probably find this passage reminiscent of Chekhov's "The Peasants" in which the women are touched to tears by incomprehensible words in the Gospel.

Guro's poetry is less successful and less original, on the whole, than her prose. The more metrical her verse, the less at ease she seems to feel; in this early book, she is already attracted by accentual verse and sometimes comes close to free verse. A certain predilection for Germanic themes (Walter von der Vogelweide, Wolfram at the coffin of Elisabeth) can be noted. Her lyric, often strongly rhythmic prose, on the other hand, shows maturity and a sure hand. Fragmentary composition is sometimes emphasized by separating portions of her "stories" from each other by dots. Guro also uses more original visual devices both for separating fragments of prose and for creating a mood: tiny drawings of leaves, fir trees, stars, or just plain circles with dots in the middle—all these placed between the lines or in the margin.

Probably the best prose in *Sharmanka* is **"Poryv" ("An Impulse")**, a story of the meeting of, and the subsequent friendship between, two women, both writers, living in the country, one of them having heart trouble. Here again there is impressionism in the way and in the order in which the story is told. At the beginning, we do not know who the characters are or exactly what is going on. Only gradually, mostly through pieces of conversation, are the relationships and situations clarified. At what would be the end, the author refuses to "terminate the tale" and leaves the whole thing up in the air. The influence of symbolism, especially of Biely, is clearly seen in the story's being told on several planes, with "eternity looking through the fir tree" and the women appearing, in a metaphysical glimpse, as "two rays of light getting hooked to each other among worlds." In addition to "Prose," "Trifles," and "Poems," there is a portion of *Sharmanka* entitled "Plays" containing two lyric dramas, **"Nishchii Arlekin" ("The Indigent Harlequin")** and **"V zakrytoi chashe" ("In a Closed Chalice")**, both well done, though completely in the tradition of Alexander Blok.

Most of Guro's next book, *Osennii son (The Autumnal Dream)*, published in 1912, is a play with the same title. It is dedicated to the memory of Guro's son who died as a child and whom she continued to think of as alive, so much so that she bought toys for him and made drawings of him as she imagined he would have looked at various stages in later life. In the drawings in *Osennii son,* he is a lanky youth of about eighteen with a dreamy, aristocratic face. The hero of the play is Baron Wilhelm Kranz, a pathetic dreamer, mocked by vulgar and prosaic people and consciously presented as another embodiment of Don Quixote, as well as an imaginary portrait of Guro's son. At the end of the play, Guro presents a rather obvious moral of the temporary victory of prosaic vulgarity over romantic idealism, though the latter is assured an eternal life. The play is followed in the book by a few pieces of Guro's typically lyric prose, as well as two poems written in free verse. One of the prose fragments, without a title, has surrealistic features: it is a description of a horselike creature with a horse name (Bulanka) who is clothed and speaks like a human being, and is attacked by *koromysla* ("yokes to carry pails with water").

Guro's third book, the posthumously published *Nebesnye*

verblyuzhata (The Baby Camels of the Sky), appeared in 1914 when Russian futurism had already reached the peak of its development. This book, with the letters of its title sprouting leaves and with two photographs of the author and many illustrations between its covers, is Guro's most typical work, and probably her best. It contains only lyric prose miniatures and several poems, mostly written in free verse; here they are not assigned to different parts of the book, as they were in *Sharmanka,* but are freely mixed so that the boundary between prose and verse is obliterated. The fragmentary character of the work is further enhanced in that titled and untitled pieces are printed in such a way that it is often difficult to determine whether a given fragment is independent or is the sequel to the one before it. We find here the familiar themes and motifs such as trees, spring, silence, earth, nature in general, faithfulness to one's youth and one's dreams, the awkward shyness of children and poets, objects with a soul, Don Quixote, and the like. Despite a certain unevenness, one finds in the book a more mature and sure hand, as well as much of that engaging purity of spirit characteristic of Guro. The first piece, **"Gazetnoe obyavlenie" ("A Newspaper Ad")**, is the keynote of the book with its combination of childish fantasy and serious overtones: it is about capturing "the baby camels in the sky," good-natured and clumsy spirits who are shorn of their fluff (from which shirts are made) and then released. Fantasies and lyric sketches of real life are freely interspersed in the book with moralistic admonitions. The final piece, entitled **"Obeshchaite!" ("Promise!")**, admonishes people not to betray their dreams and what their works represent, and was recited at Guro's funeral. In the book Guro pays tribute to the futurist predilection for neologism, though she has included very few of them; the most successful ones are created in the manner of the language of children.

Elena Guro may present a stumbling block for those who try to create a unified picture of Russian futurism. At first glance she does not look like a futurist, and some critics have been on record against her being so classified. Difficulties arise if one considers her against the background of later futurism. She lacks the iconoclastic spirit and the loudness usually associated with the movement; nor can one find in her work much verbal experiment. One may also remember that she did not sign the first important manifesto in *A Slap,* rarely participated in futurist public appearances, and refused to print her work in the second volume of *Sadok sudei* if it carried the name of "Hylaea," accepted by 1912 by practically all the rest of the futurists as the designation for their literary group. Sometimes she almost seems to belong to futurism because of her bitterness at not having been accepted by the "ruling" literary circles of symbolism: she occasionally betrays this feeling, as, for instance, in the words about her "poems no one wants to print" in *The Baby Camels in the Sky.* If, however, one accepts the idea that impressionism played an important part in the early stages of futurism, Guro easily takes her legitimate place in it. For example, her urbanism is impressionistic, rather than "classically" futuristic as found in Marinetti, Mayakovsky, and Shershenevich; this may explain the paradoxical fact that urbanism coexists with her worship of nature. One should also remember that the whole picture of Russian futurism was never smooth and clear. Some of Guro's "unfuturistic" features are shared with Khlebnikov, who also was an introvert and not much of a fighter. (One may add Guro's similarity to Khlebnikov in her fragmentary structure, in her attraction to a primeval freshness, and in her preoccupation with children's language.) But there are enough details that link Guro with the usual image of futurism. Critics (Aseyev, Khardzhiev) were right when they saw in Guro's poem **"Gorod" ("City")**, published in *Rykayushchii Parnas* (*Roaring Parnassus*), many qualities connecting her with Mayakovsky. She also made minor contribution to what is generally considered futurism's most radical creation—*zaum*, the so-called transrational language—but she did it inconspicuously, subtly, and with feminine gentleness. In her poem **"Finlandia,"** published in *The Three*, the trees *shuyat* (a word invented by Guro) rather than *shumyat* (the usual Russian word to describe the sound of trees in wind). Alexei Kruchenykh, the futurist extremist and the most ardent champion and propagandist of *zaum*, admired this innovation and wrote that coniferous trees precisely *shuyat*, whereas deciduous ones *shumyat*. Another futurist, Sergei Bobrov, saw in the same poem an imitation of the sounds of the Finnish language, and much of the Russian *zaum* was later written to imitate the sound of foreign tongues. For Kruchenykh, Guro's work was to be an example of one of the basic qualities of futurist literature, its being written for "momentary reading" or immediate comprehension (*chtoby smotrelos v mgnovenie oka*). Her attempts to illustrate her works in an original way are also similar to those of Kruchenykh and other acknowledged futurists.

It seems, however, that Guro's real stature and literary importance will be established only when she is discussed in the entire context of Russian impressionism, which is not my intention here. It is not an accident that her strongest influence is felt in Vasily Kamensky's most impressionistic book, *Zemlyanka* (*The Mud Hut*), published in 1910. The sources of Guro's impressionism, it can be suggested here, may be partly of foreign origin, but such a proposal requires careful and detailed scrutiny. It was only natural to borrow from German-Austrian literature in which impressionism had its clearest manifestation. For instance, literary miniatures, sketches, notes, pieces of dialogue, occasionally with an admixture of free verse poems, can be found in the work of the Austrian impressionist Peter Altenberg (particularly in his *Was mir der Tag zuträgt* [1901]), who, to be sure, differs from Guro in his hedonistic world outlook. But it is not hard to hear in Guro's tone echoes of some of the impressionistic works of Rainer Maria Rilke, especially in his *Aufzeichnungen des Malte Laurids Brigge;* it is in Rilke, too, that one finds Guro-like objects with a soul. Guro's sources, however, are much more complex. For example, her free verse may owe something to that of Vielé-Griffin, and her prose miniatures, to Remizov (*Posolon*). The anonymous writer in the third issue of *Soyuz molodezhi* (*Union of Youth*) tried to connect Guro with the contemporary painting of Artur von Wiesen; and Soviet scholars very convincingly saw musical composition and a system of leitmotivs in her prose, reminding the reader that Debussy, Scriabin, and Liadov were her favorite composers.

Some futurists respected Guro and tried to promote her reputation during her lifetime and after her death. Others were more restrained in their evaluation and called her work a "mixture of Maeterlinck and [Francis] Jammes made with Russian starch jelly [*kisel*]" and spoke about "the quiet melopeia of her words drained of blood, with which Guro tried to translate her astral shimmer into spoken Russian." Guro never attracted much attention on the outside, and critics began mentioning her **Sharmanka** only four years after it was published. It is interesting to note, however, that Alexander Blok himself entered in his diary on March 25, 1913: "Guro deserves attention." Soon after Guro was buried in a country cemetery near her *dacha* in Finland, her husband observed some unknown young people reading from her work near her grave. He became understandably touched and placed a bench there with a built-in shelf for Guro's books. It is not known whether such readings continued, but more than once Guro became the object of minor cults. The most extensive cult manifested itself on the pages of the periodical *Ocharovannyi strannik* (*The Enchanted Wanderer*), where appeared some of her poetry, both new and reprinted, and an essay about her as well. Poetry was published in her memory, for example, that written by Samuil Vermel, Innokenty Oksenov, and others.

Elena Guro strongly influenced the little-known poetess Ada Vladimirova; another poetess, Maria Shkapskaya, who was known in the 1920's, chose a line from Guro's play for the title of one of her verse collections (*Baraban strogogo gospodina* [*The Drum of the Strict Master*]). Guro's influence on Boris Pilnyak and Poletayev has, however, been exaggerated. As late as 1935 N. Bukharin quoted from Guro's poem in his famous speech at the First Congress of Soviet Writers, but he did not identify the author. The many-volumed *Literaturnaya Entsiklopedia*, published at that time, ignored Guro completely. The best student of futurism among Soviet scholars, N. Khardzhiev, tried to save her from oblivion several times. In 1938 he called her a "remarkable craftsman" and an innovator in prose. He also focused attention on similarities between the works of Mayakovsky and those of Guro in 1958. It may well be that in Guro's conscious effort to obliterate the difference between prose and verse lie her main historical importance and the guarantee of eventual discovery and appreciation. In her unpublished diary she left a note: "Free rhythms. Prose into verse, verse into prose. Prose that is almost verse." As a pioneer in this area, Guro deserves as much attention as Andrei Biely with his attempts to "versify" his prose: But Guro is bound to attract the attention of critics and scholars also as an impressionist (or an "intimist," as she was sometimes called) when the problem of the analysis of Russian impressionism faces literary scholarship, as it inevitably must. Someday her free verse will also become an object of study. Nor should the name of Guro be omitted in any survey of the theme of childhood in Russian literature.

Vera Kalina-Levine (essay date 1981)

SOURCE: "Through the Eyes of a Child: The Artistic Vision of Elena Guro," in *Slavic and East-European Journal*, Vol. 25, No. 2, Summer, 1981, pp. 30-43.

[In the following essay, Kalina-Levine analyzes Guro's childlike authorial voice.]

In his reminiscence about Elena Guro, Vasilij Kamenskij links Guro's poetry with a tragic event in her life, the loss of her only child. Unable to come to terms with her son's death, Guro, in Kamenskij's recollection, went on imagining her son was alive and continued to buy toys for him, maintain his room, draw his portraits, and write stories and poems for him. Although both the emphasis on biographical roots of a poet's imagination in general and Kamenskij's reminiscences in particular have to be taken *cum grano salis*, it is striking that as both a poet and a painter Guro was almost obsessively preoccupied with the world of the child. As a poetic persona, she frequently identifies with children or at least expresses her strong empathy with them by assuming a maternal stance toward life. She further confounds the issue of her parentage when she states in one of the prose sketches in **Baby Camels in the Sky** (**Nebesnye verbljužata**): "You see, I have no children, maybe that's why I love so unbearably everything that is alive. Sometimes it seems to me that I am a mother to everything." While there is uncertainty with respect to Guro's status as a parent, it is a noteworthy detail of her family background that her grandfather on her mother's side was the well-known pedagogue Čistjakov, who both wrote stories for children and was the publisher of *A Children's Journal* (*Žurnal dlja detei*) in the years 1851-1865. But whatever the specifics of their ostensible biographical underpinnings, Guro's creative interests were also clearly grounded in some of the most important trends and assumptions which gained momentum in the late nineteenth to early twentieth century, the period that nurtured Guro's literary and artistic sensibilities. One such trend was primitivism which, at the time Guro entered the literary scene in Russia, fostered an idealization of childhood and sought to legitimize its world not only in literature but also in art, psychology, philosophy, political thought, and the law.

In literature, the glorification of childhood provided a broadly based impetus for what became a central concern of the Russian Futurists, namely their endeavor to renovate language. By the time Elena Guro developed an abiding interest in the incipient Futurist or rather, Cubo-Futurist cause, heralded by the miscellany *A Trap for Judges I* (*Sadok Sudej I*) in April 1910, she had a number of published works to her credit. Most of these works were incorporated in the collection of prose, poetry, and plays entitled **The Hurdy-Gurdy** (**Šarmanka**), published in February 1909. To the extent that Guro's idealization of childhood was anticipated in her first book and as such predated her involvement with Futurism, it did not grow out of her endorsement of the Futurist demand to overthrow established forms and conventions so much as it converged with it. Within this perspective, it is pertinent that even before she turned to literature, Guro had expressed her interest in the world of the child in painting. In addition, in 1911 Guro planned to publish a book of fairy-tales, a project which, however, never came to fru-

ition because her publisher lost both the literary material and its water-color illustrations. As far as her work as a painter is concerned, Guro not only treated fairy-tale subjects on canvas, but often used simple, child-like designs (—flowers, stars, trees, et cetera) in her book illustrations. Her friend, Olga Matjušina was struck by the childish quality of Guro's drawings and watercolors:

> "A posthumous exhibit" . . . Yet everything is alive in it: cheerful puppies run, make somersaults, delicate birches quiver, a cat pricks up its ears keenly . . . Everything is painted with only a few lines, sparingly and expressively.

Giving literary and artistic expression to her interest in the infantile world, Guro made a multifaceted contribution to what was a specifically modern version of primitivism, the growing cult of childhood. This cult gained its forcefulness from the belief that childhood exemplified not only the most desirable human state but also the ideal artistic condition. Perceiving a fundamental similarity between the child and the artist, Guro viewed childhood as encapsulating the natural artistry of mankind. Her identification of childhood with genuine artistry was not unlike that of Rainer Maria Rilke who wrote, shortly before his two influential trips to Russia, that the essence of artistry lay in child-like naiveté, unselfconsciousness, openness to and instinctive trust in life.

For Guro, as for Rilke, emulation of the artistic sensibility of the child was not a mere return to the romantic ideal of the noble savage who had been praised for both his intuitive wisdom and keen sensitivity to beauty. Children in her eyes are born artists, endowed with unique perceptions

Portrait of Elena Guro by Vladimir Burliuk, 1910.

in both life and art and with a predisposition for playfulness which she considers to be at the source of all creativity. Childhood for Guro epitomizes that stage in human development in which reality is not yet divided into fixed categories or ordered by the principle of causality. The child is a symbol of wholeness, free to connect outwardly unrelated phenomena and to intermix reality with fantasy. Fascinated with the world of childhood, Guro dedicated her oeuvre to exploring it from several perspectives. The child's vision not only colors the feelings and ideas conveyed in her works but also informs the techniques and devices that shape the presentation of their thematic material. Exploiting children's language and imagery, Guro captured both the symbolizational mechanism and the freshness and immediacy of their experiences. In the process, she illuminated not only the rich fabric of the natural artistry of children but also aspects of creativity in the making.

The original freshness of the infantile world and concomitantly, the identification of the child's perceptual experiences with artistry are at the center of Guro's attention as early as her debut work entitled **"Early Spring" ("Rannja-ja vesna")**. Originally published in *An Anthology of Young Writers* (*Sbornik molodyx pisatelej*) in 1905, this story was later incorporated in Guro's book ***The Hurdy-Gurdy***, under the title **"Arrival in the Country" ("Priezd v derevnju")**. The story is a recollection of infantile perceptions. It recapitulates the patterns by which a little girl orders and apprehends the world around her. This world is based not on causal relations but mostly on sensory happenstance. Patterns emerge from relationships of surface contiguity, as they are apprehended and related to one another by the senses rather than by the intellect. In her sensory approach to life, the child or the little girl in the story is a born impressionist who dwells on her impressions solely for their pleasurable if not esthetic value. Guro's insistence on pure sensory perception, unspoiled by thought and analysis, as well as her extreme concentration on trivia, are characteristic of literary impressionism as it was practiced in the late nineteenth century by, among others, Fet in poetry and Čexov in his short stories of the 1899-1903 period.

Although the child's perceptions in **"Arrival in the Country"** are presented through the refraction of the adult persona, they preserve all their freshness and immediacy. But the persona is occasionally unable to hold back comments that point distinctly to her adult status in life, for instance: "We were then still blissfully unaware that everything is much more prosaic with adults, that they don't have the same feelings as children." In spite of the few "authorial" comments from the adult perspective, however, most of the impressions captured in the story belong to the little girl; it is the temperament of the child that puts its stamp on or filters the captured moments. Rendering reality the way it appears to her pure and immediate perception, the little girl presents at times unrealistic pictures, based on sensory illusions rather than on facts. Thus, travelling on a train, she displaces the source of motion, observing: "In the window frame, strips of earth and sky rush by quickly." Similarly, looking out of a moving carriage, it appeared to her that "the station huts swam back." However-

er, it is not only the absence of analytical knowledge but also her naiveté and inexperience that are at the source of the little girl's original vision. Capable of marvelling at even the most commonplace phenomena, she assigns nature a very special place in her scheme of life. Although she has little understanding of natural phenomena, she is intensely aware of their sensory qualities, as when, filled with delight, she wonders: "Oh, what smells with such dampness and warmth? . . . What's that light-violet little thing along the ravine?" However nature is not the only discovery that captivates the little girl. Ordinary language, the mere sounds of the most prosaic words seem to acquire new, almost mysterious dimensions, as when she overhears a conversation of adults: "Delivery of gas tar to the farmstead, a brick factory . . . —The novelty and delight from new, fresh words and names, not worn out with use and somewhat rough and hard, was being transmitted to us." The child has a unique feeling and appreciation for language. However, it is not so much the referential meaning as the totality of language that appeals to the infantile imagination. The child's emphasis on language as an autonomous whole may even lead to a dislocation of meaning. In the story, the young protagonist confuses a sequence of events as she misinterprets like sounding words: . . .

> She talked about some departures / introductions to society /. The eldest sister was "to part" / to be brought out / . And from this she kept standing before a mirror, the French girl fussed around and we were taken to the nursery.

The event that holds all the impressions together is a move to the country. This event is filled with excitement not only because the idea of it is novel and unexpected but also because the very experience of the journey is a source of an unprecedented wealth of impressions. It leads to a "newly discovered land" which is to be explored in all its sensuousness and with all the senses. In her unquenchable thirst for new perceptions, the little girl deems no color, sound, shape, or scent too trivial to notice. The child's confrontation with reality takes place mostly on the physical or sensual level. Even her apprehension of time is marked by concreteness; her awareness of the future derives from such specific actions as the covering up of furniture in preparation for the summer: "We participated in the preparation of the future, in tidying up the apartment." The little girl's life unfolds in an indistinct flow of time, interrupted by only a few special events such as Christmas or a trip to the country: "From time to time, in the dark and narrow nursery, among endless Mondays and Tuesdays, in the color of ordinary boredom, there opened up pleasantly trembling windows from which a holiday could come." Her vague awareness of temporality derives from these holidays which act as signposts in the passage of time. Their arrival is anticipated with great impatience and their proximity calculated by focusing on fixed events in life:

> We liked to while away the time until the set date; wake up in the morning with an impatiently pleasant awareness: one more day gone by and another has arrived; and there's reason to hurry and live it through faster.

Unable to consciously reckon time, the little girl views sleeping as an indicator that yet another day has elapsed. But if such attitude points to a distinctively infantile conception of time, the little girl's childishness is also reflected in her underlying egocentrism, apparent in her remark that the earth was "disobedient" as it "rocked, pushed and collapsed" under her feet. Connected with the girl's egocentric view of the world or even its direct corollary, is her tendency to animate inanimate objects. Things literally live for the sake of the little girl, and the world is nothing but an extension of her feelings and perceptions. Here the impulse to capture the infantile vision is harmoniously meshed with the use of metonymy which is so characteristic of Guro's prose. Unable to hold on to the multitude of feelings and perceptions, the little girl projects them or some striking parts and aspects of them into the surrounding world. There they are endowed with autonomous existence and as such function as the anthropomorphic reflections of the child's psyche, the psyche of an artist.

It is interesting that some thirteen years after Guro wrote her **"Arrival in the Country"** Boris Pasternak turned his attention to portraying the child as an artist in his story "The Childhood of Luvers." The similarity between Pasternak's story, particularly its first part entitled "The Long Days," and Guro's work is remarkable. Although psychologically, philosophically, and structurally much more complex, Pasternak's piece not only follows the basic plot outline but also uses some of the motifs and devices of **"Arrival in the Country."** Its very title captures the mood conveyed at the beginning of Guro's story. The long days for Ženja Luvers, as for the young protagonist in Guro's story, are times of loneliness and alienation from the incomprehensible and distant world of adults. The possibility for change and a glimpse of happiness arrive with Ženja's parents' decision to move to the country. Described at some length, the actual journey to the country gives rise to a multitude of fleeting impressions which undergo imaginative transformations in Ženja's inexperienced mind and as such attest to her innate artistic sensibility. Through Ženja-the-child, Pasternak captures the very process of creativity, the original shaping of envisioned material, leading to what Tynjanov called "a turning of vision." Like Guro, Pasternak presents his story as a recollection of childhood perceptions and experiences through the eyes of the adult persona. This persona is clearly a poet who uses densely poetic prose to capture the original vision of the child. There is no attempt to eliminate the distortions that result from the child's reliance on sensory perception rather than on facts. Like the little girl in Guro's story, Ženja attributes movement to the mountains she sees from the moving train:

> The mountainous panorama extended and kept on growing. Some were black, others were refreshed, some were obscured, others obscured. They came together and separated, they ascended and climbed down. All this moved in a sort of low circle, like the rotation of stars, with the prudent caution of giants anxious for the preservation of the earth, on the edge of catastrophe.

As for all children, abstractions make no sense to Ženja. She grasps the meaning of abstract concepts by finding their analogy among concrete, tangible phenomena. Thus, she transposes the unfamiliar concept "frontier of Asia" into an "iron balustrade placed between the public and a cage full of pumas."

In both stories, language constitutes one of the most important discoveries of childhood. Its inherent psychological significance is underscored by Ženja's panic when she is unable to identify or put a linguistic construct on the occurrence she sees in the distance. Once she learns its name, she feels comforted:

> The girl understood nothing and contentedly sucked at a falling tear. She wanted only one thing, to know the name of the unknowable—Motovilixa. That night it explained everything, for during the night the name still possessed a complete and reassuring significance for the child.

The actual object behind the word "factory" is of less interest to Ženja than the label itself. For the child, the name of a thing does not signal mere recognition but represents the very essence of that thing. The ability to designate an object by its name represents its complete mastery and therefore the expunction of the terror believed to be inherent in the unknown. Just as the little girl in Guro's story, Ženja Luvers is not under the sway of the communicative aspect of language. As a result, she easily experiences displacement in meaning, as in the following: "Later something was said in French, in the language she knew well but in a language she could not understand." To the degree that language is connected with unique perceptions of the child, it is at the source of what Pasternak called the "poetic caprice" of childhood. As Ženja matures, her life becomes prose and is transformed into fact.

Guro's interest in the child's unconventional use and understanding of language constitutes one of the most important points at which her primitivism converges with Futurism. Insofar as the child enjoys language qua language, independently of its referential or symbolic function, the child represents the prototype of the Futurist; he is the original champion of "the word as such." Indeed, the affinity between the child's inventive playfulness with language and the Futurist pursuit of neologisms and even of *zaum* was recognized by such a leading spokesman of the Futurist movement as Kručenyx and by such early Formalist critics as Šklovskij, Tynjanov, and others. The child's natural orientation toward language as such, language in its purely esthetic function, finds a particularly strong expression in children's folklore. It assumes an important role in children's play which, as Jan Mukařovský pointed out [in "Estetika jazyka," *Kapitolyz české poetiky,* Vol. 1, 1948], "is the foundation of a good part of children's folklore in which its procedures and results achieve stabilization. Here belong for instance children's counting-out rhymes which sometimes lead to an 'artificial speech,' consisting of words that have no relation to reality." But although children's play with language is essentially self-focused, it also conceals an underlying link with some practical, extra-esthetic purpose such as articulatory practice, mastery of the meaning associations between phonetically similar words, and others.

Guro's interest in the linguistic experience of children in general and her child-like predilection for phonetic innovation in particular is most clearly illustrated by the following poem entitled **"Words of Love and Warmth"** (**"Slova ljubvi i tepla"**) from her collection *Baby Camels in the Sky:* . . .

> Once upon a time there was / Bootie—tummy / Purly / Dopey / Kitty—fluffy / Feathery / Whitely / Kit-catty / Tussely . . .

Built from parallel diminutives, the poem emphasizes the phonetic interplay rather than the communicative function of the separate words. All of the rhymed nouns can be viewed as a tightly knit chain of vowels and consonants, on the one hand resembling the teasing games that children play with names, for example, Miška-šiška, Maša-kaša (Botik, from Bot, was the name of one of Guro's cats), and on the other hand, not unlike the pure sound games mentioned by Roman Jakobson in his seminal study on child language [*Child Language, Aphasia, Phonological Universals,* 1968]. These games consist of the stringing together and of the gradual modification of particular sound configurations, as in: pupsi, pipsi, titsi, tatsi, feitsa, litsa, bitsa, tatsa. However, Guro does not restrict herself to the stringing of partial similarities on the purely phonetic level; she works with meaningful word units on the one hand and utilizes the semantic potentialities of sounds on the other. The consistently used diminutive suffix *-ik,* enhances the child-like atmosphere of the poem and the particular selection of sounds phonetically reinforces the key image "kot." Out of a total of 46 consonants, there are thirteen *k,* nine *t,* but only three each *b, v, r, p, š, l;* two *ž,* and one each *d, n, č, s.* It is interesting to note that in the phonetic development of child language, the two most prominent sounds of the poem (*k* and *t*) emerge, as Jakobson pointed out, at a relatively early stage. The velar *k* is originally merged with the dental *t.* The latter (*t*) always precedes the former (*k*) in the order in which children acquire differentiated consonants. Guro's poem is based on or brings into relief the earliest consonantal phonemes of child language. As far as the organization of stressed vowels is concerned, the poem reveals an interesting pattern. Apart from the two initial *y* sounds, the entire scheme consists of the vowels *o* and *a.* The poem opens with two *o* sounds and ends with two *a* sounds, enclosing a triplicate alternation of *o - a.* It is noteworthy that in its reprinted version in the collection *The Three* (*Troe*), the entire poem is enclosed by two prose sketches in which the vowels *o* and *a* represent the distinguishing sounds of the title names, **"Kot Bot"** and **"Kot Vat."** In the prose works, as in the poem, the image of a cat serves as an impulse for the exploration of the infantile imagination. In **"Kot Bot"** Guro treats the child's ability to engender new meanings as a by-product of his play with language, for example *"U nego byl belyj, životnen'kij životik."* (He had a white, tummyzoid tummy). **"Kot Vat,"** a eulogy to Guro's cat, called here "a symbol of eternal youth," "a rising sun," borders on the ridiculous unless seen as an attempt to capture the child's enthusiasm for and ability to bestow freshness on the most ordinary objects in his environment. The three pieces together create not only a thematic sequence but also a continuity

in their phonetic patterning. The initial *o* in the name "Bot" is elaborated in the *o-a* alternation in the central poem, only to give way to the *a* sound in the title name "Vat" of the concluding prose sketch. Linked by sound and by their feline subject, the three pieces point to a common semantic denominator. To the extent that, using Kiril Taranovsky's classification of sounds, the vowels *o* and *a* are connected by the distinctive feature of compactness "usually associated with emotions of vastness, completeness, greatness, balance, strength, and power" ["The Sound Texture of Russian Verse in the Light of Phonemic Distinctive Features," *Intentional Sound of Slavic Linguistics and Poetics,* 1965], all of these emotions evoked on the level of sound, echo and expand the semantic content of the series. The phonetic level reinforces the common semantic denominator, that is, the allure, greatness, equanimity, and naive sense of omnipotence of the feline protagonist of the three pieces.

On the lexical and rhythmic levels, the poem **"Words of Love and Warmth"** draws on some of the central devices of children's folklore. The importance of diminutives and of rhymes in children's language in general and in children's poetry in particular does not require a great deal of expounding. However, if as has been observed, children's folklore has a special predilection for consecutive rhymes and for the pairing of assonant and rhymed words, Guro in her poem takes these devices to their ultimate extreme. The entire poem is built of consecutively rhymed words which, as suggested above, constitute an extended piling up of partially like configurations. Similar stringing of echoing words occurs also in a poem which, conscious of its playful and carefree origins, opens with the observation: . . .

> From summer happiness words are born! All fine words: Pondlet, watery, / fordlet, / dromedary, / bewildered, / little freighter.

Unlike this poem which accentuates the difficult *r* sound, the poem **"Words of Love and Warmth"** contains no difficult consonantal clusters, thus fulfilling the infantile need for easy pronunciation. This is in direct opposition to the Futurist demand for a "rough texture." Although some members of the extended nominal compounds function as fixed epithets of the word "kotik" ("belovatik," "pušatik," "vorkotik"), others constitute neologistic derivations from recognizable roots; they are grammatical rather than lexical innovations ("duratik," "pušončik," "košuratik," "potasik,"). Aware of children's dislike of metaphor, Guro forms her neologisms from words that denote concrete actions or attributes and which are in effect synecdoches pertaining to the single subject of the poem. The subject, a cat, represents perhaps the most popular animal figure in children's folklore, particularly in Russian lullabies. Although Guro's poem is not a lullaby, it is set in an atmosphere of drowsiness, evoked in the brief introductory passage: . . .

> The cat's ears drifted apart from warmth and laziness. Its velvet ears fell apart. And the cat became li . . . -i . . . The whitelings were rocking over the swamp.

The word *"raski . . .-is . . ."* is an onomatopoetic transformation of the word *"raskisat"* applied to an optical and dynamic occurrence; it is a phonetic and intonational accompaniment to the loss of firmness. Furthermore, echoing the word *"kiska,"* the infantile synonym for *"koška,"* it underscores the image of the cat, or rather, its singular condition. It might be said that this word epitomizes what Osip Brik meant by the term *"zvukoobraz"* (sound-image), the reproduction of a visual sensation by the inner structure of the word. For Alexej Kručenyx, word experimentation of this kind served as proof that Elena Guro was an early practitioner of *zaum,* —transrational poetry. He substantiated his contention by pointing, however, not to **"Words of Love and Warmth"** but to a much more distinctive illustration, the poem **"Finlandia,"** published in the collection **The Three.** The analogous innovation in this poem which strives to recreate the aural atmosphere of Finland, is the word *"šujat"* instead of *"šumjat"* (rustle). Kručenyx wrote that coniferous trees precisely *"šujat"* whereas deciduous trees *"šumjat."*

Closely linked with Guro's endeavor to recapture the originality of children's language was her aspiration to reproduce the freshness of their perceptions. Her fascination with the child's ability to perceive freshness in even the most commonplace phenomena is in the background of an entire section of Guro's **Hurdy-Gurdy,** called **"Trifles"** (**"Meloči"**). In these miniatures, objects are animated with feelings of joy, contentment, and stability. These feelings stem from the presumption that reality is endowed with intentionality and specifically, with benevolent intentions not only toward the child but toward all of life. A mere suggestion of strife or difficulty is resolved instantaneously and magically, either in a dream or by the power of a wish. The vision projected here is that of a fairy-tale; but instead of fantastic or supernatural beings, this fairy-tale's protagonists are the minutiae of everyday life, presented in phantasmic illumination. The simple, commonplace objects, designated by words which reflect affectionate attitude, that is, by diminutive forms, are infused with anthropomorphic life as they appear, however, not to an adult but to a child.

A different kind of fairy-tale is evoked in the poem **"Children's Hurdy-Gurdy"** (**"Detskaja šarmanočka"**), from the book that inherited part of this poem's title. The fairy-tale is enacted here on the stage of a puppet theater by such commedia del'arte figures as Harlequin and Colombine. Harlequin's song about a wondrous never-never land represents a fairy-tale within the fairy-tale which is the poem. The scene focuses on visual and auditory details, seen independently of any unifying and motivating relationship with the whole. The function of the scene is purely esthetic, but esthetic in terms of a naive onlooker, of a child. It is a spectacle which captivates the child's attention with its great variety of things taking place simultaneously: sparkles of icicles and of stars made from gold paper, snowflakes, a quadrille played on the hurdy-gurdy and danced by a cat, rope jumping by Colombine along with Harlequin and a monkey, a duel between two clowns, Harlequin's singing, and so forth. Although the spectacle with its music and multifarious movement appeals to the sensory perception of the spectator, it also reveals his emo-

tional involvement: "Oh, its thin rims rubbed off a bit!" ("Ax ee obodočki obterlis' nemnožko!").

It is noteworthy that although rhythmically the poem consists of what James Bailey defines as "strict accentual verse" ["Some Recent Developments in the Study of Russian Versification," *Language and Style,* 1972], with two- and three-ictus lines and with intervals of one to three syllables between stresses, most of the lines have a distinct trochaic cadence. To the extent that such a cadence is often found in children's poetry, the rhythmic structure of the poem enhances the infantile associations of its content. As far as rhyme is concerned, while some lines are rhymed in an alternating pattern of "exact" rhyme, other lines contain merely an "approximate" rhyme, for instance: *iskorki-igraet, obodočki-eločkoj.* In addition, almost all of the words in the poem are tied together in an intricate pattern of sound repetition, be it alliteration or assonance: *s ledjanyx-sosulek-veselen'kuju, obodočki-obterlis'-soberemsja.*

The evocation of the world of the fairy-tale is at the center of a number of other works by Guro. One poem in the collection **The Three** takes its point of departure from Puškin's poem—fairy-tale "A Tale About the Dead Tsarevna and About Seven Bogatyrs" ("Skazka o mertvoj carevne i o semi bogatyrjax"). Guro's poem is an idiosyncratic response to the question known in English as "Mirror, mirror on the wall, who is the fairest of them all," rendered in the epigraph of her poem: . . .

> Tell me, mirror / Report the whole truth / Who is here nicer than me.

This is almost a literal transcription of Puškin's lines which read as follows: . . .

> My light, mirror! say / Report the whole truth: / Am I the nicest in all the world, . . .

However, while the epigraph in Guro's poem points to its fairy-tale subtext, the poem repudiates the very premise of the fairy-tale world. Not the realm of the marvelous and of the fantastic, but concrete nature, a beautiful flower, constitutes the ideal reality in Guro's framework. Looking at the flower from several perspectives and capturing its manifold associations, the poem creates a fairy-tale of its own, a fairy-tale in which the concrete object in nature is seen under a variety of imaginative illuminations.

Guro's interest in the fairy-tale was in large part motivated by her desire to attain playful and imaginative stylization. Stylization along with the recapitulation of the child's unconventional vision enabled her to render an uncommonplace presentation of concrete reality. Apprehended by and reflecting the perceptual, linguistic, and imaginative experiences of the child, this reality was at the same time given its literary shape by an artist—the prototypical artist, created in the image and possessing the vision not of a man or woman but of the child. Portraying the artist as a child and the child as an artist, Guro achieved an effective illustration of her primitivist cult of childhood.

Milica Banjanin   (essay date 1983)

SOURCE: "Looking Out, Looking In: Elena Guro's Windows," in *Festschrift für Nikola R. Pribić,* edited by Josip Matešić and Erwin Wedel, Hieronymus Verlag Neuried, 1983, pp. 3-17.

[*In the following essay, Banjanin analyzes the use of the window motif in Guro's prose and poetry.*]

A trained painter as well as poet, Elena Guro (1877-1913) puts great emphasis on visual effects in her prose and poetry. The window is one of the commonest as well as most striking images in Guro's writings and paintings; it evolves into a unique device. Functioning not only as a visual image, the window becomes a compositional device, a physical frame, a theatrical stage, and the frame of a painting. Guro's drawings of windows help us understand the windows in her writings and the difference between the two. The "artistic" windows of the paintings imply a picture which, for the most part, shows movement in only one direction, from inside outside; her "literary" windows follow the point of view of a reader as well as of a poetic persona and allow motion in both directions, from the inside to the outside and from the outside in.

The window in Guro's literary works is seen as an opening through which the smells, sounds, visual impressions, light and air can penetrate the inner world of city rooms. The interaction between the outer and inner worlds helps create a picture of the city. The frame of the window, its glass, the window-sill, are part of the composition. One can observe the street through the window without going outside, and one can be observed from the outside. Depending on whether the curtains are drawn, or whether it is raining or the glass is dirty, the picture can change. Likewise, an open window can allow the outside world to penetrate the inner space of the room.

Images of windows and of framing appear throughout Guro's writing, but are most cleverly used to express the poet's attitude to the city, an intense and important, though short-lived theme of her work. In applying this device to her perception of the city, Guro, unlike the symbolist poets, uses the window not as a barrier that separates the poet from the outside world, and behind which the poet hides, but as a theatre, a "stage" on which the events of the outside world encounter the thoughts and emotions of the inner world. The window thus functions as a frame through which one observes and is observed; a stage that both delineates and brings together the world of the room, a symbol of the inner world and awareness, and the outside world; a cityscape that both represents reality and reflects the inner feelings of the poetic persona. The frame of the window suggests both a relationship and a limitation, but Guro determines how much is to be shown and selected. By framing and selecting specific events and emotional states from within the room (the inner world), and juxtaposing them against the sights and events of the external world, Guro forces her reader to perceive both scenes through "defamiliarized" associations. The reader has to absorb the profusion of images and details carefully before he/she is able to recombine what he/she sees into a larger picture. The reader becomes an active participant in "painting" and framing a scene, together with the poet.

Since windows are conceived as eyes open to the city, the room therefore becomes an image of the inner mood of the poetic persona. The poetic persona does not merely look out. The outside world, symbolized by the street, thrusts itself into the world of the room. As a result of this movement out/in and in/out, the room or the street becomes transformed according to the perceiver's frame of mind and self-awareness. The objects both within the room and on the street are altered as they reflect changes in the person observing them. Disparate images and fleeting perceptions of concrete reality, sensations and emotions are juxtaposed to create a picture, convey a state of mind, or merely suggest an impression. The projection of the poetic persona's emotions gives an added dimension and depth to the seemingly fragmentary world, so characteristic of Guro's writing as a whole.

Guro's idiosyncratic style is particularly well adapted to the portrayal of the fragmentary world she envisions. It is through the careful selection of individual words (or brush strokes), the weight that is given each word, its sensory texture, in both its graphic and sound aspects, typographical devices, etc., that fragments and details are combined to create larger pictures. Semantic opposition between animate and inanimate, the distinction between the outer and the inner world, is obliterated through the juxtaposing and transposing of exterior details into an inner mental vision:

> The shopowners, their dreams. The store is open. Their store is their favorite milk cow. They dream of selling out; the evening rest, the countryside, returning home, tea in the delicate twilight. Their future, their dreams flow delicately, delicately through the objects in terms of profits.

The juxtaposed heterogeneous details are brought together, combining objective reality with the imagined. The narrator, looking through a windowpane, imagines what goes on in the minds of shopowners in connection with their lives. Words evoke the visual realm (the store is open, twilight, countryside), mental perception and feeling (they dream of selling out, their dreams flow delicately through the objects), motor sensation (returning home, milk cow, the dreams flow) and a sensation of taste (tea). Guro invests the external and everyday reality with human qualities, while the inner world appears both vivid and concrete. Within the confines of a few sentences, in which the single isolated word is conceived both as complete in itself and as part of a larger whole, Guro's words are saturated with rich evocative imagery:

> Streets curve around the city without beginning or end. Windows. Droplets. Window-sills. Cats, pigeons. Ahead it unfolds, shuts itself up, opens up. Turn after turn. Reflections, resonant voices. Secrets, unknown desultory thoughts, scraps of flowers, scraps of conversation.

The self-sufficiency of the single word, the single phrase, as a fragment of the whole, is underlined. A number of seemingly disparate details (words or phrases) are combined together to convey a state of mind, a picture or a mood:

> The crowd passes like a subjugating wave. "She doesn't look bad! Ha, ha!" They pass. Women. Men. Someone's abandoned bicycle by the wall: the seat still seems hot, preserving the elasticity of the young thighs that have touched it recently. The burning beads of an amusement park. The strained voice of a singer.

Guro's fragmentary method is manifest also in the punctuation. Both in Guro's prose and poetry, sentences and lines are of irregular length, and many consist of only one or two words. Words are often repeated, and there is an abundant use of typographical devices, three dots for example. Frequently the visual or sound aspect of a word is emphasized although its denotative function is never entirely eliminated:

> Lulla, lolla, lalla-lu
> Liza, lolla, lulla-li
> Khvoi shuiat, shuiat
> Ti-i-i, Ti-i-u-u, . . .

Guro juxtaposes words to create a kind of "sound picture" in an attempt to suggest that the word is an object in its own right.

There is a stronger emphasis on individual words or sentences than on the whole. It is the word, the very sound that holds the reader's attention. Guro appears to have used one of the devices of "true Futurist poetry," attributed to her by Khlebnikov and Kruchenykh [in their "Slovokak takovoe"], that poetry should be "read in the twinkling of an eye." The emphasis is on the immediate apprehension of the pattern of internal references and on the meaning-relationship between word groups with no apparently comprehensible relation to each other. Guro has created her own fragmented lyrical prose, which resembles prose poetry. The emphasis is placed on the word itself, the image itself. Guro clarifies this point in her unpublished diary by saying:

> Free rhythms. Prose into verse, verse into prose. Prose that is almost verse . . . Sections of stories (fabula) taken as color and as leitmotifs . . . ! The story's concentrating on two or three words . . . To speak the words, as if they did not coincide with the meaning, but are provoking certain images, about which nothing at all has been said . . .

In approaching the function of windows in Guro's work we have also to be aware of the levels of consciousness on the part of the poetic persona. Guro does not merely convey the mood of her observers but also their mental experiences and associations, as well as their feelings, their inner states. Guro's personae are portrayed through several characteristic details that are repeated. Her characters are not well developed, and they all resemble each other. A change in name or in some detail is all that distinguishes them from one another. Even the men and the women are very much alike. The consciousness of her personae in her prose pieces is presented directly to the reader in a montage of often unrelated ideas and images superimposed one upon the other. The images shift back and forth in time,

while the poetic persona is generally fixed in space. This cinematic device enables Guro to represent simultaneously the inner life of her personae with outer life of the city. Within Guro's windows (frames) the details that are selected involve visual aspects of rooms or of the street, of nature, geometrical shapes as well as color, but also sounds, smells, emotions and sensations. What we are given is not a complete picture but a mosaic of details which, although they can be recombined in various ways, are all essential for what the poet/painter is evoking, whether it be a picture of the city, or its atmosphere, or the frame of mind of her personae. What is important is that Guro's images have their source in concrete reality but are presented subjectively, as a montage of fragments, rather than as a whole.

The image of the window appears most frequently in Guro's book *The Hurdy-Gurdy* (*Sharmanka*), 1909, that contains most of the city poetry and prose. The city in Guro's works, St. Petersburg, although seldom named, emerges as a contemporary confining urban environment presented in visual and sound images that are repeated throughout her works as leitmotifs. The streets and buildings are continually juxtaposed upon and intrude into city rooms: "The street asks to be allowed to enter a window." or "Furnished rooms. The street runs into them." The movement can be in the opposite direction: "I want to go out to the street."

"So Life Goes" ("Tak zhizn idet") from *The Hurdy-Gurdy,* provides an excellent example of Guro's use of the framed view. There is no plot development in this twenty-six page prose work, composed of fragments that are separated from each other by pictorial devices-dots, flowers, leaves, branches, circles. Each section, which can stand as a unit by itself, takes a real event on the street as a pretext for a remembered scene (in both the city room and on the street) that is recreated in the protagonist's memory. External reality is seen by a young girl, Nelka, who is standing on the street and waiting. The unifying element of the whole piece is Nelka's obsession with men, her awareness of male power and of the submissive role expected of women. The reader is presented with impressions that are going on in the girl's mind, as they are occurring, as if they were directly from the girl's consciousness. Almost everything happens in the realm of the mind, although the external events on the street and the happenings in city rooms are related to the main story through the reaction and sensations they evoke in Nelka, the connecting link between all the frames. Guro comes close here to the development of the stream-of-consciousness technique.

In **"So Life Goes"** there is a constant movement in memory back and forth between the city street and the rooms; the window is a frame through which the impressions of the inside and the outside alternate and converge. The actual life of the city and Nelka's perception of that life through memory and immediate impressions are delineated through the device of the window. In **"So Life Goes"** Guro had intended to write about spring in the city, about the perception of the visible through the prism of spring, both in objects and in herself. The external world and the excitement of spring on a city street are depicted through a crowd that passes like a subjugating wave (comparable to the warmth of spring that overpowers people), a crowd of elegant men whom Nelka perceives as "strict." She mentally transposes this strictness to houses and windows. The same feeling of strictness and implied fear is attributed to Nelka's stepfather who had forbidden her to go out on the street full of roar, rumble, shouts, noise, laughter, voices. Nelka feels drawn to the street, "to fly through the window to the infinite." She goes out. The windows now, as observed from the street, are colored in Nelka's perception as gray (in some instances in the story they are blue) diffusing mobile patches which represent to her someone's questions and answers. When Nelka returns to her apartment, her step-father beats her. Re-creating the beating in her memory, Nelka superimposes the image of her self-confident step-father on the other men she had seen on the street, who had symbolized for her male strength, power and dominance. Even the objects that surround Nelka begin to reflect her state of mind. The room itself becomes transformed, as the rhythm of the whip her step-father uses to beat her is introduced by the movement of the pendulum of a clock in the room. The walls are changed: "The walls watched greedily. They thirsted for the humiliation. They took pleasure in it." The lashing of the whip is associated in Nelka's mind with the crackling of lights turned on in the city. Even furniture in the room is described as reflecting the girl's inner turmoil:

> Around her, the furniture sat and stood for a long time, remaining in the same place as a witness.

Therefore it is easily understandable that when Nelka goes back to the street she feels:

> The lamps, the windows, were the same as yesterday, but now they already knew everything, like the furniture in her step-father's study. Swallowing that knowledge the lamps and windows scrutinized Nelka, becoming heavier from curiosity.

In her insistence on animating and personifying the objects and the world around her, and in forcing her reader to look at that world as if he had never seen it before, Guro comes close to the Futurist experiments, those of Mayakovsky and Khlebnikov in particular. For Guro, objects reflect not only the emotional tone of their environment, but also the environment itself.

In **"Before Spring"** (**"Pered vesnoi"**) from ***The Hurdy-Gurdy,*** the first-person narration adds credence to the narrator's actually moving in and out, and responding to the changing stimuli. In **"So Life Goes"** the movement is more a mental projection of disconnected thoughts and images triggered by present perceptions. In **"Before Spring"** it is on the street, while looking at the windows, that the poetic persona is able to day-dream about other people's lives, their secrets. Every window provides a new opportunity for guessing about the life hidden behind it. The window frame, whether that of an apartment or a shopwindow, represents a transition between the apparent and visible and the imagined. Shifts are intensified through the use of color which indicates the shifting in time. The color of the windows changes according to the lighting.

The color of windows and the inherent change in tone that is implied underlines the artistic quality of the frames/pictures, "frozen" in "spatialized" instants of time. The spatializing of time causes a momentary stop in the moving world thus allowing an image to be formed.

The window in Guro's works can be transparent, or colorful, or frozen, or dusty or empty, and can like a mirror reflect the outside world, or it can dim the contours of the external world. The sun or lights in the city at night are important in considering this aspect of the window. For example:

> Heavy and dark Petersburg plants were visible behind the dusty window-pane.

> *Sharmanka*

> The sky-blue golden morning paddles in the white blind.

> **"Morning window"**

> Bald-headed night glanced in dim windowpanes The fiery ray of the rose-colored evening glow splashed into the room. Through the flowers. The windows became lit with transparent golden-pink sparks . . .

> **"The City"**

Looking at other people's windows from the street allows the poetic persona a number of thoughts and images: "And this was already infinity, as the gray iridescent windows were leaving the street in a row. Infinity . . ." Or at night, before the lights are turned on, the "cold freezing windows" stand as if somebody had "pulled out" their soul. Both the walls and the "dim hollows of panes" project terrifying and terrible emptiness. But when the lights are turned on, as we have seen, they shed new light on the life behind windows.

In an unpublished prose piece of about twenty-six pages entitled **"The Street"** (**"Ulitsa"**), 1905-1906, the poetic persona, from whose point of view the story of the street is told, presents her impressions of the street at night. Yet is it not until the end of this open-ended prose that we find out that the poetic persona is in a room from which she has been observing the street. Her impressions are of the real motion on the street and of the visual and aural images produced by city lights and traffic: "The street flares up with rose-colored northern lights . . . The street seethes with black and fiery patches." The feeling of movement is achieved by the repetition of the verbs of motion and through the cinematographic method of shifting in rapid succession from one sight to another, from one frame to another. The memory of the persona helps her re-create the "spatialized" segments of time, presenting them in frames/pictures of city life which quickly follow one another. For example one of the street scenes is described by means of:

> Electric letters that howl at the black gaps of the sky, shouting out advertisements in red, green and yellow patches . . . The lights gallop . . .

Guro has here extracted visual signs of objects, in the manner of Cubist and Futurist art, and has transposed the elements of painting into a system of poetic imagery. Patches of color which Guro has abstracted from the illuminated words of advertisements are used to create color schemes which help make new pictures from the associations of speed and sound ("lights gallop"). Both the city itself and its lights are perceived as things gone mad, in the mind of the poetic persona. This sensation is a projection of her own inner turmoil, but we learn this only in the last segment of **"The Street,"** in which the poetic persona exclaims: "To go away, to wake up! . . ." while she is standing in a room from which she has been observing the street from a window. In **"Before Spring," "So Life Goes,"** and **"The Street,"** as we have seen, Guro has carefully used the frame of a window to show the juxtaposition of the outside world and an inner mood, and the interrelationship between the two.

Although in her prose and poetry devoted to nature the device of the window does not play as important a role as it does in her works inspired by the city, nevertheless we find several striking examples. Nature, both in the northern region of Russia (Guro was from St. Petersburg) and in Finland, which became one of the main sources of Guro's inspiration, is depicted perceptively through the device of the window:

> From the window, through the grating of the Finnish balustrade which overlooks the dark pine trees, patches of morning splendor glitter. And the promise of a return of youth. And the promise of the strained happiness of a poet's creation. The wall of silvery trunks, the sharp slope of a roof, the top of the forest. (The character of the North. Individualism. Independence. The harsh and ennobling independence of the North, like the top of a fir tree)

The external world, in this case nature with its constant renewal, is juxtaposed upon the inner world of the perceiver and her longing for the return of youth. The effect Guro achieves is not only visual, but it also takes on an added dimension through the projection of the observer's feelings.

In another prose work, **"In the Park,"** (**"V parke"**) the window becomes an extension of nature which it reflects:

> The wind lived in summer homes (*dacha*) the whole winter. The window-glass has been aired so long in the absence of human life, that even now the wind plays in it and one can hear the guttural voices of pine trees. From time to time the faces of clouds flash in the windows and stretch their faces in the manner of the forest. Nobody has frightened them here the whole winter.

The absence of curtains in the country home produces another effect: "The windows, with their huge pine-like darkness were looking into the room."

In addition to the window frame, the mental frame, the image of the frame can also be understood as the frame of a painting that depicts scenes of life in the city. The window as a painting of city life involves an artistic representation within a specific frame. A voluntarily limited objective is implied; the painting of an aspect of the city, or an event within the city, is framed within a short prose passage or a poem. These scenes, in which both visual and verbal information is conveyed, appear as small, apparently unrelated fragments, which nevertheless are part of the total picture. For example:

> An amber reflection falls on the street . . . Watery gold trembles on the ground. In polished puddles the reflection of letters from signboards and golden stripes . . . Half of a question mark in gray puddles . . .

In many instances sections of Guro's prose and poetry are separated by drawings of animals, dots, branches, leaves, etc. Pictorial devices are frequently fused with the work itself into a single visual entity. Guro's prose is at times broken into smaller units that can be read independently. Many of the smaller fragments are untitled making it difficult to determine whether they are part of a whole or not. Poetry and prose are mixed within a single piece in some instances. Impression follows impression, fragment follows fragment, often producing the effect of fleeting unconnected perceptions. What is seen does not appear as important as the impression that the observed object makes on the person who sees it. The picture is mental, rather than physical and the reader's attention is held to details of the picture; to the words, their sound. Both painting and music influenced Guro's work. Words or phrases, as sound motifs, are repeated throughout her works, creating musical effects. The frequent use of the verb *kazat'sia* (to seem) and a number of verbs of perception, particularly in **The Hurdy-Gurdy,** underline the subjective quality of the ambiguous and tenuous reality that often "appears" rather than "is" in Guro's poetic world.

The question of the "frame" (window) in Guro's paintings and drawings is also important, as a border of the representation, and as a component of the picture. This becomes particularly significant when we realize that in Guro's paintings and drawings the window often functions as a picture within a picture. The physical frame of the picture is within the space of the observer looking at the painting or drawing, while the window itself is, more often than not, within the "internal" space of the painting. In Guro's drawings of windows the position of the artist appears "internal," inside the space represented. Unlike her literary work, Guro's painting does not show as much juxtaposition and transposition between the external and the internal worlds. In Guro's art the view is more of the window itself and only in certain instances pine trees can be seen in the window, or house plants, and on one occasion other buildings and windows. Guro draws her windows in black or colored pencil, or ink, or paints them in watercolors or oil. The colors of windowpanes are predominantly bright blues; window frames range from yellow to cherry red, green, or variations of purple or blue, while the colors of the inner space are for the most part pale pastels.

The image of the window as a theatre, or a stage, represents another use of this device to depict the encounter of the outside world and the life of city rooms. "The burning squares of windows" and the streets "riddled with lighted windows" are perceived as a stage for "evening performances." These performances also take place in "the stone-clad snuff box of the city," in other words the room. The possibilities of guessing and dreaming about what is behind the walls and lighted windows, especially if they are covered with curtains, are inexhaustible.

Iron window-sills and drain pipes are an aspect of the stage setting of the city that arouses a sense of beauty in the poetic persona, because they appear "as if they were part of a musical play; as if they were on stage." The similarity between Guro and the early Mayakovsky in the language and imagery related to the city is striking. Guro's drain-pipes and window sills, among other objects, are part of the drama of the city that Mayakovsky writes about in his "nocturnes" on drain-pipes.

The effect of light on the streets and on windows is important. At night the streets are transformed, excited and tense "like a theatrical stage." The store windows, under the light of street lanterns, become a smaller stage, on which "Furs come forth glittering, as if a ball were to start." . . . The impression is that the animated objects on the lighted street, including signboards, and lighted city rooms, those "lighted corners of life," are all part of a scene of life that is being acted out in the city. The life of the city is being perceived as a theatrical performance, seen through the lighted window frame.

The handful of lights that the city "pours out" as part of its evening performance, the sounds, the wind, all of this is transformed by the morning. The smoke from chimneys becomes immobile, drain-pipes are silent, and as the city itself speaks at the end of **"Songs of the City" ("Pesni goroda")**: "my white foggy mask is quiet." It is as if everything had been put away in "long grey paper boxes." The performance is over. The windows are no longer transparent. Since window glass can be both "transparent and reflecting," the poet can see through the glass or in the glass, either the reflection of objects in the room, or reflections and representations of the world outside, as they pass through window panes.

In Guro's play **"Poor Harlequin" ("Nischii Arlekin")**, published in *The Hurdy-Gurdy,* we find the most striking example of her use of "frame" and "pictures." The play consists, in Guro's terms, of three "pictures." The word picture encompasses scenes and fragments within a selected space. At the same time the preselected fragments symbolize the life that the picture encloses and frames. The notion of the frame in **"Poor Harlequin"** has allowed Guro to present events within the "picture" from the point of view of an outsider, an external observer, and simultaneously from the point of view of the persona presented inside the picture (the Harlequin). The device of the "picture" (frame or stage) has enabled Guro to move between, in Uspensky's terms, the "external" and "internal" points of view.

As in her prose discussed above, in **"Poor Harlequin"** St. Petersburg is depicted as oscillating between reality and a stylized vision. Visual devices-dots, flowers, leaves, circles, etc.- separate sections of the play from each other. Pictorial devices and the text itself are fused into a single visual entity. The transition between the world of the pup-

pet, the Harlequin, who symbolized the plight of the poet, and the real world of the city and its inhabitants is maintained by the constant shifting of pictures. The Harlequin is seen both within the frame of his puppet stage and on the street where he addresses the passers-by. In the second "picture" of the play the Harlequin appears in the window of the children's nursery. Remaining on the window-sill, he plays with the children by displaying paper roosters. Then, frightened by the sudden appearance of the children's mother, he disappears.

In the third "picture" the Harlequin tries to perform his tricks on a crowded street, but is unsuccessful. When a gentleman from the audience climbs upon the podium to tell the Harlequin that his gaudiness is out of place on the street, we suddenly realize that the Harlequin could have all along been performing on a puppet stage. Guro has achieved the effect of distancing and framing through a skillful shift in changing "pictures." In this way Guro is able to use the point of view of an outside observer as well as the point of view of the Harlequin, who functions within the frame, to create a larger frame—the city which encompasses the drama of the poet.

As we have seen, by carefully sketching her impressions in small visual and written fragments, Guro is able to convey a colorful and vivid perception of the world around her. Each detail within her picture/frame is important in reconstructing the whole, and in perceiving a whole prose piece or a poem. In using the window, which allowed her to present the city as a montage of carefully selected details, Guro is able to touch on many of the aspects of city life that convey its nervous rhythm, mood, color, atmosphere and sounds. Her highly subjective impressions, framed within a prose piece or a poem, still remain tangible because they were imposed on the poet's senses by the real world.

The reality represented through the device of the window in Guro's works is not confined within the boundaries of a frame. The frame as a compositional device enabled Guro to select details of the external world, or the inner space of city rooms, as starting points from which she constructed a larger picture of the city. By framing objects or events within the city, Guro is forcing her reader to observe them more clearly and to combine them into new pictures.

The life that the reader senses through Guro's images is filled with typical urban problems: loneliness, alienation, prostitution, poverty, dust and dirt, crowds, noise, etc. There is a continuous movement out/in and in/out. The window in Guro's poetic world can be perceived as an object drawn from everyday life, which gives the reader both a concrete sense of the world and simultaneously the poet's own subjective insight into and experience of that world and the objects that exist in it. Details of the external world and the various objects that are used as a part of the picture help the reader understand the subjective world of the poetic persona. In selecting the objects to be framed, and in her description of them, Guro presents both a subjective view of reality and a concrete illustration of the inner states of her narrative persona. By juxtaposing elements of reality and of imagination, Guro is able to depict in concrete terms her own and her characters' perception of the interaction between the inner world and outer reality. Careful use of the window as a frame or "stage" of a seemingly incongruous and arbitrary mixture of impressions, images, events, moods, thoughts and acoustic perceptions, enabled Guro to interpret, together with the reader, the rhythm, the language and the spirit of the world that surrounded her.

Milica Banjanin (essay date 1986)

SOURCE: "Nature and the City in the Works of Elena Guro," in *Slavic and East-European Journal,* Vol. 30, No. 2, Summer, 1986, pp. 230-46.

[*In the following essay, Banjanin examines Guro's portrayal of nature and the urban world.*]

Nature attracted Guro from early childhood, and it was the original inspiration of both her poetry and her art (1900-1906). Even during the period of her interest in the city (approximately 1905-10) she continued to write about nature and to paint it. From 1910 to her death in 1913, nature is again one of the dominant themes of her writing, although we still find many entries on the city in her diaries and notebooks.

Born in Petersburg, Guro's interest in and closeness to nature go back to her childhood and youth spent in the country, in the village of Novosel'e near Pskov and at her father's estate Počinok near Luga. It was nature in this northern region and nature in Finland that became one of the main sources of her creative inspiration. Photographs of Počinok and nearby areas in Guro's archive help explain some aspects of her literary work and her art (northern pines, other trees, roots, boulders, for example). At the age of eight Guro started to write about and sketch her impressions of nature. These small visual and written fragments were to remain, throughout her life, her favorite mode of expression.

In his reminiscences of Guro, Matjušin emphasized her love of nature and her need to leave Petersburg as often as possible. According to Matjušin, an enthusiasm for nature led Guro "to transform herself, while observing, into the observed." She "gave everything to nature, all her spiritual and physical strength. And nature revealed to her, as to no one else, its secrets and its love." Matjušin thought that he had never met anyone else who had entered so intensely into a relationship with nature and had so completely dissolved in it.

What interests Guro is not the description of nature but "a sense of the lyric poetry of nature"—its inner rhythm—presented perceptively through a child's point of view that encompasses the wonder of discovery. In the prose work **"Arrival in the Country" ("Priezd v derevnju")** in *The Hurdy-Gurdy,* Guro evokes the countryside awakening from its winter sleep. After a train ride and the constant noise of the railroad, the poetic persona-narrator finds herself

> enveloped in crystal-clear silence. Everything stopped in the limpid mute air. The transparent

tops of trees looked dream-like beyond the roofs. We stood and involuntarily listened to silence.

In Guro's works, objects are frequently animated by the life hidden in them; they even have a soul, and so does nature. The country in this text is evoked through sound: the forest, horses, and earth. The sounds of falling rain, wind in the trees, the sea, blades of grass crawling out from the earth, night, falling snow—all these are part of Guro's world of nature.

In her play in four scenes *In a Closed Bowl* (*V zakrytoj čaše*), nature and poetry have a symbolic role. The play is dominated by an interplay of fantasy with the objective world. The Star-Digger, an imaginary character and a spokesman for the poetic persona, says that he does not exist because he is "the sound of rain, the heather, and smiles of mugs on a shelf " ("šum doždja, veresk, i ulybki kružek na polke"). The beauty of animated objects and nature in the play is perceived not only as the main goal of poetry but also as essential for the poet's spiritual experience. The vision of nature which the poet captures and projects artistically will live eternally, or, as Guro says in the unpublished *Poor Knight,* "the one who sees a soul everywhere, and considers everything alive" ("tot kto vidit dušu vezde, i sčitaet vse živym") will never remain in darkness.

It is usually in few strokes that Guro "paints" a picture of nature. She evokes the mood of severe winter in this description:

> Crystal-clear groves are dozing. Under their snowy dream, willow branches droop towards the earth. Under the cover of tree tops the branches blend with the white air. Lacy railings of branches are strewn with white hoarfrost, with hoarfrost as large as a fringe. Small fir trees have sunk into the snow. The bushes have also sunk into the snow, and cold reigns. In the field there is a pale blue, frozen silence.

The silence of this wintry scene suggests sleep. Hoarforst in willows evokes the picture of a fan that merges with the cold design of the air itself. So vividly has Guro re-created the mood, that we not only hear the silence of snow, but also feel the cold.

Trees are presented as living beings in Guro's writings and art: "From sheer delight small bent fir-trees place their warm snake-like stomachs on the sand and bask in the sun" ("Sognutye elki, ot naslažden'ja položili slovno zmei svoi teplye životy na pesok i nežatsja"). Guro is particularly interested in pines, and she devotes numerous drawings to them. Two pines surrounded by dunes, a scene much admired by both Guro and Matjušin, frequently are her subjects. The archive of her art contains many drawings of pines, birches, forests, tree trunks, branches, roots, and stones. Both Guro and Matjušin focused attention on the branches and roots of trees, which represented a unity "of outer form and inner structure in a single point of tension." Various sized boulders—in particular a large one on which Guro liked to sit and draw—are the subject of several canvases.

Although Guro became interested in the city and wrote

Elena Guro, circa 1912.

about it, the mechanization and constriction of urbanism drove her back from the city to nature for inspiration. A Soviet scholar writes about Guro's poetry:

> At the height of enthusiasm for urbanism in poetry and geometrization of cubism in painting, there occurs in the works of Guro a return to nature. She juxtaposes "organism" to "mechanism" and turns to the "saving earth," striving to liken the creative process to the rhythms of living nature: "Try to breathe, as the pine trees make noise in the distance, as the wind unfolds and agitates, as the universe breathes. Try to imitate the breathing of earth and the filament of clouds." [E. F. Kovtun, "Elena Guro. Poèt; xudožnik," unpublished manuscript]

Both her poetry and her art show a movement towards nature:

> If the Cubists were drawn towards inorganic forms—towards the world of crystal and stone—Guro directed her art to the forms and colors of living nature, to the world of the organic whole. Objects in her canvases, having become weightless, exist in a state of cloud-like lightness. It seems that the material substance of color,

without any residue, has been transformed into light-bearing, vibrating, gently glimmering, smoky, swirling color formations, which appear as if they were invested with a spiritual quality.

The pines that figure so prominently in Guro's literary works and art seem to stand as a link between heaven and earth. Their branches appear to reach to the skies, while their roots dig deep beneath the earth. As Guro indicates in her notebook: "The earth breathed through the trees into the nearby quiet skies" ("zemlja dyšala derev'jami v blizkoe tixoe nebo"). The heart of a tree is seen as united with the depths of the earth, while its branches are perceived as belonging to the sun and air, to the sky.

Just as Guro's early unpublished poetry (1900-1906) reveals her profound interest in nature, so too do her published works, *The Hurdy-Gurdy* and the posthumous *Baby Camels of the Sky.* Both books—with their fragmentary structure, mixture of poetry and lyric prose, and inclusion of pictorial devices—resemble Guro's unpublished diary entries, which frequently were a form of exercise for her literary and artistic endeavors. In *Baby Camels of the Sky* the poetic persona is concerned for and suffers with nature, for example, with the forest being cut down by people who do not appreciate its beauty. Guro is constantly aware of the sounds of nature, rain drops, the swaying of fragile branches of birch trees, the sounds of the earth that ask that her children be protected. This need for protection emerges in a prose poem about a pine whose core had been consumed by a fire begun in its roots:

> The tree, with a heavy curly head of immense vitality held up now by only a third of its pulp, stood deformed and deprived of its proud support and balance. It was very quiet. Doomed to a slow death, the tree was silent. . . .

The personification of the tree is emphasized by the word "curly headed," in the manner of a Russian folk song, to imply a human quality. The tree also accepts its fate and suffering in a human way. The question is asked, "Who did this to the tree?" The answer is, "I do not know." Other trees remain silent as they watch their doomed friend. The analogy with human beings is carried further by a comparison of the tree's plight to the fate of a healthy man condemned to hang.

The significance of pine trees for Guro is perhaps best seen in an unpublished prose poem, in which the poetic persona asks the pines to teach her to be a poet. In another prose poem, she says: "In the branches of pine trees and everywhere else there slumber thousands of sleepy rhythms. The pines emit so much silence that it absorbs the sounds" ("V vetvjax sosen i vsjudu dremljut tysjači sonnyx ritmov. Sosny ispuskajut stol'ko molčanija, čto ono pogloščaet zvuki"). Only a poet able to listen to silence can hear sounds in it, because the trunks of "young pines are strings" ("U junyx sosen stvoly-struny"). The pines are literally perceived as subject matter for poetry, to be molded by the poet.

Merger with nature and everything living is also found in *Poor Knight.* The best example is the lanky youth, the ethereal poor knight of the title, who completely dissolves in nature. Not only "did he become a tree, but the tree became him" ("ne tol'ko on stal derevom—derevo stalo im"). In other instances he is perceived as a cloud, or as buds on the tops of trees in spring—in other words, he is the personification of living nature.

Guro's attitude toward organic nature is similar to her relationship toward animals. She exhibits a desire "to cover the whole world with wings" ("Ja xoču pokryt' kryl'jami ves' mir"). Her love for animals appears frequently in her works. In a diary entry pertaining to *Poor Knight* there is an imaginary conversation between herself (Nora) and the knight (Wilhelm) about a sick cat. Nora takes upon herself the suffering and illness of the animal and thereby saves it. In *Poor Knight* there is a statement that those who claim to love Christ but do not love flowers, cats, mice or snakes, or plants, really do not love him.

The sympathy for animals and the love for the world as a whole that are so prominent in *Poor Knight* link it with the play *Autumn Dream* (*Osennij son,* 1912), which appears in Guro's book by the same title. The play's main character Wilhelm, a meek passive dreamer, loves both flowers and animals. He dies making himself a shield to protect a dog being shot by an officer. Guro believed that animals and trees should be respected because they carry in themselves a creative kernel and a soul. The concept of universal love for all of "God's creation" is related to Guro's view of the poet as an almost maternal figure, a giver of life, who should depict the world with a tinge of "maternal gentleness."

Guro looked upon human beings as a particular part of nature. She believed that only through carefully observing nature and its inner, hidden movement and mood can one discover its mystery. At the same time, nature reflects and corresponds to the poet's own inner mood, his or her innermost thoughts and feelings. Towards the end of Guro's life, nature evolves into a religious, moral concept. She continued to search for ways to express her attitude toward nature and the world around her, interweaving aspects and forms of poetry, prose, drawings, and paintings into a unique poetic perception of the world. The unpublished notebook for the last period of her life reveals numerous attempts to find appropriate rhythms to express in poetry different aspects of nature (e. g., wind, clouds, rain). Poetization of nature was one of the constant features of Guro's oeuvre: she remained true to the dream of a subjective, "sincere" depiction of the world.

The prose and poetry devoted by Guro to the city is confined, for the most part, to unpublished materials, *The Hurdy-Gurdy,* and the poem "The City" ("Gorod"). Although her primary interest was nature, the city plays a brief, but significant role in her work. Guro was simultaneously attracted to and horrified by the city. This attitude perhaps can be partially explained by her interest in the poetry of Blok and her familiarity with French Symbolist literature; more likely it was a direct response to Petersburg, the city she knew best.

Baudelaire's theory of "modern beauty" had shaped the Russian Symbolist interest in the city, as reflected in Brjusov and Blok's poetry. Guro had read Verlaine, Verhaeren, Vielé-Griffin; she admired Brjusov, Blok, and Belyj. (Ivanov and Blok suggested that she participate in Symbolist publications; nothing came of the venture.) Blok, in the spirit of the Petersburg literary tradition, made the city a symbolic place in which the natural and the fantastic exist with equal intensity. Most of his poems devoted to the city start with an actual event, for instance twilight, fog, a walk along the streets, weather, and city sounds; however, soon the actual acquires another meaning. The imaginary, the phantasmagoric, the elusive become as much a part of Blok's city as the concrete details. Guro's city, unlike Blok's, is not a phantasmagoric nightmare of the poet's inner turmoil. Her city does not encompass the fantastic: it is a contemporary, confining urban environment, presented in visual and musical images. The social, historical, and philosophical aspects of urban existence did not attract Guro's attention. Instead, as with her nature poetry, she chose to write about the fleeting, transitory, subjective perceptions the city aroused in her. Unlike Blok's urbanistic works, Guro's streets and buildings are continually juxtaposed upon and intrude into rooms: "The street asks to be allowed to enter a window" ("Ulica prositsja v okno").

Guro's Petersburg is refracted through highly subjective, fragmented, personal impressions, presented in cinematic flashes that convey the city's rhythm, color, mood, sounds, and atmosphere. She considered the city a source of poetry, but also of spiritual suffering, humiliation (particularly of women), constriction, male dominance, and animosity to nature.

An unpublished prose piece of about thirteen handwritten pages (both sides) entitled **"The Street"** ("Ulica," 1905-1906), which in draft versions was called **"Lanterns"** (**"Fonari"**) and **"The City"** (**"Gorod"**), clearly shows Guro's rather negative attitude towards the city. At the center is a street at night with emphasis on the blazing, rosy-red lightning and the glare of electric lights. The narrator, from whose point of view the story is told, presents her impressions of the real motion on the street, including the visual and aural images produced by city lights and traffic; she interjects into them the sense of terror that the street scene evokes in her mind. The work starts with the sentence: "The street flares up with rose-colored lightning flashes" ("Ulica vspyxivaetsja [*sic*] rozovokrasnymi spoloxami"). We are immediately thrown into the middle of a scene with lights, crowds, movement. The text is broken twice by empty lines to indicate the change in the flow of impressions. **"The Street"** has an open ending: "And silence! . . ." —a device which indicates the flow of life and which will be characteristic of Guro's published works on the city.

The street is depicted as the scene of ceaseless running of a "herd" of people enthralled by the bright lights:

> Pushing aside the lonely and alien, bumping into them, the herd runs over the ones who have fallen, runs toward brightness. The street seethes with black and fiery patches. From the secluded corners of houses, small dark insects are thrown onto the street. Immediately the crowd, and the crush of noise and shapes, rush deafeningly at them. Lost, they hurry about, failing to join the herd. In the leaping emptiness of frightened

shadows they rush about, crush each other, knock each other down. Stunned, they look for a harbor within the roaring river of the street . . .

There is an interplay between the actual motion of the crowd on the street and that of the swarming, scurrying insects attracted by city lights, and the visual effects the lights produce. The feeling of movement throughout the work is achieved by repetition of verbs of motion and by the cinematographic method of shifting in rapid succession from one sight to another.

The light of the street (referred to as "an eyeless glance" ["bezglazyj vzgljad"]), which emits "shafts of empty cold light" ("snopy pustogo xolod-nogo syeta"), contributes to the sensation of motion, as it mockingly examines people: "rapaciously, insolently looks them over, grabs them and throws them to the middle of the street" ("xiščno, naglo obsmatrivajut; xvatajut i brosajut na seredinu ulicy"). The insects tossed about and drawn by lights, and the people, who try to follow the flow of the crowd are involved in a race with time, a race for survival.

The lights are animated and personified, as is the street itself: "Many-sided, well-groomed, rouged, and hungry, the street is freshly-combed, as if it had just stepped out of a beauty parlor" ("Ulica mnogolikaja, xolenorozovaja: narumjannenaja i golodnaja . . . ulica parikma-xerski-pričesan-naja"). The street reflects the people that pass on it, as well as their traits; it actively participates in the movement it engenders. Every new shaft of light brings into focus an aspect of the life of the city street. The verbs that Guro uses: *seethe, rush, bump, push aside, rush, leap, rush about, knock down, stun, roar, tear away, pull,* suggest motion and violence, which contribute to the feeling of fright that the street arouses. The light of the street is also seen as "oppressive," as it examines passers-by as if they were goods to be weighed and handled for the profit they might bring.

Lights and signs reveal another aspect of the street scene:

> Electric letters howl at the black gaps of the sky, shouting out advertisements in red, green and yellow patches . . . The lights gallop. The street goes mad in splashes of lights and mud . . .

Here, the elements of painting are transposed into a system of poetic imagery. Visual signs of objects, in the manner of Cubist and Futurist art, become the material of poetic images. Illuminated words of advertisements are reduced to patches of color that appear at intervals, creating new color schemes and giving birth to associations of speed and sound.

In the mind of the narrative "I" the city itself becomes a thing gone mad, like the people who unsuccessfully try to keep up with the ceaseless rush of the crowd. In their madness, "houses dance in electric lights, in lightning flashes, in fiery holes. It is crowded. The houses bend down from above; they will crush us, will fall on our heads, on our brains" ("Doma pljašut v èlektričeskix ognjax, spoloxax, ognennyx dyrax. Tesno. Oni nagibajutsja sverxu, oni razdavjat, upadut na golovu, na mozg").

Madness also overcomes the city lights. "Shouting" in their fury, emitting a sound "like the tearing of calico," they begin to laugh at and mock the passers-by, suggesting that they be kicked, beaten, and driven into the street. In this projection of the growing insanity of the city that evokes the narrator's own inner turmoil, human beings lose their composure while their "ragged nerves scream [and] crucified air shouts with a cruel metallic light" ("Obodrannye nervy kričat. Raspjatyj vozdux kričit žestokim, metallíčeskim svetom"). The "ragged nerves" of the city dweller prefigure Majakovskij's "Oblako v štanax" (1915).

The madness and ugliness of Guro's city is intensified when compared to a slaughterhouse and the selling of meat, the same image Guro repeats later in the poem **"The City."** The image of the slaughterhouse is suggested by the "well-groomed meat" of women who offer themselves:

> Here, look, I am plumper from this side! Look at my breasts! I have a bust! What a bust! And I have eyes! . . . They press forward with their breasts. In a pink bare light there shine bosoms and behinds . . . They turn around in a shameless sway. There is a smell of perfume and flesh . . .

Even the color of light suggests disrobed human flesh.

The text is suddenly broken by empty lines, followed by the exclamation: "To go away, to wake up!" The narrator is in a room from which she has been observing the street. The furniture in the room is "engrossed in thought," as if time itself had stopped:

> There is only the ticking of a clock and waiting for night and sleep, and a child's bed that softly, softly sails rocking along gray swirling waves into the starless eternity . . . And silence! . . .

After depicting movement on the city street (bumping, shoving, tearing, seething, dislodging, rushing, leaping, pushing), and sharp noise (howls, roar, clank, screams, shouts), everything suddenly comes to a standstill. The words *soft, quiet, gentle,* and *silence* carry a tone opposite to that used to describe the street.

The prose work **"So Life Goes"** (**"Tak žizn' idet"**) from *The Hurdy-Gurdy* provides another excellent example of Guro's use of the city as a source for her poetic prose. As in **"The Street,"** plot development is lacking. Rather, there are descriptions and fragments of impressions of the city experienced by a young girl standing on the street. Her obsession with men, combined with an awareness of their power and of the submissive role of women, is the unifying element of the whole piece. Almost everything happens in the realm of the mind, although external happenings on the street and events within city rooms are the starting point for the re-created mental vision. The abrupt beginning and ending of **"So Life Goes"** implies the movement of life, as suggested by the title. Various sections of the twenty-six-page text are separated from each other by dots (in **"The Street"** sections are separated by lines).

"So Life Goes" starts with the statement "Nel'ka waits." The person she is waiting for is not identified. Various fragments read as a series of flashbacks in Nel'ka's memory while she waits. The sounds, the heat, the change from day to night, buildings, windows, rooms, the crowd, all are important elements in the girl's mental vision. Yet the crowd is no longer a faceless mask, a "herd," but officers, students, workers, prostitutes, sales people, men, women. Although they appear in brief flashes, they nevertheless form a picture of the city. Even though **"So Life Goes"** still encompasses large segments of city life, it is presented in a third-person omniscient narration from Nel'ka's point of view.

On the whole, **"The Street"** is closer in technique to the poetry of Symbolism. In **"The Street"** the city appears not so much as an external object, but rather as a vision, a symbol of the poet's inner anguish projected upon the outside world. The scope of the city scene in **"So Life Goes"** is larger than in **"The Street."** This is achieved through a profusion of details which, like pieces of a mosaic, suggest a whole picture:

> The street is hot. The night is deeper. Men. The air is getting heady from the perfume of passing women. The jingle of spurs is coming closer. Two officers pass with the stupid prodding step of cavalrymen. And one, lighting a cigarette, says "My Julie, ha, ha! . . . "

The night life of the city is evoked: heat, men, prostitutes, smells, and sounds. A number of leitmotifs are repeated at regular intervals in **"So Life Goes"**—the rumble of the street, for example, incessant movement, images of whips, canes and lashings, heat, sensations of subjugation and humiliation, city windows and walls. An ambiguous, tenuous, indefinite, and subjective aspect of the perceived reality that "appears" rather than "is" emerges from the repeated use of the verb *kazat'sja* (to seem), and from the verbs of perception: *saw, looked, perceived, discerned, smelled,* for example.

The story of Nel'ka is framed by a series of events and city scenes that are linked to the main story through the reactions they arouse in the girl. Her stepfather has forbidden her to go out on the street. He has beaten her twice; while she recalls the beatings, the image of her self-confident stepfather is superimposed in her mind on the other men whom she sees on the streets and who symbolize for her male strength, power, and dominance. At the same time, the lashing of the whip is connected with Nel'ka's perception of herself as a dog. The rhythmical tone of the whip used to beat Nel'ka is introduced by the movement of the pendulum of a clock in a room. The room itself is transformed, as it metonymically expresses the girl's state of mind: "The walls watched greedily; they thirsted for the humiliation. They took pleasure in it" ("Steny žadno smotreli, žaždali unizitel' nogo. Naslaždalis' !"). The lashing of the whip is associated in the girl's mind with the crackling of lights that are turned on in the city. While her stepfather is beating her, Nel'ka thinks: "He lashed at the night. The silent, black-eyed night" ("Xlestnul noč'. Molčalivuju černoglazuju noč' "). Nel'ka is represented by night, but night is "black-eyed." Between the girl and the night there is a mutual metonymical relation in which the color of her eyes is transformed to night.

In her insistence on the animation and personification of the objects and the world around her, Guro comes close to later Futurist experiments, particularly those of Xlebnikov and Majakovskij. Guro believed that objects reflect their environment and its emotional tone:

> It is *not at all by chance that I turn* constantly to *inanimate* objects; but I believe that objects, once created and thrown into the world, already interact like independent entities. Each object has its own soul, either put into it by its creator, the author, or received from later deposits upon it, from surrounding life. . . .

Guro's fragmented prose helps re-create the mental process in which the mind moves freely from one object to another, from one thought to another. Sensations alternate rapidly.

In **"So Life Goes"** time appears as a prolonged present (moment), although movement into past experience through memory is indicated. Nel'ka is fixed in space, standing on the street, waiting, while her consciousness roams freely in time. The shifting in time is indicated by the color of light reflected on the windows, which of course changes according to the hour of the day. The overall feeling is one of movement and change. Time is "spatialized"; instants of time seem to be "frozen" in a static, spatial picture. The spatializing of time causes a momentary stop, an image, in the moving world that is in a constant state of flux. These "frozen images" are close to frame shots in film. The girl's inner life, represented by memory, is shown simultaneously with the outer life, the life of the street. Reality and the city appear as sensations and experiences in perpetual flux and change.

In the previously mentioned poem **"The City,"** which in unpublished versions was entitled "Closeness" ("Tesnota") and "Urban Shame" ("Gorodskoj pozor"), the city, as in **"The Street,"** is likened to a slaughter house, which suggests sacrifice. In **"The City"** the poet meets with mockery; his song is taken as sacrifice. The poem is Symbolist in its imposition of the poet's inner being upon outer reality, and in imagery reminiscent of Blok's urban poetry. However, it also points to the poetic world of Majakovskij through the images of "blood" and "slaughterhouse," the commotion of cars, the "barking street," particularly the "tailless dog with the much-ridiculed behind," and the mockery of the poet in the city.

Although Guro did not characterize creative work as "feminine," she admitted that it seemed to her that women possessed a "special richness of light" and certain life-bearing qualities which they were able to personify in their work. For example, Nel'ka was not necessarily conceived of as a prostitute, but as a symbol of "a woman of a city street." As we saw earlier, a similar portrayal of the submission of women is given in **"The Street."** Another curious expression of Guro's attitude toward women can be found in her undated drawing in black pencil "Hysteria" ("Isterija"), which depicts a naked woman before a devil who, having ripped open her abdomen, pulls out her entrails while she smiles at him voluptuously. The woman's pose is provocative—as if she were enjoying what was happening to her. In a comment in one of his notebooks, Matjušin explains the drawing as a protest against a typical male attitude of spitting on a woman's personality after taking everything from her. According to Matjušin, the drawing expressed Guro's protest against the humiliation of the woman.

The everyday language of prose gives freshness to Guro's perception of the city. The same child-like wonder and awe can be found in her prose and poetry devoted to nature. Urbanism and the worship of nature coexist in Guro's works. The world of Petersburg, although barely named, is present with its dissonant noise, its shops, signs, crowds, and loneliness. Guro touched on many aspects of city life in terms of color, smell, and sounds. But by 1910 the city ceased to hold her attention, except in her diary. Nature presented a quieter environment in which she gave free reign to her vivid imagination and in which she communed with trees, animals, and flowers.

Guro's concept of poetry is based on her personal, subjective, emotional experience—what Roman Jakobson, in another context, calls "appropriation of reality" ["Marginal Notes on The Prose of The Poet Pasternak," in *Pasternak: Modern Judgements,* 1969]. Everything in her poetic world lives and has its own soul and character. Her task is to interpret the inanimate world and the world of nature. Although the world is reduced to the poet's subjective impressions, it is nevertheless tangible, because reality has imposed it upon the poet's senses. Guro insists repeatedly on sincerity in writing. The poet should not invent reality but should depart from it, transforming it through poetry. There is a desperate plea that the poetic persona should be able to develop her or his own style, find her or his own language, that she or he should not have to use what others have said. The inability to express the beauty of the surrounding world would be a serious flaw, as if the poet had either been unable to perceive that beauty or had not found her "real voice."

The concept of creativity in Guro's works is connected with the ability to gain an intimate knowledge of and communion with nature. Basically, the poet is conceptualized as a child-like dreamer who maintains the closest contact with the surrounding world. In the poem **"Scatterbrain, madman, soarer" ("Vetrogon, sumasbrod, letatel' ")** poetic creativity is described as the invention of both natural and spiritual phenomena, a realm where the boundaries between different artistic modes, and between art and life, do not constrain the poet:

> Scatterbrain, madman, soarer,
> maker of spring storms,
> sculptor of restless thoughts,
> driving the azure!
> Listen, you mad seeker,
> rush, dash,
> shoot past, unshackled
> intoxicator of storms. . . .

According to Matjušin, this poem is Guro's characterization of the young Futurists, her colleagues.

Guro has created her own fragmented lyrical prose in which the word itself, the image, becomes particularly important. Her prose is poetic. She clarifies this point in her unpublished diary:

> Free rhythms. Prose into verse, verse into prose.
> Prose that is almost verse . . . Sections of stories
> taken as color and leitmotifs . . . ! Concentration of the *story* in two or three words. ..

Guro's prose is concise. Its language is simple. At times she assimilates into it the language of popular speech and the street idiom. In some instances her prose is reduced to one-word sentences, which convey the essence of an idea or image:

> Streets curve around the city without beginning
> or end. Windows. Droplets. Window-sills. Cats,
> pigeons. Ahead it unfolds, shuts itself up, opens
> up. Turn after turn. Reflections, resonant voices.
> Secrets, unknown desultory thoughts, scraps of
> flowers, scraps of conversation. . . .

The fragmentation of reality achieved in Guro's poetic prose through visual imagery and, occasionally, the disordering of syntax—"The air, the city extended before her, weightless" ("Vozdux, gorod rasširjalsja pered nej, legkij")—links her work with movements of modern art.

As we have seen, nature and the city form an integral and important part of Guro's literary and artistic works. These themes represent a pattern of ideas and images that are closely related and interwoven within her poetic universe. The world of nature and of the city is appropriated and transformed in Guro's unique poetic perception and imagery into a colorful design of nuances.

FURTHER READING

Biography

Livshits, Benedikt. *The One and a Half-Eyed Archer*. Translated and annotated by John E. Bowlt. Newtonville, Mass.: Oriental Research Partners, 1977, 272 p.

> Contains brief comments on Guro's work and character from Livshits' personal journals. The book also provides a sense of the background and social milieu of Russian Futurism from an insider's perspective.

Criticism

Banjanin, M. "The Prose and Poetry of Elena Guro." *Russian Literature Tri-Quarterly*, No. 9 (1974): 303-16.

> Analyzes selected poems and fiction from Guro's *The Hurdy-Gurdy* and *Baby Camels of the Sky*.

Mirsky, Prince D. S. *Contemporary Russian Literature: 1881-1925*. New York: Alfred A. Knopf, 1926, 373 p.

> Briefly discusses Guro in a chapter on futurism. Mirsky calls *The Hurdy-Gurdy* and *The Baby Camels of the Sky* "a wonderland of delicate and unexpected expression of the thinnest tissue of experience."

Raymond Knister

1899-1932

(Full name John Raymond Knister) Canadian novelist, short story writer, poet, essayist, and critic.

INTRODUCTION

Knister was known primarily for his realistic narratives set in rural Canada. While his works were not recognized by the general public during his lifetime, Knister was a highly respected member of the Canadian literary community during the 1920s and early 1930s, and recent criticism has acknowledged him as a pioneer in establishing a distinctively modern voice in Canadian literature.

Biographical Information

Knister grew up on a farm near Comber in North Essex County, Ontario. He attended the University of Toronto, but was forced by poor health to return to his parents' farm. Around 1919, Knister began publishing critical essays, poems, and stories about rural Canadian life in various magazines. In 1922 and 1923 he worked as a reviewer for the Windsor *Border Cities Star* and the *Detroit Free Press* before moving to Iowa City to serve as editor of the avant-garde literary magazine *The Midland* and to attend Iowa State University. In 1924, Knister lived for a brief time in Chicago, where he worked as a taxi driver and published reviews for the *Chicago Evening Post* and *Poetry* magazine. Moving to Toronto in late 1924, he became a frequent contributor of articles and stories to the Toronto *Star Weekly* and made the acquaintance of several notable Canadian writers, including Morley Callaghan, Mazo de la Roche, Merrill Denison, and Charles G. D. Roberts. Knister married Myrtle Gamble in 1927, and their daughter Imogen was born in 1930. In 1931 Knister was awarded first prize in a publisher's contest for the unpublished manuscript of his novel *My Star Predominant* (1934), a fictional rendering of the life of John Keats. That same year he moved his family to Montreal where he became acquainted with such well-known writers as Leo Kennedy, Frederick Philip Grove, Dorothy Livesay, A.M. Klein, and F. R. Scott. In August, 1932, Knister drowned near Stoney Point on Lake St. Clair. Dorothy Livesay, in a memoir of Knister that was published in *Collected Poems of Raymond Knister* (1949), maintained that Knister's death was a suicide, but her conclusions have been strongly disputed by Knister's wife and daughter, and such critics as Marcus Waddington.

Major Works

Knister's best known fiction and poetry reflects his desire to capture the essence of rural Canadian life. In *White Narcissus*, Knister delineated the struggle of Richard, a successful writer, as he attempts to convince his longtime girlfriend Ada to marry him and leave her parents behind

in the small rural town where the two grew up. While the expressive prose style of *White Narcissus* has been generally well received, some critics have found Knister's use of symbolism awkward, and have faulted him for failing to fully develop the novel's themes and plots. *Collected Poems of Raymond Knister* contains such poems as "The Hawk," "Boy Remembers in the Fields," "Lake Harvest," "A Row of Stalls," and "The Plowman," which vividly depict rural experience and the Canadian landscape. In both his poetry and his fiction Knister presented sharply realistic portrayals of everyday images and events in order to illustrate their exceptional qualities, and communicated these impressions in a conversational language style. Speaking of Canadian literature and subject matter, Knister stated that "when we trust surely, see directly enough, life, ourselves, we may have our own Falstaffs and Shropshire Lads and Anna Kareninas."

PRINCIPAL WORKS

White Narcissus   (novel)   1929
My Star Predominant   (novel)   1934

CRITICISM

The New York Times Book Review   (essay date 1925)

SOURCE: "A Canadian Novel," in *The New York Times Book Review,* August 25, 1925, p. 9.

[*In the following review, the critic praises* White Narcissus *for its expressive prose style, but faults the novel's lack of substance and heavy-handed use of symbolism.*]

Raymond Knister, a young Canadian writer, has produced in **White Narcissus** a first novel of very considerable charm. It is a supremely atmospheric story, in which dark and introspective moods are developed and elaborated somewhat at the expense of the plot. Mr. Knister's prose is an excellent medium for the expression of his emotional attitudes; it never flags and never becomes clogged or difficult. The result is a novel of memorable color, and of regrettably thin substance.

Richard Miln, the protagonist of the story, is a successful advertising man, who was born in a remote and rural section of a Canadian Province. He returns from time to time to the neighborhood of his youth—partly to renew old associations and to recover the sense of his own identity. Behind the nostalgia which draws him back to the country there is a deeper motive. He always returns to renew the offer of his love to Ada Lethen, the sweetheart of his childhood. Richard is convinced of Ada's love for him, but he never quite succeeds in breaking through the emotional barriers which her strange home had erected about her. Ada was the daughter of a farmer, a man whose marked superiority had caused his neighbors to suspect and distrust him, and whose curious temperament had more than once suggested his insanity. Since a quarrel which Richard Miln could remember from his boyhood, Lethen had not spoken to his wife. For years the Lethen's had lived in bitter silence which was endurable at all only because of Ada. Thus Ada Lethen was bound to her home by a variety of emotional forces—by her love for her father and her perception of his isolation, and by her pity for her mother.

The somber atmosphere which broods over the Lethen household, and which colors the outlook of every one associated with it, is symbolized by Mrs. Lethen's white narcissi, into whose culture she had turned all the interest denied by her emotional life. Richard Miln's determination to take Ada away with him is realized after an almost hopeless struggle, and the solution involves such relatively prosaic matters as foreclosures upon mortgages and suits at law. Nevertheless, Mr. Knister preserves the atmosphere of his book intact. If the symbolism upon which it is based seems, at times, a little awkward and obvious, it has at least the merit of consistency.

Raymond Knister   (essay date 1975)

SOURCE: "Canadian Literati," in *Journal of Canadian Fiction,* Vol. IV, No. 2, 1975, pp. 160-68.

[*In the following excerpt, written before his death in 1932 and published posthumously, Knister discusses the history and development of Canadian literature, using autobiographical information to describe critical reaction to his works.*]

We have wanted to discover and create a new heaven and new earth here in Canada, and to make others see it. When we write a poem about the pines, a novel about the mounties, or paint a picture of geometric ice-floes, we hasten to ask each other, "Isn't this really Canadian? Isn't it different from the productions of efete Europe or the United States, where the people think only of dollars, paint skyscrapers, and write about stockyards. This Canada of ours is a wonderful country. Her mineral resources alone. . . ."

To be sure, different environments and modes of life do make for subtle differentiations in the human spirit. But our writers have seldom cared to probe deep enough to find them. We want to be different, but not too different. The ideal Canadian litterateur is a man who has been educated as an English gentleman, though certain New England Universities will pass; in addition he should know French and Quebec life. Nor should he forget his training, but write about Canada as accurately and sympathetically as possible from the point of view of an ominiscient tourist who, after all, knows better things. We want not so much to be different as to have had different experience about which we can talk at tea as suavely as anybody. It amounts in fact to our wanting to be American or English with an additional background which will lend *chic,* inspite of the elemental, or an unsullied outlook, according to taste. So the differences we formulate are not important or intrinsic, and our creations have only seemed to exchange trappings with those of other countries.

Again we forget that *plus ça change, plus c'est la même chose.* We forget that the differences between men are not more important than their similarities. It might be pleasant to believe that the open spaces and association with sagacious animals and noble savages have made us braver and more unselfish than other peoples, though as a matter of fact half our population has nothing directly to do with the great open spaces, not to mention the animals and savages; and those who have mostly lived on farms almost identical with farms to be found in Connecticut, Michigan, and Kansas. And we have cities that in spite of polite contrary pretensions would like to boast of skyscrapers higher than those of New York, or an underworld more sinister and ubiquitous than Chicago's.

What then of our noble determination to make an all-Canadian literature where none was? If this is the Canadian attitude, if we would like to be like Englishmen or Americans and yet we are sure we must be better because of our glorious mines and forests—how does it affect the Canadian writer who wants to write about Canadian life sincerely? We can't consider those who lightheartedly take Canada for a gold-mine of "good yarns", northerns and westerns. They are usually candid enough in their way. But what about those who have been born in Canada, have been moved by its life, tried to picture it, and become more or less worried about their failure, or the seeming impossibilities of their task? Why is it that, in spite of the able and well-known Canadian writers whose books are read in the States, American readers never think of "the Canadian novel" as they think of "the Scandinavian novel?"

The comparison is not wholly unfair, for though Norway and Sweden are older, civilization, as generally understood, has not advanced farther in them than in Canada; nor are they more open to the influence of powerful neighbors. Yet these small countries have a body of creative writers which command the respect of the world: disinterested, profound, intensely local and yet—the antithesis cannot be avoided—universal. Canada's classics (to Americans) are Ralph Connor, L. M. Montgomery, and Robert W. Service. Further comparison is not necessary.

But—what of the generations following these writers? It is thirty, fifty years since such books began to be written. Surely in that time, in a young country throbbing with energy and growth, there must have been a few young men and women who burned to give forth a microcosmic projection of what they knew, winning the favor of the gods and the praises of men? There were and there are: but their throes have not given birth to anything more nearly mountainous than the old-style pine-trees. In truth they have been in a sad way, and the conditions have not been wholly of their own making.

I may be pardoned for offering myself as *corpus vila;* it appears necessary at this point to venture into autobiography in order to explain my meaning. When I started to write, some few years ago, I was a farm lad of little academic education or worldly acquirements. I had read rather widely, not to an unheard-of quantity, perhaps one hundred volumes a year from the time I was fourteen until I was twenty-one. Long before this period I had decided that I must become an author, my only vaccilation being occasioned by a visit at the age of nine to an uncle who was a railway station agent. Well, it was getting time to start. What should I write about? It had been essays of a literary turn at first—there was one on the centenary of Froude. Then I went to Toronto University, but was unable to finish my first year, succumbing to pneumonia and pleurisy. The university magazine printed articles of mine on **"The Intellectual Mutt and Jeff "** (Don Quixote and Sancho Panza), **"The Modern Novel,"** and **"Stevenson Twenty-Five Years After,"** this latter a glowing tribute of five thousand words.

But when I got back to the farm and recovered my health by dint of working fourteen to sixteen hours in the field until autumn, I began to change my views about writing. There was something about the life that I lived, and all the other farm people round me, something that had to be expressed, though I didn't know just how. But the attempt would have to be made in the form of short stories. I had read a great many short stories from several literatures. Now for a subject; it wouldn't do to start with an autobiographical piece. One must be objective. As the days got shorter, and the time of more leisure came nearer, I looked about me earnestly.

It happened that we had a former neighbor working for us that fall. He was a tiny short old man who had sold his farm and been away for years, and now he was back among the people he had known, helping them with their crops. He and I hauled manure and cut corn in the field with sickles. He would mutter to himself amid the rustle of the stalks, though he was not ill-natured. When he was lifting staves loaded with tobacco-plants to the wagon, and had to toss them when the load became big, someone jocularly complimented him upon being a ball-player. "I'm no ball-player," he returned bitterly. "Takes a good strong man to play ball." And one night I heard him talking in his sleep from the next room, cursing shrilly at some one who had not appreciated his horses: "Nothing but a damn fool! Ever know me to run down any man's horses?"

Here was my story. When the fall work was over and the Christmas season, I sat down, on January 2nd, 1921, and wrote it. The writing was quite bad, but the composition or architecture had been given some care, and I was not surprised, though rather gratified, when **"The One Thing"** was accepted by *The Midland.* Four other magazines had rejected it. I had heard of *The Midland* through J. O'Brien's yearbooks of the short story, and I figured that it would be better to have even one cent a word and printing in such a place than the thousands dollars I had heard the popular magazines paid, and run the risk of any loss of prestige; the deuce with money! But the letter of acceptance from John T. Frederick, while it praised my story with the most ingratiating discrimination, mentioned that *The Midland* did not pay for stories. Two or three copies of the magazine were mailed to me, in which I found stories by Ruth Suckow, Walter J. Muilenburg and George Carver.

That winter I wrote several more farm stories, and also thirty or forty farm poems, with the eye on the object. These were printed at intervals in the "little" magazines, poetry journals, and expatriate quarterlies,—all American. Some little recognition came from American critics, and in London *The New Criterion* singled out a dozen of my poems from a galaxy of moderns for their "objectivity". It was this objectivity which forbade the acceptance of my work in Canadian magazines. My poems and stories were so Canadian and came so directly from the soil that Canadian editors would have nothing to do with them. The injustice was perhaps trifling; the quite modest merits of my efforts were adequately rewarded by the audience, fit though few, of the "little" magazines. But they weren't morally subversive, nor eccentric mannered, these attempts. It seemed gruesomely significant that not a Canadian editor would have anything to do with them, and that probably there were a few other young in the country writing about it with the same immediacy, who were likewise rejected. . . .

Perhaps it was mere good luck that I did not lose my sense of an indigenous life waiting to be rendered. Living in Toronto, which is a unique blend of English mannerisms and blood, pioneer Canadian puritanism, and American go-getter business tendency, I was freelancing in the magazines, doing articles chiefly, literary criticism, interviews. Also I was doing stories of farm life, very brief, and patterned according to my own liking, for the *Toronto Star Weekly,* our substitute for a Sunday newspaper. It was and is too small town to "get by" as a national weekly in another community, but its local flavor was what made it attractive to me. To be sure the editor would expostulate earnestly with me: "Mr. Knister, you make your people too real. Our readers don't want to read about real things. They want to be amused. Try to put more plot into your stories." And numbers of them came back. In fact, after I picked out half a dozen to send to Edward J. O'Brien, and he had starred or double-starred them in his *Yearbook,* all of them came back. It was disappointing, because though it was excusable in a Sunday newspaper to be determined not to be highbrow, I was sure that there were some thousands of readers of the paper who would like to see their life pictured more or less as it was, without recourse to stage types and old stuff. A new country and a new audience in the making, what an opportunity for Canadian writers! Hadn't Chekhov written in Russian papers of great and immediately increasing circulation? And in such a paper you would not have to pay any attention to the demands for a mechanical "structure" which our other magazines regarded as indispensable. . . .

I have not touched upon the Montreal scene, for example, where I am told a distinct vibration is perceptible in the air. One of *les jeunes* from that city enlisting my support for a new monthly to be published (a short-lived namesake of this magazine, by the way) expressed horror of the atmosphere of Toronto; his week-end among us had nearly stifled him, he claimed; even the liquor . . . It is amusing to contrast these hopefuls with such a reverend and idealistic man as Frederick Philip Grove, author of *A Search For America* and *Our Daily Bread,* a self-made Canadian from Scandinavia, a man of mature years and good citizenship who addresses Canadian Clubs on nationhood and kindred subjects. They might tell him that he had too many convictions. The great idea is not to have ideas, they might say, and they would be only paraphrasing the words of a greater than any to be found among us: Keats. It is not possible to know too much, but it is easy to know enough to have prejudices and opinions which may warp creation. Not that any misconception can blot out the flame of genuine creative power. With that, everything else becomes subordinate. Grove's work has genuine power.

That points, however, to the real lack in Canadian letters. We have sometimes fondly cried out for Canadian criticism, but helpful as such would be, it could do no more than clear the ground. Art must be produced, then criticism may come along and explain it. Often criticism arises from mere sense of deficiency, and is personal expression, as in this article. We have scholars in Canada who seem to know as much about writing as one can know without being a writer. It might seem fair to criticise Pelham Edgar for writing a book about Henry James instead of doing something for Canadianism, but possibly even his austere judgment has unbent to local talent and tried to get it a hearing more frequently than it has deserved. Criticism on the part of readers, yes, by all means. But not the kind which assumes that a book is going to be good or bad because it is Canadian.

When Canada is different we will have a different literature. Whether we call it lack of genuine impulse or whether we assume power that is inhibited by scapegoat inferiority complex, the fact remains that Canada has given birth to artists as clever as those of other countries, but it has not been given her to produce a figure of towering importance to the rest of the world. When she does, it is my guess that he will be found to have sprung from the soil and to have escaped the need for either a quaint regionalism or limitation of other nationalities. He will speak to men everywhere in their own tongue.

There are other standards of course besides that of relevance to "conditions". Let it not be assumed that the only expression I advocate has to do with wheat fields and stock yards. I am only pointing out that we probably will have to come to grips with reality before we shall have a literature, before Canada will mean something to the Canadian besides his own personal experience. Our next great writer may be of a different stamp altogether. If any Canadian equals *Green Mansions* or *South Wind,* not to mention *Moby Dick* in like or unlike exotic fields there will be no objection from anybody. Or if he can be as Canadian as Poe was American he may create his own world.

To round out my own story: my sapience has not availed greatly. It will not be surprising that the obstacles which were too much for the other writers I have mentioned have been overcome by myself. My first book was an anthology of Canadian short stories. My first novel might have had its scene in many countries. And let no one await a peculiarly autochthonous voice in my next: it is about the character of John Keats.

Marcus Waddington   (essay date 1975)

SOURCE: "Raymond Knister: A Biographical Note," in *Journal of Canadian Fiction,* Vol. IV, No. 2, 1975, pp. 175-92.

[*In the following excerpt, Waddington traces connections between events in Knister's life and works.*]

Knister's profound sympathy and understanding for the farming people with whom he grew up is continually revealed in his art. He believed that one of the functions of literature was to heighten cultural awareness. "When a literature has been built up from the soil of a country and the lives of its people", he wrote, "the latter become conscious in a new way of those scenes and that life" [quoted in Dorothy Livesay's "Memoir," in *Collected Poems of Raymond Knister* 1949]. He felt himself bound to express the truth about his community, the people who comprised it, and their way of life. "There was something about the life that I had lived, and all the other farm people around me, something that had to be expressed, though I didn't know just how" ["**Canadian Literati,**" Knister Papers].

Knister's poems, like his stories, show him experimenting with new shapes and forms moulded out of the raw material of country life. His early stories and poems each present an integrity of 'Image', a wholeness of life in infinitely varying patterns. They are, all of them, redolent of the earth and of the sights and sounds which greet men as they toil over it.

In the creation of his poems Knister followed what he took to be Ezra Pound's Credo, "the idea . . . that each poem should comprise an Image, and that this Image should not be blurred by extraneous matter" [*Literary Essays of Ezra Pound,* 1968]. Pound defined 'Image' as "that which presents an intellectual and emotional complex in an instant of time". He held that a good poem was one in which the emotions conjured up by the rhythms of the word were in perfect harmony with the idea or fragments of ideas expressed. The visual element or "the casting of images upon the visual imagination" provided the third dimension to the harmonious 'Image'. The majority of Knister's poems in his *Collected Poems* satisfy Pound's definition of the 'Image'.

About December, 1921, he typed out a volume of poems—*Grass Plaitings*—which he culled from his work of the two preceding years. He had read a great deal of Robert Louis Stevenson, and had been influenced by Stevenson's essay, "On Some Technical Elements of Style in Literature", which put forward many of the literary principles later popularized by Pound in his Imagist Credo. Perhaps the title, *Grass Plaitings,* alludes to Stevenson's contention that "the literary artist" ought to "plait or weave his meaning" to "make a pattern" [*Essays in the Art of Writing,* 1905]. If so, the title "Grass Plaitings" draws upon the metaphor controlling **"The Ploughman"**—the earth's blades of grass corresponding to the poet's words woven into a pattern. Seven of these poems appeared in *The Midland,* and some were later published in the *Collected Poems.*

After the publication of **"The One Thing"** in *The Midland* of January 1922 Knister turned to drama, and in March wrote *The Loading: A Play in One Act.* It was based on his story, **"The Loading"**, written the year before. He submitted this play to Bertram Forsyth, the Director of Hart House Theatre, for his consideration. In August, Knister lengthened the play to four acts and, in a letter to Forsyth, he commented on his technique and purpose:

> (I) thought I saw . . . in Strindberg's *The Father* the model for my technique . . . Particularly, how was I to render—and I wished to do so— the monotony of an existence in which a visit to the city or the eating by a sow of her farrow might seem events, save by paucity of action? A crisis, convergences in the life had to be of course, but I have tried rather to emphasize—or to show, rather—the ordinary trend. In short, my master in this piece has been Tchekov.

Forsyth was encouraging in his criticism but he declined to produce the play at Hart House Theatre. *The Loading* remained unpublished for six years until, finally, in 1928, it was published with minor changes under the title *Youth Goes West* in *Poet Lore,* a leading American magazine devoted to drama.

Yet in 1922 Knister concentrated most of his attention on short stories. In December 1921 he wrote "Indian Summer" and "Lights", both still unpublished. Then, in January, 1922 he wrote a number of more successful stories in rapid succession: **"Lapsed Crisis", "The Strawstack", "Mrs. Laneham",** and **"The Return of the Nances"**. In February 1922 he wrote **"Grapes"** and **"The Old Gestures"**, this last story much longer than any of the others. In the spring he returned to **"The One Thing"**, but unfortunately lost the manuscript sometime after. Knister attempted to publish some of these stories in a volume in June 1922.

Most of these stories draw upon farm life for their material. They bear a resemblance to the Imagist poems written during the same period. Each story is distinguished by its own tightly knit design. In each story the intellectual element, or theme, is carefully woven about the visual element, or the succession of images. The melody of emotions created by the interplay of these two elements constantly arrows toward a centre: the unfolding consciousness of the main character. In each story there is a very special moment of epiphany, when this unfolding consciousness reaches a climax and is consummated in either the expression or repression of the character's self-awareness. This moment, so crucial for the character, also becomes a crucial moment of understanding for the reader.

Knister's friendship with John T. Frederick was strengthened when in the course of his travels he met briefly with Knister and his father at the Chatham railroad station in late March. He was offered and took away Knister's volume of poetry, *Grass Plaitings.* He was "astonished by the amount of really finished work" in *Grass Plaitings,* "work of charm and, on first reading... of conviction and competence". In June, 1922, Frederick asked to have **"Lapsed Crisis"** for publication. It was altered slightly at Frederick's suggestion and published as **"Mist-Green Oats"** in *The Midland* of Aug-Sept. 1922.

While visiting Frederick at Glennie, Michigan, Knister met another young writer, Walter J. Muilenberg, and the two became fast friends. Muilenberg was a rather silent, solitary fellow; he patterned himself after Thoreau and spent his summers in a shack on an isolated part of Frederick's thousand acre farm. But a deep bond of sympathy grew up between the two young men and they would stay up till all hours discussing literary matters. While at Glennie, Knister showed his two friends a revised version of his long story "The Old Gestures" which he now called "Group Portrait".

By the fall of 1922 Knister had decided that he must become a novelist and so he applied himself to an expansion of "Group Portrait". Besides drafting a plan for his novel, he also made a deliberate effort to earn his living as a professional writer. In October he began to review books on a weekly basis for the *Border Cities Star,* a Windsor newspaper. Although resolved to do only the best work, he quickly found his creativity hampered by the 3/4 column space limit imposed by the newspaper. He needed far more scope for "a portrait"—what he thought a review ought to be. As it was he barely had room for a "snapshot-summary" or a "discursive sketch". Despite these difficulties he managed as best he could and within a year earned for the *Star* the reputation of printing one of Canada's outstanding Literary Pages.

Sometime during the winter of 1922-23 Knister was offered an editorship with *The Midland,* Frederick's proposal probably having taken shape in their summer conversations at Glennie. Meanwhile Knister was making contact with several Canadian authors, including Merrill Denison and Mazo de la Roche. He met the Toronto literary group when he attended a gathering of the Canadian Authors Association in April, 1923. Although he struck up lasting friendships with individual Canadian writers and finally got a story, **"The Strawstack"**, published in the *Canadian Forum* in October 1923, he was generally disappointed in editors of Canadian magazines. His experience had shown, with the exception of the *Forum* editors, that they "didn't know a story from a bill of lading". They seemed more receptive to literary essays, however, and perhaps with this in mind Knister wrote **"The Canadian Short Story"** in which he addressed himself to "a few beginning writers of promise . . . who must exist and who may chance on these words" [*Canadian Bookman,* August, 1923]. . . .

While serving as Associate Editor Knister also attended lectures at Iowa University, though not officially registered. He took Frederick's course in the short story for advanced students and another one in drama. He didn't, however, feel that the University system had much to contribute to his own development. As he confided to his father:

> Study the way the masters did it, and then go to
> it independent-like, and not fool around with a
> lot of courses. I'm beginning to wonder if I
> wasn't right in thinking that all along . . .

While in Iowa, Knister wrote a perceptive essay on Katherine Mansfield's stories, and another on William Wilfred Campbell's poetry. He channelled most of his energy into writing novels, however, working "furiously" during the winter months. He finally finished his first novel *Group Portrait* and revised it in March, reading it aloud as he went along. In a "Foreward" to this novel he explained that:

> The old masters, Hardy and Flaubert, achieved
> this unifying rhythm by a studied arrangement
> of exposition, background, and of scenes which
> dramatically articulated the action. And here, I
> remark without comment, I have cut directly
> across precedent: for I have given exposition and
> background in scenic form, and the drama is ar-
> ticulated by the introspection of a character
> [dated 12 March 1924, Iowa City].

He returned to Canada in October, 1924. His journey homeward became the source of one of his finest poems,

"After Exile". He meant this poem "to synthesize one individual reaction to the environment that represents his country". **"After Exile"** describes a train moving through the spreading land and unravels a ribbon of images which tells the story of the land's ongoing harvest. As these images are braided into the consciousness of the poet-observer, they are coloured by memories of his past life.

As **"After Exile"** suggests, Knister's consciousness was awakening to his old, yet new, environment. He approached it with a confident, newly matured energy. "Everything I see or hear", he told his friend, Elizabeth Frankfurth, "reminds me of something I must write". He wrote furiously and almost incessantly. During the winter he polished up *Group Portrait,* then completed a second draft of *Turning Loam* and sent both manuscripts to Hugh Eayrs, the editor of Macmillan. Although the novels were turned down, Knister remained undiscouraged. He had long ago decided and reminded himself again and again that "the only safe way to write is for one's own enjoyment". He turned his hand to short story writing too and that winter (1924-5) saw the creation of some of his best— **"Elaine"**, **"The First Day of Spring"** and **"The Fate of Mrs. Lucier"**. As well, he wrote a brilliant series of twelve poems about horses, called **"A Row of Horse Stalls"**. . . .

In the fall of 1925 Knister received the cheering, but rather ironic news that **"After Exile"** was to be published in *Voices,* an American poetry magazine edited by Harold Vinal. At the same time he wrote the first draft of **White Narcissus.** He also completed a new, enlarged version of **"The One Thing"**, a story which Knister felt was probably his most artistic attempt, embodying "not only a synthesis of one man's life, but of all the spiritual values. . . in rural living". Sometime that late fall or early winter Knister also wrote a story in celebration of the corn harvest, "Corn Husking". In November 1925 he sent Lorne Pierce a copy of his manuscript of *Windfalls for Cider* and accompanied it with such a salient statement of the problems facing the Canadian artist that it is here reproduced in its entirety:

> Perhaps nothing need be said of the form of
> these poems at this date; and I have no objection
> to the idea of any Canadian using the forms
> which traditionally belong to other litera-
> tures . . . But I seem to find an analogy in what
> some Canadian critic said at the time of the pub-
> lication of *Maria Chapdelaine,* to the effect that
> it was a pity that a native son of Quebec had not
> perceived that beauty and so embodied it. The
> difficulty would have been that in acquiring edu-
> cation and local culture he would have lost the
> courage of his environment and perhaps missed
> art in attempts at plot, action and the effects of
> current novels for the movies. It seems to me
> that the same thing has happened to many En-
> glish-speaking writers of verse, when they try to
> express the soil-spirit of this country in sonnets
> and vilanelles. To express other things, and
> themselves in so far as they are cosmopolitan
> gentlemen of the world, I repeat, is quite legiti-
> mate. Nor is it well that the writer should be ig-
> norant of other literatures. But it is not likely
> that we will reach indigenous Canadian forms at
> the first try, so that experiment has always
> seemed perilous. It will perhaps need many gen-

erations of farm boys who find a soul in the pigs they are feeding and romance in their furrows, before we produce the perfect singing voice of a Shropshire lad. It is from this sense that I would call my book *Windfalls for Cider.* Many Chattertons may come before a Burns. Burnses do not spring from the void; but undoubtedly this country will yet produce a great poet from its soil.

With so much of his creative work waiting for publication, it is not surprising that Knister [had] a series of aggressive confrontations with Canadian publishers. He considered himself first and foremost a professional writer. Publication was essential to him if he were to have an independent and regular source of income. He was entirely confident of his own ability; he had seen his stories and poems appear alongside those of the best contemporary writers in the English language. However, "it seemed gruesomely significant" to him "that not a Canadian editor would have anything to do with them" ["**Canadian Literati**"]. He addressed protests against this state of affairs to several Canadian editors and publishing houses. In June 1925 he wrote Sir John Willison, the editor of the recently established *Willison's Monthly,* that there had been "no arguable reason why some of the soundest and most original of Canadian creative work must appear in English or American periodicals". Even the *Canadian Forum,* manned as it was by "Toronto University assistant professors and visiting Oxford dons", had rejected his indigenous horse poems. In September, 1925, he introduced himself to Hodder and Stoughton by telling them that Canadian magazines were "averse from any intrinsic integrity of art", and intimating that they might improve matters. However, he fared no better with publishing houses. Hodder and Stoughton responded by inconsiderately keeping the manuscript of *Turning Loam* for six months before rejecting it.

Knister's protests to Canadian publishers were not merely self-interested. As a writer and a reader he was honestly concerned about the nature of the Canadian literary audience. He believed that there was a receptive public and body of critics if one could get by the editors. He felt, however, the heavy influx of American popular magazines was threatening to vitiate any possibility of independent Canadian taste. The Canadian magazines of mass circulation such as *Maclean's,* the *Canadian Magazine* and *Chatelaine* were in unconscionable competition with their American counterparts and for the most part featured imitative stories about a non-existent Canada. In "Canadian Letter", an essay originally intended for *This Quarter,* Knister at length dealt with the problem of a Canadian literary audience and called for the establishment of "a magazine devoted to creative work . . . chosen for vital quality, and which should give a voice to what is actually lived among us". . . .

On August 30, 1932 Knister drowned off Stoney Point, Lake St. Clair where he and his wife had taken a cottage for a brief holiday. When a man, especially such a gifted man as Knister, dies suddenly and accidentally, many people experience a need to explain his death, to dramatize it, to give it meaning. Both Dorothy Livesay and Morley Callaghan saw Knister's death as a kind of confirmation of his personal problems, of the desperation and lack of direction they claim overwhelmed him in the end.

Knister was not, in fact, in desperate financial straits toward the end of his life . . . . [His] last letter, written in a calm, rational and scholarly tone, shows no sign of anxiety or despair. It merely illustrates his continuing critical interest in Canadian literature.

Dorothy Livesay's "Memoir" of Raymond Knister is invaluable for its insight into Knister's poetry and for its vivid description of some parts of his life, especially his childhood. Livesay intimates that Knister, who was reading Maria Rainer Rilke in those last days, took Rilke's concept of the poet as a self-sacrificing martyr too much to heart and although the "Memoir" does not explicitly declare that Knister committed suicide, its implication is clear. Livesay cites passages from a *Hound and Horn* article on Rilke, which Knister had been reading, as evidence to support her interpretation. However, a reading of Knister's "Via Faust", an outline for a novel he was planning, and quite possibly the last thing he wrote, presents a different picture of his appreciation of Rilke.

Livesay assumes that "Via Faust" is autobiographical and therefore directly applicable to Knister's personal life, and she uses it to interpret Knister's life and death. Yet "Via Faust" is neither autobiographical nor factual. It is a purely fictional outline of the life of a character. Knister did not intend it to represent his own life history, although as an imaginative work it may reflect some of his own experience and feelings. Knister opens "Via Faust" by noting its "Theme, to Faust and back." He then presents an outline of the life of the protagonist, divided into four stages. Each stage marks a critical phase in the development of the protagonist's quest for spiritual knowledge and corresponds with an important period of his life. The general import of "Via Faust" is clear. As the hero moves though the stages of life, he faces hardships, but grows to overcome them. It affirms Knister's faith in the value of life beyond everything. The protagonist surrounded by death conceives of death as a necessary aspect of the earth's cycle of constant regeneration. He becomes a "good fighter" whose indomitable will has only been strengthened by the experience of sorrow.

The interpretation of Knister's death as possible suicide was repeated in a later C.B.C. radio production "Profile of Raymond Knister" written by John Wood. On this program Morley Callaghan stated that Knister was growing "rather desperate" toward the end and that he had "drowned in a curious kind of way". Wood followed suit by describing Knister's "darkening mood" and his "determination . . . slowly turning to desperation". Doris Everard, the author of the first academic thesis to be entirely devoted to Knister, has also been influenced by this interpretation. Although she does not agree with Livesay's contention that Knister committed suicide, she does discover "a darkening vision of life" in Knister's "later stories". She attributes an increasing "darkness" to a group of stories according to the chronological sequence into which she assumes that they fall, though, in fact, their chronology is not clear.

Knister possessed a healthy confidence in his own work and was conscious of its merits but he was also aware of the circumstances against which he had to struggle. On the whole he maintained a carefully balanced perspective on the relationship between his cultural environment and his work. He believed that his work was far ahead of his time, a belief now being vindicated by this publication of his hitherto unpublished stories in *The Journal of Canadian Fiction.* Knister's correspondence for the 13 year period from 1919 - 1932 reveals the consistency of his struggle to create worthwhile art and to share it with his countrymen. Knister's work follows an undeviating path of dedication to Canadian literature.

Knister's daughter comments on Dorothy Livesay's "Memoir" on her father:

I wrote to Miss Livesay to find out her reasoning, as I had always admired her poetry and did not want to misjudge her. Her appreciation of my father's work was excellent. It was only when she tried to interpret his personality and mental processes that the distortion occurred. Her interpretation was tentative at the time, but other people's enthusiastic acceptance of it created the myth of what she calls his "self-immolation to save the world." . . . Knister produced some of the most virile and sophisticated poetry, prose, and criticism of his time, but [Livesay's] stereotyped picture of him as a mentally ill "farm-boy" has killed interest in his work. Perhaps this is not what she intended but this is the impression that has been conveyed, and no one ever questioned it, up to that time. . . . I admire Dorothy Livesay for her feminism and her poetry. However I must object when the truth about a writer's life and personality is twisted in order to create a martyr or to prove a point in sociology. I'm completely certain that Raymond Knister did not die willingly. He had a tremendous love of life and a great many things he wanted to do. Also he was a very determined man and would have preferred to have had the last word.

Imogen Givens, in her "Raymond Knister: Man or Myth?" in Essays on Canadian Writing, *Fall-Winter, 1979-80.*

Peter Stevens (essay date 1976)

SOURCE: An introduction, in *The First Day of Spring: Stories and Other Prose* by Raymond Knister, University of Toronto Press, 1976, pp. xi-xxvi.

[*Stevens is an English-born Canadian poet, critic, and educator. In the following excerpt, he surveys Knister's short stories, essays, and reviews.*]

It is tempting to read the facts of Raymond Knister's life as a legend of the romantic artist, the writer whose blossoming career was cut short by early death. The parallel with someone like John Keats is uneasily apparent, particularly when one remembers that Knister wrote a novel, ***My Star Predominant,*** based on the life of Keats, and

shortly before his death Knister's wife reported in the diary she kept at that time that her husband was full of optimism about his future: he said, 'I feel just as Keats did when he said he was just coming into his powers. I feel as though I am just coming into mine.'

But the facts of Raymond Knister's life need no romantic interpretation. His life is illustrative of the role of the writer in the first decades of the twentieth century in Canada, and Knister himself seemed well aware of the difficulties involved in that role in this new country.

Raymond Knister was born in Ruscom, near Comber, in Essex County, Ontario on 27 May 1899. His father was of German stock, a man who industriously farmed the land in several places in Essex and Kent counties. There is no doubt that such a story as **'Mist Green Oats'** is autobiographical, expressing Knister's feelings of entrapment within the farming community, and the emphasis on daily chores had an obvious deadening effect on the sensitivity of the writer. And yet paradoxically much of Knister's success as poet and short story writer derives from his meticulous recording of farm life.

Early in his life he suffered a bad fall in the school playground. From that day he stammered badly and although he was given therapy and in later life practised reading poetry aloud, he never overcame this disability. It is perhaps easier in this light to understand his enthusiasm in the 1920s for the work of Wilson MacDonald, who was not only a great champion of poetry in Canada but also an inveterate public reader of his own work.

Knister's further education was ended by the influenza epidemic which followed World War I, after he had enrolled as a student at Victoria College, Toronto. He returned to live on his father's farm, but the lack of a university degree was no barrier to his own pursuits in literature. From his early days he had been an avid reader. He kept a list of the titles of the books he read from the age of fourteen to his early twenties, and his essays and reviews show a remarkable knowledge of world literature, both of the classics and of new developments in twentieth-century writing.

Early in the 1920s Knister began to concentrate on his own writing both of short stories and poems. His work was accepted and reviewed in the United States, England, and in France, in the magazine *This Quarter,* published in Paris. Eventually he moved to Iowa City, where he took some courses at the State University of Iowa and worked for the magazine *The Midland* which had accepted some of his stories and poems. The early 1920s seem to have been a fruitful period for Knister. His work was being published in reputable magazines, he was writing stories, poems, and novels and reviewing books.

By the end of 1924 he returned to Canada and continued to write in all manner of forms: poems, essays, short stories, novels, and plays. The picture of the writer that emerges here and virtually to the end of his life is of a man confident in his own abilities (although some of his letters reveal that he went through the usual depressing moods that most writers suffer). He was ready to experiment in all forms of literature, looking critically at the past in Canadian literature, trying to assess his own ideas in the light of those past writings, examining recent developments in Canada and other literatures, testing personal ideas against those he was constantly encountering in his own wide reading.

Knister worked as a free-lance writer, publishing principally in the *Toronto Star Weekly* during the years 1925-7. He also reviewed for newspapers and magazines while working on the writing he considered more literary, read widely to prepare the anthology of Canadian short stories he edited, and wrote some scholarly criticism. His first published novel, *White Narcissus*, was written in 1927 and published in 1929. The second novel, *My Star Predominant*, was awarded a prize, some of which he collected, although the publisher went bankrupt. Knister moved to Toronto in September 1926; in the winter of 1931-2 he moved to Montreal, continuing his free-lance work. It was at this time that he became acquainted with some Canadian writers then living in Montreal, most notably F.R. Scott, A.J.M. Smith, and Leo Kennedy.

His life brightened considerably when Lorne Pierce of Ryerson Press accepted his prize novel for publication and also offered Knister a position as an editor. He intended to move to Toronto in the early fall to take up his position with Ryerson. However, in August 1932 the Knisters visited Raymond's aunt and uncle, who showed them a furnished cottage they owned at Stoney Point on Lake St Clair. Knister liked the cottage and when his relatives offered it to him, he accepted gratefully, particularly as it was a short distance from his sister, Marjorie, to whom he was very attached and who was at that time living in Walkerville, a settlement now part of the city of Windsor.

On the day the Knisters were ready to leave the cottage to visit his sister for the week-end before moving to Toronto, Raymond went for a last swim in the lake. He was not a good swimmer and rowed out in a boat without an anchor. His family believe that he was pulled down while swimming by a strong undertow as the boat drifted away from him. Many boats, divers, and a plane searched for his body during the following anxious days. An entry in his wife's diary describes the final discovery: 'The divers themselves were almost pulled down into the holes by the pressure. Finally they found his body wedged in a hole at the bottom of the Lake.'

Although Raymond Knister has never been given the recognition that he deserves as one of the first truly modern writers in Canadian literature, certain portions of his work keep reappearing in standard anthologies of short stories and poetry. His first novel, *White Narcissus*, is still available in paperback and recently a limited selection of his short stories was published. His collection of poetry, first published in 1949, will be reissued in an extended form to include some previously unpublished poems.

This present edition contains the stories from that recently published selection, but also brings together a wider variety of Knister's prose, both fiction and non-fiction, long buried in magazines, together with several unpublished stories and critical statements. These last make an interesting study, for they reveal Knister's perceptive views about literature, particularly about the position of the artist in Canada and the problems facing a modern writer in relation to the development of his country's literature and the assimilation of new techniques learned from other literatures.

In his early piece about the Canadian short story (published in *The Canadian Bookman,* August 1923), Knister makes a plea for the short story as an acceptable literary genre, not one which becomes bound by commercial demands but one which embodies an author's vision of life. He shows his scepticism about the formulaic approach of the correspondence schools, touching on the inherent Americanization of Canadian stories if would-be Canadian writers follow the standards of the correspondence school which 'has its finger on the market.' Knister is much more interested in the short story as a literary form of artistic merit, stressing that good short stories will arise only out of the study of the best models, although he obviously feels that mere imitation is not enough. The writer in Canada must persevere in his studies, taking what he can from a broad selection of sources, aware that the outlets for his talents are severely limited.

In spite of all this, Knister retains a kind of spirited optimism about Canada and Canadian literature: 'It is hard to be skeptical, not to think that there are infinite spiritual possibilities in a land as huge and undeveloped as this, open to the variety and potency of influences which bear upon it.' He deals with this question with humour and yet reprimands excessive adulation of Canadian products in his 'Canadian Letter,' probably written at the same time as his article for *The Canadian Bookman*. He singles out Canadian authors he admires and shows a surprising capacity to see real merit. Perhaps the two most significant comments he makes are his rejection of a new Charles G.D. Roberts chapbook, even though he generally accepts Roberts' achievement as very good, and his acknowledgment of Arthur Stringer's early attempt in *Open Water* to make a case for free verse.

He developed these ideas later in the introduction to his anthology *Canadian Short Stories,* which ends with a tribute to the short stories of Duncan Campbell Scott. He was not afraid to criticize Scott's poetry. For example, his review of Scott's collected poems complains that one of the poems 'begins with stale afflatus like the copy for a special advertisement to be illustrated in full colour.' This kind of criticism is counterbalanced by some fulsome praise. The impression that this article, and the one devoted to Wilson MacDonald, give is of a critic who wishes to share his enthusiasm for Canadian poets with his readers. Such enthusiasm tended at times to run away with his critical sense and yet the reader is also brought up short by very telling insights and perceptions. Knister was of course writing here for a general audience and perhaps he tempered his criticism in the hope of reaching out in order to encourage a wider readership for Canadian authors.

The same is true of the monthly columns he wrote for *The New Outlook,* in which he reviewed the poems he had read in magazines and newspapers in Canada. There was some uncertainty in his views but that is understandable in a writer who is working month by month with contemporary poems. He was constantly on the look-out for fresh and invigorating material, always aware of the technical facility of a poem, even if it remained only 'pleasant and neat work' as he once summarized a Roberts poem. He emphasized the importance he placed on technique in the letter to a Miss Frankfurth included in this selection: 'Details of craftsmanship scamped or awry spoil any piece of writing for me, and it is only after the mind assents to the technical mastery that the emotion is allowed to reach me.' He labelled one poem as 'windy confusion,' and although he obviously was sympathetic to free verse his standards in that regard were rigorous: 'There is free verse in this . . . magazine, but the current notion of free verse appears to be a prose description of a poem, shredded into lines arbitrarily long and short—not a piece of work aiming at qualities of sound, of emotion and image as veritably if more directly, as metrical verse.' He usually picked out some of the better of the minor poets who were beginning to flourish in the 1920s in Canadian magazines: Edward Sapir, Joseph Schull, George Walton among others. He praised the general standard of poetry in *The McGill Fortnightly Review,* quoting with approval poems by A.J.M. Smith and F.R. Scott. He was very careful to suggest to his readers that the individual poems he chose to quote and comment on rose above the dross of much writing published in the magazines: 'Reading the output of verse appearing in Canadian magazines and newspapers is a sadly disappointing business if one is looking for the pure gold of poetry. Perhaps it is too much to expect to find several fine poems each month, but one is struck by the disproportion between our literary pretensions and our achievements.'

There speaks the reasonable voice of a critic who wants to find achievement in the current literature of his own country but who has a well-formulated sense of what is good in writing, a sense we can see at work in the short articles on E.A. Robinson and the poetry of Ireland. It is easy to read into his ideas about Robinson some of his own predilections that appear in his poetry and stories, predilections that recur in the long essay on *The Shropshire Lad.* The tone of stoicism and sadness he sensed in Housman's work applied also to his own writing. Knister suggested that Housman's poetry is the portrayal of a 'soil-loving, life-loving, inarticulate but artlessly downright yeoman' sometimes expressing 'fateful emotion combined with a zest for living.' If Housman did represent for Knister a model for his own writing about the Ontario countryside, then we must examine his work to see whether the same 'zest for living' occurs in it. Certainly these moments appear in some of the stories, even in the dourest ones, **'Mist Green Oats,'** for instance. The usual view of Knister's work as being pessimistic and emphasizing the dull routine of farm work and the killing, mind-deadening effects on the sensitive spirit is qualified not only by the epiphanies within some stories and poems, but by the sequence of journalistic sketches written mainly about a specific rural community called Corncob Corners. In this light Knister's comments on *The Shropshire Lad* give a clear indication of a tendency in him which has been overlooked.

His best and most extensive critical works are the two arti-

cles on Archibald Lampman and Wilfred Campbell. Campbell for him was a poet trapped by Victorian responses and forms: 'He reacted to the conventional stimuli in the conventional way, supplying a norm of Victorian opinion and taste in verse.' All the values in Campbell's verse were superimposed, not arising from his own vision of the scene or the individual characters he is presenting. Knister found some of the same faults in Lampman. While appreciating the observed detail of nature in Lampman's poetry, he claimed that there is no felt tension between the poet and his environment. Such tension is obviously a major ingredient in Knister's prose and poetry. He argued that Lampman's failure in this regard derives from a kind of colonial mentality: the details in the poems are Canadian, yet the general tone and form come from outside Canada. He recognized that 'to have accepted Canadian experience and written of Canada in terms of nothing else would have been, if not impossible, at least immediately fruitless and unrewarded.' He sensed a change in the later Lampman, a more modern sensibility which would have led to greater poetry for Lampman had he lived.

Again it is possible to see developing in Knister's criticism ideas which inform his own work: the specific Canadian detail with ideas embedded in an integral development of form. Certainly one can feel this process taking place in the poetry contained in the volume published in 1949. In the foreword to that volume, which he intended to be published as a preface to his projected selection of poems, he gathered together some of the notions that underlay his critical essays and reviews. One such notion was that the subject matter of poetry should be

> as real as sweating men and swilling pigs. But the feeling about them is not always so real, any more, when it gets into words. Because of that, it would be good just to place them before the reader, just let the reader picture them with the utmost economy and clearness. In the end we in Canada here might have the courage of our experience and speak according to it only.

That reality is presented in many of the stories. But Knister is not merely a direct realist; he had read too much Anderson, James, and Chekhov to rely on simple realistic detail. His essay on Katherine Mansfield made clear his belief that the realistic surface of a story should contain a symbolic depth: 'Minutiae should matter, should index ineffable inward things.' But he was not totally convinced by Mansfield's method; according to Knister, she falls into sentimental endings, and he missed local colour in some of her stories.

Local colour and surface minutiae are very much apparent in Knister's stories. He describes the atmosphere and appearance of the farm country of southwestern Ontario, and in two factual articles he wrote about Pelee Island and Long Point . . . he showed that he was aware of local history.

Much of his feeling about locality and community was expressed in the journalistic sketches about rural life published in the 1920s, mainly in the *Toronto Star Weekly.* For these pieces, set generally in his imaginary settlement of Corncob Corners, he included some of that realistic tone of the rigours of farm life, a tone which is most apparent in his longer stories about farming, but the sketches have a lighter touch. In **'Hitching Bertha to the Sled,'** for instance, the farmer's sons certainly have chores to do and the father seems something of a hard-driving taskmaster, but once he is out of the way, the boys have a great deal of fun inveigling the large calf out of the stall and hitching it to the sled. As the calf runs away, ditching the two on the sled into a snowbank, the oldest boy watches. Having been trained to take over the farm, he knows that the calf has been raised to be sold and that allowing it to run free will not put much fat on its ribs. And yet his own yearnings for freedom from the monotonous tasks of the farm are expressed in his closing exhortation to the calf, 'Go it, Bertha.' That sentiment is perhaps not so far removed from that of Len in Knister's most-anthologised story, **'Mist Green Oats,'** but the whole tone is different, for Len's thought at the end of that story is 'What's the weary use?' Even though he has experienced one or two bright moments during the depressing farm day, he has also thought about escaping to the city and has interpreted his father's demands on him as unwarranted tyranny. Len and the oldest boy in **'Hitching Bertha to the Sled'** have much in common. Len, of course, is a fuller study, and his story is one of muted despair, whereas the sketch, although it is only a simple anecdote, manages to suggest a lighter side to the bone-wearying and 'blind unwitting stupor of life' that Len experiences. This weariness is usually associated with **'Mist Green Oats'** in the version printed in anthologies. In this collection a later, slightly different version is used; the addition of two short paragraphs to the end of the story militates against the oppressive ending and indicates that Knister felt there was some hope for Len's life.

Most of the sketches proceed along similar lines. Some deal with other farm animals, most notably in the short pieces in **'A Row of Horse Stalls.'** The horses with their slow patience are held up as models for man, although Knister does not use the animals simply as moral examples, for he describes the particular characters of the horses. He makes it plain that man on the farm can retain some sense of himself in the tough battle with the land, just as the horses do. They suffer from the same blind routine as the farmer and they may also harbour thoughts of rebellion:

> If ever they become as experimentally speculative as they are contemplative, if ever a whiff of human restlessness touches them—well, the rest may be left to your imagination. There might be a conspiracy and some fine morning every man who approached a horse might be neatly despatched.

Omens of *Animal Farm!*

Other sketches focus on the eccentrics of the community, and Knister has some good-natured fun with people like Mrs Plethwick, whose obsession with birds leads to the conjecture in the village that she is a cat-killing witch. Blankenhorn, the crusty, miserly farmer, whose shrewdness and cunning are 'as arbitrary as a levelled pistol,' receives his come-uppance as the butt of a practical joke. Knister sees these people as comic characters, although he

is never malicious at their expense. He takes a delight in the way in which they get the better of officialdom in government and business, as in the story of the man fooling the customs official, and in Anthony Whicher's tribulations in trying to repair the water jacket for his mill engine. Although Whicher is buffetted, and the repair finally fails, Knister's sympathies are with him. There is something of the old pattern of country yokel caught in the trammels of the city slicker in this sketch, but it is Whicher, the yokel, who is presented as the better man.

It has become almost a cliché to regard Knister's stories as equivalent to those American stories of the mid-west with their themes of entrapment, the sensitive spirit chained in narrow-minded small-town life or fastened to the mindless activity of subsistence farming. Certainly that tone is evident in many of his stories, but the sketches tend to emphasize the irrepressible spirits of these rural people. Knister presents the young sympathetically; they are not all like Len Brinder in **'Mist Green Oats.'** Some are like Archie in **'No Gumption,'** who is subjected to the tyranny of his widowed mother. By an ironic twist he is able to convert his mother's plan to retain him for herself on the farm into a proposal of marriage to the girl he has been mooning about. Knister ends the sketch at that point: we are not given a glimpse of what might happen to Archie and his wife, for their future plays no part in this story of youth's triumph over petty authority.

A marriage also closes the sketch about Henrietta Gray. She has an impish gaiety of manner that offends the more morose and staid elders of the community, and it is fitting that she marries Hughie, whose motorcycle is a symbol of the carefree recklessness of the 1920s. This same sketch mentions in passing the community enterprises of the young—they are holding a wiener roast on the shore of Lake Erie—and Knister is at his best in these sketches in which he describes group festivities in the rural community. His account of a rural Christmas indicates how it was celebrated both in the family and in the neighbourhood. The neighbours visit for Christmas dinner and then everyone gathers on Christmas evening for a community concert. The farm chores are still to be done on the holiday, and the neighbours still discuss farm matters, and the mailman still calls on Christmas Day. Running through this is the excitement of the children as they prepare for the concert in the evening. The sketch is a simple factual account which catches the festive mood of the family in a small community with charm and without sentimentality.

The best of the sketches about community activities are those devoted to the harvest festival and the community dance. Knister deftly describes the rising excitement and jocular gossip of the farmers' wives as they prepare the harvest home supper in the church hall, which is full of the smell of 'coal-oil, fresh lumber and cooked pumpkin.' All this activity seems haphazard until suddenly the meal is under way. No characters are developed, yet the reader is allowed glimpses of some of the village people, particularly in the jocose banter about the size of some appetites. This feeling of community among the villagers is further emphasized by setting against it brief flashes of outsiders—the minister smiling meekly over his third cup of tea, the schoolteacher keeping her slightly superior attitude to the amateur performances in the concert. Knister makes clear that the performers at the concert are not star material, yet he obviously admires the community's togetherness and camaraderie.

'The Dance at Corncob Corners' best exemplifies Knister's concern with rural values. Although some 1920s dances are included, with the usual square dance, it is only the traditional ones that draw all the people together, young and old. Indeed, a stranger dancing the Charleston too vigorously is curbed by the village constable. The dance is very much a community affair: whole families attend and it is not simply a dance. Supper is served beforehand with the same gossipy tittle-tattle bandied about as at the harvest home supper. Knister stresses the participation of everyone in everything, so that the whole entertainment lasts until the small hours: 'When these people had determined upon making a night of it, a night of it they made.'

Knister also explores change and growth versus the status quo. The two old-time callers in **'The Dance at Corncob Corners'** reminisce nostalgically about dances in the past, although the author carefully includes details about the internal feuds that broke out on occasions at those dances. Knister does not sentimentalize the old days, nor does he necessarily side with the modern element. He allows both past and present to be seen in the sketch and the principal effect is one of good-natured tolerance, a tolerance which seems also to be the attitude of the community.

Nearly all Knister's stories deal with such rural communities, but included in this collection are two stories based on his years in the American mid-west and these in particular show his response to the city of Chicago. **'Hackman's Night'** conjures up that free-wheeling bootlegging legend of the windy city in the twenties with a clever use of the slang of the period that gives the story a realistic flavour. The story itself does not give much emphasis to the characters, but rather concentrates on abrupt flashes of action,

Sketch of Knister by his wife, Myrtle Gamble Knister.

the hackman in question being caught in violent confrontations between rival gangs and between criminals and police. All this action works well for the hackman, who considers himself lucky when the night is over. The story gives some sense of the sordid elements in the city, and the language used charges it with authenticity.

A much better story is **'Innocent Man.'** Almost of novella length, it describes the night spent by the protagonist, an innocent man, in the cells of a police department. The telling is determinedly realistic, reminiscent perhaps of some of Stephen Crane's Bowery tales. Ominous threat keeps emerging, sometimes anonymous, sometimes meaningless, sometimes motivated, so that at times the story takes on what amounts to a kind of Kafka-like allegory. Throughout there is an insistence on innocence, even among the others in the cells who are palpably criminal. Jack, the protagonist, is really on the border of innocence. It is established at the beginning that he is somewhat irresponsible, a great tease, and, perhaps technically, evading the legality of his contract for the ownership of his car. The effect of the story is to allow the reader to listen to the excuses and recriminations of the other prisoners. This cross-section of the population forced into cramped cells becomes a symbol of the human condition. All are protesting their innocence but the innocent along with the guilty are subjected to violence and humiliation by one of the guards. Jack in fact feels some sort of brotherhood with the other inmates, so that he can think that 'they were innocent, being men,' until he links them all together in a vision of innocence:

> Yes, they were innocent, these men, even as they had told with their lies. The comradeship, the encouragement, the little gifts they gave one another—their best. The way they strove to some ideal, the best their senses would let them recognize. The effort to win the approval of the people they had learned to admire. Weren't they all good children? Weren't they, these children, these ruffians, these men, all innocent?

The juxtaposition of 'children,' 'ruffians,' and 'men' at the end of that paragraph suggests real innocence, constantly battered by forces both within the characters themselves and also from an external, almost incomprehensible, source.

Early in the story Jack reaches the conclusion that 'when you're innocent, you've got to take what's coming,' subject as men are to 'the weird sneer of Fate.' This vision of innocence is not that of child-like idyllic existence. Indeed, somehow innocence has learned to survive in this place set within a dark and mysterious world, a state of existence that leads also to a recognition of the evil within each man: 'It seemed that right had departed from the world, that the world had departed, leaving this hell of grinning faces that saw nothing but their own evil.'

In some ways the protagonist of **'The Strawstack'** is similar to the characters in **'Innocent Man.'** He is a man carrying a burden of guilt for a 'crime' against his sister in early adolescence. As he discovers later, he is innocent of injuring his sister, but he nevertheless becomes involved with the world of real crime. Paradoxically, he remains aloof from corruption, in spite of the fact that he has committed crime: 'He had never had great faith in the evil of man.' But on his return to the farm (and the collapsed state of the farm buildings and his memory of his own wayward method of piling the straw in the stack take on symbolic implications vis-à-vis his life) the world of evil crowds in on him. The new moon stares down on him, on the run from the law, and its newness seems to him to offer an escape to a new life. Michael Gnarowski sees the story as one of a double initiation, and there is validity in that reading, although the notion of innocence lost at the strawstack and then strangely regained at the same place under the new moon is consistent with the repeated idea of innocence in Knister's stories.

If the returned man of **'The Strawstack'** has 'no great faith in the evil of man,' Mrs Lucier in **'The Fate of Mrs Lucier'** has worked herself into a state of acute distress, neurotically terrorized by visions of disasters involving herself. These imaginings could have been used to depict a rather comically pathetic woman, but Knister instead allows them to be etched realistically in Mrs Lucier's mind in order to illustrate her 'plenary terror of the world.' She is forced out into the dark, threatening landscape, and although she is saved from the consequences of her terror, she knows that she has been on the borderline of collapse.

The theme of youthful innocence fading, of the sudden revelation or vague realization of knowledge beyond innocence, runs through many of Knister's stories, whether it is, as in **'Elaine,'** a girl's gradual awareness of what kind of woman her mother is, or, as in **'Lilacs for First Love,'** a young girl's loss of her romantic notions about men. A more subtle evocation of this kind of experience occurs in **'Peaches, Peaches.'** This rather long story seems to wander without focus and yet is cleverly understated. The younger brother, Ed, is somewhat like Len Brinder: he resents the farm chores and wants to be allowed to make up his own mind about his future. He admires the jaunty self-confidence of Murray, the hired man, who is the same age as Ed, yet more at ease with the farm work and with the women hired to pick peaches. Ed agonizes about his own growing attachment to one of the helpers, Florine, and watches with uneasiness as Murray involves himself with Florine's friend, May, although Murray ignores May's apparent seriousness in her friendship with him. Ed has noticed a secret knowingness between Murray and his brother's wife, which grows in his mind without real definition. The hints are all there and by the end of the story Ed has come to a dim awareness about Murray's nature, although he himself still remains uncertain in his dealings with the opposite sex. All this personal confusion is set within the framework of late, hot summer days when there is a surfeit of peaches, giving a background of overblown fruitfulness to Ed's tension, fading away into the fall and Murray's leaving, with no resolution except that Ed is conscious of larger dimensions in human relationships and perhaps of human deceit. What on first reading seems a rather directionless story leaving conflicts unresolved becomes a cleverly oblique narrative on the nature of innocence and the discovery, perhaps inarticulate, of the dilemmas of adulthood.

'Grapes' is a similarly oblique story with a younger boy as the central character who watches an older, reserved man move tentatively towards two adolescent girls. All of them seem caught in a state of unconsciousness about their relations, and in general the unfocussed nature of this story leaves the reader somewhat dissatisfied, although Knister manages one superb scene depicting a time of tense togetherness in a water fight on a very hot day.

The notion of innocence is evoked almost imagistically in **'The First Day of Spring,'** as a father tells the story of a local girl's seduction without realizing that his own son has had romantic notions about the girl. The boy is still young and is unconscious of his own romantic admiration. But Knister includes in the story a few details seemingly unrelated to the narrative development. These details add to the realistic framework but, more than that, they point the reader to the boy's growing awareness. His romantic innocence is still strong as he hears a girl's voice (that of the cousin of the girl whose story his father is telling) in the distance. It is almost like the mysterious song of Wordsworth's solitary reaper: 'A girl's voice came from across the fields, a few words of singing, a voice with something wild and strong in it.' At the end of the story the voice returns, 'and then it stopped, as though for an answer.' The warmth of the first day of spring has vanished, the daylight disappears, 'and with the darkness Winter seemed to be returning.' Perhaps after hearing the story the boy's innocence is disappearing too, for the mysterious voice is answered to some extent by the last words of the story, spoken by the boy to the colt: " 'You're going to be broken in," I whispered. He was strangely quiet.'

Innocence is seen in a different context in **'Horace the Haymow,'** written in part in an inflated style. This style, incongruous in relation to the subject, is occasionally comic, although the story is closer to the sketches in mood and reworks the conflict between city slicker and country yokel. Again it is the city slicker who is the butt of the story, for he is an innocent in country matters.

Innocence is not the only theme Knister deals with in these stories. As mentioned earlier, Michael Gnarowski tends to see the stories in terms of initiation and maintains that in Knister's writing there are archetypal patterns derived from Frazer and Weston. Although such patterns may be in the stories, it is perhaps easier to recognize that Knister uses a variety of fictional techniques as well as archetypal patterns to develop his stories. I have already mentioned the oblique narrative method of some stories and the use of dialogue as a prime source of narrative. More generally than archetypal patterns, the stories contain symbolic detail, the details mentioned above in **'The First Day of Spring,'** for instance, and those in **'The Strawstack.'** Sometimes perhaps they are overworked and draw attention to themselves as symbols, but because Knister operates within a realistic framework, the details serve both at the realistic and symbolic levels and on the whole he controls them well.

Most of the stories of innocence focus on young people, but some have older characters as their protagonists. In these cases the theme of loss and apartness surfaces. Billy Dulckington in **'The One Thing'** allows his obsession with rearing horses to overwhelm any desire he might have for friendship, although the story indicates early on that he was never considered seriously by the women of the district. His small stature translates into a pusillanimity to such an extent that he withdraws further into himself. His farmhouse deteriorates and his farming becomes minimal, even though he retains a delight in plowing. Incidentally, a paragraph in the story offers an alternate, ironic reading for Knister's poem **'The Plowman'**:

> He liked above most things, though he did not formulate to himself any reason for the liking, the constant attempt to make each furrow straighter than the last, and, when a good furrow was attained, to keep those following it right, to have each of his 'hands' properly and symetrically shaped.

The poem is usually interpreted as a parable about the search for perfection and man's inadequacy in the face of that search. In the context of Dulckington's life the poem may be saying ironically that such a search for perfection is too obsessive and that such singlemindedness may have a warping effect; in that lies man's inadequacy. Dulckington's alienation is expressed finally by a break-down, although at least there may be in that a self-recognition of the damage his obsession has wrought. At his time of life, however, such recognition may be too late.

Alienation between people takes a different turn in **'Indian Summer.'** Knister sets up the withdrawn character of the spinster in describing her furniture and house with its 'narrow windows made narrower by curtains starched stiffly and warped perpendicularly in sentry-like columns at either side.' But, unlike Billy Dulckington, Ida Tenny is keeping hope alive, although the renewal of an old friendship keeps gossips like Mrs Lamb busy speculating and prying. Knister provides the realistic details customary in his stories, details concerned with youth and age such as the kittens and the old tomcat, the young print-clad girls passing Ida's house and the old hens in her yard.

So far the story works well enough, but the melodrama of Gregory's near death as he works in the field opposite Ida's house disturbs the quiet fabric of the story. The thought that the accident was caused because the horse was 'old and lazy' makes a nice point in relation to Ida. She must not be lazy herself, must in fact be more positive unless she wants to grow old alone. So Indian summer dawns at the end as Ida and Gregory talk, but the authorial comment in the last sentence makes the sentimentality of the ending too obvious. Knister himself was obviously dissatisfied with the ending of this story and later reworked it at greater length.

It should be apparent from this brief discussion of some of Raymond Knister's writing that he is a much more varied author than the scanty critical pronouncements maintain. Certainly many of his stories cleave to the same themes but he develops those themes in different ways. The sketches show an obverse side to the view he presents of rural life in the stories that have appeared in anthologies and selections. His criticism shows a man acutely conscious of trends in writing and with an ability to see the valuable both in earlier Canadian writing and in world lit-

erature. He is a writer willing to try his hand at many forms of writing. A play based one of his own short stories demonstrates this flexibility, and it is not his only attempt in drama—a full-length play also remains unpublished.

Margot Northey (essay date June-July 1977)

SOURCE: "Comfortably Rural," in *The Canadian Forum,* Vol. LVII, No. 672, June-July, 1977, pp. 44-5.

[*A Canadian educator and critic, Northey is the author of* The Haunted Wilderness: The Gothic and Grotesque in Canadian Fiction *(1976). In the following review, she praises Knister's diverse talents as a writer and critic, noting the authentic voice, nostalgia, and "concealed art" in* The First Day of Spring.]

In his introduction to ***The First Day of Spring: Stories and Other Prose,*** Peter Stevens claims that Raymond Knister is a much more varied author than the scanty critical pronouncements maintain. By bringing together in one volume Knister's short stories, a series of his sketches about rural life, and a number of his critical essays, Stevens allows us to assess Knister's versatility and to discover little recognized talents.

A refreshing discovery is that Knister has a sense of humour. Dorothy Livesay has remarked on the sombre tone of his fiction. but the sketches, collected under the title "Corncob Corners and Other Places," are humorous in a homespun way. At times they have a gently ironic tone reminiscent of Leacock's treatment of Mariposa; occasionally they are as corny as the title suggests.

A more important realization afforded by Stevens' volume is that Knister was an astute critic who had a sensitive finger on the literary pulse of his times. Dedicated to those modernist principles of writing little appreciated by the Canadian public in the twenties, he made some discerning analyses of contemporary writers, particularly of his fellow Canadians. Although his praise of Wilson MacDonald now seems excessive, we can easily agree with his favourable assessment of aspects of Frederick Philip Grove's fiction and Archibald Lampman's poetry, and his negative response to some of D. C. Scott's poems.

Knister's comments on the short story are especially interesting, since one can test his principles against practice merely by flipping a few pages. Decrying many Canadian writers' reliance on conventional formulae, he favours those stories of de Maupassant "in which the structure is so blended with the atmosphere and feeling that the planned element, the brick-upon-brick method which makes Maupassant a model for the correspondence school is altogether absent at first reading." Knister's own stories are notable for their lack of mechanical tricks and for their apparent plotlessness. His best live up to his credo that great art is concealed art; occasionally, as in **"Peaches, Peaches,"** his rambling narrative line is exasperating.

The similarities with Alice Munro's fiction are striking, not only in their locale but in their insistence on exact, descriptive details. Moreover both writers have a sensuous suggestiveness in their stories which leads us beyond the surface to more private and mysterious levels of experience—to a type of magic realism. Knister indicates the direction of his realism when he writes:

> What is known as realism is only a means to an end, the end being a personal projection of the world. In passing beyond realism, even while they employ it, the significant writers of our time are achieving a portion of evolution.

A recurring feature in Knister's fiction, as in Munro's, is an ambivalent regard for home and the routine of life it represents. **"Mist Green Oats"** is perhaps the most negative depiction of the dreariness and weariness of farming and its stifling effect on a youth's sensitive spirit. At the other extreme is the obvious nostalgia of the sketches, with their portraits of the old characters and customs of a farming community. In many of the stories, we feel a tension between the need for change and the appreciation of what is changeless, between the energy of new times, new ways, and new loves and the inevitability of the old cycle. Although the central character in the stories usually comes down on the side of change. Knister's attitude is less certain.

Of course not all the stories in the collection are variations on this theme, nor are they all about farm life. **"Hackman's Night"** and the lengthy **"Innocent Man"** depict the sordid underside of life in Chicago, but they are not altogether successful. Despite Knister's experience as a taxi driver in the city, the stories seem awkward and frequently inauthentic in dialogue and characterization. If these urban stories reveal another string in Knister's bow, they also suggest that in a literary, if not in a social sense, Knister felt most comfortable in the rural surroundings of his youth. Although *The First Day of Spring* convinces us of the diversity of Knister's talent, the finest parts of the collection are still those half dozen short stories about farming life for which he is already best known.

Paul Denham   (essay date 1978)

SOURCE: "Beyond Realism: Raymond Knister's *White Narcissus,*" in *Studies in Canadian Literature,* Vol. 3, No. 1, 1978, pp. 70-7.

[*In the following essay, Denham discusses the gothic and realist elements in* White Narcissus.]

A renewal of interest in Raymond Knister is evident in three recently published collections of his work. To date, however, *White Narcissus,* his only novel set in Canada and first published in 1929, has provoked little attention apart from a paperback reprint in 1962 with an introduction by Philip Child. David Arnason suggests that this neglect is probably just as well: "The novel," he writes, "will not sustain hard and sophisticated academic analysis, but it will survive it ["Preface," *Journal of Canadian Fiction,* 1975]. Much of the scant commentary on *White Narcissus* has seen it as an early experiment in realism. Desmond Pacey, for instance, links Knister with Callaghan and Grove in moving Canadian fiction away from regional and historical romance towards a realistic rendering of ordinary places and events [*Creative Writing in Canada,* 1961]. Although most critics agree that the novel has seri-

ous flaws, they usually assert that its strength lies in its rendering of the life of a particular place and time. Philip Child, for example, insists on Knister's "success in describing farm life and manners, and . . . his splendid talent for catching, with simple and vivid words in which realism and poetry are present but not at odds, the landscape of his homeland which he knew so well" ("Introduction").

White Narcissus contains undeniably realistic elements in its description of farm life, but if one reads it as a realistic novel, one is certain to find serious faults in it. Realism is not an adequate category to describe either of Knister's novels. (*My Star Predominant,* his second and last novel [1934], is a historical novel about the life of John Keats.) Margot Northey has recently suggested that the gothic and the grotesque have long traditions in Canadian fiction and are more important to that fiction than we have usually supposed [*The Haunted Wilderness: The Gothic and Grotesque in Canadian Fiction,* 1976]. *White Narcissus* confirms this view, for it contains gothic elements as well as realistic ones. Indeed it derives much of its power as a picture of life in southwestern Ontario from the tension it sets up between the two ways of seeing the world which these two traditions represent. Michael Gnarowski has also suggested that some of Knister's short stories have mythical and archetypal dimensions and that, as a product of the 1920's, when such subjects were much discussed, he probably owes as much to the work of Jessie Weston and James Frazer as to Ruth Suckow and James T. Farrell. There is some evidence in *White Narcissus* to support this claim as well. *White Narcissus* is not a great novel, but for all its faults it is a significant one, and a more complex one than we have usually thought. Its place in the tradition of Canadian fiction needs more careful definition.

Realism is a notoriously tricky term, implying both a concern for accurate representation of the surface textures of ordinary life and the necessity of getting below the surface to an interpretation of the underlying social and psychological forces that are not easily accessible to ordinary observation. In the Introduction to his collection *Canadian Short Stories* (1928), Knister uses the term in its first sense, but with a keen awareness that realism in this sense is insufficient for great art:

> In an absolute sense there is no objectivity. When Flaubert is bringing some undeniable picture to your recognition, he is doing it only to impose upon you some emotion which is part of his plan and the outgrowth of his own emotion. What is know as realism is only a means to an end, the end being a personal projection of the world. In passing beyond realism, even while they employ it, the significant writers of our time are achieving a portion of evolution (*First Day of Spring*).

One of Knister's concerns in *White Narcissus* is to assert the value of a "realistic" art as opposed to a romanticized or idealized one. Richard Milne, who is a writer and the protagonist of the novel, tends to romanticize the events of his own life and the lives of others, but he eventually abandons his romanticism. Twice Richard alludes to the story of Tristram and Iseult: once indirectly when he thinks of Ada Lethen's continuing presence as "a sword between the two [her parents], so that they could never forget the bitterness of the first few days of the quarrel"; and again, more romantically, when he perceives himself and Ada in their hopeless love for one another as "Tristram and Iseult, Lancelot and Guinevere." This tendency to think of himself as a hero of romance is also evident elsewhere: "he would bring all this [Ada's reasons for refusing him] to light; he would conquer it. He had been gathering his forces during all the month of being apart from her. Now he would test his will, his love for her, his belief in their happiness, test his whole ultimate life and hers." The fact that he does not get a chance to "test his will" at all but is prevented by an almost fortuitous resolution of Mr. and Mrs. Lethen's longstanding alienation from one another seems, from one point of view, to make for a rather abrupt and unprepared resolution to the story. Yet it constitutes a fitting comment on the inadequacy of Richard's romantic views of his own function in the plot. On the whole, however, Richard is presented sympathetically, and at several points in the novel he is aware of how unsatisfactory his romantic stance is likely to prove. Thus, when he considers the possibility that failure to win Ada may lead to his being another isolated artist, he sees the prospect not as a glamorous, Byronic one but as absurd:

> He would become after all a man essentially estranged from life, as least from the world, a romantic figure of absurd incompleteness, an unadjusted person, if successful in art, which does not demand normality, "a queer stick." All for what? "He lost a woman," one-time friends would say.

He also sees the inadequacy of his own writing about rural life; from the rather sketchy accounts we are given of it, it appears that Richard considers that his past work errs on the side of romance and hence is untrue to the life of the community he knows. Referring to the quarrel between the two neighbours, Carson Hymerson and Mr. Lethen, he "recalled the way—romantic it seemed to the real of the present—in which his writing had glossed over such differences, with all the life of which they formed part." Later he comments more extensively on his own portrayal of farm life:

> In his writing, Richard Milne had concerned himself with such people as these, typical farm characters. But while he had blinked none of their littlenesses, critics had claimed that his novels presented too roseate a picture of rural life. The reason was that he had seemed to find these temporal idiosyncrasies set off in due proportion against the elemental materials, of life. But, he reflected now, that attitude was part of the nostalgia he experienced from his own past in such scenes; and it was a form of idealism which he saw as applicable no more to this milieu than to any province of life more or less open to primal forces. He would not have idealized these in a setting of commerce or of society, and he had been wrong to blur them in a scene which his boyhood had known. Hence, he foresaw, a further development in his own art. An increasing surface hardness seemed to be an inevitable accompaniment to the progress of the significant novelists of his and an earlier day.

Knister, through his artist-figure Richard Milne, asserts the necessity of abandoning a "roseate" view of rural life, one conditioned by nostalgia for childhood, and of moving, presumably, toward a more "realistic" view. What this realistic view is to consist of, however, is not entirely clear. One possibility is that its subject is to be the reality represented by the Burnstile family—a reasonably "normal" family, with its share of squabbling and weaknesses, but one whose members function fairly harmoniously with each other and in their surroundings. This is "the daylit world of the material and of work," which for many readers is the most satisfactorily realized element of the novel. The Burnstiles belong to this "daylit world"; so, at first, do the Hymersons. But to restrict one's treatment to characters like these would indeed be to present "too roseate a picture of rural life"; mere surface realism, as Knister is aware, is not enough.

Co-existing with the daylit world, however, is another one—the world of the Lethens, whose very name evokes a world of shadow and death, thus suggesting the possibility that the novel may have a mythological dimension. Some of the elements which seem anomalous if one reads the novel as a realistic one can be accounted for in this way. Ada's pallor and her white dresses seem inappropriate to a farm girl, but not to a pure heroine of romance. Indeed, the mole on her face seems to function much as Georgiana's facial blemish does for her in Hawthorne's story "The Birthmark"—as the necessary mark of human imperfection: "it was ornament and relief. It was the most endearing feature in her face; its loss would have detracted greatly . . ." Furthermore, in the nether world from which Richard is attempting to rescue her, she seems to be a combination of Muse, Eurydice, and Persephone. He thinks of her as his Muse: "He could not hope to see the woman as others saw her. It had been one of the twin deities of his life. His urge to expression—and this. Perhaps she was at the bottom of his urge to write." There are suggestions of Eurydice, too; on his first meeting with her, " 'What is it holds you, Ada?' he asked in a choking tone, as though she were dying before his eyes." Later he catches sight of her while he is working in the field: "looking toward it [the forest], his eye caught the figure of a woman, walking, turning back, going further within its shade."

These hints of the lost Eurydice may be fortuitous, and it would be a mistake to make very much of them. But there are also hints of Persephone which resonate more clearly. Ada, like Persephone, hunts for wildflowers and is connected with the cycle of seasons. She comments, "I'm inclined not to come out very often. I think today is the first since winter that I have left the farm like this. In winter, spring, autumn, it's good to come to see that there is growth, change, and death, nothing of which is bitter or gay, simply because it does return again." Of this, too, one could make little, were it not for the central symbol of the novel, the white narcissus itself. In realistic terms, the narcissus seems and odd choice of flower to claim Mrs. Lethen's devotion; one could more readily accept a geranium or an African violet. But the Homeric *Hymn to Demeter,* on which James Frazer depended for his account of Demeter and Persephone in *The Golden Bough,* identifies the narcissus as the flower which tempted Persephone beyond the reach of help in the meadow where she was seized by Pluto. It is the narcissus' association with darkness, death, and the underworld that makes it so useful to Knister, and it tends to confirm Gnarowski's suggestion that Knister was probably aware of *The Golden Bough.* The mythological allusions (if that is indeed what they are) are the more suggestive because Knister does not use them in a mechanical way. They are barely suggested, easily overlooked; but the narcissus, the various descriptions of Ada, and the name Lethen itself all contribute to the sense of a dark and threatening underworld.

That world is one of carefully nurtured injuries and resentments, of enclosed, smothering spaces, of violence, madness, and despair. Ada has been raised from childhood in a household where the parents have not spoken to each other in years; she is afraid to leave them for Richard because what warped, narrowed emotional lives they have depend almost entirely on her. Mrs. Lethen also has her potted narcissi, which permeate the closed house with a sickly sweet smell and on which she pours out the love she should be giving to her husband and daughter. It is a world of grotesques—Mr. Lethen is described as having a "grotesque manner of broaching acquaintanceship" and as being "this weird old man with the haunted eyes." And it is described in terms which are sometimes strongly reminiscent of the conventions of gothic fiction. The town is called Lower Warping; the old hotel is closed when Richard arrives in town from the city at the beginning of the novel; the streets are empty; the garden gates are also "primly closed." This forbidding note is carried on into the description of the countryside:

> The road made fitful efforts at directness, and would ignore the swing of the high river banks, only a little farther on to skirt a depression, a sunken, rich flat, bearing rank, blue-green oats surrounded by drooping willows, elms through which only a glimpse of the brown ripples of water could be seen; again, underbrush, small maples, wild apples, green sumach came right to the road and hung over the fence, hiding the drop of the ravine. A place of choked vistas.

This landscape of "choked vistas" and "overgrown ravines" finds its focus in the Lethens' house, which looks more like the House of Usher or the Castle of Udolpho—dark, secret, moated, overgrown, and menacing—than like an Ontario farmhouse:

> The Lethen place hid the sunset, looming beyond a dredged cut to the river, like a moat, dry and overgrown with weeds. The tangle of vegetation, which in this light seemed to overlay the buildings, was in itself a quickening token to Richard Milne's remembrance, and he slowed, paused. Great evergreens shadowed the front of the place and guided his footsteps toward the lane. Dust flurried about him impotently as he reached the little leaning gate and went across the front yard, itself no haven to him: a wild expanse of grass and pine needles shadowy and whispering to his rising excitement of insuperable awaiting barriers.
>
> The house was old, its narrow windows peered dark from drapery of Virginia creeper, only the

gables showing the weathered brick expanse which towered remote as though to scan the oblivious invader below. There was something secret but secure about the air of the house, like an awareness of its life indecipherable in dark hiding of the vines. So much of its appearance Richard Milne knew more from an act of memory than by bodily sight. He had reached the low weathered wooden gate giving on the lawn, and he became unconscious of everything for that moment, of the mysteriously quickened night, the house, the trees, the dark, the pressing sky.

Later descriptions confirm this sense of secrecy and vague menace: "life went on in the rear portions of the house," and Mrs. Lethen seems to Richard to be "sinister in his mind by very reason of her appalling and helpless misery." Walking at night, Richard

> stopped before the gloom of the Lethen house, peered among its black shadows, looked to the dulled windows, the vines which were now and again carved into relief by the moonlight, and, instead of turning back, he walked past. But it was equally vain, and, coming back, he hurried past the place as though a ghost dwelt there. . . .

When the daylit world intrudes, however, the sinister element fades: "under the white glare of sunlight the Lethen place was appreciably less ominous and more dilapidated than it had appeared on the previous night."

While the major motifs of the traditional gothic romance—the fleeing maiden, the haunted castle, the depraved priest or nobleman, the unspeakable crime—often seem extravagantly silly to modern tastes, they did provide symbols for the half-apprehended terrors and dark impulses lying beneath the surface of a supposedly rational and well-ordered world. Thus the description of the house and its inhabitants not only provides a contrast with the Burnstiles; it also gives us an insight into the psychology of Richard Milne. The house appears like a gothic castle to him partly because he often thinks in literary allusions and partly because his attempt to persuade Ada to abandon her concept of duty to her parents and marry him is, indeed, the most difficult and frightening task he has ever undertaken.

Although Knister does not appear to have discussed gothic fiction in his critical writing, it may be significant that he alludes also to Nathaniel Hawthorne's *The Scarlet Letter,* a work in which gothic conventions are transmuted into great art. Richard compares himself with Arthur Dimmesdale in that both men are victims of excessive introspection and paralysis of the will:

> Phrases and images from *The Scarlet Letter* floated in his mind. He was expiating Dimmesdale's secret sin yet, after two centuries. Love could not be free yet for men and women who had taken civilization as an armour which had changed to fetters upon them. What was his whole piacular [sic] story but that of Dimmesdale—prophetic name—a delusion no longer a delusion of sin, but of impotence and analysis which belied action and love? It was the conflict

of the conscious ones of his whole generation,
this confusion of outer freedom and inner doubt.

Having fixed *The Scarlet Letter* in our minds, Knister goes
on to give us a climactic scene between Ada and Richard
which takes place in a forest and is strongly reminiscent
of Hawthorne's forest scene in which Hester Prynne persuades Dimmesdale to leave the place of his guilt and seek
a new life. In Hawthorne's story, the forest symbolizes
freedom from social codes. In *White Narcissus* it is Richard who does the persuading (the earlier parallel with
Dimmesdale is not pursued); and the forest, like the earlier
"choked vistas" of the countryside, becomes a symbol of
constraint, "the wilderness which guarded her heart,"
through which they must make their way to freedom.
That freedom, according to Richard, is to be found in the
city—not, as in so many American books, on the frontier.
Richard is a very Canadian hero: like Susanna Moodie,
Judith Gare and Sven Sandbo, Mr. and Mrs. Bentley, and
many others, he looks for freedom not in a flight from society but in a flight toward it, a re-integration with it.

Margot Northey suggests that in *Wacousta,* as in much
Canadian gothic fiction, "the deepest form of terror emanates from a demonic wilfulness" (*The Haunted Wilderness*). Knister does not take his story so far into the gothic
mode that he provides us with an instance of demonic wilfulness; Carson Hymerson's petulance hardly qualifies. Its
converse, helplessness, however, is frequently mentioned;
it is the keynote of the Lethens' lives. Ada "could not believe in freedom"; Mrs. Lethen exhibits "appalling and
helpless misery"; Mr. Lethen is unable to act against Carson Hymerson's threat to take away his farm. Richard too,
like Dimmesdale, must struggle against an inability to act.
Conversely, the keynote of the daylit world is action and
a control over externals. Richard, in his attempt to persuade Ada to abandon her parents, lectures her: "But it
is our destiny: we are bound to conquer. We must subdue
things; we've got to take from life even the emotions, the
experience, and fulfillment we need. If we shirk that we
are doing a wrong as great as that of starving in the midst
of nature's abundance." Mr. Lethen, after the accident in
which he knocks several of his wife's cherished narcissi to
the floor, stamps on them in a rage and asserts, "I did it
purposely!" It is his long-delayed ability to act "purposely" which finally ends the couple's alienation from each
other and begins a restoration of a normal relationship:
Mrs. Lethen begins to laugh. Richard's own will contributes nothing to this resolution, which is necessary to the
marriage of the lovers; but he is at least able to lead Ada
through the forest to an enclosed spot which protects
without smothering, where they consummate their love.

The elements in the novel which may be identified as gothic represent Knister's attempt to go "beyond realism," to
penetrate beneath the surface of circumstance and to
avoid Richard's mistake of presenting "too roseate a picture of rural life." One major weakness of the novel, however, is a failure to sustain the duality of the daylit world
and the dark one which Knister establishes at the beginning of the novel. Carson Hymerson is no gothic villain;
his obsessive concern to dispossess the Lethens of their
land has no motive more complicated or terrifying than
simple avarice. There is physical violence, but it is limited

to a blow or two struck in straightforward anger. Hymerson's eventual madness, which causes his removal to a
mental hospital, seems more a convenient way of resolving
the plot than an indication of the dark and violent forces
at the heart of existence. This is not a plea for more blood
and melodramatic villainy, but a suggestion that our belief
in the reality of the dark forces that the various gothic descriptions evoke is not sustained. The resolution moves the
plot firmly back into the "daylit world," but it moves it
there too easily for us to believe in the power of the dark
one; we wonder what all the fuss was about.

White Narcissus, then, is not simply a realistic novel. It
may be significant that this is a novel of southwestern Ontario, a region whose writers—from Major John Richardson to James Reaney, Graeme Gibson, and Alice
Munro—display a continuing interest in the gothic.
Speaking of the similarity of her own writing to that of the
American South, Alice Munro has remarked that "the
part of the country I come from is absolutely Gothic"
[*Eleven Canadian Novelists,* 1973]. Her novel *Lives of Girls
and Women* also presents two worlds—that of the secure
and ordered town and the violent, confusing, disordered
world of Del Jordan's Uncle Benny:

> So lying alongside our world was Uncle Benny's
> world like a troubling distorted reflection, the
> same but never at all the same. In that world
> people could go down in quicksand, be van-
> quished by ghosts or terrible ordinary cities;
> luck and wickedness were gigantic and unpre-
> dictable; nothing was deserved, anything might
> happen; defeats were met with crazy satisfac-
> tion.

The two worlds converge in one of the last images of the
book, which unites the ordinary and the mysterious: "People's lives in Jubilee as elsewhere, were dull, simple, amazing and unfathomable—deep caves paved with kitchen linoleum" (Lives). This describes the structure of *White
Narcissus* exactly. Knister juxtaposes the reality of the
Burnstiles with the reality of the Lethens; the linoleum
and the caves; a workaday, predictable world and a paralyzed, desperate, senseless one. In doing so he moves "beyond realism." If the result seems eccentric, this is partly
because we are not used to looking for gothic elements and
mythological allusions in the realistic Canadian novel. In
fact, Knister's strength is in his willingness to make use
of several modes to suggest a complex vision of the world.

Glenn Clever   (essay date 1978)

SOURCE: "Point of View in *White Narcissus,*" in *Studies
in Canadian Literature,* Vol. 3, No. 1, 1978, pp. 119-23.

[*In the following essay, Clever notes that Knister's narrative
technique in* White Narcissus, *undermines the effectiveness
of the novel.*]

[In his introduction to *White Narcissus*], Philip Child
claims that in Raymond Knister's *White Narcissus* "the
narrative is in the third person, but it is told through Richard's consciousness even though the story is more Ada's
than his." If the story were told this way, the novel would
be less disconcerting to read. In fact, Knister has little con-

trol over point of view, as Child's later comment, "In the case of Richard and Ada . . . the core of their characters is blurred by the fog of their wavering moods," tacitly acknowledges.

A casual reader looking into the book might concur with Child's first assertion. In the opening paragraphs Knister lets us into Richard's consciousness: "He found incredibly foreign the road down which he swung . . . He felt lost. . . . It was an immediate relief. . . . Milne was inclined to wonder . . ." But any closer reading soon shows the randomness of point of view. Take the statement that "a boy of eleven with yellow hair on a thin neck rushed around the corner of the house . . ." Richard could apprehend the boy's appearance, but since he does not know the boy, how does he apprehend at first glance his precise age? Or take the following passage:

> A man was tiny enough in the midst of great cities, he remembered strangely, but here it was possible to wonder how many more of these roads there were stretching away into the evening, endlessly, bearing each its strung-out farms, its weight of enigmatic human and animal circumstance.
>
> He seemed suddenly to have walked a great distance. A burden of his own past seemed to have descended upon him. How beautiful all this had been, and as the years of his boyhood slipped past without more than a dream of wider freedom, how dreary!

Here we begin listening to Richard's voice; but by the time we reach the new paragraph, the voice talking subtly changes to that of the narrator, telling us that the years of Richard's "boyhood slipped past without more than a dream. . . ." The shift in voice becomes more pronounced later on. Mrs. Hymerson, for instance, on meeting Richard starts to inquire about his family: " 'How's—,' " she begins, but then, the narrator says, she "seemed to recall that he lived apart from relatives" and asks instead, " 'How's everything in the city?' " This puts us close to her consciousness, but we get closer still in the following: " 'Quite a character' Mrs. Hymerson smiled, as though she knew and wished to take the flavour from what her husband was about to express." Similarly, we share her husband's consciousness when the narrator tells us that Mr. Hymerson "was not unaware of Richard Milne's reception" of his words.

In the novel Knister gives us only one scene from a clearly focussed point of view, when Richard from his upper bedroom window witnesses Mr. Hymerson and his son Arvin trying to fit teeth into a hayrake. He sees them down below him in the yard, hears their voices, notes their expressions, and gestures "as though he were watching a play." Knister reports to us solely through Richard's consciousness of the scene; we in turn see the three of them as though we were watching a play in which all three play their parts. In such a narrative schema the reader takes the narrator on trust, confident that the perspective from which he apprehends the unfolding drama is reliable, regardless of the credibility of the drama itself. But in *White Narcissus* as a whole such reliability falters. The voice shifts dis-

concertingly around; and the resulting uncertain relationship between reader and character is irritating, raising the question, why isn't the author consistent in his use of point of view? A consistent use of shifting perspective, dramatic or aesthetic in function, may add greatly to interest and suspense, but in *White Narcissus* the shifts occur randomly, without narrative function.

This unstructured, haphazard occurrence shows plainly in the way Knister designates his characters. He terms the protagonist variously "Richard Milne," "he," "Milne"; "Richard"; "the younger man"; "the young man"; even "the man"—just as he designates both Bill Burnstile and Mr. Hymerson. Such ambiguous distancing between reader and character jolts even more when two voices sound in one sentence, in which we hear first the distancing designation—"The young man did not reply to this"—and next listen to his consciousness—"reflecting almost with dismay that he had forgotten . . ." A similar jolt in perspective occurs in a paragraph in which the designation "the man" introduces what is practically a stream-of-consciousness passage:

> Once more the man was overcome by a sense of strangeness. He had been in his office that morning, had walked and taxied in the streets of the city and left it at noon, riding through unforgettable miles of railway yards and factories and grimy suburbs. And already he could make himself believe in the existence of such things only with an effort. For all the years in which he had struggled for success there, it seemed that the only real and personal part of his life had been lived here, surrounded by trees, fields, river, which claimed him as though he had never left them.

The reverse, from near to distant perspective, occurs in a chapter in which Ada is designated as "Ada" and "she" but ends up being termed "the tall woman." The confusion of perspective increases in a passage such as the following:

> Their mother was a red-headed, blue-eyed Scotch woman of rapid tongue and a mind of her own, which she exercised but little except when her inclinations were crossed. Bill Burnstile had run across her in the West, and, since she seemed a capable sort of woman for a housekeeper, and a good sport, he had married her. He had liked her smartness, but now she appeared to have become somewhat lackadaisical in her attitude toward life. She paid perfunctory attention to her children, and, beyond a casual word now and then to the effect that they were not to "bother Mr. Milne," she betrayed little interest in preventing them from conducting themselves as they pleased.
>
> This easy-going character showed itself in her housework as well, and if she had been inclined toward rationalization, she might have held that it manifested part of her equipment for self-preservation. For if she had tried alone to take care of the house and every need of her family, she would have been run to death.

Here we find three points of view. First, we apprehend

Mrs. Burnstile through the narrator's eyes: "red-headed, blue-eyed . . ."; next from Bill's point of view: "she seemed," "he had liked," "now she appeared"; next we see her from Richard's point of view; and finally again from the narrator's.

But to return to Child's contention that the narrative "is told through Richard's consciousness." We listen in on Richard's thoughts on a good many subjects: Ada and love, his work, and literary creation; the problems her parents pose vis-à-vis his love for Ada; the parallel of sin and guilt in Hawthorne's *The Scarlet Letter;* his mode of writing; Ada as a woman; even a long didactic interpolation about farming, cast in the form of Richard's thoughts on the topic. But this viewpoint fails to keep its focus. In his first encounter with Ada's mother, for instance, Richard's address to her is put in the context of the reader having access to the consciousness of both: ". . . he struck, with a directness which surprised them both," and "She paused, as though surprised at this revelation coming uncalled from her lips."

It is in passages on Richard and Ada that point of view shifts most disconcertingly. When Richard meets Ada we are privileged to share his most inner consciousness: "His mind refused to hope, to consider implications, overpowering, impossible, and rapt"; but we do not have access to hers—we know her inner being only through his:

> He saw the real image of her as she sat alone, while seasons passed. How else should she sit, though her reason for being in that house always had been to keep from loneliness the father and mother whose estrangement had been one of the legends of his childhood? In itself that was enough to make for loneliness, and he marvelled at her endurance, her poised good sense. With the coming of womanhood, should she not feel free? But she could not believe in freedom.

Thereafter, however, the voice shifts. The narrator lets us share her thoughts as well as his: "He made no answer, since they both knew that it was not necessary to mention why he had returned this time"; and when the narrator tells us that "she had answered so swiftly . . . that he felt he had probed her most secret dread"—that she might come to hate her estranged parents—we are to accept that we know that he knows what no one has yet told any one in the novel. When Richard meets Ada for the second time, the narrator says:

> She had kept inviolate for a few far-parted days of the year this desire to commune with nature, and had avoided the chafing with which day-by-day intercourse would have blunted her love. And this to her was everything, everything tangible of beauty beyond the poignant and trivial dullness of her days. After all, she scarcely had realized, save as a rumour, that there was another world beyond these fields. Had she not known the world of poetry, ideas, she perhaps would not have been conscious of loving them, nor ever have known the fear of love, that fear that she could grow to hate them, though her bitterness would be the mere working of monotony. Then she would wish that, like the clod-like people about her, she had never learned to love them.

In tone and in expressions such as "like the clod-like people about her" we are privileged to enter Ada's mind. Why now and not at other times?

Knister lets us become aware of Ada's possible love for Richard through the supposition on Richard's part that "she must have learned in his absence to admit to herself whether or not she loved him . . . he felt that she did love him," and this functions narratively to raise the question and leave its answer suspended dramatically in the reader's mind; but then the narrator tells us that "music . . . was the impelling passion of her life . . ." and lets us into her reminiscences:

> But even in those days the girl had begun to attempt compositions of her own. She began to be haunted by the strange tantalizings which are known to the genius of expression. She would be in despair or dullness. Or a muted ecstasy came over her, in which, so high was her vision of the beauty she wanted to embody, she did not dare attempt composition. Everything was hard for her. It was unbearable to remain silent, chilling the music from her heart with duties of the household day; and unbearable to yearn for composition, filled with ineffable impulses which she knew from old would not flower into the singing perfection of art.

This inner view makes the following outer view in which Richard questions her motives and personality, ostensibly to himself but in effect for the reader, seem merely contrivance. Similarly, when the narrator says that Richard's feelings about staying in the area after Ada's first repulse "probably arose from his sense of some appearance of the ridiculousness in his obstinacy . . ." and then adds, "in truth he was more or less dazed. . . . He had a sense of fatality . . . ," one wonders, since it makes no narrative difference, why the narrator cannot make up his mind which viewpoint he wants to use and stick to it. When Richard and Ada finally get together, the narrator comments: "There was a smile on her face he could not see;" that is, we now have a scene in which we see the action solely through the narrator's eyes, as Richard had once seen Hymerson and Arvin in the farmyard below him; but this dramatic objectivity blurs out immediately following:

> Richard Milne was silent again as she had been, withdrawn, his arms as it were galvanized, staring vindictively into the opposite darkening bank of the river. The consciousness of his complete abstraction reached them both at the same instant and he kissed her once more, automatically, and looked away, his mind engaged intensely in a struggle for relevance. She looked at him and a realization crept over her. At last, drawing an immense breath, he spoke, and his words were alien though not unfamiliar.
>
> "Perhaps you think me harsh. You know then better than I. I have never had any doubt that they are, or were, or should have been fine people. You don't object to my being open? Separately, that is." His voice revealed no humorous intention.
>
> "Why should I object to anything you may say," she murmured with a sort of contrition, almost

equivalent to repeating her declaration, as though, now, she were determined somehow to accept his love and his convictions coupled with her devotion to her parents, however troubling these commingled elements (in the calm lake of her being).

In these passages we share the thoughts of both, so that the novel draws to a close with almost a fusion of their consciousnesses, not as a necessary result of preliminary preparation, but fortuitously and without accumulative aesthetic impact.

White Narcissus deserves to be admired as a fine novel of mood and poetic description and as a turning point in the course of the Canadian novel from external to internal viewpoint; but it does leave the reader with a sense of dissatisfaction when he has finished it, and one of the main reasons for this is the lack of adequate control of point of view.

FURTHER READING

Bibliography

Burke, A. "Raymond Knister: An Annotated Checklist." *Essays on Canadian Writing* 16 (Fall-Winter 1979-1980): 20-61.
Comprehensive annotated bibliography of works by and about Knister; includes information on unpublished works collected in various archives.

Biography

Livesay, Dorothy. "Raymond Knister: A Memoir." In *Collected Poems of Raymond Knister*, by Raymond Knister, pp. xi-xii. Toronto: Ryerson, 1949.
Traces Knister's career and interprets his writings as well as events preceding his death, portraying the author as a depressed, frustrated artist and likening him to John Keats and Ranier Maria Rilke.

Criticism

Child, Philip. Introduction to *White Narcissus*, by Raymond Knister, pp. 7-16. Toronto: McClelland and Stewart, 1962.
Draws upon Livesay's memoir for biographical information and discusses symbolism, realism, and unadorned style in *White Narcissus*.

Kennedy, Leo. "Raymond Knister." *The Canadian Forum* (September 1932): 459-61.
Mostly favorable commentary on *White Narcissus* and *My Star Predominant*, praising characterization and plot development, but faulting an incomplete "embodiment of significant theme" in *White Narcissus*.

Stevens, Peter. "The Old Futility of Art: Knister's Poetry." *Canadian Literature*, No. 23 (Winter 1965): 45-52.
Surveys Knister's poetry, focusing on such themes as man vs. nature, the inadequacy of language to express the poet's vision, and analogies between farming and poetry.

Additional coverage of Knister's life and career is contained in the following source published by Gale Research: *Dictionary of Literary Biography*, Vol. 68.

Richard Middleton

1882-1911

(Full name Richard Barham Middleton) English short story writer, essayist, and poet.

INTRODUCTION

A moderately successful contributor of poetry and prose to prominent English periodicals during the early twentieth century, Middleton is best remembered for his often-anthologized story "The Ghost Ship." Throughout his career Middleton's writings revealed his frustration with what he perceived as England's indifference toward art and artists. After he committed suicide at the age of twenty-nine, he was characterized by critics as the stereotypical Romantic writer—talented, sensitive, and tragically unappreciated. Only after his death were Middleton's poems, stories, and essays collected and published in book form, gaining him posthumous popular and critical recognition.

Biographical Information

Middleton was born at Staines, Middlesex, and took pride in being related, through his mother, to Richard Harris Barham, author of *The Ingoldsby Legends*. He was an introspective and emotional student whose academic career included a year at the University of London and the passing of Oxford and Cambridge higher certificate examinations in mathematics, physics, and English. In spite of his lifelong interest in literature, Middleton did not pursue a university scholarship, choosing instead a job as a clerk in the Royal Exchange Assurance Corporation. During these years he published short stories and essays in various periodicals, and in 1905 joined the "New Bohemians," a loose-knit group of London writers. Middleton quit his office job in 1907, intending to earn his living as a writer. He spent the next few years writing pieces he described as "little articles for newspapers that don't want 'em," hoping ultimately to achieve recognition for his work as a poet. In what some commentators suggest was one of several journeys he made in search of literary inspiration and a social climate hospitable to his artistic ideals, Middleton spent the last nine months of his life in Brussels. There, in December 1911, he took his life by poisoning himself with chloroform.

Major Works

Middleton saw his writings published in such periodicals as *The Academy*, under the editorship of Alfred Douglas, and *Vanity Fair*, during the tenure of editor Frank Harris. Following Middleton's death, his friend Henry Savage gathered both unpublished manuscripts and previously published works in *The Ghost Ship, and Other Stories* and *Poems and Songs*. Additional collections of fiction, letters, sketches, and miscellanea were published by Middleton's

admirers between 1924 and 1933. His literary essays, as evidenced by those collected in *The Pantomime Man,* generally echo perspectives established by late nineteenth-century writers on topics including the women's suffrage movement, organized religion, and the state of literary art in England, while the autobiographical essays that Middleton himself arranged and titled for *The Day Before Yesterday* reveal his special aptitude for vividly representing the experiences of childhood. Traditional in subject and imagery, his verse has been likened to the lyric poetry of the 1890s in structure and tone, and his short stories, which typically center on themes of death, hardship, and poverty, often reflect the experience of lonely, neglected children in harsh circumstances. "The Ghost Ship," the story for which Middleton is best remembered, is praised for its unusual combination of humor and the supernatural.

Critical Reception

Middleton's stories and verse received little critical attention until they were collected and published after his death. Response to these posthumously published works ranges from high praise for the work of a literary genius to a dismissive appraisal of his style as unoriginal and firmly rooted in the sentimental literary tradition of the late nineteenth century. While differing in their assessments of the ultimate merit of Middleton's literary efforts, his critics, citing his graceful prose and intricately constructed verse, have generally agreed that Middleton's writings exhibit his delicate sensibility, notable literary talent, and unfulfilled promise.

PRINCIPAL WORKS

The Day Before Yesterday (essays) 1912
The Ghost Ship, and Other Stories (short stories) 1912
Poems and Songs (poetry) 1912
The District Visitor (drama) [first publication] 1924
Letters to Henry Savage (letters) 1929
The Pantomime Man (stories, sketches, and essays) 1933

CRITICISM

W. A. MacKenzie   (essay date 1912)

SOURCE: "The Works of Richard Middleton," in *The Bookman*, London, Vol. XLII, No. 250, July, 1912, pp. 172-73.

[*In the following review of* Poems and Songs *and* The Ghost Ship, and Other Stories, *MacKenzie lauds the strength of Middleton's prose while suggesting that his poetry lacks "nerve and vigour."*]

One rises from the reading of [*Poems and Songs* and *The Ghost Ship and Other Stories*] with the feeling that the end of Richard Middleton came all too soon; that his passage under the stars finished at too early an hour; that his nine and twenty years were but so much promise; and that full achievement lay just beyond the short Night he did not fear but rather sought. One feels that; and yet the feeling may be but a will o' the wisp to lead us astray; very likely it is. Must we consider the man and his work? Must we sever the work from the man? It is not given to all to know the singer, but the first man met in the street may judge the song.

I am, for the moment, concerned with Richard Middleton's song; and I confess that I find it of a monotony which may be divine, but which is—there can be no denial—wearisome. He had many rhythms—he sought variety as he sought pleasure, avidly—but the song was the same, the substance and stuff of it were ever the same: he did not sing dreams, he sang of dreams he had had. The casual reader will say at once: "Richard Middleton was a dreamer." That is just what he was not; he was a man who *said* he had had dreams, but if dreams he had he kept them jealously to himself, and the hungry of the earth want more from their poets than a disdainful or a pitiful:

I have seen God: but, hush! I may not speak.

And so, because Richard Middleton does not tell his dream, we are minded to fit him with Mr. Arthur Symons' estimate of that other strange departed sprite, Ernest Dowson: "He was not a dreamer; destiny passes by the dreamer, sparing him because he clamours for many things. He was a child, clamouring for so many things, all impossible."

In the intervals of "clamouring for so many things," Richard Middleton sang some fine things, things quite pure and exquisite. Almost perfect is this **"Nocturne"**:

> When Sleep puts on the cloak of Death,
> And in the city masquerades,
> Earth's tired children fight for breath,
> And they who sought the dreamy glades
> Fall panting on the road, and lie
> Like clods beneath the sombre sky.
>
> But when Death comes like gentle sleep,
> And takes our children to her breast,
> Our weary eyes forbear to weep—
> It is so very good to rest
> Quietly in the dreamy corn
> Until the breaking of the morn.

Almost perfect, I said; almost, but not quite; for here, twice in two stanzas, do we encounter Middleton's King Charles' head—dreamy, which, with dreams, dreaming, dreamful, was his obsession. The word, one imagines, had an uncanny fascination for him.

This **"Nocturne"** and **"The Song of the King's Minstrel,"** by their simplicity and directness, are worthy of a place in any anthology. In both these there is the true singing-stuff, elemental and inevitable. But on most occasions Middleton sang a more sophisticated strain, and once or twice he passed the bounds of current decency, as in the lines **"To C.M.,"** where he would be Peeping Tom, spying on the mysteries of the alcove, and in **"After Love"** with its "Let there be lust between us two." Of course, all that was mere braggadocio, the bantam bounce of the late 'nineties that would shock at any price the Puritan fresh from Cowper and Tennyson. And so many of us took it for bravery! Middleton, I feel, would have sacrificed these two pieces, and perhaps also **"The Rebel"** and the **"Epithalamium."** The piety of friends has preserved them. The same piety has given us an introduction to the *Poems and Songs* by Mr. Henry Savage, of which the conclusion may be quoted:

> Of his genius I am not using words idly when I say that it is of that rare quality which will sooner or later ensure him a recognised position in the front rank of English poets. Those who are not moved by the beauty of the poetry in this volume may find beauty elsewhere and had better seek it elsewhere. There is that in it beyond the reach of mere criticism. It is of the substance which lives.

Mr. Savage has the fervid courage of the devoted friend; but, honestly, I find that Richard Middleton's songs are Richard Middleton's most discreet and most trustworthy champions.

The prose volume, *The Ghost Ship* (introduced worthily and soberly by Mr Arthur Machen), is truly remarkable. It would be remarkable in any year, not only for its manner but for its matter. In quality, in fineness as in substantiality, it is far above *Poems and Songs;* and just as Middleton found himself, before the end, "drawn towards young children and people who are simple and kindly and not too clever," so it may be conceived that he was also being drawn away from the easy artificialities and affectations of prosody, and towards the more austere beauties of prose. Certainly, in prose he has done fine things. **"The Ghost Ship"** is greatly imagined—humour, pathos, fantasy, poetry, and cunning earthly philosophy—of these is it inimitably made. I *feel* that it is a masterpiece. And surely there was never a more sincere, a more poignant bit of self-revelation than **"The Great Man":** every man who has been called to letters must see himself in this faithful mirror. And for all that **"The Coffin Merchant"** may owe something to Poe and Stevenson and Ambrose Bierce, and **"The Soul of a Policeman"** a little to Anatole France; these two sketches are gripping things, eloquent in their almost bald diction, beautiful in their spare lines. Richard Middleton's prose has nerve and vigour that his verse lacks, and it has a style that should preserve it long against moth and rust. It is a prose that needs no apologist. It, and not his verse, will make live the name of this hunter after beauty, who gave up the chase ere it was full noon.

The Spectator   (essay date 1912)

SOURCE: "Richard Middleton," in *The Spectator,* Vol. 109, No. 4390, August 17, 1912, pp. 238-39.

[*In the following review, the critic characterizes* Poems and Songs *and* The Ghost Ship, and Other Stories *as "remarkable," praising Middleton's technical excellence and sensitivity.*]

Richard Middleton was a young English writer who died a year ago in Brussels at the age of twenty-nine. He had never published a book, and his work consisted of a few poems, essays, and short stories in the pages of several contemporary journals. Happily there are a few people left who appreciate good literature, and in [*The Ghost Ship, and Other Stories* and *Poems and Songs*] we have a collection of the tales and poems. They are in the highest degree remarkable; remarkable in mere accomplishment, for no younger writer of our day has excelled Middleton in the technical arts of verse and prose, and more remarkable still for their strange individuality of spirit. Our poets are apt to be propagandists and enforce, like Mr. Masefield, moral and social lessons; or they are stirred into revolt by the ironies of life, and, according to their temperament, are weeping or scoffing satirists. But Middleton cared for none of these things. His short life was spent in a ceaseless quest of beauty, beauty of sensuous form and delicate imagery, but far more that sublimated beauty of the spirit towards which all forms of art labour in vain. He was in quest of the key to the riddle of things, but it was not the obvious riddles that concerned him, but the mysteries which no "laws or kings can cause or cure." He had the metaphysician's passion for unity, the abiding sense "of something far more deeply interfused." In his wonderful

"The Story of a Book" he tells us how the common novelist was suddenly convicted of the barrenness of his work:

> He stepped out into the streets, fixing his attention on concrete objects to rest his tired mind. But he could not help noticing that London had discovered the secret which made his intellectual life a torment. The streets were more than a mere assemblage of houses, London herself was more than a tangled skein of streets, and overhead heaven was more than a meeting-place of individual stars. What was this secret that made words into a book, houses into cities, and restless and measurable stars into an unchanging and immeasurable universe?

The realist is happy among his inconsiderable details; Middleton sought always for that spiritual chemistry which transforms the material into something new and strange and lovely.

His poetry, curiously enough in such a master of melody, is less satisfying than his prose. It would be interesting to know the dates of the pieces, for some of them must have been written a long time ago. They all have Middleton's peculiar wistfulness, but they are full of false starts and blind alleys. In the absence of the dates of composition, one might hazard a guess at the kind of development they reveal. The earlier mood is frankly Pagan—not a very robust Paganism, it is true, for it lacks the complete assurance of that philosophy. It is too defiant, as in the fine **"Chant-Pagan"** and **"The Rebel,"** to be quite at ease. But the two **"Irene"** poems are a revel of sensuous beauty, and **"For He Had Great Possessions"** is a noble hymn of the worship of earth. But it is not quite the Pagan earth, and the pleasure for which all is worthy of sacrifice is not the pleasure of the flesh. In **"The Song of the King's Minstrel"** the poet is content to die in torture if only he can bring to the Queen's heart the pity of love.

> Not lightly is a king made wise,
> My body ached beneath the whips,
> And there is earth upon my eyes,
> And earth between my singing lips.
> But I sang once—and for that grace
> I am content to lie and store
> The vision of her dear, wet face,
> And sing no more.

And so presently we have his farewell to Paganism, his renunciation of splendid fancies for homely humanities. He calls it **"The New Dawn."**

> For all the rich and curious things
> That I have found within my sleep
> Are nought beside this child that sings
> Among the heather and the sheep;
> And I, who with expectant eyes
> Have fared across the star-lit foam,
> See through my dreams a new sun rise
> To conquer unachievèd skies,
> And bring the dreamer home.

This later mood, as we shall see in his prose, is very full of the ways and thoughts of children. No poet of our day has written of them so understandingly, so delicately, and, as in **"On a Dead Child,"** so poignantly. But while he seems to outgrow his dream-world—those

fair, untrodden lands,
Where summer comes not to perplex the flow-
ers,
But spring stays ever, and spring music fills
The dark and dreamy hills—

it is only fair to recognize that his best poetry is due to this
inspiration. Such are the love poems and the delicious
"Dream-Song." But the striving is always there, the chafing under more sensuous and imaginative perfection. Mysticism of the ordinary kind is a playing at fairy-tales, a
thing of the fancy; but Middleton's spirituality is far deeper and more rarefied. It appears in **"Any Lover, Any
Lass"**:

Would I might forfeit ecstasy
And find a calmer place,
Where I might, undesirous, see
Her too desirèd face.
Nor find her eyes so bright, so bright,
Nor hear her lips unroll
Dream after dream the lifelong night,
When I would love her soul.

That is the mood of his prose, his maturest and latest
work, as we learn from the introduction to these volumes.
He is now very clearly awake to the mysteries of life, and
realizes that it needs no effort of fancy to make the world
strange. His methods are various. Children fascinate him,
and in presenting the soul of a child he furnishes us with
a mirror in which we see common things in such uncommon proportions that we grow uneasy in our conventions.
"A Drama of Youth" and **"The New Boy"** are straightforward studies of a high-strung boy, first at a London day-
school and then at a public school. Their realistic power
is remarkable, but they are not specially characteristic of
the writer. But there is a group of subtler tales, tragedies
seen through childish eyes. In **"A Tragedy in Little"** a
child is puzzled at the events which follow his father's
crime. In the **"Passing of Edward"** a little girl pursues her
dead playmate, hearing him, but seeing him not. In **"The
Bird in the Garden"** a little boy in an East End slum makes
a wonderland out of the fancies of a mad uncle, and when
the sordid tragedy happens sees in very truth the coming
of the strange bird of the old man's dreams. In **"And Who
Shall Say—?"** it is murder which breaks across two children's lives, and in **"Fate and the Artist"** the fiction of the
imaginative child comes true with his death. These stories
are full of humour, but they are full, too, of an extraordinary haunting beauty. Another group might own Stevenson's "Markheim" for parent. They are psychological allegories, with a perplexing moral for art or life dancing in
the background. Such are **"The Soul of a Policeman,"**
"The Poets' Allegory," and **"The Great Man."** But best
of all we like the stories in which the writer is most fantastic—that of the conjurer who makes his wife disappear for
good and all, and of the coffin merchant who advertises
his wares in such a way as to compel men to buy—and use
them. They are madcap tales, mad with an eerie, logical,
unforgettable madness. First in this group stands **"The
Ghost-Ship,"** so good that Middleton's name deserves to
live by this tale alone. It is a wild freak of fancy, but so
soberly told that we are ready to swear that somewhere
down the Portsmouth Road there stands to-day a village
full of friendly and profitable ghosts. To the village in the

great storm in the spring of '97 was blown the ghost-ship,
Bartholomew Roberts captain. It settled in a turnip-field,
and the captain paid the debts in great gold brooches. He
held high revel with the Fairfield ghosts, and gave them
rum which was like fire and honey in the bones. Then
came a second great storm, and the ghost-ship disappeared, carrying with it nearly all the ghosts in the village:

"The wind that had been howling outside like an
outrageous dog had all of a sudden turned as melodious as the carol-boys of a Christmas Eve.

'Surely that's not my Martha!' whispered landlord, Martha being his great-aunt that lived in
the loft overhead.

We went to the door, and the wind burst it open
so that the handle was driven clean into the plaster of the wall. But we didn't think about that
at the time; for over our heads, sailing very comfortably through the windy stars, was the ship
that had passed the summer in landlord's field.
Her portholes and her bay-window were blazing
with lights, and there was a noise of singing and
fiddling on her decks. 'He's gone,' shouted landlord above the storm, 'and he's taken half the village with him!' "

**Richard Middleton was that evanescent,
shapeless thing, a meteor. . . . He
founded no school, he imitated no man, he
carried on no tradition.**

**—*S.P.B. Mais in his* From Shakespeare to
O. Henry: Studies in Literature, *1923.***

The New York Times Book Review   (essay date 1913)

SOURCE: "Poet Who Failed," in *The New York Times
Book Review,* February 16, 1913, p. 77.

[*In the following review of Middleton's verse and prose, the
critic asserts that Middleton's works were published and
given critical attention primarily because of the author's
suicide.*]

Something of the enthusiasm with which England has received Middleton's work since his death is indicated by
Henry Savage in his introduction to **Poems and Songs:**
"Of his genius I am not using words idly when I say that
it is of that rare quality which will sooner or later insure
him a recognized position in the front rank of English
poets. Those who are not moved by the beauty of the poetry in this volume may find beauty elsewhere, and had better seek it elsewhere. There is that in it beyond the reach
of mere criticism. It is of that substance which lives." This
hyperbole, for such it is as far as the present volume of
verse is concerned, must be construed as the effect of remorse for the thorough neglect which the author suffered
during his lifetime and which drove him to suicide at the
age of 29.

The quality of Middleton's poetry is well shown by the first stanza of **"Envoi"**:

> All the drear Summer time in hot and dusty
>   places
> We watched the roses die, and still our lips
> Made black by thirst, sang bravely of the ships
> That brought us to the isle of lovely faces,
> While yet our youth held all the world in fee,
> And dared the stars from an exultant sea.

Less deserving verse, perhaps, is published even in reputable magazines, but such work will give no man "a recognized position in the front rank of English poets." The wine of his song is muddy; his creative fire is of too low a temperature to perform the alchemy which brings forth poetry. The crude metal of his emotions is not transmuted. The truth is, that Middleton was not a poet in his own right; he could do no better than decorate his own material with the beauty created by greater men. Scarcely a poem in the volume is not an obvious imitation, inferior to the original. Most of them derive from Swinburne, that most dangerous of masters. In fact, however great his love of beauty may have been, Middleton had not the power of achieving it. He had not the artist's reverence of beauty, as of something divine and not to be profaned; therefore, he had no sense of the necessity of restraint, of severe simplicity, qualities which give clarity and intensity to poetic expression. This lack he tried to atone for by ornament and elaboration. Consequently, his work is without vitality, and by no means "of that substance which lives."

It is a relief to turn to his stories. Here Middleton's genius, not intense enough to command the more exacting medium of poetry, is master of the form it works in. Mr. Arthur Machen remarks in the course of the introduction which he contributes to *The Ghost Ship and Other Stories:* "It is an extraordinary book, full of a quite curious and distinctive quality." This quality is the expression of Middleton's personality, which gives the volume its interest. Middleton was a man of feelings rather than of ideas; having, unlike contemporary writers of fiction, such as Mr. Wells and Mr. Galsworthy, no theories to expound, he still adhered to the doctrine of art for art's sake. In consequence, the value of his stories lies in their charm and their well-wrought form, not in their intellectual content. Undoubtedly, Middleton knew how to tell a story. However, one meretricious device he employs only too often; that, namely, of mystifying his reader by omitting the solution to the riddle he has propounded. The effect, to be sure, is a rather pleasant fillip to the sophisticated and jaded palate, but counts against his serious pretensions as an artist. His mastery of the point of view in narrative he puts to effective use in telling his stories through the eyes of uneducated men or of children. By this means he gives half its value to his masterpiece, **"The Ghost Ship."** Like so many writers of short stories, he has a lively fancy, and he needs all his psychological insight and all his faculty for graphic corroborative detail to give the requisite "sting of reality." In **"The Ghost Ship"** his success is complete. This outrageous yarn of the spectral galleon which a tempest blew into a turnip patch at Fairfield, and which dispensed wondrous rum to the village ghosts, is told by one of the rustic witnesses with so much matter-of-fact assurance that it induces an entire suspension of disbelief. In this tale Middleton reaches his high-water mark.

Although as examples of the art of the short story his tales of children do not rank with **"The Ghost Ship,"** in them lies Middleton's best psychology. Not even Stevenson and M. Anatole France equal him in the sympathetic portrayal of the delicate fancies and the seemingly intolerable sorrows of childhood, with no touch of false sentiment and mawkishness. **"A Drama of Youth"** and **"The New Boy"** must recall to any one his rebellious loathing for his first schools, while **"Children of the Moon"** is as graceful a phantasy as one would ask. When Middleton adopts the child's point of view in telling a tragedy, he gains a poignant pathos and irony, qualities which, indeed, pervade most of his work. They are the reactions of an almost abnormally sensitive mind against the unjust suffering of the innocent.

Twice in this volume his irony rises to excellent satire. **"The Story of a Book,"** somewhat reminiscent of Mr. Bennett's **"A Great Man,"** tells how a publisher by mistake printed 5,000 copies of a commonplace novel and had to resort to strenuous advertising, with the result that the author found himself an eminent man of letters. As a sarcastic study of "best-selling" methods it deserves notice. In **"The Biography of a Superman"** Middleton discusses a celebrity by the name of Charles Stephen Dale, who corresponds in every point with Mr. Bernard Shaw. If Dale does represent Mr. Shaw, this analysis is as searching as it is diverting. In this study, moreover, Middleton shows a faculty for phrase-making:

> Dale's regrettable absence reduced what might have been an agreeable clash of personalities to an arid discussion on art. . . . He was essentially a modern, insomuch that his contempt for the writings of dead men surpassed his dislike of living authors. . . . He had drawn from the mental confusion of the darker German philosophers an image of the perfect man. . . . He generally made his readers more sorry than angry. . . . He played the part of clown with more enthusiasm than skill.

In Middleton's stories there is much autobiography, more or less open. He was a shy, unduly sensitive, unhappy boy, who never outgrew his preference for dreams rather than action. His sympathies are all with the idealist, the visionary, the weakling. His own lack of strength and vigor his work, especially his verse, shows all too plainly. That is why, though he wrote some half dozen excellent stories, he is not a commanding figure even in contemporary letters, and why his vogue, without doubt excited largely by his tragic death, cannot last.

Richard Middleton   (essay date 1913)

SOURCE: *Monologues,* 1913, pp. 9-18.

[*In the following essay, Middleton reveals his idealistic approach to writing and discusses his views on the value of the essay as a literary genre.*]

Owing to the general laxity with which men and women

use the language they inherit, in the course of years words are apt to be broadened and coarsened in their meaning. Striving against this tendency, every scrupulous writer is in danger of robbing words of a part of their birthright: through fear of letting them mean too much he makes them mean too little. Ultimately, of course, the popular meaning prevails, and we suck our fountain-pens in vain who seek to preserve a kind of verbal aristocracy; but it is a pleasant game while it lasts, and it does no one any harm.

For instance, there is this word "essay." It is used to-day loosely to mean almost any kind of prose article, especially when such articles are rescued from periodical literature and reprinted in book form. Mr. Chesterton's twisted allegories are essays, and so are Mr. Lucas's pleasant pilferings from queer books, and Mr. Shaw's dramatic criticisms. So, too, for that matter, are Earle's characters, and the Roger de Coverley papers, and Swinburne's laudations of the Elizabethan dramatists. Confronted with this embarrassing promiscuity, the critic who really wishes the word "essay" to mean something is forced to give it a purely arbitrary meaning, and this I have ventured to do in choosing a title for my lament. To say that the art of writing little articles for the newspapers and republishing them in modest volumes is decaying would be absurd; but to say that at the present time very few people are trying to write like Charles Lamb is patently true. To me, essays are such leisurely expressions of a humane and agreeable personality as we find in the works of Elia. They may criticize and rhapsodize and narrate, but the reader is always conscious of the individuality that controls the pen. A fit medium of expression for tranquil minds, they reveal with a careless generosity the mind, emotions and placid processes of thought that give them birth. The delicately-flattered reader feels that the essayist is guarding no Bluebeard's chamber of the mind. As far as the hospitable writer has himself explored it, so far are its dim corridors open to his inquiring eyes.

For of all forms of artistic expression, this is the most personal and self-revealing. It might be described as the art of expression in dressing-gown and carpet-slippers. A bad man, if there be any bad men, might endeavour to express a moment of his criminal life in a sonnet or a short story or a romance; but he would, I hope, think too highly of humanity in general to seek to reflect it in his own lost person. Yet this is the work of the essayist. "These I fear," he says with spirit, "are my meannesses, my weaknesses, my vices; but, on the other hand, I have, I think, these trivial virtues. Perhaps there are other men like me!" No bad man could write like that; he would rather believe himself unique in his villainy.

And this brings me to the quality that leads men to write essays. Being men of leisurely mind, it might naturally be presumed that they would be satisfied with dreaming, and that they would leave the drudgery of writing to men of action. But it is apparent to me that the true essayist is a man troubled with a great loneliness. He finds, doubtless, being a generous lover of his fellows, a number of acquaintances who share and even surpass his own special virtues; but he cannot discover in his personal environ-

ment those rarer beings who should also disclose his own delicate vices; and these are the men above all others with whom he wishes to come in contact. So he takes pen and paper, and, setting down his faults and his merits with a high fairness, stretches, as it were, a pair of appealing hands to his comrades in the world. This habit of analysing his own weakness gives him an introspective turn of mind. He is always lying in wait to catch himself tripping; but he would not have you ignore the other side of his character; he wishes to be fair to himself and honourable to you. He prepares a kind of balance-sheet for Judgment Day, and he is above all things anxious that it should be correct. His heart, to use a worthily hackneyed phrase, is in his work, and he appoints humanity his auditor.

Essays are written by leisurely men for leisurely readers. You cannot read Lamb as you read a romance—passionately—tearing the pages. The words flow smoothly across the printed pages, and you drift comfortably with the current, pausing here and there, as doubtless Lamb paused in the writing, to dream in some twilit backwater of thought. The nominal purpose of the voyage may be trifling; but its true purpose is as splendid as all high human endeavour. We do not really dare the great adventure in order to see Charles Lamb dreaming over the crackling of roast pork, or Mr. Max Beerbohm in rapt contemplation of his hat-box. Our autumn has its pork, and we, too, have our hat-boxes. We set out, like all great explorers, in search of ourselves, and our common sense tells us that we are most likely to get authentic news of our destination from the intellectual honesty of the essayists. Theirs is the seasoned wisdom and ripe authority of old travellers, and we realize in reading their log-books that our road does not differ greatly from theirs. Perhaps at the end of the journey we shall know that all roads are one.

I suppose that, using the word "essay" in the restricted sense I have suggested, the great essayists might easily be numbered on a baby's toes, and, as one of them still flourishes, the decay that has overtaken this form of expression may not be immediately obvious. But in the past there has always been a host of minor essayists, writers who might not achieve a great partnership between their hearts and their pens, but who did agreeable work nevertheless, and it is the absence of these minor writers of essays from the number of our modern authors that alarms me. It is true that we have our Charles Lamb, but I look in vain for our Leigh Hunt. Nor can we let ourselves be put off with some of the very able work that appears in periodicals, and has the shape and length and general outward appearance of real essays. Journalism is growing more impersonal, though by no means less egoistic, and you may search the writings even of our individual journalists, such as Mr. Chesterton and Mr. Lucas, Mr. Benson and Mr. Belloc, in vain for a decent confession of personal weaknesses. It is true they set down their petty private vices—no one who even pretends to write essays can help doing that—but they make them appear either humorously criminal, or like so many virtues in disguise, and we have seen that your true essayist is neither a sinner nor a saint, but just a common man like his readers. So while we who are ashamed of the skeletons in our waistcoat-pockets may read the writings of these gentlemen for their wit and cleverness, we will continue to turn to Lamb and Montaigne for sympathy and advice. They will bring us to the place where dreams blend with realities, and action puts on the gentle gown of thought.

The fact is, that essays are bad journalism in the literal sense of that elastic word, because they take no count of time, while it is the function of journalism to tear the heart out of to-day. A good essay should start and end in a moment as long as eternity; it should have the apparent aimlessness of life, and, like life, it should have its secret purpose. Perhaps the perfect essay would take exactly a lifetime to write and exactly a lifetime to comprehend; but, in their essence, essays—I cling to my restricted sense of the word—ignore time and even negate it. They cannot be read in railway trains by travellers who intend to get out at a certain station, for the mere thought of a settled destination will prevent the reader from achieving the proper leisurely frame of mind. Nor can they be written for a livelihood, for a man who sits down to write an essay should be careless as to whether his task shall ever be finished or not.

It may be said confidently that few persons write like this to-day; it may even be objected by sticklers for accuracy in titles that few persons have ever written like this, and I am willing to agree. But the essayist whom I have described is the perfect type—that ideal which less gifted men can only pursue to the brink of their graves; and while

in some measure this was always the ideal of periodical writers in the past, it certainly is in no wise the ideal of the journalists of to-day. They do not wish to write sympathetically of themselves; they cannot linger with leisurely trains of thought. Breathless assurance, dogmatic knowledge, and a profusion of capital "we"s help them to sing their realization of the glories of to-day, their passionate belief in the future, their indifferent contempt for the past. These are, they tell us, days of action, and dreamers can have but short shrift in a common-sense world. Probably this is true, but I notice that the literature of action does not make its readers very comfortable. Men and women are growing weary-eyed these days, and their feet stumble like those of tired runners. Their voices are growing hoarse from shouting energetic prophecies into the deaf ears of the future, and their hands are sore from their unending task of holding the round earth in its place. They cannot dream because they will not allow themselves to sleep.

It may be morbid, but I sometimes think that I can detect a note of wistfulness in the eyes of my neighbours in life, when they let them stray from their newspapers to rest for a moment on the leaves of my book. Once I discovered a tear on the cheek of a clerk in the city, and I taxed him with this mark of treachery to the life of action; but he assured me that his sorrow was due to the low price of Consols. It may have been; I do not know. But one of these

The house in the Rue de Joncker where Middleton died.

days our journalists will have to stop to take breath, and in the universal holiday perhaps some of their readers will have time to write essays.

Joyce Kilmer　(essay date 1914)

SOURCE: "A Suicide's Book," in *The New York Times Book Review,* August 16, 1914, p. 349.

[*Kilmer was an American educator, journalist, and poet. In the following review of* Monologues, *he offers a negative appraisal of Middleton's posthumously published collection of essays.*]

> It is of no use to say that people ought not to kill themselves. They will do it.

Yes, they will do it. Richard Middleton, the brilliant young poet who wrote these words, died by his own hand soon after they were published.

"Suicide and the State" is by no means the best of the essays that make up the volume called ***Monologues*** but on account of his untimely death it has special and lamentable interest. Richard Middleton was one of those essayists who gain their effects by writing seriously of trifles and flippantly of great things. Therefore it might be expected that his treatment of suicide would be fantastic, humorous; that he would write an extravagant eulogy of self-destruction and playfully consider the relative merits of shooting, drowning, and taking poison. It is true that there is occasionally a specious mirth in this essay, a humorous phrase or two thrown in as a sop to the superficial reader. But the tone of the essay is serious—deadly serious. Here was a subject on which Middleton had strong convictions, and these convictions he expressed with a fervor not easily found in his other writings.

After praising A. E. Housman's poem on this subject, Middleton called suicide the most weighty of all destructive criticisms of life, and wrote this strange apologia:

> A suicide does more than attack our persons or our pockets; he injures our self-complacency and murders our vanity. We can forgive a man for booing or creating a disturbance in the theatre of life, but we cannot forgive him for going out with a yawn before the play is over. In effect, he says: "I find your society dull and your follies do not amuse me. You are a lot of tiresome fellows!" And the devil of the business is that if the rascal is successful we cannot punish him for his impertinence. We can, and I believe sometimes do, send people to prison for failing to kill themselves, in order that they may there acquire a fuller appreciation of their fellow-human beings. But with all our wisdom we have, as yet, no certain means of chastening the untimely dead. Like the mythical woman, the suicides always have the last word in the argument, and, while we condemn their folly, we have the uncomfortable conviction that they cannot bear us.

Middleton was not playing with an idea when he wrote these words, he was expressing his real opinion. He was tragically sincere, too, when he urged that nineteen suicides out of twenty were perfectly sane and that self-

destruction was a rational act. Nor was it merely because of the novelty of the idea that he advocated "the foundation of a State department for the useful expenditure of the lives of those persons who are weary of an existence that it is hardly creditable to endure."

> There would be an office in London which would-be suicides would seek in place of the gunmaker's shop or the river. Thence, after filling up a form, they would be drafted to an establishment in which they would be maintained at Government expense, and, after a week of probation, they would be officially dead. . . . The living bodies of these dead men would then be at the service of the State. They would be available for the doctors in place of dogs and monkeys for experimental germ-breeding and vivisection; they could test high explosives and conduct dangerous chemical operations; in time of war they could man steerable torpedoes or dynamite-laden aeroplanes. In fact, they could be used in any work that involved great risk to life.

Now, this is a ridiculous idea, but it was not ridiculous to Middleton. He did not consider that dangerous and altruistic careers are easily found and entered; that humanity has its martyrs every day. Nor did he consider the fact that these martyrs go to death voluntarily, not because they hate their own lives, but because they love the lives of their fellows. Suicide is a luxury; the man who contemplates self-murder wishes to evade troublesome responsibilities and is not likely to prefer to the convenient revolver any process of death, however beneficial to society, which necessitates labor and protracted pain.

Well, it is not worth while to answer this pitiful defense of suicide. It deserves attention chiefly because it is typical, symptomatic. Middleton was an artist of remarkable ability; the essays in this book are the work of a man who knew how to give to interesting thoughts exquisite expression. His reputation as a poet has suffered since the publication, by Mr. Austin Harrison in *The English Review,* of certain bits of filthy doggerel found after his death among his papers, but the volume of his verse, published by Mitchell Kennerley, contained many lyrics of strength and beauty. But in all his writings, especially in those now under consideration, there is evident a spirit of strange discontent, which is not the powerful craving of the poet, but the nervousness, a querulousness that suggests disease.

It is hard to define this fault, it is impossible to avoid sensing it. Middleton could not write a soundly affirmative paper on any subject—not even on **"Editors"** or **"The Virtues of Getting Drunk."** He could not take a simple, generally accepted belief—an axiom—and elaborate it into a coherent and attractive structure of words. If you set before him, as a task, to develop the idea that a straight line is the shortest distance between two points, he would at once begin to rhapsodize over curves and to praise the drunken man as the poet of pedestrianism. If you gave him as a theme "Curved is the line of beauty," he would at once be irresistibly attracted by the noble austerity of the straight line.

This mental attitude, common among the younger English journalists and their American imitators, is by careless people labeled paradoxical. But this term is by no means definitive. Many paradoxes, "He that loveth his life shall lose it," for example, and many another utterance of that paradoxical Prince of Peace who came to bring a sword are as simple and necessary as light and air. The thoughts of Middleton and of others of his school are impotent because they are deliberate contradictions of life. Like many another saying, "art for art's sake" has been misunderstood. It has been taken for a motto by men who separate themselves from the common experiences of mankind, who constantly "are desirous of new things." Now the artist must be a democrat; he is successful exactly in proportion to his ability to understand and interpret the soul of mankind. And the soul of mankind is not made of fantastic denials. It is obviously and terribly affirmative.

Frank Harris   (essay date 1920)

SOURCE: "Richard Middleton: Ad Memoriam," in his *Contemporary Portraits,* Brentano's Publishers, 1920, pp. 159-77.

[*Harris was a highly controversial English editor, critic, and biographer whose fame as a critic rests primarily upon his five-volume* Contemporary Portraits *(1915-30), which contain essays marked by the author's characteristically vigorous style and patronizing tone. In the following excerpt, Harris recalls his impressions of Middleton.*]

It was in the autumn of 1907 that Edgar Jepson introduced me to Richard Middleton in the office of *Vanity Fair.* A big man and perfectly self-possessed, his burly figure, thick black beard and furrowed forehead made him look ten years older than he was: five and thirty, at least, I thought him till I caught the laughing, boyish gleam in his grey-blue eyes. He had assisted Jepson in the editing of the paper while I was in America, and on my return he helped me for some little time. He was casual, cheerfully unpunctual, careless rather than critical in correcting other men's work, and these ordinary shortcomings were somewhat harassing. One day he remarked in the air, that if he could get paid for poetry he'd prefer writing to editing. I was a little surprised: I had not thought of him as a poet; but we soon came to an arrangement. His first verses surprised me; there was the singing quality in them, a happy ease of melody, a sureness and distinction of phrase which proved that he was indeed a poet. Better still, his best verses did not echo his forerunners; imitative cadences there were, of course; a few borrowed graces; but usually the song was his own and not derived—a true poet.

One day I asked my assistant why there had been no poetry of Middleton's in the last week's impression: had he sent nothing?

"Oh, yes," was the reply, "he sent in two or three poems as usual, but they were too free, I was afraid they'd shock Mrs. Grundy, so I'm about to return them."

Needless to say that made me eager to read them: one was **"The Bathing Boy."** I published it promptly, and told Middleton what I thought, that it was finer than Herrick, with something of unsophisticated beauty in it, pure loveliness. After that my defences went down before him. I

published whatever he sent me as soon as I received it, and when he told me he wanted to do some stories, I was more than eager to see what his prose would be like; a page of it convinced me; a little too rhythmic and rounded, it had its own charm and was curiously characteristic.

"The Bathing Boy" made me want to know Middleton better. I found him deeply read in English, and of an astoundingly sure judgment in all matters of literature. His ripeness of mind excited my curiosity, and I probed further. There was in him a modern mixture of widest comprehension with a child's acceptance of vice and suffering and all abnormalities. I say a "child's" because it was purely curious and without any tinge of ethical judgment. Here is a self-revealing couplet:

> A human blossom glad for human eyes,
> Made pagan by a child's serenity.

At twenty-five Middleton had come to his full growth and was extraordinarily mature. In every respect a typical artist, he had no religious belief, death seemed to him the proper and only climax to the fleeting show, but he delighted in the pageantry of life, and the melody of words entranced him. This visible world and the passions of men and women were all his care.

Even on the practical side he was world-taught, if not world-wise; he had been educated at St. Paul's School, and then spent some years in an insurance office in the City: he had given up a large salary, he said, to write poetry. As I got to know and like him, I noticed that his head was massive, his blue eyes finely expressive, his characteristic attitude a dignified, somewhat disdainful acceptance of life's perverse iniquities.

> When I lived I sought no wings,
> Schemed no heaven, planned no hell,
> But, content with little things,
> Made an earth, and it was well.

I am anxious not to say one word more than he deserved: I never heard a new thought from him: I cannot call him, therefore, a bringer of new light; at the same time, I scarcely ever found his judgment at fault: he could have said with Heine—"I stand on the topmost wave of all the culture of my time," and perhaps that is all we can ask of the poet. He was not taken by the popular idols; Tennyson, he thought, had only written half a dozen lyrics, and "Dowson, you know, left three"; he regarded Browning as the greatest poet since Shakespeare: "he has given us a greater body of high poetry," he would say, "than any other English poet, though he never reached the magic of Keats." Blake he seemed to wince from; the poet he praised; but the prophet disquieted him, disturbed the serenity of his pagan, sad acquiescence in the mysteries of this unintelligible world.

The least one can say of Middleton is that at twenty-five he stood as an equal among the foremost men of his time in knowledge of thought and of life, and was among the first of living singers in natural endowment. He was a love-poet, too, as the greatest have been, as Shakespeare and Keats, Goethe and Dante were, and it was this superb faculty that made me hope great things from him.

Here is a verse which justifies hope, I think:

> Love played with us beneath the laughing trees,
> We praised him for his eyes and silver skin,
> And for the little teeth that shone within
> His ruddy lips; the bracken touched his knees,
> Earth wrapped his body in her softest breeze,
> And through the hours that held no count of sin
> We kept his court, until above our din
> Night westward drove her glittering argosies.

And this:

> Come, Death, and free me from these earthly
>   walls
> That heaven may hold our final festivals
> The white stars trembling under!
> I am too small to keep this passionate wonder
> Within my human frame: I would be dead
> That God may be our bed.
>
> I feel her breath upon my eyes, her hair
> Falls on me like a blessing, everywhere
> I hear her warm blood leaping,
> And life it seems is but a fitful sleeping,
> And we but fretful shades that dreamed before,
> That love, and are no more.

Though he can rise to this height of passionate utterance, the unique distinction of this book of Middleton's is that there is not a bad, hardly a weak poem in the whole volume: I know few books of which so much can be said. Middleton at twenty-seven had not only a wonderful lyrical gift: but the power of self-criticism of the masters.

Some critics have gone so far as to say that his prose was better than his verse; I do not agree with them; his prose was always the prose of a singer; but he was nevertheless a story-teller of undoubted talent. His tales of boys are among the best in the language.

His friend, Mr. Savage, tells us that "in his last year Middleton wrote scarcely any poetry at all . . . he came to love young children and people who are simple and kindly and not too clever . . . certainly he would not have written any more poems like his **'Irene'** "—poems, that is, of passion.

Well, I cannot go so far as that: I think had he lived he would have written both prose and poetry in the future as in the past: he told me more than once that he wrote stories because he found them more saleable. But the most passionate poems were his favorites as they were his best. "There is no demand for poetry," he would say, in wonder, laying stress on the word "demand," "no *demand* at all."

And here we come to the tragedy of Middleton's life as of a great many other lives. There is no "demand" in our Anglo-Saxon world for high literary or artistic work of any kind. If it is nevertheless produced, it is produced in spite of the fact that no one wants it and very few appreciate it; it must be given, therefore, and not sold, as love is given and friendship and pity and all high things. But in spite of all such arguments the tragedy remains, and the gloom of it darkens all our ways.

Reading this volume of poems now in the light of what happened, it is easy to see the attraction which Death held

for Richard Middleton, the abyss enticing him again and again. He had lived and loved, sung his songs and told his stories, and the public wouldn't listen, didn't care. Well, he doesn't care much either: life is only a dream, and this dreamer's too easily wearied to struggle, too proud to complain. A dozen poems show changing moods with the same changeless refrain:

> Too tired to mock or weep
> The world that I have missed,
> Love, in your heaven let me sleep
> An hour or two, before, I keep
> My unperturbèd tryst.

Or this, with its reminiscence of Swinburne:

> Shall tremble to our laughter,
> While we leave our tears to your hopeless years,
> Though there be nothing after;
> And while your day uncloses
> Its lorn and tattered roses,
> We shall pluck the stars from your prison bars
> And bind celestial posies.

Or this lovely verse:

> Gladly the rigging sings,
> But, oh! how glad are we,
> Lords of the dreaming sea,
> And of delicious things;
> We are more rich than kings,
> Or any men that be,
> While down eternity
> We beat with shadowy wings.

And this finally:

> No more than a dream that sings
> In the streets of space;
> Ah, would that my soul had wings,
> Or a resting-place!

As one turns the leaves one finds beauty everywhere, on every page joy in living and in love, and everywhere serenity, the sad serenity of acquiescence, and now and again the high clear note that promised so much to those who knew and loved him, and how could one help loving him if one knew him?

> For all the rich and curious things
> That I have found within my sleep,
> Are naught beside this child that sings
> Among the heather and the sheep;
> And I, who with expectant eyes
> Have fared across the star-lit foam,
> See through my dreams a new sun rise
> To conquer unachievèd skies,
> And bring the dreamer home.

And this verse, perhaps the most characteristic of all, steeped as it is in the contradictory essences of life:

> I have been free, and had all heaven and hell
> For prison, until my piteous hands grew sore
> Striking the voiceless walls; and now it is well
> Even though I be a captive evermore.
> My grateful song shall fill my hiding-place
> To find Eternity hath so sweet a face.

Ah, the "piteous hands" and "voiceless walls!"

It is over a year now since Mr. Savage called on me and told me that Richard Middleton was dead; that he had killed himself in Brussels. I stared at him unable to realize it, shocked out of thought, amazed and aching. I had never thought of Middleton as in distress or really poor: he had often spoken genially of his people, tenderly of a sister; often when he was hard up declared that he would have to go home, "retire into country-quarters for my pocket's health," meeting poverty as it should be met, with good-humor. In 1910 I noticed that his tone was a little sharper, and busied myself for him with this editor and that, and was relieved to see his contributions appearing wherever I had any influence, notably in the *Academy* and *The English Review.* In the summer of 1911 he gave me his book of poems to get published, thinking I had more influence with publishers than I possessed; I told him it would be published before the end of the year, and had good hopes in the matter. I could not conceal from him that there would be but little money in the venture, though I kept the fact to myself that the most willing publisher I could find wanted the cost of the book guaranteed. Had I been asked as to his circumstances, I should have said that Middleton was making his way slowly but surely in the esteem and affection of all good readers; that a certain number of persons already counted him as the most promising of living English poets, and that their admiration was a forecast of fame.

True, he had been ailing all through the summer; a tedious little malady, slow to get cured, plagued him with annoyance and self-disgust; true, he had talked now and then as one talks to intimate friends in moments of depression of "going out," heart-sick for the time being of the Sisyphean labor; but the weariness and disgust appeared to me to be superficial; his smile came as boyish, gay as ever; his joy in living, especially in Brussels, unvexed by the ghouls of English convention and respectability, seemed as deep as the sea. I have been told since that like Francis Adams he had tried already to kill himself, had indeed gone about for years hugging the idea that this door of deliverance was always open to him; but he had not shown me this soul-side; or perhaps I did not encourage his attempts at confession because of my own struggle with similar melancholy. Whatever the explanation may be the news of his self-murder fell on me as a shock: he would not wait for success: he had gone to death in hatred of living: the pity of it and the unavailing regret!

I was told later of those four days in Brussels which he passed in the cold, hired bedroom, four days in which he forced himself to face the Arch-Fear and conquer it. At the beginning he wrote a post card telling what he was about to do, taking farewell of his friend, in high pagan fashion, before the long journey, and then in that last awful hour, with the bottle of chloroform before him, he wrote across the card: "A broken and a contrite spirit Thou wilt not despise." The awfulness of it, and the pity deeper than tears.

> So here's an end, I ask forgetfulness
> Now that my little store of hours is spent,
> And heart to laugh upon my punishment—
> Dear God, what means a poet more or less?

Stewart Marsh Ellis   **(essay date 1922)**

SOURCE: "Richard Middleton" in his *Mainly Victorian,* Books for Libraries Press, 1969, pp. 252-56.

[*In the following excerpt from an essay originally published in* The Fortnightly Review, *October, 1922, Ellis discusses Henry Savage's assessment of Middleton's life and work.*]

Richard Middleton distinctly had a touch of genius. His fantastic stories—**"The Ghost Ship," "On the Brighton Road,"** and **"The Coffin Merchant"**—will always stand in the van of bizarre literature; his rather morbid studies of himself as a boy—**"A Drama of Youth"** and **"The New Boy"**—are marvels of introspection; and much of his poetry has beauty and charm. We were indebted to Mr. Henry Savage for collecting and supervising the publication of Middleton's work in prose and verse—five volumes, which commenced to appear a year after the young author's mournful death. The same devoted and enthusiastic friend has now come forward as the biographer of Richard Middleton [in *Richard Middleton, The Man and his Work*].

Mr. Savage's book is more a consideration and appreciation of Middleton's literary work than a biography. Mr. Savage is an able and sympathetic critic, but he lacks another equally essential quality in a biographer—the presentation in an interesting, yet accurate, way of prosaic but very necessary facts. He boasts in fact (alas! the tautophony) that during the period of his friendship with Middleton he had "an excessive contempt for facts in general." As he supposes, his memoir does suffer accordingly. For biography cannot be written without facts, and such facts as are adduced need to be related correctly, otherwise the work is valueless as biography. It is a pity that this otherwise excellent book should be marred by such elementary errors as that which speaks of the author of *The Ingoldsby Legends* as the Rev. *Thomas* Barham: a minute's research would have obviated this careless and faulty reference to Middleton's distant relative. When mentioning Middleton's schools, Mr. Savage says: "In London he seems to have gone both to St. Paul's and Merchant Taylors', the former of which was probably the scene of *A Drama of Youth.*" It is quite apparent from the story itself that Middleton describes Merchant Taylors', which is located in the old Charterhouse buildings near the Meat Markets of Smithfield: —

> For some days school has seemed to me even more tedious than usual. The long train journey in the morning, the walk through Farringdon Meat Market, which aesthetic butchers made hideous with mosaics of the intestines of animals, as if the horror of suety pavements and bloody sawdust did not suffice. . . . I saw the greasy, red-faced men with their hands and aprons stained with blood. I saw the hideous carcases of animals, the masses of entrails, the heaps of repulsive hides; but most clearly of all I saw an ugly, sad little boy, with a satchel of books on his back, set down in the midst of an enormous and hostile world. The windows and stones of the houses were black with soot, and before me there lay school, the place that had never brought me anything but sorrow and humiliation.

However, Mr. Savage might be justified in claiming that the facts of Middleton's life are unimportant, for beyond his literary work and tragic end it was singularly uneventful. After leaving school, he was, from the age of nineteen, a clerk in the Royal Exchange Assurance Corporation for six years. Clerking could hardly be expected to form a congenial career for such a brilliant, erratic spirit, whose mind during office hours was occupied with the composition of blank verse plays in the Elizabethan manner. In 1907 he resigned his position and resolved to earn his living by journalism. Two years earlier he had become a member of that literary-bohemian coterie known as "The New Bohemians," which met at "The Prince's Head" tavern, in the region of the Strand and the Street of Adventure. Here he formed his friendships with Mr. Savage, Mr. Arthur Machen, and Mr. Louis McQuilland—the trio who have consolidated his posthumous fame. On one occasion Lord Alfred Douglas came to dine with the band; owner and editor then of *The Academy,* it was he who gave Middleton the first chance of mounting the literary ladder. He accepted both articles and reviews, and, as Middleton said: "Oh, but the reviewing is great fun, an' the man Douglas is a peach with a stone in it to let me do it." Middleton established himself in two rooms at 7, Blackfriars Road, and wrote in the first flush of his aspirations: —

> My name is Richard Middleton, I'm living at
>   Blackfriars,
> Two stories up, above the street, to chasten my
>   desires;
> I have no purple heather here, no field, nor living
>   tree—
> But every night when I look out God lights the
>   stars for me.
>
>   . . . . .
>
> I am not rich nor hope to be, but mine are day
>   and night,
> And all the world to look upon, and laughter,
>   and the light,
> Where I can set my torch ablaze to make the
>   beacon burn,
> And show to God that in Blackfriars, two stories
>   up, I yearn.

Mr. Savage draws a delightful picture of the days—or rather nights—of "The New Bohemians," and, though he writes but of sixteen years ago he is already *laudator temporis acti.* The symposia at "The Prince's Head" would last until closing hour (half-past twelve in those spiritual times), and the boon companions would then continue their carouse at the rooms of one of the party until dawn. Sometimes there were walks to Hampstead, and on one occasion two of the company tore down the moonlit hill chanting Swinburne's "A Ballad of Life," "and wholly at one in our ecstasy"—much like Swinburne himself, forty years earlier, when he declaimed, with Meredith, on The Mound at Copsham, the newly discovered version by Fitz-Gerald of *Omar Khayyám.* Another adventure was in the best style of Theodore Hook. A party of the roysterers invaded the sacred precincts of the National Liberal Club, where one of them posed as a member and ordered drinks for his "guests." They were served, but a polite attendant came up to the "host," and said, "I beg your pardon, sir, but your name does not appear to be on our list of members." The visitor expressed his regret, and explained that he had mistaken the premises for those of the Athenaeum. He and his friends then made as dignified an exit as was possible. Youth will have its fling.

Middleton's attitude to love—sexual love—how much he experienced it, and how far it influenced his literary work, would provide an interesting theme of speculation. At the end of his life he wrote of a book he was contemplating: "Love I mean to leave out altogether if I possibly can, because I won't accept their damned convention. It has helped me to make a mess of things sometimes, but I don't know that it has had any great spiritual influence on my life." His biographer states that "Middleton was a man of strong passions, but what of natural desire was in him seems, so far at least as these girls were concerned, to have turned inward to be expressed in song." The girls in question, Lily and Christine, were merely commonplace young persons, apparently chorus girls of the humbler class, who were idealised by the poet. They inspired some beautiful things, preeminently **"The Silent Lover"**: —

> I cannot sing, I have no words
> To love you, hate you, make you mine—
> To win your ear like mating birds,
> To brim your veins with wanton wine;
> But all my longing senses cry
> Their faltering, broken oratory.
>
>   . . . . .
>
> I have no words, but Time shall prove
> This song of mine the best of all,
> My lips shall be as Love's, for love
> Shall make their silence musical;
> And on some rapt, enchanted night
> They shall reveal my heart's delight.

A wonderful thing that a plebeian girl like Lily (who, as Mr. Savage relates, married the lover of her choice, a news-boy, and became "the stout mother of very many children") could generate such passionate poetry as this: but, of course, she was only a symbol to the poet. Middleton wrote of his poems suggested by Lily: "I wonder whether I love Lily or youth, or is it only compassion for the little boy I never was that moves me? The doubt does not prevent my writing good verses. I want to love something or other anyhow: love kills the ego with a surfeit of egoism, and I appreciate but do not like mine."

He was right; he could write "good verses." **"The Last Serenade," "To Mélisande," "Irene," "Hylas,"** are beautiful. And he was right about his "surfeit of egoism," "the arrogance of his culture," as he called it in another place. He suffered from neuralgia, and too much alcohol at times, but his real complaint, which killed him at the last, was his morbid introspection. Shortly before his death he wrote: "Indeed, it is not hard to put a name to my disease; but one man is an egoist just as another is a negro."

> Having the thought of death
> Eternally to perplex me

he had said in one of his poems, and in another (not mentioned by Mr. Savage, though full of beauty), **"Night on Hungerford Bridge,"** he voiced the lure of suicide and oblivion: —

> Lights on the water, lights on the tide,
> And the white stars a-shiver.
> "Here is your resting, here by my side
> Forever, forever,
> And they shall forget that you lived or died."
> Thus sang the river.

In his last message to Mr. Savage, before the fatal dose of chloroform, he wrote, "I am going adventuring again." He died, in Brussels, penniless. His books, still unpublished, were going the round of publishers for rejection. *The London Magazine* had declined his finest short story, **"The Ghost Ship,"** though a week after the author's death a cable arrived to say it had been accepted by *The Century Magazine,* the payment being £25. The pity of it all resembles the tragedy of Chatterton.

S. P. B. Mais   (essay date 1923)

SOURCE: "Richard Middleton," in his *From Shakespeare to O. Henry: Studies in Literature,* revised edition, 1923. Reprint by Books for Libraries Press, 1968, pp. 221-33.

[*Mais was a prolific English writer, editor, and critic. In the following excerpt, he offers a sympathetic appraisal of Middleton's works.*]

Whether it be that famous story of **"The Ghost Ship,"** where we seem really to see the fairy barque sailing away over the turnip field, through the windy stars, its portholes and bay-windows blazing with lights to the accompaniment of singing and fiddling on deck on the part of all the village ghosts who have been inveigled away on it, or that incident in **"The Brighton Road,"** where the dead boy is eternally condemned to go on tramping—tramping . . . in all [Middleton's] stories there is an uncanny something which makes them take wing beyond the author's conception, that elusive quality which, for want of a better word, we call genius.

His stories are woven like delicate spiders' webs, besprinkled with dew; they are pure gossamer, unbelievably beautiful; but touch them and they fall to pieces in your hand. They must be read in their entirety to be appreciated: quotation in this case is like Dr Johnson's brick, no criterion whatever of the excellence of the building.

The effect is always heightened by a sure sense of humour which crops up in all sorts of unexpected places throughout his work.

What a quantity of wisdom is hidden in this paragraph on his own schooldays. "You're only here for a little spell," he said; "you'll be surprised how short it is. And don't be miserable just because you're different. I'm different; it's a jolly good thing to be different"—and then, after a pause—"All the same, I don't see why you should always have dirty nails. . . ." Or, again, in this story of the author, who, having finished his great book, "read it to his friends, who made suggestions that would have involved its re-writing from one end to the other; he read it to his enemies, who told him that it was nearly good enough to publish; he read it to his wife, who said that it was very nice, and that it was time to dress for dinner."

It is this faculty which must have so endeared him to children. Certainly no other man, Kenneth Grahame and Sir James Barrie alone excepted, ever entered so completely into the thoughts and ways of childhood.

No man has so faithfully transcribed the best moments and those hidden thoughts of our early days which we imagined were forgotten or a part of ourselves that was dead before we came across this book. How perfect and yet how characteristic is the sentence uttered almost unconsciously by the small boy in the wood. "All the wasted moonlight," he cried; "the grass is quite wet with it."

He brings back all the secret longings and untellable ecstasies of our early youth which we never breathed to the Olympians for fear of ridicule. Childhood's loves are strange loves but they are very real; uncanny to the adult mind, but so natural to the infant intelligence as scarcely to need comment. The majority of us are nowadays scarcely enamoured of the lawn-mower, but we have surely not forgotten the day when "the very appearance of the thing was cheery and companionable, with its hands outstretched to welcome mine and its coat of green more vivid than any lawn. To seize hold of its smooth handles was like shaking hands with an old friend, and as it rattled over the gravel path it chattered to me in the gruff tones of a jovial uncle. Once on the smooth lawn its voice thrilled to song tremulous and appealing and filled with the throbbings of great wings. And cheered by that song I might drive my chariot where I would. Not for me the stiff, brocaded pattern beloved of our gardener: I made curves, skirting the shadows of the tall poplars or cutting the lawn into islands and lagoons: with the cold inhumanity of youth I would marvel at the injudicious earthworms that tried to stay my progress and perished for their pains."

Surely that wakes a responsive chord in our minds of days when we burnt witches on the rubbish heap, when we coiled the garden hose round our legs, Laocoon-like, when we, too, launched our Argonauts, braving Farmer Bates' terrible wrath, by sailing past his forbidden meadow, when we too tramped through the woods in search of the magic pool by night.

There are only too few books that are able to transport us back to those golden hours when we played cricket (*real* cricket, when you were out if you hit the ball into the next garden, and stopped playing if you broke a window), owned pirate ships and magic carpets, and founded secret societies in the secrecy of the lumber-room.

Whenever we feel that nostalgia of childhood which overtakes each of us so often amid the worries and cares of life to-day, which causes us to batter vainly at fast-locked nursery doors, or to look sadly at the gaudy toy-shops, robbed by the cynical years of their fit halo, at such a time if we can find no children to play with and our hearts yearn for the fairy laughter of playing infants, to take down a volume of Richard Middleton's child fancies will do much to appease our longing and cause us to live over again those magic hours which we have now for ever lost. Everyone knows that the finest joys he experiences are just the most incommunicable: who can harness Pegasus to describe the sensation of a man who has just made a mighty, almost impossible tackle at "Rugger," brought off a long-practised shot of great difficulty at billiards, sung a song in such a way as to thrill his audience with a magnetism so great that they forget to applaud, climbed a hitherto inaccessible peak, written the last word of a play, novel or poem which he knows to be a living force, eternal, incorruptible: who, I repeat, can hope to express life's great moments even when we have reached years that perhaps have brought the power of self-expression?

How much less can we hope to regain exactly or ever to reproduce in the minds of other people the days of our Golden Age: at the most absurd moments, while hurrying into school at the last moment, while catching a train, on a route march, in the middle of worrying out a mathematical problem, some insidious sound, a cock crowing, the scrunch of a wheelbarrow, the haycutter in the fields, the pack of hounds giving tongue, some wave of recollection sweeps over us and on the instant we are back in that old garden, chasing the guinea-fowl, penetrating the meadow brook to the forbidden haunts of the pixy-ridden mill and the deep trout pool, seated in the cleft of the blasted oak looking out over Westward Ho! and Lundy for a sight of Amyas Leigh and Salvation Yeo, for John Silver and Captain Bartholomew Roberts; some friends show us over their house, and having penetrated every recess, we say, to their complete mystification: "May I see the attic now, please?" and coldly wondering at the lunatic they harbour as their guest they push us into the raftered room full of apples. In a moment we are thousands of miles away on a lonely sea, plying our raft, with rations given out and hope lost . . . when suddenly the cry goes up: "A sail! a sail!" and we are taken on board the friendly sloop and swear eternal vows of comradeship with the pirate chief, whose incarnadined face, bandage-hidden, haunts our dreams a thousand nights. Such tricks do our senses play us, and how pitiable are those (if there exist any such, which I much doubt) who are never betrayed by the smell of leaves on a November night, by the sight of a Guy Fawkes bonfire, by the chestnut roasting on All-Hallows

E'en, when they gaze into the fire and build again those gorgeous palaces which were once so real—so real . . . but I am lost myself. You see the effect of Middleton: he drives you back willy-nilly, and life becomes for a few precious moments all sunshine, laughter and innocence, and war and separation are no more.

But there is another side to Middleton which it is necessary to understand before we can pretend to have in our minds a picture of the complete man. He recurs to it again and again both in his prose and his poetry—and in its essence we might call this trait the lament of the writer, the tragedy of the artist; an overpowering sense of the inadequacy of the word-maker and the dreamer in comparison with the man of action seems an ever-present topic in the mind of Middleton as it was in the mind of Robert Louis Stevenson.

> While ordinary efficient men and women are enjoying the promise of the morning, the fulfilment of the afternoon, the tranquillity of evening, we are still trying to discover a fitting epithet for the dew of dawn. For us Spring paves the woods with beautiful words rather than flowers, and when we look into the eyes of our mistress we see nothing but adjectives. Does a handful of love-songs really outweigh the smile of a pretty girl, or a hardly-written romance compensate the author for months of lost adventure? We have only one life to live, and we spend the greater part of it writing the history of dead hours.

> Few of us are fortunate enough to accomplish anything that was in the least worth doing, so we fall back on the arid philosophy that it is effort alone that counts.

And then, in a passage pregnant with real introspection, he gives us a rare insight into his own character. It had been raining, he said, one morning, and while watching from his window he suddenly became conscious of a wet morning years before when he was eight years old, a real wet, grey day, when he heard the rain dripping from the fir-trees on to the scullery roof and the wind every now and then drove the rain down on the soaked lawn with a noise like breaking surf; he remembered thinking how nice it would be if it rained really hard and flooded the house so that they would all have to starve for three weeks, and then be rescued excitingly in boats . . . behind him in the room his brothers were playing chess and his sister was patiently beating a doll in a corner. The clock on the mantelpiece ticked very slowly and he realised that an eternity of those long seconds separated him from dinner-time.

He thought he would like to go out. The enterprise presented certain difficulties and dangers, but none that were insuperable. He would have to steal down to the hall unobserved: he would have to open the front door without making a noise and he would have to run down the front drive under the eyes of many windows. Once beyond the gate, however, he would be safe.

In the wood near the house he might meet the magician for whom he had looked so often in vain on sunny days, for it was quite likely that he preferred walking in bad weather when no one else was about. Then he thought of

Manuscript of a poem by Middleton.

the probable punishments that would ensue, but they did not trouble him much, at any rate in retrospect. And yet he did not go out: he stayed dreaming until the golden moment for action had passed and he was called back to a prosaic world by the shrieks of the chess-players, who were suddenly locked in battle. And this later morning, as he stood at the window again watching the rain, Richard Middleton indulges in the vain wish that he had then set forth to seek adventure. He would have met the enchanter in the wood and he would have taught him to conquer worlds, and to leave the easy triumphs of dreams to madmen, philosophers and poets. He would have made him a man of action, a statesman, a soldier, a founder of cities or a digger of graves.

And then comes the crucial passage. He concludes the essay thus:

> It seems to me likely enough that that moment of hesitation before the schoolroom window determined a habit of mind that has kept me

dreaming ever since. For all my life I have preferred thought to action: I have never run to the
little wood: I have never met the enchanter. And
so this morning, when Fate played me this trick
and my dream was chilled for an instant by the
icy breath of the past, I did not rush out into the
streets of life and lay about me with a flaming
sword. No: I picked up my pen and wrote some
words on a piece of paper, and lulled my
shocked senses with the tranquillity of the idlest
dream of all.

> My life, my beautiful life all wasted:
> The gold days, the blue days to darkness sunk.
> The bread was here, and I have not tasted:
> The wine was here, and I have not drunk.

I feel that in one sense this is the most tragically true, the
most artistically great of all Middleton's writing.

It is absolutely impossible to read it without transferring
the whole idea over to oneself. It is oneself who has failed,
who has stood at the window, and through inertia, panic
or for whatever cause, has let the golden moment go by,
and instead of sallying forth sword in hand to rid the
world of some abuse we have preferred the more comfortable fire and attempted to delude ourselves with the obvious lie that after all, perhaps, there was no wizard in the
wood.

Sanity, we have been told, is simply a capacity for becoming accustomed to the monstrous; and Middleton's tragedy lies as much as anything in the fact that though he refuses to call ugliness beautiful, yet he is too much of a
dreamer to sally forth sword in hand as the avenger of
wrongs.

Most of us forget our early frantic anger at the needless
horrors that abound on every side; we have our fight
against it young, are thoroughly well cowed and are lucky
if in the end we not only agree with and defend the existing
chaos and mistake it for order, light and beauty, but quite
definitely throw our whole weight on the side of ugliness
and make a religion of it. Not so Richard Middleton:

> When a young man first awakens to a sense of
> the beauty and value of life, it is natural that he
> should be overwhelmed by the ugliness of the in-
> heritance that his ancestors have forced upon
> him. He finds in the civilisation that he has had
> no place in devising a tyranny against which it
> appears almost impossible to make any resis-
> tance, a dogma which he is told everyone except
> a young fool must accept as a truth. . . . He
> may, for instance, think that it is better to grow
> and love roses in a cottage garden than to reign
> in an umbrella factory: but this briefest of the il-
> lusions of youth will be shattered forthwith by
> what appears to be the first law of civilised life:
> that a man can only earn his living by the manu-
> facture of ugliness.

He then shows you the young man turning for comfort to
latter-day prophets and philosophers, who spend their
time, he finds (in Middleton's glorious phrase), in schem-
ing little revolutions on a sound conservative basis: only
in the poets can the young man find solace.

It is unnecessary, he goes on, to point out that the dangerous revolutionary spirit which worships lovely things is
not encouraged in our national schools.

The children of the State are taught to cut up flowers and
to call the fragments by cunning names, but they are not
invited to love them for their beauty.

Their lips lisp dates and the dry husks of history, but they
have no knowledge of the splendid pageant of bygone
kingdoms and dead races.

The cheaper newspapers, which alone are read by the people, as a whole seek out and dilate on ugliness with passionate ingenuity . . . only in the poets, I repeat, can a
young man find solace.

And would you know how to be a poet in Middleton's
words?

> Take something—I would say take anything—
> and love it, and thereafter, if he were a child of
> his century, I should have to tell him of love, the
> rude, uncivilised force that has inspired all the
> deeds worth doing, that has made all the things
> worth making. I should tell him that it was non-
> sense to speak of anything or anybody being
> worthy of his love, that the question was wheth-
> er he could make his love worthy of any shadow
> of an idea that penetrates his education. I should
> tell him—to what end? That he might see life as
> he would have made it, and weep his years away;
> that he might find beauty and fail to win it; that
> he might cry his scorn of ugliness on the hills
> and have never a hearer for his pains? Pooh! It
> were kinder to let him snore with the others.
> There are too many unhappy people already.

Yet Middleton himself, with his eyes open, chose the better way: it is as a poet that he lives for the majority of his
readers, one who ever strove to keep the sun upon the
western wall.

> Roses and lilies blowing fair,
> A sunny castle in old Spain,
> A lock of my beloved's hair,
> A tale that shall be told again,
> Joy and sorrow, heaven and hell—
> These are all the wares I sell.

As one of his critics has said, the visible world and the passions of men and women were all his care.

Mr Frank Harris declares that **"The Bathing Boy"** is finer
than anything in Herrick.

His theory of poetry is to be found definitely, clearly and
finally in that remarkable passage in **"The Poet's Allegory":**

> So he pulled out his pipe and made a mournful
> song to himself of the dancing gnats and the bit-
> ter odour of the bonfires in the townsfolks' gar-
> dens. And the children drew near to hear him
> sing, for they thought his song was pretty, until
> their fathers drove them home, saying: "That
> stuff has no educational value."
>
> "Why haven't you a message?" they asked the
> boy.
>
> "I come to tell you that the grass is green be-

neath your feet and that the sky is blue over your heads."

"Oh! But we know all that!" they answered.

"Do you! Do you!" screamed the boy. "Do you think you could stop over your absurd labours if you knew how blue the sky is? You would be out singing on the hills with me."

"Then who would do our work?" they said, mocking him.

"Then who would want it done?" he retorted.

> When I lived I sought no wings,
> Schemed no heaven, planned no hell,
> But, content with little things,
> Made an earth, and it was well.
> Song and laughter, food and wine,
> Roses, roses red and white,
> And a star or two to shine
> On my dewy world at night.
> Lord, what more could I desire?
> With my little heart of clay
> I have lit no eternal fire
> To burn my dreams on Judgment Day!

But we, the great British public, had no use for song and laughter, the sweet beauty of roses in those prewar days: it is only now that poets can sell their wares and so continue to exist.

First John Davidson and then Richard Middleton—great singers both—had to leave a world grown old and cold and weary and plunge into the unknown, and in one last piteous cry Middleton takes his farewell of us:

> So here's an end; I ask forgetfulness
> Now that my little store of hours is spent,
> And heart to laugh upon my punishment.
> Dear God, what means a poet more or less?

Middleton's final note to Henry Savage:

For his friend, Henry Savage, he left a final note, written on a postcard which was found on his bed in the small room he occupied in Mme. Grey's very modest lodging-house: "Goodbye! Harry. I'm going adventuring again, and thanks to you I shall have some pleasant memories in my knapsack. As for the many bitter ones, perhaps they will not weigh so heavy as they did before. 'A broken and a contrite heart, oh Lord, thou shalt not despise.' —Richard."

from "Richard Middleton," in Authors Today and Yesterday, *edited by Stanley J. Kunitz, 1934.*

J. A. Chapman   (essay date 1929)

SOURCE: "Richard Middleton," in his *Papers on Shelley, Wordsworth & Others,* 1929. Reprint by Books for Libraries Press, 1967, pp. 128-35.

[In the following essay, Chapman offers a negative assessment of Middleton's poetry.]

> Dear God, what means a poet more or less?

Richard Middleton wrote that. He was of our time; had he not died as a young man (he was only twenty-nine), he would still be alive. He belongs to that group of latter-day English poets—Ernest Dowson, Lionel Johnson, John Davidson, and Stephen Phillips—who, if they have not this or that in common, have all of them this, that they, dying young, added their names to those others who died young; the roll, the chief names in which are Chatterton and Keats. A roll to which one may add Shelley's name, though his was a violent death, and the names of those whom the Great War took away; the last, in their fate, more fortunate, perhaps, than the others. One broods over the long list of names until one can hardly bear to think of the men any longer. What went so wrong with them? Why should Milton, Goethe, Wordsworth, Tennyson, Browning have proved so much tougher? There is perhaps a key to the mystery in a phrase in one of Richard Middleton's last letters: —'I feel drawn towards young children and people who are simple and kindly and not too clever. They give me a glimpse of the life that I have missed in my passionate search for enjoyment.'

One expects a poet to want to enjoy life, and life within rather narrow limits, and one sees that they do set out to seek enjoyment; but they mostly burn themselves out too soon. What keeps those from burning themselves out who do not do so is, I believe, this; that they care more for poetry, for the poetry that they feel they must live to write. One feels that Milton or Wordsworth would as soon have gone so far in their search for enjoyment as to incapacitate themselves for writing more poetry, as an austere priest would take the lamb from the altar, and give it to the pigs. There must be, for a man to be a great poet, and to fulfil his destiny, some cold principle in him of self-reservation; something almost like cynical calculation. Wordsworth would go only so far with his French Annette as would not prevent his writing:

> Thou dost preserve the stars from wrong,
> And the most ancient heavens through thee are
> fresh and strong.

One sees the self-reservation working most plainly in Goethe, the Goethe of whom John Sterling and Carlyle could write as this letter shows:

> Truly, as you say, one might ask the question, whether anybody did love this man, as friend does friend; especially, Whether this man did ever frankly love anybody? I think in one sense, it is very likely the answer were No to both questions; and yet, in another sense, how emphatically Yes! Few had a right to "love" this man, except in the way you mention: nay, what living man had? Schiller, perhaps to some extent; and accordingly Schiller did, to something like that extent. One does not love the Heaven's lightning, in the way of caresses altogether! This man's love, I take it, lay deep-hidden in him, as fire in the earth's centre; at the surface, —since he could not be a Napoleon, did not like to be

a broken, self-consumed Burns, —what could it do for him?

The earliest instincts of self-culture, I suppose, and all the wider insights he got in the course of that, would alike prescribe for him: Hide all this, renounce all this; all this leads to madness, indignity, Rousseauism, and will forever remain be-mocked, ignominiously crucified one way or the other, in this lower earth: let thy love, far hidden, spring up as a soul of beauty, and be itself victorious, beautiful.

The consuming eroticism of the cold North—I think one has to have lived in such a country as India to see it for what it is. It speaks in Middleton's poetry more than anything else. It is young at first; a wine, not yet a poison, and so there is a loveliness, as in this poem:

New Love

The boy weeps in the wild woods,
His bright eyes are sore,
The old inhuman solitudes
May shield his heart no more;
A maid has happened out of hell
And kissed his crimson lips too well.

Where may he hide his miseries?
Where quench the lips that burn
For scarlet love? the tangled trees,
Bramble and gorse and fern
Can hide him not, nor may he cool
His mouth in any forest pool.

Love laughs about the groves of pine,
Pan wantons in the glade,
And the boy is drunk with a new wine,
And the boy's heart is afraid;
Her lips were soft and very kind,
Her breath was like a summer wind.

Oh! wanton night, made glad with dew,
Hung with a starry veil!
The boy is lost for loving you,
The old enchantments fail.
You have led his feet to hell's gate—
To a crimson dawn and passionate.

No more in leafy solitudes,
God's paved fields among,
He shall win the peace of the wild woods
With the joy of his quiet song.
For love has found the groves of pine,
And the boy is drunk with a new wine.

There is not much sign of self-reservation in that. The maid would resent self-reservation? Very possibly, but if great poetry is to be written, or even less than great, many things must be done, I believe, that a maid would resent. I should be the last to throw stones. Seeing that we none of us know why God put it into the heart of man to be poet, *Dichter,* whether in word, stone, colour, or sound, and know as little what good or evil there is in all men's part in poetry, what it will all have amounted to before the world is done, we may be of an open mind as to the morality of any man's search for his revelation. There are moments when it seems as if the failure of most artistry of the past sprang, not from the artists' immorality, but from their morality; or as if their art had really been born in a

world in which there was neither, and suffered from having to be translated into the terms of a world in which both, alas, abound. But perhaps that is fanciful.

To go back to that poem. Poor Middleton, if his eroticism had not so filled his ear, he would have heard in his own words:

> the tangled trees,
> Bramble and gorse and fern,

and the music of them, something better to follow than his 'passionate search for enjoyment'. That is how it works with the self-reserved: they hear in their own music sweeter voices and better to follow than the voices of the sirens. But theirs is a dog's life—brooding everlastingly over the earth and the dusty ground, in the hope that a flower of poetry will peep through; brooding alone and silently.

Middleton went his own way, and one cannot say that he did not find things to justify him. They happen not to be the things that I care for most myself, and those I do care for most do not kill a man before he is thirty. This is part of a poem called **"To Irene"**:

> I think the earth was dead last night, for I,
> Keeping you in my arms, could feel no breath
> From all the slumbrous trees, it seemed that death
> Had wooed the fields, for in our ecstasy
> They had no part and where the thrushes flew
> In drowsy autumn, now no creature moved
> Across the fallen leaves, save where we loved,
> And there I heard faint wings discover you.
>
> And then you thrilled with some supreme desire
> That was not of my dreams, your pulses beat
> Time to the world, and with rebellious feet
> Your triumphing passions scaled the gates of fire;
> And lo, I was as dust! in some far place
> My soul paid tribute to tremendous kings,
> Who bowed their head before your gleaming wings
> And praised your beauty with averted face.

There is nothing as weak in that as:

> Oh! wanton night made glad with dew,
> Hung with a starry veil!

and other weak things in **"New Love,"** which it must be confessed grows steadily weaker as it moves from the inspiration with which it began; if there is nothing as weak, nothing as hackneyed and commonplace, the poem has a graver fault. What does it mean? What multitude of people, in a world already so full of beautiful poetry, can be thought of as being moved to cherish in their hearts lines with features no clearer than:

> no creature moved
> Across the fallen leaves, save where we loved,
> And there I heard faint wings discover you?

The features of this, in a piece called **"The Bathing Boy,"** are clearer:

> Till with a sudden grace of silver skin
> And golden lock he dived, his song of joy

Broke with the bubbles as he bore them in;
And lo, the fear of night was on that place,
Till decked with new-found gems and flushed of
    face,
He rose again, a laughing, choking boy.

The copy in which I have read Middleton's poems belongs to an Indian friend. He has starred two of the poems in pencil, and I take them to be the poems that have appealed most to him.

They are **"Lullaby"** and **"On a Dead Child"**. I cannot bring myself to repeat the first: it is too much the same lullaby that we have heard before many times. This is **"On a Dead Child"**:

Man proposes, God in His time disposes,
And so I wandered up to where you lay,
A little rose among the little roses,
And no more dead than they.

It seemed your childish feet were tired of stray-
    ing,
You did not greet me from your flower-strewn
    bed,
Yet still I knew that you were only playing—
Playing at being dead.

I might have thought that you were really sleep-
    ing,
So quiet lay your eyelids to the sky,
So still your hair, but surely you were peeping,
And so I did not cry.

God knows, and in His proper time disposes,
And so I smiled and gently called your name,
Added my rose to your sweet heap of roses,
And left you to your game.

It cannot have been Middleton's own child, and the man to whom the poem appealed so much cannot ever have lost a child. The loss of a man's own child is of all human experiences the very ghastliest.

Alfred Douglas (essay date 1933)

SOURCE: An introduction to *The Pantomime Man* by Richard Middleton, edited by John Gawsworth, Rich & Cowan Ltd., 1933, pp. xvii-xxi.

[*Douglas was an English poet, critic, and editor. In the following introduction to* The Pantomime Man, *he characterizes Middleton's poetry as exquisite, and contends that he, rather than* Vanity Fair *editor Frank Harris, was the first to publish Middleton's work.*]

Having been asked to write an Introduction to [*The Pantomime Man*], by the poet Richard Middleton, I hope I may be excused for informing, or reminding, my readers that, as Editor of *The Academy* in 1907, I was the first to give him recognition. I have been casting back in my mind for recollections of the man himself which, slight as they are, may have that interest which attaches to personal reminiscences of a dead poet.

Shortly after I became Editor of *The Academy* I was invited by a literary society called the "New Bohemians" to attend one of their dinners. I had never heard of the "New

Bohemians," but I was young enough in those days to be gratified by the attention, and I attended their dinner, where I met for the first time, among a lot of charming and talented people, Arthur Machen and Richard Middleton, both of whom became contributors to *The Academy.*

Middleton must have been about twenty-four then, and in spite of his black beard, he produced the effect of boyishness and, whenever I saw him at any rate, of exuberant spirits. His moods of deep depression, so often revealed in this book, were never exhibited on the few occasions when we met. He was a witty and whimsical talker and he diffused an atmosphere of gaiety and laughter.

I liked him at once, and I am proud of the fact that *The Academy* accepted for publication several poems and stories by him, among them **"A Poet's Holiday"**.

I take this opportunity of putting on record the fact that Richard Middleton was writing for me long before Frank Harris ever saw him. I mention this because Harris, who always helped himself with both hands to anything he could get hold of, either in the way of cash, credit or ideas, was given to boasting in later years that he had "discovered Richard Middleton"; as a matter of fact it was I that sent him to Harris, who gave him work on *Vanity Fair.*

Among the writers whom I met at "The New Bohemians" was the late Randal Charlton, a charming fellow, who also wrote for me on *The Academy*. Charlton did not like Middleton, and there was a sort of feud between them which broke out whenever they met. They were always girding at each other.

One day in the office of *The Academy* (round about 1909) Charlton said something deprecatory to me about Middleton, and I said, "You ought not to speak like that about him, because in the first place he is a poet, and in the second place he will not live much longer." Charlton was naturally much surprised at this dark saying, and asked me to explain what I meant by asserting that Middleton would not live much longer. I replied that I could not explain it, but that I knew it was true. I added, "He will be dead in two or three years."

I am utterly unable to account for this strange prescience on my part. Having made the remark, I forgot all about it; and if Charlton had not reminded me of it just after Middleton committed suicide, it would have entirely passed out of my mind. I saw no more of Middleton after the first year of our acquaintance. I ceased to be Editor of *The Academy* in 1910, and the last time I saw Middleton must have been about the end of 1908.

Although the present collection does not comprise any poetry, we must not forget that Middleton was, essentially and first of all, a poet; and it can, I maintain, be proved "out of the book" that all good poets also write good prose.

As a poet he belonged to the "traditional school" which, in my humble opinion, is the only school of poetry which either attracts or produces real poets. Middleton knew, and never forgot, that the art of poetry consists (as in all the arts) of putting ideas into form. The stricter and more difficult the form, the more sublime will be the result, provided always that an effect of ease and spontaneity is achieved. The finest poetry appears to be easy and inevitable, but this appearance of ease and inevitableness is the result of great art. It moves gracefully and beautifully, without apparent effort, in the strictest forms, and, though bound, it produces the illusion of perfect freedom.

Listen to this:

> If when the brown earth covers
> The bones of happy lovers,
> The tired body's ending
> Proves but the soul's amending,
> They have but little faith
> Who are afraid of Death.
>
> For all that we inherit
> Is love; and if our spirit,
> Glad from the grave and stronger,
> Clings to our dust no longer,
> We shall not grieve who treasure
> Love, beyond human measure.
>
> Though now we may not vanquish
> The joys the dead relinquish,
> And passion troubles ever
> Our unachieved endeavour,
> Sweet! be it ours to cherish
> The love that shall not perish.

There is a tremendous lot of art in this little lyric. In fact, in my opinion, it is well-nigh perfect. Even the weak rhymes, "faith" "death," "inherit" "spirit," "vanquish" "relinquish," are scarcely to be counted as blemishes. They are, I believe, deliberate ornaments of art. The poem might have been written by Swinburne at his best. Its apparent simplicity covers the skill of a master.

That anyone who could write so exquisitely (and Middleton wrote a lot of stuff on this level) should have been driven by sheer starvation and neglect to kill himself, as Middleton did, is no credit to the country of his birth.

> From the beginning when was aught but stones
> For English prophets? . . .

There is a curious mixture of the commonplace and the fantastic in some of Middleton's prose as distinct from his poetry. As one reads his laborious chroniclings in his "Journal" of everyday facts, one is occasionally inclined to wonder why he took the trouble to note all this down; but from time to time comes a flash of imagination or vision which justifies his method even in his less attractive work. At his best, as in **"The Boy Errant"** he produces a sense of fatality and poignancy. He seems to see something beyond the crude facts of life; and his art is to convey the sense of this vision to his readers. There is a phrase in **"The Pantomime Man"** which seems to me to throw a light on Middleton and to illustrate his quality as an artist. He says, "It was natural that two adults, *marooned in a turbulent sea of children,* should exchange confidences and criticisms." The words I have italicised are not only a brilliant example of "style," but they reveal something of Middleton's psychology. For Middleton was preoccupied with children, and he suffered that nostalgia of lost childhood which is shared by many poets who, at the back of their hearts, regret the fact that, against their will, they are obliged to "grow up."

This feeling has nothing in common with the arch sentimentalities of "Peter Pan." It is, on the contrary, a sad and wistful feeling. It reaches back on the one hand to the vanished kingdom of childhood, and on the other hand it makes a fierce spiritual effort towards another world "beyond the stars" where childhood may perhaps be recaptured. It is this spiritual effort which informs the art of Richard Middleton and lends magic to his written words.

Suzanne Ferguson   (essay date 1974)

SOURCE: "A Spectral Beauty: The Writings of Richard Middleton," in *English Literature in Transition: 1880-1920,* Vol. 17, No. 3, 1974, pp. 185-96.

[*Ferguson is an American educator and author of essays and reviews of modern and Victorian literature. In the following excerpt, she offers a thematic overview of Middleton's poetry, essays, and short stories.*]

An aesthete just a few years past the time when his gifts and prejudices might have been better appreciated, Middleton wrote poetry and essays that recall in general the best lyric poetry and the sophisticated magazine essays of the nineties. His imagery, in the poetry, is drawn from the most traditional of sources: sea and stars, flowers and rural landscapes, light and dark, music, especially the songs of birds, and sometimes from earlier poetic traditions, especially pastoralism. His poetic subjects are love and death; his chief influences apparently the Elizabethans, Donne and Marvell, and Keats, while the more recent models seem to be Swinburne and Dowson. Of their kind, his poems are pleasing, graceful, and even at times fairly striking. A passage will indicate some of their characteristic gestures:

> Come, Death, and free me from these earthy
>   walls
> That heaven may hold our final festivals
> The white stars trembling under:
> I am too small to keep this passionate wonder
> Within my human frame: I would be dead
> That God may be our bed.
> I feel her breath upon my eyes, her hair
> Falls on me like a blessing, everywhere
> I hear her warm blood leaping,
> And life it seems is but a fitful sleeping,
> And we but fretful shades that dreamed before,
> That love, and are no more.
>   **("Love's Mortality,"** *Poems and Songs,* First
>   Series.)

Felicitous in sound and sense, it yet lacks the distinctive personal voice associated with the great lyric poets. Middleton was, of course, very young—not quite thirty at his death—and even Yeats, at that age, had not particularly distinguished himself. Yeats' early mythologizing of his personal love into a type of ideal love and beauty, in the contexts of Irish folklore and his eclectic occultism, foreshadow the later daring experiments with literary and legendary sources that produced the characteristic images and themes of his mature poetry, if not its language. Middleton's mythologizing, such as it is, derives from literary traditions so shopworn, in his time, as to have lost nearly all force. Seemingly bound by his own prejudices as to the nature of "Beauty," Middleton is unwilling to explore individualized ways of realizing that ideal in his poems. According to Henry Savage, the poems record the progress and failure of actual love affairs. Like the poems of Dowson a decade earlier, they project these affairs as general illustrations of the frailty of human love in the matrices of materiality and time. One may conclude that the terrible despair which drove Middleton to suicide also sprang, paradoxically, from his reverence for a Beauty whose form was dictated through two millenia of Western tradition. Life never quite measured up to his high ideals.

In his essays, written for such periodicals as *The Academy* and Frank Harris's *Vanity Fair,* Middleton is no more than a verbally gifted man of his time (or perhaps of a decade earlier). Though he has a few unusual subjects, including an essay encouraging—who knows how seriously?—the state's employing of would-be suicides in high risk jobs, most of the essays tend to deal with the role of the poet in an indifferent society. Middleton's thesis outlines a Gresham's Law of Art: bad art tends to drive out good art. The titles reveal Middleton's slant: **"The Tyranny of the Ugly," "Pensions for Poets," "Traitors of Art," "The Revolt of the Philistines," "The Verdict of Posterity," "Is England Decadent?" "Poets and Critics."** These subjects, with the familiar attitudes, had been thoroughly aired in the magazines of the nineties, and Middleton had little to add to the discussion. Charming though he shows himself to be in these essays, ideas were not his forte.

Less commonplace than the others, his autobiographical essays in **The Day Before Yesterday**—assembled and titled by Middleton himself—and the autobiographical stories that open **The Ghost Ship** show a special perceptivity about a childhood that was not in its externals much different from that of most well-to-do young Englishmen: the children of the family segregated "upstairs" except for special occasions until school days; recuperations from illness in the country or at the sea; boarding school. Middleton's frank nostalgia for childhood, his idealization of children's honesty and imaginative powers, and his contempt for the pragmatic, time-serving grownups, repeat and develop in a secular way a Wordsworthian process of growth: the child comes trailing clouds of glory, not now of an immortal soul, but of appreciation of Beauty. The child enacts in his dreams and waking fantasies the role of the artist in the grownup world, seeking and creating a sustaining beauty. In these essays and in most of his stories, the aesthetic theme takes on a substance and originality that far transcend its treatment in the poetry and in the more polemical essays.

Several of Middleton's most important stories embody his central theme of the artist embattled in terms of a tension between the "real," grownup world of modern London and the ideal world of the child's mind, posited at the beginning of one of the essays:

> When a young man first awakens to a sense of the beauty and value of life, it is natural that he should be overwhelmed by the ugliness of the in-

heritance that his ancestors have forced upon him.

(Monologues)

Not that all children have the sense of the beautiful; some, in their aping of grownup ways, deny their own birthright and become philistines in miniature, and the war between the sensitive and the insensitive is often waged in little in Middleton's fiction.

The idealization of the child's consciousness adumbrated by Wordsworth had, by Middleton's time, come into its own. Besides Joyce and George Moore (in several stories of *The Untilled Field*), one thinks immediately of Kenneth Grahame, whose stories of bright, sensitive children appeared in the nineties—several of them in that bastion of decadence, the *Yellow Book.* And of Barrie, whose *Peter Pan* Middleton found a "masterpiece," the "tragedy . . . of the relationship between children and their parents . . . showing the effect of the widening experience of children as they grow up, both on the children themselves and on their parents (**The Pantomime Man**). Above all one thinks of Kipling, several of whose early stories of children seem to have inspired Middleton. Walter de la Mare's fiction continues the emphasis on child protagonists, though in a decidedly perverse and morbid strain.

An interesting corollary of the child-as-artist theme in Middleton is that of the grownup friend-to-children, always a story-teller or poet. When he appears in either the essays or stories, he is considered by the other grownups to be insane. The prime manifestation of his madness is that he has retained the freshness of the child's vision into adulthood. In one story, **"Children of the Moon,"** the lunatic friend is apprehended by his worried keeper after a pleasant evening meeting in the forest with two children. One is a boy in whom the supposed madman sees an incipient poet, the other a rich girl who, though she loves the boy's beauty and strength, will surely become a Woman. To Middleton, it is clear Woman may be an inspiration to the poet, but no poet herself, or even, in her deepest being, truly sympathetic to poetry. She is antithetical to the madman; where he remains spiritually a child, the little girl is already spiritually adult.

Middleton's stories are his most original and authentic art, and on them his claim to any but purely historical interest must rest. In them, the child-protagonist plays a very large part. Along with de la Mare, Kipling, and Joyce, Middleton was among the first to experiment with a young child's point of view, and though he was incapable of the penetration that produced Baby Stephen Dedalus, he used very young children as centers of narration in two stories written nearly a decade before the *Portrait* appeared.

Interestingly, Middleton set aside his propensity to idealize children when trying to create their point of view. In three stories, two of them among his finest, Middleton also abandoned the upper middle class milieu in which the autobiographical stories and essays take place, to exploit the matter and to some extent the manner of naturalism in order more clearly to show the bewilderment of the child in a world he assuredly never made, and from which he tries to escape through fantasy.

The story that is most experimental is finally least successful, perhaps because Middleton deviates from his obsessive tenor to explore his characteristic vehicle. Instead of the inability of the society to understand the artist, he writes of the inability of adults to understand and communicate with children. In **"A Tragedy in Little,"** a small boy observes, but does not understand, what is happening when his father's embezzlement of post office money leads to discovery, remorse, and arrest. The first scene has the boy watching from the parlor window as the mother, gardening, receives the news from her husband, whose grimaces the child regards as funny.

> . . . Jack made haste to laugh aloud in the empty room, because he knew that he was good at seeing his father's jokes. Indeed it was a funny thing that father should come home early from work and make faces at mother from the road. Mother, too, was willing to join in the fun, for she knelt down among the wet flowers, and as her head dropped lower and lower it looked, for one ecstatic moment, as though she were going to turn head over heels.

Though the boy is said to cry several times, his grief does not dispel his idea that everything is part of the new game. He wishes to laugh at his mother's absentmindedness, and at the noisily exaggerated weeping of a neighbor. When the father returns home after temporary flight, the boy acts as usual and is upset to see his father cry: "Father, the man of all jokes, the man of whom burglars were afraid and compared with whom all other little boys' fathers were as dirt, was crying like a little girl."

The most effective representation of the child's difficulty is the scene in which the father explains what he has done and what the consequences will be.

> When Jack woke up the next morning he found that the room was full of sunshine, and that father was standing at the end of the bed. The moment Jack opened his eyes, he began telling him something in a serious voice, which was alone sufficient to prevent Jack from understanding what he said. . . . Father's body neatly fitted the square of the window, and the sunbeams shone all round it and made it look splendid. . . . Every now and then father stopped to ask him if he understood, and he said he did, hoping to find out what it was all about later on. It seemed, however, that father was not going to the post-office any more, and this caused Jack to picture a series of delightfully amusing days. . . .

When the father is taken away, the boy falls into the spirit of this new game by suggesting to his mother that they help the father escape from prison.

It is not quite clear what Middleton intends in **"A Tragedy in Little."** As a technical exercise it is interesting but erratic. Though the boy is said to go to school, he seems very immature emotionally, sometimes quite babylike. His weeping seems to mean nothing to him, and while he understands almost nothing of what is going on, he asks no questions. Whether the reader, like the boy, is to take the thing as a joke or game, it is difficult to say. Since the

mother and father are such flat figures to the boy himself, as, one suspects, mothers and fathers often are to small children, the reader has little sympathy for them. The lack of developed motivation and individualization in Middleton's children is also characteristic of Walter de la Mare's; the effect is altogether different from Kipling's or Katherine Mansfield's writing about children, in which the imaginative projection of self into the child-character is much more complete, and thematic development grows out of, instead of being limited by, the image in which it is embodied. Middleton's insight that a child is likely to consider all adult behavior play, like his own, is true only up to a point. Even tiny children respond deeply to trouble or grief in their parents, though they may be easily distracted by a change of tone or scene. Middleton's boy seems mentally—or emotionally—defective.

A finer story is **"The Bird in the Garden,"** in which a boy, Toby, retreats from the brutality of his parents' world into the vague, half-real world of his probably senile Uncle John. Here the abnormality of Toby's mental processes seems a legitimate response to his environment, and his consciousness becomes the dramatic arena for the death struggle of beauty and goodness against ugliness and evil. Basically naturalistic in subject matter, the story is one of Middleton's most striking; in it his sense of the tensions between beauty and its opposite are realized powerfully and without the sentimentality that so often threatens to engulf his treatment of his obsessive theme. Middleton's manipulation of impressionist techniques in **"The Bird in the Garden"** is in advance of the literary fashion of his time, particularly in the rendering of weird visual effects that accompany Toby's fevered delirium. Unlike naturalistic rendering of settings, Middleton's descriptions are relatively spare, limited to and colored by what his centers of narration actually register from their environment. In Toby's case, the attention to realistic detail is minimal, as the mind tries to save itself from its surroundings. Of Toby's Uncle John we learn only that he is "a queer one"; of the parents and the other man, Mr. Hearn, who inhabits the basement flat, we see only the boy's impression: "dark people . . . who were apt to kick if they found you in their way, and who never laughed except at nights, and then they laughed too loudly."

When another woman comes to live in the cellar, the reader assumes it is Mr. Hearn's mistress, but in Toby's mind she is "not a dark person, but a person you could see and speak to." When he is ill, she calls him "Sonny" and tells him her name is "Mummie"; soon she, too, is cast aside with Toby, his baby sister, and Uncle John, whose pension keeps the entire ménage. Together these four await the advent of an apocalyptic bird, foretold by the uncle, "who would one day come flying through the trees—a bird of all colours, ugly and beautiful, with a harsh sweet voice." The bird's coming will herald "the end of everything."

Structurally the story is very compact. In the usual sense, there are no direct scenes, yet the dramatized narrative is presented so that the effect of actual scene is achieved, all as it passes through the screen of the child's consciousness. The narrative is organized about the image of the "garden," Uncle John's collection of boxed and tinned green plants, which he hangs from the grating that is the only source of air and light to the basement, "so that the room itself obtained very little light indeed, but there was always a nice bright green place for the people sitting in it to look at." It is to this garden that the bird will come, and when, after a particularly violent night, Uncle John and Toby find a green caterpillar, they regard it as a portent. While Toby is ill and delirious, the "garden" seems to him a forest, where he can "slip out of [Uncle John's] arms and walk among the trees and plants."

> And the place would grow bigger and bigger until it was all the world, and Toby would lose himself amongst the tangle of trees and flowers and creepers. He would see butterflies there and tame animals, and the sky was full of birds of all colours, ugly and beautiful; but he knew that none of these was the bird, because their voices were only sweet.

Recovering from his fever, Toby sees something quite different from what he has seen before: "He found himself on a heap of rags in a large cellar which depended for its light on a grating let into the pavement of the street above. On the stone floor of the area and swinging from the grating were a few sickly, grimy plants in pots."

He witnesses his mother's abuse of "Mummie." Then, when one of the men strikes the passive woman, "the old man" threatens him and is struck dead with a chair.

> Then it seemed to Toby that through the forest there came flying, with a harsh sweet voice and a tumult of wings, a bird of all colours, ugly and beautiful, and he knew, though later there might be people to tell him otherwise, that that was the end of everything.

The seeming paradox of the bird, with its harsh, sweet voice, ugly and beautiful, adequately expresses Toby's responses to life; he longs for the sweetness and beauty, yet he is not so foolish as to suppose these can come without harshness and ugliness. Still, the bird is a transcendent figure, and its coming frees Toby from the horrors of his life in reality.

"The Bird in the Garden" is one of Middleton's most successful stories because he allows his materials to find their own true resolution, rather than contriving them into allegorical form, as he does in a number of others. Even in the allegorical stories, however, an occasional situation will rise above its moral lesson. In the pretentiously titled but touching **"Fate and the Artist,"** it is the fine image of the multicolored, iridescent fish, an emblem of a slum boy's artistry as a storyteller among his fellows, that lifts the story above its didactic intent and brings it to life. In a rooftop water tank, the frail, imaginative George perceives "a spendid fish" that talks to him and appears in his dreams. A sceptical bully calls George a liar and discredits him with the other children, but when a long dry spell empties the tank, the realist sees for himself "in a shallow pool of sooty water . . . a large fish, dead, but still gleaming with rainbow colors." Unfortunately, George has also succumbed (to an illness) and does not enjoy his triumph over the unbelievers. As in **"The Bird in the Garden,"**

Middleton has used the slum setting to insist, through its powerful contrasts, on the validity of his theme.

"Fate and the Artist" is Middleton's most successful allegory of the artist's life, with one exception: the brief, bittersweet anecdote, **"The Conjuror,"** in which a less than mediocre sleight-of-hand artist in a London music hall announces that he will make his wife disappear. She does, he is a tremendous hit, and gets a year's contract on the spot. The catch is that he cannot find his wife. After searching for her at home he returns to the theater hoping for some sign or clue:

> When he was there on the stage the conjuror leaned forward suddenly and his face was filled with a wistful eagerness.
>
> "Molly!" he called, "Molly!"
>
> But the empty theatre gave him nothing but echoes in reply.

That is all; no explanations, no surmises, just the event itself, and the artist must live with his handiwork, his wish for success come horribly true. Middleton's method in **"The Conjuror,"** as in his other fantastic stories, is simply to present the possible dramatized as the actual. In this case, he succeeds; the story is poignant, but also in its particulars very funny.

The artist-versus-society motif is implicit in most of Middleton's stories of children; in them, though the children dream and fantasize, their actions and environments are for the most part realistic. In a large number of his stories with grownup protagonists, as in **"The Conjuror,"** the extra- or supernatural intrudes itself. Here again, Middleton reflects a definite vogue in English short fiction of his era (and after, as witness the fantasies of the later Kipling, of Lawrence, and A. E. Coppard, as well as the aura of extra-natural occurrences hovering about so many of Elizabeth Bowen's protagonists). Besides the theme of the embattled sensitive personality and the emphasis on a beautiful style, what Forster's stories have in common with Middleton's, what may indeed have been the element that appealed in both writers to Miss Bowen, is this element of fantasy, particularly the fantasy that projects a fear or wish of the lonely or oppressed mind.

In *The Cave and the Mountain*, Wilfred Stone has demonstrated how Forster worked out personal problems, ideological and emotional, through the acceptably formalized figures and situations of his literary fantasies. Middleton's fantasies, contemporaneous with Forster's, comprise slightly less than half the stories in *The Ghost Ship*: they were not so successfully therapeutic, if indeed they were intended to be. Middleton's characters do not transcend their situations, they succumb to them. Besides the wry horror of **"The Conjuror,"** **"The Coffin Merchant"** must be numbered among Middleton's best fantasies; it is even more macabre than the former. **"The Coffin Merchant"** is a Wellsian story about a man who receives a handbill advising him he will need a coffin in the near future, then dies suddenly after ordering one. The supernatural effect is somewhat blunted by the veiled suggestion that the protagonist is either hypnotized or poisoned (or both) by the strange coffin merchant. The power of the story derives from its simplicity of outline and the vivid representation of the settings and the two characters—the coffin merchant and his customer, or victim. A psychological interpretation of these two stories, however, suggests a strong impulse toward self-destruction, a Freudian death wish barely hidden by the inventiveness. As in the similarly morbid fantasies of Kipling ("At the End of the Passage," "The Phantom Rickshaw," or "The Wish House," for example) or of Wells ("The Door in the Wall," "The Country of the Blind"), the dark side of the unconscious makes its way to the surface as a literal impossibility that we sense to be deeply true. In one story, however, **"The Ghost Ship,"** Middleton suffused his darkness with a light that drains away nearly all its threat, making the world of death a vigorous, free, and joyous extension of living.

While **"The Bird in the Garden," "Fate and the Artist," "The Conjuror"** and **"The Coffin Merchant"** represent Middleton's most typical themes and techniques in their most interesting realizations, they take second place, finally, to his one real masterpiece. In **"The Ghost Ship"** Middleton was able to free himself almost totally from his obsession with the plight of the artist in order actually to be an artist of the kind he himself valued most. Here, the supernatural is presented as a normal and happy extension of the natural, and all the finest qualities of Middleton's writing coalesce in a high-spirited, even farcical ghost story: his "poetic" prose, his good ear for dialect, his eye for impressionist detail, and his fey, slightly morbid inventiveness. **"The Ghost Ship"** belongs to the tradition of the tall tale as well as that of the ghost story; its narrator spins his yarn with tongue-in-cheek exuberance. Only extensive quotation can possibly represent the charm and flavor of this delightful story; samples with summary will have to suffice here:

> Fairfield is a little village lying near the Portsmouth Road about half-way between London and the sea. Strangers who find it by accident now and then, call it a pretty, old-fashioned place; we who live in it and call it home don't find anything very pretty about it, but we should be sorry to live anywhere else. Our minds have taken the shape of the inn and the church and the green, I suppose. . . . Doctor says that when he goes to London his mind is bruised with the weight of the houses, and he was a Cockney born.

The narrator's story concerns the ghost ship that during a spring storm blows inland from Portsmouth and comes to rest in the tavernkeeper's turnip field. When after a time the ghosts on the ship upset the town by making the local ghosts drunk on ghost rum, the narrator and the parson go aboard the ship—which in spite of being a spirit vessel, is quite solid—to remonstrate with the captain. The narrator, given some spirits himself, is not surprised to see, through the bay window in the captain's cabin, "fishes swimming to and fro over landlord's turnips. . . . But even then I thought it was queer when I saw a drowned sailor float by in the thin air with his hair and beard all full of bubbles."

In a second storm, the night following that visit to the ship, the narrator and the tavern-keeper look out to see the ghost ship's departure:

> over our heads, sailing very comfortably through the windy stars, was the ship that had passed the summer in landlord's field. Her portholes and her bay-window were blazing with lights, and there was a noise of singing and fiddling on her decks. "He's gone," shouted the landlord above the storm, "and he's taken half the village with him."

The half the town taken by the ghost ship is the population of young male ghosts, and a half-witted live boy who returns two years later dressed as a pirate and tattooed so that "even his face looked like a girl's sampler. . . ."

> The worst of it was that he had come back as softheaded as he went, and try as we might we couldn't get anything reasonable out of him. . . . One silly tale he had that he kept on drifting back to. . . . "We was at anchor," he would say, "off an island called the Basket of Flowers, and the sailors had caught a lot of parrots and we were teaching them to swear. Up and down the decks, up and down the decks, and the language they used was dreadful. Then we looked up and saw the masts of the Spanish ship outside the harbour. Outside the harbour they were, so we threw the parrots into the sea and sailed out to fight. And all the parrots were drowned in the sea and the language they used was dreadful." That's the sort of boy he was, nothing but silly talk of parrots when we asked him about the fighting. And we never had a chance of teaching him better, for two days after he ran away again, and hasn't been seen since.

Anything much farther from the main stream of the modern short story is difficult to conceive, yet in its lovely nonsense **"The Ghost Ship"** has a timeless perfection unique in Middleton's work, and a very special place in short story literature.

It has no "theme" in the normal sense; its serious subject, death, has undergone a sea change "into something rich and strange" through the agency of wish-fulfilling fantasy. That it was Middleton's personal fantasy of rebellious freedom is suggested by a passage from an essay in *Monologues*:

> I have an ancestor, so runs the dearest of my family traditions, who was hanged as a pirate at Port Royal. How much of that priceless piratical blood of the centuries may have transmitted to me I do not know, but if I were his very reincarnation I could hardly hoist the Jolly Roger in an age that . . . does not believe in pirates.

In the first piece in his autobiographical collection, *The Day Before Yesterday,* an essay entitled **"An Enchanted Place,"** Middleton speaks explicitly of the fascination of the sea as a *Lebensraum* of the imagination:

> sooner or later our dreams always returned to the sea . . . that sea on whose foam there open magic casements, and by whose crimson tide the ships of Captain Avery and Captain Bar-

tholemew Roberts keep faithful tryst with the *Flying Dutchman.*

The enchanted place itself was simply a passage under the eaves that Middleton and his sister imagined into a pirate ship for many playtime voyages, and it is pleasant to think of **"The Ghost Ship"** as Middleton's grownup tribute to this most real part of his childhood. It was, inevitably too, an escape from the world he found increasingly intolerable, mainly, it would seem, because of the great demands he put upon the world for recognition not only of his own talent, but of aesthetic and imaginative values generally. Although the narrator of **"The Ghost Ship"** remains at home among the turnips, one mad boy goes out upon the sea, making the exchange of life for death, of reality for the world of the imagination, "not knowing any better." Like the grown but "defective" children's friend of several of the other stories and essays, the mad boy seems a projection of an important part of Middleton's self.

Middleton's experiments with the child's point of view, his beautiful prose, and his presentation, in a few stories, of the naturalist situation rendered through impressionist narration warrant his place in any historical consideration of the English short story. Whatever influence he may have had on Elizabeth Bowen and her contemporaries no doubt derives from these experiments. His greatest contribution to the genre, however, is a monument to the living imagination: **"The Ghost Ship"** itself.

FURTHER READING

Biography

Savage, Henry. "Richard Middleton: 1882-1911." *The English Review* XI (April-July, 1912): 551-55.

Recollections of Middleton by the friend who collected his works for posthumous publication.

———. *Richard Middleton, The Man and His Work.* Port Washington, N.Y.: Kennikat Press, 1972, 209 p.

Primary source of biographical information about Richard Middleton.

Criticism

Gawsworth, John. Foreword to *The Pantomime Man,* by Richard Middleton. London: Rich and Cowan Ltd., 1933, pp. vii-xiv.

Sympathetic assessment of Middleton and his work.

Starrett, Vincent. "Two Suicides." In his *Buried Caesars: Essays in Literary Appreciation,* pp. 133-145. Chicago: Covici-McGee Co., 1923.

Comparision of the lives, deaths, and literary achievements of Hubert Crackanthorpe and Richard Middleton.

Lynn Riggs

1899-1954

(Full name Rolla or Rollie Lynn Riggs) American playwright and poet.

INTRODUCTION

The author of twenty-eight plays, Riggs is best known for *Green Grow the Lilacs*, upon which the popular Rodgers and Hammerstein musical *Oklahoma!* is based. Set in Oklahoma Indian Territory during the early 1900s, Riggs's plays often depict the struggle of pioneers and Native Americans to survive as they transform a rugged natural environment into a modern municipality with the hope of achieving statehood.

Biographical Information

Riggs was born in the Cherokee Nation of Indian Territory near what is now Claremore, Oklahoma. His father was a cattleman and his mother was one-eighth Cherokee. His mother developed typhoid fever and died in 1902, and Riggs's father remarried six months later. Riggs's family never supported his interest in music and writing, and as a child he was ill-treated by his stepmother. As an adolescent Riggs acted in school plays, played guitar and sang for his friends, and gave literary readings at school. Riggs graduated in 1917 from the Eastern University Preparatory School in Claremore, and entered the University of Oklahoma in 1920. In 1923, during his senior year, Riggs exhibited signs of tuberculosis and was sent to Santa Fe, New Mexico, to convalesce. It was in Santa Fe that Riggs began writing numerous plays and poems. Gaining recognition as an accomplished playwright during the 1930s and 1940s, Riggs became popular within the social circles of American theater and film, counting actresses Bette Davis, Joan Crawford, and Jean Muir among his friends. Riggs died after a long struggle with cancer at New York City's Memorial Hospital in 1954.

Major Works

As a result of the abuse he suffered throughout his childhood, Riggs's poems and plays often contain themes of betrayal by women, youth rebellion, and loss of innocence. *Big Lake: A Tragedy in Two Parts*, the first of Riggs's plays produced in New York, depicts the trials faced by Betty and Lloyd, two teenagers who, after wandering away from a school picnic, become victims of a sinister older couple in whose cabin they seek shelter. *The Cherokee Night* deals with the problems faced by people of mixed Cherokee and white heritage, particularly the difficulties associated with maintaining tribal identities in white society. Riggs's best-known play, *Green Grow the Lilacs*, is set in the Indian Territory seven years before Oklahoma achieved statehood in 1907, and is primarily concerned with the love re-

lationship between a beautiful local woman, Laurie, and a dynamic cowboy named Curly. In his preface to *Green Grow the Lilacs*, Riggs stated that his intention in writing the play was to "recapture in a kind of nostalgic glow . . . the great range of mood which characterized the old folk songs and ballads I used to hear in my Oklahoma childhood—their quaintness, their sadness, their robustness, their simplicity, their hearty or bawdy humors, their sentimentalities, their melodrama, their touching sweetness."

Critical Reception

Critical reaction to Riggs's plays has been mixed. While some reviewers have described his treatment of such serious topics as brutality in his dramas as exaggerated and melodramatic, others have lauded his accuracy in depicting the realities of living in Indian territory and his use of regional language. Phyllis Cole Braunlich, who has written extensively on Riggs's works, has stated: "Believing that drama is 'interaction between people' and that character is destiny, [Riggs] wrote from emotion and intuition, making no attempt to write the 'traditional Western.' His plays are satisfying drama, sometimes stark, usually realistic, sometimes rich with color and pageantry, and certainly of enduring interest. In his Oklahoma plays one walks into the light of an age that has passed and there experiences the aura, mood, and folkways of times and places as authentic as memoirs."

PRINCIPAL WORKS

Knives from Syria   (drama)   1925
Big Lake   (drama)   1927
The Domino Parlor   (drama)   1928; revised version published as *Hang on to Love*, 1946
Rancor   (drama)   1928
Reckless   (drama)   [first publication]   1928
The Iron Dish   (poetry)   1930
A Lantern to See By   (drama)   1930
Roadside   (drama)   1930; later produced as *Borned in Texas*, 1945
Green Grow the Lilacs   (drama)   1931
Sump'n Like Wings   (drama)   1931
The Cherokee Night   (drama)   1932
The Son of Perdition   (drama)   1933; adapted from the novel *The Son of Perdition*, by James Gould Cozzens
The Lonesome West   (drama)   1936
Russet Mantle   (drama)   1936
The Hunger I Got   (drama)   [first publication]   1939
A World Elsewhere   (drama)   1940
The Cream in the Well   (drama)   1941
The Dark Encounter   (drama)   [first publication]   1947
Laughter from a Cloud   (drama)   1947
The Year of Pilár   (drama)   [first publication]   1947
All the Way Home   (drama)   1948
Out of Dust   (drama)   1949
Toward the Western Sky   (drama)   1951
This Book, This Hill, These People: Poems by Lynn Riggs (poetry)   1982

CRITICISM

Stanley Vestal   (essay date 1929)

SOURCE: "Lynn Riggs: Poet and Dramatist," in *Southwest Review*, Vol. 15, No. 1, Autumn, 1929, pp. 64-71.

[*In the following essay, Vestal assesses Riggs's works through 1929.*]

It has been said that all good literature—which may be interpreted to include literary drama—is in the best sense provincial. Certainly the dramas of Lynn Riggs smack of the soil where he was born and bred with an intimacy and intensity which might do credit to Thomas Hardy or some other literary lover of an English village. In this, the work of Mr. Riggs is certainly in the best tradition of English literature. For as a matter of fact the Englishman, though he may live in the ends of the earth, still thinks of his county and the immediate vicinity of his English home as his

real country. It is upon this that his thought and feeling rest and from this that his patriotism, if any, grows. One recalls an Englishman who exclaimed in amazement to an American patriot, "How can you pretend to love a country as big as the United States? Why, you haven't seen half of it!"

Mr. Riggs has spent and still spends a great deal of time in places far removed from his home town, and there are suggestions in his work at times that he would be glad to escape from the memory of it; yet the persistence with which he chooses all his themes from the life of that community, the consistency with which he lays all his scenes in the region where he was reared, are far more convincing than any superficial distaste in the man that he is in fact deeply rooted in that soil, that region. I submit that one may have a strong family feeling without spending one's days and nights in the company of one's relatives. In my opinion there is not a writer in the Southwest whose work is more deeply rooted in his native soil. . . .

Mr. Riggs was born and bred in [Oklahoma's] old Indian Territory. The contrast of his attitude toward the pioneer with that of one like myself who was reared on the west side of the state is significant of the differences which mark the two regions. Of course the old life of these two sections has been overlaid long since by the influx of a large population attracted here by the vast natural resources of the new state. The distinction is therefore largely a historical one, and no doubt must not be pushed too far; but for the understanding of Mr. Riggs' work it must not be forgotten. The region he knows is one where life has in a measure stood still, the backwoods life of small farmers and the small towns.

As Mr. Riggs sees these people, they are not romantic figures of the frontier, but baffled, discontented folk struggling against hard conditions in a harsh environment. He insists that he has not falsified the picture.

In his earlier work he concerned himself chiefly with the problems of the adolescent in such crushing surroundings: notably in his **Big Lake** he has produced a poignant tragedy at once lyrical and dramatic, full of sincerity and written with a keen sense of the poetic beauty of folk speech. Folk speech has had a great vogue in American literature in the last few years, and I am not unacquainted with the sources of much of this sort of writing. I venture to say, however, that no one has been more meticulously careful to reproduce precisely the actual rhythm and vocabulary of a specific community than has Mr. Riggs. Too often the work of writers in this medium betrays a merely literary interest; too often the speech is false. Indeed, only recently I was startled to discover in a single paragraph of a novel of one of our most celebrated folk writers three lines from a poem by Isabel Campbell, obviously lifted from *Poetry* and offered to the public as the speech of mountaineers! There is nothing of this sort of trickery in the work of Lynn Riggs. He is extraordinarily careful, even to the extent of distinguishing between the pronunciations of common words as given by different characters in the same play.

I have said that his early work deals with the problems of

adolescents in a harsh backwoods environment. Quite rightly he presents these problems from the adolescent's point of view, and the result so considered is effective and convincing, as all competent critics agree. To the mature and worldly mind, however, this method has the disadvantage that it creates a feeling of unreality almost amounting to fantasy. Yet when one scrutinizes the details of his plays, one is forced to admit that there is no falsity in incident or character, and such a criticism even seems rather absurd. Nevertheless, it is a distinct gain, in my opinion, that Mr. Riggs' later work largely abandons this method and presents the persons of his dramas as they seem to a more realistic and mature observer. The significance of the world, after all, in the long run must be the significance it has for the more mature minds; one is gratified to find that Mr. Riggs can turn from his earlier manner to something at once more powerful and more convincing.

He does this without any sacrifice of the lyrical qualities of his earlier work and with a great gain in vitality and range. His later work is not only more vivid, but more dramatic. His roots strike deeper into his native soil, and the resulting fruit is richer and juicier to the seasoned palate. However terrible the incidents, however appalling the persons of a drama may be—and Heaven knows some of Riggs' people and events are startling in these respects—characters, after all, must be presented as people and not as bogies. The characters of the greatest dramas have always been of this sort. When one reads some authors one exclaims, "What rascals human beings are!" When one reads Shakespeare, on the contrary, one comments, "How human rascals are!" It is this point of view which clearly emerges in the latest work of this Oklahoma dramatist. He has achieved a grip on his materials which enables him, without any sacrifice of vitality or truth, to present them in a broader human and even richly comic manner. This is the mark of genuinely fine drama.

All this has been his own achievement. He has never shown the slightest desire to adjust his work to the current demands of Broadway. Time after time he has refused to alter his plays even in the slightest degree in order to placate those who might have showered rewards upon him. This integrity and sincerity, I take it, is the quality which has enabled him to develop as he has and to produce plays of such fine poetic and dramatic quality. His latest plays are not only good theater and good literature, but authentic and Southwestern to the core.

Morton Dauwen Zabel   (essay date 1930)

SOURCE: "Lynn Riggs's Poems," in *The New Republic,* Vol. LXV, No. 833, November 19, 1930, p. 25.

[*Zabel was a distinguished American poet, critic, and editor of* Poetry *magazine. The following is his positive assessment of* The Iron Dish.]

The poems in Lynn Riggs's [*The Iron Dish*] fall into two groups, one of which is concerned with "this sharp incredible beauty" of which he speaks too often, the other with "the yellow calendulas and sun-baked patios of southern California and New Mexico" which his publishers adver-

tise as his native heritage, but which he employs altogether too little. In his highly decorative celebrations of beauty, Mr. Riggs is not easy to distinguish from five or six other young poets whose shining images have soon degenerated into a kind of lyric confectionery—brilliant, polished, but devoid of tone and, despite its neat epigrams, notably weak in concepts. The values and limitations of this type of lyric have been exhibited best by George O'Neil, whose ornate manner is frequently echoed in *The Iron Dish*:

> No jonquil blade is spearing up
> Through swollen earth, no silken line
> Is laid to indicate a web,
> No mouth is moving to a sign.

The brittle stanzes follow a formula which may be fundamentally different from the lyric formula of the 90's, but which provides no surer warrant of sound poetic results. It is to Mr. Riggs's credit that he handles the method with considerable restraint and dexterity, but it is not to his credit that, in employing it, he has rejected a subject matter much closer to his sympathies and better suited to his talents.

Like other young lyrists who appeared on the scene after the wholesale exploitation of American themes a dozen years ago, he has consciously turned away here from his native environmental materials. This rejection of the largely uncritical nationalism of the earlier poets was a prudent reaction, but one wonders if the recent regional verse of Mr. Frost, Malcolm Cowley, Robert Penn Warren and Allen Tate is not a timely hint to the younger men that it will be wise to return to the material of actual environment in their poetry, and to substitute for flimsy imaginative backgrounds the solid properties of real American localities. Few of Mr. Riggs's poems employ his native Southwestern forms, colors and landscapes, but those that do are easily the most convincing and graceful essays in the volume.

Horace Gregory   (essay date 1931)

SOURCE: "Lynn Riggs as Poet," in *The Nation,* New York, Vol. CXXXII, No. 3418, January 7, 1931, p. 22.

[*Gregory was a noted American poet and critic. In the following review of* The Iron Dish, *he praises Riggs's economical use of language and clear imagery in his poetry.*]

The surfaces of Lynn Riggs's poetry are clean and cool. One derives casual pleasure from the graceful gestures of his particular lyric gift. He has, however, given us little more than his quick, intelligent grasp of external design. It is not often that we find him committing himself beyond the expression of purely decorative effects. On occasions when he does cross the lines of his self-imposed limitations he is clear and vivid. Note this brief commentary:

> We will need even these stumps of cedar,
> The harsh fruit of the land.
> Our thirst will have to be slaked, if at all, by this thin
> Water on the sand.
> If we have demanded this corrosive season
> Of drought, if we have bent

Backward from the plow, asking
Even less than is sent,
Surely we may be no bitterer
Than the shrunk grape
Clinging to the wasted stem
It cannot escape.

The mood of resignation indicated throughout the volume is shown here in its last analysis and with quiet distinction. The counterpoint to this mood is a delight in sharp, hard sunlight such as may be found upon "a pink dress, a blue wagon . . . in the road . . ." all expressed in the simplest of terms and with potentialities for precision. Perhaps it is irrelevant to wish that Mr. Riggs had combined his knowledge of American Southwestern speech displayed in **Roadside** with the formal economy that distinguishes the poems in **The Iron Dish.** He has made the poet and the dramatist two distinct and separate personalities. An indication of what may be accomplished in the fusion of the two is shown in a poem called **"Santo Domingo Corn Dance."** The poem is a neat and highly original interpretation of an Indian motif. Here is a selection that illustrates Mr. Riggs's ability in handling the theme:

The Song of the Bodies

I am
Naked before
You, High One—look! Hear me!
As I stamp this ground worn smooth
By feet.
Not as
A supplicant
I shake the doors of earth—
Let the green corn spring to meet
My tread!

Mr. Riggs's promise seems to lie in a direction away from the florid and strikingly poetic phrase; it finds its best expression in the clean-cut image and in an austere economy of words.

Mark Van Doren (essay date 1931)

SOURCE: "Oklahoma and the Riviera," in *The Nation*, New York, Vol. CXXXII, No. 3423, February 11, 1931, pp. 164-65.

[*Van Doren was a highly respected and prolific American poet, novelist, short story writer, playwright, editor, and critic. In the following review of* Green Grow the Lilacs, *he asserts that the play's predictability and lack of plot development allow the audience to focus on Riggs's use of the dialect of Oklahoma.*]

Much has been made of the novelty which Lynn Riggs slipped into Broadway through one of its many side doors when the Theater Guild last week put on his Indian Territory folk-play, **Green Grow the Lilacs.** . . . It was indeed a novelty, but I suspect that the discussion of it has for the most part lacked the proper emphasis. There has been a tendency, for instance, to say that Mr. Riggs with one puff blew artifice out of the theater, replacing it with the strong, free, natural air of life as it is lived, or was lived, in one very real portion of this inhabited continent. If there was something naive and undramatic about the

piece, that didn't at all matter—in fact, it made it what it was, and stood for nothing less than a guaranty of the author's sincerity, and if his desire to bring a full-bodied population into the region of thin wings.

But **Green Grow the Lilacs** was packed with devices that are very old on this or any other stage; it thronged with easily recognizable properties; it was one of the least natural pieces imaginable. The hero, for instance, was a cowboy—and might not one have expected that he would be fine and hearty, rough but good, with a grand flow of words on every occasion except that of his wooing, when of course he would be stricken dumb? Might not one have foreseen, given as setting an Oklahoma farmhouse, the presence there of somebody's old aunt, a woman with a kind and knowing heart but with a pretty tart tongue? Couldn't one have looked forward to seeing a lovely, timid heroine threatened by a dark, designing villain with a dirty mind—a hired man, perhaps? What would be surprising about the arrival of a Jewish peddler with a derby on his ears and with a pack of trinkets at his feet which he ges-

---

Lynn Riggs on being a playwright:

I honestly haven't any theories, any very definite aims (except to be a good dramatist), and I don't know any rules. All I am sure of is this: Drama to me, in full, is simply the effect of person upon person. Put two people in a room, and there's drama. . . . No one could be more surprised than I at some of their incalculable actions. . . . I feel almost that all I know about people I learned from writing plays. For once having started a scene between living people, the dramatist, it seems to me, must step aside, self-abnegating whether he will or no, and listen to his creations.

You know yourself how much concerned I am about poetry, and the rhythms of speech. That's the reason I continue to write about Oklahoma people, and especially backwoods or unlettered people. Or *part* of the reason, at least—for I find it difficult to give up using that flavorous, that lustrous imagery, that beautiful rhythmic utterance. The main reason, of course, is that I know more about the people I knew in childhood and youth than any others. But it so happens that I knew mostly the dark ones, the unprivileged ones, the ones with the most desolate fields, the most dismal skies. And so it isn't surprising that my plays concern themselves with poor farmers, forlorn wives, tortured youth, plow hands, peddlers, criminals, slaveys—with all the range of folk victimized by brutality, ignorance, superstition, and dread. And will it sound like an affectation (it most surely is not) if I say that I wanted to give voice and a dignified existence to people who found themselves, most pitiably, without a voice, when there was so much to be cried out against?

Lynn Riggs, in a letter to Walter S. Campbell, 13 March 1929, excerpted in Haunted By Home: The Life and Letters of Lynn Riggs, *by Phyllis Cole Braunlich, 1988.*

ticulatingly recommended? Might there not also be a fat, ridiculous neighbor girl whose gaucherie would contrast with the rather miraculous grace of the heroine, though both were farmer misses? And wouldn't such a contrast make a pleasant parallel to the contrast already established between the sunny-hearted cowboy and the dark-minded hired man? Nor would a rustic dance be out of order, or a set of local songs.

Of such things was Mr. Riggs's piece composed. Which is not saying at all that it was anything less than it should be. It should have been, and decidedly was, a play that could be thoroughly enjoyed in the theater. The theater is not an exhibit hall for nature, it is hardly convertible into a museum of ethnology. Mr. Riggs must have known very well what he was about when he refrained from taxing the powers of his audience's attention in the mere matter of plot. He made his story conventional so that we could be free to listen to his language. That was his novelty, and that deserves the praise. I haven't the slightest idea whether the speeches he put into his people's mouths were authentic or not, nor do I care; but I know that they were good to hear—rich, full, and carefully flavored. After the first few minutes, in which they seemed a bit forced, we became accustomed to them and soon got to listening for only them. It is really an event on Broadway when the audience grows interested in the language of a play. In that sense *Green Grow the Lilacs* was a triumph, and an important one. . . .

J. Brooks Atkinson   (essay date 1932)

SOURCE: "Riggs Worships Great Spirit," in *The New York Times,* June 21, 1932, p. 19.

[*As drama critic for* The New York Times *from 1925 to 1960, Atkinson was one of the most influential reviewers in America. In the following mixed review of* The Cherokee Night, *he praises the play's universal themes and Riggs's ability to express the desperation and confusion felt by his characters.*]

From *Green Grow the Lilacs* . . . Lynn Riggs has passed bravely on to *The Cherokee Night.* . . . Although it is a perplexing drama, which holds the conventional theatre forms in fine contempt, it has an exaltation of spirit that is honest, solid and moving, and this footloose department feels well repaid for the journey involved in seeing it.

For it is Mr. Riggs's thesis that the Cherokee blood plagues those who inherit it. In a phantasmagoria of scenes, badly related and bewildered in their time sequence, he shows the Cherokee half-breeds and quarter-breeds fumbling through a world to which they do not belong. Cast adrift in a white man's world, they degenerate into desperadoes and loose livers, robbers and prostitutes without losing their Cherokee pride of spirit. The full-blooded Cherokees abide by the pagan instincts of their tribe. In a society of restless bunglers, both white and red, the full-blooded Cherokees retain a laconical peace of spirit.

All this Mr. Riggs evokes in seven scenes laid in various parts of Oklahoma, which is the land he knows and loves. He leaps with baffling versatility from 1915 to 1931, back

to 1908, up to 1919; and then, taking a firm stance, he clears all hurdles back to 1895. As a result his characters are never more than fugitive shadows, and what relation they bear to the whole is something in which this column refuses to be examined.

"The intent of the play," says Mr. Riggs in a program note, "is meant to carry the play forward in space in exactly the same way as the mind—dealing with a subject—drawa out of past or future or present, impartially, the verbal or visual image which will serve best to illustrate and illumine a meaning."

Let this column state categorically that Mr. Riggs's principle is one of the worst by which a play can be written. It gives a muddled mind the authority of an artist.

But amid the sycamore trees that shade the Hedgerow Theatre and with a mill stream singing just beyond the cyclorama, you can bear with a few major infractions of the rules. For the anguished mood of *The Cherokee Night* is a purging one. . . . And before the play is well started you begin to realize that this story of a lost tribe is no isolated episode. It is the story of a world that has lost its heritage. The Cherokee tragedy is the universal complaint.

John Anderson   (essay date 1941)

SOURCE: "*Cream in the Well* Opens at the Booth: Martha Sleeper and Leif Erickson Appear in Rustic Tragedy with Oklahoma Setting," in *New York Journal-American,* January 21, 1941.

[*In the following review, Anderson offers a negative assessment of* The Cream in the Well.]

Though Lynn Riggs has brought to the theatre such mature work as *Green Grow the Lilacs* and *Russet Mantle,* his latest play . . . *The Cream in the Well,* seems to be the sophomoric tragedy about incest every fledgling playwright is supposed to get out of his system early in his career.

[*The Cream in the Well*] is a gritty and uninteresting study of abnormal passion, tritely gloomy and uninspired.

Since most of it sounds like a heavy prologue to the short final scene of death and spiritual redemption, it has the general appearance of a one-act play that has been expanded by putting long drawn out sighs between the lines.

For his scene and his people Mr. Riggs goes to the Indian Territory of his birth and shows us the family Sawters living on Big Lake, near Verdigris Switch, A. D. 1906. Things hain't a-doin' so well on the farm, what with Clabe gone off to the Navy, and poor Pa Sawters with just his own two hands, and that extra eighty acres to work.

But poor Pa don't know the half of it. It was his own daughter, Julie, who sent her brother away when she found him sobbing one day on a mossy bank by the lake because he was going to marry Opal, the girl from the other shore.

Julie says she sent him away because Opal wasn't good enough for him, and he had to see the world, but, as Mr.

Doodles Weaver says in "Meet the People," "We know, don't we."

In any case, Julie's repressed desires made her a lady hellcat and she couldn't rest until she drove Opal to suicide, married Gard Dunham, Opal's left-over husband, out of twisted revenge on her guilty love and drove him to drink. By this time the Sawters seemed nearly as depressed as I was.

Then Clabe came back. He told Julie how he had degraded his own love and proposed that they frankly accept their incestuous fate. Julie, however, said everything would be all right if she just walked out into the lake far enough, which was a good idea, only I thought Clabe should have gone wading fatally with her. Curtain.

To expand such dark and tangled passion into drama of necessary dimension and tragical release, demands, of course, great power and writing of uncommon concentration. Though Mr. Riggs is a poet there is neither much sensitiveness nor perception in the dialogue, or enough real strength in drawing the characters. He never illuminates these blasted lives with compassionate understanding, or lifts the events of the play above a humdrum and obvious level to the pitch of grieving fatefulness. . . .

Richard Lockridge   (essay date 1941)

SOURCE: *"The Cream in the Well,* Psychological Drama, Opens at the Booth," in *New York Sun,* January 21, 1941.

[*In the following review, Lockridge asserts that the plot and characters in* The Cream in the Well *lack depth, and that "instead of appearing to tell of something which had to happen, [the play] tells a mighty gloomy story that the author just thought up."*]

A dark, disturbing play by Lynn Riggs was performed with slow intensity last evening at the Booth Theater. In a world confused by external happenings, Mr. Riggs retains a probing interest in the human mind and in the long shadows cast over it by the taboos which so largely govern human life. His *The Cream in the Well* comes close to psychological tragedy, and is utterly unrelenting.

But it is, I think, only partially successful and in treating the matters of which Riggs is here writing, partial success is not enough. His story of peculiarly star-crossed lovers is steadily, grimly interesting. The form in which he has cast his play, if a long way from perfect, provides telling scenes and a reasonable intensification of mood. But if as a playwright you plan to delve into the darker recesses of the human spirit you need to be more than interesting, and more than competent.

Mr. Riggs's lovers are a brother and sister, living on a farm in the Indian Territory in 1906. The sister, tormented and bitter, is there throughout the play. Only toward the end does the brother return from wandering, drawn back by the love he fears and abhors. Only in the final moments of the play do the brother and sister face the fact of their love, made horrid to both by one of the race's oldest taboos. And they find no solution except suicide.

It is this love, for a long time hinted at and finally openly described, which is the center of Riggs's play. He is interested in it chiefly as it affects the participants. But through them, as the knowledge of it festers in them, it affects others. It leads to broken lives, to the suicide of a girl who had threatened to come between them and to the destruction of a young farmer who is undone by his love of the sister. It makes the sister a driven, haunted creature, dangerous to all about her. It makes the brother one of those mythical men—Mr. Riggs slips into routine here—who visit the more notorious sinks of iniquity to drown their bitter memories.

And it makes—well, call it an interesting play; call it minor-league O'Neill. Mr. Riggs's investigation of the psychological problems involved is no doubt exact, but it is never particularly deep. He enables you to understand Julie and Clabe, but does not make you feel with them. With the emotions thus left free, you have time to notice that the story is neatly arranged and that the situations are arbitrary. Instead of appearing to tell of something which had to happen, *The Cream in the Well* tells a mighty gloomy story that the author just thought up. It tells it too much in duologues, and rather too slowly.

Joseph Wood Krutch   (essay date 1941)

SOURCE: "Tragedy Is Not Easy," in *The Nation,* New York, Vol. 152, No. 5, February 1, 1941, pp. 136-37.

[*Krutch is widely regarded as one of America's foremost literary and drama critics. A conservative and idealistic thinker, he was a consistent proponent of human dignity and the preeminence of literary art. In the following essay, he asserts that although* The Cream in the Well *"is good it is not quite good enough to meet the requirements of the most difficult and exacting of dramatic forms."*]

Some ten years ago when Lynn Riggs's *Green Grow the Lilacs* was a current production of the Theater Guild its author was commonly set down as a more than usually promising young playwright who had chosen to cultivate the "folk play" rather than any one of the other more popular genres. Broadway has not been especially hospitable to the folk play (vide Paul Green), and despite two subsequently produced works Mr. Riggs rather fell out of sight. Now he has reappeared with an extremely ambitious and solemn piece called *The Cream in the Well.* . . . Here the time is 1906 and the scene Indian Territory—which is familiar ground for the author. But *The Cream in the Well* is not really folk drama. It is, in intention at least, high tragedy. It does not, that is to say, exist for the purpose of exhibiting the "manners" of a particular scene but for the sake of the passions portrayed, and Indian Territory in 1906 is merely a local habitation. The scene might be New York City or Singapore without essentially changing the play, and, as a matter of fact, the remoteness and relative unfamiliarity of the setting tend only to make the whole seem almost abstract.

The central character is the hellion daughter of a benevolent and hard-working farmer couple on a Cherokee allotment. Before the play begins she has already succeeded in separating her brother from his fiancée and in sending him upon an adventurous as well (one gathers) as a somewhat debauched career with the United States Navy. During the action she further succeeds, before her ultimate suicide, in driving the deserted fiancée to her death and in making a drunkard out of the weakling she herself has contemptuously consented to marry. Rather early in the play the audience has begun to realize what, it later appears, the principal parties concerned also understand, namely, that the girl is in love with her own brother and that her malice springs from conflict and frustration. In fact, near the end, the brother actually suggests that it would be better for them to yield to their impulses, that even unnatural love is less destructive than hate. But she is not able to face that possibility and prefers self-destruction instead.

Mr. Riggs writes, not only with obvious sincerity but also on a rather high level of literacy and competence. The result is that he holds the interest and commands respect. Yet it is impossible not to feel that the whole thing is somehow gratuitous, to ask what the play "means," why it was written, what it is ultimately "about." I have already said that it is not a folk play whose *raison d'être* is the presentation of a local culture. Neither is it primarily a psychological study, since the interest is not really centered in the psychological problem. And that leaves one asking for the sake of what it does exist.

Mr. Riggs, to be sure, might reply with a rhetorical question. "What," he might ask, "do *Oedipus* and *Agamemnon* mean?" "What, for that matter, did Mr. O'Neill's *Desire Under the Elms* or his *Mourning Becomes Electra* mean?" Such questions, however, suggest their own answers. Obviously it is not necessary for a play to "mean" anything in the sense in which the word is here being used, provided that the passions revealed are really convincingly intense to a superlative degree. But they must be intense and convincing for beyond anything that is necessary in another kind of play. We easily grant our cooperation to the writer who is managing to amuse us. We demand somewhat more if he is presenting an interesting thesis, if he is proposing to demonstrate some truth we want to know. But we demand most of all of the author who invites us to a high tragedy. We resist it as we resist all things which are even superficially unpleasant or painful.

What's Hecuba to us or we to Hecuba? As the tired business man says, we have troubles enough of our own. We must, if the tragedy is really to succeed, be caught up and carried away in spite of ourselves. We must find ourselves concerned whether we want to be or not, too moved to ask why we should care. And if Mr. Riggs commands respect and holds attention without quite stilling question or complaint, the reason probably is simply that though his play is good it is not quite good enough to meet the requirements of the most difficult and exacting of dramatic forms. . . .

Thomas Erhard (essay date 1970)

SOURCE: *Lynn Riggs: Southwest Playwright,* Steck-Vaughn Company, 1970, 44 p.

[*Erhard is a prolific American playwright, educator, and critic. In the following excerpt from his critical biography of Riggs, he surveys Riggs's career as a playwright.*]

Knives from Syria was staged successfully by the Santa Fe Players in 1925 and became [Riggs's] first published play in 1927. A slim one-act comedy with a deus-ex-machina ending, *Knives from Syria* was nevertheless important as a preparatory work. In the play Mrs. Buster, a widow, says her daughter (Rhodie, 18) must marry the hired man (Charley, 33). But Rhodie wants to marry an itinerant Syrian peddler. Charley, breathless, comes in one night and says someone has tried to kill him; tension builds as Charley goes off in the dark to seek his assailant. The peddler arrives, acts mysteriously, and shows off his collection of Syrian knives, "good for cutting the throats of men." Mrs. Buster, terrified, permits Rhodie to pledge her troth to the peddler. But when Charley announces that the would-be killing was just a joke by some of his friends, Mrs. Buster finds herself backed into a corner; she has given Rhodie to the peddler. The play ends with the implication that Mrs. Buster can now have Charley for herself. Everyone, presumably, will live happily ever after.

Although Riggs handles the suspense well, characterizations are thin, and the comedy is only mildly amusing. The playlet, however, shows us a genial middle-aged woman without a man, a romantic young woman, a hired man, a peddler who is both mysterious and comic, and a group of young men bent upon playing tricks in the dark. Thus one can find in this early play the seeds of *Green Grow the Lilacs.* The romantic young girl also appears later as the main character in *Roadside,* where the braggart hero reappears as a wandering Texan instead of a Syrian peddler. The play not only anticipates Riggs's best works, especially with its theme of beauty in rebellion, but it echoes earlier folk drama as well. The anthologist S. Marion Tucker reminds us that *Knives from Syria* strongly resembles John Millington Synge's *In the Shadow of the Glen.*

Encouraged by his play's success . . . Riggs began an incredibly active five-year period in which he wrote almost a dozen plays. His first full-length play was *The Primitives,* a satire on life in Santa Fe. Unhappy with it, he destroyed the script; but in 1925 he also wrote *Sump'n Like Wings* and *Big Lake,* both full-length plays. In the fall of 1926 Riggs returned to Chicago, where he almost managed to get *Knives* produced; failing, he accepted Kenneth Macgowan's invitation to come to New York, where he wrote *A Lantern To See By.* He spent the summer of 1926 on playwright Hatcher Hughes's farm in Connecticut. Producer Otto Kahn optioned *Sump'n Like Wings,* and Riggs received a $500 advance. He wrote home exultantly, "When the play opens, of course, I begin making $200 or $300 a week for as long as the play runs. . . . I am quite happy of course that at last I am to be what the world calls a success, and that I have done the thing I like best." But Kahn dropped his option, and the play was never done in New York. Again and again in the following years, Riggs thought he would have a hit in New York, only to meet disappointment. Riggs stayed solvent in 1926 by writing for the First National Motion Picture Company in New York.

Riggs did reach New York (but not Broadway) when *Big*

Lake, a poetic tragedy, was staged by George Auerbach at Richard Boleslavsky's American Laboratory Theatre on April 8, 1927. The now-renowned critic and scholar Francis Fergusson had a bit part, and Stella Adler, later one of the Group Theatre's most famous actresses, played the major role of Elly. The ALT was a highly considered semiprofessional experimental troupe, and Riggs received considerable notice. Sidney Howard, the noted realistic playwright of the 1920's, offered Riggs much encouragement. Barrett Clark recommended him to the John Simon Guggenheim Foundation, and Riggs was the first Oklahoman to receive a Guggenheim Fellowship. Riggs became known as one of the most promising American playwrights, unaware that the tag would come to be more curse than blessing.

Big Lake, a simple, powerful tragedy, shows youthful sensitivity snuffed out meaninglessly by evil. In the first part, subtitled "The Woods," Betty and Lloyd, two high school students, have come out to Big Lake in rural Oklahoma before dawn in order to be alone with their romantic fancies before their class holds a breakfast picnic. Betty becomes terrified: "It's like the woods wuz waitin' . . . to git us." Betty wants to find a rowboat, to escape the terror of the woods, but Lloyd suggests instead an old cabin nearby.

In the cabin are Butch, a bootlegger who has stabbed a man; and his mistress, Elly. Butch, afraid that his victim did not die before giving evidence, tells Elly he will use the two young people for an alibi. But Elly is strongly moved by the innocent appearance of the young people; and when Betty and Lloyd borrow their rowboat, Elly urges Butch to save the young people: "Wuzn't you ever jist startin' life? Wuzn't you ever innocent and good . . . you cain't kill a thing like that." When the sheriff arrives, Butch shouts that the murderer has taken a girl onto the lake to rape her. The sheriff and his deputies rush out; when Elly calls Butch a beast, he replies, "Mebbe I am one . . . this place we're livin' in—what's it? It's the woods, Elly. It's the dark woods."

In the second portion of the play, subtitled "The Lake," the sheriff shoots Lloyd from the shore, and Betty falls overboard and drowns. The play ends with Elly saying slowly, "It's alwys the way . . . boats leak, guns go off . . . they's wild animals—sump'n happens, sump'n alwys happens. It cain't be helped."

The inevitability smacks of Greek tragedy; and there is rich irony in that the lake, symbol of beauty and freedom to the young people, is actually more murderous than the threatening woods. Symbolically, one theme is loss of innocence. The evil in the woods (everyday life) overtakes innocence even out on the lake (the romantic world that people would like to live in). Although melodramatic, *Big Lake* avoids excessive sentimentality. Burns Mantle, reviewing in *The New York Daily News,* said, "If you foster any belief that you are a real student of the theatre this *Big Lake* is one of the exhibits worth your study." He added, *"Big Lake* gives young Riggs a definite place among the native poets with a feeling for drama. Almost anything may come of this developing talent." Barrett H. Clark, in his 1928 *Study of the Modern American Drama,* called Eu-

gene O'Neill, Paul Green, and Riggs the equal of any of the European dramatists. And at that time Rigg's reputation rested solely on *Big Lake.*

Two months after the production, Riggs went to Yaddo, at Saratoga Springs, New York, for the summer. There he wrote his one-act play *Reckless,* which was later to become the first scene of the full-length *Roadside.* He also wrote *The Lonesome West,* an autobiographical drama which featured a domineering stepmother and three sons who try to get away from the farm. Producers praised the script, but it was not actually produced until 1936, when the Hedgerow Theatre gave it a few performances. In the fall of 1927 Riggs returned to New York City and wrote *Rancor,* the story of an ambitious woman who becomes trapped in marriage to a weak farmer in isolated rural Oklahoma. The play was produced on July 12, 1928, at Hedgerow, and was one of its more successful repertory offerings. . . .

Sump'n Like Wings is the story of Willie Baker, a beautiful young tomboy and coquette chafing under the rule of her mother, who runs the restaurant in her uncle's hotel in Claremont (Claremore). The time is 1913. Willie runs off with a married man who gets her pregnant and deserts her; and in Act Two Willie is back home again, once more enduring the restrictions set up by her mother. Frustrated, Willie runs away a second time. But again she is deserted, her baby dies, and Willie returns to a rundown rooming house of dubious reputation. Willie's uncle tries to talk her into coming home, but Willie refuses: "There's more to life than sump'n to eat and a bed, I guess . . . they's sump'n in you 'at has to be free—like a bird, or you ain't livin'." The play ends with Willie barricading her rooming-house door with chairs in order to keep the drunken males out. There is hope that Willie will finally become her own woman, but Riggs provides a superb irony: Willie, who was always locked in by her mother, now must lock herself in if she is to have any meaningful freedom. The simply plotted plays says, with some effectiveness, that people are always locked in, somehow, by someone, even if only by themselves.

Buoyed by nibbles from many producers on several plays, Riggs next wrote *A Lantern to See By* in 1928. This powerful play was also optioned for Broadway, but was dropped before rehearsals could begin. As with *Sump'n Like Wings,* it was published and later produced at the Detroit Playhouse on September 25, 1930. Broadway was not opening its doors.

A Lantern to See By is a tragedy of the old Indian Territory, near Claremore, and shows the darker side of the rural Southwest. Jodie Harmon is the sensitive oldest son in a large farm family, and he resents the way his often-drunk father brutally treats his mother. The father (John) smashes Jodie in the head with a pinch-bar and tells him that the only way anyone gets anything in life is by fighting for it. The mother dies. Jodie falls in love with the young Annie, who comes in as housekeeper, and he goes off on a road job to earn money to marry her. His father takes Annie as a mistress, however; and when Jodie returns, a play-party is in progress and Annie has just learned that John does not intend to pay wages for her varied services.

Jodie, infuriated because his own wages had been sent back to his father by his employer, responds to Annie's angered goading and kills his father with the pinch-bar. Jodie shouts, "I had to. He'd a-killed me. He's *been* a-killin' me—all my life—slow." Jodie gives himself up to the hushed guests. Despite the stark ending, a ray of hope is left open when one of the guests says Jodie will not hang but only go to jail.

Felix Sper, in his fine book on regional theatre *From Native Roots,* has noted the similarities between *Lantern* and Eugene O'Neill's *Desire Under the Elms. Lantern* has catharsis at the end and has comic relief (which O'Neill often found difficult) in the squabbling early scenes of the many brothers on the farm. Tension is maintained throughout, and the simply plotted, highly unified script moves rapidly. Further, the play attains poetic power because of its myth-like theme straight out of basic folklore: the son must kill the father in order to become a man himself. By setting the play in one of the more primitive backwaters of American civilization, Riggs achieves a folk play of no small effectiveness. Not surprisingly, however, no one in New York has ever staged the play.

The year 1928 brought two additional recognitions to Riggs. The August issue of *Poetry Magazine* printed eight of his poems, and the Guggenheim Fellowship allowed him to travel and write in Europe. He wrote a one-act play, *On a Siding,* which he later destroyed; and in late 1928 began *Green Grow the Lilacs* in Paris. Annoyed with the climate, he moved south and finished *Lilacs* on the Mediterranean coast early in 1929. While there he began *Roadside,* which he finished in New York late in 1929.

Suddenly everything seemed to fit together for Riggs, and he appeared on the verge of a spectacular writing career. He went to Hollywood in the spring of 1930 as a screenwriter for Pathe Pictures and wrote a war movie, *Beyond Victory* (starring James Gleason), one of the early talkies. Later he did the movie script for *The Siren Song.* He wrote home, "If we get a good director, I'm hoping it will be a sensation." He then summered at Provincetown, where he began writing *The Cherokee Night.* On September 25, 1930, *A Lantern to See By* opened in Detroit; on September 26, 1930, he had his first Broadway opening with *Roadside;* his book of poems, *The Iron Dish,* came off the press; and later that fall the Theatre Guild put *Green Grow the Lilacs* into rehearsal. . . .

Roadside is the most high-spirited of all Riggs's plays; and critics have remarked on its frontier humor that relates it to the folk literature of Paul Bunyan, Davy Crockett, Mike Fink, and to the writings of Mark Twain. Alan S. Downer, in his *Fifty Years of American Drama,* even says it "might be described as the great American comedy." It is both a tall tale and a takeoff on a tall tale. Riggs himself said of it, "It is a comedy about the impossible dream man has always had: complete freedom, the right to be lawless, uncircumspect, gusty and hearty, anarchic, fun loving, chicken-stealing if necessary (for where there is no ordinary morality, there is of course no crime)."

The comedy takes place in the Indian Territory, near and in Verdigris Switch, in the summer of 1905. Hannie, "a buxom girl of twenty with black-snapping eyes and a rich earthy humor," has run away from her timid farmer-husband, Buzzey, and is once again crossing the countryside with her father, Pap Rader, in his covered wagon. "Men is s' crazy," she says. "Some wants to set on a farm till they dry up and blow away—like Buzzey here. Or some wants to go streakin' across the country, hell-bent for high water—like Paw. If they was jist a half-way crazy man who liked to streak, and liked to set—*both.* A nonsensical strappin' man who had a good time settin' or streakin'—but who had a *good time.*" This man of course does turn up, in the person of Texas, who has just torn the roof off the Verdigris Switch jailhouse. "I hate rules, and I hate fences," he says, and tells his new friends that Texas was named after him. "I ain't ever been licked by mortal man. Onct a whole *crowd* of mortal men—cowpunchers—*tried* to lick me, and they was seventy-three of 'em by count, and they all had shootin' arns." This is as American as Davy Crockett and as universal as the braggart warriors in ancient classical comedy.

Hannie has a comic love duel with Texas; and, disconsolate at thinking he has lost her, Texas allows the marshal to take him back to Verdigris Switch. But in the courtroom again, when Texas realizes that Hannie does care for him, he breaks free once more in a manner long-since clichéd in Hollywood's Western films. "My, I like that feller," shouts Pap when Texas pops the marshal on the jaw and escapes.

Back at the wagon Texas tells Hannie, "We're sump'n alike . . . you're crazy and reckless and wild. You make a feller wonder big and step fur." When Hannie replies, "I'd blister you 'th my tongue ever couple of days. I'd cripple you—" Texas retorts, "I'd hate you 'f you didn't!" He and Hannie drive off with Pap. "Good-bye, you all! I bet you wish you was us!" shouts Texas, and the marshal watches with a slow, admiring grin.

S. Marion Tucker (in *Twenty-Five Modern Plays*) likens the play to a ballad: "*Roadside* is casual about exposition, about the logic of events, or about the unities. Instead, the playwright, like the ballad singer, chooses to talk most about the parts of the story that interest him—the gusty

Riggs relaxing in Spain in July, 1928, on his way to France during his Guggenheim fellowship year in Europe.

comedy of the courtroom scene, for instance, for which the well-made play could ill spare the time." Tucker adds, "The structure of *Roadside* grows out of its material; it is lanky, casual, and rich in speech and feeling, like its characters. Like them, it is earthy and elemental." Riggs conceived of the play first as a brief sketch of Hannie casting off Buzzey (the portion published as *Reckless* in 1928), and gradually built the tale into a full-length play.

Alan Downer sets *Roadside* into another extremely basic framework: the rebel against established society. He writes: "What distinguishes this play from the usual melodrama about the West is obviously the freshness and poetry of the speech, and the warm humanity of the characters." Downer adds that, even more important, the year 1905 was not the time of a free frontier. Railroads and farms were crowding out the wanderers; thus the theme was of serious importance. Downer concludes:

> *Roadside* is about liberty, the liberty of individuals, about human importance and dignity. This is a subject with which modern drama has often been preoccupied, but often in terms more didactic than dramatic. By turning to folk materials, which can be felt more than intellectually comprehended, Riggs appeals to the instinct dormant in most Americans to live close to nature. He thus states his theme by indirection, by character in action awakening the nostalgia of his audience. It is not only the marshal who grins admiringly in reply to Texas' farewell, 'Bet you wish you was us!' . . .

Theatre Arts Monthly said [*Green Grow the Lilacs*] hovered on the edge of song, and Riggs himself wrote in the preface to the printed version:

> It must be fairly obvious from seeing the play that it might have been entitled *An Old Song.* The intent has been solely to recapture in a kind of nostalgic glow (but in dramatic dialogue more than in song) the great range of mood which characterized the old folk songs and ballads I used to hear in my Oklahoma childhood—their quaintness, their sadness, their robustness, their simplicity, their hearty or bawdy humors, their sentimentalities, their melodrama, their touching sweetness. For this reason it seemed wise to throw away the conventions of ordinary theatricality—a complex plot, swift action, etc.—and try to exhibit luminously, in the simplest of stories, a wide area of mood and feeling.

Riggs also said that all his plays had a slight edge beyond realism and that he believed in the symphonic nature of a play.

Mark Van Doren, reviewing in *The Nation* (February 11, 1931) said, "It is really an event on Broadway when the audience grows interested in the language of a play. In that sense *Green Grow the Lilacs* was a triumph, and an important one." Interestingly, just before the play opened in New York Riggs had written in *The New York Evening Post* (January 24, 1931):

> The fact is that far from idealizing the poetic quality of that speech, I haven't equaled it. I have an aunt . . . who naturally speaks a much more highly charged poetic language than I can contrive to write. . . . From morning until night she will comment on the affairs of the household, on the state of the weather, on the goings-on of the neighbors, in a language that would gladden the heart of any poet who loved apt and spontaneous word-images. And this was generally true of the Oklahoma folk of thirty years ago, whom I have written about. These people talked poetry without any conscious effort to make beautiful language. . . . Because of the external poverty and sameness of their lives they felt the need of richness and variety in their thoughts. . . . I let my characters write their own speeches, the language which was familiar to my boyhood years. Whatever poetry may be found in the play is to the credit of my neighbors, not of myself.

Aunt Eller, of course, was really his Aunt Mary Riggs Brice; and Laurey was patterned on his sister, Mrs. Mattie Cundiff, the person he was closest to throughout his entire life. She was the only person to whom he could communicate his inner tensions and lonelinesses.

When we look at the script, we see that *Green Grow the Lilacs* is a natural foundation for the later *Oklahoma!* We have a gallant, romantic Western hero (Curly), a beautiful, bantering, and romantic heroine (Laurey), a comic confidante for Laurey (Aunt Eller), a melodramatic villain (Jeeter Fry), a comic supporting man (The Peddler), and extras which include a fiddler, a banjo player, cowboys, and girls. The cast of *Lilacs* already reads like that of a musical.

Set in the Indian Territory in 1900, the play actually opens with a song, as Curly comes to the farmhouse and greets Aunt Eller. Both the language of the song and Riggs's first stage direction, "It is a radiant summer morning several years ago," plus several other speeches about the beauty of the day provide the basis for Rodgers and Hammerstein's opening *Oklahoma!* number, "Oh, What a Beautiful Mornin'." Curly's first words to Aunt Eller, "I wouldn't marry you ner none of yer kinfolks . . . and you c'n tell 'em that, *all* of 'em, includin' that niece of your'n, Miss Laurey Williams," create the tone of love-duel comedy and hint of course, that Curly and Laurey *will* end up together. Laurey comes in, "Heared a voice a-talkin' rumbly," and we begin the first love duel. The device, popularized in British Restoration comedy, is still a staple of modern musical comedy. In his early plays Riggs was heavy-handed in his dialect use, although it reflected accurately the illiteracy of the Indian Territory settlers. But by now the language has mellowed in Riggs's memory, has become more poetic, and is only a step away from the lyrics of musical comedy.

Curly invites Laurey to the play-party at Old Man Peck's, but she has already promised—out of fear—to go with Jeeter. Curly then says he has hired transportation from over at Claremore to take her to the party: "A bran' new surrey with fringe on the top four inches long—and *yeller!* And two white horses a-rarin' and faunchin' . . . and this yere rig has got four fine side-curtains, case of rain. And isinglass winders to look out of! And a red and green lamp set on the dashboard, winkin' like a lightnin' bug!" The lyrics were already there for Rodgers and Hammerstein's "Surrey with the Fringe on Top."

In the second scene, in Laurey's bedroom, Riggs uses sentimentalism effectively as preparation for the finale when he has Laurey say, "If we ever had to leave this here place, Aunt Eller, I'd shore miss it. I like it. I like the thicket down by the branch whur the 'possums live, don't you? And the way we set around in the evenings in thrashin' time, a-eatin' mushmelons and singin'. . ." The Territory is idealized and softened from Riggs's earlier plays. But evil is still present, and Laurey's worry to Aunt Eller is an effective plant for later: "What if Jeeter set the house on fire. . . . Sump'n black a-pilin' up. Ever since a year ago. Sump'n boilin' up inside him—*mean.*"

Ado Annie and the Peddler now arrive, with the latter a direct descendant from Riggs's early **Knives from Syria.** Ado Annie's making up to the peddler is also an echo from **Knives.** The entire scene contains the basis for Annie's song in *Oklahoma!,* "I'm Just a Girl Who Can't Say No."

Scene Three, in the smokehouse, home of Jeeter Fry (Jud Fry in *Oklahoma!*), increases the tensions. Curly, resembling Texas in **Roadside,** tells Jeeter, "My name's Curly . . . I break broncs, mean uns. I bull-dog steers. I ain't never been licked. . . ." Curly and Jeeter play cards, and we see the dark side of Jeeter, who warns Curly to stay away from Laurey. Curly replies, "In this country, they's two things you c'n do if you're a man. Live out of doors is one. Live in a hole is the other . . . why don't you do sump'n healthy onc't in a while, 'stid of stayin' shet up here a-crawlin' and festerin'!" Curly's comments form the basis for the song, "Pore Jud Is Daid," in *Oklahoma!* Jeeter's characterization is not deep and is melodramatic. Riggs, in ominous moments in his plays, often turns to oldfashioned melodrama. But most musicals don't have time for in-depth characterization of villains, and Riggs provided a ready-made character for *Oklahoma!* The first half of the play ends ominously as the Peddler comes into the smokehouse and sells Jeeter a frogsticker to "kill a frog or a bastard" with; and, as with any good melodrama, we in the audience sense that the frogsticker will be used later.

Scene Four is the play-party at Old Man Peck's, and Riggs uses three old Territory songs to open, climax, and close the scene. He has all but written in the big "production number" of most modern musicals, and Rodgers and Hammerstein had little structural altering to do as they prepared their version twelve years later. Jeeter comes in, filled with passion for Laurey; and Riggs, who usually did not aim toward "box office," used a commercial device here: the lustful passions are put into the heart of the antagonist, and the always-outwardly-proper theatre audience can root righteously against the villain. In most of his tragedies, however, Riggs either did not realize or did not choose to acknowledge the fact that audiences embarrass easily; and when he put unusual passions and desires into the hearts of his protagonists, he made his audiences uncomfortable.

Through the play-party scene Riggs effectively juxtaposes the boisterous festivity with the undercurrent of tension between Jeeter and Laurey and Curly. Laurey accepts Curly's proposal, but Jeeter's ugly, drunken threats keep the tension strong. Rodgers and Hammerstein did improve the play-party scene, but they remained extremely faithful to Riggs and his regional background. The scene in *Oklahoma!* begins with a song, "The Farmer and the Cow Man Should Be Friends." One character says, "I'd like to say a word for the farmer; he come out West and made a lot of changes." This is countered by a rancher: "He come out West and built a lot of fences . . . right acrost our cattle ranges." The conflict was true to life in Riggs's own boyhood; this addition in the musical does not detract from the Lynn Riggs flavor.

Another addition is an interesting improvement. Rodgers and Hammerstein have people at the party bid for anonymously prepared lunch baskets. Curly and Jud, however, learn which basket is Laurey's, and they bid furiously. Although the actual contest is for a lunch basket, it really is for Laurey herself, and it adds excellent suspense. Curly's successful bid further motivates Jud in his desire for revenge.

Scene Five, the climax of **Lilacs,** begins lyrically as Curly and Laurey return home from their wedding. But they are met with the bawdy shivaree, frightening enough in itself, and then by Jeeter, who burns the haystack onto which the roisterers have pushed Curly and Laurey. Curly and Jeeter fight, and Jeeter falls on his own frogsticker and dies. Melodrama, yes; but Riggs creates a rich mood from the old-time Territory customs that build plausibly into the play's climax.

Scene Six, the finale, echoes **Roadside** in romantic heroics. Curly escapes from jail, where he is awaiting the hearing on Jeeter's death. But in this play Riggs places the escape in the final moments instead of in the first act, and he creates additional sympathy over and above the anti-law heroics with Curly's intense desire to consummate his marriage. Aunt Eller takes over the Texas role for a moment as she outtalks Old Man Peck, who has been deputized to arrest Curly. Curly is given permission to spend the night with Laurey, and indications are that he will be cleared when he reports to court in the morning.

Rodgers and Hammerstein alter *Oklahoma!* slightly at the end. Aunt Eller suggests that "any good law can be bent a little," and they hold an informal trial at once, freeing Curly immediately in order to eliminate the escape from jail. Thus the *Oklahoma!* ending is a little more clear-cut in its lightness than the almost bitter-sweet **Lilacs;** but Rodgers and Hammerstein undoubtedly wanted to build to a crescendo of exhilaration as the musical ended.

Riggs blends the outlaw-philosophy with the compromises necessary in a civilized country, and the freedom theme of **Roadside** is mellowed. In **Roadside,** Texas won his showdown with the marshal, and he continued to roam as the spirit moved him. **Lilacs,** however, shows a shift. Laurey says, "I'll stand it—if they send you to the pen fer life." Instead of the rebel Hannie, who wants to run, Laurey will stay and assume responsibility. And Curly adds, "It come to me settin' in that cell of mine. Oh, I got to be a farmer, I see that! Quit a-thinkin' about dehornin' and brandin' and th'owin' the rope, and start in to git my hands blistered a new way. Oh, things is changin' right and left . . . country a-changin', got to change with it." Riggs is saying good-bye to the old days of the Territory. Civilization has finally taken over.

One reviewer greeted *Green Grow the Lilacs* with this affirmation: "It is a folk piece of this fertile American earth . . . in these days we are grown-up enough to write, mount, and enjoy such pieces, to consider them discriminately. Our theater will not be full-rounded until it gives them just place" *(American Drama and Its Critics).* But Broadway did not give place to Lynn Riggs. He was not to attain another New York production for five more years. *Lilacs* was rumored for the Pulitzer Prize, but the award went to Susan Glaspell for *Alison's House,* the sensitive portrayal of the poet Emily Dickinson. Riggs was happy for Miss Glaspell: "I am very glad . . . for it will mean that her interest in the American theatre will receive a stimulant. . . . She has the sort of creative mind that is needed in the theatre. . . . Susan Glaspell requires this sort of encouragement to continue." Riggs, who at this time said, "It is awfully exciting to work on a play," did not receive this kind of encouragement with Broadway and its critics.

But in 1931 Riggs's future looked bright. On April 19 he had a public reading of the unfinished *The Cherokee Night* in the Carolina Playmakers' Theatre, then went to Oklahoma to soak up added background for further revisions of the play which was to become his favorite. While in Oklahoma he said about New York theatre: "Passion, honesty, truth and glamour have been lost in a straining after smartness, after the commercial thing." He then went on to Santa Fe for his first extended stay since 1925, worked further on *The Cherokee Night,* did a dramatic adaptation of James Gould Cozzens' novel *Son of Perdition,* and directed *Rancor* at the Santa Fe community theatre in December, 1931.

He finished *The Cherokee Night,* and Jasper Deeter produced it at Hedgerow on June 18, 1932, with Riggs directing. Never to be produced on Broadway, the play was done at the University of Iowa and at Northwestern, with Riggs again directing both of these; and in the summer of 1936 it was performed ten days off-Broadway at the Provincetown Theatre by a training unit of the Federal Theatre. Ironically, despite the lack of Broadway blessing, *The Cherokee Night* may, in the long run, prove to be his greatest play.

Quite different in structure from any of Riggs's other dramas, *The Cherokee Night* is virtually a series of seven one-act plays which depict the disintegration of the western branch of the Cherokee tribe. The story takes place between 1895 and 1931 in the Indian Territory and later the State of Oklahoma. The scenes are not presented chronologically, and in them we see some half a dozen characters at different ages in their lives. Despite the seeming jumble, however, the play is artistically unified and builds to a powerful finale, although Brooks Atkinson, in *The New York Times* of June 21, 1932, carped at the structure when he first saw it: " 'The intent of the play,' says Mr. Riggs in a program note, 'is meant to carry the play forward in space in exactly the same way as the mind . . .

draws out of the past or future or present, impartially, the verbal or visual image which will serve to illustrate and illuminate a meaning.' Let this column state categorically that Mr. Riggs's principle is one of the worst by which a play can be written." Even as late as the 1930's, critics demanded the comfortable, Ibsenian well-made play.

Atkinson, however, was won over by Riggs's theme. His review ended, "You begin to realize that this story of a lost tribe is no isolated episode. It is the story of a world that has lost its heritage. The Cherokee tragedy is the universal complaint." By far the most poetic of all Riggs's plays, *The Cherokee Night* says, in essence, that for an Indian to deny his "Indian-ness" is to diminish himself as a human being. It also shows the corruption of the Cherokees by both the whites and the neighboring Osage Indians, and it shows vividly and poignantly the tormented lives and prejudice that mixed-breeds face in our twentieth century Southwest.

The opening scene shows four couples, all of part-Cherokee blood, on a picnic near old Claremore Indian Mound. Old Man Talbert, the local "crazy man," appears out of the darkness and frightens them with tales of visits that the spirits of dead Cherokees have made to him on the old mound. The spirits have chanted to him, "Are you sunk already to the white man's way . . . night—*night*—has come to our people." Subsequent scenes show how the four young couples degenerate to prostitutes, criminals, informers, ne'er-do-wells, or simply people who stagnate intellectually and spiritually. The ways of the white man, even the strongly religious, corrupt; and the most terrifying scene shows one of the half-breed young men "evangelized" by a splinter group of ardent fundamentalists who end up by chaining him in their church and torturing him. The scene is among the most powerful in all of Riggs's writing and has symbolic overtones beyond its powerful realism.

When the degeneration of all the half-breeds is complete, Riggs flashes back in the final scene to an earlier day and an Indian hut on Claremore Mound. The half-breed Spench rushes in fleeing from a white posse, and old Gray-Wolf asks him why he has committed his many crimes. Spench replies, "I tried everything. Tried to farm. Too restless. Cattle herdin', ridin' fence. Sump'n always drove me on . . . sump'n inside—no rest, I don't know—bad blood. Too much Indian, they tell me," but old Gray-Wolf counters with, "Not enough Indian." The posse shoots Spench in cold blood and then warns Gray-Wolf, "You Indians must think you own things out here. This is God's country out here—and God's a white man." The dead man's woman sits by the body and mourns, as the play ends, "Sleep, rest now . . . but here's your son. In him your trouble. It goes on. In him. It ain't finished." And the audience realizes that throughout the earlier scenes they have, indeed, been seeing the trouble going on and on, and the evils brought about by prejudice and greed. The play is still highly topical; by particularizing and showing us one small corner of the old Southwest, Riggs has shown us man in all places and all ages. This powerful and meaningful play could, in today's tense times, be a smash hit in

New York if ever a farsighted producer would "discover" it. . . .

[*Russet Mantle* is a] bittersweet comedy [that] gains much from local color, being set in the portal of a ranch just outside Santa Fe, a setting that was almost home for Riggs. Four major characters face up to life in the play, and a fifth continues to hide from it. Horace and Susannah Kincaid, both about fifty and unhappy with each other, are trying to raise apples and chickens on their ranch after losing their money in the stock market crash. They host Susannah's sister, Effie, and Effie's daughter, Kay, both from Louisville. Into this household arrives the young militant poet, John Galt, seeking a job. At times the play sounds as modern as the 1960's: Horace tells John that he will soon adjust to the world, but John retorts, "The world will do a little adjusting, too . . . my generation will see to that. They were born desperate enough, and searching, and the taste of rage is in their mouths." John also adds, "How can I consider my own bread and butter important? My life is worth nothing, nothing at all, unless I'm part of the agony that's beating and tearing the world."

In the second act Susannah warns John to stay away from young Kay. Later, Horace does exactly the same. In the two conversations, both Horace and Susannah reveal the emptiness of their marriage and how they have put masks over reality. Kay overhears these speeches, and she and John are horrified: "They don't even know now what defeated them. They've lied to themselves so long."

As Act Three begins, Kay is pregnant by John. The assembled group tries to find a solution. Kay's mother, Effie, wants to return to Louisville and act as if nothing happened. She will wear the mask of conformity to the end. John, however, faces up to responsibility; and he and Kay prepare to go live in the world as it is. When they leave, Kay urges her Uncle Horace, "Imagine you're young again," and John adds, "And the world is beginning for you." The play ends with Susannah saying to Horace, "Let's try." Riggs's epigraph, from *Hamlet*, epitomizes not only the New Mexico setting but the major theme: "But look, the morn, in russet mantle clad, walks o'er the dew of yon high eastward hill." The play is one of rebirth, and is definitely part of the mainstream of social comedy in the Depression era that looked ahead to a better world.

Riggs was more at home with his comedy in *Russet Mantle* than with his serious theme. Edith Isaacs, in *Theatre Arts Monthly,* said, "You are a little ashamed not to have recognized before the full depth of Lynn Riggs's sense of humor." And *Time* said that Riggs "flabbergasted Broadway by revealing an unsuspected talent for grade A comic characterization." Stark Young spoke for the majority of critics when he said in *The New Republic,* "It breaks down in the serious-poetic speeches given to the young roles. The effect becomes sententious and in a tone false to the remainder of the play." Today the theme seems too openly expressed and too sugar-coated, but we must remember that the decade was not one of disillusion, and the postwar cynicism was still far in the future. It is to Riggs's credit that he said something meaningful in his comedy rather than merely providing frothy fun. . . .

Finished in 1938, *The Year of Pilár* is a powerful tragedy of an upper-class Yucatecan family and, through them, of their entire social group. The family deteriorates morally and is killed by the rebelling Indians, who regain some of their rightful lands from the earlier Spanish conquerors.

Riggs centers the play around Pilár, one of the daughters in the Crespo family, which has moved back from New York City to the old plantation after admitting defeat in trying to carve out a meaningful life in the United States. Pilár, despite a stronger idealism and higher moral code than the rest of the family, meets a rape-torture death at the hands of the Indians. As with most of Riggs's serious plays, *Pilár* is powerful and ritual-like. Riggs has a sure touch when he writes about primitive ethnic groups, and in this play he echoes some of the same stresses that he saw as a boy between Cherokees and whites in the old Indian Territory. *The Year of Pilár* is about prejudice and freedom from oppression, and it remains pertinent in today's world. Although published, it has never been staged professionally.

The play also has a strong under-theme of sexuality. Pilár is terrified, yet drawn to her orgiastic death; and many of the other characters exhibit similar split feelings of outer aversion toward sex and inner compulsion to it. Many critics have deliberately turned their heads away from this often-recurring motif in Riggs's plays; a number of them would prefer to think of Riggs solely as the writer of congenial comedies down on the farm. But Riggs was also keenly interested in the turbulent sexual desires masked under the hypocritical exteriors of most humans. . . .

Riggs returned to Broadway on January 20, 1941, with his most powerful play, but it was attacked by the New York critics. Martin Gabel co-produced and directed Riggs's tragedy, *The Cream in the Well,* in an excellently staged production at the Booth Theatre, with sets by Jo Mielziner. It closed after twenty-four performances and a damnation rarely seen in theatrical journalism. The New York newspapers had the following things to say about it: "merely a morbid excursion into an unpleasant subject" (*World-Telegram*); "Mr. Riggs has dropped down to the low of his career" (*PM*); "minor-league O'Neill" (*Sun*); "sophomoric tragedy" (*Journal-American*); "the kind of play one would be glad to forget . . . balderdash of a curdling sort, sadly ineffectual" (*Herald Tribune*); and even Brooks Atkinson (*Times*) asked, "Why?" Bitterly hurt, Riggs fled to Santa Fe to lick his wound for almost a year, and didn't write another line with a regional flavor for seven years.

The Cream in the Well, Ibsenian in its constantly unfolding exposition, takes place in the isolated Big Lake area near Verdigris Switch in 1906. Joseph Wood Krutch synopsizes it best:

> The central character is the hellion daughter of ·
> a . . . hard working farmer couple on a Cherokee allotment. Before the play begins she has already succeeded in separating her brother from his fiancée and in sending him upon an adventurous as well . . . as . . . debauched career with the . . . Navy. During the action she further succeeds, before her ultimate suicide, in

driving the deserted fiancée to her death and in making a drunkard out of the weakling she contemptuously consented to marry. . . . The girl is in love with her own brother . . . and her malice springs from conflict and frustration. In fact, near the end, the brother actually suggests that it would be better for them to yield to their impulses, that even unnatural love is less destructive than hate. But she is not able to face that possibility and prefers self-destruction instead ("Tragedy Is Not Easy").

Despite the sincerity and power of the play, it was condemned. Riggs had dared to write about incest; and incest was not to become "box office" until a decade later in the relaxed postwar mores. Ironically, **The Cream in the Well** is in good taste and is far more artistic than much of the contemporary Theatre of Violence. The play is Greek-like in its intensity and passion, and it belongs in the same category as O'Neill's *Desire Under the Elms* and Owen Davis's *Icebound*—inevitable tragedies stemming out of the tensions of living in rural isolation. Riggs has created his own doomed House of Atreus in the backwoods by Big Lake. The particularized regional setting provides the background for a universal tragedy. The lack of sophistication of the rural characters adds credibility as they fumble toward awareness of the explosive situation. It is not merely folk drama; it is high tragedy.

Krutch puts his finger on why the newspaper reviews joined in their cry of outrage: "We demand most of all of the author who invites us to high tragedy. We resist it as we resist all things which are even superficially unpleasant or painful" ("Tragedy Is Not Easy"). In other words, turbulent, culturally-tabooed feelings that lurk too close to home must be exorcised at once. **The Cream in the Well** never had a chance with the still hypocritically Puritan Broadway audiences of 1941.

Only one month after the production of **The Cream in the Well**, Riggs had an article in *Theatre Arts* in which he urged the necessity for the tributary theatre, far from Broadway. The timing of this article, originally a speech in San Diego the year before, was bitterly ironic, and it ended, "I should think we would take the theatre seriously. I should think we would take life seriously." But Broadway refused to the bitter end to take Lynn Riggs seriously. . . .

Dark Encounter, published but never produced, showed Riggs's concern about world problems. Taking place in an isolated house on Cape Cod on D-Day, the play is the story of a young woman (Gail) and a stranger (Karl) who suddenly appears. Riggs creates powerful suspense because we think that Karl may be a German saboteur, but we discover that he has applied for American citizenship and is distraught because his brother is fighting in the Nazi army. Coast Guardsmen and Gail's crippled Army-veteran fiancé try to kill Karl, but another man is killed by mistake. Karl is a victim of circumstantial evidence, but a Portuguese girl witness switches to the truth at the last moment. Although we have a happy love ending between Gail and Karl, the play is a strong outcry against racial and national prejudices, and hatreds of all kinds. Karl says, "Everything fought for has been lost. . . .

God! Look at the dissension, the bigotry and mistrust! Look at youth—the youth that is to be the future of the race . . . making their guttural animal sounds instead of lucid speech. The beast walks over the earth! The beast . . . man . . . !" Riggs, with a strong sense of human responsibility, was part of the outcry being made by Robert Sherwood, Lillian Hellman, and the young Tennessee Williams, as they all wrote with fear that the brutes would conquer the sensitive. By placing his play on the day of the most pivotal battle of World War II, Riggs gained thematic impact. . . .

Perhaps [Riggs's] work is best summed up by John Gassner, in his *Best American Plays*:

> Lynn Riggs was one of the most gifted writers ever to write for the American stage, to which he brought a vivid memory, a compassionate spirit, and a poet's soul. It was impossible for him to cut his cloth to the requirements of show business, and I cannot recall anything he ever wrote . . . to which it was possible to attribute anything less than total integrity of observation and imagination . . . with his lively yet fine regional feeling, he also helped to give the American theatre some status for a while as a national institution rooted in the land.

In his reply to the citation given him by the University of Oklahoma, Riggs had some interesting things to say about himself:

> Actually, I have done little in life except try to discover who I am and what my relation to the world I know consists of.

> In the world itself I have never really felt at home. How can anyone feel at home in a world of unparalleled stupidity and cruelty, a world aching with hunger and despair? Can one be at peace with the economic and social and political organization of a world that makes man fear living, hate his neighbor, revile the sources of his being, and boast of his allegiance to violence and destruction? I do not think so.

> And turning from the consideration of the outer world in dismay, I look at myself. And what do I find there? Weakness. Lack of discipline. Feeble attempts at understanding. Ignorance. Vanity. Waywardness and conceit.

> I find, however, five working senses. And by great good luck I am able to see that these are tools that can perhaps be made to work for good instead of evil, that if I can refine them enough—these five senses—if I can use them enough *truthfully,* they may relate things to me that will give me strength and enough hope to go on when I find myself and the world impossible. Perhaps—if I am lucky, if I make declarations strong enough through work or through living—other people, too, may find the way less hard.

This quiet, unpretentious man who had only four plays produced on Broadway was nevertheless the greatest playwright to come out of the Southwest. Had there been vigorous regional professional theatre in his lifetime, his fame would have been assured, for he wrote with sensitivity and charm about the passions and foibles of the people he knew in the old Indian Territory.

Phyllis Cole Braunlich on Riggs's Career:

Lynn Riggs is still the only playwright to tell the world of the joys and conflicts of early Oklahoma life as Indian Territory shed adolescence to become a state in 1907. He attempted only to tell individual stories out of his experience, not to write historical dramas; yet his writings contain truths of time, place, and people that can be found nowhere else. Nonetheless, if his musical, emotionally charged poetry were his only literary legacy, it should earn for him a solid place in American letters. His courage and conviction, his firm but tender love of the word, are an example for writers everywhere who believe in their material, and who know that what they have to say must be said, in spite of all.

Phyllis Cole Braunlich, in her Haunted By Home: The Life and Letters of Lynn Riggs, *1988.*

Phyllis Cole Braunlich   (essay date 1988)

SOURCE: "*The Cherokee Night* of R. Lynn Riggs," in *The Midwest Quarterly,* Vol. XXX, No. 1, Autumn, 1988, pp. 45-59.

[*Braunlich is an American biographer and critic whose works include* Haunted By Home: The Life and Letters of Lynn Riggs *(1988). In the following essay, she provides a detailed analysis of* The Cherokee Night.]

"An absorbed race has its curiously irreconcilable inheritance. It seems to me the best grade of absorbed Indian might be an intellectual Hamlet, buffeted, harrassed, victimized, split, baffled—with somewhere in him great fire and some granite. And a residual lump of stranger things than the white race may fathom" (Letter to [Barrett H.] Clark, 10 March 1929). This statement by part-Cherokee playwright Lynn Riggs recognized, early on, the failure of the assimilation policy for Native Americans. The theme of the play he was writing, ***The Cherokee Night,*** might also be stated thus: the combination of American Indian and white blood in his veins, like the combination of American Indian and white cultures in his life, set the "absorbed" Indian, or part-Indian American at war within himself as well as within society. The combinations refused to mix and cancelled out each other.

Riggs saw that the pure-blood Indian people had known who they were and where they had come from—but their mixed-blood descendants were tragic figures between two worlds. Whatever options his characters chose in order to cope—violence, crime, alcohol, apathy, or denial of their origins—only led them further into tragedy. The characters articulate this theme variously in the seven scenes of the play, each of which is like a separate vignette; five characters introduced as young adults in the first act are seen in various stages of their lives, from infancy, when the

father of two of them dies as a fugitive from the law, to middle age when one sister lives in poverty, while the other has denied her heritage to live in a wealthy white man's world.

Riggs's controversial theory is commonly accepted today. The United States had tried a sequence of Indian policies, from annihilation to separation, and back to assimilation: annihilation in early wars, then separation to reservations and Indian Territory, then the opening of Indian lands to resettlement, undermining tribal authority. A typical policy statement was made by Thomas J. Morgan, new Commissioner of Indian Affairs in the Department of the Interior in 1899:

> The Indians must conform to "the white man's ways," peaceably if they will, forcibly if they must. They must adjust themselves to their environment, and conform their mode of living substantially to our civilization. . . . They can not escape it, and must either conform or be crushed by it. [*Now That the Buffalo's Gone: A Study of Today's American Indians,* Alvin M. Josephy, Jr., 1982]

American Indian children were systematically removed from their tribal homes and sent to white schools. "The boarding schools were often effective in their short-term goals of teaching English to Indian youth, moving children away from intimate contact with tribal/reservation conditions, and conversion to Christianity," wrote Sally J. McBeth, [in *Ethnic Identity and the Boarding School Experience of West-Central Oklahoma American Indians,* 1983]. "Historical factors such as the breakdown of reservations in Oklahoma and land allotment were also at work promoting the eventual disintegration of the tribe and complete assimilation. This assimilation, however, did not and has not occurred.

But Native Americans refused to vanish as a people. The boarding school, intended as separation, became a pan-Indian unifying force. For the first time, members of various tribes shared a common language, English, and became self-conscious as Indians."At the same time, the retention of one's Native language in Oklahoma continued to be a positive affirmation of the desire to maintain one's heritage despite immense pressures to the contrary." Riggs's play demonstrates the failure of assimilation policy, through the havoc it wreaked on individual lives.

Riggs (1899-1954) did not live to see the eventual rebellion in the 1960s and later, when Indian people and other American ethnic groups resolved to reclaim their culture and take pride in their racial and historical heritage. But this play, the only one he wrote that dealt with his Cherokee heritage, powerfully demonstrates the uniquely tragic situation of young part-Indian people such as he knew during the early years of this century. He is best known as writer of ***Green Grow the Lilacs,*** a 1931 Theater Guild hit on Broadway, which in 1943 was revised as the musical *Oklahoma!* At the time, Americans knew little of Indian ways, except for the Hollywood movie stereotypes Riggs abhorred. None of his twenty-five plays dealt directly with Indianness except ***The Cherokee Night,*** a play which ought to be recognized for its insights as well as its dramatic intensity.

Although this play was performed only in college and experimental theaters, it was published by Samuel French in 1936, and it deserves attention as authentic American Indian literature. I will analyze both the play and some of Riggs's concerns, expressed in his own notes about the performances he directed at the University of Iowa in 1932. Riggs said in informal notes that the scenes illustrate these qualities of the Cherokees: "bravery, sense of ritual, independence, pride, cunning, fierceness, aesthetic sense, in sum their authentic glory . . . [and] present perversion of these qualities."

First, let us review briefly the situation of the Cherokees in northeastern Oklahoma leading up to the time of the play, 1895-1931. Although many had died on the "Trail of Tears" which forced their resettlement in the mid-nineteenth century, the Cherokees in Oklahoma had reestablished their tribal government, founded both a male and female seminary, and using Sequoyah's written syllabary of their language, had published a newspaper in Tahlequah, *The Cherokee Advocate*. But the Civil War again devastated the tribe, physically, politically, and economically. They lost thousands of their cattle and were then forced to give up large tribal land holdings for resettlement. The Cherokees freely intermarried with non-Indians, at least seven hundred of them as early as 1877.

Into this social upheaval Riggs brings his part-Indian characters, taking them from infancy or childhood into their thirties, then reverting in the final scene to 1895 and a full-blood chief, the dignified forebear of the tragedies to come. One-sixteenth Cherokee himself, Riggs saw in the psyche of the early twentieth-century, mixed-blood Cherokee a unique form of modern alienation, a stream of natural emotion that had been thwarted and turned aside by the overriding white culture. The resulting inner conflicts tore at the banks of his stability, his energy, his hope.

Throughout the play Riggs used the landmark Claremore Mound as a visual symbol, seen either as the immediate location of a scene or as a distant feature of the horizon: in an 1817 territorial war on this broad, flat-topped hill, Cherokee warriors massacred residents of an Osage village. This bloody last battle between the tribes is well remembered. Legends are told relating to the battle, which ended many things, including a way of life based on tribal loyalty.

In addition to the book's explanatory prologue, Riggs wrote pages of detailed directions. Among his papers in the Lynn Riggs Memorial Collection at Rogers State College, Claremore, Oklahoma, are informal notes listing: what characteristics of the Cherokee are portrayed; costumes, reflecting for the most part the clothing of the poor, rather than stereotyped "Indian" garb; and a "drum plot" giving directions for an off-stage drum beat, varying in intensity with the drama and making transitions between scenes. Written for a production he directed at the University of Iowa in 1932, these notes shed much light on his intentions in this experimental play. It was also presented in 1932 at Hedgerow Theatre near Philadelphia, in 1934

at Syracuse University, and in a 1936 Federal Theatre production in New York City.

Riggs said on several occasions that he considered the nonchronological sequence of the play's seven scenes essential to his meaning, to the cyclical causes and effects which visit the frustrations and failings of the fathers on the sons from generation to generation. When urged to structure the play more traditionally, he refused, although popular audiences of the Thirties found it somewhat confusing. The play as structured, though presenting much action, is more symbolic than realistic, and thus experimental.

His introduction to the published version explains:

> They are citizens without a state. They are wayfarers on a dark road—and the dangers without are as nothing to the devils within. Driven as they are by urges impossible for them to understand, their actions are apt to be incalculably inadequate, or, on occasion, theatrically violent—like a river clawing at and destroying a countryside. . . . And his night is usually black with storm, and unlighted by lamp or star.

He wrote that though the play takes place in Indian Territory before Oklahoma statehood, "it might have been about any Indian tribe or about any strong racial strain, especially those whose emotional equipment is rich and complicated."

Although the scenes of the play are arranged nonchronologically, for the sake of clarity I will discuss them in chronological order.

Scene VII, 1895, titled "The Cherokee Night," takes place in and around the cabin of John Gray-Wolf, who is playing a Cherokee song on a drum for his eight-year-old orphaned grandson. A wounded outlaw, Edgar Spench (also known as Edgar Breeden) stumbles in and Gray-Wolf tries to stop the bleeding in his side. Spench raves, "Sump'n always drove me on. . . . Bad blood. Too much Indian, they tell me" [*Busset Mantle and The Cherokee Night: Two Plays by Lynn Riggs*, 1936].

"Not enough Indian," Gray-Wolf says. "I'm full-blood Cherokee. I live peaceful. I ain't troubled. I remember the way my people lived in quiet times. Think of my ancestors. It keeps me safe. You, though—like my boy. He's dead. He was half white, like you. They killed him, *had* to kill him. Not *enough* Indian.

When the white posse arrives and kills Spench, his wife Marthy, mother of their small son Gar, and Florey, who is carrying Spench's illegitimate daughter (Bee) arrive. Marthy says to her dead husband, "You was hounded day and night, inside and outside. By day, men. At night, your thoughts. Now it's over. . . . But here's your son. In him your trouble. It goes on. In him. It ain't finished. . . . Your disgrace, your wickedness, your pain and trouble live on a while longer. In her child, in my child. In all people born now, about to be born. . . . Someday, the agony will end. . . . Maybe not in the night of death, the cold dark night, without stars. Maybe in the sun."

Riggs's stage notes in the published play close the denouement: "A far-away look is in Gray-Wolf's eyes, a quality of magnificent dignity and despair as if he mourned for his own life, for the life of his son, for his grandson, for Spench, for the women, for a whole race gone down into darkness." With a drumbeat like a slow pulse, the cabin interior fades and the snow-dusted Claremore Mound looms again in the background.

Riggs's informal notes said that scene VII means

> Cherokee night, epitomized by the desperado, who fulfills in himself both defeat from the whites, and defeat from within. Finally shot in cold blood, perhaps not caring very much, *because of the loss of blood, literally.*

> Projection of the strain—in the unborn child, Bee, the absent child, Gar, and the little grandson. Projection of application beyond race, beyond personal interpretation. . . .

In Scene IV (1906), three boys, Gar Breeden, Hutch Moree, and Art Osburn, explore "The Place Where the Nigger Was Found," a black man who was murdered the night before in a gambling game on Claremore Mound. The language expresses the attitudes of white Oklahomans at the time, when blacks had been "run out of Claremore." Art, a dark, brooding character, says "Niggers'll kill—and not keer!" The boys whip up a mock frenzy to show their own bravado about bloodshed—but then they find an Ace of Spades, a tin cup, and, pushing aside leaves, they find blood on their hands. As they run terrified, the ghostly form of a large, black man rises from among the leaves and yawns as if very much at home. Riggs commented in his notes: "Cherokee remnants of blood-lust become terrifying to the possessor. White strain makes its expression imaginatively impossible." He contrasts this blockage with the Negroes' apparent "natural lithe functioning."

Scene V, "The High Mountain" (1913) demonstrates the spiritual fervor of a fundamentalist white sect in a church on Eagle Bluff, overlooking the Illinois River and the town of Tahlequah—an Indian town, seat of the Cherokee Nation. Gar Breeden, now 18, being chased by a shotgun-toting white man, seeks refuge in the church. His entry disturbs the ecstatic chants of worship, led by the preacher, Jonas.

Gar tells the preacher privately, "It's all shut up in me, it's drivin' me crazy!" He had been expelled from Oklahoma A&M College, where his guardian had sent him, but no longer felt he belonged in Claremore. "No place for me anywhere! Come down to Tahlequah yesterday to see if—to see—I thought this bein' the head of—Listen, I'm half Cherokee. I thought they could help me out here, I thought they—Old men sittin' in the square! No tribe to go to, no Council to help me out of the kind of trouble I'm in. Nuthin' to count on!"

Seeing possibilities in the intense young man, Jonas tries to persuade him to accept the faith and to join the sect he calls—ironically—"People of the Lost Tribe, God's Chosen." He also offers to train Gar to succeed him as preacher, saying: "There's no help from the Cherokees. They're dying out. They're hardly a Tribe any more. They have no order of life you could live. Their ways are going. Their

customs change. That part of you can never be fulfilled. What's left? You must look to heaven! Like us!"

When Gar refuses, Jonas tells the people to chain him to a post and they threaten to kill him—but the Klaxon horn of an approaching car signals his rescue. The sect members have stolen goods and livestock from the Cherokees in Tahlequah and must look to their own safety. This scene represents the climax of the play, revealing that there is neither spiritual nor physical refuge for the Cherokees. It is followed by the tragic denouement in Gray-Wolf's cabin, even though the scenes are out of chronological order by 18 years.

Much non-fiction has been written, pro and con, about the white man's effort to capture the American Indian's fundamentally religious spirit. Many believed—correctly—that the "heathen" religions of the tribes must be rejected if the Indian were ever to assimilate.

> Historically, there was no such thing as a single Indian religion; spiritual concepts and systems differed from tribe to tribe. All of them, however, served the same individual and collective purposes, working for the survival, unity and well-being of the people, ensuring order, balance and harmony. . . . (Josephy).

But instead of the tribal council, Gar finds only the sterile remnants, "Old men sittin' in the square."

Josephy agreed with Riggs that the various Indian religions were imprinted in racial memory,

> awesomely pervasive and relentless, the inner skein of collective and individual life. . . . To individual Indians, deep spiritual feelings and reverence for all of creation were as much a part of their being as their physical features and personality. Spiritual power flowed like energy from their bodies, guiding their thoughts and actions by day and entering their dreams at night. It counseled and directed them throughout their lives, endowing them with values and a world view that gave meaning to their existence. . . .

> In general, however, Congress and the administrations in Washington regarded them [missionaries] as the best civilizing influence and came to rely on them increasingly as agents to guide the Indians toward assimilation.

Scene I, "Sixty-Seven Arrowheads," introduces six part-Indian young adults having a picnic on Claremore Mound in 1915. They are Gar Breeden, Hutch Moree, and Art Osburn, whom we met as children, Bee Newcomb (the unborn child of Florey met earlier, now a waitress, but turning to prostitution), Viney Jones, a schoolteacher, and Audeal Coombs, a "beauty operator" not heard of later.

A ghostly teepee and muffled drumbeat introduce the scene, which again is haunted by the spirits of past bloodlettings. Gar says the others should feel what he feels—a spiritual presence because they are "sitting on the graves of a lot of dead Cherokees." Old Man Talbert is discovered nearby, chopping at the ground in search of arrowheads. He tells them a ghost story, of the Cherokee spirits he has seen charging over the Mound, returning with long-haired Osage scalps "swishin' and drippin'" at every Cherokee belt. To a drum-beat accompaniment, Talbert recites a poetic message he received from the ghostly Cherokee chief in the form of a traditional Native American oration. The specter says (through Talbert): "Now you've saw, you've been showed. *Us*—the Cherokees—in our full pride, our last glory! This is the way we are, the way we was meant to be!" He recounts the glory of the battle:

> But this was moons ago; / We, too, are dead. / We have no bodies, / We are homeless ghosts, / We are made of air!

"Who made us that, Jim Talbert? Our children—our children's children! They've forgot who we was, who *they* are!" Saying the young have "sunk already to the white man's way," he adds,

> The grass is withered. / Where the river was is red sand. / Fire eats the timber. / Night— *night*—has come to our people!

Talbert, in a fearful frenzy, says because of the ghosts he must dig up the mountain if necessary, till he finds sixty-seven arrowheads and gives them to the Cherokees. "When they touch 'em, they'll remember. *The feel of flint in their hands!*" But saner minds know that even the touch of flint cannot bring back the life that was.

In the next three chronological scenes, we catch up with Hutch Moree in 1919, Art Osburn and Bee Newcomb in 1927, and Viney Jones in 1931.

Scene VI, "The White Turkey," 1919: Hutch, a light-haired, slow-witted oil field teamster, has moved in with nineteen year-old Kate Whiteturkey, on her family farm near Bartlesville. Strong-willed, spoiled, wearing expensive but gaudy clothes, Kate tells Hutch's brother George not to try to get Hutch away from her. "I got three Stutzes, and I'm gonna have an airplane next month." Newly rich from Osage oil lands, she has bought Hutch ten silk shirts, six pairs of shoes, and his own Stutz Bearcat car. Her family farms no more. She drives her cars everywhere, but is bored with places. She tells George, "It's just his [Hutch's] hard luck to be born part-Cherokee instead of full-blood Osage. He might just as well be white trash for all the good bein' Indian does him."

George, who has been away finishing college, says, "He's got 80 acres of land, his allotment, in Rogers County. Good land, too." When Hutch enters, George tells him, "They're making that new road from Claremore north through Vinita and on up to the Kansas line. It would be a good job for you, get you away from this—all this. Your teams are in the pasture, idle. They ought to be working. *You* ought to be working." Hutch loses his new-found confidence, returns to his former stuttering, but still resents his brother's call back to responsibility. He is not strong enough to take up the hard road again.

Scene II, "The Hatchet": In 1927, Bee is put in the Rogers County Jail cell next to Art's cell. Supposedly charged with drunkenness, Bee is being paid to get a confession from Art that he killed his Osage wife. He confesses that he hated the older woman whom he married for security.

When they were going up the river, he beat her with a hatchet and dumped her out of the boat to drown. His confession is recorded, and he will hang. Bee feels guilty, but takes her $25 and leaves. Riggs noted that the scene illustrates "Cherokee hate—and maladjustment because of it. Also rancor, bitterness, sadism, wildness, cupidity."

Scene III, "Liniment," 1931: Viney, 41, no longer a schoolteacher but wife of the mayor of Quapaw, visits the humble home of her sister Sarah after ten years of silence between them. Sarah's daughter Maisie, a child-wife at 17, has been hoping for fifty cents to buy liniment for her mother's rheumatic knees. But Sarah's pride will not let her accept the money from critical Viney. She says to Viney, "Be mean and cunning and full of hate, like the Indian. Be greedy and selfish the way the white man is. None of what's good. . . ." The sisters will probably not see each other again. Both ways of life have failed these women. Riggs noted informally that Viney's resilience, which made her white, was in this case, "a defeat also, because it cheats her, makes her life thin and fictitious." His finale to these life stories was to return to the dignified Gray-Wolf and a better time but a bitter prophecy.

Riggs's notes direct his play to open with drum beats, the basic unit of Indian music: "Bass drum 6 beats; baritone drum 4; Pause." This rhythm recurs at the end of Scene IV, just before the intermission, recalling the audience to the beginning and thus reiterating the timelessness of the scenes. Scene II begins with an unaccented bass beat "like rain on the roof." The baritone drum then mingles its "8-to-the-bar" beat with the recorded hymn, "My Faith Looks Up to Thee." Recorded bird whistles join the drum at the end of this Scene II, and both sound at the beginning of the next. Switching register, the bass drum beat opens Scene IV and comes to a crescendo with the violent expressions of the boys. In the midst of Scene VI, one loud bass-drum exclamation blends to a two-beat measure, then to an unaccented beat, the play ending with the pattern of the beginning: "Bass 6, baritone 4, Pause. . . ." He was this specific because untrained non-Indians are unable to imitate these patterns extemporaneously. Obviously Riggs, an accomplished singer and guitarist, used this tribal rhythm to connect his non-chronological scenes. The patterns will recall anyone who has ever heard an authentic Indian drum to the scene of unfamiliar rituals.

In the Thirties, New York audiences seemed bewildered. Playwright Sidney Howard, in a 1936 letter to theatre historian Barrett H. Clark, wondered if the movies would be the best vehicle for this play. Perhaps the stage for *Cherokee Night* exists best between book covers, where the characters are easier to follow.

In October 1933, almost a year after the first productions of *Cherokee Night*, Riggs reviewed his work to see whether the imperatives of his material were misdirecting the play. Often accused of being, though original, too inflexible, Riggs wrote his friend and agent Barrett Clark at Samuel French, Inc.

> The point of my doing the production at Iowa was to see whether the play worked that way or not. It did work—nearly everybody will testify to that. Some day the producers will learn that

if a play has a certain structure there is a reason
for it. . . . However, I'll try to see how much
I can feel the play some other way. I doubt if I
can.

And of course, he couldn't. The play begins with young
adults, takes them to mid-life, back to childhood, and in
the end to the generation before their birth.

Riggs also gave directions for the costuming. At the 1915
picnic, impudent Bee wears a richly-colored dress and silk
stockings. The men wear wide-beaded belts and moccasins
with their blue jeans and work shirts. Viney wears a hat,
middy blouse, and long skirt. More prosperous in 1931 at
her sister's house, Viney wears a Eugenie hat and fur coat.
But Sarah, who is poor, wears a Mother Hubbard dress
and gray knitted shawl. In 1919, Kate Whiteturkey, the
Osage woman newly rich from oil headrights, has a modern rich-colored short dress, expensive but not in good
taste. Hutch, who lives with her, wears a white silk shirt
with red stripes, detachable silk collar, and necktie. Nothing especially Indian here, except for beaded belts and
comfortable moccasins. Riggs's point was that these twentieth-century Indians most often wore the clothing of the
poor, not the feathers or breech-cloths of movie Indians.

Although the play is essentially tragic, Riggs was happy
in its creation, begun in France as he was finishing **Green
Grow the Lilacs** in 1930, on a Guggenheim Fellowship.
Working on it later in Provincetown theatre colony on 20
October 1930, he wrote Clark that the old Indian, a real
nobleman, in his "triumphant comprehension . . . makes
the whole play dignified and austere beyond my first feeble
calculation." Therefore, Gray-Wolf's declaration had to
be his denouement.

Riggs saw in the situation of the Cherokee in this century
the universal problem of alienation that has occupied
modern writers. Like the Indians, exiles in their own
homeland, mankind's vital stream of natural emotion has
been dammed by modern society—and therefore, the
stream tears at the banks of his psyche.

Riggs's people in **Cherokee Night** are in many ways like
himself. He spent many childhood hours playing by the
imposing Claremore Mound, close by the country grave
of his Cherokee mother, who died when he was a toddler.
He often felt, as he said of the Cherokee, that his strongest,
most primitive emotions had no outlet. Covertly homosexual, he, too, was often driven by urges impossible for him
to understand, his actions apt to be, as he said, "incalcula-
bly inadequate." Although completely non-violent, a genial person with many friends, Riggs in his plays and especially his poems recognized always that underground
stream. He was frequently withdrawn and moody, and at
these times conscious of "devils within."

Riggs makes abundant mention in this play of Oklahoma's
native flora and fauna, as well as Cherokee history and legend. Gray-Wolf, for example, tells his grandson about the
brave warrior who put his soul in the top of a sycamore
tree for safety while he went into battle. But bravery also
includes stoic acceptance in his advice to his grandson:
"When death wants you, it's better to sit and wait."

Noted playwright Paul Horgan said in a 1981 interview

that this is the greatest of Riggs's many Oklahoma plays
and should be revived. At the very least, it should be read,
for its insight into its part-Cherokee characters and its historical perspective on their Indian Territory/Oklahoma
life in the first third of this century.

Phyllis Cole Braunlich   (essay date 1990)

SOURCE: "The Oklahoma Plays of R. Lynn Riggs," in
World Literature Today, Vol. 64, No. 3, Summer, 1990,
pp. 390-94.

*[In the following essay, Braunlich provides an overview of
Riggs's dramatic works.]*

Rollie Lynn Riggs (1899-1954) is without doubt the greatest playwright from Oklahoma to write plays about Oklahoma. To be specific, he dramatized life in Indian Territory just before and after statehood, which came in 1907. He
is best known for his successful 1931 play **Green Grow the
Lilacs,** produced on Broadway by the Theatre Guild. The
same group produced the play in a musical version by
Richard Rodgers and Oscar Hammerstein in 1943, titled
Oklahoma! The phenomenal success of this play, which
is still performed internationally, would alone be sufficient
to establish Lynn Riggs's reputation as an outstanding
Oklahoma writer. However, he also wrote twenty other
full-length plays, twelve of which were published and
eight produced though unpublished. He also published
one-act plays, screen and television plays, short stories,
and two volumes of poetry.

Thirteen of Riggs's full-length plays tell of the colorful
people of his Oklahoma childhood, who struggled against
hard conditions to settle and develop a new territory. Nine
of these are tragedies: **Big Lake, Sump'n Like Wings, A
Lantern to See By, The Lonesome West, Rancor, The
Domino Parlor, The Cherokee Night, The Cream in the
Well,** and **Out of Dust.** The other four are comedies:
Roadside, Green Grow the Lilacs, All the Way Home, and
Some Sweet Day. Those plays marked with an asterisk
were published by Samuel French, Incorporated of New
York. In my 1988 biography of Riggs, *Haunted by Home,*
I append a list of all his writings, with the record of play
productions and the present locations of manuscripts.

New York producers and audiences often found Riggs's
subject matter shocking and unbelievable; the Ideal West
of romantic American fiction is what they expected, and
they could not believe that life as recently as 1910 could
have been as hard and deprived as it was for many of this
playwright's characters. Riggs, however, was devoted to
truth above popularity and was determined to tell authentic stories from his early years in Claremore, Oklahoma.
Still, it was not his intention to illustrate history; he was
interested in young Indian Territory people and their individual struggles for a better life. Nearly all his characters
were based on actual persons. He once said he felt uneasy
when people commented that they knew a lot about Oklahoma from his plays: "The range of life there is not to be
indicated, much less its meaning laid bare, by a few people
in a few plays. Some day, perhaps, all the plays I will have
written, taken together, may constitute a *study* from

which certain things may emerge and be formulated into a *kind of truth* about people who happen to be living in Oklahoma."

Speaking of his Oklahoma taciturnity, Riggs attributed this characteristic to lack of education and also to the fact that

> . . . the people who settled Oklahoma were a suspect fraternity, as fearful of being recognized by others as they were by themselves. Gamblers, traders, vagabonds, adventurers, daredevils, fools. Men with a sickness, men with a distemper. Men disdainful of the settled, the admired, the regular ways of life. Men on the move. Men fleeing from a critical world and their own eyes. Pioneers, eaten people. And their descendants have the same things in them, changed a little, grown out of a bit, but there, just the same. And so they don't speak. Speech reveals one. It is better to say nothing. And so these people, who had been much admired and much maligned, have been *not quite known.*

Riggs added that he hoped to speak for them, however imperfectly, in his plays. He wrote in his own "intuitive" style, following the development of emotions. If his plots did not follow traditional formulas, they expressed the truths of life as he saw it in early Oklahoma. His heroes were often small and always human; perhaps the "anti-hero" of modern literature better describes some of his characters. Although he found the reality of life dramatically stronger than artificial invention, he had trouble convincing producers that his Oklahoma rascals and victims were believable.

The dark mood varied, however; some of his plays were full of light, hope, and the energetic recklessness with which people on the plains and rocky hills found their fun. He said while working on **Green Grow the Lilacs,** a story of courtship and bravado, that these rarer Oklahomans "were not parsimonious of speech and ordinarily, not parched in their fruity enjoyment of life." He took special delight in their poetic speech, whose melodious flow and metaphoric aptitude are uniquely preserved in his plays. Let us look at each of his Oklahoma plays in the order of their creation and briefly describe their themes.

The American Laboratory Theatre produced **Big Lake,** a tragedy, on Broadway in 1927. Two adolescents, Betty and Lloyd, wander away from a school picnic and seek shelter in a dugout house with an evil couple. Butch, a bootlegger, has just murdered an informer and schemes to pin the murder on Lloyd. He looks upon Betty with lust. After the two escape from the situation and return to their friends, the ugly accusations of their classmates and teacher repel them. They flee out onto the lake, where death pursues them. Parts of the play use children's game songs from Riggs's childhood. He protests the inability of innocence to survive in a world of evil adults and malicious gossipers.

Big Lake has enjoyed a long and perplexing popularity, since its action is slow and old-fashioned. It continues to be offered for productions in the Samuel French catalogue, along with **Green Grow the Lilacs, Hang On to**

Love (formerly **The Domino Parlor**), **Roadside,** and **Russet Mantle** (a New Mexican comedy). Critics praised the play's poetic quality and evocation of mood, but some called it an amateurish first attempt. Barrett Clark, Riggs's agent and friend who later became a renowned theatre historian, saw a new "winged lightness" in Riggs's dialogue. He wrote in his introduction to the play (1925): "I am sure that in Lynn Riggs our American theatre has found a poet who can bring to it an authentic note of ecstasy and passion, expressed in terms of drama. He is one of the few native dramatists who can take the material of our everyday life and mould it into forms of stirring beauty." Reviewing the work for the *Daily Oklahoman* in October 1927, Ben A. Botkin praised "the poetic appeal of lines whose rhythmic and emotional values make it a contribution to literature as well as to the theatre." He cited Riggs's use of symbolism and contrast in employing the grim incongruity of the children's songs and cited the lyric qualities of the play's dialogue as reminiscent of the playwrights Synge and O'Neill.

Riggs next wrote **Sump'n Like Wings** in Santa Fe in 1925, while he was struggling to find his own wings and to test them on his flight to Broadway. In the Oklahoma town of "Claremont" just after statehood, Willie, aged sixteen, seeks something more than her monotonous life in her mother's home. Unconventional and untrained in the social graces, she places her faith in lovers and is twice disappointed. She decides she has to take care of herself, to be independent, declaring, "It's the way people are made that's to blame" for what they become. She is made to desire a freer life and to rise above her poverty and lack of education. It is Willie's ambitious and hard-working spirit that transformed many poor, uneducated pioneers into the builders of a new civilization in the wilderness, in Oklahoma as elsewhere.

Riggs wrote **A Lantern to See By** in 1926 in New York. The hero in this tragedy, nineteen-year-old Jodie Harmon, is the sensitive son of a tyrannical farmer. After his overworked mother dies, Jodie's father hires Annie Marble to do the domestic work, but she sees a way to escape the drab farm life by becoming a prostitute. When Jodie, who loves Annie purely, discovers his father's illicit relationship with her, he kills his father, then is shocked to learn of Annie's consent to the relationship. This powerful tragedy raises the question of why there is often an offspring in a given family whose nature does not follow the family type but whose character makes a difference in the family's destiny.

A Lantern to See By was among many of Riggs's plays to make their professional debut at the famed Hedgerow Theater outside Philadelphia. A critic wrote in the *Philadelphia Ledger* on 13 July 1931: "It shows Lynn Riggs gifted with a flair for bringing out touches of character, for molding earthy native types, making them human, virile and alive yet escaping coarseness; building scenes of intense dramatic value and filling them with words that need no battery to galvanize them to pulsating power." When the play was published in 1928, critic David Russel wrote in the *Dallas Morning News:* "Here is tragedy and realism caught in a form of haunting and moving beauty. No one who wishes to follow the best that is being written in the theater today can afford to miss reading these plays." Even so, stark tragedy countered the usually celebrative mood of Broadway playgoers. Riggs's Oklahoma tragedies were produced in off-Broadway and university theatres but seldom ran on Broadway. It was his comedies that eventually brought him popular success.

Riggs hoped that another tragedy, *The Lonesome West,* would be his masterpiece, but it was never published and ended in obscurity. An autobiographical play whose action takes place on the eighty-acre farm of the Bingham family near "Blackmore," Oklahoma, the work employs a set designed to resemble the farm buildings of the author's early childhood. The children—Marthy, twenty-five, Ed, who is married, and Sherman, eighteen—correspond closely to Riggs's family group, and the stone-hearted step-mother, Kate Chambers, resembles his own step-mother.

In the playwright's next tragedy, *Rancor,* Dorie Bickel is plagued with a husband, Ned, and a son, Julius, who neglect farming in favor of hunting and loafing. They fall in love with a mother and daughter, Maggie and Loochie, who are equally unambitious. While Dorie earns the family's living out of the truck farm and a restaurant, Julius drops out of business school to marry Loochie. Ned, rejected by Maggie, commits suicide. Although deeply hurt, Dorie realizes she must depend only on herself for success in life, much like Riggs's earlier heroine, Willie. Riggs explained that Dorie's jealousy of her husband drives her to get ahead, to shame him for his laziness and unfaithfulness. Increasing "rancor" between them drives him to Maggie for consolation, and the son's defection adds to her isolation. He wrote, "The bond between Dorie and Ned is one of those terrible ones—senseless, of course—that are so current in life: two people who love each other, but can't move or speak without causing each other pain."

Riggs next wrote a picaresque comedy, *Roadside,* which went through several metamorphoses but continued—and continues—bumping along the road, a play with too much life in it to die. Pretty and unruly Hannah and her rascally father Pap Rader wander the country roads in their early version of a recreational vehicle. They meet wild and reckless Texas, just the "world-slingin', star-traipsin' son-of-a-gun" that Hannie has been waiting for, one able to match her restless spirit and eschew roots and regulations. She has already left her ineffectual husband Buzzy and the farm near Verdigris. Since no jail can hold Texas, a comic courtroom scene ends well, with the larger-than-life couple hitting the road happily, even though they recognize that civilization is quickly fencing in the wild frontier and their days of free wandering may soon be limited.

The delight of both critics and audiences was cowboy Texas's declaration that at his mythical birth he was full-grown, wearing a ten-gallon hat, boots, and chaps, and "coming out shooting"! The Shakespearean quality of the play requires the urban audience to use imagination, to forfeit realism for its comedy and romance. Drama historian Alan S. Downer praised *Roadside* especially for the poetic quality of its rustic dialogue. He cited, for example,

Hannie's explanation to her divorced husband Buzzy of how she came to marry him in the first place.

> All I c'n recollect was once about two year ago it was Spring, and Pap and me stopped by that little branch than run th'ough yore cow pasture. And you come down to set the dogs on us. When you seen me—you didn't. So I fell in a daze er sump'n—and when I come to, it seemed like I was kinda married to you—All on account of it bein' Spring, and you not settin' the dogs on us—and one other thing. I was all set to marry *someone* along about then—and I never thought to be picky and choosy.

This artfully naïve tall tale, called a country version of *The Taming of the Shrew,* had only a brief run on Broadway in 1930, but it has delighted and continues to delight audiences in amateur productions. Rumors persist that *Roadside* will be updated as a musical play. It celebrates the wild and free life in harmony with nature—nature as it was before interstate highway systems crisscrossed the prairies.

Folkways and folk songs are preserved in Riggs's greatest play, *Green Grow the Lilacs* (1931), the most authentic and immortal stage work yet to spring from Oklahoma soil. Riggs planned the climax around a shivaree, a raucous mock-serenade given a couple on their wedding night. A fight breaks out during the shivaree, and the villain of the story is killed, with the hero accused of his murder. The play revolves around the brave-young-love story of Laurie and the dashing cowboy Curly. Much of the action takes place at a "play-party," an early Oklahoma house party with music, song, and dancing. Riggs wished to preserve the many old songs which he collected and sang, accompanying himself on his guitar. Cowboys sang them in the play and in front of the curtain, between acts. In the old song "Green Grow the Lilacs" a suitor is haughtily rejected by his ladylove, like the bantering rejection between the lovers in the play: Laurie forgets this pretense, however, when she is frightened by the unwelcome advances of Jeeter, the hired hand. The play closes with declarations of the exciting future in the brand new state of Oklahoma for those who are "hearty" and willing to work hard.

Both *Green Grow the Lilacs* and *Oklahoma!* continue in performance. *Oklahoma!,* long an international favorite, has enjoyed several revivals in New York and is still a popular movie. The musical ran on Broadway for five years and nine months beginning in 1943, breaking all previous records. It revitalized war-weary audiences with its freshness, gaiety, poetry, humor, and courage. The team of Richard Rodgers and Oscar Hammerstein gave Riggs full credit for the plot and dialogue, most of which were retained in their musical version. Hammerstein told the *New York Times* after the opening, "Mr. Riggs' play is the wellspring of almost all that is good in *Oklahoma!* I kept most of the lines of the original play without making any changes in them for the simple reason that they could not be improved upon—at least not by me."

The Hedgerow Theater near Philadelphia, an "angel" to Riggs and other new or experimental play-wrights, premiered his unique play *The Cherokee Night* in June 1932. Critics were divided on the work's merits, puzzled by its use of strong language, but few could deny that something important had been preserved in it. Literature about American Indians, up to this point, either idealized the child of nature or focused on the interracial wars for winning the West. Neither of these themes is found in the plays of Lynn Riggs. *The Cherokee Night* tells the experience of the Cherokee after intermarriage made him a mixed-breed, an anomaly in the twentieth century, bereft of the culture of his past yet unable to fit into the white man's culture of the present. Riggs said the play is a study of certain qualities, strains, and emotions that are particularly strong in a mixed race. He himself was part Cherokee and knew prototypes of his characters in Oklahoma. Unlike some of his dramas, this one becomes more contemporary with the passage of time; it illustrates the failure of the assimilation policy, the loss of tribal and individual identity, and the concomitant loss of "Cherokee pride," a necessity to Cherokee functioning.

Published in a volume with *Russet Mantle* in 1936, *The Cherokee Night* makes haunting reading. The people, outsiders in the white man's culture but no longer protected by leaders of their own, choose crime, drunkenness, laziness, and prostitution in their despair. The play closes with the earliest scene chronologically, in which Gray Wolf, an old chief, mourns with magnificent dignity for his people, "for a whole race gone down into darkness." Riggs saw this scene as the denouement, after the climactic death of a criminal in a church, and thus explains the experimental disorder of the scenes. The play makes reference to Oklahoma flora and fauna as well as to Cherokee history and legends.

In *The Domino Parlor* (1928) men gathered at the Mission Club, joked and cursed, drank alcoholic beverages, gambled at dominoes, and witnessed two fights, a shooting, two murders, and the return of a hardened blues singer, who attempted to rekindle an old love. Critics expressed shock at the low language and moral tone, the amounts of "bootleg liquor and bootleg love" found in a recreation parlor in "dry" Oklahoma, where the sale of alcoholic beverages was still against the law. However, the play was again based on a real place in Claremore, on real characters and events. Published in 1948 as *Hang On to Love,* the work is a blues song filled with regret.

Riggs's next Oklahoma play, *The Cream in the Well,* was received with astonishment and disgust on Broadway. He was stunned by this response, though he knew the work packed dramatic power. It closed after twenty-four performances in New York in 1941, but it was published in *Four Plays* in 1947. Set on the shores of Big Lake, near Verdigris Switch, Indian Territory, the play tells the story of the Sawter family and especially their mean and neurotic daughter Julie. Because of her possessive, incestuous love for her brother Clabe, she drives him away to the Navy, drives to suicide a woman in whom he shows interest, marries a widower and drives him to alcoholism, and finally drowns herself to end the unnatural passion.

The title is taken from the common Territory custom of using the cool depths of a well to store perishable foods, especially milk and cream. Like a well on the Sawter place, Julie, instead of fulfilling the function of preserving, sours everyone and every situation. In *Commonweal* a critic wrote on 31 January 1941, "Mr. Riggs wants to write Greek tragedy with Oklahoma farmers in place of kings and queens. . . . It just can't be done." The play apparently fails to win the sympathy of the audience for the characters, yet Riggs saw them as being just as tragic as kings and queens. *The Cream in the Well* reflects to some extent the madness that afflicted many pioneer women, especially educated ones such as Julie, in their isolated and frustrated lives. The life of Riggs's own educated stepmother, whose name was Juliette, has some parallels to this play. Riggs again was puzzled that actual life situations were not believable to Eastern audiences. The latter preferred to believe that the backwoods were benign, harboring no evil spirits. Joseph Wood Krutch praised Riggs for his attempt, if unconvincing, saying that tragedy is a more difficult genre than comedy. Riggs's dialogue was ingeniously written, with highly speakable lines, and held the audience in a dramatic grip in spite of the violent and sordid theme. For the reader, *The Cream in the Well* is powerful dramatic literature.

Eloise Wilson thought *All the Way Home* and *Out of Dust* (1948) were Riggs's greatest plays, works in which he "uses an abundance of rich folk material and shows love, for the first time, in its finest aspects; also, he achieves taut dramaturgy." Taking his major characters from his Aunt Mary's family, he presents in *All the Way Home* the older generation (Mary and her two cousins) and the younger, Mary's three daughters Tessie, Libby, and Doll, who visit their mother from "Tulsey-town" (early Tulsa) for her birthday in 1910. The drama centers on a mysterious picture in the mother's photo album, a love story, and an all-night refuge in the storm cellar. Family possessions and folkways are incorporated into the play, which was performed in summer theatres in 1948 but never reached Broadway. An interesting technique used by Riggs was the intermittent tableau, which introduced the characters in pairs held immobile in the spotlight for a moment, as in a photograph. The work might better have been titled *Family Photo Album.*

Out of Dust is a powerful Western drama set on the cattle drive along the Shawnee Trail from Oklahoma to the railroad at Baxter Springs, Kansas. Old Man Grant heads the family of three sons: Teece, who ineffectively protects his wife Maudie against the advances of the father; Bud, who has been in trouble with the law and as a result is in financial debt to his father; and Jeff, young and sensitive, who plans to meet his betrothed, Rose, in Baxter Springs, to marry her and stay there, away from the domination and corruption of his father. An Iago-like character, King, the sub-boss, incites the sons to murder the father. The hot, dry, unrelenting hardships of the trail form a fitting background for the cruelty of Teece, who despises his sons' weakness as he keeps them weak, torments them with their bondage to him, and taunts them by threatening to withhold their inheritance. The innocent Rose, who rides out to meet Jeff, is drawn into the drama. This exciting play illustrates the techniques of the cattle drive and deserves a hearing again. A manuscript is now in the Beinecke Library at Yale University. Charles Aughtry called it "an excellent example of the stark power of regional drama at its best."

Riggs's final Oklahoma comedy, *Some Sweet Day,* tells the delightful odyssey of eight-year-old Duncan, who runs away from his stepmother's cruelty and waits for the train in Claremore to go to his "Granmaw's house" in Sapulpa. He makes new friends in the "wagon yard," a rustic hostelry provided in many Oklahoma towns for those who were visiting overnight, seeking shelter from a snowstorm, or waiting for the train to come. People parked and lived in their wagons, cooked over a campfire, cared for their animals and children, and took refuge when needed inside a crude building warmed by a woodstove. Some of the drama centers on the cyclical return of Halley's Comet in 1910, a phenomenon that was received with great fear at the time.

Some Sweet Day was revised for television production in 1953, with happy, lyric songs and dances. Duncan is aided in his journey by the cowboy Buck and meets an assortment of people waiting for the temporarily disabled train, including a schoolteacher going to Sapulpa to teach and a circus family on their way to Joplin to perform. The manuscript includes the words to numerous songs: love songs, a jail song, a riddle song, and advice to a growing boy are among them. In a theme song Buck advises people, if they're going to take the comet's pass for a sign (possibly the end of the world), to take it for a *good* sign. He anticipates the comet's next return about eighty years hence, when it is sure to find "better women and better men," plenty of food, and freedom for all. This fanciful musical play, with the right production, could rival *The Wizard of Oz* for its optimistic enchantment. In addition, it memorializes the wagon yard and the comet's reception, bits of Americana that have almost been lost from memory.

Riggs was stagestruck early in life, having a secret desire to be an actor. Had he not been so enamored of drama, had he written novels instead, his work would have been more accessible to the general public and easier to find today. Since he did not, anyone wishing to find him must look in libraries for out-of-print books and in special collections such as the Beinecke Library at Yale for unpublished manuscripts.

Taken as a whole, Riggs's Oklahoma plays tell much about early Oklahoma life and people. His problem was to make the tragedies dramatically appealing to audiences, where critics said he often failed. Riggs was unable to contrive gratuitous happy endings, but his comedies were well received. No one questions, however, that he authentically reproduced the rhythm and poetic quality of Oklahoma speech with an accuracy unmatched before or since by any other writer. He wrote prolifically; most of his plays were published, many of the others were performed, and in addition he made numerous contributions to poetry and prose. His characters were varied, genuine, and unique.

Riggs's originality was both his genius and his curse, since it was sometimes perceived as "regional" or "experimental." Believing that drama is "interaction between people" and that character is destiny, he wrote from emotion and intuition, making no attempt to write the "traditional Western." His plays are satisfying drama, sometimes stark, usually realistic, sometimes rich with color and pageantry, and certainly of enduring interest. In his Oklahoma plays one walks into the light of an age that has passed and there experiences the aura, mood, and folkways of times and places as authentic as memoirs.

FURTHER READING

Biography

Braunlich, Phyllis Cole. *Haunted By Home: The Life and Letters of Lynn Riggs.* Norman, Okla.: University of Oklahoma Press, 1988, 233 p.

> Full-length biography of Riggs with excerpts from his poetry and letters.

"Lynn Riggs, Playwright." *Theatre Arts Monthly* XXII, No. 7 (July 1938): 528.

> Brief overview of Riggs's life and career through 1938.

Criticism

Clurman, Harold. A review of *Borned in Texas*, by Lynn Riggs. *New Republic* 123, No. 10 (4 September 1950): 23.

> Brief review in which Clurman suggests that the play does not lend itself to successful production in New York, stating: "*Borned in Texas* is literally a country piece, like a delicate cowboy song or an engaging minor poem—very slight in texture—which can only be given for a small audience wholly congenial to its material."

Additional coverage of Riggs's life and career is contained in the following sources published by Gale Research: *Contemporary Authors,* Vol. 145 and *Native North American Literature.*

Le petit prince (The Little Prince)

Antoine de Saint-Exupéry

The following entry presents criticism of Saint-Exupéry's *Le petit prince* (1943; *The Little Prince*). For information on Saint-Exupéry's complete career, as well as additional commentary on *The Little Prince*, see *TCLC*, volume 2.

INTRODUCTION

Although renowned in his native country for his reflective, humanistic stories of the early days of aviation, Saint-Exupéry is best known in English-speaking countries for *The Little Prince*. Considered both a fantasy for children and a philosophically sophisticated allegory for adults, this story has attained the stature of a classic fairy tale, praised for its poignant story, poetic language, and whimsical illustrations.

Biographical Information

Saint-Exupéry was born into an aristocratic family in Lyons, France. From 1917 to 1919 he attended the Ecole Bossuet and the Lycée Saint-Louis, both naval preparatory schools, and later studied at a school for air cadets at Avord. He served in the French Army Air Force from 1921 to 1926 and became instrumental in the dangerous task of establishing mail routes across the African deserts and over the Andes mountains in South America, recounting his experiences during these treacherous flights in such works as *Courrier sud* (*Southern Mail*), *Vol de nuit* (*Night Flight*), and *Terre des hommes* (*Wind, Sand, and Stars*). By 1934 he was serving as a publicity agent for Air France, and beginning in 1935 he served as a foreign correspondent for various newspapers. While flying for the French Air Force during World War II, Saint-Exupéry was shot down over enemy territory and escaped to the United States, where he became a lecturer and freelance writer as well as an important force in the French Resistance. It was also during this period that he wrote *The Little Prince*. Saint-Exupéry returned to active duty and flying in 1943; he was reported missing in action and presumed dead in July of the following year.

Plot and Major Characters

Written amidst the horror and confusion of the war, *The Little Prince* is widely viewed as a reaffirmation of Saint-Exupéry's belief in the importance of friendship, altruism, love, and imagination. The story is narrated by a pilot who has crashed in the desert and is attempting to repair his plane before his supplies run out. A child abruptly appears, and, as the two spend time together, the pilot learns the story of the boy, a prince who has come from an asteroid called B 612. Having left his asteroid to escape the tyrannical demands of his only companion there, an animate rose, the prince has visited six planets before coming to

Earth, and the narrative of his experiences on those planets forms a catalog of human weaknesses and failings. During his travels, the prince discovers the true nature of his relationship with his rose: that it is his responsibility to the rose, rather than any intrinsic property of beauty or goodness, that makes her special to him. In order to return to his asteroid to be reunited with her, he allows himself to be bitten by a serpent, which will kill his body but free his spirit.

Critical Reception

Commentators have noted that *The Little Prince* contains sophisticated philosophical concepts that differentiate the work from most children's literature. In emphasizing the responsibility of the individual for the well-being of others, for example, Saint-Exupéry created a compelling argument for many of the altruistic activities in which he was involved, while the prince's experiences on other planets are widely viewed as an indictment of the types of behavior that cause society to require such remedies. Critics often focus on Saint-Exupéry's motive for writing the story, analyzing its autobiographical elements and its expression of the author's fears for the fate of Europe under fascism. Although some see such elements as detrimental to its role as children's fiction, *The Little Prince* is generally acknowledged as a successful allegory which can be enjoyed by children and adults. Maxwell A. Smith has written: "Because of its poetic charm, . . . its freshness of imagery, its whimsical fantasy, delicate irony and warm tenderness, it seems likely that *The Little Prince* will join that select company of books like La Fontaine's *Fables*, Swift's *Gulliver's Travels*, Carroll's *Alice in Wonderland* and Maeterlinck's *Blue Bird*, which have endeared themselves to children and grown-ups alike throughout the world."

CRITICISM

Katherine S. White   (essay date 1943)

SOURCE: A review of *The Little Prince* in *The New Yorker*, Vol. 19, May 29, 1943, p. 52.

[*In the following review, the reviewer describes Saint-Exupéry's* The Little Prince *as overelaborate and confusing.*]

The critics of children's books have a tendency to greet with joyous cries of welcome any juvenile written by an author who has a name in a wider field of writing. This is natural enough, considering the number of books they must read in a year by writers without talent, and often there is real cause for rejoicing over a great name on the title page. Not always, though. This spring, for example, the cries of welcome have been for *The Little Prince,* written and illustrated by Antoine de Saint-Exupéry. Whatever the merits of the book, it seems to be news: it has had a rush of publicity, it is on the best-seller lists, some reviewers announce that it has already taken its place among the children's classics, others call it a book only for subtle-minded adults, and all unite in praise and in rather solemn analysis of its overtones of meaning. I therefore feel strangely alone, since, to my mind, *The Little Prince* is not a book for children and is not even a good book. It can be described as a philosophical fairy tale, or, if you prefer the word so often used of Saint-Exupéry, a metaphysical one. The only youthful appraisal I can offer is that of a twelve-year-old boy, who likes almost all kinds of books and usually reads at top speed. After dragging through this one, he said, "He seems to be writing about grownup things in a childish way." Possibly this judgment has some merit because, when you come to think of it, the best children's books are those which treat childlike things in an adult way. *The Little Prince* unquestionably has its moments of charm and point and its naïve drawings have occasional humor and grace, but as a fairy tale, whether for adults or children, it seems to me to lack the simplicity and clarity all fairy tales must have in order to create their magic, and too often its charm turns into coyness and its point is lost in cloudy and boring elaboration.

Anne Carol Moore   (essay date 1943)

SOURCE: A review of *The Little Prince* in *The Horn Book Magazine*, Vol. XIX, No. 3, May-June 1943, pp. 164-65.

[*Moore was an American librarian and author of children's story books who often wrote on the topic of children's literature. In the excerpt below, she characterizes* The Little Prince *as a work as applicable to adults as to children.*]

By one of the happy chances of advance publication, Antoine de Saint-Exupéry's *The Little Prince* came to me on the eve of Hans Christian Andersen's birthday. I read it at once, not as a reviewer, but as a gift for a day which grows more significant every year that I live.

All life—its poetry and philosophy, its humor and pathos, its poverty and riches, as seen by Andersen from the earth over which he wandered more than a century ago—was the theme of those dramas in miniature: The Snow Queen, The Nightingale, The Garden of Paradise, Thumbelina, The Rose-Elf. If I were to be cast away, not on the proverbial desert island—there are no more desert islands—but in the dreariest of all places during this World War (which might be a schoolroom), I have always felt my one book would be Andersen's *Fairy Tales*. No; I should beg for a companion volume and its title is *The Little Prince.*

From its magical frontispiece, picturing the escape of the Little Prince from his tiny planet, with the aid of a migrating flock of wild birds, to his flowers and his volcanoes, I am held, as I believe many children will be, by the pictures—pictures which are an integral part of the dramatic and philosophic story; pictures so childlike and free, yet as suggestive of the ageless Primitives as the text, which, with all its fresh imagery and originality, is a reminder of Hans Christian Andersen and his supreme gift of giving life to the inanimate. "Saint-Exupéry has written a book to please the child he was and still is," I said to myself, "just as W. H. Hudson did in *A Little Boy Lost.*" It may be disturbing to some readers that a snake should play a part in returning the Little Prince to his planet. Readers who feel that way may well re-read *A Little Boy Lost* for a different attitude toward snakes, as well as Andersen's *Fairy Tales* for a fresh illumination of life in a world which has never been in such need of the water of life to which we must ever look for fresh wellsprings of imagination. Saint-Exupéry has personally experienced the hunger and thirst, the dangers and loneliness of the world he not only lives in but in which he continues to fly up to the stars.

No one who has been as deeply moved as I have been by the recurrence of his childhood memories as recorded in *Wind, Sand and Stars* and *Flight to Arras* can be expected to deal objectively with *The Little Prince.* I have been interested but not impressed by most of the adult reviewers and commentators who have attempted to place the book. Is it for adults or for children? they ask. Who shall say?

I look upon it as a book so fresh and different, so original yet so infused with wisdom as to take a new place among books in general. I predict that the children who like it will like it very much for its magical quality and the direct approach of the Little Prince to "matters of consequence." Children who have never held communication with the stars, with flowers, with desert foxes or with a stranded aviator may find it perplexing. The same holds good for adult readers who look upon philosophy as a subject for scholars rather than an experience of childhood. Those in whom the flower of imagination was never nourished and tended will probably wonder what it is all about when "reality" should be our first concern at this time. . . .

To the children of France the Little Prince should stand as a symbol of their deliverance from bondage in the 20th century. To many children of other countries the Little Prince will share the secret imparted to him by the fox he tamed in the desert. "It is only with the heart one can see rightly; what is essential is invisible to the eye." . . .

The Little Prince seems to me the most important book of many years. . . .

Maxwell A. Smith (essay date 1956)

SOURCE: *Knight of the Air: The Life and Works of Antoine de Saint-Exupéry,* Pageant Press, Inc., 1956, pp. 189-200.

[*Smith was an American educator and critic who specialized in French literature. In the following essay, he provides a highly favorable assessment of* The Little Prince.]

The Little Prince was published in New York in the spring of 1943 in both English and French editions but was not well known to French readers until the Gallimard edition of 1946. Unique among all of his writings, it is a delicate and ethereal fairy tale apparently addressed to children although its wide philosophical overtones as a parable will be understood only by adults. There has been much discussion concerning the author's purpose in writing this charming fable. Was it a brief relaxation from the anguish concerning his country which tormented him in his American exile, a bit of playful and poetic whimsey for the entertainment of children, particularly for the child he once had been and which in some respects he had fortunately never ceased to be? Was it chiefly a pretext for the lovely sketches and aquarelles which for years he had been drawing for his own delight? Was it rather like the *Lettre à un otage* intended primarily for the consolation of his beloved compatriots, an opportunity to lift them for a moment from their blackness of despair? To justify the latter theory, one might mention the dedication to his friend, Léon Werth, "This grown-up who lives in France where he is cold and hungry and has great need of being consoled."

It is possible, of course, for imaginative youngsters of all ages from eight to eighty to enjoy this delightful fantasy without bothering themselves too much concerning the motivation of the author. It would be pleasant for most readers to share the theory of the late Professor Eliot Fay [*Modern Language Journal*, November, 1948], based on an interview with Consuelo de Saint-Exupéry, the author's wife, that this is an allegory of their love. Just as the Little Prince, tiring of his love for his beloved flower had left his tiny planet to wander through celestial space, so Saint-Ex, after seven years of married life, had suddenly informed his wife that he needed to be alone to travel and

seek adventure throughout the world, but would some day return to her and settle down to a regular conjugal state. According to Consuelo, he did return three years later just as he had promised, a short time before the outbreak of the war. (There seems to be a slight inconsistency of dates in this account, since they were married in 1931 and this would make him return two years after the outbreak of hostilities.) Mr. Eugene Reynal, Saint-Exupéry's friend and American publisher, rejects completely, however, this romantic theory concerning the composition of *The Little Prince.*

According to a letter from Mr. Reynal, the book

> had its origin in a little drawing made as a joke on the margin of Bernard Lamotte's original sketch for the illustrations in *Flight to Arras.* It was a little winged figure looking something like himself which he became intrigued with and which he kept drawing over and over again in different forms for his own amusement. As he played with it, it grew in form and I suppose set his mind to work with the little stories about the figure which finally emerged as a book. We kept after him to work on the drawings with a book in mind without having any more idea of the form the story might take than I am sure he had at that time. He would call us up excitedly at different times to show us how the drawings were coming along. When we suggested color, he started experimenting with that. I am quite sure the pictures and the book developed together in his mind and I am also sure they provided him with a new medium for expressing his own philosophy as well as a form of relaxation in this new departure for his work.

In many other ways, moreover, we may seek in *The Little Prince* a deeper revelation of the author's life and personality than is to be found in the purely factual references to his childhood and maturity of his other books. Guillain de Benouville, the famous leader of the Resistance Movement, tells in *Confluences* of his friendship with Saint-Ex in Algiers during May, 1944, and of the latter's handing to his friends a copy of *The Little Prince* which he evidently considered to be his autobiography. "He held it out with a smile, almost as if he had given us his photograph." Louis Barjon, who knew Saint-Ex well at this time, states in the same work that few books have given us a more faithful and profound picture of the real Saint-Ex, and even goes so far as to say that he could easily show how the physiognomy of the little prince reproduces that of the author, feature by feature. (The reader thinks at once of the scarf which flew behind the little prince, and which was such an inseparable part of the author's attire.) Albérès likewise in his *Saint-Exupéry* finds in this autobiography "all his imagery and symbolism, the deserted planets and the marvelous flame of the man and his friendship, all this waking dream in which Saint-Exupéry lived and whose most touching image he gives us the day on which he assumed the paternity of the little prince. For in this book he has put the whole of himself."

Many readers likewise will have noticed in several of his earlier books premonitions or hints of the figure of the little prince. As early as *Southern Mail,* for instance, the hero, Bernis, was confronted with the "phantom of a tender urchin," the child which he had once been, and his death on the desert sands underneath the vertical star in which the treasure glittered resembles that of the little prince. In the chapter called "The Secret Garden" of *Wind, Sand and Stars* we encounter the little princesses with their tame snakes beneath the floor, and in the conclusion of the same volume we recall the episode in which the author feels compassion for the little Polish emigrant. "I leaned over this smooth forehead, over these sweetly pouting lips and I said to myself: this is the face of a musician, this is the child-Mozart, this is a beautiful promise of life. The little princes of legends were not different from him." So deeply a part of himself indeed is the concept of the little prince that P. L. Travers has written: "Each of his books has been a path leading across the sand dunes to the prince's citadel" [*New York Herald Tribune Weekly Book Review,* April 11, 1943].

"Please draw me a sheep." As Saint-Exupéry, trying to mend his broken motor in the midst of the Sahara, looked up startled at this abrupt request, he had his first glimpse of the little prince, with whom he was to become so much better acquainted during the next eight days. At the age of six, Saint-Ex had proudly drawn the picture of a boa constrictor which had swallowed an elephant, but his grown-up friends had taken it for the picture of a hat. When he had made another drawing showing the elephant inside, his adult advisers had rudely suggested that he devote himself to geography, history, arithmetic and grammar, thereby causing him to abandon a magnificent career as a painter. However, when he now made the same drawing for the little prince, he was astonished to see this astute little mind recognize at once that it was not a hat but a boa which had swallowed an elephant, neither of which animals, however, answered his request for a sheep. After several unsuccessful attempts to please him with a sheep, Saint-Ex in desperation finally drew a box and when he told the little prince that the sheep was inside, the prince could not only divine the presence of the animal but also the fact that he was asleep.

Saint-Ex soon learned that his little friend came from a tiny planet called Asteroid B612. This planet had first been discovered by a Turkish astronomer in 1908, but since he wore an outlandish foreign costume, no one believed him. Fortunately a few years later a Turkish dictator forced his people to adopt modern dress, so that in 1920 when the same scholar made his demonstration in fashionable attire his discovery was accepted. This is the first of many amusing shafts of irony directed at the foibles of grown-ups by the author. "Grown-ups love numerals. When you tell them that you have made a new friend, they never ask you any questions on essential matters. They never say to you, 'What does his voice sound like? What games does he love best? Does he collect butterflies?' Instead they demand: 'How old is he? How many brothers has he? How much does he weigh? How much money does his father make?' . . . If you were to say to grown-ups: 'I saw a beautiful house made of rosy bricks, with geraniums in the windows, and doves on the roof,' they would not be able to get any idea of that house at all. You would have

to say to them, 'I saw a house that cost $20,000.' Then they would exclaim, 'Oh, what a pretty house that is!'

"Just so, you might say to them, 'the proof that the little prince existed is that he was charming, that he laughed, and that he wanted a sheep. If anybody wants a sheep that is a proof that he exists.' They would shrug their shoulders and treat you like a child. But if you said to them: 'The planet he came from is Asteroid B612,' then they would be convinced and leave you in peace from their questions. That's the way they are. One must not hold it against them."

Soon the author learned that the little prince had on his planet three volcanoes (including one which was extinct) which he cleaned out every day, a multitude of baobab bushes which he extirpated daily (it was to avoid this heavy chore that he had asked for the sheep) and the most beautiful rose, absolutely unique in the world, which he watered and put under glass at night with the greatest tenderness. Alas, finding his flower to be both vain and mendacious, he had decided after a quarrel to take advantage of the migration of some wild birds to leave his planet and his beloved rose.

As the wandering prince visits Asteroids 325 to 330 in his vicinity, the author, with gentle irony, resumes his attacks on the vagaries of contemporary man. The first planet was occupied only by a king, dressed in royal purple and ermine, who in his solitary majesty saw in the little prince only a subject whom he could order around. When the prince yawned, the king first forbade such insolence, but when the little prince was unable to obey, the king ordered him to yawn. Anxious to retain this subject, the king offered him the post of Minister of Justice, which would allow him to judge an old rat, but since there was only one, it would be necessary to pardon him after each conviction, in order to make him last. When the little prince insisted on leaving, the king, with a great air of authority, appointed him his ambassador.

The second planet was inhabited by a conceited man who insisted that the little prince clap his hands in admiration so that he could take off his hat and bow. At first this was very entertaining but after five minutes the exercise grew monotonous and the prince departed.

Planet 3 was occupied by a drunkard who was drinking to make himself forget that he was ashamed of drinking. The fourth planet contained a businessman who was counting so hard the number of stars which he possessed that his cigarette had gone out and he did not have time to relight it. "I am concerned with matters of consequence," said the businessman, "I administer them, count them and recount them." When asked what he did with the stars he replied, "I write the number of my stars on a little paper, then I put this paper in a drawer and lock it with a key." The little prince considered this amusing and even rather poetic but he realized that he had different ideas from adults about what is serious. The fifth planet was a very tiny one, with barely enough space for a street lamp and a lamplighter. Ordered to light up every evening and extinguish at dawn, the poor man had to perform both of these functions every minute because a change in the planets had now caused his to revolve faster and faster. This is the first man whom the little prince did not regard as ridiculous because, despite his laziness, he was performing his duty—the only one who paid any attention to anything but himself. The sixth and last planet was occupied by a geographer, who was unable to answer any questions because he was waiting for an explorer to bring him information on which he could write books. At the suggestion of the geographer, the little prince now goes to visit the Earth.

In comparison with these tiny planets, the Earth is surely a mighty place for it counts no less than one hundred and eleven kings (including the Negro kings, of course), seven thousand geographers, nine hundred thousand businessmen, seven and a half million drunkards and thirteen hundred and eleven million vain people, a total of two billion grown-ups. Yet as Saint-Ex points out (ever conscious of the tiny place which human beings take up on the vast surface of the earth) these two billion could easily be placed on a tiny island of the Pacific twenty miles square.

Landing on the Earth in the African desert, the little prince was surprised at first to find no men, only a friendly serpent. After much wandering he came to a magnificent garden of five thousand roses, all of them as beautiful as the rose which he had loved, believing it unique in the world. No wonder that, disillusioned, he lay down in the grass and wept. Then he learned from a little fox the great lesson of friendship—only when he has tamed the fox will they both have need of each other and will consider each other unique in the world. This then is what made his beloved rose unique, for he had tamed the rose by watering her and tending her, and now she was like no other rose in the world. When he came to say goodbye to the fox, the latter confided in him the great secret: "It is only with the heart that one can see rightly; what is essential is invisible to the eye."

"What is essential is invisible to the eye," the little prince repeated, so that he would be sure to remember.

"It is the time you have wasted for your rose that makes your rose so important . . . Men have forgotten this truth," said the fox. "But you must not forget it. You become responsible forever for what you have tamed. You are responsible for your rose."

And now we come perhaps to the loveliest and most poetical passage of this little fable, when on the eighth day the author and his diminutive friend set out in search for water. "What makes the desert beautiful," said the little prince, "is that somewhere it hides a well."

"I was astonished by a sudden understanding of that mysterious radiation of the sands. When I was a little boy I lived in an old house, and legend told us that a treasure was buried there. To be sure, no one had ever known how to find it; perhaps no one had ever even looked for it. But it cast an enchantment over that house. My home was hiding a secret in the depth of its heart.

" 'Yes,' I said to the little prince. 'The house, the stars, the desert—what gives them their beauty is something that is invisible.'

" 'I am glad,' said he, 'that you agree with my fox.'

"As the little prince dropped off to sleep I took him in my arms and set out . . . It seemed to me that I was carrying a very fragile treasure. It seemed to me, even, that there was nothing more fragile on all the Earth. In the moonlight, I looked at his pale forehead, his closed eyes, his locks of hair that trembled in the wind and I said to myself: what I see here is nothing but a shell. What is most important is invisible.

"And, as I walked on so, I found the well, at daybreak."

What made the water taste like something far sweeter than ordinary water was the walk under the stars, the song of the pully, the effort of his arms: "It was good for the heart like a present. When I was a little boy, the lights of the Christmas tree, the music of the midnight mass, the tenderness of smiling faces used to make up, so, the radiance of the gifts I received." It is because men are blind and do not seek with the heart that they fail to find what they are looking for, which awaits them in a rose or in a little water.

But alas, the next day was the anniversary of the date when the little prince had descended from his star, exactly in this spot of the desert. Just as the author has succeeded in repairing his motor the little prince tells him that he has persuaded his friend, the serpent, to bite him with his deadly poison so that he can leave behind him his body, like an old shell, and go back to his distant star. "You know my flower . . . I am responsible for her . . . And she is so weak! She is so naive! She has four thorns of no use at all to protect herself against the world."

"There was nothing there but a flash of yellow close to his ankle. He remained motionless for an instant. He did not cry out. He fell as gently as a tree falls. There was not even any sound because of the sand."

For a time Saint-Ex was deeply saddened by the loss of his little friend. At daybreak, however, when he did not find his body, he knew that the little prince was safely back in his star. And each night as he looks at the heavens he seems to hear the laughter of the little prince, like four hundred million little bells. But alas he remembers that although he had drawn a muzzle for the sheep, he had forgotten to draw a leather strap. He asks himself with great anxiety, will the little prince remember each night to put a glass over his flower, or will he forget sometime, and in that case will the sheep eat the rose? "And no grown-up will ever understand that this is a matter of so much importance!"

To analyze in detail so lovely and fragile a tale would be like removing the petals of a rose to try to discover its charm. For that reason I have preferred to quote at length from the original so that the reader too may "see with the heart." It is perhaps too early to predict what part of Saint-Exupéry's works will achieve immortality. Because of its poetic charm, however, its freshness of imagery, its whimsical fantasy, delicate irony and warm tenderness, it seems likely that *The Little Prince* will join that select company of books like La Fontaine's *Fables,* Swift's *Gulliver's Travels,* Carroll's *Alice in Wonderland* and Maeterlinck's *Blue Bird,* which have endeared themselves to children and grown-ups alike throughout the world.

André Maurois   (essay date 1966)

SOURCE: "Antoine de Saint-Exupéry," in *From Proust to Camus: Profiles of Modern French Writers,* by André Maurois, translated by Carl Morse and Renaud Bruce, Doubleday & Company, 1966, pp. 201-23.

[*An extremely versatile French writer, Maurois made his most significant contribution to literature as a biographer. In the following excerpt from an overview of Saint-Exupéry's career, he commends* The Little Prince *for its enigmatic blend of lucid and obscure symbolism.*]

I shall certainly not try to "explain" *Le Petit Prince.* That children's book for grownups is alive with symbols which are beautiful because they seem, at the same time, both lucid and obscure. The essential virtue of a work of art is that it has its own significance, without reference to abstract concepts. A cathedral does not require commentaries, the starry vault does not require footnotes. I believe that *Le Petit Prince* may be an incarnation of Tonio as a child. But as *Alice in Wonderland* was at the same time a tale for little girls and a satire on the Victorian world, *Le Petit Prince,* in its poetic melancholy, contains a whole philosophy. The king is obeyed only when he orders what would, in any case, occur. The lamplighter is respected because he is occupied with other things besides himself; the businessman is scoffed at because he thinks that stars or flowers can be "possessed"; the fox lets himself be tamed in order to recognize a footstep that will be different from all others. "One only knows the things that one tames, says the fox. Men buy things already made in the stores. But as there are no stores where friends can be bought, men no longer have friends." *Le Petit Prince* is the work of a wise and tender hero who did have friends.

Robert H. Price   (essay date 1967)

SOURCE: *"Pantagruel* and *Le petit prince." Symposium* Vol. XXI, No. 3, Fall, 1967, pp. 264-70.

[*In the essay below, Price compares* The Little Prince *in style and theme to François Rabelais's* Gargantua and Pantagruel.]

Any attempt to determine whether one writer has influenced another when the only proof that can be adduced is similarity of thought and expression is risky business at best. One must refrain from yielding to the ever-present temptation to see literary influences at work when, in all likelihood, discoverable parallels are simply coincidental or, as is often the case, one is dealing with kindred souls thinking alike but independently of each other. Nevertheless, comparative studies of strangely similar works do have their place in literary criticism. Apart from any attempt to suggest influence, they can be valuable in that they often serve to make the ideas contained in each of the works more meaningful, for what André Gide said about imitators also holds true in some measure for writers who, unknowingly, deal with age-old questions of universal im-

port in ways similar to those of their predecessors: "Souvent une grande idée n'a pas assez d'un seul grand homme pour l'exprimer, pour l'exagérer tout entière; un grand homme n'y suffit pas; il faut que plusieurs s'y emploient, reprennent cette idée première, la redisent, la réfractent, en fasse valoir une dernière beauté" ["De l'influence en littérature," *OEuvres completes,* 1932-39].

Among all the French writers in the great tradition of the imaginary voyage, two seem to stand out as particularly kindred souls: Rabelais and Saint-Exupéry. What a fine case for literary influence could be made here if only Saint-Exupéry or one of his biographers mentioned Rabelais! We could then immediately ascribe the striking parallels to direct and conscious influence and thereby validate the internal evidence, just as it is possible to do with Pascal's *Pensées* and Saint-Exupéry's *Citadelle* on the basis of Dr. Pélissier's first-hand knowledge of Saint-Exupéry's favorite authors [*Les Cinq Visages de Saint-Exupéry,* 1951]. But there is no external evidence of any kind to support such a conjecture in the present instance and, however plausible it may seem, we cannot make the claim that Saint-Exupéry had Rabelais' fourth and fifth books of *Pantagruel* in mind when he wrote *Le Petit Prince.* We must content ourselves with seeing how the evident parallels in these works tend to throw into sharper relief certain otherwise enigmatic features of their shared theme of fanciful voyage and alienation from reality. The thematic and stylistic parallels also serve to underscore the essential spiritual kinship of these two profoundly humanistic authors, each of whom was a writer by avocation suffering in exile at the time he conceived of the work in question. The big prince, Pantagruel, at sea, and the little prince, in space, were seeking, as were their creators, reassurance and solid ground—a basis upon which to construct an ideal.

Both works can be read and enjoyed on two levels, and their authors insist that we not neglect the higher one. "L'abstracteur de quinte essence" [Rabelais] tells the reader in the prologue to *Gargantua* fourteen years before the appearance of the partial edition of *Le Quart Livre* that "l'habit ne faict pas le moyne"—that we must not judge on the basis of external appearances—for who, he asks, would have given a piece of onion for Socrates "tant laid il estoit de corps et ridicule en son maintien . . . rustiq en vestimens . . ." [*OEuvres completes,* 1962]. Yet beneath that deceptive and unpromising exterior, he assures us, was a wealth of understanding, virtue, courage, sobriety, equanimity and assurance. Rabelais goes on to declare, "c'est pourquoy fault ouvrir le livre et soigneusement peser ce que est deduict." He exhorts the reader to look beyond the literal meaning and to seek a higher meaning. To do this, one must follow the example of Plato's philosophical dog and "rompre l'os et sugcer la sustantificque mouelle."

Similarly, Saint-Exupéry, in order to stress the need to see beneath the surface of things, uses the device of the open and closed boa constrictor drawings at the beginning of *Le Petit Prince.* He also tells us of the Turkish astronomer who discovered in 1909 asteroid B 612, the little prince's home, but whom nobody believed at the International Congress of Astronomy because of his outlandish Turkish clothes. If, despite these examples and others, there is still any doubt left in the reader's mind about the author's intentions, he states unequivocally and with a touch of acerbity: "[...] je n'aime pas qu'on lise mon livre à la légère."

Rabelais in exile in Metz in 1546-47 and Saint-Exupéry in New York in 1942 were each going through a particularly trying period in their lives and were seeking equilibrium and peace of mind in a world which had turned topsy-turvy for them. These two men of action, each having cause to be concerned about his professional career, were cast adrift emotionally and spiritually, far from friends and home. The problem of how to bear up under the strains and frustrations of life was foremost in their thoughts.

The dual nature of Rabelais' *Le Quart Livre* and of Saint-Exupéry's **Le Petit Prince** is probably a reflection of the very dual nature of life as experienced by the two authors in exile. There are, according to both these spiritual humanists, two levels of reality in life, and it is the deeper or, from the spiritual point of view, the higher level to which man must aspire if he is to arrive at ultimate truth. The conception of reality as expressed by Plato in his parable of the cave is analogous. But whereas for Plato, value exists independently of a valuator, for Saint-Exupéry, and doubtless for Rabelais, there is no such thing as *a priori* value. Rather, *man* is the measure of all things, and the world takes on meaning and value for him only insofar as he puts meaning and value into it by his involvement with, and contributions to, his fellow men. This conception is foreign neither to Renaissance thought nor to certain schools of twentieth-century French thought. Indeed, relativism is one of their basic characteristics and establishes an often overlooked affinity between two eras widely separated in time.

The peregrinations of the two princes illustrate the nature of this type of quest for individual truth. Rabelais chooses a long sea voyage (already announced, to be sure, earlier in 1546, near the end of *Le Tiers Livre*) to symbolize his alienation from familiar reality and a quest for solid spiritual ground, for the trip was not undertaken solely for the purpose of finding out whether Panurge should marry or not; it was essentially a voyage of self-discovery. Whereas Saint-Exupéry, the aviator, naturally chooses the medium of space, Rabelais, in view of the then current popularity of navigation accounts, chooses the sea, although he did announce a trip to the moon for his hero in the last chapter of his first work, *Pantagruel Roy des Dipsodes* (1532), and later, near the end of *Le Tiers Livre* (Chapter LI), foresaw the possibility of interstellar travel.

In reading these fanciful philosophical travel accounts we must always be aware of the fact that each author projects himself into a personified alter ego in which he mirrors his personal growth. Pantagruel, whom Rabelais now rarely reminds us is a physical giant, gradually becomes during the course of the voyage a superior being—a giant in *moral* stature—the symbol of human potentiality. Likewise, the little prince through his encounter with the fox eventually discovers the answers to the great questions in life and rids his spirit of torment and uncertainty. In dealing with this process of spiritual growth, both authors use

physical thirst as a symbol of spiritual thirst. Pantagruel and his companions in seeking the Dive Bouteille are really in quest of the Pierian Spring or, indeed, the very well-spring of their being, as is the little prince when he and the author set out across the desert in search of a well.

As seekers thirsting for ultimate truth, neither Rabelais nor Saint-Exupéry wrote from a dogmatic or even systematic point of view. Neither one was installed in a philosophical or theological system. They both insisted on freedom from preconceptions and prescriptions in their search for truth. And, likewise, it was in the very process of writing that their thoughts, and the form in which they expressed them took shape and direction. . . .

Saint-Exupéry in maintaining that existence or creation precedes the plan is very close to existentialism. In all his works, it is evident that he insists on the vital need for man to grow and to define himself on the basis of his acts. And, according to Saint-Exupéry, man can meet this need only insofar as he establishes bonds of responsibility with his fellow men. The little prince learns that he is responsible for his rose and that it is the time and energy that he devotes to the care of his rose that endows it with value and meaning, thus giving him purpose and direction in life. It is unlikely that Rabelais, the dedicated and skilled physician, felt any differently about man's role in life. He detested the monastic ideal of withdrawal from life and everything else that he deemed to be a hindrance to man's physical, mental, and spiritual growth. The irrepressible Frère Jean des Entommeures is indication enough that Rabelais felt, as did Saint-Exupéry, that man, if he is to give meaning to his existence, must act in such a way as to be able to give meaning to his actions. Man is what he does, and if he can ascribe no significant and satisfying purpose to what he does, he can only drift aimlessly on the sea of life.

Pantagruel and the little prince do not drift during their voyages. They continually define themselves and become increasingly aware of their direction in life as they discover and disengage that "structure which alone matters." To be sure, Rabelais and Saint-Exupéry were seekers during their entire lifetime. But each one was, at the same time, quite clear in his own mind about what constituted obstacles to man's attempts to realize his full potential and promise as a human being. Neither Rabelais nor Saint-Exupéry had any patience with stupidity, superstition, preconceptions, and prejudices which thwart the growth of human dignity and rob man of his rightful equanimity and nobility of spirit. The *escales* or stopping-off places in both works (islands in one and planets in the other) afford the authors the opportunity to represent in the inhabitants the enemies of the ideal they had in mind. Allegorical social satire in the form of grotesque caricaturization shows how strongly the two authors felt about certain human preoccupations, attitudes, and vices. The reader is confronted with a series of ludicrous and frequently harmful cases of monomania which prevent man from extending his horizons. Constrained by intellectual and spiritual blinders, the various freaks fail even to glimpse the vision of their potential stature as men. The monomaniacs on the islands and planets are victims of their own simplistic and distorted views of life. Erich Auerbach sums it up nicely [in his *Mimesis*, 1957]: "Thick-headedness, inability to adjust, one-track arrogance which blinds a man to the complexity of the real situation are vices to Rabelais. This is the form of stupidity which he mocks and pursues." The same appraisal, of course, holds true for Saint-Exupéry.

There can be little doubt that Rabelais believed self-discovery to be the most vital knowledge to which man can attain. Echos of Socrates are to be found throughout his writings. Besides mentioning the philosopher specifically in the prologue to *Gargantua* and elsewhere, Rabelais frequently alludes in various ways to the Socratic (or more properly, the Delphic) precept, "Know thyself."

The message of the Dive Bouteille (even though we cannot be sure that Rabelais is the author of that part of the fifth book which deals with the oracle) can be viewed in the same light. The priestess Bacbuc interprets the oracle by telling Panurge and the others to *drink*—not read—the gloss out of a large book-shaped silver flask and by explaining at the same time that "Trinch" means "Buvez" and that in wine there is hidden truth. She then adds, "La dive Bouteille vous y envoye, soyez vous mesmes interpretes de vostre entreprinse."

To many of Rabelais' readers, this episode, unless it is understood properly, seems anticlimactic—as well as trivial and disappointing to a man who has come thousands of miles at risk of life and limb to seek help. Jean Plattard was right when he pointed out that instead of interpreting the oracle to mean "Bois aux sources du savoir" we should consider it to be a "conseil pratique"—"une solution de simple bon sens." But, just as one must look beneath the cover of the book-shaped flask and beyond the literal contents of that flask, so too must one look even beyond common sense and discover that ultimately we are dealing with the deeper knowledge of self, for it is precisely such knowledge which *enables* one to exercise that most uncommon commodity of common sense. Panurge was incapable of heeding reasonable advice before undertaking the voyage because he had not yet acquired self-knowledge, for Pantagruel had told him essentially the same thing as Bacbuc when he first brought up the question of whether or not he should get married: "N'estez vous asceuré de vostre vouloir? Le poinct principal y gist: tout le reste est fortuit, et dependent des fatales dispositions du ciel." The advice, at that point, as we know, fell on deaf ears, and the voyage of self-discovery was absolutely necessary before Panurge could know his own mind.

Self-knowledge, then, is the *sine qua non* of human endeavor, for to know one's own mind, it is necessary first to know one's own self. Man must make the attempt to find out what he is before he can know what he wants—before he *can* make meaningful and satisfying choices and thus live life to the fullest. The little prince after drinking from the well in the desert commented on its meaning to him and on the ultimate meaning of all things in life by repeating the lesson that the fox had taught him: "Voici mon secret. Il est très simple: on ne voit bien qu'avec le coeur. L'essentiel est invisible pour les yeux." The author of the chapters devoted to the Dive Bouteille would likewise have us understand that final answers must come from within and that we are what we make of ourselves.

In times of rapid change—such as the sixteenth and our own century—in which man advances on so many fronts but is also confronted with seemingly insurmountable obstacles (and is not that the real significance of the dreadful tempest in *Le Quart Livre?*) the need for equanimity grounded on self-knowledge is most pressing. And if Pantagruelism is, as Rabelais defined it in the prologue to the definitive edition of *Le Quart Livre*, "[une] certaine gayeté d'esprit conficte en mepris des choses fortuites," it is obviously needed as much today as it was in Rabelais' time. But Rabelais realized early that such an outlook does not result from shutting oneself off from life and its problems. On the contrary, man must become involved and must grapple with adversity, for his *engagement* is the only valid test of his worth. The optimistic stoicism combined with gaiety is the fruit of his victory and the hallmark of genuine humanity.

The quest for self-knowledge and definition is perhaps one of the most salient commonly-shared features of sixteenth and twentieth-century French thought. An admirer of Saint-Exupéry, André Gide, who rarely traveled without his copy of Montaigne's *Essais,* is certainly an outstanding example of devotion to that quest. But there are other names, too, in the twentieth century in addition to those of Saint-Exupéry and Gide: Sartre, Camus, Malraux, Montherlant—all of whom have preached a similar, if not identical, message: that it is imperative that man, through the most complete exposure to life and involvement with it, discover and indeed *create* what he is—for life can become meaningful and fruitful only through a concomitant awareness of self.

Brian Masters　(essay date 1972)

SOURCE: *"Le petit prince,"* in *A Student's Guide to Saint-Exupéry,* Heinemann Educational Books Ltd., 1972, pp. 84-91.

[*Masters is an English educator and critic. In the following excerpt, he discusses themes of love, maturity, and responsibility in* The Little Prince.]

Le Petit Prince was published in New York in 1943, only a few months after *Lettre à un Otage.* It purports to be a story for children (and can be read as such), but the story illustrates the eternal truths which Saint-Exupéry had been at pains to convey in his other books, and which the 'grown-ups' who read them had been too stupid to understand.

In addressing his book to children, and making frequent, gently sarcastic remarks about the obscurantism of the adults, the author wishes to point out that his book has much to teach the 'grandes personnes', if only they would listen. Perhaps it is for the children to explain to them?

The author has crashed his aircraft in the desert. He is busy repairing it, when he is quite suddenly approached by a charming little prince with blond hair, who says to him, 'S'il vous plaît . . . dessine-moi un mouton . . .'

The author obliges, and friendship between the two unlikely castaways is established. The Little Prince tells how he is in love with a rose, on the planet where he lives, but her vanity and fickleness hurt him, so he decided to travel far from his planet. Before leaving, he was careful to collect all the seeds of the baobab trees, which threatened to spread all over the planet, and to sweep out his three volcanoes. Then he journeyed from one planet to another.

On one planet, he met a monarch without subjects, who enjoyed playing at being king, and was delighted to have the Little Prince as a temporary subject whom he could command. On another, there was the narcissist, whose only pleasure was to be admired. He, too, was alone on his planet, so his only admirer was himself. The third planet was the home of the drunkard, who was ashamed of being alcoholic, and drowned his shame in drink. The fourth planet sheltered the businessman, counting his money, making calculations, and claiming ownership of the stars. The final planet which the Little Prince visited was so small that day and night were each only a few minutes long. Here there lived a lamplighter, whose entire life was taken in lighting and putting out his lamp to keep time with the swift rotation of his planet. However absurd and frustrating it may seem, the Little Prince felt respect for the lamp-lighter, because of all those he had visited, he was the only one who was looking after something other than himself.

Eventually, the Little Prince landed on earth, and was surprised to find it empty. He met a fox, who explained to him that the important thing in life is to 'tame' people, make friends with them, create ties with them, and then the world becomes orderly around them. 'On ne voit bien qu'avec le coeur,' says the fox, 'l'essentiel est invisible pour les yeux.'

You are forever responsible for the thing that you have tamed, says the fox. The Little Prince realizes that he is responsible for his rose, left alone on his planet; once he has offered and accepted love, he has accepted responsibility.

Disappointed with earth, where the inhabitants turn in giddy circles and get nowhere because they have no sense of purpose or direction, the Little Prince leaves, as suddenly as he came, but not before telling the airman that his life may also henceforth have a sense, because somewhere, in one of those stars, is a little prince who is his friend.

In *Terre des Hommes,* Saint-Exupéry had written,

> Mais la verité, vous le savez, c'est ce qui simplifie le monde, et non ce qui crée le chaos. La vérité, c'est le langage qui dégage l'universal.

In *Le Petit Prince,* he set out to 'simplify the world'.

A. The Rose

The rose with which the prince is in love is a vain and capricious creature:

> —Ah! je me réveille à peine . . . Je vous demande pardon. . . . Je suis encore toute décoiffée . . .
>
> Le Petit Prince, alors, ne put contenir son admiration:

> —Que vous êtes belle!

> —N'est-ce pas, répondit doucement la fleur. Je suis née en même temps que le soleil.

Her unreliability and contradictory nature causes him pain and heartache. He is too young to have learned the lesson that flowers are not to be heeded—they are to be cherished for their beauty alone:

> il ne faut jamais écouter les fleurs. Il faut les regarder et les respirer.

It is obvious that the flower is symbolic of the feminine temperament which Saint-Exupéry never fully understood. It has been suggested that the prince's flower is, more precisely, a symbol of Consuelo, the author's wife. Their marriage had certainly been at once touchingly and childishly romantic, and at times tempestuous. Consuelo was, moreover, a striking beauty universally admired.

Such can only be conjecture. Yet it is interesting to note how little Saint-Exupéry's bewilderment in the presence of women had changed over the years. The Little Prince's rose echoes very clearly the only other feminine character in his work, Geneviève in *Courrier Sud*:

> Sans doute l'aimait-elle toujours, mais il ne faut pas trop demander à une faible petite fille.

> (*Courrier Sud*)

It is instructive also to read the letters which Saint-Exupéry addressed to Renée de Saussine in his youth, in which the slightly hurt tone of one who does not comprehend the vagaries of the female heart is similar to that of the Little Prince:

> C'est bien la première fois depuis Dakar que je puis vous parler sans amertume. Je vous en ai bien voulu! C'est curieux comme vous savez ne rien comprendre quand vous voulez.

> (*Lettres de Jeunesse*)

And yet, when the Little Prince has 'apprivoisé' his flower, he is prepared to sacrifice himself for her. Were he not to return to his planet, his rose would have no one to water her and protect her; she is so weak and naive, she would be helpless without him. She would wither and die. The prince accepts his responsibility for her; his duty is to 'seem to die' (*avoir l'air de mourir*) for her sake, in recognition of the bond which ties her to him.

B. Les Grandes Personnes

The grown-ups are short-sighted, mean, petty, selfish. They cannot understand anything intuitively, because they lack imagination, but must needs always have things explained. They have a veritable passion for facts and figures:

> Les grandes personnes ne comprennent jamais rien toutes seules . . . elles ont toujours besoin d'explications.

> Et les hommes manquent d'imagination. Ils répètent ce qu'on leur dit.

The Little Prince's greatest pleasure is watching the sunset, which he can do as often as he likes on his small planet, simply by moving his chair a little. But grown-ups know no such pleasure. With their facts and figures, they are so busy taking themselves seriously, that they have no time for the simple beauties of life:

> Je connais une planète où il y a un Monsieur cramoisi. Il n'a jamais respiré une fleur. Il n'a jamais regardé une étoile. Il n'a jamais aimé personne. Il n'a jamais rien fait d'autre que des additions. Et toute la journée il répète comme toi: 'Je suis un homme sérieux! Je suis un homme sérieux!' et ça le fait gonfler d'orgueil. Mais ce n'est pas un homme, c'est un champignon!

The planets which the prince visits before his arrival on Earth are inhabited by men who each represent the follies and vices of mankind which Saint-Exupéry most regrets; the taste for power (the king), vanity (the narcissist), acquisitiveness (the businessman). They are all inward-looking, self-regarding, prisoners of their own imperious needs. Only the lamplighter leads a life devoted to something outside himself; his task, though apparently ludicrous, has a sense which theirs does not:

> Celui-là, se dit le petit prince, tandis qu'il poursuivait plus loin son voyage, celui-là serait méprisé par tous les autres, par le roi, par le vaniteux, par le buveur, par le businessman. Cependant c'est le seul qui ne me paraisse pas ridicule. C'est, peut-être, parce qu'il s'occupe d'autre chose que de soi-même.

Children intuitively understand the world in all its simplicity. Most men, when they cease to be children, forget the truths which they once knew with such clarity, and spend the rest of their lives contributing to chaos and confusion. They believe they know everything, as the sum of their 'knowledge' increases with age; but they have facts, not comprehension. Children do not need facts:

> Mais, bien sûr, nous qui comprenons la vie, nous nous moquons bien des numéros!

Saint-Exupéry, in *Le Petit Prince,* wants us to make a supreme effort to return to the essential truth of childhood. In that way, perhaps we may finally understand:

> Piètre non-sens: les enfants qui ne comprennent point—c'est-à-dire seuls comprennent.
>
> (*Carnets*)

C. L'Apprivoisement

'Apprivoiser', says the fox, means 'to create bonds'. 'Si tu m'apprivoises, nous aurons besoin l'un de l'autre . . . ma vie sera comme ensoleillée.' The fox asks the Little Prince to tame him, so that they might be bound to each other by mutual need. Only then will their solitude cease:

> On ne connaît que les choses que l'on apprivoise, dit le renard. Les hommes n'ont plus le temps de rien connaître. Ils achètent des choses toutes faites chez les marchands. Mais comme il n'existe point de marchands d'amis, les hommes n'ont plus d'amis. Si tu veux un ami, apprivoise-moi!

Just as the pilots of the Line, united in mutual need, are responsible for each other, so the Little Prince will be re-sponsible for the fox, as he is already for his rose. Disinterested love carries the heaviest responsibility:

> Les hommes ont oublié cette vérité, dit le renard. Mais tu ne dois pas l'oublier. Tu deviens responsable pour toujours de ce que tu as apprivoisé. Tu es responsable de ta rose. . . .

The fox shares with the Little Prince his own secret of life. It is a very simple secret, as all truth is simple, but it is important because men have lost sight of it. It is a secret which Saint-Exupéry tried to impart, in more high-blown language, in *Pilote de Guerre.* It is this:

> Voici mon secret. Il est très simple: on ne voit bien qu'avec le coeur. L'essentiel est invisible pour les yeux.

Is this not identical with the message of *Pilote de Guerre,* that the intelligence is incapable of perceiving reality, which is revealed only to one who sees with the spirit? Substitute *Esprit* for *coeur,* and *intelligence* for *yeux* in the above passage, and the lesson is the same.

What Saint-Exupéry is saying is this: childhood has much to teach manhood, because a child has the gift of spontaneous, intuitive understanding of what matters in the world. The child tells us that we must learn to penetrate appearances in order to discover hidden realities which the intelligence, with its analytic methods, is incapable of perceiving. The child is closer to poetic truth than we; with divine and simple grace, and without any fuss, the child understands the world through love:

> L'intelligence ne vaut qu'au service de l'amour.
>
> (*Pilote de Guerre*)

Surprisingly, this graceful and blazingly simple book has been subjected to the most diverse interpretations. Some critics, impervious to its message, have set their intellectual faculties to work in an effort to analyse it out of existence, and are thus guilty of an unconscious irony which, one suspects, would have greatly amused its author. Renée Zeller, for example, considers the two active volcanoes on the prince's planet to be symbolic of Charity and Hope, while the extinct volcano, which the prince none the less still tends, symbolizes Saint-Exupéry's lost religious faith! For Yves Le Hir, the disabled aircraft which the narrator is trying to put in order when the Little Prince first appears, is a symbol of the author's soul. R.-M. Albérès, whose whole thesis looks like an attempt to establish the author's impotence, suggests that the Little Prince is 'the child that Saint-Exupéry never had'. While Pierre de Boisdeffre is simply dismissive. The book, he says, excites teachers, but bores children to death ('enthousiasme les instituteurs et assomme les enfants'). Rumbold and Stewart see the book as a satire on those aspects of American life which Saint-Exupéry found most distasteful.

Jean-Claude Ibert comes closest to an understanding of the author's intention. He says that Saint-Exupéry was enchanted by the child's capacity to see things with an interior, subjective vision, and by his unshakeable confidence that what he saw was indeed so. A child cannot be deterred by argument, for truth, as he sees it, has nothing to do with reason:

Ce qui l'enchantait, chez les enfants, c'est surtout leur adhésion totale à leurs croyances, leur singulière aptitude à situer le possible au coeur même de ce qui paraît être impossible, et leur merveilleuse disponibilité affective qui leur permet de donner de l'âme à ce qui est, par définition, inanimable. Il décelait en eux, à l'état naturel, cet élan d'amour incontrôlé qui doit conduire les hommes à s'accomplir dans une quête de pureté où se trouvent exprimés à la fois la valeur de leur condition et le sens de leur universalité. Les enfants ont des choses une vision intérieure, subjective: ils les *apprivoisent*. Saint-Exupéry s'est efforcé de nous montrer comment nous pouvions adopter leur *point de vue*.

(Saint-Exupéry, by J. C. Ibert)

And, as if to help us see matters from a child's point of view, he illustrated the book himself with the drawings of a child.

One thing is sure: there is a large element of autobiography in *Le Petit Prince.* Both Saint-Exupéry and his creation felt isolated and at loggerheads with a world which would not see the truth. Saint-Exupéry, who retained the charm of infancy well into his manhood, was never at ease 'on earth'. His imagination took flights of fancy which lifted him into the world of make-believe and left his friends far behind. He would have been happy, one suspects, on the Little Prince's planet, shifting his chair to watch the sunset.

Joseph Andrew Casper   (essay date 1983)

SOURCE: "I Never Met a Rose: Stanley Donen and *The Little Prince*," in *Children's Novels and the Movies,* edited by Douglas Street, Frederick Ungar Publishing Co, 1983, pp. 141-50.

[*Casper is an English educator and critic. In the excerpt below, originally published in his* Stanley Donen *in 1983, he compares the mixed critical reaction surrounding Saint-Exupéry's* Little Prince *to the similar reception of the 1974 film adaptation by Hollywood musical director Stanley Donen.*]

In the literary season of 1943, one of the warmest critical welcomes was accorded Antoine de Saint Exupéry's *The Little Prince,* a "parable for grown people in the guise of a simple story for children," as it was appropriately described by the *New York Times* reviewer. Only the *New Yorker's* critic remained aloof, claiming the piece was neither a children's book nor a good book since it lacked the simplicity and clarity all fairy tales need to create their magic. Readers, however, didn't feel that way at all, and they made the book a bestseller. Although the fairy-tale form was a new medium of expression for Saint Ex, *The Little Prince,* like his other works, was a reflection of his own life, personality, philosophy and vision.

Born in Lyons in 1900 into a stuffy bourgeois household where adults mistook his sketch of an elephant swallowing a boa constrictor for a hat, Saint Ex received a thorough schooling in the humanities. Military training ended a bit of bohemia at Paris' École des Beaux Arts. While in the service, he spent all his pocket money and free time in aviation lessons, thus making his childhood dream of flying come true. Taking note, his superiors sent him to flying school in Morocco where he obtained his civilian pilot's license at the age of twenty-one. Writing essays on aviation relieved the boredom of the various jobs that followed his demobilization. In 1926, however, he was hired to fly the mail route from France to her North African colonies and went on to become chief of Juby Airport, where rescue missions were the rule of the day. Antiquated World War I Bréguets planes, dissident Arabs, sand storms, desert heat and hurricanes made these pioneer days of flying even more treacherous. During his vigils, Saint Ex wrote his first novel, *Southern Mail* (1929), an impressionistic blend of the adventures and romance of an aviator hero—the archetypical Saint Exupery protagonist—subsequently adapted for the screen by French director Pierre Billon in 1937.

In 1929, Saint Exupery joined a new mail line, opening up the first air routes between France and South America. *Night Flight* (1932), his second and much more assured fiction, detailed this hair-raising job. This aesthetic and commercial success underwent MGM's high gloss treatment a year later at the hands of producer David O. Selznick, house director Clarence Brown and stars Clark Gable, Lionel and John Barrymore and Helen Hayes heading an illustrious cast.

As war clouded over Europe, Saint Exupery was charged with various propaganda missions in North Africa—a period which provided the spatial and temporal setting for his *The Little Prince.* With France at war Saint Exupery saw active service on and off. During one of his self-exiles, this time in America, he brooded on his recent reconnaissance missions over Germany and the defeat of France in *Flight to Arras* (1942). Then, confronting the child within—the child which was always part of himself and which, he insisted, must be part of every man—in *The Little Prince* he tweaked contemporary man's callous materialism, pusilanimity and selfishness and went on to assert the significance of man as a spiritual being while defending the values of participation in life, friendship, love, empathy, courage, duty to something beyond oneself, and self-sacrifice.

Henri Peyre, in his study of *The Contemporary French Novel* (1955), predicted immortality for Saint Exupery as a "pioneer who has annexed the virgin dommain of aviation to letters . . . and a thoughtful writer who has formulated anew, with force and beauty, some of the baffling problems facing man . . ." And Peyre's prediction seems to have come true, at least in regard to *The Little Prince,* which has been translated into some thirty languages and kept constantly in print. In addition, from the beginning this slim volume of whimsey has tantalized filmmakers from Walt Disney to Orson Welles—predictably too, since film, with its phantasmagoric abilities, has always held a natural affinity for fantasy. But it wasn't until the late sixties—when fantasy became, once again, a necessary antidote to the turmoil of the times—that serious work was begun on a film version of *The Little Prince;* the film itself was released in 1974.

A. Joseph Tandet, a theatrical lawyer and sometime producer, who had represented a playwright who had at one time optioned the property, shelled out six figures for the rights owned by Saint Exupery's widow and Paris publisher Gallimard. Because the work was envisioned as a musical film, Alan J. Lerner was approached. An old friend of Tandet's and the celebrated librettist and lyricist of such Broadway hits as *Brigadoon* (1947), *Paint Your Wagon* (1951), *An American In Paris* (1951), *My Fair Lady* (1956), *Gigi* (1958) and *Camelot* (1962), Lerner, at this time, was under contract to Paramount to produce a total of five musical extravaganzas. (The inordinate success of Warner Brothers' *My Fair Lady* (1964), Disney's *Mary Poppins* (1964), and especially Fox's *The Sound Of Music* (1965) convinced Hollywood that the spectacular musical was the newest vein to be mined.) Extremely enthused Lerner wrote a screenplay in the midst of production chores on *Paint Your Wagon* and *On A Clear Day You Can See Forever.*

Recalling that Frederick Loewe, Lerner's former collaborator and now a Palm Springs retiree, had independently expressed an interest in the work, Tandet sent him the scenario. Loewe was hooked immediately and began composing a score with Lerner.

Robert Evans, Paramount's production vice-president, gave Saint Exupery's book to director Stanley Donen, one of the top builders of the Hollywood musical (*On The Town,* 1949, *Singin' In The Rain,* 1952, *Seven Brides For Seven Brothers,* 1954, *The Pajama Game,* 1957, and others). Donen, recently returned to the West Coast in search of projects after having been independently based in London for the past dozen years while fashioning such witty, elegant and deft film comedies as *Indiscreet* (1957), *Charade* (1963), *Two For The Road* (1967) and *Bedazzled* (1968), was quite touched by the Exupery work and equally eager to make another musical. Moreover, he had already collaborated with Alan Lerner—and quite successfully—when he replaced Charles Walters in the shooting of *Royal Wedding* in 1951.

Donen was elated that Lerner's script retained the novel's narrative form, the day-night format and above all, Saint Ex's engaging dialogue. The book's first-person point of view became first-person voice-over narration in the screenplay as the aviator recalled his own childhood, his meeting with the Prince after his aircraft went down in the Sahara Desert, and then the Prince's own chronicle of adventures within the aviator's narrative. Throughout the novel and the script, day, regarded as a time for action, alternated with night, the period of contemplation. And, as in the original, all the encounters in the adaptation were essentially dialogic: ingenuous, concise, poetic speech. The Frenchman had used words beyond the accepted range of children, for he believed that children accept and are tantalized by new and even long words, invariably asking their meaning and assimilating them with ease. Neither Lerner nor Donen had difficulty utilizing the vocabulary.

Lerner's adaptation also preserved practically all of the Prince's major encounters. Recaptured for the screen were his confrontations with his beloved coquetish Rose on his own asteroid, his meetings on a pilgrimage to other planets with the power-obsessed Monarch (rewritten as the more visually appealing royal obsession with boundaries), with the Businessman who keeps account of the stars as if they were his alone, with the Snake who offered a means to return home, and with the Fox, the little wanderer's teacher of friendship.

Scratched from the screenplay were the Conceited Man, always insisting that the Prince applaud him; the Tippler drinking away the shameful memory of his dependence upon the bottle; the Railway Switchman sorting out travelers and sending them on their way; and the Merchant dispensing thirst-quenching pills to save folks time. Lerner pointed out that the satire in these episodes was not sufficiently sharp and Donen concurred. In any case, it was felt that the script contained enough examples of the folly and vanity of modern man.

In an attempt to make the satire more immediately topical, the novel's Geographer—unable to answer any questions because he was waiting for an explorer to supply him with the information to fill his volumes—became in the film an Historian who fabricated events. To reflect to antiwar sentiment of the early seventies, Lerner concocted a Militarist who proclaimed that dying was life's *raison d'être.* The character of the Lamplighter, the first the Little Prince does not think ludicrous since he is the only one paying attention to something other than himself, was included in the original screenplay and a sequence was filmed in which he was a life-size puppet on a six-foot planet on which night and day rapidly alternated as the Prince, moon-like, hovered about. However, unsatisfactory optical work forced Donen eventually to delete these scenes from the finished movie.

What Stanley Donen did object to in the script was Lerner's ending in which the Prince returned to the Snake, fell asleep, and merely disappeared. Eager to make all of the fable's points come through, Donen demanded that Lerner keep the author's original ending. Ironically, Saint Exupery himself had had trouble persuading his publishers that the story could end with the Little Prince's death by snakebite. Children accept all natural things, the novelist argued, whereas adults distort the natural. And for Saint Exupery, death was not an end but a means by which the pilgrim may return from whence he came. . . .

Critics loved or hated the film it seemed—no one took the middle ground. And viewers were equally divided. The motion picture was a commercial failure. Paramount didn't know how to market this property efficiently and eventually simply decided to walk away from it. Besides, they had on their financial minds Francis Ford Coppola's big-budget *Godfather Part II,* which was released in tandem with **The Little Prince** during the same Christmas season. They opted to rally one hundred percent behind *The Godfather II* in the hope of filling the tills with greenbacks and the shelves with nominations and possible awards. Since its release, the filmed **The Little Prince,** mirroring its literary namesake, has achieved something of a cult status, frequently appearing on the art house revival circuit and the college campus. This witnesses to an immortality for Antoine de Saint Exupery and his intriguing narrative of an aviator and a little prince who tamed him.

Joy D. Marie Robinson   (essay date 1984)

SOURCE: *Antoine de Saint-Exupéry,* Twayne Publishers, 1984, pp. 120-42.

[*In the following excerpt, Robinson provides an analysis of* The Little Prince.]

[*Le Petit Prince*], so often mistaken for "only" a children's book, is in fact a delicate crystallization of Saint-Exupéry's philosophy of life, in allegorical form. The success of this book has been so great that Saint-Exupéry is often thought of simply as "the author of the *Little Prince,*" and the book itself has become a beginning French reader in America. It is, indeed, sad that such sensitive, exquisitely wrought writing should be subjected to the impatient deciphering of beginning students, as a butterfly being dissected to see what makes it fly. As Maxwell Smith says: "To analyze in detail so lovely and fragile a tale would be like removing the petals of a rose to discover its charm" [*Knight of the Air,* 1956].

It is perhaps surprising to find this gentle allegory written at a time when Saint-Exupéry was so agonizingly concerned for his country, yet there are many signs of the gradual growth of the figure of the Little Prince in the author's thoughts. On a copy of *Pilote de guerre,* Saint-Exupéry sketched a child standing on a cloud, watching the burning of Arras. To the suggestion that the child be made to reveal his thoughts, Saint-Exupéry replied, "No, not his thoughts. They are too melancholy." Fleury also mentions the frequent sketching of *un petit bonhomme* leaning from a cloud; and, on a letter to Léon Werth, reproduced in *Icare,* there is again "a little fellow" on a cloud, quietly watching a country road, while a Messerschmitt plane approaches menacingly. Reynal, the editor, claims that the book originated in a drawing of a little winged figure, made as a joke on the margin of Lamotte's sketch for the illustrations in *Flight to Arras:* Reynal kept urging Saint-Exupéry to write a book on the figure, finally suggesting a children's book for Christmas 1942. Yet, as Pélissier points our, the book rapidly progresses from its childlike beginning to become a philosophical fable [Smith]. Just as the drawings of the Little Prince can be traced back over several years, it will be seen that many of the ideas expressed so poignantly in *Le Petit Prince* have their source in earlier writings.

Le Petit Prince begins with the well-known pair of drawings which the narrator, Saint-Exupéry himself, discouraged in his childhood artistic attempts, now uses whenever he meets an apparently lucid adult to see if he really has understanding. Drawing number one is of a boa constrictor which has swallowed an elephant whole; most grown-ups see a hat shape, for they cannot see beyond the exterior. For them, he produces his drawing number two, the open snake, so that they may see the elephant inside. Now that they have failed the test, Saint-Exupéry comes down to their level and talks to them of politics, bridge, and neckties, instead of virgin forests and stars. So the theme is proclaimed that "grown-ups" have lost the gift of per-

ception and only those who keep the child alive within them can continue to see through the exterior to the essence which lies within. As the *Time* review of the book recognized, this "fairy-tale for grown-ups . . . challenges man the adult and deplores the loss of the child in man [26 April 1943]. Saint-Exupéry laments that "Grown-ups never understand anything alone, and it is tiring for children always, always to give them explanations," a comment which recurs as a leitmotif, with variations, at the end of many chapters.

After living for many years alone in the world of grown-ups, Saint-Exupéry is stranded one day in the desert, trying to repair his plane, when suddenly the Little Prince miraculously appears and demands "Please, draw me a sheep." Accepting the mystery, Saint-Exupéry starts to draw but first he sketches his drawing number one, and the Little Prince immediately protests that he does not want an elephant in a boa constrictor. At last, here is someone who does understand; and so Saint-Exupéry starts to draw a sheep for him. The Little Prince rejects each attempt until, at last, Saint-Exupéry simply draws a box in which the sheep might be. Then the Little Prince is content for he sees the sheep inside the box and even sees that it is asleep.

So begins the gentle friendship between the Little Prince and the narrator, Saint-Exupéry. Little by little, the pilot learns about his new friend's life, but always by indirect allusion, for the Little Prince never tells about himself and never answers questions, although he is always asking them. Soon Saint-Exupéry discovers that his little visitor fell from the sky and that the planet from which he came was very small.

As Saint-Exupéry puzzles over the Little Prince's appearance, he concludes that he must have come from one of the small asteroids. To satisfy the grown-ups, Saint-Exupéry gives the number of the asteroid, B 612, but he would rather have begun his story like a fairy-tale: "Once upon a time there was a little prince who lived in a planet hardly any bigger than he was and who needed a friend."

One day Saint-Exupéry discovers the story of the baobab trees on the Little Prince's planet. Their powerful seeds take root and, unless one carefully weeds them out each day, soon giant trees will take over the planet. Besides the daily discipline of weeding baobab shoots, there was also the responsibility of sweeping out the planer's three volcanoes to avoid chimney fires. It would be easy to analyze this episode as a morality tale but, following Maxwell Smith's advice, we will not tear the rose apart.

On the fourth day, Saint-Exupéry realizes the Little Prince's melancholy, revealed by an ingenuous reference to the sunsets which the Prince could see so often on his tiny planet. The Little Prince confides that when he is sad he likes to watch a sunset; and one day he had watched forty-three sunsets. Nostalgically, Saint-Exupéry wishes that, like the Little Prince, he could just move his chair to see the sun setting in France, but "sadly, France is much too far away."

Suddenly, on the fifth day, Saint-Exupéry discovers the secret of the Little Prince's melancholy; it is the beautiful, temperamental Rose, which grew unexpectedly on his planet and so tormented him with her whims that he finally decided to leave. When the Little Prince first mentions his Rose, however, Saint-Exupéry is so concerned with the plane which he still cannot repair, and with his dwindling water supply, that he casually dismisses the Little Prince's questions about flowers, thorns, and sheep, with the almost unpardonable remark, "I am concerned with serious things." Immediately, the Little Prince accuses him of speaking like a grownup and compares him to the red-faced man he had met, who loved nobody and cared only for numbers. He, declares the Little Prince, was not a man but a mushroom! Then the Little Prince launches into a passionate, beautiful proclamation of what is truly important in life: "And if I know a flower unique in the world, which exists nowhere except on my planet and which a little sheep can annihilate in one stroke . . . without realizing what he is doing, isn't that important?" Suddenly he bursts into tears, and Saint-Exupéry, recalled to a realization of what is truly important, forgets his tools, his plane, thirst, and death. "There was on one star, on one planet, my planet the Earth, a little prince to console." And he takes him in his arms to console him.

Soon Saint-Exupéry comes to know about the beautiful, coquettish Rose who had tormented the Little Prince by her moody vanity. Only when, driven to despair by her tantrums, the Little Prince had decided to leave his planet, did the Rose finally admit that she loved him; and as the Little Prince now recognizes he was foolish not to have understood: "I ought to have judged her on acts and not on words. She perfumed me and illumined me. . . . I ought to have guessed her affection behind her poor wiles . . . But I was too young to know how to love."

Many critics maintain that the Rose symbolizes Consuelo, and this theory was encouraged by Consuelo herself. However, it must be remembered that Saint-Exupéry had also deeply loved his fiancée, Louise de Vilmorin, when he was indeed "too young" to understand. Carlo François points out an interesting parallelism between the description of the Rose and that of Geneviève in the semiautobiographical *Courrier sud,* written before Saint-Exupéry met Consuelo. It is also conceivable that Saint-Exupéry had loved other women, of whom we know nothing, so that the Rose could represent a composite portrait. She is best understood, perhaps, in the old, literary tradition of the *Roman de la rose,* as an allegorical image of the loved one. As the Little Prince grows in wisdom, he learns to love simply for what the Rose is in her essence, and she becomes unique for him because of his love for her.

The Little Prince sets out on his travels, aided by a flight of migratory birds, and he visits a number of other planets before he reaches the Earth of men. Each planet is inhabited by a unique, solitary figure, who comes to represent some aspect of men, foible or quality. There is first the King, who eagerly adopts the Little Prince as a subject whom he can command. He believes that he rules over the whole universe, obeyed by the very stars, but his authority is reasonable, based only on what can be expected. When the Little Prince, named minister of justice by the King, protests that there is nobody on the planet to judge, the monarch replies: "You will judge yourself. . . . It is the most difficult. . . . If you succeed in judging yourself, you must be a true sage."

On the second planet the Little Prince finds the Vain Man, who sees in his visitor only an admirer. The Little Prince soon tires of applauding him and travels on, declaring, "Grown-ups are decidedly very strange." On the third planet he meets the pathetic Drunkard, caught in his vicious circle of drinking to forget that he is ashamed of drinking. The Little Prince is even more puzzled.

Arriving on the fourth planet, the Little Prince meets a more formidable species, the Businessman (the English term is used in the French text). This man can do nothing but count his riches, uncertain even of what he thinks he possesses. To the Little Prince's insistent question, he replies that he is counting those "little gold things in the sky which make the lazy folk dream," for he believes that he owns the stars, simply by writing down their numbers. Like the King, he believes that the stars are his; like the Drunkard, he is caught in a vicious circle, for he explains that the purpose of being rich in stars is simply to buy more stars. At every interruption by the Little Prince, he repeats, "I am serious, I have no time to waste." Here, indeed, is the red-faced man, the "mushroom" whom the Little Prince had accused Saint-Exupéry of resembling. The Little Prince finds the Businessman rather foolish in his belief that he can possess anything by recording the number on a paper. He remembers his own precious possessions, the flower which he waters and the volcanoes which he sweeps, realizing "It is useful to my volcanoes, it is useful to my flower, that I should possess them."

Traveling on to the fifth planet, the Little Prince finds the enigmatic, poetic figure of the Lamplighter who, as his planet turns faster and faster, must continuously light and extinguish his lamps. For the Little Prince, this seemingly senseless work has a meaning and is useful because it is beautiful: "When he lights his lamp, it is as though he brought to life another star, or a flower." This man, who would seem ridiculous to the King or to the Businessman, is lovable to the Little Prince because he is faithful to his task. He alone does not seem ridiculous, for he is concerned with something other than himself. The Lamplighter is perhaps related to the church sacristan mentioned in *Pilote de guerre*: "the love of his God, in the sacristan, becomes the love of lighting the candles . . . he is satisfied to make the candelabras flower." The Lamplighter is, in fact, for the Little Prince, the only one of his new acquaintances of whom he could have made his friend.

On the sixth planet, the Little Prince meets the Geographer, who spends his time writing about what others have discovered, while he stays at his desk. Here is truly the antithesis of Saint-Exupéry's conviction that only by participating can he have the right to speak; and, in his journal, Saint-Exupéry had commented on the Geographer who "separates thought from action." Here, however, the Little Prince meets some new ideas: he has his first inkling of mortality, when the Geographer refuses to record flowers because they are "ephemeral"; and when the Geographer defines that term as meaning "threatened with future disappearance," the Little Prince knows his first feeling of regret and thinks of his flower. Especially, it is the Geographer who recommends that he visit the Earth, which has a good reputation.

The Earth is, therefore, for the Little Prince, the seventh planet, a number of perhaps biblical significance. Perhaps biblically again, he is greeted by the Serpent, who speaks in enigmas: "I am more powerful than the finger of a king. . . . I can carry you away further than a ship." He promises to help if some day the Little Prince yearns to return to his planet. Like Saint-Exupéry the Little Prince is looking for mankind. He inquires of a flower, who considers men too rootless, then climbs a mountain peak, where only the echo answers him.

Suddenly in his quest he comes to a garden filled with roses and he is deeply disappointed, for his Rose had always said that she was unique. Reflecting sorrowfully, "I believed myself rich in a unique flower and I possess only an ordinary rose," the Little Prince lies down in the grass and weeps.

Now the little Fox appears, who will console the Little Prince and teach him his secrets, as the little desert fox had comforted Saint-Exupéry when he was stranded in the desert, and had taught him wisdom. The Little Prince is looking for friends, but the Fox says that, before he can become his friend, he must be "tamed." (Here, we encounter a problem of translation, for the one English word "to tame" translates two very different French one: *domestiquer* in the sense of training an animal to behave suitably, and *apprivoiser* in the sense of creating bonds of affection between man and animal. The French text here is *apprivoiser*.) When the Fox explains that *apprivoiser* means that, "If you tame me, we shall need each other. I shall be for you unique in the world," the Little Prince begins to understand that his Rose has "tamed" him. The Little Prince is at first too impatient to tame the Fox, for he is in a hurry to discover more friends, but the wise Fox explains that "one only knows those things which one tames." Then the Fox teaches the Little Prince the slow, gentle patience of making friends, not by words, for "language is the source of misunderstanding," but just by coming closer every day. Every day, too, he must come at the same time, so that one hour may become unique; and so the Fox teaches the importance of ritual.

When, at last, the Little Prince must leave to continue his quest, the Fox sends him first to visit the garden of roses again. There the Little Prince suddenly understands, and he exclaims: "You are nothing yet. Nobody has tamed you and you have tamed nobody. . . . You are beautiful but you are empty. One cannot die for you. . . . My Rose alone is more important than all of you, for it is she whom I have watered. . . . Since she is my Rose." Then he returns to the Fox, who gives him his three-fold secret, "One sees well only with the heart. The essential is invisible to the eyes. . . . It is the time which you have spent for your rose which makes your rose so important. . . . You become responsible for always for whatever you have tamed."

Enriched with this vital secret, the Little Prince leaves the Fox to continue his journey. He meets a railway switch-man, sending trains to left and right, and wonders what the busy travelers are seeking. "Nothing at all," says the switch-man, pointing out that only the children look out of the windows. The Little Prince agrees, saying: "Only children know what they are seeking." Then the Little Prince meets a merchant of antithirst pills designed to save the time usually spent on drinking, and the puzzled Little Prince reflects that, if he had that time to spend he would walk quietly toward a fountain.

It is now the eighth day of Saint-Exupéry's breakdown in the desert, and he has drunk the last drop of water. Still the Little Prince cannot understand his anxiety, for "it is good to have had a friend, even if one is going to die." Then he suggests, simply, though rather unreasonably, that they start looking for a well. Gradually, as they walk on the sand beneath the stars, the Little Prince imparts the Fox's secret to Saint-Exupéry, distilling it in quiet phrases: "Water can also be good for the heart. . . . The stars are beautiful because of a flower which one does not see . . . what makes the desert beautiful is that it hides a well somewhere." Suddenly, Saint-Exupéry understands the mysterious radiance of the sand, he remembers his childhood home, enchanted by the legend of a treasure hidden in its heart, and he discovers the secret: "Whether it concerns a house, stars or the desert, what makes their beauty is invisible." When the Little Prince falls asleep and Saint-Exupéry carries him, he realizes that he sees only the shell, for the important is invisible. "What moves me so much about this little sleeping prince is his faithfulness to a flower, it is the image of a rose which radiates within him like the flame of a lamp."

Miraculously they do find a well in the desert, a simple village well, and Saint-Exupéry draws up the bucket on the groaning pulley. When the Little Prince says "I am thirsty for that water," Saint-Exupéry understands the quality of the water: "It was born of the walk beneath the stars, of the song of the pulley, of the effort of my arms. It was good for the heart, like a gift." Gently meditating on the blindness of men, the Little Prince teaches Saint-Exupéry that what they keep seeking could be found in a single rose or in a drop of water.

Suddenly the Little Prince starts to talk of his planet, anxiously asking Saint-Exupéry to draw a muzzle on the sheep to protect his Rose, and Saint-Exupéry realizes that the Little Prince is intending to return home. Quietly the Little Prince dismisses him to work on his plane, while he seeks the help of the Serpent. First, however, he gives the lonely Saint-Exupéry a special gift: just as all the stars flower for the Little Prince because of his Rose, so will all the stars ring with laughter for Saint-Exupéry, because of the Little Prince's laughter. "Since I will laugh in one of them, it will be for you as though all the stars were laughing. . . . It will be as though I had given you, instead of stars, a mass of little sleigh-bells which can laugh."

Bravely then, the Little Prince speaks of his coming return to his star, his death by the Serpent. To lessen Saint-Exupéry's grief, he tells him not to mourn over his body: "I will look as though I am dead, but it will not be true. . . . I cannot carry that body away. It is too heavy. . . . Old, empty shells are not sad." Just like Saint-

Exupéry's young brother, François, the Little Prince affirms that his body is not his essential self. The Little Prince walks toward the Serpent, there is a flash of yellow, and he falls like a tree. The reader is reminded of Bernis's death in *Courrier sud,* when "a lost child filled the desert," and of Fabien's death in the desert when "two children seem to sleep." Here, though, is the enigma of the book which is never explained, for, at day-break, Saint-Exupéry does not find the Little Prince's body.

Six years later, as Saint-Exupéry tells his story, he wonders over this enigma. A little consoled by time, he can enjoy listening to the stars at night; but, because he forgot to add a fastening to the muzzle he drew for the sheep, he always wonders whether the Rose is safe. This unanswerable mystery can change the stars' laughter to tears. "But no grown-up will ever understand that it is of such importance."

Saint-Exupéry had difficulty persuading his publishers to accept the death of the Little Prince, but he argued that children accept all natural things. He insists, perhaps, on the idea of the continued life of the spirit, by his plea to his readers to let him know if by chance they meet the Little Prince in the desert. Perhaps, too, the mysterious disappearance of the body is a suggestion, even subconscious, of resurrection. After all, Saint-Exupéry, without being a practicing Catholic, frequently claimed the enriching influence of his religious upbringing which teaches that belief.

The Little Prince was probably Saint-Exupéry's favorite book of all his writings, with the possible exception of *Citadelle.* Benouville, who knew Saint-Exupéry in Algiers, writes that Saint-Exupéry seemed to consider the book his autobiography and that he gave it to his friends as he might offer his photo ["Saint-Exupéry fraternal," *Conflueres,* 1947]. Albérès says that the Little Prince is Saint-Exupéry's alter ego [*Saint-Exupéry,* 1961]. "This resolute, courageous and hopelessly sentimental little fellow, standing on his miniscule planet, is indeed his double who lived in the astral world while Saint-Exupéry's body lived among men." The Little Prince, says Albérès, is the symbol of life, the discoverer of all the essential values of life; he is, indeed, the child whom Saint-Exupéry never had. But this comes too close to the analysis which "tears the rose apart." Borgal more simply recognizes that *Le Petit Prince* is "a long fable in which the principal themes of Saint-Exupéry's thoughts are transfigured into the most delicate poetry. . . . This book is the purest masterpiece of exupérian art [*Saint-Exupéry, mystique sanc foi,* 1965]. The immediate reaction to *The Little Prince* was hesitant, perhaps confused, for, as the critic, Binsse, realized, it did not fit into the category in which the public had placed the author. Yet, as Smith foresaw in 1956, the book would perhaps become one of the immortals with La Fontaine's *Fables,* Swift's *Gulliver's Travels,* Carroll's *Alice,* and Maeterlinck's *Blue Bird.*

FURTHER READING

Biography

Cate, Curtis. *Antoine de Saint-Exupéry: His Life and Time.* New York: Putnam, 1970, 608 p.
    Detailed overview of Saint-Exupéry's life.

Rumbold, Richard, and Stewart, Lady Margaret. *The Winged Life: A Portrait of Antoine de Saint-Exupéry, Poet and Airman.* New York: David McKay Company, Inc., 224 p.
    Biographical study emphasizing Saint-Exupéry's aviation experiences.

Criticism

Arnold, James W. "Musical Fantasy: *The Little Prince.*" In *Shadows of the Magic Lamp: Fantasy and Science Fiction in Film,* edited by George Slusser and Eric S. Rabkin, pp. 122-40. Carbondale: Southern Illinois University Press, 1985.
    Summarizes the plot of *The Little Prince* and discusses director Stanley Donen's film adaptation of the novel.

Balakian, Nona. "Poet of the Air—and Earth: Antoine de Saint-Exupéry." In her *Critical Encounters: Literary Views and Reviews, 1953-1977,* pp. 142-45. New York: The Bobbs-Merrill Company, Inc., 1978.
    Overview of Saint-Exupéry's career with brief commentary on *The Little Prince.*

Review of *The Little Prince. Commonweal* XXXVII, No. 26 (16 April 1943): 644-45.
    Compares *The Little Prince* to the works of eighteenth-century French moralists, but calls the book more "witty, revolutionary and cerebral."

Sherman, Beatrice. "A Prince of Lonely Space." *The New York Times Book Review* (11 April 1943): 9.
    Favorable review of *The Little Prince.*

"Adult Fairy Tale." *Time* XLI, No. 17 (26 April 1943): 100.
    Characterizes *The Little Prince* as a challenging work for adults.

Additional coverage of Saint-Exupéry's life and career is contained in the following sources published by Gale Research: *Children's Literature Review,* **Vol. 10;** *Contemporary Authors,* **Vols. 108, 132;** *Dictionary of Literary Biography,* **Vol. 72;** *Major Authors and Illustrators for Young Adults; Major 20th-Century Writers; Something about the Author,* **Vol. 20;** *Twentieth-Century Literary Criticism,* **Vol. 2; and** *World Literature Criticism.*

Arthur van Schendel

1874-1946

Dutch novelist and short story writer.

INTRODUCTION

Considered the greatest Dutch prose writer of his day, Schendel is best known for a series of works set in nineteenth-century Holland and the Dutch colonies in Indonesia. Conveying a sense of nostalgia, Schendel's novels are well-regarded for their minutely detailed settings and romantic characters.

Biographical Information

Schendel was born in Batavia, the capital of the Dutch East Indies (now Indonesia), where his father served as an officer in the army and his mother's family had lived for several generations. In 1879 his family moved to Holland, where Schendel's father died in 1880. Schendel attended a variety of schools, including an acting school, and became qualified to teach French and English. His earliest novels were love stories set in medieval Italy. The first of these works, *Drogon*, was published in 1896, the same year that he left Holland to study and teach in Tuxford, England. By 1905 he had returned to Holland. During the 1920s and 1930s, Schendel lived in Italy, where he produced the majority of his works. Schendel returned to Amsterdam in the 1940s and suffered a fatal heart attack in 1946.

Major Works

Schendel's novels are distinguished by vivid characterizations, a simple prose style, and engaging plots. The first of his series of Dutch novels, *Het fregatschip Johanna Maria* (*The Johanna Maria*), for example, is the tale of a sailmaker's love for the ship on which he serves. The narrative relates the protagonist's sense of helplessness when the sailing vessel is rendered obsolete in the emerging era of steamships. *The Johanna Maria* is typical of Schendel's novels in its focus on a character who struggles unsuccessfully against a rapidly changing world. According to Frans van Rosevelt, "What shines forth in Van Schendel's work is essentially the detached tone of his prose that is suddenly disrupted by a character's insights and emotions."

PRINCIPAL WORKS

Drogon (novel) 1896
Een zwerver verliefd (novel) 1904
Angiolino en de lente (novel) 1923
Oude italiaansche steden (novel) 1924
Merona, een edelman (novel) 1927
Florentijnsche verhalen (novel) 1929
Het fregatschip Johanna Maria (novel) 1930
  [*The Johanna Maria*, 1935]
Jan Compagnie (novel) 1932
  [*John Company*, 1983]
De waterman (novel) 1933
  [*The Waterman*, 1963]
Een Hollandsch drama (novel) 1935
  [*The House in Haarlem*, 1940]
De grauwe vogels (novel) 1937
  [*Grey Birds*, 1939]
De wereld een dansfeest (novel) 1938
De Nederlanden (poetry) 1945
Het oude huis (novel) 1946
Herdenkingen (autobiography) 1950
Verzameld werk. 8 vols. (novels and short stories) 1976-78

CRITICISM

Fred T. Marsh   (essay date 1935)

SOURCE: A review of *The Johanna Maria,* by Arthur van Schendel, in *The New York Times Book Review,* October 13, 1935, pp. 7, 21.

[*In the following review, Marsh praises* The Johanna Maria *for its artistry and simplicity.*]

[*The Johanna Maria*] is the story of an old-time sailorman and an old-time full-rigged ship. It is a slight tale, but it is also a chip of the old epic tradition. Its bald and factual bits of narration of events and explanations of people, its high seriousness and its concealed but conscious artistry combine to render it poetic, a little Dutch miniature of an epic in cleanly patterned prose—if we may guess from the translation.

The ship is the Johanna Maria, launched 1865 out of the port of Amsterdam, tall of mast, ready to compete with the best the English have to offer, Captain Jan Wilkens. Many, many years later she is docked in old Amsterdam, her faring days over, a home for an old sailorman who has waited all the years for the chance to buy her and make her his own. In the years between she has made a hundred voyages, known a thousand sailormen, borne a half-dozen different names under a score of captains of various nationalities. But the old logs remain intact, the marks of carpentry, each with its history, can still be seen, and every inch of her tells a story to her first sailmaker, Jacob Brouwer.

This Brouwer was a waif before he ran away at sea, stowing away in a ship where he learned the art of mending sails along with all the arts of the sea. A full-fledged sailmaker, he fell in love with the Johanna Maria on her maiden voyage. A quiet, homeless man of the sea, he stuck to the ship, despite the enmity of poor Captain Wilkens, who gradually sank under the tragedy of his home life, took to drink, and one night, after making his peace with Brouwer, disappeared overboard. He stuck to her until she was sold into foreign hands. Growing older, he began to skimp and save, to do a little private trading between ports on his own account, to invest in cargoes on a larger scale, always keeping in mind his dream of some day buying the ship of his heart.

In foreign keeping the Johanna Maria fell into evil hands, passing from one set of exploiters to another. But Jacob Brouwer keeps track of her. Steam is crowding sail off the seas. And the time comes when the price of the Johanna Maria has fallen so low and the savings of the sail-maker have risen so high that his seemingly absurd dream actually comes true.

That is the outline of the tale. But many a yarn of men and other ships, of characters and events, livens the way. However highly one might be tempted to place this well-known Dutch novel out of Holland's seafaring tradition (and I cannot go all the way with Quiller-Couch, who writes a seriously pleasant introduction for literarily minded folk), one can see no reason for any one failing to enjoy so can-

didly naïve, four-square, very neat and exemplary, craftsmanlike a tale of the Dutch seas and the Dutch sailors. In quality it will, perhaps, remind the American reader first of all of Dana's *Two Years Before the Mast*—although there seems no obvious reason for comparing the two. It is certainly neither of Smollett nor Cooper nor Marryat nor Conrad. In its precision and simplicity lie such poetry and such romance (by no means inconsiderable) as it has to offer.

Rob Nieuwenhuys   (essay date 1972)

SOURCE: "The World Beyond," in his *Mirror of the Indies: A History of Dutch Colonial Literature,* edited by E. M. Beekman, translated by Frans van Rosevelt, The University of Massachusetts Press, 1982, pp. 154-66.

[*In the following essay, which was originally published in Dutch in 1972, Nieuwenhuys praises* John Company *for its unity but compares it unfavorably with Schendel's other novels, faulting its lack of "real human and dramatic content."*]

Arthur van Schendel's *John Company* is a historical novel dealing, from a Dutch perspective, with the first Dutch settlement in the Indies. The novel shows a great deal of unity throughout. No doubt Van Schendel, while unfolding an important phase in Dutch colonial history, aimed at monumentality.

His novels, especially those written after 1930, have a broad perspective and a carefully worked-out plot. The critic Jan Greshoff, in his *Notes concerning "John Company" and "The Waterman"* (*Aanteekeningen over Jan Compagnie en De Waterman,* 1934), compared Van Schendel's *John Company* to a mural. The comparison, when one thinks of it, makes a great deal of sense, especially because it illustrates so well how carefully Van Schendel went to work.

> [*John Company*] is a detailed portrayal of the colorful first years in the history of the United East Indies Company. One mural, as it were, depicts the young city of Amsterdam and its growing port, its trade, and its rivalries. Placed in the foreground, and somewhat more clearly outlined than the other figures, we see a lively, overconfident young fellow who is anxious to escape the narrow confines of the town and who heads for the Indies.
>
> The second mural reveals the Dutch establishing themselves in the Banten area on Java's West Coast. And again, among a multitude of natives, Chinamen, Englishmen, and Hollanders, we discern the more pronounced figure of De Brasser, soldier, corporal, and sergeant. The third tableau gives us a marvelous view of the Moluccas. It shows us the descendants of the Portuguese living their amiable, naive lives among the natives but it also shows all too well the servants of the Company destroying their idyll through fire and sword in order that they may send even more pepper and cloves back to Europe. The central figure here too is that of Jan de Brasser, now a free man, a landowner, a planter and mer-

chant, who with care and hard work makes his fortune. He also makes it a point to remain as morally upright and just as circumstances allow.

In conclusion, the fourth mural shows the city of Amsterdam again, now much more crowded, greater, more colorful and richer, as the center of European commerce. Against this great national backdrop, old De Brasser stands out again as somebody not quite at home there, albeit for a different reason this time. As we look around us and examine one tableau after another in this manner, hundreds of details begin to stand out, far too many to describe here. Van Schendel shows us an amazing variety and number of things but he has managed to arrange them in such a way as to make them into a harmonious whole. All the parts contribute and are essential to this larger concept, and for that reason, whenever *John Company* comes to mind, I invariably think of it as one, inseparable whole.

Greshoff, aiming to praise Van Schendel, considers his prose devoid of "literary embellishments," but this does in no way mean that Van Schendel uses a lively and natural prose that follows the vagaries of the human heart, as does Multatuli's, for example. On the contrary, Van Schendel employs a stylized, classical, and somewhat archaic Dutch, which certainly reveals a good deal of literary preoccupation on his part. His style is cool and most effective whenever it contrasts with a dramatic incident, which is the case in most of his novels. Even when the dramatic element is lacking, however, his prose retains this quality of always progressing slowly and steadily, but its effectiveness is then diminished or lost altogether. This is the case in *John Company,* where his sober style could not quite function to effect, because the story lacks real human and dramatic content. For that reason, *John Company* does not quite measure up to an earlier novel like *The Frigate "Johanna Maria"* (*Het Fregatschip Johanna Maria*), and even less to his subsequent tragic novels. Greshoff has a different opinion and tries to forestall any criticism of this kind in the last few pages of his critique. He finds *John Company* just as successful a novel as Van Schendel's *The Waterman,* or his *A Dutch Drama* (*Een Hollands drama*), or *Gray Birds* (*Grauwe vogels*), or *The World is Dancing* (*De wereld een dansfeest*).

The critic H.'s-Gravesande, in his 1949 monograph dealing with Arthur van Schendel, regrets the fact that there is relatively little biographical information available. Van Schendel was a man little inclined to reveal private details of his life, to be sure, but we do know quite a bit about him even so. For our purposes it is interesting to know that Van Schendel was born in Batavia in 1874. His father was an officer there and took his family back to the Netherlands when Arthur was just five years old. The formative years that any child spends in the Indies are quite decisive, however. 'S-Gravesande informs us that Van Schendel's father died when the child was still quite young, which meant that he was largely brought up by his mother. Hers was a family with long-standing ties with the tropics, a colonial family, so to speak, which meant an Indies family with Indies traditions, Indies aunts and uncles, nephews, nieces, and so on. If not distinguishable from the Holland-

ers by their looks, they must surely have stood out on account of their different way of speaking, their way of life, in short, through their different habits. Van Schendel must have known these people, also in later life, after they had returned to the Netherlands, "repatriated," as they called it. His mother's family must have been quite close to him afterwards in Holland too. He was part of them, while he could at the same time stand back far enough to see how typically Indies and different they were, living in Holland but according to their own cultural pattern. Even so, Van Schendel wrote remarkably little about his family. For one thing, he did not emulate Couperus's habit of modeling his fictional characters after living family members.

Once, in *The World is Dancing,* he introduces an Indies lady whom he draws admirably, mostly by just allowing us to overhear her talk. Her authenticity leaves little doubt that she is modeled after one or several members of his Indies "clan." This remarkable portrait of a lady should be seen within its proper framework, or within the whole gallery of portraits called *The World is Dancing.* This novel deals with the tragic history of the dancing couple Marion and Daniël as told by nineteen different people who knew them at various stages in the past. One of these people is the Indies lady, Mrs. Hadee, "née Odilie Harings." ("How old am I? Oh, Sir, I've quite forgotten that.") She is the piano teacher of Marion, Mr. Ringelinck's little daughter. She talks about her relationship with Ringelinck in a self-satisfied and coquettish sort of way ("I'm not sure whether I could really accept such a present, people so quickly jump to the wrong conclusions. But then again, Ringelinck never did give me the idea that I ought to be careful, he is such a thoroughly respectable gentleman.") She is flattered by his attentions but she feels that his friends insult her: "My God, the number of insufferable men in this world, always after something." Her speech is a mixture of cunning and innocence, the somewhat romantic jargon of so many older Indies ladies ("What a dear, what a pretty!"), larded with French words and exclamations. What characterizes her most as an Indies lady is her particular tone of voice. Van Schendel conveys it admirably.

J. J. A. Mooij   (essay date 1972)

SOURCE: "On Literature and the Reader's Beliefs (with Special Reference to *De Waterman* by Arthur van Schendel)," in *Dichter und Leser: Studien zur Literatur,* edited by Ferdinand van Ingen, and others, Wolters-Noordhoff, 1972, pp. 143-50.

[*In the following essay, Mooij discusses psychological beliefs evidenced in* De Waterman.]

[Nearly] all novels, including *De Waterman,* appeal to beliefs in that they merely suggest or hint at the motives and causes which underlie certain acts performed by the characters. Of course, the novelist may deliberately try to make the behaviour of his characters incomprehensible, but this is done, I think, only in a minority of cases.

One prominent example in *De Waterman* is the behaviour of the grown-up people in Gorkum towards the boy Maarten. Apparently there is here some connection between religion, parochialism, and severity in education; a connection which is indeed not altogether out of the common. On the basis of his beliefs as to human psychology the reader should be able to gather that such a connection exists: the author does not explicitly tell him so.

Maarten's reactions also, especially his rebelliousness, his feeling of guilt, his urge to self-destruction, and his role (in Northrop Frye's terminology) as a 'pharmakos in reverse' [Northrop Frye, *The Anatomy of Criticism,* 1951] are largely understandable as a possible effect of his education. His father's saying to him 'That boy no longer belongs here', together with many other things done to him may have affected Maarten's psyche to the end of his life. This is hardly ever explicitly indicated but for the greater part implicitly given to understand. That is to say that beliefs as to psychological mechanisms are appealed to. The intricate pattern of psychological connections can only be confidently conjectured on the basis of such beliefs. Of course, I do not want to suggest that Maarten's grown-up life is completely rectilinear. There are some influential contingencies, such as his love for a Roman Catholic girl, his meeting with Koppers and Wuddink, the death of his child. But again, beliefs held in real life are bound to play a role in the acceptance of the after-effects of these contingencies.

Nor is Maarten the only main character whose behaviour and development must be regarded in the light of certain psychological views, vague and indefinite though they may be. The same applies to Aunt Jans (Juffrouw Goedeke). The reader is invited to largely accept her own account of her life at the end of chapter 12. This would mean that he has to believe that her psychological state of mind in her latter days is after all a natural (though not in the least a predictable) outcome of her life experience. Moreover, and more importantly, to understand and appreciate her story the reader should know something about the way people see themselves and their own life in retrospect (and this involves memory, the sentiment of 'lost time' and lost opportunities, etc.). The story of Juffrouw Goedeke also appeals to the belief that there is a rather general human striving after social respectability and honour and power; without such a belief Maarten's behaviour cannot be seen as in any way deviating.

Many of the psychological beliefs relevant to a proper understanding of *De Waterman* are in the category of what [Henry David] Aiken calls 'cultural beliefs' in so far as they are somehow connected with the scientific commitments of a particular culture or age. The relevant beliefs with respect to the natural world, however, are mostly 'natural beliefs' [in M. C. Beardsley and H. M. Schuller, eds., *Aesthetic Inquiry: Essays on Art Criticism and the Philosophy of Art,* 1967]. But this need not always be so. The physical knowledge appealed to can be of a much more sophisticated type than in *De Waterman.*

Lastly, I should like to point out that the deeply melancholy, even tragic character of the novel is based on certain general notions which are part of a (perhaps only incompletely articulated) world view.

Apparently the novel appeals to feelings of sympathy towards Maarten. More especially, the reader is expected to recognize Maarten's attitude and abilities as things which ask for benevolent attention to begin with (which of course does not quite exclude the possibility of moral censure). It is presupposed that Maarten is, in many senses, a gifted boy whose whole life—difficult, wayward, and in the end unhappy—is presented from this basic perspective.

The above would imply that the reader is expected to have more or less definite beliefs with respect to the moral value of certain acts, attitudes, abilities and feelings. Moreover, he should view life as irrevocable and definitive; he should agree that acts and experiences cannot be undone. Ideas such as these emotionally colour the thoughts and remarks of the characters as to what might have been different, if certain things had not happened. These obstacles, however, could not possibly be removed, so the characters think; and the reader is invited to think so, too.

Frans van Rosevelt   (essay date 1983)

SOURCE: An introduction in *John Company* by Arthur van Schendel, edited by E. M. Beekman, translated by Frans van Rosevelt, The University of Massachusetts Press, 1983, pp. 1-12.

[*In the following essay, van Rosevelt discusses themes and characters of* John Company, *and its similarities to* The Johanna Maria.]

There is no better introduction to the everyday experiences of men and women during the early days of the East Indies Company than *John Company.* It provides a first-hand account of the perils at sea and in the newly discovered Indonesian Islands. To Arthur van Schendel, its author, the work represented a journey back, both to Indonesia, where he had been born, and to Amsterdam, where he spent his youth during a time when that city was also young and growing.

John Company is considered one of the five best books that the prolific Van Schendel wrote between 1930 and 1935. It was preceded by *The "Johanna Maria" (Het Fregatschip Johanna Maria)* and followed by *The Waterman (De Waterman), A Dutch Tragedy (Een Hollands Drama), The Rich Man (De Rijke Man),* and *The Gray Birds (De Grauwe Vogels).* These novels are considered to belong to the writer's "Dutch Period" and deal with strong-willed characters who are often driven by fate, heredity, or their own convictions to a tragic end. *John Company* shares a number of these characteristics, but it is exceptional in its scope and breadth and in its foreign setting. This biographical and historical chronicle of the confrontation of East and West is neither an apology for nor a defense of what was to become a colonial situation. The novel's perceptive response to Indonesia is an *histoire de mentalités* and places Arthur van Schendel among writers such as Multatuli, Joseph Conrad, and Maria Dermoût.

The youngest of five children, Arthur van Schendel was born on March 5, 1874, in Batavia, the capital of the Netherlands East Indies. His father, George, was a lieutenant colonel who had risen from the ranks in the colonial army. His mother, Johanna Lippe, came from a family that had been in the Indies for several generations. When Arthur was five years old, the Van Schendels moved to the Netherlands, and a year later, in 1880, his father died. Restlessness or, more likely, her frequent inability to pay the rent caused his mother to move often after that, and Arthur lived at four different addresses in as many years in Haarlem alone.

The historian and critic of Indies literature, Rob Nieuwenhuys, tells us that Van Schendel must have learned about Indies manners and mannerisms from his mother and her family. Be that as it may, Arthur did not stay with his mother for very long; essentially he had left home and was looking after himself by the time he was fourteen years old. (This reminds us of the child Jan de Brasser in the novel, who can mend his own clothes when he is six and already has taught himself to read.)

Because of his mother's peregrinations, Arthur attended a variety of secondary schools in Amsterdam without finishing at any. He applied to acting school in 1891 and found himself accepted as the best of a dozen applicants. Fellow students remembered him as a very tall, kind boy with a lot of kinky blond hair, who was given to teasing. Apparently he did this without malice, as a way of testing the sincerity and convictions of his classmates. He was well over six feet tall, and he may have been considered too tall to become an actor. In any case, he abandoned his training and instead studied for and obtained a diploma to teach French. He admired the poet Verlaine, and later, in 1927, he wrote an essay about him. Before that, however, Van Schendel was "discovered" through a poem he had written, and he became acquainted with a group of literary people. While still at acting school, he had already started work on his first novel. It appeared to good reviews in 1896, when Arthur van Schendel had just turned twenty-two.

That year he also began to study for a diploma to teach English and left to teach at a grammar school in Tuxford, England. He came to know the language well enough to consider writing in it. In one of his few autobiographical essays, **"The Grammar School,"** he describes this stint, where he ended up teaching a wide variety of subjects. He lived in and near London for several years and also spent a year in Wales, but he left there just after the turn of the century because he could not find anyone with whom to speak English.

In England still, in 1902, he married Bertha Zimmerman. They had two children, but one died and Bertha herself died back in Holland in 1905. Three years later, Van Schendel married Annie de Boer, and they stayed in the Netherlands until 1920, when, for reasons of health, she had to spend winters in southern Europe. The Van Schendels never settled in Holland again. They lived near Florence, Italy, where the author E. du Perron stayed with them in 1929, then near Paris, where their children attended the Sorbonne. They spent most of the thirties and the ensuing war years in the seaside town of Sestri Levante near Genoa, Italy, although Van Schendel usually went to Amsterdam and Brussels around Christmas time. His friend and biographer G. H.'s-Gravesande has described Van Schendel's return to a bleak postwar Amsterdam, a return made more poignant by the arrival of the few survivors of its once extensive Jewish population. Weakened by a fractured hip, Arthur van Schendel died of a heart attack on September 11, 1946, at the age of seventy-two.

Van Schendel's letters to the celebrated young poet Willem Kloos have a forthright and self-assured tone and give evidence that he had early set his mind on becoming a writer. Kloos supported his work, and they became friends. Van Schendel's determination can be seen in his work; he produced an average of almost one book a year, working up his research into newspaper articles. Of his more than forty novels, those written before 1930 generally have a medieval, southern European setting in the manner of the pre-Raphaelites. This inclination stems in part from Van Schendel's admiration for the neo-romantic poetry of Kloos, Perk, and Gorter. By 1930, however, Van Schendel had brought out a novel that showed a departure, in its period and setting, from this neo-romantic and Italianate preoccupation. That year he published **The "Johanna Maria,"** which was translated into English by Brian Down in 1935.

The "Johanna Maria" became Van Schendel's best-known book. Widely translated, it was to overshadow much of his earlier and subsequent work. It is the story of Jacob Brouwer, a boy who becomes enchanted by a ship from the very moment he sees it launched. He spends his life with the frigate, first in its service, then in pursuit of it, and finally as its owner, but by that time this type of ship has become a rarity and lies idle among the newfangled steamers in Amsterdam's harbor. One winter, old Brouwer slips from her rigging and suffers a fatal fall. This account of a man's single-minded passion, of the end of his kind and the end of his ship, is rendered in an even and unassuming prose. Yet this somewhat archaic style harbors many instances of longing, courage, and wonder.

Much of this is also true of **John Company.** What shines forth in Van Schendel's work is essentially the detached tone of his prose that is suddenly disrupted by a character's insights and emotions. Where the marvelous occurs as unexpectedly as it does here, in the everyday world of men at work, we know ourselves to be in the realm of the fairy tale. For that reason, the bar of raisins a worker gives young De Brasser is nothing short of miraculous. This fairy-tale quality is enhanced by the elements that show the unexpected workings of fate and point out how time reveals the true natures of men. The roles of Manuel Silva and Yen Pon—agents of good fortune who personify the reward for good deeds—come to mind. There is, in addition, a great sense of longing that suffuses this and subsequent novels, a longing traceable to the author's youth spent on the quays and among the waterways of Amsterdam. The critic Stuiveling has suggested that Van Schendel's nostalgia became increasingly stronger as the writer grew older and continued to live abroad.

In 1931, one year after the publication of **The "Johanna Maria,"** the Society of Dutch Literature insultingly awarded Arthur van Schendel, who was fifty-seven years old at the time and a well-established author of more than sixteen books, a prize generally considered to be only for the youngest authors. The critic and poet Marsman was quick to point out the absurdity of that so-called award, but the affront was presumably made up for in 1938 when three Dutch professors nominated Van Schendel as their national candidate to receive a Nobel prize. Van Schendel received a Dutch medal in 1939.

In 1931, Van Schendel was busy writing *John Company,* which was to appear the following year. Before that he brought out a brief novel called *South Sea Island* (*Het Eiland in de Zuidzee*), a retelling of the mutiny on the *Bounty,* which in subject matter was closely related to the issues dealt with in *John Company*—of rebellion and life in the Pacific. 'S-Gravesande suggests that the shorter work was a spin-off from the research done for *The "Johanna Maria,"* which is plausible enough. It is also possible that Van Schendel wrote this chronicle in emulation of Simon Vestdijk's historical novel set in Jamaica, *Rum Island* (*Rumeiland*), which Van Schendel greatly admired.

More closely related to the Pacific, in general, and to Java and the Moluccan Islands, in particular, is the material he gathered and preserved in a series of brief essays. Together they comprise some two dozen pieces, and although not published until 1936, they are clearly related to his research for *John Company.* The essays are about Henry the Navigator, Portuguese India, Sir Francis Drake (who visited the Moluccas on his circumnavigation), and related subjects. Van Schendel's introduction to this collection of essays, called *Explorers* (*Avonturiers,* reissued in 1980), refers to the very same themes of fortune, fate, and the yearning for distant places found in most of his work, particularly in *John Company.*

> The longing for adventure lives in each and every human heart, even though there is little of it left in those of us who have learned to keep to the beaten track. Countless are the ways in which this longing manifests itself: Running away to sea, to far away places, is only the simplest. . . . Comfort and orderliness provide a safe shelter to dwell in but it so happens that the human heart needs more than security. It continues to long for the unknown that lies beyond. It probably sounds farfetched, maybe even a little foolish, inasmuch as nature burdens us with no more and no less than we can bear, but I do think that without that kind of longing there would not be any hope left in the world. It is only a small flame but one that cannot even abide the laws of gravity. Who knows, that very same longing for adventure may one day be observed to exist among the stars.

John Company was written in Ascona, Switzerland, where Van Schendel completed it in March 1932, before going to live in Sestri Levante, Italy. Van Schendel wears his scholarship lightly, and he nowhere openly informs, let alone instructs his reader. Such would have run counter to his narrative intent, of course, which is ever detached. The novel is a self-contained, autonomous whole that includes a wealth of information which closely parallels the growth of the Dutch East Indies Company from infancy to early adolescence.

Toward the end of the sixteenth century, the United Netherlands were fighting their protracted war of independence from Spain. Their trade routes to the Mediterranean and Portugal were closed, and their brave attempts to reach the Indies via the Arctic had ended in disaster. What they needed were accurate charts showing the way to the Indies, as well as the encouraging news, which proved not entirely accurate, that the Portuguese hold on Asia was far weaker than had been believed. Jan Huyghen van Linschoten was the man who got them what they needed.

Van Linschoten, who had worked for and spied on the Portuguese in Lisbon and in Goa, India, over a number of years, provided his countrymen with an *Itinerario,* that is, descriptions and charts that would guide them to the Indies. As early as 1595, Cornelis Houtman, taking a copy of the *Itinerario* with him, reached the Indies and made a treaty with the Muslim Sultan of Bantam (or Banten), whose strongholds commanded the Sunda Straits between the large islands of Sumatra to the west and Java to the east. The Dutch base of operations soon shifted some fifty miles further east along the north coast of Java, where the city of Batavia, now Jakarta, was founded. By 1598, Dutch fleets reached the Moluccan Islands and there traded on the islands of Banda, Ternate, and Amboina (modern spelling: Ambon). Amboina was small, situated to the south of the islands of Buru and Ceram. The Moluccas lie to the west of New Guinea, the world's second-largest island, and to the east of the starfish-shaped island of Celebes. The distance from Jakarta to Amboina is some 3,000 kilometers or 1,800 miles across the increasingly deeper Java, Flores, and Banda seas. These Spice Islands had been important Muslim centers, and they were on bad terms with the proselytizing Portuguese. Competition between the English, Portuguese, Dutch, and other merchants prompted the local rulers to increase their prices and tariffs; when this was done, the Dutch consolidated their various trading companies into the "Vereenigde Oost-Indische Compagnie," the United East Indies Company, whose initials "VOC" were soon superimposed on its flag and coinage. In some remote areas of New Guinea, now Irian Jaya, a Dutchman is still referred to as "orang kompenie," or man of the Company.

Like the warlike Papuans from New Guinea, the Dutch too undertook punitive or "hongi-" raids, a *hongi* being a heavily armed fleet of *praos* with which the Company went to cut down nutmeg trees in those areas where they were deemed superfluous. The Company sought first to establish a monopoly in the spice trade, then to keep prices up by controlling the supply.

Whereas its younger rival, the Dutch West Indies Company, held sway over the New Netherlands, its Caribbean islands, Guyana, and Brazil, the East Indies Company at its apogee had trading posts in Ghana, the African Cape, the island of Mauritius, and Basra on the Persian Gulf. On the Indian subcontinent it had "factories" in Vasanur, Malabar, Mysore, and the Coromandel Coast, held the islands of Ceylon and Taiwan, and had strongholds scattered across the more than three thousand islands comprising the Indonesian archipelago. After the expulsion of the Portuguese for religious reasons, the Company continued to trade with Japan from its tiny post in the Bay of Nagasaki, which explains the Japanese presence in *John Company.* Considering its enormous investments and profits,

its vast domain, and its many enemies, the Company was an empire unto itself. Controlled by the Lords Seventeen, it was also a fairly humane and efficient enterprise and continued to be so for a long time, both in terms of its own period and our own.

As the title suggests, the novel is not about its protagonist Jan de Brasser so much as about the early growth of the East Indies Company, "John Company" being the name given to anyone associated with it. Jan de Brasser is to some degree symbolic of all those who left Holland to seek their fortune in the East. The Dutch meaning of his name implies that he is a spendthrift. Van Schendel diminished the importance of his main character by introducing a great many other characters to the cast who help illustrate the ups and downs of those serving the Company.

The novel has a number of characteristics typical of the 1930s. For example, it is rather programmatic and ambitious in its historical portrayal of an era. It deals with several themes that do not seem to be sufficiently integrated into the framework of the story. In this novel one also becomes conscious of Van Schendel's portrayal of themes such as the eastward flow of empire, youth and old age, East and West, black and white, war and peace, and profit and loss, as well as the rise and fall of cities, all on a vast historical scale. Indeed, the suggestion that the overall composition of *John Company* resembles a mural was made by Van Schendel's friend and critic Jan Greshoff. Greshoff, whose remarks are also to be found in Rob Nieuwenhuys's *Mirror of the Indies*, calls *John Company*

> a detailed portrayal of the colorful first years in the history of the United East Indies Company. One mural, as it were, depicts the young city of Amsterdam and its growing port, its trade and its rivalries. Placed in the foreground, and somewhat more clearly outlined than the other figures, we see a lively, overconfident young fellow who is anxious to escape the narrow confines of the town and who heads for the Indies.

Greshoff goes on to praise Van Schendel's prose for its absence of "literary embellishments," but this does not mean that Van Schendel uses a lively and natural prose. As Nieuwenhuys points out:

> His style is cool, and most effective whenever it contrasts with a dramatic incident, which is the case in most of his novels. Even when the dramatic element is lacking, however, his prose retains this quality of always progressing slowly and steadily but its effectiveness is then diminished or lost altogether. This is the case in *John Company,* where his sober style could not quite function to effect because the story lacks real human and dramatic content.

This is only partially correct. Certainly Van Schendel cannot be taken to task for the things he chose not to write about. Where the alleged lack of dramatic elements is concerned, it is true that the novel has no developed love interest or much sexual passion, for example. We feel we hardly know De Brasser's wife and that she remains superficial. However, that may have been Van Schendel's intention, and he might just as well be accused of having drawn a stereotype of a pretty but superficial and supersti-

tious Indies girl. Of course, sometimes his prose is altogether too predictable and repetitive, as when we are told once again how many houses are being put up or how many dances and dinners are being prepared. It is true that sometimes we are told too much and shown too little, but Van Schendel can also surprise us with a chapter where understatement is most eloquent. For example, when he intimates the horrors of the bestial mass execution in which Draet is forced to participate, the soldier's remorse and its consequences are profoundly tragic. In contrast, some of his scenes are as quietly undramatic as a painting by Jan Vermeer, such as the tranquil scene just before Jan de Brasser turns the corner and comes home again.

It has been argued, and with some merit, that the characters remain too sketchy and that Jan de Brasser himself is, paradoxically, too much of a synthesis. He seems to lack the deeper psychological and emotional motivations that propel Jacob Brouwer in *The "Johanna Maria."* This is something Van Schendel must have realized but wanted, however. Moving all those characters from east to west and back again left little space in which to develop De Brasser the way he could develop Brouwer.

What Van Schendel could and did develop in *John Company* are the qualities Jan de Brasser embodies, which form the essence of the book. De Brasser has the tenacity and the courage to face up to the tyranny of time, heredity, and circumstance. The novel deals essentially with De Brasser's single-minded pursuit of making amends and doing justice to his mother and his uncle. He is a man who endures, as indeed his valiant mother did before him. At times more a figure than an individual, he suffers pain and injustice, for he is a man shaped and conditioned by his class and by his past. The muddled religious disputes back home concern the same subject. In fact, his uncle "considered it a cruel thing to decree that a sinner who was not of the elect could not hope to mend his ways and redeem himself through good deeds," and this opinion keeps business from his shop and compels Jan to leave. In the process, Jan goes on to redeem himself on a secular level exactly as his uncle might have wished, and against all odds. Van Schendel does not hold with the pretense of religious salvation of one kind or another: Jan de Brasser is fated to be who he is and what he is, no matter where he goes. No sooner does he seem to be thriving in a new environment than Maartensz shows up again to thwart him or to blow the whistle on him. De Brasser remains a loner, on the outside of the colorful world of the Mardijkers, and the only true passion he knows is loyalty, to them, to his newly found brother, and to the people in Amsterdam. De Brasser reasons as best he can, another form of courageous action, and he persists where others have given up or gone mad.

The novel's well-wrought and restrained language suggests more than it actually describes. What passions exist in the book derive from De Brasser's attempt to hold on to his sanity in the face of many injustices. His restraint comes far from easily, however. A great deal of the book's tension stems from an overall sense of pent-up emotion. Van Schendel makes the volcanic nature and the beauty of the Moluccas complement the emotions of his characters. De Brasser does come close, also, to running amuck after Draet's suicide. Isabel, De Brasser's wife, is not the only one who is superstitious, but she senses and expresses, more than any other character, the general feeling of dread. It is not fate, but dread, an unnamed fear that pervades her life and that of the others.

The book has suffered from pointless comparisons to *The "Johanna Maria,"* but it is true that the books have a great deal in common. For one thing, they share the same ironic vision. In *John Company,* even persistence and courage are ultimately defeated by time, and only stoicism can brave such odds. The world of *John Company,* although its setting is among the most beautiful in the world, is a world where the life of man is insignificant, lonely, and often wasteful. De Brasser's life is most significant in his small interactions with naturally decent or gracious people, and not in terms of religion, morality, corporate policies, or causes. The critic Ter Braak is correct in saying that Arthur van Schendel refused to be fashionable and that his aim was to portray tragedy. But it is tragedy with a difference, and that difference is irony. In the book's final scene, which is a showcase of Van Schendel's ability to indicate the passage of time, Asjie, the little blue cockatoo whose antiquated language no one can understand anymore, has the last word.

Lev Shestov

1866-1938

(Pseudonym of Lev Isaakovich Schwarzmann) Russian-born philosopher, critic, and essayist.

INTRODUCTION

Often compared to Danish philosopher Søren Kierkegaard, Shestov is known for his religious existentialist thought in which he rejects empirical science as a valid means for revealing truths concerning human existence. Shestov viewed reason as a "restraint" on freedom, maintaining that truth is not objective but subjective, and is accessible to the individual only through faith in God and a deep commitment to biblical teachings. Shestov's philosophical and critical essays are often praised for their coherent presentation of ideas and vigorous prose style.

Biographical Information

Shestov was born in Kiev to an upper-middle class Jewish family. His early education in Hebrew and Jewish literature, folklore, and religious teachings at the gymnasium in Kiev would later become central to his work. Studying mathematics and law at the University of Moscow, Shestov finished as a Candidate of Laws but never entered law practice because his dissertation was not approved by the Committee of Censors due to its controversial topic dealing with the Russian labor force. He went to work for his father's textile firm, and during this time began writing articles for avant-garde publications. One of his earliest essays, "Georg Brandes and Hamlet," was published in the journal *Kievskoe slovo* in 1895, and became the basis of his first book, *Shakespeare i yevo kritik Brandes* (*Shakespeare and His Critic Brandes*). During this period, Shestov decided to devote himself exclusively to the study of philosophy, and he read the works of Socrates, St. Augustine, Plotinus, Blaise Pascal, Martin Luther, Baruch Spinoza, and G. W. F. Hegel, as well as the Bible. In 1919 he left Russia permanently with his family, and in 1921 settled in Paris, where he taught philosophy at the Institut des Etudes Slaves and lectured at an extension program of the Sorbonne. While lecturing in Amsterdam in the 1920s he met German philosopher Edmund Husserl, and it was at Husserl's suggestion that Shestov began to read Kierkegaard, in whose work he discovered parallels with his own thought. Shestov died in 1938.

Major Works

Shestov's early writings examine philosophical and religious implications in the works of William Shakespeare, Leo Tolstoy, Friedrich Nietzsche, Anton Chekhov, and Feodor Dostoevsky. In his first major work, *Shakespeare and His Critic Brandes*, Shestov attacks the materialism and nationalism of Danish literary critic Georg Brandes.

In his next critical study, *Dobro v uchenii Tolstovo i Nietzsche* (*The Good in the Teachings of Count Tolstoy and Nietzsche*), Shestov discusses Tolstoy's moralistic equation of God with goodness and Nietzsche's nihilistic declaration that "God is dead." This work also generated controversy as a result of Shestov's acknowledgment of Nietzsche's honesty, courage, and spiritual quality. In *Dostoevski i Nietzsche* (*Dostoevsky and Nietzsche: The Philosophy of Tragedy*), Shestov viewed Dostoevsky's *Notes from Underground* (1864) as the most poignant statement regarding the human experience. *Apofeoz bezposhvennosti* (*The Apotheosis of Groundlessness*), a work which was vilified for its "libertinism," consists of over 160 brief essays dealing with science, philosophy, and literature. Shestov's religious works expound on his major premise that "to find God, one must tear oneself away from the seductions of reason" because reason and faith are essentially incompatible. *Na vesax Iova* (*In Job's Balances*) uses the plight of Job in the Old Testament to exemplify the inherent tragedy of life and argue that only through faith does one discover freedom, for "faith is the ultimate source of man's deliverance from despair."

PRINCIPAL WORKS

Shakespeare i yevo kritik Brandes [*Shakespeare and His Critic Brandes*] (criticism) 1898

Dobro v uchenii Tolstovo i Nietzsche: Filosofiya i propoved' [*The Good in the Teachings of Count Tolstoy and Nietzsche: Philosophy and Preaching*] (criticism) 1900

Dostoevski i Nietzsche: Filosofiya tragedii [*Dostoevsky and Nietzsche: The Philosophy of Tragedy*] (criticism) 1901

*Apofeoz bezpochvennosti [*The Apotheosis of Groundlessness*] (essays) 1905

†Nachala i kontsy [*Beginnings and Ends*] (essays) 1908

Velikie kanuny [*Great Vigils*] (essays) 1912

Vlast' kliuchei: Potestas clavium [*The Power of the Keys*] (essays) 1919

La nuit de Gethsémani (essay) 1923

Les Révélations de la mort: Dostoievski-Tolstoi (criticism) 1923

La Philosophie de la tragédie: Dostoievski et Nietzsche (criticism) 1926

Sur les confins de la vie: L'apothéose du dépaysement (essays) 1927

Na vesax Iova [*In Job's Balances*] (essays) 1929

Skovannyi Parmenid: Ob istochnikakh metafizicheskikhistin [*The Shackled Parmenides: On the Sources of Metaphysical Truth*] (essays) 1931

Kierkegaard i eksistentsialnaya filosofiya: Vox clamantis in deserto [*Kierkegaard and Existential Philosophy*] (criticism) 1936

Athènes et Jérusalem (essays) 1938

Umozrenie i otkrovenie: Religioznaya filosofiya Vladimira Solovyovai drug'lie stat'i [*Speculation and Revelation: The Religious Philosophy of Vladimir Solovyov and Other Essays*] (essays) 1964

Sola fide—tolko veroyu [*By Faith Alone*] (essays) 1966

---

*This volume was published as *All Things are Possible* in 1920.

†The English translation of this collection of essays was published in London in 1916 as *Anton Chekhov and other Essays* and in Boston as *Penultimate Words*.

CRITICISM

The Times Literary Supplement (essay date 1917)

SOURCE: "A Sceptic with a Purpose," in *The Times Literary Supplement*, No. 784, January 25, 1917, p. 40.

[*Below*, The Times Literary Supplement *offers a thematic analysis of the critical essays collected in* Anton Tchekov and Other Essays.]

Mr. Shestov is evidently a remarkable critic, and these essays of his were well worth translating. He is, Mr. Murry tells us in his introduction, fifty years old and has written little. Criticism with him is not a hand-to-mouth business. He does not choose a subject and then to begin to wonder what he can find to say about it. His criticism is philosophy expounded by means of a particular example, and rather hinted at than expounded. One feels that he has strong convictions but is shy of proclaiming them. Mr. Murry says that he is afraid of being dogmatic. If so it is not a cowardly fear, but a desire to leave the reader to draw his own conclusions. He will lead him to the water and trust in his thirst. Mr. Murry tells us also that, when Shestov began to write nearly twenty years ago, "Karl Marx was enthroned and infallible" in Russia, and that he has always been in reaction against dogmatic materialism. His business is to hint a doubt and hesitate dislike of it. Perhaps he hints and hesitates too much; but he seems to us to make his points clearly enough, just because he leaves them to make themselves.

The first essay on Tchekov may reassure those who wonder whether all Russians are like the people in Tchekov. He was, Mr. Shestov says, a specialist in hopelessness. Something must have happened to him which killed hope in him; and after it he wrote about a world from which hope had been removed. "He refused in advance every possible consolation, material or metaphysical. Not even in Tolstoi, who set no great store by philosophical systems, will you find such keenly expressed disgust for every kind of conceptions and ideas as in Tchekov. . . . Finally, he frees himself from ideas of every kind, and loses even the notion of connexion between the happenings of life." One can see that Mr. Shestov has a sympathy for this utterly destructive criticism, which is hardly criticism but rather a mode of experience. It was something that happened to Tchekov, not a pose that he assumed for artistic purposes; and therefore the fact that he was able to make real works of art out of this mode of experience is itself valuable. He did, in his negative way, prove something—namely, the supremacy of the spirit of man over its own hopelessness. And he proved it all the more surely because he was not trying to do so. He really was hopeless, and wished that he wasn't. There is no luxury of woe in him. He doesn't want to rub the gilt off the gingerbread, but for him there is no gilt on the gingerbread to begin with. And yet he is interesting and must have interested himself, or he would not have continued to write. He had, by no effort of thought, but by mere calamity, attained to the last scepticism, the disbelief in, and, more, the lack of any sense of, any kind of universal whatever. "In all the thoughts, feelings, and ideas," he says himself, "which I form about anything there is wanting the something universal which could bind all these together in one whole." To him every man is merely himself and has nothing in common with other men; and he remains the artist of men seen so.

That is the point; he does remain an artist, just as Schopenhauer remained a philosopher, although he denied all value to the contents of space and the subject matter of thought. But Tchekov is more sincere than Schopenhauer, for he takes no pleasure in his denial; it is something that has happened to him, and he does not even hail it as truth. But still he writes. It is a kind of undramatic tragedy. The worst that can happen to a man has happened to him; and yet the tragic beauty is wrung out of it. Mr. Shestov refuses to judge Tchekov by the moral conclusions that might be drawn from his works, because he knows that in fact they are not drawn. They ought to be devitalizing, but they are not, for there never is any poison in sincerity; and at last he tells us what is Tchekov's secret. "The only philosophy which Tchekov took seriously, and therefore seriously fought, was positivist materialism—just the positivist materialism; the limited materialism, which does not pretend to theoretical completeness." Above all things he hated the conviction that in the face of nature man must "always adapt himself and give way, give way, give way." He seems to submit to it in his stories, but "the submission is but an outward show; under it lies concealed a hard, malignant hatred of the unknown enemy." And with this hatred, Mr. Shestov hints, he proves more than the idealists and metaphysicians ever prove. He proves the irreconcilability of man to this tyranny of things. If there is nothing but adaptation, then the fact remains that man has not adapted himself. Hope and faith may be merely adaptation; but these characters of Tchekov, and Tchekov himself, have neither. They rebel utterly against all illusions that nature may try to impose on them; they will not be adapted; and by their rebellion they prove that adaptation is not everything, that in their case at least "great, unerring Nature once goes wrong." And so with their despair the whole theory of adaptation falls to the ground. They are, in fact, the real martyrs of a faith which they seem not to possess and yet possess more deeply than those who profess it.

That is the conclusion to which Mr. Shestov leads us, but with his peculiar method he leaves us to draw it. Mr.

Murry says that he is hardly a philosopher, and yet we think he is nothing else; only with his method he makes the reader philosophize for him. He seems the most complete sceptic; but he is not the cause of scepticism in others. His scepticism is all really an attack on materialism, which itself began by pretending to be scepticism, as tyrants begin by pretending to be demagogues. Materialism pretended to be the free choice of man's mind; but then it told him that he had no choice—that nature itself forced him to believe it. Mr. Shestov tells us that nature forces us to believe nothing. His scepticism, all the more because it seems impartial, is directed against the reigning tyrant. Let us get rid of him at least, and then we can think about a constitution. Above all, he wants to destroy man's sense of status, upon which all his tyrant delusions are based. "Christ knew that men could renounce all things save the right to superiority alone, to superiority over one's neighbours, to that which Nietzsche calls the patent of nobility." He seems to believe that Christ himself did not think it possible to take from men their hope of distinction. But there is inherent in Christianity the doctrine that men must utterly strip themselves of this hope; and this doctrine is what Mr. Shestov preaches. Because of it he is angry with the famous speech of Dostoevsky on Pushkin, which is included in the pages from the journal of an author.

D. H. Lawrence   (essay date 1920)

SOURCE: Preface to *All Things Are Possible,* in *Selected Literary Criticism,* edited by Anthony Beal, 1955. Reprint by Viking Press, 1955, pp. 242-44.

[*Lawrence was an English novelist, short story writer, poet, essayist, critic, translator, and dramatist, who is known for his controversial and outspoken ideas on such topics such as religion, psychology, and sex. In the following essay, which was originally published in 1920 as a preface to* All Things Are Possible, *he identifies Shestov as the disseminator of culture that is distinctively Russian, devoid of the influence of Western Europe.*]

In his paragraph on The Russian Spirit, Shestov gives us the real clue to Russian literature. European culture is a rootless thing in the Russians. With us, it is our very blood and bones, the very nerve and root of our psyche. We think in a certain fashion, we feel in a certain fashion, because our whole substance is of this fashion. Our speech and feeling are organically inevitable to us.

With the Russians it is different. They have only been inoculated with the virus of European culture and ethic. The virus works in them like a disease. And the inflammation and irritation comes forth as literature. The bubbling and fizzing is almost chemical, not organic. It is an organism seething as it accepts and masters the strange virus. What the Russian is struggling with, crying out against, is not life itself: it is only European culture which has been introduced into his psyche, and which hurts him. The tragedy is not so much a real soul tragedy, as a surgical one. Russian art, Russian literature after all does not stand on the same footing as European and Greek or Egyptian art. It is not spontaneous utterance. It is not the flowering of a

race. It is a surgical outcry, horrifying, or marvellous, lacerating at first; but when we get used to it, not really so profound, not really ultimate, a little extraneous.

What is valuable is the evidence against European culture, implied in the novelists, here at last expressed. Since Peter the Great Russia has been accepting Europe, and seething Europe down in a curious process of catabolism. Russia has been expressing nothing inherently Russian. Russia's modern Christianity even was not Russian. Her genuine Christianity, Byzantine and Asiatic, is incomprehensible to us. So with her true philosophy. What she has actually uttered is her own unwilling, fantastic reproduction of European truths. What she has really to utter the coming centuries will hear. For Russia will certainly inherit the future. What we already call the greatness of Russia is only her pre-natal struggling.

It seems as if she had at last absorbed and overcome the virus of old Europe. Soon her new, healthy body will begin to act in its own reality, imitative no more, protesting no more, crying no more, but full and sound and lusty in itself. Real Russia is born. She will laugh at us before long. Meanwhile she goes through the last stages of reaction against us, kicking away from the old womb of Europe.

In Shestov one of the last kicks is given. True, he seems to be only reactionary and destructive. But he can find a little amusement at last in tweaking the European nose, so he is fairly free. European idealism is anathema. But more than this, it is a little comical. We feel the new independence in his new, half-amused indifference.

He is only tweaking the nose of European idealism. He is preaching nothing: so he protests time and again. He absolutely refutes any imputation of a central idea. He is so afraid lest it should turn out to be another hateful hedge-stake of an ideal.

"Everything is possible"—this is his really central cry. It is not nihilism. It is only a shaking free of the human psyche from old bonds. The positive central idea is that the human psyche, or soul, really believes in itself, and in nothing else.

Dress this up in a little comely language, and we have a real ideal, that will last us for a new, long epoch. The human soul itself is the source and well-head of creative activity. In the unconscious human soul the creative prompting issues first into the universe. Open the consciousness to this prompting, away with all your old sluice-gates, locks, dams, channels. No ideal on earth is anything more than an obstruction, in the end, to the creative issue of the spontaneous soul. Away with all ideals. Let each individual act spontaneously from the forever incalculable prompting of the creative well-head within him. There is no universal law. Each being is, at his purest, a law unto himself, single, unique, a Godhead, a fountain from the unknown.

This is the ideal which Shestov refuses positively to state, because he is afraid it may prove in the end a trap to catch his own spirit. So it may. But it is none the less a real, living ideal for the moment, the very salvation. When it becomes ancient, and like the old lion who lay in his cave and whined, devours all its servants, then it can be dispatched. Meanwhile it is a really liberating word.

Shestov's style is puzzling at first. Having found the "ands" and "buts" and "becauses" and "therefores" hampered him, he clips them all off deliberately and even spitefully, so that his thought is like a man with no buttons on his clothes, ludicrously hitching along all undone. One must be amused, not irritated. Where the armholes were a bit tight, Shestov cuts a slit. It is baffling, but really rather piquant. The real conjunction, the real unification lies in the reader's own amusement, not in the author's unbroken logic.

Benjamin De Casseres   (essay date 1920)

SOURCE: "Shestov's Challenge to Civilization," in *The New York Times Book Review,* October 3, 1920, p. 19.

[*In the following review of* All Things Are Possible, *De Casseres discusses the unique Russian character of Shestov's philosophy.*]

Leo Shestov, a Russian still living at the age of 50, belongs in the high line of iconoclasts. His book, ***All Things Are Possible,*** just translated from the Russian by S. S. Koteliansky with a brilliantly written foreword by D. H. Lawrence, is a sheaf of 166 pensées on life, literature, European civilization, Russia, and, in fact, all things. His style is clear, uncollegiate and literary.

There is, nevertheless, a unity in the nihilism of Shestov, as there is in all his great predecessors. The unity of the skeptical thinkers is never in the brain. It is in the sensibility. Thought-siftings take on the fibre of the sieve, and our sensibility is a sieve of the external and internal universes. Our thoughts and judgments are created by our feelings and instincts. Spinoza says that every ideal is based on a physical need. Among the great negationists, like Shestov, the need is also physical—it is the search for Ultimate Well-Being, which idealists call Truth.

Mr. Lawrence tells us that Shestov is "preaching nothing." He is only "tweaking the nose of European idealism." His work is a protest against all present-day solutions of anything. A conviction is in a jail. In the infinite combinations of mind and matter all things are possible. Whatever is is only provisionally true. The "great teachers" are merely temperament superimposed on mystery. "Panaceas" are the art of sticking diamonds in our wounds. Illusion is Grace (Did not Emerson say, "Illusion is God's method"?) The Sphinx says, "Ask me no questions and I'll tell you no lies." What we call "progress" is only a return to the deeps of memory. What gardens, what prospects, what vistas in life! It is all memory.

What remains? Your consciousness, your self—the Recorder of the transitory, the aesthetic onlooker. The universe was invented so that the soul of a Shestov—or you or me—could enjoy the spectacle. The individual is the final criterion of all things—if we must have a criterion. This ultimate is the instinctive worship and divinization of master souls by the herd. In social and artistic and political evolution the part is greater than the whole. The cultured superman is the pinnacle—call him Shakespeare,

Napoleon, Beethoven, the Galilean or Montaigne—the "message" is nothing; the vision is all.

So, in wandering through this fascinating intellectual addenda to a profoundly Russian and modern sensibility one always feels one is in direct contact with a Man, not with a "message," a "solution" or a patent social or artistic nostrum. There are so many persons writing today, but individuals are few. Most of our up-to-date "philosophers" and "thinkers" quote authorities to stand on. Shestov quotes them to deny them. The difference reminds me of an anecdote told about the late William James. After a month spent at Chautauqua, among the goodly Disciples of Sweetness and Light, he hurried back to New York with the exclamation, "Where can I find some crooks? I want to rub elbows with life!" A splendid parable by our pluralistic Paul, who was trying to find the road out of Damascus.

The disease of Russia, Shestov avers impliedly, is that it has never dared to assert itself. It is sick because it has put on the spiritual, mental, social and religious mask of European civilization. There is no self-reliance, no healthy egotism in the Russian. He lives on borrowed clothes and borrowed food. He has conceived himself as he is not, and as he can never be. His soul is imported. He has not yet discovered that the Kingdom of God is within him. He is Hamlet-Don Quixote because he has not the courage to be simply Russian. He is neither Teuton, Gaul nor Anglo-Saxon, and the tragi-comedy of Russia today is caused by the pathetic attempts to ape the thought and manners of these Uitlanders. Mr. Lawrence is right when he says, echoing Shestov, "Russia will laugh at us before long; meanwhile she goes through the last stages of reaction against us, kicking away from the old womb of Europe."

Shestov gives one of the final kicks. "A plague on both your houses!" he thunders, which might be paraphrased into "A plague on all your houses!" But he smiles a veiled smile withal, as who should say:

"We Russians may be the finale of crowns in the drama of Christian civilization!"

David Gascoyne   (essay date 1949)

SOURCE: "Lev Shestov After Ten Years Silence," in *Horizon,* London, Vol. 20, No. 118, October 1949, pp. 213-29.

[*Gascoyne is an English poet, translator, critic, memoirist, dramatist, novelist, short story writer, and editor. In the following essay, he explicates basic tenets of Shestov's thought, comparing and contrasting his unique form of existentialism with that of Heidegger, Kierkegaard, and Sartre.*]

As far as it is possible to judge, there exists at present among the intelligent reading public in England only a dim and confused conception of the significance of Existential Philosophy and its situation in relation to the rest of contemporary thought. It is unlikely however that the confusion that reigns here in people's minds with regard to this philosophic movement is anything like the dense and inextricable confusion regarding it that must by this time have become general in France. Intellectual discursivity, having sensed the menace to itself that a proper understanding of the essential thought of the philosophers who may rightly be described as existential would represent, seems to have found the topic of *Existentialisme* more stimulating than any other to have cropped up in France for a long while and to have set about muddling the crucial issues involved with a dogmatizing polemical gusto such as is fortunately seldom equalled on this side of the Channel. Here, stifling our resentment at being as usual about a decade behind the intellectual development of the rest of Europe, we generally miss the real point, pass on garbled accounts of what it is all supposed to be about and are wearily deprecating in our comments on it.

When I refer here to Existential Philosophy, I should like it to be quite clear from the start that I do not mean this expression to be understood to designate the philosophy associated with the movement headed by the brilliant ex-professor, publicist and playwright Jean-Paul Sartre. If one would form a just estimate of the distance that separates Sartre's *Existentialisme* from the kind of thought that in what I am going to say I shall refer to as existential, one should try to imagine Pascal writing a poetic novel about the gulf that he felt to be yawning at his side all the time towards the end of his life. Existentialism is the post-experimental intellectual exploitation of the experience of existing. The kind of philosophy that I wish to discuss is actual spiritual activity. Not all that goes on within man is what the Marxists call 'mere reflection'.

Frequently heard and familiar enough though the names of the representatives of Cartesian Existentialism have become, it is extremely seldom that anyone refers to the one great modern thinker who can justly be described as a representative of authentically existential philosophy, Leon Chestov. For every mention of Chestov's name during the ten years that have passed since his death, there have been I should imagine at least five hundred references to Jean-Paul Sartre. While it would be untrue to say that Chestov remains quite unknown in this country, since three books of his have been translated and published here—*Anton Chehov and Other Essays,* with an introduction by Middleton Murry, in 1916, *All Things are Possible,* introduced by D. H. Lawrence, in 1920, and in 1932, introduced by Richard Rees, *In Job's Balances,* a book uniting in one volume several representative short works—it is still necessary to say that this great, profoundly disturbing Russian thinker, whose message for the present time is quite as significant as his friend Berdyaev's, is unjustly neglected and his importance altogether underestimated.

Leon Chestov, exiled after 1920 by the Soviet Polit-bureaucratic revolutionaries to whom his philosophy was insufficiently optimistic to be useful to their purposes, was a Voice Crying in the Wilderness his whole life long. *Vox Clamantis in Deserto* is the sub-title of one of his last works, *Kierkegaard and Existential Philosophy,* published in French translation a year or two before the first appearance of Sartre, who has always resolutely ignored him, though the world described with such long-drawn-out repugnance in his own imaginative works is certainly a desert. It is not surprising, however, that Chestov's voice has remained inaudible to one who has declared, during

a discussion of the epistemological foundations of Existentialism, that the Absolute is in Descartes. The Absolute that is to be found in Descartes's Cogito is absolute self-sufficiency, and if this produces a desert, Sartre's superb intelligence can still reign supreme in it and immediately reduce to silence all voices crying 'Prepare ye . . .'.

Coming as the most recent successor of two or three of the most original and significant thinkers of the nineteenth century—Kierkegaard, Nietzsche, Dostoievsky—Chestov may be considered to have made it possible at present to think of Existential Philosophy as such, that is to say to see it as a distinct current of thought with special distinguishing characteristics and central preoccupations, with a task and destiny to fulfil in the history of the spiritual crisis of Western man in the present age. The *Existentialisme* of Sartre does not belong to this current of thought. It is a perversion of the thought that inspired Kierkegaard and Dostoievsky (the Knight of Faith and the Underground Man) based on a typically French Cartesian misunderstanding of the essence of the special contribution of these solitary individualists to European philosophical speculation. Heidegger's position in relation to this situation is a quite special one, which I cannot begin to discuss here, but it should not be confused with Sartre's, simply on the supposition that they are both 'atheists', as innumerable facile vulgarizers and subtle casuists have attempted to do during the last five or ten years. What critics really mean when they state, as for instance Mr. J. V. Langmead-Casserley does in *The Christian in Philosophy,* that 'in writers like Heidegger and Sartre we are confronted by an existentialism which is specifically atheist', is simply that the assumption of these philosophers is that contemporary man is not a conscious believer in God. To assume this does not make one an atheist; and when Sartre does also announce himself as being specifically an atheist, this is a professional naïveté on his part. The now universal state of human existence cannot be said to be one of continual, profound, everyday faith in the living God. To have real faith in God is not at present natural to man in the world. To be a wholehearted and practically consistent believer is to be an exception to the normal condition of man in the twentieth century. It is the universal, *a priori* condition of human existence that is the subject existentialism undertakes to describe, to begin with, and the exceptions can only have significance in relation to a 'normal' or 'ordinary' state that has been first properly defined and analysed. It becomes clear after the initial examination of the ordinary state of man's existence has been made that there exists in it a tendency towards something else, which is ordinarily resisted in ways which Heidegger in particular subjects to detailed analysis. This something else is the state which results from a change of the 'ordinary' state of existence into a more highly developed state. The state of the conscious and deliberate atheist and the state of the authentic Christian both represent a higher development of existence than that of the ordinary. The only thing that any existentialist philosopher could be said to set out to convert anyone to is responsible choice. The important point that Sartre misses is that neither belief nor disbelief can be taught to anyone, and atheism, as soon as it becomes specific, is a belief: a belief in the non-existence of the spiritual dimension of reality, resting on a refusal to recognize that there is a Ground of Being.

'Socrates spent the month following his verdict in incessant conversations with his pupils and friends. That is what it is to be a beloved master and to have disciples. You can't even die quietly,' wrote Leon Chestov in 1905, thirty-four years before his own death. 'The best death is really the one which is considered the worst,' he wrote: 'to die alone, in a foreign land, in a poor-house, or, as they say, like a dog under a hedge.'

Chestov did not die in a poor-house, but otherwise he may be said to have achieved this ambition. His only disciple in 1939 was the Roumanian-born Jewish poet and philosopher Benjamin Fondane, who was destined to a death in the gas-chambers at Birkenau six years later. At the end of his life, Chestov was resigned to being neglected or mischievously misinterpreted by his contemporaries, who if ever they referred to him, did so to pour scorn on his crazy 'anti-rationalism', being unable to observe that few thinkers in the history of philosophy have had so realistic a respect for the power of human reason, even though this was a respect tempered by a realization of its limitations and of its hypnotic influence over those whom it enslaves. He did not want disciples—he did not even want to have pupils or a class of students, which for a philosopher in these days is rare. He believed philosophical activity to consist in absolutely undivided truth-seeking, and this he could not reconcile with telling people they need seek no more, should they happen also to be seeking Truth, but simply attend his classes and pay attention while he told it [to] them, the proper fee at the end of the term, and the maximum amount of lip-service to the importance of his ideas. To adopt the role of a teacher of this kind, would have been altogether in contradiction with the inner position, the adoption of which is a necessary prerequisite of Existential Philosophy, properly so-called. It is perfectly extraordinary how this simple fundamental distinction which makes Existential Philosophy *existential* is still so universally and completely ignored, particularly by professors.

It was not unintentionally that in introducing Leon Chestov I began by referring to his death. In Chestov's philosophical writings the thought of death is like a constant ground-note; death was to him a starting point as well as the ultimate goal for speculative thought. The first and most indispensable prerequisite for whoever would undertake the task of philosophy was for Chestov not the rational faculty or cogitative power, but courage. All advances in the realm of human thought are the result of a victory over fear. The justification of Socratic doubt, which questions the foundedness of all commonly accepted truths as a matter of discipline, is in the realization that we are ever apt to use our faculty of rational thinking less for the purpose of arriving at the truth than for that of protecting ourselves from fear of the unknown.

Chestov addressed his philosophy not to a class of passive students, but to an individual reader, his interlocutor. With regard to the fruitfulness of the normal master-pupil relationship, or what has become in the modern world the normal relationship between teacher and taught, he was

from the very beginning completely sceptical; but if he had not had some faith in the possibility and efficacy of communicating real philosophic thought he would hardly have continued to the end of his life to publish books in which an interlocutor is continually stimulated to reconsider the views of other great philosophers as well as his own views of them.

Chestov in many of his works leads his interlocutor through a careful and penetrating analysis of certain of the writings of Tolstoy, Dostoievsky and Chekhov to the possible recognition of the startling and difficult fact that there exist certain situations and states, such as have to be passed through at least once by all who are mortal, wherein a man may suddenly have to admit that the ordinary, reassuring truths and assumptions upon which we all base our everyday life and which it might well seem outrageous even to question publicly, are no longer able to satisfy him, but seem to the contrary to have been simply the easily available, conventionally legitimized means whereby men commonly stupefy themselves so as to continue to be able to remain fast asleep even when wide awake and busily occupied in carrying on very competently their no doubt highly important and altogether worth-while daily affairs.

For most of us, this moment of dislocation, of panic, of abrupt unfamiliarity and questionableness of everything hitherto regarded as certain, is throughout our whole lives postponed, evaded, and its possibility and implications absolutely denied and ignored. But as Chestov took pains to make vivid to his interlocutor, with the approach of death, this moment may become increasingly difficult to postpone. For it is in part the moment of fully recognizing the truth of the fact of Death itself, and of its immense enigmatic significance for the whole of the human life that leads to it.

It would be a great mistake to regard Chestov's preoccupation with Death as a gloomy aberration or morbidity; it is in fact a throughly normal and healthy preoccupation for a philosopher, and it is the ordinary current attitude to the darker aspect of reality that is morbid. It is generally far too easily forgotten today, in discussions of modern philosophy, that there have been in the history of thought few definitions of philosophy's purpose which more deserve serious attention, the attention of our second thoughts, than the Platonic-Socratic 'preparation in view of death'. Most modern philosophers, restlessly haunted by the ambition of succeeding in the enterprise of making philosophy an important department of the imposing edifice of Materialist Science, or rather the indispensable epistemological handmaid of an authoritative world-hegemony of laboratory and classroom workers and mathematicians, do not care, it would seem, to be reminded of this supposedly nonsensical formulation of the purpose of speculative thought; indeed, they seem unanimously to take it for granted that we should all be inarticulately resigned to being dead already.

In this respect, Heidegger's philosophy is an exception; in it the way all men regard Death most of the time they are alive, or rather the quasi-universal Western educated habit of evading real seriousness—and an appearance of seriousness is more than almost anything else made to serve to facilitate this evasion—has been treated as the subject of a rigorous, detailed analysis. For Heidegger, resolution-in-view-of-death is an experienced reality that is to be regarded as the necessary foundation of all human life having personal authenticity. Until we have undergone the realization that comes with a moment of the kind I tried to describe just now, we shall be all the time as it were running away from our true self, unable to accept life in its complete seriousness, continually anxious to keep always to the most superficial level of experience where everything is a matter of course and nothing new or difficult ever disturbs the unexceptional monotonously humdrum normality of a mediocre existence.

Martin Heidegger, in making the analysis to be found in *Sein und Zeit* of everyday banality and the inauthentic conception of death that is based on hearsay and clichés and not on a profound personal realization, was partly inspired originally by a story of Tolstoy's, *The Death of Ivan Ilyitch.* It happens that this story was among the later writings of Tolstoy that Chestov examines at some length in his book **The Revelations of Death,** in an essay entitled **'The Last Judgement'.** The moral to which Chestov's reflections on Tolstoy's greatest short story led him, he has expressed in what seems to me a rather more cogent form than that given it in that essay, in another of his writings, **'Revolt and Submission',** where he says:

> Despite his reason man is a being subject to the power of the moment. And even when he seeks to consider all things *sub specie aeternitatis,* his philosophy is usually *sub specie temporis*—indeed, of the present hour. This is why men reckon so little with death, as though death did not exist. When a man thinks on his dying hour—how do his values and standards change! But death lies in the future, which will not be—so every one feels. And there are many similar things of which one has to remind not only the common herd but also the philosophers who know so much that is superfluous and have forgotten, or have never known, what is most important.

After I had been reflecting quite recently on these words of Chestov and was beginning to plan the present dissertation, I happened idly to pick up an anthology of old English poetry, and on the page at which I opened it, this is the poem I found:

> A good that never satisfies the mind,
> A beauty fading like the April showers,
> A sweet with floods of gall that runs combined,
> A pleasure passing ere the thought made ours,
> An honour that more fickle is than wind,
> A glory at opinion's frown that lowers,
> A treasury that bankrupt time devours,
> A knowledge than grave ignorance more blind,
> A vain delight our equals to command,
> A style of greatness, in effect a dream,
> A swelling thought of holding sea and land,
> A servile lot, decked with a pompous name
> Are the strange ends we toil for here below
> Till wisest death makes us our errors know.

Several of the fourteen lines of this sonnet of Drummond of Hawthornden, seem to me to refer specifically to illu-

sions which today as much as ever are particularly influential, illusions of the kind which without our being in the least aware of it may colour and modify the whole of our outlook, fundamental ideas and behaviour, with the result that we become unreal human beings, maladapted to the real world we live in, absurdly confident of our sanity, common sense and grip on things, all the while being objectively no more than inefficient bunglers, wasters, and self-deceivers.

Those who are familiar with Kierkegaard's life and thought will recall that his real career as a serious philosopher with a great vocation did not begin until he had gone through the experience of what he called 'the great earthquake'. Now there is no doubt that this terrible and profoundly effective experience which forced upon him certain essential realizations about himself which it may be he could not have reached by any less drastic way, was a crisis precipitated by the death of his father. Thus, it may be said, then, that Existential Philosophy as we know it today had its origin in the death of the philosopher's father. There is a deep connexion between this fact and the truth expressed by Chestov in another passage from the work I quoted from just now in which he says:

> As soon as man feels that God is not, he suddenly comprehends the frightful horror and the wild folly of human temporal existence, and when he has comprehended this he awakes, perhaps not to the ultimate knowledge, but to the penultimate. Was it not so with Nietzsche, Spinoza, Pascal, Luther, Augustine, even with St. Paul?

There cannot be for the Christian any reality in Christ's resurrection unless he really believes in it. Not very long after Kierkegaard's campaign against the high-toned insincerity of the Churches representing the social acknowledgement of God's reality in the clever, busy, highly respectable bourgeois world of the mid-nineteenth century, Nietzsche proclaimed to European thinking men, who had succeeded in banishing all real religious consciousness from everyday life completely, 'God is dead!'

When he has comprehended this, man awakes, perhaps not to the penultimate knowledge, but to the prepenultimate. I believe that the ultimate, or penultimate knowledge will be found to be the beginning of all really transparent apprehension of the world which scientific knowledge decomposes. This is because I have the faith of a Christian and really believe in the truth and presently imminent reality of the Resurrection, so far as I understand it.

> The ancients, to awaken from life, turned to death. The moderns flee from death in order not to awake and take pains not even to think of it. Which are the more 'practical'? Those who compare earthly life to sleep and wait for the miracle of the awakening, or those who see in death a sleep without dreamfaces, the perfect sleep, and while away their time with 'reasonable' and 'natural' explanations? This is the basic question of philosophy, and he who evades it evades philosophy itself.

It might be said that philosophy as Chestov envisaged it

was, instead of being as it is supposed to be, a part of one's education, a subject studied in a course having its place in the curriculum of a university, a necessary *antidote* to one's education. Philosophy in this sense—truly Existential Philosophy, which aims, not at making as complete and rational a discursive exposition as possible of the purely conceptional problems of existence, but at launching individuals into a more fully conscious and authentic real existence of their own, is really the beginning and foundation of a second education, one that continues throughout the lives of all of whom it might ultimately be said that they attained anything like wisdom. To begin with, it brings one to the realization that the knowledge of the world, of man, of history, of reality, with which one has been equipped by one's education, the picture one has of the reality which is the contingent context of one's life, is only a structure of more or less ready-made and on the whole passively accepted *ideas,* corresponding to the objective real world with a degree of accuracy that no one could ever hope to calculate.

The most outstanding characteristics of Chestov's philosophy are its anti-idealism and its anti-rationalism. Now both these expressions require immediate modificatory definition. Chestov was not a disbeliever in the invisible, nor anti-metaphysical in the sense in which the Logical Positivists are anti-metaphysical. Philosophy can never dispense with ideas or with the use of the rational faculty. But a self-critical philosophy can become conscious that the individual thinker's ideas are necessarily only approximate and partial reflections not to be confused with what they reflect, and that the Reason with the deificatory capital R is only a collective reflection of the individual's faculty of thinking rationally re-reflected in the minds of individuals.

Idealism in the sense in which Chestov's philosophy understands the word is thinking which treats ideas as though they were the completed final end-product of thinking, whereas they can for the existing individual never be more than the means by which he thinks, convenient approximate reflections from which the thinker should continually re-detach himself and what they reflect.

To some extent, everyone is an idealist, in the sense of the word which I have been attempting to define. Undoubtedly everyone has an idea of the world we live in which is only a very approximate, and to a large extent second-hand, hearsay idea of it, and just as undoubtedly we rely on this idea that we have cultivated and allowed to grow up in our minds and come to accept it just as though it really corresponded to the actual world in its unknowable objectivity. And unless we are continually conscious of the difference between knowing a thing and thinking one knows it before having had an opportunity to do so, we are thus in danger of becoming secured against reality, which *in reality* is inevitably mysterious, being only very incompletely knowable through any one individual's experience, unaccountable in fact and perhaps still full of astonishing surprises and things of which we had never dreamed. It is only too easy to become comfortably secured against reality in this way, secured against it by an

ideal reality which a kind of universal tacit agreement among us allows us to regard as identical with the only true reality, though the reason we tolerate it as a substitute is that it is what we call normal, average, safe, readily accountable, domesticated in fact to fit in with our own ordinarily egotistical purposes.

Only with a full realization of the extent to which we are all idealists of this kind, only, that is to say, with a proper realization of our actual state of Socratic ignorance, for which there can be no *a priori* truths until we have found out what they are for ourselves, can the autocritical habit of mind indispensable to a genuine philosopher begin to develop.

Anti-idealism is the result of a realization of how fatally easy it can always be to confuse an idea of a thing that one has in one's mind that came to be there as the result of our having read or been told something about someone or something, with an idea that we might have developed of the same thing if we had actually experienced knowledge of it ourselves. We remain very largely ignorant of the extent to which our knowledge is in reality knowledge of the knowledge of others. Education fosters this sort of confusion and ignorance, unless a conscious anti-idealism enables us to be continually on our guard against it. We cannot possibly do without the knowledge of others, but it is most useful to us when we are fully conscious that it is not the result of our own experience when we remember it. As soon as we become aware of the extent to which we are conditioned by and dependent on ideas, we become perceptibly more realistic and objective; at the same time we become more open-minded, tolerant, pacific and cooperative. We cease to think of ourselves as the elect, to whom the last word on our special subjects has been specially divulged by grace of the goddess of Reason; for an orderly but after a while dusty permanent model scheme of basic assumptions for referring to about Everything, we exchange a new habit, that of having a thorough spring-clean and stocktaking of all our ideas regularly at not-too-long intervals.

It may be that Chestov himself nowhere expresses what I have called his anti-idealism in quite the bald form in which I have presented it; it may be, too, that what I have said either reveals the quintessence of Chestov, or is, to the contrary, a misrepresentation of him resulting from my having used Chestov's name merely as a cover under which to pass off some idea or attitude of my own. If the latter were actually the case, I might still argue with a grain of truth that in this I had at least given an illustration of Chestov's method. At any rate, Chestov did himself express quite clearly enough the anti-idealism I have spoken of, in the following words:

> Even the blind, one would think, must arrive at the conviction that matter and materialism are not the crucial issue. The most deadly enemy of the spirit everywhere is not inert matter, which in fact, as the ancients taught, and as men teach today, exists either not at all, or only potentially as something illusory, pitiable, powerless, suppliant to all—the most deadly and pitiless enemies are ideas. Ideas, and ideas alone, are that

with which every man must do battle who would overcome the falsehood of the world.

I think I may add here, that he who would overcome the false materialist philosophy which has so often been denounced as the real reason for the present situation in our relations with Leon Chestov's native land, the philosophy of the Communist intellectuals leading the great Party which claims to represent the toiling Russian masses, the philosophy which drove Chestov into exile after 1920, will be unable to get very far until he sees that Materialist Idealism, which does not yet realize that it ought truly to be thus so-called, confuses reflection and reflector. Certainly, there cannot be a reflection without a reflector for it to be seen in, but it is a naïve and fatal error to confuse the two on account of their being inseparable in living experience, although easily separable in reflected or theoretical experience by the (immaterial) experimenter.

It might also be added that Christian philosophy properly so-called is anti-idealist in just the sense I have been discussing, or otherwise can be only a quasi-Christian philosophy, as most philosophies since Christ, with the possible exception of such philosophy as might in a certain sense be called Socratic, have inevitably been. 'The Sabbath was made for man and not man for the Sabbath' is the classic maxim which might serve as the type for an authentically Christian anti-idealism.

For a Christian existential philosopher, all we highly rational, educated men are in reality all we still to a very large extent ignorant and unconscious men, just as all we respectable citizens are in reality all we miserable sinners.

'For we must disrobe ourselves of all false colours, and unclothe our Souls of evil Habits,' says Thomas Traherne, in the *Centuries of Meditations;* 'All our Thoughts must be Infantlike and clear; the Powers of our Soul free from the Leaven of this World, and disentangled from men's conceits and customs. Grit in the eye or yellow jaundice will not let a Man see those Objects truly that are before it. And therefore it is requisite that we should be as very Strangers to the Thoughts, Customs and Opinions of men in this World, as if we were but little children.'

And Kierkegaard tells us very much the same thing, in an entry in his *Journals:*

> *Truth is naked.* In order to swim one takes off one's clothes—in order to aspire to the truth one must undress in a far more inward sense, divest oneself of all one's inward clothes, of thoughts, conceptions, selfishness, etc., before one is sufficiently naked.

This attitude of continual auto-criticism, which I have characterized as Anti-Idealism, is recognizably the same as that which Chestov expresses in the following passage from his *All Things Are Possible:*

> There is no mistake about it, nobody *wants* to think. I do not speak here of logical thinking. That, like any other natural function, gives man great pleasure. For this reason philosophical systems however complicated, arouse real and permanent interest in the public provided they only require from man the logical exercise of the

mind, and nothing else. But to think—really to think—surely this means a relinquishing of logic. It means living a new life. It means a permanent sacrifice of the dearest habits, tastes, attachments, without even the assurance that the sacrifice will bring any compensation.

What superficial commentators have unanimously described as 'anti-rationalism' and even 'irrationalism' in Chestov, is really nothing of the sort, but a necessary implication of his anti-idealism and a result of his unusual objectivity of mind, or what amounts to the same thing, of his highly auto-critical habit of thought (prior to the actual approximate formulation of his thought in writing, that is to say). A thinker who is above all aware of his own ignorance and uncertainty, who is not deceived by his ability to discover and repeat impressively sounding formulae into supposing that he has solved a problem and said the last word on a subject, who is constantly asking questions, and questioning where it is the rule to see nothing questionable, will not be satisfied for long with the criteria which simple-minded rationalists regard as the sole supreme arbiters of their thought. This does not mean that he must therefore despise Reason or logic; it simply indicates that he is not limited by the common confusion between what man has discovered, and what he has invented for purposes of convenience, in his mind.

No. 267 of Pascal's *Pensées* may relevantly be quoted here:

'The last proceeding of reason is to recognize that there is an infinity of things which are beyond it. It is but feeble if it does not see so far as to know this. But if natural things are beyond it, what will be said of supernatural?'

Also No. 272:

'There is nothing so conformable to reason as this disavowal of reason.'

The individual human reason becomes more rational as a result of losing its idealist awe of the Cartesian Goddess of Reason, who is never satisfied until everything has been reduced to clarity and distinctness, even if by artificial means; in recognizing its inevitable limitations and in liberating itself from the delusory self-sufficiency of the Cartesian cogitator, reason transcends itself and can become reintegrated with the creative imagination.

In a previous quotation, Chestov asks whether real thinking does not mean a relinquishing of logic. That he means by this an emancipation from complete dependence on logic is obvious from the following passage from the same book (*All Things Are Possible*):

> To discard logic as an instrument, a means or aid for acquiring knowledge, would be extravagant. Why should we? For the sake of consequentialism? i. e. for logic's very self? But logic, as an aim in itself, or even as the *only* means to knowledge, is a different matter. Against this one must fight even if he has against him all the authorities of thought—beginning with Aristotle.

Existential Philosophy cannot be understood unless it is seen to be a protest and a struggle, fighting against not only Aristotle, but also against, for instance, Descartes, Spinoza, Hegel, Spencer, Husserl and Carnap. Its objectively critical attitude to the notion of Pure Reason and its refusal to make itself dependent on any predetermined method or criteria is related to its preoccupation with the problem of Original Sin and the hypothesis that the present condition of man is a fallen and not a supernatural one. Since man began to become civilized, his condition has been necessarily an unnatural one. Reason, the use of which has led to the progressive development of human civilization, is nevertheless not an entirely unmixed blessing. It is the blessing promised to Eve by the serpent and comes from the tree of which the fruit is death and limitation, not life and freedom. Existential Philosophy is a struggle for liberation. With it, an essentially Christian philosophy, as distinct from a nominally and superficially Christian philosophy, enters the history of Western thought. This is true even of Nietzsche, if not of the whole of Nietzsche (in whom the 'will to stupidity' and the 'will to power' not infrequently come into stultifying conflict), at least of that part of his thought which still remains creatively valuable; for Christianity had become by Nietzsche's time so profoundly self-contradictory on account of the predominance of pagan ethical principles in European thought surviving even Luther and the Reformation (the Renaissance and the secularization of classical learning putting back with one hand what the Lutheran Reformation had taken away with the other) that the genuinely Christian liberation in thought had to assume the guise of Anti-Christ. It is Nietzsche's greatest fault and weakness that he failed to understand this situation and his relation to it anything like as fully as he might have done.

Chestov is of all the great existential philosophers—the others are Pascal, Kierkegaard and Nietzsche—the one who is nearest to us; and he is of all recent philosophers the one who is most necessary to a true understanding of the significance of existential philosophy in general and of its role in the crisis of modern thought. He is the philosopher of Tragedy and of Paradox; a seeker after the 'one thing needful', a solitary thinker whose despair does not counsel us to come to terms with defeatist resignation, but can inspire in those capable of it the violence with which alone is the Kingdom of Heaven to be taken. His message is just that which is needed as a corrective to the dispassionately impotent, science-seduced teaching of present-day British Academic philosophy. 'The don is the eunuch,' as Kierkegaard wrote in his *Journals,* 'but he has not emasculated himself for the sake of the Kingdom of Heaven, but on the contrary, in order to fit better into this characterless world.' Chestov never made the slightest attempt to fit in with the characterless modern world; perhaps that is why he has been so largely ignored by the intellectual representatives of this world till now; but it is also the reason why one can be confident that he will eventually be heard, nevertheless, for such thinking as his is for modern philosophy increasingly 'the one thing needful'.

'Power without wisdom is dangerous,' Bertrand Russell went so far as to admit in a broadcast talk not long ago, 'and what our age needs is wisdom, even more than knowledge. Given wisdom, the power conferred by science can bring a new degree of well-being to all mankind; without wisdom, it can only bring destruction.' This would appear to indicate a belated readiness on the part

of an authoritative representative of scientifically aspiring materialist Thought to turn at last to the consideration of what [Miguel de] Unamuno has called 'the most tragic problem of philosophy', or at least to concede that scientific thought and wisdom are two quite different things, since they became separated by the University dictatorship of the professoriat, which exiles human subjectivity and silences the private feelings of the individual's heart. The utterances of Bertrand Russell in view of the crisis of contemporary society should be compared with the answer of the old professor to the young student whose personal crisis drives her to seek his wise advice in Chekhov's *A Dreary Story.*

Supposing the philosophers who speak in the name of scientific materialism do gradually become aware of their lack of wisdom, and begin to try to become philosophers in the true sense of the word (the etymological definition is 'one who loves wisdom'), where are they to turn? Existential Philosophy does not give itself out to be wisdom; though it looks rather as though Sartre, for instance, would have no objection to the public making use of his philosophy as though it were. Existential philosophers may be said to be in general agreement, however, with Pascal's saying: 'I can only approve of those who seek with lamentation'. Should anyone turn to Chestov for wisdom, this is what he has to say to him:

> Although there have been on earth many wise men who knew much that is infinitely more valuable than all the treasures for which men are ready even to sacrifice their lives, still wisdom is to us a book with seven seals, a hidden hoard upon which we cannot lay our hands. Many—the vast majority—are even seriously convinced that philosophy is a most tedious and painful occupation to which are doomed some miserable wretches who enjoy the odious privilege of being called philosophers. I believe that even professors of philosophy, the more clever of them, not seldom share this opinion and suppose that therein lies the secret of their science, revealed to the initiate alone. Fortunately, the position is otherwise. It may be that mankind is destined never to change in this respect, and a thousand years hence men will care much more about "deductions" theoretical and practical, from the truth than about truth itself; but real philosophers, men who know what they want and at what they aim, will hardly be embarrassed by this. They will utter their truths as before, without in the least considering what conclusions will be drawn from them by the lovers of logic.

In case the end of this passage should seem to lend itself to any ambiguity, I think I may add that it is unlikely that Chestov, in speaking of 'real philosophers', was thinking of the representatives of bourgeois materialism, thinkers who also certainly 'know what they want and at what they aim', i. e., knowledge, i. e., power.

Bernard Martin   (essay date 1966)

SOURCE: An introduction to *Athens and Jerusalem* by

Lev Shestov, translated by Bernard Martin, Ohio University Press, 1966, pp. 9-44.

[In the following excerpt, Martin discusses the basic tenets of Shestov's most important work as representative of his philosophical thought.]

In his last years Shestov brooded incessantly over what he called, in a letter to [Sergei] Bulgakov, "the nightmare of godlessness and unbelief which has taken hold of humanity." He was convinced that only through "the utmost spiritual effort," as he termed it, could men free themselves from this nightmare. His own life concentrated on a passionate struggle against the "self-evident" truths of speculative philosophy and positivistic science which had come to dominate the mind of European man and made him oblivious to the rationally ungrounded but redeeming truths proclaimed in the Bible. This struggle is most fully reflected in his last and greatest book, the monumental *Athens and Jerusalem,* on which he worked for many years and completed just a year before his death.

Athens and Jerusalem is the culmination of Shestov's entire lifetime of intellectual inquiry and spiritual striving. It brings together all the diverse strands that had appeared in his earlier writings. His largely negative work of thirty years before, such as *The Apotheosis of Groundlessness,* may be regarded in retrospect as prolegomena and preparation for the positive message of the great work on which Shestov's permanent fame as a religious thinker will undoubtedly rest. In it he set himself the task of critically examining the pretension of human reason to possession of the capacity for attaining ultimate truth—a pretension first put forth by the founders of Western philosophy in Athens two and a half millennia ago, maintained ever since by most of the great metaphysicians of Europe, and still defended by many philosophers today. This pretension, he concluded, must be firmly rejected. Reason and its by-product, scientific method, have their proper use and their rightful place in obtaining knowledge concerning empirical phenomena, but they cannot and must not be allowed to determine the directions of man's metaphysical quest or to decide on the ultimate issues—issues such as the reality of God, human freedom and immortality.

The scientists and most of the philosophers, Shestov repeatedly insists in *Athens and Jerusalem* as well as in some of his earlier works, have been concerned with discovering self-evident, logically consistent, or empirically verifiable propositions which they take to be eternal and universal truths. For them, man is merely another link in the endless chain of phenomena and lives in a universe totally governed by the iron laws of causal necessity. They assume, whether they say so explicitly or not, that human liberty is largely an illusion, that man's freedom to act and his capacity for self-determination are sharply limited by the network of unchangeable and necessary causal relationships into which he has been cast and which exercise an insuperable power over him. Consequently, the path of both virtue and wisdom for man, they believe, lies not in useless rebellion against necessity but in submissive obedience and resignation.

European man, according to Shestov, has languished for centuries in a hypnotic sleep induced by the conviction that the entire universe is ruled by eternal, self-evident truths (such as the principles of identity and non-contradiction) discoverable by reason, and by an everlastingly unalterable and indifferent power which determines all events and facts. This power is commonly known as "necessity." God Himself, for a thinker like Spinoza, has no power to transcend the necessary structures that express His being. And Spinoza is only the culmination of the mechanistic philosophy that has dominated European metaphysics since Aristotle. To be sure, there have been solitary figures here and there, Shestov points out, who have protested against the pretensions of reason and its self-evident truths and have stubbornly refused to accept the dictates of the natural sciences concerning what is possible and what is impossible, but theirs were voices "crying in the wilderness." Tertullian's was such a voice, and so also was St. Peter Damian's. In modern times, Shestov declares, it is Dostoevsky who, in his passionate *Notes from the Underground,* has presented the strongest and most effective "critique of reason." The world as logic and science conceive it, governed by universal and immutable laws and constrained by the iron hand of necessity, is for Dostoevsky a humanly uninhabitable world. It must be resisted to the utmost, even if the struggle seems a senseless beating of the head against a stone wall. Shestov finds an immense nobility and heroism in the cry of Dostoevsky's protagonist in his *Notes from the Underground:*

> But, good Lord, what do I care about the laws of nature and arithmetic if I have my reasons for disliking them, including the one about two and two making four! Of course, I won't be able to breach this wall with my head if I'm not strong enough. But I don't have to accept a stone wall just because it's there and I don't have the strength to breach it.
>
> As if such a wall could really leave me resigned and bring me peace of mind because it's the same as twice two makes four! How stupid can one get? Isn't it much better to recognize the stone walls and the impossibilities for what they are and refuse to accept them if surrendering makes one too sick?

To resist the self-evident truths of science and philosophy, to stop glorifying and worshipping them, however, is not necessarily an exercise in futility. If man will attend to the ancient message of the Bible, Shestov maintains, he will find there a conception of God, of the universe and of himself that not only lends meaning to such resistance but also makes of it the first and most essential step in becoming reconciled with God and regaining his freedom. For the Bible, in opposition to Western science and philosophy, proclaims that God is the omnipotent One for whom literally nothing is impossible and whose power is absolutely without limits, and that He stands not only at the center but at the beginning and end of all things. God, according to the Bible, created man as well as a universe in which there is no defect, a universe which—indeed—He saw to be "very good." Having created man, God blessed him, gave him dominion over all the universe and bestowed upon him the essentially divine and most precious of all gifts, freedom. Man is not, unless he renounces his primordial freedom (as all men, in fact, tend to do in their obsession with obtaining rational explanation and scientific knowledge) under the power of universal and necessary causal laws or unalterable empirical facts. Unlike both traditional philosophy and science, which have sought to transform even single, non-recurring facts or events into eternal and unchangeable truths, the Bible refuses to regard any fact as ultimate or eternally subsistent but sees it rather as under the power of God who, in answer to man's cry, can suppress it or make it not to be. For biblical faith, knowledge—whether it is concerned with what have been called "truths of reason" or "truths of fact"—is not, as it is for traditional philosophy and science, the supreme goal of human life. Against their assumption that knowledge justifies human existence, the existential philosophy which takes its rise from the Bible will insist that it is from man's living existence and experience that knowledge must obtain whatever justification it may have.

There can be no reconciliation, Shestov contends, between science and that philosophy which aspires to be scientific, on the one side, and biblical religion, on the other. Tertullian was right in proclaiming that Athens can never agree with Jerusalem—even though for two thousand years the foremost thinkers of the Western world have firmly believed that a reconciliation is possible and have bent their strongest and most determined efforts toward effecting it. The biblical revelation not only cannot be harmonized with rationalist or would-be "scientific" metaphysics but is itself altogether devoid of support either from logical argument or scientific knowledge. For biblical man based his life totally and unreservedly on faith, which is not, as has often been suggested, a weaker form of knowledge (knowledge, so to speak, "on credit," for which proofs, though presently unavailable, are anticipated at some future time), but rather a completely different dimension of thought. The substance of this faith, emphatically denied both by science and philosophy, is the daring and unsupported but paradoxically true conviction that all things are possible. Shestov was haunted for years by the biblical legend of the fall. As he interpreted it, when Adam ate the fruit of the tree of knowledge, faith was displaced by reason and scientific knowledge. The sin of Adam has been repeated by his descendants, whose relentless pursuit of knowledge has led not to ultimate truth but to the choking of the springs of life and the destruction of man's primordial freedom.

According to Shestov, speculative philosophy beginning in wonder or intellectual curiosity and seeking to "understand" the phenomena of the universe, leads man to a dead end where he loses both personal freedom and all possibility of envisioning ultimate truth. It is, in a sense, the Original Lie which has come into the world as a consequence of man's disobedience of God's command to refrain from eating of the tree of knowledge. Its narrowness, its lack of imagination, its preoccupation with "objectivity" and its wish to extrude from thought all human emotion, its conviction that there is nothing in the world that is essentially and forever mysterious and rationally inexplicable, its refusal even to entertain the possibility of a universe in which the rules of traditional logic (such as the principles of non-contradiction and identity) do not hold sway—all

this condemns it to sterility. If philosophy is to serve the human spirit rather than destroy it, it must—Shestov maintains—abandon the method of detached speculation and disinterested reflection (what Husserl called *Besinnung*); it must become truly "existential" in the sense of issuing out of man's sense of helplessness and despair in the face of the stone walls of natural necessity. When philosophy becomes, as it must, a passionate and agonized struggle against the self-evident, necessary truths that constrain and crush the spirit, when it refuses, for instance, to refrain from drawing any distinction between the propositions, "the Athenians have poisoned Socrates" and "a mad dog has been poisoned" and to regard both with the same "philosophic" indifference—then it may make man receptive to the supernatural revelation of Scripture and to the possibility of redemption that is to be found there. "Out of the depths I cried unto Thee, O Lord" and "My God, my God, why hast Thou forsaken me?" —the experience reflected in these agonized cries of the Psalmist, Shestov maintains, must be *the starting point of true philosophy.*

Lev Shestov was a philosopher who philosophized with his whole being, for whom philosophy was not an academic specialty but a matter of life and death. He was a man with an *idée fixe.* His independence of the tendencies of the time in which he lived was astonishing. He sought God and the liberation of man from the power of necessity.

—*Nikolai Berdyaev in his* "The Fundamental Ideas of the Philosophy of Lev Shestov," *translated by Bernard Martin, 1982.*

When his philosophy has taught man to reject all *veritates aeternae* as illusions, to confront unflinchingly the horrors of his historical existence, to experience his despair authentically and without evasion, to realize his mortality and his insignificance in a universe that seems bent on his destruction, then it may perhaps succeed in preparing him for that act of spiritual daring which is faith and which can bring him to the God who will restore to him not only a center of meaning for his life but also his primordial freedom. As Shestov states it in *Athens and Jerusalem:*

> . . . to find God one must tear oneself away from the seductions of reason, with all its physical and moral constraints, and go to another source of truth. In Scripture this source bears the enigmatic name "faith," which is that dimension of thought where truth abandons itself fearlessly and joyously to the entire disposition of the Creator: "Thy will be done!" The will of Him who fearlessly and with sovereign power returns to the believer, in turn, his lost power:

" . . . what things so ever you desire . . . you shall have them." (Mark 11:24)

Faith, for Shestov, is *audacity,* the daring refusal to accept necessary laws, to regard anything as impossible. It is the demand for the absolute, original freedom which man is supposed to have had before the fall, when he still found the distinction between truth and falsehood, as well as between good and evil, unnecessary and irrelevant. Through faith, Shestov seems to suggest, man may become, in a sense, like God himself for whom neither intellectual nor moral grounds and reasons have any reality. "Groundlessness," he writes,

> is the basic, most enviable, and to us most incomprehensible privilege of the Divine. Consequently, our whole moral struggle, even as our rational inquiry—if we once admit that God is the last end of our endeavors—will bring us sooner or later (rather later, much later, than sooner) to emancipation not only from moral evaluations but also from reason's eternal truths. Truth and the Good are fruits of the forbidden tree; for limited creatures, for outcasts from paradise. I know that this ideal of freedom in relation to truth and the good cannot be realized on earth—in all probability does not need to be realized. But it is granted to man to have prescience of ultimate freedom.

> Before the face of eternal God, all our foundations break together, and all ground crumbles under us, even as objects—this we know—lose their weight in endless space, and—this we shall probably learn one day—will lose their impermeability in endless time.

But Shestov's God—the God of whom the Bible speaks and before whom all human foundations crack and crumble—is not the God of Spinoza or of Kant or of Hegel. Against all metaphysical and rationalist theologies, Shestov declares, "We would speak, as did Pascal, of the God of Abraham, the God of Isaac, the God of Jacob, and not of the God of the philosophers. The God of the philosophers, whether He be conceived as a material or ideal principle, carries with Him the triumph of constraint, of brutal force." The God of the Bible is not to be found as the conclusion of a syllogism. His existence cannot be proved by rational argument or inferred from historical evidence. "One cannot demonstrate God. One cannot seek Him in history. God is 'caprice' incarnate, who rejects all guarantees. He is outside history, like all that people hold to be *to timôtaton.*" How shall one arrive at this *Deus absconditus,* this hidden God? "The chief thing," says Shestov, "is to think that, even if all men without exception were convinced that God does not exist, this would not mean anything, and that if one could prove as clearly as two times two makes four that God does not exist, this also would not mean anything." To the complaint that it is not possible to ask men to take a position which negates a universal conviction of the race and flies in the face of logic, Shestov replies "Obviously! But God always demands of us the impossible . . . It is only when man wishes the impossible that he remembers God. To obtain that which is possible he turns to those like himself."

Shestov suggests, as we have already indicated, that modern man can perhaps reach the God of the Bible only by first passing through the experience of his own nothingness and by coming to feel, as did Nietzsche and others, that God is not. This feeling is a profoundly ambiguous one, capable of leading men in diametrically opposite directions.

> Sometimes this is a sign of the end and of death. Sometimes of the beginning and of life. As soon as man feels that God is not, he suddenly comprehends the frightful horror and the wild folly of human temporal existence, and when he has comprehended this he awakens, perhaps not to the ultimate knowledge, but to the penultimate. Was it not so with Nietzsche, Spinoza, Pascal, Luther, Augustine, even with St. Paul?

Our task, if we would enter upon the road which leads to true reality and ultimately to the God revealed in Scripture, consists "in the Psalmist's image, in shattering the skeleton which lends substance to our old ego, melting the 'heart in our bowels.' "

Experiencing the abyss that opens before him when all his laws, his "eternal truths" and his self-evident certainties are taken away, the desperate soul feels that "God is not, man must himself become God, create all things out of nothing; all things; matter together with forms, and even the eternal laws." When he has experienced this complete abandonment to himself and to boundless despair, then a man—as such irreconcilable enemies as St. Ignatius Loyola, the founder of the Jesuits, and Luther, the renegade monk, both have testified—may, through faith, direct his eyes toward ultimate reality and see the true God who will restore to him the limitless freedom with which he was created and again make all things possible for him.

Man, Shestov concludes, must choose: Athens *or* Jerusalem. He cannot have both. Athens—with its constraining principles, its eternal truths, its logic and science—may bring man earthly comfort and ease but it also stupefies, if it does not kill, the human spirit. Jerusalem—with its message of God and man for both of whom nothing is impossible, with its proclamation that creativity and freedom are the essential prerogatives of both the divine and human—terrifies man, but it also has the power of liberating him and ultimately transforming the horrors of existence into the joys of that paradisiacal state which God originally intended for His creatures.

Shestov has been dismissed by some critics as a wild irrationalist, a willful protagonist of the absurd, who wished to abandon reason entirely in order to make room for a trans-rational revelation. But the case is hardly so simple as this. His polemics against scientific knowledge and reason, as even the most superficial reading of his work reveals, are themselves peculiarly lucid and rational. They are also based on a masterful knowledge of the entire Western philosophical tradition. Shestov, as ***Athens and Jerusalem*** and his other books powerfully attest, was completely at home in the thought of all the great European philosophers from Heraclitus to Husserl. Furthermore, given his predilection for irony and overstatement and his proclaimed intent forcibly to awaken his readers, to drive them through shock out of comfortable ruts into new and unfamiliar paths, it may be doubted that he meant categorically to reject objective knowledge, i.e., logic and science, as such. His real concern seems to have been rather to emphasize that these are hardly the unmixed blessing they have commonly been taken to be and that they assuredly do not exhaust the possible approaches to truth. What they tend, rather, to do is to lead those who concentrate on them away from the ultimate reality given in revelation.

In addition to the partial and preliminary truths of science and logic, Shestov wished to make it clear, there are infinitely more significant "personal" and "subjective" truths which can neither be objectively demonstrated nor empirically verified, and among these are the biblical affirmations concerning God and human freedom. If the latter are declared absurd before the bar of reason and experience, then the truths approved by these judge are themselves foolishness before God.

What Shestov was fundamentally concerned with doing throughout his lifetime was to criticize the timidity and lack of imagination of traditional philosophy, with its view that metaphysical truth flows solely from obedience and passive submission to the structures of being given in experience, and to insist instead that ultimate reality transcends the categories of rationalist metaphysics and scientific method and that the truth about it is to be discovered through the untrammeled soaring of the spirit and through daring flights of the imagination. It may be said that so to insist is to abandon philosophy for poetry and art, but Shestov himself always maintained that philosophy is indeed, or rather should be, more art than science.

Shestov criticized science because it subordinates man to impersonal necessity. But it is fairly clear that he did not mean to question the preliminary value and significance of scientific knowledge in everyday life. What he insisted, rather, was that the limits of science must be clearly understood and that the scientists and the would-be scientific philosophers must not pretend that their essentially "soulless and indifferent truths" alone will satisfy the ultimate needs of the human spirit. More than anything else Shestov was troubled by the tendency of the scientists and the rationalist philosophers to bless and glorify their "constraining truths." Granted that there is a great deal of physical constraint in the world, why must man worship and adore it? Why should he not rather fiercely resent and ceaselessly challenge its authority? To sing praises not only to that measure of necessity and constraint that obviously exists but to go further and maintain that everything in the universe is necessarily and eternally as it is—this tendency of rationalist thought, he contended, does the greatest violence to the spirit. Furthermore the belief, inculcated by scientism and rationalism, in an eternally necessary and unchangeable order of things is, in a sense, a "self-fulfilling" conviction. Men who accept it will do nothing to affirm even that degree of creative freedom which they have within the limits of natural necessity, much less expand it; and their freedom, as well as their capacity for attaining that realm of authentic being which— Shestov believed—lies forever beyond "reasonable explanation," will consequently atrophy and disappear. That true, existential philosophy must be a continuous and ago-

nizing struggle against constraint, against the immoderate pretensions of the most valuable motifs in Shestov's thought.

Shestov also performed a useful service in forcibly and repeatedly drawing our attention to the fact that not all questions are of the same kind. A physical question such as "What is the speed of sound?" differs essentially and in kind from a metaphysical question such as "Does God exist?" Against the positivists he maintained that questions such as the latter are genuine and, indeed, of ultimate importance, but that their significance lies precisely in the fact that they do not admit of ordinary answers, that such answers kill them.

In the specifically religious thought of his mature and final period, Shestov seems to have been motivated basically by an unremitting awareness of what Mircea Eliade has appropriately called "the terror of history." He was obsessed by the fact that Socrates, the best and wisest of men, was poisoned by the Athenians and that, in the understanding of historicist and rationalist philosophies, this fact is on the same level as the poisoning of a mad dog. The despair which an awareness of the terror of history entails can be overcome, he concluded, only through faith. In this he was in complete agreement with Eliade who has written [in his *Cosmos and History*, 1959]:

> Since the "invention" of faith, in the Judaeo-Christian sense of the word (for God all is possible), the man who has left the horizon of archetypes and repetition can no longer defend himself against that terror except through the idea of God. In fact, it is only by presupposing the existence of God that he conquers, on the one hand, freedom (which grants him autonomy in a universe governed by laws or, in other words, the "inauguration" of a mode of being that is new and unique in the universe) and, on the other hand, the certainty that historical tragedies have a transhistorical meaning, even if that meaning is not always visible for humanity in its present condition. Any other situation of modern man leads, in the end, to despair.

Faith in God was, for Shestov, the ultimate source of man's deliverance from despair and the guarantee of his own freedom in a universe all of whose energies seem bent on denying it. Such faith, he held, as we have seen, lies beyond proofs and is in no way affected by logical argument. In this he was surely right. Like Kierkegaard, he recognized that faith can no more be destroyed by logical impossibility than it can be created by logical possibility. If faith is not pre-existent, if it does not precede all of a man's reasoning and argumentation, then these will never lead him to God. Scripture itself, he pointed out, does not demand faith; it presupposes it.

But the question may be raised—How is faith obtained? By man's own wishing and striving for it? Though Shestov's definition of faith as "audacity" seems to suggest that it is produced by an affirmation of human will, he plainly denied that man can by himself obtain faith. Faith is a gift of God, a manifestation of His grace. Echoing the Calvinistic doctrine of predestination and applying it to faith, Shestov seems to have believed that it is mysteriously given to some and denied to others by God. Even one to whom it is given may, of course, reject it, but none by his own unaided endeavor can obtain it. Must it be sought in order to be found? Yes, according to Shestov. The first movement of faith, he wrote, [in *In Job's Balances*] involves "a spiritual exertion" on the part of man and, as we have already heard him say, "to find God one must *tear oneself* away from the seductions of reason." Man must begin by questioning all laws, by refusing to regard them as necessary and eternal. But whether Shestov believed that even this can be done without the grace of God is something that is not altogether clear.

For modern man—Shestov, as we have seen, suggested—God may perhaps be reached only by first passing through the experience of despair, through a sense of utter abandonment. But if one feels that "God is not, man must himself become God, create all things out of nothing; all things; matter together with forms, and even the eternal laws"—what guarantee is there that this will not end in pagan titanism? Is there any assurance that man will not arrogantly put himself in the place of God, or that he will go beyond self-exaltation and recognize God as his own and the universe's Lord and Creator? Indeed, Shestov himself seems at times to blur any ultimate distinction between God and the individual who is in the condition of faith. Through faith, he appears to have believed, man becomes—in an important sense—like God. For the man of faith, too, "all things are possible," and this, according to him, is the operational definition of God.

Has this notion of radical, unlimited freedom, this conception that *all* things may become possible for man, any validity or significance? We may agree with Shestov that science and rationalist philosophy have, indeed, often exceeded their proper bounds and manifested an unjustified tendency to pronounce arbitrary judgment over what is possible and what is impossible. We may agree also that science has deliberately overlooked "miracles" and wilfully ignored much that is fortuitous, extraordinary, and incapable of being assimilated into its accepted categories of explanation. But does this entitle us to go to the opposite extreme and deny, as Shestov at times appears to do, that there are any norms, principles or laws governing the phenomena of the universe? Shestov may also be right in holding that scientific knowledge has often tended to enslave man or at least diminish his freedom to act, and we may concur in his suggestion that, by transcending science and returning to the biblical outlook, man may find the scope of his liberty greatly enlarged and discover that many things he formerly believed impossible are quite possible. But does his freedom thereby become, as Shestov seems to believe, absolute and unlimited? Faith, he claims, gives man absolute freedom. But how? By what means does faith produce this astounding result? And can Shestov, or anyone else who accepts the literal truth of the promise proclaimed in Mark XI, 23-24, point to anyone either in the past or present in whom this promise has been fully actualized? And furthermore, should he not in all fairness have conceded that while science (or rather, an excessive worship of science) may have at times enslaved man, it has also given him a greater measure of power over nature and thereby broadened the range of his freedom?

Faith, Shestov maintained, results in the liberation of man not only from all physical compulsion but also from all moral constraint. In faith man, to employ the terminology of Nietzsche, moves "beyond good and evil." He is freed from subjection to all ethical principles and moral valuations, and returns to the paradisiacal state in which the distinction between good and evil and between right and wrong is non-existent. But, granted that man's awareness of moral distinctions imposes heavy burdens upon him and restricts his freedom, is a return to the condition of Adam before the fall possible? And granted also that the God of the Bible is degraded and, indeed, denied if He is reduced to the position of guarantor of bourgeois morality, with the selfishness and cruelty that it has often served to cloak, can it be denied that the biblical God is in fact represented as a Lawgiver who has a moral will for man and that man's freedom in the Bible is understood as his capacity to respond affirmatively or negatively to God's call? Aside from the question whether he has, in his concept of "moral freedom," fairly portrayed the character of the God of Abraham, Isaac and Jacob of whom he purported to speak, it may be asked of Shestov whether it makes any sense to assert that man can live entirely without ethical norms or principles. Or was it, perhaps, his belief that a life "beyond good and evil" cannot be lived in man's present existence but only in some transcendent realm? On this he is not clear. In any case, the tendency to formless anarchism that is to be discerned in his friend Berdyaev and that seems to have been part of the mental furniture of a good many other Russian thinkers and writers of his time did not leave him untouched.

For all its ambiguities, exaggerations and inconsistencies, Shestov's work remains of vital contemporary significance. Here was a thinker thoroughly schooled in the Western philosophical tradition who rejected that tradition with passionate intensity when he discovered the deadly threats to the human spirit implicit in it and who, in the style of the prophet, not the theologian or religious apologist, summoned men to turn away from Athens and seek their salvation in Jerusalem.

Not only to the irreligious and non-religious man of the Twentieth Century, but also to him who claims to live by the faith of the Bible yet whose understanding of that faith has inevitably been encumbered and distorted by centuries of rationalist philosophical and theological commentary, Shestov offers a fresh appreciation of the terror and promise of the biblical message. In his own lifetime his was "a voice crying in the wilderness," but it is time that this voice be heard again.

Arthur A. Cohen   (essay date 1967)

SOURCE: "Lev Shestov: *Athens and Jerusalem,*" in *Commonweal,* Vol. LXXXV, No. 22, March 10, 1967, pp. 661-62.

[*Cohen is an American novelist, critic, editor, and author of nonfiction works dealing with Jewish theology. In the following review of* Athens and Jerusalem, *he concludes that Shestov is "innocently, marvelously, accurately on target about the human condition."*]

Lev Isaakovich Schwarzmann, the son of a prosperous Jewish merchant of Kiev, chose early to be known by the pseudonym, Shestov. Shestov concealed the man Schwarzmann; the passionate, inflammatory prose of Shestov's French and Russian critical and philosophic writing, though it seems autobiographical, reveals nothing about the man Schwarzmann, though it tells us ever so much about the pseudonymous person, Shestov. Indeed, reading *Athens and Jerusalem,* the last work Shestov was to complete shortly before his death in 1938, one is struck by the fact that Shestov is to Schwarzmann no less a device of revelation than were the mnemonic names which the prophets of Israel often assumed, concealing their real identity in order better to arouse, agitate, and dismay the contented ignorant.

Alas, the device fails (or does it?) for few know Shestov, much less Schwarzmann. Shestov is unknown in the United States and England. Only four of his books have ever been translated into English; his works are generally out of print even in France, where he lived in self-imposed exile from 1919 until his death; and though a complete edition is promised in France and Germany, his works are generally unread. However, to be unread does not always mean to be without influence. *Many* people do not make a reputation—one will do if it is the right one (remember Joseph and Pharaoh or Isaiah and King Hezekiah). Enough then to note that it was D. H. Lawrence who introduced S. S. Koteliansky's translation of Shestov's, *Apotheosis of Groundlessness* (published under the title, *All Things are Possible,* 1920) and Albert Camus who devoted a long interpretative section of *The Myth of Sisyphus* to Shestov's vision of the ultimate absurdity of rationalism and the revolt of man's primordial freedom against necessity and the irremediable.

Already it may be said I have read Shestov before. I have read him in Kierkegaard or Heidegger, in Sartre or in Dostoevsky. Shestov is only another existentialist bell-ringer; he tricks himself out with false names like Kierkegaard's Johannes Climacus; he tells us everything in a loud, clangorous, unrelenting voice, with repetitions and with aphorisms, with shouts and with wheedles, a veritable *vox clamans in deserto*. Perhaps, perhaps, but much more, for D. H. Lawrence is right in one important respect regarding him: Shestov does administer one of the last kicks to the ailing body of the West. He is the best of Russia (the historian of Russian philosophy, V. V. Zenkovsky, regards him as more "profound and significant" than even Berdyaev), for he incapsulates as well all that is vague, imprecise, and unsystematic in Russian thought.

Unlike many among his academic predecessors, Shestov has absolutely no enthusiasm for the achievement of western rationalism or empiricism. It not only bores him, it scandalizes him. If philosophy, he declares, does not enable man to tap the limitless resources of his own freedom, a freedom which is itself not outside, but within contradiction and illogicality, then it is a false freedom, in fact, it is the incarnation of unfreedom. More radically than Kierkegaard (whose work he only began to read late in his life at the suggestion of his friend and philosophic enemy, Edmund Husserl), Shestov affirms the necessity of breaking

outside all the canons of thought—not the particular, subjective, concrete man against the System as Kierkegaard would suggest, but simply Man, who is neither particular nor general except insofar as one feels obliged to defend his existence against universal claims of reason.

Kierkegaard, however much beloved to Shestov, is a sell-out, for Kierkegaard feels obliged to polemicize against the System with the rhetoric of the System. Actually, every thinker whom it might be thought would be congenial to Shestov is finally anathema to him—Socrates and Plato, St. Augustine and Plotinus, Meister Eckhardt and Angelus Silesius, in part, even Dostoevsky and N. N. Berdyaev. They all give in, surrendering the treasure of their freedom for a portion in the kingdom of knowledge and ends. Shestov rejects all these and stands alone, completely and courageously solitary.

Athens and Jerusalem, Shestov's philosophic masterpiece, excellently translated and introduced by Bernard Martin, comes to us now, as Shestov comes to us now, out of place and date. Had it been published in the forties, before the time of existentialism, crisis theology, death of god marathons, secular city barterings and situation ethics, Shestov might have stood a chance. He might even have been launched as Leslie Fiedler launched Simone Weil, another Jew in distemper, but, as it is, Shestov is too late. It is however his very lateness that makes him all the more important. The very fact that he defined the absurdity of reason well before its hegemony had been compromised by both existentialists and logical analysts makes his polemic all the more valuable.

Athens and Jerusalem makes it clear: man can't have it both ways. On the one hand he cannot affirm the sovereign independence of reason, the autonomy of the will, the irrelevance of God and his judgments upon human history and continue to ask that history have meaning, that life be fulfilled and death overcome, that pain and suffering be banished, that freedom and intelligence be unconfined. One, but not both, Shestov insists with what Camus calls his "admirable monotony." You can have Athens and its legacy of luminous reason, a reason which vindicates the decision of Adam to taste the fruit, but makes Adam and his descendants forever dependent upon the necessity of reason or you can take Jerusalem in which man lives and sins before a God whose very divinity is defined by his ability to compass, invade, and overturn all human invention and contrivance.

It is man who makes necessity rule, not God. For God there can only be freedom and destiny, never necessity and fate. Human freedom must destroy the untruth of thought—a radical contradiction in itself—precisely because Shestov does not consider the truths produced by thought to be true. They are approximations to thought, they comport with logic, they follow from reason, but their truth is not within life. Indeed Shestov would argue that the only truths which can liberate are those which are born within the contradictions of life, canceling out logic and reason. And is this not precisely the point to which the thought of our day has come: rational ethics have disappeared, dogmatic theology has disappeared, metaphysics have all but vanished and in their place men come to think about themselves only in the context of today and tomorrow, the immediacy of the moment, the free address and the free act, the liberated body and the unanalyzed mind.

Shestov is a great contemporary and will probably always be contemporary as long as our civilization continues its disintegration. He is neither hopeful nor despairing—on such issues as cause men to hope and despair, he is strangely silent. Indubitably he is a mystic, but only in the sense that he never tells us from where comes his assurance of his own ultimate ground. But that doesn't matter. We don't have to ask such questions just yet. What counts throughout the dithyrambic repetition of his *Athens and Jerusalem* liturgy is that he seems appallingly right—all the philosophers (Socrates, Descartes, Spinoza, Kant, Hegel) seem in his version of their doctrine to be unbelievably self-deceiving and the Bible (for Shestov the Old and the New Testaments) seems innocently, marvelously, accurately on target about the human condition.

R. M. Davison on Shestov's existential philosophy:

Shestov's attack upon reason draws him close to existentialism. He acknowledged himself in his work on Kierkegaard that he had an astonishing affinity with the founding father. Long before he knew Kierkegaard's works Shestov was writing in their language.

In considering the existentialist implications of Shestov's thought we must return to his view of reason as a restraint on man's freedom to his view of knowledge as captivity. He declines to be coerced by objective evidence and asserts the right of the individual to his own interpretation of the world against all comers. An extreme example of this is Shestov's defence of the greater "truth" of the way in which, contradicting common sense and the universal judgment of reason, we see each other when in love. Because the judgment of a love is that of a small minority against a huge majority it does not mean that he must be wrong. Truth is not a matter of counting heads and weighing the evidence; it is a matter of what is believed or is thought to have been revealed.

R. M. Davison, in his "Lev Shestov: An Assessment," Journal of European Studies, *December, 1981.*

Louis J. Shein (essay date 1967)

SOURCE: "Lev Shestov: A Russian Existentialist," in *The Russian Review,* Vol. 26, No. 3, July, 1967, pp. 278-85.

[*Russian-born Shein is a Canadian editor, translator, former Presbyterian minister, and author of works on theology and philosophy. In the following essay, he presents an overview of Shestov's work and stresses the relevance of his philosophical thought for contemporary readers.*]

Lev Shestov is a strange and in some respects a rather unique phenomenon in the history of Russian philosophic thought. He was a man whose whole being was dominated by a "single Idea." This all-embracing idea was a passionate desire to liberate man from the tyrannical power of necessity in order to find the truth that is beyond the limits of necessity.

Shestov's personal friend Nicholas Berdyaev, himself a religious existentialist, says that Shestov was a philosopher who philosophized with his whole being, for whom philosophy was a matter of life and death. It is rather difficult to account for Shestov's anti-rationalism. A. M. Lazarev, another personal friend, hints at some "tragic avalanche" in Shestov's life which may have caused him to turn his back on rationalism. We are not told what that "avalanche" was, but it really does not matter in the final analysis. Berdyaev probably comes closer to the core of Shestov's problem when he tells us [in *Put,* No. 50] that "for Shestov, the sources of philosophy were the human tragedy, the horrors and sufferings of human life and the sense of hopelessness."

Lev Isaakovich Shwartzman, who wrote under the pseudonym of Shestov, was born in Kiev in 1865. He graduated from the Law Faculty of the University of Kiev. He moved to St. Petersburg and later to Moscow and devoted his time and energy to literary and philosophic writings. After the Revolution he emigrated to Paris, where he taught at the Sorbonne and continued to write on various subjects until 1938, the year of his death.

Shestov was the product of Russian and European culture. In addition, he was steeped in Cabalistic and Hassidic literature, which undoubtedly greatly influenced his existentialist thinking. He was an excellent literary critic. His essays on Tolstoy, Dostoyevsky, Chekhov, and others are literary masterpieces. His large book on Shakespeare is undoubtedly one of the best on the subject. He wrote a great number of books on philosophical themes, among which are: *All Things Are Possible, Beginnings and Ends, The Power of the Keys, On Job's Balances, Athens and Jerusalem,* and *Speculation and Revelation.* He also wrote a large number of articles which appeared in *Sovremennye zapiski.* Only a few of his works have appeared in English translation, and most of these are out of print. While Shestov is well known in European intellectual circles, he is practically unknown on the North American continent.

Shestov's anti-rationalism and his paradoxical method of posing problems often gave rise to misunderstandings. Many of his contemporaries regarded him as an obscurantist and an "intellectual maverick." D. H. Lawrence, in his foreword to *All Things Are Possible,* has this to say:

> What the Russian is struggling with, crying out against, is not life itself: it is only European culture which has been introduced into his psyche, and which hurts him. . . . What is valuable is the evidence against European culture, implied in the novelists, here at last expressed . . . In Shestov one of the last kicks is given . . . He is only tweaking the nose of European idealism. He is preaching nothing: so he protests time and again. "Everything is possible"—this is his really central cry. It is not nihilism. It is only a

shaking free of the human psyche from old bonds. The positive central idea is that the human psyche, or soul, really believes in itself, and in nothing else.

We know that Lawrence nursed a strong bias against anything Russian, but the above quotation shows a complete misunderstanding of Shestov's position. While Shestov was deeply concerned with man's destiny, his chief concern was with man's relationship to God. God, not man, was central.

It must be emphasized that Shestov was not an obscurantist. His point of departure is his critique of rationalism and scientism, the evil twins in modern society. He insisted that philosophy was the result of "magnanimous despair" rather than of speculative thought. This "magnanimous despair" was deeply rooted in his psyche. Like Miguel de Unamuno, Shestov was deeply conscious of the "tragic sense of life." He was perplexed and distressed by the human tragedy and the horrors of human suffering, and was searching for a balance between suffering and justice, but could not find it on the human plane. He came to the conclusion that such a balance can only be maintained by God "with whom all things are possible."

We must think of Shestov as a religious existentialist akin to the Danish thinker Soren Kierkegaard, whom he read rather late in life, but in whom he found a kindred spirit. He accepts Kierkegaard's definition of philosophy, namely, that "the task of philosophy is to free oneself from the power of rational thinking and to find courage to look for the Absurd and the Paradox. He then asks, Was Hegel right when he stated that "the real is rational and the rational real"? His answer to this question is, "When every certitude that is possible for man speaks of impossibility, there begins a new, no longer a rational, but a 'mad' struggle about the possibility of the impossible." Kierkegaard defines this struggle as existential philosophy—a philosophy that seeks the truth not in Reason with its limited possibilities, but in the Absurd that knows no limits. Shestov applies this definition to his own type of existentialism.

Shestov's *Weltanschauung* can only be understood against the background of Russian philosophic thought during the nineteenth century. [In *A History of Russian Philosophy,* 1953] V. V. Zenkovsky rightly points out that

> Shestov's work is powerful evidence that the problem of secularism has actually been *fundamental* in the development of Russian thought . . . His creative activity is a kind of culmination of the long and intense struggle of Russian thought against secularism. Shestov is the high point in this basic movement of Russian thought; and in this lies his inestimable significance for the history of Russian philosophy . . .

It is possible that the "tragic avalanche" which Shestov experienced was due to the fact that he became aware of the dehumanization and depersonalization inherent in modern society thanks to the tyrannical dominance of Reason. He witnessed with horror and dismay the pantheon of false gods created by Reason. These gods were useful gods, and therefore more dangerous than the ancient "graven images." It should be pointed out that Shestov was not against reason or science in daily life. This was not his problem. What he rebelled against was the claim made by reason and science, namely, that they are the sole authority in this world.

Science and Reason, according to Shestov, have arrogated unto themselves an authority which is not rightly theirs. Neither science nor reason can deal with ultimate problems, such as the existence of God, the nature of man, immortality, etc. Shestov was concerned with "what matters most." It is for this reason that Philo, Spinoza and Hegel were his *bêtes noires.* They were the perpetrators of the "big lie," namely, that Reason is the sole and supreme authority in the universe. The original culprit was of course, Thales, the father of the "big lie." He recalls for us in this connection the story of the young Thracian woman, who, when she saw Thales fall into a well while searching heaven for its secrets, was seized with an uncontrollable laughter that has reverberated throughout the centuries. For here was a philosopher who was so busy searching heaven for its secrets that he failed to see the well in front of his feet. What Shestov is saying [in his *In Job's Balances,*] is that philosophy must never try to be a science. "The certainty that the existing order is immutable is for certain minds synonymous with the certainty that life is nonsensical and absurd."

In attacking philosophy and science, which base their premises on reason alone, Shestov was speaking from a personal experience of an existence beyond the limits of reason—the realm of faith. Both philosophy and science fail to see the dilemma inherent in the law of causality. The dilemma according to Shestov is this: If we admit that the law of causality knows no exceptions, how are we to explain Jesus' last words on the cross, "My God, my God, why hast Thou forsaken me?" How can one account for the crucifixion of the most perfect being on earth? Are philosophy and science more indispensable in this life than truth? Shestov insists that truth is the indispensable principle in life.

The claim that science is merely concerned with facts indicates a complete misunderstanding of the nature of science. Science is not concerned with facts as such; it demands proof for every statement it makes. Even such sciences as zoology and botany are not concerned with mere facts; they are concerned with theory, with making judgments. In short, reason decrees what may or may not be. Reason seeks to be both law-giver and judge, but it fails to deal with ultimate truths. Ultimate truths, according to Shestov, are absolutely unintelligible, but not inaccessible. Even the so-called "middle" truths, such as joy, pain, light, heat, humiliation, etc., are unintelligible, but are accessible.

> It is possible to understand the arrangement of a locomotive. It is also legitimate to seek an explanation of an eclipse of the sun, or of an earthquake. But a moment comes . . . when explanations lose all meaning and are good for nothing any more. It is as though we were led by a rope—the law of sufficient reason—to a certain place and left there.

The *leitmotif* that runs through all his writings and thinking is liberation from the tyranny of necessity. The antinomies are not between religion and atheism, but between faith and reason. Faith is a new dimension, a "second sight." To illustrate what he means by faith, he recalls a legend about the Angel of Death, who

> when he comes for a soul, sees that he has come too soon, so he does not take the soul away, but leaves the man one of the innumerable pairs of eyes with which his body is covered. And then the man sees strange and new things, more than other men see and more than he himself sees with his natural eyes . . . But since all our other organs of sense, and even our reason, agree with our ordinary sight . . . the new vision seems to be outside the law, ridiculous . . . it seems only a step short of madness . . . not poetic madness . . . but the madness for which men are pent in cells.

The man of faith is in essence the "underground man" whose passionate desire is to escape from the "cave" where laws, principles, and self-evident truths are supreme. The struggle is between the two kinds of vision. In a sense the "underground man" is "everyman" desperately struggling against the "Euclidean mind" that insists that "twice two is four." It is this passionate search for truth and freedom that led Shestov to his uncompromising anti-rationalistic position. His distrust of reason also led him to place the blame for human sufferings on knowledge. When man stopped feeding upon the tree of life and began to feed upon the tree of knowledge, he embarked upon a self-destructive course from which he is unable to extricate himself.

As a religious existentialist who believed in a God who is "limitless possibility" and who stands in opposition to reason and necessity, he could no longer trust reason. By uniting reason with revelation, the God of the Bible was exchanged for the God of the philosophers and theologians. In short, the medievalists replaced Tertullian's *credo quia absurdum est* with *credo ut intelligam.* Shestov accepts Tertullian's position, for "one can and one must sacrifice everything in order to find God." Like Kierkegaard's "leap of faith," Shestov says that "one must be daring to speak of a real God who is called the Creator of heaven and earth both in the Scriptures and in the Symbol of faith." Faith for him is not a self-evident truth, but is predicated on the existence of a living all-perfect Being, not bound by reason of necessity.

In his last two books, **Speculation and Revelation,** and **Athens and Jerusalem,** Shestov deals at greater length with the relation of faith to reason. Athens stands for reason, while Jerusalem stands for faith, and the two are mutually exclusive. Science, for example, is concerned with facts in order to construct a theory. It therefore proceeds to "create" truth in order to validate its premises. Faith on the other hand, is concerned with finding the truth in God, which in his view needs no rational proof, and in fact cannot provide a rational proof for the existence of God. Faith enables man to "see" God existentially. Like Luther and St. Paul he insists on *sola fide* (by faith alone).

Although Shestov left his mark on some of his European contemporaries, especially on Camus, Sartre, and Merleau-Ponty, generally speaking, he was a voice crying in the wilderness. While dark clouds were already gathering

---

An excerpt from *Dostoevsky, Tolstoy and Nietzsche*

Now we approach the philosophy of Tolstoy's antipode, Nietzsche. With him, as with Count Tolstoy, the initial cause of the shaking of his soul was the discovery of the great event that "God is dead," as he himself later expressed it, or that "God is the good," as Tolstoy now says, assuring us that in just this lies the essence of Christianity and the religious consciousness of our time. As proof that the statements "God is the good" and "God is dead" are equivalent, and that Tolstoy and Nietzsche set out from the same point of view, we quote the following words of Nietzsche: "The best means of beginning each day well is to think on awakening whether one cannot give joy to at least one person this day. If this could be regarded as a substitute for the religious habit of prayer, our neighbors would only gain by the change." Or again: "There is too little love and goodness in the world to give any of it away to imaginary beings."

To the Russian reader, who has always heard about the cruelty of the antichrist and immoralist Nietzsche, these words must seem remarkable. Nevertheless, in them we find the explanation of all his future tendencies of mind. These two aphorisms are taken from *Human, All Too Human*—the book in which Nietzsche for the first time freed himself from the metaphysics of Schopenhauer. Henceforth metaphysics, which had determined the content of his first work, *The Birth of Tragedy*—this typical model of learned *causerie,* full of talent, in the pessimistic style—is for him only a science "which deals with the basic errors of men, but as if they were basic truths." He no longer seeks enlightenment in this "science." He flees from his theory of the esthetic interpretation of tragedy at the moment precisely when he appears most to need it, for tragedy, which up until then had occurred only in the souls of Prometheus, Oedipus, and the other heroes of the dramas of Sophocles and Aeschylus, now occurs in his own soul. He understands now that a great misfortune cannot be justified by the fact that one can recount it beautifully and sublimely. The art which embellishes human sorrow is no longer of any use to him. He seeks another refuge where he hopes to find salvation and to escape from the horrors which pursue him. He hastens toward the "good" which he has become accustomed to consider as all-powerful, as able to replace everything, as God, as even above God; it seems to him that man will only gain if, instead of turning toward God, he reserves all his love for his neighbor. As the reader can see, the idea is purely Tolstoyan. There is only this difference: at that time Nietzsche had still not experienced any testing of fate, and believed with all his soul in salvation through love and that his entire fate depended on the results which this belief could bring him.

Lev Shestov, in his Dostoevsky, Tolstoy and Nietzsche, *translated by Bernard Martin, Ohio University Press, 1969.*

over Europe, there was still some naive hope in certain intellectual circles that reason would ultimately triumph. However, only one year after Shestov's death the world was plunged into a global conflagration by a country where Kant and Hegel elevated Reason to the level of the Absolute. Reason found expression in genocide, concentration camps, and general destruction. It seems that Shestov's anti-rationalism was fully vindicated. At any rate, the events that have been taking place in the three decades since Shestov's death have shaken man in his implicit trust in the supremacy of reason. Man in the sixties can no longer be so optimistic about the ultimate triumph of reason in human relations, judging by the irrational behavior of nations, great and small.

The claims of reason frightened Shestov. He wanted to save man from the tyranny of reason and to preserve his dignity. He wanted to establish a point of view that would take seriously the idea that God *is*. In short, he wanted to provide a basis for an evaluation of life in terms of personal existence in relation to God. To use Martin Buber's idea, he sought to provide a basic for an "I and Thou" relationship. He fought relentlessly against Karamazovism, which advanced the idea that since God does not exist, "all things are allowable." To this blasphemous idea he reacted with a resounding affirmation that since God exists, "all things are possible with God." He wanted to rescue God from the rational and scientific straight jacket into which He was placed by philosophers and theologians.

Shestov's keen analysis of the malaise of modern society with its culture predicated on the supremacy of reason and science is undoubtedly one of his great contributions to social and philosophic thought. His ideas would be more congenial to the mood of *our* generation that is seeking values to give meaning and purpose to life in a depersonalized society. We would like to conclude our exposition with a quotation from a well-known Russian philosopher [V. V. Zenkovsky, in his *A History of Russian Philosophy,* Vol. 2], who stated that "Shestov's unforgettable contribution lies in his anti-secularism and his ardent preaching of a religious philosophy built upon faith and revelation." Whether or not we fully accept Shestov's "either-or" position, we can no longer ignore him, for he has something vital to say to our generation.

Michael Wyschogrod   (essay date 1968)

SOURCE: A review of *Athens and Jerusalem,* in *Jewish Social Studies,* Vol. XXX, No. 4, October, 1968, pp. 291-92.

[*German-born Wyschogrod is a professor of philosophy and author who specializes in Jewish theology. In the following review, he offers a mixed assessment of* Athens and Jerusalem.]

Lev Shestov was a Russian Jewish philosopher who lived in Paris from 1920, the year he was forced to flee his homeland for France because of the Bolshevik revolution. He very quickly won considerable fame on the continent and, though philosophically in total disagreement, Husserl and Shestov became close friends. It was in Husserl's home that Shestov met Heidegger in 1929. At Husserl's sugges-

tion, Shestov began reading Kierkegaard under whose influence he remained for the rest of his life.

[*Athens and Jerusalem*] is an excellent translation of Shestov's last and most important work. It is fundamentally an attack on philosophy which, in Shestov's view, is enslaved to the notion of necessity. Philosophy seeks understanding and considers this goal achieved only when it has subsumed any given phenomenon under some law. Once this is done, the phenomenon is seen as necessary in terms of the law or laws appropriate to it. In this way philosophy destroys freedom. Freedom is possible only where there is a God who is the creator of the laws that govern the world but who is himself not bound by these laws. Shestov thus pits philosophy against the Bible and opts unequivocally for the latter.

The most curious aspect of this book is the index. There are numerous entries under Kant, Spinoza, Socrates and many other philosophers but there are almost no entries under any biblical heading. Shestov obviously knows much more about philosophy, the villain of the book, than about the Bible, its hero. The Bible that Shestov champions is somewhat remote. We get very little specific insight into biblical theology. One is even at a loss to say whether it is the Jewish Bible or the Christian one that Shestov is championing. For this reason Shestov cannot be considered a Jewish philosopher in any but the most general sense.

Viewed as comments on the history of philosophy, this is an interesting book. It is marred by a tendency toward the unhistorical, as in the following: "But everything that seems unclear to us, debatable and incomplete in Socrates' doctrine can be completed and clarified from Spinoza's work."

Robert L. Strong, Jr.   (essay date 1971)

SOURCE: A review of *Dostoevsky, Tolstoy, and Nietzsche,* in *The Russian Review,* Vol. 30, No. 3, July, 1971, pp. 314-15.

[*Below, Strong gives a mixed appraisal of* Dostoevsky, Tolstoy, and Nietzsche.]

Beginning his adult life as a lawyer, Lev Shestov (1866-1938) came to philosophy by way of literary criticism. His first book (1898) dealt with Shakespeare and was soon followed by the two long essays which have been translated for the present volume, ***The Good in the Teaching of Tolstoy and Nietzsche: Philosophy and Preaching*** (1900) and ***Dostoevsky and Nietzsche: The Philosophy of Tragedy*** (1903). Written in a rambling, non-rigorous, and impressionistic style, they nevertheless convey aesthetic power. The subtitle of the second essay indicates a similarity to the interpretation given Dostoevsky by Berdyaev and Rozanov. It is, furthermore, in the tragic view of life that the key to these two works may be found. For, despite their early successes, all three writers under discussion experienced moral crises during their middle years, (a torment evidently undergone by Shestov himself during the 1890s). The metaphor of "gazing into the abyss" is employed, and the horrors of the human condition which they saw there impelled each man to seek salvation.

Tolstoy's solution (too harshly condemned, I think by Shestov) was to equate God with "the good" and to preach fraternal love. Dostoevsky's radically egotistical Underground Man, as embodied in Raskolnikov, for example, had to be saved by Orthodox Christianity. And Nietzsche, for whose courage Shestov expresses the greatest admiration, eventually succumbed to the doctrines of *amor fati* and the *Übermensch*. Within our space limitations here, Shestov's own philosophy must briefly be summarized as anti-idealistic and anti-rationalistic. In a sense, it was at least tangential to religious existentialism. Late in life, moreover, Shestov wrote a book on Kierkegaard, and an English translation has recently appeared.

Bernard Martin's introduction is competent, though overly long (thirty pages) because of many needless quotations from the texts which follow. One puzzling omission is Shestov's real family name (Schwarzman). A knowledge of this thinker's Jewish background would provide another dimension to Shestov's passionate moral fervor and to his own solution: belief in a predominantly Old Testament God for whom "one must sacrifice everything."

Czesław Miłosz (essay date 1973)

SOURCE: "Shestov, or the Purity of Despair," in *Emperor of the Earth: Modes of Eccentric Vision*, University of California Press, 1977, pp. 99-119.

[*Recipient of the 1980 Nobel Prize in literature, Lithuanian-born Miłosz is known for his contributions to the development of Polish poetry. In the following essay, originally published in the journal* Tri-Quarterly *in 1973, Miłosz examines the defining characteristics of Shestov's work, and compares him to other philosophers and literary critics, in particular Kierkegaard and Simone Weil.*]

Lev Shestov (pen name of Lev Isaakovich Schwarzman) was born in Kiev in 1866. Thus by the turn of the century he was already a mature man, the author of a doctoral dissertation in law, which failed to bring him the degree because it was considered too influenced by revolutionary Marxism, and of a book of literary criticism (on Shakespeare and his critic Brandes). His book *Dobro v uchenii grafa Tolstogo i Nitsshe—filosofia i propoved (The Good in the Teaching of Count Tolstoy and Nietzshe: Philosophy and Preaching)* was published in 1900. In the same year he formed a lifelong friendship with Nikolai Berdyaev, one that was warm in spite of basic disagreements that often ended in their shouting angrily at one another. His friendship with Berdyaev and Sergei Bulgakov places Shestov in the ranks of those Russian thinkers who, about 1900, came to discover a metaphysical enigma behind the social problems which had preoccupied them in their early youth. Shestov's philosophy took shape in several books of essays and notes written before 1917. His collected works (1911) can be found in the larger American libraries. The fate of his writings in Russia after the revolution, and whether their meaning has been lost for new generations, is hard to assess. In any case Shestov expressed himself most fully, it seems to me, in his books published

abroad after he left Russia in 1919 and settled in Paris, where he lived till his death in 1938. These are *Vlast' klyuchei: Potestas Clavium (The Power of the Keys)*, 1923 and *Na vesakh Iova (In Job's Balances)*, 1929; those volumes which first appeared in translation, *Kierkegaard et la philosophie existentielle*, 1938 (Russian edition, 1939), and *Athènes et Jérusalem: un essai de philosophie religieuse*, 1938 (Russian edition, 1951); lastly those posthumously published in book form, *Tol'ko veroi: Sola Fide (By Faith Alone)*, 1966, and *Umozreniïe i otkroveniïe: religioznaya filosofia Vladimira Solovyova i drugïie stat'i (Speculation and Revelation: The Religious Philosophy of Vladimir Solovyov and Other Essays)*, 1964.

Shestov has been translated into many languages. Yet in his lifetime he never attained the fame surrounding the name of his friend Berdyaev. He remained a writer for the few, and if by disciples we mean those who "sit at the feet of the master," he had only one, the French poet Benjamine Fondane, a Rumanian Jew later killed by the Nazis. But Shestov was an active force in European letters, and his influence reached deeper than one might surmise from the number of copies of his works sold. Though the quarrel about existentialism that raged in Paris after 1945 seems to us today somewhat stale, it had serious consequences. In *The Myth of Sisyphus*—a youthful and not very good book, but most typical of that period—Albert Camus considers Kierkegaard, Shestov, Heidegger, Jaspers, and Husserl to be the philosophers most important to the new "man of the absurd." For the moment it is enough to say that though Shestov has often been compared with Kierkegaard, he discovered the Danish author only late in his life, and that his close personal friendship with Husserl consisted of philosophical opposition—which did not prevent him from calling Husserl his second master after Dostoevsky.

I am not going to pretend that I have "read through" Shestov. If one is asked whether one has read Pascal, the answer should always be in the negative, no matter how many times one has looked at his pages. In the case of Shestov, however, there are obstacles other than density. His *oeuvre* is, as Camus defined it, of "admirable monotony." Shestov hammers at one theme again and again, and after a while we learn that it will emerge inevitably in every essay; we also know that when the theme emerges, his voice will change in tone and sustain with its usual sarcasm the inevitable conclusion. His voice when he enters an argument is that of a priest angry at the sight of holy vessels being desecrated. Convinced that he will not be applauded because his message seems bizarre to his contemporaries, he does nothing to diminish our resistance, which is provoked most of all by what Lévy-Brühl, in a polemic with him, called "hogging the covers." Shestov was often reproached for finding in Shakespeare, in Dostoevsky, and in Nietzsche much that is not there at all, and for too freely interpreting the opinions of his antagonists (numerous, for these included practically all the philosophers of the past three thousand years). He dismissed the reproach with a laugh: he was not such a genius, he would say, that he could create so many geniuses anew. Yet the reproach is not without validity.

He knew he was not understood; probably he did not want to be overly clear. But the difficulty in assimilating him is not caused by any deviousness on his part or by any levels of ironic meaning or aphoristic conciseness. He always develops a logical argument in well-balanced sentences which, especially in their original Russian, captivate the reader with their scornful vigor. Shestov is probably one of the most readable philosophic essayists of the century. The trouble lies in his opposition to those who separate the propositions of a given man from his personal tragedy—to those who, for instance, refuse to speak of Kierkegaard's sexual impotence or of Nietzsche's incurable disease. My guess is that Shestov, too, had his own drama, that of lacking the talent to become a poet, to approach the mystery of existence more directly than through mere concepts. And although he does not mix genres, or write "poetic prose," one feels that at a given moment he falls silent and leaves much unsaid because the border of the communicable has been crossed. That is why in self-defense he sometimes quotes Pascal: *"Qu'on ne nous reproche donc plus le manque de clarté, puisque nous en faisons profession"*— "Then let people not blame us any more for our lack of clarity, since we practice this deliberately."

To associate Shestov with a transitory phase of existentialism would be to diminish his stature. Few writers of any time could match his daring, even insolence, in raising the naughty child's questions which have always had the power to throw philosophers into a panic. For that reason such questions have been wrapped in highly professional technical terms and, once placed in a syntactic cocoon, neutralized. The social function of language is, after all, both to protect and to reveal. Perhaps Shestov exemplifies the advantages of Russia's "cultural time lag": no centuries of scholastic theology and philosophy in the past, no university philosophy to speak of—but on the other hand a lot of people philosophizing, and passionately at that, on their own. Shestov was a well-educated man, but he lacked the polite indoctrination one received at Western European universities; he simply did not care whether what he was saying about Plato or Spinoza was against the rules of the game—that is, indecent. It was precisely because of this freedom that his thought was a gift to people who found themselves in desperate situations and knew that syntactic cocoons were of no use any more. Sorana Gurian after all was an agnostic, largely beyond the pale of religious tradition, and not a philosopher in the technical sense of the word. Whom could she read? Thomas Aquinas? Hegel? Treatises in mathematical logic? Or, better still, should she have tried solving crossword puzzles?

What does a creature that calls itself "I" want for itself? It wants to be. Quite a demand! Early in life it begins to discover, however, that its demand is perhaps excessive. Objects behave in their own impassive manner and show a lack of concern for the central importance of "I." A wall is hard and hurts you if you bump against it, fire burns your fingers; if you drop a glass on the floor, it breaks into pieces. This is the preamble to a long education the gist of which is a respect for the durability of "the outside" as contrasted with the frailty of the "I." Moreover, what is "inside" gradually loses its unique character. Its urges, desires, passions appear to be no different from those of other members of the species. Without exaggeration we may say that the "I" also loses its body: in a mirror it sees a being that is born, grows up, is subject to the destructive action of time, and must die. If a doctor tells you that you are dying of a certain disease, then you are just another case; that is, chance is a statistical regularity. It is just your bad luck that you are among such-and-such a number of cases occurring every year.

The "I" has to recognize that it is confronted with a world that follows its own laws, a world whose name is Necessity. This, according to Shestov, is precisely what lies at the foundations of traditional philosophy—first Greek, then every philosophy faithful to the Greeks. Only the necessary, the general, and the always valid will merit investigation and reflection. The contingent, the particular, and the momentary are spoilers of unity—a teaching that dates back to Anaximander. Later Greek thinkers exalted the all-embracing Oneness and represented individual existence as a crack in the perfectly smooth surface of the One, a flaw for which the individual had to pay with his death. From a Shestovian perspective, Greek science and morality both follow the same path. The sum of the angles in a triangle equals two right angles; the general, eternal truth reigns high above breeding and dying mortals just as eternal good does not change whether or not there is a living man to aspire to it.

The "I" is invaded by Necessity from the inside as well, but always feels it as an alien force. Nevertheless the "I" must accept the inevitable order of the world. The wisdom of centuries consists precisely in advising acquiescence and resignation. In simple language, "Grin and bear it"; in more sophisticated language, *"Fata volentem ducunt, nolentem trahunt"*—"The Fates lead the willing man, they drag the unwilling." Stoicism, whose very essence is to curb the shameful pretense of transitory individual existence in the name of universal order (or, if you prefer, Nature), was the final word of Graeco-Roman civilization. But, says Shestov, stoicism has survived under many disguises and is still with us.

Shestov simply refuses to play this game of chess, however, and overturns the table with a kick. For why should the "I" accept "wisdom," which obviously violates its most intense desire? Why respect "the immutable laws"? Whence comes the certainty that what is presumably impossible is really impossible? And is a philosophy preoccupied with *ho anthropos,* with man in general, of any use to *tis anthropos,* a certain man who lives only once in space and time? Isn't there something horrible in Spinoza's advice to philosophers? *"Non ridere, non lugere, neque detestari, sed intelligere"*—"Not to laugh, not to weep, not to hate, but to understand"? On the contrary, says Shestov, a man should shout, scream, laugh, jeer, protest. In the Bible, Job wailed and screamed to the indignation of his wise friends.

Shestov (and he was not the first, for Rozanov had already made the same suggestion) believed that Dostoevsky's most significant work was *Notes from Underground,* and considered the major novels that followed as commentaries and attempts to solve the riddle set forth in the *Notes.* He expressed this opinion in an essay written in

1921 for the hundredth anniversary of Dostoevsky's birth. Shestov believed that the true critique of pure reason was not Kant's achievement but Dostoevsky's, and in the *Notes* specifically. He admired Dostoevsky's philosophical genius without reservation—and accepted as true the disparaging rumors about his personal life, rumors spread mostly by Strakhov. It also suited his purpose to see such characters as the Underground Man, Svidrigailov, Ippolit in *The Idiot,* Stavrogin, and Ivan Karamazov as Dostoevsky's true spokesmen, and even to a large extent autobiographical portraits; and to dismiss Father Zosima and Alyosha as *lubok* (cheap block prints). To Shestov peace of mind was suspect, for the earth we live on does not predispose us to it. He loved only those who, like Pascal, *"cherchent en gémissant"*—who "seek while moaning." This approach to Dostoevsky should appeal to those critics who believe the *Notes* reveal much that this conservative publicist and orthodox Christian tried to stifle in himself. There is, however, one basic difference between Shestov and those who think of Dostoevsky as a humanist, often mentioning the vision of earthly paradise (modeled on Claude Lorrain's painting "Acis and Galatea" in the Dresden gallery) in his later writings. The vision, they believe, is proof that a young Fourieriest was still alive in the conservative author of *The Diary of a Writer.* Shestov does not agree with this "humanistic" interpretation.

The narrator of Dostoevsky's *Dream of a Ridiculous Man* visits in his sleep, in a state of anamnesis perhaps, a humanity living in the Golden Age before the loss of innocence and happiness. Now for Shestov the story of the Garden of Eden, because of its unfathomable depth and complexity, spoke for the super-human origin of the whole Scripture. Explanations of the Fall advanced by both theologians and the popular imagination seemed childish to him when compared with chapters 2 and 3 of Genesis. Dostoevsky's intuition enabled him, Shestov felt, to guess at a *metaphysical state* of man before the Fall, not just to visualize a happy Rousseauistic society: "their knowledge was higher and deeper than the knowledge we derive from our science; for our science seeks to explain what life is and strives to understand it in order to *teach others how to live* [the italics are mine], while they knew how to live without science. I understood that, but I couldn't understand their knowledge. They pointed out the trees to me, and I could not understand the intense love with which they looked on them; it was as though they were talking with beings like themselves. And, you know, I don't think I am exaggerating in saying that they talked with them!" (David Magarshack's translation). Shestov doesn't hesitate to speak of man before he tasted from the tree of knowledge of good and evil as possessing omniscience and absolute freedom. What, then, was the Fall? A choice of an inferior faculty with its passion for a *distinguo* and for general ideas, with pairs of opposites: good, evil; true, untrue; possible, impossible. Man renounced faith in order to gain knowledge. Shestov names his enemy: Reason. He even says the fruits of the forbidden tree could just as well be called synthetic judgments a priori. And if Dostoevsky's *Notes from Underground* occupies a central place for Shestov, it is because the hero screams "No!" to "two and two make four" and wants "something else."

According to Shestov, Hellenistic civilization could accept neither the God of the Old Testament nor Christ of the New Testament. It had to adapt the scandalous particularity of a personal God to its general ideas, shaped as they were through speculation. "The good is God," "Love is God"—to such equations the Hellenized citizens of the Roman Empire could give assent. But the equations are nonsensical, says Shestov, for here the abstract is put before the living. He reminds us with relish that Saint Augustine hated the Stoics as much as Dostoevsky hated the liberals; both the Stoics and the liberals recommended a morality of self-sufficing Reason.

The gnosis, when it absorbed Christian elements, was nothing more than an attempt to trim the Scriptures of their "capriciousness," of their antigenerality equated with untruth. The heresy of Marcion in the beginning of the second century, inspired by the gnosis, altogether rejects the Jehovah of the Old Testament as an evil demiurge because his *incomprehensible* behavior seems offensive to an enlightened mind. But similar Hellenization of the Scriptures continued throughout the Middle Ages. Where the Scholastics affirmed that God created the universe by making use of some preexisting laws of Nature (two and two make four, the principle of contradiction, and so on, as eternal principles) they in fact put Necessity (universal laws) above the God of Genesis. They paved the way for the modern attitude that calls religion before the tribunal of Reason. The modern mind, Shestov affirms, is completely under the spell of formulas found in their most perfect form in two representative thinkers: Spinoza and Hegel. The latter said: "In philosophy religion receives its justification. Thinking is the absolute judge before whom the content of religion must justify and explain itself." And the reader who does not share Shestov's belief in the Garden of Eden should be aware of the basic issue; by voicing his disbelief he takes the side of knowledge against faith.

Shestov opposed Jerusalem to Athens in a most radical, uncompromising manner. Those names stood for faith versus reason, revelation versus speculation, the particular versus the general, a cry *de profundis* versus the ethics of, as Ivan Karamazov said, "accursed good and evil." Shestov liked to quote Tertullian:

> *Crucifixus est Dei filius; non pudet, quia pudendum est. Et mortuus est Dei filius; prorsus credibile est, quia ineptum est. Et sepultus resurrexit; certum est quia impossibile est*—The Son of God was crucified; this does not bring shame, because it is shameful. And the Son of God died; again this is believable because it is absurd. And having been buried, he rose from the dead; this is certain because it is impossible.

Contemporaries of Tertullian, perhaps no less than their remote descendants of the twentieth century, disliked everything in the New Testament which was in their eyes *"pudendum," "ineptum," "impossibile."* Shestov's men were Pascal because he had faith in the God of Abraham, Isaac, and Jacob, and not in the God of philosophers;

Martin Luther because he relied on "faith alone" and because he used to say that blasphemy is sometimes dearer to God than praise; Nietzsche because he saw through the speculative nature of ethics devised to supplant the killed God; and, finally, Kierkegaard.

> **I emphasize the point: contemporary philosophy does not recognize and cannot endure the problematic and, consequently, also the metaphysics of knowledge. To everyone knowledge presents itself as if standing outside of all problems.**
>
> *—Lev Shestov, in his* "Myth and Truth: On the Metaphysics of Knowledge," *translated by Bernard Martin, 1982.*

Shestov's articles attacking Edmund Husserl in *La Revue Philosophique* had an unexpected effect: a meeting of the two men, at the philosophical congress in Amsterdam in 1928, which developed into a friendship. They respected each other, always stressing that they stood at opposite poles in their concept of philosophy. It was Husserl who literally forced Shestov to read a thinker with whom he himself disagreed—Kierkegaard. Shestov thus found out that he was less a maverick than he had thought. It must have been quite a surprise for him to learn that Kierkegaard saw the source of philosophy not in amazement, as did the ancients, but in despair, and that he too opposed Job to Plato and Hegel. Those were Shestov's own most cherished thoughts. A remark by Kierkegaard testifying to his stake in the Absurd, "Human cowardice cannot bear what insanity and death have to tell us," could have been made by Shestov as well. From Kierkegaard he took the name applicable *ex post* to his own meditation, "existential philosophy" as distinguished from speculative philosophy.

No wonder Camus in *The Myth of Sisyphus,* when invoking the protagonists of paradox and the Absurd, mentioned Kierkegaard and Shestov first of all. The similarities, however, between the Parisian existentialism of the 1940s and 1950s on the one hand, and Kierkegaard and Shestov on the other, are superficial. Camus, it is true, was perhaps no less fascinated than was Shestov with Dostoevsky's *Notes from Underground,* even to the extent that his last book, *The Fall,* is essentially the *Notes* rewritten. Yet Shestov, convinced as he was that the Underground Man deserved salvation because of his longing after "something else," would not leave him a victim of his desperate, crazy, solitary ego. Certainly he was skeptical of the alternatives proposed by Dostoevsky—the peasant pilgrim Makar Dolgoruky, Father Zosima, Alyosha. Nevertheless, he was a man of the Scriptures. He would probably have gladly accepted the epithet Plato often hurled at his opponents in a dispute—*Misologos,* a hater of reason—but only to stress the absurd of the human condition, which is masked by Reason. There was a way out: "The good is not God. We must seek that which is higher than

the good. We must seek God." Which means that the despair that seizes us when we are faced with the Absurd leads us beyond good and evil to an act of faith. There is nothing impossible for God and for those who truly believe in him. An absurd affirmation, for who ever saw a mountain moved by prayer? But do we have a choice? The fruits of the tree of knowledge bring only death. It should be noted that Shestov was not a preacher; he tried only to present a dilemma in all its acuteness. Most definitely he was neither a moralist nor a theologian.

For Camus, despair was not a point of departure but a permanent state of existence not excluding happiness. He wanted us to believe that even Sisyphus could be happy. He was drawn thus by the French moralistic tradition toward some sort of accommodation with a world deprived of meaning. Perhaps it sounds strange, but his atheist existentialism is less radical than Shestov's precisely because of that moralistic (Greek, after all) bent. To Camus Shestov's God seemed capricious, wicked, immoral, and as such was rejected. "His [God's] proof is in his inhumanity." For the humanist this was unacceptable. In *The Myth of Sisyphus* Camus defines the difference between his Parisian contemporaries' position and that of Shestov: "For Shestov reason is useless, but there is something beyond reason. For the absurd mind, reason is useless and there is nothing beyond reason." Camus preserved that complete bereavement till the end. In *The Fall,* his last book, the narrator and hero settles down in a bar near the port of Amsterdam in an underground private hell where there is no aspiration and no promise.

Either/or. Shestov's categorical opposition between faith and reason reminds one of the theory of two parallel truths, elaborated in the thirteenth century; but, in fact, he rejects the truth of reason completely; the world of the "laws of Nature" is, as he says, a nightmare from which we should waken. His criticism is directed primarily against those who eschew the fundamental "either/or" and who, even though they pronounce themselves for faith, imperceptibly move to the side of their adversary. Thus the case of all devisers of theodicy: since the world created by God is not a very happy place, something should be done to lift from God the responsibility for evil—and thence the attempts at a "justification of God" accomplished by means of human reason. This aspect of Shestov's struggle is well represented by his essays on Vladimir Solovyov and Nikolai Berdyaev in his posthumous volume ***Umozreniïe i otkroveniïe.*** Let us concede that his severe, unornamented style makes Solovyov sound by contrast verbose if not wooly, and Berdyaev, frequently rhetorical. But Shestov also argues well. Without detracting from Solovyov's imposing stature, he accuses him of nothing less than an unintentional falsity. He "placed on his banner a philosophy of Revelation, but practiced, like Hegel, a dialectical philosophy." "The idea of a 'philosophy of Revelation' seduced Solovyov as if it were itself the Revelation and, without his noticing it, took the place of the Revelation, just as for Hegel the rational took the place of the real." What happened to Solovyov had happened before; when a mind introduces rational order into the Revelation which defies order ("For the wisdom of this world is foolishness with God," I Corinthians 3:19) it ends by taking refuge in an ethical system, in a moral ideal, to be realized of course in some future kingdom of God on earth. Solovyov, contends Shestov, came gradually to conclusions quite similar to the moralistic and antimetaphysical teachings of Tolstoy—then woke up and took fright. Solovyov's last book, *Three Conversations* (1900), is a complete reversal. It is directed at Tolstoy, but perhaps the author really settles accounts with himself. After all, its focus is the story of the Antichrist who comes disguised as a lover of mankind. Such a change in Solovyov's orientation was to Shestov's liking. The pivotal points in his interpretation of the Scriptures were the Fall and the renewal of man by his partaking from the tree of life as promised in the Apocalypse. The last event was to occur, however, in a metaphysical rather than purely historical dimension. We cannot be more specific, because we simply do not know what Shestov meant in his references to the Revelation of St. John; we have to respect his silence. In any case, Solovyov was guilty in Shestov's opinion of an inadmissable attachment to ethics at the expense of the sacred and of bowing before the tribunal of reason, as had Spinoza and the German idealistic philosophy.

The essay on Berdyaev is most revealing. The exaltation of human freedom gave to Berdyaev's writings their tone of unbridled optimism; mankind called to collaborate with God would attain "Godmanhood" ("Bogochelovechestvo"); in this respect he may be counted among many of Teilhard de Chardin's predecessors. But for Berdyaev, the belief that free action can transform the face of the earth had its roots in the eschatological and apocalyptic orientation of the Russian nineteenth-century mind, continuing the line of Slavic messianism. When in the last pages of *The Russian Idea* Berdyaev praises the Polish messianic philosopher August Cieszkowski and his voluminous work *Our Father,* he confirms this estimation. It is precisely this lofty notion of human freedom and man's unlimited possibilities in the pursuit of good that Shestov attacks. He suspects that for his friend freedom is an expedient means of explaining away the horror of existence. Evil in the world results from man's freedom, man could only have been created free, thus Berdyaev does not go beyond the Christian doctrine. Yes, but his teachers are German mystics—Meister Eckhardt, Jakob Boehme, Angelus Silesius—who affirm that a sort of dialectical movement *preceded* the creation of the universe. The ideas of these mystics were to inspire the whole of German idealistic philosophy which Shestov belabors now in the person of its precursors. According to the German mystics man's freedom—meaning the possibility of evil, which has existed since before the beginning of time—is due to the dark force of the preexisting Naught that limits the power of God. Indeed, above God the mystics put *Deitas,* an eternal law. But this is the gnosis!, exclaims Shestov. In striving to equate the good with God, Berdyaev made God depend on man in his struggle against a dark preexisting nothingness to such an extent that man, absolutely necessary to God, began to play the central role. Why should "Godmanhood" succeed where God fails? Why not transform "Godmanhood" into "Mangodhood"? And that, Shestov feels, is what Berdyaev does in fact. His philosophy of freedom, presumably an existential philosophy, deals with the illusory, exaggerated freedom of the Pelagians and is not existential; the latter is a philosophy *de profundis* recognizable

by its refusal to explain away suffering and death, no matter which "dynamic process" is supposed to achieve the victory of the good. When Ivan Karamazov says that the tear of a child outweighs all the possible harmony of the universe, he cannot and should not be answered with historical dynamism.

Perhaps Shestov in his polemic with Berdyaev "pulls the blanket to his side" a little. Yet if we compare his essay on Berdyaev with his essay on Husserl (his last, written in 1938 to honor the memory of his friend who had just died) we must conclude that, contrary to appearances, Shestov probably had more in common with Husserl than with Berdyaev, even though in the Great "either/or" Husserl opted for science. Husserl thus intended Reason to be an instrument for discovering absolute and eternal truths untouched by relativism, truths valid for gods, angels, and men, on earth and in the universe. By "more in common" I mean the sternness proper to both men. Shestov admired Husserl precisely because he was a man ready to accept a verdict of reason even if it provided him with no comfort at all. If he himself chose the Scriptures, it was not because they brought him comfort but because he believed them to contain the truth.

Future studies of Shestov, it seems to me, should not devote more than a very limited space to the French intellectual scene, even though Shestov lived in Paris for nearly two decades. There is one exception, however. The *oeuvre* of Simone Weil throws some of his propositions into relief, and conversely Shestov enables us to see her basic premises better. Not that they knew each other. Perhaps Shestov used to pass her in the Latin Quarter when she was a student at the Ecole Normale Supérieure. Her colleague there was Simone de Beauvoir, and the fate of these two women provides us with an awe-inspiring lesson. Simone de Beauvoir was responsive to the intellectual and literary fashions of the day and became a famous but not first-rate writer, one of those who make a lot of splash in a life-time but are soon forgotten. Simone Weil—antimodern, aloof, quixotic, a searcher for the ultimate truth—died in London in 1943 at the age of thirty-four completely unknown, but her notes and maxims published posthumously secured her a permanent place in the history of religious ideas. My mention here of Simone de Beauvoir is not totally arbitrary. Immediately after World War II she, with Sartre and Camus, was promoting the "existentialist movement." Yet the very problems that concerned Shestov remained outside her sphere of interest. To apply any epithet to Weil's philosophy would be futile; that she, as it seems, read some Shestov is not material either. What matters is a similarity of temperament in the two thinkers, expressing itself in their classicism and nakedness of style, and in general in the same attitude toward time. Shestov wrangled not only with Spinoza as if he were his contemporary, but also with Plato, and saw the last three thousand years practically as one short moment. Simone Weil's notebooks are full of quotations in the original Greek, of mathematical equations, and of references to Hinduism, Zen, and Taoism—which did not hinder her in her passionate twentieth-century commitments. But there is something else that authorizes us to speak of Shestov and Simone Weil in one breath. It is the central theme of their thought, the phenomenon of suffering and death. These are her words:

> A Discourse of Ivan in the Karamazovs. Even if that immense factory brings the most extraordinary marvels and costs only a single tear of a single child, I refuse. I adhere completely to that feeling. No matter which motive people might offer me, nothing could compensate for the tear of a child and nothing will make me accept that tear. Nothing, absolutely nothing conceivable by intelligence. One thing only, intelligible only to supernatural love: God willed it thus. And for that reason I would also accept a world of pure evil, the consequences of which would be as bad as one tear of a child. [*Cahiers,* III]

Shestov could have written these lines, but they would have had a different meaning to him.

Although Simone Weil was Jewish, she was raised in an areligious family and was unacquainted with Judaism. In Kiev Shestov absorbed Jewish religious literature, including legends and folklore, at an early age. Simone Weil's sacred book was Homer's *Iliad;* her thought was inspired by Plato, later by the New Testament. She was as thoroughly Hellenized as it was possible for pupils of the French *lycées* in the early decades of our century to be. And, had Shestov lived to read her work, he would have quoted her as an example confirming his thesis about the irreconcilable feud between Athens and Jerusalem. With the exception of the Book of Job, Simone Weil did not venerate the Old Testament and spoke harshly of the God of the Old Testament and of the Jews, reproaching them for cruelty and superstition. She was totally on the side of Athens; besides, she believed Greek and Hindu metaphysics to be identical in essential points. Her God was Greek. She even hinted at the possibility of Dionysus having been an incarnation of God, before Christ. And the gnostic penchants typical of early Hellenized Christians can be easily detected in her work. For instance, in her historical essays the indignation with which she describes the French crusade against the Albigensians and the conquest of the land speaking Oc, meaning Occitan (now the south of France), is due not only to her sympathy for the massacred and the oppressed but in large part to her identification with Albigensian Christianity related through Manichaeism to the gnosis of Marcion.

Future investigation—and I do not doubt that there will be one—should be centered in the first place on Shestov's and Weil's concept of Necessity as well as on different treatments of the relationship between Oneness and the particular. For Shestov, universal Necessity was a scandal. He felt that its horror was best described by Dostoevsky in *The Idiot* where there is talk of Holbein's painting of the *Deposition from the Cross:*

> Looking at that picture, you get the impression of Nature as some enormous, implacable, and dumb beast, or, to put it more correctly, much more correctly, though it might seem strange, as some huge engine of the latest design which has senselessly seized, cut to pieces, and swallowed up—impassively and unfeelingly—a great and priceless Being, a Being worth the whole of Na-

ture and all its laws, worth the entire earth, which was perhaps created solely for the coming of that Being! The picture seems to give expression to the idea of a cold, insolent, and senselessly eternal power to which everything is subordinated.

Shestov wanted man to oppose that beast with an unflinching "No."

Simone Weil's attitude, on the other hand, was similar to the wonder a mathematician feels when confronted with the complexities of numbers. A few quotations [from *La pesanteur et la gráce,* 1946] will suffice to show this: "Necessity is a veil of God"; "God entrusted all phenomena without exception to the mechanism of the world"; "In God not only is there an analogy of all human virtues, but also an analogy of obedience. In this world he gives necessity free play"; "The distance between necessity and the good is the very distance between the Creation and the Creator"; "The distance between necessity and the good. To contemplate it without end. A great discovery made by the Greeks. Undoubtedly the fall of Troy taught them this"; "God can be present in Creation only in the form of absence"; "God is not omnipotent because he is the Creator. Creation is an abdication. But he is omnipotent in the sense that his abdication is voluntary; he knows its effects and wants them."

For Simone Weil the "terrifying beauty" of the world was mysteriously linked to mathematical Necessity. Yet she would not disagree with Shestov when he denounced "the beast," since she believed that the determinism of Nature is the domain of the Prince of this World acting on God's authority. But as a philosopher (also a college professor of philosophy) whose intellectual antecedents were essentially Greek, she would not turn against Reason. Applying ideas of reduction, she conceded as much as possible to the immutable structure of the world. The power of God to act through Grace is, by his own will, infinitely small but sufficient to save man. It is the mustard seed of the Gospel (or the silence of Christ in the "Legend of the Grand Inquisitor"). It makes it possible for us to accept an existence which, when looked at rationally and soberly, is unbearable. Shestov fumed against Greek wisdom which led to stoical resignation. He even reproached Nietzsche, whom he esteemed, with *amor fati,* a final blessing given to fate. Simone Weil interpreted "Thy Kingdom come" as a prayer asking for the end of evil, for the end of the world, and "Thy will be done" as an assent to the existence of a world bound by the laws of Necessity. Moreover, that heroic assent was in her view the very core of Christianity: "just as a child hides from his mother, laughing, behind an armchair, so God plays at separating himself from himself through the act of Creation. We are God's joke"; "To believe that reality is love, seeing it for what it is. To love what is impossible to bear. To embrace iron, to press one's body against the cold of hard metal. That is not a variety of masochism. Masochists are excited by fake cruelty. For they do not know what cruelty is. One must embrace, not cruelty, but blind indifference and blind brutality. Only in such a manner does love become impersonal."

Why should love become impersonal? Here again Shestov

would not agree. In the Jansenist *"Le moi est haïssable"*—
"the I is hateful"—of Pascal, with whom he otherwise
agreed, he suspected a glimmer of the old Greek nostalgia
for the immutable, eternal, general Oneness in which the
particular disappears. Why should we hate "I"? Was it not
the "I" of Job that complained and wailed? Was not the
God who would demand such an impossible detachment
from us a God of philosophers rather than a God of
prophets? Simone Weil's response to these questions
points to her latent Platonism and to the Platonic myth
of the world as a prison of souls longing after their native
land, the empyrean of pure ideas. Many of her maxims
amount to a confession of guilt, the basic guilt of existing,
and to a desire for self-annihilation. "My existence diminishes God's glory. God gave it to me so that I may wish
to lose it." She was aware that a self-imposed renunciation
of the "I" was nearly impossible, and yet she rated the
very aspiration to achieve renunciation as a high spiritual
attainment. She referred more than once to two lines in
Racine's *Phèdre* (again we are in a Jansenist climate):

> *Et la mort à mes yeux ravissant la clarté*
> *Rend au jour qu'ils souillaient toute sa pureté.*

> [And death, ravishing the light from my eyes,
> Gives all purity back to the day they defiled.]

This is, however, an essay on Shestov, not on Simone Weil.
Their judgments often converge, yet in general these two
move in realms that bear only a tangential relationship to
each other. Not only was she passionately interested in social problems (she worked as a laborer in the Renault factory and participated in the Spanish civil war) but her religious, even mystical, experience was drawing her to
Roman Catholicism and to a discussion of religion as an
institution. For very personal reasons she decided not to
receive the sacrament of baptism. Nevertheless, Catholic
theology and the history of the Roman Catholic church
occupy a prominent position in her writings. Shestov was
dominated by a violent scorn for speculative philosophy
because he believed that although it pretends to bring solace, in truth its consolations are illusory. Paradoxically
he waged his war as an antirationalist using rational argument as his weapon. We know nothing about his confes-
sional options and not much about the intensity of his personal faith.

What could Sorana Gurian, a young woman dying of cancer, get from her reading of Shestov? Not the promise of
a miraculous cure. He did not maintain that you can
knock down the wall of Necessity by beating your head
against it. To the sober-minded who criticized the Absurd
of Kierkegaard and his faith in the impossible, he used to
reply that Kierkegaard knew perfectly well the weight of
reality: Regina Olsen would not be restored to him. Yet
there is a great difference between our looking at ourselves
as ciphers on a statistical sheet and our grasping our destiny as something that is personal and unique. Simone Weil,
though she advocated the voluntary renunciation of the
"I," also considered the destruction of the "I" by an external force as a sign of utter misfortune: prisoners and prostitutes are compelled by *others* to visualize themselves as
objects, statistical ciphers, interchangeable units. Shestov
did not fight science. Yet in his rebellion against philoso-

phy we may sense an implied rejection of the terror exert-
ed by a whole purely quantitative, scientific *Weltanschauung.* Such a scientific code of self-perception, imposed by
education and the mass media, eats up our individual substance from the inside, so to speak.

To Sorana the God of the Scriptures defended by the stern
priest Shestov would probably not have meant an afterlife
and a palm tree in Heaven. He must have appeared to her
as he did to the Russian author, as pure anti-Necessity.
The question was not the existence of Heaven and Hell,
not even the "existence" of God himself. Above any notions, but revealed by his voice in the Scriptures, he is able
to create anything, even a personal heaven and earth for
Sorana Gurian. Or for each one of us.

James M. Curtis   (essay date 1975)

SOURCE: "Shestov's Use of Nietzsche in His Interpretation of Tolstoy and Dostoevsky," in *Texas Studies in Literature and Language,* Vol. XVII, 1975, pp. 289-302.

*[Curtis is an American professor of Russian and author of
works on Russian literature.]*

Lev Shestov wrote two books whose titles contain a reference to Nietzsche: *The Good in the Teaching of Count
Tolstoy and F. Nietzsche* (1900) and *Dostoevsky and
Nietzsche: The Philosophy of Tragedy* (1903). It often
seems to the critic who wishes to do justice to these works,
Shestov's second and third respectively, that such an undertaking merely shows why Nietzsche never believed in
the adequacy of any single logical statement. The three
were fashionable figures in the *fin de siécle* mood of the
time; but the rigor and intellectual integrity of Shestov's
thought transcends the age of impressionistic criticism in
which he wrote. His interpretation of literary works as autobiographical documents links him to the nineteenth century; but he never takes the artists' statements as dogmas,
and an implicit skepticism about the relevance of conscious intentions pervades his writing. While these two
books probably constituted the turning point in his own
intellectual development, the present state of Shestov
studies precludes anything more than sheer speculation on
the inviting topic of Nietzsche's importance in Shestov's
mature works. Although Shestov was a philosopher, a free
spirit in Nietzsche's sense, he distinguished himself as a
critic. Obviously, then, the present article can address itself only to the problems of Shestov's use of Nietzsche in
these two books.

But to do this fully, one would like to characterize Shestov's place in Russian and European Nietzscheanism, and
here again, single statements consistently prove inadequate. Although we are beginning to recognize Shestov as
the foremost interpreter of Nietzsche at the time, he had
little in common with Viacheslav Ivanov's pontifications
on the artist as myth-maker, and even less with the exploitation of Nietzsche's ideas in the prose of Gorky, Artsy-
bashev, and Sologub. Although David Thatcher found
enough material on early English reactions to the concept
of the *Übermensch* to justify devoting a whole book (*Nietzsche in England, 1890-1914*) to this topic alone, Shestov
explicitly and emphatically rejects it, as well as anything

else that smacks of hero worship. As for Nietzsche himself, his much-vaunted, dazzling style made little impact on Shestov, although he did admire it. Where Nietzsche often relies on paradoxes for effect, and achieves a lofty tone by avoiding extended historical analyses, Shestov explains what he means in a flat, nonrhetorical style, and relates abstract principles to specific problems. This last point, in fact, summarizes Shestov's use of Nietzsche: although one can often find sources in Nietzsche for Shestov's statements, Shestov never simply repeats him. Shestov so completely assimilated what Nietzsche was doing that he could transmute Nietzsche's challenging aphorisms into elements of a larger, coherent analysis. Thus, we should say, not that Nietzsche "influenced" Shestov but that Shestov found a conceptual paradigm of great power in Nietzsche's work, and applied that paradigm with consummate skill and insight to some of the greatest works of world literature.

Although Shestov refers to virtually all of Nietzsche's works at one time or another, he found the essence of the conceptual paradigm in the tripartite historical analysis of *The Birth of Tragedy.* Typically, however, Shestov does not use the famous terms "Apollonian" and "Dionysian" in his criticism; rather, he repeats Nietzsche's emphasis on the innate complementarity of these two opposed principles which—precisely because of their opposition—formed a unity in the great age of Greek tragedy. Nietzsche writes [in *Sämtliche Werke,* Vol. 70]:

> And thus the double nature [*Doppelwesen*] of the Aeschylean Prometheus, his conjoint Dionysian and Apollonian nature can be expressed in the conceptual formula: "Everything that exists is just and unjust and in both cases is equally justified."

For our present purposes, this kind of logic, in which two opposed elements form a totality, will be called binarism; Shestov himself follows Nietzsche in referring to binary thinking as "tragedy," which he equates with philosophy toward the end of his book on Dostoevsky.

But, as is well known, Nietzsche argues in *The Birth of Tragedy* that Socrates, through Euripides, brought about the individuation of the binary nature of tragedy, and the Apollonian and the Dionysian split apart:

> Here *philosophical thought* overgrows art and forces it to cling close to the trunk of dialectic. The Apollonian tendency has withdrawn into logical schematism, as in Euripides something analogous is to be noticed in the transformation of the Dionysian into naturalistic effect. [*Sämtliche,* 70]

The very fact that Socrates could ask "What is the good?" implies a preference for Apollonian reason over Dionysian frenzy, and implies the existence of fixed values. Since everything is equally justified in the binary world of tragedy, terms like "good" and "bad" have little meaning; but positing the existence of fixed values creates the necessity for making judgments—a key idea in Shestov's criticism. And since (as Nietzsche never tired of pointing out) no one can give empirical proof of the existence of fixed values, any

system that implies any fixed values whatsoever amounts to some form of idealism.

Both Shestov and Nietzsche consider Kant's philosophy the culmination of idealism, and thus the quintessential description of the situation of modern man. Moreover, both our thinkers agree that when the fixed values of idealism, as in Kant's categorical imperative, block the dynamics of the will to power, cruelty results. Nietzsche had suggested in *The Genealogy of Morals* that "the categorical imperative reeks of cruelty," and Shestov developed the thought:

> It [idealism] has equipped itself with the categorical imperative, which has given it the right to consider itself an autocratic monarch, and to see all who refuse it obedience as insolent rebels who deserve torture and execution. And what refined cruelty the categorical imperative has manifested every time its demands were violated! [*Dostoevsky and Nietzsche*]

This cruelty may mask itself as service to mankind, but Shestov, following Nietzsche, disregards the mask. Thinking of Nietzsche's dictum that "what justifies a man in his reality—it will always justify him," Shestov declares:

> In a philosophical system, in addition to cruelty, you will in the last analysis definitely find something incomparably more valuable and significant: the author's self-justification, and together with that an accusation as well, an accusation of all those who by their life in one way or another arouse doubts as to the unconditional justness of the system and to the high moral qualities of the author.

Logically, then, a philosophical system shuns real introspection in order to seek converts, and seeks them by what Shestov calls "preaching." He takes the term from Nietzsche's definition of "altruistic moral preaching in service of individual egotism" as "one of the most common *falsehoods* of the nineteenth century." Shestov thus concludes that "preaching, like many other forms of man's spiritual activity, does not have and cannot seek, any goal outside itself." Man exists alone; idealism simply uses preaching as a means of pretending that he does not.

However, neither Nietzsche nor Shestov considers individuation, with its consequent idealism, an inherently permanent state; for them, certain individuals occasionally, and usually briefly, transcend it. They thus create tragedy anew, as the third stage of the process which Nietzsche outlines in *The Birth of Tragedy.* For the early Nietzsche at least, this occurs in Wagner's *Gesamtkunstwerk.* Whereas Nietzsche tends to discuss the art work itself, for Shestov, tragedy occurs only in individuals; art works merely express the tragic awareness of these individuals. We may consider it the crucial difference between Shestov and Nietzsche that Shestov applies to all art (at least to all the artistic works he discusses) Nietzsche's explanation of the title of his book *Human, All Too Human:* "Idealism is inappropriate for me: The title says, 'Where you see ideal things, I see—human, ah only the all too human'."

The urgency and directness of Shestov's criticism stem from his ability to analyze even the three men whom he admires most as human, all too human; all individuals have both strengths and weaknesses. We must believe him when he asserts that "my goals lie outside the realm of accusations and justification." Thus, he is describing, not criticizing, when he gives the following gloss to Nietzsche's thought that "unity (monism) [is] a need for inertia."

> The contemporary mind cannot endure a philosophy which offers it several basic principles. It strives for monism at any cost—for a unifying . . . single principle. It even has difficulty enduring dualism [i. e., binarism]. To carry two principles seems to it too large a burden.

The ability to "carry two principles" implies a certain alienation from the contemporary mind: the sickness of the artist. Nietzsche had written [in *Sämtliche,* 78] "there are exceptional states which govern the artist . . . so that it does not seem possible to be an artist and not be sick." Whereas most of Nietzsche's admirers even today consider this sickness, and the creativity that it can produce, an accomplishment—a feat to be emulated or envied— Shestov does not. He emphasizes that "no one enters the world of tragedy voluntarily." Or, more specifically:

> Dostoevsky, like any man, did not want tragedy for himself, and tried to avoid it in any way he could; if he did not avoid it, it was *against* his will, as a result of external circumstances beyond his control.

Parting with one's ideals (Shestov and Nietzsche also use the term "convictions") involves such pain that an individual does so only under the duress of external circumstances. In general terms, Shestov finds that Tolstoy never abandoned idealism, but that Dostoevsky did, particularly in *Notes from the Underground* and *The Brothers Karamazov.*

Although he never says so openly, Shestov models his contrast between Tolstoy and Dostoevsky on Nietzsche's contrast, in *The Birth of Tragedy,* between Homer, the Apollonian artist, and Archilochus, the Dionysian artist. Nietzsche begins his comments on Homer [in his *Sämtliche,* 70] by stating: "That overwhelming dismay before the titanic forces of nature, that Moira enthroned inexorably over all knowledge— . . . was again and again overcome by the Greeks through that artistic *middle world* of the Olympians." He associates the artist who creates this middle world with Schiller's "naive" artist, of whose harmony with nature he says that it is not a state "which we *must* encounter at the threshold of every culture, like a paradise of mankind; only an age which sought to make an artist of Rousseau's Emile and imagined that it found in Homer an artist reared in the heart of nature could believe in it." Shestov makes no statements about whether or not this state of nature is necessary, but he certainly has no doubts about Homer's naiveté, to which he adds that of Tolstoy.

> *War and Peace* is a truly philosophical work; in it Homeric and Shakespearean "naiveté" predominates, that is, the absence of any desire to give retribution for good and evil, the consciousness that one must seek the responsibility for human life higher, outside ourselves. [***The Good***

in the Teaching of Count Tolstoy and F. Nietzsche]

While Shestov admits that Tolstoy judges Napoleon and Sonia, he insists that "no one who lived, no matter how he lived, even immorally, tastelessly, or crudely, evoked Count Tolstoy's indignation." Shestov extends this to *Anna Karenina,* where he considers Levin's undeserved happiness and Anna's equally undeserved suicide as signs of Tolstoy's ability to accept the existence of both good and evil in the world.

However, we find significant shifts in the statements about Tolstoy's naiveté in ***Dostoevsky and Nietzsche,*** where Shestov concludes that "he [Tolstoy] does not achieve that Homeric, patriarchal naiveté which is ascribed to him, although he strives for it with all his might." Shestov now discerns an internal tension in Tolstoy; just as the naive art of Homer enabled the Greeks to forget about the horrors of reality, so

> His [Tolstoy's] activity as a writer is one continual striving somehow or other—by force, cleverness, or deceit—to conquer a stubborn enemy who undermines the possibility of a happy and luminous existence in its very basis. And he is successful at this to a significant degree. [***The Good***]

Tolstoy's need to deny the reality of evil, the "stubborn enemy," makes him an idealist, and a Kantian. Thinking of Nietzsche's remark [in *Sämtliche,* 73] that the most important thing of all for Kant was to make "the moral 'kingdom' unassailable, or intangible to reason," Shestov now says that "this is the task of Tolstoy's art, this is the meaning of Kantian idealistic philosophy: to transfer all the disturbing questions of life in one way or another to the realm of the unknowable." As always, Shestov does not remain content with abstractions, but shows how this "task" determines the nature of characterization in Tolstoy; noting such scenes in *War and Peace* as the one in which Natasha simply does not react at all to the burning of Moscow, Shestov comments:

> In Count Tolstoy his heroes never cease to believe in the "beautiful" and the "sublime"—even in those moments when the disjuncture of reality and ideals becomes clear to them: they allow reality to enter into its rights, but never cease for a minute to revere ideals. [***Dostoevsky and Nietzsche***]

Yet how do Tolstoy's characters continue to "revere" ideals even in the face of death? Shestov's answer to this question, his analysis of the deaths of Prince Andrei and Ivan Ilyich, is of considerable interest.

Shestov finds that Tolstoy solves this problem in a Kantian manner, by portraying death "not from the point of view of those who are departing, but from the point of view of those who remain on earth." Or, more technically:

> Death is present as something quite different from life, and therefore quite unfathomable for the living. As he dies, Prince Andrei loses his human individuality, which, gradually dissolving and becoming dissipated, sinks into something different from everything which we can

imagine. This something different, this *Ding an sich* or "will" is in any case something that derives from Kant and Schopenhauer and is the "immortality" which awaits men. For the living, such a grandiose horizon seems like an interesting spectacle.

In short, by refusing to let the threat of pain and death shake an individual's ideals (something which, incidentally, Tolstoy also does in other death scenes in *War and Peace*), "he has found his *Ding an sich* and his synthetic a priori judgements, that is, he has learned how people get away from everything that is problematical, and how firm principles by which a man can live are created."

It would seem that "The Death of Ivan Ilyich" provides a perfect fictional illustration of the way sickness can lead to a "re-evaluation of all values," and Shestov does call it [in **The Good**] "a question mark, marked out with such strong black paint that it shows through all the layers of the new rainbow colors of the sermon with which Tolstoy wanted to force us to forget all our former doubts." Although Ivan Ilyich's sufferings do distance him from his family and from his former ideals—ideals in the Nietzschean sense—Shestov observes that there is a hole in the black sack into which Ivan Ilyich feels that someone is pushing him, and that through that hole "something shines through." When we read in the story that "there was no fear of death, because there was no death," Tolstoy has merely exchanged one set of ideals for another; the essential mode of abstraction and depersonalization of suffering remains:

> How does Count Tolstoy explain in his soul this horrible tragedy of a completely innocent man? His answer is a sermon: Love your neighbor and work. . . . After reading Ivan Ilyich, we are not at all interested in finding out how we are to save ourselves from his horrible fate.

Thus, Shestov develops a concept of the function of art which is the exact opposite of that which Tolstoy developed in *What Is Art?* Whereas Tolstoy felt that art should infect the reader with the artist's feelings of love and brotherhood, Shestov is convinced that truly great art—tragedy—challenges the reader's monism, that it shakes him out of the inertia of his idealism. With this essential difference in mind, we may conclude these comments on Shestov's analysis of Tolstoy by noting some of his observations on Tolstoy's crisis.

Shestov makes much of Tolstoy's admission, in the article on his experiences in Moscow flophouses during the census of 1881, that it made him feel good when others saw him giving money to a poor prostitute. In the Nietzchean manner, Shestov denies all moral and altruistic value to Tolstoy's later publicistic writings, insisting that he did everything he did in order to justify his own actions. Thus, Tolstoy found relief from his anxieties in the comforting absolutes of the categorical imperative.

> This principle is now the most valuable of all for Count Tolstoy. "To serve the good" is not only not a burden for him, it is a release from a burden. . . . And duty, pure Kantian duty, in that form which allows no doubts whatsoever about what one "may" and "may not" do, lies at the basis of Count Tolstoy's teaching.

Kantian idealists preach; in Tolstoy's case, the preaching often took the form of violent denunciations of all those who, even implicitly, challenge "the high moral qualities of the author": "Count Tolstoy cannot take a step without calling an enormous quantity of his neighbors immoral." Shestov finds the cruelty which the categorical imperative always implies, but attempts to conceal, implicit in this highly judgmental attitude.

Yet Shestov does not judge Tolstoy in turn; rather, he applies to Tolstoy the strain of generosity and charity which is present in Nietzsche, but which most people ignore. Nietzsche had written in *Beyond Good and Evil*:

> Whoever has looked deeply into the world has understood well what wisdom lies in the fact that men are superficial. It is its [wisdom's] instinct of preservation that it teaches them to be flighty, frivolous, and false. . . . Let no one doubt that whoever *needs* the cult of the superficial in this manner, has at one time gone beyond it.

Shestov therefore impresses on the reader that both Tolstoy and Dostoevsky—as well as Nietzsche himself—needed the comfort of idealism, and that all three of them resorted to preaching at various times.

> I do not wish to say this as a rebuke to Dostoevsky, Nietzsche, and Count Tolstoy. . . . They could no longer live without an answer to their questions—and any answer was better than nothing. This is the "superficiality born of depth," as Nietzsche says. It is impossible to exist always and unvaryingly looking into the eyes of frightful specters.

As a result of Tolstoy's stubborn refusal to admit the role of evil in the world, "we have [in him] a unique example of a great man striving at any cost to compare himself with mediocrity, to become a mediocrity himself." Thus arises the question which Shestov poses a few pages later [in **Dostoevsky and Nietzsche**]: "The a priori exists only for mediocre natures. What remains for Dostoevsky?" In Shestov's interpretation, what remains for Dostoevsky is tragedy—but tragedy experienced and expressed only when he could do nothing else.

In **The Good in the Teaching of Count Tolstoy and F. Nietzsche,** Shestov finds Tolstoy and Dostoevsky more similar than he does three years later in his book on Dostoevsky. In his book on Tolstoy, he makes an analogy between Tolstoy's normative pronouncements in *What Is Art?* and Dostoevsky's treatment of Raskolnikov:

> The basic idea in *Crime and Punishment* is virtually stated in the very title of the novel. Its essence is that a violation of a rule cannot be allowed under any circumstances—even when a man does not understand for what purpose the rule has been thought up.

In 1900, then, Shestov considers *Crime and Punishment,* especially the conclusion, an affirmation of fixed values—a clinging to idealism. Possibly under the impact of Nietzsche's *The Will to Power* (published posthumously in 1901) to which he makes several implicit references, Shestov changes his mind about *Crime and Punishment* in *Dostoevsky and Nietzsche.*

In *Dostoevsky and Nietzsche,* Shestov pays noticeably more attention to individual texts, and noticeably less attention to theoretical issues. Early in the book, he gives the following account of Dostoevsky's career:

> Dostoevsky's literary activity can be divided into two periods. The first one begins with *Poor Folk* and ends with *Notes from the House of the Dead.* The second one begins with *Notes from the Underground* and ends with the Pushkin speech, that dark apotheosis of Dostoevsky's entire work.

Shestov develops this general thesis with his usual penetration. While he interprets the first period as one of preaching and the second as one of tragedy, he finds both preaching and tragedy in each period.

In treating Dostoevsky's early career, Shestov emphasizes the manner in which Dostoevsky acquired his ideals from Belinsky, and characterizes the break with Belinsky in the late forties as a foretaste of the pain that would force Dostoevsky to enter the realm of tragedy with *Notes from the Underground.* Of the stories themselves, he has little to say except that "reality, of course, is dark and unsightly . . . but the ideals are clear and bright." Rather, he directs our attention to Dostoevsky's own reports that he cried while creating Makar Devushkin, and attributes to Dostoevsky the desire to make all mankind cry for his lovesick clerk—a desire characteristic of preaching, and, obviously, one very much in keeping with Tolstoy's attitudes in *What Is Art?*

Passing rapidly to the post-exile works, Shestov devotes more space than one might expect to *The Village of Stepanchikovo* and *Notes from the House of the Dead,* because he adduces them as evidence of the durability of ideals, and considers them Dostoevsky's attempts to deny to himself the impact of his prison experiences. Although Shestov asks, "Are there really such incorrigible idealists who will continue to fuss around with their ideals no matter what people do to them, and who can turn any hell into paradise?," he later notes flashes of doubt even here, as in the narrator's statement in *Notes from the House of the Dead* that the prison contained "the most gifted, the strongest of all our people." Shestov cites this famous passage not as evidence of Dostoevsky's humanism, as sentimental civic critics would have it, but as a rejection of idealistic belief in the intelligentsia as "the best people in Russia" in exchange for a new respect for the prisoners, whose sufferings had brought them close to tragedy.

"Notes from the Underground is a soul-rending scream of horror torn from a man who has suddenly become convinced that he has lied his whole life." Thus Shestov characterizes Dostoevsky's first tragic work. As we know, entering the realm of tragedy means renouncing one's former ideals, and Shestov locates this renunciation precisely—in the scene in Part II in which the narrator insults Liza by giving her a five-ruble note. Shestov identifies Liza with the woman in the Nekrasov poem (a prime example of preaching) which serves as the epigraph.

It was not Liza that he drove away. He needed the image of Liza only in order to spit at and stamp into the mud the "idea," that same idea which he had served over the course of his whole life.

Moreover, the underground man's rebellion against the wall in Part I also belongs with this renunciation of ideals; for Shestov, the wall is a physical realization of the Kantian absolute. After quoting the underground man's ironic words to the effect that "the wall has something calming, morally reassuring and finally perhaps even something mystical," Shestov extends this attitude to the author himself:

> The language is different, of course, but who does not recognize the Kantian a priori placed in front of the *Ding an sich?* You see, "eternal" truths were thought up by wise men not so much for those who need comfort, as for the comforters, that is, for themselves. Dostoevsky is horrified at this thought.

In order to understand Shestov's reading of *Notes from the Underground* in its philosophical, Nietzschean, context, we need to recall his association of monism with idealism, and binarism with tragedy; thus, Shestov is saying that the underground man rejects monism for binarism, the constant interplay of the Apollonian and the Dionysian.

When he discusses *Crime and Punishment,* Shestov naturally begins with the now well-known analogy between Raskolnikov's article and Nietzsche's concept of a life beyond good and evil. But for once Shestov is so eager to point out tragic elements in the work that his remarks strike us as schematic. Presumably reasoning that guilt of any kind implies judgments, and thus idealism, Shestov assumes that in tragedy no real guilt is possible. Not only does he not ask the standard question, "Why does Raskolnikov commit the murders?" he seems to fly in the face of the text, and denies Raskolnikov's guilt at all: "Raskolnikov is not a murderer; he committed no crime. The story about the pawnbroker and Lizaveta is a fiction, an addition, a nonsense tale." For Shestov, all of Dostoevsky's major heroes are merely idealists who have become convinced of the fallacy of idealism.

> It is these criminals *without crime,* these gnawings of conscience *without guilt* that comprise the content of Dostoevsky's numerous novels. He himself is in this, reality is in this, real life is in this; everything else is "teaching."

Perhaps he is overcompensating for what he now considers a lapse of taste in his earlier remarks on *Crime and Punishment,* or perhaps he has in mind something like the tragic flaw of the protagonists of Greek tragedy, and assumes that it precludes real, personal guilt. To be sure, Shestov's statement that Raskolnikov "committed no crime" takes literally an actual passage in the text; when he is confessing to Sonia, Raskolnikov does say, "I didn't kill the pawnbroker; I killed myself." But when Shestov calls the account of the murder "a fiction," the common sense and sobriety which are the hallmarks of his criticism have deserted him.

When, in the passage on "criminals without crime," Shestov says, "everything else is 'teaching,' " he is doing a typical thing. He is refusing to idealize Dostoevsky; he tells us that even Dostoevsky could not remain in the realm of tragedy indefinitely, and cites a number of characters from the later novels whom he considers examples of preaching, such as Myshkin and Father Zosima. He does not, however, really analyze any of them in detail. But he does discuss "The Legend of the Grand Inquisitor" at some length, and he has some unusual things to say about it.

Claiming that Dostoevsky laughs at himself from time to time in the later works, Shestov writes:

> What is the legend of the Grand Inquisitor about? Who is the cardinal from whose hands the people accepts its wafers? Is this legend not a symbol of the prophetic "activity" of Dostoevsky himself? The miracle, the secret, the authority—after all, it was from these, and only from these, elements that his sermon was compiled.

Of all the interpretations of the Legend, this is surely the first, and probably the only one which suggests that in it Dostoevsky is parodying himself. But we need neither accept nor reject this relationship between Dostoevsky and the Grand Inquisitor to accept Shestov's reading of the character himself, which perhaps represents his finest application of rigorous personalism.

> What would have happened to the Grand Inquisitor if he had not had the proud faith that without him all mankind would perish. . . . He does not know that it is not *the people* who are obliged to *him,* but *he to the people* for his faith, that faith which at least partially justifies in his eyes his long, tiresome, tortured, and lonely life.

Here Shestov reverses the generally accepted view of things, as he so often does. The usual interpretation attributes to the Grand Inquisitor a certain grandeur and martyrlike quality, since he is living a lie for the sake of the people, who cannot endure the truth. Denying altruism once again, Shestov suggests that he *needs* to believe that he is doing so, in order to find self-justification; in short, he is an idealist. The confrontation between Christ and the Grand Inquisitor thus becomes a confrontation between tragedy and idealism; one could also say that Christ's silence during the Grand Inquisitor's sermon represents the absence of a judgmental quality in tragedy.

Since Shestov deals with Dostoevsky at relatively greater length and in relatively greater detail than with Tolstoy, it seems convenient to assess his critical practice in these two books by considering his treatment of Dostoevsky. It gives us a certain measure of Shestov's achievement as a critic when we realize that the seven decades of Dostoevsky scholarship which have accumulated since 1903 often corroborate his findings, or at least the attitudes which remain nascent in them. We would now say, for example, that Shestov misses the irony in the presentation of Makar Devushkin, and the parody of sentimentalism in *Poor Folk,* but Shestov found self-parody in the Grand Inquisitor, and it does no violence to the general tenor of his thought to extend this self-parody back to Dostoevsky's first work. Thus, one could say that Dostoevsky was paro-

dying his own utopian ideals, although he had not suffered enough to give them up.

Furthermore, in 1903 Shestov could not have known that a quarter century after he wrote, Yury Tynianov would demonstrate that Dostoevsky parodies Gogol in *The Village of Stepanchikovo,* and that he parodies a classic example of preaching in Shestov's sense—*Selected Passages from Correspondence with Friends.* After all, Shestov emphasizes that detachment from one's past constitutes a necessary first step for those who enter the realm of tragedy, and Gogol obviously played a crucial role in Dostoevsky's literary past. Nor is the suggestion, made some time ago, that in the Grand Inquisitor Dostoevsky is parodying Belinsky inconsistent with Shestov's reading, for the young Dostoevsky found in himself a strong response to his champion's impassioned rhetoric. If he wished to mock the ideals of his youth, he would naturally have chosen Belinsky as a model.

It would also repay the effort to investigate the patterns by which Dostoevsky's characters acquire ideals, and then reject them after intense suffering. If we remember that Shestov called Father Zosima a teacher, and cited him as an example of Dostoevsky's preaching, we can understand Alyosha's despair, when Zosima's body begins to stink, as the despair which occurs as the initial stage in the rejection of ideals. Finally, detailed studies such as Robert Belknap's *The Structure of "The Brothers Karamazov"* have shown that the complex symbolism of the novel links the Karamazovs with both good and evil; when Kolya Krasotkin shouts "Hurrah for Karamazov!" he is expressing a tragic awareness of the coexistence of good and evil in the world.

In more general terms, we can consider Shestov's book on Dostoevsky the first mature, full-length work of a distinctly modern criticism in Russia. Shestov reacted against nineteenth-century civic criticism in various ways which make him in a certain sense a predecessor of Formalism. While the Formalists' practice of criticism would differ considerably from his, Shestov does anticipate them in denying the role of ideology in a work while asserting the need for rigorous analysis. Like the Formalists, Shestov has no patience with the concept of the critic as someone who completes and corrects the artist's work, the attitude which he formulates in these words: "Artists don't do their work sufficiently consciously; it's necessary that someone check, explain and essentially supplement them." Likewise, Shestov is at one with the Formalists in his stress on the way in which the art work changes the reader's perception:

> The task of art is not at all to submit to regulation and normative attitudes thought up by various on one basis or another, but to break the chains that bind the human mind which is straining toward freedom.

One has only to state that art does this through images, not binary concepts, to have a description of Shklovsky's *ostranenie.*

Finally, when we survey twentieth-century criticism for analogous works, we find that Shestov was so far ahead of his time that we have to come up almost to the present to find them. Two French works, Lucien Goldmann's *The Hidden God* (on Pascal and Racine) and Sartre's *Saint Genet,* provide examples of works which also combine exhaustive knowledge of the texts with comparable philosophical acumen. Although it would be out of place here, a comparison of Goldmann's and Shestov's work would show numerous affinities in their concept of the tragic, and in their use of binarism (which Goldmann calls "dialectical thought" and needlessly associates with Marx). It is no exaggeration, then, to say that Shestov can take his place in intellectual history as the foremost interpreter of Nietzsche in Europe at the time, and as one of the major Russian critics of the Symbolist period. One can only hope that an awareness of the stature and richness of Shestov's literary criticism will stimulate further interest in the cosmopolitan, eclectic age which he both represents and transcends.

Lev Shestov on reason and faith:

Reason teaches piety and obedience. If, then, faith also taught piety and obedience, there would be no distinction between reason and faith. Why then does Spinoza affirm so insistently that "there is no connection between philosophy and faith" and that they "are totally different"? And why did Luther, for his part, attack reason so violently? I recall that Luther—who in all things followed Scripture and particularly St. Paul, who in turn relied on Isaiah—every time he pronounced judgments that were particularly audacious and offensive to reason was convinced, like Spinoza, that man's will is not free. And I would add to this that the source of their conviction, in both cases, was their inward experience. Finally—and this is the most important thing—these "immediate deliverances of consciousness" caused them a mad terror. Both of them experienced something akin to what a man buried alive feels: he feels that he is living, but he knows that he can do nothing to save himself, and that all that remains to him is to envy the dead who do not have to be concerned with saving themselves. Not only *De servo arbitrio* and *De votis Monasticis judicium* but all of Luther's works speak to us of the boundless despair that seized him when he discovered that his will was paralyzed and that it was impossible for him to escape his downfall. Spinoza does not speak freely of what takes place inside himself, and yet, calm and reserved as he appears, he at times allows confessions to escape that permit us to catch a glimpse of what his philosophical "happiness" cost him.

Lev Shestov, in his Athens and Jerusalem, *translated by Bernard Martin, 1966.*

James P. Scanlan   (essay date 1976)

SOURCE: A review of *In Job's Balances: On the Sources of the Eternal Truths,* in *Slavic Review*, Vol. 35, No. 4, December, 1976, pp. 752-53.

[*Scanlan is an American educator and author of works con-*

cerning Russian philosophy. Below, he discusses problems with the translation of *In Job's Balances.*]

In light of the debt owed the Ohio University Press for making available in English over the past ten years an entire series of works by the Russian existentialist philosopher and critic, Lev Shestov (1866-1938), only a churl could greet the present (seventh) volume without at least a show of gratitude. The fact is, however, that *In Job's Balances* has been available in English for a long time. Indeed, portions of the work have already appeared in other volumes of the Ohio University Press series. The chapter "What Is Truth?" was appended to the Press's edition of *Potestas Clavium* in 1968, and for this reason has been excluded from the present volume. However, other, shorter sections included here have also appeared earlier in the *Shestov Anthology* published by the Press in 1970.

It is, of course, useful to have the whole work once again in print, but even that boon has its blemishes. The 1932 translation used here—without revision—was done indirectly from a German translation. The resulting English text, though collated with the Russian and accurate in a general way, is not only remote from the original stylistically but is capable of promoting some unfortunate misunderstandings. Thus, to render Shestov's "dostovernost' sama po sebe, a istina sama po sebe" as "certainty and truth each exist independently" is to suggest, first, that there *is* such a thing as certainty—which is precisely the illusion Shestov seeks to dispel—and second and perhaps still worse, that this (genuine) certainty should be sought independently of truth. Minor omissions, gratuitous additions, and simple slips are also a persistent problem; for example, "laws of human evolution" unaccountably become "laws of human thought," and so on.

None of this is to say that the "pilgrimages through souls" (as Shestov called them) which make up the book are in themselves anything short of spellbinding. The essays are vintage Shestov: the old irrationalist's campaign against the logical intellect is at its most brilliant and compelling height, and the "souls" he traverses in waging this campaign—Spinoza, Pascal, Plotinus, and above all Dostoevsky and Tolstoy—are remarkably illuminated by the attendant spiritual commotion. Bernard Martin's new introduction is competent and informative, as usual, and there is an added bonus for this edition in the form of a newly-translated letter from Shestov to his daughters, in which he comments further on Tolstoy.

Still, because the primary text of the present volume offers no improvement on a known, existing resource, its value is regrettably limited. Students of Russian thought will welcome it, but will reserve their enthusiasm for the announced next volume of the series, which promises not only additional unpublished letters and fragments but the first English translation of Herman Lowtzky's biography of Shestov, as well as the first publication in any language of Shestov's 1918-19 Kiev lectures on the history of Greek philosophy.

David Patterson   (essay date 1978)

SOURCE: "Shestov's Second Dimension: *In Job's Bal-*

ances," in *Slavic and East-European Journal,* Vol. 22, No. 2, Summer, 1978, pp. 141-53.

[In the following essay, Patterson examines Shestov's use of biblical imagery and discusses his interpretations of the fiction of Tolstoy, Dostoevsky, and Nietzsche in his In Job's Balances.*]*

In his introduction to Lev Šestov's **Umozrenie i otkrovenie** Nikolaj Berdjaev tells us that Šestov was a man for whom philosophy was a matter of life and death, for whom human tragedy, terror, and suffering form the starting point of philosophy in such a way that "the conflict of biblical revelation and Greek Philosophy became the fundamental theme of his thought." Although Albert Camus believed that Šestov "had only begun to move into that desert where all certainties are turned to stone," in *Le mythe de Sisyphe* he describes Šestov by saying:

> In the course of striving with admirable monotony Shestov struggled incessantly toward the same truths, seeking to demonstrate without respite that the most self-contained system, the most universal rationalism always ends by foundering on the irrationality of human thought. Not a single piece of ironic evidence or derisive contradiction which may debilitate reason escapes him. His one point of interest is the exception that lies within the history of the heart or the spirit. Regarding the experiences of a Dostoevsky condemned to death, the frustrated spiritual adventures of a Nietzsche, the imprecations of a Hamlet, or the embittered aristocracy of an Ibsen, he tracks down, clarifies, and magnifies the human rebellion against the irremediable.

Looking at the spiritual renaissance which occurred in Russia during the late nineteenth and early twentieth centuries, A. N. Latynina [in his "Dostoevskij i èkzistencializm," *Dostoevskij—xudožnik i myslitel,* edited by K. N. Lumonov, 1972] places Šestov among the literary-aesthetic figures, including Rozanov, Merežkovskij, and Ivanov, rather than among those whose interests were predominately philosophical, such as Solov'ev, Bulgakov, and Berdjaev. V. V. Zenkovskij considers Šestov the high point of the movement against secularism that had been initiated by the Slavophiles, explaining that Šestov's

> creative contribution to Russian philosophic searchings lies not in the often devastating force of the ironical comments which are scattered throughout his works, but in the fearless disclosure of all the falsities of ancient, modern, and contemporary rationalism, as manifestations of secularism, and the disclosure that the autonomy of reason ("transcendentalism") inevitably becomes a tyranny of reason, so that everything that does not fall into the system of rationalism drops from the field of vision. [*A History of Russian Philosophy,* trans. George G. Klein, 1953]

Sidney Monas has pointed out that in spirit Šestov was one of the Hassidim—those philosophers who emphasized unique and mystical experience and who were fond of paradox and mystery. Although Šestov is often identified with irrationalism, his irrationalism forms "a *secondary* stratum of his creativity. His *religious* world must be considered primary." Having been a part of the general religious direction taken up by Solov'ev, which reacted against the so-called historical Christianity that ignores the "mystery of life," Šestov himself glimpsed the terrible mystery when in September of 1894, at the age of twenty-eight, he experienced a transformation of some kind—a "hidden catastrophe," as Zenkovskij calls it—which led him to break with reason and all the truths he had previously upheld. Although the details of the occurrence remain hidden, Šestov appears to allude to it in an entry from his "Dnevnik myslej" dated 11 May 1920: "This year it is twenty-five years since the 'disintegration of the bond of ages,' or more precisely, it was twenty-five years last fall at the beginning of September. I'm writing it down so I won't forget. The most important events in one's life—and no one else knows anything about them—are easily forgotten."

Šestov had originally been a student of mathematics, graduating in 1889 with a law degree from the University of Moscow. Given his Jewish heritage, the law meant much more to him than simply a legal code, and if we may identify "the bond of ages" with the law, its disintegration was indeed catastrophic. It was during this period of spiritual cataclysm that Šestov began reading Nietzsche, who, as J. H. Dubbink has indicated [in his "L. Šestov and L. Tolstoj," *Dutch Contributions to the Sixth International Congress of Slavieists,* edited by A. F. G. Van Holk, 1968], was Šestov's first teacher and caused him his first great difficulties. In 1900 Šestov published a comparative study of Tolstoj and Nietzsche, and three years later his book on Dostoevskij and Nietzsche came out.

In 1921, about a year after his self-imposed exile, *La Nouvelle Revue Française* published Šestov's essay on Dostoevskij, **"La lutte contre les évidences."** Latynina has pointed out that this essay, in addition to his earlier studies of Dostoevskij, signifies one of the first approaches to Dostoevskij in the spirit of existential philosophy. It is included in his key work **Na vesax Iova (In Job's Balances,** 1929) and is the one piece that first called widespread attention to him. The essay characterizes a further development of Šestov's earlier approach to Dostoevskij (whom he often referred to as Kierkegaard's double), and explains what it is like to philosophize like the underground man.

The Tolstoj essay, **"Na strašnom sude,"** ("The Final Judgment") which also appears in **In Job's Balances,** is more than a further development of an earlier approach, however. It marks a complete change in Šestov's attitude toward Tolstoj. In the study of Tolstoj and Nietzsche published in 1900 Šestov maintained that Tolstoj reached the abyss only to shy away from it. He claimed that Tolstoj resorted to preaching, where "the aim is not in the first place to bring about a conversion of others, but a self-defense of Tolstoj against the intruding forces of the 'podpol'e'." James M. Curtis notes that Tolstoj in *What is Art?* thought that art should infect the reader with the artist's feelings of love and brotherhood, while "Shestov is convinced that truly great art—tragedy—challenges the reader's monism, that it shakes him out of the inertia of his idealism." In the essay in **In Job's Balances,** on the other hand, Šestov sees Tolstoj a profound thinker who painfully abandoned everything in order to place himself before the Last Judgment. Dubbink explains that the change in Šestov's attitude was largely the result of having read Tolstoj's posthumous works, with the essay in *In Job's Balances* dating from 1921-22: "This brings a new aspect of Death into Šestov's philosophy. In his former works Death came as a thief in the night, unannounced. But now it looks as if a sort of preparation is possible and desirable."

The publication of *In Job's Balances* in 1929 falls immediately prior to Šestov's discovery of Kierkegaard, yet by this time he had already laid the groundwork for his existential philosophy. As Viktor Erofeev puts it [in his "Ostaetsia odno: proizvol," *Voprosy literatury,* 1975] from the beginning of Šestov's philosophical endeavor Nietzsche was his teacher and Kierkegaard his double. Like Kierkegaard, Šestov was engaged in a struggle against that philosophy which takes reason to be the sole authority in determinations of truth. Bernard Martin in this connection writes:

> The central concern of Shestov's own agitated and impassioned striving in the last decades of his life was to restore to men the freedom he believed they had forfeited in their obsession with rational knowledge and the God who had primordially granted this freedom to them and who alone can give it back to them. This God was the living God of the Bible—not the God of the philosophers who is a principle or a postulate, an idea deduced by speculative thought from an examination of nature or the processes of history. [Introduction to *In Job's Balances*]

Also like Kierkegaard, says Berdjaev, Šestov's main philosophical adversary was Hegel, although the philosophers whom Šestov addresses in *In Job's Balances* are Spinoza, Pascal, and Plotinus, and Spinoza is his opponent.

The essays on Pascal ("**Gefsimanskaja noč' "**) and Spinoza ("**Synov'ja i pasynki vremeni**") first appeared in 1924 and 1925, respectively, in *Sovremennye zapiski,* and the Plotinus chapter ("**Neistovye reči**") in 1926 in *Versti.* Šestov viewed Spinoza as a man who took up "the dreadful task of murdering God, i.e. the God of biblical faith—and this by none other than God Himself." Šestov saw Pascal, on the other hand, as a man who was concerned only with the salvation of the soul, and this could come only from the God of the Bible, not the God of the philosophers. In spite of the radical differences between Pascal and Plotinus, Šestov believed that certain important aspects of the two are closely related. He generally ignored Plotinus' ethics and theodicy, for example, as well as his attempts to reconcile Plato and Aristotle. "What is of ultimate significance," Martin explains, "is Plotinus' conviction that one must struggle against the enchanting power that has persuaded men to accept 'natural necessity' and to believe in the infallibility of reason with its offer of eternal and universally valid truths." Thus Šestov rejected the rationality of Athens and pursued the passion of Jerusalem.

[In Job 6: 2-3] Job cried out, and still he cries, "Oh that my grief were thoroughly weighed and my calamity laid in the balances together! For now it would be heavier than

the sand of the sea: therefore my words are swallowed up." This, of course, is the passage to which the title of Šestov's collection refers. Here he probes the limits of speculative thought in an effort to reach the second dimension of thought (*vtoroe izmerenie myšlenija*), as he calls it, where words are swallowed up. In *Umozrenie i otkrovenie* he explains that the difference between stopping where thought leaves off and going beyond, into a "second dimension," may be seen in Kant's reaction to Job opposite that of Kierkegaard. For Kant, the focus of the Book of Job is the moral argument between Job and his friends. Reason knows there is no helping Job, that he ought to accept and calmly bear his afflictions. The only satisfaction he can count on is ethical; it is his moral stance in the face of catastrophe and revilement that we must look to. Kant ignores the twofold return of all Job had lost, because reason does not allow such a thing. Kierkegaard, however, emphasizes this above all other aspects of the story. According to him, the key lies in the repetition or the resurrection that comes in faith, and not the Greek recollection that comes in rational speculation on the ethical. If Kant is right, says Šestov, then Job is lost. Rather, Job's outcry, not his moral posture, opens the way to the second dimension of thought, which in turn reveals a new way of looking at truth whereby all things are possible. If there is a world to be seen in a grain of sand, there is another realm to behold in a tear of lamentation. But for this new eyes are required.

In the essay on Dostoevskij in *In Job's Balances* Šestov tells us that the Angel of Death sometimes visits a man not to take him but to leave him with a new set of eyes, to make him mad, not in the poetic sense, where the individual is beset with eros or ecstasy, but truly mad. Before such an encounter with death can occur there must be a self which can meet with death in such a way that the encounter throws the self back upon itself. This means that the individual must have acquired a sense of harmony and balance in existence, must have constructed a coordinate system that provides the self with direction and definition. Because the system defines the individual from without, in terms of his coordinates in the universal, it acknowledges no individual existence; until the internal life of the individual is externalized and situated within the system it is deemed either illegitimate or nonexistent. Instead of relating itself to itself, the self prior to the encounter relates to the harmony of the order so that there is in fact no self, but merely the potential for self. Here the greatest good is to discourse daily and rationally about virtue, and to will to do otherwise is worse than error—it is madness, the madness induced by the Angel of Death.

According to Šestov, the encounter with the Angel of Death did not occur for Dostoevskij when he faced the firing squad or during his stay in prison. The turning point, rather, comes in *Zapiski iz podpol'ja (Notes from the Underground),* in which the reign of reason and conscience comes to an end as he discovers that the hope had been supporting the doctrine and not the doctrine the hope. He falls into a state of confusion, says Šestov [in *Na vesax iova*]; he rushes ahead without knowing where he is going and awaits something without knowing what it is. For Dostoevskij the encounter with death comes as a revelation which assumes the form not of answers but of questions.

Beginning with *Zapiski iz podpol'ja* the theme dominating Dostoevskij's work is that "twice two is four" is a principle of death. However, it is only after adopting the principle that one may come to see it as a principle of death. The forbidden Fruit must be consumed in order to see that the Tree of Knowledge is not that of Life; it is the fallen man who encounters death. Thus the encounter which leads to a break with speculative thought posits itself only at the instant it occurs; it cannot happen until it happens, and this is what gives it the abruptness which evokes the horrified "Can it be?" The hand that reaches for the Fruit is the hand that refuses to be drained of life; the Fruit is consumed, we see the life draining, and again, more desperately than ever, we refuse. For life we plead with death.

Šestov asserts, therefore, that one aim of Dostoevskij was to come to terms with the Fall, which awakens man to the "stone wall" of reason and knowledge. "The essence of knowledge," Šestov writes, "is limitation; this is the meaning of the biblical legend. Knowledge is a capacity, a constant preparedness to look around, ahead, and behind. It is the result of the fear that if you do not look to see what is around you, you will fall prey to a dangerous and insidious enemy." Knowledge defines a field of vision; the eyes are opened with the eating of the Fruit. So it was that after he had fallen into a well while walking along and looking up at the heavens, Thales resolved to never wander about wherever God may lead him, but to always look carefully for the ground beneath his feet. And "as long as a person feels the ground under his feet, he does not dare to deny obedience to reason and ethics."

Here one may ask where the ground comes from. Šestov explains that once the Fruit becomes the forbidden Fruit, freedom becomes more than man can bear, and the fear that arises in freedom is a fear of groundlessness, of chaos, of unlimited possibility. The only way to gain the ground and the ability to see whether it is there is to do that which is forbidden, thus providing a sense of direction; the prohibition becomes the single point of reference. Thus, if it is the fallen man who encounters death, it is equally the man who has exchanged the terrors of freedom for the reassurance of necessity; yet the encounter awakens a new terror, one which arises from the very necessity that had promised firm ground. The horror, as Šestov expresses it [in ***Umozrenie***], emerges when we discover that "in the Bible God created a living man from dust, but our reason strives with all its might to return the living man to lifeless dust." Hence the fear revealed in a handful of dust.

Šestov believed and stated in ***In Job's Balances*** that the goal of knowledge or speculative thought is to maintain a unidimensional image of the world; reason seeks to banish from existence all that is abrupt or unexpected, for only then will man cease to question and become as God. To posit a self, however, is to reveal the lie of the system erected on reason, ethics, and natural necessity, since in the first instance the self stands apart from the system. It is only within the context of this isolated, internal immediacy that the sudden can arise. The encounter with death is therefore an internal encounter, sudden because it can

not be externalized to fit into the universal order. Where the individual had visualized himself in the mirror of the system, he must now listen for himself in the darkness of death. When he hears nothing he struggles to fill the silence with his own outcry, in the passion of which eternal truths are swallowed up. The sudden appears, for example, when Tolstoj is overwhelmed by a fear of death one night in Arzamas, an incident retold in *Zapiski sumasšedšego (Notes of a Madman)* which Šestov takes to be the key to everything Tolstoj wrote after his fiftieth year. This is what led Tolstoj "to pose questions whenever and wherever our whole being is convinced that no such questions may be asked, for there are no answers and there never will be." When questions with no answers arise, reality and illusion exchange places—the ground crumbles and with it the self. The individual falls into despair, and as he seeks to bring the self into a relationship to itself, the transformation of thought begins.

While speculative thought has its origins in curiosity or wonder, the second dimension of thought is rooted in despair. In despair the individual is transfixed by the monolithic reality of death, riveted to the impotence of himself. The self loses the temporal arrangement of itself and with it the finite world, but this does not mean the individual has been set adrift in the eternal; rather, he is held over its edge by the heels—life is both his salvation and his damnation. Death is no longer a nebulous something which the future holds in store: it shrouds the present and the life of the self in the present with disjunction. Here arises the question of authenticity. For the first time the self confronts itself as a task, and the task is to relate itself to itself and thus create itself. In the impotence of despair, however, the individual is unable to meet the task, and herein lies his guilt. He is like a man with a wooden leg—he cannot take a step without reflection.

Insofar as action establishes a bond between the individual and the finite world, the impotence to act isolates the individual, and still another question appears: "Forlornness, abandonment, impenetrable darkness, chaos, the impossibility of foresight, complete ignorance—can a man endure *this?*" Yet this is exactly what the man in despair must endure, and the forlornness of despair assumes its most abbreviated form in the *lama sabachthani*. Whereas the encounter with death had thrown time out of joint, the *lama sabachthani* dissolves objective time altogether; the next day becomes nothing and the instant everything. Furthermore, the instant is no longer an atom of time but of eternity, the point where eternity meets tangentially with time. In objective time one moment leads to and cannot be separated from the next; in subjective time, or the lifetime of the individual self, one instant does not follow the other, for there is only the one instant, the decisive instant. Lifetime, in other words, is precisely the instant. Here the self must relate itself absolutely not only to itself but to the absolute. Because the individual's spiritual essence is now determined by this relationship, it is only in terms of the instant that his eternal life is called into question; immortality lies in the instant. The "what" of the eternal condition comes in the form of a judgment, and since there is just the one instant, there is only one judgment, the Last Judgment.

Thus the question which is embodied in the despair of the *lama sabachthani* must be revolved in a Last Judgment in which the individual is qualitatively measured against his relationship to the absolute. So it was that Ivan Il'ič, who despaired of the absence and cruelty of God, faced a judgment unlike any he had known as a judge; as Šestov points out, it was a Last Judgment. The cries of Job, then, like those of Ivan Il'ič, provide the occasion for a Last Judgment, and in this connection Šestov writes: "Reason presents its demands without regard to the heart, and so does the heart without regard to reason. What is this mysterious 'heart'? With Job it says: if my grief were laid in the balances, it would be heavier than the sand of the sea. Reason replies: the grief of the whole world cannot outweigh even a single grain of sand." The task remaining, therefore, is to find a way to tip the balances, and here begins the struggle for possibility.

In his book on Berdjaev and Šestov James Wernham points out [in his *Two Russian Thinkers,* 1968] that "one cannot without circularity argue for reason. One cannot without circularity argue against reason. But one can decide for it or against it." This is in fact one of the main points of Šestov's peculiar philosophical investigation: he seeks a dimension of thought which embraces contradiction and paradox, rather than reason and the law of contradiction. "The 'reason' by which the 'general world' is supported," says Šestov, "and which gives truth to 'twice two is four' and 'nothing happens without a cause,' not only fails to justify Tolstoj's new fears and anxieties, but it *judges* them in the most ruthless way to be '*without cause,*' founded on nothing, arbitrary, and therefore unreal, illusory." The second dimension of thought thus strives to sustain the questions with no answers, over and against reason's search for the answers to the inquiries of curiosity and its efforts to dismiss the outcries of despair.

In an attempt to bring out the distinction between the two dimensions of thought, Šestov sets Spinoza's "laugh not, weep not, curse nothing, but understand" against Pascal's "seek with lamentation." As Šestov sees it, Spinoza teaches us to view the world as one which functions according to eternal, immutable, and rational laws, and even God is not exempt from those laws; whatever is real is rational, and whatever is rational is necessary. Contrary to thought which is rooted in despair and takes its impetus from torment, Spinoza seeks to eliminate torment and despair, pursuing instead the equilibrium of the equation which only reason and ethics can provide. For Spinoza, it is the ignorant, weak, uncomprehending man who is engulfed by the fear of death one night in Arzamas, or who, like Ivan Karamazov, is agonized by the sufferings of the children.

Turning to Pascal, Šestov tells us, "For Pascal, any kind of 'calm' that comes to people from reason or morality signifies the end, nonexistence, death. Thus his enigmatic, 'methodological' rule, seek with lamentation." To seek with lamentation is to discard reason and necessity as the keepers of the keys or the sole authorities of truth precisely because of the peace of soul they bring; this "peace" is the sleep induced by the Fruit, the sleep of Peter in Gethsemane. To seek with lamentation is to make Job's words our

own and his sufferings contemporary. Reason declares: here is the sand, but the grief of Job has long since faded away. Lamentation replies: here is the grief of Job despite the passing of the sand. But the power of reason is formidable, as long as we are under its spell, life seems impossible without it. Šestov therefore viewed Pascal's attempt "to free himself from the power of reason" as the most striking aspect of his philosophy. In the light of Spinoza's assertion [in his *Ethics,* translated by William Hale White; edited by James Gutmann; revised by Amelia Hutchinson Stirling, 1949] that "it is not the nature of reason to consider things as contingent but as necessary," we see in Pascal's struggle against reason the struggle for possibility unlimited by necessity—the second dimension of thought.

If there is a single definitive characteristic about Pascal's struggle it is this: by all that is conceivable, the endeavor is doomed to miscarriage from the start. Paraphrasing Pascal, Šestov writes, "If today the truth were revealed from beneath all veils and presented to man, he would not recognize it, for according to the 'criteria' for truth, i.e. the conjunction of those signs which, according to our convictions, separate lie from truth, he would be compelled to call it a lie. And above all he would be convinced that it is not only useless, but harmful to people." The language of Pascal is in fact more that of a prophet than a philosopher; he proceeds more from revelation than from speculation. As Šestov has pointed out, "the prophets, contrary to the philosophers, never know peace. They are the incarnation of distress. . . . To the prophet, the all-powerful God, Creator of heaven and earth, is above all things, and then comes truth. To the philosopher, truth is above all things, and then comes God." So described, we would have to take Pascal to be a prophet. And in the realm of the prophet, the realm of the abyss, lies the second dimension of thought.

From the earliest times men have tried to capture the "irrational residue of being" by dressing it in the garb of reason; but when revealed truth is scratched into stone, it is lost to the stone. In the logic of language and speculative thought truth becomes universal and necessary, but in the struggle for possibility the universal and necessary must be left behind and the individual stranded in the silence of passion. We may glimpse the truth, the mystery at the limits of thought, but as soon as we try to communicate it, Šestov says, we begin to see as the world sees and to speak as it demands. It is the business of knowledge to label and categorize, but as Šestov indicates in ***Afiny i Ierusalim,*** Plotinus understood that knowledge enslaves, and he thus "began to seek a way out, a salvation beyond knowledge." In ***In Job's Balances*** we read, "Plotinus fled from wisdom; he fled from reason. And he arrived at the utterly unfounded, the totally groundless 'sudden'." Therefore, instead of looking for arguments in Plotinus' *Enneads,* we must, again, strive to make his voice our own. Karl Jaspers notes, for example [in his *Die gvossen philosophen,* 1957], that the truth of such thinking (thinking within the second dimension of thought), lies not in logical operations but in our own existence; we agree or disagree to the extent that we perceive our own existential potentiality.

We now have to ask what it is like to inhabit the realm where thought is transfigured. In this connection Šestov relates Abbot Boileau's account of how Pascal reached the point where he was perpetually afraid to turn his gaze to his left for fear of the abyss awaiting him there; whenever he sat down he would move his chair a bit to the right in order not to fall into the void. Šestov, however, makes an amendment to Boileau's anecdote: the abyss was indeed there, but it was not to Pascal's left—it was beneath his feet. While Tolstoj at the end of *Ispoved' (Confession)* found himself hanging over the abyss in a dream, Pascal lived in the continual presence of it. Men like Pascal and Nietzsche, Šestov declares, are of another world; they dwell above the abyss, but we inhabit the earth. We seek the center, the path of least resistance; they lived in daily torment. The abyss is the nebulous condition formed by questions with no answers; the task is to sustain rather than eliminate them, and this is the daily torment—we must keep the abyss beneath our feet.

Although the movement into the second dimension of thought carries us over the abyss, it is possible only in the presence of the questions and the torment. The annihilation of speculation is therefore propelled by passion. The individual kicks loose the life that had held him by the heels and in so doing regains a new life supported not by the groundwork of reason, ethics, and necessity, but by the passion. Death is chosen for the sake of a new life so that the encounter with death is now qualified by choice, by the decisiveness of the instant. The focus of existence is thus shifted from the result to the process; the agony is the sole guarantee.

Loyola and Luther were irreconcilable enemies, Šestov tells us, yet "both taught that only the person who is lost in eternity and has been left to himself and his fathomless despair is capable of directing his eyes toward the final Truth." Here begins the shift from speculative philosophy to biblical philosophy as Šestov conceived it. In the former category he places Aristotle, Spinoza, Kant, and Hegel; in the latter Pascal, Kierkegaard, Dostoevskij, and Tolstoj. In more fundamental terms, the distinction which Šestov makes is that which Thorleif Boman describes [in his *Hebrew Thought Compared with Greek*, translated by Jules L. Moreau, 1960] as the difference between Greek and Hebrew thought: "If Israelite thinking is to be characterized, it is obvious first to call it dynamic, vigorous, passionate, and sometimes explosive in kind; correspondingly Greek thinking is static, peaceful, moderate, and harmonious in kind." If Boman's distinction should appear too simplistic, one may recall Erich Auerbach's comparison of Homer with the Abraham-Isaac story. In Homer, says Auerbach, language serves to reveal thought, while in the story of the sacrifice of Issac language only conceals thought. In the Greek style everything is in the foreground, while in the Hebrew all is moved to the background.

The second dimension of thought is directed inward; its task is to internalize. It is subjective, concentrating on the inward life of the thinking subject; for the second dimension of thought, then, the internal is superior to the external. Perhaps we may now see in what sense the sufferings of Job weigh heavier than the sand of the sea, heavier than the external reality with all its necessary and universal truths. Whereas the universal nature of the rational and the ethical provides us with direction, there is no direction for the man who seeks with lamentation, and he cannot make himself understood. Like Abraham raising the knife over his son, he cannot state his case without losing his case, and must set out without knowing where he is going. This is what so amazed Šestov about Tolstoj's departure from home one night in 1910. "He grew sick of all his achievements, all his glory," as Šestov sees it. "Everything grew heavy, agonizing, unbearable. It is as if he tears his venerability away from himself with a trembling and impatient hand . . . along with all the symbols of his wisdom and status as a teacher, in order to stand before the final Judgment with a light, or at least a lighter soul; he was compelled to forget and renounce the sum of his great past." Thus everything must be sacrificed for nothing.

Finally, it must be asked why Šestov calls the second dimension a dimension of *thought* when he sees it as something which is beyond language. Might it not be considered as something other than thought? We have seen that speculative thought is indifferent to the existence of the thinking subject. Its object is to relate the individual to truth, where the attention is focussed on whether or not the thing related to is indeed the truth; its emphasis is on the outcome rather than the process, on the being rather than the becoming, and it proceeds from the individual outward. The second dimension of thought, however, puts everything into a process of becoming and omits the outcome. It proceeds from the subject inward, where the emphasis is not on the content of thought as such but on what happens to the individual while thinking. Under the second dimension of thought, for example, reflection is not concerned with the problem of whether its object is the true God but whether the individual is related to the object in such a manner that the relationship is truly a God relationship. Because the second dimension of thought is thus rooted in inwardness, it culminates in the passion of the individual and not in the language of the world. And passion finds its expression in paradox: if my grief were laid in the balances it would weigh heavier than the sand of the sea.

Since speculative thought cannot bring us to the second dimension of thought, we can only break through with a leap, an infinite movement which must be effected by passion. Yet the passion launching us into the second dimension cannot be distinguished from it, so that it appears to be a passion and not a dimension of thought after all. In terms of Šestov's biblical philosophy, it is the passion of faith, and the temptation that would prevent the movement of faith is that of reason, ethics, and natural necessity—the temptation of the serpent. Thus in the passion of faith, where thought leaves off, Job came to declare [in Job 19:27-28]: "And though after my skin worms destroy this body, yet in my flesh shall I see God: Whom I shall see for myself, and mine eyes shall behold, and not another; though my veins be consumed within me."

FURTHER READING

Criticism

Coates, Carrol. "A New Look at Shestov." *Books Abroad* 42, No. 3 (Summer 1968): 385-87.

Thematic analysis of Shestov's critical writings on Dostoevsky, Chekhov, Nietzsche, and Tolstoy.

Davison, R. M. "Lev Shestov: An Assessment." *Journal of European Studies* 11, No. 4 (December 1981): 279-84.

Examines the fundamental principles of Shestov's thought, his opposition to reason in favor of faith, and the similarities between his ideas and other philosophical traditions and teachings.

Monas, Sidney. Reviews of *Dostoevsky, Tolstoy and Nietzsche* by Lev Shestov and *A Shestov Anthology*, edited by Bernard Martin. *Slavic Review* 30, No. 4 (1971): 909-11.

Favorable review of the insights and writing style of *Dostoevsky, Tolstoy and Nietzsche*; however, Monas identifies problems with several of the translations and Bernard Martin's editing and organization of the *Anthology*.

Murry, John Middleton. "The Honesty of Russia." In his *The Evolution of an Intellectual*, pp. 26-37. London: Jonathan Cape, 1927.

Analyzes the distinctively "Russian" aspect of Shestov's ideas.

Shein, Louis J. Review of *Potestas clavium* by Lev Shestov. *Canadian Slavic Studies* 3, No. 1 (1969): 149-50.

Defines Shestov's philosophical position within the scope of Russian European culture, describing the essays collected in *Potestas clavium* as a continuation of his "earlier polemic against rationalism and scientism."

Wernham, James C. S. "Shestov." In his *Two Russian Thinkers: An Essay in Berdyaev and Shestov*, pp. 57-109. Toronto: University of Toronto Press, 1968.

Compares and contrasts aspects of Shestov's life and philosophy to that of his friend and colleague, Russian philosopher and proponent of Christian Existentialism, Nikolay Berdyaev.

César Vallejo

1892-1938

(Full name César Abraham Vallejo) Peruvian poet, short story writer, essayist, playwright, journalist, and novelist.

INTRODUCTION

Vallejo is considered one of the most important poets in modern Spanish American literature. Influenced by various political, intellectual, and aesthetic events and movements of the late nineteenth and early twentieth centuries—including communism, the Spanish civil war, Darwinism, and Spanish Modernism—his works are marked by inventive wordplay and stylistic experimentation. Thematically, Vallejo's poems are often concerned with social and political injustice, alienation, and the conflict between physical desire and spirituality.

Biographical Information

The youngest of eleven children, Vallejo was born into a lower middle-class family in Santiago de Chuco, Peru. He attended Trujillo University, where he earned his B.A. in 1915 as well as a degree in law; during this time he also published his first works in local newspapers. Associated with *Nuestra epoca,* a short-lived journal noted for its radical political opinions, he was implicated in the vandalism that occurred during a 1919 demonstration. Vallejo was imprisoned the following year and during his incarceration wrote several of the poems included in the 1922 volume *Trilce.* He left Peru in 1923 and settled permanently in Paris. He made several trips to Spain, where he met prominent writers and thinkers of the Generation of 1927, including Rafael Alberti and Federico García Lorca. A supporter of Loyalist forces in the Spanish civil war, Vallejo additionally helped establish the Spanish journal *Nuestra España* and wrote of his love and hopes for the country in *España, aparta de mí este cáliz* (*Spain, Let This Cup Pass from Me*). A registered Communist, he also made several trips to Russia; his experiences there as well as his leftist ideology are documented in the essay collection *Rusia en 1931* and *El tungsteno,* a novel focusing on capitalistic abuses inflicted on Peruvian miners. Vallejo died in Paris in 1938 at the age of forty-six.

Major Works

Vallejo's first poetry collection, *Los heraldos negros* (*The Black Heralds*), focuses on his memories of childhood, the landscape surrounding his birthplace, and the Indians indigenous to Peru. Noted for its use of decorative language, *The Black Heralds* is often considered to be largely influenced by Spanish *modernismo,* which derived many of its characteristic themes and stylistic traits from the French Symbolist and Decadent movements of the late nineteenth century. *Trilce,* Vallejo's second collection of poems, rep-

resents a marked shift in development and world view. Conveying the bitterness stemming from his prison experience and the anguish he associated with existence, *Trilce* concerns what Vallejo perceived as a conflict between humanity's animal nature and its constant struggle for—and inability to achieve—pure love, spiritual transcendence, and social harmony. In order to convey his vision of an absurd and hostile world, Vallejo shunned traditional poetic diction in favor of a more personal, "raw" language. For example, Vallejo used distorted syntax and unusual orthography to suggest disparate images and concepts in the posthumously published *Poemas humanos* (*Poemas humanos/Human Poems*), which emphasizes the plight of the poor and the individual's search for identity and purpose in a dehumanizing world.

Critical Reception

Despite the highly individualistic and idiosyncratic nature of his writings, Vallejo's poetry is considered to be of universal relevance. D. P. Gallagher has observed: "For Vallejo a poem is essentially a statement about Vallejo or about the human problems of which Vallejo is a microcosm. Language is not wrenched in order to achieve a new, unprecedented decorativeness, but rather in order to discover the man that has been hitherto hidden behind its decorative façades." Because of Vallejo's emphasis on ambiguity and manipulation of conventional standards of spelling and grammar, his writings are not readily accessible to English-language audiences. Nevertheless, among Spanish-speaking readers, he is frequently considered one of the greatest poets of the twentieth century.

PRINCIPAL WORKS

Los heraldos negros [*The Black Heralds*]   (poetry)   1918
Trilce   (poetry)   1922
Escalas melografiades   (novellas and short stories)   1923
Rusia en 1931: Reflexiones al pie del Kremlin   (essays)   1931
El tungsteno: La novela proletaria [*Tungsten*]   (novel)   1931
Poemas humanos [*Poemas humanos/Human Poems*]   (poetry)   1939
España, aparta de mí este cáliz [*Spain, Let This Cup Pass from Me*]   (poetry)   1940
Novelas y cuentos completos   (novellas and short stories)   1967
Obra poética completa   (poetry)   1968
César Vallejo: The Complete Posthumous Poetry   (poetry)   1978
Teatro completo   (dramas)   1979

CRITICISM

James Higgins   (essay date 1965)

SOURCE: "The Conflict of Personality in César Vallejo's *Poemas Humanos*," in *Bulletin of Hispanic Studies*, Vol. XLIII, No. 1, January, 1965, pp. 47-55.

[*In the excerpt below, Higgins discusses Vallejo's* Human Poems, *contending that this work demonstrates Vallejo's preoccupation with the theme of "the individual . . . continually at war with himself."*]

[Vallejo's] last and definitive book of verse, *Poemas humanos,* was published posthumously in 1939 and most of the poems were written in the latter years of Vallejo's life. Even the most superficial reading of this volume is enough to reveal what Guillermo de Torre [in "Reconocimiento critico de César Vallejo," *Revista Iberoamericana*, XXV (1960)] has called 'la propensión al desdoblamiento, al verse a sí mismo como un otro'. One is struck by the number of poems in which Vallejo is engaged in dialogue with himself:

> Tú surfres de una glándula endocrínica, se ve.
> Y bien? Te sana el metaloide pálido?

In other poems the poet dissociates himself completely from the figure of César Vallejo:

> Yo no sufro este dolor come César Vallejo.
>
> . . . . .
>
> César Vallejo, te odio con ternura!
>
> . . . . .
>
> César Vallejo ha muerto.

Elsewhere he puts his own existence in doubt and envisages the possibility of his being someone else:

> A lo mejor, soy otro.

At one point he speaks of himself as being two different people:

> Sé que hay una persona
> que me busca . . .
> Sé que hay una persona compuesta de mis
>   partes,
> a la que integro cuando va mi talle
> cabalgando en su exacta piedrecilla.

As [Xavier Abril in his *César Vallejo o la teoría póetica,* 1963] suggests, there appears to be some connexion between the theme of the double of 1923 and Vallejo's concern in the later years of his life to present himself as a personality in conflict: '*Poemas humanos* ratifica, con su obsesión del "otro," el motivo del "doble" revelado en **"Fabla salvaje"**.

What is the connexion? Is one to assume that Vallejo himself was a schizophrenic like Balta Espinar? It is well known that psychological factors, notably a mother fixation, a persecution complex and a tendency to obsessions played an important role in Vallejo's life and work. On the other hand, his poetry contains no references to schizophrenia as such, and from the little that is known of his life there is no evidence of the illness. While Vallejo is obviously working out his own personal problems to some extent in his poetry, it seems certain he did not suffer from the illness known as schizophrenia. The poet himself warns us against such a conclusion and offers us a clue to the interpretation of this conflict of personality:

> Pues de lo que hablo no es
> sino de lo que pasa en esa época, y
> de lo que ocurre en China y en España, y en el
>   mundo.
> (Walt Whitman tenía un pecho suavísimo y re-
>   spiraba
> y nadie sabe lo que él hacía cuando lloraba en su
>   comedor).

Vallejo is here claiming that this poetry, like Whitman's, is not concerned with his private preoccupations but with the situation of modern man. The implication is that this conflict of personality is not a mental illness but a moral condition he shares with other men. It would seem plausible that in 1923 Vallejo was interested in the mental illness of Balta Espinar because he saw in it the image of a moral illness affecting the whole of mankind. By the time he came to write *Poemas humanos* he had become obsessed with this idea and he presents man as a being at war with himself. This is confirmed by a line defining man as

> el bimano, el muy bruto, el muy filósofo

Thus, it is man, torn by the different parts of his nature—in this case by the conflict between body and spirit—rather than the poet himself, who is pursued and haunted by a double.

For Vallejo the tragedy of man is that he aspires to an integrated, unified existence, but finds himself divided in a state of inner discord. There is in man an essential duality: the divergent parts of his nature are in constant conflict and are never able to fuse together and harmonize. Basically, Vallejo sees this conflict as one between that part of man which longs to be free to develop its potentialities and to forge an existence which will be spiritually fulfilling, and that part of him which is determined and limited by forces outside his control: heredity, environment, education, physical and psychological needs. This is the theme of the prose poem **"Algo te identifica"** where technical features—parallel sentences, each term of the one corresponding and standing in opposition to a term in the other; the opposition of terms within a sentence—contribute to the picture of forces in conflict. The personality that aspires to liberty cannot break free from the claims of the predetermined personality:

> Algo te identifica con el que se aleja de ti, y es la
> facultad común de volvver: de ahí tu más grande pesadumbre.

Neither can it conform to the limits imposed upon it:

> Algo te separa del que se queda contigo, y es la esclavitud común de partir: de ahí tus más nimios regocijos.

The result is that the individual is continually at war with himself, one part of him yearning to move off in search of freedom and fulfilment but held back by the inert weight of the other. To convey this idea Vallejo employs one of his most characteristic techniques: the juxtaposition of words which contradict each other. Men, he says,

> yacen marchando al son de las fronteras o, simplemente, marcan el paso inmóvil en el borde del mundo.

This conflict is occasionally presented in terms of the tension between the natural and the civilized man. The individual seeks to develop the fundamental tendencies of his nature, to build up his own personal style of life, but the social man has to conform to the claims of society. He is forced to play the role of businessman, schoolteacher or labourer, adopting the habits and the uniform of the part:

> . . . el hombre procede suavemente del trabajo
> y repercute jefe, suena subordinado.

For Vallejo all social activity is based on postures. Man rises in the morning and does not start living until he has dressed himself in a personality which he wears all the waking day:

> He aquí que hoy saludo, me pongo el cuello y vivo.

Thus dressed, he is ready to face the world and to attend to his affairs, but in so doing he has lost contact with the essential part of himself and produced a split in his personality.

> Tal me recibo de hombre, tal más bien me despido.

In general, however, it is on the conflict between man's spiritual nature and the physical, between the 'filósofo' and the 'bruto', that Vallejo fixes his attention. As André Coyné has pointed out [in his *César Vallejo y su obra poética,* 1958], *Poemas humanos* is characterized by 'la obsesión de la animalidad.' Vallejo makes references to Darwin and, in accordance with his theory of evolution, considers man to be little more than an advanced animal species. This attitude leads him to employ the names of animals to designate man. The latter is varyingly described as 'mamífero', 'mono', 'paquidermo', 'cetáceo', 'plesiosaurio', 'kanguro', 'jumento', 'conejo', 'elefante', but perhaps the most crushing epithet is that of 'antropoide'. For if, instead of taking anthropoid to mean an animal of the ape family, one interprets it literally, one arrives at the ultimate irony of seeing man classified as an animal resembling man.

> **For Vallejo the tragedy of man is that he aspires to an integrated, unified existence, but finds himself divided in a state of inner discord. There is in man an essential duality: the divergent parts of his nature are in constant conflict and are never able to fuse together and harmonize.**
>
> **—James Higgins**

Rarely can a poet have insisted so much on the human organism and on the role it plays in the life of man. *Poemas humanos* contains no less than ninety-nine different nouns referring to the human anatomy and there are times when the reader requires the aid of a medical dictionary. What emerges is a picture of man dominated by bodily appetites and functions. Food appears as man's primary need and hunger—or rather a state of utter privation, a dark night of the body in which bread assumes an almost mystical significance—is one of the great themes of the book. In **"Parado en una piedra"** Vallejo shatters the myth of the triumph of mind over matter by showing the effect of hunger on the individual. Hunger brings on delirium, interfering with the reasoning faculty and causing man to rave: his only reaction is blind unthinking rage against the world:

> cómo clava el relámpago
> su fuerza sin cabeza en su cabeza!

The poet also reacts against idealized conceptions of human love. In his poetry all romantic transcendence is reduced to an elemental sensuality, or, as Coyné puts it, to a 'sensación general de bienestar córporeo'. The sexual act itself is stripped of all refinement and presented in the crudest terms, as when the poet describes himself

> . . . ascendiendo y sudando
> y haciendo lo infinito entre tus muslos.

He equally brushes aside the conventions of polite speech and poetic language to impress on the reader the importance that the acts of excretion assume in his life. At one point he is to be found 'al pie de un urinario' at another 'pujando, / bajandome los pantalones.'

Poemas humanos reveals, too, the depths of degradation to which a man can fall when his bodily needs are not satisfied. Driven by starvation, he grabbles for a few scraps like a rat in a rubbish heap:

> . . . busca en el fango huesos, cáscaras.

He wallows in filth and, losing all sense of his own dignity, becomes accustomed to it:

> . . . sienta, ráscase, extrae un piojo de su axila,
> mátalo.

Exposed to malnutrition, cold and dirt, he succumbs to illness:

> . . . tiembla de frío, tose, escupe sangre.

The final blow to human dignity is when man, the highest creature in the universe, is laid low by microbes:

> acaban los destinos en bacterias

For Vallejo there is no greater proof of the insignificance and the limitations of man.

Man, then, is an animal, but he is also a spiritual being. If he were simply an animal he would enjoy the uncomplicated existence of an unthinking beast, the sublime, baja perfección del cerdo. He is an animal who thinks and feels and aspires to rise above his animal state. His greatest suffering springs from his inability to do so. In this sense the title of one of his poems is significant: **"El alma que sufrió de ser su cuerépo."** Man aspires to an existence which will fulfil his deepest spiritual needs but the limitations of his physical nature deny him such fulfilment. Thus Vallejo observes:

> éste es mi brazo
> que por su cuenta rehusó ser ala.

He feels his body to be an immense inert weight anchoring him to the ground and preventing him from rising to the heights:

> Reanudo mi dìa de conejo,
> mi noche de elefante en descanso.

He strives after the spiritual and is condemned to the material. Just as Christ was crowned with thorns, man suffers the affliction of his animal nature, of his 'corona de carne.'

An essential feature of *Poemas humanos* is the attempt to surmount the state of duality to which man is condemned. At times Vallejo sees it as a question of transcending the personality imposed on man by forces outside him. This is the theme of **"Palmas y guitarras"** in which he speaks of love as a means of attaining to spiritual plenitude. The poet here invites the woman to come with her two personalities to him with his two personalities:

> Ahora, entre nosotros, aquí,
> ven conmigo, trae por la mano a tu cuerpo.

He invites her to unite with him in the act of love through which she will transcend her imposed personality and life as it is ordinarily lived, thus discovering her true essence and reaching a higher plane of existence where her spiritual aspirations will be satisfied:

> Ven a mí, si, y a ti, sí
> con paso par, a vernos a los dos con paso impar,
> marcar el paso de la despedida.
> Hasta cuando volvamos! Hasta la vuelta! . . .
>
> . . . . .
>
> Hasta cuando volvamos, despidámonos!

Xavier Abril [in his *Vallejo: Ensayo de aproximación critica,* 1938] has shown that Quevedo exercised a major influence on Vallejo and indeed the Peruvian was much more steeped in the writings of the Spanish Golden Age than is normally recognized. Here he employs a series of paradoxes reminiscent of the Spanish mystics and *conceptistas.* These paradoxes put the reader face to face with a number of contradictions—in coming to the poet, the woman is coming to herself; through an act which is a part of the normal course of life, the lovers go above and beyond the normal; the union of the lovers is a parting—and by demanding of him an effort of thought, force him to realize that the contradictions are only apparent and that there exists a plane of reality beyond the limits of contradiction. The act of love is thus seen as a journey to another world on which the lovers' spiritual personalities embark, leaving their imposed personalities behind in this world:

> Hoy mismo, hermosa, . . .
>
> . . . . .
>
> saldremos de nosotros, dos a dos.

Though in this poem Vallejo speaks of transcending his physical condition, it is obvious that the act of love implies the harmonious fusion of the physical and the spiritual. Much of his work is concerned with the attempt to achieve unity, with 'la persecución apasionada de una unidad en la cual se reconciliarían todos los contrarios'. In **"Oye a tu masa,"** Vallejo urges man to take account of the duality of his nature:

> Oye a tu masa, a tu cometa, escúchalos . . .
> oye a la túnica en que estás dormido,
> oye a tu desnudez, dueña del sueño.

Man must take into account his animal nature (masa) and the spiritual (cometa), his social personality (symbolized by the tunic and which forces the individual's intimate personality to lie dormant) and his intimate personality (symbolized by nakedness and which takes over in sleep when the consciousness is no longer in control). He must seek to achieve a balance between the divergent parts of his nature, allowing no one to dominate:

> Bestia dichosa, piensa;
> dios desgraciado, quìtate la frente.

Luego, hablaremos,

Only in this way, by balancing the conflicting forces within him, can man become a unified, integrated personality.

"Oye a tu masa" speaks of the necessity for equilibrium as a basis for unity and **"Palmas y guitarras"** of the possibility of achieving unity through love but in *Poemas humanos* only three poems—**"Al fin, un monte,"** **"Entre el zolor y el placer,"** and **"Hallazgo de la vida"**—offer any evidence of the actual attainment of such a state. What emerges is rather a conviction that duality is permanent and irremediable. In the poem **"Nómina de huesos"** which is a kind of litany of human limitations, it is found to be impossible to compare man with himself, to harmonize his conflicting personalities:

Se pedía a grandes voces:

. . . . .

—Que le comparen consigo mismo.
Y esto no fue posible.

No matter how much the poet might strive to overcome the division within him, he keeps coming back to his reality as a personality in conflict with himself:

Y aun
alcanzo, llego hasta mí avión de dos asientos.

The plane, symbol of the poet's aspirations and strivings, comes back to its starting point like a boomerang. Significantly it has two seats: the number two, with its connotations of duality, recurs again and again in the poetry of Vallejo.

It is on the conflict between man's spiritual nature and the physical, between the 'filósofo' and the 'bruto', that Vallejo fixes his attention. Vallejo makes references to Darwin and, in accordance with his theory of evolution, considers man to be little more than an advanced animal species.

—James Higgins

Not only does the poet fail to escape from division but he comes to realize that fragmentation goes beyond a simple duality. In **"Cuatro conciencias"** he speaks of four separate forces struggling for domination within his mind. Juan Larrea [in his *César Vallejo o Hispanoamérica en la cruz de su razón,* 1957] has suggested a parallel between this poem and William Blake's *Vala, or the Four Zoas,* a psychological poem which takes place in the human brain where Tharmas, Luvah, Urizen and Los, symbols of instinct, emotion, intellect and imagination, wage war on one another for mastery of the mind. It seems valid to interpret Vallejo's poem in this light, but what is really interesting from our point of view is the dawning of the insight

that the fragmentation of the human personality is not simple but multiple:

Cuatro consciencias
simultáneas enrédanse en la mía!

. . . . .

No puedo concebirlo; as aplastante.

In this course of *Poemas humanos* one becomes aware that not only is fragmentation multiple but that it multiplies, that it is not a state but an unending process. To a certain extent Vallejo was sustained by his humanitarian-political beliefs, by his immense love of his fellow men, his deep sense of solidarity with the rest of suffering humanity, his belief in the need for united action to combat evil and injustice. In the main, however his poetry is the poetry of a man crushed by life and obsessed by the horror of death and for whom experience has meant a progressive demoralization of his personality. This becomes obvious from a reading of the poem **"La paz, la avispa, el taco, las vertientes"** where the poet records a premonition of his impending death. In his terror he feels the whole universe to be collapsing about him and himself to be disintegrating with it. He is surrounded by chaos and chaos is rooted in his being. Since the logic of ordinary language would falsify such an experience, Vallejo seeks to express it by babbling a seemingly senseless enumeration of words. The first stanza enumerates a series of nouns, the second a series of adjectives, the third a series of gerunds, the fourth a series of adverbs and indefinite expressions, and the fifth a series of substantivized adjectives. The only coherence lies in that all of the these words appear to refer in some way to death and to the sentiments it arouses in the poet. Thus the third stanza seems to refer to the poet reviewing his situation at the moment of death and leaves us with the impression of a personality that has gone completely to pieces:

Ardiendo, comparando,
viviendo, enfureciéndose,
golpeando, analizando, oyendo, estremeciéndose,
muriendo, sosteniéndose, situándose,
llorando . . .

Vallejo reacts to the injustice of such an existence as the poor man reacts to the injustice of society—with rage. But such rage is impotent and, unable to find an object to strike at, turns inwards, consuming him like a poison and bringing about further disintegration:

La cólera que al árbol quiebra en hojas,
a la hoja en botones desiguales
y al botón, en ranuras telescópicas;
la cólera del probe
tiene dos ríos contra muchos mares.

The final irony is that man's only defence completes his demoralization.

In conclusion, then, it may be said that the protagonist of **"Fabla salvaje,"** a man haunted by a double, foreshadows man as he appears in *Poemas humanos:* a being who aspires to unity and is condemned to duality, and who undergoes a deterioration of his condition until division becomes complete disintegration.

Keith A. McDuffie   (essay date 1968)

SOURCE: "César Vallejo: Profile of a Poet," in *Proceedings: Pacific Northwest Conference on Foreign Languages,* Vol. XIX, April 19-20, 1968, pp. 135-43.

[*In the following overview of Vallejo's poetry, McDuffie examines the thematic and stylistic features of* Trilce, Black Heralds, *and* Human Poems, *as well as Vallejo's place in twentieth-century Hispanic literature.*]

The poetry of César Vallejo has received increasing attention both within and without the Hispanic world since the premature death of the Peruvian *mestizo* poet on the eve of World War II. Now, nearly seventy-five years since his birth in a small town of the Peruvian sierra, Santiago de Chuco, and thirty years since his untimely death on Good Friday of 1938 in Paris, his reputation continues to grow. Evidence of his international stature is the fact that he has attracted the attention of critics writing in Italian, Portuguese, German, English, Swedish, Hebrew, Russian and French, and translations of his poetry exist in most of these languages.

It is our purpose here to trace briefly the poetic development of Vallejo as represented in his three books of poems, *Los heraldos negros, Trilce* and the posthumous *Poems humanos.* By placing Vallejo's work within an historical perspective we may arrive at a clearer evaluation of his originality and position in the panorama of Twentieth Century Hispanic-American poetry.

At least two distinct concepts of poetic style characterize Vallejo's first book of poems, *Los heraldos negros.* One concept immediately recongizeable may be traced to those Modernists writing principally between 1900 and 1916, primarily the Leopoldo Lugones of *Lunario sentimental* and above all the Uruguayan poet Julio Herrera y Reissig. These influences are hardly surprising for a young poet writing between 1915 and 1918, the latter date marking the publication of the first edition in Lima. Vallejo employs luxurious ornament, refined colors, religious imagery defining the profane posture of the *poète maudit,* nervous crises, morbid flights of melancholy into a world of synesthesias and exotic half-tones—in short, all the poetic apparatus of one phase of Modernism, with its roots in Baudelaire, Laforgue, Samain, Verlaine, Mallarmé and Poe, passing through Darío to Lugones and Herrera y Reissig.

Most of the poems exhibiting these characteristics are love poems, which comprise fully half of Vallejo's first work. Despite their derivative quality, they do not disguise the poet's anguished search for permanence in a world of change, and his developing concept of death as the only real solution to the limitations of material existence.

The second and more original concept of poetic expression to be found in *Los heraldos negros* is best exemplified in those poems in which the poet evokes memories of his native sierra, of his family and childhood home, and especially of his mother; or those poems in which he expresses

a growing sense of compassion for the suffering of his fellow men. In such poems Vallejo discards the luxurious ornamentation and refined vocabulary inherited from the Modernists in favor of images and vocabulary drawn from everyday experience. In addition, there is a tendency to move away from fixed verse and stanza forms toward freer rhythms more closely approximating those of speech. Poetic form is increasingly dictated by the expressive requirements of the material, rather than being imposed from without by exterior patterns.

Beginning his poetic career firmly in the path of tradition, Vallejo left behind the poetics inherited from certain Modernist poets, but continued the spirit of Modernism by declaring in *Trilce* absolute freedom for the poet.

— *Keith A. McDuffie*

At its farthest remove from the effete cosmopolitanism of the love poems, this new voice of the poet attains a bewildered, child-like innocence:

> Y en esta hora fría, en que la tierra
> trasciende a polvo humano y es tan triste,
> quisiera yo tocar todas las puertas,
> y suplicar a no sé quién, perdón,
> y hacerle pedacitos de pan fresco
> aquí, en el horno de mi corazón . . . !
> ("El pan nuestro")

A deceptively simple diction conveys deep emotion, as in a poem to his dead brother:

> Hermano, hoy estoy en el poyo de la casa,
> donde nos haces una falta sin fondo!
> ("A mi hermano Miguel")

The imagery and the distortion of normal linguistic patterns show increasing boldness and effectiveness:

> Y mi madre pasea allé en los huertos,
> saboreando un sabor ya sin sabor.
> Está ahora tan suave,
> tan ala, tan salida, tan amor.
> ("Los pasos lejanos")

Humble images take on transcendental implications:

> Ya nos hemos sentado
> mucho a la mesa, con la amargura de un niño
> que a media noche, llora de hambre, desvelado . . .
> Y cuándo nos veremos con los demás, al borde
> de una mañana eterna, desayunados todos!
> ("La cena miserable")

This transcendental hunger for life reflects the fact that the roots of the poet's affliction are beyond the physical, are indeed metaphysical:

> Hay un vacío
> en mi aire metafísico

que nadie ha de palpar:
el claustro de un silencio
que habló a flor de fuego.

Yo nací un dìa
que Dios estuvo enfermo.

("Espergesia")

Los heraldos negros is a transitional work; pointing backward to a period which the consensus of critics consider to have ended by 1916, the year of Rubén Darìo's death. But the most original poems point toward Vallejo's second book *Trilce,* which appeared in 1922, shortly before he left Peru permanently for Europe. An example of the continuity between *Los heraldos negros* and *Trilce* is the poem *"Trilce* III":

Las personas mayores
a qué hora volverán?
Da las seis el ciego Santiago,
y ya está muy oscuro.
Madre dijo que no demoraría.

Aguedita, Nativa, Miguel
cuidado con ir por ahí, por donde
acaban de pasar gangueando sus memorias
dobladoras penas,
hacia el silencioso corral, y por donde
las gallinas que se están acostando todavía,
se han espantado tanto.
Major estemos aquí no más.
Madre dijo que no demoraría.

The colloquially intimate expression of this poem reminds us again of Vallejo's poem to his dead brother Miguel, the poem with which *Los heraldos negros* closes:

Miguel, tú te escondiste
una noche de agosto, al alborear;
pero, en vez de ocultarte riendo, estabas triste.
Y tu gemelo corazón de esas tardes
extintas se ha aburrido de no encontrarte. Y ya
cae sombra en el alma.

Oye, hermano, no tardes
en salir. Bueno? Puede inquietarse mamá.

("A mi hermano Miguel")

To a greater or lesser extent, this tone and style are employed in *Trilce* when Vallejo deals with certain intimate themes, such as memories of his mother and his childhood, and in two instances, his youthful experiences of love.

But like *Los heraldos negros, Trilce* is a work characterized by two different concepts of poetic expression, and it is the second of these that led the distinguished critic Enrique Anderson Imbert to term *Trilce* a work of pure poetic rebellion, a literary explosion in which the poet blows to bits all literary traditions [*Historia de la literature hispano-americana* (1961)]. The description is hyperbolic, but effectively indicates the predominance of this style in the work as a whole. Other critics have called *Trilce* "surrealistic," forgetting that it was published two years before André Breton published the *Surrealist Manifesto* in 1924. That *Trilce* was strongly influenced by the various literary "Isms" following the First World War is unquestionable: above all, the Hispanic movements: *ultraísmo,* headed by Jorge Luis Borges, and Vicente Huidobro's *creacionismo.*

More than influencing Vallejo in specific poetic techniques, however, these movements created a mood of iconoclastic freedom which gave impetus to the direction in which Vallejo was moving in *Los heraldos negros.* The importance awarded the metaphor as the basic element of poetic creation in both *ultraísmo* and *creacionismo* does not apply to *Trilce.* Huidobro had said in his "Arte poética": "Por qué cantáis la rosa ¡oh Poetas! / Hacedla florecer en el poema." The concept was not new with Huidobro. In 1893 the Cuban poeta Julián del Casal had echoed his master Baudelaire when he declared in the poem "En el campo" [which was included in Julio Caillet Bois's 1965 edition of *Antología de la poesía hispano-americano*]:

Más que la voz del pájaro en la cima
de un árbol todo en flor, a mi alma anima
la música armoniosa de una rima.

The superiority of human creation to Nature amounted to a program for much vanguard poetry; in Vallejo, Nature is hardly more than an expressionistic reflection of human emotions. Rather than create his own poetic world in *competition* with exterior Nature, Vallejo is more concerned with discovering his own inner nature, using frequently elements of Nature to do so.

In Vallejo, Nature is hardly more than an expressionistic reflection of human emotions. Rather than create his own poetic world in competition with exterior Nature, Vallejo is more concerned with discovering his own inner nature, using frequently elements of Nature to do so.

— Keith A. McDuffie

[In his 1962 *César Vallejo o la teoría poética,* the] poet and critic Xavier Abril considers the primary influence on *Trilce* to be Mallarmé's poem "Un coup de dés," entitled "Una jugada de dados jamás abolirá el acaso" in the Spanish translation published by the Sevillian critic Rafael Cansino-Assens in 1919. The characteristics of this influence, according to Abril, are the psychological rather than the logical use of words, the tendency of the poetic anecdote to resolve itself into an abstraction and the creation of images, particularly those based on numbers, which evoke a concept of the absolute as a means of escaping temporal limitations.

But already in *Los heraldos negros,* published prior to the appearance of Mallarmé's poem in Spanish, Vallejo was moving toward a poetics that was to predominate in his second work. In the poem **"Absoluta"** the poet begins:

Color de ropa antigua. Un Julio a sombra,
y un Agosto recién segado. Y una
mano de agua que injertó en el pino
resinoso de un tedio malas frutas.

We are close here to the technique of *Trilce.* Vallejo's

imagination has assimilated natural elements and returned them in a new order based on emotional, not logical, necessity. The specific poetic procedure here is that of representing abstract emotions concretely. *"Trilce XVII"* is an example of the same technique:

> Junio, eras nuestro. Junio, y en tus hombros
> me paro a carcajear, secando
> mi metro y mis bolsillos
> en tus 21 uñas de estación.

Frequently Vallejo reverses the process, making abstract what was concrete, as in *Trilce* XX:

> . . . Pues apenas
> acerco el 1 a 1 para no caer.

At times both processes are joined in dizzying leaps from the concrete to the abstract and back again. An example is *"Trilce* LV":

> Ya la tarde pasó diez y seis veces por el
>
> subsuelo empatrullado,
> Y se está casi ausente
> en el número de madera amarilla
> de la cama que está desocupada tanto tiempo
> allá
> enfrente.

The great majority of poems, in their rejection of rational and logical order in favor of an emotional interpretation of reality, reflect the author's profoundly pessimistic view of the world in which he finds himself: a world where absurdity and injustice are perpetuated by unassailable logic. Language is the poet's only weapon, and it is bent to his own purposes as he attempts to express his experience of life: ". . . esta existencia que todaviza / perenne imperfección," as Vallejo exclaims in *"Trilce* XXXVI".

[In his 1958 *Valoración de Vallejo* the] Argentine critic Saul Yukievich has dismissed certain poems of *Trilce* either as antipoetry by definition or as automatic writing in the most orthodox surrealist manner. But the latter observation ignores the fact that André Bretón did not define automatic writing until two years after the appearance of *Trilce.* A more accurate criticism of the most difficult poems is that their emotional unity seems insufficiently molded for the reader to penetrate their hermetic surfaces. The word "seems" is used advisedly, for it is possible that many of their secrets may yet be clarified by sympathetic analysis.

Trilce, published three years before Pablo Neruda unleashed the verbal chaos of his *Tentativa de un hombre infinito,* and nine years before Vicente Huidobro published *Altazor,* was an historic declaration of poetic freedom in Spanish America. It was and remains a startling work, full of private images, capricious spellings, distorted syntax, deliberate violations of grammar, as well as a great number of archaic, neologistic and colloquial expressions. But unlike so much vanguard poetry, *Trilce* retains a human element under all its linguistic and typographical peculiarities, its liberal use of scientific and technical vocabulary, its torrent of invented words and plays with pure sound. This element is primarily an emotional concept of man as essentially an orphan who must search relentlessly for his

redemption in love. In his second work, Vallejo had turned primarily inward upon his own condition, but in the last years of his life, his gaze turned outward. In his final work, *Poemas humanos,* he was to give definitive expression to his emotions of love and compassion for his fellow men.

Poemas humanos shows an intensified preoccupation with the animal misery of his own life, the last years of which were spent in Paris in a descending cycle of poverty and ill health. At the same time, Vallejo developed a greatly intensified feeling of compassion for the poor and oppressed he saw everywhere about him. The style of these poems is the seed that *Trilce* planted, now full-grown and flowered into a more direct, less hermetic expression. In their totality, the poems are a concatentation of men, animals and things that absorb into themselves the poet's intense emotions, until they lose their original natures and become extraordinary symbols of the poet's psychic life:

> Jamás, hombres humanos,
> hubo tanto dolor en el pecho, en la solapa en la
>   cartera,
> en el vaso, en el carnicería, en la aritmética!
> Jamás tanto cariño doloroso,
> jamás tan cerca arremetió lo lejos,
> jamás el fuego nunca
> jugó mejor su rol de frío muerto!
>
> Jamás señor ministro de salud, fue la salud
> más mortal
> y la migrana extrajo tanta frente de la frente!
>
> Y el mueble tuvo en su cajón, dolor,
> el corazón, en su cajón, dolor,
> la lagartija, en su cajón, dolor.
>   **("Los nueve monstruos")**

The poet's suffering has its roots in the basic human condition:

> Tengo un miedo terrible de ser un animal
> de blanca nieve, que sostuvo padre
> y madre, con su sola circulación venosa,
> y que, este dìa espléndido, solar y arzobispal,
> dìa que representa así a la noche,
> linealmente
> elude este animal estar contento, respirar
> y transformarse y tener plata.

But his own anguish does not obscure the suffering of others:

> Hay gentes tan desgraciadas, que ni siquiera
> tienen cuerpo; cuantitativo el pelo,
> baja, en pulgadas, la genial pesadumbre;

Considering the plight of so much of mankind, most of the preoccupations of Western culture seem irrelevant, even frivolous:

> Un cojo pasa dando el brazo a un niño
> Voy, después, a leer a André Bretón?
>
>   . . . . .
>
> Otro busca en el fango huesos, cáscaras
> Cómo escribir, después, del infinito?

Before such scenes, poetic expression seems inadequate:

Un albañil cae de un techo, muere, y ya no al-
    muerza
Innovar, luego, el tropo, la metáfora?

The poet's rage at injustice contains at its center an immense tenderness for his fellow man:

La cólera que quiebra al hombre en niños,
que quiebra al niño, en pájaros iguales,
y al pájaro, después, en huevecillos;
la cólera del pobre
tiene un aceite contra dos vinagres.

His desire to participate in the founding of a new order led
Vallejo to join the Communist party, a choice made by
many intellectuals during the Thirties, for reasons similar
to those Vallejo expresses in his book *Rusia en 1931. Al
pie del Kremlin.* But the latter is a journalistic defense of
Communism, and it is not accurate to call either Vallejo
the poet or his poetry Communist, as has been done by
critics with certain extraliterary considerations in mind.
Vallejo himself stressed the fact that the artist, since he is
first of all a human being, is a political subject, but that
his purpose is not to propagandize any catechism or collection of specific ideas. Instead, it is to create political
ideals in the broadest sense, that is to say, humane ideals
and desires in men.

> **Vallejo was one of the first Hispanic-
> American poets to incorporate into his
> concept of poetry the most lasting message
> of the numerous artistic movements
> following the First World War: the
> breakdown of the old order and the absurd
> materialistic logic on which it was based,
> and the concomitant need to attempt a
> reintegration of reality which would award
> priority to the deepest emotional needs of
> man.**
>
> **— *Keith A. McDuffie***

Vallejo saw in the outcome of the Spanish Civil War
Spain's and the world's hope for a better future, and in a
series of poems entitled *España, aparta de mí este cáliz,*
he raised a call to battle and self-sacrifice, hailing the common man's opportunity to redeem himself by dying so that
his posterity might truly live. The epic tradition of the de-
casyllable is invoked in the tercets of the **"Redoble fúnebre
a los escombros de Durango":**

Padre polvo que vas al futuro,
Dios te salve, te guíe y te dé alas,
padre polvo que vas al futuro.

But the Falangist troops were winning as the hour of Vallejo's death grew near. As if unable to do anything more
for Spain and his fellow man, Vallejo could only express
his community with them in death: "En suma, no poseo
para mi vida sino mi muerte." It came to him April 15,
1938, in Paris.

Beginning his poetic career firmly in the path of tradition,
Vallejo left behind the poetics inherited from certain Modernist poets, but continued the spirit of Modernism by declaring in *Trilce* absolute freedom for the poet. He was one
of the first Hispanic-American poets to incorporate into
his concept of poetry the most lasting message of the numerous artistic movements following the First World
War: the breakdown of the old order and the absurd mate-
rialistic logic on which it was based, and the concomitant
need to attempt a reintegration of reality which would
award priority to the deepest emotional needs of man. In
his final poems he catalogued his own physical disintegration and spiritual anguish as he watched the social and
moral disintegration of a Europe rushing headlong toward
its second major upheaval of the century. But at the same
time, Vallejo declared his passionate faith in man's ability
to overcome his animal nature, with all its limitations, in
order to progress spiritually. In the willingness of the common man to redeem life on this earth by sacrificing himself
for the common good, Vallejo found his only hope for a
better world. This was essentially the message he left in his
final poems, expressed in a more immediately intelligible
style than he had employed in *Trilce,* so that all men
might hear and understand him.

> **Vallejo and Spain:**
>
> [Vallejo's] archetype was the infantile complex be-
> queathed to Peru by mother Spain, a colonization with-
> out resolution, a complex that seeks to be reabsorbed,
> that searches out its own dispersion, its death. Vallejo's
> journey was from mother to Mother, Spain was his Eu-
> ropean center of gravity; it is as if he crawled there to de-
> posit his gold. In Vallejo the poetry of a scourged coun-
> try seeks its rapist, to return to the rapist the very life
> that was defiled, and this return is made as the rapist it-
> self is dying; in this sense is there a mesh, that profound
> resolution we feel is archetypal, and to put it this way of
> course says very little about the personal César who wan-
> dered in Europe for fifteen years, making five trips to
> Spain interspersed with three trips to Russia, all of them
> from his base in Paris. He went to Paris, he tells us, "to
> be a son," yet the French could not really baptise him,
> or, to put it another way, it was only in the revolutionary
> crossfire of Spain and Russia that the eternal Peruvian
> boy, magnetized to the art center of the Western World,
> was able to *become* a son.
>
> *Clayton Eshleman, in his "César against Vallejo," in*
> Parnassus: Poetry in Review, *Spring-Summer, 1973.*

The Times Literary Supplement (essay date 1969)

SOURCE: "Visions of Solidarity," in *The Times Literary
Supplement,* No. 3526, September 25, 1969, p. 1098.

[*In the following review of* Poemas humanos/Human
Poems, *the critic provides an overview and comparison of*
The Black Heralds, Trilce, *and* Human Poems.]

The Peruvian poet César Vallejo died in Paris on April 15,

1938, leaving behind him in manuscript the ninety-four poems first published in the following year under the title of *Poemas Humanos.* Many of these poems were written or revised only a few months before his death; together with his other volumes, *Los Heraldos Negros* (1919), *Trilce* (1922) and the sequence of fifteen poems, *España, aparta de mi este cáliz,* inspired by the Spanish Civil War, they form a highly original body of verse which establishes Vallejo beyond any doubt as a major twentieth-century poet, whose continuing influence in the Spanish-speaking countries is comparable only to that of Neruda.

Though his three principal collections are markedly different from one another, they present an impressive continuity of both themes and technique. Many of the poems in his first volume, *Los Heraldos Negros,* take their vocabulary and mood from slightly older Latin-American poets, notably from Rubén Darío. Yet, despite the conscious imitation of prevailing modes, there are already signs of a strong personality in the process of finding its own forms. The experience behind the best of these poems is deeply rooted in Vallejo's native Peru: the tensions of adolescence, set in the framework of a conventional Catholic upbringing, horror at the exploitation of native labour, and nostalgia for the dying grandeur of the pre-Columbian heritage. These things converge at times in a sense of the pointlessness of human suffering and a conviction that God, if he exists, must himself be an imperfect, suffering being.

In *Trilce,* the rhetoric which occasionally flaws the earlier poems is completely discarded; expression is cut down to the bone, resulting in a language which, though often obscure, is wholly authentic and original. The technique of these poems has sometimes been described as Surrealism *avant la lettre;* it would be more accurate to say that Vallejo's deliberate rejection of logical discourse comes from a deeply personal need to explore the sources of his anguish at their most primitive and pre-articulate level. At this stage, Vallejo's poetry is haunted by the feeling of being orphaned in an absurd universe, in which any desire for individual redemption seems doomed to failure. The intricate number symbolism which plays a large part in these poems embodies the sense that life is a process of constant and progressive fragmentation: that the ideal unity of being is continually broken in existence, and that time develops in a proliferation of separate units which is ended only by death. The most moving poems in *Trilce,* however, arise directly from Vallejo's own circumstances: the death of his mother, which was to remain a constant obsession in his work, and the break-up of his childhood home, are transmuted, with no loss of concrete detail, into an analogy of the human condition itself.

The full implications of this do not appear until *Poemas Humanos.* The two collections are separated by a gap of sixteen years, during which Vallejo lived in Paris, often under conditions of poverty and illness, and became increasingly interested in Marxism. (The experience of two trips to Russia and his meetings with Russian writers of the time, including Mayakovsky, are recorded in his prose-work *Rusia en 1931,* which forms an important source for the understanding of his later poetry.) In terms

of his verse, Vallejo's Marxism seems a natural climax, rather than a sudden conversion: the vision of human solidarity which appears in his later poems owes as much to the Christian notion of brotherly love and to the now magnified image of the childhood home as to any strictly Communist ideology. Compared with *Trilce,* the rhythms of *Poemas Humanos* are generally more sweeping and, except in the superb final poems, less intense. Nevertheless, it is remarkable how much of the very individual language of *Trilce* is carried over, as Vallejo moves from the analysis of his personal fears to that of the human situation as a whole, a transition made possible by the complete lack of self-regard which is one of the most striking features of his work.

Perhaps the greatest virtue of Mr. Eshleman's edition [of *Poemas Humanos/Human Poems*] is that it contains what is probably the best available text of Vallejo's own poems. As for his translations, he has wisely resisted the temptation to "re-create" the originals, and has provided a literal version which should be very helpful to any reader with a moderate knowledge of Spanish who is prepared to tackle the poems themselves. The problems of translating Vallejo are in any case formidable, though recent versions by Robert Bly, Charles Tomlinson and others show that certain poems, at least, can be brought over effectively into English. Much of his work, however, allows the translator very little scope for manoeuvre, so closely is the actual sound of the language implicated in the expression. As an American poet, Mr. Eshleman has clearly been encouraged by the exponents of Projective Verse, whose own experiments in the physiological basis of poetic utterance have something in common with Vallejo's practice. Inevitably, his versions often fall short of the musical assurance which lends conviction to the originals, even where one can only grope for the meaning.

More seriously, there are occasional errors of translation which make for unnecessary obscurity. Thus, the climax of one poem it spoilt by the rendering of its final line: "la cantidad enonme de dineroque cuesta el ser pobre" means, not "the enormous quantity of money it costs the poor being", but "the enormous quantity . . . it costs to be poor". Similarly, another crucial line—"tan puro de miseria está el creyente"—is made to mean its exact opposite: not "the believer is so full of malice", but "the believer is so free from malice". There are about a dozen mistakes of this order, all of which could easily be revised. However, this qualification apart, Mr. Eshleman's book, with its informative introduction, should supply many readers with an excellent introduction to one of the most compassionate and verbally inventive poets of this century.

D. P. Gallagher   (essay date 1973)

SOURCE: "César Vallejo (Peru, 1892-1938)," in *Modern Latin American Literature,* Oxford University Press, London, 1973, pp. 11-38.

[*In the essay below, Gallagher provides an overview of Vallejo's career.*]

Vallejo's first book of poems, *Los heraldos negros* (1918), is at first sight a derivative work, and one or two poems in it could easily have been written by Rubén Darío, others by Herrera y Reissig or Lugones. Take the opening stanza of 'Nochebuena' ('Christmas Eve'):

> Al callar la orquesta, pasean veladas
> sombras femeninas bajo los ramajes,
> por cuya hojarasca se filtran heladas
> quimeras de luna, pálidos celajes

> ['When the orchestra falls silent, veiled / female shadows stride beneath the branches / through whose foliage are filtered / frozen whims of moon, pallid skyscapes.']

—a purely decorative description that parades all the portentous hush, the hectically contrived mystery of fleeting feminine presences, the subtly filtered light effects, the delicate pallors of *modernista* rhetoric. Silk appears predictably in the next stanza, deployed for an equally predictable synaesthesic effect:

> Charlas y sonrisas en locas bandadas
> perfuman de seda los rudos boscajes.

> ['Chats and smiles in wild flocks / perfume the rugged woods with silk.']

In fairness 'Nochebuena' is an exception, the only poem in the book that could have fitted easily in Darío's *Prosas profanas* (1896). More common are the poems that imitate Herrera y Reissig, whom we noted as the exponent of a more intense, more imagistic *modernismo* who was, however, equally affected, equally a concocter of literary exercises wholly lacking in emotional urgency. These poems, like Herrera y Reissig's, are almost obligatorily set in a pastoral dusk. Portentous poplars, 'like imprisoned hieratic bards', decorate a landscape charged too conspicuously with idyllic significance. Even the supposedly innovatory poems about the Indians of the Peruvian sierra where Vallejo was born read in parts like mere exercises in exotic decoration, and the fact that the landscape is one Vallejo knew well, unlike the Basque country which was so dear to Herrera y Reissig although he never visited it, seems quite accidental:

> La aldea . . . se reviste
> de un rudo gris, en que un mugir de vaca
> se aceita en sueño y emoción de huaca.
> Y en el festín del cielo azul yodado
> gime en el cáliz de la esquila triste
> un viejo coraquenque desterrado.

> ['The village . . . is decked / in rugged grey. The bellowing of a cow / is annointed in dreams and the emotion of a *huaca* tomb. / And in a feast of blue, iodic sky / an old exiled *coraquenque* groans from the chalice of a cattle-bell.']

Dreamy sounds, a melancholy that feels very self-imposed, a contrived wistfulness all add up to a meekly derivative literary exercise, not an authentic description of the sierra and its Indians. The cycle of poems called 'Nostalgias imperiales', from which the above passage is quoted, and another one called 'Terceto autóctono', also about the sierra and the Indians, have, in general, the glossy feel of exotica set up for the tourist, much as do the Indians that Darío occasionally evoked.

The *modernista*—especially the late *modernista*—roots of much of *Los heraldos negros* have been expertly charted by André Coyné in his *César Vallejo y su obra poética*. We should not, of course, be surprised by them. They are present in the first efforts of all the best poets of Vallejo's generation, in Neruda and Borges for instance, who felt the call of duty to describe the dusk as assiduously as Vallejo did. What is remarkable about *Los heraldos negros* is the sense one gets now and then of a personal voice emerging, far more assertively than it does, say, in Neruda's *Crepusculario* (1923). In many of the poems, Vallejo's own experiences, his own personality, begin confidently to express themselves, and with them there tentatively burgeons a new language, the beginnings of maybe the most original voice in Latin American poetry.

The most predominant type of poem in *Los heraldos negros* is the love poem—the setting and the idiom are very often *modernista,* but the poems are already beginning to tell a personal story, the story of Vallejo's own attitudes, fears, and hopes. Thus whereas their religious-cum-erotic imagery has strong *modernista* overtones, it begins to take on connotations that are not purely decorative.

For Vallejo a poem is essentially a statement about Vallejo or about the human problems of which Vallejo is a microcosm. Language is not wrenched in order to achieve a new, unprecedented decorativeness, but rather in order to discover the man that has been hitherto hidden behind its decorative façades.

— D. P. Gallagher

Vallejo was born and brought up in an intensely Catholic environment in the primitive Andean town of Santiago del Chuco, in the north of Peru. It is indeed said that he was sometimes under pressure from his family to become a priest. It is not surprising, therefore, that when sexual experience is seen in some of his poems in a religious context, a personal dilemma is being worked out far removed from any mere literary influence:

> Linda Regia! Tus pies son dos lágrimas
> que al bajar del Espíritu ahogué,
> un Domingo de Ramos que entré al Mundo,
> ya lejos para siempre de Belén.

> ['Gorgeous girl! Your feet are two tears / which I drowned when I descended from the Spirit / one Palm Sunday that I entered the World / already distant, for ever, from Bethlehem.']

Throughout his work, the erotic is treated by Vallejo with ambivalence, and he shifts back and forth from sheer disgust with it to a hope that it will stimulate some sort of spiritual fulfilment. Either way, its points of reference are spiritual, he will not allow himself any sheer physical *enjoyment* from it.

The ambivalence is stressed in a punning line from **'Nervazón de angustia'** (**'Nervous Gust of Anguish'**). A 'sweet Hebrew girl' to whom the poem is addressed (echoing the biblical tone that was dear to Herrera y Reissig) is asked to *'unnail his nervous tension'*. Then 'Tus lutos trenzan mi gran cilicio / con gotas de curare'—'Your mourning braids my great hairshirt / with drops of curare.' She is thus either the poison that magnifies and finalizes his agony, or its cure, the ultimate executioner, or the redeemer. Or both, because that fundamental conceit of the Spanish mystics, that life is the beginning of death and that death is the beginning of life, is central to Vallejo's early poetry. And copulation consequently implies both annihilation and rebirth, crucifixion (which its posture resembles) and resurrection. Thus in **'Ascuas'** (**'Embers'**):

> sangrará cada fruta melodiosa
> como un sol funeral, lúgubres vinos,
> Tilia tendrá la cruz
> que en la hora final será de luz.

> ['Each melodious fruit will bleed / like a funereal sun, gloomy wines, / Tilia will have the cross / which in the final hour will turn to light.']

Each noun ('fruit', 'sun', 'wine') suggests achievement; each verb or adjective ('will bleed', 'funereal', 'gloomy') suggests the struggle involved in its path, the blemishes that still mar it, until the final struggle, the crucifixion, leads to an ultimate light. Similarly in **'El poeta a su amada'** (**'The Poet to His Beloved'**), the 'sacrifice' involved in love-making 'sobre los dos maderos curvados de mi beso' ('upon the two curved beams of my kiss') is a mere prelude to a more satisfactory relationship that will follow death, where

> . . . ya no habrán reproches en tus ojos benditos;
> no volveré a ofenderte. Y en una sepultura
> los dos nos dormiremos, como dos hermanitos.

> ['There will be no more reproaches in your blessed eyes; / I shall not offend you again. And in a tomb / the two of us shall sleep, like a little brother and sister.']

Death thus purifies a relationship which during life has been sinfully profane, and sets him free from his sanctimonious fear of copulation. 'Love, come to me fleshless', he asks in **'Amor'**,

> y que yo a manera de Dios, sea el hombre
> que ama y engendra sin sensual placer.

> ['And may I, in the manner of God, be the man / who loves and begets without sensual pleasure.']

In the poem **'Deshora'** (**'Untimely Moment'**) he hankers after a

> Pureza amada, que mis ojos nunca
> llegaron a gozar. Pureza absurda—

> ['Beloved purity, which my eyes never / managed to enjoy. Absurd purity.']

a pre-pubertal purity 'en falda neutra de colegio' ('in a neutral school skirt'). This ideal is frequently contrasted to a more lustful form of sexual experience of which his memories are always guilty ones, memories of masculine violence imposed on a female whose purity is thereby irrevocably savaged. Thus in **'Heces'** (**'Dregs'**), amidst the dreary rain of Lima, he remembers

> las cavernas crueles de mi ingratitud;
> mi bloque de hielo sobre su amapola
> más fuerte que su 'No seas así.'

> ['The cruel caves of my ungratefulness; / my block of ice upon your poppy / more potent than your "Don't be like that.' "]

One of the central obsessions within this very personal statement that thus begins to emerge from the poems of *Los heraldos negros,* and which is developed with a far more eloquent anguish in his next book, *Trilce* (1922), is the memory of one single traumatic act: Vallejo's departure from his family up in Santiago del Chuco, and his consequent initiation into worldliness. Like the idyll of a pure, fleshless love, the idyll of the rural home is evoked in poems like **'Idilio muerto'** in deliberate contrast to Lima or 'Byzantium', a stifling Babylon where it rains drearily, where the air asphyxiates and the blood goes to sleep. Not only does he regret the fact that he has lost a pastoral paradise for the sake of a rotten city; he feels guilty about it:

> Hay soledad en el hogar; se reza;
> y no hay noticias de los hijos hoy.
> Mi padre se despierta, ausculta
> la huída a Egipto, el restañante adios.
> Está ahora tan cerca;
> si hay algo en el de lejos, seré yo.

> ['There is loneliness back home; they're praying / and there's no news of the children today. / My father wakes up, listens for / the flight into Egypt, the staunching farewell. / He is so near now. / If there's something far in him, it must be me.']

Yet always the memory of the home town, in particular of the archetypally beautiful mother is summoned as a consolation, as something to latch on to even now, and the home town and family elicit from Vallejo his first wholly genuine poetry, underivative, untainted by literary postures. In 'Canciones del hogar' ('Home songs'), a cycle of five poems that closes *Los heraldos negros,* a wholly new idiom emerges, only glimpsed at in most of the other poems of the book, and such as had not been seen before in Latin American poetry. For one gets a sense reading these final poems that they really had to be written, and that the sentiments they need to convey are really more important than the style in which they are expressed. It is as if Vallejo for the first time felt he no longer needed to enlist the aid of Darío or Herrera y Reissig, felt he could manage on his own. And the deeply felt emotions unwittingly produce a new language: directly simple, free of posturing decoration, yet always under strict control, with the result that the poems often risk reaching the brink of sentimentality yet yet hold back and are able, as few poems can, to be moving about the most ordinary things without bathos. Thus Vallejo remembers playing hide-and-seek with his brother Miguel (**'A mi hermano Miguel'**), who is now dead:

Miguel, tú te escondiste
una noche de agosto, al alborear;
pero, en vez de ocultarte riendo, estabas triste.
Y tu gemelo corazón de esas tardes
extintas se ha aburrido de no encontrarte. Y ya
cae sombra en el alma.

Oye, hermano no tardes
en salir. Bueno? Puede inquietarse mamá.

['Miguel, you hid / one August night, at day-break; / but instead of laughing you were sad. / And your twin heart of those faded / evenings has grown weary of not finding you. And already / a shadow is falling on my soul. / Listen brother, hurry / out. All right? Mother might start worrying.']

There are a few other poems here and there which are written in this direct, unpretentious manner. Usually they are poems that express a genuine confused awkwardness, a sense that life is somehow bigger and more elusive than he had bargained for. Thus the title poem that opens the book:

Hay golpes en la vida, tan fuertes . . . Yo no sé!
Golpes como del odio de Dios; como si ante
ellos,
la resaca de todo lo sufrido
se empozara en el alma . . . Yo no sé!

['There are blows in life that are so heavy . . . I don't know! / Blows like the hatred of God; as though in face of them / the dregs of all suffering / were stagnating in the soul . . . I don't know!']

Or the poem **'Agape'** where a sense of pain and loneliness is kept this side of self-pity with the occasional mocking irony: 'Perdóname Señor: qué poco he muerto' ('Lord forgive me: how little I've died').

Vallejo is, indeed, always effective in *Los heraldos negros* when shouting sardonic defiance at God, as though in liberating himself from his devotional guilt he were liberating himself too from the clogging postures of an inherited idiom:

Dios mío, si tú hubieras sido hombre.
hoy supieras ser Dios;
pero tú, que estuviste siempre bien,
no sientes nada de tu creación.
Y el hombre sí te sufre: el Dios es él!

['God, if you'd been a man / you'd know how to be God; / but you who were always all right / have no feeling for your creatures. / Yet man must endure you: *he* is God.']

It should be remembered that *Los heraldos negros* was written by a very young man indeed, by a young provincial, moreover, who had nothing but the limited *modernista* tradition to fall back on. Even so, and even in his blatantly *modernista* poems, he is able to surpass the *modernistas*. The book, of course, must have been useful anyway as a literary exercise, as an apprenticeship. Most of the metres that the *modernistas* introduced into Spanish poetry for the first time are mastered with assurance. All of the poems are written moreover with a discipline rare before then in Spanish American poetry: within the limitations of the idiom in which they are written, the poems perpetrate very few redundant lines.

And yet *Los heraldos negros* is a paltry work in comparison with the book that followed it in 1922, *Trilce.* What happened to Vallejo in the three or four years that separated the two volumes? What developments explain his passage from the elegant correctness of *Los heraldos negros* to the utterly unprecedented innovatory power of the new book?

Certainly a few experiences enriched that unpromising background to *Los heraldos negros* which had consisted merely of a quiet life in Santiago del Chuco, a thesis on **'Romanticism in Spanish Poetry'** in Trujillo, soul-searching conversations with provincial intellectuals there, and a perhaps marginally more fruitful impecunious loneliness in Lima.

In 1918 his mother died, with the consequence that there could no longer be any hope of recovering the forsaken idyll. Definitely on his own, the fragile balance that seemed to hold his neuroses just about at bay in *Los heraldos negros* began to crack. He returned to Santiago del Chuco in 1920, yet became involved almost immediately in a local political dispute which culminated in the burning down of the town's general store. Vallejo's role appears to have been merely conciliatory, yet he managed to get himself imprisoned in Trujillo for some three and a half months, accused of being the 'intellectual instigator' of the incident.

One can safely imagine that conditions in a Trujillo prison in 1920 were not congenial. Certainly, both the injustice of the sentence and the rough loneliness of the cell appear to have left a marked impression on Vallejo, who was obviously a most hypersensitive man. And it is important to note that many of the poems in *Trilce* were in fact written in prison, the circumstance contributing greatly, no doubt, to their sometimes frenzied anguish.

Trilce is so different a book from *Los heraldos negros* that it is hard to believe it was written by the same man. Whereas *Los heraldos negros* is either politely literary or, at best, starkly direct, *Trilce* is an intensely difficult work. For in freeing language from the received rhetoric of *modernismo* or even of colloquial directness Vallejo presents us the word in the raw, disconnected, thrust upon us in isolation or, more often perhaps, under the guise of a syntax which, though deceptively conventional, appears, at first sight anyway, to add up to no recognizable meaning. All the decorative aspects of *Los heraldos negros* are, moreover, abandoned. There is no question any longer of Vallejo allowing himself to sit back and describe a landscape. Indeed he allows himself nothing in *Trilce* that does not appear to be urgently important personally, just as he grimly shuns all temptation to indulge in a 'beautiful' turn of phrase.

There is a revealing poem in the book—poem [*'Trilce LV'*]—that suggests how he now thinks his poetry should be behaving:

Samain diría el aire es quieto y de una
contenida tristeza.
Vallejo dice hoy la Muerte está soldando

cada lindero a cada hebra de cabello perdido,
desde la cubeta de un frontal, donde hay algas,
toronjiles que cantan divinos almácigos en guar-
dia,
y versos antisépticos sin dueño.

['Samain would say the air is quiet, of a / composed sadness.

Vallejo says Death today is welding each limit
to each thread of lost hair; from the cask of a
frontal, where there is sea weed, balm-gentle
singing divine vigilant seedlings and antiseptic
verses without an owner.']

Thus the delicate cadences and preciously fragile melancholy of a French Symbolist like Samain (who was a decisive influence on Lugones and Herrera y Reissig) are dismissed, replaced by a self-parodying effusion of harsh 'antiseptic' contradictions, 'verses without an owner', without the spurious backing of received ideas or a received
idiom. Moreover, the announced lack of 'ownership' underlines the extent to which the poetry of *Trilce* involves
a 'letting the language speak'. The man gives way to the
words that are unsuspectedly buried within him, the
words more than the images, for Vallejo's enterprise is
not, fundamentally, a surrealist one. Vallejo seems to be
seeking to find himself not in the *images* of his unconscious, but rather in the *language* of his unconscious. He
is perhaps the first Latin American writer to have realized
that it is precisely in the discovery of a language where literature must find itself in a continent where for centuries
the written word was notorious more for what it concealed
than for what it revealed, where 'beautiful' writing, sheer
sonorous wordiness was a mere holding operation against
the fact that you did not dare really say anything at all.
The summoning of unprecedented, raw language involves
in Vallejo a process of self-discovery, therefore, a fact
worth noting all the more simply because Vallejo's frequently cited debt to Mallarmé can thereby be put into
perspective. The reason is that for Vallejo a poem is never
a mere verbal object, a cluster of sparsely connected words
that seek to refer to nothing but themselves. For Vallejo
a poem is essentially a statement about Vallejo or about
the human problems of which Vallejo is a microcosm.
Language is not wrenched in order to achieve a new, unprecedented decorativeness, but rather in order to discover the man that has been hitherto hidden behind its decorative façades. The discovery is not a pleasant one, and the
noise the poems make is consequently aggressive and not
beautiful.

Let us take the love poems, almost as predominant in *Trilce* as in *Los heraldos negros.* Much the same sexual ambivalence as was displayed in *Los heraldos negros* can be
found, yet again, in *Trilce.* Again there is a hankering after
a pure, innocent love which may have been possible in the
past and which is now out of reach:

. . . Es el rincón
donde a tu lado, leí una noche,
entre tus tiernos puntos,
un cuento de Daudet. Es el rincón
amado. No lo equivoques.

['It's the corner / where at your side I read one

> **It is a curiously subtle, menacing world
> that Vallejo has left us in his mature
> works, and he has conveyed it in a
> language that has been very carefully
> selected, a language which is perpetually
> just off centre, which has the appearance
> often of correctness, yet which it is never
> quite possible to pin down.**
>
> — *D. P. Gallagher*

night / amidst your sweet polka dots / a Daudet
story. It's the beloved / corner. Don't mistake
it.']

One notes that there is no need felt here to complicate the
language. Indeed there are one or two things that Vallejo
appears to be so sure of—a pure forsaken love, his family,
his mother—that he does not have to grapple with their
meaning within himself, and he expresses them therefore
unabashedly in the direct language of 'Canciones del
hogar'. But where the erotic becomes tortured, guilt-
ridden, the language becomes contorted, as though Vallejo
felt that he could maybe get to the complex truth of his
experience if only he could find the right idiom to define
it.

Clayton Eshleman has written [in the foreword to the
1969 English language version of *Poemas humanos*] that
'In Vallejo the amount of physical suffering is the alteration that it seeks.' This is indeed so, the main problem
being worked out in the erotic poems in *Trilce* being therefore that his dissatisfaction with sexual experience is usually a direct result of the great deal he expects from it. The
splendour that he hopes to extract from copulation always
runs aground against the inevitable limitations of copulation itself. In ['*Trilce* LIX'] his vast hopes are mirrored by
the 'Pacific, immobile, glass, bulging / with all the possi-
bles', only to be countered by the great wall of the 'Andes,
cold, inhumanable, pure'. The vastness of his expectations
would seem, therefore, to be the cause of his ultimate disgust with 'aquel punto tan espantablemente conocido'
('that point so horrifierly known'—presumably the vagina?) and the cause in general of his failure to obtain satisfaction:

Y me retiro hasta azular, y retrayéndome
endurezco, hasta apretarme el alma!

['And I retire until I'm blue, and in the act of
withdrawal / I harden, until my soul grows
tight'.]

Now and then the erotic poems start hopefully. Thus IX:

Vusco volvver de golpe el golpe.
Sus dos hojas anchas, su válvula
que se abre en suculenta recepción
de multiplicando a multiplicador,
su condición excelente para el placer,
todo avía verdad.

['I wish to retturn the blow by blow. / Its two broad leaves, a valve / that opens in succulent reception / from multiplied to multiplier / its excellent ability to please / everything promises truth.']

A hectic effort is, indeed, announced in the first line, but there seems no reason why it should not be rewarded. Then:

> Busco volvver de golpe el golpe.
> A su halago, enveto bolivarianas fragosidades
> a treintidós cables y sus múltiples,
> se arrequintan pelo por pelo
> soberanos belfos, los dos tomos de la Obra,
> y no vivo entonces ausencia,
> ni al tacto.

['I wish to retturn the blow by blow. / In its honour I impose mountain on Bolivarian crags / at thirty-two cables and their multiples, / hair by hair, there is a contraction / of glorious blubber-lips, the two volumes of the Book, / and I live no absence then, / not even touching.']

Craggy Andean heights worthy of Bolívarand enigmatic cables of probably very high tension are dizzily deployed on (presumably?) a receptive vagina whose lips are no less than the two volumes of *the Book,* and the enterprise succeeds in abolishing 'absence'.

But the poem ends with a characteristic statement of failure, despite the effort and initial optimism:

> Fallo bolver de golpe el golpe.
> No ensillaremos jamás el toroso Vaveo
> de egoísmo y de aquel ludir mortal
> de sábana,
> desque la mujer esta
> ¡cuánto pesa de general!
>
> Y hembra es el alma de la ausente.
> Y hembra es el alma mía.

['I fail to repay [sic] the blow by blow. / We shall never saddle the robust shlabering / of selfishness and of that mortal rubbing / of the sheet / ever since this woman here / how much she weighs of general! / And the soul of the absent woman is female. / And my soul is female.']

The failure—indeed the horror ('that mortal rubbing of the sheet')—looks as if it is about to be explained, even blamed on the woman ('desque da mujer esta . . .'). Yet what is the explanation? An exclamation which seems to be a *non sequitur* (unless he is blaming her for a sort of contingent weightiness, for having too much *body* and not enough soul), followed by two lines which are surely merely enigmatic, offering the appearance of explanatory meaning, but remaining ultimately irreducible.

Most of the poetry in *Trilce* is indeed ultimately too irreducible for it to have been fair even to have offered the sort of exegesis I have attempted to offer of this poem, which may, after all, not have been intended to have the sexual connotations suggested at all. One thing though, is I think clear: the poem is about effort of some kind, effort to surpass some sort of limitation, marred in the end by failure.

The gap that separates aspiration from execution is indeed the central concern of *Trilce,* whatever form it takes. Always Vallejo is bashing his head against some limit, trying to wrench himself through what is given, trying to free himself, in general, from the limitations imposed by time and by space. The man who can write that 'La muerte está soldando cada lindero a cada hebra de cabello perdido' [*'Trilce* LV'] and that men are 'the corpses of a life that never was' [*'Trilce* LXXV'] is also the man who announced that we must 'fight to thread ourselves through the eye of a needle', or who declares:

> . . . traspasaré mi propio frente
> hasta perder el eco
> y quedar con el frente hacia la espalda.

['I shall pass through my own forehead / until I loose the echo / and end up with my forehead turned towards my back.']

Impressive though it is to manage to pass through one's own forehead, it is maybe no improvement to end up with one's forehead turned towards one's back, and indeed very often Vallejo's efforts to surpass limits end with him falling flat on his face. Very often Vallejo introduces a sort of nightmare arithmetic to dramatize the battleground. Numbers, of course, have their own relentless logic, and for Vallejo they symbolize the relentlessness of fate and of time. If only we could change the rules of arithmetic, maybe we could also change our destiny! Thus in [*"Trilce* LIII"] he seems to be hoping that by dint of a 'cabezazo brutal' (a brutal blow of the head) he might convert eleven into an even number:

> Como si las hubiesen pujado, se afrontan
> de dos en dos las once veces.

['As though they'd been pressured the eleven times / confront each other two by two.']

In the end, the enterprise is marred by an inability to surpass the 'eternal three hundred and sixty degrees', and by the return of a menacing 'frontier', which interposes itself, like an 'itinerant conductor's baton' ('ambulante batuta') between ambition and its fruition. Vallejo in the end is always being cut down to size by frontiers, by demarcation lines in general (*fronteras, linderos*), and none are more definitive than the four walls of his cell in Trujillo. Like all his frontiers, they too are relentlessly numerical:

> Oh las cuatro paredes de la celda.
> Ah las cuatro paredes albicantes
> que sin remedio dan al mismo número.

['Oh the four walls of the cell. / Ah the four bleaching walls / which give the same number without fail.']

Whereas to grapple with the limitations of numerals and spaces may seem a somewhat abstract enterprise, the cell does indeed give Vallejo good reason to feel cut down to size. Similarly, whereas it is somewhat abstract to aspire to thread oneself through the eye of a needle, Vallejo has some very tangible ambitions too, and they often relate to his mother, first abandoned, and now dead and buried in Santiago del Chuco.

In *Los heraldos negros* mere separation from the mother gave Vallejo the sense that he had become an orphan. In

Trilce, where the mother is finally dead, we get a sense of his growing resentment at having to cope on his own with a hostile environment that holds no promise any longer of a potential return to the cosy security of the family fold. Yet this anguished orphanhood is not set up self-pityingly as a merely personal problem. It is to become—it had already begun to in *Los heraldos negros*—the orphanhood of mankind in general abandoned by God, or more specifically of the toiling masses abandoned by their employers. And the sense of 'orphanhood' felt by the man from the sierra in a hostile Lima is of course not one on which Vallejo need have a monopoly. The drama of the *serrano* emigrating to Lima in the hope of making good there, and finding instead exploitation, unemployment, and homelessness, is one that has long bedevilled Peru. Vallejo summarizes the intimidated feelings of the *serrano* who arrives in Lima in a poem ['*Trilce* XIV'] in which he expresses his awe at 'that manner' the *limeño* has 'of walking on trapezes'. And in another poem ['*Trilce* VI'] he wistfully evokes the absence of a washerwoman (his mother?) who used to wash his clothes. The objects on his bedside table are no longer his. If only, in his loneliness, he knew that one day she would return:

> a entregarme las ropas lavadas, mi aquella
> lavandera del alma. Qué mañana entrará
> satisfecha, capulí de obrería, dichosa
> de probar que sí sabe, que sí puede
> ¡COMO NO VA A PODER!
> azular y planchar todos los caos.

['To hand over the washed clothes, laundress / of my heart. What morning will she enter all satisfied, a good job done, happy / to show that yes, she knows how, she can / HOW COULD SHE NOT! / bleach and iron all the chaoses.']

Life is now ordinary, automatic, full of mere 'loving and carrying on', of mere 'this and that' ['*Trilce* LVII']: 'Every day I wake up blind / to work for a living: and I have breakfast / without tasting a drop of it, every morning' ['*Trilce* LVI']. Food without his mother is not worth tasting, even if he shares it with another happy family. What's the use when it is not *his* family?

> El yantar de esas mesas así, en que se prueba
> amor ajeno en vez del propio amor,
> torna tierra el bocado que no brinda la
> MADRE,
> hace golpe la dura deglusión; el dulce.
> hiel; aceite fúnereo, el café.

['Having supper at tables like that, where you taste / the love of others instead of your own / turns the mouthful that the MOTHER hasn't provided to dirt / and the painful swallowing becomes a slap; the sweet / becomes icy; the coffee, a funereal oil.']

Such are the rewards of the 'futile coming to age of being a man'—'esta mayoría inválida de hombre' ['*Trilce* XVIII'].

Throughout *Trilce,* Vallejo contrasts the drabness, the limitations, the loneliness he has landed himself in with the forsaken paradise of the sierra. Sometimes he allows himself desperately to conjecture that nothing has happened at all, that he has not left, or otherwise that he is returning to find everything the same as before. In these poems Vallejo drops linguistic complications once more and achieves a tone similar to that of [the sequence] 'Canciones del hogar', only it is more effective now because the fragile idyll is seen to be on the point of cracking.

> Las personas mayores
> a qué hora volverán?
> Da las seis el ciego Santiago,
> y ya está muy oscuro.
>
> Madre dijo que no demoraría.
>
>   ['*Trilce* III']

['The grown-ups / what time will they come back? / Blind Santiago strikes six / and it has got very dark. / Mother said she wouldn't be long.']

In another poem, after evoking his family desperately, as though by writing about them he could bring them back to life, he eventually gives in and opts instead for a sort of bravado irony:

> Todos están durmiendo para siempre,
> y tan de lo mas bien, que por fin
> mi caballo acaba fatigado por cabecear
> a su vez, y entre sueños, a cada venia, dice
> que está bien, que todo está muy bien.
>
>   ['*Trilce* LXI']

['All of them are now for ever asleep / and so very fine, that at last / my horse grows tired and starts to nod off / himself, and half asleep, every time he bows, he says / that it's fine, that it's all just fine.']

In the end, even the mother-son relationship is doomed to succumb to the logic of arithmetic. Thus in ['*Trilce* XVIII'] Vallejo appeals to his mother, 'lovable keeper of innumerable keys', to help him against the four walls of the cell.

> Contra ellas seríamos contigo, los dos,
> más dos que nunca. Y ni lloraras,
> di, libertadora!

['Against them you and I would be, the two of us, / more two than ever. And you wouldn't even cry, / tell me now, deliverer!']

The appeal has a defiant hopefulness, but the mother is dead.

Two is set up as an ideal number in *Trilce* and it seems to me to stand for the ideal pairing of mother and son. Yet how can you keep two from becoming three? How can you preserve a 'dicotyledon' intact and stave off its 'propensiones de trinidad'—'propensities towards trinity'? In a strange poem on the 'grupo dicoteledón' (dicotyledon group—['*Trilce* V']) there is a desperate plea that the dicotyledon should remain unmultiplied ('A ver. Aquello sea sin ser más'), undisturbed ('y crome y no sea visto'), and safe from catastrophe ('Y no glise en el gran colapso'), and that 'the betrothed be betrothed eternally' ('los novios sean novios en eternidad'), unmarried and therefore free of progeny ('trinity').

This poem (which one must admit is so potentially obscure that any 'explanation' of it such as my own may be wide of the mark) seems to contain most of the obsessions of *Trilce,* and perhaps suggests ways of tying them up. For is not this hankering after a pure, sexless love that we also found in *Los heraldos negros* really a search for a mother-son relationship? One would be perhaps going too far if one were to suggest that his fear of 'trinity', of a 'third party', signified a fear of an intruding father. The important fact is that Vallejo appears to be seeking in the love affairs of *Trilce* (a neologistic title which ominously suggests three) a blissful, pure, eternal 'togetherness' which he may only have achieved with his mother, an unprecedented ecstasy which he certainly seems to think copulation unable to provide. And certainly the most dearly remembered lovers are often more maternal than sexy, such as the *amada* in [*'Trilce* XXXV'] busily preparing him lunch, sewing a button on his shirt, and sewing his 'flank' ('costado': ribs?) to hers. Alas, no togetherness, no 'dicotyledon', can last; there is no number which will not multiply, roll into the next, and then the next:

> Pues no deis I, que resonará al infinito.
> Y no deis O, que callará tanto,
> hasta despertar y poner de pie al I.
>
> [Trilce V']

['So don't give I, for it will resound unto infinity. / And don't give o, for it will be silent, / until it awakens and gives rise to i.']

Such is the logic of arithmetic, of unstoppable time, of nature, of all those things Vallejo battles against in *Trilce,* a startling, pent-up, dramatic book which is also relentlessly authentic, free of even a momentary lapse into easy phrase-making, and free too of illusions, despite the vastness of its quests.

In June 1923 Vallejo left Peru for Europe, arriving in Paris a month later. He was never to return.

During his first decade in Paris Vallejo appears to have written very few poems, although the dating of his poetry subsequent to *Trilce* is very difficult indeed. None at all appeared in book form until his death, *Poemas en prosa, Poemas humanos,* and *España aparta de mí este cáliz* having all been published posthumously by his French widow, Georgette. According to her, Vallejo tended to date his poetry when he had finished revising it, often many years after writing, so that certainly many poems in *Poemas humanos* that have often been thought to have been written as late as 1937 were probably first drafted much earlier.

From 1925 to 1930 Vallejo did write frequent articles on literature in two Peruvian publications, *Mundial* and *Variedades,* and in a review which he himself helped to set up in Paris, *Favorables-Paris-Poemas.* A selection was published several decades later under the title *Literature y arte.* None of these articles is particularly distinguished as such, yet they provide useful insights into Vallejo's attitude to poetry at the time and, I think one can safely say, for the rest of his life. In them he seeks primarily to expose what he sees as the sham nature of contemporary poetry. According to Vallejo, for poetry to be innovatory, its newness must spring from a genuinely original sensibility, not from some arbitrary decision to be original. Instead poets seem to think that by just naming new inventions like the

aeroplane and the telegraph they are being original and modern whereas only a genuinely sensitive assimilation of new things will create a new poetry. Ultimately 'most writers who opt for the *avant-garde* do so out of cowardice or indigence', out of self-defence in order to conceal the poverty of their talent. Cocteau, for instance, 'is deep down a conservative, despite his modernist efforts and poses. His postures are all make-up; his acrobatics are those of a clown—false ones.' Similarly lapidary statements are made about contemporary Spanish American poets, such as Neruda and Borges and Gabriel Mistral. The diatribes are often unjust, and never well documented, but they reveal a reluctance to be satisfied which was always to stand him in good stead, because he never failed to apply it to his own work. Other articles can be revealing in a more general way. Thus he says of the colour black that it can symbolize 'according to the hemisphere and the time, sadness or joy, death or epiphany', and that 'each thing potentially contains all the energies and directions of the universe. Not only is man a microcosm. Each thing, each phenomenon is also a microcosm on the march.' Neither of these statements is particularly profound, but they remind one of the extent to which the 'things' evoked in Vallejo's poetry are above all things, and never components of a decipherable 'code'. If an object in a poem by Vallejo is symbolical it is symbolical in so many directions that one is forced in the end to contemplate the object itself for its own sake.

If an object in a poem by Vallejo is symbolical it is symbolical in so many directions that one is forced in the end to contemplate the object itself for its own sake.

— D. P. Gallagher

The articles also reveal a growing political awareness in Vallejo, the beginning of a process which culminated, in 1928, in the first of three trips to the Soviet Union. Vallejo came to be an extremely militant, indeed rather dogmatic, Communist in the thirties—he is said to have greeted the advent of the Spanish Republic with wary indifference, because he did not believe in the compromises of Popular Front regimes. His militance can best be observed in works like *Rusia en 1931,* a book of observant but often sycophantic reportage, some little-known plays, and *El tungsteno* (1931), a novel that sought to expose the exploitation of Peruvian tungsten miners by an American company. None of these works is particularly distinguished, their purpose being wholly didactic, though none is ineffective as propaganda, because a clearly very genuine passion sustains them. What is remarkable is that Vallejo never let his political faith significantly affect his poetry. Politics are present in many of the poems in *Poemas humanos,* but always as just one new element in Vallejo's consciousness. Unlike Pablo Neruda, who as we shall see in the next chapter was prompted by militance wholly to abandon the hermetic, neurotic vision of *Residencia en la tierra,* Vallejo regards Communism, in **Poemas humanos** and **'España aparta de mí este cáliz',** as just one more component of an essentially unchanged vision, just the vague sighting of a way out from a world that nevertheless remains as hermetically frontier-bound as that of **Trilce.** It would seem that Vallejo was too rigorous a man to believe in miracles; or conversely, that political affirmation outside his poetry was mostly just a necessary and convenient way of preserving his sanity. In order to arrive at the self-discovery that he was aiming for in his poems, he had to keep all his options open, however terrible. In his ordinary life he could take time off from so dangerous an enterprise and choose the option that seemed most promising to him. How else can one explain the almost schizophrenic gap that separates the relentless affirmations of the prose from the tortured neurosis of the poetry?

Poemas humanos is Vallejo's most remarkable book. Unlike **Trilce,** it develops logically from its predecessor. There is the same struggle against limitations as in **Trilce,** the same neurosis, and in particular the same search for an unprecedented language that rarely allows itself the luxury of facility, yet never indulges in complexity for its own sake. The writing is difficult because what has to be said is difficult, and what has to be said has to be said truthfully, undistracted by literary formulae, unfalsified by too easy a flow of words.

What strikes one most about **Poemas humanos** is the very personal, almost eccentric nature of Vallejo's sensibility. The poems are nearly all about neurosis, about suffering in general, but the specific problems described are always very precise, very subtle. Vallejo seems to be trying to locate the exact shape of a malaise that nevertheless remains elusively intangible despite the precise but enigmatic forms it takes. It is not quite illness, not quite the fear of death, not quite, say, hunger, which Vallejo knew very well in his early days in Paris, not quite the passing of time, yet it is related to all these things. It is an ontological malaise, beyond specific cause. In a prose poem ironically called **'Voy a hablar de la esperanza'** (**'I Am Going to Speak of Hope'**), he writes,

> I hurt now without explanation. My pain is so deep it had no cause any longer, nor does it lack cause . . . My pain is from the north wind and from the south wind, like those neuter eggs some rare birds lay in the wind. If my girlfriend had died, my pain would be the same. If they'd cut out my throat from the root, my pain would be the same. If life were finally of a different order, my pain would be the same. Today I suffer from further up. I just suffer today.

How does this pain manifest itself? In a manner that is at once precise and deviously enigmatic. It is like 'the pencil I lost in my cavity', like an unknown something quivering in one's tonsil's, like 'plastic poisons' in the throat, like a splinter, like something that 'slips from the soul and falls to the soul'; it is 'as if they'd put earrings' on him, it is 'below, above, right here, far', and it stands

> . . . oblique to the line of the camel,

fibre of my crown of flesh

—a subtle location and a subtle texture!

Indeed everything in **Poemas humanos** is subtly off centre, or ex-centric, and everything gets intangibly under the skin. Even his hopes are distinctly odd, in poems where stolidly political lines like 'Let the millionaire walk naked, stark naked' are undermined by a flurry of whimsically nonsensical ones like 'let a candle be added to the sun' or 'let the naked strip / let the cloak dress in trousers'. In another poem, he expresses his longing for love, 'a vast political longing for love', yet the love he wishes to manifest turns out to be strikingly personal:

> Ah querer, éste, el mío, éste, el mundial,
> interhumano y parroquial, proyecto!
> Me viene al pelo,
> desde el cimiento, desde la ingle pública,
> y, viniendo de lejos, da ganas de besarle
> la bufanda al cantor,
> y al que sufre, besarle en su sartén,
> al sordo, en su rumor craneano . . .

> ['Ah to love, this, my, this, the world's / interhuman and parochial, project! / Just what I wanted, / from the foundation, from the public groin, / and, coming from **afar**, I'd like to kiss / the singer on his muffler, **/ to** kiss the sufferer on his frying pan, / the **deaf** man on his noisy cranium.']

It is as though he wanted deliberately to invalidate its more sensible propositions with a touch of uncompromising madness:

> Quiero, para terminar . . .
> cuidar a los enfermos enfadándolos,
> comprarle al vendedor,
> ayudarle a matar al matador—cosa terrible—
> y quisiera yo ser bueno conmigo
> en todo.

> ['I'd like, finally / to care for the sick infuriating them, / to buy from the salesman, / to help the killer kill—a terrible thing—/ and I'd like to be good with myself / in everything.']

The strangely precise intangibility of **Poemas humanos** manifests itself often in descriptions of Vallejo's own body. Just as things outside him seem relentlessly to be slipping away from any recognizable centre, support, or point of reference, so Vallejo's own body begins to fall apart from itself, in poems that make a very personal contribution to that venerable literary topic, the *doppelganger.* Thus in **'Poema para ser leído y cantado'** (**'Poem to Be Read and Sung'**):

> Sé que hay una persona
> que me busca en su mano, día y noche,
> encontrándome, a cada minuto, en su calzado.

> ['I know there's a person / who looks for me day and night in his hand / and finds me all the time in his shoes.']

Men flee from their feet, from their 'rough, caustic heels', Vallejo flies to himself 'in a two-seater plane', the body separates itself from itself in order merely to end up scurrying enigmatically around 'a long disc, an elastic disc', and these disengagements occur precisely at those moments when his normal hold on things breaks down, and the intangible malaise in the form of a bristle or a splinter or whatever takes over.

In the end, Vallejo is attempting to describe, in *Poemas humanos,* that sense of indefinable confusion which he announced as far back as the title poem of *Los heraldos negros* with the statement 'Hay golpes en la vida, tan fuertes . . . Yo no sé!' ('There are blows in life which are so strong, I don't know'). The confusion is such that nothing seems to belong anywhere in particular, things just happen without cause, or just *are,* one after another, without hierarchy, without purpose:

> La paz, la avispa, el taco, las vertientes,
> el muerto, los decílitros, el buho,
> los lugares, la tiña, los sarcófagos, el vaso, las
>   morenas,
> el desconocimiento, la olla, el monaguillo,
> las gotas, el olvido,
> la potestad, los primos, los arcángeles, la aguja,
> los párrocos, el ébano, el desaire,
> la parte, el tipo, el estupor, el alma . . .

> ['Peace, wasp, heel, watershed, / corpse, decilitres, owl / places, wringworm, sarcophagi, glass, brunettes, / ignorance, stewpot, choirboy, / drops, oblivion, / jurisdiction, cousins, archangel, needle, / vicars, ebony, insult, / part, type, stupor, soul . . .']

Abstract qualities are indistinguishable from concrete ones, wholes from parts, people from things, and subtle menaces ('drops', 'the needle') are never absent. I mentioned that it is wrong to expect anything to symbolize anything specific in Vallejo—for him the world is too contingent for it to be possible to extract a definitive sign from it. There are indeed poems that seek to emphasize the point that a thing is, after all, merely a thing, that life is, merely, life, 'Just life, like that: quite a thing' ('Solo la vida, así, cosa bravísima'); for a 'house, unfortunately, is a house', nothing more. In the end, the fact that things are merely 'there' is the heart of the problem, for there is nothing that Vallejo can do against their oppressive contingency, or against their ordinariness, for we live in the end 'by the comb and the stains on the handkerchief' ('por el peine y las manchas del pañuelo'), and there is nothing more to it. But their very contingency makes them enigmatically menacing. If we cannot perceive their significance, who knows what terrible ones they might not be concealing? At any rate we are lucky in the end if we can pull ourselves together (quite literally) just enough to face one more day:

> Ya va venir el día: da
> cuerda a tu brazo, búscate debajo
> del colchón, vuelve a pararte
> en tu cabeza, para andar derecho.
> Ya va venir el día, ponte el saco.

> ['The day is on its way wind / up your arm, look for yourself under / the mattress, stand again / on your head, in order to walk straight. / The day's on its way, put on your coat.']

One would have thought that the problem of facing another day was one a Bolshevik might have overcome more easily. It is a measure of Vallejo's honesty that he knew it was not that easy, just as he knew, too, that Bolshevism had no answer to death, no way of countering time. It is not surprising that when depicting a Russian Bolshevik in 'Salutación angélica' ('Angelic greeting') he should place him on a forbidding pedestal and then give the impression that *he* could never scale it. Vallejo declares that the Bolshevik has a 'soul perpendicular to' his own, and then tells us how he would like to share the 'fervour' of the Bolshevik's 'faith'. If one is to judge from his poems, Vallejo's faith was to remain 'bristled' and 'splintered'.

It is a measure of Vallejo's unusual authenticity and rigour that **'España aparta de mí este cáliz'** (**'Spain, remove this chalice from me'**), his poem on the Spanish Civil War, is possibly his finest work, and it is doubtful if a better poem was ever written about the Spanish Civil War, at any rate in Spanish. For Vallejo's account of that episode is wholly his own—it was not written according to any political or aesthetic prescription—and it deploys the same unique idiom of *Poemas humanos.*

There is no poet in Latin America like Vallejo, no poet who has bequeathed so consistently personal an idiom, and no poet so strictly rigorous with himself.

— D. P. Gallagher

It must have been as difficult to write about the Spanish Civil War in 1937 as it is to write about Vietnam now. Most poetry about tragic contemporary wars is marred by the fundamental bad faith of the enterprise, unless the poet happens to have participated as a combatant. For otherwise the poetry often consists of the working out, explicitly or not, of a rather too self-indulgent guilt on the part of the poet that he didn't fight himself. If Vallejo ever felt such guilt, he certainly did not impose it on his readers. He had himself probably suffered too much to need to feel it anyway. Another shortcoming of poetry about contemporary events in general is that it is often too much circumscribed by the episode in question, and there is maybe too much gesturing desire on the part of the poet to record the right emotion at the right time about the right thing. With Vallejo it is different because for him the Spanish Civil War is much more than a political event—it is suffering and death, it is that dismemberment of unity which we have seen him observing even in his own body, and it is in general a manifestation of that very intangible malaise that we noted was central to *Poemas humanos.*

Thus in the section on Málaga, disaster is depicted in much the same terms as when it befalls Vallejo's own body, for the curse of the *doppelganger* afflicts that city too:

> Málaga caminando tras de tus pies, en éxodo,

bajo el mal, bajo la cobardía, bajo la historia cón-
cava, indecible
con la yema en tu mano: ¡tierra orgánica!
y la clara en la punta del cabello: ¡todo el caos!

['Malaga, walking behind your feet, in exodus,
/ in evil, in cowardice, in concave history, unut-
terable, / the yolk in your hand: organic land! /
And the white on your hair's end: the entire
chaos!']

That disrupted egg could easily have messed up Vallejo's
own hair, in his own room! Death, in **'Imagen española de
la muerte' ('Spanish Image of Death')**, is just death, not
merely the death inflicted by a specific enemy in a particular war; and like all things that menace in Vallejo's poetry,
it is intangible, yet subtly, elusively precise:

¡Ahí pasa! ¡Llamadla! ¡Es su costado!
Ahí pasa la muerte por Irún;
sus pasos de acordeón, su palabrota,
su metro del tejido que te dije,
su gramo de aquel peso que he callado . . . ¡sí
son ellos!

'There she goes! Call her! It's her flank! / There
goes death through Irún; / her accordeon step,
her four-letter word, / her metre of the fabric I
told you about, / her gram of that weight I kept
to myself . . . Yes it's them!'

That is not a foe you can fight with rifles, or with anything,
even though Vallejo appeals desperately that we should
try, that we should pursue it to the foot of the enemy
tanks: 'Hay que seguirla / hasta el pie de los tanques en-
emigos.'

In the end, **'España, aparta de mí este cáliz'** is a work concerned less with specific causes than with an endemic
human condition and with *individual* suffering. Although
we know where Vallejo's heart is, his hatred of the Nationalist intervention being indeed all the more effective for
not being spelt out, a compassion for mankind far wider
than the issues involved informs the whole work and contributes to its greatness. His compassion is most moving
when it is directed at individual victims: now and then, for
instance, he will give us a portrait of a specific dead hero,
such as Pedro Rojas, or he will trace the individual destiny
of a soldier on the battlefront, such as Ramón Collar
(**'VIII'**).

Ramón Collar, yuntero
y soldado hasta yerno de su suegro,
marido, hijo limítrofe del viento Hijo del Hombre!
Ramón de pena, tú, Collar valiente,
paladín de Madrid y por cojones. ¡Ramonete,
aquí,
los tuyos piensan mucho en tu peinado!

['Ramón Collar, plough-boy / and soldier to the
son-in-law of his father-in-law, / husband, border son of the wind Son of Man, / Ramón of sadness, you, brave Collar / paladin of Madrid and
with your balls. Ramonete, / your family are
thinking about your hair-style.']

At first sight, we seem to be in the presence of an archetypal eulogy. Then characteristically, in brutal contrast to

Ramón's heroics, we glimpse the family absurdly reminiscing about his hair-style, or we glimpse the pathos of his
absence from home: 'Tu pantalón oscuro, andando el
tiempo, / sabe ya andar solísimo, acabarse' ('Your dark
trousers, as time goes by / already know how to walk quite
alone / how to waste away'). Vallejo's personal touch is
never absent even when he is dealing with the most notorious events of the war, such as for instance the battle of
Guernica:

¡Lid a priori, fuera de la cuenta,
lid en paz, lid de las almas débiles
contra los cuerpos débiles, lid en que el niño
pega,
sin que le diga nadie que pegara,
bajo su atroz diptongo
y bajo su habilísimo panal,
y en la que la madre pega con su mal, con su
grito, con el
dorso de una lágrima
y en que el enfermo pega con su mal, con su pastilla y su hijo
y en que el anciano pega
con sus canas, sus siglos y su palo
y en que pega el prebístero con dios!

['*A priori* contest, beyond reckoning, / contest of
peace, contest of weak souls / against weak bodies, contest in which a child hits out / without
anyone telling him to / with his atrocious diph-
thong, / and with his most able nappy / and in
which a mother hits out with her wrong, with
her scream, with the back of a tear / and in
which a sick man hits out with his wrong, with
his pill and his son / and in which an old man
hits out / with his grey hairs, his centuries, and
his stick / and in which a priest hits out with
God.']

All this indignation, all this retaliatory violence on the
edge of despair, is expressed in a language that never lets
up on its ability to deliver surprises which however never
distract from the urgency of what is being said.

Neruda, in his poem on the Spanish Civil War, 'España
en el corazón' ('Spain in the heart'), often lapses into a
pious idiom, a sort of socialist anthem rhetoric. Vallejo always avoids piety—maybe he has too few illusions. There
is always a note of sardonic irony even in his most tragic
passages, with the consequence that they always remain
this side of bathos:

Herido mortalmente de vida, camarada,
camarada jinete,
camarada caballo entre hombre y fiera,
tus huesecillos de alto y melancólico dibujo
forman pompa española,
laureada de finísimos andrajos . . .

['Mortally wounded with life, comrade, / comrade horseman, / comrade horse half-man half-
beast / your little bones, a lofty sad design, / are
a Spanish pageant, / crowned with the finest
rags.']

Vallejo, one can see, is writing in the jestingly ironical and
macabre tradition of the war-song, not the piously wide-
eyed one of the socialist anthem.

There is no poet in Latin America like Vallejo, no poet who has bequeathed so consistently personal an idiom, and no poet so strictly rigorous with himself. It is a curiously subtle, menacing world that he has left us in his mature works, and he has conveyed it in a language that has been very carefully selected, a language which is perpetually just off centre, which has the appearance often of correctness, yet which it is never quite possible to pin down. Perhaps one would have to analyse Vallejo's syntax in order to grasp the manner in which his language works. One might start with his use of adverbs, prepositions, and conjunctions. In normal syntax these words are supposed to qualify or link given concepts. Yet in Vallejo's poetry we meet adverbs that have lost sight of their verbs, prepositions that have been left stranded by an unknown noun, conjunctions that have found their way to the wrong sentence. His poetry is full of stranded loose words like 'after', 'then', 'now', 'which', 'this', 'that', 'but', 'for', 'beneath', which never quite seem to know what word to latch on to, or if they do latch on to one it is usually a stridently enigmatic neologism, or a word they seem fated to contradict, or one that itself seems stranded out of context. Often the poems simply break up into inane exclamations: 'Oh for so much! Oh for so little! Oh for them', 'No! Never! Never yesterday! Never later!', 'So much life and never!', 'So many years and always, always, always', 'No? Yes but no?':

> After, these, here,
> after, above,
> maybe, while, behind, so much, so never,
> under, perhaps, far,
> always, that, tomorrow, how much,
> how much!

Such helpless inanities express the ultimate stage of Vallejo's statement of fundamental bewilderment, initiated in the cry of *Los heraldos negros*—'yo no sé.'

Vallejo died on 15 April 1938 at the age of forty-six of an illness that was never diagnosed. Legend has it that half an hour before he died he uttered the words 'Me voy a España'—'I'm off to Spain.' Yet according to his widow Georgette, his last words were more enigmatic and more trivial: 'Palais Royal'. To judge from his poetry, the latter version is the more likely, and he no doubt would have been grateful—and perhaps amused—that his widow has corrected a legend whose banality he would surely never have allowed himself.

Alfred J. MacAdam (essay date 1980)

SOURCE: "¡Viva Vallejo! ¡Arriba España!" in *The Virginia Quarterly Review*, Vol. 56, No. 1, Winter, 1980, pp. 185-92.

[*In the review below, MacAdam favorably assesses* César Vallejo: The Complete Posthumous Poetry, *discussing thematic and stylistic features of Vallejo's verse and the translation problems posed by his writings.*]

"There is no problem as consubstantial with literature and its modest mystery as translation." This is the first sentence of Jorge Luis Borges' meditation on various English translations of Homer, beginning with Chapman and ending with Samuel Butler. Borges concludes in "The Homeric Versions" (1932) that: (1) all texts are, in the widest sense of the word, translations; (2) all texts, even the final, printed version, are drafts; (3) there is no "definitive" text; and (4) no translation is, in the last analysis, better than any other. Even the worst translation may succeed in communicating to the reader some aspect of the original absent in the "better" translation.

As we read Borges, we wonder how there can be so many translations of Homer. Did the English learn more Greek over the centuries? Was one age closer in spirit to the age of Homer or to Homer himself than another? Do Pope's heroic couplets really put Homer in corsets, or are we blinded by our post-Romantic prejudice to 18th-century elegance? No other literary act demonstrates so clearly the simultaneously historic and nonhistoric nature of the literary text and how the act of reading is inherently ironic, a transformation of what we see into what we want to see.

And as problematic as translation is, it is no more ambiguous than the translator himself. The translator has always had a subaltern role in the world of letters because translation has always been a subaltern act. It was part of the poet's apprenticeship, or, at best, an opportunity for a known poet to show his skill. Pope and Dryden lend dignity to all translators, but they were famous before they were known as translators. Of course, there have always been those who produce ponies, but their work represents the seamy side of literary life and has scant relation to translation taken as a species of esthetic production. Nevertheless, even the trot transforms its chosen text into something else.

We may, then, question the myth of the facing texts, the device we assume keeps translators honest. The fact is that while the purpose of the facing texts is to show the difference between texts in different languages, they actually serve only as trots, aids to those whose knowledge of a language is deficient. The person who knows enough of a language to read a text in the original doesn't need the translation; for the person totally ignorant of the work's original language the translation is all that is necessary. And yet the picture of the reader turning his eyes from one side of the book to the other, reading the same text in two different languages again stands as an icon for Borges' thoughts: as we read we translate a text (even if it is already in our own language) into our own experience; we interpret it. The text I read at 16 changes when I read it at 35 because I have changed. No act shows the provisional nature of reading and writing as does translation, a series of decisions and revisions themselves subject to infinite questioning and revising. "The concept of the *definitive text* pertains only to religion or fatigue." [In discussing *César Vallejo: The Complete Posthumous Poetry* we] must take these ideas into account in considering the heroic efforts made by Clayton Eshleman and José Rubia Barcia to translate César Vallejo, one of the most "difficult" poets to write in Spanish in the 20th century.

There are a few facts about Vallejo we ought to have in mind as we think of his poetry. First, that he was born in a remote village in north-central Peru of parents of mixed blood: he was neither Indian nor white in a society where the shade of one's skin determined one's place in the world. Second, his poverty: he was one of eleven children and had to struggle to educate himself, to make himself more than he was. Third, we must take into account the Catholic faith he was born into and from which he lapsed: the religious images in his poetry and the sense of guilt we also find there derive from that lost faith. Finally, we must understand the moral outrage of a man who had educated himself above his origins but who always remembered the squalor of both his family and the even less well-off peasants in the countryside. Vallejo was a well-known poet in Peru when he moved to Paris in 1923 at the age of 31. He had already published *The Black Heralds* in 1919, poems in the *fin-de-siècle* vein, and *Trilce* in 1922, the most idiosyncratic avant-garde poetry written in Spanish. At 46, heartbroken over the Spanish Civil War, he died in Paris.

[*César Vallejo: The Complete Posthumous Poetry*] contains the poetry Vallejo wrote and rewrote between 1923 and 1938, a mixture of lyric poetry, much of it imbued with social consciousness (he joined the Spanish Communist Party in 1931), and the stunning collection of war poetry, *Spain, Take This Cup From Me* (1937-1938). This translation is important not only because it provides us with annotated versions of Vallejo's later poetry but also because it enables us to see how a poet maturing in the 20's and 30's was drawn irresistibly into politics. The poets of the Anglo-American world divided on the issue of the Spanish Civil War into right and left, as did the French, while in the Hispanic world, the best poetic voices, Vallejo and Pablo Neruda among them, were militantly left-wing.

Before passing on to the poetry itself, we should note that this is Clayton Eshleman's third attempt to bring Vallejo into English: in 1968, he published with Grove Press the *Poemas humanos/Human Poems,* and in 1974, *Spain, Take This Cup From Me,* again with Grove. His reasons for trying yet once more are many, among them: the availability of improved texts (printed versions compared with manuscripts), more and better scholarship (we simply know more about Vallejo and his writings), and changes in the translator himself. In José Rubia Barcia, a Spaniard in exile in the United States since the Spanish Civil War, Eshleman found not only a person who could help him understand Vallejo's Spanish but also one who could help keep his semantic speculations about particular passages within fixed bounds. Eshleman assumes complete responsibility for the results, but he notes that Rubia Barcia's presence helped him to make his decisions. The results have impressed many: the translation won a National Book Award in 1979.

The poetic tradition into which Vallejo was born, and which shaped his first book, *The Black Heralds,* was the moribund combination of Romanticism and Symbolism called in Spanish America *Modernismo. Modernismo* was an attempt to bring poetry in Spanish back into the mainstream of the Western literary tradition, from which it had drifted during the war-torn years of the first half of the 19th century. Thus, Vallejo in 1919 is melancholic, maudlin, and euphonic:

> *Hay golpes en la vida, tan fuertes . . . ¡Yo no sé!*
> *Golpes como del odio de Dios; como si ante ellos,*

> *la resaca de todo lo sufrido*
> *se empozara en el alma . . . ¡Yo no sé!*

> *Son pocos; pero son . . . Abren zanjas oscuras*
> *en el rostro más fiero y en el lomo más fuerte.*
> *Serán tal vez los potros de bárbaros atilas;*
> *o los heraldos negros que nos manda la Muerte.*

There are blows in life, so strong . . . I don't know!
Blows like God's hate; as if when we face them
the undertow of all we've suffered
flowed into our souls . . . I don't know!
They are few; but they exist . . . They open dark furrows
in the fiercest face and in the strongest back.
Perhaps they are the ponies of barbarous attilas;
or the black heralds Death sends to us (my translation)

There is a lot of post-Nietzschean depression in this poem, a trait that becomes constant in Vallejo, but there is also a melodramatic posturing—the "I don't know!" refrain—that marks the poem (of which these are the first two stanzas) as being under the influence of *Modernismo*. There is, again, much we will see in later Vallejo: the almost masochistic sense of having been brutalized by life, a religious sense, if not a religious belief, and the ubiquity of Death, always personalized as it is here.

In the first book-length division of the Eshleman translation, "Nómina de huesos" (1923-1936) "Payroll of Bones" (1923-1936), we find a poem that show the continuity and the evolution of Vallejo's style: **"Piedra negra sobre una piedra blanca," "Black Stone on a White Stone."** By the 30's, Vallejo had already passed through an avant-garde phase of poetic experiment, a search for a personal poetic language. This search culminated in *Trilce* (1922), written in a code so dense and personal it defies "translation" of any kind. The poems of the 30's retain some of that hermeticism, but they modify it in order to express a personal yet comprehensible vision of the world.

Like the poem quoted above from *The Black Heralds,* **"Piedra negra sobre una piedra blanca"** is a meditation on death:

> *Me moriré en París con aguacero,*
> *un día del cual tengo ya el recuerdo.*
> *Me moriré en París—y no me corro—*
> *talvez un jueves, como es hoy, de otoño.*

> *Jueves será, porque hoy, jueves, que proso*
> *estos versos, los húmeros me he pueso*
> *a la mala y, jamás como hoy, me he vuelto,*
> *con todo mi camino, a verme solo.*

> *César Vallejo ha muerto, le pegaban*
> *todos sin que él les haga nada;*
> *le daban duro con un palo y duro*

> *también con una soga; son testigos*
> *los días jueves y los huesos húmeros,*
> *la soledad, la lluvia, los caminos . . .*

Eshleman translates this sonnet in this way:

> I will die in Paris with a sudden shower,
> a day I can already remember.
> I will die in Paris—and I don't budge—

maybe a Thursday, like today is, in autumn.

Thursday it will be, because today, Thursday,
   when I prose
these poems, the humeri that I have put on
by force and, never like today, have I turned,
with all my road, to see myself alone.

César Vallejo has died, they beat him,
everyone, without him doing anything to them;
they gave it to him hard with a stick and hard

also with a rope; witnesses are
the Thursday days and the humerus bones,
the loneliness, the rain, the roads . . .

There is a here-and-now quality in the Spanish that is attenuated in the English, and there are some interpretations I would question, even though Eshleman explains some of them in his notes. Eshleman's second verse, "a day I can already remember," does not correspond precisely to *"un día del cual tengo ya el recuerdo,"* which, literally, is "a day of which I already possess the memory." It is not only remembering that matters here, but the fact that the memory of the future is possessed, filed away in memory. The aside in verse three Eshleman translates as "—and I don't budge—," but *"y no me corro"* could mean (since the verb *correr* means other things besides running) "and I don't get upset." In the second stanza, Eshleman translates *"estos versos"* as "these poems." This might better have been translated literally as "these verses," since the sonnet dramatizes the moment of writing, a moment we readers ironically share. It is as if the poet were present, and because of this the poem becomes, as epitaphs did among the Romantics, the voice of the dead poet coming back to life through the reader. In the sixth and seventh lines, we find the curious statement, *"los húmeros me he puesto / a la mala,"* which Eshleman renders "the humeri that I have put on by force," but which might also be translated as "my shoulders, which pain me terribly." In the same stanza, Vallejo says *"me he vuelto / con todo mi camino, a verme solo,"* which Eshleman makes "never like today, have I turned, / with all my road, to see myself alone." The verse might also be translated, "and, but never like today, I have seen myself again with all my road, alone."

The poetic tradition into which Vallejo was born, and which shaped his first book, *The Black Heralds,* was the moribund combination of Romanticism and Symbolism called in Spanish America *Modernismo.*

— *Alfred J. MacAdam*

Seen in this way, the poem gives the poet's vision of his own death, of a message being sent to him by his worn-out body, and of this being one of a series of intimations of mortality. The same Christ-like figure is here that is present in the early poem, the same *persona* with his fixations: stones (to be carved, tombstones, missiles), the dreariness of rain, and the beaten body, itself a *memento mori*. Here is Vallejo the pilgrim, the ironic pilgrim whose road leads only to death.

This singer of his miserable self is not alone in the poetry of the post-Symbolist era which was, among other things, a resurrection of the Romantic ego repressed by the Symbolists. But that same ego abandoned its self-indulgence at a critical moment, the agonizing death of liberal aspirations in the Spanish Civil War. In his last book, Vallejo achieves a union with humanity on a collective scale: he becomes a prophet, a voice speaking for the people.

The title of **Spain, Take This Cup From Me** comes, of course, from Jesus' agony in the garden, here described in Matthew 26:39: "And he went a little further, and fell on his face, and prayed, saying, O my Father, if it be possible, let this cup pass from me; nevertheless, not as I will, but as thou wilt." Here Vallejo again takes on a Christlike role, ironically twisting Christ's prayer: it is not to God Vallejo speaks, but to Spain, begging Spain not to require him to drink the death draught of civil war. The prayer to "Mother Spain" (called so in the poem **"Spain, Take this Cup from Me"**) is empty because Spain cannot answer it. Unlike Jesus, who accepts the will of God and makes His sacrifice willingly, Vallejo imbues his war poetry with the vertiginous horror of civil violence in a land breeding only death.

But Vallejo's poetry is not all despair. Like most of the poets who wrote on the Spanish Civil War (Auden and Neruda included), Vallejo's poems in this book tend either toward the ode or the elegy. That is, when he attempts to be hortatory and to glorify the arms of the Republic, he writes odes, or that special form of ode in which the poet takes on the chanting voice of the collectivity, the hymn. The poems in **Spain, Take This Cup From Me** should not be confused with patriotic ditties. Vallejo sacrifices none of his obscurity, his totally personal style even though he attempts to speak for all. Like Neruda in *Spain in My Heart* (1938), Vallejo changes his subject matter—he wants to speak for humanity in favor of the Republic and no longer merely express himself—but he does so in his own style.

The final poem of the collection, the one that provides the title for the entire collection, shows that moment when ode and elegy blend. It exhorts the children of the world to carry on, to live out the humanitarian ideals the Republic had come to symbolize to the liberal imagination:

> . . . if mother
> Spain falls—I mean, it's just a thought—
> go out, children of the world, go and look for
>   her! . . .

Spain then may cease to exist as a Republic, as a nation, but it must continue to exist as an idea: the poem is elegiac in its meditation on political defeat and an ode in that it attempts to move, through apostrophe, a younger generation to greater things.

Stephen Hart   (essay date 1984)

SOURCE: "César Vallejo's Personal Earthquake," in *Romance Notes,* Vol. XXV, No. 2, Winter, 1984, pp. 127-31.

[*In the essay below, Hart discusses historical and religious references in the poem "Terremoto."*]

César Vallejo's poem **"Terremoto"** has received little critical attention in the past. [In the 1976 *César Vallejo: The Dialectics of Poetry and Silence*] Jean Franco discusses how the poem 'destroys any sense of presence in order to replace this by relativity and function', but she does not bring out the relevance of the historical figures to the imagery used. Américo Ferrari gives a longer critical discussion of **"Terremoto"** [in the 1972 *El universo poético de César Vallejo*], showing how it is characterized by opposites of various kinds, but confessing ignorance at the meaning of certain phrases such as 'horizonte de entrada' and the relevance of certain names such as Atanacio and Isabel. Clayton Eshleman goes one step further in this disregard for the resonance attached to historical figures by remarking [in *César Vallejo: The Complete Posthumous Poetry*] that the proper names mentioned in **"Terremoto"** "have no particular meaning for a Spanish reader." In this article, I show how the historical figures form a vital part of the argument of the poem, without which the poem cannot be understood. As we shall see, **"Terremoto"** manipulates, in an allusive and subtle manner, arguments about religious heterodoxy, such as Arianism and the Incarnation, which once troubled Christendom. These religious debates are related creatively to the personal spiritual anguish experienced by the poet. Before a discussion of these strands of religious controversy, the poem must be quoted in entirety:

> Hablando de la leña, callo el fuego?
> Barriendo el suelo, olvido el fósil?
> Razon,
>
> mi trenza, mi corona de carne?
> (Contesta, amado Hermeregildo, el brusco;
> pregunta, Luis, el lento!)
>
> ¡Encima, abajo, con tamaña altura!
> ¡Madera, tras el reino de las fibras!
> ¡Isabel, con horizonte de entrada!
> ¡Lejos, al lado, astutos Atanacios!
>
> ¡Todo, la parte!
> Unto a ciegas en luz mis calcetines,
> en riesgo, la gran paz de este peligro,
> y mis cometas, en la miel pensada,
> el cuerpo, en miel llorada.
>
> ¡Pregunta, Luis; responde, Hermeregildo!
> ¡Abajo, arriba, al lado, lejos!
> ¡Isabel, fuego, diplomas de los muertos!
> ¡Horizonte, Atanacio, parte, todo!
> ¡Miel de miel, llanto de frente!
> ¡Reino de la madera,
> corte oblicuo a la línea del camello,
> fibra de mi corona de carne!

The main opposition around which the whole poem is constructed is that between body and soul, as Ferrari has suggested. The references to historical figures of the past are used as means of exploring this basic antithesis. Luis

and Isabel are political figures, the first being perhaps Louis II Le Bègne (846-879), reputed a stammerer, which would explain why Vallejo calls him "el lento"; and the latter being Isabel I (1451-1504), Queen of Castile. The other two historical characters are mainly known for their spiritual preeminence. Vallejo writes "Hermeregildo", although the normal spelling in Spanish is "Hermenegildo (San)" (d. 585), the Visigothic Prince who was converted to Catholicism in 573 and who was executed after twice attempting to murder his father. Vallejo's description of him as 'Hermeregildo, el brusco' is, thus, quite apt. The fact that Vallejo mis-spells this saint's name need not trouble us. It is no doubt quite deliberate. In **'Los nueve monstruos',** for example, as the fascimile of the original typescript shows, Vallejo's mis-spells Jean-Jacques Rousseau's name as "Russeau". The fourth figure mentioned is 'Atanacio' which, again, should be spelled rightly 'Atanasio (San)' (296-373), one of the fathers of the Christian Church and patriarch of Alexandria. Vallejo introduces Saint Hermenegild and Saint Athanasius into his poem because they were both renowned for their defence of the orthodox faith against Arianism. Saint Hermenegild rebelled against his father Leovigild precisely because the latter was an Arian. Saint Athanasius fought successfully, for his part, against Arianism in the Council of Nicaea (325). Arianism, about which debate raged in the 4th century and even later, in stressing the absolute divinity of God and the humanity of Christ, tended to produce a split between the physical and spiritual realms which proved unacceptable to orthodox Christianity.

An enquiry into this fundamental philosophical issue lies at the heart of Vallejo's poem. Thus, in the first stanza, the poet asks whether, when reasoning, he should forget "my braid, my crown of flesh." In other words, Vallejo seems to be saying, should we ever think of our mind and body as separate entities? Similarly, Vallejo asks whether he should forget "the fossil" (i. e. the inevitability of physical death) while "sweeping the ground" (i. e. thinking). The same parallelism underpins the metaphor which opens the poem where 'wood' (body) is contrasted with 'fire' (soul). This particular analogy of fire burning and consuming the wood appears to come from Hugh of St Victor, though Vallejo may have found it elsewhere, and a very beautiful example of it occurs in Luis de León. As will become clearer, Vallejo is also referring—albeit obliquely—to another related debate which perturbed early Christendom.

In the second half of the poem, Vallejo underlines that the relations he is alluding to are in the nature of a synecdoche. Thus, he begins line eleven with the exclamation "¡Todo, la parte!". The relation between part and whole can be compared to that between soul and body. One image which acts as a go-between linking the two levels is the "wood". The greatest key to its precise resonance in Vallejo's poem appears in the at first enigmatic line, "¡Isabel, fuego, diplomas de los muertos!" Since Isabel I holds the dubious distinction of having founded the Spanish Inquisition, I take this line to be an evocation of the traditional means by which heretics were executed, namely the *auto-de-fe.* The reference to fire, or burning at the stake, along with the background of Arianism, a persistent heretical creed, in the poem, would seem to strengthen this interpretation. That fire should be described as "diplomas of the dead" is no doubt a reference to the belief that, through fire, the sinner's soul should be purged of evil, and, therefore, as it were, obtain the certificate necessary to enter the Kingdom of Heaven. This gives a rather graver significance in retrospect to the opening line of the poem, "Hablando de la leña, callo el fuego?"

Because so many of the images ultimately stem from the antithesis body-soul, it comes as no surprise that Vallejo is also reviving the debate in early Christendom concerning the mystery of how the components of body and soul are joined in the Incarnation. The fathers of the Church themselves compared this transcendent fusion to that of, *inter alia*, wine, honey, water, fire and iron. Vallejo, indeed, quite often used the idea of admixture to define spiritual relationships. Thus, in **"Los desgraciados"**, he speaks of "el hacha en que están presos / el acero y el hierro y el metal" which seems to be a reference to the Trinity of the Father, Son and Holy Spirit administered in Mass. In a similar vein, in **"Batallas II"**, Vallejo writes of how "a lo largo del mar que huye del mar, / a través del metal que huye del plomo, / al ras del suelo que huye de la tierra" to suggest the spiritual fragmentation caused in matter itself by the Spanish Civil War. The most common admixture in Vallejo's poetry occurs between water and wine, which again symbolizes the body-soul pair. In **"Despedida recordando un adiós"**, for example, Vallejo bids farewell to "wine that is in the water like wine" and to "alcohol that is in the rain". In **"Me viene, hay días, una gana ubérrima, política. . . ."** Vallejo speaks of the "king of wine" and the "slave of water". In **"Terremoto"**, many of these various poetic strands are woven together. In particular, honey, fire and water (or tears) are employed as images to signify the dialectic of body and soul. In the third stanza, for example, body and soul are described as two different kinds of honey, the first of which is "miel llorada", the second being "miel pensada". In the final three lines of the poem, all these connotations are brought triumphantly together in a *summa* reminiscent of Golden Age verse:

> ¡Reino de la madera,
> corte oblicuo a la línea del camello,
> fibra de mi corona de carne!

Here, Vallejo compares once more his flesh to wood. His flesh is seen at once as a crown (of thorns), like the one Christ wore before crucifixion, and also wood (which is reminiscent, given the context, of the wood of the cross on which Christ was crucified). Again, this symbolism was quite common in Vallejo's poetry. In **"Un pilar soportando consuelos . . . "**, for instance, Vallejo had spoken of "las tablas de esta frente". The final image of **"Terremoto"**, thus, combines various levels of suffering and sacrifice. The poet is also kneeling in prayer. The wood of his flesh has been cut back, as a result of intense suffering, to "la línea del camello", namely, the kneeling position characteristic of camels at rest. The image of the honey which appeared earlier on in the poem can also be taken as a grotesque reference to the poet's flesh which, through the purgation of fire, begins to melt. Vallejo seems to take an almost masochistic pleasure in these images of self-destruction (or rather, martyrdom), represented variously as burning wood, melting honey and the unavoidable fossil.

"Terremoto," as we see, employs historical figures and the religious ideas associated with them to express a personal spiritual dilemma. It is a complex poem, more demanding intellectually and emotionally than critics have hitherto assumed.

In much of Vallejo's poetry, metaphor has come under the sway of philosophic and scientific modes of knowledge; hence, poetic particulars are openly substituted one for the other, wresting them from one sphere and relocating them in another.

—*Christiane von Buelow, in her "The Allegorical Gaze of César Vallejo," in* Modern Language Notes, *March 1985.*

Stephen Hart   (essay date 1985)

SOURCE: "The World Upside-Down in the Work of César Vallejo," in *Bulletin of Hispanic Studies,* Vol. LXII, No. 2, April, 1985, pp. 163-77.

[In the following excerpt, Hart explores Vallejo's treatment of the theme of the world turned upside-down, asserting that his early poetry and prose convey a "desire to return to a silent paradise of animal simplicity," while his writings after his conversion to Communism depict both a world gone wrong and the hope for a future utopia.]

The desire to turn the world upside-down, as expressed in the *Trilce* poems, is to be viewed as a modern example of a *topos* that has enjoyed a rich and varied tradition in European literature, especially in the avant-garde. For the search is ultimately directed towards a prelapsarian state. But, as we find so often in Vallejo's poetry, this poetical device is used for specifically personal ends. In Vallejo's early work (up until about 1925), this *topos* is used to characterize a pre-edenic state in which the poet is fully integrated with his animal self or *anima* (soul). But later on, the same *topos*, through revitalization with the Marxian dialectic, is used to represent the world of capitalism as a political world the wrong way up. Towards the end of Vallejo's life, a means of escaping this impasse by reverting the world to its original harmony seemed possible through the heroic efforts of the Republicans during the Spanish Civil War.

The search for the other side of reality is present in the very first poem of *Trilce* thus setting the mood for the whole collection. The fundamentally animal quality of the poetic experience expressed is evident if we consider that the poem is essentially about excrementation. The epiphany achieved by means of full integration with the biological function of the body is equally one of silence:

> Y por la península párase
> por la espalda, abozaleada, impertérrita
> en la línea mortal del equilibrio.

Poetic inscape, here symbolized by *península*, is muzzled (*abozaleada*), and therefore silent. It is equally backwards to our normal conception of reality ('por la espalda'). Epiphany, as we see, reveals the hidden reverse of reality, transporting the poetic subject into a prelapsarian bliss that is totally animal and silent.

It should be pointed out at this stage that for Vallejo to search for a pre-verbal state of animal simplicity by using words is, of course, a paradox in itself. Indeed, the frustration springing from this desire to express the inexpressible often leads Vallejo to turn his destructive energy on words themselves. He pulls them to bits, vents his anger on their inexpressive object-like opacity. The best example of this is, perhaps, '*Trilce* LX,' where the phrase 'busco volver de golpe el golpe' is massacred to produce respectively 'vusco volvvver de golpe el golpe (. . .) busco vol ver de golpe el golpe (. . .) fallo bolver de golpe el golpe'. Vallejo's friends remember him as taking a fiendish delight in annihilating words. Juan Espejo Asturrizaga recalls how Vallejo once read one of Francisco Villaespesa's poems and began pulling it to pieces, changing the words in the poem: Eracomo meterse dentro del poema y jugar en su interior hasta dejarlo deshecho [in his *César Vallejo: Itinerario del hombre,* 1965]. Ernesto More, commenting on the same mannerism, concludes that 'Vellejo jugaba con las palabras igual que un muchacho con sus juguetes, hasta destrozarlas' [in his *Vallejo en la encrveljáda del drama pervano,* 1968]. Interestingly enough, the madman of Vallejo's short story "**Los Caynas**" (1923) has a very similar mannerism:

> Luis Urquizo habla y se arrebata, casi chorreando sangre el rostro resurado, húmedos los ojos. Trepida; guillotina sílabas, suelda y enciende adjetivos.

He guillotines syllables, solders and lights up adjectives, treating language in a way similar to Vallejo himself. Luis Urquizo is also a man who sees the world upside-down:

> Aquel hombre continuó viendo las cosas al revés, trastrocándolo todo, a través de los cinco cristales ahumados de sus sentidos enfermos.

Not only does he destroy language, and see the world upside-down, but he is also totally at one with the animal side of human nature. He and his relatives 'eran víctimias de una obsesíon común, de una misma idea, zoológica, grotesca, lastimosa, de un ridículo fenomenal; se creían monos, y como tales vivían' [in *Novelas y cuentos completos,* 1970]. Luis Urquizo is, as it were, the paradigm of the other self which the poems of *Trilce* attempt to body forth—a human animal living in a world that is back to front and pre-verbal.

Often, this other mysterious self is suggested through the symbolic use of the mirror. In '**Fabla salvaje,**' a short story of the same period, the protagonist, Balta Espinar, is perpetually haunted by the eerie reflection of himself in mirrors and water. A similar desire to go through the magic looking-glass forms the core of a poem '**Hay un lugar que yo me sé**' published in *España* in 1923:

> Mas el lugar que yo me sé
> en este mundo, nada menos

> hombreado va con los reversos.
> —Cerrad aquella puerta que
> está entreabierta en las entrañas
> de ese espejo . . .

The mirror becomes symbolic of a door onto the beyond. A similar idea is expressed in '*Trilce* VIII:'

> Pero un mañana sin mañana
> entre los aros de que enviudemos,
> margen de espejo habrá
> donde traspasaré mi propio frente
> hasta perder el eco
> y quedar con el frente hacia la espalda.

The poetic subject will pass through the looking-glass to become totally at one with the reverse image of the self contained in the mirror. That other realm behind the mirror defies the Kantian categories of time ('un mañana sin mañana') and space ('quedar con el frente hacia la espalda'). In its evocation of a silent and timeless immobility, this poem brings to mind the canvas *La Reproduction interdite* by the Belgian artist René Magritte, in which a man is gazing, into a mirror, at the back of his own head. Vallejo's poem, like Magritte's canvas, shows us a topsy-turvy world that is strange and mysterious.

A preoccupation with the wonderland behind the mirror, evident in different writers such as Paul Valéry, Paul Éluard, and Julio Cortázar, appears in others of the *Trilce* poems, particularly 'LXXV', 'LXVII' and 'XL.'

Just as the image reflected in the mirror seems to hint at a mysterious other world, so too does the sound of music. Thus, in '*Trilce* XLIX,' for example, the sound of a piano revolutionizes the poet's conception of reality:

> Piano oscuro a qué atisbas
> con tu sordera que me oye,
> con tu mudez que me asorda?
> Oh pulso misterioso.

The roles of the poet and piano have been exchanged. Rather than the more normal situation of the poet hearing the piano, we are presented with the piano which hears the poet. The second proposition of the stanza obeys, equally, the law by which all is rendered topsy-turvy. The *mudez* of the piano deafens the poet. Thus, not only is the piano—hearer relationship reversed, turning the piano from passive to active participant, but the realms of sound and silence are likewise interchanged. Silence takes some of the character of sound. It is deafening!

In other poems we find a similar reversal of the values of sound and silence. In '*Trilce* XLVIII' for instance, the 'penultimate coin', itself a symbol of transcendence, is evoked as a resonant silence:

> Ella, vibrando y forcejando
> pegando gritttos,
> soltando arduos, chisporroteantes silencios,
> orinándose de natural grandor,
> en unánimes postes surgentes,
> acaba por ser todos los guarismos,
>   la vida entera.

Those silences which encapsulate the brief transcendent glimpse of 'la vida entera' are 'chisporroteantes' and related to natural biological processes ('orinándose de natural grandor'). This realm of 'entire life' is strictly that of the inner world. In *'Trilce V'* for example, the intense subjectivity of Vallejo's search is brought into focus. In the second stanza of this poem, Vallejo suggests how the transcendence of binary opposition leads to an inward kingdom, silent and invisible:

> A ver. Aquello sea sin ser más.
> A ver. No transcienda hacia afuera,
> y piense en són de no ser escuchado,
> y crome y no sea visto.
> Y no glise en el gran colapso.

The poet wishes his experience to remain as it is, within the self as a thought which cannot be heard, as a color which cannot be seen. If not, the experience of triunine epiphany will slip into the great collapse, the Fall of the objective world. The prelapsarian bliss which the poet longs to attain is, thus, situated not in a distant past but within the self. Paradise, Vallejo seems to be saying, is there if only we could see it. For it is the animal reality of man.

The paradox behind this insight—which is at once archetypal and local—derives from the fact that, were man to become fully integrated with his animal self, then the world would surely be turned upside-down. Such, at any rate, seems to be the idea expressed in *'Trilce XIII.'* The poem concludes by exulting the epiphany of the sexual act, when man is at one with his animal destiny:

> Oh Conciencia,
> pienso, sí, en el bruto libre
> que goza donde quiere, donde puede.
> Oh, escándalo de miel de los crepúsculos.
> Oh estruendo mudo.
> ¡Odumodnuertse!

The sexual act is seen as scandal which, in its total rejection of Consciousness, turns the world back to front. Thus Vallejo writes 'estruendo mudo' backwards in the final exclamation of the poem. This attitude of vital acceptance of the animal and sexual reality of mankind, so admirably expressed in this poem, may well have been catalyzed, if not inspired, by the poetry of Walt Whitman, whom Vallejo was reading from at least 1917 onwards.

This full integration with the animal reality of the human psyche often leads, in Vallejo's prose and poetry of the early period, to an obsession with incest. On a subconscious level, this preoccupation is linked to silence since, as Claude Lévi-Strauss has shown, one of the basic desires of the primitive mind involves escaping the social laws controlling the exchange of women and words, thereby returning to incest and silence. In *Muro antártico* (1923), for example, incestual desire is depicted as an idyllically pure emotion:

> ¡Oh carne de mi carne y hueso de mis huesos!
>
> . . . ¡Oh hermana mía, esposa mía, madre mía!

In one of his prose poems, **'El buen sentido'**, no doubt written shortly after his arrival in Paris in 1923, Vallejo describes with undeniably sexual overtones a future reunion with his mother:

> Mi adiós es un punto de su ser, más externo que el punto de su ser al que retorno. Soy, a causa del excesivo plazo de mi vuelta, más el hombre ante mi madre que el hijo ante mi madre.

In this Oedipal *regressus ad uterum,* the normal conception of linear time can have no place:

> La mujer de mi padre está enamorada de mí, viniendo y avanzando de espaldas a mi nacimiento y de pecho a mi muerte. Que soy dos veces suyo: por el adiós y por el regreso.

Notice how the mother is described as 'advancing backwards'. This particular version of the world upside-down is, as we shall see, common in Vallejo's poetry.

A similar uncanny encounter with the mother figure is the central incident in another of Vallejo's short stories, 'Más allá de la vida y la muerte' (1921). Vallejo sees the meeting with his dead mother as an event that elides the logical categories of space, life and death:

> ¡Meditad sobre este suceso increíble, rompedor de las leyes de la vida y de la muerte, superador de toda posibilidad; palabra de esperanza y de fe entre-el absurdo y el infinito, innegable deconexión de lugar y de tiempo; nebulosa que hace llorar de inarmónicas armonías incognoscibles!

In this sudden unexpected visitation from beyond the grave, the world is turned back to front. The protagonist becomes as a father to his own mother:

> como si a fuerza de un fantástico trueque de destino, acabase mi madre de nacer y yo viniese, en cambio, desde tiempos viejos, que me daban una emoción patternal respecto de ella.

In *Trilce* also, Vallejo often uses the image of journey in a backward direction to express the eeriness of the poetic experience as life's secrets are suddenly revealed. In *'Trilce X,'* for example, Vallejo is desperately searching for a hidden transcendent meaning to his life:

> Cómo detrás desahucian juntas
> de contrarios. Cómo siempre asoma el guarismo
> bajo la línea de todo avatar.

Numerical harmony (*quarismo*) surfaces beneath what at first seemed like non-consequential events. In the following verse, this line of transformations ('línea de todo avatar') is seen as a gradual quintessentialization of life:

> Cómo escotan las ballenas a palomas.
> Cómo a su vez dejan el pico
> cubicado en tercera ala.
> Cómo arzonamos, cara a monótonas ancas.

Whales are reduced to doves, themselves archetypal symbols of the Ideal. Then the doves' beaks are cubed to produce the third wing ('tercera ala')—again with implications of transcendence in the image of the trinity. The stanza concludes with the final stage of this series of transformations—a state in which our normal conceptions of reality are stood on their head. The poet is riding on a donkey's back, but he is facing in the direction of the rump! A similar image of inversion appears in 'Trilce LXXI,' but here it is sexual experience which turns the world topsy-turvy:

> Vanse los carros flagelados por la tarde,
> y entre ellos los míos, cara atrás, a las riendas
> fatales de tus dedos.

The *carros* which are a symbol of the linear consecutivity of events are different from those of the poet ('los míos'), which are facing in the opposite direction ('cara atrás').

In these two *Trilce* poems, Vallejo uses a spatial image to evoke the world upside-down. In the prose poem **'Lánguidamente su licor,'** however, Vallejo manages to suggest reversal on the temporal as well as the spatial level:

> Un tiempo de rúa, contuvo a mi familia. Mamá
> salió, avanzando inversamente y como si hubiera
> dicho: las partes.

As in **'El buen sentido,'** Vallejo's mother is 'advancing backwards'. This spatial reversal also implies the reversal of time, for the scene takes place in 'un tiempo de rúa'. Such is the meaning of the conclusion of the poem. The children, like the hen's eggs, go backwards in time. They return to their point of origin:

> Fue una gallina vieja, maternalmente viuda de
> unos pollos que no llegaron a incubarse. Origen
> olvidado de ese instante, la gallina era sus hijos.
> Fueron hallados vacíos todos los huevos. La
> clueca después tuvo el verbo.

Vallejo subverts Euclidean space not only in a horizontal sense but in a vertical sense as well. Thus, in **'*Trilce* LXVIII,'** for example, it begins to rain not downwards but upwards:

> Y llueve más de abajo ay para arriba.

Similarly, in **'*Trilce* LXXVI,'** Vallejo joins hands with Heraclitus, Saint John of the Cross, and the surrealists, in seeing upward and downward movement as one and the same:

> No subimos acaso para abajo?

In the prose poem **'Existe un mutilado . . .',** Vallejo clearly links the animal reality of man with the backward movement into a different spatio-temporal continuum already described. It is indeed in this prose poem that the difference between the 'otherness' experienced by Vallejo and that espoused by the Christian tradition is made most explicit. The *mutilado* is an invalid not because he is unable to grasp the intellectual meaning of the world but because his fundamentally animal reality is unable to find expression in the human world:

> El mutilado de la paz y del amor, del tronco y
> del orden y que lleva el rostro muerto sobre el
> tronco vivo, nació a la sombra de un árbol de es-
> paldas y su existencia transcurre a lo largo de un
> camino de espaldas.

Human consciousness, symbolized by 'el rostro', is merely a dead outer growth of the inner animal reality of the body, in turn symbolized by 'el tronco vivo'. Notice how this deep animal reality of man is associated with an upside-down world. For this specific invalid was born in the shade of 'un árbol de *espaldas*', and his life continues along 'un camino de *espaldas*' (my emphasis). In the remainder of the poem, Vallejo explores poetically the duality of mind and body, ultimately ascribing value to the animal side of man, with images that echo closely one of Whitman's poems translated into Spanish as 'Canto el cuerpo eléctrico':

> Como el rostro está yerto y difunto, toda la vida
> psíquica, toda la expresión animal de este hom-
> bre, se refugia, para traducirse al exterior, en el
> peludo cráneo, en el tórax y en las extremidades.
> Los impulsos de su ser profundo, al salir, re-
> troceden del rostro y la respiración, el olfato, la
> vista, el oìdo, la palabra, el resplandor humano
> de su ser, funcionan y se expresan por el pecho,
> por los hombros, por el cabello, por las costillas,
> por los brazos y la piernas y los pies.

Despite the fact that this human animal is unable to find adequate expression in the higher human senses—smell, hearing, speech—nevertheless, he is complete in himself:

> Mutilado del rostro, tapado del rostro, cerrado
> del rostro, no obstante, está entero y nada le hace
> falta. No tiene ojos y ve y llora. No tiene narices
> y habla y sonrìe. No tiene frente y piensa y se
> sume en sì mismo. No tiene mentón y quiere y
> subsiste. Jesús conocìa al mutilado de la función,
> que tenìa ojos y no veìa y tenìa orejas y no oìa.
> Yo conozco al mutilado del órgano, que ve sin
> ojos y oye sin orejas.

Christ's parable contains the implicit assumption that man, when looking at the world or listening to the Word, should be able to see a mystic meaning beneath the surface. The function required is an intellectual one—man's divine ability to perceive spiritual truth beneath the apparent. The man not blessed with this ability is a 'mutilado de la función'. The *mutilado* Vallejo is describing, however, is mutilated for very different reasons. For it is his deep animal being, rather than his intellectual faculties, which is unable to function freely. For this reason, he is a 'mutilado del órgano', like the poet himself:

The unanimous message, thus, which emerges from the early period (including the short stories, *Trilce* and the prose poems) is that Vallejo is searching for an inner experience that is at once intensely animal and characterized by silence. We have seen how, in order to give this radical insight the desired impact on the reader, Vallejo employs the *topos* of the world upside-down. Later on in Vallejo's poetic career, however, we find a new system of values emerging. While in 1926, Vallejo could still be regarded as an avant-garde writer (he contributed in the June and October issues of *Favorables Paris Poema*), by the following year, he had cut most of his ties with the avant-garde movement. Thus, on 7 May 1927, in an article published in *Variedades,* no. 1001, **'Contra el secreto profesional: a propósito de Pablo Abril de Vivero',** Vallejo accused avant-garde artists of being so out of 'cowardice' or 'poverty'. Vallejo, at this time, was gaining interest in politics. By at least August 1927, he was reading *L'Humanité,* the official organ of the French Communist Party. Further reading soon followed. Before long, Vallejo was quoting and discussing political thinkers such as Marx, Lenin, Trotsky, Stalin, Bukharin, Plekhanov, among others. Vallejo's political studies profoundly revolutionized his poetic style in one significant way, for they introduced him to the

Hegelian-Marxian dialectic, and particularly its intuition of how each term or phenomenon destroys itself while changing into its opposite. Vallejo had an inkling of this idea by at least early 1927. In March of that year, Vallejo published an article which discusses the physical laws of the universe in dialectical terms:

> No hay que atribuir a las cosas un valor belinge-rante de mitad, sino que cada cosa contiene posiblemente virtualidad para jugar todos los roles, todos los contrarios, pudiendo suceder, en consecuencia, que el color negro simbolice a veces, según los hemisferios y las épocas, el dolor y el placer, la muerte y la epifanìa (. . .) Y esto prueba que toda cosa posee una gran multiplicidad de valores vitales y que, por ejemplo, un frìo puede llegar a ser tan fuerte que producirìa la combustión. Cada cosa contiene en potencia a todas las energìas del universo.

When Vallejo came to introduce this revolutionary insight into his poetry, he did so through images that themselves encapsulate dialectical mobility. In this Vallejo was not alone. The politicization of surrealism led many French surrealists independently along a similar path of poetic experimentation. One of the first examples of the dialectical image in Vallejo's poetry is to be found in **'Sombrero, abrigo, guantes'**, a poem written perhaps as early as late 1926. In the last stanza of the poem, Vallejo explores a train of thought in which opposites are presented dynamically:

> Importa oler a loco postulando
> ¡qué cálida es la nieve, qué fugaz la tortuga,
> el cómo qué sencillo,' qué fulminante el cuándo!

Not only do we meet with a logically impossible fusion of opposites ('qué fugaz la tortuga'), but also one of Vallejo's favourite antitheses (used as an example in the article quoted above) of hot and cold. 'How hot the snow is!', Vallejo exclaims. While the image of 'icy fire' is a traditional one, Vallejo uses it here, as elsewhere, in a dialectical sense. Thus, in **'Salutación angélica',** he speaks of the bolshevik's 'calor doctrinal, frìo' in 'Esto . . . ' of a 'frìo incendio', and in **'Los desgraciados',** he exhorts the socially deprived in the following terms—'atiza / tu frìo, porque en él se integra mi calor'. In **'Sermón sobre la muerte',** we hear of how 'se quema el precio de la nieve', and in **'Despedida recordando un adiós'** of the 'del Frìo frìo y frìo del calor'.

Though used sporadically in his earlier poetry, the dialectical image in which relations between things are reversed came to constitute a cornerstone of Vallejo's poetic style from about 1927 onwards. Thus, the antitheses between upward and downward movement, though in evidence in *Trilce* as we have seen, achieved greater flexibility in the post-vanguard period, through catalyzation by the Hegelian-Marxian dialectic. In **'Gleba',** for instance, the labourers descend 'por etapas hasta el cielo', and in **'Y si después de tántas palabras . . . ',** we are presented with the possibility of '¡Levantarse del cielo hacia la tierra'. In **'Los mineros salieron de la mina . . . ,'** the miners are able to climb down looking up and to climb up looking down, while, in **'Himno a los voluntarios de la República,'** Vallejo exclaims:

> ¡Unos mismos zapatos irán bien al que asciende
> sin vìas a su cuerpo
> y al que baja hasta la forma de su alma!

In a similar vein, Vallejo plays off dialectical pairs such as night/day, moon/sun and light/dark in **'Ouedéme a calentar la tinta . . . ', 'Tengo un miedo terrible . . . ', 'Ello es el lugar . . . '** and **'Algo te identifica . . . '.** In other poems, such as **'Oye a tu masa . . . '** and **'Qué me da . . .',** Vallejo explores the dialectical tension of death and life.

Just how deep-rooted the dialectical method became in Vallejo's poetic style is suggested by the frequency with which the rhetorical structure of the poem itself is of a dialectical kind, as in, for example, **'Confianza en el anteojo . . . ', 'Un hombre pasa . . . ', 'Cuídate España. . .'** and especially **'Yuntas'** as the title indicates. Occasionally, the dialectical method informs the semantic pattern, image and rhythm of a poem, as is the case with **'De puro calor . . .',** which opens as follows:

> ¡De puro calor tengo frìo,
> hermana Envidia!
> Lamen mi sombra leones
> y el ratón me muerde el nombre,
> ¡madre alma mìa!

Beginning with the hot-cold antithesis we have already met, Vallejo subsequently unfolds a train of thought in which everything calls forth its opposite. Lions do what mice usually do and vice-versa. This topsy-turvy world is further delineated in the following stanza:

> ¡Al borde del fondo áoy,
> cuñado Vicio!
> La oruga tañe su voz,
> y la voz tañe su oruga,
> ¡padre cuerpo mìo!

Of special interest are the third and fourth lines of the stanza where Vallejo reverses the order of the noun phrase and verb, thereby generating a totally new idea; 'caterpillar' and 'voice' exchange grammatical positions. Dialectical intertextuality works, indeed, not only within the stanza itself but also between the stanzas of the poem. Thus, *hermana* of the first verse is antithetical to *cuñado,* of the second, as *madre* is to *padre,* and *alma* to *cuerpo.* Constant oppositions such as these, in the post-vanguard poetry, tend to produce a dynamic and tightly woven poetic fabric which articulates a dialectical world-view.

An acquaintance with the Hegelian-Marxian dialectic apparently sharpened Vallejo's political vision. During those years in which Vallejo's political commitment deepened, from 1927 until the apex of enthusiasm for Soviet communism in 1930-31, he continued to view the world as the wrong way up. Whereas, before, in *Trilce,* Vallejo subverted the given in order to create a poetic universe unhampered by the straitjacket of reason, now he sought to uncover the workings of the world according to political rather than purely artistic formulae. Throughout the *Poemas humanos,* which were written over a period of roughly eleven years from 1926 until 1937, Vallejo portrayed, apart from isolated examples, a cruel inhuman world based on social injustice. Like Marx a century before, who regarded his contemporary world as a world the wrong way up, Vallejo came more and more to see the political reality of his own era as a grotesque distortion of an ideal world. Such is the political meaning of the first stanza of **'Los desgraciados'**, a poem written in the midst of the economic despair of the thirties:

> Ya va a venir el dìa; da
> cuerda a tu brazo, búscate debajo
> del colchón, vuelve a pararte
> en tu cabeza, para andar derecho.

These lines express the Marxian insight that alienated labor, in a capitalist society, 'alienates from man his own body'. The worker feels his own body as something reified, a mere object. Like a machine, it must be wound up and, as an object separate from the worker's being, it must be looked for under the mattress. The injustice of the worker's plight is expressed neatly by the *topos* of the world upside-down, for, in order to walk straight, the *desgraciado* must stand on his head. In a politically unjust world, all is back to front.

This terrifying political vision of the world the wrong way round is nowhere better delineated than in **'Los nueve monstruos'**, a poem which was again written in the thirties. The suffering caused by social inequality produces a topsy-turvy world which borders on a nightmare:

> crece el mal por razones que ignoramos
> y es una inundación con propìos lìquidos,
> con propio barro y propia nube sólida!
> Invierte el sufrimiento posiciones, da función
> en que el humor acuoso es vertical
> al pavimento,
> el ojo es visto y esta oreja oìda,

The cloud becomes solid, water stands upright, the eye is seen and the ear is heard. As the poem goes on to suggest, one of the reasons for this topsy-turvy world is capitalism:

> ¡Cómo, hermanos humanos,
> no deciros que ya no puedo y
> ya no puedo con tánto cajón,
> tánto minuto, tánta
> inversión, tánta lejos y tánta sed de sed!

The word *inversión* is a focal point of the whole poem. Apart from its obvious meaning of 'inversion', this word also has the meaning of 'investment'—a lexical item which is catalyzed into existence through proximity to the word *cajón* (safe). As a pun, *inversión* thereby identifies the inverted world with a political system based on safes, investments, in short, capitalism. As the character called 'La masa' makes quite clear in Vallejo's play **Lock-Out,** written some years before (in 1931), but relevant to the context of the later poem:

> ¡Hay una revolución! . . . ¡La revolución! . . .
> ¡Sì, la revolución! . . . ¡ La revolución que inver-
>   tirá todas esas injusticias! . . .

Two poems collected in **Poemas humanos** are especially noteworthy in that they map out what such an ideal world would be like were it to come into being. They were typed up towards the end of Vallejo's life, barely six months before his death, on 19 November 1937, and are entitled **'Ande desnudo . . . '** and **'Viniere el malo . . . '**. In the first of these two poems, Vallejo projects a world in which

misfortune belongs to the rich rather than the poor, and in which the poor give up their labours and rest:

> ¡Ande desnudo, en pelo, el millonario!
> ¡Desgracia al que edifica con tesoros su lecho de
>   muerte!
> ¡Un mundo al que saluda;
> un sillón al que siembra en el cielo;

In **'Viniere el malo . . . '**, Vallejo imagines a world in which everything is reversed, even creation itself:

> Comenzare por monte la montaña,
> por remo el tallo, por timón el cedro
> y esperaren doscientos a sesenta
> y volviere la carne a sus tres tìtulos . . .

Our normal world in which mountains, through erosion, one day become hills, in which stalks grow to form trees which are eventually turned into oars, in which the wood of cedar trees is used to make tillers, is completely turned on its head in Vallejo's poem. Would that flesh itself, as Vallejo goes on to say, 'return to its three titles', the Father, the Son and the Holy Ghost. Perhaps most significant of all, the upside-down world is one in which death no longer holds sway. As we read in the following stanza:

> Sobrase nieve en la noción del fuego,
> se acostare el cadáver a mirarnos,
> la centella a ser trueno corpulento
> y se arquearan los saurios a ser aves . . .

Beginning with the heat-cold antithesis familiar by now, Vallejo strives to will into being a world in which the 'corpse might lay down to watch us' rather than the reverse, the thunder precede the flash of lighting, and in which saurians, defying the deterministic laws of evolution, 'might arch to become birds'. The revolution at stake is, thus, not only political but one which would upturn the structure of the very universe. It is perhaps the truest kind of revolution since it would actually entail reversing evolution itself!

When the Spanish Civil War broke out in June 1936, Vallejo immediately understood that the Republican cause was a genuine grass roots revolution of the people. In the sheaf of fifteen poems which composed **España, aparta de mì este cáliz,** Vallejo departed from rigid communist orthodoxy in depicting the revolution of the Spanish working class in religious terms. Again the *topos* of the world upside-down flowed freely from Vallejo's pen. The apocalyptic vision announced in **'Himno a los voluntarios de la República'**, especially, possesses great affinities with the prophecies of Isaiah who predicted that 'sera el pueblo como el sacerdote, el siervo como el señor, la sierva como la señora, el vendedor como el comprador (. . .)' (24:2). Sometimes the language of Vallejo's poem follows Isaiah's text quite closely:

> Asì tu criatura, miliciano, asì tu exangüe cria-
>   tura,
> agitada por una piedra inmóvil,
> se sacrifica, apártase,
> decae para arriba y por su llama incombustible
>   sube,
> sube hasta los débiles,
> distribuyendo españas a los toros,
> toros a las palomas . . .

We notice immediately that the sacrifice of the *miliciano* leads to a reversal of the laws of gravity ('decae para arriba') in a way by now familiar. The evocation of bull and dove living in harmony can be compared to Isaiah's prophecy of eternal peace within the animal kingdom:

> El lobo habitará con el cordero, la pantera se
> tenderá con el cabrito, el novillo y el cachorro
> pacerán juntos. (11:6)

This future paradise of the world the right way up entails a miraculous transfiguration of earthly laws:

> ¡Enterlazándose hablarán los mudos, los tullidos
>   andarán!
> ¡Verán, ya de regreso, los ciegos
> y palpitando escucharán los sordos!

This fragment of Vallejo's poem is almost a *verbatim* transcription of Isaiah:

> Entonçes se abrirán los ojos de los ciegos y los
>   oìdos
> de los sordos se abrirán, el
> cojo saltará como ciervo y la lengua del mudo
>   gritará
> de gozo.
>
> (35:5-6)

The following line of Vallejo's **'Himno a los voluntarios de la República'** has a beautiful symmetrical grace about it:

> ¡Sabrán los ignorantes, ignorarán los sabios!

In the second clause, we detect once more the presence of the Jewish prophet, who predicted that 'fracasará la sabidurìa de los sobios, se ocultará la inteligencia de los inteligentes' (26:14). In the bliss upon earth which the militiamen are struggling to body forth, death will nor kill but itself will die:

> ¡Sólo la muerte morirá!

This imminent topsy-turvy world is again a reminiscence of Isaiah who prophesied that the Lord 'destuirá la muerte por siempre' (25:8).

The Revolution which the Republicans stand for is, thus, as much a spiritual as a concrete social transformation. It comes as no suprise, therefore, that those poems composed in the last years of Vallejo's life chart a gradual movement away from the previous emphasis on animality. In **"Batallas II"** for example, the animal plane is superseded by the strictly human plane. The poem calls for a humanization of everything—animals, trees and even the sky:

> para que todo el mundo sea un hombre, y para
> que hasta los animales sean hombres,
> el caballo, un hombre,
> el reptil, un hombre,
> el buitre, un hombre honesto,
> la mosca, un hombre, y el olivo, un hombre
> y hasta el ribazo, un hombre
> y el mismo cielo, todo un hombrecito.

Perhaps the most striking and original use of the *topos* of the world upside-down occurs with reference to poetic creation itself. In **'Pequeño responso a un héroe de la República'**, we find an image that, in effect, turns the Creation back to front:

> y un libro, yo lo vi sentidamente,
> un libro, atrás un libro, arriba un libro
> retoño del cadaver ex abrupto.

From the Republican hero's body, there springs a book, thus reversing the Genesis when, according to St. John, 'the Word became flesh' (1:14). The flesh of the *miliciano* is turned back into Word; his fame lives on in Vallejo's verse.

The *topos* of the world upside-down was used in a variety of ways by Vallejo throughout his life. In **Trilce,** the prose poems and the short stories, this poetic device is a sign connotative of Vallejo's desire to return to silent paradise of animal simplicity. Later on, and specifically because of his political conversion to communism, the *topos* is employed either to depict the social *status quo* as a world the wrong way up, or to describe the future religious and political utopia of 'paz indolora'. Despite Vallejo's changing preoccupations, this particular poetic device remained with him throughout.

Vallejo is concerned with the fiction that preoccupies many modern writers, namely, the "I" that perceives nature and creates meaning.

—*Christiane von Buelow, in her "The Allegorical Gaze of César Vallejo,"* in Modern Language Notes, *March, 1985.*

Lorna Close   (essay date 1987)

SOURCE: "Vallejo, Heidegger and Language," in *Words of Power: Essays in Honour of Alison Fairlie,* edited by Dorothy Gabe Coleman and Gillian Jondorf, University of Glasgow Publications in French Language and Literature, 1987, pp. 163-86.

[*In the essay below, Close analyzes the linquistic richness of Vallejo's poetry, noting his innovative use of syntax, spelling, wordplay, and ambiguity. Noting similarities between Vallejo's verse and Heidegger's theories of language, the critic also relates Vallejo's focus on the nature of language and his attempt to address its limitations in order "to project a more accurate and authentic view of the human condition, of man's 'being-in-the-world.' "*]

The reader coming to the poetry of César Vallejo, the Peruvian poet who died in Paris in 1938 at the age of 44, is at once confronted by and locked in struggle with linguistic difficulty. Words appear as no mere symbols, but have the density, timbre, impact, weight and opacity of physical objects, recalling what Gerard Manley Hopkins said of language in his essay on 'Rhythm and other Structural Parts of Rhetoric-Verse' [in the 1959 *The Papers and Journals of Gerard Manley Hopkins*]: 'We may think of words as heavy bodies, as indoor and out of door objects of nature and man's art'. To Hopkins, as to Vallejo, language has a corporeal character, a substantiality that cannot be effaced by the formalities of meaning. In Vallejo's verse, one is made conscious of the anarchic associative drive and energy of words, and has a sensual, indeed sexual awareness of their independent identity—we are never allowed to forget, in Vallejo, that Spanish is a language particularly rich in obscene or comic double meanings that subvert the decorum of some of the commonest words in usage. Language in Vallejo is in rebellion. In his second collection of poems, *Trilce,* published in 1922, he says 'La creada voz rebélase y no quiere / ser malla ni amo' (*"Trilce, V"*). It is rebelling unpredictably even here, because through phonetic identity in pronunciation between b and v in Spanish, what appears orthographically as 'rebélase'—*rebels,* with a b, is indistinguishable from 'revélase'—*reveals itself,* with a v. This single example is typical of a systematic and far-reaching habit of word-play of every kind in Vallejo's work. Writing in *El arte y la revolución,* the poet had claimed for himself considerable licence in the handling of language: 'La gramática, como norma colectiva en poesìa, carece de razón de ser. Cada poeta forja su gramática personal e intransferible, su sintaxis, su ortografia, su analogìa, su prosodia, su semántica . . . El poeta puede hasta cambiar, en cierto modo, la estructura literal y fonética de una misma palabra, según los casos'.

Writing of *Trilce,* Jean Franco has said [in the 1976 *César Vallejo: The Dialectics of Poetry and Silence*]: 'a volcanic eruption has taken place, destroying the hierarchies of the past, leaving man to confront a universe in which he has no special purpose or importance'. This 'volcanic eruption' expresses itself in a radical dislocation of the common procedures of language: Vallejo disrupts syntax, mingles different registers of discourse, abruptly shifting from the familiar trivia of meaningless colloquialism ('qué me importa', 'qué se va a hacer', 'anda', etc.) which are the daily currency of speech, to scientific, technical or musical terminology. Poetic archaisms rub shoulders with arcane number symbolism. The result of this idiosyncratic and incongruous mingling is to slow down our rate of reading, violently disturbing our comprehension, making each word starkly distinct, so that we are forced back to that childhood state of having to grapple with meaning half-understood, making us recapture the primal impact of the *strangeness* of words. Unexpected departures from the familiar are also found in the coining of neologisms: 'tristura' for 'tristeza', sadness; 'dulcera' instead of 'dulce', sweet, or 'dulzura', sweetness; or in sudden shifts in orthography—often only affecting one letter—e.g. 'excrementido' for 'excrementado (covered in excrement); 'toz' with a z for 'tos' (a cough). Further, Vallejo abandons formal verse-structures in most poems—each poem has its own organic form, as it were generated by its content.

In considering Vallejo's practice as a writer, and his ideas on language, I suggest that it is illuminating to compare these with the German philosopher Heidegger's conception of man's being and of language—especially poetic language. The latter are first explored in *Sein und Zeit* (1927), then in an essay on 'Hölderlin and the Essence of Poetry' (1935), to become an increasingly major preoccupation of the writings published in the 1940s and 1950s (such as *Über den Humanismus* (1949), and *Unterwegs zur Sprache* (1959). In some senses it may be said that Vallejo wrestles with two conundrums that have equally concerned twentieth-century philosophers such as Heidegger or Sartre: the enigma of what Neruda termed man's 'Residencia en la tierra' (in Heideggerian terminology man's 'being-in-the-world') coupled with the enigma of language. I do not wish to suggest a direct influence of Heidegger's thought on Vallejo, rather to point to an interesting coincidence of attitude between philosopher and poet.

To Heidegger, man is defined not by essence or spirit but by his habitation on earth, and in this he sees three elements as intimately interrelated—dwelling, building and being. He bases this intuition etymologically on the association between Old High German *buan*—to dwell, to live in a place, with *bauen,* to build, which is in turn related to the first person singular of the verb to be—*ich bin.* In this context he says [in 'Building Dwelling Thinking' in *Poetry, Language, Thought,* 1975]: 'to be a human being means to be on earth as a mortal, it means to dwell. Dwelling is the basic character of Being in keeping with which mortals exist, and 'building belongs to dwelling and receives its nature from it'. In other words, the familiar trappings of human existence, houses, tools, etc. are the unself-conscious expression of human need, in function, and collectively arrived at. In the fullest sense these are extensions of man's being, in relation to which he defines the contours of self. Buildings—for example a bridge—are human constructs, but have autonomous reality, exist in themselves, not just as objects of perception. A bridge is not simply *placed* in a location, it *makes* or marks out a location, changes a landscape by 'gathering' together elements in a relationship that could not otherwise exist. Buildings are products of human activity that map out human topography, give a definition of the relevant space surrounding a human being. Space is not to be understood in terms of a void 'out there', it is comprehensible only in terms of a clearing within boundaries, in relation to what is given in terms of things and locations: 'When we speak of man and space it sounds as though man stood on one side, space on the other. Yet space is not something that faces man. It is neither an external object nor an inner experience. Space is no more than the medium of man's 'stay' in the world: 'The relationship between man and space is none other than dwelling, strictly thought and spoken.' Things and locations are the expression and measure of the boundaries of man's being on earth, they at once contain and express him.

What has this to do with language? First, language is equally a human construct, but is the creation of no single individual. Language speaks *through* us because it is communal and pre-existent; it is therefore a perversion of the proper order of things to regard the individual as the master of language—language is the master of man, he is its vehicle. Secondly, for Heidegger there is a strict correlation between dwelling/building/being/speech. The relationship between man and space—his dwelling—*demands* to be spoken, hence Heidegger can say, in a famous aphorism: 'Language is the house of being' (*Über den Hu-*

manismus, 1949). The interaction between humanity and the world is essentially linguistic: 'Only when there is language is there a world' ['Hölderlin and the Essence of Poetry', in *Existence and Being,* 1949]. Language is essentially speech, conversation: 'The being of man is founded in language, but this only becomes actual in conversation. Conversation 'gathers' people into communal existence, as a bridge or building may be said to 'gather' landscape. Communal existence is at the same time our experience of dwelling among a world of things. Paradoxically, it is in poetry that we find the most intense expression of speech. Common speech is 'dead' poetry that can be revivified in verse. Poetry is not to be thought of as a 'higher' form of diction, but [he writes in 'Language', in *Poetry, Language, Thought*] as a 'presencing' of language, in the sense of showing, disclosure, revelation. In his essay on the poetry of Georg Trakl, 'Language in the Poem', he says: 'The dialogue of thinking with poetry aims to call forth the *nature* of language, so that mortals may learn again to live within language. In poetry we encounter not the language of signs, but the *being* of language—language as an immediate presence that surrounds and incorporates us as our clothes or dwelling might: 'Poetry builds up the very nature of dwelling. Poetry and dwelling not only do not exclude each other; on the contrary, poetry and dwelling belong together, each calling for the other ['. . . Poetically Man Dwells . . .', in *Poetry, Language, Thought*]. Poetry is also a measuring of what it means to be human, and the first 'measure' of existence is the awareness that man is mortal. In projecting a view of the language of speech and poetry as not primarily rational, Heidegger is reacting against those alienating habits of usage that treat language as a mere conceptual tool, a logical, categorising instrument which divorces linguistic signification from being, lived experience. [In the 1974 *Modern Poetry and the Idea of Language* Gerard] Bruns sees Heidegger's own style as a 'calculated affront to such speech, and even more is it an affront to the tradition of philosophical utterance . . . For Heidegger is a philosopher who makes us aware of the presence of language. His speech is never transparent: it never proceeds according to the decorum of clarity that distinguishes logical discourse . . . Like the poet . . . Heidegger is concerned to transform language in a way that releases it from or opposes it to conventional usage'.

To return to Vallejo: throughout his poetry, and especially in **Poemas humanos,** his posthumously published collection of verse, there is an acutely exacerbated consciousness of the body and bodily functions; a sense of the structure, the weight, mass and behaviour of the human body in relation to its daily environment, and in particular to the banality of its surroundings. As much as is the case in the poetry of Quevedo, the seventeenth-century poet with whom he had considerable affinity, house and body become interchangeable terms to express earthly existence.

Thus in 'Canciones del hogar' in his first published collection of poems, **Heraldos negros** (1919), recollections of childhood and family relationships are inseparable from the spatial context of the house that was their setting, with its pictures of saints on the walls, its ancient armchair, the corridors and rooms where the child played, the stone bench marking the boundary between indoors and out-

side. The loving warmth of his mother's body, and the expression of that love in the giving of sustenance are evoked by transforming that body into an oven: 'Tahona estuosa de aquellos mis bizcochos' ('**Trilce XXIII**'). And in '**Trilce LXV**' his dead mother, immortalised by memory, takes on the monumental grandeur of a cathedral: 'Me esperará tu arco de sombra / las tonsuradas columnas de tus ansias / que se acaban la vida . . . Así, muerta immortal. / Entre la columnata de tus huesos / que no puede caer ni a lloros:' Life itself is defined by the spatial context in which it takes place, as in '**Santoral**' (*Heraldos negros*): 'Llegué hasta la pared / de enfrente de la vida. / / Y me parece que he tenido siempre / a la mano esta pared.' Environment and being are inseparable [in **'Ello es que el lugar donde me pongo'**]: 'Mi casa, por desgracia, es una casa, / un suelo por ventura, donde vive / con su inscripción mi cucharita amada, / mi querido esqueleto ya sin letras, / la navaja, un cigarro permanente'. It is significant that these lines with their ironic evocation of the familiar human dwelling-place as a fragile, if comforting refuge from the threat of the void should be the prelude to consideration of the nature of life, mortality and human suffering, expressed with the colloquial directness of speech. To Vallejo, a house is essentially a dwelling, inextricably associated with being, bearing the marks of human habitation and presence as intimately as shoes or the tomb wear the imprint of the human body: 'Una casa viene al mundo, no cuando la acaban de edificar, sino cuando empiezan a habitarla. Una casa vive únicamente de hombres, como una tumba. De aquí esa irresistible semejanza que hay entre una casa y une tumba' Here, as characteristically in Vallejo, man's dwelling on earth is measured with the yardstick of mortality. At times, too, the impossibility of escaping the constricting and delimiting confines of the given is a cause for despair: 'En el campo y en la ciudad, se está demasiado asistido de rutas, flechas y señales, para poder perderse. Uno está allí indefectiblemente limitado, al norte, al sur, al este, al oeste. Uno está allí irremediablemente situado.. . a mí me ocurre en la ciudad amanecer siempre rodeado de todo, del peine, de la pastilla de jabón, de todo. Amanezco en el mundo y con el mundo y conmigo mismo . . . Esto es desesperante' [**Contra el secreto profesional**].

To turn now to language: in her studies of Vallejo's use of language [the 1973 *Poetry and Silence: César Vallejo's 'Sermon Upon Death'* and the 1976 *César Vallejo; The Dialectics of Poetry and Silence*], Jean Franco gives an extensive analysis of the poet's work, which she sees as typically modern in exemplifying a breakdown of faith in the power of the Word, showing the inoperability of traditional images and metaphors, the speciousness of 'harmony', in the Modernist sense. Professor Franco sees in Vallejo's poetry in part a rebellion against the alienating power of language and logic, in part an expression of frustration over the impotent poverty of language to adequately express experience. So she says of **Trilce** 'Words and phrases suggest new images as if creation itself obeyed half-voluntary processes and as if the poet's apparent sense of direction were constantly being undermined by the ambiguity of words. Thus language does not so much denote experiences or objects as show that a limited number of words and expressions must cover a wide and even contradictory range of experience'. Of *Poemas humanos* she writes: 'it is impossible to read the *Poemas humanos* and still doubt that Vallejo was profoundly concerned with the failure of both script and speech to replace the Christian Logos'. Only in such 'social' poems as **'Los mineros'** and **'Gleba'** in *Poemas humanos,* and in the poems written about the Spanish Civil War in *España, aparta de mí este cáliz* does she see Vallejo showing confidence in the possibility of once again restoring expressive power to speech. I would argue rather that paradoxically it is in struggling with the very frustrations and inadequacies of language that Vallejo both attempts to project a more accurate and authentic view of the human condition, of man's 'being-in-the-world', and offers a critique of language which shows how the very nature of language itself reveals that 'being' to us. I will analyse two of Vallejo's best-known poems from *Poemas humanos* in support of my argument.

'intensidad y altura'

Quiero escribir, pero me sale espuma,
quiero decir muchísimo y me atollo;
no hay cifra hablada que no sea suma,
no hay pirámide escrita, sin cogollo.

Quiero escribir, pero me siento puma;
quiero laurearme, pero me encebollo.
No hay toz hablada, que no llegue a bruma,
no hay dios ni hijo de dios, sin desarrollo.

Vámonos, pues, por eso, a comer yerba,
carne de llanto, fruta de gemido,
nuestra alma melancólica en conserva.

Vámonos! Vámonos! Estoy herido;
Vámonos a beber lo ya bebido,
vámonos, cuervo, a fecundar tu cuerva.

A common theme of twentieth-century writing is a dialectic in which the compulsion to speak is set against the impossibility of expression. In Samuel Beckett's words: 'The expression that there is nothing to express, nothing with which to express, nothing from which to express, no power to express, no desire to express, together with the obligation to express' ['Dialogue between Samuel Beckett and Georges Duthuit,' *Transition,* No. 5 (1949)]. It is ironic that Vallejo's confession of inarticulacy should be couched in the strictly formal terms of the sonnet, with all its connotations of compression, concision and control of expressive means. Further, it is full of overt parallelism: 'Quiero—pero' and 'Quiero—y', four times repeated, are exactly balanced and negated by 'no hay—que' in the third and the seventh lines of the first and second quatrains, and 'no hay—sin' in the fourth and eighth lines. Terms evocative of writing: 'escribir' and 'escrita' alternate with or are balanced by those suggestive of speech: 'decir', 'hablada'. There is a strict rhyme scheme in '-uma' and '-ollo' in the quatrains and '-va' and '-ido' in the tercets, end-stopping every line and effectively putting a halt to forward movement or thought. However, if we look at the first eight lines of the sonnet, it becomes clear that there is no 'mot-thème' in Saussure's terms, from which the other words may be said to spring. The rhyming words certainly demonstrate high phonetic similitude—'espuma—suma—puma—bruma', and 'atollo—cogollo—encebollo—desarrollo', but it would be difficult, not to say

arbitrary, to designate one word of the respective chains a key-word. Each refers backwards and forwards in a circular pattern of resonances. The relentless dominance of the rhyme-scheme is strongly reminiscent of seventeenth-century satirical and burlesque sonnets—especially those of Quevedo—which show great ingenuity in rhyming words ending in unlovely sounds or with coarse associations—'ajo', 'ujo', 'ote', 'azo', etc. In fact the sonnet is both a poem about inarticulacy and a controlled ironic burlesque of literary form.

There is further apparent symmetry in the use of reflexive forms of the verb in the first two lines of each quatrain. Yet the apparent syntactic parallelism does not mask an incongruous distortion of syntax in line six. We begin with three true reflexives: 'me sale' (suggestive of action outside the control of the speaker—cf. 'me sale sangre'—'blood pours out of me'); 'me atollo'—figuratively 'to be in a jam', 'to get stuck', has also very concrete associations, because the verb literally means 'to be blocked or clogged' (as of gutters); 'me siento' is straightforward and requires no comment. However, 'laurearme' in the next line is odd, since it does not exist as a reflexive verb. It is, in fact, an example of the so-called 'ethical dative', common in colloquial speech; the use of a reflexive form when not strictly necessary to give affective, emphatic or personal value to a statement (compare English use of 'up', 'down' with the verb in such constructions as to eat *up,* drink *down,* with, e.g. 'comer*se* una manzana' as distinct from 'comer una manzana'). If this construction is possible with 'laurear', it sounds highly incongruous with 'encebollar', a verb used only transitively meaning 'to cook something with a garnish of onion'. It is typical of Vallejo to exploit the possible confusions and ambiguities of the reflexive form, which in Spanish can be used to express the passive, to make impersonal statements, and is also found colloquially, in the 'ethical dative', as well as the true reflexive. By diverging from the norm, he makes us acutely aware of the unconsciously expected patterns of syntactical usage.

A similar disruption of linguistic norms occurs at the lexical level with the neologism 'toz' in the seventh line. As we read in the **'Advertencia'** of *César Vallejo, Obra Poética Completa—Edición con facsímiles* with reference to this word: 'Ante la imposibilidad de saber si quiso escribir *tos* o *voz,* se ha dejado como está el sétimo verso del soneto de la página 347'. S and z are pronounced identically by perhaps a majority of Latin-American speakers, but by removing the orthographic distinction between them, the neologism conflating 'tos' and 'voz' suggests their intrinsic synonymity, that inarticulate cough and voice are one. Further, 'toz' brings to mind a variety of other terms: *tozo,* small, dwarfish, tubby; *tozudo,* stubborn; *tozar,* to come upon, to be stubborn; *tozuelo,* the back of the head; *tozotada,* a heavy blow on the nape of the neck. This may remind us of the fact that individual words may themselves evoke a succession of images independent of and even irrelevant to their context, as Sartre observes in *L'idiot de la famille:* 'le graphème, par sa configuration physique et avant tout traitement éveille des résonances.' So 'le château d'Amboise' may suggest 'framboise', 'boisé', 'boiserie', 'Ambroisie', 'Ambroise'—not a private range of associations, but objective connotations that can be potentially apprehended by any reader, allowing him to range beyond the confines of the text.

Another term with confusing multiple meanings is 'cogollo' which may signify 1) vegetable heart; 2) cream, summit, choice part of something, e.g. the 'cream' of society; 3) nucleus or centre of something. The fact that it is not immediately obvious to the reader from the context which is the appropriate sense of the word adds to the disorientating effect of the poem as a whole.

The major and central notion of the sonnet is the discrepancy and discontinuity between man's sentient, physical, animal nature, and his desire to achieve controlled expression through speech or writing—a desire always doomed to frustration. A dialectical tension is set up within the poem between two levels or sets of associations: on the one hand there are images and patterns of order—pyramid, cypher, sum, the controlled form of the sonnet and the verbal symmetries within it. On the other, animal and vegetable imagery, expressions of involuntary and innocent ejaculation—*espuma, llanto, toz, gemido*—together with a network of anarchically proliferating free associations. In this, language becomes a self-generative process, without beginning or end. As Michel Foucault puts it, referring to modern literature as a whole [in the 1966 *Los Mots et us choses*]: 'Car maintenant il n'y a plus cette parole première, absolument initiale par quoi se trouvait fondé et limité le mouvement infini du discours: désormais le langage va croître sans départ, sans terme et sans promesse. C'est le parcours de cet espace vain et fondamental que trace de jour en jour le texte de la littérature'.

I have already suggested that the rigidity of the rhyme-scheme sets in train a causal pattern that is in part responsible for the apparently arbitrary and certainly arresting choice of terms—'encebollo', 'cogollo', 'puma', etc. But the notion that association is by homophony or the independent meaning of words outside the line of strictly logical argument is far-reaching in the poem. The implicit analogy/contrast between a stately geometrical construct—a pyramid, empty within, and the clustering leaves of cabbage or lettuce, layer upon layer packed around nothing (suggesting perhaps that there can be no formal construct without vulnerable organic heart), gives rise to a chain reaction of unpredictably metamorphosing vegetable association. So the evocation of the poet's crowing 'laurearme' is appropriate within the context of the poem, but the onion garnish of 'me encebollo' brings aspiration mockingly down to earth, while also transposing to a vegetable the idea of layers clustering tightly on one another. The vegetable theme is continued in **'Vámonos, pues, por eso, a comer yerba'**—become like the beasts cropping grass in the knowledge of one's impotence—but this also has biblical overtones of the story of Nebuchadnezzar, who in his madness gave way to eating grass; and he was driven from men, and did eat grass as oxen, and his body was wet with the dew of heaven, till his hairs were grown like eagles' feathers, and his nails like birds' claws.' The fleeting evocation of a once-proud king brought to the level of the beasts contrasts sharply with the preceding line's allusion to the son of God as the procession of God, the Verbum, or the Word made flesh. The biblical-

vegetable theme continues with the expression of human sorrow and travail—man the fruit brought forth, like the children of Eve in grief and lamentation. However, at this point the heightened language with its echoes of the Psalms, Ecclesiastes and the Book of Job is undermined and mocked by the anarchically mutating shift from fruit (figurative and metaphorical) to literal fruit in cans—'en conserva'.

In much the same way, the allusions to animality mutate bizarrely from the suggestion of potent energy and latent menace of the puma, the Amerindian tribal sacred animal, to the subliminal echo of Christ, the bridegroom in the guise of the wounded hart seeking his beloved in St. John of the Cross's *Cántico espiritual* evoked by the urgency of 'Vámonos! Vámonos! Estoy herido;' an association which I suggest is sparked off by the preceding biblical allusions. In his commentary on the lines from the *Cántico espiritual* '. . . el ciervo vulnerado / por el otero asoma', St. John of the Cross writes: 'Y es de saber que la propiedad del ciervo es subirse a los lugares altos, y cuando está herido vase con gran priesa a buscar refrigerio a las aguas frías . . .'. Here, however, it is not cool water brooks that the wounded lover will drink, but stale water, and the faint subliminal shadow of the 'ciervo' yields place by phonetic shift to 'cuervo', the crow, bird of ill-omen and death. It is possible too to see, in the last line, with its injunction to the crow to make his mate fecund, a sardonic reminder of the Spanish proverb which warns against misplaced, self-destructive and self-defeating generosity: 'Críacuervos y te sacarán los ojos'.

While it is possible to trace a train of associations in this fashion, we do not have satisfyingly purposive exploration of extended metaphor, whose implications are exhaustively worked out, as in, say, a seventeenth-century 'metaphysical' sonnet, but rather, to pursue the train metaphor, a series of deflections into sidings that lead no further, save in indirect and haphazard fashion. Thus the mocking analogy in lines seven and eight: 'as soul is to body, so fruit is to the can, one contained within the other', appears to be merely a banal and unilluminating comparison, a parallel simply stated, whose appropriateness is not elucidated, as is, for example, Donne's 'spider love, which transubstantiates all, / And can convert manna to gall' ('Twickenham Garden'), a brilliantly illuminating conceit, which triumphantly succeeds in convincing the reader of the aptness of yoking together such opposites as 'spider' and 'love'. Relationships between images are not arbitrary, but function at the level of the fluid interaction of words, whose momentum seems self-generated, and whose associations appear haphazard and non-functional, not elucidated in terms of controlled metaphor, and therefore not predominantly rational.

The opacity of the images in the sonnet has much to do with their being banal, familiar, everyday, anti-poetic, resistant to symbolisation; 'given' objects with no ready-made intrinsic meaning or point. A clogged drain, lettuce heart, onion garnish, cough, canned fruit, lack the dignity and resonance of assuagingly familiar literary allusion. Such terms pose the problem of the discrete existence of *things*, challenging the attempt to incorporate them by language or understanding. The incongruous mingling of the banality and trivia of existence defeats the aspiration that would attempt to transcend it, and this defeat is conveyed at the level of language, through the autonomy, the unpredictable twists and turns of words. The poem itself in all its use of expressive means is an exemplification of its theme of frustration: the impulse to act, to give definition to expression is negated, dissipated, absorbed in inertia or brute sentient, but irrational being. A series of impulses is generated, only to end in self-defeat, frustrating the reader to whom *feeling* is conveyed clearly enough, while individual elements of the poem remain opaque, resistant to comprehension. The poem's final paradox is that it eloquently succeeds in conveying the experience of inarticulacy, reminding us of Heidegger's view [in *Being and Time]* that 'in "poetical" discourse the communication of the existential possibilities of one's state-of-mind can become an aim in itself and this amounts to a disclosing of existence'. Through language, Vallejo has achieved the exact mirroring of a state of mind, full of inconsistencies, waywardness and contradiction.

'considerando en frío, imparcialmente . . . '

Considerando en frío, imparcialmente,
que el hombre es triste, tose y, sin embargo,
se complace en su pecho colorado;
que lo único que hace es componerse
de días;
que es lóbrego mamífero y se peina:

Considerando
que el hombre procede suavemente del trabajo
y repercute jefe, suena subordinado;
que el diagrama del tiempo
es constante diorama en sus medallas
y, a medio abrir, sus ojos estudiaron,
desde lejanos tiempos,
su fórmula famélica de masa . . .

Comprendiendo sin esfuerzo
que el hombre se queda, a veces, pensando,
como queriendo llorar,
y, sujeto a tenderse como objeto,
se hace buen carpintero, suda, mata
y luego canta, almuerza, se abotona . . .

Considerando también
que el hombre es en verdad un animal
y, no obstante, al voltear, me da con su tristeza
en la cabeza . . .

Examinando, en fin,
sus encontradas piezas, su retrete,
su desesperación, al terminar su día atroz,
borrándolo . . .

Comprendiendo
que él sabe que le quiero,
que le odio con afecto y me es, en suma,
indiferente . . .

Considerando sus documentos generales
y mirando con lentes aquel certificado
que prueba que nació muy pequeñito . . .

le hago una seña,
viene,
y le doy un abrazo, emocionado

¡Qué más da! Emocionado. . . Emocionado . . .

This poem enacts a dialectical debate between two attitudes to man, implicit in two different registers of language. The first is impartial, impersonal, conceptual, legal, scientific or pompously pedantic; the language of documents, of detached official modes of classification. Thus we have man defined as a lugubrious mammal—'lóbrego mamífero'—a pedantic coupling of *esdrújulo* words, stressed on the antepenultimate syllable, uncommon in Spanish and found mostly in Classical or foreign loanwords (cf. also 'fórmula famélica'). Human time is charted by diagram, and man is measured in terms of formula and mass, his activities determined by the Cartesian subject-object relationship. Contrasting with this, we have a truly comprehensive view of man as a being in the pathos of his animal nature—inconsequential, lacking in self-awareness, yet darkened in his existence by the intermittent capacity for thought, as instinctive and uncontrollable as weeping. Vallejo's half-compassionate, half-mocking view of man as an animal condemned to suffer because of his consciousness is frequently expressed in *Poemas humanos,* as in '**El alma que sufrió de ser su cuerpo'**: 'Tú sufres, tú padeces y tú vuelves a sufrir horriblemente / desgraciado mono, / jovencito de Darwin . . . y a tu ombligo interrogas: dónde? cómo?' Man is a prisoner of existence, 'cautivo en tu enorme libertad'.

The poem here analysed ends with a touching abdication of the power of words in favour of the silent eloquence of behaviour and gesture, as the poet embraces his fellow-man, eliminating the distance between them, to stand as equals communicating and showing true comprehension, like animals, through touch.

The poem is remarkable for the complex pattern of alliteration, assonance and harmony it contains: triste—tose; complace—componerse—colorado; suavemente—suena subordinado; diagrama—diorama; fórmula famélica. More important though than sound patterns set up independent of meaning are firstly, association of meaning through homophony; and secondly, a complex use of words with double, often unrelated meanings. Thus:

se complace = takes pleasure in, but also suggests complacency

componerse = (little used) to be made up of, to comprise; also to dress up, adorn oneself

suavemente = softly, gently; also meekly, weakly

fórmula = recipe/scientific formula/model

masa = mass (weight)/mass (number)/dough

voltear = to tumble; also to be tossed, thrown in the air as by a bull

encontradas = opposing or alternating, but also past participle of 'encontrar', to find

piezas = parts, pieces/theatrical plays/rooms
retrete = retreat, inner sanctuary, but primarily now used to signify 'lavatory'

sujeto = a person/to be subject to/syntactical subject of a sentence.

So 'fórmula famélica de masa', for example, may be read as either 'famished formula of mass-man' or 'hungry recipe for dough', and 'sus encontradas piezas, su retrete' may be either 'his opposing parts, his retreat', or 'his discovered rooms, his lavatory', or a combination of either. Ambiguity of meaning is therefore far-reaching in the poem, encouraging a doubleness of vision in the reader, who must hold two equally significant meanings in focus. It is perhaps appropriate that the poem should speak of a diorama, for this form of scenic representation lighted from above and viewed through an aperture was made up usually of transparent canvases painted on both sides, and by varying the intensity of light on the canvases, it was possible to transform the same scene from dark to light, day to night, or to highlight different elements in the same scene, allowing for a variety of different perspectives of the same representation, in other words.

All the way through the poem, man's being, the poem's subject, is related to his habitation and his unselfconsciousness and revealing behaviour. Man's being is circumscribed by his dress, the tools and adornments of his daily routine of toilet and work. The very parts of his body are interchangeable with the rooms he inhabits; his place of intimate retreat is the lavatory, where he performs the most basic of animal bodily functions.

In his **'Apuntes para un estudio'**, notes for a study of contemporary literature that was never completed, under a series of headings such as Romanticism, Realism, Symbolism, etc., Vallejo classifies himself and the Chilean poet Pablo Neruda under the heading of 'Verdadismo'. We may remember in this context Neruda's manifesto in the first issue of *Caballo verde para la poesía* in 1935, where he announces his intention to write 'impure poetry'—'une poesía sin pureza'—'like a suit of clothes, like a human body, with food stains and shameful gestures, with wrinkles, observations, dreams, vigils, prophecies'. Neruda's stated aim was to record, as far as possible unselectively, all the traces and minutiae of human existence, convey its confused diversity in an intellectually 'impure', sensual, material form of verse that should have the physical consistency of wood, iron, flower, water, flesh. To Neruda, the poetic act is an act of constant mingling with the physical world, and he comes to be seen by his contemporaries as the prophet of unashamed acceptance of the body in all its animality, its ordinariness and even shabbiness. We have already seen how Vallejo's poetry conveys an equally intense awareness of the human body, but his 'verdadismo' goes further in compassionately recording the vulnerable inconsequentiality, the inconsistency of human behaviour. So, he can place conscious human activity, whether in work or in acts of violence ('se hace buen carpintero, suda, mata'), on the same plane as, and in the context of, the habitual daily routine of eating, dressing, singing a song ('y luego canta, almuerza, se abotona'), or can project a view of man as an absurd, clownish tumbling animal, yet one whose very tumbling is oppressively sad. Man's life is no more than the accumulation of days; existence, whose mere tool or object he is, and which he can neither control nor comprehend, fills him intermittently with despair and grief. In general terms, the poem can be seen as a progressive shedding of the position of detached,

official observer, considering and examining the human condition, checking on latrines and documents like a government inspector to an *understanding* that is effortless—'sin esfuerzo'—because it is emotional identification with the erratic vagaries of human feeling, expressed through direct physical contact that speaks for itself without need of words.

Vallejo's 'verdadismo', the capacity to capture 'un timbre humano, un latido vital y sincero, al cual debe propender el artista', as he wrote in an article in *Variedades,* 7th May (1937), is no less evident in his use of language in the poem, for here language may truly be said to speak *through* man, in Heideggerian terms, to be possessed of independent energy. The poem gives the impression that the forward unfolding of thought is generated by patterns of association sparked off by chance by the words themselves. So 'repercute' leads to 'suena', paralleling the symmetrical association between 'jefe' and 'subordinado'. 'Diagrama' by phonetic similitude suggests 'diorama'. The ambiguity of meaning of 'fórmula' anticipates and is linked with that of 'masa', and the punning word-play of 'encontradas *piezas*' provides the momentum that generates 'retrete'. That 'sujeto' should naturally bring to mind 'objeto' calls into play a whole series of relationships in which the syntactical categories are a mirror in philosophical terms of the Aristotelian/Cartesian distinction between perceiving self and perceived object, and in sociopolitical terms encapsulates the Marxist view of the capitalist relationship of employee to boss, already touched on in the poem. If, as Vallejo wrote in an article in *Mundial,* 11th March (1927) 'Cada cosa contiene en potencia a todas las energìas y direcciones del universo. No sólo el hombre es un microcosmos, cada fenómeno de la naturaleza es también un microcosmos en marcha', then each word which is used to convey such a reality should also contain a protean associative energy. By forcing us to acknowledge the anarchic self-generative associative drive of words, Vallejo directs us to the nature and being of language as an immediate presence, like the world of 'given' material objects we find ourselves in. To use Heidegger's term, Vallejo 'presences' language in the sense that he reveals its true nature and function.

In this poem as elsewhere in his verse, Vallejo shows a grasp of the fluid dynamic potential of language and thought. Thus, though man and the poet himself can only avail themselves of an 'alfabeto gélido' to answer the questions posed by 'el bimano, el muy bruto, el muy filósofo . . . saber por qué tiene la vida este perrazo, / por qué lloro, por qué, / cejón inhabil, veleidoso, hube nacido / gritando . . .' we are left with the paradox that pessimistic awareness of the limitations of language can have a corrective and liberating effect, for as he wrote in **'Autopsia del superrealismo'**, pessimism and despair are mere stages in a quest, not its goal: 'El pesimismo y la desesperación deben ser siempre etapas y no metas. Para que ellos agiten y fecunden el espíritu, deben desenvolverse hasta transformarse en afirmaciones constructivas'.

Having recognised the extent of language's power to alienate and to schematise, he intensifies sensitivity to the way the writer can succeed in overcoming this alienation, finding a register of poetic discourse that will more authentically convey the nature of the human condition, true to his own injunction in his 1936/37 notebook: 'Cuidado con la substancia humana de la poesía'. The independent associative logic of words through which is heard the voice of the community, the 'gathering' power of language, in Heidegger's phrase, reflects the form of the human mind, either in expressing dialectical opposition between contraries or in sequential, self-generative, unpredictable evolution of terms. Like the material objects that map out the terrain of human dwelling—shoes, clothes, articles of toilet, eating implements; like human habitations, whether house or tomb; like the awareness of death against which life is measured, language gives evidence of human weakness, poverty and imperfection, but at the same time testifies to its energy and indomitable creative persistence. Vallejo's language, full of inconsistencies, paradox and contradiction faithfully reflects the confused inconsequentiality of human animal behaviour, as it also succeeds in conveying the inflections of speech. As Jean Franco says, '[the] counterpoint between the solitude of print and the immediacy of the spoken word provides the *Poemas humanos* with much of their energy . . . his '**Sermon upon Death**' and many others of the *Poemas humanos* represent astonishing efforts to make print translate the presence of the human voice'. In this, Vallejo's practice would appear to bear out Heidegger's paradox that it is in poetry that we find the most intense expression of speech. Further, if Heidegger could say, as we have already seen, that 'the dialogue of thinking with poetry aims to call forth the *nature* of language, so that mortals may learn again to live within language', it is paradoxically by demonstrating the autonomy of language that Vallejo achieves a reconciliation between man and the word—not the Christian Logos, the divinely uttered Word made flesh—but the word as it emerges from its essentially human context, for as he says, 'El intelectual revolucionario desplaza la fórmula mesiánica, diciendo "mi reino es de este mundo" '. By using language to testify to the mundane truth of human behaviour and thought processes which are ignored by systems of

thought—whether philosophical, psychological, scientific or aesthetic, as he suggests in 'Un hombre pasa con un pan al hombro' in *Poemas humanos*—Vallejo restores the word to its human function, true to the spirit of his own dictum: 'Hacedores de imágenes, devolved las palabras a los hombres'. The punning 'rebélase' of *Trilce* has proved to be prophetic, for in rebelling, words have truly revealed themselves as they are.

Christiane von Buelow   (essay date 1990)

SOURCE: "César Vallejo and the Stones of Darwinian Risk," in *Studies in Twentieth Century Literature*, Vol. 14, No. 1, Winter, 1990, pp. 9-19.

[*In the excerpt below, von Buelow assesses Vallejo's treatment of Darwinian and Marxist theory in his short story "Los caynas."*]

The young man who narrates César Vallejo's short story **"Los caynas"** (1923) is shocked and terrified when he enters the house of a village family to find that those living there more closely resemble monkeys than they do humans. The narrator recoils from the howling and shrieking acrobatics of a woman whose "anthropoid image" is at once mechanical, child-like and bestial. This "regressive zoological obsession" comes as the third and final manifestation of what the narrator vaguely calls "the mysteries of reason [that] become thorns and well up in the closed and stormy circle of a fatal logic." Earlier episodes anticipate this singular species regression with an oblique, mysterious logic. A young man named Urquizo from the same village family falls prey to a peculiar form of madness: he boasts to those assembled at a bar that his horse has the extraordinary capacity to defy gravity and ride inverted, hooves pointing upward. Meeting Urquizo in the street one day, the narrator accidentally slips and bumps into him and evokes the angry protest, "Are you mad?" This last episode of "seeing things in reverse" appears to the shaken narrator as a "more transcendent [madness], nothing less than a ratiocination." The madman's psychic projection and the very certainty with which he insists on his own sanity threaten to overwhelm the secure boundaries of rationality within which reality is recognizable. Reason and madness are in danger of reversing positions, of exchanging places. And, Vallejo implies, these sensory and psychic reversals or inversions proceed according to a deterministic or "fatal logic" towards the eventual collective retrogression of species.

In what sense, though, should we term the imagined or real species mutation a reversal? For apes to be considered the reversal or inversion of human beings, a Darwinian logic must prevail. What Darwin called "propinquity of descent" amounts to the spatial representation (in family trees or classificatory lineages) of a thoroughly temporalized notion of species; hence, what a species "is" depends on the ancestral (pluralized) species from which it descends. The people of Cayna mime the species from which, according to evolutionary theory, they are descended: the anthropoid apes, the apes whose name derives from their close resemblance to man. As long as the transformation into monkeys can be described as a "resemblance" or "simulation of the anthropoid," as long as the victims are prey to a mental disequilibrium or madness and not to an actual empirical mutation of the species, rationality can be said to lie with the permanence of species self-identity and not, as Darwin maintained, with species mutation. However, as it becomes evident that this regression is communal—no one in Cayna escapes the real or imagined species mutation—so it becomes inevitable that the narrator, who tells us he is "distantly related" to Urquizo's family, will succumb to the unavoidable contagion. In the final coda to the story, the narrator is incarcerated in an insane asylum for his "unreasonable" belief in the fixity of the human species ("Poor thing! He thinks he is a man!"). Reason and madness have obviously reversed positions; less evident perhaps is what this reversal entails: reason and species mutation have become synonymous.

Obviously we are witness to no ordinary natural scientific species mutation. Vallejo's "regressive zoological obsession" deliberately reverses a progressive Darwinian species adaptation to environment. Why would Vallejo represent the life of Peruvian indigenous people as a retrogression of species? The answer to this question is as complex and manifold as the wide-ranging reaches of Darwinism itself. We know, thanks to Jean Franco's [1976 book on Vallejo entitled *César Vallejo—The Dialectics of Poetry and Silence*], that the author read the influential popularizer of Darwin, Ernst Haeckel, and that **"Los caynas"** in particular registers "the shattering effect evolutionist theory had on him." Haeckel's writings help us to situate the barely concealed terror of Vallejo's narrator as the villagers of Cayna teeter between a mental aberration, in which they closely *resemble* monkeys, and a Darwinian "law of change," in which a species *is* its genealogical descent. Haeckel had stressed that nature's "law" was Darwinian natural selection, and further, that this law preserved the unity of nature by controlling the physiological functions of heredity (which preserved features between generations) and adaptation (which modified features according to environment). Precisely this reciprocal action of heredity and adaptation is operating in Vallejo's short story: the law of heredity dictates the narrator's ever-closer capitulation to the inevitable effects of consanguinity; in recognition of the law of adaptation to the environment, he reports with anthropological detachment on the isolated and backward conditions that coincide with the extinction of human civilization.

Haeckel [in his *The Riddle of the Universe,* 1900] cites Robert Hartmann's *The Anthropoid Apes,* which he says reveals the "unprejudiced findings" of comparative anatomy, these being that "the body of man and anthropoid ape are the same in every respect." Haeckel turns Darwinian materialism into a doctrine that eliminates all metaphysical atavism; seeking an open confrontation with theology, he cites the eighteenth-century natural historian, Buffon: "If we do not take the soul into account, [the orangoutan] lacks nothing that we posses." Reading Haeckel, we sense that Vallejo recapitulates the polemical ferocity of the whole late nineteenth-century intellectual climate when he rather characteristically confronts religious transcendence with the most unrelentingly nominalist materialism—summarized perfectly by the title of the poem from *Poe-*

mas humanos, **"On the Soul That Suffered from Being Its Body."** . . .

It is the name of the popular Victorian, Herbert Spencer, which we for good reason most closely associate with the Malthusian principle "survival of the fittest." . . . Spencer explicitly identified survival of the fittest in nature with strongly individualist principles and laissez faire capitalism. Just as in nature the struggle for existence operates to remove the sickly, the malformed and the unfit, Spencer argued, so in society competition eliminates the ignorant, the improvident and the lazy. Reading **"Los caynas"** according to Spencerian principles, then, we could say that the villagers are clearly the least powerful and least adapted of all "variations" to the stern discipline of individualist self-differentiation and economic competition; the retrogression of the species in this case would correspond to the elimination of inferior varieties in the natural environment. Through such individualist and capitalist principles are strongly antithetical to Vallejo's most deeply held beliefs, in one respect at least, as we shall see shortly, the text suggests that the author surreptitiously seeks to distance himself from those "primitive" village origins denigrated by the metropolis.

Though there is no necessary correlation between Darwinian principles and the racist and laissez faire assumptions of social evolutionism—Marx, after all, wished to dedicate the second volume of *Capital* to Darwin—it was nevertheless this conservative, "scientistic" strain of thought that provided the ideological impetus to a whole generation of Latin American positivists. Although conditions varied from country to country, these positivist "reformers" were united in their allegiance to progress and science, viewing these as the means to remedy the perceived economic, militaristic and cultural debilities of their nations. They sought a social order dedicated to the educational and material well-being of its citizens and, toward that end, they gladly sacrificed political liberty, which they identified with anarchy. As avid Spencerians, they identified the march of progress and civilization with the individualist dominance of the fittest in the economic and political realm. According to the Mexican Justo Sierra, for example, Latin America must develop quickly from a military to an industrial power in order to ward off the insatiable colossus to the north. The dubious logic of substituting a freely accepted "adaptation" to the colonizer in order thus to avoid an imposed colonization clothes in legitimizing Darwinian garb: unless they disavow their own history, Mexicans will become the unfit, "a proof of Darwin's theory . . . in the struggle for existence" [Leopold Zea in *Las ideas en*]. Many Latin American positivists adopted the racist ideologies of their European counterparts in order to justify military defeats. The Argentine, J. B. Alberdi, like Justo Sierra, identified the indigenous Indian population with passive domesticated barbarity—an atavism that must be renounced in favor of development and the accumulation of industrial wealth.

In Peru, positivism's greatest impetus came from the disastrous war with Chile in 1879. Peru's "feudal servitude," "its weak-willed [Indian] race," could be no match for Chile's modern nationalist liberalism, according to

Mariano Cornejo. At every step of cornejo's argument, social selection adapts continents in the same way that Darwinian natural selection adapts organisms to their planetary ends. Professing the evolutionary laws of Darwin, Cornejo hardly veils his disgust for those who have been proven unfit:

> I don't know how in seven centuries of bowing down so much we have not acquired a hunchback as a distinguishing mark.

"Los caynas" could be read as an allegory or fable in which the unfit are made literally to acquire the "distinguishing mark" that has made them victims in the struggle for the survival of the fittest. The stark alternatives of civilization or barbarism, Enlightenment progress or retrogressive servitude: these are the familiar terms of the eminent Argentine positivist, Domingo Sarmiento. In Vallejo's short story the struggle for existence has been lost and "civilization" proves to be imminently reversible into literal "barbarism." However, given the fact that much of Vallejo's writing makes very clear his political commitments to the oppressed indigenous population of Peru, we would want to argue that the very literalness of the story's species mutation seeks to satirize the Positivists' pseudoscientific ideals of development and progress. The story would then be a critical allegory seen from the perspective of the social evolutionism that brands those outside "the march of civilization" as barbaric, unfit, or, in more contemporary terms, underdeveloped. Compelling as such an interpretation is in most respects, one aspect of the story remains outside its purview.

Vallejo's writings call for a dialectical interpretation that registers the power and authority of the natural scientific model and recognizes in turn that this model will ironically undermine any transfer of natural history to humanly constructed social and political bonds.

— *Christiane von Buelow*

When the narrator returns to his village after years of absence to pursue his studies, he witnesses an eerie environment of "inexplicable destruction" and unending silence. Remembering the "anthropoid image" of his distant ancestor, the narrator admits to being "guided by a secret attraction" toward some terrible end. Following immediately on this admission, the dreaded but alluring "origin of the species" confronts the narrator most immediately: "the face of my father! . . . a monkey!" He proceeds to call his progenitor a caged gorilla and identify himself again and again as the bearer of civilizing light. All artificial light, including fire, has been eradicated and the narrator's efforts to reach his father of old ("I thought I had made a light in him") are mistaken for the natural light of a star ("Light! Light! . . . A star!" the anthropoid babbles between hair-raising screams). In the next and last en-

counter with his father, a whole tribe of monkeys defiantly extinguishes the matches struck by the young man assuming the role of Prometheus. Certainly it could be argued that the "secret attraction," the alluring but fearful image, consists of seeing his own father prey to this retrogression of species. An Oedipal struggle appears to underlie the narrators's wish to usurp the parental "civilizing" role in relation to his father. There are after all several *Trilce* poems that dwell on the fall of the child into consciousness' knowledge and time as a result of the betrayal by the instruments of "civilizing light," speech and the alphabet. And, to seal the case for a necessary psychoanalytic component to our interpretation, the narrator has cast himself as progenitor of the father who conceived him (the son). The young man's reminder to the father of their familial bond serves as the redeeming catalyst momentarily transforming the monkey into a man of the greatest gentleness:

> —My father! —I broke in to beg him, impotent and helpless to throw myself in his arms.
>
> My father then suddenly laid aside his diabolical manner, calmed his wild appearance and seemed in one single impulse to rescue the night of his mind. He immediately slipped toward me, gentle, soft, tender, sweet, transfigured; a man as he must have approached my mother on the day in which their deeply human embrace extracted the blood with which they filled my heart and made it beat in time to the temples of my head and the soles of my feet.

The narrator has himself created the "human" father in the very moment of the sexual encounter that engendered himself, the son. In so doing, the son has placed himself in the position of the "humanizing" mother, whose embrace transforms the "diabolical" male. The fantasy appears to be one of self-engenderment, asserting a freedom from biological generation as such. For even though the son superficially owes his life to the parents' beneficent extraction of blood for their offspring, here, as in one of Vallejo's [*Poemas humanos*] the consanguineous bonds have been inverted such that the son "sustained father / and mother solely with [his] veiny circulation" ("sostuvo padre / y madre, con su sola circulación venosa").

A fragment from the notebooks attributes the longevity of a biblical patriarch to the author's father, while making the son's response to that powerfully enduring presence quite clear:

> I was far from my father for two hundred years and they wrote to me that he was living forever. But a profound sense of life produced in me the intimate and creative necessity to believe him dead. (*Contra el secreto profesional*, 1973.)

Focus on a psychoanalytic interpretation of "Los caynas" directs us to reexamine the climactic verdict delivered by a father against his son: "Poor thing! He thinks he is a man! He is mad!" The father's words in this reading thinly veil a patriarch's defiant resistance to his son's maturity and autonomy; a father denies that his son is man by virtue of being his father, while the son proves his manhood by bestializing his father and casting himself in the role of civilizing liberator. The Darwinian allegory, in this reading them, signifies the author's attempt to "put to death" or drive to extinction his own indentured origins.

Critical attention to this externalized narrative's one moment of quickly displaced self-recognition and interior reflection—"guided by a secret attraction . . . [to] the face of my father! . . . a monkey!"—produces a reading that clearly stands in polar opposition to the communitarian principles of a critical socio-political interpretation. Such a politically engaged interpretation is nevertheless preserved by the total trajectory of the story and in the semantic ambiguity of the father's climactic verdict ("Poor thing! He thinks he is a man! He is mad!"). The father, in such a reading, sardonically refers to the denial of humanity imposed on the Peruvian masses under the harsh capitalist exploitation legitimized by the scientist slogan, the "survival of the fittest." And the narrator at the end of the story is declared mad precisely because he insists he is a man (and not a monkey). Thus, in this reading, it is the Latin American's "mad" (quixotic?) nobility to insist inalterably on his culture and his history, all social evolutionists and positivists to the contrary.

The two interpretations are not easily reconcilable with one another, though Vallejo's text quite simply contains both adaptations of Darwinism to the social order: the dialectical materialism that destroys all systems of entrenched national and class privilege as well as a model of competitive individualism, albeit one displaced to the realm of the unconscious. The narrator's manifest desire that his father forget their Darwinian kinship with the beasts (or, allegorically, the expressed wish that they resist submission to the injustice of "inhuman" class domination) is tempered by a latent struggle with and rejection of the father and, by extension, a rejection of the isolated and backward life that the father represents. In **"Los caynas,"** an individualist struggle against paternal authority and the internalization of the unacknowledged judgment of the colonizer within the colonized disrupt the univocity of the socio-political interpretation. The psychoanalytic and the socio-political interpretations together do not so much create a critical pluralism as they do a fruitful dialectic in which political solidarity does not cancel out the destructive wish fantasies of the unconscious, nor do the textual fissures of the Oedipal struggle vitiate the political outrage of those perpetually branded as the servile, primitive and child-like ancestors of "advanced" capitalism.

This final scene of **"Los caynas"** registers all the ambivalence that the phrase "the human" entailed for Vallejo. The pressure of natural science to conceive of all human experience in materialist, if not entirely monistic terms, leads a complex and ambivalent life in Vallejo's writings. In **"The Soul that Suffered from Being its Body,"** for example, the common man fighting during the Spanish Civil War suffers to the point of becoming an "unfortunate monkey, Darwin's little one" ("desgraciado mono, jovencito de Darwin"). This bestial retrogression appears interchangeable with a monistic reduction of the spiritual aspects of human being to a sum of bodily organs ("You suffer from an endocrine gland," "Tú sufres de una glándula endócrcnica"). Though diminished to the size and stature

of an "atrocious microbe," this reduction of the human to materialist origins and causes carries with it a set of associations not entirely negative. The enormity of the bestial suffering expunges the boundaries of the individual ego and produces a gratuitous heroism of interchangeable proper names ("nicolás or santiago, this one or that one" "nicolás o santiago, tal o cual") and an unaccountable strength, "an autonomous hercules," that memorializes the common man, the "unfortunate monkey." When the humansoul suffers from being its body, historically situated suffering ("in the year '38") has turned into the utter subjection to natural history. It is as though Vallejo must reduce what is human to an unrelenting animal suffering incapable of experiencing relief in cognition or memory in order then to raise up and redeem that suffering only momentarily in some unexpected reassertion of the properly historical and human.

The question of how to read Vallejo's Darwinism captures a central interpretive problematic raised by the poetry and prose writings alike: Is history as a human construct distinct from evolutionary natural history? How should we read Vallejo's relentless monist insistence on the constitution of reality by unmitigated temporal succession—literally or ironically? As an adoption of Haeckel's destructive monism? Or as an ironic intensification of reductive monism and thus a critique of Spencerian and Positivist social models? Vallejo's writings call for a dialectical interpretation that registers the power and authority of the natural scientific model and recognizes in turn that this model will ironically undermine any transfer of natural history to humanly constructed social and political bonds.

In a short fragment from the notebooks, Vallejo reflects on the crucial issue of whether Darwin or Marx is the correct interpreter of history. Is history simply another version of nature, a mirror reflection of evolutionary natural science?

> Before the stones of Darwinian risk of which the palaces of Tuileries, Postdam, Quirinal, the White House and Buckingham are constructed, I suffer the pain of a megatherium that meditates motionless, hind legs on Hegel's head and front legs on Marx's head. [*Contra el secreto profesional*]

Great historical empires have now been reduced to extinction in a perpetual struggle of the fittest. The monumental permanence of famous seats of political power has eroded into the ruins of natural history. The scene is frozen into the motionless rigidity of an allegorical emblem. The observing "I" appears paralyzed into thoughtful silence. His meditation on this destruction brands him a megatherium, a large and long extinct mammal—the very animal whose bones Darwin dug up at Punta Alta on the Voyage of the *Beagle*. The "I" is rooted in (the heads of !) nineteenth-century dialectical thought at the same time that it has been rejected by natural selection. In many ways this piece recapitulates the antinomies of Vallejo's Darwinism: on the one hand, the human subject is completely immersed in the unprivileged species—being of unredeemed nature; on the other hand, the possibility of a collective human self-transformation, though not actualized, is always held open.

FURTHER READING

Criticism

Franco, Jean. "Vallejo and the Crisis of the Thirties." *Hispania* 72, No. 1 (March 1989): 42-8.

    Discusses Vallejo's political and aesthetic beliefs, his modernist and avant-garde influences, and elements of his work.

Von Buelow, Christiane. "Vallejo's *Venus de Milo* and the Ruins of Language." *PMLA* 104, No. 1 (January 1989): 41-52.

    In-depth analysis of "*Trilce* 36." Noting Vallejo's relationship to the avant-garde and modernist movements of the early twentieth century and applying Walter Benjamin's theories of the symbol and the allegory to "*Trilce* 36," von Buelow argues that "Vallejo's poetry goes beyond simply renouncing 'the cult of the beautiful' in symbolist poems . . . and affects a critical decomposition of what might be called 'the aesthetics of the symbol.' "

Additional coverage of Vallejo's life and works is contained in the following sources published by Gale Research: *Contemporary Authors,* Vol. 105; *Hispanic Literature Criticism,* Vol. 2; *Hispanic Writers*; and *Twentieth-Century Literary Criticism*, Vol. 3.

Robert Wiene

1881-1938

German film director and screenwriter.

INTRODUCTION

Wiene is best known for *Das Kabinett des Dr. Caligari* (*The Cabinet of Dr. Caligari*), one of the most famous silent films ever made. Distinctive for its highly stylized sets and acting techniques, *The Cabinet of Dr. Caligari* represents both the earliest and the most complete manifestation of German Expressionism in film. Critics have variously characterized it as an extremely influential film that has inspired countless later filmmakers or as an anomaly in film history, a unique work with few imitators.

Biographical Information

Wiene was born in Sasku, Saxony, a region of eastern Germany. His father was a well known actor in Dresden, and Wiene's college education was in theater history. His career in film began in 1914 as a scriptwriter for the independent producer Oskar Messter. During the First World War, Wiene directed his first films, which were primarily sentimental melodramas starring Henny Porten, who became known as "the darling of the German silent cinema." *The Cabinet of Dr. Caligari* was made in 1919 from a script by Carl Mayer and Hans Janowitz, and was initially assigned by producer Erich Pommer to director Fritz Lang. Unable to direct due to a prior commitment, Lang proposed major script revisions to his replacement, Wiene, who endorsed them despite the objections of Mayer and Janowitz. Wiene also differed with the screenwriters in the choice of set designer. Mayer had suggested that Alfred Kubin, an illustrator and writer with a hallucinatory aesthetic vision, design the sets, but Wiene, in the interest of keeping production costs to a minimum, instead chose Walter Röhrig, Hermann Warm, and Walter Reimann—three prominent artists and designers in the Expressionist movement—who conceived ideas that could be realized inexpensively. Integrating the visual designs of these artists with the script's narrative, Wiene developed an acting style to complement both and guided the production of what is considered the first great horror film. Although he enjoyed a long and prolific career, Wiene never repeated the success he achieved with *The Cabinet of Dr. Caligari*. In 1934 Wiene left Germany to avoid Nazi persecution and settled in France. He died in 1938 while working on a film called *Ultimatum*.

Major Works

Wiene's reputation rests almost exclusively on *The Cabinet of Dr. Caligari*. The film opens with a young man named Francis sitting in a garden telling another man a story about Jane, a woman with whom he was once romantically involved. What follows is the visualization of Francis's story. A fair has come to the town of Holstenwall, and a doctor named Caligari applies to a local official for permission to show his "creature," a somnambulist named Cesare. The official grants him permission, but does so in a rude, humiliating way. That night the official is murdered. At the fair the next day, Francis, his friend Alan, and Jane enter Caligari's tent. Seeing that Cesare is making predictions about the future, Alan asks: "How long shall I live?" Cesare answers "until dawn" and that night sneaks into Alan's room and kills him. Suspicious of Caligari, Francis investigates Alan's death as well as other recent mysterious murders. On visiting Caligari's tent one night, he sees what he thinks is Cesare sleeping in a coffin. At the same time, however, Cesare is shown sneaking into Jane's bedroom; unable to bring himself to kill her, he abducts her and flees across the rooftops of Holstenwall. Francis and the police find that both Cesare and Caligari are missing. Francis also discovers that Caligari is really the director of a local insane asylum, and a search of his office reveals that he has modeled himself after an eighteenth-century hypnotist who used one of his subjects to commit a series of murders. Meanwhile, Cesare, still carrying Jane, has been chased through town by an angry mob and dies of exhaustion. Francis confronts Caligari with the corpse of his somnambulist, whereupon the doctor deteriorates into raving lunacy and is placed in a straitjacket. The narrative then returns to Francis in the garden, which is revealed to be part of Caligari's asylum, where Francis is an inmate. The story he told is thus revealed to have been the hallucination of a madman. Ending on a note of hope, a kindly looking Caligari declares that he now knows how to cure Francis.

The Cabinet of Dr. Caligari introduces themes, characters, and styles of lighting, set design, and acting that not only became staples of horror cinema but also influenced other genres as well. For example, the figure of an odd, sinister stranger who comes to town with a grotesque assistant began with Caligari and Cesare and became familiar to movie audiences through *Frankenstein, Dracula*, and related horror films of the 1930s and 1940s. Similarly, the presentation of madness received its first major cinematic treatment in *The Cabinet of Dr. Caligari*, and critics have observed that much of the film's power to terrify derives from its emphasis on the fragility of identity and the tenuous nature of reason. Indeed, Siegfried Kracauer has argued that the themes of irrationality and restored authority in *The Cabinet of Dr. Caligari* reflect a "mass psychological predisposition" in the German people to accept the fascist government of Adolf Hitler in the 1930s. Finally, the thematic and stylistic influence of *The Cabinet of Dr. Caligari* on subsequent films has been observed in the Expressionist elements of such horror films as *Frankenstein* and *Dracula* as well as the shadowy lighting and darkly imaginative set design of films noir, the taut, psychological thrillers of the 1940s that depict a world of fear and terror populated by neurotic, often deranged characters.

Wiene's subsequent works include *Genuine*, a fantasy concerning an oriental princess sold in a slave market who is intent on revenging herself; *Raskolnikow (Raskolnikov)*, an adaptation of Fyodor Dostoevsky's *Crime and Punishment*; and *INRI (Crown of Thorns)*, the story of Christ set within a framing story of political assassination. The best known and most acclaimed of his later films is *Orlacs Hände (The Hands of Orlac)*, the tale of a concert pianist who loses his hands in a railway accident and, through surgery, is given new hands that he begins to suspect once belonged to a murderer.

Critical Reception

At the time of its opening, *The Cabinet of Dr. Caligari* impressed most critics with its striking stylization. Röhrig, Warm, and Reimann's sets depicting twisting streets and angular buildings earned the film its reputation as the European cinema's first work of art. Wiene's direction of the two principal actors—Werner Krauss as Dr. Caligari and Conrad Veidt as Cesare—is said to complement the bizarre sets and reinforce the film's aura of dread and terror. In later years, much critical attention has focused on the narrative, specifically the question of the authorship and meaning of the film's framing device, which places Francis in the garden and reveals at the end that it is he who is insane, not Caligari. As written by Mayer and Janowitz, the story ended with Caligari descending into madness. It was Lang who proposed the twist ending, arguing that without restoring a sense of moral authority at the end, audiences would find the film too disturbing. Kracauer, whose arguments parallel those made by Mayer and Janowitz at the time, has contended that the ending precludes the possibility of interpreting the story as an anti-authoritarian political allegory and abets a conservative, indeed fascist, love of authority and order. As other critics point out, however, the ending is far more ambiguous than Kracauer's argument suggests. Logic would dictate that when the madman's story ends, that is, when Francis is revealed to be insane, the set design should reflect the return to normality. However, the sets at the end are just as fantastic as those corresponding to Francis's story. Thus, the restoration of a sense of rational order is undermined and the audience is left to reconcile conflicting signs.

PRINCIPAL WORKS

Arme Eva [with W. A. Berger]   (film)   1914
Die Konservenbraut   (film)   1915
Die Liebesbrief der Königin   (film)   1916
Der Mann im Spiegel   (film)   1916
Die Räuberbraut   (film)   1916
Das wandernde Licht   (film)   1916
Ein gefährliches Spiel   (film)   1919
Die drei Tänze der Mary Wilford   (film)   1920

Genuine   (film)   1920
Das Kabinett des Dr. Caligari [*The Cabinet of Dr. Caligari*]   (film)   1920
Die Nacht der Königin Isabeau   (film)   1920
Höllische Nacht   (film)   1921
Salome   (film)   1922
INRI [*Crown of Thorns*]   (film)   1923
Raskolnikow [*Raskolnikov*; also released as *Crime and Punishment*]   (film)   1923
*Orlacs Hände [*The Hands of Orlac*]   (film)   1925
Die Königin von Moulin-Rouge   (film)   1926
Der Rosenkavalier   (film)   1926
Die berühmte Frau [*The Dancer of Barcelona*]   (film)   1927
Die Frau auf der Folter [*A Scandal in Paris*]   (film)   1928
Der Andere   (film)   1930
Panik in Chicago   (film)   1931
Polizeiakte 909   (film)   1934
†*Ultimatum* [with Robert Siodmak]   (film)   1938

*This film was remade in the United States as *Mad Love* in 1935.

†Wiene died during the production of this film, which was completed by Siodmak.

CRITICISM

Siegfried Kracauer   (essay date 1947)

SOURCE: "Caligari," in *From Caligari to Hitler: A Psychological History of the German Film*, Princeton University Press, 1947, pp. 61-76.

[*A German philosopher as well as a social and arts critic, Kracauer emigrated to the United States when the Nazis came to power. In the following excerpt, he examines the production history, themes, and techniques of* The Cabinet of Dr. Caligari, *arguing that this film best exemplifies his thesis that German popular culture provided evidence of a "mass psychological predisposition" in the German people to accept and embrace Adolf Hitler's fascism.*]

[The original story of ***The Cabinet of Dr. Caligari***] is located in a fictitious North German town near the Dutch border, significantly called Holstenwall. One day a fair moves into the town, with merry-go-rounds and side-shows—among the latter that of Dr. Caligari, a weird, bespectacled man advertising the somnambulist Cesare. To procure a license, Caligari goes to the town hall, where he is treated haughtily by an arrogant official. The following morning this official is found murdered in his room, which does not prevent the townspeople from enjoying the fair's pleasures. Along with numerous onlookers, Francis and Alan—two students in love with Jane, a medical man's daughter—enter the tent of Dr. Caligari, and watch Cesare slowly stepping out of an upright, coffinlike box. Caligari tells the thrilled audience that the somnambulist will answer questions about the future. Alan, in an excited state, asks how long he has to live. Cesare opens his mouth; he seems to be dominated by a terrific, hypnotic power emanating from his master. "Until dawn," he answers. At dawn Francis learns that his friend has been stabbed in exactly the same manner as the official. The student, suspicious of Caligari, persuades Jane's father to assist him in an investigation. With a search warrant the two force their way into the showman's wagon, and demand that he end the trance of his medium. However, at this very moment they are called away to the police station to attend the examination of a criminal who has been caught in the act of killing a woman, and who now frantically denies that he is the pursued serial murderer.

Francis continues spying on Caligari, and, after nightfall, secretly peers through a window of the wagon. But while he imagines he sees Cesare lying in his box, Cesare in reality breaks into Jane's bedroom, lifts a dagger to pierce the sleeping girl, gazes at her, puts the dagger away and flees, with the screaming Jane in his arms, over roofs and roads. Chased by her father, he drops the girl, who is then escorted home, whereas the lonely kidnaper dies of exhaustion. As Jane, in flagrant contradiction of what Francis believes to be the truth, insists on having recognized Cesare, Francis approaches Caligari a second time to solve the torturing riddle. The two policemen in his company seize the coffinlike box, and Francis draws out of it—a dummy representing the somnambulist. Profiting by the investigator's carelessness, Caligari himself manages to escape. He seeks shelter in a lunatic asylum. The student follows him, calls on the director of the asylum to inquire about the fugitive, and recoils horror-struck: the director and Caligari are one and the same person.

The following night—the director has fallen asleep—Francis and three members of the medical staff whom he has initiated into the case search the director's office and discover material fully establishing the guilt of this authority in psychiatric matters. Among a pile of books they find an old volume about a showman named Caligari who, in the eighteenth century, traveled through North Italy, hypnotized his medium Cesare into murdering sundry people, and, during Cesare's absence, substituted a wax figure to deceive the police. the main exhibit is the director's clinical records; they evidence that he desired to verify the account of Caligari's hypnotic faculties, that his desire grew into an obsession, and that, when a somnambulist was entrusted to his care, he could not resist the temptation of repeating with him those terrible games. He had adopted the identity of Caligari. To make him admit his crimes, Francis confronts the director with the corpse of his tool, the somnambulist. No sooner does the monster realize Cesare is dead than he begins to rave. Trained attendants put him into a strait jacket.

This horror tale in the spirit of E. T. A. Hoffmann was an outspoken revolutionary story. In it, as Janowitz indicates, he and Carl Mayer [the screenwriter] half-intentionally stigmatized the omnipotence of a state authority manifesting itself in universal conscription and declarations of war. The German war government seemed to the authors the prototype of such voracious authority. Subjects of the Austro-Hungarian monarchy, they were in a better position than most citizens of the Reich to pene-

trate the fatal tendencies inherent in the German system. The character of Caligari embodies these tendencies; he stands for an unlimited authority that idolizes power as such, and, to satisfy its lust for domination, ruthlessly violates all human rights and values. Functioning as a mere instrument, Cesare is not so much a guilty murderer as Caligari's innocent victim. This is how the authors themselves understood him. According to the pacifist-minded Janowitz, they had created Cesare with the dim design of portraying the common man who, under the pressure of compulsory military service, is drilled to kill and to be killed. The revolutionary meaning of the story reveals itself unmistakably at the end, with the disclosure of the psychiatrist as Caligari: reason overpowers unreasonable power, insane authority is symbolically abolished. Similar ideas were also being expressed on the contemporary stage, but the authors of *Caligari* transferred them to the screen without including any of those eulogies of the authority-freed "New Man" in which many expressionist plays indulged. . . .

Since [Robert Wiene's] father, a once-famous Dresden actor, had become slightly insane towards the end of his life, Wiene was not entirely unprepared to tackle the case of Dr. Caligari. He suggested, in complete harmony with what [Fritz Lang, who had been originally assigned to direct *The Cabinet of Dr. Caligari*] had planned, an essential change of the original story—a change against which the two authors [Hans Janowitz and Carl Mayer] violently protested. But no one heeded them.

The original story was an account of real horrors; Wiene's version transforms that account into a chimera concocted and narrated by the mentally deranged Francis. To effect this transformation the body of the original story is put into a framing story which introduces Francis as a madman. The film *Caligari* opens with the first of the two episodes composing the frame. Francis is shown sitting on a bench in the park of the lunatic asylum, listening to the confused babble of a fellow sufferer. Moving slowly, like an apparition, a female inmate of the asylum passes by: it is Jane. Francis says to his companion: "What I have experienced with her is still stranger than what you have encountered. I will tell it to you." Fade-out. Then a view of Holstenwall fades in, and the original story unfolds, ending . . . with the identification of Caligari. After a new fade-out the second and final episode of the framing story begins. Francis, having finished the narration, follows his companion back to the asylum, where he mingles with a crowd of sad figures—among them Cesare, who absent-mindedly caresses a little flower. The director of the asylum, a mild and understanding-looking person, joins the crowd. Lost in the maze of his hallucinations, Francis takes the director for the nightmarish character he himself has created, and accuses this imaginary fiend of being a dangerous madman. He screams, he fights the attendants in a frenzy. The scene is switched over to a sickroom, with the director putting on horn-rimmed spectacles which immediatcly change his appearance: it seems to be Caligari who examines the exhausted Francis. After this he removes his spectacles and, all mildness, tells his assistants that Francis believes him to be Caligari. Now that he understands the case of his patient, the director concludes, he will be able to heal him. With this cheerful message the audience is dismissed.

Janowitz and Mayer knew why they raged against the framing story: it perverted, if not reversed, their intrinsic intentions. While the original story exposed the madness inherent in authority, Wiene's *Caligari* glorified authority and convicted its antagonist of madness. A revolutionary film was thus turned into a conformist one—following the much-used pattern of declaring some normal but troublesome individual insane and sending him to a lunatic asylum. This change undoubtedly resulted not so much from Wiene's personal predilections as from his instinctive submission to the necessities of the screen; films, at least commercial films, are forced to answer to mass desires. In its changed form *Caligari* was no longer a product expressing, at best, sentiments characteristic of the intelligentsia, but a film supposed equally to be in harmony with what the less educated felt and liked.

If it holds true that during the postwar years most Germans eagerly tended to withdraw from a harsh outer world into the intangible realm of the soul, Wiene's version was certainly more consistent with their attitude than the original story; for, by putting the original into a box, this version faithfully mirrored the general retreat into a shell. In *Caligari* (and several other films of the time) the device of a framing story was not only an aesthetic form, but also had symbolic content. Significantly, Wiene avoided mutilating the original story itself. Even though *Caligari* had become a conformist film, it preserved and emphasized this revolutionary story—as a madman's fantasy. Caligari's defeat now belonged among psychological experiences. In this way Wiene's film does suggest that during their retreat into themselves the Germans were stirred to reconsider their traditional belief in authority. Down to the bulk of social democratic workers they refrained from revolutionary action; yet at the same time a psychological revolution seems to have prepared itself in the depths of the collective soul. The film reflects this double aspect of German life by coupling a reality in which Caligari's authority triumphs with a hallucination in which the same authority is overthrown. There could be no better configuration of symbols for that uprising against the authoritarian dispositions which apparently occurred under the cover of a behavior rejecting uprising.

Janowitz suggested that the settings for *Caligari* be designed by the painter and illustrator Alfred Kubin, who, a forerunner of the surrealists, made eerie phantoms invade harmless scenery and visions of torture emerge from the subconscious. Wiene took to the idea of painted canvases, but preferred to Kubin three expressionist artists: Hermann Warm, Walter Röhrig and Walter Reimann. They were affiliated with the Berlin Sturm group, which, through Herwarth Walden's magazine *Sturm,* promoted expressionism in every field of art.

Although expressionist painting and literature had evolved years before the war, they acquired a public only after 1918. In this respect the case of Germany somewhat resembled that of Soviet Russia where, during the short period of war communism, diverse currents of abstract art enjoyed a veritable heyday. To a revolutionized people expressionism seemed to combine the denial of bourgeois traditions with faith in man's power freely to shape society and nature. On account of such virtues it may have cast a spell over many Germans upset by the breakdown of their universe.

"Films must be drawings brought to life": this was Hermann Warm's formula at the time that he and his two fellow designers were constructing the *Caligari* world. In accordance with his beliefs, the canvases and draperies of *Caligari* abounded in complexes of jagged, sharp-pointed forms strongly reminiscent of gothic patterns. Products of a style which by then had become almost a mannerism, these complexes suggested houses, walls, landscapes. Except for a few slips or concessions—some backgrounds opposed the pictorial convention in too direct a manner, while others all but preserved them—the settings amounted to a perfect transformation of material objects into emotional ornaments. With its oblique chimneys on pell-mell roofs, its windows in the form of arrows or kites and its treelike arabesques that were threats rather than trees, Holstenwall resembled those visions of unheard-of cities which the painter Lyonel Feininger evoked through his edgy, crystalline compositions. In addition, the ornamental system in *Caligari* expanded through space, annuling its conventional aspect by means of painted shadows in disharmony with the lighting effects, and zigzag delineations designed to efface all rules of perspective. Space now dwindled to a flat plane, now augmented its dimensions to become what one writer called a "stereoscopic universe."

Lettering was introduced as an essential element of the settings—appropriately enough, considering the close relationship between lettering and drawing. In one scene the mad psychiatrist's desire to imitate Caligari materializes in jittery characters composing the words "I must become Caligari"—words that loom before his eyes on the road, in the clouds, in the treetops. The incorporation of human beings and their movements into the texture of these surroundings was tremendously difficult. Of all the players only the two protagonists seemed actually to be created by a draftman's imagination. Werner Krauss as Caligari had the appearance of a phantom magician himself weaving the lines and shades through which he paced, and when Conrad Veidt's Cesare prowled along a wall, it was as if the wall had exuded him. The figure of an old dwarf and the crowd's antiquated costumes helped to remove the throng on the fair's tent-street from reality and make it share the bizarre life of abstract forms.

If Decla [the company that produced the film] had chosen to leave the original story of Mayer and Janowitz as it was, these "drawings brought to life" would have told it perfectly. As expressionist abstractions they were animated by the same revolutionary spirit that impelled the two scriptwriters to accuse authority—the kind of authority revered in Germany—of inhuman excesses. However, Wiene's version disavowed this revolutionary meaning of expressionist staging, or, at least, put it, like the original story itself, in brackets. In the film *Caligari* expressionism seems to be nothing more than the adequate translation of a madman's fantasy into pictorial terms. This was how many contemporary German reviewers understood, and relished, the settings and gestures. One of the critics stated with self-assured ignorance: "The idea of rendering the notions of sick brains . . . through expressionist pictures is not only well conceived but also well realized. Here this style has a right to exist, proves an outcome of solid logic."

In their triumph the philistines overlooked one significant fact: even though *Caligari* stigmatized the oblique chimneys as crazy, it never restored the perpendicular ones as the normal. Expressionist ornaments also overrun the film's concluding episode, in which, from the philistines' viewpoint, perpendiculars should have been expected to characterize the revival of conventional reality. In consequence, the *Caligari* style was as far from depicting madness as it was from transmitting revolutionary messages. What function did it really assume?

During the postwar years expressionism was frequently considered a shaping of primitive sensations and experiences. Gerhart Hauptmann's brother Carl—a distinguished writer and poet with expressionist inclinations—adopted this definition, and then asked how the spontaneous manifestations of a profoundly agitated soul might best be formulated. While modern language, he contended, is too perverted to serve this purpose, the film—or the bioscop, as he termed it—offers a unique opportunity to externalize the fermentation of inner life. Of course, he said, the bioscop must feature only those gestures of things and of human beings which are truly soulful.

Carl Hauptmann's views elucidate the expressionist style of *Caligari.* It had the function of characterizing the phenomena on the screen as phenomena of the soul—a function which overshadowed its revolutionary meaning. By making the film an outward projection of psychological events, expressionist staging symbolized—much more strikingly than did the device of a framing story—that general retreat into a shell which occurred in postwar Germany. It is not accidental that, as long as this collective process was effective, odd gestures and settings in an expressionist or similar style marked many a conspicuous film. *Variety,* of 1925, showed the final traces of them. Owing to their stereotyped character, these settings and gestures were like some familiar street sign—"Men at Work," for instance. Only here the lettering was different. The sign read: "Soul at Work."

After a thorough propaganda campaign culminating in the puzzling poster "You must become Caligari," Decla released the film in February 1920 in the Berlin Marmorhaus. Among the press reviews—they were unanimous in praising *Caligari* as the first work of art on the screen—that of *Vorwärts,* the leading Social Democratic Party organ, distinguished itself by utter absurdity. It commented upon the film's final scene, in which the director of the asylum promises to heal Francis, with the words: "This film is also morally invulnerable inasmuch as it evokes sympathy for the mentally diseased, and comprehension for the self-sacrificing activity of the psychiatrists and attendants." Instead of recognizing that Francis' attack against an odious authority harmonized with the Party's own antiauthoritarian doctrine, *Vorwärts* preferred to pass off authority itself as a paragon of progressive virtues. It was always the same psychological mechanism: the rationalized middle-class propensities of the Social Democrats interfering with their rational socialist designs. While the Germans were too close to *Caligari* to appraise its symptomatic value, the French realized that this film was more than just an exceptional film. They coined the term *"Caligarisme"* and applied it to a postwar world seemingly all upside down; which, at any rate, proves that they sensed the film's bearing on the structure of society. The New York première of *Caligari,* in April 1921, firmly established its world fame. But apart from giving rise to stray imitations and serving as a yardstick for artistic endeavors, this "most widely discussed film of the time" never seriously influenced the course of the American or French cinema. It stood out lonely, like a monolith.

Caligari shows the "Soul at Work." On what adventures does the revolutionized soul embark? The narrative and pictorial elements of the film gravitate towards two opposite poles. One can be labeled "Authority," or, more explicitly, "Tyranny." The theme of tyranny, with which the authors were obsessed, pervades the screen from beginning to end. Swivel-chairs of enormous height symbolize the superiority of the city officials turning on them, and, similarly, the gigantic back of the chair in Alan's attic testifies to the invisible presence of powers that have their grip on him. Staircases reinforce the effect of the furniture: numerous steps ascend to police headquarters, and in the lunatic asylum itself no less than three parallel flights of stairs are called upon to mark Dr. Caligari's position at the top of the hierarchy. That the film succeeds in picturing him as a tyrant figure of the stamp of Homunculus and Lubitsch's Henry VIII is substantiated by a most illuminating statement in Joseph Freeman's novel, *Never Call Retreat.* Its hero, a Viennese professor of history, tells of his life in a German concentration camp where, after being tortured, he is thrown into a cell:

> Lying alone in that cell, I thought of Dr. Caligari; then, without transition, of the Emperor Valentinian, master of the Roman world, who took great delight in imposing the death sentence for slight or imaginary offenses. This Caesar's favorite expressions were: "Strike off his head!"—"Burn him alive!"—"Let him be beaten with clubs till he expires!" I thought what a genuine twentieth century ruler the emperor was, and promptly fell asleep.

This dreamlike reasoning penetrates Dr. Caligari to the core by conceiving him as a counterpart of Valentinian and a premonition of Hitler. Caligari is a very specific premonition in the sense that he uses hypnotic power to force his will upon his tool—a technique foreshadowing, in content and purpose, that manipulation of the soul which Hitler was the first to practice on a gigantic scale. Even though, at the time of *Caligari,* the motif of the masterful hypnotizer was not unknown on the screen—it played a prominent role in the American film *Trilby,* shown in Berlin during the war—nothing in their environment invited the two authors to feature it. They must have been driven by one of those dark impulses which, stemming from the slowly moving foundations of a people's life, sometimes engender true visions.

One should expect the pole opposing that of tyranny to be the pole of freedom; for it was doubtless their love of freedom which made Janowitz and Mayer disclose the nature of tyranny. Now this counterpole is the rallying-point of elements pertaining to the fair—the fair with its rows of tents, its confused crowds besieging them, and its diversity of thrilling amusements. Here Francis and Alan happily join the swarm of onlookers; here, on the scene of his triumphs, Dr. Caligari is finally trapped. In their attempts to define the character of a fair, literary sources repeatedly evoke the memory of Babel and Babylon alike. A seventeenth century pamphlet describes the noise typical of a fair as "such a distracted noise that you would think Babel not comparable to it," and, almost two hundred years later, a young English poet feels enthusiastic about "that Babylon of booths—the Fair." The manner in which such Biblical images insert themselves unmistakably characterizes the fair as an enclave of anarchy in the sphere of entertainment. This accounts for its eternal attractiveness. People of all classes and ages enjoy losing themselves in a wilderness of glaring colors and shrill sounds, which is populated with monsters and abounding in bodily sensations—from violent shocks to tastes of incredible sweetness. For adults it is a regression into childhood days, in which games and serious affairs are identical, real and imagined things mingle, and anarchical desires aimlessly test infinite possibilities. By means of this regression the adult escapes a civilization which tends to overgrow and starve out the chaos of instincts—escapes it to restore that chaos upon which civilization nevertheless rests. The fair is not freedom, but anarchy entailing chaos.

Significantly, most fair scenes in *Caligari* open with a small iris-in exhibiting an organ-grinder whose arm constantly rotates, and, behind him, the top of a merry-go-round which never ceases its circular movement. The circle here becomes a symbol of chaos. While freedom resembles a river, chaos resembles a whirlpool. Forgetful of self, one may plunge into chaos; one cannot move on in it. That the two authors selected a fair with its liberties as contrast to the oppressions of Caligari betrays the flaw in their revolutionary aspirations. Much as they longed for freedom, they were apparently incapable of imagining its contours. There is something Bohemian in their conception; it seems the product of naïve idealism rather than true insight. But it might be said that the fair faithfully reflected the chaotic condition of postwar Germany.

Whether intentionally or not, *Caligari* exposes the soul wavering between tyranny and chaos, and facing a desperate situation: any escape from tyranny seems to throw it into a state of utter confusion. Quite logically, the film spreads an all-pervading atmosphere of horror. Like the Nazi world, that of *Caligari* overflows with sinister portents, acts of terror and outbursts of panic. The equation of horror and hopelessness comes to a climax in the final episode which pretends to re-establish normal life. Except for the ambiguous figure of the director and the shadowy members of his staff, normality realizes itself through the crowd of insane moving in their bizarre surroundings. The normal as a madhouse: frustration could not be pictured more finally. And in this film, as well as in *Homunculus,* is unleashed a strong sadism and an appetite for destruc-

tion. The reappearance of these traits on the screen once more testifies to their prominence in the German collective soul.

Technical peculiarities betray peculiarities of meaning. In *Caligari* methods begin to assert themselves which belong among the special properties of German film technique. *Caligari* initiates a long procession of 100 per cent studio-made films. Whereas, for instance, the Swedes at that time went to great pains to capture the actual appearance of a snowstorm or a wood, the German directors, at least until 1924, were so infatuated with indoor effects that they built up whole landscapes within the studio walls. They preferred the command of an artificial universe to dependence upon a haphazard outer world. Their withdrawal into the studio was part of the general retreat into a shell. Once the Germans had determined to seek shelter within the soul, they could not well allow the screen to explore that very reality which they abandoned. This explains the conspicuous role of architecture after *Caligari*—a role that has struck many an observer. "It is of the utmost importance," Paul Rotha remarks in a survey of the postwar period, "to grasp the significant part played by the architect in the development of the German cinema." How could it be otherwise? The architect's façades and rooms were not merely backgrounds, but hieroglyphs. They expressed the structure of the soul in terms of space.

Caligari also mobilizes light. It is a lighting device which enables the spectators to watch the murder of Alan without seeing it; what they see, on the wall of the student's attic, is the shadow of Cesare stabbing that of Alan. Such devices developed into a specialty of the German studios. Jean Cassou credits the Germans with having invented a "laboratory-made fairy illumination," and Harry Alan Potamkin considers the handling of the light in the German film its "major contribution to the cinema." This emphasis upon light can be traced to an experiment Max Reinhardt made on the stage shortly before *Caligari.* In his *mise-en-scène* of Sorge's prewar drama *The Beggar* (*Der Bettler*)—one of the earliest and most vigorous manifestations of expressionism—he substituted for normal settings imaginary ones created by means of lighting effects. Reinhardt doubtless introduced these effects to be true to the drama's style. The analogy to the films of the postwar period is obvious: it was their expressionist nature which impelled many a German director of photography to breed shadows as rampant as weeds and associate ethereal phantoms with strangely lit arabesques or faces. These efforts were designed to bathe all scenery in an unearthly illumination marking it as scenery of the soul. "Light has breathed soul into the expressionist films," Rudolph Kurtz states in his book on the expressionist cinema. Exactly the reverse holds true: in those films the soul was the virtual source of the light. The task of switching on this inner illumination was somewhat facilitated by powerful romantic traditions.

The attempt made in *Caligari* to co-ordinate settings, players, lighting and action is symptomatic of the sense of structural organization which, from this film on, manifests itself on the German screen. Rotha coins the term "studio constructivism" to characterize "that curious air of completeness, of finality, that surrounds each product of the German studios." But organizational completeness can be achieved only if the material to be organized does not object to it. (The ability of the Germans to organize themselves owes much to their longing for submission.) Since reality is essentially incalculable and therefore demands to be observed rather than commanded, realism on the screen and total organization exclude each other. Through their "studio constructivism" no less than their lighting the German films revealed that they dealt with unreal events displayed in a sphere basically controllable.

In the course of a visit to Paris about six years after the première of *Caligari,* Janowitz called on Count Etienne de Beaumont in his old city residence, where he lived among Louis Seize furniture and Picassos. The Count voiced his admiration of *Caligari,* terming it "as fascinating and abstruse as the German soul." He continued: "Now the time has come for the German soul to speak, Monsieur. The French soul spoke more than a century ago, in the Revolution, and you have been mute. . . . Now we are waiting for what you have to impart to us, to the world."

The Count did not have long to wait.

Lotte H. Eisner   (essay date 1969)

SOURCE: "The Beginnings of the Expressionist Film," in *The Haunted Screen: Expressionism in the German Cinema and the Influence of Max Reinhardt,* translated by Roger Greaves, University of California Press, 1969, pp. 17-38.

[*Widely recognized as an eminent film critic, Eisner began her career in Germany in the mid-1920s, then fled to France in the 1930s following the rise of nazism. In the following excerpt, which is reprinted from the 1969 translation and revision of the 1952 French version of her* The Haunted Screen, *Eisner examines the Expressionist aspects of* The Cabinet of Dr. Caligari.]

The leaning towards violent contrast—which in Expressionist literature can be seen in the use of staccato sentences—and the inborn German liking for chiaroscuro and shadow, obviously found an ideal artistic outlet in the cinema. Visions nourished by moods of vague and troubled yearning could have found no more apt mode of expression, at once concrete and unreal.

This explains why the first films of second-rate directors such as Robert Wiene or Richard Oswald misled people into thinking them remarkably gifted. These works blithely married a morbid Freudianism and an Expressionistic exaltation to the romantic fantasies of Hoffmann and Eichendorff, and to the tortured soul of contemporary Germany seemed, with their overtones of death, horror and nightmare, the reflection of its own grimacing image, offering a kind of release.

In 1817, in a letter to the archetypal Romantic Rahel Varnhagen, Astolphe de Coustine wrote: 'Behind the lives and writings of the Germans there is always a mysterious world whose light alone seems to pierce the veil of our atmosphere; and the minds disposed to ascend towards that world—which ends with the beginning of this one—will always be alien to France.'

It was in this mysterious world, attractive and repugnant at the same time, that the German cinema found its true nature.

The making of *Caligari* was strewn with incidents, which have been variously reported by the different people responsible for it.

We know from the comments of one of the authors of the scenario—quoted by Kracauer in *From Caligari to Hitler* (1947)—that the prologue and epilogue were added as an afterthought in the face of objections from both authors. The result of these modifications was to falsify the action and ultimately to reduce it to the ravings of a madman. The film's authors, Carl Mayer and Hans Janowitz, had had the very different intention of unmasking the absurdity of asocial authority, represented by Dr Caligari, the superintendent of a lunatic asylum and proprietor of a fairground side-show.

Erich Pommer, who used to claim to have 'supervised' *Caligari,* alleges that the authors submitted the scenario to him and informed him of their intention of commissioning the sets from Alfred Kubin, a visionary designer and engraver whose obsessed works seem to arise from a chaos of light and shadow. Kubin's *Caligari* would certainly have been full of Goyaesque visions, and the German silent film would have had the gloomy hallucinatory atmosphere which is unmistakably its own without being sidetracked into the snares of abstraction. For Kubin, like Janowitz, came from Prague, a mysterious town whose ghetto, with its tortuous back-alleys, was a survival from the Middle Ages. Like Janowitz, Kubin knew all the horrors of an in-between world. In a half-autobiographical, half-fantastic tale, *Die Andere Seite,* published in 1922, he describes his wanderings through the dark streets, possessed by an obscure force which led him to imagine weird houses and landscapes, terrifying or grotesque situations. When he entered a little tea-shop, everything seemed bizarre. The waitresses were like wax dolls moved by some strange mechanism. He had the feeling that his intrusion had disturbed the few customers sitting at the tables; they were completely unreal, like phantoms hatching satanic plots. The far end of the shop, with its barrel-organ, seemed suspicious, a trap. Behind that barrel-organ there was surely a bloody lair wreathed in gloom . . . It is a pity that so vivid a painter of nightmares was never commissioned for *Caligari.*

The practical Pommer relates that while Mayer and Janowitz were 'talking art' at him, he for his part was considering the scenario from a very different point of view. 'They wanted to experiment,' he wrote in 1947, 'and I wanted to keep the costs down.' Making the sets in painted canvas was a saving from every point of view, and largely facilitated production in days when money and raw materials were scarce. On the other hand, at a time when Germany was still going through the indirect consequences of an abortive revolution and the national economy was as unstable as the national frame of mind, the atmosphere was ripe for experiment. The director of *Caligari,* Robert

Wiene, subsequently claimed in London to be responsible for the film's Expressionist conception.

Yet it is difficult to be sure of the true details of these remote events. . . .

Today we know that Fritz Lang, who was chosen as the director of *Caligari* before Robert Wiene (he refused because he was still engaged in the filming of *Die Spinnen*), suggested to the production company that a good way of not scaring off the public would be to bring in a kind of *Rahmenhandlung* (framing-treatment), a prologue and epilogue in conventional settings supposed to take place in a lunatic asylum. Thus the main action, related in a conversation between two lunatics sitting in the asylum garden, became the elaborate invention of a fantastic world seen through the eyes of a madman.

When Abel Gance, that eternal pioneer, had made his own attempt at filming a world seen through the eyes of a madman he had gone about it in a quite different way. In *La Folie du Dr Tube*, knowing nothing of anamorphic lenses, he borrowed several concave and convex mirrors from a Hall of Mirrors in a nearby amusement-park and filmed the reflections of people and objects, occasionally obtaining, in addition to 'stretching' effects, mere blobs and wavy lines. This was a fundamentally Impressionistic use of the camera; the distortions of *Dr Caligari* lie in the basic graphic idea, and can therefore be termed *Expressionistic*.

The sets of *Caligari*, which have often been criticized for being too flat, do have some depth nonetheless. As Rudolph Messell says in *This Film Business* (1928), 'the background comes to the fore'. The depth comes from deliberately distorted perspectives and from narrow, slanting streets which cut across each other at unexpected angles. Sometimes also it is enhanced by a back-cloth which extends the streets into sinuous lines. The three-dimensional effect is reinforced by the inclined cubes of dilapidated houses. Oblique, curving, or rectilinear lines converge across an undefined expanse towards the background: a wall skirted by the silhouette of Cesare the somnambulist, the slim ridge of the roof he darts along bearing his prey, and the steep paths he scales in his flight.

In *Expressionismus und Film*, Rudolf Kurtz points out that these curves and slanting lines have a meaning which is decidedly metaphysical. For the psychic reaction caused in the spectator by oblique lines is entirely different from that caused in him by straight lines. Similarly, unexpected curves and sudden ups and downs provoke emotions quite different from those induced by harmonious and gentle gradients.

But what matters is to create states of anxiety and terror. The diversity of planes has only secondary importance.

In *Caligari* the Expressionist treatment was unusually successful in evoking the 'latent physiognomy' of a small medieval town, with its dark twisting back-alleys boxed in by crumbling houses whose inclined façades keep out all daylight. Wedge-shaped doors with heavy shadows and oblique windows with distorted frames seem to gnaw into the walls. The bizarre exaltation brooding over the synthetic sets of *Caligari* brings to mind Edschmid's statement that 'Expressionism evolves in a perpetual excitation'. These houses and the well, crudely sketched at an alley-corner, do indeed seem to vibrate with an extraordinary spirituality. 'The antediluvian character of utensils awakens,' says Kurtz. This is Worringer's 'spiritual unrest' creating the 'animation of the inorganic'.

The Germans, used as they are to savage legends, have an eerie gift for animating objects. In the normal syntax of the German language objects have a complete active life: they are spoken of with the same adjectives and verbs used to speak of human beings, they are endowed with the same qualities as people, they act and react in the same way. Long before Expressionism this anthropomorphism had already been pushed to the extreme. In 1884 Friedrich Vischer, in his novel *Auch Einer*, talks about 'the perfidy of the object' which gloats upon our vain efforts to dominate it. The bewitched objects in Hoffmann's obsessed universe appear in the same light.

Animate objects always seem to haunt German narcissism. When couched in Expressionist phraseology the personification is amplified; the metaphor expands and embraces people and objects in similar terms.

So we frequently find German-speaking authors attributing diabolical overtones to, for example, the street: in Gustav Meyrink's *Golem*, the houses in the Prague ghetto, which have sprouted like weeds, seem to have an insidious life of their own 'when the autumn evening mists stagnate in the streets and veil their imperceptible grimace'. In some mysterious way these streets contrive to abjure their life and feelings during the daytime, and lend them instead to their inhabitants, those enigmatic creatures who wander aimlessly around, feebly animated by an invisible magnetic current. But at night the houses reclaim their life with interest from these unreal inhabitants; they stiffen, and their sly faces fill with malevolence. The doors become gaping maws and shrieking gullets.

'The dynamic force of objects howls their desire to be created,' Kurtz declared, and this is the explanation of the overpowering obsessiveness of the *Caligari* sets.

But light, atmosphere, and distance are not the only determinants of the object-distortion which we find in Expressionist art. There is also the power of Abstractionism. Georg Marzynski informs us in his book *Methode des Expressionismus* (1920) that a selective and creative distortion gives the artist a means of representing the complexity of the psyche; by linking this psychical complexity to an optical complexity he can release an object's internal life, the expression of its 'soul'. The Expressionists are concerned solely with images in the mind. Hence oblique walls which have no reality. For, as Marzynski says, it is one of the characteristics of 'imagined images' to represent objects on the slant, seen from above at an acute angle; this viewpoint makes it easier to grasp the whole structure of the image.

The Germans love watching the reflections of distorting mirrors. The Romantics had already observed certain formal distortions. One of Ludwig Tieck's heroes, William Lovell, describes the impression of an unstable, ill-defined universe: 'at such times the streets appear to me to be *rows of counterfeit houses* inhabited by madmen . . . ' The streets described by Kubin or Meyrink and those of the *Caligari* sets find their perfect echo in this phrase.

The abstraction and the total distortion of the *Caligari* sets are seen at their most extreme in the vision of the prison-cell, with its verticals narrowing as they rise like arrow-heads. The oppressive effect is heightened by these verticals being extended along the floor and directed at the spot where the chain-laden prisoner squats. In this hell the distorted, rhomboid window is a mockery. The designers succeed in rendering the idea of a goal-in-the-absolute, in its 'most expressive expression'.

Hermann Warm stated that 'the cinema image must become an engraving'. But the German cinema's use of light and shade did not issue from this affirmation alone. The serial film *Homunculus,* made three years earlier, clearly demonstrates the effect that can be obtained from contrasts between black and white.

A lack of continuity is apparent between the Expressionistic sets and the utterly bourgeois furniture—the chintzy armchairs in Lil Dagover's sitting-room or the leather armchair in the madhouse yard. The break in style is fatal. Similarly, the façade of the asylum is not distorted, yet the end of the film is seen in the same weird décor. It is hard to say which is the more responsible for this: the Expressionist tendencies of the designers, or the parsimony of the producer.

The stylization of the acting is dictated by the sets. Yet Werner Krauss in the part of the satanic Dr Caligari and Conrad Veidt in that of the sinister somnambulist are the only actors who really adapt themselves to it, and—in Kurtz's words—achieve a 'dynamic synthesis of their being', by concentrating their movements and facial expressions. Through a reduction of gesture they attain movements which are almost linear and which—despite a few curves that slip in—remain brusque, like the broken angles of the sets; and their movements from point to point never go beyond the limits of a given geometrical plane. The other actors, on the other hand, remain locked in a naturalistic style, though, owing to the old-fashioned way in which they are dressed (cloaks, top hats, morning-coats), their outlines do achieve an element of the fantastic.

The characters of Caligari and Cesare conform to Expressionist conception; the somnambulist, detached from his everyday ambience, deprived of all individuality, an abstract creature, kills without motive or logic. And his master, the mysterious Dr Caligari, who lacks the merest shadow of human scruple, acts with the criminal insensibility and defiance of conventional morality which the Expressionists exalted.

S. S. Prawer   (essay date 1980)

SOURCE: "The Iconography of the Terror-film: Wiene's *Caligari,*" in *Caligari's Children: The Film as Tale of Terror,* Oxford University Press, Oxford, 1980, pp. 164-200.

[Prawer is a German-born English critic and educator specializing in German literature, particularly the work of

Heinrich Heine. In the following excerpt, taken from his book which examines the masterpieces of Gothic cinema and theorizes on the function and significance of the artistic expression of horror, he provides an extended discussion of the thematic, narrative, and stylistic innovations of The Cabinet of Dr. Caligari *and assesses its influence on subsequent films and filmmakers.]*

The Cabinet of Dr. Caligari invites its audience to explore a *mise en scène* that sets live actors and solid furniture into stylized exterior and interior sets obviously painted on to theatrical flats and photographed by a camera which moves relatively little. Its flowing narrative does, however, make significant though sparing use of cross-cutting, flash-back, reductions and expansions of the image-field, high-angle shots, low-angle lighting, split screen, quickly flashed or long-held images, and other devices of the early film, as its tells the story baldly summarized in *The Oxford Companion to Film* as follows:

> Caligari is a hypnotist whose somnambulist, Cesare, kills the hero's friend and carries off his girl. Having exposed Caligari, the hero is himself revealed as an inmate of a lunatic asylum where Caligari is director.

And the *Companion* adds:

> The original outline by MAYER and JANOWITZ represented Caligari unequivocally as the insane villain: the framework, which by representing the hero as mad reverses the authors' intentions, was added by POMMER.

Whether Pommer [Erich Pommer, the film's producer] or another was responsible for the alteration need not concern us now. We should remember, however, that unlike *Dr. Jekyll and Mr. Hyde* and *Vampyr,* *Caligari* did not begin with a specific literary work that had to be adapted for the screen. Its authors conceived it, from the beginning, as a film. The difference between their conception and the finished work can now be studied with great accuracy; for the Deutsche Kinemathek in Berlin has acquired from the estate of Werner Krauss, and has kindly allowed me to see, a typescript of the original screen-play. From this it appears that a 'framework' was envisaged by the authors, but that it was a framework of a different kind. At the opening of the typescript we meet Francis, the narrator, not in a lunatic asylum, as it turns out in the film, but as a prosperous 'Dr. Francis' inhabiting a country house, where he recounts to a happy, punch-drinking group of friends the tale of Caligari and his somnambulist in which he had been involved some twenty years before. Among those who listen to him is Jane, the very Jane who also plays a central part in the Caligari story, and who is now happily married to Francis. Francis's memory has been reactivated by the sight of some gipsies travelling to a fair—but throughout his narration his present distance from the world of Caligari and his somnambulist is to be kept before us by intertitles that pointedly use the epic preterite: 'When, the next day, we went to the fair, we had no idea that in the meantime a terrible crime had been committed.' Nothing in this version leaves any room for doubt that the events recounted actually occurred—we are even shown an official plaque put up by the town of Holstenwall to mark the spot where Caligari's cabinet had once stood! Through the introduction of a sympathetic disciple as well as various other signs, including unmistakable signals in the projected intertitles, the typescript asks us to regard Caligari as a dedicated scientist whose mind has given way, as a man to be pitied, as a tragic figure. It offers little support for Kracauer's thesis of a revolutionary or anti-tyrannical tendency that those who made the actual film then perverted. The Pirandellian ambiguities introduced into the film by the altered framework, by the substitution of a narrator who may or may not be insane for one who recollects long-past unhappy events in the tranquillity of domestic happiness, seem to me a distinct improvement, a deepening of the film's import, a just reflection of historical and social uncertainties characteristic of the time just after the First World War. They take wing from one brief hint in the typescript, one passing suggestion, soon dismissed, of a less than completely reliable narrator: 'And then I felt', the typescript makes the narrator say at one point, 'as though I myself had lost my reason.'

It has become all too fashionable of late to dismiss *Caligari* as a cinematic backwater. I believe, on the contrary, that it presents a veritable anthology of figures, themes, and images which later directors have re-used, varied, expanded, and developed further, without even now exhausting their possibilities. . . .

At the centre of the film is the sinister figure of Werner Krauss's Caligari, with his unforgettable shuffling walk, his obsequious showman's gestures, his leering glances through round spectacles, his weird Biedermeier costume, his gloves with their three black stripes matching the patterning of his straggling hair and the converging lines painted on to the scenery and the floors of the film-set. The significance of this figure is worth pursuing in some detail.

This Caligari is, first of all, a piece of scene-design: part of an over-all visual pattern which gains its meaning from a larger whole. In *The Cabinet of Dr. Caligari,* as in later films of terror, this point is driven home, unobtrusively but constantly, by the composition of the frames, the relation of the actor to the scenery and to his fellow-actors as conveyed by stance, costume, and camera angle.

Secondly, Caligari is a showman whose deliberately weird get-up and exaggerated gestures are designed to induce an audience to attend the thrilling spectacle that awaits it in his fairground tent. Here, clearly, we have a reflection, within the film, of what has brought us into the cinema to watch the film. Before and during its original showing it was, in fact, advertised, by its distributors and exhibitors in Berlin and elsewhere, with considerable showman's flair; the advertising campaign included posters and newspaper graphics whose design resembled that of the poster which Werner Krauss's Caligari unrolls from a cross-bar stuck to a pole to advertise, within the film, the exhibition of his somnambulist. The fascination which films of this kind may exert on the individual spectators as well as the group is symbolized within *The Cabinet of Dr. Caligari* first by the crowd that attends Caligari's spectacle when Francis and Alan pay their fateful visit, and then by Jane's reactions to the solo performance Caligari maliciously arranges for her. . . . [Many] later terror-films, from *Mark of the Vampire* and *Mad Love* to *Peeping Tom,* make some of their subtlest effects by reminding their audiences of the kind of attraction that has brought them to watch what they are in fact watching. Wiene's film does this too, and in the process it jogs us into remembering that not so long ago the cinema itself, which is here self-consciously entering the realm of art, was a fairground side-show.

A French critic, C. B. Clément, writing in *Communications* in 1975, has seen a strong sexual connotation in the scene, already mentioned, in which Caligari lures the terrified and fascinated Jane into his deserted fairground booth to give her a private view of his rigid somnambulist. What we see is a malevolent old man, a demonic bourgeois, attracting a young girl by flipping open two flaps to show her something behind the scenes ('ob-scene'?)—the 'exhibitor' as 'exhibitionist'! But perhaps we had better leave that interpretation to hard-line Freudians.

Caligari is shown, thirdly, to be a multiple personality, two of whose facets are indicated by the distinct costuming and make-up which we also associate with *Jekyll and Hyde* films. As 'Caligari' he is a fairground showman, pushed around by authorities whom he has to cajole and coax, dependent on audiences whom he has to attract. The menace that comes from him in that guise is the menace of the underdog who is eager to take his revenge for social slights and oppression. As director of the mental home he is—well, dual again, for Alan sees him, and we see him for a time, as a power-obsessed maniac who belongs in a strait-jacket more surely than his patients, while the final scenes suggest that he may be an urbane and benevolent healer of sick minds. This kind of presentation of different views of the same personality, or different aspects of the same personality, through changes in the acting style and make-up and lighting of the same actor, has become a staple of the terror-film since *Jekyll and Hyde* was first made into a movie in 1908. It is no accident, of course, that Caligari is a doctor—or, more precisely, an alienist; the complex feelings he provokes were familiar to contemporaries of Charcot and Freud, 'healers' who moved among hysterics and conducted experiments with hypnotism.

Caligari is shown, fourthly, as an early victim of that favourite affliction of so many recent terror-films, culminating in *The Exorcist* and *The Heretic:* demonic possession. The original Caligari, we learn from the film, was an eighteenth-century 'mystic' (the religious associations of that term are highly significant in this context); the director of the mental home reads about him and becomes obsessed with him. For weeks before the film opened in Berlin, advertisements proclaimed in strange, jagged, hieroglyphic-like lettering: DU MUSST CALIGARI WERDEN ('You have to become Caligari'): and these letters in fact appear in the film superimposed upon the scenery to show the alienist's obsession with, and take-over by, the long-dead Caligari. 'Possession', here, comes by way of printed or written words, by means of a book and letters appearing on a wall, rather than a picture, a painted portrait, as in Corman's *The Haunted Palace* and other, similar, works. The first time we ever see Caligari, he is clutching a book! In Fritz Lang's *The Testament of Dr. Mabuse,* the director of another mental home, Dr. Baum, was to be taken over in a parallel way by the spirit of a man still alive, the super-criminal Dr. Mabuse, incarcerated as a madman and scribbling down unceasing plans for crimes and world-domination. Dr. Baum thus fulfils, in Lang's film, the functions of Caligari *and* Cesare in Robert Wiene's. In Lang, the 'taking-over', the 'possession', of Dr. Baum is shown by superimposition; in *The Exorcist,* its principal (and certainly most effective) mark is a change of voice. For many of us the real 'star' of this crude and unpleasant movie was the unseen Mercedes McCambridge, who lent the demon her voice, though no regular cinema-goer could be quite impervious to the aura around Max von Sydow, playing the title role: an aura deriving in part from his appearance as the tormented hero of many a Bergman film, and in part from his appearance as Jesus in *The Greatest Story Ever Told* (1965).

The fifth iconographic aspect of the Caligari figure for which important parallels may be found in later films of the same genre is that he is shown as a dreamer within the dream-like movie that bears his name. We see the director of the mental home in his bed, tossing in uneasy sleep, perturbed (we surmise) by dreams of persons and events that we have been seeing, and are seeing, in the film of which he is part. Such images of the dreamer within a dream, or the dreamer and his dream, will recur in many of the most successful terror-films of later times—in Cavalcanti's *Dead of Night,* for instance.

Caligari is shown, as has already been said, as a stranger who disrupts the normal lives of the inhabitants of a small town: he and his somnambulist are marked out as strangers by idiosyncracies of costume and movement that set them to some extent apart from the rest of the cast. This is one of a cluster of themes and images which Paul Monaco, in *Cinema and Society,* has analysed in a large number of German films as 'symbols of Germany's obsession with the loss of the war of 1914-18': Monaco lists 'betrayal, the foreigner as evil-doer, guilt, racing against time, dangerous streets'. In itself, however, the image of the 'disruptive stranger' is central to the terror-film of many nations, just as it had been to a great many literary and sub-literary terror-fictions: we need think only of the part which it plays in such classics as *Dracula,* for instance, where the menace comes to England from Transylvania, or in *The Mummy,* where it comes from Egypt. This helps to explain, among other things, why so many of the most successful terror-stars of the American sound-cinema betrayed by their speech that they hailed from England or from the continent of Europe. In Robert Florey's *Murders in the Rue Morgue,* which starred Bela Lugosi, this is brought out into the open when the customers lured into Dr. Mirakle's fairground tent comment explicitly on Mirakle's foreign modes of speech: 'Did you notice his accent? I have never heard one like it.'

There is a Hoffmannesque twist, however, to this story of Caligari the 'stranger': for just as in Hoffmann's 'The Sandman' the sinister itinerant vendor of spectacles is identified with a respected local lawyer, so Caligari, as it turns out, is very much part of the little town he terrorizes in the inner story. He is, after all, the director of one of the town's most necessary institutions. Here we should

perhaps remember that Caligari's outer appearance was suggested to the script-writers by a photograph of the philosopher Arthur Schopenhauer in his old age. In many a later film will we find some connection made between the terror-makers that fill the screen and small-town German life.

The Cabinet of Dr. Caligari features a number of striking images which show its eponymous hero combining qualities that were destined to play—in this particular combination—a vital role in later terror-films. On the one hand we see him as a doctor in elegant morning-dress attended by subordinate colleagues in white coats as he examines his patients; on the other we see him as an adept of curious lore, who rummages in old volumes of 'mystical' texts and is seen clutching one of them to his bosom in an extravagant gesture of delight. The combination of scientist and 'mystic' adept, exhibited as deadly and dangerous in *Caligari,* in Ulmer's *The Black Cat* (1934), and elsewhere, is however, the very combination needed to fight the forces of evil in other films: one need think only of the Van Helsing figure in such films as *Dracula, The Mummy,* and their progeny.

Another aspect of Caligari may be illuminated by a passage from Heinrich Heine's *The Romantic School* in which the poet talks about attacks made by German 'supernaturalists' on the rationalists of the Enlightenment. In their hatred of the rationalists, Heine declares, these people

> resemble the inmates of a madhouse who, though they are afflicted with the most diverse kinds of madness, manage to accommodate themselves with one another tolerably well, but who are filled with bitterest hatred of the man whom they regard as their common enemy: the alienist who wants to restore their reason.

Heine's perspective is clear, and the framing action of *Caligari* would seem to suggest a similar perspective to its spectators. Béla Bálazs tells us that at one time the film even appeared with the sub-title 'How a madman sees the world'. Yet a question mark continues to hang over the figure of Krauss's Caligari. He directs a madhouse—but is he not himself deluded? Is the insanity we seem to see breaking out in him simply a projection from one of his patients who externalizes in the director the madness that is 'really' in himself? Or is Francis, whatever his own state of mind, seeing truly? Who will guard the guardians? What happens when those who should cure us are themselves in need of cure? What do we do when those who should protect us are driven to persecute us? The political and social resonance of such questions is immediately apparent—as is the fact that Wiene's film, and Krauss's performance, owe a good deal of their force to their ability to raise them in our minds. They are emphasized by the very rhythm of the film, which ends (in unmutilated copies) on a long-held, puzzling close-up of Krauss's face—the longest-held close-up in the whole work.

To this disturbing portrait Krauss adds another nuance by insinuating—mainly through Caligari's shuffling walk supported by a stick—that there may also be something physically wrong with him; that he is, in some not immediately tangible way, a cripple. We are therefore free to see his lust for power and desire for revenge as in part at least an attempt to compensate for physical inferiority as well as for some real or imagined social slight. This impression, however, which many a modern viewer undoubtedly gains, may well be contrary to the film-makers' intentions. What Werner Krauss is probably attempting, with his hobbling walk, is to find a dynamic equivalent for the static distortions of the scenery—just as his hand and arm movements, when clutching a book or miming hallucination, are as deliberately exaggerated and twisted as the painted perspectives before which they are enacted. The gait and gestures of the soberly clad director of the asylum are noticeably less extravagant than those of the showman in his high hat.

Above all, however, as Noel Carroll has so convincingly shown in 'The Cabinet of Dr. Kracauer' (*Millenium Film Journal*, 1978), Krauss's movements are 'literalizations' of the metaphor that he is morally twisted—just as the sets suggest by their 'bending buildings, crooked street-lamps and cracked walls' that the world into which he enters is about to collapse on to its inhabitants, and by their many knife-like or stiletto-like shapes that this world is hostile and threatening.

Caligari owes the power that he wields to his mastery of hypnosis. He thus becomes—and this is clearly a further, most significant, aspect of the character that Wiene, Mayer, and Krauss project—the mesmerist, the controller from afar, the man who can kill without ever being seen to raise the knife himself, the man who can induce others to act or be acted upon in the way a puppetmaster manipulates his marionettes. This is shown symbolically by the way Cesare awakes on Caligari's command in the fairground tent, and by the dummy which takes Cesare's place when the latter is sent out on a murderous mission. The film's intertitles make the master-slave relationship explicit:

> 'Cesare! Do you hear me? It is I calling you: I,
> Dr. Caligari, —your master—Awaken for a
> brief while from your dark night'——;

they emphasize, too, the idea of unholy experimentation on helpless human beings:

> 'Now I shall be able to prove whether a som-
> nambulist can be compelled to do things of
> which he knows nothing, things he would never
> do himself and would abhor doing if he were
> awake . . .'

The social, political, and moral implications of all this have been imaginatively explored in another medium by Thomas Mann's *Mario and the Magician*. There is a clear connection here with hypnotist figures favoured by non-German film-makers too—from silent American versions of *Trilby* to the Hammer *Dracula* films, directed by Terence Fisher, where the vampire-count acquires a whole bevy of minions whom he induces to act for him in the way Renfield does in the original novel. We [may see] how in zombie-movies, from Halperin's *White Zombie* of 1932 to John Gilling's *The Plague of the Zombies* in 1965, the image takes on an additional economic menace: zombies are used by their masters and controllers not just as instru-

ments of mayhem, but also as a source of cheap labour. The symbol would, I am sure, have delighted Karl Marx.

The ultimate significance of Caligari's hypnotizing powers, and of the way in which at his very first introduction his gaze is directed outwards towards the viewer, has been perceptively glossed by Roland Barthes in his seminal essay 'On Leaving the Cinema' (*Communications*). Here Barthes has rightly drawn attention to the hypnotizing function of the cinema-screen itself, with its immobile but flickering light watched by intent spectators in the dark. Mark Nash, whose book on Carl Dreyer refers to Barthes's essay, rightly adds that

> hypnosis has a privileged place in early cinema:
> e.g. *The Cabinet of Dr. Caligari,* the representa-
> tions of the doctor with his thick spectacles and
> his gaze into camera, who *sees* into psychologi-
> cal (and supernatural) problems; Lang's *Dr. Ma-
> buse;* the doctor in *Vampyr* where the result of
> the hypnosis is Gray's uncanny dream (central
> to vampirism) of losing his own blood.

When Nash goes on to liken the whole experience of watching Dreyer's film—'its slowness, its controlled rhythm, its silences'—to the experience of being hypnotized, he could just as well be talking about *Caligari,* or *Tired Death* (*Destiny*), or (*Warning*) *Shadows,* or many another German film of the Weimar period.

The scene in which Caligari substitutes a dummy for the somnambulist whom he has sent out on his murderous mission suggests another aspect of this figure which was to have a long subsequent history in the terror-film. It shows him as a man who can manipulate the phenomenal world in such a way that we think we are seeing what is not, in reality, 'there'. Fritz Lang and Thea von Harbou, in *The Testament of Dr. Mabuse,* invented an aural equivalent of this visual illusion: a gramophone rigged up in such a way that when the handle of Dr. Baum's locked study door is tried at a time when he is out on nefarious business, his voice will call from inside the room: 'I do not wish to be disturbed! I have given express orders that I am not to be disturbed!' The complex delights offered by images and sounds of this nature derive in part, once again, from the cinema-experience itself. The cinema, after all, constantly shows us men and women who are not 'really' there, and lets us hear voices whose owners—if they dwell in the land of the living at all—are many miles away.

This recognition leads us to yet another important role the figure of Caligari plays in Wiene's film. One of his functions is to suggest monsters arising from the subconscious; figures who may have a socially and historically significant original outside the mind, but whose appearance and actions are shown by the framework story to be inevitably coloured by the nature of the mind that apprehends them.

Kracauer saw Caligari as a 'tyrant' figure—a view that is justified if one looks at the role he plays in controlling his somnambulist and possibly his role as director of the madhouse. In other respects, however—in his attitude to duly constituted authorities and to the Holstenwall establishment—he is, like Lang's Mabuse, a dangerously subversive force. Nor can he simply be seen as a negative figure. Even if he is taken for the murderous 'mad scientist' Francis sees in him, our reaction to him must be complex and ambiguous. He is, after all, the one character who does what his nature leads him to do, regardless of the consequences; who lives to the full, and whose fall—if fall there is—has something of tragic grandeur about it. If he has to cringe to authority, as so many of his fellow-Germans had to do, then he does so in a deliberately exaggerated, almost mocking manner and takes his revenge afterwards. He is an artist in his way, far removed from the petty criminal whom we see languishing in the city gaol: like Mabuse and Haghi he avoids the drabness, the half-measures of ordinary lives, he defies convention, rises above the mass, and thus inspires admiration and envy.

Lastly: the image of Caligari which we see on the screen is, unmistakably, the image of an actor, Werner Krauss; an actor who will later embody a whole gallery of sinister creations, from Jack the Ripper (or 'Springheeled Jack') in Paul Leni's *Waxworks* to Süss's Jewish 'co-conspirators' in Veit Harlan's revolting *Jew Süss*. Those of us who know these performances—as well as such more sympathetic creations as the troubled professor in Pabst's *Secrets of a Soul* or the ageing actor in Willi Forst's *Burgtheater* (1936)—find that the aura with which they have surrounded Krauss in our memory will, for good or ill, enter into our appreciation of his Caligari in Wiene's classic film. That aura has, in fact, radiated far beyond the Weimar cinema, as a characteristic passage from Jean Renoir's autobiography may help to attest.

> It was Werner Krauss who taught me to understand the importance of actors. I greatly admired him and that is why I asked him to play the part of Count Muffat in *Nana*. My admiration dated from *Caligari*. I had also seen him in other films and in a stage production of Ibsen's *Wild Duck*. What impressed me about him was in the first place his technical skill, his knowledge of makeup and the use he made of small physical peculiarities. After a number of experiments he devised a Count Muffat who was not Werner Krauss and yet was him . . .

Even though Renoir came to believe, later, that such 'skill in the physical presentation of a character is not the root of the actor's business, and that although a convincing outward appearance is certainly a help, it can never be more', his early films helped to perpetuate the kind of performance that Krauss had pioneered in *Caligari* and that penetrated the U.S.A. with successive waves of German immigrants. The same goes for Conrad Veidt, whose make-up in *Caligari* strongly influenced Jack Pierce in his horror-creations for Universal; variations on it turn up, sporadically, in other terror-cycles.

> In *Usher* I bleached my hair white and wore pure white makeup with black eyebrows—I don't think anybody had done that since Conrad Veidt—there was this whole extraordinary thing that he was ultrasensitive to light and sound, so I tried to give the impression he'd never been exposed to the light, someone who had just bleached away. Now Roger dug this entirely . . . he found it very exciting that the actor could bring [into the film] a visual creation that complemented his.

The speaker here is Vincent Price, interviewed for *Films and Filming* in 1969; the version of Poe's *The Fall of the House of Usher* he is talking about is that directed by Roger Corman in 1960, which introduced to the public Price's conception of the terror-maker as Dandy, whose roots in the German cinema he here suggests.

Vincent Price's dictum has already brought before us another figure we must examine in the context of **The Cabinet of Dr. Caligari:** the somnambulist Cesare, Caligari's victim and instrument. As played by Conrad Veidt, Cesare is a 'drawing brought to life' in an even more obvious sense than his master: his black upper garment is streaked with the same white paint as that used on the scenery, and when he walks along a shadowed wall, arm upraised, it looks as though the wall had exuded him. And like his master, Cesare anticipates and comprehends a whole cluster of attributes and qualities that were to be of immense importance in the history of the terror-film. Let us examine a few of these.

In the first place, the Cesare we see on the screen in **The Cabinet of Dr. Caligari** is the first fully developed example of what was to be explored further by the two Lon Chaneys, by Boris Karloff, and by Barbara Steele: the monster whose deeds and appearance may terrify, but who is also pitiable and lovable. Wiene has stressed this side of Conrad Veidt's creation by the last glimpse he allows us of Cesare: a tall, black-clad, lonely figure gently stroking the white petals of a flower. This reminds us of an ambiguity in the figure of Cesare which matches that already analysed in the figure of Caligari: is he, in fact, simply the gentle inmate of a mental institution, transformed into a murderous monster in the mind of another inmate, or does he really have the lethal capabilities attributed to him by Francis and exhibited before our very eyes in the film in which he plays a central part? Ambiguities and tensions of this kind are, of course, the very stuff of the suspense engendered by terror-movies as well as *films noirs*.

Connected with all this is [an archetypal image of the terror-film] . . . : the confrontation of dark monster and white-clad bride. In **Caligari** this confrontation leads Cesare, for the only time, to thwart the will of his evil master: he stays his hand and abducts the girl instead of killing her. *Frankenstein, King Kong, The Mummy,* and countless other terror-films were to introduce modified versions of this confrontation, whose mythical resonances were well brought out by the last lines spoken in the 1933 *King Kong:*

> OFFICER: The airplanes got it.
>
> DENHAM: Oh no, it was not the airplanes. . . .
> It was beauty killed the beast.

Many strands lead over from this to the fairy-tale film *Beauty and the Beast,* on which Jean Cocteau, René Clément, and Christian Bérard collaborated in 1946 and which has, in its turn, greatly enriched the iconography of fantastic terror. Those disembodied arms which jut out of walls (and up from tables) holding lights have proved their fascination over and over again as other film-makers borrowed and varied them.

In its archetypal confrontation scene between Cesare and Jane *The Cabinet of Dr. Caligari* once again subtly modifies and—I believe—improves what had been envisaged in the original screen-play. The directions in the screen-play preserved in the Deutsche Kinemathek clearly insinuate that what happens when Cesare stays his hand is that a blind sexual impulse overpowers the equally blind impulse to obey his master. In the film Cesare's disobedience is not so crudely motivated: we have just a glimpse, in Jane's bedroom, of the more gentle, pathetic creature susceptible to beauty who is so unforgettably presented in the final scene which shows him caressing a flower—another scene, we should remember, which was added after the screenplay left its authors' hands. It is wholly in keeping with all this that Cesare is not required, in the film, to perform any of the common fairground strong-man tricks (like breaking an iron chain) envisaged in the screen-play.

Cesare's irruption into the peace and privacy of Jane's bedroom is preceded by another image on whose significance I have had occasion to remark . . . : that of the watcher with evil intent who peers out from the darkness of some hiding-place at his unsuspecting victim. The menacing image of the 'watcher at the window' is common to *Caligari, Frankenstein, Vampyr,* and many, many successors. Here, once again, we cannot but be conscious of implied analogies with the cinema-goer as *voyeur.*

The figure of Cesare that we see on the screen in *The Cabinet of Dr. Caligari* is also related, through his bearing and movement, to two further familiar figures of the later terror-film. The first of these, obviously, is the zombie: the being which is neither alive nor dead, which we surmise to be in some in-between state of consciousness that is not known to ordinary living men. The second is a figure which has moved into the mainstream of terror-cinema as the zombie moved out of it: the automaton, the machine with 'human' qualities that thwarts its maker and controller at some crucial moment. In this sense Cesare is the forerunner of that multitude of robots in or out of human form, from *Metropolis* onwards, which culminates in the computers that play such a banefully 'human' part in *2001* and *The Demon Seed.* But Cesare is a tragic figure in a way the robot can never be. He is a human being robbed of an essential part of his humanity: his consciousness and his will. He is a human dreamer forced, by a malevolent agency, to lose himself in his dream.

When Cesare is out on his murderous expeditions, a dummy is substituted for him in his coffin-like box; and this substitution brings us into those regions of the uncanny which are populated by such simulacra of human beings as dolls, puppets, marionettes, and waxworks. The dummy 'stands in' for Cesare symbolically as well as physically, just as Madame Tussaud figures 'stand in' for the men they represent in Leni's *Waxworks,* the doll with the crushed head for the central figure of *Whatever Happened to Baby Jane?,* and voodoo dolls for the necromancer's victim in *White Zombie, The Plague of the Zombies,* and the 'Sweets to the Sweet' episode of *The House that Dripped Blood* (1970).

Cesare is also shown, in a wholly cinematic way, as a figure that acts out another's dark desires. This is suggested, not only by the fact that we know him to be sent by Caligari to execute the latter's commands ('dreaming but murderous unconsciousness', to use F. D. McConnell's formulation, at the service of 'waking but malevolent reason'); but also by the vigour with which Francis, telling his story to others, imitates the stabbing motions we saw Cesare's shadow make with a dagger in an earlier scene. It is surely significant that before Cesare murders Alan, we have been told that Alan is Francis's rival for Jane's affections! The possibilities inherent in the brilliant 'shadow' episode of *Caligari* were to be developed to the full by Arthur Robison in (*Warning*) *Shadows.* In this last-named film a *montreur d'ombres* demonstrates to a cultivated and elegant group what dangerous potentials their character and situation hold by making their shadows act out—and thus literary 'foreshadow'—what would happen if such potentials were translated into actually. Cesare's shadow may be seen, like those in Robison's later film, as a 'Shadow' in Jung's sense; it insinuates that Cesare, like his master, is a monster from the subconscious.

Right at the beginning of *The Cabinet of Dr. Caligari* we see Cesare taking on the function of yet another figure whose uncanny potentialities have fascinated the makers of terror-films and their audiences: the clairvoyant. Cesare's prediction that Alan will die before the next night is over terrifies us, not only by the threat this poses to the sympathetic young man, but also, more particularly, because we sense that the prophecy will come true and that Cesare is therefore exercising paranormal powers. The fear that may be engendered by such powers, not only in those whose future is seen as black, but also in the clairvoyants themselves, is powerfully communicated in the framework action of *Dead of Night,* where the future seems to be shown by a dream, and in John Farrow's *Night has a Thousand Eyes* (1948), where the character played by Edward G. Robinson tries desperately to avert a catastrophe whose advent has been communicated to him in an unsought and undesired vision.

Finally, Cesare is seen, like his master, as a 'stranger' who comes into the community from outside, with the travelling fair; and he is seen to be the actor Conrad Veidt who would later impersonate such ominous characters as Ivan the Terrible in *Waxworks,* Jekyll and Hyde in *The Head of Janus,* Orlac in *The Hands of Orlac,* the Grand Vizier in *The Thief of Baghdad* (1940), and the Nazi officer in *Casablanca.*

An intelligent and articulate man, Veidt analysed his own performances on more than one occasion, stressing two aspects which he thought particularly significant. The first of these was the intensity with which he sank himself into whatever part he played.

> For days or even weeks before filming I withdraw into myself, contemplate my navel, as it were, concentrating on a kind of infection of the soul. And soon I discover how the character I have to portray grows in me, how I am transformed into it. The intensity of the process almost frightens me. Before long I find, even before the cameras begin to turn, that in my daily life I move, talk, look and behave differently. The inner Conrad Veidt has become that other

person whom I have to portray, or rather into whom my self has changed by autosuggestion. This state could best be described as one of being 'possessed'.

The metaphor of 'possession' which Veidt uses, in this interview with Paul Ickes that was first published in 1927, has an obvious connection with the kind of film in which he appeared. Two years later, in 1929, we find Veidt again commenting on his characterizations, this time in a Berlin film-magazine to whose readers he explained why he liked to portray 'evil' characters:

> Characters called 'evil' are not as bad as they appear on the surface; if I enjoy playing them, it is not because their destructiveness attracts me, but rather because I want to show the remnant of humanity which is hidden in even the most evil evildoer.

That could have been said by Karloff and Lugosi, by Cushing, Lee, and Klaus Kinski, as easily as by Conrad Veidt.

The final image we have of Veidt's Cesare in *The Cabinet of Dr. Caligari*—a black-clad, sad-visaged figure caressing a flower with beautiful, long-fingered hands—suggests that we are here in the presence of an actor who could play non-horrific roles with equal panache. This augured well for a future described by Béla Bálazs:

> Not only romantic acting went out of fashion but romantic faces as well. Especially among the male stars, popularity was diverted to those who had commonplace faces. Conrad Veidt's romantic, exalted, almost expressionist head, which brought him world success in the years immediately following the first world war, no longer appealed to the public. Not only was he crowded out by ordinary commonplace faces—he himself did his best to tone down his eccentric appearance and look as commonplace as possible, in order to be able to compete with rival stars. [*Theory of the Film: Character and Growth of a New Art*]

Veidt could never look or sound commonplace—but it is significant that after fulfilling his long-cherished ambition to play Victor Hugo's Gwymplaine in *The Man Who Laughs* (1928), he did not allow himself to be drawn into the 'grotesque horror' business. Inevitably, like so many refugee actors, he played Nazi persecutors in such Hollywood entertainments as *Escape* and *Casablanca;* but he also showed himself, in German, English, and American sound-films, a leading man whose romantic appeal was only increased by that suggestion of the sinister, of possible menace, which remained an inseparable part of his personality.

The last word on all this may be left with Veidt himself who declared, in his Hollywood years: 'No matter what roles I play, I can't get *Caligari* out of my system'.

Even before introducing Veidt's Cesare, *The Cabinet of Dr. Caligari* has given us a disconcerting image of zombie-like presence and absence, of existence in a limbo between life and death, through the appearance of the heroine, Jane, walking slowly towards the camera while staring straight ahead with unseeing eyes. This happens in the very opening scene, which R. V. Adkinson, in his account of the film for the Classic Film Scripts series, has described as follows:

> A cold, sombre atmosphere pervades the opening scene of the film. Francis and an older man are sitting on a bench by a high forbidding wall which curves away into shadow. The leafless branches and twigs of a tree hang down above the heads of the two men; dead leaves carpet a path in front of them, emphasizing the lifeless, still quality of the setting. On the opposite side of the path to the bench are a couple of stunted fir-trees: winter is in the air. Both the men on the bench are dressed in black; their eyes gape wildly from pale faces. The older man leans over towards his young companion to speak to him; Francis, apparently not very interested, responds by staring blankly skyward [. . .]

> As he turns to speak to Francis, the eyes of the older man, beneath a pair of bushy grey eyebrows, are dilated with horror or fear.

> TITLE: *'Everywhere there are spirits. . . . They are all around us. . . . They have driven me from hearth and home, from my wife and children.'*

> The older man continues his monologue, while the boughs from the overhanging tree move about his face. We see that the wall behind him is painted with a bizarre leaf and line pattern.

> Francis turns suddenly to look down the path past his older friend. As he turns he makes a sudden movement of surprise: the figure of a young woman, Jane, has just emerged from the shadow at the end of the path.

This description suggests how the *mise en scène* of the opening sequence slides us from a 'normal' world to the distorted one presented in the stylized settings that are yet to come. The wall and the path we see at first seem to be an actual wall, an actual garden or park, with natural branches and leaves—the painted pattern to which Adkinson refers towards the end of his description looks to me like the not unusual staining of a garden wall. The older man's opening words, in the first of the intertitles that appear in the film, act as a preparation for a different *mise en scène*: one that presents living actors and normal pieces of furniture in an unrealistic setting which yet conveys, unmistakably, the ambience of small German towns. They also announce one of the great themes of the terror-film: that of being shaken out of one's familiar world, the world of hearth and home, wife and children, by the intrusion of a 'spirit' world which is always there, always waiting, but does not always spring upon us. The words may be those of a man whom the world writes off as 'mad'; but may not such madness bring insights as well as deprivation? The old man's words have a theological, philosophical, and social resonance that cannot be simply shut off. Many a later terror-film—*The Uninvited, The Haunting, The Exorcist, The Sentinel*—will attempt further probings of the themes so powerfully suggested in the first intertitle of *The Cabinet of Dr. Caligari,* which might be more accurately translated as: 'Spirits exist . . . they are around us everywhere . . . They have driven me from hearth and home, from my wife and children.'

The opening scene described by R. V. Adkinson is part of the much-discussed and much-debated 'framework action' of Wiene's film—the frame which makes the tale of Caligari and Cesare appear, not an account of 'real' horrors, but the fantasies of a madman. Whether this was suggested by Pommer, or Lang, or Wiene, is now of little moment; it has become an inseparable part of the film and hence of cinema-history. Two points need to be made, however. The first of these is that even if we do take the story of Caligari and his dark doings as a madman's fantasy, we must surely feel that this fantasy has a great deal of symbolic truth; the symbolic truth of the Expressionist plays its scenery and acting-style recall, which brought out in fantastically heightened and concentrated form what men and women felt about the world-order, felt about lives in a specific time and a specific place. The 'revelation', when the frame is completed by the ending of the film, that what we have been seeing all this while may well have been a madman's fantasy, distances the story, certainly, makes us reflect on it more, but it does not lead us to write off the symbolic import of the images the director and script-writers and designers and actors have brought before us. And that leads to the second point which has to be made. The frame never closes entirely; though we go back, briefly, to the two speakers of the opening, on their park bench, the final scenes take place in the same expressionistic sets as those used in Francis's tale. The floor of the 'cell' in which we see Francis incarcerated is a stage-floor and its walls are painted cardboard; it holds nothing like the suggestions of a 'real' world conveyed by the earthy path, the autumnal or wintry leaves and branches, and the solid-looking wall, which we had been shown in the opening scene. We are, therefore, still within the world of Francis's tale when the house lights go up.

Critics have always been quick to condemn framework devices of this kind as a 'cop-out'; the general reaction to Fritz Lang's *The Woman in the Window* (1944) showed this clearly. In Lang's film the frame closes in a neater way than it does in Wiene's; in precisely the way, in fact, which he later claimed to have suggested for *Caligari* itself. [As Lang recalled in Peter Bogdanovich's book *Fritz Lang in America*]:

> Erich Pommer offered to me **The Cabinet of Dr Caligari** . . . which I was eventually unable to do . . . It was really the work of three painters . . . who wanted to make a kind of expressionist picture; the whole story had been written, and the only contribution I made was that I said to Pommer, 'Look, if the expressionistic sets stand for the world of the insane, and you use them from the beginning, it doesn't mean anything. Why don't you, instead, make the Prologue and Epilogue of the picture normal?' So the film begins in the garden of an asylum and is told normally; then when the story is told from the viewpoint of one of the inmates, it becomes expressionistic; and at the end it becomes normal again and we see that the villain of the picture, Dr Caligari, is the doctor of the asylum.

Now what else is the ending of *Caligari*—where we meet people we've seen in 'the dream'—but the ending of *Woman in the Window*? And this was unconscious—I didn't even *think* I was copying myself at the time I had the idea for *Woman in the Window.*

Lang clearly had not seen *Caligari* for a long time when he opined that 'at the end it becomes normal again'; but even in *The Woman in the Window,* his own variant on Wiene's film, the story of the Professor's temptation and fall is not devalued by the revelation that 'it was all a dream'. What Lang shows us are possibilities latent in his hero's character, possibilities conditioned, to an important extent, by the social world in which he lives—and acting them out in a dream may help him as much as seeing them acted out may help us. Here, once again, what we see in the film reminds us of what we are doing when we watch the film: the act of waking up, mimed for us by Edward G. Robinson, corresponds to the end of the film and the going-up of the house lights. What we have seen on the screen, however, was ordered by a waking intelligence that is not ours, though it may have spoken to us in the manner of our dreams. As Susanne Langer has rightly said,

> The moving picture takes over [the dream mode], and [thereby] creates a virtual present. In its relation to the images, actions, events, that constitute the story, the camera is in the place of the dreamer.
>
> But the camera *is* not a dreamer. We are usually agents in a dream. The camera (and its complement, the sound track) is not itself in the picture. It is the mind's eye and nothing more. Neither is the picture (if it is art) likely to be dream-like in its structure. It is a poetic composition, coherent, organic, governed by a definitely conceived feeling, not dictated by emotional pressures. *(Feeling and Form. A Theory of Art)*

As so often, one of the most important functions of similarity is to remind us of differences.

Caligari, as we have seen, differs from Lang's film in that its frame does not close as decisively, does not leave us back in our 'normal' world as unequivocally, as *The Woman in the Window.* In this it resembles *Dead of Night,* directed by Cavalcanti, Dearden, Hamer, and Crichton. The five stories united in that film, a veritable anthology of terror-film motifs, are linked by a sixth, a framing tale, which shows us an architect woken from a nightmare by a phone call from a prospective client whom he has never met. As he approaches the client's house he recognizes the scenery of his nightmare, and once inside the house he realizes that every one of its guests and inhabitants are part of his nightmare too. When he tells them this, they recount the stories of their own contact with the inexplicable; but everything which occurs, including the story-telling, is foreseen by the architect, who dreads what he knows must come: his murder of one of the guests, a sceptical psychiatrist. One way of looking at what happens at the end of the film is excellently exemplified by Ivan Butler in *Horror in the Cinema:*

> The linking story is handled with a skill apt to be overshadowed by the more flamboyant epi-

sodes. The gradual encroachment of strangeness and menace upon the complete normality of the opening party indicated by the growing distortion of viewing angles, the slow fading of day to dusk . . . are still impressive today. After the killing of the Doctor, when the horror is come upon us, all reality vanishes. Dominated, ingeniously, by the innocent fancy-dressed children from the party scene, the terror of nightmare is created in a wild swirl of distorted staircases and passages, the camera swinging and twisting about as Craig himself does in his efforts to wake up.

The subtlest touch of the film, however, is a momentary shot almost at the very end. We finally leave Craig in exactly the position that we first found him—arriving at Foley's house in his car. *Dead of Night,* then, like Joyce's *Finnegans Wake,* is circular—it will go on for ever, ninety per cent dream, ten per cent awake. So, but for this one shot, it might appear. Before leaving his house, however, Craig has been speaking to Foley on the telephone. As he speaks, we see— for just a few frames—Foley himself, at his house, on the other end of the telephone. That shot tells us the truth. The film throughout has been seen from Craig's viewpoint. Even the stories, where he was not present, are seen as told to him. Now suddenly *we* see Foley. Craig has not met him. The dream has faded. He does not know what Foley and his house look like. Now, we see Foley. He really is there, waiting. This tiny shot is the most frightening in the film, for through it the dream becomes reality. This time, it is really happening. There will be no waking relief for Craig. This time, he drives to his doom. In no other medium but the film could the situation be so briefly yet devastatingly made clear.

Dead of Night stands, unmistakably, in the tradition of the English ghost-story from which the plots of its constituent episodes directly or indirectly derive; but in its use of a disorientating framework, in its play with psychiatry and occultism, and in its climactic confrontation of ventriloquist and dummy, it betrays no less clearly its descent from Wiene's *Caligari.*

As in *Dead of Night,* so in *Caligari* the framework story is indelibly associated with one character whom the camera presents to us but whose limited vision we are also made to share. As a student, not yet fully integrated into bourgeois life, Francis is a marginal man—but he is the exact opposite of that other marginal man . . . , David Gray. Where David Gray drifts through the action of *Vampyr* like a sleep-walker, Francis is constantly on the move in the inner story, constantly enlisting the help of the authorities while tirelessly seeking and following out clues on his own initiative. 'I will not rest', one of the intertitles has him say, 'until I have fully fathomed the terrible things that are happening around me.' His problem is that of the seeker after truth; and what happens at the end is that his own competence is called into question, like everything else in the shifting perspectives of the film. How far has he been externalizing, projecting his own inner turmoil on to whatever world there may be outside? How far has he seen truly? What symbolic truth might his vision, whatev-

er their experiential status, have for audiences in the world within which the film was conceived, or in that in which it is viewed by other, later audiences? These are questions which still concern us—they are raised by the film in its final form more powerfully and directly than by the more conventional frame, the recollection-in-tranquillity pattern, of the original screen-play.

In the form its director and designers actually gave it, *The Cabinet of Dr. Caligari* impressively demonstrates the cinematic possibilities opened up by an abrupt change of perspective. Having looked at certain 'events' through the eyes of a story-teller who presents himself as a participant, we are suddenly made to look at that story-teller and ask ourselves whether we have not in fact been sharing a lunatic's delusions. Later directors have played many variations on this. Herk Harvey's *Carnival of Souls* (1962), for instance, shows us a young woman surviving a car-accident and returning to a world in which people behave like stiff puppets, refusing to talk to her or even acknowledge her presence. More and more desperately she tries to make contact; and she seems, at last, to succeed when a wraith-like, corpse-like group embraces her and draws her away in a dance. Then comes the change of perspective: we see ordinary people towing a car from the bay in which our heroine sits dead at the wheel. She did not survive the accident after all; the film had been set in *la zone,* the limbo between life and death. Behind the structure of Harvey's film we perceive not only *The Cabinet of Dr. Caligari* but also a distinguished literary work: Ambrose Bierce's 'An Occurrence at Owl Creek Bridge', itself made into an eerily impressive film by Robert Enrico in 1964.

Abrupt changes of perspective have an underground relation to the décor of *Caligari* which we can best discern through a study of Rudolf Kurz's celebrated book on Expressionism and the German film. Writing in 1926, Kurz described the settings of *Caligari* as follows:

> Perpendicular lines tense towards the diagonal, houses exhibit crooked, angular outlines, planes shift in rhomboid fashion, the lines of force of normal architecture, expressed in perpendiculars and horizontals, are transmogrified into a chaos of broken forms . . . A movement begins, leaves its natural course, is intercepted by another, led on, distorted again, and broken. All this is steeped in a magic play of light, unchaining brightness and blackness, building up, dividing, emphasizing, destroying.

Why the designers chose this style is given a psychological explanation.

> It is a simple law of psychological aesthetics that when we feel our way into certain forms exact psychic correspondences are set up. The straight line guides our feelings differently from a crooked one; startling curves affect our souls in other ways than smoothly gliding lines; the rapid, the jagged, the suddenly ascending and descending calls forth responses that are different from those evoked by the silhouette of a modern city with its richness of transitions.

The abrupt change of perspective at the end of *Caligari,* at whatever stage it was introduced, may be seen as just as 'rapid', 'jagged', and 'suddenly . . . descending' as the scenic design.

There is still one other aspect of the ending of *Caligari,* however, which deserves closer attention than it has so far received. We leave Francis, it will be remembered, strait-jacketed in a cell, while the director holds out hopes of a cure. The final 'title' reads: 'At last I understand the nature of his madness. He thinks I am that mystic Caligari—! Now I can also see the way to cure him.' An ominous conclusion, surely—for what these words show is that the director has either not understood, or that he is wilfully misrepresenting, Francis's beliefs. Francis does not think, by any means, that the director 'is' 'that mystic Caligari'. On the contrary: the film has shown us beyond any doubt that Francis, despite his cry: 'He is Caligari . . . Caligari . . . Caligari!', knows the 'mystic Caligari' to have been an eighteenth-century figure, quite distinct from the sinister showman encountered many years later. What he does believes is that the director has become obsessed by this Caligari to the extent of assuming his name and repeating his crimes with the help of the same kind of instrument that the original Caligari used: a somnambulist under his hypnotic control. Francis does not believe, in other words, that the director 'is' 'that mystic Caligari'; he knows that the director is the director, but believes him to have used his position to obtain an instrument essential to the reenactment of another's crimes. If this is a delusion then the director has failed to diagnose it correctly; if it is not a delusion, then the director is deliberately pulling wool over his colleagues' eyes. All this must be in our minds as we watch that famous long-held shot of Werner Krauss's ambiguous expression which ends the film; as must also the fact that we never, at any stage, learn the real name of the director who, in the inner story, disguises his appearance and takes on the name of Caligari. He remains as nameless as Frankenstein's monster.

The ambiguity I am trying to highlight here has been described in a different though related way by F. D. McConnell. 'We do not, of course, know', McConnell writes in *The Spoken Seen,*

> what the doctor's curative treatment will be—and we need not be familiar with recent developments in behaviorist psychotherapy to fear that the remedy may be as bad as, or worse than, the disease. But more centrally, we are disturbed by the sight of Krauss's face itself, that face which the fantasy-center of the film has taught us to associate with malevolent, irrational destructiveness. We remember . . . what the explicit story of the film has taught us to forget: the potential evil and dehumanization of official authority. And it is this tension between memory and forgetfulness . . . that constitutes . . . lasting horror.

In the iconography of the terror-film the madhouse plays an important part. It does so partly because madness is indeed terrifying—Hitchcock's *Psycho* and Polanski's *Repulsion* are dedicated to that proposition—but it does so also because in a madhouse authority may be exercised over others in a particularly frightening or humiliating way; and because the madhouse is a closed institution in which the problems of a particular society, the wounds inflicted and the violence unleashed by that society, can be depicted in heightened, concentrated, and frequently symbolic form. From Val Lewton's *Bedlam* to Alain Jessua's *Shock Treatment,* the film has often treated the madhouse in this way. A particularly interesting use of this setting was made by Gordon Douglas and his team in *Them;* here doubt is cast, first on the existence and then on the hiding-place of the giant mutants to which the title refers because those who volunteer helpful information on these points are found in a mental home and an alcoholics' ward. And then, of course, there is Samuel Fuller's *Shock Corridor* (1963), of which Raymond Durgnat has said:

> The film's tense, hard, muscular style resumes the American variation of German expressionism. Carried to Hollywood by such directors as Murnau, Leni, Lang and other exiles, expressionism was blended with its apparent antithesis, the tough deadpan, by the American *films noirs* from the late '30s to the mid-'50s. But Fuller's paroxystic situations and style reveal the tough deadpan as a kind of psychic delirium and restore an expressionistic world.

Many other closed institutions have been pressed into the service of the terror-film: an island laboratory in *The Island of Lost Souls,* a prison in *The Walking Dead* (1936), a provincial school in *Les Diaboliques,* and even a (very peculiar) dancing academy in Dario Argento's *Suspiria* (1977). The last-named film is especially important in this context because it experiments once again—less radically than *Caligari*—with stylized sets that occasionally resemble stage-flats. Above all there is the clinic or hospital—Franju's *Eyes Without a Face,* Robert Day's *Corridors of Blood* (1962), David Cronenberg's *Rabid* (1976), and countless other films have made use of a setting which played on our fear of operations as well as the terror-movie's traditional suspicion of science and scientists.

The very title of *The Cabinet of Dr. Caligari* refers us, however, to a quite different, an apparently more 'open', institution: the travelling fair or carnival, home of the earliest cinema-shows, traditional scene of thrilling entertainments, whose roller-coasters, ghost-trains, and freak-shows have proved so attractive to the makers of terror-films because they too deal in *Angstlust,* in thrills that cause delight by playing on fear. When handbills announcing the fair appear on the screen in *Caligari:*

> LATE EXTRA!
> Holstenwall Fair,
> including sideshows of all kinds,
> and marvels
> NEVER SEEN BEFORE!

cinema-goers smile with recognition—for it is precisely promises of this kind which lure us into the cinema. Paul Leni's *Waxworks,* Robert Florey's *Murders in the Rue Morgue,* Erle C. Kenton's *House of Frankenstein* (1944), Hitchcock's *Strangers on a Train,* and Freddie Francis's *Torture Garden* show some of the more sinister uses to which fairground settings were put in the wake of *Caligari.* Through it all rings the fairground barker's patter: Bela Lugosi's in *Rue Morgue:*

I am Dr. Mirakle, and I am not a sideshow charlatan; if you are looking for the usual hocus-pocus, just go to the box-office and get your money back . . .

or Boris Karloff's in *House of Frankenstein:*

Believe me, my friends, this is no fake. Before your very eyes is all that remains of a vampire, one of the world's Undead. Dare I but remove the stake from where his heart once beat, he would rise from the grave in which he lies and turn into a bat, a vampire bat, and would feed hideously upon the living whose veins pulsate with warm and vibrant blood. Ladies and gentlemen, the skeleton of Count Dracula the vampire!

Who could miss the link of these and other passages with the terms in which the makers of *Rue Morgue* and *House of Frankenstein* advertised their wares! Four of the films just mentioned also play on a potent contrast first explored by Wiene: the open space occupied by the fair with its many attractions, all for sale—and the 'cabinet', the showman's booth or tent, into which spectators have to be inveigled. After the opening narration *Caligari* leads us, in fact, into a more and more enclosed space: from the patently painted and studio-built town to the fair, thence to the 'cabinet', thence to Cesare's box: and from that ultimate enclosure, reminding us of all men's ultimate enclosure in a coffin, forces are sent into the more open world outside to wreak terrifying havoc. The final scenes then lead us back into enclosure: first that of the mental home, then that of the cell and that of the strait-jacket confining Francis, whose visions we have been sharing. Our resistance to claustrophobia is thus put to a severe test in a setting where we have a greater chance of passing the test than in the 'real' world outside the cinema.

One aspect of the fair in *Caligari,* the first one we are shown, has rightly attracted the attention of several commentators: the turning roundabout. A significant scene begins with an unusual iris-in: a small circle is isolated near the right-hand corner of the screen, in which we see an organ-grinder's hand turning a barrel-organ on which a chained monkey squats. Then the iris opens out to reveal, not only the organ-grinder, but also a fairground set dominated by two roundabouts in full revolution. These may be and have been felt, not only as a synecdoche for the fair itself, but also as multivalent symbols which speak, in their context, of the innocent pleasures of childhood, the turning of the wheel of fate or history, the spin of life, the obsessive circularity of the narrator's thoughts; they have also suggested, to some observers, a simulacrum of experience—like the cinema itself. All this is deliberately associated with another 'turning' image, the organ-grinder cranking his instrument; an image whose symbolic import one of the greatest German *Lieder,* the final song of Schubert's *Winter Journey,* has indelibly impressed on the cultural consciousness of Germany and the world. It is through this symbol-charged set that Krauss's Caligari makes his way towards his 'cabinet'.

One of the merits of Kracauer's pioneering book *From Caligari to Hitler* is that it conveyed to English-speaking readers something of the readiness with which German audiences responded to symbolic suggestions. Symbols, by definition, are multivalent, unlike allegories, in which there is a one-to-one correspondence; and an 'allegorical' reading of *Caligari* is therefore bound to be inadequate or worse. 'In Germany', Fritz Lang said to Peter Bogdanovich, 'we worked with symbols'; and prompted by his interviewer, he added: 'A symbol shouldn't reinforce, it should *make* the point'.

Between the madhouse and the fair Wiene shows us the little town of Holstenwall, in which most of the characters live. This is partly, as we have already seen, the cosy familiar world into which strangers bring disaster when they break into the tiny room inhabited by Alan or the more opulent bedroom of Jane. It is also, however, through the crazy perspectives of its streets, the jagged, knife-like projections of its scenery (particularly its windows), and the insubstantiality of its theatrical flats, itself felt as threatening; and some of the menaces it contains are clearly shown in the two interiors which are not domestic. The first of these is the office of the town clerk, to which Caligari repairs for his showman's licence. We soon perceive this office to be the setting for an enjoyment of power less flamboyant but no less intense than Caligari's own. At the entrance and again on the furniture the symbol '§' has been painted several times—not, as R. V. Adkinson seems to think, a 'cabbalistic' sign, but simply the indication of a 'paragraph' in the German civil and criminal code. Under the protection of this sign the ill-tempered licensing-official lords it, on his high stool, over his subordinates and petitioners. The expressiveness and truth-value of images of this kind are in no way devalued by the film's frame. The complement of this sinister office is the even more sinister prison cell in which a criminal sits chained and immured. With its white lines all converging on to the manacled, scowling figure of Rudolf Klein-Rogge, and its one tiny, crazily angled window, high above the imprisoned man's reach, it is the other end of the chain of legal paragraphs that begins in the town clerk's little kingdom, and presents itself as a symbol of social constriction—necessary social constriction, perhaps, but none the less terrifying for that—which matches in intensity the complementary image of the madman's cell and the strait-jacket at the end of the film. Terror is not simply 'brought in by strangers', as the simplest view of the story would have it; terror is inherent in the social structure which the 'stranger' finds when he gets there and which fires in him a resentment that releases more terror. Nor, as we have already found, is the 'stranger' really a stranger: the madhouse over which he presides is as much part of Holstenwall as the town clerk's office and the prison cell.

Can all that be written off as a madman's vision? Have not these distorted perspectives, rather, succeeded in conveying the insolence of office, and the horror of being imprisoned and confined, more powerfully than naturalistic settings could have done? There are other ways, of course, of achieving such effects. The makers of *Caligari* could have followed the lead of Abel Gance in *The Madness of Dr. Tube* (1915), where distortion was achieved, not by means of painted scenery, but by a system of convex and concave mirrors. They might have tried to use distorting lenses, as Murnau did some six years after *Caligari* in a famous sequence of *The Last Laugh.* They might also have used unusual camera angles, as the Russians did in so many of their silent films, or as Pabst did, or Duvivier. Later makers of terror-films, with far more sophisticated equipment and much more money to spend than the makers of *Caligari,* have produced visual distortions of a kind that even Gance and Murnau never dreamed of; one thinks of the fly's-eye view of Kurt Neumann's *The Fly* (1958), the robot's-eye view in Michael Crichton's *Westworld,* or the special effects that made us share the tortured vision of Corman's *Man with X-Ray Eyes* in 1963. But the method employed in *Caligari* works excellently, and cannot be condemned simply because it was pioneered by stage-designers or because it conflicts with dogmatic notions that the cinema must photograph unstylized reality in such a way that the result has style. By what compulsion must it? *Caligari* can still excite and grip its audience today, where many a stylish photoplay causes nothing but fatigue and irritation.

The social meaning of *Caligari* has been the subject of a good deal of comment—particularly after Siegfried Kracauer's *From Caligari to Hitler* had tried to show

> that during their retreat into themselves the Germans [of the period just after the First World War] were stirred to reconsider their traditional belief in authority. Down to the bulk of Social Democratic workers they refrained from revolutionary action; yet at the same time a psychological revolution seems to have prepared itself in the depths of the collective soul. The film reflects this double aspect of German life by coupling a reality in which Caligari's authority triumphs with a hallucination in which this same authority is overthrown . . .

Though one may deny, as I do, that a collective 'soul' manifests itself in film-plots in the simple way Kracauer would have us believe, and that 'reality', in *Caligari,* can be hived off neatly from 'hallucination', there can be little doubt that the uncertainties and fears the film conveys in its final form have a good deal to do with uncertainties and fears felt in the young Weimar Republic, in a Germany that had just lost a war and seen the apparent collapse of its traditional authoritarian structure. But this too must be seen in a wider context: a context sketched by David Thomson when he said of *Caligari* that it is one of the first films to exploit the resemblance between watching films and dreaming, and that it therefore asks, with particular force, 'the basic question that confronts a movie audience: are we watching reality or fantasy?' When they face us, inescapably, with this question, later terror-films can, once again, be seen as repeating, or developing further, what *Caligari* pioneered.

The literary affinities of *Caligari* . . . are with German Romanticism in general and *Schauerromantik* in particular; and the nineteenth-century costumes worn by most of the characters serve to stress these affinities. They should not, however, be allowed to obscure the fact that it also has unmistakable affinities with literary Expressionism. Expressionist drama is recalled by the conflict of generations suggested in *Caligari*—Krauss's director is an evil father-figure for Cesare and Francis, and appears linked to older traditions, older generations, through his assump-

tion of the personality of the original Caligari. It is recalled, too, by the film's violence and stylization of gesture, and by its deliberate employment of the grotesque. In this last respect it also resembles Expressionist fiction and poetry: the mingling of menace with the ridiculous in Krauss's performance recalls many a grotesque bourgeois in the stories of Kafka or the poems of Alfred Lichtenstein as well as the plays of Carl Sternheim. And if one now reads the description of the Angel of Death which Jakob van Hoddis, whose poem 'End of the World' is frequently said to have inaugurated German Expressionism, penned in 1914:

> Der Todesengel harrt in Himmelshallen
> Also wüster Freier dieser zarten Braut.
> Und seine wilden, dunklen Haare fallen
> Die Stirn hinab, auf der der Morgen graut.
>
> Die Augen weit, vor Mitleid glühend offen
> Wie trostlos starrend hin zu neuer Lust,
> Ein grauenvolles, nie versiegtes Hoffen,
> Ein Traum von Tagen, die er nie gewusst.
>
> (The angel of death waits in heavenly halls
> A fearsome wooer of this tender bride.
> And his wild dark hair falls
> Down his forehead, on which a grey dawn
>   breaks.
>
> Wide open, glowing with pity, his eyes
> Stare inconsolably towards new desired delight,
> A ghastly hope that never quite dried up,
> A dream of days he never knew)—

may one not see in it an almost point-by-point anticipation of Conrad Veidt's Cesare, as he appears, not in heavenly halls, but in the white virginal expanses of Jane's room, which Francis so fervently desires to enter?

Wiene's film is also remarkable for the way in which it brings the language of twentieth-century painting into the cinema. The city-impressions of Feininger, Meidner, and Kubin, the triangular shapes of Cubism, the hysterical wavy lines and angular portraits of Munch, and even the tendril shapes of *art nouveau,* all find meaningful equivalents. As this list may serve to suggest, the designer's style is not *purely* Expressionist—and it is interesting to note in this connection that the Mayer-Janowitz typescript has none of the consciously Expressionist stylization of language that characterizes Mayer's later writings for the cinema. Nevertheless the visual style of *Caligari* has enough affinity with Expressionist painting and drawing to justify the usual label. When a later terror-film, Jack Gold's *The Medusa Touch,* imports actual paintings into its setting—Caravaggio's *Medusa,* Munch's *The Cry,* the claustrophobic shapes of Francis Bacon—these only serve to underline the film's visual and thematic banality. In *Caligari,* however, the painters' images are fully at home, harmonize perfectly with the work's theme and style: with its attempt to make the film's physical setting a hieroglyph of inner experience, its suffusion of landscapes and townscapes with feelings and states of mind.

One important set of hieroglyphs has, alas, been lost to the film as shown to English audiences. The letters that compose the original main title and intertitles exhibit the characteristic *Caligari* shapes as surely as the painted sets; the way they are formed, the directions in which they slope, how they relate to one another or vary in size, the jagged or snake-like ornamentations that accompany them, indicate and control the film's tone, mood, and atmosphere. In this too the example set by *Caligari* has been followed . . . by other films that have among their principal ingredients the attempt to depict, evoke, and convey terror.

Within its stylized settings *Caligari* introduces a multitude of visual motifs that later terror-films were to elaborate. The huge staring eyes of Veidt's Cesare, filling the screen in the most intimate close-ups of the whole film, matched by the glare of Caligari's spectacles; the shadow of a murderer, showing his nefarious work without showing his body; the clutching, warding-off hands of a murder-victim; the arrest which brings an 'explanation' that explains nothing; the pursuit over roof-tops and along winding paths that leads to an unexpected terrifying goal—these are only some of the images that later films have drawn from the rich store of this seminal film. Commenting, in 1920, on Wiene's imaginative use of shadows on a wall to make murder visible, Kurt Tucholsky singled out an aspect of *Caligari* which is worth recalling in face of the ever greater explicitness that audiences and film-makers have demanded in recent years. 'This demonstrates again', Tucholsky writes, 'that what is guessed at is more terrible than anything that can be shown. No film can come up to our imagination.' The thoughts *Caligari* here inspires in Tucholsky were later to be restated, and put into practice, by Fritz Lang and the Val Lewton team.

A structural analysis of the plot of *Caligari* would distinguish the following stages:

(A. Opening of frame)

1. We are introduced to a story-teller, a listener, a mysterious female figure. A perspective is established: that of the story-teller.

(B. Inner story)

2. A close-knit society is penetrated by an enemy from outside.

3. By means of an innocent but lethal helper, the enemy strikes at an eminent member of the society he now menaces, and at one member of the group with which the audience, caught in the story-teller's perspective, identifies: the trio hero—beloved heroine—friend.

4. The hero alerts the authorities to the source of the danger to society, but investigators are baffled.

5. The enemy strikes at the heroine; she is saved by the incompleteness of his control over his lethal helper, and the enemy is tracked by the hero to a domain where the enemy has authority—an authority conferred on him by society.

6. With the help of subordinate members of the enemy's domain he is unmasked and rendered harmless by the hero, whose resolute action has thus saved society from a murderous onslaught.

(C. 'Closing' of frame)

7. The dramatis personae of section B are now seen in the domain in which the action of stage 6 had taken place—but under a new aspect. The enemy has *not* been defeated; he and his helper are still alive and his power is unbroken. Our point of view can therefore no longer be unequivocally that of the storyteller 'hero'.

8. The 'hero' attacks the 'enemy' and is rendered harmless in exactly the same way the 'enemy' had been rendered harmless at stage 6, and with the aid of the same subordinates.

9. The 'enemy' speaks as a friend and is left poised to 'help' the 'hero'. It is he and not the 'hero' who preserves society from potentially destructive members. Or is it?

A glance at this structure, and at the quotation and question marks that invade it at stages 8 and 9, shows up immediately the profound disorientation the film conveys, the questions it leads us to ask about authority, about social legitimation, about the protection of society from disrupting and destructive influences, and about the shifting points of view that convert enemies into friends into enemies, whose origins may well be sought in the German situation after the First World War. Like any genuine work of art, *The Cabinet of Dr. Caligari* has its roots deep in the society of its time; but its significance, its appeal, and its influence far transcend its origins.

What a structural summary like that just attempted fails to reveal is the over-all rhythm of the film: the rhythm commended by Louis Delluc in a passage Lotte Eisner used as the epigraph of her *Caligari* chapter in *The Haunted Screen*—a slow beginning, breathtaking acceleration, and the slowing-up of the long-held close-up before the word *Ende* appears on the screen in that angular *Caligari*-script which the original audiences came to know so well. All credit for this must go to Robert Wiene; for as Fritz Lang once said, the peculiar rhythm that every worthwhile film may be felt to have is the distinctive contribution of its director.

The influence of *Caligari* on later film-makers has often been indirect rather than direct, mediated rather than unmediated. In Japan, for instance, it would have come for the most part by way of Kinugasa's *A Page of Madness* rather than by way of Wiene's original. It is also incontestable that important elements of later terror-movies in Germany and abroad derived from early Scandinavian films, from early Hollywood movies, from *Nosferatu, Mabuse,* and *Metropolis,* rather than *Caligari;* that the complete control over *all* elements of our visual experience sought by Wiene's studio-bound film (in which even light and shade were painted on to the scenery!) has been consciously abandoned by most later film-makers; that sixty years of further development have added themes, images, and technical devices, as well as an explicitness in the treatment of sex and violence that would have been inconceivable to Wiene and his collaborators. It is also incontestable that the use of theatrical flats imposed limitations on camera angles and camera mobility that most film-makers came to find excessively irksome. Acting-styles have changed too: we shall not find in this early German film anything like the amused self-parody, the tongue-in-cheek attitude, that Vincent Price, for instance, brings to his flamboyant roles in *The Abominable Dr. Phibes, Dr. Phibes Rises Again* (1972), and *Theatre of Blood* (1973). Nevertheless, if we look closely enough we shall discover that the majority of the themes, images, and devices which distinguish the cinematic tale of terror may be detected, in rudimentary or developed form, in **The Cabinet of Dr. Caligari;** and that far from being irrelevant to the subsequent history of the motion picture, this masterly document of the Germans' search for ever new ways of articulating and presenting the fantastic is a work no student of the terror-film, and no lover of the cinema, can afford to pass by.

Thomas Elsaesser   (essay date 1982)

SOURCE: "Social Mobility and the Fantastic: German Silent Cinema," in *Wide Angle,* Vol. 5, No. 2, 1982, pp. 14-25.

[*Elsaesser is an English film scholar and educator who has done extensive research on German cinema. In the following excerpt, he examines the various ways in which* The Cabinet of Dr. Caligari *can be interpreted.*]

In **Dr. Caligari,** . . . the initial situation contains a social aspect involving class and status differences. Caligari, asking deferentially for a permit to put up his tent show, is treated by the town clerk and his subordinates in a brusque, humiliating and insulting manner. There can be little doubt that this scene transmits to the spectator an identifiable, realistic experience of the arbitrary and haughty behavior that a militarist bureaucracy (which is what the civil service was even during the Weimar Republic) displayed towards civilians. What we all at some stage of our lives have murmured under our breath—"I could have killed him"—Caligari acts out. He takes revenge on the hated town clerk by way of his medium Cesare, thus setting off the chain of events which make up the narrative. But here too, any analysis of the origins and causes of such an all-powerful but at the same time petty bureaucracy is blocked and displaced. Instead we find a commensurate magic omnipotence—one which in effect overcompensates. Thus, in Caligari's medium Cesare, as in *The Golem,* a force is set free which at least in part escapes its creator's control. Cesare is Caligari's double and the embodiment or condensation of rebellious, anti-authoritarian drives which stand in direct contradiction to his own authoritarianism. What makes the film significant is less its striking decor as such but the degree to which the decor permits a particularly complex and contradictory narrative to articulate itself within the space of one fiction. There has been much debate about the meaning of the framing device but it seems to me that it is only one—albeit an important one—of the many strategies in the film for sustaining a multi-perspectival narrative. Perhaps the easiest way to locate these strategies is to ask some simple questions such as why does Francis, the narrator in the frame and protagonist of the story who tracks down Caligari, "go mad"? Or, what is the relation between the murder of the town clerk and the murder of Allen, Francis' friend? These rather naive questions, which doubtless would be asked by every spectator if the film were a "realistic" film, somehow seem irrelevant. And that is, I think,

because questions of motivation and causality have, in the process of editing the film into such static, self-contained tableaux, become almost illegible. It would lead too far to enter into the full history of the tableau-scene as a form of "negative" dramaturgy (one finds its theory in Diderot), but as part of a rhetoric of muteness and self-repression it is the most direct link between bourgeois drama and melodrama of the stage, and the silent German cinema. This illegibility of both temporal and causal sequence in the film, the opaqueness of the emotional relationship between, for example, Francis, Jane, Allen, and the breaking off or fading out of several scenes in mid-gesture, on a note of suspension, is in fact evidence of the dynamic interplay of forces between reality and filmic form, the work of resistances without which there would be no narrative and no narrator. The act of narration per se establishes itself in **Dr. Caligari** and subsequently in countless films of the classic German cinema (with their frame tales, their narrator figures, their nested narratives) as a field of force, as a struggle for control over the intensities of discourse itself.

The static quality of this, as of other films, therefore, should not be mistaken for clumsiness of mise-en-scène, or the primitive state of film form, but rather as the containment of an agitation which, banished from articulating itself in a linear fashion such as we are used to from classical narrative, creates a different kind of economy of the filmic signifier. **Dr. Caligari** displaces not only its social themes by making them into enigmas whose resolutions lead elsewhere (thereby creating the conditions for narration, for there being "texts" that need deciphering), it also displaces an already constituted cinematic narrative: the subtext in **Dr. Caligari** is the genre of the detective serial, extremely popular in Germany in the early Twenties (e.g., Joe Deeb, Stuart Webb).

The particular, and perhaps unique, economy of **Dr. Caligari** shows itself, if one tries to answer the question of what motivates the characters, by putting it in slightly different terms: namely, who narrates the story, whose story is it, and to whom is it narrated? If one follows accounts like Kracauer's, it is the story of Caligari, the mad doctor, the premonitory materialization of a long line of tyrants, the faithful image of German military dictatorship and its demonic, mesmerizing hold over others. But can we construct for Caligari's behavior a certain motivational logic, a certain coherence within the story? The doctor, researching in his archives, finds the secret of somnambulism and brings a patient under his control. Disguising himself as a fairground operator, he uses his power to avenge himself on his enemies (the town clerk) and subsequently to lure a young woman into his tent. He beckons Jane inside, shows her the upright box, flings it open with a leer to reveal the rigid figure of Cesare, who, as she gets closer, opens his eyes, whereupon she stands transfixed in fascination, until she breaks away with a terrified, distraught expression on her face. The sexual connotations of the scene are unmistakable, and here Caligari's powers compensate a kind of impotence; his behavior towards Jane is the very epitome of the "dirty old man" exposing himself: showing Cesare is literally an "exhibition." Cesare's abduction of the girl strengthens this particular interpretation: the medium becomes, as it were, the detachable part of Caligari, not so much his double as his tool. Caligari's story would be centered on a disturbed relationship to sexuality and political power in which impotence is being overcompensated by exhibition ("I'll show you"), but where showing involves an alternation of hiding and revealing, i.e., flashing, blinking.

It is interesting that Cesare, unlike the Golem and other "creatures," does not turn against his master. Instead, when pursued by Francis, he drops the girl, becomes weak, withers or fades away, or as the inter-text puts it, he dies of exhaustion. In this respect he is rather similar to Nosferatu, fading with daylight (like overexposed film stock). When Cesare does return to his creator the very sight of him and the necessity to recognize him as part of himself makes Caligari go mad, as if the limit-point of the narrative was the acknowledgement of a relation and the establishment of an identity.

But is it possible to see the film centered on Caligari? The story is initiated by Francis, and in this sense it is his story, too, of how he came to be at the place from which he tells it, as the recollection of a series of events whose memory is activated by the sight of a figure in white passing by, who subsequently turns out to be Jane. What, then, is Francis' story; and why does he go mad? It is essentially the tale of a suitor who is ignored or turned down: the narrative comes full circle when Francis pleads with Jane to marry him and she replies that "we queens may never choose as our hearts dictate." In the story itself, the choice is between Francis and Allen. After the visit to the fairground, where Allen is told by Cesare that he has only until dawn to live, the friends part with the remark: "we must let her choose. But whatever her choice, we shall always remain friends." In this situation of rivalry the main beneficiary of Allen's death seems to be Francis, a benefit which his horror both suppresses and expresses.

This moment of recognition (in the script it appears as "a look of comprehension") is itself turned into an enigma (i.e., disavowed): "I shall not rest until I get to the bottom of these events," and it opens up the detection narrative, with its false trail-false suspect strategy, in which substitution plays a major part. In this respect Cesare is Francis' double: he kills the rival and abducts the bride, thus acting out his secret desires. The fact that throughout the rape/abduction scene both Francis and Caligari sit stupidly in front of Cesare's dummy not only accentuates the gesture of disavowal, it also establishes a parallelism of desire between Francis and Caligari underlined later by the repetition of an identical composition and shot: first Caligari is put in a straightjacket and locked into a cell, and then Francis is shown in the same position. The investigation of the series of crimes thus culminates in the visual statement that the criminal is the alter ego of the detective—the story of Oedipus, in other words, but itself held in suspense by the reversibility which the framing of the tale imposes on any attempt at decipherment.

Yet it is equally possible to read *The Cabinet of Dr. Caligari* as Jane's story, in which case her doctor-father and Dr. Caligari feature as doubles of each other, and Cesare as the disavowed phallus-fetish of a curiosity which the

scene in Caligari's tent marks as explicitly sexual. One recalls that she is motivated to visit Caligari by "her father's long absence." In the face of Francis' protestations that it could not have been Cesare who abducted her, Jane insists vehemently on being right, as if to defend *her* version against the rival claims of Francis.

What implications can one draw from this? It would appear that in *The Cabinet of Dr. Caligari* a visual form and a mode of narration has been found where several different "versions" or narrative perspectives converge or superimpose themselves on the same fictional space: its economy is that of condensation, itself the outcome of a series of displacements which de-center the narrative, while at the same time creating entry points for a number of distinct and different spectator fantasies, centered on male and female Oedipal scenarios. Technically, this is accomplished by a dis-articulation of action time in favor of narrated time, and (supported by the decor, but by no means confined to it) the projection of a purely interior space organized to visually bring to the fore the repetition and parallels which the narrative elides and mutes. What we see is a lacunary, elliptical text in which the figures of the fantastic can be seen as a particular textual economy of narrative perspectivism and spectator projection: paradoxically, this economy (which has the force of repression) here works both towards opening up the text and at the same time condensing its elements into a tight Oedipal logic.

Dr. Caligari thus posits a very strong internal system of relations between the different characters, wherein they act as substitutes for each other, either as doubles or (fetishized) part-objects. The narrative effects these forms of containment by a repression of desire, so that in the language of such an (Oedipalized) fantasy a specifically bourgeois renunciation of desire legitimates itself. The "political" nature of the psychic repression is named, shown, hinted at, only to become in turn the object of further repression. It is as if the social motifs are being substituted by sexual motifs, but these are themselves distorted by the force of narration itself, so that the film offers "solutions" which leave everything open, or rather, produce radically equivocal textual ensembles. It would therefore be inaccurate to say that in the German silent cinema all social conflicts become internalized, "psychologized"—unless one added that this interiorization is of such a virulent kind that it tends to threaten and disturb the very process of psychological containment or resolution.

Nancy Ketchiff   (essay date 1984)

SOURCE: "Dr. Caligari's Cabinet: A Cubist Perspective," in *The Comparatist*, Vol. VIII, May, 1984, pp. 7-13.

[*In the following excerpt, Ketchiff argues that* The Cabinet of Dr. Caligari *is more significantly Cubist than Expressionistic and suggests that the film's manipulation of space mirrors its main themes.*]

The Cabinet of Dr. Caligari is an early example of a rejection of early cinematic tradition with its stress of illusion and narrative. The film attempts to maintain a sequential unfolding of narrative while introducing the self-conscious mode of self-reflexion. Narrative had previously demanded illusion, and the makers of *Caligari* were forced to face the dilemma of modernist painters. A dialectic arose in which the thingness of the film as medium was juxtaposed to the reality of the sequential narrative. To articulate this dialectic *Caligari*'s makers were forced to deny illusion, and they did so in a way that has affinities with the solutions effected by Cubism from 1907-14.

The same problem confronting these German filmmakers in 1919 had earlier confronted Braque and Picasso. These artists sought to maintain the tangibility of forms, the painters' "narrative," but denied the traditional way by which this had been achieved. From the Renaissance on, the reality of objects had been achieved on the canvas by obfuscating the surface itself. Linear perspective became a means to replicate the external world, but it did so at the expense of the picture plane. We look through the surface of a Renaissance work as we look through a window. To the Cubists, the tangible reality of the canvas had to be maintained along with the depiction of the palpability of forms rendered upon that surface. Braque and Picasso achieved a dialectic which pivoted on the denial of illusion. Using facetted planes, simultaneity, and dislocation, the Cubists denied recession, the mainstay of illusionistic space, and linear perspective. With recession into space ignored, the tangibility of objects was evoked through simultaneity. This meant that various angles of objects could be rendered on the single plane of the canvas surface. Light, which to the Renaissance artist had come from a single naturalistic source, became more arbitrary for the Cubists. Douglas Cooper points out that for Picasso painted light was manipulated like light falling on a statue. Rather than creating the illusion of single source light which meant certain parts of forms had to be obscured by shadow, Picasso saw light only as the means to clarify the totality of the object. In this way, the anti-illusionistic light of the Cubists complemented their use of simultaneity and their denial of recession.

In short, Braque and Picasso faced a dilemma. They considered illusion to be a stumbling block for a self-reflexive visual art, but they recognized that illusion had been for centuries the only method available for painters like themselves who wanted to render the palpability of external forms. Braque and Picasso cut this Gordian knot by equating illusion with recession. By denying recession into the canvas through the avoidance of consistent light and the use of simultaneity, the artists discovered they could give form to their dialectic: both the tangibility of the canvas and that of the objects portrayed upon it were rendered.

In *The Cabinet of Dr. Caligari* a recognition like that of the Cubists that illusion and spatial recession were intimately linked is the first step toward the denial of traditional illusionistic ways of showing narrative. The theme of *Caligari* revolves around a questioning of reality and, at one level, this confusion stems from the fact that *Caligari*'s audience is confronted not with the simple illusionistic story reality common to traditional films, but with two realities—the story and the film itself. Narrative exists but does not obscure the tangibility of the film itself. Compounding this dialectic is the fact that we ultimately

learn that the reality of the narrative has been true only in the eyes of a madman; we have trusted an unreliable narrator. *Caligari* thus becomes a tribute to the constancy of art (the self-reflexive film) over the fallibility of external reality—and this revelation further repudiates the use of illusion as a means to truth.

This very acknowledgment of the fictive nature of the story and the tangibility of the medium introduces an ironic mode to *Caligari* that is not compatible with German Expressionism, the movement with which the film is usually linked. Chronologically *The Cabinet of Dr. Caligari* does fall into the period called Expressionist. Moreover, the theme, dealing as it does with insanity and "medieval" superstitions, corresponds to the subject matter favored by Expressionist artists. But it must be remembered that insanity and superstitions are only the superficial themes of the film; the narrative actually serves to illustrate the theses that illusion is fallible and art is true. This theme is far more Cubist than Expressionistic, particularly because the latter, as I mentioned, is temperamentally opposed to irony and the former is ironic by its very nature. Expressionism, as opposed to Cubism, is a utopian movement sympathetic to social reform. Its adherents hoped to spotlight what was amiss in the world in order that it could be seen and changed. Because it is messianic, German Expressionism distorts, exaggerates, and deals with strident emotions—all things are on the brink of disaster. And, seemingly in line with Expressionism, *Caligari*'s actors roll their eyes, beat their breasts, and convey their parts with melodramatic fervor. But this hand wringing is actually used less to evoke Expressionist emotionalism than to emphasize the fictive character of Jane, Caligari, and the narrator; their exaggerations remind the audience of their roles as actors. They are equally part of the art of the film and part of the narrative.

A by-product of the acknowledgment of the actors as actors is a profound lessening of empathy between the audience and the characters of the *Caligari* narrative. We are interested in and surprised by the story of the film, but at no point are we upset, for example, in a personal way by Cesare's death or by the unveiling of the narrator as a madman. This effect is more Cubist than Expressionist in spirit. For example, in synthetic Cubism's collages (the 1912-17 papiérs collés of Braque and Picasso) pieces of external reality were pasted to the canvas surface. Newspaper, chair caning, and simulated wood grain paper were introduced into the painting and assumed a dual significance. They were real, namable things with a role within the still life "story" and yet were also parts of the canvas itself. Like *Caligari*'s actors, the dual role of the collages' pasted materials stemmed from the dialectic the work of art established. Another notable feature is that the added materials of the Cubist collage are not interesting by themselves; that is, we have no empathy with them. They are interesting in their relationship to the dialectic of realities confronting us. The repudiation of illusion in *Caligari* and in Cubist canvases carries with it a repudiation of empathy. This is, it seems, unconscious and was not a motivation for the denial of illusion.

Technical details and effects in *Caligari* reinforce the Cubist analogy. In the opening credits themselves one experiences an element which superficially looks Expressionistic but which can be fruitfully interpreted in light of Cubist practices. The credits and the German titles of the silent film were done in a medieval Gothic script—a typeface amenable to the Expressionists' love of German medieval art. (The medieval motif is implicit in the film's content also. Early in the film the audience learns the story of *Caligari* comes from the eleventh century and the evocation of this hoary legend lends the properly mystical tone to the film). The German script of the titles does more than simply help create a medieval ambience for the story that follows. By using a highly "artful" Gothic script whose flourishes and details stress its value as a design as well as function as words that relate the action of the story, *Caligari* again shows affinities with early synthetic Cubism where words and lettering are included on the canvas in an attempt to further deny recession.

This interpretation of the function of lettering comes alive in *Caligari* in the scene after the narrator finds the doctor at the madhouse and we are "told" Caligari runs outside screaming: the word "Caligari" is written all over the image. This is an interesting device because the printed word seems synaesthetically to create a screaming sound; but, more importantly, it makes us very aware of the dialectic between art and narrative because the words exist outside of the illusion of the frame. They float on the surface as decoration, losing their function as signifiers. A rupture has occurred that destroys any remnants of illusion. Letters and words are read and things that are read exist on flat surfaces. *Caligari*'s type face emphasizes this surface orientation as the Cubists' use of words strengthens the tangibility of the canvas by emphasizing the picture plane. In both cases the impulse is toward a self-reflexion that helps deny illusion.

Caligari's makers, therefore, have attempted in the film's theme and visual details to clarify a dialectic between narrative and self-reflection that bears affinities to Cubism. These similarities may well transcend in importance Expressionist characteristics of the film. In fact, the Expressionistic elements of *Caligari* are, for the most part, extrinsic ones—they are embellishments that would have made the film more acceptable (at least to the avant-garde) as a product of modernist Germany. The Cubist character of *Caligari* is intrinsic: its dialectical theme comes from the same temperament evidenced in Braque and Picasso. The practitioners of both mediums realized that illusion must be destroyed in order to have a self-reflexive art that could retain some sense of a traditional narrative. This is the point at which Cubism diverges from the abstract art of Kandinsky or Mondrian. Where nonrepresentational art discovers equivalents to inner states of mind in a wholly self-reflexive way, the Cubist "object" translates into thematic narrative. The makers of *The Cabinet of Dr. Caligari* wanted to retain narrative without illusion in the same way that Braque and Picasso sought to depict the three-dimensional palpability of objects without illusion. The Cubists' solution to this problem sheds light on the method in *Caligari.*

Earlier, I mentioned that the anti-illusionistic Cubists es-

chewed recession in order to assert simultaneously the picture plane (the canvas surface) and the objects depicted. In *Dr. Caligari* this same annihilation of recession is utilized in order to achieve the same ends of self-reflexion and anti-illusionism, while still permitting a narrative to unfold. The lettering devices of the titles are a clue to this spatial manipulation through its insistence on surface. But it is in *Caligari*'s use of the Cubist denial of recession that the film most fully achieves its goal of presenting a narrative without illusion.

When *Caligari* begins, the sets are obviously Expressionistic in their distortion. Chairs are too tall, or small, or odd; walls lean into rooms, windows are unbalanced parallelograms. But the actors seem able to function within these visually strange surroundings with remarkable ease. There is however, one disjunction the viewer notices: the actors' clothing is not from the same era as their surroundings. The modernist tone of the furnishings speaks of a contemporary ethos, but the clothing is dated, as though the actors were "real" people, but real people in costumes. There is, therefore, an immediate disjunction, a lack of continuity, and we might say a lack of empathy between the participants in the narrative and their physical environment.

This disjunction prepares us for a curious and significant spatial characteristic of *Dr. Caligari*—in scene after scene there is no middle ground. Lacking a middle ground, there can be no recession into the space of the presented scene. Thus, there can be no illusion of a "real" environment because the space cannot be entered. The lack of empathy a viewer feels for the characters of *Caligari* is transformed by this spatial manipulation from an abstract to a concrete effect. The flatness of the scenery asserts the reality of the film as a medium, on the surface of which the narrative is played out. The lack of interaction between "story" and set allows each an importance, an independent existence— something illusion does not allow.

The disjunction of the early scenes becomes more forceful when we first see the carnival entrance, the ticket seller, and his monkey. There is a clear foreground with actors, but the background—so obviously painted—is separated by a railing from those "carriers of the story." Some figures descend the stairs that we assume are obscured by the railing to go to the carnival, but in terms of space we cannot really perceive where they go. Certainly, they do not go into the background, yet no middle ground exists; consequently, no illusion is permitted. The set is a self-conscious cipher—a symbol for the "place" of the action but one whose self-consciousness never lets us forget that it is a function of the art-form itself.

It is thematically appropriate that when the carnival is introduced space is obscured, empathy denied, and the dialectic clarified, because throughout the film the carnival symbolizes both good and evil. A carnival is an ambiguous social setting where success is measured by the effectiveness of shams, of illusions. Cesare himself, under less malevolent hands than Caligari, would be a simple fraud, the product of magician's illusions that trick his audience. The lack of illusionism in the set complements the oddity of this particular carnival which deals with the real, not with magic or illusion—at least we perceive it that way in the beginning.

That the spatial disjunction of *Caligari*'s sets parallels that of Cubist canvases is most clear in the scene in which Cesare abducts Jane and runs off into the hills with her limp body over his shoulder. Instead of running recessively into the distant space, Cesare very literally seems to hit the mountains after three or four steps. What looked far away was, in fact, close. The vista we defined as the distance asserts its surface in the same manner as a Cubist canvas. It also shifts abruptly from looking real, like a distant scene, to looking false and "artificial." A dialectic arises from this deliberate denial of illusionism. This undercutting of illusionistic reality is strikingly similar to that which occurs in synthetic Cubism's collages. In both, expectations are established only in order not to be fulfilled. This process accents the shifts from a discrete narrative to a discrete medium, the two poles of the dialectic. The annihilation of illusion is perhaps more strident in the film than in the collage because Cesare not only cannot enter the space of the setting, but dies as he makes the attempt.

Another denial of expectation occurs at a point which is the fulcrum of *Caligari*—the moment when we first question the reliability of the narrator. At this point the question of illusionism emerges as central to the whole of the film because everything we have thus far believed is revealed to be the illusion of a madman. The narrator has gone to the asylum to find the evil doctor, believing that he is the Caligari of the carnival. Suddenly, as he arrives at the piazza before the hospital, we are struck by what seems to be the spaciousness of the scene. Rather than the denial of a middle ground, we have an emphasis upon it. The open piazza leads to a classical tripartite arch, an architectural formation common in the Renaissance and admired for its grace, precision, and logic. But compare the rendering of piazza and arch in a work as clearly Renaissance as Raphael's *School of Athens* to its replication in *Caligari.* Raphael's painting literally shows us how linear perspective recedes from the foreground in orthogonals which meet at the vanishing point in the background through the arrangement of tiles in the piazza. In *Caligari,* this perspective is reversed. It is the narrator who stands at the vanishing point—but it is not in the background, but rather in the foreground. Distance irrationally advances. It is this illogical spatial disjunction which alerts us to the irrational viewpoint of the now suspect narrator. And, when he dashes to the building, it suddenly is not in the distance at all. The entire scene is middle ground; there is no transition. Front and back are rejected and the action is forced to occupy a spatial limbo without connections. This lack of connection between narrator and environment accents the newly revealed chaos of his mind.

Space and manipulations of that space are central to the intertwined themes and ideas of *The Cabinet of Dr. Caligari.* And these spatial solutions for the problem of illusionism have very clear Cubist affinities, as does the ultimate decision to attempt a rendering of a dialectic between the narrative and its vehicle, the film. There are details within the film that are Expressionistic; at the first glance

the distortions and jagged edges of the sets seem to be pure products of German aesthetics ca. 1900-20. But the expressionism of *Dr. Caligari* was relatively superficial. It provided the film with an appropriate "modern" tone. The Cubist orientation of *Caligari,* on the other hand, while less obvious, is more substantive and innovative. A Cubist perspective provided means by which film broke with the tradition it had recently felt such a great need to develop. Analyzing that perspective sheds greater light on the fact that the film is a palimpsest, that there are layers of "meanings" and "realities" in it. Ironically, one dimension of meaning is a Cubist meaning which asserts pluralistic reality.

Mike Budd   (essay date 1990)

SOURCE: *"The Cabinet of Doctor Caligari:* Production, Reception, History," in *Close Viewings: An Anthology of New Film Criticism,* edited by Peter Lehman, The Florida State University Press, 1990, pp. 333-52.

[*Budd is an American film scholar and educator who has written extensively on* The Cabinet of Dr. Caligari. *In the following excerpt, which summarizes much of his previous scholarship on the film, he places* The Cabinet of Dr. Caligari *in its historical and artistic contexts.*]

Films, like other cultural products, are made and received within particular historical situations. Thus close analyses of film texts will be most revealing when they demonstrate how textual operations and processes are implicated in larger historical processes. Rather than reified objects dissected by the critic, films are dynamic processes in which we as viewers make meaning and pleasure and knowledge—help make our own lives—but not under conditions of our own choosing. These conditions include the discourses and institutions that construct the complex matrix of alternatives within which we make history; they also often determine and disguise our choices. A truly democratic culture requires a critical history, which expands and clarifies present alternatives by reconstructing their bases in the past. This essay aims to contribute to such a critical history through an examination of the production, textual, and reception processes of *The Cabinet of Doctor Caligari* (1920). . . .

The Cabinet of Doctor Caligari was made within a commercial studio system and shown initially in commercial theaters. But the production of such an unusual film only became possible through a special set of historical conditions within the institutions of classic realist cinema in Germany. Dependent on exports, German film executives constantly looked for ways to sell in foreign markets. They were aided in this in the late teens and early twenties, when a period of inflation and currency devaluation followed Germany's defeat in World War I and further encouraged exports by making its products relatively cheap. But during the war Hollywood had become dominant internationally; in order to compete German films would have to be different. An artistically oriented cadre of studio personnel made possible one kind of product differentiation: an artistic stylization that contrasted with the usual realism of U.S. films. "Artistic" films never constituted more than a small percentage of Germany's total output. Yet to bolster exports the German film industry for several years after the war was unusually open to experimentation labeled "artistic" and thus ordinarily excluded from the discourse of classic realism, with its rigid demands for the largest possible market.

In postwar Germany, "artistic" often meant expressionism, a movement in many arts that was part of the larger movement of cultural modernism. In the early decades of the twentieth century a revolution of international modernism took place in virtually all the arts. Cubism and surrealism in France, expressionism in Germany, futurism in Italy, and constructivism in the Soviet Union were all diverse and cross-cultural movements in themselves but part also of an international assault on traditional artistic processes and styles. Painting as a window on the world, poetry as a genteel mirror of cultural order, the well-made play with its plausible characters and naturalistic situations, the realist novel—these and other time-honored forms and conventions were attacked, ridiculed, and ignored by modernist artists. In quite divergent ways they often promoted disunity over unity, montage and collage over continuity, and shocking and subjective new styles over the conventional representation of an "objective" external world.

Yet as a modernist movement German expressionism was a profoundly contradictory, unstable, and transitional phenomenon. It was strongly influenced by the subjectivist traditions of nineteenth-century German romanticism, which glorified the unified vision of an isolated and rebellious artist. On the other hand, it developed the radical disjunction and abstraction of emergent modernist forms. Expressionism carried these contradictions within itself. It combined an intense desire to overthrow authority and change the world with a rejection of and retreat from the world into a grotesque realm of subjective expression. Many artists and writers hated the bourgeois forms of their political and cultural fathers, yet in their romantic idealism were often unable actively to support contemporary social (and socialist) movements for democratic change. Influenced by expressionism, many of them, including *Caligari* 's scriptwriters, Carl Mayer and Hans Janowitz, registered their political ambivalence in their work, often unintentionally.

The expressionist movement began in painting and poetry around 1910, spread first to literature and the theater, then to the most expensive arts—opera, architecture, and film. In the years immediately following World War I, wealthy art patrons, theater audiences and critics, government sponsors, and advertising and the mass media began to accept and promote expressionism. Yet at the precise moment of this acceptance, expressionism as an avant-garde phenomenon was dialectically transformed into its opposite and successor, the *Neue Sachlichkeit,* the new sobriety or sanity. The destruction and trauma of the war, cooptation by established institutions, and its own internal contradictions by 1924 transmogrified expressionism in the art world just as it found its public everywhere else. In the visual arts, for example, the characteristic distorted and angular shapes and bright, almost deranged colors

gave way to the cool, geometric forms and subdued colors of the new sobriety. More generally, expressionism's anguished protest against authority and its subjective expression of intense emotion became rationalized, calm, "objective." The tensions and contradictions of expressionism were the preconditions for its historical change; as an institutionalized discourse its gaps and stress points would appear especially in its intersection with other discourses.

One of these discourses was the classic realist cinema, and in *The Cabinet of Doctor Caligari* this dominant mode comes into incompatible juxtaposition with a carefully limited version of expressionism. We can specify *Caligari* 's relation to expressionism and explore the consequences of the film's uneasy place between dominant and oppositional discourses and institutions by locating three areas of differential influence by expressionism: theme, narrative form, and setting. Thematically, *Caligari* seems to be characteristic not only of expressionism but also of older and more popular German cultural traditions. Insanity, the grotesque and uncanny, the outcry against an older generation and against authority—expressionism, and *Caligari,* drew these themes largely from traditions of German romanticism in literature, theater, and the visual arts.

But it is only when we leave these thematic generalities, these results of interpretation, and examine the bases for interpretation in the specificities of narrative and setting that we approach *Caligari* and expressionism concretely. In 1919 and 1920 literary expressionism was changing. The world war that lasted from 1914 to 1918 shocked many writers and others with its new scale of mindless technological barbarity. The abortive, compromised revolution in Germany that ended the war embittered many who had sought peace and social justice. Disillusioned, writers like Franz Werfel, Hanns Johst, and Paul Kornfeld rejected not only the socially activist themes of their earlier work but also their innovations (or imitations of innovations) in form. Late expressionism became antisubjective, antiromantic; following Goethe in rejecting modernism as sickness, all but a few writers by 1920 had either rediscovered the conservative forms of German literature or moved toward the sober style of the *Neue Sachlichkeit.*

At the same time that the romantic rejection or political critique of society by the modernist artist was becoming untenable for many expressionist writers, the movement was being accepted by the cultural establishment. At this moment expressionism began to find a carefully limited place in the commercial discourse of cinema. This acceptance was only possible because *Caligari,* like most other films influenced by expressionism, ignored the (largely antinarrative) avant-garde in favor of a conventional narrative form. In fact, *Caligari* 's unconventional aspects—the expressionist settings and plot reversal at the end—emerge from and are dependent on the largely conventional form of the film's classic realist narrative. Before it is anything else, *Caligari* is a story, told in the "invisible" discourse of classic realism for smooth consumption. Viewers may experience some disorientation because of the strange images, yet editing and cinematography help construct a reassuringly stable space and time where recognizable characters act out a story. (Indeed, when the film opened in New York in 1921, several reviewers noted how the initial sense of strangeness passed as one settled into the story.) Francis's tale, which comprises most of the film, is that most typical of realist narratives, the detective story. Thus it includes diversionary subplots (the attempted murderer imprisoned by the police), suspenseful chases (Francis following Caligari to the asylum), and the female character, Jane, used as token of exchange and power by the male characters. These strategies help subordinate style to narration and to produce what seems to have been for many exciting, largely commercial, and patriarchal cinema. But as narrative form, all this is very far from expressionist literature or drama, which was highly disjunctive, episodic, and modernist.

Whereas the narrative form of *Caligari* places it among the most advanced developments of the commercial realism of its time and seems virtually untouched by expressionism, the settings, derived from expressionist painting and theatrical set design, introduce the most disturbing and modernist elements. For whatever reason, the visual design of *Caligari* shows clearly the cubist influence on expressionism, specifically the styles of Robert Delaunay, Lyonel Feininger, and the painters associated with the *Brücke* (Bridge) group. In France the aesthetically radical principles of cubism would be applied to the overall formal design of a film in *Ballet Mécanique* (1924), for example. But from its inception the modernist qualities of *Caligari* were largely confined to its settings—to the angular, splintery shapes, the tilted houses, the distortions that can seem to infuse the world of the film with strangeness and dread. Disturbing, yet able to be coopted, *Caligari* exists in that anomalous cultural space between a modernist avant-garde and the capitalist institutions of mass-produced culture.

At the same time, *Caligari*'s visual style resembled what was appearing elsewhere in the German mass media. The film's designers—Hermann Warm, Walter Röhrig, and Walter Reimann—were part of the group around *Der Sturm,* Herwarth Walden's commercially successful Berlin magazine and publicity apparatus then riding the crest of the expressionist wave. How logical, then, for them to work for Erich Pommer, the film's producer, another businessman with an eye for exploiting a fashion. The capitalist corporation that Pommer supervised could exploit expressionism as international modernism, carefully containing its more radical dimensions. This was the corporation's way of differentiating its product as "artistic" though still (barely) within the relatively narrow parameters of a commercial cinema.

As a part of making history, film viewing is an active and dynamic process in which people construct their experience and their relation to the text in different ways. And as a model for and part of the historical process of generating (and closing down) emancipatory alternatives, film viewing is a reading, a working on and playing with a text that is nothing but the encoded traces, the mediations of the historical conditions and conflicts of its own production. Thus reading as making meaning and pleasure underlies usually unexamined processes of film viewing, and

a crucial aspect of this activity is the revision of the narrative's past (what has been read) and predictions for the narrative's future (what will be read) in light of a changing present (what's being read); to read is to reread. Limited to being always at only one point in the temporal progression that is the phenomenal event of a film, viewers' minds nevertheless range constantly across their experience of the film so far and across expectations of what it will be. They compare, correct, specify, place, and predict, noting patterns of similarity and difference, of rhyming and progression. The classical narrative cinema attempts to rationalize and administer this process of consumption as it does the production of films. The management of such a closed system demands the projection of a semblance of continuity and coherence, so gaps and contradictions are for most viewers contained in a seemingly smooth production and consumption of narrative questions and answers. The rereading performed while viewing the film the first time can thus become a justification for not viewing it, not rereading it, again. In general, commercial films are made and presented as products that seem to be used up or consumed in the experience of "entertainment." For the film to become a commodity consumable in one viewing, rereading must be carefully contained, minimizing unsolved narrative or other puzzles that might prompt reflection or critical examination.

What then of *The Cabinet of Doctor Caligari,* which near its end throws into question the status or truth-value of what has come before by revealing that its protagonist-narrator is mad? With its twist ending and expressionist settings the film virtually *demands* rereading. Although realist and commercial films, especially mysteries, commonly provide minor shocks of revelation that may prompt some more ambitious viewers to reread for narrational clues and deceptions, such rereadings usually seem to confirm and augment the managed pleasures of consumption. A film like *Caligari,* on the other hand, can radically *activate* rereading, can make it more than the tying up of loose narrative ends. One might try to explain, for example, the expressionist settings as the visions of the mad narrator, Francis. But the same settings are present in the frame story! Indeed, the more one tries to make everything fit, reconsidering the film retrospectively, the more difficult and problematic it becomes. These difficulties may prompt a more thorough, critical, and active rereading, even with the first viewing. Such an active rereading would be a re-cognition, a radical problematization of the first, consumerist rereading.

A restrospective rereading of *Caligari* might take this radical path, or it might stay within the safe boundaries of the consumer of narrative. Insofar as it is a classical narrative, the film tries to guide us into the latter course. In order to do this it must accomplish two difficult things at the same time. It must fool us into believing that Francis is sane until the end of a first, "naive" reading. Yet it must also avoid any narrational inconsistencies or contradictions that might become apparent with the closer inspection of a retrospective rereading. The following analysis will show, however, that such contradictions are unavoidable in *Caligari* and thus can lead to a more radical rereading. Crucial aspects of the film are *necessary* in order to make both the first, "naive" reading and subsequent retrospective readings possible. Neither wholly conventional/classical nor simply transgressive/modernist, these aspects intimately intermingle the two. [In a footnote, Budd states: "Few film 'landmarks' have been so thoroughly associated with a single influential reading as has *The Cabinet of Doctor Caligari* with Siegfried Kracauer's *From Caligari to Hitler*. Supposedly added against the screenwriters' wishes, the frame story for Kracauer simply cancels out the attack on authority in Francis's story: 'A revolutionary film was thus turned into a conformist one . . . by putting the original into a box, this version faithfully mirrored the general retreat into a shell.' Noting but failing to account for the continuation of expressionist settings in the frame story, Kracauer claims the hypnotic and tyrannical Caligari to be a premonition of Hitler.

In implicit opposition to Kracauer, Noël Burch and Jorge Dana (in their 'Propositions,' *Afterimage*, Spring 1975) propose a modernist reading of the film. For them, *Caligari* becomes 'the first self-reflexive filmic work' through a subversion of codes of illusionist representation that in 1919 were newly established. I propose to shift the terms of analysis in order to subsume these readings within a consideration of what processes and structures set the historical conditions of possibility for these and other readings and interpretations."]

The contradictory demands of advancing and retrospective readings center on settings, since these are the most obviously modernist or transgressive aspects of a film that is primarily classical. . . . In classic realist cinema, dream sequences or stories told by the insane are usually clearly marked internally through stylistic elements such as setting, color, or acting in order to differentiate them from the naturalized, self-effacing discourse of realism. But the unexamined assumption that because setting functions to support narrative, the setting's level of stylization should be consistent with the narrative's "degree of reality" is precisely what *Caligari* makes problematic. And it becomes so problematic because, unlike more radically modernist films like the surrealist *Un Chien Andalou* (1928), disturbing anomalies appear in what otherwise appears to be a relatively conventional narrational system. . . . [We] can identify stresses that prevent this system from attaining equilibrium and harmony.

1. In order to help explain Francis's story retrospectively as fantasy, the level of visual stylization of the frame and narrated segments must be as *different* as possible. This helps explain, for example, the relative bareness of the garden decor in which Francis tells his story. The garden contrasts with the deranged perspectives of Holstenwall that immediately follow it in opening the tale. The film begins again causally at this point to help create a "naive" first reading, to induce forgetting of frame and telling; it seems also to start over *visually*, but in support of a retrospective reading.

2. Regardless of whether or not one sees the settings as motivated by Francis's madness, the implicit classical principle of consistency and homogeneity must keep the various settings of the frame story—garden, courtyard, and cell—on the *same* level of stylization, since they are proximate within the story space. This principle is even stronger in a reading that visually separates frame from framed, since that separation depends on the consistency of opposed parts.

3. Finally—and it is at this point that major stresses within the system of decor in *Caligari* emerge—a third contradictory stylistic pressure makes itself felt. The courtyard setting occurs in *both* frame and tale, thus holding those two levels *together* and working in diametrical opposition to attempts to keep them apart.

Architectonically, then, the system is unbalanced, out of true, a narrative and stylistic puzzle in which all the pieces don't fit. The film implicitly offers to explain one of its transgressions (the expressionist settings) with the other (the insane narrator), but only at the price of inconsistency. The attempted distinction between settings . . . is necessarily compromised and inconsistent, since to distinguish clearly between "normal" and "mad" worlds from the outset is to give the game away. In classical narrative most told stories are not stylistically different from their frames. Thus the minimalism of the garden decor—a wall and bench, a few bushes and "branches"—wants to be read, relatively superficially the first time, as suggesting some continuity with the settings that follow while also retrospectively suggesting discontinuity. Of necessity both the same and different from the expressionist settings that follow, this minimalism ends up splitting the difference while trying to avoid salience. Attempting to accommodate two contradictory readings, the text produces a mild but functional heterogeneity, an inconsistency probably overlooked by most viewers in the realist effect of unity and continuity. The analysis here demonstrates that this inconsistency, this aporia of rereading, *is not a mistake but a necessary contradiction. Caligari* generally follows the realist subordination of style to narration while allowing one element of style, setting, to get uppity; it also promotes an active rereading that may disrupt the positioning of the viewer as consumer. [In a footnote, Budd continues: "Several commentators have pointed out the film's heterogeneity of acting styles, usually assuming it to be an error or inadequacy. The acting ranges from the expressionist stylization of Werner Krauss as Caligari and Conrad Veidt as Cesare, through the conventional silent film histrionics of Francis and Jane, to the restrained and relatively naturalistic portrayal of the white-coated doctors in the asylum. Yet this disjunction of acting styles is no accident, but like the settings a symptomatic contradiction produced by the conflicting projects of the film. On the one hand, there is the necessity for stylistic consistency between setting and character (as defined by acting, costume, and make-up). This consistency is limited to Caligari and Cesare, whose sharp, angular gestures, furtive lines, and stylized costumes and make-up mark them as one with their expressionist surroundings. On the other hand, there is the necessity for stylistic *in*consistency between setting and character. The text needs a stable reference point of sanity in a narration that suddenly reverses itself, shifting its ascription of madness from Caligari to Francis. With no stylistic relation to their surroundings, the asylum doctors, and especially the older one, constitute this reference point, since they are the only characters whose psychological traits are the same in both Francis's story and the frame that encloses it. Thus escaping from a reading of the film's expressionist aspects as motivated by the narrator's madness, these icons of objective science become virtually the last alibis for the invisible authority of classic realist narration itself; they become the stable ground that makes intelligible the sudden reverses of figures reread."]

We may restate the problem of *Caligari* by pointing to another, compounding contradiction. If the relation of garden setting to Holstenwall setting is, as argued, a kind of strategic compromise covering a contradiction, visually both similar and different, then we might expect that the courtyard in the frame story would appear different—but not too different—from its appearance in Francis's story, in order to support both advancing and retrospective readings. The difference would help suggest, retrospectively, that Francis had constructed his mad tale by transforming his "real" environment. Why, then (asks your narrator), is the courtyard setting unchanged on its reappearance in the frame story?

The answer lies again in the difficult demands of a retrospective narration. Narratively, the final courtyard scene is a crucial one: the film's very intelligibility depends on the clear reversal and revelation that Francis has lied, that he is an inmate in the same asylum he virtually directs in his own tale. This point *prevents* any ascription of the setting to Francis's madness. But in order to ensure that the audience understands that this is the asylum, the courtyard must look the same in both frame and tale. The moment of shock in the realization of the narrator's unreliability, the temporary vertigo that may disturb the secure, knowing processing of the viewer as customer—this effect demands that the courtyard be *immediately recognizable*. Consider the alternative: if the courtyard *were* different, our difficulty would be increased intolerably; we would be genuinely puzzled as to the relative statuses of the parts; we might ask if Francis were right, the frame a lie; we might even begin to see the inadequacy of character as an explanation and move toward problems of how character is represented. But the film for most viewers probably contains these speculations, unless those viewers already have some theoretical and historical knowledge. It can still shock and disturb, not only in its relatively conventional elements of horror and the uncanny (as one of the links between the iconography of German romanticism and the Hollywood horror genre) but also in the stresses of an architectonic that must be traversed again, reconsidered, "where something past comes again, as though out of the future; something formerly accomplished as something to be completed." That "something past" includes unexamined realist assumptions about narrational authority and neutrality, about a fixed and unchanging relation between segments designated "telling" and "tale," and about "the narrative's degree of reality."

Perhaps because of the heightened conflict of dominant and oppositional discourses that became the conditions of its production, *Caligari* condenses and mediates those conditions with unusual force and clarity. Yet production and text do not exhaust the moments in the history of a film; with *Caligari* the conflict of institutions is rearticulat-ed in its conditions of reception, producing a fascinating reception history, only part of which we can sketch here.

As perhaps the most difficult and modernist of the German expressionist films of the twenties, *Caligari* was advertised and sold on the basis of its artistic innovations and prestige. In Paris it was an immediate and long-lasting success, playing for years there and even inspiring the term "Caligarisme" to designate "a postwar world seemingly all upside down" (Kracauer in *From Caligari to Hitler*). In the United States the film was distributed by Samuel Goldwyn, opening at the Capitol Theatre in New York, one of the largest and most prestigious houses, on 3 April 1921. After breaking house records there for a week it played at a number of theaters in other cities, but it did not enjoy the general commercial success of the more conventional German imports of the time—Ernst Lubitsch's historical dramas *Madame DuBarry* (released in the United States as *Passion*) and *Anna Boleyn* (*Deception*).

Three aspects, three discourses of the publicity apparatus of the culture industries became important in the U.S. reception of *Caligari*: advertising, exhibition, and reviews. First, ads aggressively attempted to shape the film's reception in their own image, foregrounding characters and stars, making expressionism into a novelty, touting the suspenseful story, and trying to keep the whole thing dignified, as befitted a European art film. They also obsessively reproduced images of Cesare threatening Jane and tried to make *Caligari*'s expressionism into a continental clothing fashion with which to sell Goldwyn's new female stars to U.S. women. These strategies took up the film's construction of Jane as object of desire for the male characters (and perhaps viewers), trying to assimilate it to the discourses of publicity.

Because of widespread anti-German prejudice, advertising called the film's origins "European," obscuring *Caligari*'s artistic as well as national context. Expressionism's extreme subjectivism attributed its representational distortion, abstraction, and fragmentation to the pure emotional expression of a transcendent artist. Thus it was of all styles in the modernist pantheon perhaps the most vulnerable to a naturalization and psychologization in which the transcendent artist becomes a character, whose pure expression becomes, in turn, madness. Mystification of the film's origins prepared it for insertion into the culture of commodities, but still word got out that it was a German film, a product of the diseased Hun mind, as some reviewers implied. [In a footnote, Budd quotes a reviewer who stated that *Caligari* "is one of those screen dissipations to be indulged in only once in a lifetime. The Germans, who seem still convinced that they won the war, are getting morbid over it. We've got more evidence on our side, but we want to get away from ghastliness as much as possible. Any second picture of this type would be like artistic slime"]. Thus, ironically, the naturalization of expressionism helped make possible the irrational attribution of madness to a whole nation.

But to make the film consumable, advertising was not enough. The text itself had to be changed in the exhibition situation. This was the age of the picture palace, the industry's attempt to attract more middle-class viewers and to

make moviegoing itself a stable, profitable institution beyond the success or failure of any individual film. Fragments of high and mass culture were melded together in
the larger theaters into presentations of which the feature
film was only one part: selections from classical music
played by a live orchestra, ballet or other dance numbers,
newsreels and film shorts, and staged prologues and epi-
logues to the feature were all part of these presentations.

As organized by Sam "Roxy" Rothafel, who managed the
Capitol Theatre and was one of the leading impresario-
exhibitors in the country, the presentation for *The Cabinet
of Doctor Caligari* was typically lavish but also somewhat
unusual, with a live, *narrative* prologue and epilogue that
essentially placed a second frame onto Francis's story.
The curtain opened on two characters, Cranford and Jane,
sitting in front of a cozy fireplace. Cranford tells a story
of walking through thick foliage into a garden where he
encounters Francis ("like a man sleepwalking in a horrid
nightmare"), who begins to tell him the story of "The
Cabinet of Doctor Caligari." Then the curtains close, the
lights fade, and this staged prologue slides seamlessly into
the opening of the film. At the end, after the doctor has
examined Francis and exclaimed in the final title, "I think
I know how to cure him now," we return to the stage,
where Cranford reassures (?) us that Francis, cured, today
leads a happy, normal life, unable to remember his hallucination.

It's difficult to imagine a more blatant attempt to force a
problematic text into conventional form, to contain its excesses in a frame of authoritarian and commodifying realism. The character who listens to Francis's story in the
film is a potentially problematic one, since he seems to be
an inmate of the asylum but must also serve as stand-in
for the viewer at the crucial moment of the revelation of
Francis's madness, when he recoils at the protagonist's
ravings as a cue for our own response. The added second
frame attempts to contain the sliding of this function,
probably invisible to most viewers anyway, by making the
listener a sane "anchor," an authoritative reference point
outside the original text. The discourse of the film is attributed to a responsible source, since doubt is cast from the
outset on Francis's sanity. With the problems and disturbances of the film not so much solved as enclosed, re-
framed, the limits of the culture industry's cooptation of
Caligari were seemingly reached: the ruthless functional-
ism of this second frame tries to reestablish the hierarchy
of discourses in realism, with style subordinate to (and dissolving into) narration, fantasies subordinate to (and de-
marcated from) a narrow, ideological concept of the real.

Though the trade paper *Motion Picture News* claimed that
the prologue and epilogue "were used by practically every
exhibitor who has shown the picture," reviewers ignored
the second frame and wrote about the film. Not that reviewers' comments were any more enlightening or less formulaic than they are today: in keeping with the pseudo-
high culture milieu of the Capitol and other picture palaces, many reviewers and critics tried to spiritualize and
mystify *Caligari.* Imitating the discourse of quasi-religious
celebration used by reviewers of the higher arts, they posited a realm of gentility for this film, blessed by its separa-

tion from the material world of commodities and exchange. Yet as Herbert Marcuse has pointed out, this "affirmative culture" is not so far from the mundane world
of capitalism:

> As in material practice the product separates it-
> self from the producers and becomes indepen-
> dent as the universal reified form of the "com-
> modity," so in cultural practice a work and its
> content congeal into universally valid "values."

The ideas of the powerful are often the most powerful
ideas. During this period the U.S. cultural establishment
began to take a serious interest in the movies, and *Caligari,*
like other German imports, became evidence for arguments by reviewers and others that film could be an art
form, with all the prestige and mystification that nomina-
tion entails. In the stock exchange of cultural legitimation,
Caligari 's deracinated expressionism and its limited modernist innovations became values that encouraged cultural
"investment" in the new medium of film. Thus valued,
such innovations also reciprocally added to the "cultural
capital"—the power to *define* aesthetic value and status—
of dominant social groups.

FURTHER READING

Criticism

Budd, Michael. "Contradictions of Expressionism in *The
Cabinet of Dr. Caligari." Indiana Social Studies Quarterly*
XXXIV, No. 2 (Autumn 1981): 19-25.
    Argues that *The Cabinet of Dr. Caligari* exemplifies the
    characteristic contradictions within German Expres-
    sionist works between nineteenth- and twentieth-cen-
    tury themes and aesthetic forms.

——. "Modernism and the Representation of Fantasy:
Cubism and Expressionism in *The Cabinet of Dr. Caligari."*
In *Forms of the Fantastic: Selected Essays from the Third In-
ternational Conference on the Fantastic in Literature*, edited
by Jan Hokenson and Howard Pearce, pp. 15-21. New York:
Greenwood Press, 1982.
    Discusses the influence of Cubism and German Expres-
    sion on the presentation of fantastic subject matter in
    The Cabinet of Dr. Caligari.

——. "Authorship as a Commodity: The Art Cinema and
The Cabinet of Dr. Caligari." Wide Angle 6, No. 1 (1984): 12-
19.
    Examines *The Cabinet of Dr. Caligari* as "an early exam-
    ple of art cinema, a mode of cinematic discourse which
    differentiates itself in limited modernist directions from
    the dominant mode of classical narrative, but which nev-
    ertheless is produced and consumed largely *within* the
    commodity relations of advanced capitalist societies."

——. "The National Board of Review and the Early Art
Cinema in New York: *The Cabinet of Dr. Caligari* as Affirmative Culture." *Cinema Journal* 26, No. 1 (Fall 1986): 3-18.
    Analyzes an early review of *The Cabinet of Dr. Caligari*
    in order to "suggest some of the complexity and thick-
    ness of the matrix of determinations within which cul-

tural products like films—and film reviews—are received."

Lennig, Arthur. "*Caligari* as a Film Classic." In *The Classic Cinema: Essays in Criticism*, edited by Stanley J. Solomon, pp. 56-63. New York: Harcourt Brace Jovanovich, 1973.

General discussion of the themes, characters, and stylistic techniques of *The Cabinet of Dr. Caligari*.

Peary, Danny. "*The Cabinet of Dr. Caligari*." In his *Cult Movies 3: 50 More of the Classics, the Sleepers, the Weird, and the Wonderful*, pp. 48-51. New York: Simon and Schuster, 1988.

Offers an account of the production history of *The Cabinet of Dr. Caligari* and traces its influence on later horror films.

Pegge, C. Denis. "*Caligari*: Its Innovations in Editing." *Quarterly of Film, Radio, and Television* XI, No. 2 (Winter 1956): 136-48.

Excerpt from a "postshooting script" that Pegge composed from the print of *The Cabinet of Dr. Caligari* distributed by the British Film Institute.

Rubenstein, Lenny. "*Caligari* and the Rise of Expressionist Film." In *Passion and Rebellion: The Expressionist Heritage*, edited by Stephen Eric Bronner and Douglas Keliner, pp. 363-73. New York: Universe Books, 1983.

Survey of the stylistic and thematic influence of German Expressionism on *The Cabinet of Dr. Caligari* and several later films.

Orlando

Virginia Woolf

(Full name Adeline Virginia Stephen Woolf) The following entry presents criticism of Woolf's novel *Orlando: A Biography* (1928). For discussion of Woolf's complete career, see *TCLC*, Volumes 1 and 5; for discussion of her novel *Mrs. Dalloway*, see *TCLC*, Volume 20; for discussion of her essays, see *TCLC*, Volume 43.

INTRODUCTION

One of the most prominent literary figures of the twentieth century, Woolf is best known for her technical innovations in the novel, most notably her development of stream-of-consciousness narrative in such works as *Jacob's Room* (1922), *Mrs. Dalloway* (1925), and *To the Lighthouse* (1927). Her novel *Orlando* comprises the fantasy biography of an English nobleman who survives numerous adventures, undergoes a mysterious sex change, and lives more than three centuries. A high-spirited, satirical consideration of nearly four centuries of English literary and social history, *Orlando* is also a tribute to Vita Sackville-West, an aristocrat and author who served as the model for Woolf's protagonist.

Plot and Major Characters

Subtitled "A Biography," *Orlando* traces its aristocratic hero through more than three centuries, opening in the Elizabethan era when the eponymous protagonist is sixteen years old. In the novel, decades unaccountably and swiftly pass as Orlando pursues his literary aspirations, is awarded a peerage, engages in a love affair with a Russian princess, and is named ambassador to Constantinople. After falling into a trance during a siege of that city in the seventeenth century, Orlando revives, transformed physically into a woman, although otherwise unaltered. Fleeing to England, Orlando engages in a legal battle to regain the property she had held as a man. In the eighteenth century she becomes acquainted with such prominent literary figures as Joseph Addison, Jonathan Swift, and Alexander Pope. She marries in the nineteenth century and subsequently struggles to reconcile her desire to write with Victorian notions of feminine duty. The novel concludes in 1928 as Orlando publishes the poem she has been revising for more than three centuries, is reunited with her husband, and achieves a unifying vision of life.

Major Themes

Several themes in *Orlando* reflect concerns that pervade Woolf's works, including marriage and the equality of the sexes, the difference between chronological time and a person's age as determined by wisdom and experience, and the enigma of individual personality. The novel was inspired in part by Woolf's desire to "revolutionize" bio-graphical writing—a genre in which her father, Sir Leslie Stephen, had achieved considerable success during the Victorian era—and in part by Woolf's romantic liaison with Vita Sackville-West. Drawing a portrait of Sackville-West through a combination of fact and imagination, *Orlando* parodies Victorian biography, particularly in its mockery of documentary evidence. The androgynous character of Orlando—particularly the fact that Orlando's essential character is not altered though he changes from male to female—is seen to demonstrate Woolf's belief that each individual has both male and female characteristics and that intellectually men and women are indistinguishable. Similarly, Woolf's unconventional presentation of time allows an examination of the character of Orlando in the context of English social history. In rendering each historical period Woolf adopted a narrative style to reflect the predominant literary and social conventions of the times, and in each, humor is largely achieved through exaggeration and ironic contrast.

Critical Reception

Woolf noted that writing *Orlando* provided her with a light-hearted "writer's holiday" after completing *To the Lighthouse,* and the novel impressed many early readers and critics as little more than an entertainment written to amuse Woolf's family and friends. Nevertheless, initial assessments of *Orlando* were generally favorable, noting in particular the fine descriptive writing in such passages as the depiction of the Great Frost of 1604 and of the thaw that followed. Most early commentators, however, placed the novel outside Woolf's main body of work, a judgment with which numerous critics have since disagreed, viewing *Orlando* as the fictional complement to her feminist essay *A Room of One's Own* and seeing in its themes and its rejection of literary conventions similarities with her more prominent works.

CRITICISM

Arnold Bennett   (essay date 1928)

SOURCE: A review of *Orlando,* in *Virginia Woolf: The Critical Heritage,* edited by Robin Majumdar and Allen McLaurin, Routledge & Kegan Paul, 1975, pp. 232-34.

[*An English novelist, short story writer, and essayist of the early twentieth century, Bennett is credited with bringing techniques of European Naturalism to the English novel. He is best known as the author of* The Old Wives' Tale *(1908) and the* Clayhanger *trilogy (1910-16), realistic novels depicting life in an English manufacturing town. In the following excerpt, which originally appeared in the* Evening Standard *in November 1928, Bennett unfavorably reviews* Orlando.]

You cannot keep your end up at a London dinner-party in these weeks unless you have read Mrs Virginia Woolf's *Orlando.* For about a fortnight I succeeded in not reading it—partly from obstinacy and partly from a natural desire for altercation at table about what ought and ought not to be read. Then I saw that Hugh Walpole had described it as 'another masterpiece', and that Desmond MacCarthy had given it very high praise.

I have a great opinion of the literary opinions of these two critics. So I bought the book and read it. I now know exactly what I think of it, and I can predict the most formidable rumpuses at future parties.

It is a very odd volume. It has a preface, in which Mrs Woolf names the names of 53 people who have helped her with it. It has, too, an index. I admit some justification for the preface, but none for the index.

Further, the novel, which is a play of fancy, a wild fantasia, a romance, a high-brow lark, is illustrated with ordinary realistic photographs, including several of Vita Sackville-West (a Hawthornden prize-winner), to whom the book is dedicated. The portraits of Miss Sackville-West are labelled 'Orlando'.

This is the oddest of all the book's oddities. . . .

Orlando at the end of the book has achieved an age of some four centuries. Which reminds one of the Wandering Jew and the Flying Dutchman. Half-way through the story he changes into a woman—and 'stays put'. Which reminds one of *Seraphita,* the dullest book that Balzac ever wrote.

I surmise that Orlando is intended to be the incarnation of something or other—say, the mustang spirit of the joy of life, but this is not quite clear to me.

The first chapter is goodish. It contains vivacious descriptions of spectacular matters—such as a big frost, royal courts, and the love-making of Orlando and a Muscovite girl in furs and in the open air amid the fiercest frost since the ice-age. Mrs Woolf almost convinces us of the possibility of this surely very difficult dalliance.

The second chapter shows a startling decline and fall-off. Fanciful embroidery, wordy, and naught else!

The succeeding chapters are still more tedious in their romp of fancy. Mrs Woolf does not seem to have understood that fancy must have something to play *on.* She has left out the basic substance. For example, Orlando, both as man and as woman, is said to have had many lovers, but details are given of only one love.

I shall no doubt be told that I have missed the magic of the work. The magic is precisely what I indeed have missed.

The writing is good at the beginning, but it goes to pieces; it even skids into bad grammar. Mrs Woolf has accomplished some of the most beautiful writing of the modern age, including paragraphs that Nathaniel Hawthorne himself might have signed. *Orlando,* however, has nothing anywhere near as good as her best.

The theme is a great one. But it is a theme for a Victor Hugo, not for Mrs Woolf, who, while sometimes excelling in fancy and in delicate realistic observation, has never yet shown the mighty imaginative power which the theme clearly demands. Her best novel, *To the Lighthouse,* raised my hopes of her. *Orlando* has dashed them and they lie in iridescent fragments at my feet.

Conrad Aiken (essay date 1929)

SOURCE: A review of *Orlando,* in *Virginia Woolf: The Critical Heritage,* edited by Robin Majumdar and Allen McLaurin, Routledge & Kegan Paul, 1975, pp. 234-36.

[*An American man of letters best known for his poetry, Aiken was deeply influenced by the psychological and literary theories of Sigmund Freud, Havelock Ellis, Edgar Allan Poe, and Henri Bergson, among others, and is considered a master of literary stream of consciousness. In the following review, which was originally published in the* Dial *in February 1929, Aiken comments on form, tone, and theme in* Orlando.]

That Mrs Woolf is a highly ingenious writer has been made glitteringly obvious for us in *Mrs Dalloway* and *To the Lighthouse*: which is not in the least to minimize the fact that those two novels also contained a great deal of beauty. That she is, and has perhaps always been, in danger of carrying ingenuity too far, is suggested, among other things, by her new novel, or 'biography', *Orlando.* What ever else one thinks about this book, one is bound to admit that it is exceedingly, not to say disconcertingly, clever. In England as well as in America it has set the critics by the ears. They have not known quite how to take it—whether to regard it as a biography, or a satire on biography; as a history, or a satire on history; as a novel, or as an allegory. And it is at once clear, when one reads *Orlando,* why this confusion should have arisen; for the tone of the book, from the very first pages, is a tone of mockery. Mrs Woolf has expanded a *jeu d'esprit* to the length of a novel. One might almost say, in fact—when one notes in the index that there are precisely seven references to 'The Oak' (a poem which plays an important part in the story—and which in a sense is almost its ghostly protagonist) and when one recalls that Knole, a famous English house, is at Sevenoaks, (clearly the house described in the novel) that *Orlando* is a kind of colossal pun. More exactly, one might compare it with *Alice in Wonderland;* for if the latter is an inspired dream, organized with a logic almost insanely unswerving, so the former is a kind of inspired joke, a joke charged with meanings, in which the logic, if not quite so meticulous, is at any rate pressing.

There is thus an important element of 'spoof' in *Orlando*: Mrs Woolf apparently wants us to know that she does not herself take the thing with the least seriousness—that she is pulling legs, keeping her tongue in her cheek, and winking, now and then, a quite shameless and enormous wink. With all this, which she accomplishes with a skill positively equestrian, she is obliged, perforce, to fall into a style which one cannot help feeling is a little unfortunate. It is a style which makes fun of a style: it is glibly rhetorical, glibly sententious, glibly poetic, glibly analytical, glibly austere, by turns—deliberately so; and while this might be, and is, extraordinarily diverting for a chapter or two, or for something like the length of a short story, one finds it a little fatiguing in a full-length book. Of course, Mrs Woolf's theme, with its smug annihilation of time, may be said to have demanded, if the whole question of credibility was to be begged, a tone quite frankly and elaborately artificial. Just the same, it is perhaps questionable whether she has not been *too* icily and wreathedly elaborate in this, and taken her Orlando in consequence a shade too far towards an arid and ingenious convention. Granted that what she wanted to tell us was a fable, or allegory: that she wanted to trace the aesthetic evolution of a family (and by implication that of a country) over a period of three hundred years: and that she had hit upon the really first-rate idea of embodying this racial evolution in one undying person: need she quite so much have presumed on our incredulity? One suspects that in such a situation an ounce of ingenuousness might be worth ten times its weight in ingenuity; and that a little more of the direct and deep sincerity of the last few pages, which are really beautiful and really moving, might have made *Orlando* a minor masterpiece.

As it is, it is an extremely amusing and brilliant *tour de force*. It is as packed with reference, almost, as 'The Waste Land'. Some of the references, it is true, are too esoteric—for one not in the enchanted circle—to be universally valid; and this may or may not be thought a mistake. One's private jokes and innuendoes are pretty apt to become meaningless, with the passage of time and the disappearance of the *milieu* which gave them point. This, again, is of a piece with Mrs Woolf's general air of high spirits; of having a lark; of going, as it were, on an intellectual spree; and that there is far too little of this spirit in contemporary literature we can cheerfully admit. But here too one feels inclined to enter a protest. For the idea, as has been said, is first-rate, an idea from which a poet might have evoked a profusion of beauty as easily as the djinn was released from his bottle. Mrs Woolf does indeed give us a profusion of beauty and wisdom: but it is beauty and wisdom of a very special sort. Her roses are cloth roses, her scenes are scenes from a tapestry, her 'wisdom' (that is, her shrewd and very feminine comments on men and things) has about it an air of florid and cynical frigidity, a weariness wrought into form; as if—to change the image—she were stringing for her own entertainment a necklace of beautifully polished platitudes. If only—one thinks—she could have brought an Elizabethan freshness to this admirable theme—if she could have worked her mine a little deeper, a little more honestly, a little less for diversion's sake, and a little more for poetry's; and if, finally, she were not quite so civilized, in the Kensington Gardens sense of the word, or so burdened with sophistication, or could admit now and then, if for only a moment, a glimpse into the sheer horror of things, the chaos that yawns under Bloomsbury—but then this book would not have been the charming *jeu d'esprit* that it is; it would have been something else.

Elizabeth Bowen   (essay date 1960)

SOURCE:"Prefaces: *Orlando,*" in her *Seven Winters: Memories of a Dublin Childhood and Afterthoughts,* Alfred A. Knopf, 1962, pp. 130-39.

[*Bowen was an Anglo-Irish fiction writer and critic. Often compared with the fiction of Virginia Woolf, her novels and short stories display a similar stylistic control and subtle insight in the portrayal of human relationships. Bowen is also noted for her series of supernatural stories set in London during World War II. In the following excerpt, which was originally published as the foreword to the Signet Classics edition of* Orlando, *she recalls her initial impressions of the novel upon its publication in 1928 and reconsiders it within the context of Woolf's career.*]

Virginia Woolf's **Orlando** was first published in London in October of 1928. I remember the book was regarded with some mistrust by one generation—my own, at that time "the younger." We, in our twenties during the twenties, were not only the author's most zealous readers, but, in the matter of reputation, most jealous guardians. Her aesthetic became a faith; we were believers. We more than admired, we felt involved in each of her experimental, dazzling advances. Few of us (then) knew the still-conservative novels of her first period; a minority had informed itself of **The Mark on the Wall** and **Kew Gardens,** handprinted and issued in 1919 by the original Hogarth Press. She broke full upon us, it would be correct to say, with **Jacob's Room,** 1922, on which followed **Mrs. Dalloway,** 1925; then, while we were still breathless, **To the Lighthouse,** 1927. What now, what next? Next came **Orlando.**

It was *Orlando*'s fate to come hard on the heels of the third of those masterpieces, of which each had stimulated a further hope. We regarded this book as a setback. Now, thirty-two years later, I wonder why this should have been so.

One trouble was, I imagine, our peculiar attitude to this writer's art. Defending it as we did against all comers—"stupids," dissidents, or the unseeing critic—we were ready, should so desperate a need arise, to defend it against the artist herself. Never had we foreseen that we might require to. The virtue of the art was, for us, its paradox: sublimating personality into poetry, it had, as art, the chastity of the impersonal. Before we had read *Orlando,* indeed for some time before it was "out," we scented the book as a transgression. Unofficial publicity was unfortunate, the more so because it was unofficial. This *Orlando*—we did not care for the sound of it. The book was, we gathered, in the nature of a prank, or a private joke; worse still, its genesis was personal. Inspired by a romantic friendship, written for the delectation of the romantic friend, it was likely to be fraught with playful allusion. Nor was that all—a distinguished, sympathetic, and "special" coterie had contributed to the invention known as *Orlando.* That Virginia Woolf should have intimates was a shock.

Most of us had not met Virginia Woolf; nor did we (which may seem strange) aspire to. She did not wish to be met. Her remoteness completed our picture of her, in so far as we formed a picture at all. Exist she must (or writing could not proceed from her), but we were incurious as to how she did. What she looked like, we had not a remote idea; authors' photographs did not, then, ornament book jackets. Our contentment with not knowing Virginia Woolf today would appear extraordinary, could it even be possible. We visualized her less as a woman at work than as a light widening as it brightened. When I say, "She was a name, to us," remember (or if you cannot remember, try to imagine) what a name *can* be, surrounded by nothing but the air of heaven. Seldom can living artists have been so—literally—idealized.

Malevolent autumn of twenty-eight—it taunted us with the picture of a lady given to friends, to the point of fondness, and jokes, to within danger of whimsicality. Ourselves, we were singularly uncoordinated, I see now, as generations go. When I hear it said, as sometimes I do today, that Virginia Woolf's reputation was built up by a sophisticated coterie, I ask myself: "Whom can they possibly mean?" We, the ardent many, were rank-and-file provincials, outlanders, free lances, students (to me, in 1922, reading *Jacob's Room,* Bloomsbury meant University College, London). We ran, if into anything, into floating groups, loose in formation, governed by vague affinities. Then scorning fringes of coteries, we have remained, I notice, unwilling to form their nucleus in our later days—not, I hope, hostile, but non-attachable. Nevertheless, what we heard of *Orlando* galled us. We were young enough to feel out of it.

What we loathed was literary frivolity. So this was what Virginia Woolf could be given over to, if for an instant we took our eye off her—which, to do us justice, we seldom did. Cloak-and-dagger stuff. The finishing touch was the success the book enjoyed with our elders—*Orlando* charmed its way into the forts of middle-aged folly. "Your Mrs. Woolf has so often puzzled us. But *this* book of hers is delightful! We see what you mean!" Betrayed. . . .

We, naturally, read *Orlando.* We knew neither how to take it nor what to make of it; it outwitted us. Up to this year, I had never read it again.

The position as to *Orlando* has now changed. Or, better, the book itself has a position it lacked before—it belongs to what is central and main in the writer's work, instead of appearing, as it once did, to hover on the questionable periphery. There has been time, since Virginia Woolf's death, to stand back and view her work as a whole—still more, to see the whole as a thing of structure (in so far as an artist's whole art is like a building) or of inevitable growth (in so far as a whole art is like a tree). Though what does one mean by "a whole art"? Seldom does a writer lay down his pen or a painter his brush with calculated finality, saying: "This is forever; I have done!"

Death, other than in very old age, is an arbitrary interruption, the snipping of a cord at what seems often a fortuitous point. Rather, in Virginia Woolf's case, say her achievement within her fifty-nine years of life seems more, rather than less, significant now that we judge it steadily, *as* a whole. Up to 1941—that is, while she was living and at work—judgment was bound to be piecemeal, book by book. Temporary mists, misprisions, prejudices, sometimes intervened. From those mists' evaporation nothing she did gains more than *Orlando.* That *Orlando* was beautiful nobody doubted: what we now see is that it is important—and why.

It was important to the writer. She was the better, one feels certain, for writing it; in particular, for doing so when she did. More irresponsible than the rest of her work in fiction, it has the advantage of being less considered and more unwary. This book corresponds with a wildness in her, which might have remained unknown of—unless one knew her. This was a rebellion on the part of Virginia Woolf against the solemnity threatening to hem her in. *Orlando* is, among other things, rumbustious; it is one of the most high-spirited books I know.

Personal memories of Virginia Woolf cast, for me, their own light upon *Orlando,* though I certainly never spoke to her of the book, heard her speak of it, or attempted to find my way back to it while I knew her. Friendship with her—chiefly laughter and pleasure, and an entering, in her company, into the rapture caused her by the unexpected, the spectacular, the inordinate, the improbable, and the preposterous—filled out nine years of the lengthy interval between my first and second readings of *Orlando.* From her I learned that one can be worse than young and foolish; for she was the epitome of the young and foolish; it is among the glories of *Orlando* that it is in some ways a foolish book. It is not disorganized—on the contrary, it is a miracle of "build"—but it is rhapsodical. Halfway through her creative life, she desired a plaything—also a mouthpiece. Shyness is absent from *Orlando*; in what sometimes are rhetorical exclamations, sometimes lyrical flashes like summer lightning, she voices herself on the subjects of art, time, society, love, history, man, woman. The book is a novelist's holiday, not a novel.

By definition, *Orlando* is a fantasy. What is that? A story that posits "impossible" circumstances and makes play with them. Fantasy may juggle with time and space, and ignore, for instance, the law of gravity. Infinitely less fortunate is the novel, a work of imagination fettered to earthly fact and subject to dire penalty if it break the chain—one slip on the part of the novelist as to "reality" and his entire edifice of illusion totters and threatens to tumble down. At the same time, the licence accorded the fantasist is not boundless—the probable must enter his story somewhere. Should it fail to do so, interest is lost. Against extraordinary events, he must balance (in some sense) ordinary, or at least credible, characters. Where would *Wonderland* and *Through the Looking-Glass* be without the prim, dogmatic lucidity of the temperamentally *un*adventurous Alice? Virginia Woolf, whom the "musts" of the novel bored, fell in without complaint with the laws of fantasy. Her Orlando—that is, her central character—though redeemed by grace, genius, and breeding from being "ordinary," is *as a character* absolutely convincing. To the change of sex, to the mysterious flight of time—centuries slipping by like months in the country—he-she reacts in a manner one cannot challenge—psychologically, all is extremely sound. And the more transitory, lesser cast are touched in, manipulated, with great adroitness. Nothing in *Orlando,* other than the outright impossible, seems improbable. Ironically, fantasy made Virginia Woolf a more thoroughgoing "straight," one might say assiduous, novelist than she was wont to be. The entire thing was a pleasure—she did not "have to"; she was out of school.

What a performance *Orlando* is, simultaneously working on amazement and suspending disbelief! At the start, a sixteen-year-old aristocrat, male, proffering a bowl of rose water to the ancient Queen Elizabeth I; at the close, a woman of thirty-six, still Orlando, under an oak tree in the moonlight, in the reign of Britain's King George V—the month October, the year 1928, the exact day probably that of the publication of *Orlando.* The change of sex took place in Constantinople, where Orlando was being ambassador, towards the end of the seventeenth century. The longing to be a poet which consumed the youth has been realized by the woman, who has combined this with giving birth to a son. Exquisite social comedy has enjoyed a run of—roughly—three and a half centuries, partly in London, partly in the great Kentish country house. The Victorian age has been survived. Love has seared its way into a young breast, never to be forgotten, always to be associated with a Jacobean Thames ice carnival lasting a winter. Among the series of grand effronteries with which *Orlando* handles English history, there appear to be a few inadvertent errors—surely St. Paul's Cathedral acquires a dome sooner than it did? The enormous sense of release that runs through the book is partly an affair of effortless speed, mobility, action—carriages dashing, whips cracking, mobs swaying, ice islands twirling doomfully down the river. By contrast, I remember Virginia Woolf—back to being a novelist, writing *Between the Acts*—coming down the garden path from her studio, saying: "I've spent the whole of the morning trying to move people from the dining-room into the hall!"

I have a theory—unsupported by anything she said to me, or, so far as I know, to anyone—that Virginia Woolf's writing of *Orlando* was a prelude to, and in some way rendered possible, her subsequent writing of *The Waves,* 1931. Outwardly, no two works of fiction could be more different; yet, did the fantasy serve to shatter some rigid, deadening, claustrophobic mould of so-called "actuality" which had been surrounding her? In *To the Lighthouse* (coming before *Orlando*), she had reached one kind of perfection. This she could not surpass; therefore, past it she could not proceed. In *Orlando,* delicacy gives place to bravura, to rhetoric. It was a breaking point and a breathing space at the same time, this fantasy. She returned to the novel, to *The Waves,* with—at least temporarily—a more defiant attitude to the novel's "musts."

Captive in the heart of the book *Orlando,* in the midst of the splendid changing and shifting scenes, are accounts of the sheer sensation of writing, more direct than this writer has ever given us. For instance:

> At this moment . . . Orlando pushed away her chair, stretched her arms, dropped her pen, came to the window, and exclaimed, "Done!"
>
> She was almost felled to the ground by the extraordinary sight which now met her eyes. There was the garden and some birds. The world was going on as usual. All the time she was writing the world had continued.
>
> "And if I were dead, it would be just the same!" she exclaimed.

There is a touch of hallucination about "reality"; creative Orlando was right, so was his-her creator. Virginia Woolf's vision conferred strangeness, momentarily, on all it fell on; it was, I believe, her effort to see things as they were apparent to *other* people that wore her down. The bus, the lamp-post, the tea-cup—how formidable she found them, everyday things! Nothing of an ordeal to her, however, were melodrama or panorama—she was at home with, or within, either.

Orlando, about which we who were then young were so stupid in 1928, is, I perceive, a book for those who are young. How does it strike those who are young now?

Ralph Samuelson   (essay date 1961)

SOURCE: "Virginia Woolf, *Orlando,* and the Feminist Spirit," in *The Western Humanities Review,* Vol. XV, No. 1, Winter, 1961, pp. 51-8.

[*In the following excerpt, Samuelson discusses Woolf's "defiant feminist spirit" in* Orlando.]

Orlando is virtually the only work of Virginia Woolf's in which critical questions about her "feminism" have not repeatedly arisen. Moreover, the problem of what "type" of literature it belongs to has been with us since its appearance in 1928. Its method is fantasy, of course; the work begins with Orlando, the hero, a young man during the late 1580s, but in the middle of it all, Orlando's sex magi-

Vita Sackville-West's comments after reading *Orlando;* from a letter to her husband, Harold Nicolson:

Now that I have finished [*Orlando*] I still think it an absolutely enchanting book. Do you? Do you notice the craft of it,—how the style changes from the florid exaggeration of Elizabethan times to the purer directness of the 18th cent.—and so down to the vividness and psychological turmoil of modernity? The style and texture of it seem to me to be above reproach, as also the beauty, wit, and imaginativeness. The only criticism I have is this: (and you must keep this *entirely* to yourself . . .)—that the general inference is too inconclusive. I mean, she has slightly confused the issues in making Orlando 1) marry, 2) have a child. Shelmerdine does not really contribute anything either to Orlando's character or to the problems of the story, (except as a good joke at the expense of the Victorian passion for marriage) and as for the child it contributes less than nothing, but even strikes rather a false note. Marriage & motherhood would either modify or destroy Orlando, as a character: they do neither. Nor is the marriage with Shelmerdine offered as a satisfactory solution for the difficulties of matrimony. The nearest approach to a solution of the total study, is when Orlando realizes the value of Ecstasy, i.e., of Life as opposed to Literature. There is one other objection to Shelmerdine; and that is, that one does not know how to fit Shelmerdine into it. Will he be immortal too? if not, one has to face the unpleasant fact that one day he will die & Orlando be left desolate. No, I think Shelmerdine, *as a husband,* was a mistake.

Vita Sackville-West, in a letter to Harold Nicolson, dated 12 October 1928, reprinted in Twentieth Century Literature, *Vol. 25, Nos. 3-4, Fall-Winter, 1979, p. 349.*

cally changes, and the novel ends with Orlando a woman, thirty-six years old, in the late 1920s.

Of this novel, covering more than three hundred years' time during which the same person changes from a man to a woman, most of the critics have suggested that the work is apparently doing no more than playing facetiously with notions of Bergsonian flux. But the trouble is that a good deal more is involved in the sex change than would be necessary to do merely this. Orlando's sex change occurs fairly early in the novel, and is introduced in such a way as to suggest there exists no essential difference between men and women, other than the physical. This point is made very carefully:

> We may take advantage of this pause in the narrative to make certain statements. Orlando had become a woman—there is no denying it. But in every other respect, Orlando remained precisely as he had been. The change in sex, though it altered their future, did nothing whatever to alter their identity.

As a woman, Orlando finds herself confronted with a host of new problems, of which, when she was a man, she had been unaware:

> "Lord! Lord!" she cried again at the conclusion of her thoughts, "must I then begin to respect the opinion of the other sex, however monstrous I think it? If I wear skirts, if I can't swim, if I have to be rescued by a bluejacket, by God!" she cried, "I must!"

Here is certainly the feminist spirit asserting itself, under a thinly disguised veil of the "humor" involved in a situation wherein a man turns into a woman. The point is that there is no essential difference between the sexes, but that women are treated as if there were. In the general situation of the novel (and revelatory in the following quotation) there exists an enactment of revenge on the world of men, with Orlando himself serving as the sacrificial vessel. For in turning into a woman, Orlando sees how inconvenient it becomes to exercise her freedom, and is presumably dogged by the notion that her former male self is partially responsible for creating this world in which she is now so imprisoned spiritually.

> She remembered how, as a young man, she had insisted that women must be obedient, chaste, scented, and exquisitely apparelled. "Now I shall have to pay in my own person for those desires," she reflected; "for women are not (judging by my own short experience of the sex) obedient, chaste, scented, and exquisitely apparelled by nature. . . ."

Orlando, of course, is also a writer—a poet—and when he becomes a woman, his vocation becomes a special problem it had not been before. Soon after the sex change from man to woman, Orlando finds herself with a camp of gypsies. The desire to write is still with her as strongly as ever. However, "slowly, she began to feel that there was some difference between her and the gypsies which made her hesitate sometimes to marry and settle down among them." And the difference is not that she is English, but that she is a writer and a woman.

She returns to England. Her life is relatively pleasant for a time, but gradually Orlando unconsciously takes on certain of the attributes she knows women are supposed to have. She plays her role as a woman, and that this will do real harm to her writing is the clear implication. Certain "changes" take place in her:

> For example, it may have been observed that Orlando hid her manuscripts when interrupted. Next, she looked long and intently in the glass. . . . She was becoming a little more modest, as women are, of her brains, and a little more vain, as women are, of her person.

Soon the eighteenth century has arrived, and while Orlando is delighted to find herself in the witty company of Swift, Pope, and Addison, the passage Virginia Woolf chooses to quote from one of Addison's *Spectator* papers—a clear implication of male superiority and dominance—shows the effect the eighteenth century must have had on a woman's spirit of independence.

It is the nineteenth century, however, which is the worst

for women: the century is characterized by doubt, confusion, by thick, black clouds—fitful gusts of rain "which were no sooner over than they began again." The weather turns chilly; beards appear on men; women spend all their lives bearing children, and have time for nothing but this and raising them. The roles they play seem more constricting than ever. "Mrs. Bartholomew nodded. The tears were already running down her cheeks but as she wept she smiled. For it was pleasant to weep. Were they not all of them weak women?"

The third finger of Orlando's left hand begins to itch unnaturally for a ring. Orlando begins to desire not a "lover" as she (and he) always had in the past, but a "husband." Finally, Orlando gives way to her desire for a ring. She marries, and the conflict between her marriage and her writing comes immediately to the fore. Is this really marriage, she asks herself, "if one still wished, more than anything in the whole world, to write poetry."

This is followed by a facetious scene in which the writer wins out over the wife for possession of Orlando. Sitting at a desk, she decides to see if it is actually possible to write while married.

> But she would put it to the test. She looked at the ring. She looked at the ink pot. Did she dare? No, she did not. But she must. No, she could not. What should she do then? Faint, if possible. But she had never felt better in her life.

She finally determines to go ahead and write something, and as she dips her pen in ink, she is amazed that "there was no explosion."

Always, however, it is the nineteenth century—the century of Virginia Woolf's childhood—which is returned to with the greatest seriousness. We are told, for instance, that

> Orlando had inclined herself naturally to [other periods]. But the spirit of the nineteenth century was anti-pathetic to her and broke her, and she was aware of her defeat at its hands as she had never been before.

These last are almost embarrassingly serious words, and utterly out of harmony, again, with the intended "humor" of Orlando's general plight, and with the popular critical opinion that the only reason Virginia Woolf has Orlando change from a man into a woman is to reveal that the sexes in some vague and delightful manner "intermix." On the contrary, it is rather the serious combat of the female Orlando versus "the world" that underlies the more consciously wrought, surface texture of the novel.

As readers of literature, we can be thankful, once again, that Virginia Woolf took very seriously what Aileen Pippett saw as her "problem"—thankful that Virginia Woolf saw it and used it in the way any writer uses any experience. As James Baldwin has said [in *Notes of a Native Son*], "Any writer . . . finds that the things which hurt him and the things which helped him cannot be divorced from each other; he could be helped in a certain way only because he was hurt in a certain way. . . ." That this is true of a great many writers of first-rate talent attests to the fact—obvious to writers themselves—that out of a dy-

namism between personality and environment comes literature.

In *Orlando,* at times, the feminist point of view is often giving vent merely to embarrassingly aggressive tendencies. . . . At its best, however, the feminist spirit has nothing to do with all this, but shows rather Virginia Woolf's strong desire simply to be herself, and among other things to be true to a point of view representative of some of the experiences and feelings of her sex. It is not by accident that one of the characters in Virginia Woolf's first novel *The Voyage Out* makes the penetrating observation that Jane Austen may be the best woman novelist because she is the only woman novelist who did not try to write like a man. This spiritual recognition of Jane Austen as one of her true forbears was an exceedingly good thing to have happened to Virginia Woolf. Without the selfconscious awareness of her sex as reflected in *Orlando* and elsewhere, we would lose immensely—lose the compellingly poetic, almost mystical intuitions experienced, for instance, by Mrs. Ramsay and Mrs. Dalloway. And to return to the work at hand: it is not quite an accident that the reader remembers Orlando as a woman, not a man—certainly not a combination of both—and not by accident that such a subject as a sex change would present itself to Virginia Woolf as the tool for evolving a sometimes comic, sometimes deadly serious, satire on one phase of her relations with her world.

Howard German and Sharon Kaehele (essay date 1962)

SOURCE: "The Dialectic of Time in *Orlando,*" in *College English,* Vol. 24, No. 1, October, 1962, pp. 35-41.

[*In the following essay, German and Kaehele examine Woolf's presentation of "the dialectic of time" in* Orlando.]

Signs of the twentieth century's preoccupation with time can be readily discerned in the frequency with which the modern novel develops a dialectic between the ephemeral and the enduring. Virginia Woolf's *Orlando* is an illustration, although a somewhat unconventional one, of this concern, for it examines "the two forces which alternately, and what is more confusing still, at the same moment, dominate our unfortunate numbskulls-brevity and diuturnity." A fantastic and farcical variant of such family novels as *The Way of All Flesh* and *The Forsyte Saga, Orlando* traces through more than three centuries a protagonist whose life is loosely based upon the careers of various members of the Sackville family. In following Orlando through such an extended interval, Mrs. Woolf is able, despite her use of fantasy and farce, to depict the distinctive qualities of four centuries of English history and to examine the effects of the individual ages upon literature, human nature, and the relationship between the sexes. But of greater significance in the novel are her presentation of the subjective qualities of time and her analysis of the individual's attempt to resolve the conflict between the forces of "brevity and diuturnity."

Despite the longevity of *Orlando*'s Tiresias-like protagonist, the time span supports the argument for "brevity" in the novel's dialectic of time: as living conditions and customs are modified with the centuries, as Orlando alters some of her habits and beliefs, and as her acquaintances and servants disappear with the years, the power of time over man and his creations becomes quite apparent. Other details in the novel, however, are undoubtedly more effective in creating a subjective sense of time within the reader. In a way that a limited cataloguing can only suggest, *Orlando* is permeated with images of flight and flowing and with descriptions of and references to objects (such as water, birds, candles, and feathers) suggesting movement and transience. Daily acts are compared to "the passage of a ship in an unknown sea"; happiness is rarely achieved because "dark flows the stream" of life; consciousness returns "like a tide, the red, thick stream of life again, bubbling, dripping." Frightened by a sense of time's relentlessness, Orlando walks carefully across "the narrow plank of the present, lest she would fall into the raging torrent beneath." Orlando thinks of Sasha as "the spring and green grass and rushing waters"; when dubious of Sasha's fidelity. Orlando thinks of himself as a great fish "rushed through waters unwillingly." Birds serve as symbols of Love, Lust, Happiness, and the ineffable, uncapturable secret of life. As a part of nearly every landscape, birds are frequently described in a way that likens their actions and transience to that of man: "There were sparrows; there were starlings; there were a number of doves, and one or two rooks, all occupied after their fashion. One finds a worm, another a snail. One flutters to a branch, another takes a little run on the turf. . . . Clouds pass, thin or thick. . . . The sun dial registers the hour in its usual cryptic way." Sasha compares Orlando to a "million-candled Christmas tree" because he looked "as if he were burning with his own radiance, from a lamp within." When happy, Orlando feels that the "birds sang; the torrents rushed"; when bewildered, she thinks of herself as "a feather blown by the gale." Shelmerdine's name awakens in Orlando's mind images of "the steel blue gleam of rook's wings, the hoarse laughter of their caws, and the snake-like twisting descent of their feathers in a silver pool."

The delineation of the inner life of the individual in *Orlando* also draws attention to the ephemeral and the flowing. In addition to emphasizing the "extraordinary discrepancy between time on the clock and time in the mind," Mrs. Woolf makes clear that the comforting objectivity and regularity of historical and clock time are almost irrelevent in view of the individual's greater dependence upon his subjective sense of time. Moreover, in a passage describing this "extraordinary discrepancy," she refers to the mortality of animals and plants and, by inference, to the dissolution of man's mind, the vital recorder of human time: "But time . . . though it makes animals and vegetables bloom and fade with amazing punctuality has no such simple effect upon the mind of man. . . . An hour once it lodges in the queer element of the human spirit, may be stretched to fifty or a hundred times its clock length; on the other hand, an hour may be accurately represented on the timepiece of the mind by one second." In its subjective reaction to temporal reality the mind comprehends time as a continuous flow. The chaotic, fleeting, impalpable quality of mental life is demonstrated in several passages of Chapter Six in which Mrs. Woolf resorts to the stream-of-con-

sciousness technique for rendering Orlando's thoughts. Musing on her present status and personality, for example, Orlando thinks aloud: "What then? Who then. . . . Thirty-six, in a motor car; a woman. Yes, but a million other things as well. A snob am I? The garter in the hall? The leopards? My ancestors? Proud of them? Yes, greedy, luxurious, vicious? Am I?" For Mrs. Woolf, this sense of flow is so much the normal state of the mind that she condemns experiences which make consciousness discontinuous. She comments, as does E. M. Forster in *Howards End,* upon the unassimilable quality of rapid travel: "After twenty minutes [of traveling] the body and mind were like scraps of torn paper tumbling from a sack and, indeed, the process of motoring fast out of London so much resembles the chopping up small of body and mind, which precedes unconsciousness and perhaps death itself that it is an open question in what sense Orlando can be said to have existed at the present moment."

This focusing of attention upon details of flow, change, and transience is inevitably accompanied by explicit statements about and reactions to the transitoriness of human life. Mrs. Woolf's comment upon Orlando's philandering during the Elizabethan Age, for example, emphasizes not only the way *mores* alter with time but also the unalterable fact of human mortality: "Are we to blame him? The Age was the Elizabethan; their morals were not ours, nor their poets, nor their vegetables even. Everything was different. . . . The poets sang beautifully how roses fade and petals fall . . . and what the poets said in rhyme, the young translated into practice. Girls were roses and their seasons were as short as the flowers'. Plucked they must be before nightfull; for the day was brief and the day was all." On several occasions Orlando is overwhelmed by a morbid realization of death's inexorableness. Even when happy in the company of Sasha, he is likely to be overcome with melancholy and "fling himself face downward on the ice and look into the frozen water and think of death." Watching a performance of *Othello,* Orlando thinks "Ruin and death . . . cover all. The life of man ends in the grave. Worms devour us." But the best illustration of the usual effect of transience upon Orlando's consciousness is found in the last section of the novel when she feels terror and panic on several occasions because of her awareness of the present moment. Orlando's reactions on these occasions would seem absurd had not the novel's stress on transitoriness made understandable her fear that "every time the gulf of time gaped and let a second through some unknown danger might come with it."

In conflict with all these reminders of "brevity" are the forces which contribute to "diuturnity." "Diuturnity," of course, does not mean the eternal posited by orthodox Christianity, for the novel makes no claim for such an escape from time—one feels that Mrs. Woolf, like Orlando, believes in "no immortality." *Orlando* does imply, however, that there are forces in the mind and certain perspectives that can temporarily free the individual from the tyranny of time. Surely one of the forces that resist time's flow is the human memory: Mrs. Woolf's delineation of Orlando's consciousness shows it to be compounded of sense impressions, emotions, and recollections and suggests that the mind's ability to recall the past is a mode of escaping the onrush of the present manner. Speculating about love, for example, Orlando finds his thoughts so linked with memories of Sasha that, for him, love is "all ambered over with snow and winter; with log fires burning, with Russian women, gold swords, and the bark of stags. . . . Every single thing, once he tried to dislodge it from its place in his mind, he found thus cumbered with other matter like the lump of glass which after a year at the bottom of the sea, is grown over with bones and dragonflies, and coins and the tresses of drowned women." Armed with memory, the individual is able to deal with the present moment so that it need not create a "violent disruption" in his consciousness. But memory is unfortunately an uncertain ally. By enveloping objects in the present with associations, memory can produce a state of confusion in which "nothing is any longer one thing"; indeed, when the associations invoke powerful emotions, the present may be obliterated completely by the past. The more successful "practitioners of the art of life" are able, Mrs. Woolf implies, to avoid such extreme flights from the present as Orlando takes when a "whiff of scent" reminds her of Sasha's treachery. Memory, furthermore, has its limitations in the individual's struggle against time because it is so uncontrollable: "Memory is the seamstress, and a capricious one at that. Memory runs her needle in and out, up and down, hither and thither. We know not what comes next, or what follows after."

However capricious it may be, memory, with its associational ties, gives proof that the individual has a self or identity which resists flux. Late in the novel Orlando observes that "she had been a gloomy boy, in love with death as boys are; and then she had been amorous and florid, and then she had been sprightly and satirical, and sometimes she had tried prose and sometimes she had tried the drama. Yet through all these changes she had remained, she reflected, fundamentally the same." Although fundamentally the same, Orlando is still not simply a single self. The variety of qualities contained within the individual can be seen, for example, in Orlando's use of three different names for Shelmerdine, each one reflecting a mood of her own. This multiplicity of selves is presented with comic exaggeration by Mrs. Woolf when she speculates that each individual has as many as two thousand and fifty-two selves which are "built-up, one on top of the other as plates are piled in a waiter's hand, have attachments elsewhere, sympathies; little constitutions and rights of their own . . . so that one will come only if it is raining, another in a room with green curtains, another when Mrs. Jones is not there." But Mrs. Woolf adds that among these disparate selves is a Key Self which has the power to amalgamate and control the other selves, though it itself is unresponsive to conscious, willed control. With the seemingly fortuitous addition of the Key Self, Orlando becomes a "real self," an integrated whole which "darkened and settled" and became silent since "when communication [among her various selves] is established, there is nothing more to be said." When integrated by the Key Self, Orlando is able to observe reality with greater satisfaction "as if her mind had become a fluid that flowed round things and enclosed them completely"; even more important, she finds the present moment less frightening,

"for she was now one and entire and presented, it may be, a larger surface to the shock of time."

The characteristics and power of the Key Self equate it with a quality or part of the mind that is described by a different metaphor in another passage in the novel. At one point when Orlando, "strung up by the present moment," is further distressed by seeing a carpenter's nailless thumb, she feels "faint for a moment, but in that moment's darkness, when her eyelids flickered, she was relieved of the pressure of the present." The shadow projected by her mind destroys the terror and confusion of the present and makes the moment tolerable and comprehensible. Mrs. Woolf later describes this shadow deepening into a pool at the back of Orlando's mind, "a pool where things dwell in darkness so deep that what they are we scarcely know. She now looked down into this pool or sea in which everything is reflected—and, indeed, some say that all our most violent passions and art and religion are the reflections which we see in this dark hollow at the back of the head when the visible world is obscured for the time." Under the influence of this inner vision, Orlando finds external reality altered so that "everything was partly something else and each gained an odd moving power from the union of itself so that with this mixture of truth and falsehood her mind became like a forest in which things moved: lights and shadows changed, and one thing became another. . . . She forgot the time." Clearly, then, the mind is a powerful antagonist to time, not only through the power of memory which gives the individual an identity or self, but through this organizing, creative function which alters or shapes external reality and is responsible for literature, religion, and our most violent passions.

By means of statement and imagery, the novel identifies certain perspectives or concerns which, because of their appeal to the inner "pool," enable the individual to escape from the domination of time. Of course, no one antidote for time is continuously effective. For example, nature, one of Orlando's sources of the timeless, is also a reminder of transitoriness since trees lose their leaves and birds their feathers; furthermore, nature occasionally seems at war with literature, another mode of timelessness. Nevertheless, as Orlando's reactions to the oak tree show, nature frequently provides him with a feeling of stability: "He loved, beneath all this summer transience, to feel the hard root of the earth's spine; for such he took the hard root of the oak tree to be; or, for image followed image, it was the back of a great horse that he was riding; or the deck of a tumbling ship. . . . He felt the need of something which he could attach his floating heart to. . . . To the oak tree he tied it and as he lay there gradually the flutter in and about him stilled itself." The image of the roots of the oak tree beneath the earth's surface suggests the image of the "pool" at the back of the Orlando's mind and makes clear the part of Orlando to which nature appeals. The roots, firm beneath all the "summer transience," provide the individual with an awareness of an impersonal perspective outside of human time. It is only from a point beside the oak tree (i. e., from a perspective influenced by nature) that Orlando, although able to see her elaborate manor house, itself a symbol of centuries of English history, is able to accept the argument of the old gypsy, Rustum, about the insignificance of possessions, family, and race.

On two occasions in the novel nature not only dispels Orlando's fear of death but helps to convert her sense of brevity into a feeling of extreme joy. In one instance, Orlando, while walking over the moor, watches a feather fall into a mysterious silver pool and suddenly feels a strange exultation and a desire for the forgetfulness of death and a merging with nature. She senses the same ecstasy on another occasion when sailing a penny steamer in the Serpentine. Identifying the toy boat with her husband's brig, she agonizes when a "white crest with a thousand deaths arched over it"; when the boat rights itself and reappears, she is ecstatic. She suddenly decides that "it is not articles by Nick Greene on John Donne nor eight-hour bells nor covenants nor factory acts that matter; it's something useless, sudden, violent; something that costs a life; red, purple; a spirit; a splash; like those hyacinths (she was passing a fine bed of them); free from taint, dependence, soilure of humanity or care of one's kind; something rash, ridiculous, 'like my hyacinth, husband I mean, Bonthrop: that's what it is—a toy boat on the Serpentine, it's ecstasy—ecstasy'." In both instances the "pool" imagery relates these exultant moments to a particular part of Orlando's mind. The reason for this feeling of ecstasy and for Orlando's love of nature is suggested by the phrase "a splash; like those hyacinths," which recalls the Greek myth of Hyacinthus, and by Orlando's slip of the tongue, "my hyacinth, husband I mean, Bonthrop," which identifies Shelmerdine with the Greek youth and the flower. By these details Mrs. Woolf implies that Orlando, for the moment, finds nothing terrifying in a death which promises a metamorphosis like that of Hyacinthus into the beauty of nature. Both the Greek myth and the annual rebirth of the flower argue for a continuity in nature which Orlando has sensed as the oak tree's roots lying beneath the summer transience. When Orlando is powerfully moved by the beauty of nature or strongly desires to escape the temporal, egocentric limitations of self, the prospect of a union with nature after death is not merely a consolation; it can be conducive to an ecstasy comparable to that she experiences when she is reunited with Shelmerdine after a long separation.

Literature, which promises immortality for the creator and a timeless or universal point of view for the reader, is quickly seized upon by Orlando as a mode of escaping time. His penchant for writing is strengthened when he contrasts the fleeting fame achieved by his ancestors through their military exploits with the immortality of Sir Thomas Browne and his works. The reason for the instinctive appeal which literature has for Orlando is suggested by the imagery which relates it to the inner "pool" by which the individual conquers time. One of the images that continually recur to Orlando is that of a man, probably Shakespeare, whom she saw writing at a table; she imagines him as "a man who sees ogres, satyrs, perhaps the depths of the sea." The power of literature to allay distress is seen when Orlando, returning from Turkey, is overcome with memories of Sasha, thoughts of her own change in sex, and apprehension about the freedom she is giving up. Suddenly the image of Shakespeare appears to

her and spreads, "like the risen moon on turbulent waters, a sheet of silver calm"; when she recalls her own poem, "The Oak Tree," her fears vanish completely. Because of the timeless perspective both literature and nature provide, it is appropriate that Orlando's most successful poem should deal with nature. The similarities between literature and nature are seen in the following passage in which literature is described as an expression of nature's appeal to the inner "pool" of the mind: "Was not writing poetry a secret transaction, a voice answering a voice? . . . What could have been more secret, she thought, more slow, and like the intercourse of lovers, than the stammering answer [her poem] she had made all these years to the old crooning song of the woods, and the farms and the brown horses?"

Orlando finds, however, that literature and nature are incapable of satisfying all the needs of the individual. Despite the disparity between poetry and the personality of a poet like Nick Greene, Orlando needs someone with whom she can talk about books and her own poetry; despite the ludicrousness of the Archduke Harry as a lover, she occasionally feels the need for "life and a lover," and despite the fact that her reaction to society is usually one of disgust, she feels at times a need for the company of other people. The most successful demonstration of the "timeless" value in human relationships is shown by Orlando's relationship with Shelmerdine. Their relationship illuminates Mrs. Woolf's ideas of androgyny, her belief that "different though the sexes are, they intermix. In every human being a vacillation from one sex to the other takes place." (This concept is shown in comic exaggeration by Orlando's change of sex in the middle of the novel.) Both Orlando and Shelmerdine are clearly androgynous, and the harmony between them seems based upon the ability conferred by this trait to understand the opposite sex intuitively. (Some hints of the androgynous basis between lovers is seen in Orlando's early uncertainty about Sasha's sex and in Orlando's burlesque affair with the Archduchess-duke Harriet-Harry.) The correspondence between Shelmerdine's actual career and Orlando's boyish dreams suggests that in Shelmerdine Orlando has found a lover whose overt masculine traits match her own submerged masculinity. Marriage to Shelmerdine makes it possible for Orlando to resist the Victorian efforts to suppress the independence of women, and it also enables her to enjoy a union somewhat like that effected within herself by the addition of the Key Self. The importance and power of the relationship between male and female is dramatized by the comic but climactically situated final reunion between Orlando and Shelmerdine; on this occasion, Orlando again achieved a perspective that enables her to convert her fear of the "cold breeze of the present" into a feeling of ecstasy.

This analysis of the conflict between the ephemeral and the timeless has still to explain fully the profound appeal that such antagonists to time as nature, literature, and love have for the inner "pool" of the mind. The basis for this appeal can be seen in those episodes in which a power in the mind succeeds in forcing Orlando to lose consciousness at moments of great inner turmoil. The force which causes Orlando to faint when she sees Sasha in the arms of the Russian sailor operates more powerfully to produce his seven-day sleep when Sasha deserts him. Although offered ironically as rhetorical questions because of the improbability of this episode, Mrs. Woolf's comments about Orlando's sleep are illuminating:

> But if sleep it was, of what nature . . . are such sleeps as these? Are they remedial measures—trances in which the most galling memories, events that seem likely to cripple life for ever, are brushed with a dark wing which rubs their harshness off and gilds them, even the ugliest and basest, with a lustre, an incandescence? Has the finger of death to be laid on the tumult of life from time to time lest it rend us asunder? Are we so made that we have to take death in small doses or we could not go on with the business of living? And then what strange powers are those that penetrate our most secret ways and change our most treasured possessions without our willing it?

These questions imply that among the diverse traits of the dark inner "pool" is a powerful instinct for death which is capable of exerting itself whenever the present moment is fraught with excessive emotional pain for the individual. In some cases this force is powerful enough to destroy consciousness; in other instances it may merely alter the individual's view of reality so that the experience becomes tolerable. The desire for death within the mind of the individual accounts in part for the appeal of the timeless, impersonal perspectives offered by nature, literature, and love.

An excerpt from *A Writer's Diary*

"I shall let myself dash this in for a week"—I have done nothing, nothing, nothing else for a fortnight; and am launched somewhat furtively but with all the more passion upon *Orlando:* **a Biography.** It is to be a small book and written by Christmas. . . . I walk making up phrases; sit, contriving scenes; am in short in the thick of the greatest rapture known to me; from which I have kept myself since last February, or earlier. Talk of planning a book, or waiting for an idea! Then one came in a rush. . . . I had very little idea what the story was to be about. But the relief of turning my mind that way was such that I felt happier than for months; as if put in the sun, or laid on a cushion; and after two days entirely gave up my time chart and abandoned myself to the pure delight of this farce; which I enjoy as much as I've ever enjoyed anything; and have written myself into half a headache and had to come to a halt, like a tired horse, and take a little sleeping draught last night. . . . I am writing *Orlando* half in a mock style very clear and plain, so that people will understand every word. But the balance between truth and fantasy must be careful. It is based on Vita, Violet Trefusis, Lord Lascelles, Knole, etc.

Virginia Woolf, in a diary entry of October 22, 1927, in her A Writer's Diary: Being Extracts from the Diary of Virginia Woolf, *edited by Leonard Woolf, 1953. Reprint by Harcourt Brace Jovanovich, 1954.*

This explanation of the way in which the individual's fear of death is assuaged by an unconscious desire for death clarifies Mrs. Woolf's statement about the manner in which "our unfortunate numbskulls" are dominated by the conflicting forces of brevity and diuturnity.

Jean Guiguet   (essay date 1962)

SOURCE: *Virginia Woolf and Her Works,* translated by Jean Stewart, Hogarth Press, 1965, 488 p.

[*In the following excerpt, Guiguet draws on Woolf's diary entries to examine her intentions in writing* Orlando *and to assess the significance of the novel to her literary development.*]

On December 20, 1927, two and a half months after she has started on *Orlando,* the first half of which has already been drafted, Virginia Woolf writes in the Diary:

> How extraordinarily unwilled by me but potent in its own right, by the way, *Orlando* was! as if it shoved everything aside to come into existence. Yet I see looking back just now to March that it is almost exactly in spirit, though not in actual facts, the book I planned then as an escapade; the spirit to be satiric, the structure wild. Precisely.

One must note in this passage the three characteristics of *Orlando* (mentioned moreover in various terms in almost every paragraph of the Diary that refers to it) which yield the whole secret of that work, disconcerting enough in other respects and full of pitfalls for an unwary reader. First and foremost, it is a book which was "unwilled"; it willed itself. Although the element of artifice and tension in Virginia Woolf's novels has often been exaggerated or misinterpreted, it is difficult to deny it entirely. *Orlando,* on the contrary, is essentially spontaneous. But here again one must not confound spontaneity with externality, as the author herself frequently invites us to do. The externality is entirely superficial, it lies in the manner not in the matter; it is a refusal to go deep, which is not the same thing as a rejection of depth. *Orlando* is spontaneous, in so far as it imposed itself upon her, its necessity lay within itself, that is to say it was not the fruit of a deliberate purpose or an idea, but an inevitable gesture, an urgent need of the whole being.

One might refer here to that "summa" which Virginia Woolf, like all great artists, constantly dreamed of writing, from *Mrs Dalloway* to *Between the Acts.*

Yet it is not true to say that the author has poured all her experience into it, but rather that all her experience underlies it and sometimes comes to the surface. We can see here a reversal of the creative process which demands a reversal of the method of interpretation. Instead of seeking in this work the final stage of a train of thought, the result of a working out process, which should be if not a conclusion at least the ultimate term of a pursuit, we should see in it the immediate data, in their simplest form, the fund of ideas, interests and preoccupations which constitute the manifold starting-points for those explorations in depth, her other novels.

As a joke Virginia Woolf labelled *Orlando* a "biography". Among those composite titles with which she was always trying to define her books, when she felt them overflowing the frame-work of the novel, perhaps the one that best suits *Orlando* is, as we shall see, "Essay-novel". For the time being we might suggest "Conversation piece" or "In confidence". Indeed, through that kind of spontaneity I have defined, these three hundred pages are one long rambling discussion in which the author confides in us, now inspired by some chance remark, now in a long development where fanciful wit does not preclude seriousness, now with an exaggeration which is sometimes playful, sometimes provocative, sometimes ironical, sometimes a hypothesis and sometimes a disguise for sincerity, and sometimes all these together. In this respect *Orlando* offers a wealth of revelations—and it is also extremely difficult and risky to make use of in this respect. Its tone requires a constantly alert attention. After all it is only a book, but we have to re-create in it the author's total presence: the inflexion of the voice, the liveliness of the eyes, and even the gestured and attitude of the whole body. We need to confirm every sentence, almost every word, with some sign that would guarantee its "truth". A book can only be read that way—if "reading" is the right word—if one is intimately acquainted with its author. And even considering that Leonard Woolf himself took *Orlando* "more seriously than [she] had expected"—should one add, than she took it herself? —I would go so far as to say that only the person to whom it was dedicated, for whom, actually, it was written—Vita Sackville-West—can solve the riddle of it. She was its point of departure: in her alone it reaches its destination. For her it has its meaning; for us it offers only signs. Let us admit straight away that this is certainly a weakness, the chief weakness of *Orlando.* If its author, for all her usual lucidity, never discovered this clearly, she none the less felt and expressed it indirectly. In the first place, it is "a writer's holiday"—a release for the artist who, essentially, speaks to the general public—and for this Virginia Woolf felt some reluctance before she finally yielded to it. Then the terms "farce", "joke" recur constantly in her descriptions of the book. But while farces and jokes are never purely such, and this is certainly the case with *Orlando,* they are always to some extent a closed book to the uninitiated.

However, although this deep seated hermetic quality makes any systematic interpretation dubious and therefore invalid, the novel has characteristics which ensure for it an honourable, if a rather special, place among the author's works. These are the two aspects stressed in the passage quoted above: the spirit of satire, whose verve, combined with the lively pace of the story and the brio of the fantasy, carries the reader along through the paths of history and literature and the mazes of the human soul, all so entangled and at the same time so vigorously drawn that he is continually losing his way and then finding it again, without really being sure of anything. These two traits, satire and fantasy, fun and freedom, comprise the surface but also the whole bearing of the book; they confer on it that vigour and that somewhat turbulent charm that distinguish it from the other novels and yet cannot be dismissed as mere accident, artifice or caprice. Dense and polyvalent beneath the clarity and apparent lightness of its style, *Orlando* is, both in detail and taken as a whole, more ambiguous and elusive than its hero-heroine. Its complexity can best be suggested by applying to it those lines with which Virginia Woolf tries to prepare a reader for the mysteries of another fantasy which, beneath obvious dissimilarities, is related to her own by manifold and close links:

> In reading *The Faery Queen* the first thing, we said, was that the mind has different layers. It brings one into play and then another. The desire of the eye, the desire of the body, desires for rhythm, movement, the desire for adventure— each is gratified. And this gratification depends upon the poet's own mobility. He is alive in all his parts. He scarcely seems to prefer one to another.

From what we have just said, it is easy to imagine that, in this supposed "Defoe narrative", the essentially picaresque story which the author pretends—without deceiving herself or anyone else—to tell without allowing herself to be distracted from her purpose, is only a pretext and an occasion.

Orlando, born of a noble and illustrious family about 1570, is 16 years old on the first page; in his dress, his actions, his feeling and thoughts he represents the perfect type of those "strange Elizabethans" who yet "had a face like ours". His biographer follows him up to his thirty-sixth year, that is to say until 1928. Thus crudely reported, the fact that the centuries sit as lightly on the hero as the decades may cause some surprise. But when we follow him from the court of Elizabeth to that of James I, from the banks of the Thames to the shores of the Bosphorus, from a love affair with Sasha, the passionate Muscovite lady, to marriage with the romantic adventurer and, eventually, highly modern aviator, Marmaduke Bonthrop Shelmerdine—for in the mean-time Orlando has changed sex—we realise, in fact, that time has impaired neither his youth nor his beauty nor his zest for life. All that one can say is that this hero-heroine takes part in the life of each century with an admirable flexibility and openmindedness: that is no doubt the secret of his perpetual youth; violent and passionate in the Elizabethan atmosphere, under James I he blossoms forth at court and then, in disgrace, retires to his estate to brood like Hamlet or Sir Thomas Browne; in Turkey he is more Turkish than the Turks; and when he, or rather she returns to the London of Addison, Dryden and Pope, the interest she takes in these figures is fully equal to that taken by other people of her class. Just as the young man Orlando frequented the court when this was the only place where life seemed worth living, so the young woman Orlando frequents salons under Queen Anne, still in pursuit of the same treasure—life—which at that time is only to be found there. Under Victoria, how can she live? By putting on a large number of petticoats and, eventually, getting married: let us add, "by loving nature, and being no satirist, cynic or psychologist". Luckily this is only a brief interlude: the twentieth century arrives and Orlando collects her thoughts before venturing at last into the maelstrom of trains, cars, shops and society lunches; and she asserts her unity and her continuity in a last symbolic gesture by publishing *The Oak Tree,* a poem on which she has been working since her Elizabethan adolescence.

It is pointless to dwell on the fantastic character of the hero and the story. It can only disconcert us if we forget that we have here simultaneously a biography, a narrative *à la* Defoe, contemporary memoirs, a satire, and finally, a fantasy or joke in which the author's verve, imagination and humour are given free rein without any further aim than the fun of writing. Thus *Orlando* cannot be confined within any of the genres in which it participates, and whatever certain critics may say we have to recognize it as a novel of the same type, if not in the same vein, as the rest of Virginia Woolf's novels. Like them, it rejects literary conventions, and like them it seeks, with apparent casualness but in all sincerity, to grasp the essence of a fluid and complex reality which our habits of speech, confused with our habits of thought, have unduly solidified and simplified. And this is because this search is Virginia Woolf's sole problem and because even in fun, even when playing truant, she cannot give it up. Indeed, *Orlando* provides the soundest possible argument against those who accuse Virginia Woolf of artificiality and accuse her of wearing herself out in Byzantine refinements of form and technique at the expense of the real and living content of her work. Even when she casts off all concern for form and technique indeed when she makes fun of them in herself as in others, we see that her object remains the same, and the fundamental subject of her book remains the same; which allows one to assert that both of these represent the essence of her being, the direction of her entire inner life, and not simply the superficial curiosity of a sterile intellectual.

Orlando is a biography in so far as the hero's life is consubstantial with history; in other ways it is no more of one than any novel in which a historical character plays a leading part. The Preface leaves no doubt about the element of parody in the work, and moreover the so-called biographer loses no opportunity of pointing out the obstacles that frustrate her scholarship and the pitfalls that ensnare her art. Indeed, she takes a mischievous delight in displaying and exploiting the weaknesses of that literary genre which, being neither art nor science, is only a technique, as she explains more seriously elsewhere. The destruction of some essential documents, the dubious character of certain others, the respect for propriety, and even more farfetched reasons—such as the simple fact that Orlando starts to think—are constantly referred to by the author as excuses for her lacunae, her flights of fancy, her digressions, and even the blank spaces which, in imitation of Sterne, she leaves us free to fill as we choose. And in fact *Orlando* reminds one of *Tristram Shandy* rather than of *Robinson Crusoe* or *Moll Flanders*. It is not a story any more than a biography. That "on with the story" with which Virginia Woolf summed up the brisk movement of *Moll Flanders* recurs constantly, either in these very terms or disguised in other forms; but far from preventing interruptions, it merely closes them. If certain episodes, particularly at the beginning when her enthusiasm was overflowing and her pen racing along, flow with the same swift rhythm as the action described, the movement in general comes from elsewhere, being less a consequence of the adventure than a characteristic of the hero. In fact, it is not

so much the story as the protagonist that reminds us of Defoe, and one might say of Orlando what Virginia Woolf said of Moll Flanders: ". . . life delights her, and a heroine who lives has us all in tow."

Another project of the author was to write the memoirs of her contemporaries. The Diary even specifies certain names; the keys are there, but are we therefore entitled to play the parlour game they suggest? The sight of the manifold changes undergone by the principal character is discouraging. Did the author even follow up her original intention? Before starting the book she talks about Lytton (Strachey), Roger (Fry), Duncan (Grant), Clive (Bell), Adrian (Stephen); and since none of these lives is "related", as promised in the same passage, one may assume that this aspect was discarded. A fortnight after the book was begun—that is to say, at most, when she was finishing the first chapter—Virginia Woolf notes that "it is based on Vita, Violet Trefusis, Lord Lascelles, Knole etc."

"Based on" is already vaguer than the biographical narratives announced a month previously. The fact that subsequently we do not read of any names in connection with her remarks about Orlando, may be due to judicious cutting by Leonard Woolf. I believe, however, that it can be explained simply by a change of orientation in the book. The fantasy which, partly to make fun of History, had plunged the author's friend into remote historic distances, was now caught up in the trammels of its own artifice; History had taken its revenge by asserting its authority, and Nick Greene and Pope had ousted from the stage the friends whom Virginia Woolf had thought of introducing on to it. Nick Greene, indeed, appears as a typically twentieth-century figure, and "this gentleman, so neat, so portly, so prosperous", with such definite ideas about literature, is surely some influential critic from the author's circle. But even admitting that this may be so, this portrait which may have amused the Woolfs and their friends by reference to its original has enough comic virtue as an unnamed type to render unnecessary any curiosity about the model that inspired it. Even if he owes to that model his way of pronouncing "Glory"—Glawr—and other characteristics, his fictional identity with the Nick Greene of the second chapter is far more important that his actual status. The hunt for keys may have a historic interest and may sometimes shed light on the process of literary creation; in the case of *Orlando* it is doubtful whether it presents either advantage, and even whether the data for the sport exist. Later, when studying *Orlando* as a fantasy, I shall examine the relations between reality and the imaginary world, of which the problem of keys, rightly understood, is only one particular aspect. For the moment I must conclude that, starting from the project of writing the memoirs of her contemporaries, Virginia Woolf quickly dropped this scheme in favour of what one might subtitle "the memory of contemporaries". And the pun reveals the whole distance between a subject which, all things considered, was alien to the author, since memoirs belong to the order of facts and actions, and an essentially Woolfian subject. But before approaching the content of the book, let us finish examining the form under which it is disguised.

Satire and fantasy, inseparable, since they are derived from one another, are the dominant features of *Orlando.* They define the humour which gave rise and constant sustenance to this "half laughing, half serious" work. In that passage written in March 1927, to which the author refers, half-way through her task, to observe the identity of her achievement with her conception, we read: "Satire is to be the main note—satire and wildness. . . . My own lyric vein is to be satirised. Everything mocked." We have already seen that the story-teller's art and that of the biographer are imitated only to be parodied. Yet considering that Virginia Woolf believes neither in the continuity of a story, nor in the unity of a personality circumscribed in space and time, a postulate essential to the biographer, there is nothing surprising about her mockery. But she is too lucid and too intelligent to stop short at irony; she dares to be humorous. Her habitual state of tension may make us forget her capacity for this amused detachment; yet all her favourite heroines, from Mrs Ambrose to Mrs Ramsay, have had this gift, relieving their essential seriousness. If Lord Orlando is somewhat lacking in it—no doubt because it is rarely a masculine virtue—Orlando has enough of it to reduce her impulses of enthusiasm and passion to their right proportions. But it is above all the story-teller's humour that compels our attention. It is shown throughout in the mischievous glance that deflates fine sentiments, diminishes grand gestures, trips up a flight of eloquence with an aside, breaks the lyrical flow of a description with an incongruous detail or simply a dissonant word. At every line the writer makes fun of writing, she parodies herself page after page, indicts her own habits—her use of symbols, her exaggerated concern with detail and her excess of imagination, her fondness for interior analysis and her love of words. Even traits which are characteristic of her as a person rather than as a writer are not spared: her changing moods, her alternate fits of self-confidence, enthusiasm and discouragement, the way she oscillates between love of society and love of solitude, between zest for life and despair, between a taste for action and a passion for literature and the contemplative life, even the conflict between her masculine and feminine sides. The manifold oppositions of her nature are an inexhaustible store-house: set side by side, they prove mutually destructive by ridicule. This play of contrasts is one of the forms that fantasy takes in *Orlando*; the other is exaggeration. This pervades the book, in its totality as in its detail, in action as in speech, in its characters and in its objects. It might almost be set down in figures: Orlando's age is multiplied by ten, and everything, roughly, is in proportion. The list of furnishings for the great house with its 365 bedrooms is shorter than that which inspired it, in Vita Sackville-West's *Knole and the Sackvilles*: but the figures are inordinately swollen: the Spanish blankets are increased from two to fifty, and so are the chandeliers; the stools from three to sixty, the walnut-tree tables from two to sixty-seven, and so forth. The great frost in James I's reign, the mists of the Romantic period, the Victorian damp, Orlando's love affairs, his slumbers, Nick Greene's vanity and spite, the devastating effect of Pope's wit, Marmaduke's courage, are all enlarged to gigantic, extravagant proportions. One is inevitably reminded of Cervantes, Rabelais, Sterne, Swift; Virginia Woolf borrows from all these masters of the heroic-comic vein. But if the book has the charm and the defects of a pot-pourri, it possesses a twofold unity, external and internal, which fuses imitations and tones down artifice. Exaggeration cannot destroy its proportions; here things and places, time and events are on the same scale as the human beings involved with them. The expansion of a moment or the shrinking of centuries, the spreading panoramas and the spectacular transformations, the ephemeral love affairs and the enterprises that are part of history, all are so perfectly in keeping that fantasy takes on the look of reality—too much so, perhaps, so that one forgets and ceases to be astonished. And on the surface, the same voice is constantly heard, in a self-parody that sometimes seeks to parody others. The writing in *Orlando,* swift, easy and yet vigorous, remains—throughout all the vicissitudes of the subject—faithful to its spontaneity, to its playful tone, constantly obliterating the stroke it has just set down, asserting only to deny the moment after, creating and destroying its own creation in a rhythm which is perhaps the most profound expression of her whole personality ever given us by Virginia Woolf.

Orlando provides the soundest possible argument against those who accuse Virginia Woolf of artificiality and accuse her of wearing herself out in Byzantine refinements of form and technique at the expense of the real and living content of her work.

—*Jean Guiguet*

Yet if the style of Orlando, in the most general sense of the term, reproduces the essential personal style of Virginia Woolf, that way of being and acting that is displayed in every aspect and action of an individual, the teeming wealth of ideas, hinted at or exploited to the full, in the form of witty paradox or argument, transposed into images or embodied in dramatis personae, makes this book an authentic repository of the author's thought.

Orlando: courtier, diplomat, poet; Orlando: man, woman; three centuries, thirty years; the culture of a whole nation, the experience of an individual; a family tree, a single being; Orlando is either, or both, as you like. As you like it, not merely because Orlando was born in Shakespeare's day, but because the complexity of a personality is an elusive and incommunicable mystery to which there is no other answer. That is the essence of this book, which is everywhere in it and nowhere in particular; the versatility of the form and that of the hero, the fantastic train of events, the intermittence of the commentary. It is each of these elements and none of them in particular, for they all hold together to express a vision of a human being. And this vision is expressed both through the hero and through his story—which gives us the novel; and also through the digressions and asides that accompany it: which gives us the essay. And I have suggested essay-novel to characterise this book, for its two aspects are not simply juxtaposed, although it is easy to distinguish the limits of each; they react profoundly on one another; thought has stylized the novel, and the novel lends its fantasy to the essay. This explains, furthermore, apart from the other reasons that she may have suggested, the satisfaction that Virginia Woolf found in writing it: her intelligence and her sensibility found equal vent.

Already in *The Voyage Out,* the human personality was seen as overflowing the narrow bounds within which Hirst sought to confine it. What line could circumscribe the "two thousand and fifty-two" different personalities within each of us? And how can one follow or disentangle the "seventy-six" kinds of time "all ticking in the mind at once"? Here, humorously expressed, we recognize preoccupations with which the earlier novels had already made us familiar. The fantastic, changeable, ambiguous and irrational character of Orlando is merely the diversity that lies within each of us, given that intensification which is at the base of the novel.

The relations of this hero with people and things are disconcerting not only because they emanate sometimes from one self, sometimes from another, but also because they oscillate constantly between the behaviour dictated by the conventions (or as Virginia Woolf would say, the spirit of the time) and that to which his essential nature impels him. One may wonder, as with Mrs Dalloway, if he really is his superficial or his deeper self. And as with Clarissa, the answer is that he is neither one nor the other, but the fusion of both in a rhythm that makes him shift constantly from one to the other—or more simply still, that "he is".

[In *Orlando* the problem of time] provides both the structure of the book and part of its substance. It is approached now in the form that was characteristic of *Mrs Dalloway,* now in that with which Virginia Woolf had experimented in *To the Light-house.* Space, as well as time, is compressed within one individual's consciousness; and the inward eye that can look back through tens and hundreds of years has the same power of spanning space, from the English Channel to Snowdon, or calling forth the greenness of an English landscape on the arid slopes of Mount Athos, and vice versa. Faced with such confusion (a crossing of the lines) one asks, like Orlando: "What is appearance, what is reality amidst all this?" The riddle that haunts Orlando's mind, and his creator's, is the same as that for which the heroine of *The Voyage Out* had sought an answer. Here, the cruise is replaced by a dream-journey, but the same instinctive aspiration inspires this illusory quest, this pursuit of phantom figures—love, friendship, truth. And when all is said and done, "is this . . . what people call life?" And what is life? And does not this fruitless quest recur in each of Virginia Woolf's books? Surely it is the dominant aspect of her own being? The phantom, "the great fish who lives in the coral groves", the "wild goose", the impossible, inaccessible truth, seems to have been grasped by the end of the book, but its capture fails to elucidate its mystery. As in the earlier books, it is an incommunicable experience, the presence of a being wholly comprised within a name, a call,

a cry: "Rachel, Rachel!" "Clarissa!" "Mrs Ramsay!" and now "She!" And as the whole book has merely catalogued that disparate collection of "scraps of torn paper tumbling from a sack" that each of us is, without ever discovering "the Key self, which amalgamates and controls them all" the answer can only be another, final invitation to further search. Orlando's ecstasy brings us to the same point as Lily Briscoe's vision. Both leave us on the threshold across which no word can take us: yet if we can learn to see and to love, we may perhaps be granted our own "vision", our own revelation.

This central problem involves an infinity of others. Amongst those most closely associated with personality, we should consider memory, which, in Orlando's case, combines with heredity to make him transcend time and space; and above all, sexual ambiguity. Since the brief reference to Sapphism made on March 14, 1927, when Virginia Woolf was planning *The Fessamy Brides,* this aspect had gained considerable importance. Standing between the feminist preoccupations of *Night and Day* (1919) and the pamphlet *A Room of One's Own, Orlando* reveals the living substance that fed Virginia Woolf's feminism. If Orlando's bisexuality is due to the resemblance between Vita Sackville-West and the Hon. Edward Sackville, whose portrait by Cornelius Nuie serves as frontispiece to the original edition; if it is also due to certain characteristics of Vita herself, yet one may safely assert that it is chiefly due to the author's own dual nature. Without entering the field of biographical hypotheses, unconfirmed at the present time by any evidence, and restricting one-self to questions of character and temperament, it is undeniable that Virginia Woolf was compact of elements which an over-simplified conception, largely obsolete today but still prevalent in 1927, would have divided between the two sexes. And the whole of her dual nature gives weight to her assertion of human ambisexuality:

> Different though the sexes are, they intermix. In every human being a vacillation from one sex to the other takes place, and often it is only the clothes that keep the male or female likeness, while underneath the sex is the very opposite of what it is above.

The energy and vitality of the hero-heroine suffice, with the aid of the author's verve, to solve the difficulties to which this ambiguity gives rise. In this Orlando really plays the role of a hero, the creator of an attitude. He proves and affirms by being and living. *A Room of One's Own,* and later, *Three Guineas* deal with the problem from a logical point of view without being any more convincing.

The difficulty of communicating with another person and of understanding human beings is only a direct consequence of the complexity of the individual. The gulf seems deepened, at times, by differences which extend beyond the individuals themselves and spring from a whole network of circumstances which can be summed up by the word "culture". Such is the case in Orlando's relations with Sasha, the Russian girl, or with the Greek gipsies, but in fact he is equally remote from Nick Greene, whether in his seventeenth- or his twentieth-century form, or from the Archduke.

A special sort of communication, but one which assumes capital importance both for the poet-hero and still more for his biographer-novelist, is the problem of literary expression. The vicissitudes of inspiration, the pitfalls of language, those of imitation, the influence of the period, the bondage of technique, are so many aspects of literary activity which, although the tone and treatment are playful, are none the less described with a penetration and authenticity which are reinforced by many parallel passages in the Diary. We may note, on the one hand, the conclusion that emerges from Orlando's literary experience and, on the other, that which emanates from the book itself, and which is expressly formulated. The first brings out the identity of motive between artistic creation and action: both are directed towards reality, they are the two convergent ways taken alternately by the human being in his pursuit of an inexpressible and inaccessible truth. When he suffers a setback on one path, Orlando starts off along the other. This is surely the same rhythmical alternation we noticed in Virginia Woolf herself. If the motives are identical, so too are the results. Action leaves us disappointed and dissatisfied; and the paths of art do not lead us to the secret that we are seeking:

> Having asked then of man and of bird and the insects, for fish, men tell us, who have lived in green caves, solitary for years to hear them speak, never, never say, and so perhaps know what life is—having asked them all and grown no wiser, but only older and colder (for did we not pray once in a way to wrap up in a book something so hard, so rare, one could swear it was life's meaning?) back we must go and say straight out to the reader who waits a-tiptoe to hear what life is—alas, we don't know.

Nevertheless, disappointment and frustration do not mean despair; they are the condition of life itself, its torment but also its driving impulse.

Knowledge, revelation, communication can only be attained in silence. And we remember both that book of silence that Hewett in *The Voyage Out* wanted to write, and Mrs Ramsay's longing "to be silent, to be alone . . ."

Every age, in its own way, tries to *be* and to formulate its being. The masterly portrayals of successive periods in *Orlando* express the success and failure of these attempts. Shakespeare and Sir Thomas Browne, Pope, Addison and Swift survive not through what they found but because they sought, and because we follow their footsteps on man's eternal quest. We should note in passing the almost total omission of the writers of the nineteenth century, very characteristic of Virginia Woolf's dislike of this period, which in her view was not moved by human anxiety and did not "seek".

One evident consequence of this conception of literary creation is the inadequacy of that criticism which distributes praise and blame in accordance with some textbook rules, and even more of that which studies the author rather than his work. If we can recognize, in the figure of Nick Greene, the attitude of some of Virginia Woolf's detractors, yet her satire goes far beyond these. Basically criticism and all other subsidiary aspects of literature, from the patronage of former days to modern commercialization, including literary fame and that apparently ineluctable phase, the public fate of the printed work, are unrelated to art. For the work of art is a profoundly personal gesture, at most "a secret transaction, a voice answering a voice".

If the relations between one human being and another, and those more special relations between an artist and his public, are neither easy nor satisfying, how much less so are social relations in general. If Orlando, like Virginia Woolf, was for a while seduced by fashionable life, like her he plumbed its emptiness; the evening endured at Lady R.'s bears a curious likeness to the luncheon party described by the author in her diary, November 30, 1927.

Thus, despite Orlando's numerous love affairs and the crowds with which he mingles, loneliness is his lot. Not the solitude in which he sometimes chooses to withdraw and which gives him the opportunity to try out those great themes beloved of Virginia Woolf, the Sea, the Air, the Forest, the Earth, in a vein of parody to be sure, yet not without a secret enjoyment—but the basic loneliness of the Outsider. I may be accused of unjustifiably and anachronistically annexing Virginia Woolf for Existentialism. And yet the absurd, atomized world into which she plunges her hero and to which he cannot give any unity but his own, without even being certain of his own unity, is singularly akin to that of Camus.

I have tried to elucidate this book which, under a style that is "very clear and plain, so that people will understand every word" has indubitably a hidden meaning, because it is at the same time a book, a mask and a confidential message, and one is never quite sure with which of the three one is dealing. However, whereas I have frequently pointed out its connection with the author's personal experience, and even insisted on the hero's kinship with his creator, there remains one point on which a scrupulous reader is entitled to demand enlightenment: the faithfulness of the portrait to its model. Even if the fantastic nature of the treatment and the general trend of modern art may lessen the importance of this problem, they cannot wholly deprive it of meaning.

In an earlier section I reported the little that is known about the friendship between Virginia Woolf and Vita Sackville-West. It scarcely enables one to establish any deeper connection between the novel and reality. Vita's books should not be neglected: *Knole and the Sackvilles,* already mentioned, from which Virginia Woolf borrowed certain details, and the poem *The Land,* a few lines of which are quoted as being part of Orlando's *The Oak Tree.* And it should also be mentioned that certain other characters may, from time to time, have come between the painter and her model, mingling their features with the latter's. Sir John Harington for instance, whom Lytton Strachey sketches in a few pages; a great favourite with the ladies, who welcomed Queen Elizabeth for a day in that vast Somerset manor to which periodically, when out of the royal favour, he would retire to seek consolation with his dog and to translate Ariosto's *Orlando Furioso.* But these are merely superficial elements. We are forced by our ignorance of the facts to return to the work itself. Beneath the ideological pessimism we discovered in it, it is a paean to life, it speaks of joy. And this joy is not only derived from the artist's sense of deliverance, as she relaxes in easy creativity; it is a feeling that springs from a deeper source; it is the whole of that "singularly happy autumn" of 1927. In the whole of the Diary, this is the only time we find so wholly unclouded a statement, such a completely expansive note. Three months spent writing *Orlando,* living *Orlando,* living in him—in her. And one may venture the hypothesis that Virginia Woolf found in her model, and put into her book, not only herself, as we have seen, but her complement: all that was lacking in herself, and to which she aspired—vigour and robustness, a sort of unselfconsciousness and a sort of greatness which her fragility and introspectiveness forbade her. Whereas "twilight and firelight were her own illumination" she gave Orlando a solar brilliance. She loved Vita for all that they had in common, she admired her for the qualities she would have liked to have; she made Vita her hero-heroine, which was one way of fulfilling herself through her friend. If, as is likely, Vita Sackville-West was thinking of *Orlando* when she defined Virginia's penetration and the use she made of it for her art, this passage confirms the truthfulness of the portrait, unaffected by the embellishments of fancy and the glow of inward vision:

> She could also create fabulous tapestries out of her peculiar vision of her friends, but at the same time, I always thought her genius led her by short cuts to some essential point which everybody else had missed. She did not walk there: she sprang.

How, then, are we to judge this book, so intimate and yet so external? If we remain on the purely literary plane we shall see nothing but the artifice, the "fabulous tapestries". And *Orlando,* considered thus, is too contrived a book. If the author follows her whim, its wayward wanderings are too cunningly traced, and it seems deliberately devised to mystify the reader, even though it frequently instructs while it entertains him. In general, when *Orlando* first appeared, critics did not go below the surface of the book. Indulgent or sarcastic, they tempered their disapproval by praising either its satire or its fantasy.

Others, at a later date, considering it in its proper perspective, in relation to the rest of her work, have probed its ideological implications, stressing this or that according to their own temperament and thus reaching what might be called the middle strata of the work. Thus they have admitted its serious significance and a certain value which their predecessors had denied it. One might feel justified in going no further, by Virginia Woolf's own comments. Once she had got the book out of her system, her own judgment, as almost always, anticipates with great soundness that of her critics:

> . . . I think it lacks the sort of hammering I should have given it if I had taken longer; is too freakish and unequal, very brilliant now and then. As for the effect of the whole, that I can't judge. Not, I think, "important" among my works.

This last phrase is a revealing one; it stresses the particular, unique character of *Orlando,* while the inverted commas limit the sense of the word *important.* If *Orlando* is thus diminished, not to say condemned as a "work", it may perhaps have "importance" of another sort—that which I have attempted to bring out, which is only to be discovered by probing below the middle strata. But in that case it must be admitted that *Orlando* becomes an esoteric work which can only yield its whole secret to a handful of initiates. Without claiming to be one of these, I have approached it with all the circumspection required by an obscure document, lacking the context of notes, appendices and references which would have shed full light on it.

Reproaching herself for the futility of *Orlando,* the author seems to forget that she has been on holiday. Or was it because Virginia Woolf never took a holiday? Already on November 20, 1927, in the middle of that marvellous period of unconstrained writing, she asks herself: "Do I learn anything?" For the time being she experiences only the delight of this unbridled style, and she promises herself to hand over her pen to the artist anxiously whispering over her shoulder, who must shape all this random chatter into a work of art. We have just seen that Virginia Woolf was later to consider this recasting as hastily and inadequately done. In any case, not until a year later does she reply to the question put by her more exacting self: "*Orlando* taught me how to write a direct sentence; taught me continuity and narrative and how to keep the realities at bay." This formal gain, however, fails to satisfy her (yet another argument against those who accuse her of being exclusively preoccupied with form and technique): " . . . I did not try to explore. And must I always explore? Yes I think so still." Exploring, for her, means that research in depth through which form and substance are fused in indestructible unity, and which, as I have pointed out, was lacking in *Orlando*: that research in depth which, for Virginia Woolf, is the very essence of artistic creation and which alone entitles a work to be called "important". . . .

N. C. Thakur   (essay date 1965)

SOURCE: *The Symbolism of Virginia Woolf,* Oxford University Press, London, 1965, 171 p.

[*In the following excerpt, Thakur analyzes symbolism in* Orlando.]

Talking about *Orlando,* David Daiches says [in *The Novel and the Modern World*], 'It would be a weary task to disentangle the profoundly symbolic from the deliberately irresponsible . . .', and, I would add, the historically true. Yet it is a fascinating study to see how from the available factual material Virginia Woolf has created a delightful novel, though, like Defoe and Fielding who name their novels 'The Life, Adventures and Pyracies of . . .', and 'The History of . . .', she calls it 'A Biography'.

It is based upon Victoria Sackville-West, Knole, and the Sackvilles. The heraldic leopard, the swaying tapestry, the gilded furniture, and the depth of mirrors that Virginia Woolf mentions in *Orlando,* are directly taken from Victoria Sackville-West's book *Knole and the Sackvilles.* Hall, the falconer; Giles, the groom; Mrs. Grimsditch, the house-keeper; and Mr. Dupper, the chaplain, are all in *Knole and the Sackvilles* having their dinner at the Parlour Table or the Long Table of 'the Right Honourable Richard, Earl of Dorset, in the year of our Lord 1613'. The character and temperament of Orlando changes according to the temperaments of the various Sackvilles who lived during the different ages—the Elizabethan, the Restoration, and the Victorian—and he/she reflects their several tastes and pleasures. *Orlando* no doubt is, as Stephen Spender says [in *World within World*], 'a fantastic meditation on a portrait of Victoria Sackville-West'. In spite of all this it is not a merely biographical novel. Just as *To the Lighthouse* goes beyond the biographical notes of Sir Leslie Stephen and his family to reflect Virginia Woolf 's ideas about 'reality' and its intuitive realization, *Orlando,* besides fantastically portraying the Sackville-West family, symbolizes Virginia Woolf 's ideas about time, personality, literature, and the art of biography.

Orlando begins with the closing reign of Queen Elizabeth who was growing 'old and worn and bent', and closes on 'the twelfth stroke of midnight, Thursday, the eleventh of October, Nineteen hundred and Twenty Eight'. Orlando, its protagonist, living through this long period—more than three hundred years—attains the age of thirty-six years. This extraordinary discrepancy symbolizes Virginia Woolf 's idea about the two different ages of man, which are determined by 'time on the clock and time in the mind', and not by a sort of 'bogus "time" ' which, according to Wyndham Lewis [in *Men without Art*], the Bloomsbury people have created 'to take the place of the real "Time" '. Writing about time, Virginia Woolf says:

> . . . time, unfortunately, though it makes animals and vegetables bloom and fade with amazing punctuality, has no such simple effect upon the mind of man. The mind of man, moreover, works with equal strangeness upon the body of time. An hour, once it lodges in the queer element of the human spirit, may be stretched to fifty or a hundred times its clock lengths; on the other hand, an hour may be accurately represented on the timepiece of the mind by one second. (*Orlando*)

So of Orlando she writes that it 'would be no exaggeration to say that the he would go out after breakfast a man of thirty and come home to dinner a man of fifty-five at least'.

The age of a person, as determined by 'time in the mind' varies according to the poetic temperament and the imaginative faculty of that person. The unimaginative, she feels, 'live precisely the sixty-eight or seventy-two years allotted them on the tombstone'. Imaginative people

> are hundreds of years old though they call themselves thirty-six. The true length of a person's life, whatever the *Dictionary of National Biography* may say, is always a matter of dispute. (*Orlando*)

Orlando who, being modelled after Victoria Sackville-West, is a poet and thirty-six years of age according to the time on the clock, is more than three hundred years old according to the time in the mind. Victoria Sackville-West had evidently lived the past in her imagination because in

addition to *Knole and the Sackvilles* she wrote, at the age of thirteen, 'an enormous novel' about Edward Sackville and his two sons. She loved Knole, and in the old house 'the past mingled with the present. . . .'

> The house is not haunted, but you require either an unimaginative nerve or else a complete certainty of the house's benevolence before you can wander through the state-rooms after nightfall with a candle. The light gleams on the dull gilding of furniture and into the misty depths of mirrors, and startles up a sudden face out of the gloom; something creaks and sighs; the tapestry sways, and the figures on it undulate and seem to come alive. [*Knole and the Sackvilles*]

This quality of having lived the past imaginatively Virginia Woolf portrays symbolically by making Orlando a fantastic character who lives through the Elizabethan, Restoration and Victorian ages and yet is only thirty-six in nineteen hundred and twenty-eight.

De Quincey compares the human brain to a palimpsest:

> What else than a natural and mighty palimpsest is the human brain? Such a palimpsest . . . oh reader! is yours. Everlasting layers of ideas, images, feelings, have fallen upon your brain softly as light. Each succession has seemed to bury all that went before. And yet, in reality, not one has been extinguished.

Virginia Woolf appears to agree with De Quincey that ideas, images, feelings, like the words on a palimpsest, continue to live in one's brain. While writing about William Hazlitt in 1930, only two years after the publication of *Orlando,* she says,

> He loves to grope among the curious depths of human psychology and to track down the reason of things. He excels in hunting out the obscure causes that lie behind some common saying or sensation, and the drawers of his mind are well stocked with illustrations and arguments. . . . He is speaking of what he knows from experience when he exclaims, 'How many ideas and trains of sentiments, long and deep and intense, often pass through the mind in only one day's thinking or reading!' Convictions are his life blood; ideas have formed in him like stalactites, drop by drop, year by year. [*The Times Literary Supplement,* 18 September 1930]

Orlando's fantastic age represents the idea that the impressions gathered by Victoria Sackville-West and the emotions she experienced while walking through Knole at night with a taper in her hand and while musing in the family chapel alone, formed into imperishable stalactites and left an indelible imprint on the palimpsest of her mind.

Orlando's being as old as the Sackville family suggests another train of thought. In *Mrs. Dalloway* and *To the Lighthouse,* two novels immediately preceding *Orlando,* and in *The Waves,* immediately following it, Virginia Woolf repeats her idea about the continuance of life after death. Clarissa Dalloway feels that she will survive in the trees at home and in the house there, in other people, and especially in the people she knew best. Mrs. Ramsay believes that she will survive in others as long as they live. Bernard puts it more pithily when he says, 'we are the continuers, we are the inheritors'. By making the long line of the Earls and Dukes of Dorset and the Lord Sackvilles live in Orlando, Virginia Woolf makes him a symbol, if not of the whole racial and collective unconscious described by Jung, at least of that part of it which we may name 'the family unconscious'. All these ideas make the fantasy about Orlando's age highly symbolical.

Orlando's change of sex, also, is used symbolically to suggest another group of ideas. In *Symbols of Transformation* Jung mentions that 'Among the primordial water which was in the beginning' was known as 'the father of fathers, the mother of mothers'. He also mentions that in Egyptian and Babylonian mythologies the 'generative primal matter' and 'the primordial mother' are both bisexual by nature. Talking about 'anima' Jung says,

> Since the anima is an archetype that is found in men, it is reasonable to suppose that an equivalent archetype must be present in women; for just as the man is compensated by a feminine element, so woman is compensated by a masculine one.

In support of his thesis he quotes Edward Maitland and Nicholas of Flüe, two Christian mystics, who saw reality in a bisexual form—'Mother as well as Father', and as 'majestic father', and 'majestic mother'. Poets and philosophers, too, have believed in the androgynous state of man. Virginia Woolf herself, while discussing the 'Unity of mind', questions 'whether there are two sexes in the mind corresponding to the two sexes in the body'. She comes to the conclusion that

> in each one of us two powers preside, one male, one female; and in the man's brain the man predominates over the woman, and in the woman's brain the woman predominates over the man. (*A Room of One's Own*)

This idea of a person's being both 'Hee and Shee', Virginia Woolf also mentions in *The Waves,* though on a slightly different plane, when she makes Bernard say, 'nor do I always know if I am man or woman'. Orlando's being first a man and then a woman, besides suggesting man's being androgynous, represents the change in the historical character represented by Orlando.

> It was a change in Orlando herself that dictated her choice of a woman's dress and of a woman's sex. . . . Different though the sexes are, they intermix. In every human being a vacillation from one sex to the other takes place. . . .

> For it was this mixture in her of man and woman . . . that often gave her conduct an unexpected turn. The curious of her own sex would argue, for example, if Orlando was a woman, how did she never take more than ten minutes to dress? And were not her clothes chosen rather at random, and sometimes worn rather shabby? . . . Yet again, they noted, she detested household matters, was up at dawn and out among the fields in summer before the sun had risen. No farmer knew more about the crops

than she did. She could drink with the best and liked games of hazard.

This lack of a feminine concern for clothes, and having a manly interest in farming, drinks and games of hazard, show the predominance of man in Orlando. But at another time the feminine in her—giving birth to and bringing up children, and the running of the household, as represented by her buying 'sheets for a double bed' becomes uppermost.

In *Knole and the Sackvilles* Victoria Sackville-West, describing Charles, the Sixth Earl, says,

> . . . let us call him the Restoration Earl—the jolly, loose-living, magnificent Maecenas, 'during the whole of his life the patron of men of genius and the dupe of women, and bountiful beyond measure to both' . . . he disturbed London by a rowdy youth; he was reported to have passed on his mistresses to the king. . . .

When it comes to John Frederick Sackville, she describes him as follows:

> He belonged to an age more delicate, more exquisite; an age of quizzing glasses, of flowered waistcoats, of buckled shoes, and of slim bejewelled swords.

A little earlier in that book she also mentions how the rowdy way of life of the Restoration had changed to the 'good breeding, decency of manners, and dignity of exterior deportment of Queen Anne's time'. This change in the Sackvilles from the robust masculine to the delicate more feminine behaviour of a later age along with the fact that on the death of the Duchess Arabella Diana 'her estate devolved upon her two daughters, Mary and Elizabeth'—from male to female descendants—are other points of significance in Orlando's change of sex.

In *Orlando* the house, nine acres of stone, massed like a town with 'stables, kennels, breweries, carpenters' shops, wash-houses, places where they make tallow candles, kill oxen, forge horse-shoes, stitch jerkins', like the broad-backed moors and the Parthenon in *Jacob's Room,* and like the house and the 'Noble Barn' in *Between the Acts,* becomes a symbol of historical time against which Virginia Woolf shows the passage of different ages. The house and the oak tree still stand after generations of Sackvilles, having played their parts, have departed. Virginia Woolf seems to believe with Sir Thomas Browne, whom she mentions in *Orlando,* that 'the irregularities of vain-glory, and wilde enormities of ancient magnanimity . . . must diminish their diameters and be poorly seen in Angles of Contingency'. She externalizes this idea by describing the crypt of the family chapel, where Orlando's ancestors lay, coffin piled upon coffin, for ten generations together.

> The place was so seldom visited that the rats had made free with the lead work, and now a thigh bone would catch at his cloak as he passed, or he would crack the skull of some old Sir Malise as it rolled beneath his foot. It was a ghastly sepulchre; dug deep beneath the foundations of the house as if the first Lord of the family, who had come from France with the Conqueror, had wished to testify how all pomp is built upon cor-

ruption; how the skeleton lies beneath the flesh; how we that dance and sing above must lie below; how the crimson velvet turns to dust; how the ring (here Orlando, stooping his lantern, would pick up a gold circle lacking a stone, that had rolled into a corner) loses its ruby and the eye which was so lustrous shines no more.

The crypt with the lead work destroyed by the rats, and with the thigh bone and skulls rolling about suggests death, decay and corruption. The destruction of the symbols of pomp, power, and glory—the crimson velvet turning to dust, the ring losing its ruby, and the eye its lustre—heightens the sense of the transitoriness of human life and glory.

Virginia Woolf feels that if an individual life, and even the glory of an age, is so transient, there is no reason for anyone to be proud of pomp and power. (This idea is dealt with again . . . in *Between the Acts.*) The absurdity of having 365 bedrooms which had been in the possession of the family for four or five hundred years, and of being proud of having earls, or even dukes as one's ancestors, is high-lighted by mentioning the simple gipsy whose family went back two or three thousand years, whose ancestors had built the Pyramids centuries before Christ was born, and who lived a life of 'making a basket' or 'skinning a sheep', and laughed at the 'vulgar ambition' of earls and dukes who snatch land or money from people and accumulate 'field after field; house after house; honour after honour'.

Victoria Sackville-West was a novelist and a poet. She had won the Hawthornden Prize for her poem, *The Land.* Many of her ancestors were poets and writers. Orlando, reflecting their various talents, becomes a symbol of the literary traditions of the family. During the Elizabethan Age, like Thomas Sackville the first Earl of Dorset, who contributed to *Gorboduc* and *The Mirror of Magistrates,* he writes *Aethelbert: A Tragedy in Five Acts;* like Richard Sackville who was a friend and patron of Beaumont, Ben Jonson, Fletcher, and Drayton, he is a great lover of scholars. Victoria Sackville-West once offered hospitality to a poet, a friend of General Franco, who afterwards, according to Stephen Spender [in *World within World*], wrote against her; Orlando patronizes Mr. Nicholas Greene of Clifford's Inn, a poet, who in return for his hospitality writes 'a very spirited satire' about a visit to a nobleman in the country. Nick Greene, the 'sardonic loose-lipped man' whose ridicule of Orlando's tragedy had not only hurt Orlando but also made him destroy his fifty-seven poetical works, stands for the 'irresponsible' reviewer whose reviews affect the sensibility of authors.

Ultimately Orlando swears, 'I'll write, from this day forward, to please myself', and indulges in profound thoughts as to the nature of obscurity. In this he resembles his creator. 'I write,' Virginia Woolf says, 'what I like writing and there's an end on it.' At another place she records, 'I'm the only woman in England free to write what I like,' and she has described the advantages of 'obscurity' to a writer in *A Room of One's Own.*

Orlando, the writer, like Lily Briscoe, the artist in *To the Lighthouse,* and Miss La Trobe, the producer in *Between the Acts,* becomes a symbol of a creative artist, and reflects the 'rigours of composition'. He 'wrote and it seemed good; read and it seemed vile'; he alternated between ecstasy and despair, and wondered whether he was 'the divinest genius or the greatest fool', and these feelings, reflecting Virginia Woolf's own as we find them scattered throughout her diary, attain symbolic value.

In *Orlando* Virginia Woolf also portrays the successive ages of English life and letters, which she was to develop again in *The Years* and *Between the Acts.* Whereas in *Between the Acts* she describes them in a more terse and symbolic way through the pageant, in *Orlando* she is more explanatory, and uses atmosphere and seasons as symbols, a method that she was to employ again in *The Years.* About the Elizabethan Age in *Orlando* she says:

> . . . their morals were not ours; nor their poets; nor their climate; nor their vegetables even. Everything was different. . . . Sunsets were redder and more intense; dawns were whiter and more auroral. Of our crepuscular half-lights and lingering twilights they knew nothing. . . . The sun rose and sank. The lover loved and went.

The redder and more intense sunsets symbolize the ardent poets and the lovers of the 'garden flower' and of 'the wild and the weeds', and the bold and free manners of men and women who narrate 'how Jakes had lost his nose and Sukey her honour'.

One important result of the Augustan Age was to produce a style of exemplary clarity, to write 'as Locke recommended lucidly and without mystifying aura'. Virginia Woolf describing the change in Orlando's style says,

> His floridity was chastened; his abundance curbed; the age of prose was congealing those warm fountains. The very landscape outside was less stuck about with garlands and the briars themselves were less thorned and intricate. Perhaps the senses were a little duller and honey and cream less seductive to the palate.

The duller scenes and senses, contrasting with the 'ingrained habit of colour and passion' of the Elizabethans, become apt symbols of the Age of Reason.

Similarly Virginia Woolf uses frost, the darkness of night, clouds and dampness, and the clear and uniform skies, as symbols to suggest the temper of an age, or the state of mind of an individual. The Great Frost, when 'birds froze in mid-air and fell like stones to the ground', not only provides an occasion for Virginia Woolf to indulge in her flights of fantasy, and a place for the escapades of Orlando and the revelries of the new king, but also serves as a symbol of the callousness of the court: 'while the country people suffered the extremity of want', the capital, because the new king wanted to 'curry favour with the citizens', enjoyed a carnival of utmost brilliancy. The river, which had frozen, was 'to be swept, decorated and given all the semblance of a park or pleasure ground'.

The darkness and blackness, which Virginia Woolf mentions fifteen times in six pages, and which make the night of 'so inky a blackness that a man was on you before he could be seen', creating a sinister atmosphere, becomes symbolic of the deceit of Sasha, the Muscovite, and of the black mood of Orlando, the cheated. When 'with an awful and ominous voice, a voice full of horror and alarm', St. Paul's struck the stroke of midnight, Orlando, standing in the doorway of an inn near Blackfriars, knew that his doom was sealed.

> He stood in the doorway in the tremendous rain without moving. As the minutes passed, he sagged a little at the knees. The downpour rushed on. In the thick of it, great guns seemed to boom. Huge noises as of the tearing and rending of oak trees could be heard. There were also wild cries and terrible inhuman groanings.

The 'huge noises' and the 'wild cries' and 'inhuman groanings', symbolize the lacerating of Orlando's heart and his anguished cry at being cheated by Sasha. Similarly the 'turbulent yellow waters', the mere look of which was 'enough to turn one giddy', which Orlando saw instead of 'the solid ice' the river had been for three months, become symbols of the riot and confusion of his mind.

When he saw the ship of the Muscovite Embassy standing out to sea, Orlando flung himself from his horse, and in his rage tried to breast the sea:

> he hurled at the faithless woman all the insults that have ever been the lot of her sex. Faithless, mutable, fickle, he called her; devil, adulteress, deceiver; and the swirling waters took his words, and tossed at his feet a broken pot and a little straw.

The broken pot and the little straw, remnants of a wrecked home and a nest destroyed, that the sea tossed at his feet, become symbols of his shattered dreams of a comfortable home that he wanted to found with Sasha.

After describing how Orlando met Pope, Addison, Swift, and Lord Chesterfield, and saw Dr. Johnson, Mr. Boswell, and Mrs. Williams, Virginia Woolf closes the chapter with a description of the spreading clouds.

> At length she came home one night after one of these saunterings . . . and stood there . . . looking out of the window. . . . She could see St. Paul's, the Tower, Westminster Abbey, with all the spires and domes of the city churches. . . . Upon this serene and orderly prospect the stars looked down, glittering, positive, hard, from a cloudless sky. In the extreme clearness of the atmosphere the line of every roof, the cowl of every chimney was perceptible. . . . She heard the far-away cry of the night watchman—'Just twelve o'clock on a frosty morning'. No sooner had the words left his lips than the first stroke of midnight sounded. Orlando then for the first time noticed a small cloud gathered behind the dome of St. Paul's. As the strokes sounded, the cloud increased and she saw it darken and spread with extraordinary speed. . . . With the twelfth stroke of midnight, the darkness was complete. A turbulent welter of cloud covered the city. All was darkness; all was doubt; all was confusion. The Eighteenth century was over; the Nineteenth century had begun.

'The extreme clearness of the atmosphere', the 'cloudless sky', the 'glittering, positive, hard' stars, and the 'orderly prospect', evoking the lucid style and the extreme rationalism of Addison, Pope, and Swift, become symbolic of the Age of Reason. Similarly the spreading clouds, and the 'doubt' and 'confusion' symbolize Romanticism and the Victorian Age, which had, as Lytton Strachey says, 'barbarism and prudery', and 'self-complacency and self-contradiction'. Virginia Woolf further expresses her ideas about the Victorian Age by using the ever increasing dampness and ivy as symbols.

> But what was worse, damp now began to make its way into every house—damp, which is the most insidious of all enemies, for while the sun can be shut out by blinds, and the frost roasted by a hot fire, damp steals in while we sleep; damp is silent, imperceptible, ubiquitous. Damp swells the wood, furs the kettle, rusts the iron, rots the stone.

This dampness makes men feel 'the chill in their hearts; the damp in their mind'. This condition of the moral and mental state of the Victorians is taken up again and dealt with exhaustively in *The Years* and *Three Guineas.* The dampness makes ivy grow in 'unparalleled profusion'. It smothers the bare stones of the houses in greenery. This concealing of even the bare stones by the ivy suggests the 'evasions and concealments' that were sedulously practised by both the sexes, and the prudery of the Victorian Age. The dampness not only makes ivy grow, but also makes vegetation become 'rampant'. Cucumbers 'came scrolloping across the grass', and 'giant cauliflowers' tower deck above deck. This 'fecundity of the garden, the bedroom and the henroost' becomes symbolic of the large Victorian families. This fecundity, which is the spirit of the age, is expressed when Orlando, now wearing a crinoline and a plumed hat in the Victorian fashion, wants someone to 'lean upon'.

The cloudy sky, that had engendered dampness and ivy, bearded men, and even muffled furniture, changes with the changing eras.

> It was no longer so thick, so watery, so prismatic now that King Edward . . . had succeeded Queen Victoria. The clouds had shrunk to a thin gauze; the sky seemed made of metal, which in hot weather tarnished. . . . It was a little alarming—this shrinkage. Everything seemed to have shrunk.

This shrinkage in King Edward's time is symbolic of the change that took place in the dress, manners, and tastes of the age. The dresses became short and less cumbersome, women grew narrow 'like stalks of corn, straight, shining, identical'. Men's faces became 'bare as the palm of one's hand'. The curtains and covers became frizzled up and the walls became bare to be decorated by 'brilliant coloured pictures of real things'. The families, coming within the grip of shrinkage, also ceased to grow large.

In spite of the fact that Virginia Woolf did not have good health and being very sensitive was depressed by the inhuman wars, she was, Clive Bell records [in *Old Friends*], 'the gayest human being', and she saw 'life itself as a vast Shakespearean Comedy' [according to David Garnett in

The Flowers of the Forest]. Thus she is able to create delightful comedies in *Orlando* and *Between the Acts,* to see the brighter side of life, and believe in progress. Her last two novels, even though they were written under the shadow of war, show the same spirit of hope and progress. This spirit is symbolized in *The Years* through the young couple and the rising dawn, and in *Between the Acts* through the birth of a new life and the raising of the curtain for a new play. In *Orlando* it is expressed through another symbol:

> . . . as she was thinking this, the immensely long tunnel in which she seemed to have been travelling for hundreds of years widened; the light poured in. . . . And so for some seconds the light went on becoming brighter and brighter, and she saw everything more and more clearly and the clock ticked louder and louder until there was a terrific explosion right in her ear. . . . Ten times she was struck. In fact it was ten o'clock in the morning. It was the eleventh of October. It was 1928. It was the present time.

The long tunnel stands for time. The light becoming brighter as the end—the present time—approaches is a symbol of Virginia Woolf's delight in the progress the world has made. This is both material progress—from the muffled overcrowded Victorian houses with their 'small tin bath tubs' to the sanitary and convenient modern houses with their shower baths, from travelling 'for hours with one's feet in dirty straw dragged along the streets by horses' to riding in omnibuses and motor-cars—and also the progress towards mental and spiritual freedom, for Orlando, in contrast to the mothers and unpaid housekeepers of the previous age, is now free to write poetry and win prizes, and to be her own mistress.

As Virginia Woolf calls *Orlando* a biography, she also presents in it symbolically her ideas about the art of biography. She seems to believe with Lytton Strachey and Victoria Sackville-West, that the function of a biographer is to be truthful. Desmond MacCarthy sums up Lytton Strachey's ideal about the art of biography in the following words:

> . . . biography must aim at being a truthful record of an individual life, composed as a work of art. [*Memories*]

Victoria Sackville-West feels that to write a biography is not 'to write a panegyric'. Virginia Woolf symbolically expresses these ideas through Our Ladies of Purity, Chastity, and Modesty. Like De Quincey's Ladies of Sorrow who address a new born child, they address the newly changed Orlando. These Ladies, who 'cover vice and poverty', and all those things that are 'frail or dark or doubtful', saying 'speak not, reveal not', and who hide behind 'ivy and curtains', sing in unison thus:

> Truth come not out from your horrid den. Hide deeper, fearful Truth. For you flaunt in the brutal gaze of the sun things that were better unknown and undone; you unveil the shameful; the dark you make clear, Hide! Hide! Hide!

This exhortation of theirs that Truth should hide rather than unveil the shameful makes them symbolic of that school of biographers who mention only 'those performances and incidents which produce vulgar greatness' and who, thinking it 'an act of piety', try to hide the faults and failings of the men they portray by not leading the thoughts into their 'domestic privacies' and the 'minutest details' of their private lives.

An excerpt from *Orlando*

[Orlando returns home for the first time as a woman.]

It was a fine evening in December when she arrived and the snow was falling and the violet shadows were slanting much as she had seen them from the hill-top at Broussa. The great house lay more like a town than a house, brown and blue, rose and purple in the snow, with all its chimneys smoking busily as if inspired with a life of their own. She could not restrain a cry as she saw it there tranquil and massive, couched upon the meadows. As the yellow coach entered the park and came bowling along the drive between the trees, the red deer raised their heads as if expectantly, and it was observed that instead of showing the timidity natural to their kind, they followed the coach and stood about the courtyard when it drew up. Some tossed their antlers, others pawed the ground as the step was let down and Orlando alighted. One, it is said, actually knelt in the snow before her. She had not time to reach her hand towards the knocker before both wings of the great door were flung open, and there, with lights and torches held above their heads, were Mrs. Grimsditch, Mr. Dupper, and a whole retinue of servants come to greet her. But the orderly procession was interrupted first by the impetuosity of Canute, the elk hound, who threw himself with such ardour upon his mistress that he almost knocked her to the ground; next, by the agitation of Mrs. Grimsditch, who, making as if to curtsey, was overcome with emotion and could do no more than gasp Milord! Milady! Milady! Milord! until Orlando comforted her with a hearty kiss upon both her cheeks. After that, Mr. Dupper began to read from a parchment, but the dogs barking, the huntsmen winding their horns, and the stags, who had come into the courtyard in the confusion, baying the moon, not much progress was made, and the company dispersed within after crowding about their Mistress, and testifying in every way to their great joy at her return.

No one showed an instant's suspicion that Orlando was not the Orlando they had known. If any doubt there was in the human mind the action of the deer and the dogs would have been enough to dispel it, for the dumb creatures, as is well known, are far better judges both of identity and character than we are. Moreover, said Mrs. Grimsditch, over her dish of china tea to Mr. Dupper that night, if her Lord was a Lady now, she had never seen a lovelier one. . . .

Virginia Woolf, in her Orlando, *Harcourt, Brace and Co., 1928.*

James Naremore   (essay date 1973)

SOURCE: *The World without a Self: Virginia Woolf and the Novel,* Yale University Press, 1973, 259 p.

[*In the following excerpt, Naremore discusses Woolf's attempt in* Orlando *to devise a new type of biography that evokes personality through a combination of fact and fiction.*]

In the interval between the demanding tasks of *To the Lighthouse* and *The Waves,* Virginia Woolf was occupied with *Orlando,* a mock biography inspired partly by her romantic friendship with Vita Sackville-West. The emphasis on fantasy allowed free rein to her naturally ornate, erotic style, and provided good material for sketches of vast, generalized landscapes. Perhaps more important, in pretending to write a biography Mrs. Woolf gave her prose some breathing room above the subjective deeps. As usual, she describes her central character in the third person and from an omniscient perspective; but here she chooses to look down through the eyes of a voluble, often unreliable narrator, a "biographer" who indulges in digressions and flights of description like the famous accounts of the Great Frost or the damp cloud descending over Victorian England. The voice of this narrator is highly flexible, capable of adapting with ease to all the inner emotional rhythms of Orlando's life; at times, however, particularly in the first parts of the book, it stands at a marked distance, observing its subject's behavior with wonder, puzzlement, or even blatant incomprehension. Orlando's conversations with herself are reported, but usually as well-ordered, logical meditations. In general, *Orlando* employs the techniques of conventional omniscient narration, and, on the surface at least, its existence might imply that Mrs. Woolf had temporarily lost interest in the flow of mental life. Even the plot, granting its outrageousness, is more conventionally "novelistic" than Mrs. Woolf's previous work—certainly no one could charge that nothing happens in this book.

Ultimately, however, *Orlando* is as much about the inner life as any of Virginia Woolf's other novels. The difference is that here she chose to represent a chiefly internal, implicit experience as if it were objective and explicit. Instead of dealing with an inner life which is at least generally bound by an ordinary circumstantial context, she chose to imagine the racial or family memory in a character much like Vita Sackville-West, and then depicted that memory as a sequence of actual events. . . . [She] was fascinated with the mind's ability to think back to times before it even existed, and travel to places it has never been. Thus when Mrs. Ramsay sinks into a "core of darkness," she feels that she can go anywhere: "Her horizon seemed to her limitless. There were all the places she had not seen; the Indian plains; she felt herself pushing aside the thick leather curtain of a church in Rome." Orlando's experience has precisely this sort of limitless possibility, but it is presented straightforwardly, in a book that purports to be a biography.

This fanciful device, like all of Mrs. Woolf's experiments, represented another attempt to overcome the problem of isolation; it allowed her to suggest that the envelope surrounding individual lives is in some sense permeable, permitting some contact with what lies "outside." Hence we encounter a recognizable stream of consciousness only in the later chapters of *Orlando,* and find there that Virginia Woolf is no longer satisfied with the ordinary flotsam of the internal monologue—she is approaching those deeper, more communal regions Joyce treats in some parts of *Ulysses* and in *Finnegans Wake:*

> "Sheets for a double bed," Orlando repeated dreamily, for a double bed with a silver counterpane in a room fitted with taste which she now thought a little vulgar—all in silver; but she had furnished it when she had a passion for that metal. While the man went to get sheets for a double bed, she took out a little looking-glass and a powder puff. Women were not nearly as roundabout in their ways, she thought, powdering herself with the greatest unconcern, as they had been when she herself first turned woman on the deck of the *Enamoured Lady.* She gave her nose the right tint deliberately. She never touched her cheeks. Honestly, though she was now thirty-six, she scarcely looked a day older. She looked just as pouting, as sulky, as handsome, as rosy (like a million-candled Christmas tree, Sasha said) as she had done that day on the ice, when the Thames was frozen and they had gone skating—
>
> "The best Irish linen, Ma'am," said the shopman, spreading the sheets on the counter,—and they had met an old woman picking up sticks. Here, as she was fingering the linen abstractedly, one of the swinging doors between the departments opened and let through, perhaps from the fancy-good departments, a whiff of scent, waxen, tinted as if from pink candles, and the scent curved like a shell round a figure—was it a boy's or was it a girl's?—young, slender, seductive—a girl, by God! furred, pearled, in Russian trousers; but faithless, faithless!

As the story of Orlando's "life" reaches its conclusion, every sensation evokes a web of associations. The effect is extraordinary: the fall of every "atom"—the shopkeeper's talk, the glimpse of a reflection in a hand mirror, the scent drifting in through an open door—activates a "tremour of susceptibility." The previous events of the tale are gathered up in a single moment, and, like Bernard in *The Waves,* Orlando knows the feeling of time "whizzed back an inch or two on its reel"; also like Bernard, she participates in other selves, even other sexes. In one sense the moment is poignant, because Sasha and youth are gone—yet in another sense it is a joyful and triumphant experience, because all time, all distinctions, all finality seem to have been overcome.

Such passages reveal the basic similarity between *Orlando* and Mrs. Woolf's other work—again she presents a victory over time and death, again she insists on the unity of experience. In this case, however, she was directly concerned with *historical* consciousness, and with an attack on the deadening empiricism of most biographical literature. If she felt that the novels of Bennett and Galsworthy had been weighted down by a superficial realism, she found the typical biography, with its slavish attention to facts, even more burdensome. The biographer's work is grounded in a tight little realm of detail and distinction, much like the everyday reality that grows up around characters in *The Waves*; biography, as it is usually practiced, deals with our "shell," not our soul, with our temporal, not our eternal being. In one sense, then, the historian's facts threaten our survival, so that Mrs. Woolf's playful satire of historicism in *Orlando* represents a perfectly serious attempt to show us a world which cannot be explained by fact, a world in which the changes wrought by historical process become merely "what you see us by."

All this is not to say that Virginia Woolf was disinterested in conventional historical writings—on the contrary, like everyone else in Bloomsbury, she was fascinated by them. But in *Orlando,* as in most cases where she deals with historical subject matter, she tries to create an imaginative unity between past and present, and in so doing exposes the relative emptiness of empirical data. Humanity, she seems to say, has always shared a common life; only the external circumstances of time and place make us seem different. She had touched on this theme many times before, especially in her essays. In **"The Pastons and Chaucer,"** for example, she refuses to take the impersonal, scholarly point of view of a writer who is forever removed from medieval England. Instead she shows us how John Paston felt as he sat alone reading:

> For sometimes, instead of riding off on his horse to inspect his crops or bargain with his tenants, Sir John would sit, in broad daylight, reading. There, on the hard chair in the comfortless room with the wind lifting the carpet and the smoke stinging his eyes, he would sit reading Chaucer, wasting his time, dreaming—or what strange intoxication was it he drew from books? Life was rough, cheerless, and disappointing. A whole year of days would pass fruitlessly in dreary business, like dashes of rain on the window-pane. There was no reason in it as there had been for his father; no imperative need to establish a family and acquire an important position for children who were not born . . . But Lydgate's poems or Chaucer's, like a mirror in which figures move brightly, silently, and compactly, showed him the very skies, fields, and people whom he knew, but rounded and complete. Instead of waiting listlessly for news from London or piecing out from his mother's gossip some country tragedy of love and jealousy, here, in a few pages, the whole story was laid before him.

"The Pastons and Chaucer" is no excavation of dead relics from the past. It recreates Paston before our eyes, presenting him as a character like Rachel Vinrace or Mrs. Ramsay, a sensitive person who exchanges rough life for dreamy solitude. Paston is also like the characters in *Between the Acts* who are troubled by the fragmentary quality of ordinary life; he feels dependent on the piecemeal facts of "news" or "gossip," which have to travel across time and space. But when he retreats from active life and gives himself over to imagination, he can understand "the whole story." Moreover, just as the imagination of Chaucer redeems Paston, so the imagination of Virginia Woolf, who has absorbed both Paston and Chaucer, helps to redeem us. As we sit reading Mrs. Woolf's essay, we half

share in Paston's experience. Like him, we overcome boundaries and seem to understand a life "rounded and complete." Without leaving our chairs, we take imaginative possession of an event that occurred hundreds of years before our birth.

> **Ultimately *Orlando* is as much about the inner life as any of Virginia Woolf's other novels. The difference is that here she chose to represent a chiefly internal, implicit experience as if it were objective and explicit.**
>
> **—James Naremore**

This kind of triumph over space and time can be found everywhere in Virginia Woolf's writing, but in essays like **"The Pastons and Chaucer,"** in *Orlando,* and subsequently in *Between the Acts,* it becomes more specifically the triumph of imagination over the historical process. Thus the many evident similarities between *Orlando* and *Between the Acts*: both deal with the realm of action and affairs and treat that realm with a good deal of comic irony; both use a magnificent country estate as a focal point, and end with night scenes in which a man and a woman move toward each other across a timeless, otherworldly landscape. In both Mrs. Woolf employs bits of parody and doggerel language, and adapts her familiar style to new techniques, with less emphasis on the watery language and single ghostly voice of her previous novels. Finally, both books present history as a kind of pageant, where the costumes change but the actors remain essentially the same.

Between the Acts, however, is occasioned by the events leading up to World War II, so that its darker moments always contain the tension of an impending brute violence. *Orlando* is in every sense a happier book, chiefly because it was prompted by a love for Vita Sackville-West and by Mrs. Woolf's long-standing interest in biographical literature. Indeed, to appreciate *Orlando* fully, to understand a few of the motives behind its technical peculiarities, one needs to know something of its background. One should recognize, for example, that it refers back to Leslie Stephen's *Dictionary of National Biography*, that it is contemporary with Lytton Strachey's anti-Victorian life studies and his quasi-fictional *Elizabeth and Essex,* and that it looks forward to Virginia Woolf's own attempt at biography in *Roger Fry.* In addition, there are two less widely-known Bloomsbury biographies which have a more direct bearing on what Mrs. Woolf called her "writer's holiday": Harold Nicolson's *Some People,* and his wife Vita Sackville-West's *Knole and the Sackvilles.* To read these books, together with Mrs. Woolf's writings on biography, is to see that *Orlando* is not just "about" her friends; it is, in part, both a response to their work and a commentary on the relationship between "fact" and imagination.

The only critic who has written at length about the "biographical" subject of *Orlando* is Leon Edel. In his Alexander Lectures, published as *Literary Biography,* Professor Edel offers a long digression on what he calls Virginia Woolf's "fable for biographers":

> The idea for the work appears to have been given to Virginia Woolf by Lytton Strachey. One day at lunch, he told her . . . "You should take something wilder and more fantastic, a framework that admits of anything, like *Tristram Shandy.*" This fictional biography thus stems from a preeminent figure in modern biography. The acknowledgement . . . carries not only Strachey's name, but also that of another biographer, Harold Nicolson . . . who was to write a little volume on biography published by Leonard and Virginia Woolf at the Hogarth Press. The plot thickens considerably when we note that Sir Harold Nicolson's wife is none other than Vita Sackville-West. And if we remind ourselves that Virginia Woolf's father, Sir Leslie Stephen, was the editor of the *Dictionary of National Biography,* we have a vision of Orlando in the cradle, grandfathered and uncled by a group of biographers.

Edel might have added that Orlando also has an "aunt," since Vita Sackville-West was herself a talented biographer, and since *Knole and the Sackvilles* is Virginia Woolf's primary source for historical detail. Moreover, while Lytton Strachey may have planted the seeds that matured into Mrs. Woolf's book, her immediate inspiration was apparently Harold Nicolson's series of character sketches, *Some People.* The Elizabethan adventures in *Orlando* and even the use of illustrations in the early Hogarth editions probably owe something to Strachey's *Elizabeth and Essex,* but it is difficult to say just how much; both books were published in 1928, though Strachey had begun work in 1925, two years before *Orlando* was conceived. It was in October, 1927, that the specific idea for *Orlando* came to Mrs. Woolf. On Wednesday, October 5, she wrote in her *Diary:* "having done my last article for the *Tribune* . . . instantly the usual exciting devices enter my mind: a biography beginning in the year 1500 and continuing to the present day, called *Orlando*: Vita, only with a change about from one sex to another." The "last article" she mentions was an essay-review of *Some People,* which appeared in the New York *Herald Tribune* on October 30, under the title **"The New Biography."** Just as the feminist didactics of *Orlando* can be connected with *A Room of One's Own* (1928), so the comic, hyperbolic style and the biographical satire can be demonstrated to follow from what Virginia Woolf had just written about Nicolson. But while the relationship between *Orlando* and *A Room of One's Own* has often been noted, the essay on Nicolson and the similar but later discussion of Strachey, entitled **"The Art of Biography,"** need more emphasis.

Virginia Woolf's review of *Some People* opens with an analogy which would ultimately produce the title *Granite and Rainbow* for one of her collections of essays: "if we think of truth as something of granite-like solidity and of personality as something of rainbow-like intangibility and reflect that the aim of biography is to weld these two into one seamless whole, we shall admit that the problem is a stiff one and that we need not wonder if biographers have for the most part failed to solve it." In this sentence, Mrs. Woolf outlines the thesis that would preoccupy her in *Orlando* and in her subsequent essay on Strachey. Indeed, the dichotomy she presents here between biographical truth and human personality, between granite and rainbow, is akin to other antithetical structures at the heart of her writings—surface and depths, masculine and feminine, day and night, fact and imagination—and it cannot be underemphasized. The first term of each pair of contrasts always refers to something solid, distinct, mundane, and perishable; the second points to something disembodied, misty, visionary, and nearly eternal. The one is represented by Mr. Bennett, the other by Mrs. Brown. This kind of opposition is touched upon when Rachel Vinrace contemplates the difference between her inner life and the everyday world where "things went round and round quite satisfactorily to other people," or when the speaker in **"The Mark on the Wall"** contrasts the sea-green depths of consciousness with the Table of Precedency, or even when Mrs. Ramsay reads poetry while Mr. Ramsay enjoys Walter Scott. In the context of the essay on Harold Nicolson, the familiar antithesis is posed as a problem for biographers: the biographer serves the world of factual truth, but his aim, in the words of Sidney Lee, is the " 'transmission of personality.' " Is it ever possible, Mrs. Woolf asks, to bring these conflicting notions together?

Some of her most intimate friends were trying to solve the problem by combining the roles of biographer and creative artist; in her essays on biography she applauded their efforts, even though she obviously did not believe they had succeeded. At least, she wrote, they had improved on the Victorian authors of what she calls the "old" biography. Both her review of *Some People* and her essay on Lytton Strachey make essentially the same points about the Victorians: nineteenth-century biographers distorted the personalities of their subjects because they were ploddingly factual and "dominated by the idea of goodness." J. A. Froude's biography of Carlyle had helped alter the current fashion for ignoring the subject's sex life and permitting him "only a smooth superficial likeness to the body in the coffin"; and Edmund Gosse had dared to show that even his father had imperfections. But in Mrs. Woolf's eyes the first true revolutionary was Strachey, who was basically irreverent and possessed of "gifts analogous to the poet's," even if he did not have the poet's "inventive power." Nevertheless, Mrs. Woolf argues that Strachey was successful only in *Queen Victoria. Eminent Victorians* she calls a set of "caricatures," whereas *Elizabeth and Essex,* one of Strachey's most ambitious works, she thinks went too far in flouting the limitations of biography. Victoria's life had been scrupulously authenticated, but Strachey indulged himself in fictions about Elizabeth, who inhabited a strange and relatively obscure age. Thus, Mrs. Woolf says, Strachey's Elizabeth "moves in an ambiguous world, between fact and fiction, neither embodied nor disembodied." Strachey had not achieved a synthesis of rainbow and granite, had not managed the fruitful exchange between the two worlds that Mrs. Woolf works for everywhere in her writings. In fact, she says, a true dialectic between those worlds is probably impossible. If the biographer "invents facts as an artist invents them—facts that no one else can verify—and tries to combine them with facts of the other sort, they destroy each other."

Harold Nicolson's work revealed the same problems as Strachey's, though in certain ways it evidently struck her as more experimental and intriguing. His *Some People* is an eccentric but charming hybrid of a book, redolent of a secure English gentility more remote today than the mountains of the moon. It contains a series of character sketches based on Nicolson's experiences in the diplomatic service, and the early editions are prefaced with this brief, Puckish note: "Many of the following sketches are purely imaginary. Such truths as they may contain are only half-truths." Like *Orlando, Some People* is a playful book, though not outrageously so. If it lacks high seriousness, it does convey some of the pleasures of light, sophisticated literature. Thus we meet such characters as Jeanne de Hénant, who is seen quoting Verlaine through the languid plumes of her cigarette smoke; Jeanne's mother, listening to the Alexandrine her daughter has quoted and "scratching the top of her bald brown head with a table fork," mumbles "Tu as des ideés saugrenues." Years later, Nicolson was to explain that Jeanne and her mother are "an exact description of a French family in which I lived while preparing my examination for the Diplomatic Service . . . nothing fictional has been introduced." But the character of Jeanne is really no less vivid than the essentially fictional "Miss Plimsoll," a governess whose nose was "sharp and pointed like that of Voltaire. . . . When the thermometer fell below 60 it turned scarlet: below 50 it assumed a blue tinge with a little white morbid circle at the end; and at 40 it became sniffly and bore a permanent though precarious drop below its pointed tip."

Virginia Woolf admired Nicolson's book even though she recognized its essential slightness and fragility. Nevertheless, she was troubled by the presence of characters like Miss Plimsoll, whom she suspected were fictional: "Even here," she wrote, "where the imagination is not deeply engaged, when we find people we know to be real, like Lord Oxford or Lady Colefax, mingling with Miss Plimsoll . . . , whose reality we doubt, the one casts suspicion upon the other. Let it be fact, one feels, or let it be fiction; the imagination will not serve under two masters simultaneously." Thus, although she regarded Nicolson as an important example of the biographer as artist, who had indicated a "possible direction," there remained for Virginia Woolf no author "whose art is subtle and bold enough to present that queer amalgamation of dream and reality, that perpetual marriage of granite and rainbow" which is the essence of a truthful depiction of personality.

As I have said, Mrs. Woolf began *Orlando* with these issues very much in mind. In a letter to Vita Sackville-West concerning the new book, she remarked, "it sprung upon me how I could revolutionize biography in a night." Of course she did not even write a biography, much less revolutionize the form, and it is difficult to say just how seriously she went about this task. But clearly the ideas she had outlined in her essay on Nicolson are central to *Orlando*; indeed, even the granite-rainbow metaphor appears in one of the narrator's more significant digressions. Speaking of the difficulty of transmitting Orlando's personality, the biographer-persona comments:

> Nature, who has played so many queer tricks upon us, making us so unequally of clay and diamonds, of rainbow and granite, and stuffed them into a case, often of the most incongruous, . . . nature, who has so much to answer for besides the perhaps unwieldy length of this sentence, has further complicated her task and added to our confusion by providing . . . a perfect rag-bag of odds and ends within us . . . [and] has contrived that the whole assortment shall be lightly stitched together by a single thread.

The narrator of *Orlando,* while trying to do his (or her) duty as a biographer, is much troubled by all the complexities in human personality that we typically find in Mrs. Woolf's novels. In fact, *Orlando* is largely devoted to conflicts between the biographer and the artist—conflicts from which the artist always emerges victorious.

Even so, the book does have a kind of basis in biographical fact. To see how Mrs. Woolf has adapted her historical sources, one need only read Frank Baldanza's brief but excellent account in "*Orlando* and the Sackvilles" [*PMLA*, March 1955]. As Baldanza shows, Virginia Woolf drew heavily on Vita Sackville-West's *Knole and the Sackvilles* (1922), a biography of the grand country estate which had been in possession of the Sackville family since 1566. The details used to describe Orlando's home, even down to the imagery itself, are mostly taken from Miss Sackville-West's account of Knole, although they have been freely adapted to the services of fiction. The person of Orlando is a composite of the Sackville family, merged at last into the figure of Vita Sackville-West, who, in 1927, won the Hawthornden Prize for her poem "The Land," which is quoted in *Orlando* and retitled "The Oak Tree." The early Orlando bears a superficial resemblance to Thomas Sackville, poet and author of *Gorboduc,* who was appointed treasurer to Elizabeth and presented with Knole because, as legend has it, the Queen "wished to have him nearer to her court and councils." Like Charles Sackville, the second Duke of Dorset, Orlando briefly loves a mysterious Russian lady. The gypsy girl he later takes for a wife in Constantinople is based on a real Pepita, a Spanish dancer who was Vita Sackville-West's grandmother and, like Orlando after his sex change, the subject of extensive litigation to determine the true heir of Knole. [The critic adds in a footnote: "The history of Pepita is not found in *Knole and the Sackvilles,* but in a later book by Vita Sackville-West, *Pepita.*"] Even the household servants at Orlando's estate—Mrs. Grimsditch, Mr. Dupper, Mrs. Stewkly, Nurse Carpenter, and Grace Robinson the blackamoor—can be found in *Knole and the Sackvilles:* they are listed in a catalog of the household at Knole under Richard Sackville, the seventeenth-century Earl of Dorset.

But *Knole and the Sackvilles* was more than a sourcebook, and it seems to me that Baldanza's careful research does not indicate its full significance. Vita Sackville-West herself was too modest about the possible influence of her book. In 1955, she wrote that *Orlando* was inspired by Virginia Woolf's "own strange conception of myself, my family, and Knole . . . They satisfied her acute sense of the continuity of history." The "strange conception" was indeed Virginia Woolf's own, but it was echoed and doubtless stimulated by what she had read in *Knole and the Sackvilles,* like this passage about the garden at the estate:

> . . . the garden, save for one small section where the paths curve in meaningless scollops among the rhododendrons, remains today very much as Anne Clifford knew it. . . . The white rose which was planted under James I's room has climbed until it now reaches beyond his windows on the first floor; the great lime has drooped its branches until they have layered themselves in the ground of their own accord and grown up again with fresh roots into three complete circles all sprung from the parent tree . . . the magnolia outside the Poet's Parlour has grown nearly to the roof, and bears its mass of flame-shaped blossoms like a giant candelabrum; the beech hedge is twenty feet high; four centuries have winnowed the faultless turf. . . . The soil is rich and deep and old. The garden has been a garden for four hundred years.

Here was an ultracivilized representation of that nearly timeless but often frightening natural unity Virginia Woolf tried to suggest in all her novels. In *Orlando* itself there is a whimsical reference to the oak tree which the hero has known since "Somewhere about the year 1588," and which is "still in the prime of life."

Vita Sackville-West's comments on the significance of her family history must also have struck a responsive chord in Mrs. Woolf: "Such interest as the Sackvilles have," she wrote, "lies . . . in their being so representative. From generation to generation they might stand, fully equipped, as portraits from English history, . . . let them stand each as the prototype of his age, and at the same time as a link to carry on, not only the tradition but also the heredity of his race, and they immediately acquire a significance, a unity." Such a notion is a step—a large step perhaps, but only a step—from Virginia Woolf's fanciful conception of "portraits from English history" rendered through the life of a single person. Yet Miss Sackville-West continues in this vein, until a kind of sexual transformation seems implicit in what she says about her forebears. Not only were they a family of lovers and would-be poets, but the masculine side of the family had ceased to dominate by the eighteenth century. Looking at the portrait gallery in Knole, she writes:

> You have first the grave Elizabethan, with the long, rather melancholy face, emerging from the oval frame above the black clothes and the white wand of office . . . You come down to his grandson: he is the Cavalier by Vandyck . . . hand on hip, his flame-coloured doublet slashed across by the blue of the Garter . . . You have next the florid, magnificent Charles, the fruit of the Restoration, poet, and patron of poets, prodigal, jovial, and licentious . . . in his Garter robes and his enormous wig, his foot and fine calf well thrust forward . . . the crony of Rochester and Sedley, the patron and host of Pope and Dryden . . . you come down to the eighteenth century. You have on Gainsborough's canvas the beautiful,

sensitive face of the gay and fickle duke . . . You have his son, too fair and pretty a boy, the friend of Byron, . . . the last direct male.

I do not mean to suggest that the sexual theme of *Orlando* derives wholly or even chiefly from *Knole and the Sackvilles*; but a passage like this one must have provided food for Mrs. Woolf's imagination. There are no female portraits here, yet when one reads this description, it is as if a slow metamorphosis were overtaking a single representative of the Sackvilles, taking him through the ages and making him gradually more feminine in the progress.

If *Knole and the Sackvilles* supplied Virginia Woolf with historical detail and perhaps even suggested the themes and plot of *Orlando,* it also stood as another example of a biography to which she might respond. Like the "new" biography, *Knole and the Sackvilles* is a very personal book, characterized by what Mrs. Woolf called a "lack of pose, humbug, solemnity." It is far from comic, but it talks fairly openly about the sex life of the Sackvilles, and focuses on domestic events rather than public careers. Miss Sackville-West is clearly more interested in her ancestors' poetry than in their politics, and hence her book is different from Victorian biography, where, as Virginia Woolf wrote, chapter headings such as "life at college, marriage, career" make "arbitrary and artificial distinctions." Like the new biography as Mrs. Woolf later described it, *Knole and the Sackvilles* is a small volume in which "the author's relation to his subject is different. He is no longer the serious and sympathetic companion, toiling . . . slavishly in the footsteps of his hero. Whether friend or enemy . . . he is an equal."

But Vita Sackville-West's personal, sometimes even poetic little book about her family home is filled nearly to the brim with odd facts. One of the fascinations of *Knole and the Sackvilles* for anyone interested in English history is the large number of minor documents it quotes—letters; amateur poems; diaries; catalogs of members of the household; account-books with expenses dutifully entered in the margins; petitions; menus; inventories; official reports of parliament; receipts; even a sort of dictionary of thieves' slang, dated 1690, which was found scribbled on the back of an official paper. These quaint but often sober details are sometimes cited at great length, and even though Virginia Woolf had written that biographical "fact" gave "rest and refreshment" to the imaginative faculties, at least once in *Orlando* she clearly makes fun of Vita Sackville-West's charming pedantry. The source of her amusement is the fifth chapter of *Knole and the Sackvilles,* where, among sundry other documents, we find a list of "household stuff" dated July, 1624, and including "a pair of Spanish blankets, 5 curtains of crimson and white taffeta, the valance to it of white satin embroidered with crimson and white silk," "a yellow satin chair and 3 stools, suitable with their bukram covers," "a said bag, wherein are 9 cups of crimson damask laid with silver parchment lace," "2 brass branches for a dozen lights apiece," "6 pairs of mats to mat chambers with at 30 yards apiece," "2 walnut tree tables," and "a box containing 3 dozen of venice glasses." The list goes on for about two pages, after which Miss Sackville-West apologizes, "I fear lest the detailing of these old papers should grow wearisome." In

Orlando this passage is openly mocked; when the hero takes an interest in refurbishing his estate, Mrs. Woolf's biographer-persona attempts to verify the truth of his report by quoting a document:

> He now set to work in earnest, as we can prove beyond a doubt if we look at his ledgers. Let us glance at an inventory of what he bought at this time, with the expenses totted up in the margin—but these we omit.
>
> "To fifty pairs of Spanish blankets, ditto curtains of crimson and white taffeta; the valence to them of white satin embroidered with crimson and white silk. . . .
>
> "To seventy yellow satin chairs and sixty stools suitable with their buckram covers to them all. . . .
>
> "To sixty seven walnut tree tables. . . .
>
> "To seventeen dozen boxes containing each dozen five dozen of Venice glasses. . . .
>
> "To one hundred and two mats, each thirty yards long. . . .
>
> "To ninety seven cushions of crimson damask laid with silver parchment lace and footstools of cloth of tissue and chairs suitable. . . .
>
> "To fifty branches for a dozen lights apiece. . . ."
>
> Already—it is an effect lists have upon us—we are beginning to yawn.

A passage like this one leads quite naturally to the issue of parody in *Orlando.* Only with respect to this list can *Orlando* be considered a parody of *Knole and the Sackvilles.* In fact it is a parody at all only in a very limited sense, the prose style undergoes some changes, but the book has relatively little in common with Joyce's "Oxen of the Sun." At most, one can point to the mock preface and index, which mimic the form of scholarly biography, and a few passages which allude to other writings without really trying to imitate them. Here, for example, is a probable reference to *Lady Chatterley's Lover,* which was distributed privately in England in 1928:

> Surely, since she is a woman, and a beautiful woman, . . . she will soon give over this pretense of writing and thinking and begin at least to think of a gamekeeper . . . And then she will write him a little note . . . and make an assignation for Sunday dusk . . . all of which is, of course, the very stuff of life and the only possible subject for fiction. . . . love—as the male novelists define it—and who, after all, speak with greater authority? —has nothing whatever to do with kindness, fidelity, generosity, or poetry. Love is slipping off one's petticoat and—But we all know what love is.

And here Mrs. Woolf makes fun of her own writing in a reference to the novel she had just published:

> He saw the beech trees turn golden and the young ferns unfurl; he saw the moon sickle and then circular; he saw—but probably the reader can imagine the passage which should follow and how every tree and plant in the neighborhood is described first green, then golden; how moons rise and suns set; how night succeeds day and day night; how things remain much as they are for two or three hundred years or so, except for a little dust and a few cobwebs which one old woman can sweep up in half an hour; a conclusion which, one cannot help feeling, might have been reached more quickly by the simple statement that "Time passed" (here the exact amount could be indicated in brackets) and nothing whatever happened.

And yet, while mocking references do not make a parody, *Orlando* did serve to liberate Mrs. Woolf's prose; the author seems conscious throughout of the comic potential in her inherently ornate language. At one extreme, the style has a lively but slightly archaic quality, almost like an imitation of an eighteenth-century comic novel: "many a time did Orlando, pacing the little courtyard, hold his heart at the sound of some nag's steady footfall on the cobbles"; "Seizing the pen with which his little boy was tickling the cat's ears, and dipping it into the egg-cup which served for inkpot, Greene dashed off a very spirited satire there and then". At the other extreme—what might be called the extreme of modernity—are two curious passages in the last chapter, where the narrator drifts into a sort of nonsense-language full of doggerel. It is as if the speaker were out on the edge of a mysterious terrain, talking aloud just to save the book from extinction. The first passage occurs when Orlando sits down to write and the biographer finds that there is nothing to say:

> Let us go, then, exploring, this summer morning, when all are adoring the plum blossom and the bee. And humming and hawing, let us ask the starling (who is a more sociable bird than the lark) what he may think on the brink of the dustbin, whence he picks among the sticks combings of scullion's hair. What's life, we ask, leaning on the farmyard gate; Life, Life, Life! cries the bird, as if he had heard.

The second passage precedes the birth of Orlando's child. Here is a portion of it:

> Oh yes, it is Kew! Well, Kew will do. So here we are then at Kew, and I will show you to-day (the second of March) under the plum tree, a grape hyacinth, and a crocus, and a bud, too, on the almond tree; so that to walk there is to be thinking of bulbs, hairy and red, thrust into the earth in October, flowering now; and to be dreaming of more than can rightly be said, and to be taking from its case a cigarette or cigar even, and to be flinging a cloak under (as the rhyme requires) an oak, and there to sit, waiting the kingfisher.

Mrs. Woolf seemed fond of this new style. She wrote in her *Diary,* "I feel more and more sure that I will never write a novel again. Little bits of rhyme come in." And though of course she did continue to write novels, her interest in the strange new manner stayed with her; consider, for example, the oddly trivialized language she used later in *Between the Acts.* Significantly, the doggerel passages in *Orlando* occur when the biographer is faced with the problem of describing poetic and sexual creativity. In both cases he makes some attempt to represent mysterious powers which seem beyond his power or will to invoke directly; we have, for example, the bird's cry of "Life," and the highly sexual "bulbs, hairy and red, thrust into the earth." Perhaps in the largest sense, the narrator's babble signifies the inadequacy not only of biography, which cannot explore the most intimate and important parts of the subject's life, but also of language itself. There are suggestions of this idea elsewhere in Mrs. Woolf's fiction, particularly when her characters undergo a "dissolution." In *Orlando* there are similar moments, when the hero-heroine is described asleep, in a state of sexual rapture, or sunk in intense imaginative concentration. Toward the end of the book, these moments are described in a language that is almost as disembodied as Orlando herself, as if the biographer had come to the end of the tether. At one point Orlando seems to comment on the significance of the phenomenon: " 'And if I were dead,' she exclaims upon rising from the poem she has been composing, 'it would be just the same!' "

The typical writer of "old" biography, as described in Mrs. Woolf's essays, might echo Orlando's sentiments, though for different reasons: in his view, so long as the heroine is writing a poem instead of fighting a war or running for office, she might as well be a corpse. But the biographer of *Orlando* is not typical, though he sometimes claims to be. Even when he sounds most pompous or naive, one cannot be sure that he is unaware of his own ironies. At first he welcomes the opportunity to write about an aristocratic man of action: "Happy the mother who bears, happier still the biographer who records the life of such a one! Never need she vex herself, nor he invoke the help of novelist or poet. From deed to deed, from glory to glory, from office to office he must go, his scribe following after, till they reach whatever seat it may be that is the height of their desire." In the next breath, however, the narrator confesses that Orlando is hardly the subject for a pedant's vicarious fantasies; Orlando wants to go to war, but he also has a poetic and feminine side: "Directly we glance at eyes and forehead, we have to admit a thousand disagreeables which it is the aim of every good biographer to ignore." The narrator of *Orlando* is certainly not a "good" biographer, and by the time we reach the end of the book, he has committed all sorts of heresies against scientific objectivity. Toward the end he remarks, "The true length of a person's life, whatever the *Dictionary of National Biography* may say, is always a matter of dispute. For it is a difficult business—this time-keeping; nothing more quickly disorders it than contact with any of the arts."

Orlando's biographer is probably best described as a mask, a pose which Mrs. Woolf can assume or drop at will. Thus chapter 2 opens with an ironic apology for the biographer's "difficulty": "Up to this point . . . documents, both private and historical, have made it possible to fulfill the first duty of a biographer, which is to plod, without looking to right or left, in the indelible footprints of truth . . . on and on methodically till we fall plump into the grave and write *finis* on the tombstone above our heads." But the previous chapter has not been concerned

with "documents," and the biographer, there as elsewhere, seems more inclined to poetry than to history. For example, when Orlando drops off to sleep in the first chapter, overtaken by one of those hypnotic moods Mrs. Woolf depicts so often, we are told that "his limbs grew heavy on the ground; . . . by degrees the deer stepped nearer and the rooks wheeled round him and the swallows dipped and circled and the dragon flies shot past, as if all the fertility and amorous activity of a summer's evening were woven web-like about his body." Later in the chapter, the brilliantly hyperbolic description of the Great Frost is supposedly based on the evidence of "historians." But these historians are very different from ours; they tell us that "Birds froze in mid-air and fell like stones to the ground," and that in Norwitch, "a young country woman started to cross the road . . . and was seen by the onlookers to turn visibly to powder and be blown in a puff of dust over the roofs."

The official evidence of biographers, historians, and eye-witnesses is consistently mocked. In chapter 3, when Orlando is given a dukedom and the ambassadorship to Constantinople, where he "had a finger in some of the most delicate negotiations between King Charles and the Turks," we are, or should be, on the familiar public ground of the "old" biography. And yet, while the author previously related the details of Orlando's amours and the most intimate of his thoughts, at this stage in the hero's life "we have the least information to go upon." It seems that all the important documents relating to Orlando's career have been destroyed. "Often the paper was scorched a deep brown in the middle of the most important sentence." Obviously, the comparative dullness of public lives is being satirized here, but the author is perhaps making another point as well. In her essay on Strachey, Virginia Woolf had commented on the perishable quality of biography: "Micawber and Miss Bates" she wrote, "will survive Lockhart's Sir Walter Scott and Lytton Strachey's Queen Victoria. For they are made of more enduring matter. The artist's imagination at its most intense fires out what is perishable in fact; but the biographer must accept the perishable, build with it, imbed it in the very fabric of his work. Much will perish; little will live." Hence rainbow turns out to be more durable than granite, just as, in a more famous antithesis, Mrs. Ramsay's spirit is more nearly eternal than Mr. Ramsay's reputation can ever be.

The biographer of *Orlando* occasionally tries to do justice to the facts, but maintains the pose only briefly. Likewise, he cannot be a servant of Victorian morality; Orlando's sex-change is reported in spite of the blandishments of Purity, Chastity, and Modesty. Even some of the more lively didactic passages are treated half-jokingly: "these moralities belong, and should be left to the historian, since they are as dull as ditch-water." Although there are occasions when Virginia Woolf's own literary mannerisms are made the butt of the narrator's jokes, the interests of the would-be biographer are usually no different from Mrs. Woolf's typical concerns. For example, consider the book's fascination with the workings of consciousness. " 'What a phantasmagoria the mind is and meeting-place of dissemblables!' " Orlando declares to herself. The narrator has already confirmed this point by noting the "disorderly and circuitous way" the mind works and by describing in great detail the relations between sensations and ideas. When Orlando's attempts at composition are frustrated by images of his "lost Princess," we are given a long digression on the workings of memory. Later there is an almost equally long discussion of the effects of duration, where we are told that "An hour, once it lodges in the queer element of the human spirit, may be stretched to fifty or a hundred times its clock length." But after noting that the disparity between clock time and mental time "deserves further study," the narrator feels he must hurry on: "the biographer, whose interests are . . . highly restricted, must confine himself to one simple statement: when a man has reached the age of thirty, as Orlando now had, time when he is thinking becomes inordinately long."

Toward the end of the book, in a passage where the biographer's mask is securely in place, the narrator speaks contemptuously of mere thought. But Virginia Woolf's irony could not be more transparent:

> Life, it has been agreed by everyone whose opinion is worth considering, is the only fit subject for novelist or biographer; life, the same authorities have decided, has nothing whatever to do with sitting still in a chair and thinking. Thought and life are as the poles asunder. . . . If only subjects, we might complain (for our patience is wearing thin), had more consideration for their biographers! What is more irritating than to see one's subject, on whom one has lavished so much time and trouble, slipping out of one's grasp altogether and indulging—witness her sighs and gasps, her flushing, her palings—what is more humiliating than to see all this dumb show of emotion and excitement gone through before our eyes when we know that what causes it—thought and imagination—are of no importance whatsoever.

Virginia Woolf wrote **Orlando,** of course, partly to demonstrate the importance of thought and imagination. The biographer-persona, in spite of his disclaimers, does not ignore the imaginative or sexual life, nor even those oddly disembodied moments that are so much a part of Mrs. Woolf's novels; and for these reasons the book is neither a consistent parody of official Victorian biography nor a simple satire. The narrator may claim to have the instincts of a biographer, but he begins the book like a novel, in the midst of an action, and his attention is always focused on Orlando's private selves. Obviously, the book is meant to poke fun at the "old" biography in a good many ways. I have already mentioned the use of comic paraphernalia like the mock preface and index, the occasional pretended distrust of imagination, and the abortive attempts at pedantry; more important, instead of a chaste history of the public life of an English peer, the narrator unfolds the imaginative and sexual life of a sensitive youth who is miraculously transformed into a woman overnight. If, in spite of the narrator's fascination with personality, Orlando never seems as fully-developed as Miss Plimsoll or Queen Victoria, that is partly because Mrs. Woolf's characters always tend to merge with the narrator and become slightly disembodied, and partly because her book is a critique of all biography, both old and new. Perhaps at some

point she really intended to make **Orlando** a model for the "new" biography. But from the start the book was controlled by a playful fantasy, and the result is reminiscent of any of Mrs. Woolf's novels: an exploration into a realm where it is hard to determine whether character or novelist is speaking, where radical distinctions and discontinuities (as between the eighteenth century and the nineteenth) are more apparent than real, where granite gives way almost entirely to rainbow.

Ultimately, Virginia Woolf does little to revolutionize biography and much to break new ground for writers of imaginative literature. In a far less comprehensive and ambitious sense, **Orlando** describes some of the same phenomena as *Finnegans Wake;* it accounts for vast periods of history through the experience of a single person who, we are told, has "a great variety of selves to call upon," and it openly declares that "the most successful practitioners of the art of life, often unknown people by the way, somehow contrive to synchronize the sixty or seventy different times which beat simultaneously in every normal human system."

In her essays, Virginia Woolf acknowledged the importance of the biographer and showed her deep interest in his craft. But she placed him always after the artist, since in her mind "fact" was always inferior to imagination. To the question her contemporaries and friends were asking—whether biographical and imaginative truths could be combined, whether granite could be fused with rainbow—her answer was always a regretful negative. **Orlando** is another of these negative replies, since at every turn it is meant to show us the futility of biographical fact and the necessity for art in the depiction of personality.

A similar pattern lies, I think, behind the sexual theme of **Orlando,** about which I have said rather little because it has been treated so extensively elsewhere. The book is often described as "androgynous," chiefly on the strength of Mrs. Woolf's plea for an "androgynous mind" in *A Room of One's Own.* Certainly Orlando is, from the moment we first see him, a sexually ambiguous figure; and certainly the author is concerned to show that the "masculine" and "feminine" temperaments are and should be mixed in every person. But could anyone argue that the mind that produced **Orlando** is truly androgynous, whatever its intentions? If Mrs. Woolf regarded Shakespeare as an androgynous mind and found "a little too much of a woman" in Proust, what must we say of her work? **Orlando** pays tribute to the active, outgoing character, but ultimately it celebrates an introspective, poetic sensibility. Here, as in *A Room of One's Own,* Virginia Woolf's argument rests on the assumption that there are two inherently different worlds, masculine and feminine. She believed that these worlds ought to coexist; she fought discrimination against women, and she quite wisely observed that they would need money to write books. But at the same time she was attracted to the passive, dreamy experiences which she repeatedly associated with femininity. Sometimes she was able to range back and forth between the two worlds of rainbow and granite (as in writing her biography of Roger Fry), but one of her major weaknesses is that she was never quite able to synthesize them. In the last analysis, she prefers one order of experience over the other.

Hermione Lee   (essay date 1977)

SOURCE: *The Novels of Virginia Woolf,* Holmes and Meier Publishers, 1977, 237 p.

[*In the following excerpt, Lee discusses Woolf's use of the life and writings of Vita Sackville-West as inspiration for* Orlando.]

Orlando has a different quality from all Virginia Woolf's other novels, though it is interestingly comparable to many of them, particularly to *Jacob's Room* and *Between the Acts.* The difference in quality is suggested by its subtitle, 'A Biography': it is an attempt to represent the character of a real person. Though *To the Lighthouse* was also, in a sense, biographical, it was not written *for* the characters who are evoked in the novel. *Orlando,* by contrast, is a personal offering, dedicated to Vita Sackville-West in a spirit of love and fascination and also of irony.

In writing the book, Nigel Nicolson suggests [in his *Portrait of a Marriage*], 'Virginia had provided Vita with a unique consolation for having been born a girl.' *Orlando* is meant to console Vita not only for her sex, but also for her loss of Knole, the ancestral home of the Sackvilles, which came about because she was a woman and could not inherit. Vita had passionate and bitter feelings of possession and loss for Knole, which one can see expressed in her novels *The Heir* (1922) and *The Edwardians* (1930) and in her letters to [her husband, Harold Nicolson]: 'Oh God, I do wish that Knole hadn't got such a hold on my heart! If only I had been Dada's son, instead of his daughter!' In *The Heir* (subtitled 'A Love Story') a quiet little man from Wolverhampton suddenly finds himself in possession of a Kentish Elizabethan manor house. The story describes his increasingly possessive love for the place, which is heavily mortgaged and has to be auctioned. The hero, Chase, finds the thought of losing the house more and more unbearable, for 'The house *was* the soul; did contain and guard the soul as in a casket . . . the soul of England.' At the sale he finds himself 'fighting to shield from rape the thing he loved' and buys it back in a defiant gesture 'to cast off the slavery of the Wolverhamptons of this world.' The language of the story is equally emotional throughout, and accurately reflects Vita's passion for family property, and her idea of herself as part of the tradition she inherits:

> If could take my England, and could wring
> One living moment from her simple year,
> One moment only, whether of place or time,
> . . . Then should my voice find echo in English
>   ear;
> Then might I say, 'That which I love, I am.'

> [*The Land*]

'I loved it,' she says of Knole in *Knole and the Sackvilles,* 'and took it for granted that Knole loved me.' The phrase is suggestive of the aristocratic pride which united a distaste for the Wolverhamptons of this world with a strong local feeling for family, house and land. In *The Edwardi-*

ans, published two years after *Orlando,* Vita recreates her childhood at Knole ('Chevron'). Chevron's beauty dominates the book, and the thought of its becoming national property (as Knole did in 1941) is anathema to the hero. But in *The Edwardians* the way of life made necessary by the place is treated with some reservations. The hero's sister is a socialist and 'regards our love for Chevron as a weakness.' Chevron's way of life is threatened, and the book is tinged with Vita's wistful acceptance of that fact—a quality similar to the tender nostalgia at the end of *Orlando.* As in *Orlando,* too, genders overlap. The brother and sister of *The Edwardians* are called Sebastian and Viola, and both are in love with the same character. It is interesting that Vita, by this reference to Shakespeare's sexually ambiguous twins, should have followed the consolation for the loss of Knole provided by *Orlando.* There, Knole is Orlando's because she has been a man; in *The Edwardians,* Chevron is Vita's because she is a man as well as a woman. Vita's masculine sexuality, which she herself fictionalized in the melodramatic and romantic *Challenge* (written in 1919 but at the time unpublished), is closely related to her feelings about her family home, and this is made apparent both in her own novel about Knole and in *Orlando.*

Virginia Woolf understood and admired Vita's feelings for her house and her land, and was interested in the link between those feelings and Vita's sexuality, a link which she recognized as being central to Vita's character. By making Orlando's life span over 300 years and include a change of sex she suggests that Vita's personality was formed equally by its androgyny and by its inheritance from the past. The novel's general themes of history and sexual identity are thus at every point directed towards a description of personality. The historical periods that have created the house have also created Orlando. The book necessitates a double reading; its fantasy and pageantry are being used as the material of a love letter which tells the loved one the writer's opinion of her. As the book goes on, it becomes increasingly concerned with what Vita is like. Virginia Woolf feared that the book, which she had 'begun as a joke,' lacked 'unity.' There is some truth in this; the serious concentration on Orlando's personality is at odds with the very materials and techniques used to create it. The idealization of the character (which Quentin Bell remarks on [in his *Virginia Woolf: A Biography*]; criticizing it for its nearness to 'the glamorous creations of the novelette') gives an oddly romantic air to a book which partly sets out to be an instrument of ridicule and satire.

For the subtitle is also a joke. The personal emphasis of *Orlando* is couched in parodic terms; the study of Vita's character is presented through the medium of a literary *jeu d'esprit.* The game takes various forms. Overall, the techniques of the historical biographer are being ridiculed, very much as in *Jacob's Room.* What is life? the narrator asks, giving throughout the implied answer that life is not what the biographers make of it, 'since a biography is considered complete if it merely accounts for six or seven selves, whereas a person may well have as many thousand.' The serious experiment in *Jacob's Room* of 'following hints' in order to get at the truth of life and character is refashioned here into a less arduous and more entertaining shape. Many of the techniques are the same. The biographer is as much in evidence, hanging 'like the hawk moth' 'at the mouth of the cavern of mystery,' periodically standing back to generalize or comment about life and art, speaking to the reader more often and more directly than Orlando does. In *Jacob's Room,* however, the difficulty of discovering Jacob produced a sense of sadness, anticipating his death. *Orlando* provides a comic version of the same difficulty. The ironic disparity between the jaunty, factual attempt at biography and the shifting, ambiguous quality of life is parodic rather than elegiac.

The elusiveness of the principal character is not the central theme. Orlando is far closer to us than Jacob; her thoughts frequently overlap with the biographer's. They voice, indistinguishably, questions asked by women and by writers: 'Which is the greater ecstasy? The man's or the woman's?'; 'What then, was Life?'; 'What has praise and fame to do with poetry?' Unlike Jacob, Orlando is a self-conscious participant in the biographer's quest for personality, and at times speaks for her:

> 'Hair, pastry, tobacco—of what odds and ends are we compounded,' she said (thinking of Queen Mary's prayer book). 'What a phantasmagoria the mind is and meeting-place of dissemblables!'

The biographer is wily. The quaintness of Orlando's vocabulary and the humorous conclusion to her meditation ('she threw her cheroot out of the window and went to bed') prevent us from taking too seriously a platitude with which the biographer is very much in agreement. The light tone avoids solemnity and at the same time allows for flexibility; at any moment we may find that it is the biographer rather than Orlando who is speculating:

> Had Orlando, worn out by the extremity of his suffering, died for a week, and then come to life again? And if so, of what nature is death and of what nature life? Having waited well over half an hour for an answer to these questions, and none coming, let us get on with the story.

Here the character of a pompous biographer is being assumed in order for it to be mocked. This satire on traditional biography (which owes a debt to Lytton Strachey's work in the same field) is carried out in various ways, all aimed at showing up the dichotomy between factual biography and true life. The predicament of the biographer whose subject does nothing but write (and whose reader may consequently ask for his money back) is wittily described; the absurdities of 'Acknowledgements' and 'Indexes' are mocked; and the solemn use of historical records is made fun of: 'We have done our best to piece out a meagre summary from the charred fragments that remain; but often it has been necessary to speculate, to surmise, and even to use the imagination.' Orlando's career at this point is given to us through the diary of 'John Fenner Brigge, an English naval officer' and 'Miss Penelope Hartopp, daughter of the General of that name.' Though the pastiche on 'source material' is meant to amuse, it also arises naturally from Virginia Woolf's tendency to create scenes and characters through different observers; Penelope Hartopp's account of events is reminiscent of Ellie

Henderson's view of Clarissa's party. In all the literary jokes made in *Orlando* there is a similar sense of Virginia Woolf's pleasure and natural inclination. Brief satires on legal parlance, ridiculous accounts and examples of Victorian literature, pastiches of Sir Thomas Browne or Jane Austen, sidelong digs at D. H. Lawrence and his gamekeeper or at Hemingway and his monosyllables, burst out energetically from within the general parodic vein. Virginia Woolf does not pursue the parodic line which Joyce takes in 'The Oxen of the Sun' section of *Ulysses,* where the development of the foetus is imaged in a gargantuan parody of the major styles of English literature from Anglo Saxon to the future time. But there is in *Orlando* a more moderate form of the same idea. Each historical period, which in itself illustrates or sets off a part of Orlando's character, is invoked by literary or artistic allusions which may (as in the references to Sir Thomas Browne) move towards actual stylistic parody. Usually, however, the allusions suggest rather than imitate the tone of the period.

A major element in the book's humour is the satire directed against Vita herself, and Vita's work. Clearly, we are allowed to view with irony the inconsistency in Orlando which allows him to be 'unaccountably ashamed of the number of his servants and of the splendour of his table' when he is with Nick Greene, and to describe 'with some pride' when she is with Rustum the gipsy 'the house where she was born, how it had 365 bedrooms and had been in

Angelica Bell, "The Russian Princess as a Child," from the first edition of Orlando.

the possession of her family for four or five hundred years.' This fond satire on Vita's personal characteristics incorporates a literary debunking of *Knole and the Sackvilles,* which Vita published in 1922. 'I am reading *Knole,'* Virginia Woolf writes to Vita '. . . you have a rich dusty attic of a mind.' The use she makes of Vita's book on Knole is well suggested by the illustrations which she chose, in consultation with Vita, for the first edition of **Orlando.** Three of these are photographs of Vita, posed and dressed to suggest Orlando in the eighteenth, nineteenth and twentieth centuries. One is a photograph of Angelica Bell in outlandish costume, representing Sasha; and three are historical portraits of 'the Archduchess Harriet,' of 'Marmaduke Bonthrop Shelmerdine' and of 'Orlando as a boy,' which is the portrait of the young Edward Sackville, son of the fourth Earl of Dorset, one of the illustrations to *Knole and the Sackvilles.* The combination of photographs of Vita and historical portraits reflects Virginia Woolf's treatment of her subject. In part **Orlando** really is the history of the Sackvilles at Knole. Many of the details that Vita records are used in **Orlando.** These may be small matters like the names of the servants, the descriptions of the bowls of potpourri, the mention of King James's silver brushes or of the gallery 'whose floor was laid with whole oak trees sawn across.' But more important themes are also incorporated. Orlando's early tragedies call to mind not only Vita's juvenile historical novels and plays but also Charles Sackville's *Gorboduc;* Orlando's relationship with Nick Greene refers to the Sackvilles' patronage of the arts; the allusions to Shakespeare echo Vita's attempts to forge some connection between Shakespeare and Knole; Vita herself speaks in *Knole* of 'the disadvantage of fine birth to a poet.' Vita's desire to 'resurrect the Sackvilles' in her guidebook, to destroy the concept of the house as a historic monument to the dead, is close in spirit to Orlando's wistful sympathy for the house at the end of the book:

> The house, with its exits and entrances, its properties of furniture and necessities . . . the house demands its population. Whose were the hands that have, by the constant light running of their fingers, polished the paint from the banisters? . . . Who were the men and women that, after a day's riding or stitching, lay awake in the deep beds, idly watching between the curtains the play of the firelight, and the little round yellow discs cast upon walls and ceiling through the perforations of the tin canisters standing on the floor, containing the rush lights?
>
> Thus the house wakes into a whispering life, and we resurrect the Sackvilles. [*Knole and the Sackvilles*]

. . . . .

> Rows of chairs with all their velvets faded stood ranged against the wall holding their arms out for Elizabeth, for James, for Shakespeare it might be, for Cecil, who never came. The sight made her gloomy. . . . Chairs and beds were empty; tankards of silver and gold were locked in glass cases. The great wings of silence beat up and down the empty house. . . . The gallery stretched far away to a point where the light almost failed. It was as a tunnel bored deep into

the past. As her eyes peered down it, she could see people laughing and talking. . . . [*Orlando*]

Orlando is an attempt to resurrect the Sackvilles. But it does not treat Vita's literary monument to them as sacrosanct. The game Virginia Woolf plays with *Knole* is that of exaggerating all its details, taking her cue from Vita's descriptions of the house as having the look of 'a medieval village,' of containing within its 'four acres of building' seven courts, corresponding 'to the days of the week; and in pursuance of this conceit . . . fifty-two staircases, corresponding to the weeks in the year, and three hundred and sixty-five rooms, corresponding to the days.' Vita admits that she has not verified this count, but the elaborate grandeur of the claim (particularly because of the sense it gives of Knole as a House of Time) attracts Virginia Woolf's attention, and sets the tone for the passage in which she describes Orlando's refurnishing of Knole. Every item in the list of Orlando's expenses is taken from the inventories and lists of 'household stuff' given in the chapter 'Knole in the reign of Charles I'; but the numbers of Spanish blankets, walnut-tree tables, cushions of crimson damask, are wildy exaggerated. Vita's apology for her lists ('I fear lest the detailing of these old papers should grow wearisome') is taken up: 'Already—it is an effect lists have upon us—we are beginning to yawn.'

But though the effect is satirical, it is also creative of atmosphere. Knole is vividly, marvellously realized, partly through the parodic treatment of Vita's book, partly through more lyrical descriptive passages. Such changes of approach are characteristic of **Orlando;** its interest, and also its weaknesses, arise from the attempt to use several styles and several approaches interchangeably. Her diary notes on the writing of **Orlando** lay stress on this attempt. It is to be written, she says, in 'a mock style very clear and plain'; but then again 'it has to be half laughing, half serious; with great splashes of exaggeration.' In the end she decides that **Orlando** is not a complete success: it is 'too freakish and unequal, very brilliant now and then.' Presumably she would, in **Orlando,** feel open to the charge she herself levels against the purple patch—'not that it is purple but that it is a patch.'

The diary entries point to two of the stylistic variations in **Orlando,** that between satire and lyricism, and that between the early fantasy and later seriousness of the book. But there are further refinements. Each historical period is evoked in a fluent essayist's style, distinct from the satiric tone used for the pedantic biographer, or from the impressionistic, lyrical style which attempts to reach the heart of **Orlando**'s personality and the nature of life. Even within the 'clear and plain' historical style there are variations. The spirit of each age requires a different literary treatment. Rich, clear, sharp, energetic details evoke the Elizabethan period like a Breughel painting; the vitality, passion and pageantry of the age are encapsulated in the personality of Queen Elizabeth, and in Orlando's affair with Sasha. The literary climate is suggested by a generalized paraphrase of all Elizabethan poetry: 'The moment is brief they sang; the moment is over; one long night is then to be slept by all.' If one turns from this first chapter to the description of the eighteenth century in Chapter Four, one finds different techniques at work. The spirit of the age is preserved in the minds of its major literary figures; as a result the chapter consists largely of anecdotes and quotations, and is summed up by a silhouette portrait of Johnson, Boswell and Mrs Thrale. The nineteenth century, by contrast, is expansively caricatured; the emphasis is on grotesque parody, whether in the generalized account of the country's rising damp or its three-volume novels, or in the exchange about wedding rings between Orlando and Mrs Bartholemew ('The muffins is keepin' 'ot,' said Mrs Bartholemew mopping up her tears, 'in the liberry'). The pictorial images for the age are a Turner cloudscape and an object which suggests a mixture of the Albert Memorial and Crystal Palace:

> Draped about a vast cross of fretted and floriated gold were window's weeds and bridal veils; hooked on to other excrescences were crystal palaces, bassinettes, military helmets, memorial wreaths, whiskers, wedding cakes, cannon, Christmas trees, telescopes, extinct monsters, globes, maps, elephants, and mathematical instruments—the whole supported like a gigantic coat of arms on the right side by a female figure clothed in flowing white; on the left, by a portly gentleman wearing a frock-coat and sponge-bag trousers.

The list is impressionistic and elephantine, and far removed in tone from the bizarre precision and archaic tone of the list that describes, as the climax to a series of brilliant descriptive passages, the breaking of the Great Frost:

> Many perished clasping some silver pot or other treasure to their breast; and at least a score of poor wretches were drowned by their own cupidity . . . furniture, valuables, possessions of all sorts were carried away on the icebergs. Among other strange sights was to be seen a cat suckling its young; a table laid sumptuously for a supper of twenty; a couple in bed; together with an extraordinary number of cooking utensils.

Cutting transversely across these linear, historical changes in style is the fluctuation between wit and lyricism in the treatment of Orlando. Where Virginia Woolf is concentrating on the absurdities of the biographer who attempts to create Orlando, or on the relation between Orlando and the spirit of the age, or on Orlando's moments of action, the style is witty, 'clear and plain.' Where she is concentrating, as she does increasingly, on the true, inward nature of personality, the style is lyrical and impressionistic. But a serious tone is never allowed to dominate; the light-fantastic is compulsively reintroduced. This is necessary if Virginia Woolf is to sustain all the levels of the book at once, but it is often rather irritating. It seems at times as though, in making Orlando at once a creature of fantasy who lives for centuries and changes her sex, and at the same time a complex person to be used as the spokesman (like Mary Seton in *A Room of One's Own*) for women and for women writers, Virginia Woolf has set herself an almost impossible task.

> When the sailors began chanting, 'So good-bye and adieu to you, Ladies of Spain,' the words echoed in Orlando's sad heart, and she felt that however much landing there meant comfort,

meant opulence, meant consequence and state (for she would doubtless pick up some noble Prince and reign, his consort, over half Yorkshire), still, if it meant conventionality, meant slavery, meant deceit, meant denying her love, fettering her limbs, pursing her lips, and restraining her tongue, then she would turn about with the ship and set sail once more for the gipsies.

> Among the hurry of these thoughts, however, there now rose, like a dome of smooth, white marble, something which, whether fact or fancy, was so impressive to her fevered imagination that she settled upon it as one has seen a swarm of vibrant dragon-flies alight, with apparent satisfaction, upon the glass bell which shelters some tender vegetable.

The dome shape is a recurring image of comfort and fulfilment in Virginia Woolf, used here to express the contrast between Orlando's new feelings of restriction at being a woman and the consolation of writing. The process of thought is an extremely serious one—indeed it contains the argument of *A Room of One's Own.* But seriousness is kept within the realm of fantasy by the artificial rhythms and repetitions of the first paragraph and the elaborate image of the second part. The writer chooses to be winsome and entertaining rather than solemn or didactic; and thereby succeeds only in sounding whimsical and affected.

Though the book's carefully preserved lightness of tone may not always be interesting or persuasive, its serious, innermost intention—the analysis of Orlando's character—is convincingly achieved. Orlando, who is both man and woman, also stands in a dual relation to time. We partly feel that, although Orlando takes over 300 years to reach the age of thirty-six, she does not change. Her essential qualities are already formed when she is an Elizabethan boy of sixteen and continue, over the centuries, to express themselves in her poem, 'The Oak Tree':

> How very little she had changed all these years. She had been a gloomy boy, in love with death, as boys are; and then she had been amorous and florid; and then she had been sprightly and satirical; and sometimes she had tried prose and sometimes she had tried drama. Yet through all these changes she had remained, she reflected, fundamentally the same. She had the same brooding meditative temper, the same love of animals and nature, the same passion for the country and the seasons.

It is important that there should be a 'sameness' about Orlando. Although the character becomes more self-possessed and aware as a mature woman than as a young man, he/she is always sulky, beautiful, clumsy, impetuous, devoted to nature and solitude and 'afflicted with a love of literature.' It is by this means that Virginia Woolf emphasizes Orlando's natural androgyny: she is the same character whether she is a man or a woman, and it is evident from the first line of the book that Orlando's man/womanly characteristics overlap. Orlando's 'sameness' enables Virginia Woolf eventually to attack the nineteenth century, the only age to which Orlando cannot adapt her bisexual personality, since it forces men and women into unnaturally rigid marital roles. Ironically, then, the major change in Orlando's life comes not when she turns from man into woman, but when she has to adapt herself to the Victorian age:

> Orlando had inclined herself naturally to the Elizabethan spirit, to the Restoration spirit, to the spirit of the eighteenth century, and had in consequence scarcely been aware of the change from one age to the other. But the spirit of the nineteenth century was antipathetic to her in the extreme, and thus it took her and broke her, and she was aware of her defeat at its hands as she had never been before. For it is probable that the human spirit has its place in time assigned to it; some are born of this age, some of that; and now that Orlando was grown a woman, a year or two past thirty indeed, the lines of her character were fixed, and to bend them the wrong way was intolerable.

That Orlando should have permanent qualities, 'fixed lines,' rather than a changing, developing character, is necessary too if we are to bear in mind that the fantasy of Orlando's moving through time is a lighthearted metaphor for her historical consciousness. By the end of the book we think of Orlando as an achieved and real personality, dominated by her powerful feelings of the past history of her house and family. We concentrate, finally, on her consistency, not on the changes she has 'lived' through. This is emphasized in the remarkable passage about the true self and the Captain self which draws to a conclusion our consideration of Orlando/Vita.

> She was . . . changing her selves as quickly as she drove . . . as happens when . . . the conscious self, which is the uppermost and has the power to desire, wishes to be nothing but one self. This is what some people call the true self, and it is, they say, compact of all the selves we have it in us to be; commanded and locked up by the Captain self, the Key self, which amalgamates and controls them all.

At a cursory reading the passage suggests that the conscious or true self is the *same* as the Captain self. But the Captain self is rather the guardian of the true self, standing in the same relationship to it as does the biographer to his subject. Virginia Woolf is the Captain self of the novel who 'amalgamates and controls' all the selves of Orlando. But Orlando too has a Captain self which searches for her true self, the combination of all her identities, with such questions as these:

> 'What, then? Who, then?' she said. Thirty-six; in a motor-car; a woman. Yes, but a million other things as well. A snob, am I? The garter in the hall? The leopards? My ancestors? Proud of them? Yes! Greedy, luxurious, vicious? Am I? (here a new self came in). Don't care a damn if I am. Truthful? I think so. Generous? Oh, but that don't count (here a new self came in).

The passage continues to delineate all her qualities, though the Captain self does not succeed in finding the true Orlando until she passes through the lodge gates to her house. The questionings suggest Orlando's infinite variety, but they also confirm the reader's sense that Orlando has a recognizable, consistent personality. Because Virginia Woolf wanted to write a lighthearted, not a serious biography, she chose to build Orlando's 'true self' out of a fantastic time sequence rather than out of a day-in-the-life, as with Mrs Dalloway, or out of a sequence from childhood to old age, as with Bernard, who, at the end of *The Waves,* is a Captain self calling for his true self in manner very similar to Orlando's.

The historical organization of *Orlando* is, then, a means of showing how Orlando stays the same, not how she changes. Similarly, the sex change does not alter Orlando's character, but her perceptions and her social behaviour. Her perceptions are enriched by it—'She was man; she was woman; she knew the secrets, shared the weaknesses of each'—but her social behaviour is restricted. Because she understands both sides, but has to behave as a woman, she is both enlightened and frustrated. She thus becomes the ideal spokesman for the androgynous argument also being evolved at this time in *A Room of One's Own,* which, though a more public and straightforward statement than *Orlando,* uses some of the same techniques, such as the mingling of a chronological account of women through the centuries with the fantasy of Shakespeare's sister. In *A Room of One's Own,* as in *Orlando* (and as in the later and less engaging *Three Guineas*) women are encouraged to cherish and make use of their special qualities, which arise from centuries of oppression:

> 'Better it is,' she thought, 'to be clothed with poverty and ignorance, which are the dark garments of the female sex; better to leave the rule and discipline of the world to others; better be quit of martial ambition, the love of power, and all the other manly desires if so one can more fully enjoy the most exalted raptures known to the human spirit, which are,' she said aloud, as her habit was when deeply moved, 'contemplation, solitude, love.'

Virginia Woolf says that this train of thought leads Orlando into 'the extreme folly . . . of being proud of her sex,' but the comment is perhaps not quite true to the tone of the passage from which it arises. A comparison with *A Room of One's Own* is invited. Here she states that 'it is fatal for anyone who writes to think of their sex. It is fatal to be a man or a woman pure and simple; one must be woman-manly or man-womanly.' Though the need for such impartiality is applied equally to both sexes, there is in her account of the two imaginary writers, Mary Carmichael and Mr A, a definite preference for the woman, insufficiently androgynous though she may be. Orlando is supposed to balance equally the qualities of both sexes, as is shown in this charming analysis of Vita which expresses very clearly Virginia Woolf's feelings about her:

> For it was this mixture in her of man and woman, one being uppermost and then the other, that often gave her conduct an unexpected turn. The curious of her own sex would argue, for example, if Orlando was a woman, how did she never take more than ten minutes to dress? And were not her clothes chosen at random, and sometimes worn rather shabby? And then they would say, still, she has none of the formality of a man, or a man's love of power. She is excessive-

ly tender-hearted. She could not endure to see a donkey beaten or a kitten drowned. Yet again, they noted, she detested household matters, was up at dawn and out among the fields in summer before the sun had risen.

But Orlando is more a critic of men than of women, and she does in fact become more womanly—'a certain change was visible in Orlando' deeper than the change of clothes. Though she is described as an androgynous personality, her female characteristics seem to dominate. It would be hard to imagine an *Orlando* in which the sex change was the other way round. Only if Orlando had ended up as a man would the enthusiasm for the hermaphrodite mind be absolutely unbiased. Not until *The Waves* does the androgynous spokesman become a man. In *Orlando* the emphasis is feminist; Orlando really does fall into the folly of 'being proud of her sex.'

She is hauled back from such folly, however, by a consideration of the word 'love.' The satisfaction Orlando finds in her relationship with Shelmerdine (far greater than any she enjoyed in her egotistical masculine affairs) is reminiscent of Katharine and Ralph's achievement in *Night and Day* (and suggestive of Vita's adaptable *modus vivendi* with Harold Nicolson). Orlando's sense of freedom and excitement in the relationship provides her with those moments of ecstasy which result, here and elsewhere in Virginia Woolf's work, from the personality's being transcended:

> It is not articles by Nick Greene or John Donne nor eight-hour bills nor covenant nor factory acts that matter; it's something useless, sudden, violent; something that costs a life; red, purple, blue; a spurt; a splash; like those hyacinths (she was passing a fine bed of them); free from taint, dependence, soilure of humanity or care for one's kind; something rash, ridiculous, like my hyacinth, husband I mean, Bonthrop; that's what it is—a toy boat on the Serpentine, ecstasy—it's ecstasy that matters.

Colours, movements and natural objects are preferred to the masculine world of administration, articulacy and philanthropy. Orlando thrives on an incoherent plane (described in the terms of an abstract painting) where her love for one person is a mixed part of her intense susceptibility to immediate experience. Such ecstasy can only result from an emancipating relationship in which sexual characteristics are blended. The tone and structure of Orlando do not, however, lend themselves to a study of relationships. Shelmerdine is a flimsy and fantastic creature, only serviceable as an agent for the moments of ecstasy, or as an instrument of satire on the nineteenth-century matrimonial instinct, to which Orlando falls an unwilling victim. His return in an aeroplane at the end indiscreetly forces a renewal of the book's fantasy level, which, since the striking of the present time, has been abandoned in favour of a conclusive search for Orlando's 'true self.'

This self lies not in her relationships with other people, but in her relationship with her house and with her writing. The closest analogy between Orlando and her biographer is that both are struggling to find a way of expressing life (or truth, or reality: the terms are frequently interchange-able) in art. Orlando's attempts to write are, like her character, partly evolved from and partly at odds with the historical periods through which she lives. When an Elizabethan, she writes tragedies like *Gorboduc*; when a seventeenth-century ambassador she reads Sir Thomas Browne and meditates upon tombstones (shrinking from 'the cardinal labour of composition which is excision'); in the eighteenth century she becomes a lover of the picturesque; and in the nineteenth century has to wrestle with the spirit of the age which would have her write 'in the neatest sloping Italian hand . . . the most insipid verse she had ever read in her life.' In the end Orlando writes Vita's poem *The Land*—not perhaps a very startling departure from Victorianism, but the result of 'the transaction between a writer and the spirit of the age' which 'is one of infinite delicacy.'

The difficulty of making the transaction when the writer is unsympathetic to his age is only one of the several difficulties which obstruct Orlando in her natural desire to write. Orlando is an aristocrat, by tradition a patron rather than a writer; to become the latter she must 'substitute a phantom' (literature) 'for a reality' (her house and lands). In substituting phantom for reality she is faced with the essential task of every writer (not least of Orlando's biographer, who is much preoccupied with it), that of translating reality into words. 'Life? Literature? One to be made into the other? But how monstrously difficult!'

Like all books about writers, *Orlando* reflects itself: the book, and the biographer's explanations of her difficulty in writing it, is a mirror, as well as a framework, for Orlando's poem, and her difficulty in writing it. Throughout, the biographer and Orlando both have to tackle again and yet again what it means to have to write; to have, for instance, to try to turn 'green' from a thing into an idea:

> He was describing, as all young poets are forever describing, nature, and in order to match the shade of green precisely he looked (and here he showed more audacity than most) at the thing itself, which happened to be a laurel bush growing beneath the window. After that, of course, he could write no more. Green in nature is one thing, green in literature another. Nature and letters seem to have a natural antipathy; bring them together and they tear each other to pieces. The shade of green Orlando now saw spoilt his rhyme and split his metre.

At this early stage in Orlando's literary career he abandons the problem precipitately, and the biographer has done no more than crudely to impress on us the untransferability of greenness into poetry. In the second assault on the same problem, both Orlando and the biographer are more sophisticated. Orlando is at the stage of rejecting all elaboration, all rhetoric, all figures of speech. Let words be things themselves, not other things. But nature itself, he finds, does not invite such treatment, for all its things can be seen as other things. Looking at nature—even before one has written about it—must mean using metaphor. Again he abandons the problem:

> So then he tried saying the grass is green and the sky is blue . . . Looking up, he saw that, on the contrary, the sky is like the veils which a thou-

sand Madonnas have let fall from their hair; and the grass fleets and darkens like a flight of girls fleeing the embraces of hairy satyrs from enchanted woods. 'Upon my word,' he said . . . 'I don't see that one's more true than another. Both are utterly false.' And he despaired of being able to solve the problem of what poetry is and what truth is, and fell into a deep dejection.

Always, when Orlando returns to the attempt at representation, she works through images, as does her biographer. As the period changes, so too do the figures of speech. In the eighteenth century, 'green' is more formally decorated: 'She compared the flowers to enamel and the turf to Turkey rugs worn thin. Trees were withered hags, and sheep were grey boulders. Everything, in fact, was something else.' But the problems of mimesis remain unsolved, and cannot be solved, since new ways of making 'green' be literature have endlessly to be struggled for. Lightheartedly, and in miniature, *Orlando* thus suggests the necessity for Virginia Woolf's own unceasing literary experimentation.

In the struggle, the writer has to establish and sustain integrity. Orlando must learn to ignore the flattery or abuse of such as Nick Greene, and come to the point of saying: 'Bad, good, or indifferent, I'll write, from this day forward, to please myself.' All writers, of course, not only those who are also aristocrats or women, have to struggle for that defiant statement, which arises, or should arise, from the continuous tension between exposure and privacy in the writer's life.

> While fame impedes and constricts, obscurity wraps about a man like a mist; obscurity is dark, ample, and free; obscurity lets the mind take its way unimpeded.

It is an obvious enough conflict—*A Writer's Diary* bears evidence to it on almost every page—but not a simple one. Though the writer's initial, and essential, integrity, can be established by sloughing off external influences, there follows the pull towards the outside world, the desire for fame. Orlando has to reject Nick Greene after their first encounter in order to become her own literary master and judge. But she needs him again in his later incarnation (as a man of letters modelled on Sir Edmund Gosse) so that he can give her manuscript what it needs: 'It wanted to be read. It must be read. It would die in her bosom if it were not read.' Only then, after the intercourse with public life, can the writer, justified, withdraw again into obscurity into the centre of her 'true self,' which, for Orlando, is found in her relationship with her house and land:

> What has praise and fame to do with poetry? . . . Was not writing poetry a secret transaction, a voice answering a voice? So that all this chatter and praise and blame and meeting people who admired one and meeting people who did not admire one was as ill suited as could be to the thing itself—a voice answering a voice. What could have been more secret, she thought, more slow, and like the intercourse of lovers, than the stammering answer she had made all these years to the old crooning song of the woods, and the farms and the brown horses

standing at the gate, neck to neck, and the smithy and the kitchen and the fields, so laboriously bearing wheat, turnips, grass, and the garden blowing irises and fritillaries?

> So she let her book lie unburied and dishevelled on the ground, and watched the vast view, varied like an ocean floor this evening with the sun lightening it and the shadows darkening it. . . .

The passage gently humanizes the 'crooning' landscape, and treats Orlando's meditation romantically—with a tender allusion to Vita's poem (' . . . the springing grass / Was dulled by the hanging cups of fritillaries'). It is a serious and restrained conclusion to a book which has been witty, extravagant, even flashy, in tone and manner. The biographer, at this point in full possession of Orlando's true self, creates a mood of sober sympathy for her heroine, and, giving up tricks and jests, herself discreetly disappears.

An excerpt from *A Writer's Diary*

The sun is out again; I have half forgotten *Orlando* already, since L. [Woolf's husband, Leonard] has read it and it has half passed out of my possession; I think it lacks the sort of hammering I should have given it if I had taken longer; it is too freakish and unequal, very brilliant now and then. As for the effect of the whole, that I can't judge. Not, I think, "important" among my works. L. says a satire.

L. takes *Orlando* more seriously than I had expected. Thinks it in some ways better than the *Lighthouse:* about more interesting things, and with more attachment to life and larger. The truth is I expect I began it as a joke and went on with it seriously. Hence it lacks some unity. He says it is very original. Anyhow I'm glad to be quit this time of writing "a novel"; and hope never to be accused of it again.

Virginia Woolf, in a diary entry of May 31, 1928, in her A Writer's Diary: Being Extracts from the Diary of Virginia Woolf, *edited by Leonard Woolf, 1953. Reprint by Harcourt Brace Jovanovich, 1954.*

Harold Skulsky (essay date 1981)

SOURCE: "Virginia Woolf's *Orlando:* Metamorphosis as the Quest for Freedom," in his *Metamorphosis: The Mind in Exile,* Cambridge, Mass.: Harvard University Press, 1981, pp. 195-222.

[*In the following excerpt, Skulsky examines Orlando's transformation from male to female.*]

Unlike Gregor Samsa's abrupt descent into the bondage of the carapace, Orlando's transformation into a woman is the initial stage of a gradual unfolding of comprehensive personal freedom, an unfolding that coincides with Virginia Woolf's narrative as a whole. Transformation in this extended sense has much the rhythm of an organic process—the butterfly's evolving declaration of independence. Orlando traces, by her efflorescence, the outlines of an intricate ideal of freedom. This, at all events, is the general view I should like to defend in what follows. The constraint Orlando manages to overthrow is largely intellectual; it consists of certain shibboleths of what we may broadly describe as bourgeois common sense—the dichotomies of the real and the imaginary, the actual and the possible, the masculine and the feminine. I shall proceed by discussing each of these matters in turn and then offering a general assessment of their connections with the central theme of transformation.

Orlando begins his career, as a young Elizabethan patrician, by presuming on a freedom he has not yet achieved: freedom to explore the imaginary without being put out of countenance by the real: "He was describing, as all young poets are forever describing, nature, and in order to match the shade of green precisely, he looked (and here he showed more audacity than most) at the thing itself, which happened to be a laurel bush growing beneath the window. After that, of course, he could write no more. Green in nature is one thing, green in literature another. Nature and letters have a natural antipathy: bring them together and they tear each other to pieces. The shade of green Orlando now saw spoilt his rhyme and split his metre." At this point we are evidently being invited by the ironical narrator to suppose that the hero has caught himself out in a silliness to which the antidote is a certain gruff realism; he has been turning love of literature and of its practitioners into an idolatry: "To his imagination it seemed as if even the bodies of those instinct with such divine thoughts must be transfigured. They must have aureoles for hair, incense for breath, and roses must grow between their lips." Unfortunately, the love of literature is itself a "disease" whose "fatal nature" is "to substitute a phantom for reality, so that Orlando, to whom fortune had given every gift—plate, linen, houses, men-servants, carpets, beds in profusion—had only to open a book for the whole vast accumulation to turn to mist." Here, for the moment at least, the fantastic prevails and the real betrays an underlying flimsiness; Lamia, in effect, is having her brief revenge.

Yet it is the solidity of Orlando's ancestral domain, we learn, that usually consoles him for the volatility of his phantoms: "He opened his eyes, which had been wide open all the time, but had seen only thoughts, and saw lying in the hollow beneath him, his house." It is a little ominous, perhaps, that thoughts and material things are put on a par here as being equally objects of seeing; and indeed it turns out that what Orlando chiefly "sees" in the hollow beneath him is a moralized parade of images:

> For after all, he said, kindling as he looked at the great house on the greensward below, the unknown lords and ladies who lived there never forgot to set aside something for those who come after; for the roof that will leak; for the tree that will fall. There was always a warm corner for the old shepherd in the kitchen; always food for the hungry; always their goblets were polished, though they lay sick, and the windows were lit though they were dying. Lords though they

were, they were content to go down into obscurity with the molecatcher and the stonemason.

The landscapes we encounter in Woolf's romance are rarely without such phantom embellishments as the molecatcher and the stonemason. As Orlando moves through his preternaturally slow ripening, each century of English experience somehow generates the setting and conditions required by its characteristic notion of the real. Thus in the Enlightenment "the very landscape outside was less stuck about with garlands and the briars themselves were less thorned and intricate. Perhaps the senses were a little duller and honey and cream less seductive to the palate." In the Renaissance "the weather itself, the heat and cold of summer and winter, was, we may believe, of a different temper altogether. The brilliant amorous day was divided as sheerly from the night as land from water. Sunsets were redder and more intense; dawns were whiter and more auroral. Of our crepuscular half-lights and lingering twilights they knew nothing. The rain fell vehemently or not at all. The sun blazed or there was darkness." The inauguration of the nineteenth century shows once again parallel changes of outer and inner climate: "As the ninth, tenth, and eleventh strokes struck, a huge blackness sprawled over the whole of London. With the twelfth stroke of midnight, the darkness was complete. A turbulent welter of cloud covered the city. All was dark; all was doubt; all was confusion." The mocking account of the young poet's discomfiture by "the thing itself," it is eventually borne in on us, was an irony at our expense; things are not to be brought to bay "in themselves," and if nature proves to be no less a phantom of communal prejudice than its poetic image, the charade of Augustan social "reality" virtually cancels itself out: "This is one of the cases where truth does not exist. Nothing exists. The whole thing is a miasma—a mirage." "At one and the same time therefore, society is everything and society is nothing. Society is the most powerful concretion in the world, and society has no existence whatsoever."

And reality has its geographical as well as its historical variability, as Orlando unsettlingly discovers during her sojourn among the Turkish gypsies, who cannot abide her transcendentalist inclinations:

> It sprang from the sense they had (and their senses are very sharp and much in advance of their vocabulary) that whatever they were doing crumbled like ashes in their hands. An old woman making a basket, a boy skinning a sheep, would be singing contentedly at their work, when Orlando would come into the camp, fling herself down by the fire and gaze into the flames. She need not even look at them, and yet they felt, here is someone who doubts; (we make a rough-and-ready translation from the gipsy language) here is someone who does not do the thing for the sake of doing; nor looks for looking's sake; here is someone who believes neither in sheepskin nor basket; but sees (here they looked apprehensively about the tent) something else.

The gypsies disagree profoundly not only with Orlando's refusal to accept nature as the ultimate reality but with what they regard as her vapid sentimentality about nature itself: "The elder men and women thought it probable that she had fallen into the clutches of the vilest and cruelest among all the Gods, which is Nature. Nor were they far wrong. The English disease, a love of Nature, was inborn in her, and here where Nature was so much larger and more powerful than in England, she fell into its hands as she had never done before." "[Rustum el Sadi] had the deepest suspicion that her God was Nature. One day, he found her in tears. Interpreting this to mean that her God had punished her, he told her that he was not surprised. He showed her the fingers of his left hand, withered by the frost; he showed her his right foot, crushed where a rock had fallen."

The root of these quarrels is simply that the disputants hold (or wish to hold) differing theories of appearances on which they substantially agree; so far, at least, reality takes its place among the discredited phantoms of the narrative:

> No passion is stronger in the breast of man than the desire to make others believe as he believes. Nothing so cuts at the root of his happiness and fills him with rage as the sense that another rates low what he prizes high. Whigs and Tories, Liberal Party and Labour Party—for what do they battle except their own prestige? It is not love of truth, but desire to prevail that sets quarter against quarter and makes parish desire the downfall of parish. Each seeks peace of mind and subservience rather than the triumph of truth and the exaltation of virtue—But these moralities belong, and should be left to the historian, since they are as dull as ditchwater. "Four hundred and seventy-six bedrooms mean nothing to them," sighed Orlando. "She prefers a sunset to a flock of goats," said the gipsies.

As Lycius under Lamia's tutelage awakens from one trance into another, Orlando congratulates herself paradoxically at one point on her spiritual progress: " 'I am growing up,' she thought . . . 'I am losing some illusions . . . perhaps to acquire others'."

The moral that Orlando eventually draws from these reflections is emphatically not the lotus-eating romanticism that the narrator mercilessly parodies at one point, and that rather suggests a caricature of Keats's diatribe against Apollonius:

> A man who can destroy illusions is both beast and flood. Illusions are to the soul what atmosphere is to the earth. Roll up that tender air and the plant dies, the colour fades. The earth we walk on is a parched cinder. It is marl we tread and fiery cobbles scorch our feet. By the truth we are undone. Life is a dream. 'Tis waking that kills us. He who robs us of our dreams robs us of our life—(and so on for six pages if you will, but the style is tedious and may well be dropped).

Orlando is little less adroit than the gypsies in getting her bearings among physical objects—sheepskins, baskets, or mountains; on an elementary level, her inventory of such objects matches that of her hosts. What she comes to reject is the interpretation of such reassuring agreements embodied in realism, whether the naive realism of the gypsies

or the sophisticated version purveyed to Bloomsbury by G. E. Moore.

In Moore's version, which is a useful foil to Orlando's emerging view, all objects of perception, including sensible qualities, are outside the mind:

> Whenever I have a mere sensation or idea, the fact is that I am then aware of something which is equally and in the same sense *not* an inseparable aspect of my experience. The awareness which I have maintained to be included in sensation is the very same unique fact which constitutes every kind of knowledge; "blue" is as much an object, and as little a content of my experience, when I experience it, as the most exalted and independent real thing of which I am ever aware. There is, therefore, no question of how we are to "get outside the circle of our own ideas and sensations." Merely to have a sensation is already to *be* outside the circle. It is to know something [for example, "blue"] which is as truly and really not a part of my experience as anything which I can ever know.

To say that an expanse of sensible color is "outside" or is "not a part" of its respective sensation is to deny any necessity for such expanses to be sensed in order to exist; for what would such a necessity be like? Not, surely, the necessity with which the incidence of evenness depends on that of number, or of loudness on that of sounds. It may be that properties like evenness or loudness are necessarily restricted to qualifying some kinds of things and cannot otherwise occur, but there is no useful analogy to be drawn from this fact. For the object of an awareness is not a property of the awareness at all. A sensation of blue, for example, need not itself be blue. Perhaps, indeed, it *cannot* be blue, for a sensation is simply an act of sensing, and there is room at least for doubt that one can sense bluely. It is, for Moore, a fallacy to consider that sensations are not acts but images—images whose likeness or unlikeness to external objects is a plausible subject for dispute. [In his *Philosophical Studies,* Moore states:] "We have no reason for supposing that there are such things as mental images at all."

Orlando's evolving view is very nearly the denial of all this, and the heart of it is the conviction that our mental images all too eloquently vindicate their own existence, though their role in sensations is not quite the one Moore so easily dismisses. If one were to distill a formal position from the meditative passages I shall be considering in a moment, the result, I think, would be roughly as follows. Sensations, to be sure, are not acts varying somehow by color and shape; but this is because they are not acts at all, with objects whose independence of being acted on could serve to show the ease with which we may get outside the circle of our experience. When we say that someone has a sensation of a round blue patch we mean that he is in a particular state of mind—for that is the sort of thing a sensation is—and that this particular species of sensation accompanies one's seeming to see the round blue surface of a physical object. *Being of a round blue patch* is the analogue in sensation of *being round and blue* in physical appearance. For these appearances the only evidence is the sensations that accompany them, but conceptually the appearances have priority; reports about physical objects in themselves are simply confidently elliptical reports of appearances. It is these objects, in short, and not images, whose status is in doubt; for the consciousness that encircles us is less diaphanous than Moore allows.

No doubt the sequence of appearances and images that occur to Orlando tallies in part with the experience of others, and defines the order that common sense ascribes to real things. But to dichotomize the world into the real and the apparent or imaginary is to fall into the demoralizing error of regarding consciousness as at best a spyhole into a world from which the mind is essentially excluded. A real object is simply an apparent object that has met a test of coherence with other appearances, and it is as imaginary as any hallucination in the radical sense that, as it happens, without images there are no appearances—no conceptual episodes of seeming to see physical objects. The natural environment of such seemings consists of images, and while certain practicalities are served by discounting the latter, an important freedom and an important truth are redeemed, for the artist especially, by surrendering to their ubiquity.

The spiritual transformation by which Orlando reaches this view is, at the outset, embarrassed by realist misgivings. The callow Jacobean poet deprecates his inability to focus on the real: "Every single thing, once he tried to dislodge it from its place in his mind, he found thus cumbered with other matter like the lump of glass which, after a year at the bottom of the sea, is grown about with bones and dragon-flies, and coins and the tresses of drowned women." Even his current thought, Orlando reflects to his annoyance, is encumbered with metaphors expressing the same sort of impertinent matter:

> "Why not simply say what one means and leave it?" So then he tried saying the grass is green and the sky is blue and so to propitiate the austere spirit of poetry whom still, though at a great distance, he could not help reverencing. "The sky is blue," he said, "the grass is green." Looking up, he saw that, on the contrary, the sky is like the veils which a thousand Madonnas have let fall from their hair; and the grass fleets and darkens like a flight of girls fleeing the embraces of hairy satyrs from enchanted woods. "Upon my word," he said . . . "I don't see that one's more true than another. Both are utterly false." And he despaired of being able to solve the problem of what poetry is and what truth is and fell into a deep dejection.

This odd mixture of compassion and mockery is characteristic of Virginia Woolf's treatment of the adolescent Orlando's frustrations. The metaphorical turn of mind, as it blesses or afflicts the young man, is simply the habit of transcribing the text of subjective history without the deletions required to make it intersubjective:

> He loved, beneath all this summer transiency, to feel the earth's spines beneath him; for such he took the hard root of the oak tree to be; or, for image followed image, it was the back of a horse that he was riding; or the deck of a tumbling

ship—it was anything indeed, so long as it was hard, for he felt the need of something which he could attach his floating heart to; the heart that tugged at his side; the heart that seemed filled with spiced and amorous gales every evening about this time when he walked out.

What Orlando feels the need of, at this stage, is the notion of a physical world that transcends appearances, possible or actual; it is the need of something he will eventually recognize as chimerical: "Hair, pastry, tobacco—of what odds and ends are we compounded . . . What a phantasmagoria the mind is and meeting place of dissemblables."

The context of the physical items Orlando mentions is the mind, or minds, of which they are ingredients, and the result of contemplating physical appearances in their mental context is phantasmagoria: "Everything was partly something else, and each gained an odd moving power from this union of itself and something not itself so that with this mixture of truth and falsehood her mind became like a forest in which things moved; lights and shadows changed, and one thing became another." At least once we are offered an illustration of precisely how something becomes nothing; when, on her homeward voyage from Turkey, Orlando surveys the English coast, she is affected by a puzzling visual image:

> There now rose, like a dome of smooth, white marble, something which, whether fact or fancy, was so impressive to her fevered imagination that she settled upon it as one has seen a swarm of vibrant dragonflies alight, with apparent satisfaction, upon the glass bell which shelters some tender vegetable. The form of it, by the hazard of fancy, recalled that earliest, most persistent memory—the man with the big forehead in Twitchett's sittingroom . . . The truth was that the image of the marble dome which her eyes had first discovered so faintly that it suggested a poet's forehead and thus started a flock of irrelevant ideas, was no figment, but a reality; and as the ship advanced down the Thames before a favouring gale, the image with all its associations gave place to the truth, and revealed itself as nothing more and nothing less than the dome of a vast cathedral rising among a fretwork of white spires.

Notably, the image does not give way to truth by withdrawing; what it reveals as "reality" is only itself in a new guise or under a new interpretation. It transpires that the "fancy" is of the kind that prompts us by the dense texture of fancies that cohere with it to announce the presence of a "reality."

Licensed by this phenomenalism, Woolf's narrator rejects the view that history—the account of what happens to perceiving selves—is to be restricted to the "objective," and hence to the partial. An epoch of hyperbolic feelings is better and more accurately served by reproducing its own hyperbolic vision of itself, as the narrator serves the Jacobeans in a surreal and rather Ovidian bagatelle:

> The Great Frost was, historians tell us, the most severe that has ever visited these islands. Birds froze in mid-air and fell like stones to the ground. At Norwich a young country-

woman . . . was seen by the onlookers to turn visibly to powder and be blown in a puff of dust over the roofs . . . The fields were full of shepherds, ploughmen, and little bird-scaring boys all struck stark in the act of the moment, one with his hand to his nose, another with the bottle to his lips, a third with a stone raised to throw at the raven who sat, as if stuffed, upon the hedge within a yard of him . . . The court was at Greenwich, and the new King seized the opportunity that his coronation gave him to curry favour with the citizens. He directed that the river, which was frozen to a depth of twenty feet and more for six or seven miles on either side, should be swept, decorated, and given all the semblances of a park or pleasure ground, with arbours, mazes, alleys, drinking booths, etc., at his own expense.

. . . . .

Near London Bridge, where the river had frozen to a depth of some twenty fathoms, a wrecked wherry boat was plainly visible, lying on the bed of the river where it had sunk last Autumn, overladen with apples. The old bumboat woman, who was carrying her fruit to market on the Surrey side, sat there in her plaids and farthingales with her lap full of apples, for all the world as if she were about to serve a customer, though a certain blueness about the lips hinted the truth. 'Twas a sight King James liked to look upon, and he would bring a troupe of courtiers to gaze with him.

Here, at any rate, is the Jacobean myth vividly illuminated: the fascination with freaks and pageants, with life conceived as a brilliant and intricate masque, with death conceived as a dance of grotesquely ornate drollery. And the style of description, a series of pictorial flashes of macabre transformation and elemental caprice, is in the same idiom as Ovid's *jeux d'esprit* on the flood of Deucalion and the effects of the Gorgon's stare. In *Orlando,* however, the idiom is at the disposal not of a despairing ironist but of a chronicler of the imagination for whom accuracy consists, in effect, in framing the sketch of a room with a suspicion of the side of the sketcher's nose, or perhaps (if he is sitting) with a foreground of his hands and lap. To explode the myth of the thing in itself is, for Orlando the poet, to justify the autonomous exercise of the imagination, and hence to regain an essential freedom.

Talk of regaining a freedom runs the risk of misunderstanding, so I shall take this opportunity of emphasizing that the phenomenalist interpretation of experience we have been considering is hardly a piece of cultural subversion, or a precursor of late twentieth-century *anomie.* One might as plausibly cast in that ideological role Prospero's conviction that we are such stuff as dreams are made on. The point, once again, is not so much to dethrone the real as to exalt the imaginary by showing that, for the hardest-headed among us as for the dreamers, the reading of "see" on which "he sees an oak tree" is consistent with the tree's nonexistence is more fundamental than the reading that implies its existence; in either case one has to do with an image. For their own legitimate purposes, common sense and science partition experience into the objective and the subjective, and this proceeding becomes perverse only if it is allowed to impoverish our sense of reality. Common sense, tradition, even conventional social manners (if prevented from tyrannizing) are good things in their place— beside and not over against the creatures of the mythic imagination. *Orlando* is too history-haunted, too private, too libertarian a romance to reflect the iconoclasm of an ideologue. Its mischief has nothing in common with vandalism.

The narrative demonstrates a different sort of freedom, I think, in its ambiguous handling of time; for we are left to contend as best we can with the fact that the central figure, among others, has lived through more than three centuries of varied history by the end of the narrative while growing no older than thirty-six. This is easily enough accounted for if we assume that the years are measured in intersubjective or public time and the centuries in private; the sense of duration, as the narrator delights in reminding us, is wonderfully elastic:

> An hour, once it lodges in the queer element of the human spirit, may be stretched to fifty or a hundred times its clock length; on the other hand, an hour may be accurately represented on the timepiece of the mind by one second. This extraordinary discrepancy between time on the clock and time in the mind, is less known than it should be and deserves fuller investigation.

. . . . .

> All which [that is, Orlando's lionization by Victorian society] is properly enclosed in square brackets, as above, for the good reason that a parenthesis it was without any importance in Orlando's life. She skipped it, to get on with the text. For when the bonfires were blazing in the market place, she was in the dark woods with Shelmerdine alone. So fine was the weather that the trees stretched their branches motionless above them, and if a leaf fell, it fell, spotted and gold, so slowly that one could watch it for half an hour fluttering and falling till it came to rest at last on Orlando's foot.

. . . . .

> And indeed, it cannot be denied that the most successful practitioners of the art of life, often unknown people by the way, somehow contrive to synchronise the sixty or seventy different times which beat simultaneously in every human system so that when eleven strikes all the rest chime in unison, and the present is neither a violent disruption nor completely forgotten in the past. Of them we can justly say that they live precisely the sixty-eight or seventy-two years allotted them on the tombstone. Of the rest, some we know to be dead, though they walk among us; some are not yet born, though they go through the forms of life; others are hundreds of years old though they call themselves thirty-six.

The times not registered by clock or tombstone apparently divide up the units of public time into arbitrary units of private; presumably, the general rule is that the more eventful or highly valued a span of experience, the swifter it seems in the having and the longer in retrospect, and the reverse with empty or oppressive time. On this interpretation, the narrator has simply chosen to ignore the conventional hierarchy of precision or objectivity among measures of duration. The resulting paradox is a variation on Rosalind's metaphysical impudence toward quite another Orlando in *As You Like It:*

> ROSALIND. Time travels in divers paces with divers persons. I'll tell you who time ambles withal, who time gallops withal, and who he stands still withal.
>
> ORLANDO. I prithee, who doth he trot withal?
>
> ROSALIND. With a priest that lacks Latin, and a rich man that hath not the gout; for the one sleeps easily because he cannot study, and the other lives merrily because he feels no pain; the one lacking the burthen of lean and wasteful learning, the other knowing no burthen of heavy tedious penury. These time ambles withal.
>
> ORLANDO. Who doth he gallop withal?
>
> ROSALIND. With a thief to the gallows; for though he go as soft as foot can fall he thinks himself too soon there.
>
> ORLANDO. Who stays it withal?
>
> ROSALIND. With lawyers in the vacation; for they sleep between term and term, and then they perceive not how Time moves.

The operative word, on what we may call the Shakespearean model of the vagaries of time, is "perceive"; and as applied to the narrative attitude toward the real or objective in **Orlando,** we shall understand that the clock is only one measure—the public measure—among others, all rooted in perception and subject to its contingencies.

The difficulty with this approach is that the Shakespearean model clarifies only part of what Virginia Woolf's narrator is enabled to say by his treatment of time; that Orlando's public years are private minutes does not by itself palliate the miracle that she manages to live through three hundred years of public events, beginning as an Elizabethan and still carrying on in the reign of George V, and the historical evocations are too elaborate and highly charged to be the machinery of a pointless joke. I should like to suggest that the subject of the historical part of **Orlando**'s temporal paradox is not the status of *fact,* but the multiple *possibilities* of the central figure. For these are not all-inclusive; we may reasonably entertain not only the innocuous claim that it is logically possible for Orlando to have lived in any one of several epochs, but also the more interesting claim that given Orlando's essential character the roles she would respectively have played in them are as they are represented in the narrative. Construed in this way, the narrator's flight of fancy turns out to have the assurance and complexity typical of informed claims about what would be true in circumstances that happen not to hold.

With its ellipses filled in, the current claim would, I think, take roughly the following form: there are alternative schemes of things, or total states of past, present, and future affairs—possible worlds, shall we say—that are very similar to the actual world in the things they contain, their laws of nature, and what happens in them. In those similar worlds that the narrator, at least, would pick out as especially similar to the actual world, Orlando never figures as an Elizabethan nobleman without also having the experiences we are reading about. On this interpretation, each historical episode in the narrative is the main clause of a conditional sentence contrary to fact with the if-clause and the subjunctive mood suppressed: "Orlando (would have) aspired to piratical adventure (if he had been a young Elizabethan nobleman)." The "biography" is a direct exploration of what we may call Orlando's historical possibilities. But if this reading is sound, why does the narrator drop the prefix "it is possible that" or "it would have been the case that," and dart from one alternative world to another—from one in which Orlando is Elizabethan to another in which she is Augustan—as if they were all on a par with the actual world?

The answer seems to be that this is precisely the insidious point of the narrative; that the dethronement of the actual is part of the same subversive libertarian program as the dethronement of the real. For the entities that are the fundamental bearers of truth and possibility—the so-called propositions—are no respecters of worlds. That Orlando is an Elizabethan nobleman is true in some possible worlds and false in others, just as it is true at some moments and false at others that Orlando is in Turkey. "Now" and "actually" are not (as common sense would have it) the labels of a privileged moment and world; they are not labels at all, but expressions that vary in reference with the moments and worlds in which sentences containing them are uttered. To evaluate a particular utterance of "Orlando is now in Turkey," one notes the time of utterance and then ascertains whether Orlando is in Turkey at that time. Thus the narrator uses "the present moment" archly here and there as if just one date could be so described, but permits the date mentioned to vary ironically.

To contemplate the possible truth of a proposition on this view is to enjoy a kind of freedom of which the utterance in some particular world of "now" or "actually" is a crass interruption. To measure truth by reference to such interruptions is to allow them to immure the self in but one of the universes to which it is native, and since "now" names no moment, being taken in by the hallucination of a Present Moment par excellence is an experience of peculiar dread, a confrontation with the void.

The narrative is strewn with such dread confrontations:

> Her thoughts became mysteriously tightened and strung up, as if a piano tuner had put his key in her back and stretched the nerves very taut; at the same time her hearing quickened; she could hear every whisper and crackle in the room, so that the clock ticking on the mantelpiece beat like a hammer. And so for some seconds the light went on becoming brighter, and she saw everything more and more clearly, and the clock ticked louder and louder until there was a terrible explosion right in her ear. Orlando leapt as if she had been violently struck in the head. Ten times she was struck. In fact it was ten o'clock in the morning. It was the eleventh of

October. It was nineteen twenty-eight. It was the present moment. No one need wonder that Orlando started, pressed her hand to her heart and turned pale. For what more terrifying revelation can there be than that it is the present moment? That we survive the shock at all is only possible because the past shelters us on one side, and the future on the other.

. . . . .

She saw with disgusting vividness that the thumb of Joe's right hand was without a fingernail and there was a raised saucer of pink flesh where the nail should have been. The sight was so repulsive that she felt faint for a moment, but in that moment's darkness, when her eyelids flickered, she was relieved of the presence of the present. There was something strange in the shadow that the flicker of her eyes cast, something which (as anyone can test for himself by looking now at the sky) is always absent from the present—whence its terror, its nondescript character—something one trembles to pin through the body with a name and call beauty, for it has no body, is as a shadow and without substance or quality of its own, yet has the power to change whatever it adds itself to. This shadow now while she flickered her eye in her faintness in the carpenter's shop stole out, and attaching itself to the innumerable sights she had been receiving, composed them into something tolerable, comprehensible.

The shadow that the self casts on the moment it contemplates, and that subdues its terror, is the sense of unity, of transcending any particular moment or possible state of affairs. The enjoyment of this unity, I think, is ultimately connected with the narrative insistence on counterfactual history, and the strange egalitarianism with which it presents the incompatible worlds it contemplates.

Our way of determining from the outside what shall count as an individual is a matter of convention. If our problem is to decide whether Orlando the Elizabethan courtier and his namesake the Caroline Ambassador are one and the same, we look for a schedule of continuous passage between the point and moment at which the courtier was last located and the point and moment at which the Ambassador was first located such that each point-moment position on the schedule was occupied by one or the other of them. Continuity in space and time will allow us to identify the courtier with the Ambassador even though it would be logically permissible to take two consecutive positions on the schedule as those respectively on which one individual ceases to exist and a second begins; indeed, if the contrast between the courtier and the Ambassador were as catastrophic as that between Gregor and the beetle, an outsider might be tempted to embrace the latter alternative with some enthusiasm. Even the narrator, who knows better, verges once on treating Orlando's change in sex as if it were a question of identifying distinct parts of a whole consisting of two successive individuals:

Orlando had become a woman—there is no denying it. But in every other respect, Orlando remained precisely as he had been. The change of

sex, though it altered *their* future, did nothing whatever to alter *their* identity. *Their* faces remained, as *their* portraits prove, practically the same. His memory—but in future we must, for *convention's* sake, say "her" for "his" and "she" for "he"—her memory then, went back through all the events of her past life without encountering any obstacle. (emphasis added)

From the inside, however, from Orlando's perspective, it is simply axiomatic that if she has a memory at all, it is an awareness "of *her* past," the past of an indivisible subject; there is ultimately no danger of her shrinking away, as perceiver, into the nothingness of the present and the actual. Terms like "Elizabeth's favorite courtier" or "the Caroline Ambassador to Turkey"—the terms of merely conventional statements of identity—are descriptions that change their reference from moment to moment or from one possible world to another; in this respect they are no different from "now," "actually," "the English monarch in 1590" (variable from world to world), or "the English monarch" (variable from time to time and world to world). Proper names and their associated pronouns, on the other hand—in the narrator's ordinary usage, at any rate—do not vary at all in the context of "now" or "it is possible (is actually the case) that." The entire point of our being told, concerning Orlando, that "she reviewed . . . the progress of her own self along her own past" depends on our understanding that the reference of the pronouns "she," "her own self," and "her" is identical despite contextual differences in tense and mood. In the current jargon phrase, the terms are all "rigid designators."

It is true that side by side with pronominal "self" or "herself" we find "self" and "Orlando" serving as common nouns in the plural, and that this may suggest a flirtation with anxieties about the unity of the person:

For she had a great variety of selves to call upon, far more than we have been able to find room for, since a biography is considered complete if it merely accounts for six or seven selves, whereas a person may well have as many thousand. Choosing, then, only those selves we have found room for, Orlando may now have called on the boy who cut the nigger's head down; the boy who sat on the hill; the boy who saw the poet; the boy who handed the Queen the bowl of rose water; or she may have called upon the young man who fell in love with Sasha; or upon the Courtier; or upon the Ambassador; or upon the Soldier; or upon the Traveller; or she may have wanted the Woman to come to her; the Gipsy; the Fine Lady; the Hermit; the girl in love with life; the Patroness of Letters . . . All these selves were different, and she may have called on any of them.

Perhaps; but what appeared certain (for we are in the region of "perhaps" and "appears") was that the one she needed most kept aloof; for she was, to hear her talk, changing her selves as quickly as she drove—there was a new one at every corner—as happens when, for some unaccountable reason, the conscious self, which is the uppermost, and has the power to desire, wishes to be nothing but one self. This is what some people call the true self, and it is, they say, compact of all the selves we have it in us to be; commanded and locked up by the Captain self, the Key self, which amalgamates and controls them all."

The list of Orlando's "selves" consists not of individuals but of individual concepts or roles satisfied by the same "she" at different times in different possible worlds. They are her possibilities of transformation, the selves she has it in her to be. Certain traits, on the other hand, are essential to the role-*bearer* or "Captain self"; for "through all those changes she had remained, she reflected, fundamentally the same. She had the same brooding meditative temper, the same love of animals and nature, the same passion for the country and the season." There is thus an opportunity of choosing to be an essential or "true" self—to play in one's imagination a role that epitomizes the rest; though the motive for such an averaging, is, says the narrator, "unaccountable." To rejoice imaginatively in the rich multiplicity of one's "selves," it is clear, is to celebrate the unity and energy of the protean Self that, by its joint presence in more than one possible world, impersonates them all.

Suppose—to explore the contrasting possibility—that we deny Orlando's axiom, as in effect Stevenson's Dr. Jekyll tries to do, by assuming that one cannot intelligibly ask whether the Jekyll of one moment is literally the same as the Jekyll of the next; they are distinct objects—stages, let us say—that pass our conventional test (of resemblance and continuity) for parts of the whole that is Jekyll *tout court,* a whole that (like a relay race or dynasty) is extended in time as well as space. In Jekyll's exceptional case, unfortunately, the whole is not continuous; stages of Jekyll periodically end in stages of Hyde. To make matters worse, each stage of Jekyll is also a stage of his submerged *alter idem,* of a Hyde in hiding—"the cavern in which [the mountain bandit] conceals himself from pursuit."

It is, indeed, ostensibly with a view to ending this agonizing duality that Jekyll first resorts to chemical means of achieving an antiseptic alternation between respective stages of the "polar twins": "The unjust might go his way . . . and the just could walk steadfastly . . . no longer exposed to disgrace and penitence." But the plan, on Jekyll's account, has gone wrong; as before, Hyde is unadulterated, and Jekyll "a mere polity of multifarious, incongruous, and independent citizens." In another respect, however, on the assumption that Jekyll and Hyde are not and cannot be identical, the experiment appears to be partly successful: though Jekyll concedes that he is guilty of conniving at Hyde's infamy, "even now I can scarce grant that I committed it"; connivance is presumably far less burdensome to conscience than commission. The "depravity," after all, is merely "vicarious."

As the insistent irony of Stevenson's tale makes clear to us, this account will not do. Connivance is itself a form of commission, that "heresy of Cain" to which (in its venial form) the narrative *raisonneur* Utterson confesses in Stevenson's prologue: "I let my brother go to the devil in his own way." But not all such heresies are venial. To release Hyde—to let him go despite the horror of his "way"—is

clearly to go with him. But what is worse, Jekyll is lying. His language betrays him. Far from being vicarious, his sadistic pleasures are simply "the secret pleasures that I had enjoyed in the disguise of Hyde." "Hyde," in short, is the name Jekyll goes by in disguise, under the influence of the drug that both disfigures him and relieves him of his inhibitions; he is no more subject to multiplication by the number of his conflicting urges or transformations than is the drunkard with whom he compares himself. The monster whose deeds he remembers performing is *ipso facto* himself, as he fitfully realizes. To sum up "my life as a whole," for Jekyll, is to include the life of Hyde.

And yet the lie of the exculpatory third person persists to the end: "He, I say—I cannot say, I." The amateur of "transcendental medicine" remains the dupe of his own intellectual quackery, and especially of his muddled ontology of the self as process rather than as the subject of process. But what Jekyll so strenuously denies, his story forbids us to overlook: under whatever name or condition or disguise, Jekyll endures from stage to stage of his history. It is only the stages endured that are necessarily distinct. There is, in short, a crucial difference between the delusive multiplicity of selves in which Jekyll seeks refuge from his responsibility and the imaginative multiplicity of roles in which Orlando and Jekyll himself (to his grief) find opportunities for the exploration of their freedom.

The "biographer" whom Virginia Woolf has provided for Orlando, if I am thus far right, by blithely renouncing conventional narrative fidelity to the real and the actual, demonstrates (to his own satisfaction at least) a more inclusive fidelity to concrete human experience and its alternative possibilities. To achieve liberty, one must take liberties; and of all the conventions with which such liberties are taken in **Orlando,** none is more mischievously derided than the convention that one's sex ordains how one ought properly to think, to behave, and above all to be treated. The allegorical figures who act out their masque of disapproval and departure in the bedchamber where the sleeping Orlando is changing sex are in effect the three goddesses of sexual propriety: Purity, Modesty, and Chastity, supercilious idols of "those who prohibit; those who deny; those who reverence without knowing why; those who praise without understanding; the still very numerous (Heaven be praised) tribe of the respectable; who prefer to see not; desire to know not; love the darkness."

For the "tribe of the respectable," Orlando's sexual transformation is socially null—a case not covered by the gender-specific rules for responding to persons; hence their enthusiasm for finding ways to avoid acknowledging it: "The change seemed to have been accomplished painlessly and completely and in such a way that Orlando herself showed no surprise at it. Many people, taking this into account, and holding that such a change is against nature, have been at great pains to prove (1) that Orlando had always been a woman, (2) that Orlando is at this moment a man." In the same spirit, the legal case against her right to her own inheritance charges her in desperation with being dead as a male and disqualified as a female from holding property: "Thus it was in a highly ambiguous condition, uncertain whether she was alive or dead, man or woman, Duke or nonentity, that she posted down to her country seat, where, pending the legal judgement, she had the Law's permission to reside in a state of incognito or incognita as the case might turn out to be." One is unknown, insoluble, without the conventional label that defines the roles of those one has to do with.

Orlando's new acquaintance with being a woman permits her, of course, to compare the advantages of the feminine and masculine labels. At first, on her sea voyage home from Turkey, she supposes, like Ovid's Teiresias, that in some respects the feminine lot is the more agreeable:

> Then she had pursued, now she fled. Which is the greater ecstasy? The man's or the woman's? And are they not perhaps the same? No, she thought, this is the most delicious (thanking the Captain [for the offer of a slice of corned beef] but refusing), to refuse, and see him frown. Well, she would, if he wished it, have the very thinnest, smallest sliver in the world. This was the most delicious, to yield and see him smile. "For nothing," she thought, regaining her couch on deck and continuing the argument, "is more heavenly than to resist and to yield; to yield and to resist. Surely it throws the spirit into such a rapture that nothing else can. So that I'm not sure," she continued, "that I won't throw myself overboard, for the mere pleasure of being rescued by a bluejacket after all." (It must be remembered that she was like a child entering into possession of a pleasaunce or toycupboard; her arguments would not commend themselves to mature women, who have had the run of it all their lives.)

The sardonic parenthesis, as it turns out, is grotesquely understated; the game with which Orlando has allowed herself to be beguiled is stultifying to both sides:

> "To fall from a mast-head," she thought, "because you see a woman's ankles; to dress up like a Guy Fawkes and parade the streets, so that women may praise you; to deny a woman teaching lest she may laugh at you; to be the slaves of the frailest chit in petticoats, and yet to go about as if you were the Lords of Creation. —Heavens!" she thought, "what fools they make of us—what fools we are!" And here it would seem from some ambiguity in her terms that she was censuring both sexes equally, as if she belonged to neither.

The full insidiousness of the prescribed roles emerges only when Orlando's critical neutrality wavers and threatens to give way to the delusion that the roles are more than a game: "Do what she would to restrain them, the tears came to her eyes, until, remembering that it is becoming in a woman to weep, she let them flow." "That men cry as frequently and as unreasonably as women, Orlando knew from her own experience as a man; but she was beginning to be aware that women should be shocked when men display emotion in their presence; and so, shocked she was."

All this, it is true, has the makings of comedy, and nowhere more than when Orlando feels obliged by Purity, Modesty, and Chastity to register shock:

Here she turned to present the Archduchess with the salver, and behold—in her place stood a tall gentleman in black. A heap of clothes lay in the fender. She was alone with a man.

Recalled thus suddenly to a consciousness of her sex, which she had completely forgotten, and of his, which was now remote enough to be equally upsetting, Orlando felt seized with faintness.

"La!" she cried, putting her hand to her side, "how you frighten me!" "Gentle creature," cried the Archduchess, falling on one knee and at the same time pressing a cordial to Orlando's lips, "forgive me for the deceit I have practised on you!"

Orlando sipped the wine and the Archduke knelt and kissed her hand.

In short, they acted the parts of man and woman for ten minutes with great vigour and then fell into natural discourse.

But the comedy takes an acrimonious turn as Orlando comes to see that the convention of femininity entails not only irksome restrictions but deeply insulting dispensations. To get rid of her unwanted lover, Orlando tries to persuade him of her unworthiness by grossly cheating him at a game; to her irritation, she is eventually spared the punishment she has worked so hard to deserve:

> To love a woman who cheats at play was, he said, impossible. Here he broke down completely. Happily, he said, recovering slightly, there were no witnesses. She was, after all, a woman, he said. In short, he was preparing in the chivalry of his heart to forgive her and had bent to ask her pardon for the violence of his language, when she cut the matter short, as he stooped his proud head, by dropping a small toad between his skin and his shirt.
>
> In justice to her, it must be said that she would infinitely have preferred a rapier. Toads are clammy things to conceal about one's person a whole morning. But if rapiers are forbidden, one must have recourse to toads.

There is clearly as much outrage as mischief in the bestowal of the toad; it is a substitute for the home thrust of a rapier.

As Orlando proceeds on her tour down the centuries, she pauses at the eighteenth to collect perennial canards about women like a connoisseur of grievances culling specimens. To Addison, we are informed, woman is "a beautiful romantic animal"; to Lord Chesterfield, a child "of a larger growth." Another eighteenth-century wit declares that "when they lack the stimulus of the other sex, women can find nothing to say to each other. When they are alone, they do not talk; they scratch." Still another, that "women are incapable of any feeling of affection for their own sex, and hold each other in the greatest aversion." In the nineteenth century, the injustice of sexual convention begins to be somewhat more evenhanded: "Men felt the chill in their hearts; the damp in their minds. In a desperate effort to snuggle their feelings into some sort of warmth one subterfuge was tried after another. Love, birth, and death were all swaddled in a variety of fine phrases. The sexes drew further and further apart. No open conversation was tolerated. Evasions and concealments were sedulously practised on both sides." Victorian marriage in particular is an institution of stifling dependency into which men and women are herded by the morbid roles imposed on them, roles that in the case of women require a wardrobe calculated to constrain free movement and an array of obligatory phobias (such as the fear "lest there should be robbers in the wainscot") with the same effect: "All these things inclined her, step by step, to submit to the new discovery, whether Queen Victoria's or another's, that each man and each woman has another allotted to it for life, whom it supports, by whom it is supported, till death them do part. It would be a comfort, she felt, to lean, to sit down; yes, to lie down; never, never, never to get up again."

And the twentieth-century Lawrentian reaction against propriety, Orlando finds, has scarcely been an improvement; in the name of a vital freedom it has merely substituted a new decorum by which the self is confined (especially in the official paradigm of femininity) to harping on the single note of *eros,* and a dehumanized *eros* at that:

> Surely since [Orlando] is a woman, and a beautiful woman, and a woman in the prime of life, she will soon give over this pretence of writing and thinking and begin to think, at least, of a gamekeeper (and as long as she thinks of a man, nobody objects to a woman thinking). And then she will write him a little note (and as long as she writes little notes nobody objects to a woman writing, either). And make an assignation for Sunday dusk; and Sunday dusk will come; and the gamekeeper will whistle under the window—all of which is, of course, the very stuff of life and the only possible subject for fiction. Surely Orlando must have done one of these things? Alas, —a thousand times, alas, Orlando did none of them. Must it then be admitted that Orlando was one of those monsters of iniquity that do not love? She was kind to dogs, faithful to friends, generosity itself to a dozen starving poets, had a passion for poetry. But love—as the male novelists define it—and who, after all, speak with greater authority? —has nothing whatever to do with kindness, fidelity, generosity, or poetry. Love is slipping off one's petticoat and—But we all know what love is.

Behavior is not the only slave of the sexual role, whimsical artifact though the latter is; unfortunately for Orlando, one cannot go through the motions of conformity for long without losing one's inner autonomy; the flimsiness of the eighteenth-century gown, the weight of the Victorian crinoline are in the end a very efficient means of subjecting the mind and the body:

> Vain trifles as they seem, clothes have, they say, more important offices than merely to keep us warm . . . There is much to support the view that it is clothes that wear us and not we them; we may make them take the mould of arm or breast, but they mould our hearts, our brains, our tongues to their liking . . . If we compare the picture of Orlando as a man with that of Orlando as a woman we shall see that though both

are undoubtedly one and the same person, there are certain changes. The man has his hand free to seize his sword; the woman must use hers to keep the satins from slipping from her shoulders. The man looks the world full in the face, as if it were made for his uses and fashioned to his liking. The woman takes a sidelong glance at it, full of subtlety, even of suspicion. Had they both worn the same clothes, it is possible that their outlook might have been the same too.

Each of these costumes carries with it a particular limitation on outlook, on the range of experience. In the eighteenth century, Orlando accordingly defends her freedom by a tactical transvestism: "Her sex changed far more frequently than those who have worn only one set of clothing can conceive; nor can there be any doubt that she reaped a two-fold harvest by this device; the pleasures of life were increased and its experiences multiplied. From the probity of breeches she turned to the seductiveness of petticoats and enjoyed the love of both sexes equally."

If the identification of probity with being male and of seductiveness with being female is indeed a fiction ordained by convention and subtly reinforced by the symbolism of dress, then the narrator's talk of "the mixture in her of man and woman" can hardly be taken on its face; it is a parody of the same ludicrously false dichotomies that underlie the hesitations of Orlando's friends about how to classify her:

> The curious of her own sex would argue how, for example, if Orlando was a woman, did she never take more than ten minutes to dress? And were not her clothes chosen rather at random, and sometimes worn rather shabby? And then they would say, still, she has none of the formality of a man, or a man's love of power. She is excessively tenderhearted. She could not endure to see a donkey beaten or a kitten drowned. Yet again, they noted, she detested household matters, was up at dawn and out among the fields in summer before the sun had risen. No farmer knew more about the crops than she did. She could drink with the best and liked games of hazard. She rode well and drove six horses at a gallop over London Bridge. Yet again, though bold and active as a man, it was remarked that the sight of another in danger brought on the most womanly palpitations. She would burst into tears on slight provocation. She was unversed in geography, found mathematics intolerable, and held some caprices which are more common among women than men, as, for instance, that to travel south is to travel down hill.

For the mentality that regards every strength or weakness of character or intellect as an essential peculiarity of one sex or the other, Orlando's biological nature will hardly determine her sex; her inability or refusal to sustain a consistent role implies the lack of any definite nature at all. Orlando, as her biographer twice warns us, is sometimes a little at odds with our expectations, sometimes "a trifle clumsy": "Yet it is true that there was an absentmindedness about her which sometimes made her clumsy; she was apt to think of poetry when she should have been thinking of taffeta; her walk was a little too much of a stride for a woman, perhaps, and her gestures, being abrupt, might endanger a cup of tea on occasion."

One might gather from all this that the ideal of "clumsiness" being burnished by Orlando's biographer is a kind of bisexual aestheticism in thin disguise. That the suggestion is far too narrow is sufficiently indicated by the pains the biographer takes to provide that clumsiness with a foil in the freakishness of Orlando's admirer and fellow transvestite Harry Archduke of Finster-Aarhorn, who throws off his pretense to confess

> that he was a man and always had been one; that he had seen a portrait of Orlando and fallen hopelessly in love with him; that to compass his ends, he had dressed as a woman . . . that he had heard of her change and hastened to offer his services (here he teed and heed intolerably). For to him, said the Archduke Harry, she was and would ever be the Pink, the Pearl, the Perfection of her sex. The three p's would have been more persuasive if they had not been interspersed with tee-hees and haw-haws of the strangest kind. "If this is love," said Orlando to herself, looking at the Archduke on the other side of the fender and now from the woman's point of view, "there is something highly ridiculous about it."

There is something highly ridiculous in a charade of romanticized prurience. It may be, as the biographer speculates, that the romance and the prurience in love are "so strictly joined together that you cannot separate them"; but in the Archduke it is grotesquely obvious which is the directing impulse: "It was Lust the vulture, not Love the Bird of Paradise that flopped, foully and disgustingly, upon [Orlando's] shoulders." The egoism and impersonality of the Archduke's obsession are stupidly confining, and so far in sharp contrast to the inclusiveness of experience and sympathy the biographer eventually celebrates on the eve of Orlando's motherhood: "Hail, happiness! kingfisher flashing from bank to bank, and all fulfillment of natural desire, whether it is what the male novelist says it is; or prayer; or denial; hail! in whatever form it comes, and may there be more forms, and stranger."

Orlando's continuing fascination with a person of her own sex, unlike the Duke's harlequinade, is presented to us as something serious, validated by inner kinship, and made tragic by betrayal:

> As all Orlando's loves had been women, now, through the culpable laggardry of the human frame to adapt itself to convention, though she herself was a woman, it was still a woman she loved; and if the consciousness of being of the same sex had any effect at all, it was to quicken and deepen those feelings which she had had as a man. For now a thousand hints and mysteries became plain to her that were then dark. Now, the obscurity, which divides the sexes and lets linger innumerable impurities in its gloom, was removed, and if there is anything in what the poet says about truth and beauty, this affection gained in beauty what it lost in falsity.

. . . . .

Here, as she was fingering the linen abstractedly, one of the swing-doors between the departments opened and let through, perhaps from the fancy-goods department, a whiff of scent, waxen, tinted as if from pink candles, and the scent curved like a shell round a figure—was it a boy's or was it a girl's—furred, pearled, in Russian trousers—young, slender, seductive—a girl, by God! but faithless, faithless!

The sexual duality (by the conventional standard) of the people Orlando loves—not only of the Elizabethan aristocrat's mistress but of the twentieth-century poet's husband—seems to me to be offered, like Orlando's transformation itself, both as a reversal of the process by which "the sexes drew further and further apart," and more fundamentally as the pattern for a general response to the doubt that behind another's behavior lie feelings like one's own. It is a doubt one cannot plausibly reason away by appealing to the likeness of behavior in the Other to what in oneself invariably accompanies feeling of such and such a kind; this would be to generalize from a single instance (oneself). Perhaps one might proceed by noting that the sum of one's characteristics is clearly *enough* to produce or admit of the pairing of behavior and inner events one observes in oneself and seeks assurance of in others. Among these characteristics some will be necessary to such pairing. The more like oneself the others are, the more likely it is (by the uniformity of nature) that they too satisfy these necessary conditions. If one could eliminate one's differences from a given class of others without finding an alteration in the pairing, then one would know that these differences at least had not disqualified the others from sharing one's feelings, and indeed perhaps had qualified them to have other sorts of feelings as well, of which one had had no suspicion. But of course, most of the changes required by the experiment are quite impossible: "There are a great many properties of which I cannot divest myself and a great many that I cannot acquire; and among them are properties which are peculiar to me, or peculiar to some other person." But an experiment in empathic transformation that cannot be conducted in fact can still (perhaps) be conducted in imagination; and the poet Orlando is peculiarly fitted to conduct it.

For the rest, those who, like Orlando and her husband, have emancipated themselves from artificial norms of sexuality, find that their most fragmentary utterances hold no mystery for their partners—that at a profound level their minds turn out to be formed on the same pattern: " 'Are you positive you aren't a man' he would ask anxiously, and she would echo, 'Can it be possible that you're not a woman?' and then they must put it to the proof without more ado. For each was so surprised at the quickness of the other's sympathy, and it was to each such a revelation that a woman could be as tolerant and free-spoken as a man, and a man as strange and subtle as a woman, that they had to put the matter to the proof at once." The only matter they are putting to the proof here is their physical difference; tolerance and subtlety have turned out not to be criteria of sex at all.

Orlando rebels against the tyranny of the real, the actual, and the stereotypical by casually trespassing on bounda-

403

ries she comes to regard as artificial; her transformation is simply the temporal emblem of her multiple residence in universes that are held by common sense to be mutually inaccessible. But the sequence of universes we look into is far from arbitrary; they turn out at last to have been framed in the awareness of the twentieth-century woman who alone among Orlando's avatars is able, like Eliot's Teiresias, to achieve a synoptic vision. The worlds in which that vision occurs may not enjoy a privileged status of actuality, but they alone are the scene of Orlando's maturity and fulfillment, and they alone are the measure of likeness among possible worlds that gives meaning to the counterfactual idiom of Orlando's "biography" (in all like worlds in which Orlando enjoys a given form, her experiences in that form are as registered in the world of the mature woman's awareness). In this sense the subject of that "biography" is a woman, and the earlier sequences of the book are perversely misleading. Why is the womanhood of the most inclusive Orlando reserved by the device of transformation as a surprise? Why, for that matter, does the tone of the narrative as a whole mislead us by transforming itself by degrees from fantasy to mimesis, from parody to directness?

The answer, I think, is that part of the subversive function of Orlando's transformation is craftily rhetorical. To be taken seriously, in the face of rooted prejudice, as the heroine of a quest for creative mastery, it is as well for the heroine to begin by introducing herself as a hero; for "the truth is," says her biographer with more than a touch of irony, "that when we write of a woman, everything is out of place—culminations and perorations; the accent never falls where it does with a man." The Shakespearean mistress of an earlier Orlando is able to exercise the full force of her personality, to take command of her play, only after she assumes the disguise of a gentleman, and drops the name of "Rosalind" for the questionable *nom de guerre* of "Ganymede." Virginia Woolf's Orlando refines the stratagem by acting under a far more valiant name—Orlando is Roland—and retaining it even when she has thrown off her disguise. Now, however, it is inalienably the name of a woman. By taking command of a literary kind reserved by prejudice for men, Orlando achieves still another freedom of the imagination for herself and for us.

Susan M. Squier   (essay date 1986)

SOURCE: "Tradition and Revision in Woolf's *Orlando*: Defoe and 'The Jessamy Brides'," in *Women's Studies: An Interdisciplinary Journal*, Vol. 12, No. 2, 1986, pp. 167-77.

[*In the following excerpt, Squier analyzes* Orlando *as Woolf's challenge to the tradition of realistic novels initiated by Daniel Defoe.*]

On March 14, 1927 Virginia Woolf recorded in her diary the symptoms of an "extremely mysterious process . . . the conception last night between 12 & one of a new book."

> I sketched the possibilities which an unattractive woman, penniless, alone, might yet bring into being. . . . It struck me, vaguely, that I might write a Defoe narrative for fun. Suddenly be-

tween twelve & one I conceived a whole fantasy to be called "The Jessamy Brides"—why, I wonder? . . . No attempt is to be made to realise the character. Sapphism is to be suggested. Satire is to be the main note—satire & wildness.

That Woolf's sixth novel represents an act of comic tribute to her loving friend Vita Sackville-West has been well documented. However, a return to the diary record of *Orlando*'s conception suggests that the work was more than the playful tribute to Sackville-West or the escape from works of a more "serious poetic experimental" nature which some critics, following Woolf's lead, have judged it to be. Instead, *Orlando* completes the labor of self-creation which Woolf began in her autobiographical novel, *To the Lighthouse* (1927). In that earlier novel, she laid to rest the ghosts of her parents, establishing herself as an adult woman independent of their potentially eclipsing examples. In *Orlando* (1928), which, [according to Helen MacAfee in the *Yale Review,* 1929], bears "the clear stamp of her mind in its maturity," and "might in a sense have been called an autobiography," Woolf went further. Claiming her *literary* majority, she confronted the influence of both literal and literary fathers to reshape the novel, and so to create a place for herself in the English novelistic tradition which was their legacy to her. *Orlando* may be read as a serious work of criticism as well as a love-tribute, then, and its major concerns are prefigured in Woolf's diary entry of March 14, 1927: the confrontation with one's literary precursors and the impact of gender upon literary genre.

With *Orlando*'s subtitle, "A Biography," Woolf issued a challenge both to her father, Sir Leslie Stephen—who had achieved his prominence as the editor of the *Dictionary of National Biography*—and more broadly to the patrilineal tradition of English literature which Stephen traced in his important volume, *English Literature and Society in the Eighteenth Century.* Preeminent in that tradition was Daniel Defoe, who to Leslie Stephen was the father of the English novel. Stephen wrote of Defoe as typifying the middle class values which led to the rise of the novel as genre; individualism, nationalism, and resourceful pragmatism. But Defoe was also the aesthetic father of *Orlando.* To Woolf, Defoe led the list—as the announced in the Preface to *Orlando*—of those "dead and so illustrious that I scarcely dare name them, yet no one can read or write without being perpetually in their debt." Woolf's homage to Defoe, like her relationship with Leslie Stephen, was far from simple, however; consideration of Defoe's role as acknowledged precursor of *Orlando* will reveal the scope and nature of Woolf's designs on the English novel. In acknowledging her debt to Defoe, Woolf was also subverting his influence and challenging the genre of the realistic novel which he initiated. Moreover, by challenging that genre, she framed a gender-based critique of the patriarchal ideology in which the novel has its origins.

In her bicentenary essay on Daniel Defoe, Woolf wrote of him as "one of the first indeed to shape the novel and launch it on its way." This position of precedence makes itself felt in *Orlando,* which in both narration and plot recalls Defoe's *Moll Flanders.* As early as 1919 Woolf had praised that novel for the "briskness of the story," and her own *Orlando*—written less than a decade later—shares the light picaresque mode and brisk pacing of Defoe's novel, as well as its episodic plot. Aspects of the characters also resemble each other: both novels have protagonists who disguise themselves as men; who consort with prostitutes and gipsies; who are experienced and capable international travellers; who are mothers (Moll, repeatedly); and who explore the different strata of London society. Yet their stories seem to be inverse mirror images: Moll Flanders develops from a position of social marginality (as a pickpocket, whore, and bigamist) to a penitent identification with conventional social values, while Orlando moves from a position of privileged centrality (due to his aristocratic lineage, great hereditary wealth, and masculine prerogative) to a position of social marginality as a woman and poet, a position both character and novel affirm. Despite the characters' different developmental paths, Woolf's comments in **"Defoe"** suggest that she borrowed the spirit of *Orlando* from *Moll Flanders,* for she asserts there that Defoe's work contained a subterranean affirmation of his protagonist which the author's overt moralizing belied.

> The interpretation that we put on his characters might . . . well have puzzled him. We find for ourselves meanings which he was careful to disguise even from himself. Thus it comes about that we admire Moll Flanders far more than we blame her. Nor can we believe that Defoe had made up his mind to the precise degree of her guilt, or was unaware that in considering the lives of the abandoned he raised many deep questions and hinted, if he did not state, answers quite at variance with his professions of belief.

In choosing a "Defoe narrative" as her model for *Orlando,* Woolf was engaged in the same technique of revisionary reading that she demonstrated in **"Defoe."** She chose to find in Defoe's novel meanings which, while they might have puzzled him, were nonetheless crucial to her at that stage of her artistic development. Admiring Moll rather than blaming her, Woolf found in the character qualities upon which she modeled her own literary emancipation, for that was the task at hand following her completion of *To the Lighthouse.*

As Woolf understood *Moll Flanders,* the novel's admirable spirit of briskness was due "partly to the fact that having transgressed the accepted laws at a very early age she [Moll] has henceforth the freedom of the outcast." The idea that alienation could liberate was appealing to Woolf, who from her early years had struggled with feelings of exclusion from social and literary London. By the time she wrote **Three Guineas** (1937) she firmly believed that the outsider position was the best vantage point from which to work for peace and sexual equality. However, roughly ten years earlier her mind was not yet made up on this issue, and she found in *Orlando* an opportunity to try out the outsider's experience—not only in the person of her protagonist, but also in the novel's very form and style. Like *Moll Flanders, Orlando* transgresses "accepted laws," but those laws are not only social, but literary.

Consideration of the rules of characterization which *Orlando* contravened demonstrates the novel's liberating re-

vision of the genre "launched" by Defoe. A crucial challenge to writers in the novel's early years was the creation of individuated characters, rather than the stock characters, allegorical figures, or types which peopled earlier literary genres. Four techniques contributed to the creation of this new character, according to Ian Watt [in *The Rise of the Novel: Studies in Defoe, Richardson, and Fielding*]: a detailed presentation of characters in relation to their environment; the use of past experience as cause of present action (in contrast to the earlier stress on disguise and coincidence in plotting); a more minutely discriminated time scale; and finally the use of realistic proper (first and last) names, rather than emblematic or conventional single names. Woolf's earliest plans for *Orlando* expressed her opposition to the cardinal tenet of the developing novel tradition, the creation of individuated characters: "No attempt," she specified in her diary entry of March 1927, "is to be made to realise the character." Moreover, throughout *Orlando* she maintained her opposition to traditional novelistic practice, by inverting all of the techniques for character creation in order not to emphasize identity, but to call the very concept into question. So, Orlando's single name (hereditary titles aside) makes him/her the very type of comic gender reversal, in its allusion to Shakespeare's *As You Like It.* The more minutely discriminated time scale of the realistic novel here becomes a life of more than five hundred years which alternately flash by without commentary and creep along second by second. While in the realistic novel the plot introduced a new logic of cause and effect; in *Orlando* the preeminent dramatic action—Orlando's gender change—seems uncaused by any previous event, and is accompanied both by coincidence (the trance occurs at the same time as the Turkish revolt against the Sultan) and disguise (Orlando passes for a Turkish boy and a gipsy after the gender change). Finally, the realistic novel's careful presentation of character in relation to environment becomes, in *Orlando,* a survey of the protagonist's contrasting experiences of Elizabethan, Jacobean, Carolinean, Restoration, Augustan, Victorian and Modern England, as well as of Constantinople before and after the Sultan's fall. This extensive topographical and temporal detail, far from increasing our belief in Orlando as an actual person, rather causes us to view him/her as the type of symbol of the British poet, nobleman/woman, and statesman.

Woolf's treatment of Orlando's character thus demonstrates her divergence from what she has seen, in 1919, as the key ingredient of the Defoe narrative—the conviction that "the novel had to justify its existence by telling a true story," or what Ian Watt has defined as the principle of "formal realism":

> the premise, or primary convention, that the novel is a full and authentic report of human experience and is therefore under an obligation to satisfy its reader with such details of the story as the individuality of the actors concerned, the particulars of the times and places of their actions, details which are presented through a more largely referential use of language than is common in other literary forms.

Intimations of Woolf's motives for so diverging from

Defoe's novelistic technique appear in her 1919 essay. There, she wrote of Defoe's works as "prosaic," characteristic of the "great plain writers, whose work is founded upon a knowledge of what is most persistant, though not most seductive, in human nature." Her view recalls Leslie Stephen's indictment of Defoe for "absence of any passion or sentiment," and his dry judgement that "the merit of De Foe's narrative bears a direct proportion to the intrinsic merit of a plain statement of the facts." Yet a more recent and deeply felt influence than Leslie Stephen's prompted Woolf to subvert Defoe's realism and plain speaking. The sexual metaphor buried in the prose of both father and daughter—the notion of Defoe as lacking a certain sexual quality, as being neither seductive, passionate, nor full of sentiment—suggests that sexuality or gender may have played a part in Woolf's decision to revise Defoe's style. Indeed, a connection may be made between Defoe's prose style and character creation and the world view of the literary tradition Defoe fathered, suggesting that it was a desire to reevaluate the patriarchal literary tradition and culture—under the influence of her new love for Vita Sackville-West—which promoted the form and style of *Orlando.*

When Vita first read *Orlando,* in October 1928, she wrote to Virginia Woolf, "I am completely dazzled, bewitched, enchanted, under a spell." The novel's style brought to her mind "a robe stitched with jewels." Sackville-West's comments indicate the elements in *Orlando* which most fully subvert the influence of Defoe: *Orlando*'s unrealistic, even fantastical and magical plot and character, and *Orlando*'s ornate diction. Moreover, Vita's comments suggest Woolf's reason for challenging the patriarchal bias of the novel genre in *Orlando:* her novel's celebration of qualities unacceptable to traditional realism. The eighteenth century fathers of the novel adhered to a strictly referential use of language, corollary to the commitment to formal realism which aligned them with the realist philosophers. That this linguistic probity had moral and cultural ramifications for them was most tellingly expressed in Locke's observation, in the *Essay Concerning Human Understanding,* that "eloquence, like the fair sex, involves a pleasurable deceit." This assumed connection between eloquence, deceit and femininity which lay at the basis of formal realism would have made such a technique inappropriate for *Orlando,* a novel written to celebrate the seductive, passionate character of Vita Sackville-West, by a writer who admitted, "It is true that I only want to show off to women. Women alone stir my imagination." For if Defoe's realism eschewed elaborate diction as deceitful, seductive, and above all feminine, Woolf turned in *Orlando* to elaborate diction and fanciful plotting precisely because it could best embody the complex woman poet to whom the novel paid homage. Woolf turned the realistic novel on its head in *Orlando,* playing with distinctions between reality and fantasy, truth and lying, masculinity and femininity. Her challenge to the conventions of realism, boldy emphasized by her prefatory tribute to Defoe, reflects the realization that the rules of genre are shaped by the politics of gender. As Nancy Miller has pointed out:

> The attack on female plots and plausibilities assumes that women writers cannot or will not

obey the rules of fiction. It also assumes that the truth devolving from *veri*similitude is male. For sensibility, sensitivity, "extravagance"—so many code words for feminine in our culture that the attack is in fact tautological—are taken to be not merely inferior modalities of production but deviations from some obvious truth. The blind spot here is both political (or philosophical) and literary. It does not see, nor does it want to, that the fictions of desire behind the desiderata of fiction are masculine and not universal constructs. ["Emphasis Added: Plots and Plausibilities in Women's Fiction," *PMLA,* January 1981]

Challenging the universality of the "fictions of desire" basic to the realistic novel, Woolf was both following and subverting her literary and literal fathers. Not only did she contravene Defoe's style of moralistic truth-telling nearly point-for-point, but she also revised Stephen's approach to literary criticism, in which he had been—according to Noel Annan [in *Leslie Stephen: His Thought and Character in Relation to His Time*]—the first writer to consider the impact of changing social classes upon the production of literature and the development of new literary genres. By shifting her index from his focus on economic and social class to her own interest in sex class, Woolf subverted her father's approach in order to consider specifically the impact of *gender* upon *genre.* While all of *Orlando* is a meditation upon this issue, perhaps the most pointed statement of Woolf's concern comes near the novel's end, in one of the "biographer's" numerous asides to the reader (and we might mark Woolf's sly glee at putting such a speech in the mouth of one of her father's fellow biographers):

> we must here snatch time to remark how discomposing it is for the biographer that this culmination and peroration should be dashed from us on a laugh casually like this; but the truth is that when we write of a woman, everything is out of place—culminations and perorations; the accent never falls where it does with a man.

With the veiled allusion to other sorts of climaxes, Woolf intimates the sexual and gender-related motives for her revision of her father's art as biographer and literary critic. To the novelist/biographer writing of a woman, "truth" takes a different form than it does with a man. Woolf's metaphor encompasses not only the multiple climaxes of the female orgasm, but the multiple high-points of Orlando's life—the birth of her child, the publication of "The Oak Tree," her marriage, winning the Burdett Coutts' Memorial Prize for her poem. Furthermore, Woolf's metaphor suggests that language, like the shape of a literary work, shifts when it is called upon to describe not the man around whom a novel or biography is typically composed, but rather the woman who discomposes it. Working in the *spirit* of her father's criticism, Woolf subverted the *matter,* calling into question both gender divisions and the literary form enshrining them.

The sexually liberating nature of *Orlando*'s homage to Defoe—and the realistic novel he fathered—lies in the fact that to challenge the constraints of the literary canon is to confront the deepest politics or philosophy linking gender to genre. As Nancy Miller has pointed out, both style and character creation reflect ideology:

> To build a narrative around a character whose behavior is deliberately idiopathic . . . is not merely to create a puzzling fiction, but to fly in the face of a certain ideology (of the text and its context), to violate a grammar of motives that describes while prescribing . . . what wives, not to say women, should or should not do.

In beginning with the idea of "an unattractive woman, penniless, alone," Woolf in her choice of a heroine defied the ideology ascribing to a woman value depending upon her worth to a man. It is this ideology which Mrs Ramsay espouses, in *To the Lighthouse,* when she urges "Minta must, they all must marry, since . . . an unmarried woman has missed the best of life." And by settling on Orlando, a character whose gender changes midway through the novel, Woolf further violates the ideology shaping patriarchal culture itself: what Gayle Rubin has termed the "sex/gender system." Woolf both invoked and defied this system when she first planned to title the novel "The Jessamy Brides." "Jessamy," "a man who scents himself with perfume or who wears a sprig of Jessamine in his buttonhole . . . a dandy, a fop," had by the time Woolf wrote *Orlando* been paired conceptually with an equally transgressive parallel term, "Amazon," a woman whose stature and physical prowess were more conventionally masculine than feminine. In its evocation of the gender line crossings embodied by a foppish male bride, a feminine man, and an "Amazonian" woman, the initial title for Orlando prefigures Woolf's protagonist, who in the course of a long life loved both sexes passionately, contracted a marriage to a man whom she jokingly suspected of being a woman (and who entertained the corresponding suspicion that Orlando was a man), and who at the novel's conclusion summons herself ("Orlando?") only to be answered by a multiplicity of selves—of both genders and sexual orientations. The provisional title also brings to mind the lovingly unorthodox marriage of Vita Sackville-West and Harold Nicolson, which encompassed homosexual affairs for both parties while remaining their primary and most honored tie. In its allusions to a variety of unorthodox marriages, "The Jessamy Brides" not only embodies the disobedient briskness which Woolf admired in *Moll Flanders,* but it replicates Woolf's own defiance of social conventions in her love affair with Vita Sackville-West.

That love affair was already underway when Woolf finished her autobiographical novel, *To the Lighthouse,* and she gave Vita an elaborately bound copy of the novel enscribed, "Vita from Virginia (In my opinion the best novel I have ever written.)" Yet when Vita opened the expensively bound volume, she found only blank pages. This gesture of the blank-paged book both encompasses the past and anticipates the future, supporting what Louise DeSalvo has cogently documented: that the relationship with Vita was for Woolf an important artistic turning point. Underscoring the homage to Woolf's two mothers, Julia Stephen and now Vita Sackville-West, in its evocative blank pages this gift also intimates the coming challenge to two fathers, Leslie Stephen and Daniel Defoe, in the rupture with the patriarchal novelistic tradition to come. For the gift of this blank-paged book suggests that whatever Woolf's "best novel" is to be, if it is to reflect her love for Vita Sackville-West it will be unreadable within the patriarchal tradition of English literature and culture. And indeed, even the conception of that novel still to come challenged the form at the heart of *To the Lighthouse,* "father and mother and child in the garden." For having found herself "virgin, passive, blank of ideas" for a number of weeks following the completion of *To the Lighthouse,* Woolf on that mysterious March night of 1927 found stirring within her *Orlando*—the consummation of her love for Vita. In its defiance of the "Defoe narrative" as in its evocative embodiment of another form for both gender and genre, *Orlando* stands not only as a serious work of criticism *in and of* the tradition of Leslie Stephen, but as Woolf's gesture of literary emancipation.

Pamela L. Caughie   (essay date 1989)

SOURCE: "Virginia Woolf's Double Discourse," in *Discontented Discourses: Feminism/Textual Intervention/Psychoanalysis,* edited by Marleen S. Barr and Richard Feldstein, University of Illinois Press, 1989, pp. 41-53.

[*In the following essay, Caughie challenges feminist readings of* Orlando.]

Written by a feminist (Virginia Woolf), for a bisexual (Vita Sackville-West), about an androgyne (Orlando), the novel *Orlando* would seem to be the quintessential feminist text. And that, indeed, is what it is in danger of becoming, just as Woolf is in danger of becoming the acclaimed Mother of Us All. In promoting Virginia Woolf's *Orlando* as a feminist work, feminist critics have picked the right text, but for the wrong reasons. *Orlando* works as a feminist text not because of what it says about sexual identity but because of what it manages not to say; not because of what it reveals about the relation between the sexes but because of what it does to that relation; not because its protagonist is androgynous but because its discourse is duplicitous. With its eponymous character who changes from a man to a woman halfway through the novel, with its capricious narrator who at times speaks in the character of Orlando's male biographer and at others sounds suspiciously like *Orlando*'s female author, this novel assumes what Jane Gallop [in *The Daughter's Seduction: Feminism and Psychoanalysis*] calls a "double discourse." This double discourse is one that is oscillating and open, one that "asserts and then questions," "a text that alternately quotes and comments, exercises and critiques." By drawing on the Lacanian readings of Jane Gallop and Shoshana Felman, I want to offer a reading of *Orlando* that will explore its functioning as a feminist text and that will expose many feminist critics' appropriation of it.

Orlando is a biographical novel about a poet who lives and loves for over three centuries (and who is likely to live and love three more), changing from a man to a woman halfway through the novel, somewhere around the end of the seventeenth century. When discussing this novel, one must begin with this caution: anything you can say about *Orlando* can be used against you. For *Orlando* defies conclusions. The text of **Orlando** is as unstable as the sex of Orlando. The first words of the novel shake our certainty about anything in this text. We read, "He—for there could be no doubt of his sex . . . ," and immediately our doubt is aroused. The emphasis on what should be obvious makes it seem unnatural. The emphasis on an innocent pronoun makes it suspect. This novel abounds in qualifications ("Change was incessant, and change perhaps would never cease"), paradoxes ("the [blank] space is filled to repletion"), and contradictions (the androgyne itself). This sexual and textual indeterminacy links language and identity. As the androgynous Orlando brings the question of sexual identity to the fore, the obtrusive narrator brings the textual language to the fore by intruding to discuss his own art, to mock his own method, and to characterize his own readers. Orlando is identified with writing throughout: she is read like a book; she concludes that she is "only in the process of fabrication"; and she writes at her poem through four centuries, borrowing indiscriminately, from different literary ages, all the while questioning "What's an 'age,' indeed?"

This novel, then, is a text about writing, about constructing lives, histories, identities, and fictions. Its desire is for expression itself, as Orlando says, for the fulfillment of desire "in whatever form it comes, and may there be more forms, and stranger." This fulfillment of desire, this desire for expression, encourages us to read androgyny not in terms of some innate bisexuality but in terms of the situation of desire, the subject's situation in a signifying chain. One must assume a sexual identity in order to take one's place in language, in order to express anything. Sexual identity is assumed in language; it is, as Felman says [in "Rereading Femininity," *Yale French Studies,* 1981], "conditioned by the functioning of language." Woolf brings out the arbitrariness of that identity, the arbitrariness of language itself, through Orlando's switching from one sex to the other, and from one poetic language to another, as well as through the shifting of her own rhetoric in this novel.

Just as Orlando's identity swings from the extreme of conventionality—Orlando as a boy slicing at the swinging Moor's head—to the extreme of eccentricity—Orlando as a woman discovering she has three sons by another woman—so the language of the text shifts from the transparent conventionality of clichés—to put it in a nutshell, by the skin of his teeth—to the opaque originality of Orlando and her lover Shel's cypher language—Rattigan Glumphoboo. Just as the bombastic masque of the Three Sisters hyperbolizes Orlando's sex change, the self-conscious diction maximizes the language of the text, not just the self-conscious diction of Orlando's extravagant metaphors (he calls his lover a melon, a pineapple, an olive tree, a fox in the snow), but the self-conscious diction of the biographer's narrative as well (he describes Orlando's betrothed as fair, florid, and phlegmatic). Just as the sexual differences are put into confusion ("You're a woman, Shel!" "You're a man, Orlando!"), so are the extremes of rhetoric. For as Woolf reveals by mocking her own "Time Passes" section of *To the Lighthouse,* what is highly original in one context can, in another, be a tedious, grandiloquent way of saying simply "time passed." What is con-

ventional and what is original, what is mainstream and what is marginal change, like Orlando's sex, with time and circumstance. We see that identity is as variable as language, language as vulnerable as identity. Woolf's rhetoric in **Orlando** is no more chaste than is her protagonist.

What is novel expresses, then, is the difficulty of reaching conclusions about identity or language. Both are based on making distinctions, yet these distinctions are not fixed by reference to anything outside them. There is nothing "out there" to measure them against. What Woolf shares with a writer like Lacan is his verbal play meant to undercut his own position as the one presumed to know. What Woolf admires in and shares with writers like Browne, De Quincey, and Montaigne is their willingness to entertain a variety of opinions, their contentment to remain in uncertainties, and their use of qualifying language to avoid "the rash assumptions of human ignorance" (**"Montaigne,"** *The Common Reader*). And so, in **Orlando,** "we are now in the region of 'perhaps' and 'appears'." To speak directly and with certainty on any matter is beyond the novelist Woolf as it is beyond the poet Orlando. Desperately seeking the irreducible linguistic episteme, Orlando discovers that one cannot simply say what one means and leave it: "So then he tried saying the grass is green and the sky is blue and so to propitiate the austere spirit of poetry. . . . 'The sky is blue,' he said, 'the grass is green.' Looking up, he saw that on the contrary, the sky is like the veils which a thousand Madonnas have let fall from their hair; and the grass fleets and darkens like a flight of girls fleeing the embraces of hairy satyrs from enchanted woods. 'Upon my word,' he said, . . . 'I don't see that one's more true than another. Both are utterly false'."

As Orlando discovers, poetry and nature, language and identity, must be learned together. This is the point of the vacillating rhetoric and the epicene protagonist of Woolf's novel. Orlando's identity, like her poem, is a palimpsest. It is "compounded of many humours," composed of "odds and ends," a "meeting-place of dissemblables." Orlando continually wavers between beliefs, changes or disguises her sex, moves in harmony with and at odds with the times. So too Woolf's novel offers support for differing positions without arguing for any one. She writes: "Society is the most powerful concoction in the world and society has no existence whatsoever"; there is not much difference between the sexes, for Orlando remains "fundamentally the same" throughout, and the difference is "one of great profundity"; "Clothes are but a symbol of something hid deep beneath," and clothes "wear us," changing "our view of the world and the world's view of us." Such oscillations on the thematic and narrative levels of this novel are presented metaphorically in the recurring image of the perpetually swaying arras and in the alternation of light and dark in Orlando's cab ride with Alexander Pope. It is in the midst of all these contrarieties, in the midst of such violent shifts in viewpoint, that Woolf offers her famous androgynous statement, not as a metaphysical or feminist theory, not as a resolution to or a synthesis of contrarieties, but as a way to remain suspended between opposed beliefs: "For here again we come to a dilemma. Different though the sexes are, they intermix. In every human being a vacillation from one sex to the other takes place, and often it is only the clothes that keep the male or female likeness, while underneath the sex is the very opposite of what it is above." Androgyny embodies this oscillation between positions. It figures a basic ambiguity, not only a sexual ambiguity but a textual one as well. Androgyny is a refusal to choose.

And yet so many critics choose androgyny as the appropriate textual strategy or the appropriate sexual identity. In praising Woolf's *Orlando* for its presentation of transsexualism and its theory of androgyny, most critics have tended to take Woolf's statements out of their context in this novel and to cite them as unambiguous truths about sexual identity or modernist-feminist novels. The androgynous Orlando is appropriated as a symbol of the more unified self, or as a resolution to the problem of true self and conventional self. "Androgynous wholeness" is the phrase Sandra Gilbert uses. Androgyny becomes a form of self-mastery, a metaphor for the autonomous self, a freedom from history, society, language. Yet such readings fail to grasp the concept of identity in *Orlando* because they fail to attend to its rhetoric.

In *Orlando,* androgyny and transsexualism call into question not just conventional assumptions about sexuality, but, more important, conventional assumptions about language itself. In its rhetorical transports, Woolf's novel challenges the reference theory of meaning. In particular, it questions the notion that words get their meanings from things they refer to; the definition of words and categories by their essential traits; and the isolation of words and statements from their contexts of use in order to interpret them. The point of focusing on the marginal case (e. g., the transsexual) is to reveal the crucial decisions made in the application of a term or in the assumption of an identity. We can see this point most clearly in the famous clothes philosophy passage in Chapter Four, the passage often cited as Woolf's theory of androgyny.

Now a woman and living in the eighteenth century, Orlando in this chapter is becoming acutely aware of her sex as she faces a legal challenge to her property rights, as she parries the advances of the ship's captain and the Archduke, and as she contends with "the coil of skirts about her legs." Initially unchanged by the sex change, or so her biographer tells us, Orlando is now assuming a more feminine nature. Her biographer writes: "The change of clothes had, some philosophers will say, much to do with it. Vain trifles as they seem, . . . they change our view of the world and the world's view of us." According to this philosophy, our identity is as changeable as our apparel. Clothes make the man, or the woman. The difference between men, and between men and women, would seem to be a superficial one. However, the biographer continues: "That is the view of some philosophers and wise ones, but on the whole, we incline to another. The difference between the sexes is, happily, one of great profundity. Clothes are but the symbol of something hid deep beneath. It was a change in Orlando herself that dictated her choice of a woman's dress and a woman's sex." That is, clothes don't *make* the woman, clothes *mark* the woman beneath. But again, the biographer continues, and two sentences later we find the famous androgyny passage cited above:

"For here again, we come to a dilemma. Different though the sexes are, they intermix. In every human being a vacillation from one sex to the other takes place, and often it is only the clothes that keep the male or female likeness, while underneath the sex is the very opposite of what it is above."

Placed in its context, this paragraph not only contradicts the earlier assertion that Orlando's sex change had not affected his/her identity, and that other philosophy that says we put on our identity with our clothing, but it also contradicts itself. For the biographer begins by saying that clothes are a symbol of something deep beneath, that is, one's nature or identity, and ends by remarking that often what is deep beneath is the opposite of the clothing above. In other words, the passage asserts both that clothes are natural and fitting and that clothes are arbitrary and deceiving. Such a self-contradiction is not in the least surprising in this particular novel. What is surprising is that in appropriating this statement as Woolf's theory of androgyny, critics pass over the contradictions, accepting the statement at face value, taking the biographer at his word, which is to take his discourse for granted.

If we consider this passage within its eighteenth-century context, we see that Woolf is not arguing for one of two ontological theories—that is, that identity is fixed or it is changeable, that sexual differences are natural or they are learned—but presenting two positions in eighteenth-century thought which come out of a particular conception of language. On the one hand, we have Samuel Johnson's position: thought must be distinguished from rhetoric, the content from the form, the man from his attire. On the other hand, we have Alexander Pope's position: the rhetoric makes the thought, the form and content are inseparable, the man must dress to advantage. On the one hand, clothes are vain trifles and rhetoric is superfluous; on the other hand, clothes are expressive and rhetoric is essential.

But these apparently opposing views are grounded in the same assumptions about language and identity. To speak of rhetoric as either revealing or concealing, to speak of appearance as either natural or contrived, is to set up a false opposition. It is to assume that we can get beyond or beneath the linguistic paradigm, in which rhetorical and sexual differences function. Such assumptions about language and identity imply the possibility of a natural or naked state or status. Thus, when Sandra Gilbert offers us the choice of stripping away "costumes (and selves) to reveal the pure, sexless (or third-sexed) being behind gender and myth," she assumes a pure, free ontological essence which we can locate and define prior to its insertion into language, society, culture. Proving the contrary is precisely the point of the vacillating rhetoric and epicene protagonist of Woolf's novel.

In *Orlando,* clothing, identity, and rhetoric are not an ornamentation of something prior, but an orientation to something else. What matters is not what they mask or mark, but what they enable the protagonist or the writer to accomplish. That is, what matters is not the *nature* of the sign, the transsexual, but its position and function within a particular discursive situation. And so, we must attend to the production of the androgynous Orlando, not to her properties. If we return to that clothes philosophy passage, we see that in trying to distinguish the ways in which Orlando has changed with the sex change and how Orlando embodies traits of both sexes, the biographer ends up making stereotypical remarks, for he can make such sexual distinctions only by relying on conventional assumptions about sexual difference. His only recourse, then, is to look at the particular case: "but here we leave the general question [of sexual difference] and note only the odd effect it had on the particular case of Orlando herself." We, too, must attend to the particular case rather than the general category. What we need in order to read this novel is a conceptual model that enables us to discuss the androgyne not in terms of its relation to the self beneath or the world beyond, but in terms of the multiple and shifting relations among signifying systems, such as rhetoric, fashion, gender, and genre.

Thus, we must attend not only to the various relations among changing historical periods and rhetorical styles, but also to the changing sexual metaphors as well. By employing three metaphors for sexual identity in *Orlando*—androgyny, transvestism, and transsexualism—Woolf shows us that there are different ways of talking about identity, different kinds of appropriateness, different functions of language. When we fail to specify the kinds of distinctions we are relying on (as Sandra Gilbert does in equating these metaphors), our conclusions become suspect. Woolf knows all too well that any language she can use is already embroiled in certain conventional assumptions about gender and identity. Her solution, changing metaphors for sexual identity, is less a freedom from a gendered reality than a freedom from referential thinking. Such freedom comes about by a change in our conception of language. What is at issue here is a language that sets up opposing alternatives and one that plays out various relations. Such an epicene novel is possible when different functions of language are tested out rather one being taken for granted.

The androgyne, as Felman says, is "constituted in ambiguity" and therefore is not representative of any "single signified." The androgyne threatens meaning by breaking down those oppositions that allow us to make meaningful distinctions. It calls attention to and calls into question one way of making meaning, the institution of representation. Androgyny is not a freedom from the tyranny of sex, as Maria DiBattista says, so much as a freedom from the tyranny of reference. The shifting and blurring of sexual identities, like the shifting and blurring of literary genres, periods, and styles, disrupts meaning brought about by fixed polarities, by defined standards, by rigid categories, by "rhetorical hierarchy" (Felman's phrase). Sex and text are rhetorical terms; they function not only according to certain grammatical and syntactical patternings and social norms but also rhetorically and historically. They are constructed according to a particular model of language. To put sexual identity and textual meaning into confusion, as Woolf does in *Orlando,* is to disclose the dependence of sexual traits and literary standards on certain kinds of discourse. Because one cannot locate innate sexual traits or essential literary values in the face of changing attitudes,

conventions, and paradigms (whether scientific, literary, or psychological), one must continually posit and undermine, affirm and doubt, "yield and resist." Oscillation is the rhythm of *Orlando*; oscillating exploration is its method.

Far from defeating sexual difference, as many feminist critics claim, *Orlando* enacts it, enshrines it, exploits it, makes a spectacle of it, but as a playful oscillation not a stable opposition. The androgynous self in *Orlando* is a metaphor for the dramatic, the role-playing self. Androgyny is a metaphor for change, for openness, for a self-conscious acting out of intentions. It is not an ideal *type,* but a contextual *response.* Identity is always disguised in *Orlando* not because the "true self" is running around "incognito or incognita as the case might turn out to be" but because identity is a series of roles. And successive roles subvert referential poles (Felman). In this sense, *Orlando* presents a Lacanian view of identity. Woolf no more than Lacan tries to *define* female identity, for any identity assumed finally, definitively, essentially will be constraining; any identity deemed authentic, appropriate, natural will be illusory. Yet Orlando does not *transcend* identity any more than Woolf advocates a gender-free reality, as Sandra Gilbert asserts. For one cannot deny the reality of gender or the necessity of identity. "Identity," Gallop writes, "must be continually assumed and immediately called into question," just as expression must be exercised and at once critiqued. Divesting Orlando of property and patronym, putting her paternity and propriety into question, Woolf does not liberate her identity but refuses the categories by which it is fixed, determined, legalized. *Orlando* "compromises the coherence" of sexuality and textuality (see Felman). Its open-endedness, its openness to other literary texts, resists closure and containment, refuses to provide a conclusive and thus an exclusive statement. *Orlando* shows us how sexuality and textuality perform in the world; it does not tell us what they are or what they should be. What Woolf defies in this novel is any attempt to *define* writing or identity by definitive standards to which it conforms or from which it deviates.

In her diary Woolf refers to *Orlando* as her "play side." It refuses to stop the play of speculation with a consistent argument or theory. The play side is concerned with writing as pleasure, not as production. As Woolf wrote in her typescript of **"Professions for Women"**: "When people said to me what is the use of your trying to write? I could say truthfully, I write not for use, but for pleasure" (*Pargiters*). When Orlando admires the anonymous writers who built the house of literature, she means those writers who wrote with no practical purpose in mind, whether to protest or to proselytize, but only out of the love of writing. For too long we have downplayed the play side of Virginia Woolf as displayed in such works as *Orlando, A Room of One's Own,* and *Flush.* We have turned her play side into a meaningful representation, into an alternative or an appropriate form. But as Ionesco once cautioned, any established form of expression can become a form of oppression, can become authoritative, can become, in Gallop's words, "a position and a possession." Orlando and Woolf neither reject past aesthetic standards nor prescribe new ones. They take from the literary past what is useful to them, use up standards, dispose of them, and thus expose them as provisional and changeable, disclose their dependence on certain contexts. Enacting a type of discourse rather than codifying one, as Woolf does in *Orlando,* exposes the supposed universality of aesthetic standards of value. By questioning various metaphysical positions, by testing out various narrative strategies, Woolf produces not "stable assumptions" but "contextual associations." (Gallop 64). She disrupts our tendency to see language as the transparent medium of communications; she defies our habit of looking through discourse to representation. It is not that *Orlando*'s playful surface has no point to it; its point is its playful surface. It is time this play side of Woolf's writing be accounted for in terms of different conceptions of self, language, and reality—in terms of a dramatic self not an appropriate one, in terms of a performative view of language not a cognitive one, in terms of a rhetorical reality not a referential one.

It is not, then, that the appropriate identity is androgynous, but that the androgyne defies an appropriate, a definable, identity. Androgyny in *Orlando* is not so much a psychosexual category as a rhetorical strategy, less a condition than a motive. Androgyny does not *substitute for* anything; for that would be to fix it, possess it, universalize it. The androgyne defeats the norm, the universal, the stereotype that Woolf feared becoming, as she so often expresses in her diaries: "I will go on adventuring, changing, opening my mind and my eyes, refusing to be stamped and stereotyped" (*A Writer's Diary*). The stereotype, says Roland Barthes, is "the word repeated without any magic, any enthusiasm, as though it were natural, as though by some miracle this recurring word were adequate on each occasion for different reasons" (*The Pleasure of the Text*) or, I might add, on different occasions for the same reason. To continue with Barthes's terminology, the androgyne, unlike the stereotype or the norm, is neither consistent nor insistent; it is perverse.

By taking the androgynous personality out of its context in this novel, by turning it into an alternative to or a substitute for the conventional character of the traditional novel or for the conventional self of patriarchal society, so many feminist critics run the risk of reducing it to a platitude. They risk turning a text that works to undo norms, stereotypes, and standards into a new norm, what Gallop calls a "normalizing moralism" or "a comforting representation." The problem with the platitude, the norm, the stereotype is not that they are false or trite in themselves but that they are false or trite in being detached from the contexts that gave rise to them. As Woolf shows in *Orlando,* what enables Alexander Pope's scathing remark on the character of women (a remark so famous that the narrator need not repeat it) to survive to shape future attitudes toward women is its being loosed from its generating context, which was this: Orlando inadvertently offended Mr. Pope by dropping a sugar cube "with a great plop" into his tea. A witty remark may be a petty retort. Unmoored from their contexts, literary standards, sexual traits, and social values appear to be incontestable; yet they are responses to particular historical and rhetorical situations. Taking Woolf's statement about androgyny out of its context in *Orlando,* repeating it as an unambiguous truth

about human nature, trivializes it. What gives the concept its force are the contextual, textual, and sexual relationships in which it plays its part. "If you cannot give something up for something of like value," Gallop writes, "if you consider it nonsubstitutable, then you don't possess it any more than it possesses you." We need to look at what Woolf *does* in a particular text and context, not at what her writing *represents* for all times or for all women.

Like Orlando herself, her critics must avoid the tyranny or folly of sex pride. They must avoid setting up a feminist referential in place of a masculinist one. They must resist reestablishing a natural, even necessary, relation between self and narrative when they have exposed such a relation as arbitrary and provisional in conventional novels.

What *Orlando* presents, then, is not a metaphysical theory but a play of forms. Woolf's androgynous vision affirms Gallop's "permanent alternation," a persistent oscillation, as our binocular vision allows us to see both duck and rabbit in Wittgenstein's sample sketch (*Philosophical Investigations, II*). The double discourse of *Orlando* enables Woolf to set up exchanges between opposing positions, between different orders of discourse. What appears to be an opposition between positions is tolerated as difference without belligerence, as different options on a spectrum of possibilities, not a *choice* of position but a *doubling* of vision. The double discourse enables Woolf to present a bistable vision, not a univocal theory. This double discourse does not deny a feminist reading. As Gallop says, "This problem of dealing with difference without constituting an opposition may just be what feminism is all about." Woolf's gesture in *Orlando* is much like Gallop's in *The Daughter's Seduction*: she undercuts her own writing, or as Woolf puts it, mocks her own lyric vein (*Writer's Diary*); she changes her viewpoint; she alters her narrative voice. The ironic, mocking tone, the vacillating narrative voice, and the pastiche of literary allusions in *Orlando* check our efforts to read for a personal argument, check our tendency to take Woolf at her word, which is to take her discourse for granted. The double discourse, in Felman's terms its "play of undecidability," encourages us to suspend our analytical, judicial, end-seeking, purposive reading for the delight in speculation, equivocation, rhetoric, and play. Feminist readings of *Orlando* read only the law, or the counterlaw, of this novel, not its desire. They stress the purposive and polemical over the playful and pleasurable. They would suppress the very multiplicity and flexibility by means of which Woolf defies authority, systems that shut out (*Writer's Diary*), and "the desire to make others believe as [she] believes". *Orlando* is feminist not in what its language says but in what its discourse achieves. *Orlando* gives us not a theory of androgyny but a performance.

If androgyny were a triumph over the tyranny of sex (Maria DiBattista), a resolution to the contradictions between female and male (Rachel DuPlessis), or a transcendence of a gendered reality (Sandra Gilbert), then in writing *Orlando* Woolf would more than likely have defeated the need for literature, for sex cannot be separated from text, the grammatical from the gendered. Orlando's androgyny and diuturnity are not a testament to some essential and enduring human nature but an affirmation of adaptation and change and of the life-sustaining impulse to create fictions. The novel ends at the present moment, the moment of Woolf's writing ("Thursday, the eleventh of October, Nineteen Hundred and Twenty-eight"), with Orlando's sighting of the wild goose: "It is the goose!" Orlando cried. "The wild goose . . ." The wild goose and the ellipsis assure us that nothing is concluded, that the chase will continue. We can only respond, "Encore!"

FURTHER READING

Biography

Bell, Quentin. "June 1925–December 1928." In his *Virginia Woolf: A Biography*, Vol. II, pp. 109-40. New York: Harcourt Brace Jovanovich, 1972.
> Covers the period during which Woolf conceived of, wrote, and published *Orlando.*

Pippett, Aileen. *The Moth and the Star: A Biography of Virginia Woolf.* Boston: Little, Brown, and Co., 1955, 368 p.
> Includes an account of the writing of *Orlando* and initial response to the novel.

Criticism

Alexander, Jean. "*Orlando.*" In her *The Venture of Form in the Novels of Virginia Woolf*, pp. 127-46. Port Washington, N.Y.: Kennikat Press, 1974.
> Discusses symbol and structure in *Orlando* within the context of Woolf's career.

Baldanza, Frank. "*Orlando* and the Sackvilles." *PMLA* LXX, No. 1 (March 1955): 274-79.
> Draws parallels between the "biography" of Orlando and the history of the Sackville family.

Blackstone, Bernard. "*Orlando* (1928)." In his *Virginia Woolf: A Commentary*, pp. 131-38. London: Hogarth Press, 1949.
> Plot summary and interpretation.

Gorsky, Susan Rubinow. "People and Characters." In her *Virginia Woolf*, pp. 67-96. Boston: Twayne, 1978.
> Discusses *Orlando* in a survey of Woolf's novels that treat "the problem of how to write about a person (living or dead, real or fictitious)," including *Jacob's Room, Mrs. Dalloway, Roger Fry,* and *Flush.*

Green, David Bonnell. "*Orlando* and the Sackvilles: Addendum." *PMLA*, LXXI, No. 1 (March 1956): 268-69.
> Links the sex change in Orlando to the extinction of the male line of Sackville heirs and the inheritance of the family estate into the female line, the Sackville-Wests.

Hoffman, Charles G. "Fact and Fantasy in *Orlando*: Virginia Woolf's Manuscript Revisions." *Texas Studies in Literature and Language* X, No. 3 (Fall 1968): 435-44.
> Contrasts the manuscript version of *Orlando* with the published version, noting differences "which are worth examining because they help clarify Virginia Woolf's intentions, particularly in relation to the various aspects of Orlando's character and the history of the Sackville family."

Holtby, Winifred. "Two in a Taxi." In her *Virginia Woolf,* pp. 161-85. London: Wishart & Co., 1932.
> Summarizes and explicates *Orlando* and compares its consideration of literature, time, and sex with that in *A Room of One's Own* (1929). According to Holtby: "Different as they are in form, the two books are complementary. *Orlando* dramatizes the theories stated more plainly in the essay. The essay makes clear the meaning of the allegory."

Johnson, Manly. "*Orlando* and *The Waves.*" In his *Virginia Woolf*, pp. 77-91. New York: Frederick Ungar, 1973.
> Summarizes the plot of *Orlando* and comments: "Despite its capriciousness, *Orlando* is a substantial work of fiction. The impressionistic rendering of three centuries of English manners and literary history would alone give it a permanent interest. But in addition, it offers felicities of style, delights of parody, and thematic subtleties."

Kushen, Betty. "'Dreams of Golden Domes': Manic Fusion in Virginia Woolf's *Orlando.*" *Literature and Psychology* 29, Nos. 1-2 (1979): 25-33.
> Examines the significance and success of Woolf's movement from "a predominantly depressive position in *To the Lighthouse,* a meditation in mourning of the lost Mrs. Ramsay, to an overtly manic effort in *Orlando,* an attempt at dazzling exuberance."

Love, Jean O. "*Orlando* and Its Genesis: Venturing and Experimenting in Art, Love, and Sex." In *Virginia Woolf: Revaluation and Continuity,* edited by Ralph Freedman, pp. 189-218. Berkeley and Los Angeles: University of California Press, 1980.
> Recounts Woolf's relationship with Vita Sackville-West and its literary record in *Orlando.*

Moore, Madeline. "Virginia Woof's *Orlando*: An Edition of the Manuscript." *Twentieth-Century Literature* 25, Nos. 3-4 (Fall/Winter 1979): 303-55.
> Includes introductory commentary, manuscript text, and letters by Woolf, Vita Sackville-West, and Harold Nicolson regarding *Orlando.*

Philipson, Morris. "Virginia Woolf's *Orlando*: Biography as a Work of Fiction." In *From Parnassus: Essays in Honor of Jacques Barzun,* edited by Dora B. Weiner and William R. Keylor, pp. 237-48. New York: Harper & Row, 1976.
> Discusses Woolf's artistic strategy in *Orlando,* defining the basis of the work as "two extended metaphors, one regarding longevity and the other sexuality. Both are employed in order to demonstrate formative influences, to arrive at an understanding of the essence of the subject of the biography—poetically."

Richter, Harvena. "Three Modes of Time." In her *Virginia Woolf: The Inward Voyage,* pp. 149-79. Princeton: Princeton University Press, 1970.
> Examines Woolf's manipulation of time in *Orlando, The Waves,* and *The Years.*

Roessel, David. "The Significance of Constantinople in *Orlando.*" *Papers on Language & Literature* 28, No. 4 (Fall 1992): 398-416.
> Suggests that the significance of Constantinople in the lives and works of Woolf and Vita Sackville-West and in political events of the 1920s led Woolf to situate Orlando's sex change in that city.

Rosenthal, Michael. "*Orlando*." In his *Virginia Woolf,* pp. 128-41. New York: Columbia University Press, 1979.

Maintains that "Orlando's discovery of her essential artistic self marks the appropriate conclusion for a book which is finally less concerned with Vita Sackville-West than with depicting Woolf's own sense of the workings of the creative imagination. . . . The strains of parody, biography, and satire fall away and Woolf is left, as always, endorsing the life-giving energies of art."

Rubenstein, Roberta. "*Orlando*: Virginia Woolf's Improvisations on a Russian Theme." *Forum for Modern Language Studies* IX, No. 2 (April 1973): 166-69.

Cites Orlando's romance with Sasha as an allegorical representation of Woolf's fascination with Russia and Russian literature.

Sackville-West, Vita. "Virginia Woolf and *Orlando*." *The Listener* 53 (27 January 1955): 157-58.

Traces the writing of *Orlando* through personal letters and includes an excised portion of the original manuscript.

Steele, Philip L. "Virginia Woolf's Spiritual Autobiography." *Topic* IX (Fall 1969): 64-74.

Suggests that "Orlando is Woolf's spirit, her sensibility, set down in a confused and tumultuous world trying to discover the reality, the value, the meaning of life. The world with which Virginia Woolf had to come to terms, as the world of an intellectual, spanned several centuries of life and literature. All the ideas, the alternatives, the questions with which she wrestled in moving between isolation and society, masculine or feminine attitudes, romanticism or restraint in writing, are projected into the four centuries of Orlando's career."

Stewart, Jack F. "Historical Impressionism in *Orlando*." *Studies in the Novel* V, No. 1 (Spring 1973): 71-85.

Relates Woolf's subjective treatment of history in Orlando to the impressionist style in painting. According to Stewart, "As impressionist painters like Monet tried to catch the play of sunlight transfusing objects, as pointillists like Seurat created a porous texture out of stipple dots, so Virginia Woolf highlights the flow of historical consciousness by dissolving the tyranny of time, accelerating change, and breaking the bonds of nuclear biography."

Whittemore, Reed. "Biography and Literature." *Sewanee Review* C, No. 3 (Summer 1992): 382-96.

Considers the significance of *Orlando* in the development of modern biography.

Wilson, J. J. "Why Is *Orlando* Difficult?" In *New Feminist Essays on Virginia Woolf,* edited by Jane Marcus, pp. 170-84. Lincoln: University of Nebraska Press, 1981.

Defines *Orlando* as an anti-novel. According to Wilson, "Of the many genres into which *Orlando* could fit (*Bildungsroman,* picaresque, quest novel, satire, fantasy, fairy story, *conte philosophique,* feminist pamphlet, literary history, or even that which it purports to be, a biography), the anti-novel seems the least Procrustean and describes best its origins and functions."

Twentieth-Century
Literary Criticism

Cumulative Indexes
Volumes 1-56

How to Use This Index

The main references

> **Calvino, Italo**
> 1923-1985.....CLC 5, 8, 11, 22, 33, 39,
> 73; SSC 3

list all author entries in the following Gale Literary Criticism series:

BLC = Black Literature Criticism
CLC = Contemporary Literary Criticism
CLR = Children's Literature Review
CMLC = Classical and Medieval Literature Criticism
DA = DISCovering Authors
DC = Drama Criticism
HLC = Hispanic Literature Criticism
LC = Literature Criticism from 1400 to 1800
NCLC = Nineteenth-Century Literature Criticism
PC = Poetry Criticism
SSC = Short Story Criticism
TCLC = Twentieth-Century Literary Criticism
WLC = World Literature Criticism, 1500 to the Present

The cross-references

> See also CANR 23; CA 85-88;
> obituary CA 116

list all author entries in the following Gale biographical and literary sources:

AAYA = Authors & Artists for Young Adults
AITN = Authors in the News
BEST = Bestsellers
BW = Black Writers
CA = Contemporary Authors
CAAS = Contemporary Authors Autobiography Series
CABS = Contemporary Authors Bibliographical Series
CANR = Contemporary Authors New Revision Series
CAP = Contemporary Authors Permanent Series
CDALB = Concise Dictionary of American Literary Biography
CDBLB = Concise Dictionary of British Literary Biography
DLB = Dictionary of Literary Biography
DLBD = Dictionary of Literary Biography Documentary Series
DLBY = Dictionary of Literary Biography Yearbook
HW = Hispanic Writers
JRDA = Junior DISCovering Authors
MAICYA = Major Authors and Illustrators for Children and Young Adults
MTCW = Major 20th-Century Writers
NNAL = Native North American Literature
SAAS = Something about the Author Autobiography Series
SATA = Something about the Author
YABC = Yesterday's Authors of Books for Children

Twentieth-Century Literary Criticism
Cumulative Author Index Errata

References in this index to the following series are either missing or incorrect: *Native North American Literature, Poetry Criticism, Short Story Criticism, Something about the Author Autobiography Series, Something about the Author, Twentieth-Century Literary Criticism, World Literature Criticism, Yesterday's Authors of Books for Children.*

Correct citations are given below for authors appearing in both *Twentieth-Century Literary Criticism* and other Literary Criticism Series titles. For further references to authors appearing in Literary Criticism Series titles, please see either the individual indexes for each series or the current *Contemporary Authors Cumulative Index*.

A.E.	TCLC 3,10
Adams, Andy	TCLC 56
Adams, Henry	TCLC 4, 52; DA
Ady, Endre	TCLC 11
Agee, James	TCLC 1,19
Akutagawa Ryunosuke	TCLC 16
Alain	TCLC 41
Alain-Fournier	TCLC 6
Alas, Leopoldo	TCLC 29
Aldanov, Mark	TCLC 23
Aleichem, Sholom	TCLC 1,35
Anderson, Maxwell	TCLC 2
Anderson, Sherwood	TCLC 1, 10, 24; DA; SSC 1; WLC
Andrade, Mario de	TCLC 43
Andreas-Salome, Lou	TCLC 56
Andreyev, Leonid	TCLC 3
Annensky, Innokenty Fyodorovich	TCLC 14
Anwar, Chairil	TCLC 22
Apollinaire, Guillaume	TCLC 3, 8, 51; PC 7
Arlt, Roberto	TCLC 29; HLC
Artaud, Antonin	TCLC 3, 36
Artsybashev, Mikhail	TCLC 31
Asch, Sholem	TCLC 3
Ahterton, Gertrude	TCLC 2
Auerbach, Erich	TCLC 43
Austin, Mary	TCLC 25
Azuela, Nariano	TCLC 3; HLC
Babel, Isaak	TCLC 2, 13; SSC 16
Babits, Mihaly	TCLC 14
Bacovia, George	TCLC 24
Baker, Ray Stannard	TCLC 47
Balmont, Konstantin	TCLC 11
Barbellion, W. N. P.	TCLC 24
Barbusse, Henri	TCLC 5
Barea, Atruro	TCLC 14
Baring, Maurice	TCLC 8
Baroja, Pio	TCLC 8; HLC
Barres, Maurice	TCLC 47
Barrie, J. M.	TCLC 2
Barry, Philip	TCLC 11
Baum, L. Frank	TCLC 7
Beard, Charles A.	TCLC 15
Beerbohm, Max	TCLC 1, 24
Belasco, David	TCLC 3
Bell, James Madison	TCLC 43; BLC
Belloc, Hilaire	TCLC 7, 18
Bely, Andrey	TCLC 7
Benavente, Jacinto	TCLC 3
Benchley, Robert	TCLC 1, 55

Benet, Stephen, Vincent	TCLC 7; SSC 10
Benet, William Rose	TCLC 28
Bengtsson, Frans	TCLC 48
Benjamin, Walter	TCLC 39
Benn, Gottfried	TCLC 3
Bennett, Arnold	TCLC 5, 20
Benson, E. F.	TCLC 27
Benson, Stella	TCLC 17
Bentley, E. C.	TCLC 12
Bergson, Henri	TCLC 32
Bernanos, Georges	TCLC 3
Besant, Annie	TCLC 9
Betti, Ugo	TCLC 5
Bialik, Chaim Nachman	TCLC 25
Bierce, Ambrose	TCLC 1, 7, 44; DA; SSC 9; WLC
Bjornson, Bjornstjerne	TCLC 7, 37
Black Elk	TCLC 33
Blackmore, R. D.	TCLC 27
Blackwood, Algernon	TCLC 5
Blasco Ibanez, Vicente	TCLC 12
Blok, Alexander	TCLC 5
Bloy, Leon	TCLC 22
Boas, Franz	TCLC 56
Bodenheim, Maxwell	TCLC 44
Borchert, Wolfgang	TCLC 5
Borowski, Tadeusz	TCLC 9
Bosman, Herman Charles	TCLC 49
Bosshere, Jean de	TCLC 19
Bourget, Paul	TCLC 12
Bourne, Randolph S.	TCLC 16
Bradford, Gamaliel	TCLC 36
Brancati, Vitaliano	TCLC 12
Brandes, Georg	TCLC 10
Brecht, Bertolt	TCLC 1, 6, 13, 25; DA; DC 3; WLC
Brennan, Christopher John	TCLC 17
Bridges, Robert	TCLC 1
Bridie, James	TCLC 3
Broch, Hermann	TCLC 20
Bromfield, Louis	TCLC 11
Brooke, Rupert	TCLC 2, 7; DA; WLC
Brown, George Douglas	TCLC 28
Bryusov, Valery Yakovlevich	TCLC 10
Buchan, John	TCLC 41
Bulgakov, Mikhail	TCLC 2, 16
Bulgya, Alexander Alexandrovich	TCLC 53
Bunin, Ivan Alexeyevich	TCLC 6; SSC 5
Burroughs, Edgar Rice	TCLC 2, 32
Butler, Samuel	TCLC 1, 33; DA; WLC
Cabell, James Branch	TCLC 6

Cable, George Washington	TCLC 4; SSC 4
Campana, Dino	TCLC 20
Campbell, Roy	TCLC 5
Campbell, Wilfred	TCLC 9
Capek, Karel	TCLC 6, 37; DA; DC 1; WLC
Carducci, Giosue	TCLC 32
Carman, Bliss	TCLC 7
Carnegie, Dale	TCLC 53
Carossa, Hans	TCLC 48
Carr, Emily	TCLC 32
Cary, Joyce	TCLC 1, 29
Casely-Hayford, J. E.	TCLC 24; BLC
Cather, Willa	TCLC 1, 11, 31; DA; SSC 2; WLC
Cavafy, C. P.	TCLC 2, 7
Chambers, Robert W.	TCLC 41
Chandler, Raymond	TCLC 1, 7
Chapman, John Jay	TCLC 7
Chatterji, Saratchandra	TCLC 13
Chekhov, Anton	TCLC 3, 10, 31, 55; DA; SSC 2; WLC
Chesnutt, Charles W.	TCLC 5, 39; BLC; SSC 7
Chesterton, G. K.	TCLC 1, 6; SSC 1
Chopin, Kate	TCLC 5, 14,; DA; SSC 7
Claudel, Paul	TCLC 2, 10
Colette	TCLC 1, 5, 16; SSC 10
Comstock, Anthony	TCLC 13
Connor, Ralph	TCLC 31
Conrad, Joseph	TCLC 1, 6, 13, 25, 43; DA; SSC 9; WLC
Coppard, A. E.	TCLC 5
Coppee, Francois	TCLC 25
Corelli, Marie	TCLC 51
Corvo, Baron	TCLC 12
Cotter, Joseph Seamon Sr.	TCLC 58; BLC
Couperus, Louis	TCLC 15
Cram, Ralph Adams	TCLC 45
Crane, Hart	TCLC 2, 5; DA; PC 3; WLC
Crane, Stephen	TCLC 11, 17, 32; DA; SSC 7; WLC
Crawford, F. Marion	TCLC 10
Croce, Benedetto	TCLC 37
Crofts, Freeman Wills	TCLC 55
Crothers, Rachel	TCLC 19
Crowley, Aleister	TCLC 7
Csath, Geza	TCLC 13
Cullen, Countee	TCLC 4, 37; BLC; DA
Cunha, Euclides da	TCLC 24

Literary Criticism Series
Cumulative Author Index

A.
See Arnold, Matthew

A. M.
See Megged, Aharon

A. R. P-C
See Galsworthy, John

Abasiyanik, Sait Faik 1906-1954
See Sait Faik
See also CA 123

Abbey, Edward 1927-1989...... **CLC 36, 59**
See also CA 45-48; 128; CANR 2, 41

Abbott, Lee K(ittredge) 1947-...... **CLC 48**
See also CA 124; DLB 130

Abe, Kobo 1924-1993..... **CLC 8, 22, 53, 81**
See also CA 65-68; 140; CANR 24; MTCW

Abelard, Peter c. 1079-c. 1142 ... **CMLC 11**
See also DLB 115

Abell, Kjeld 1901-1961............ **CLC 15**
See also CA 111

Abish, Walter 1931-.............. **CLC 22**
See also CA 101; CANR 37; DLB 130

Abrahams, Peter (Henry) 1919- ..... **CLC 4**
See also BW 1; CA 57-60; CANR 26;
DLB 117; MTCW

Abrams, M(eyer) H(oward) 1912-... **CLC 24**
See also CA 57-60; CANR 13, 33; DLB 67

Abse, Dannie 1923-................ **CLC 7, 29**
See also CA 53-56; CAAS 1; CANR 4;
DLB 27

Achebe, (Albert) Chinua(lumogu)
1930- ..... **CLC 1, 3, 5, 7, 11, 26, 51, 75;**
BLC; DA
See also BW 2; CA 1-4R; CANR 6, 26;
CLR 20; DLB 117; MAICYA; MTCW;
SATA-Obit 38, 40; YABC

Acker, Kathy 1948- .... **CLC 45**
See also CA 117; 122

Ackroyd, Peter 1949-.......... **CLC 34, 52**
See also CA 123; 127

Acorn, Milton 1923-.............. **CLC 15**
See also CA 103; DLB 53

Adamov, Arthur 1908-1970 ...... **CLC 4, 25**
See also CA 17-18; 25-28R; CAP 2; MTCW

Adams, Alice (Boyd) 1926- ... **CLC 6, 13, 46**
See also CA 81-84; CANR 26; DLBY 86;
MTCW

Adams, Douglas (Noel) 1952- ... **CLC 27, 60**
See also AAYA 4; BEST 89:3; CA 106;
CANR 34; DLBY 83; JRDA

Adams, Francis 1862-1893...... **NCLC 33**

Adams, Richard (George)
1920-.................. **CLC 4, 5, 18**
See also AITN 1, 2; CA 49-52; CANR 3,
35; CLR 20; JRDA; MAICYA; MTCW;
SATA-Obit 7, 69

Adamson, Joy(-Friederike Victoria)
1910-1980 .... **CLC 17**
See also CA 69-72; 93-96; CANR 22;
MTCW; SATA-Obit 11, 22

Adcock, Fleur 1934-.............. **CLC 41**
See also CA 25-28R; CANR 11, 34;
DLB 40

Addams, Charles (Samuel)
1912-1988 .... **CLC 30**
See also CA 61-64; 126; CANR 12

Addison, Joseph 1672-1719 .... **LC 18**
See also CDBLB 1660-1789; DLB 101

Adler, C(arole) S(chwerdtfeger)
1932-.................... **CLC 35**
See also AAYA 4; CA 89-92; CANR 19,
40; JRDA; MAICYA; SATA 15;
SATA-Obit 26, 63

Adler, Renata 1938-............ **CLC 8, 31**
See also CA 49-52; CANR 5, 22; MTCW

Aeschylus
525B.C.-456B.C........ **CMLC 11; DA**

Afton, Effie
See Harper, Frances Ellen Watkins

Agapida, Fray Antonio
See Irving, Washington

Aghill, Gordon
See Silverberg, Robert

Agnon, S(hmuel) Y(osef Halevi)
1888-1970 .... **CLC 4, 8, 14**
See also CA 17-18; 25-28R; CAP 2; MTCW

Aherne, Owen
See Cassill, R(onald) V(erlin)

Ai 1947-................... **CLC 4, 14, 69**
See also CA 85-88; CAAS 13; DLB 120

Aickman, Robert (Fordyce)
1914-1981 .... **CLC 57**
See also CA 5-8R; CANR 3

Aiken, Conrad (Potter)
1889-1973 .... **CLC 1, 3, 5, 10, 52**
See also CA 5-8R; 45-48; CANR 4;
CDALB 1929-1941; DLB 9, 45, 102;
MTCW; SATA-Obit 3, 30; TCLC 9

Aiken, Joan (Delano) 1924-........ **CLC 35**
See also AAYA 1; CA 9-12R; CANR 4, 23,
34; CLR 1, 19; JRDA; MAICYA;
MTCW; SATA 1; SATA-Obit 2, 30, 73

Ainsworth, William Harrison
1805-1882 .... **NCLC 13**
See also DLB 21; SATA-Obit 24

Aitmatov, Chingiz (Torekulovich)
1928- .... **CLC 71**
See also CA 103; CANR 38; MTCW;
SATA-Obit 56

Akers, Floyd
See Baum, L(yman) Frank

Akhmadulina, Bella Akhatovna
1937-...................... **CLC 53**
See also CA 65-68

Akhmatova, Anna
1888-1966 .... **CLC 11, 25, 64**
See also CA 19-20; 25-28R; CANR 35;
CAP 1; MTCW; SAAS 2

Aksakov, Sergei Timofeyvich
1791-1859 .... **NCLC 2**

Aksenov, Vassily................. CLC 22
See also Aksyonov, Vassily (Pavlovich)

Aksyonov, Vassily (Pavlovich)
1932-...................... **CLC 37**
See also Aksenov, Vassily
See also CA 53-56; CANR 12

Alarcon, Pedro Antonio de
1833-1891 .... **NCLC 1**

Albee, Edward (Franklin III)
1928- ...... **CLC 1, 2, 3, 5, 9, 11, 13, 25,**
53; DA
See also AITN 1; CA 5-8R; CABS 3;
CANR 8; CDALB 1941-1968; DLB 7;
MTCW; YABC

Alberti, Rafael 1902-.............. **CLC 7**
See also CA 85-88; DLB 108

Alcala-Galiano, Juan Valera y
See Valera y Alcala-Galiano, Juan

Alcott, Amos Bronson 1799-1888 .. **NCLC 1**
See also DLB 1

Alcott, Louisa May
1832-1888 .... **NCLC 6; DA**
See also CDALB 1865-1917; CLR 1;
DLB 1, 42, 79; JRDA; MAICYA; YABC;
1

Aldanov, M. A.
See Aldanov, Mark (Alexandrovich)

Aldington, Richard 1892-1962...... **CLC 49**
See also CA 85-88; CANR 45; DLB 20, 36,
100

Aldiss, Brian W(ilson)
1925-.................. **CLC 5, 14, 40**
See also CA 5-8R; CAAS 2; CANR 5, 28;
DLB 14; MTCW; SATA-Obit 34

Alegria, Claribel 1924-............ **CLC 75**
See also CA 131; CAAS 15; HW

Alegria, Fernando 1918-........... **CLC 57**
See also CA 9-12R; CANR 5, 32; HW

Aleixandre, Vicente 1898-1984 ... **CLC 9, 36**
See also CA 85-88; 114; CANR 26;
DLB 108; HW; MTCW

Alepoudelis, Odysseus
See Elytis, Odysseus

Aleshkovsky, Joseph 1929-
See Aleshkovsky, Yuz
See also CA 121; 128

Aleshkovsky, Yuz................. CLC 44
See also Aleshkovsky, Joseph

Alexander, Lloyd (Chudley) 1924- .. **CLC 35**
See also AAYA 1; CA 1-4R; CANR 1, 24,
38; CLR 1, 5; DLB 52; JRDA; MAICYA;
MTCW; SATA-Obit 3, 49

Arany, Janos 1817-1882........ **NCLC 34**

Arbuthnot, John 1667-1735.......... **LC 1**
See also DLB 101

Archer, Herbert Winslow
See Mencken, H(enry) L(ouis)

Archer, Jeffrey (Howard) 1940- .... **CLC 28**
See also BEST 89:3; CA 77-80; CANR 22

Archer, Jules 1915- .... **CLC 12**
See also CA 9-12R; CANR 6; SATA 5;
SATA-Obit 4

Archer, Lee
See Ellison, Harlan

Arden, John 1930- .... **CLC 6, 13, 15**
See also CA 13-16R; CAAS 4; CANR 31;
DLB 13; MTCW

Arenas, Reinaldo
1943-1990 .... **CLC 41; HLC**
See also CA 124; 128; 133; HW

Arendt, Hannah 1906-1975 .... **CLC 66**
See also CA 17-20R; 61-64; CANR 26;
MTCW

Aretino, Pietro 1492-1556 .... **LC 12**

Arghezi, Tudor.................... **CLC 80**
See also Theodorescu, Ion N.

Arguedas, Jose Maria
1911-1969 .... **CLC 10, 18**
See also CA 89-92; DLB 113; HW

Argueta, Manlio 1936-............ **CLC 31**
See also CA 131; HW

Ariosto, Ludovico 1474-1533......... **LC 6**

Aristides
See Epstein, Joseph

Aristophanes
450B.C.-385B.C.... **CMLC 4; DA; DC 2**

Armah, Ayi Kwei 1939- .... **CLC 5, 33; BLC**
See also BW 1; CA 61-64; CANR 21;
DLB 117; MTCW

Armatrading, Joan 1950-.......... **CLC 17**
See also CA 114

Armstrong, Jeannette 1948-.......... **PC X**

Arnette, Robert
See Silverberg, Robert

Arnim, Achim von (Ludwig Joachim von
Arnim) 1781-1831 .... **NCLC 5**
See also DLB 90

Arnim, Bettina von 1785-1859.... **NCLC 38**
See also DLB 90

Arnold, Matthew
1822-1888 .... **NCLC 6, 29; DA**
See also CDBLB 1832-1890; DLB 32, 57;
SAAS 5; YABC

Arnold, Thomas 1795-1842 ...... **NCLC 18**
See also DLB 55

Arnow, Harriette (Louisa) Simpson
1908-1986 .... **CLC 2, 7, 18**
See also CA 9-12R; 118; CANR 14; DLB 6;
MTCW; SATA-Obit 42, 47

Arp, Hans
See Arp, Jean

Arp, Jean 1887-1966.............. **CLC 5**
See also CA 81-84; 25-28R; CANR 42

Arrabal
See Arrabal, Fernando

Arrabal, Fernando 1932- ... **CLC 2, 9, 18, 58**
See also CA 9-12R; CANR 15

Arrick, Fran.................... **CLC 30**

Arthur, Ruth M(abel) 1905-1979.... **CLC 12**
See also CA 9-12R; 85-88; CANR 4;
SATA-Obit 7, 26

Arundel, Honor (Morfydd)
1919-1973 .... **CLC 17**
See also CA 21-22; 41-44R; CAP 2;
SATA-Obit 4, 24

Ash, Shalom
See Asch, Sholem

Ashbery, John (Lawrence)
1927- ...... **CLC 2, 3, 4, 6, 9, 13, 15, 25,
41, 77**
See also CA 5-8R; CANR 9, 37; DLB 5;
DLBY 81; MTCW

Ashdown, Clifford
See Freeman, R(ichard) Austin

Ashe, Gordon
See Creasey, John

Ashton-Warner, Sylvia (Constance)
1908-1984 .... **CLC 19**
See also CA 69-72; 112; CANR 29; MTCW

Asimov, Isaac
1920-1992 ...... **CLC 1, 3, 9, 19, 26, 76**
See also BEST 90:2; CA 1-4R; 137;
CANR 2, 19, 36; CLR 12; DLB 8;
DLBY 92; JRDA; MAICYA; MTCW;
SATA-Obit 1, 26, 74

Astley, Thea (Beatrice May)
1925- .... **CLC 41**
See also CA 65-68; CANR 11, 43

Aston, James
See White, T(erence) H(anbury)

Asturias, Miguel Angel
1899-1974 .... **CLC 3, 8, 13; HLC**
See also CA 25-28; 49-52; CANR 32;
CAP 2; DLB 113; HW; MTCW

Atares, Carlos Saura
See Saura (Atares), Carlos

Atheling, William
See Pound, Ezra (Weston Loomis)

Atheling, William, Jr.
See Blish, James (Benjamin)

Atherton, Lucius
See Masters, Edgar Lee

Atkins, Jack
See Harris, Mark

Atticus
See Fleming, Ian (Lancaster)

Atwood, Margaret (Eleanor)
1939- ..... **CLC 2, 3, 4, 8, 13, 15, 25, 44,
84; DA**
See also AAYA 12; BEST 89:2; CA 49-52;
CANR 3, 24, 33; DLB 53; MTCW;
SAAS 8; SATA-Obit 50; TCLC 2; YABC

Aubigny, Pierre d'
See Mencken, H(enry) L(ouis)

Aubin, Penelope 1685-1731(?)........ **LC 9**
See also DLB 39

Auchincloss, Louis (Stanton)
1917- .... **CLC 4, 6, 9, 18, 45**
See also CA 1-4R; CANR 6, 29; DLB 2;
DLBY 80; MTCW

Auden, W(ystan) H(ugh)
1907-1973 ...... **CLC 1, 2, 3, 4, 6, 9, 11,
14, 43; DA**
See also CA 9-12R; 45-48; CANR 5;
CDBLB 1914-1945; DLB 10, 20; MTCW;
SAAS 1; YABC

Audiberti, Jacques 1900-1965 ...... **CLC 38**
See also CA 25-28R

Auel, Jean M(arie) 1936-.......... **CLC 31**
See also AAYA 7; BEST 90:4; CA 103;
CANR 21

Augier, Emile 1820-1889 .... **NCLC 31**

August, John
See De Voto, Bernard (Augustine)

Augustine, St. 354-430.......... **CMLC 6**

Aurelius
See Bourne, Randolph S(illiman)

Austen, Jane
1775-1817 ..... **NCLC 1, 13, 19, 33; DA**
See also CDBLB 1789-1832; DLB 116;
YABC

Auster, Paul 1947-............... **CLC 47**
See also CA 69-72; CANR 23

Austin, Frank
See Faust, Frederick (Schiller)

Autran Dourado, Waldomiro
See Dourado, (Waldomiro Freitas) Autran

Averroes 1126-1198 .... **CMLC 7**
See also DLB 115

Avison, Margaret 1918-.......... **CLC 2, 4**
See also CA 17-20R; DLB 53; MTCW

Axton, David
See Koontz, Dean R(ay)

Ayckbourn, Alan
1939- .... **CLC 5, 8, 18, 33, 74**
See also CA 21-24R; CANR 31; DLB 13;
MTCW

Aydy, Catherine
See Tennant, Emma (Christina)

Ayme, Marcel (Andre) 1902-1967... **CLC 11**
See also CA 89-92; CLR 25; DLB 72

Ayrton, Michael 1921-1975........ **CLC 7**
See also CA 5-8R; 61-64; CANR 9, 21

Azorin........................ **CLC 11**
See also Martinez Ruiz, Jose

Baastad, Babbis Friis
See Friis-Baastad, Babbis Ellinor

Bab
See Gilbert, W(illiam) S(chwenck)

Babbis, Eleanor
See Friis-Baastad, Babbis Ellinor

Babel, Isaak (Emmanuilovich)
1894-1941(?) ..... **TCLC 16; WLC 2, 13**
See also CA 104

Babur 1483-1530................. **LC 18**

Bacchelli, Riccardo 1891-1985 ..... **CLC 19**
See also CA 29-32R; 117

Bach, Richard (David) 1936-....... **CLC 14**
See also AITN 1; BEST 89:2; CA 9-12R;
CANR 18; MTCW; SATA-Obit 13

Bachman, Richard
See King, Stephen (Edwin)

Bachmann, Ingeborg 1926-1973..... **CLC 69**
See also CA 93-96; 45-48; DLB 85

Bacon, Francis 1561-1626 .... **LC 18**
See also CDBLB Before 1660

Badanes, Jerome 1937-............ **CLC 59**

Bagehot, Walter 1826-1877 ...... **NCLC 10**
See also DLB 55

Bagnold, Enid 1889-1981.......... **CLC 25**
See also CA 5-8R; 103; CANR 5, 40;
DLB 13; MAICYA; SATA-Obit 1, 25

Bagrjana, Elisaveta
See Belcheva, Elisaveta

Bagryana, Elisaveta
See Belcheva, Elisaveta

Bailey, Paul 1937- .... **CLC 45**
See also CA 21-24R; CANR 16; DLB 14

Baillie, Joanna 1762-1851 .... **NCLC 2**
See also DLB 93

Bainbridge, Beryl (Margaret)
1933- .... **CLC 4, 5, 8, 10, 14, 18, 22, 62**
See also CA 21-24R; CANR 24; DLB 14;
MTCW

Baker, Elliott 1922- .... **CLC 8**
See also CA 45-48; CANR 2

Baker, Nicholson 1957- .... **CLC 61**
See also CA 135

Baker, Russell (Wayne) 1925-...... **CLC 31**
See also BEST 89:4; CA 57-60; CANR 11,
41; MTCW

Bakhtin, M.
See Bakhtin, Mikhail Mikhailovich

Bakhtin, M. M.
See Bakhtin, Mikhail Mikhailovich

Bakhtin, Mikhail
See Bakhtin, Mikhail Mikhailovich

Bakhtin, Mikhail Mikhailovich
1895-1975 .... **CLC 83**
See also CA 128; 113

Bakshi, Ralph 1938(?)-............ **CLC 26**
See also CA 112; 138

Bakunin, Mikhail (Alexandrovich)
1814-1876 .... **NCLC 25**

Baldwin, James (Arthur)
1924-1987 ...... **CLC 1, 2, 3, 4, 5, 8, 13,
15, 17, 42, 50, 67; BLC; DA; DC 1**
See also AAYA 4; BW 1; CA 1-4R; 124;
CABS 1; CANR 3, 24;
CDALB 1941-1968; DLB 2, 7, 33;
DLBY 87; MTCW; SATA-Obit 9, 54;
TCLC 10; YABC

Ballard, J(ames) G(raham)
1930- .... **CLC 3, 6, 14, 36**
See also AAYA 3; CA 5-8R; CANR 15, 39;
DLB 14; MTCW; TCLC 1

Balzac, Honore de
1799-1850 .... **TCLC 5; DA**
See also DLB 119; NCLC 5, 35; YABC

Bambara, Toni Cade
1939- .... **CLC 19; BLC; DA**
See also AAYA 5; BW 2; CA 29-32R;
CANR 24; DLB 38; MTCW

Bamdad, A.
See Shamlu, Ahmad

Banat, D. R.
See Bradbury, Ray (Douglas)

Bancroft, Laura
See Baum, L(yman) Frank

Banim, John 1798-1842 .... **NCLC 13**
See also DLB 116

Banim, Michael 1796-1874 ..... **NCLC 13**

Banks, Iain
See Banks, Iain M(enzies)

Banks, Iain M(enzies) 1954- .... **CLC 34**
See also CA 123; 128

Banks, Lynne Reid .... **CLC 23**
See also Reid Banks, Lynne
See also AAYA 6

Banks, Russell 1940- .... **CLC 37, 72**
See also CA 65-68; CAAS 15; CANR 19;
DLB 130

Banville, John 1945-............ **CLC 46**
See also CA 117; 128; DLB 14

Banville, Theodore (Faullain) de
1832-1891 .... **NCLC 9**

Baraka, Amiri
1934- .... **CLC 1, 2, 3, 5, 10, 14, 33;
BLC; DA**
See also Jones, LeRoi
See also BW 2; CA 21-24R; CABS 3;
CANR 27, 38; CDALB 1941-1968;
DLB 5, 7, 16, 38; DLBD 8; MTCW;
SAAS 4

Barbera, Jack (Vincent) 1945-...... **CLC 44**
See also CA 110; CANR 45

Barbey d'Aurevilly, Jules Amedee
1808-1889 .... **NCLC 1**
See also DLB 119

Barclay, Bill
See Moorcock, Michael (John)

Barclay, William Ewert
See Moorcock, Michael (John)

Barfoot, Joan 1946- .... **CLC 18**
See also CA 105

Barker, Clive 1952- .... **CLC 52**
See also AAYA 10; BEST 90:3; CA 121;
129; MTCW

Barker, George Granville
1913-1991 .... **CLC 8, 48**
See also CA 9-12R; 135; CANR 7, 38;
DLB 20; MTCW

Barker, Harley Granville
See Granville-Barker, Harley
See also DLB 10

Barker, Howard 1946-........... **CLC 37**
See also CA 102; DLB 13

Barker, Pat 1943-............... **CLC 32**
See also CA 117; 122

Barlow, Joel 1754-1812 .... **NCLC 23**
See also DLB 37

Barnard, Mary (Ethel) 1909-...... **CLC 48**
See also CA 21-22; CAP 2

Barnes, Djuna
1892-1982 .... **CLC 3, 4, 8, 11, 29**
See also CA 9-12R; 107; CANR 16; DLB 4,
9, 45; MTCW; TCLC 3

Barnes, Julian 1946-............. **CLC 42**
See also CA 102; CANR 19; DLBY 93

Barnes, Peter 1931- .... **CLC 5, 56**
See also CA 65-68; CAAS 12; CANR 33,
34; DLB 13; MTCW

Baron, David
See Pinter, Harold

Baron Corvo
See Rolfe, Frederick (William Serafino
Austin Lewis Mary)

Barondess, Sue K(aufman)
1926-1977 .... **CLC 8**
See also Kaufman, Sue
See also CA 1-4R; 69-72; CANR 1

Baron de Teive
See Pessoa, Fernando (Antonio Nogueira)

Barreto, Afonso Henrique de Lima
See Lima Barreto, Afonso Henrique de

Barrett, (Roger) Syd 1946- .... **CLC 35**
See also Pink Floyd

Barrett, William (Christopher)
1913-1992 .... **CLC 27**
See also CA 13-16R; 139; CANR 11

Barrington, Michael
See Moorcock, Michael (John)

Barrol, Grady
See Bograd, Larry

Barry, Mike
See Malzberg, Barry N(athaniel)

Bart, Andre Schwarz
See Schwarz-Bart, Andre

Barth, John (Simmons)
1930- ...... **CLC 1, 2, 3, 5, 7, 9, 10, 14,
27, 51**
See also AITN 1, 2; CA 1-4R; CABS 1;
CANR 5, 23; DLB 2; MTCW; TCLC 10

Barthelme, Donald
1931-1989 ...... **CLC 1, 2, 3, 5, 6, 8, 13,
23, 46, 59**
See also CA 21-24R; 129; CANR 20;
DLB 2; DLBY 80, 89; MTCW;
SATA-Obit 7, 62; TCLC 2

Barthelme, Frederick 1943-........ **CLC 36**
See also CA 114; 122; DLBY 85

Barthes, Roland (Gerard)
1915-1980 .... **CLC 24, 83**
See also CA 130; 97-100; MTCW

Barzun, Jacques (Martin) 1907- .... **CLC 51**
See also CA 61-64; CANR 22

Bashevis, Isaac
See Singer, Isaac Bashevis

Bashkirtseff, Marie 1859-1884 ... **NCLC 27**

Basho
See Matsuo Basho

Bass, Kingsley B., Jr.
See Bullins, Ed

Bass, Rick 1958-................. **CLC 79**
See also CA 126

Bassani, Giorgio 1916-............ **CLC 9**
See also CA 65-68; CANR 33; DLB 128;
MTCW

Bastos, Augusto (Antonio) Roa
See Roa Bastos, Augusto (Antonio)

Bataille, Georges 1897-1962 .... **CLC 29**
See also CA 101; 89-92

Blunden, Edmund (Charles)
1896-1974 . . . . CLC **2, 56**
See also CA 17-18; 45-48; CAP 2; DLB 20,
100; MTCW

Bly, Robert (Elwood)
1926- . . . . CLC **1, 2, 5, 10, 15, 38**
See also CA 5-8R; CANR 41; DLB 5;
MTCW

Bobette
See Simenon, Georges (Jacques Christian)

Boccaccio, Giovanni 1313-1375 . . . . TCLC **10**
See also CMLC 13

Bochco, Steven 1943- . . . . CLC **35**
See also AAYA 11; CA 124; 138

Bodker, Cecil 1927- . . . . CLC **21**
See also CA 73-76; CANR 13, 44; CLR 23;
MAICYA; SATA-Obit 14

Boell, Heinrich (Theodor) 1917-1985
See Boll, Heinrich (Theodor)
See also CA 21-24R; 116; CANR 24; DA;
DLB 69; DLBY 85; MTCW

Boerne, Alfred
See Doeblin, Alfred

Bogan, Louise 1897-1970 . . . . . CLC **4, 39, 46**
See also CA 73-76; 25-28R; CANR 33;
DLB 45; MTCW

Bogarde, Dirk . . . . CLC **19**
See also Van Den Bogarde, Derek Jules
Gaspard Ulric Niven
See also DLB 14

Bogosian, Eric 1953- . . . . CLC **45**
See also CA 138

Bograd, Larry 1953- . . . . CLC **35**
See also CA 93-96; SATA-Obit 33

Boiardo, Matteo Maria 1441-1494 . . . . LC **6**

Boileau-Despreaux, Nicolas
1636-1711 . . . . LC **3**

Boland, Eavan (Aisling) 1944- . . . CLC **40, 67**
See also CA 143; DLB 40

Boll, Heinrich (Theodor)
1917-1985 . . . . CLC **2, 3, 6, 9, 11, 15, 27,
39, 72**
See also Boell, Heinrich (Theodor)
See also DLB 69; DLBY 85; YABC

Bolt, Lee
See Faust, Frederick (Schiller)

Bolt, Robert (Oxton) 1924- . . . . CLC **14**
See also CA 17-20R; CANR 35; DLB 13;
MTCW

Bomkauf
See Kaufman, Bob (Garnell)

Bonaventura . . . . NCLC **35**
See also DLB 90

Bond, Edward 1934- . . . . CLC **4, 6, 13, 23**
See also CA 25-28R; CANR 38; DLB 13;
MTCW

Bonham, Frank 1914-1989 . . . . CLC **12**
See also AAYA 1; CA 9-12R; CANR 4, 36,
JRDA; MAICYA; SATA 3;
SATA-Obit 1, 49, 62

Bonnefoy, Yves 1923- . . . . CLC **9, 15, 58**
See also CA 85-88; CANR 33; MTCW

Bonnin, Gertrude 1876-1938 . . . . PC **X**

Bontemps, Arna(ud Wendell)
1902-1973 . . . . CLC **1, 18; BLC**
See also BW 1; CA 1-4R; 41-44R; CANR 4,
35; CLR 6; DLB 48, 51; JRDA;
MAICYA; MTCW; SATA-Obit 2, 24, 44

Booth, Martin 1944- . . . . CLC **13**
See also CA 93-96; CAAS 2

Booth, Philip 1925- . . . . CLC **23**
See also CA 5-8R; CANR 5; DLBY 82

Booth, Wayne C(layson) 1921- . . . . . CLC **24**
See also CA 1-4R; CAAS 5; CANR 3, 43;
DLB 67

Borel, Petrus 1809-1859 . . . . NCLC **41**

Borges, Jorge Luis
1899-1986 . . . CLC **1, 2, 3, 4, 6, 8, 9, 10,
13, 19, 44, 48, 83; DA; HLC**
See also CA 21-24R; CANR 19, 33;
DLB 113; DLBY 86; HW; MTCW;
TCLC 4; YABC

Borrow, George (Henry)
1803-1881 . . . . NCLC **9**
See also DLB 21, 55

Boswell, James 1740-1795 . . . . LC **4; DA**
See also CDBLB 1660-1789; DLB 104, 142;
YABC

Bottoms, David 1949- . . . . CLC **53**
See also CA 105; CANR 22; DLB 120;
DLBY 83

Boucicault, Dion 1820-1890 . . . . . . NCLC **41**

Boucolon, Maryse 1937-
See Conde, Maryse
See also CA 110; CANR 30

Bourjaily, Vance (Nye) 1922- . . . . CLC **8, 62**
See also CA 1-4R; CAAS 1; CANR 2;
DLB 2, 143

Bova, Ben(jamin William) 1932- . . . . CLC **45**
See also CA 5-8R; CAAS 18; CANR 11;
CLR 3; DLBY 81; MAICYA; MTCW;
SATA-Obit 6, 68

Bowen, Elizabeth (Dorothea Cole)
1899-1973 . . . . . . CLC **1, 3, 6, 11, 15, 22**
See also CA 17-18; 41-44R; CANR 35;
CAP 2; CDBLB 1945-1960; DLB 15;
MTCW; TCLC 3

Bowering, George 1935- . . . . CLC **15, 47**
See also CA 21-24R; CAAS 16; CANR 10;
DLB 53

Bowering, Marilyn R(uthe) 1949- . . . CLC **32**
See also CA 101

Bowers, Edgar 1924- . . . . CLC **9**
See also CA 5-8R; CANR 24; DLB 5

Bowie, David . . . . CLC **17**
See also Jones, David Robert

Bowles, Jane (Sydney)
1917-1973 . . . . CLC **3, 68**
See also CA 19-20; 41-44R; CAP 2

Bowles, Paul (Frederick)
1910- . . . . CLC **1, 2, 19, 53**
See also CA 1-4R; CAAS 1; CANR 1, 19;
DLB 5, 6; MTCW; TCLC 3

Box, Edgar
See Vidal, Gore

Boyd, Nancy
See Millay, Edna St. Vincent

Boyd, William 1952- . . . . CLC **28, 53, 70**
See also CA 114; 120

Boyle, Kay 1902-1992 . . . . . CLC **1, 5, 19, 58**
See also CA 13-16R; 140; CAAS 1;
CANR 29; DLB 4, 9, 48, 86; DLBY 93;
MTCW; TCLC 5

Boyle, Mark
See Kienzle, William X(avier)

Boyle, Patrick 1905-1982 . . . . CLC **19**
See also CA 127

Boyle, T. C.
See Boyle, T(homas) Coraghessan

Boyle, T(homas) Coraghessan
1948- . . . . CLC **36, 55**
See also BEST 90:4; CA 120; CANR 44;
DLBY 86; TCLC 16

Boz
See Dickens, Charles (John Huffam)

Brackenridge, Hugh Henry
1748-1816 . . . . NCLC **7**
See also DLB 11, 37

Bradbury, Edward P.
See Moorcock, Michael (John)

Bradbury, Malcolm (Stanley)
1932- . . . . CLC **32, 61**
See also CA 1-4R; CANR 1, 33; DLB 14;
MTCW

Bradbury, Ray (Douglas)
1920- . . . . CLC **1, 3, 10, 15, 42; DA**
See also AITN 1, 2; CA 1-4R; CANR 2, 30;
CDALB 1968-1988; DLB 2, 8; MTCW;
SATA-Obit 11, 64; YABC

Bradley, David (Henry, Jr.)
1950- . . . . CLC **23; BLC**
See also BW 1; CA 104; CANR 26; DLB 33

Bradley, John Ed(mund, Jr.)
1958- . . . . CLC **55**
See also CA 139

Bradley, Marion Zimmer 1930- . . . . . CLC **30**
See also AAYA 9; CA 57-60; CAAS 10;
CANR 7, 31; DLB 8; MTCW

Bradstreet, Anne 1612(?)-1672 . . . LC **4; DA**
See also CDALB 1640-1865; DLB 24;
SAAS 10

Bragg, Melvyn 1939- . . . . CLC **10**
See also BEST 89:3; CA 57-60; CANR 10;
DLB 14

Braine, John (Gerard)
1922-1986 . . . . CLC **1, 3, 41**
See also CA 1-4R; 120; CANR 1, 33;
CDBLB 1945-1960; DLB 15; DLBY 86;
MTCW

Brammer, William 1930(?)-1978 . . . . CLC **31**
See also CA 77-80

Brancato, Robin F(idler) 1936- . . . . . CLC **35**
See also AAYA 9; CA 69-72; CANR 11,
45; CLR 32; JRDA; SATA 9;
SATA-Obit 23

Brand, Max
See Faust, Frederick (Schiller)

Brand, Millen 1906-1980 . . . . CLC **7**
See also CA 21-24R; 97-100

Branden, Barbara . . . . CLC **44**

Brandys, Kazimierz 1916- . . . . CLC **62**

Catton, (Charles) Bruce
1899-1978 .... **CLC 35**
See also AITN 1; CA 5-8R; 81-84;
CANR 7; DLB 17; SATA-Obit 2, 24

Cauldwell, Frank
See King, Francis (Henry)

Caunitz, William J. 1933- .... **CLC 34**
See also BEST 89:3; CA 125; 130

Causley, Charles (Stanley) 1917-..... **CLC 7**
See also CA 9-12R; CANR 5, 35; CLR 30;
DLB 27; MTCW; SATA-Obit 3, 66

Caute, David 1936-............... **CLC 29**
See also CA 1-4R; CAAS 4; CANR 1, 33;
DLB 14

Cavallo, Evelyn
See Spark, Muriel (Sarah)

Cavanna, Betty .... **CLC 12**
See also Harrison, Elizabeth Cavanna
See also JRDA; MAICYA; SATA 4;
SATA-Obit 1, 30

Caxton, William 1421(?)-1491(?)..... **LC 17**

Cayrol, Jean 1911-................ **CLC 11**
See also CA 89-92; DLB 83

Cela, Camilo Jose
1916- .... **CLC 4, 13, 59; HLC**
See also BEST 90:2; CA 21-24R; CAAS 10;
CANR 21, 32; DLBY 89; HW; MTCW

Celan, Paul .... **CLC 53, 82**
See also Antschel, Paul
See also DLB 69; SAAS 10

Celine, Louis-Ferdinand
.... **CLC 1, 3, 4, 7, 9, 15, 47**
See also Destouches, Louis-Ferdinand
See also DLB 72

Cellini, Benvenuto 1500-1571 .... **LC 7**

Cendrars, Blaise
See Sauser-Hall, Frederic

Cernuda (y Bidon), Luis
1902-1963 .... **CLC 54**
See also CA 131; 89-92; DLB 134; HW

Cervantes (Saavedra), Miguel de
1547-1616 .... **TCLC 12; DA**
See also LC 6, 23; YABC

Cesaire, Aime (Fernand)
1913-.............. **CLC 19, 32; BLC**
See also BW 2; CA 65-68; CANR 24, 43;
MTCW

Chabon, Michael 1965(?)- .... **CLC 55**
See also CA 139

Chabrol, Claude 1930- .... **CLC 16**
See also CA 110

Challans, Mary 1905-1983
See Renault, Mary
See also CA 81-84; 111; SATA-Obit 23, 36

Challis, George
See Faust, Frederick (Schiller)

Chambers, Aidan 1934- .... **CLC 35**
See also CA 25-28R; CANR 12, 31; JRDA;
MAICYA; SATA 12; SATA-Obit 1, 69

Chambers, James 1948-
See Cliff, Jimmy
See also CA 124

Chambers, Jessie
See Lawrence, D(avid) H(erbert Richards)

Chang, Jung 1952- .... **CLC 71**
See also CA 142

Channing, William Ellery
1780-1842 .... **NCLC 17**
See also DLB 1, 59

Chaplin, Charles Spencer
1889-1977 .... **CLC 16**
See also Chaplin, Charlie
See also CA 81-84; 73-76

Chaplin, Charlie
See Chaplin, Charles Spencer
See also DLB 44

Chapman, George 1559(?)-1634...... **LC 22**
See also DLB 62, 121

Chapman, Graham 1941-1989 ...... **CLC 21**
See also Monty Python
See also CA 116; 129; CANR 35

Chapman, Walker
See Silverberg, Robert

Chappell, Fred (Davis) 1936-.... **CLC 40, 78**
See also CA 5-8R; CAAS 4; CANR 8, 33;
DLB 6, 105

Char, Rene(-Emile)
1907-1988 .... **CLC 9, 11, 14, 55**
See also CA 13-16R; 124; CANR 32;
MTCW

Charby, Jay
See Ellison, Harlan

Chardin, Pierre Teilhard de
See Teilhard de Chardin, (Marie Joseph)
Pierre

Charles I 1600-1649 .... **LC 13**

Charyn, Jerome 1937- .... **CLC 5, 8, 18**
See also CA 5-8R; CAAS 1; CANR 7;
DLBY 83; MTCW

Chase, Mary (Coyle) 1907-1981 ...... **DC 1**
See also CA 77-80; 105; SATA-Obit 17, 29

Chase, Mary Ellen 1887-1973....... **CLC 2**
See also CA 13-16; 41-44R; CAP 1;
SATA-Obit 10

Chase, Nicholas
See Hyde, Anthony

Chateaubriand, Francois Rene de
1768-1848 .... **NCLC 3**
See also DLB 119

Chatterje, Sarat Chandra 1876-1936(?)
See Chatterji, Saratchandra
See also CA 109

Chatterji, Bankim Chandra
1838-1894 .... **NCLC 19**

Chatterton, Thomas 1752-1770 .... **LC 3**
See also DLB 109

Chatwin, (Charles) Bruce
1940-1989 .... **CLC 28, 57, 59**
See also AAYA 4; BEST 90:1; CA 85-88;
127

Chaucer, Daniel
See Ford, Ford Madox

Chaucer, Geoffrey
1340(?)-1400 .... **LC 17; DA**
See also CDBLB Before 1660

Chaviaras, Strates 1935-
See Haviaras, Stratis
See also CA 105

Chayefsky, Paddy .... **CLC 23**
See also Chayefsky, Sidney
See also DLB 7, 44; DLBY 81

Chayefsky, Sidney 1923-1981
See Chayefsky, Paddy
See also CA 9-12R; 104; CANR 18

Chedid, Andree 1920-............. **CLC 47**

Cheever, John
1912-1982 ...... **CLC 3, 7, 8, 11, 15, 25,
64; DA**
See also CA 5-8R; 106; CABS 1; CANR 5,
27; CDALB 1941-1968; DLB 2, 102;
DLBY 80, 82; MTCW; TCLC 1; YABC

Cheever, Susan 1943-.......... **CLC 18, 48**
See also CA 103; CANR 27; DLBY 82

Chekhonte, Antosha
See Chekhov, Anton (Pavlovich)

Chekhov, Anton (Pavlovich)
1860-1904 .... **TCLC 2; DA; WLC 3, 10,
31, 55**
See also CA 104; 124; YABC

Chernyshevsky, Nikolay Gavrilovich
1828-1889 .... **NCLC 1**

Cherry, Carolyn Janice 1942-
See Cherryh, C. J.
See also CA 65-68; CANR 10

Cherryh, C. J..................... **CLC 35**
See also Cherry, Carolyn Janice
See also DLBY 80

Chesnutt, Charles W(addell)
1858-1932 ... **TCLC 7; BLC; WLC 5, 39**
See also BW 1; CA 106; 125; DLB 12, 50,
78; MTCW

Chester, Alfred 1929(?)-1971....... **CLC 49**
See also CA 33-36R; DLB 130

Chesterton, G(ilbert) K(eith)
1874-1936 .... **TCLC 1; WLC 1, 6**
See also CA 104; 132; CDBLB 1914-1945;
DLB 10, 19, 34, 70, 98; MTCW;
SATA-Obit 27

Chiang Pin-chin 1904-1986
See Ding Ling
See also CA 118

Ch'ien Chung-shu 1910-............ **CLC 22**
See also CA 130; MTCW

Child, L. Maria
See Child, Lydia Maria

Child, Lydia Maria 1802-1880 .... **NCLC 6**
See also DLB 1, 74; SATA-Obit 67

Child, Mrs.
See Child, Lydia Maria

Child, Philip 1898-1978 .... **CLC 19, 68**
See also CA 13-14; CAP 1; SATA-Obit 47

Childress, Alice
1920- .... **CLC 12, 15; BLC; DC 4**
See also AAYA 8; BW 2; CA 45-48;
CANR 3, 27; CLR 14; DLB 7, 38; JRDA;
MAICYA; MTCW; SATA-Obit 7, 48

Chislett, (Margaret) Anne 1943-.... **CLC 34**

Chitty, Thomas Willes 1926-....... **CLC 11**
See also Hinde, Thomas
See also CA 5-8R

Chomette, Rene Lucien 1898-1981 .. **CLC 20**
See also Clair, Rene
See also CA 103

Chona, Maria 1845(?)-1936 . . . . PC X

Chopin, Kate . . . . . . **TCLC 8; DA; WLC 5, 14**
See also Chopin, Katherine
See also CDALB 1865-1917; DLB 12, 78

Chopin, Katherine 1851-1904
See Chopin, Kate
See also CA 104; 122

Chretien de Troyes
c. 12th cent. - . . . . **CMLC 10**

Christie
See Ichikawa, Kon

Christie, Agatha (Mary Clarissa)
1890-1976 . . . . . . **CLC 1, 6, 8, 12, 39, 48**
See also AAYA 9; AITN 1, 2; CA 17-20R;
61-64; CANR 10, 37; CDBLB 1914-1945;
DLB 13, 77; MTCW; SATA-Obit 36

Christie, (Ann) Philippa
See Pearce, Philippa
See also CA 5-8R; CANR 4

Christine de Pizan 1365(?)-1431(?) . . . . **LC 9**

Chubb, Elmer
See Masters, Edgar Lee

Chulkov, Mikhail Dmitrievich
1743-1792 . . . . **LC 2**

Churchill, Caryl 1938- . . . . **CLC 31, 55**
See also CA 102; CANR 22; DLB 13;
MTCW

Churchill, Charles 1731-1764 . . . . **LC 3**
See also DLB 109

Chute, Carolyn 1947- . . . . **CLC 39**
See also CA 123

Ciardi, John (Anthony)
1916-1986 . . . . **CLC 10, 40, 44**
See also CA 5-8R; 118; CAAS 2; CANR 5,
33; CLR 19; DLB 5; DLBY 86;
MAICYA; MTCW; SATA-Obit 1, 46, 65

Cicero, Marcus Tullius
106B.C.-43B.C. . . . . **CMLC 3**

Cimino, Michael 1943- . . . . **CLC 16**
See also CA 105

Cioran, E(mil) M. 1911- . . . . **CLC 64**
See also CA 25-28R

Cisneros, Sandra 1954- . . . . . . **CLC 69; HLC**
See also AAYA 9; CA 131; DLB 122; HW

Clair, Rene . . . . **CLC 20**
See also Chomette, Rene Lucien

Clampitt, Amy 1920- . . . . **CLC 32**
See also CA 110; CANR 29; DLB 105

Clancy, Thomas L., Jr. 1947-
See Clancy, Tom
See also CA 125; 131; MTCW

Clancy, Tom . . . . **CLC 45**
See also Clancy, Thomas L., Jr.
See also AAYA 9; BEST 89:1, 90:1

Clare, John 1793-1864 . . . . **NCLC 9**
See also DLB 55, 96

Clarin
See Alas (y Urena), Leopoldo (Enrique
Garcia)

Clark, Al C.
See Goines, Donald

Clark, (Robert) Brian 1932- . . . . **CLC 29**
See also CA 41-44R

Clark, Curt
See Westlake, Donald E(dwin)

Clark, Eleanor 1913- . . . . **CLC 5, 19**
See also CA 9-12R; CANR 41; DLB 6

Clark, J. P.
See Clark, John Pepper
See also DLB 117

Clark, John Pepper 1935- . . . . **CLC 38; BLC**
See also Clark, J. P.
See also BW 1; CA 65-68; CANR 16

Clark, M. R.
See Clark, Mavis Thorpe

Clark, Mavis Thorpe 1909- . . . . **CLC 12**
See also CA 57-60; CANR 8, 37; CLR 30;
MAICYA; SATA 5; SATA-Obit 8, 74

Clark, Walter Van Tilburg
1909-1971 . . . . **CLC 28**
See also CA 9-12R; 33-36R; DLB 9;
SATA-Obit 8

Clarke, Arthur C(harles)
1917- . . . . **CLC 1, 4, 13, 18, 35**
See also AAYA 4; CA 1-4R; CANR 2, 28;
JRDA; MAICYA; MTCW;
SATA-Obit 13, 70; TCLC 3

Clarke, Austin 1896-1974 . . . . **CLC 6, 9**
See also CA 29-32; 49-52; CAP 2; DLB 10,
20

Clarke, Austin C(hesterfield)
1934- . . . . **CLC 8, 53; BLC**
See also BW 1; CA 25-28R; CAAS 16;
CANR 14, 32; DLB 53, 125

Clarke, Gillian 1937- . . . . **CLC 61**
See also CA 106; DLB 40

Clarke, Marcus (Andrew Hislop)
1846-1881 . . . . **NCLC 19**

Clarke, Shirley 1925- . . . . **CLC 16**

Clash, The . . . . **CLC 30**
See also Headon, (Nicky) Topper; Jones,
Mick; Simonon, Paul; Strummer, Joe

Clavell, James (duMaresq)
1925- . . . . **CLC 6, 25**
See also CA 25-28R; CANR 26; MTCW

Cleaver, (Leroy) Eldridge
1935- . . . . **CLC 30; BLC**
See also BW 1; CA 21-24R; CANR 16

Cleese, John (Marwood) 1939- . . . . . **CLC 21**
See also Monty Python
See also CA 112; 116; CANR 35; MTCW

Cleishbotham, Jebediah
See Scott, Walter

Cleland, John 1710-1789 . . . . **LC 2**
See also DLB 39

Clemens, Samuel Langhorne 1835-1910
See Twain, Mark
See also CA 104; 135; CDALB 1865-1917;
DA; DLB 11, 12, 23, 64, 74; JRDA;
MAICYA; 2

Cleophil
See Congreve, William

Clerihew, E.
See Bentley, E(dmund) C(lerihew)

Clerk, N. W.
See Lewis, C(live) S(taples)

Cliff, Jimmy . . . . **CLC 21**
See also Chambers, James

Clifton, (Thelma) Lucille
1936- . . . . **CLC 19, 66; BLC**
See also BW 2; CA 49-52; CANR 2, 24, 42;
CLR 5; DLB 5, 41; MAICYA; MTCW;
SATA-Obit 20, 69

Clinton, Dirk
See Silverberg, Robert

Clough, Arthur Hugh 1819-1861 . . **NCLC 27**
See also DLB 32

Clutha, Janet Paterson Frame 1924-
See Frame, Janet
See also CA 1-4R; CANR 2, 36; MTCW

Clyne, Terence
See Blatty, William Peter

Cobalt, Martin
See Mayne, William (James Carter)

Coburn, D(onald) L(ee) 1938- . . . . . . **CLC 10**
See also CA 89-92

Cocteau, Jean (Maurice Eugene Clement)
1889-1963 . . . . **CLC 1, 8, 15, 16, 43; DA**
See also CA 25-28; CANR 40; CAP 2;
DLB 65; MTCW; YABC

Codrescu, Andrei 1946- . . . . **CLC 46**
See also CA 33-36R; CAAS 19; CANR 13,
34

Coe, Max
See Bourne, Randolph S(illiman)

Coe, Tucker
See Westlake, Donald E(dwin)

Coetzee, J(ohn) M(ichael)
1940- . . . . **CLC 23, 33, 66**
See also CA 77-80; CANR 41; MTCW

Coffey, Brian
See Koontz, Dean R(ay)

Cohen, Arthur A(llen)
1928-1986 . . . . **CLC 7, 31**
See also CA 1-4R; 120; CANR 1, 17, 42;
DLB 28

Cohen, Leonard (Norman)
1934- . . . . **CLC 3, 38**
See also CA 21-24R; CANR 14; DLB 53;
MTCW

Cohen, Matt 1942- . . . . **CLC 19**
See also CA 61-64; CAAS 18; CANR 40;
DLB 53

Cohen-Solal, Annie 19(?)- . . . . **CLC 50**

Colegate, Isabel 1931- . . . . **CLC 36**
See also CA 17-20R; CANR 8, 22; DLB 14;
MTCW

Coleman, Emmett
See Reed, Ishmael

Coleridge, Samuel Taylor
1772-1834 . . . . **NCLC 9; DA**
See also CDBLB 1789-1832; DLB 93, 107;
YABC

Coleridge, Sara 1802-1852 . . . . **NCLC 31**

Coles, Don 1928- . . . . **CLC 46**
See also CA 115; CANR 38

Colette, (Sidonie-Gabrielle)
1873-1954 . . . . . **TCLC 10; WLC 1, 5, 16**
See also CA 104; 131; DLB 65; MTCW

Collett, (Jacobine) Camilla (Wergeland)
1813-1895 . . . . **NCLC 22**

Collier, Christopher 1930- . . . . **CLC 30**
See also CA 33-36R; CANR 13, 33; JRDA;
MAICYA; SATA-Obit 16, 70

Collier, James L(incoln) 1928- . . . . . **CLC 30**
See also CA 9-12R; CANR 4, 33; JRDA;
MAICYA; SATA-Obit 8, 70

Collier, Jeremy 1650-1726 . . . . **LC 6**

Collins, Hunt
See Hunter, Evan

Collins, Linda 1931- . . . . **CLC 44**
See also CA 125

Collins, (William) Wilkie
1824-1889 . . . . **NCLC 1, 18**
See also CDBLB 1832-1890; DLB 18, 70

Collins, William 1721-1759 . . . . **LC 4**
See also DLB 109

Colman, George
See Glassco, John

Colt, Winchester Remington
See Hubbard, L(afayette) Ron(ald)

Colter, Cyrus 1910- . . . . **CLC 58**
See also BW 1; CA 65-68; CANR 10;
DLB 33

Colton, James
See Hansen, Joseph

Colum, Padraic 1881-1972 . . . . **CLC 28**
See also CA 73-76; 33-36R; CANR 35;
MAICYA; MTCW; SATA-Obit 15

Colvin, James
See Moorcock, Michael (John)

Colwin, Laurie (E.)
1944-1992 . . . . **CLC 5, 13, 23, 84**
See also CA 89-92; 139; CANR 20;
DLBY 80; MTCW

Comfort, Alex(ander) 1920- . . . . **CLC 7**
See also CA 1-4R; CANR 1, 45

Comfort, Montgomery
See Campbell, (John) Ramsey

Compton-Burnett, I(vy)
1884(?)-1969 . . . . . . **CLC 1, 3, 10, 15, 34**
See also CA 1-4R; 25-28R; CANR 4;
DLB 36; MTCW

Conan Doyle, Arthur
See Doyle, Arthur Conan

Conde, Maryse 1937- . . . . **CLC 52**
See also Boucolon, Maryse
See also BW 2

Condon, Richard (Thomas)
1915- . . . . **CLC 4, 6, 8, 10, 45**
See also BEST 90:3; CA 1-4R; CAAS 1;
CANR 2, 23; MTCW

Congreve, William
1670-1729 . . . . **LC 5, 21; DA; DC 2**
See also CDBLB 1660-1789; DLB 39, 84;
YABC

Connell, Evan S(helby), Jr.
1924- . . . . **CLC 4, 6, 45**
See also AAYA 7; CA 1-4R; CAAS 2;
CANR 2, 39; DLB 2; DLBY 81; MTCW

Connelly, Marc(us Cook)
1890-1980 . . . . **CLC 7**
See also CA 85-88; 102; CANR 30; DLB 7;
DLBY 80; SATA-Obit 25

Conrad, Joseph
1857-1924 . . . . . **TCLC 9; DA; WLC 1, 6,**
13, 25, 43
See also CA 104; 131; CDBLB 1890-1914;
DLB 10, 34, 98; MTCW; SATA-Obit 27;
YABC

Conrad, Robert Arnold
See Hart, Moss

Conroy, Pat 1945- . . . . **CLC 30, 74**
See also AAYA 8; AITN 1; CA 85-88;
CANR 24; DLB 6; MTCW

Constant (de Rebecque), (Henri) Benjamin
1767-1830 . . . . **NCLC 6**
See also DLB 119

Conybeare, Charles Augustus
See Eliot, T(homas) S(tearns)

Cook, Michael 1933- . . . . **CLC 58**
See also CA 93-96; DLB 53

Cook, Robin 1940- . . . . **CLC 14**
See also BEST 90:2; CA 108; 111;
CANR 41

Cook, Roy
See Silverberg, Robert

Cooke, Elizabeth 1948- . . . . **CLC 55**
See also CA 129

Cooke, John Esten 1830-1886 . . . . . **NCLC 5**
See also DLB 3

Cooke, John Estes
See Baum, L(yman) Frank

Cooke, M. E.
See Creasey, John

Cooke, Margaret
See Creasey, John

Cooney, Ray . . . . **CLC 62**

Cooper, Henry St. John
See Creasey, John

Cooper, J. California . . . . **CLC 56**
See also AAYA 12; BW 1; CA 125

Cooper, James Fenimore
1789-1851 . . . . **NCLC 1, 27**
See also CDALB 1640-1865; DLB 3;
SATA-Obit 19

Coover, Robert (Lowell)
1932- . . . . **CLC 3, 7, 15, 32, 46**
See also CA 45-48; CANR 3, 37; DLB 2;
DLBY 81; MTCW; TCLC 15

Copeland, Stewart (Armstrong)
1952- . . . . **CLC 26**
See also Police, The

Coppola, Francis Ford 1939- . . . . **CLC 16**
See also CA 77-80; CANR 40; DLB 44

Copway, George 1818-1869 . . . . **PC X**

Corbiere, Tristan 1845-1875 . . . . . **NCLC 43**

Corcoran, Barbara 1911- . . . . **CLC 17**
See also CA 21-24R; CAAS 2; CANR 11,
28; DLB 52; JRDA; SATA-Obit 3, 77

Cordelier, Maurice
See Giraudoux, (Hippolyte) Jean

Corman, Cid . . . . **CLC 9**
See also Corman, Sidney
See also CAAS 2; DLB 5

Corman, Sidney 1924-
See Corman, Cid
See also CA 85-88; CANR 44

Cormier, Robert (Edmund)
1925- . . . . **CLC 12, 30; DA**
See also AAYA 3; CA 1-4R; CANR 5, 23;
CDALB 1968-1988; CLR 12; DLB 52;
JRDA; MAICYA; MTCW;
SATA-Obit 10, 45

Corn, Alfred (DeWitt III) 1943- . . . . **CLC 33**
See also CA 104; CANR 44; DLB 120;
DLBY 80

Cornwell, David (John Moore)
1931- . . . . **CLC 9, 15**
See also le Carre, John
See also CA 5-8R; CANR 13, 33; MTCW

Corrigan, Kevin . . . . **CLC 55**

Corso, (Nunzio) Gregory 1930- . . . **CLC 1, 11**
See also CA 5-8R; CANR 41; DLB 5, 16;
MTCW

Cortazar, Julio
1914-1984 . . . . . . **CLC 2, 3, 5, 10, 13, 15,**
33, 34; HLC
See also CA 21-24R; CANR 12, 32;
DLB 113; HW; MTCW; TCLC 7

Corwin, Cecil
See Kornbluth, C(yril) M.

Cosic, Dobrica 1921- . . . . **CLC 14**
See also CA 122; 138

Costain, Thomas B(ertram)
1885-1965 . . . . **CLC 30**
See also CA 5-8R; 25-28R; DLB 9

Costantini, Humberto
1924(?)-1987 . . . . **CLC 49**
See also CA 131; 122; HW

Costello, Elvis 1955- . . . . **CLC 21**

Couch, Arthur Thomas Quiller
See Quiller-Couch, Arthur Thomas

Coulton, James
See Hansen, Joseph

Court, Wesli
See Turco, Lewis (Putnam)

Courtenay, Bryce 1933- . . . . **CLC 59**
See also CA 138

Courtney, Robert
See Ellison, Harlan

Cousteau, Jacques-Yves 1910- . . . . . . **CLC 30**
See also CA 65-68; CANR 15; MTCW;
SATA-Obit 38

Coward, Noel (Peirce)
1899-1973 . . . . **CLC 1, 9, 29, 51**
See also AITN 1; CA 17-18; 41-44R;
CANR 35; CAP 2; CDBLB 1914-1945;
DLB 10; MTCW

Cowley, Malcolm 1898-1989 . . . . **CLC 39**
See also CA 5-8R; 128; CANR 3; DLB 4,
48; DLBY 81, 89; MTCW

Cowper, William 1731-1800 . . . . **NCLC 8**
See also DLB 104, 109

Cox, William Trevor 1928- . . . **CLC 9, 14, 71**
See also Trevor, William
See also CA 9-12R; CANR 4, 37; DLB 14;
MTCW

Cozzens, James Gould
1903-1978 . . . . **CLC 1, 4, 11**
See also CA 9-12R; 81-84; CANR 19;
CDALB 1941-1968; DLB 9; DLBD 2;
DLBY 84; MTCW

Davie, Donald (Alfred)
1922- .... CLC **5, 8, 10, 31**
See also CA 1-4R; CAAS 3; CANR 1, 44;
DLB 27; MTCW

Davies, Ray(mond Douglas) 1944- .. CLC **21**
See also CA 116

Davies, Rhys 1903-1978.......... CLC **23**
See also CA 9-12R; 81-84; CANR 4;
DLB 139

Davies, (William) Robertson
1913- ..... CLC **2, 7, 13, 25, 42, 75; DA**
See also BEST 89:2; CA 33-36R; CANR 17,
42; DLB 68; MTCW; YABC

Davies, Walter C.
See Kornbluth, C(yril) M.

Davis, Angela (Yvonne) 1944- ...... CLC **77**
See also BW 2; CA 57-60; CANR 10

Davis, B. Lynch
See Bioy Casares, Adolfo; Borges, Jorge
Luis

Davis, Gordon
See Hunt, E(verette) Howard, Jr.

Davis, Harold Lenoir 1896-1960.... CLC **49**
See also CA 89-92; DLB 9

Davison, Frank Dalby 1893-1970 ... CLC **15**
See also CA 116

Davison, Lawrence H.
See Lawrence, D(avid) H(erbert Richards)

Davison, Peter (Hubert) 1928- ..... CLC **28**
See also CA 9-12R; CAAS 4; CANR 3, 43;
DLB 5

Davys, Mary 1674-1732............. LC **1**
See also DLB 39

Dawson, Fielding 1930- .... CLC **6**
See also CA 85-88; DLB 130

Dawson, Peter
See Faust, Frederick (Schiller)

Day, Thomas 1748-1789............. LC **1**
See also DLB 39; 1

Day Lewis, C(ecil)
1904-1972 .... CLC **1, 6, 10**
See also Blake, Nicholas
See also CA 13-16; 33-36R; CANR 34;
CAP 1; DLB 15, 20; MTCW

de Andrade, Carlos Drummond
See Drummond de Andrade, Carlos

Deane, Norman
See Creasey, John

**de Beauvoir, Simone (Lucie Ernestine Marie
Bertrand)**
See Beauvoir, Simone (Lucie Ernestine
Marie Bertrand) de

de Brissac, Malcolm
See Dickinson, Peter (Malcolm)

de Chardin, Pierre Teilhard
See Teilhard de Chardin, (Marie Joseph)
Pierre

Dee, John 1527-1608 .... LC **20**

Deer, Sandra 1940-................ CLC **45**

De Ferrari, Gabriella .... CLC **65**

Defoe, Daniel 1660(?)-1731 ...... LC **1; DA**
See also CDBLB 1660-1789; DLB 39, 95,
101; JRDA; MAICYA; SATA-Obit 22;
YABC

de Gourmont, Remy
See Gourmont, Remy de

de Hartog, Jan 1914-............. CLC **19**
See also CA 1-4R; CANR 1

de Hostos, E. M.
See Hostos (y Bonilla), Eugenio Maria de

de Hostos, Eugenio M.
See Hostos (y Bonilla), Eugenio Maria de

Deighton, Len .... CLC **4, 7, 22, 46**
See also Deighton, Leonard Cyril
See also AAYA 6; BEST 89:2;
CDBLB 1960 to Present; DLB 87

Deighton, Leonard Cyril 1929-
See Deighton, Len
See also CA 9-12R; CANR 19, 33; MTCW

Dekker, Thomas 1572(?)-1632...... LC **22**
See also CDBLB Before 1660; DLB 62

de la Mare, Walter (John)
1873-1956 ...... TCLC **14; WLC 4, 53**
See also CDBLB 1914-1945; CLR 23;
DLB 19; SATA-Obit 16; YABC

Delaney, Franey
See O'Hara, John (Henry)

Delaney, Shelagh 1939- .... CLC **29**
See also CA 17-20R; CANR 30;
CDBLB 1960 to Present; DLB 13;
MTCW

Delany, Mary (Granville Pendarves)
1700-1788 .... LC **12**

Delany, Samuel R(ay, Jr.)
1942-............. CLC **8, 14, 38; BLC**
See also BW 2; CA 81-84; CANR 27, 43;
DLB 8, 33; MTCW

De La Ramee, (Marie) Louise 1839-1908
See Ouida
See also SATA-Obit 20

de la Roche, Mazo 1879-1961...... CLC **14**
See also CA 85-88; CANR 30; DLB 68;
SATA-Obit 64

Delbanco, Nicholas (Franklin)
1942-..................... CLC **6, 13**
See also CA 17-20R; CAAS 2; CANR 29;
DLB 6

del Castillo, Michel 1933- .... CLC **38**
See also CA 109

Delibes, Miguel................ CLC **8, 18**
See also Delibes Setien, Miguel

Delibes Setien, Miguel 1920-
See Delibes, Miguel
See also CA 45-48; CANR 1, 32; HW;
MTCW

DeLillo, Don
1936- ..... CLC **8, 10, 13, 27, 39, 54, 76**
See also BEST 89:1; CA 81-84; CANR 21;
DLB 6; MTCW

de Lisser, H. G.
See De Lisser, Herbert George
See also DLB 117

Deloria, Ella Cara 1888-(?) .... PC **X**

Deloria, Vine (Victor), Jr. 1933-.... CLC **21**
See also CA 53-56; CANR 5, 20; MTCW;
SATA-Obit 21

Del Vecchio, John M(ichael)
1947- .... CLC **29**
See also CA 110; DLBD 9

de Man, Paul (Adolph Michel)
1919-1983 .... CLC **55**
See also CA 128; 111; DLB 67; MTCW

De Marinis, Rick 1934-........... CLC **54**
See also CA 57-60; CANR 9, 25

Demby, William 1922-....... CLC **53; BLC**
See also BW 1; CA 81-84; DLB 33

Demijohn, Thom
See Disch, Thomas M(ichael)

de Montherlant, Henry (Milon)
See Montherlant, Henry (Milon) de

Demosthenes 384B.C.-322B.C. .... CMLC **13**

de Natale, Francine
See Malzberg, Barry N(athaniel)

Denby, Edwin (Orr) 1903-1983..... CLC **48**
See also CA 138; 110

Denis, Julio
See Cortazar, Julio

Denmark, Harrison
See Zelazny, Roger (Joseph)

Dennis, John 1658-1734........... LC **11**
See also DLB 101

Dennis, Nigel (Forbes) 1912-1989.... CLC **8**
See also CA 25-28R; 129; DLB 13, 15;
MTCW

De Palma, Brian (Russell) 1940-.... CLC **20**
See also CA 109

De Quincey, Thomas 1785-1859 ... NCLC **4**
See also CDBLB 1789-1832; DLB 110; 144

Deren, Eleanora 1908(?)-1961
See Deren, Maya
See also CA 111

Deren, Maya .... CLC **16**
See also Deren, Eleanora

Derleth, August (William)
1909-1971 .... CLC **31**
See also CA 1-4R; 29-32R; CANR 4;
DLB 9; SATA-Obit 5

de Routisie, Albert
See Aragon, Louis

Derrida, Jacques 1930-........... CLC **24**
See also CA 124; 127

Derry Down Derry
See Lear, Edward

Dersonnes, Jacques
See Simenon, Georges (Jacques Christian)

Desai, Anita 1937- .... CLC **19, 37**
See also CA 81-84; CANR 33; MTCW;
SATA-Obit 63

de Saint-Luc, Jean
See Glassco, John

de Saint Roman, Arnaud
See Aragon, Louis

Descartes, Rene 1596-1650 .... LC **20**

De Sica, Vittorio 1901(?)-1974 ..... CLC **20**
See also CA 117

Destouches, Louis-Ferdinand
1894-1961 .... CLC **9, 15**
See also Celine, Louis-Ferdinand
See also CA 85-88; CANR 28; MTCW

Deutsch, Babette 1895-1982 .... CLC **18**
See also CA 1-4R; 108; CANR 4; DLB 45;
SATA-Obit 1, 33

Doyle, A. Conan
See Doyle, Arthur Conan

Doyle, Arthur Conan
1859-1930 . . . . . **TCLC 12; DA; WLC 7**
See also CA 104; 122; CDBLB 1890-1914;
DLB 18, 70; MTCW; SATA-Obit 24;
YABC

Doyle, Conan 1859-1930
See Doyle, Arthur Conan

Doyle, John
See Graves, Robert (von Ranke)

Doyle, Roddy 1958(?)- . . . . **CLC 81**
See also CA 143

Doyle, Sir A. Conan
See Doyle, Arthur Conan

Doyle, Sir Arthur Conan
See Doyle, Arthur Conan

Dr. A
See Asimov, Isaac; Silverstein, Alvin

Drabble, Margaret
1939- . . . . **CLC 2, 3, 5, 8, 10, 22, 53**
See also CA 13-16R; CANR 18, 35;
CDBLB 1960 to Present; DLB 14;
MTCW; SATA-Obit 48

Drapier, M. B.
See Swift, Jonathan

Drayham, James
See Mencken, H(enry) L(ouis)

Drayton, Michael 1563-1631 . . . . **LC 8**

Dreadstone, Carl
See Campbell, (John) Ramsey

Drexler, Rosalyn 1926- . . . . **CLC 2, 6**
See also CA 81-84

Dreyer, Carl Theodor 1889-1968 . . . . **CLC 16**
See also CA 116

Drop Shot
See Cable, George Washington

Droste-Hulshoff, Annette Freiin von
1797-1848 . . . . **NCLC 3**
See also DLB 133

Drummond, Walter
See Silverberg, Robert

Drummond de Andrade, Carlos
1902-1987 . . . . **CLC 18**
See also Andrade, Carlos Drummond de
See also CA 132; 123

Drury, Allen (Stuart) 1918- . . . . **CLC 37**
See also CA 57-60; CANR 18

Dryden, John
1631-1700 . . . . **LC 3, 21; DA; DC 3**
See also CDBLB 1660-1789; DLB 80, 101,
131; YABC

Duberman, Martin 1930- . . . . **CLC 8**
See also CA 1-4R; CANR 2

Dubie, Norman (Evans) 1945- . . . . . . **CLC 36**
See also CA 69-72; CANR 12; DLB 120

Du Bois, W(illiam) E(dward) B(urghardt)
1868-1963 . . **CLC 1, 2, 13, 64; BLC; DA**
See also BW 1; CA 85-88; CANR 34;
CDALB 1865-1917; DLB 47, 50, 91;
MTCW; SATA-Obit 42; YABC

Dubus, Andre 1936- . . . . **CLC 13, 36**
See also CA 21-24R; CANR 17; DLB 130;
TCLC 15

Duca Minimo
See D'Annunzio, Gabriele

Ducharme, Rejean 1941- . . . . **CLC 74**
See also DLB 60

Duclos, Charles Pinot 1704-1772 . . . . . **LC 1**

Dudek, Louis 1918- . . . . **CLC 11, 19**
See also CA 45-48; CAAS 14; CANR 1;
DLB 88

Duerrenmatt, Friedrich
. . . . **CLC 1, 4, 8, 11, 15, 43**
See also Duerrenmatt, Friedrich
See also DLB 69, 124

Duerrenmatt, Friedrich
1921-1990 . . . . . . **CLC 1, 4, 8, 11, 15, 43**
See also Duerrenmatt, Friedrich
See also CA 17-20R; CANR 33; DLB 69,
124; MTCW

Duffy, Bruce (?)- . . . . **CLC 50**

Duffy, Maureen 1933- . . . . **CLC 37**
See also CA 25-28R; CANR 33; DLB 14;
MTCW

Dugan, Alan 1923- . . . . **CLC 2, 6**
See also CA 81-84; DLB 5

du Gard, Roger Martin
See Martin du Gard, Roger

Duhamel, Georges 1884-1966 . . . . **CLC 8**
See also CA 81-84; 25-28R; CANR 35;
DLB 65; MTCW

Dumas, Alexandre (Davy de la Pailleterie)
1802-1870 . . . . **NCLC 11; DA**
See also DLB 119; SATA-Obit 18; YABC

Dumas, Alexandre
1824-1895 . . . . **NCLC 9; DC 1**

Dumas, Claudine
See Malzberg, Barry N(athaniel)

Dumas, Henry L. 1934-1968 . . . . . **CLC 6, 62**
See also BW 1; CA 85-88; DLB 41

du Maurier, Daphne
1907-1989 . . . . **CLC 6, 11, 59**
See also CA 5-8R; 128; CANR 6; MTCW;
SATA-Obit 27, 60

Dunbar, Paul Laurence
1872-1906 . . . . **TCLC 8; BLC; DA;
WLC 2, 12**
See also BW 1; CA 104; 124;
CDALB 1865-1917; DLB 50, 54, 78;
SAAS 5; SATA-Obit 34; YABC

Dunbar, William 1460(?)-1530(?) . . . . **LC 20**

Duncan, Lois 1934- . . . . **CLC 26**
See also AAYA 4; CA 1-4R; CANR 2, 23,
36; CLR 29; JRDA; MAICYA; SATA 2;
SATA-Obit 1, 36, 75

Duncan, Robert (Edward)
1919-1988 . . . . **CLC 1, 2, 4, 7, 15, 41, 55**
See also CA 9-12R; 124; CANR 28; DLB 5,
16; MTCW; SAAS 2

Dunlap, William 1766-1839 . . . . **NCLC 2**
See also DLB 30, 37, 59

Dunn, Douglas (Eaglesham)
1942- . . . . **CLC 6, 40**
See also CA 45-48; CANR 2, 33; DLB 40;
MTCW

Dunn, Katherine (Karen) 1945- . . . . . **CLC 71**
See also CA 33-36R

Dunn, Stephen 1939- . . . . **CLC 36**
See also CA 33-36R; CANR 12; DLB 105

Dunne, John Gregory 1932- . . . . **CLC 28**
See also CA 25-28R; CANR 14; DLBY 80

Dunsany, Edward John Moreton Drax
Plunkett 1878-1957
See Dunsany, Lord
See also CA 104; DLB 10

du Perry, Jean
See Simenon, Georges (Jacques Christian)

Durang, Christopher (Ferdinand)
1949- . . . . **CLC 27, 38**
See also CA 105

Duras, Marguerite
1914- . . . . . . **CLC 3, 6, 11, 20, 34, 40, 68**
See also CA 25-28R; DLB 83; MTCW

Durban, (Rosa) Pam 1947- . . . . **CLC 39**
See also CA 123

Durcan, Paul 1944- . . . . **CLC 43, 70**
See also CA 134

Durrell, Lawrence (George)
1912-1990 . . . . **CLC 1, 4, 6, 8, 13, 27, 41**
See also CA 9-12R; 132; CANR 40;
CDBLB 1945-1960; DLB 15, 27;
DLBY 90; MTCW

Dutt, Toru 1856-1877 . . . . **NCLC 29**

Dwight, Timothy 1752-1817 . . . . . . **NCLC 13**
See also DLB 37

Dworkin, Andrea 1946- . . . . **CLC 43**
See also CA 77-80; CANR 16, 39; MTCW

Dwyer, Deanna
See Koontz, Dean R(ay)

Dwyer, K. R.
See Koontz, Dean R(ay)

Dylan, Bob 1941- . . . . . . **CLC 3, 4, 6, 12, 77**
See also CA 41-44R; DLB 16

Eagleton, Terence (Francis) 1943-
See Eagleton, Terry
See also CA 57-60; CANR 7, 23; MTCW

Eagleton, Terry . . . . **CLC 63**
See also Eagleton, Terence (Francis)

Early, Jack
See Scoppettone, Sandra

East, Michael
See West, Morris L(anglo)

Eastaway, Edward
See Thomas, (Philip) Edward

Eastlake, William (Derry) 1917- . . . . . **CLC 8**
See also CA 5-8R; CAAS 1; CANR 5;
DLB 6

Eberhart, Richard (Ghormley)
1904- . . . . **CLC 3, 11, 19, 56**
See also CA 1-4R; CANR 2;
CDALB 1941-1968; DLB 48; MTCW

Eberstadt, Fernanda 1960- . . . . **CLC 39**
See also CA 136

Echeverria, (Jose) Esteban (Antonino)
1805-1851 . . . . **NCLC 18**

Echo
See Proust, (Valentin-Louis-George-Eugene-)
Marcel

Eckert, Allan W. 1931- . . . . **CLC 17**
See also CA 13-16R; CANR 14, 45;
SATA-Obit 27, 29

Epstein, Leslie 1938- .... **CLC 27**
See also CA 73-76; CAAS 12; CANR 23

Equiano, Olaudah
1745(?)-1797 .... **LC 16; BLC**
See also DLB 37, 50

Erasmus, Desiderius 1469(?)-1536.... **LC 16**

Erdman, Paul E(mil) 1932- .... **CLC 25**
See also AITN 1; CA 61-64; CANR 13, 43

Erdrich, Louise 1954-......... **CLC 39, 54**
See also AAYA 10; BEST 89:1; CA 114;
CANR 41; MTCW

Erenburg, Ilya (Grigoryevich)
See Ehrenburg, Ilya (Grigoryevich)

Erickson, Stephen Michael 1950-
See Erickson, Steve
See also CA 129

Erickson, Steve .... **CLC 64**
See also Erickson, Stephen Michael

Ericson, Walter
See Fast, Howard (Melvin)

Eriksson, Buntel
See Bergman, (Ernst) Ingmar

Eschenbach, Wolfram von
See Wolfram von Eschenbach

Eseki, Bruno
See Mphahlele, Ezekiel

Eshleman, Clayton 1935-........... **CLC 7**
See also CA 33-36R; CAAS 6; DLB 5

Espriella, Don Manuel Alvarez
See Southey, Robert

Espriu, Salvador 1913-1985........ **CLC 9**
See also CA 115; DLB 134

Espronceda, Jose de 1808-1842... **NCLC 39**

Esse, James
See Stephens, James

Esterbrook, Tom
See Hubbard, L(afayette) Ron(ald)

Estleman, Loren D. 1952- .... **CLC 48**
See also CA 85-88; CANR 27; MTCW

Eugenides, Jeffrey 1960(?)- .... **CLC 81**
See also CA 144

Euripides c. 485B.C.-406B.C. .... **DC 4**
See also DA

Evan, Evin
See Faust, Frederick (Schiller)

Evans, Evan
See Faust, Frederick (Schiller)

Evans, Marian
See Eliot, George

Evans, Mary Ann
See Eliot, George

Evarts, Esther
See Benson, Sally

Everett, Percival L. 1956-........ **CLC 57**
See also BW 2; CA 129

Everson, R(onald) G(ilmour)
1903-...................... **CLC 27**
See also CA 17-20R; DLB 88

Everson, William (Oliver)
1912-................... **CLC 1, 5, 14**
See also CA 9-12R; CANR 20; DLB 5, 16;
MTCW

Evtushenko, Evgenii Aleksandrovich
See Yevtushenko, Yevgeny (Alexandrovich)

Ewart, Gavin (Buchanan)
1916-.................... **CLC 13, 46**
See also CA 89-92; CANR 17; DLB 40;
MTCW

Ewing, Frederick R.
See Sturgeon, Theodore (Hamilton)

Exley, Frederick (Earl)
1929-1992 .... **CLC 6, 11**
See also AITN 2; CA 81-84; 138; DLB 143;
DLBY 81

Eynhardt, Guillermo
See Quiroga, Horacio (Sylvestre)

Ezekiel, Nissim 1924-............. **CLC 61**
See also CA 61-64

Ezekiel, Tish O'Dowd 1943- .... **CLC 34**
See also CA 129

Fadeyev, A.
See Bulgya, Alexander Alexandrovich

Fadeyev, Alexander
See Bulgya, Alexander Alexandrovich
See also WLC 53

Fagen, Donald 1948-............. **CLC 26**

Fainzilberg, Ilya Arnoldovich 1897-1937
See Ilf, Ilya
See also CA 120

Fair, Ronald L. 1932-............. **CLC 18**
See also BW 1; CA 69-72; CANR 25;
DLB 33

Fairbairns, Zoe (Ann) 1948- .... **CLC 32**
See also CA 103; CANR 21

Falco, Gian
See Papini, Giovanni

Falconer, James
See Kirkup, James

Falconer, Kenneth
See Kornbluth, C(yril) M.

Falkland, Samuel
See Heijermans, Herman

Fallaci, Oriana 1930-............. **CLC 11**
See also CA 77-80; CANR 15; MTCW

Faludy, George 1913-............. **CLC 42**
See also CA 21-24R

Faludy, Gyoergy
See Faludy, George

Fanon, Frantz 1925-1961..... **CLC 74; BLC**
See also BW 1; CA 116; 89-92

Fanshawe, Ann .... **LC 11**

Fante, John (Thomas) 1911-1983 ... **CLC 60**
See also CA 69-72; 109; CANR 23;
DLB 130; DLBY 83

Farah, Nuruddin 1945-....... **CLC 53; BLC**
See also BW 2; CA 106; DLB 125

Farigoule, Louis
See Romains, Jules

Farina, Richard 1936(?)-1966 .... **CLC 9**
See also CA 81-84; 25-28R

Farley, Walter (Lorimer)
1915-1989 .... **CLC 17**
See also CA 17-20R; CANR 8, 29; DLB 22;
JRDA; MAICYA; SATA-Obit 2, 43

Farmer, Philip Jose 1918-....... **CLC 1, 19**
See also CA 1-4R; CANR 4, 35; DLB 8;
MTCW

Farquhar, George 1677-1707....... **LC 21**
See also DLB 84

Farrell, J(ames) G(ordon)
1935-1979 .... **CLC 6**
See also CA 73-76; 89-92; CANR 36;
DLB 14; MTCW

Farrell, James T(homas)
1904-1979 .... **CLC 1, 4, 8, 11, 66**
See also CA 5-8R; 89-92; CANR 9; DLB 4,
9, 86; DLBD 2; MTCW

Farren, Richard J.
See Betjeman, John

Farren, Richard M.
See Betjeman, John

Fassbinder, Rainer Werner
1946-1982 .... **CLC 20**
See also CA 93-96; 106; CANR 31

Fast, Howard (Melvin) 1914- ...... **CLC 23**
See also CA 1-4R; CAAS 18; CANR 1, 33;
DLB 9; SATA-Obit 7

Faulcon, Robert
See Holdstock, Robert P.

Faulkner, William (Cuthbert)
1897-1962 ..... **CLC 1, 3, 6, 8, 9, 11, 14,
18, 28, 52, 68; DA**
See also AAYA 7; CA 81-84; CANR 33;
CDALB 1929-1941; DLB 9, 11, 44, 102;
DLBD 2; DLBY 86; MTCW; TCLC 1;
YABC

Fauset, Jessie Redmon
1884(?)-1961 .... **CLC 19, 54; BLC**
See also BW 1; CA 109; DLB 51

Faust, Irvin 1924-................. **CLC 8**
See also CA 33-36R; CANR 28; DLB 2, 28;
DLBY 80

Fawkes, Guy
See Benchley, Robert (Charles)

Fearing, Kenneth (Flexner)
1902-1961 .... **CLC 51**
See also CA 93-96; DLB 9

Fecamps, Elise
See Creasey, John

Federman, Raymond 1928- ...... **CLC 6, 47**
See also CA 17-20R; CAAS 8; CANR 10,
43; DLBY 80

Federspiel, J(uerg) F. 1931-........ **CLC 42**

Feiffer, Jules (Ralph) 1929-.... **CLC 2, 8, 64**
See also AAYA 3; CA 17-20R; CANR 30;
DLB 7, 44; MTCW; SATA-Obit 8, 61

Feige, Hermann Albert Otto Maximilian
See Traven, B.

Fei-Kan, Li
See Li Fei-kan

Feinberg, David B. 1956-.......... **CLC 59**
See also CA 135

Feinstein, Elaine 1930-............ **CLC 36**
See also CA 69-72; CAAS 1; CANR 31;
DLB 14, 40; MTCW

Feldman, Irving (Mordecai) 1928-.... **CLC 7**
See also CA 1-4R; CANR 1

Fellini, Federico 1920-1993 .... **CLC 16**
See also CA 65-68; 143; CANR 33

Fournier, Henri Alban 1886-1914
See Alain-Fournier
See also CA 104

Fournier, Pierre 1916-............ **CLC 11**
See also Gascar, Pierre
See also CA 89-92; CANR 16, 40

Fowles, John
1926-.... **CLC 1, 2, 3, 4, 6, 9, 10, 15, 33**
See also CA 5-8R; CANR 25; CDBLB 1960
to Present; DLB 14, 139; MTCW;
SATA-Obit 22

Fox, Paula 1923-................... **CLC 2, 8**
See also AAYA 3; CA 73-76; CANR 20,
36; CLR 1; DLB 52; JRDA; MAICYA;
MTCW; SATA-Obit 17, 60

Fox, William Price (Jr.) 1926-..... **CLC 22**
See also CA 17-20R; CAAS 19; CANR 11;
DLB 2; DLBY 81

Foxe, John 1516(?)-1587 .... **LC 14**

Frame, Janet .... **CLC 2, 3, 6, 22, 66**
See also Clutha, Janet Paterson Frame

Francis, Claude 19(?)- .... **CLC 50**

Francis, Dick 1920-........ **CLC 2, 22, 42**
See also AAYA 5; BEST 89:3; CA 5-8R;
CANR 9, 42; CDBLB 1960 to Present;
DLB 87; MTCW

Francis, Robert (Churchill)
1901-1987 .... **CLC 15**
See also CA 1-4R; 123; CANR 1

Frank, Elizabeth 1945-............ **CLC 39**
See also CA 121; 126

Franklin, Benjamin
See Hasek, Jaroslav (Matej Frantisek)

Franklin, Benjamin 1706-1790... **LC 25; DA**
See also CDALB 1640-1865; DLB 24, 43,
73

Fraser, (Lady) Antonia (Pakenham)
1932-...................... **CLC 32**
See also CA 85-88; CANR 44; MTCW;
SATA-Obit 32

Fraser, George MacDonald 1925-.... **CLC 7**
See also CA 45-48; CANR 2

Fraser, Sylvia 1935-.............. **CLC 64**
See also CA 45-48; CANR 1, 16

Frayn, Michael 1933-...... **CLC 3, 7, 31, 47**
See also CA 5-8R; CANR 30; DLB 13, 14;
MTCW

Fraze, Candida (Merrill) 1945-..... **CLC 50**
See also CA 126

Frazer, Robert Caine
See Creasey, John

Frazer, Sir James George
See Frazer, J(ames) G(eorge)

Frazier, Ian 1951-............... **CLC 46**
See also CA 130

Frederic, Harold 1856-1898...... **NCLC 10**
See also DLB 12, 23

Frederick, John
See Faust, Frederick (Schiller)

Frederick the Great 1712-1786...... **LC 14**

Fredro, Aleksander 1793-1876..... **NCLC 8**

Freeling, Nicolas 1927- .... **CLC 38**
See also CA 49-52; CAAS 12; CANR 1, 17;
DLB 87

Freeman, Judith 1946-............ **CLC 55**

Freeman, Mary Eleanor Wilkins
1852-1930 .... **TCLC 1; WLC 9**
See also CA 106; DLB 12, 78

French, Marilyn 1929-..... **CLC 10, 18, 60**
See also CA 69-72; CANR 3, 31; MTCW

French, Paul
See Asimov, Isaac

Freneau, Philip Morin 1752-1832.. **NCLC 1**
See also DLB 37, 43

Friedan, Betty (Naomi) 1921-...... **CLC 74**
See also CA 65-68; CANR 18, 45; MTCW

Friedman, B(ernard) H(arper)
1926-....................... **CLC 7**
See also CA 1-4R; CANR 3

Friedman, Bruce Jay 1930-.... **CLC 3, 5, 56**
See also CA 9-12R; CANR 25; DLB 2, 28

Friel, Brian 1929-........... **CLC 5, 42, 59**
See also CA 21-24R; CANR 33; DLB 13;
MTCW

Friis-Baastad, Babbis Ellinor
1921-1970 .... **CLC 12**
See also CA 17-20R; 134; SATA-Obit 7

Frisch, Max (Rudolf)
1911-1991 ..... **CLC 3, 9, 14, 18, 32, 44**
See also CA 85-88; 134; CANR 32;
DLB 69, 124; MTCW

Fromentin, Eugene (Samuel Auguste)
1820-1876 .... **NCLC 10**
See also DLB 123

Frost, Frederick
See Faust, Frederick (Schiller)

Frost, Robert (Lee)
1874-1963 .... **CLC 1, 3, 4, 9, 10, 13, 15,
26, 34, 44; DA**
See also CA 89-92; CANR 33;
CDALB 1917-1929; DLB 54; DLBD 7;
MTCW; SAAS 1; SATA-Obit 14; YABC

Froude, James Anthony
1818-1894 .... **NCLC 43**
See also DLB 18, 57, 144

Froy, Herald
See Waterhouse, Keith (Spencer)

Fry, Christopher 1907-....... **CLC 2, 10, 14**
See also CA 17-20R; CANR 9, 30; DLB 13;
MTCW; SATA-Obit 66

Frye, (Herman) Northrop
1912-1991 .... **CLC 24, 70**
See also CA 5-8R; 133; CANR 8, 37;
DLB 67, 68; MTCW

Fuchs, Daniel 1909-1993 .... **CLC 8, 22**
See also CA 81-84; 142; CAAS 5;
CANR 40; DLB 9, 26, 28; DLBY 93

Fuchs, Daniel 1934-.............. **CLC 34**
See also CA 37-40R; CANR 14

Fuentes, Carlos
1928-...... **CLC 3, 8, 10, 13, 22, 41, 60;
DA; HLC**
See also AAYA 4; AITN 2; CA 69-72;
CANR 10, 32; DLB 113; HW; MTCW;
YABC

Fuentes, Gregorio Lopez y
See Lopez y Fuentes, Gregorio

Fugard, (Harold) Athol
1932-.... **CLC 5, 9, 14, 25, 40, 80; DC 3**
See also CA 85-88; CANR 32; MTCW

Fugard, Sheila 1932- .... **CLC 48**
See also CA 125

Fuller, Charles (H., Jr.)
1939-............ **CLC 25; BLC; DC 1**
See also BW 2; CA 108; 112; DLB 38;
MTCW

Fuller, John (Leopold) 1937-....... **CLC 62**
See also CA 21-24R; CANR 9, 44; DLB 40

Fuller, Margaret .... **NCLC 5**
See also Ossoli, Sarah Margaret (Fuller
marchesa d')

Fuller, Roy (Broadbent)
1912-1991 .... **CLC 4, 28**
See also CA 5-8R; 135; CAAS 10; DLB 15,
20

Fulton, Alice 1952-.............. **CLC 52**
See also CA 116

Fussell, Paul 1924-.............. **CLC 74**
See also BEST 90:1; CA 17-20R; CANR 8,
21, 35; MTCW

G. B. S.
See Shaw, George Bernard

Gaboriau, Emile 1835-1873...... **NCLC 14**

Gadda, Carlo Emilio 1893-1973.... **CLC 11**
See also CA 89-92

Gaddis, William
1922-........ **CLC 1, 3, 6, 8, 10, 19, 43**
See also CA 17-20R; CANR 21; DLB 2;
MTCW

Gaines, Ernest J(ames)
1933-.............. **CLC 3, 11, 18; BLC**
See also AITN 1; BW 2; CA 9-12R;
CANR 6, 24, 42; CDALB 1968-1988;
DLB 2, 33; DLBY 80; MTCW

Gaitskill, Mary 1954-............. **CLC 69**
See also CA 128

Galdos, Benito Perez
See Perez Galdos, Benito

Galeano, Eduardo (Hughes) 1940-... **CLC 72**
See also CA 29-32R; CANR 13, 32; HW

Galiano, Juan Valera y Alcala
See Valera y Alcala-Galiano, Juan

Gallagher, Tess 1943-.......... **CLC 18, 63**
See also CA 106; DLB 120; SAAS 9

Gallant, Mavis 1922-........ **CLC 7, 18, 38**
See also CA 69-72; CANR 29; DLB 53;
MTCW; TCLC 5

Gallant, Roy A(rthur) 1924- .... **CLC 17**
See also CA 5-8R; CANR 4, 29; CLR 30;
MAICYA; SATA-Obit 4, 68

Gallico, Paul (William) 1897-1976... **CLC 2**
See also AITN 1; CA 5-8R; 69-72;
CANR 23; DLB 9; MAICYA;
SATA-Obit 13

Gallup, Ralph
See Whitemore, Hugh (John)

Galt, John 1779-1839............ **NCLC 1**
See also DLB 99, 116

Galvin, James 1951-.............. **CLC 38**
See also CA 108; CANR 26

Gann, Ernest Kellogg 1910-1991.... **CLC 23**
See also AITN 1; CA 1-4R; 136; CANR 1

Garcia, Cristina 1958- .... **CLC 76**
See also CA 141

Garcia Lorca, Federico 1898-1936 .... **DC 2**
See also CA 104; 131; DA; DLB 108; HLC;
HW; MTCW; SAAS 3; WLC 1, 7, 49;
YABC

Garcia Marquez, Gabriel (Jose)
1928- .... **CLC 2, 3, 8, 10, 15, 27, 47, 55;
DA; HLC**
See also Marquez, Gabriel (Jose) Garcia
See also AAYA 3; BEST 89:1, 90:4;
CA 33-36R; CANR 10, 28; DLB 113;
HW; MTCW; TCLC 8; YABC

Gard, Janice
See Latham, Jean Lee

Gard, Roger Martin du
See Martin du Gard, Roger

Gardam, Jane 1928-.............. **CLC 43**
See also CA 49-52; CANR 2, 18, 33;
CLR 12; DLB 14; MAICYA; MTCW;
SATA 9; SATA-Obit 28, 39, 76

Gardner, Herb.................... **CLC 44**

Gardner, John (Champlin), Jr.
1933-1982 ..... **CLC 2, 3, 5, 7, 8, 10, 18,
28, 34**
See also AITN 1; CA 65-68; 107;
CANR 33; DLB 2; DLBY 82; MTCW;
SATA-Obit 31, 40; TCLC 7

Gardner, John (Edmund) 1926-..... **CLC 30**
See also CA 103; CANR 15; MTCW

Gardner, Noel
See Kuttner, Henry

Gardons, S. S.
See Snodgrass, W(illiam) D(e Witt)

Garfield, Leon 1921-.............. **CLC 12**
See also AAYA 8; CA 17-20R; CANR 38,
41; CLR 21; JRDA; MAICYA;
SATA-Obit 1, 32, 76

Garner, Alan 1934-............... **CLC 17**
See also CA 73-76; CANR 15; CLR 20;
MAICYA; MTCW; SATA-Obit 18, 69

Garner, Hugh 1913-1979 .... **CLC 13**
See also CA 69-72; CANR 31; DLB 68

Garnett, David 1892-1981 .... **CLC 3**
See also CA 5-8R; 103; CANR 17; DLB 34

Garos, Stephanie
See Katz, Steve

Garrett, George (Palmer)
1929-.................. **CLC 3, 11, 51**
See also CA 1-4R; CAAS 5; CANR 1, 42;
DLB 2, 5, 130; DLBY 83

Garrick, David 1717-1779 .... **LC 15**
See also DLB 84

Garrigue, Jean 1914-1972 .... **CLC 2, 8**
See also CA 5-8R; 37-40R; CANR 20

Garrison, Frederick
See Sinclair, Upton (Beall)

Garth, Will
See Hamilton, Edmond; Kuttner, Henry

Gary, Romain .... **CLC 25**
See also Kacew, Romain
See also DLB 83

Gascar, Pierre .... **CLC 11**
See also Fournier, Pierre

Gascoyne, David (Emery) 1916- .... **CLC 45**
See also CA 65-68; CANR 10, 28; DLB 20;
MTCW

Gaskell, Elizabeth Cleghorn
1810-1865 .... **NCLC 5**
See also CDBLB 1832-1890; DLB 21, 144

Gass, William H(oward)
1924- .... **CLC 1, 2, 8, 11, 15, 39**
See also CA 17-20R; CANR 30; DLB 2;
MTCW; TCLC 12

Gasset, Jose Ortega y
See Ortega y Gasset, Jose

Gautier, Theophile 1811-1872 ..... **NCLC 1**
See also DLB 119

Gawsworth, John
See Bates, H(erbert) E(rnest)

Gaye, Marvin (Penze) 1939-1984 ... **CLC 26**
See also CA 112

Gebler, Carlo (Ernest) 1954-....... **CLC 39**
See also CA 119; 133

Gee, Maggie (Mary) 1948-........ **CLC 57**
See also CA 130

Gee, Maurice (Gough) 1931-....... **CLC 29**
See also CA 97-100; SATA-Obit 46

Geiogamah, Hanay 1945-........... **PC X**

Gelbart, Larry (Simon) 1923- ... **CLC 21, 61**
See also CA 73-76; CANR 45

Gelber, Jack 1932-........ **CLC 1, 6, 14, 79**
See also CA 1-4R; CANR 2; DLB 7

Gellhorn, Martha (Ellis) 1908- .. **CLC 14, 60**
See also CA 77-80; CANR 44; DLBY 82

Genet, Jean
1910-1986 ... **CLC 1, 2, 5, 10, 14, 44, 46**
See also CA 13-16R; CANR 18; DLB 72;
DLBY 86; MTCW

Gent, Peter 1942-................. **CLC 29**
See also AITN 1; CA 89-92; DLBY 82

Gentlewoman in New England, A
See Bradstreet, Anne

Gentlewoman in Those Parts, A
See Bradstreet, Anne

George, Jean Craighead 1919-...... **CLC 35**
See also AAYA 8; CA 5-8R; CANR 25;
CLR 1; DLB 52; JRDA; MAICYA;
SATA-Obit 2, 68

Georges, Georges Martin
See Simenon, Georges (Jacques Christian)

Gerhardi, William Alexander
See Gerhardie, William Alexander

Gerhardie, William Alexander
1895-1977 .... **CLC 5**
See also CA 25-28R; 73-76; CANR 18;
DLB 36

Gerstler, Amy 1956-.............. **CLC 70**

Gertler, T. .... **CLC 34**
See also CA 116; 121

Ghalib 1797-1869 .... **NCLC 39**

Ghelderode, Michel de
1898-1962 .... **CLC 6, 11**
See also CA 85-88; CANR 40

Ghiselin, Brewster 1903- .... **CLC 23**
See also CA 13-16R; CAAS 10; CANR 13

Ghose, Zulfikar 1935-............. **CLC 42**
See also CA 65-68

Ghosh, Amitav 1956- .... **CLC 44**

Gibb, Lee
See Waterhouse, Keith (Spencer)

Gibbons, Kaye 1960- .... **CLC 50**

Gibson, William 1914-........ **CLC 23; DA**
See also CA 9-12R; CANR 9, 42; DLB 7;
SATA-Obit 66

Gibson, William (Ford) 1948- ... **CLC 39, 63**
See also AAYA 12; CA 126; 133

Gide, Andre (Paul Guillaume)
1869-1951 ...... **TCLC 13; DA; WLC 5,
12, 36**
See also CA 104; 124; DLB 65; MTCW;
YABC

Gifford, Barry (Colby) 1946-....... **CLC 34**
See also CA 65-68; CANR 9, 30, 40

Gilbreth, Frank B., Jr. 1911-....... **CLC 17**
See also CA 9-12R; SATA-Obit 2

Gilchrist, Ellen 1935-........... **CLC 34, 48**
See also CA 113; 116; CANR 41; DLB 130;
MTCW; TCLC 14

Giles, Molly 1942-............... **CLC 39**
See also CA 126

Gill, Patrick
See Creasey, John

Gilliam, Terry (Vance) 1940-....... **CLC 21**
See also Monty Python
See also CA 108; 113; CANR 35

Gillian, Jerry
See Gilliam, Terry (Vance)

Gilliatt, Penelope (Ann Douglass)
1932-1993 .... **CLC 2, 10, 13, 53**
See also AITN 2; CA 13-16R; 141; DLB 14

Gilman, Charlotte (Anna) Perkins (Stetson)
1860-1935 .... **TCLC 13; WLC 9, 37**
See also CA 106

Gilmour, David 1949-............. **CLC 35**
See also Pink Floyd
See also CA 138

Gilpin, William 1724-1804....... **NCLC 30**

Gilray, J. D.
See Mencken, H(enry) L(ouis)

Gilroy, Frank D(aniel) 1925-........ **CLC 2**
See also CA 81-84; CANR 32; DLB 7

Ginsberg, Allen
1926- .. **CLC 1, 2, 3, 4, 6, 13, 36, 69; DA**
See also AITN 1; CA 1-4R; CANR 2, 41;
CDALB 1941-1968; DLB 5, 16; MTCW;
SAAS 4; YABC 3

Ginzburg, Natalia
1916-1991 .... **CLC 5, 11, 54, 70**
See also CA 85-88; 135; CANR 33; MTCW

Giono, Jean 1895-1970.......... **CLC 4, 11**
See also CA 45-48; 29-32R; CANR 2, 35;
DLB 72; MTCW

Giovanni, Nikki
1943- ...... **CLC 2, 4, 19, 64; BLC; DA**
See also AITN 1; BW 2; CA 29-32R;
CAAS 6; CANR 18, 41; CLR 6; DLB 5,
41; MAICYA; MTCW; SATA-Obit 24

Grass, Guenter (Wilhelm)
1927- . . . . . **CLC 1, 2, 4, 6, 11, 15, 22, 32, 49; DA**
See also CA 13-16R; CANR 20; DLB 75, 124; MTCW; YABC

Gratton, Thomas
See Hulme, T(homas) E(rnest)

Grau, Shirley Ann 1929- . . . . **CLC 4, 9**
See also CA 89-92; CANR 22; DLB 2; MTCW; TCLC 15

Gravel, Fern
See Hall, James Norman

Graver, Elizabeth 1964- . . . . **CLC 70**
See also CA 135

Graves, Richard Perceval 1945- . . . . **CLC 44**
See also CA 65-68; CANR 9, 26

Graves, Robert (von Ranke)
1895-1985 . . . **CLC 1, 2, 6, 11, 39, 44, 45**
See also CA 5-8R; 117; CANR 5, 36; CDBLB 1914-1945; DLB 20, 100; DLBY 85; MTCW; SAAS 6; SATA-Obit 45

Gray, Alasdair 1934- . . . . **CLC 41**
See also CA 126; MTCW

Gray, Amlin 1946- . . . . **CLC 29**
See also CA 138

Gray, Francine du Plessix 1930- . . . . **CLC 22**
See also BEST 90:3; CA 61-64; CAAS 2; CANR 11, 33; MTCW

Gray, Simon (James Holliday)
1936- . . . . **CLC 9, 14, 36**
See also AITN 1; CA 21-24R; CAAS 3; CANR 32; DLB 13; MTCW

Gray, Spalding 1941- . . . . **CLC 49**
See also CA 128

Gray, Thomas 1716-1771 . . . . **LC 4; DA**
See also CDBLB 1660-1789; DLB 109; SAAS 2; YABC

Grayson, David
See Baker, Ray Stannard

Grayson, Richard (A.) 1951- . . . . **CLC 38**
See also CA 85-88; CANR 14, 31

Greeley, Andrew M(oran) 1928- . . . . **CLC 28**
See also CA 5-8R; CAAS 7; CANR 7, 43; MTCW

Green, Brian
See Card, Orson Scott

Green, Hannah
See Greenberg, Joanne (Goldenberg)

Green, Hannah . . . . **CLC 3**
See also CA 73-76

Green, Henry . . . . **CLC 2, 13**
See also Yorke, Henry Vincent
See also DLB 15

Green, Julian (Hartridge) 1900-
See Green, Julien
See also CA 21-24R; CANR 33; DLB 4, 72; MTCW

Green, Julien . . . . **CLC 3, 11, 77**
See also Green, Julian (Hartridge)

Green, Paul (Eliot) 1894-1981 . . . . . . **CLC 25**
See also AITN 1; CA 5-8R; 103; CANR 3; DLB 7, 9; DLBY 81

Greenberg, Ivan 1908-1973
See Rahv, Philip
See also CA 85-88

Greenberg, Joanne (Goldenberg)
1932- . . . . **CLC 7, 30**
See also AAYA 12; CA 5-8R; CANR 14, 32; SATA-Obit 25

Greenberg, Richard 1959(?)- . . . . **CLC 57**
See also CA 138

Greene, Bette 1934- . . . . **CLC 30**
See also AAYA 7; CA 53-56; CANR 4; CLR 2; JRDA; MAICYA; SATA 16; SATA-Obit 8

Greene, Gael . . . . **CLC 8**
See also CA 13-16R; CANR 10

Greene, Graham
1904-1991 . . . . **CLC 1, 3, 6, 9, 14, 18, 27, 37, 70, 72; DA**
See also AITN 2; CA 13-16R; 133; CANR 35; CDBLB 1945-1960; DLB 13, 15, 77, 100; DLBY 91; MTCW; SATA-Obit 20; YABC

Greer, Richard
See Silverberg, Robert

Greer, Richard
See Silverberg, Robert

Gregor, Arthur 1923- . . . . **CLC 9**
See also CA 25-28R; CAAS 10; CANR 11; SATA-Obit 36

Gregor, Lee
See Pohl, Frederik

Gregory, J. Dennis
See Williams, John A(lfred)

Grendon, Stephen
See Derleth, August (William)

Grenville, Kate 1950- . . . . **CLC 61**
See also CA 118

Grenville, Pelham
See Wodehouse, P(elham) G(renville)

Greve, Felix Paul (Berthold Friedrich)
1879-1948
See Grove, Frederick Philip
See also CA 104; 141

Grieve, C(hristopher) M(urray)
1892-1978 . . . . **CLC 11, 19**
See also MacDiarmid, Hugh
See also CA 5-8R; 85-88; CANR 33; MTCW

Griffin, Gerald 1803-1840 . . . . **NCLC 7**

Griffin, John Howard 1920-1980 . . . . **CLC 68**
See also AITN 1; CA 1-4R; 101; CANR 2

Griffin, Peter . . . . **CLC 39**

Griffiths, Trevor 1935- . . . . **CLC 13, 52**
See also CA 97-100; CANR 45; DLB 13

Grigson, Geoffrey (Edward Harvey)
1905-1985 . . . . **CLC 7, 39**
See also CA 25-28R; 118; CANR 20, 33; DLB 27; MTCW

Grillparzer, Franz 1791-1872 . . . . . . **NCLC 1**
See also DLB 133

Grimble, Reverend Charles James
See Eliot, T(homas) S(tearns)

Grimke, Charlotte L(ottie) Forten
1837(?)-1914
See Forten, Charlotte L.
See also BW 1; CA 117; 124

Grimm, Jacob Ludwig Karl
1785-1863 . . . . **NCLC 3**
See also DLB 90; MAICYA; SATA-Obit 22

Grimm, Wilhelm Karl 1786-1859 . . **NCLC 3**
See also DLB 90; MAICYA; SATA-Obit 22

Grimmelshausen, Johann Jakob Christoffel
von 1621-1676 . . . . **LC 6**

Grindel, Eugene 1895-1952
See Eluard, Paul
See also CA 104

Grisham, John 1955(?)- . . . . **CLC 84**
See also CA 138

Grossman, David 1954- . . . . **CLC 67**
See also CA 138

Grossman, Vasily (Semenovich)
1905-1964 . . . . **CLC 41**
See also CA 124; 130; MTCW

Grubb
See Crumb, R(obert)

Grumbach, Doris (Isaac)
1918- . . . . **CLC 13, 22, 64**
See also CA 5-8R; CAAS 2; CANR 9, 42

Grundtvig, Nicolai Frederik Severin
1783-1872 . . . . **NCLC 1**

Grunge
See Crumb, R(obert)

Grunwald, Lisa 1959- . . . . **CLC 44**
See also CA 120

Guare, John 1938- . . . . **CLC 8, 14, 29, 67**
See also CA 73-76; CANR 21; DLB 7; MTCW

Gudjonsson, Halldor Kiljan 1902-
See Laxness, Halldor
See also CA 103

Guenter, Erich
See Eich, Guenter

Guest, Barbara 1920- . . . . **CLC 34**
See also CA 25-28R; CANR 11, 44; DLB 5

Guest, Judith (Ann) 1936- . . . . **CLC 8, 30**
See also AAYA 7; CA 77-80; CANR 15; MTCW

Guild, Nicholas M. 1944- . . . . **CLC 33**
See also CA 93-96

Guillemin, Jacques
See Sartre, Jean-Paul

Guillen, Jorge 1893-1984 . . . . **CLC 11**
See also CA 89-92; 112; DLB 108; HW

Guillen (y Batista), Nicolas (Cristobal)
1902-1989 . . . . . **CLC 48, 79; BLC; HLC**
See also BW 2; CA 116; 125; 129; HW

Guillevic, (Eugene) 1907- . . . . **CLC 33**
See also CA 93-96

Guillois
See Desnos, Robert

Gunn, Bill . . . . **CLC 5**
See also Gunn, William Harrison
See also DLB 38

Harris, MacDonald
See Heiney, Donald (William)

Harris, Mark 1922- . . . . **CLC 19**
See also CA 5-8R; CAAS 3; CANR 2;
DLB 2; DLBY 80

Harris, (Theodore) Wilson 1921- . . . . **CLC 25**
See also BW 2; CA 65-68; CAAS 16;
CANR 11, 27; DLB 117; MTCW

Harrison, Elizabeth Cavanna 1909-
See Cavanna, Betty
See also CA 9-12R; CANR 6, 27

Harrison, Harry (Max) 1925- . . . . . . **CLC 42**
See also CA 1-4R; CANR 5, 21; DLB 8;
SATA-Obit 4

Harrison, James (Thomas)
1937- . . . . **CLC 6, 14, 33, 66**
See also CA 13-16R; CANR 8; DLBY 82

Harrison, Kathryn 1961- . . . . **CLC 70**
See also CA 144

Harrison, Tony 1937- . . . . **CLC 43**
See also CA 65-68; CANR 44; DLB 40;
MTCW

Harriss, Will(ard Irvin) 1922- . . . . . . **CLC 34**
See also CA 111

Harson, Sley
See Ellison, Harlan

Hart, Ellis
See Ellison, Harlan

Hart, Josephine 1942(?)- . . . . **CLC 70**
See also CA 138

Hart, Moss 1904-1961 . . . . **CLC 66**
See also CA 109; 89-92; DLB 7

Harte, (Francis) Bret(t)
1836(?)-1902 . . **TCLC 8; DA; WLC 1, 25**
See also CA 104; 140; CDALB 1865-1917;
DLB 12, 64, 74, 79; SATA-Obit 26;
YABC

Hartley, L(eslie) P(oles)
1895-1972 . . . . **CLC 2, 22**
See also CA 45-48; 37-40R; CANR 33;
DLB 15, 139; MTCW

Hartman, Geoffrey H. 1929- . . . . **CLC 27**
See also CA 117; 125; DLB 67

Haruf, Kent 19(?)- . . . . **CLC 34**

Harwood, Ronald 1934- . . . . **CLC 32**
See also CA 1-4R; CANR 4; DLB 13

Hass, Robert 1941- . . . . **CLC 18, 39**
See also CA 111; CANR 30; DLB 105

Hastings, Hudson
See Kuttner, Henry

Hastings, Selina . . . . **CLC 44**

Hatteras, Amelia
See Mencken, H(enry) L(ouis)

Hatteras, Owen
See Mencken, H(enry) L(ouis); Nathan,
George Jean
See also WLC 18

Havel, Vaclav 1936- . . . . **CLC 25, 58, 65**
See also CA 104; CANR 36; MTCW

Haviaras, Stratis . . . . **CLC 33**
See also Chaviaras, Strates

Hawes, Stephen 1475(?)-1523(?) . . . . . **LC 17**

Hawkes, John (Clendennin Burne, Jr.)
1925- . . . . . . **CLC 1, 2, 3, 4, 7, 9, 14, 15,
27, 49**
See also CA 1-4R; CANR 2; DLB 2, 7;
DLBY 80; MTCW

Hawking, S. W.
See Hawking, Stephen W(illiam)

Hawking, Stephen W(illiam)
1942- . . . . **CLC 63**
See also BEST 89:1; CA 126; 129

Hawthorne, Nathaniel
1804-1864 . . . . **TCLC 3; DA**
See also CDALB 1640-1865; DLB 1, 74;
NCLC 39; YABC; 2

Haxton, Josephine Ayres 1921- . . . . **CLC 73**
See also CA 115; CANR 41

Hayaseca y Eizaguirre, Jorge
See Echegaray (y Eizaguirre), Jose (Maria
Waldo)

Haycraft, Anna
See Ellis, Alice Thomas
See also CA 122

Hayden, Robert E(arl)
1913-1980 . . **CLC 5, 9, 14, 37; BLC; DA**
See also BW 1; CA 69-72; 97-100; CABS 2;
CANR 24; CDALB 1941-1968; DLB 5,
76; MTCW; SAAS 6; SATA-Obit 19, 26

Hayford, J(oseph) E(phraim) Casely
See Casely-Hayford, J(oseph) E(phraim)

Hayman, Ronald 1932- . . . . **CLC 44**
See also CA 25-28R; CANR 18

Haywood, Eliza (Fowler)
1693(?)-1756 . . . . **LC 1**

Hazlitt, William 1778-1830 . . . . . . **NCLC 29**
See also DLB 110

Hazzard, Shirley 1931- . . . . **CLC 18**
See also CA 9-12R; CANR 4; DLBY 82;
MTCW

Head, Bessie 1937-1986 . . . **CLC 25, 67; BLC**
See also BW 2; CA 29-32R; 119; CANR 25;
DLB 117; MTCW

Headon, (Nicky) Topper 1956(?)- . . . **CLC 30**
See also Clash, The

Heaney, Seamus (Justin)
1939- . . . . **CLC 5, 7, 14, 25, 37, 74**
See also CA 85-88; CANR 25;
CDBLB 1960 to Present; DLB 40;
MTCW

Hearne, Vicki 1946- . . . . **CLC 56**
See also CA 139

Hearon, Shelby 1931- . . . . **CLC 63**
See also AITN 2; CA 25-28R; CANR 18

Heat-Moon, William Least . . . . **CLC 29**
See also Trogdon, William (Lewis)
See also AAYA 9

Hebbel, Friedrich 1813-1863 . . . . . **NCLC 43**
See also DLB 129

Hebert, Anne 1916- . . . . **CLC 4, 13, 29**
See also CA 85-88; DLB 68; MTCW

Hecht, Anthony (Evan)
1923- . . . . **CLC 8, 13, 19**
See also CA 9-12R; CANR 6; DLB 5

Hecht, Ben 1894-1964 . . . . **CLC 8**
See also CA 85-88; DLB 7, 9, 25, 26, 28, 86

Hegel, Georg Wilhelm Friedrich
1770-1831 . . . . **NCLC 46**
See also DLB 90

Heidegger, Martin 1889-1976 . . . . . . **CLC 24**
See also CA 81-84; 65-68; CANR 34;
MTCW

Heifner, Jack 1946- . . . . **CLC 11**
See also CA 105

Heilbrun, Carolyn G(old) 1926- . . . . . **CLC 25**
See also CA 45-48; CANR 1, 28

Heine, Heinrich 1797-1856 . . . . **NCLC 4**
See also DLB 90

Heinemann, Larry (Curtiss) 1944- . . **CLC 50**
See also CA 110; CANR 31; DLBD 9

Heiney, Donald (William)
1921-1993 . . . . **CLC 9**
See also CA 1-4R; 142; CANR 3

Heinlein, Robert A(nson)
1907-1988 . . . . . . **CLC 1, 3, 8, 14, 26, 55**
See also CA 1-4R; 125; CANR 1, 20;
DLB 8; JRDA; MAICYA; MTCW;
SATA-Obit 9, 56, 69

Helforth, John
See Doolittle, Hilda

Hellenhofferu, Vojtech Kapristian z
See Hasek, Jaroslav (Matej Frantisek)

Heller, Joseph
1923- . . . . **CLC 1, 3, 5, 8, 11, 36, 63; DA**
See also AITN 1; CA 5-8R; CABS 1;
CANR 8, 42; DLB 2, 28; DLBY 80;
MTCW; YABC

Hellman, Lillian (Florence)
1906-1984 . . . . . . **CLC 2, 4, 8, 14, 18, 34,
44, 52; DC 1**
See also AITN 1, 2; CA 13-16R; 112;
CANR 33; DLB 7; DLBY 84; MTCW

Helprin, Mark 1947- . . . . . **CLC 7, 10, 22, 32**
See also CA 81-84; DLBY 85; MTCW

Helyar, Jane Penelope Josephine 1933-
See Poole, Josephine
See also CA 21-24R; CANR 10, 26

Hemans, Felicia 1793-1835 . . . . . . **NCLC 29**
See also DLB 96

Hemingway, Ernest (Miller)
1899-1961 . . . . **CLC 1, 3, 6, 8, 10, 13, 19,
30, 34, 39, 41, 44, 50, 61, 80; DA**
See also CA 77-80; CANR 34;
CDALB 1917-1929; DLB 4, 9, 102;
DLBD 1; DLBY 81, 87; MTCW;
TCLC 1; YABC

Hempel, Amy 1951- . . . . **CLC 39**
See also CA 118; 137

Henderson, F. C.
See Mencken, H(enry) L(ouis)

Henderson, Sylvia
See Ashton-Warner, Sylvia (Constance)

Henley, Beth . . . . **CLC 23**
See also Henley, Elizabeth Becker
See also CABS 3; DLBY 86

Henley, Elizabeth Becker 1952-
See Henley, Beth
See also CA 107; CANR 32; MTCW

Hennissart, Martha
See Lathen, Emma
See also CA 85-88

Henry, O.............. **TCLC 5; WLC 1, 19**
  See also Porter, William Sydney
  See also YABC

Henry, Patrick 1736-1799 .... **LC 25**

Henryson, Robert 1430(?)-1506(?).... **LC 20**

Henry VIII 1491-1547............. **LC 10**

Henschke, Alfred
  See Klabund

Henson, Lance 1944-............... **PC X**

Hentoff, Nat(han Irving) 1925-..... **CLC 26**
  See also AAYA 4; CA 1-4R; CAAS 6;
  CANR 5, 25; CLR 1; JRDA; MAICYA;
  SATA-Obit 27, 42, 69

Heppenstall, (John) Rayner
  1911-1981 .... **CLC 10**
  See also CA 1-4R; 103; CANR 29

Herbert, Frank (Patrick)
  1920-1986 .... **CLC 12, 23, 35, 44**
  See also CA 53-56; 118; CANR 5, 43;
  DLB 8; MTCW; SATA-Obit 9, 37, 47

Herbert, George 1593-1633......... **LC 24**
  See also CDBLB Before 1660; DLB 126;
  SAAS 4

Herbert, Zbigniew 1924-........ **CLC 9, 43**
  See also CA 89-92; CANR 36; MTCW

Herbst, Josephine (Frey)
  1897-1969 .... **CLC 34**
  See also CA 5-8R; 25-28R; DLB 9

Herlihy, James Leo 1927-1993 ...... **CLC 6**
  See also CA 1-4R; 143; CANR 2

Hermogenes fl. c. 175-........... **CMLC 6**

Hernandez, Jose 1834-1886...... **NCLC 17**

Herrick, Robert 1591-1674 ..... **LC 13; DA**
  See also DLB 126; SAAS 9

Herring, Guilles
  See Somerville, Edith

Herriot, James 1916-............. **CLC 12**
  See also Wight, James Alfred
  See also AAYA 1; CANR 40

Herrmann, Dorothy 1941-........ **CLC 44**
  See also CA 107

Herrmann, Taffy
  See Herrmann, Dorothy

Hersey, John (Richard)
  1914-1993 .... **CLC 1, 2, 7, 9, 40, 81**
  See also CA 17-20R; 140; CANR 33;
  DLB 6; MTCW; SATA-Obit 25; SC 76

Herzen, Aleksandr Ivanovich
  1812-1870 .... **NCLC 10**

Herzog, Werner 1942-............. **CLC 16**
  See also CA 89-92

Hesiod c. 8th cent. B.C.-......... **CMLC 5**

Hesse, Hermann
  1877-1962 .... **CLC 1, 2, 3, 6, 11, 17, 25,
  69; DA**
  See also CA 17-18; CAP 2; DLB 66;
  MTCW; SATA-Obit 50; TCLC 9; YABC

Hewes, Cady
  See De Voto, Bernard (Augustine)

Heyen, William 1940- .... **CLC 13, 18**
  See also CA 33-36R; CAAS 9; DLB 5

Heyerdahl, Thor 1914-........... **CLC 26**
  See also CA 5-8R; CANR 5, 22; MTCW;
  SATA-Obit 2, 52

Heym, Stefan 1913-............. **CLC 41**
  See also CA 9-12R; CANR 4; DLB 69

Hibbert, Eleanor Alice Burford
  1906-1993 .... **CLC 7**
  See also BEST 90:4; CA 17-20R; 140;
  CANR 9, 28; SATA-Obit 2; SC 74

Higgins, George V(incent)
  1939-.............**CLC 4, 7, 10, 18**
  See also CA 77-80; CAAS 5; CANR 17;
  DLB 2; DLBY 81; MTCW

Highet, Helen
  See MacInnes, Helen (Clark)

Highsmith, (Mary) Patricia
  1921-............**CLC 2, 4, 14, 42**
  See also CA 1-4R; CANR 1, 20; MTCW

Highwater, Jamake (Mamake)
  1942(?)-..................... **CLC 12**
  See also AAYA 7; CA 65-68; CAAS 7;
  CANR 10, 34; CLR 17; DLB 52;
  DLBY 85; JRDA; MAICYA;
  SATA-Obit 30, 32, 69

Highway, Tomson 1951-............. **PC X**

Hijuelos, Oscar 1951- ...... **CLC 65; HLC**
  See also BEST 90:1; CA 123; HW

Hikmet, Nazim 1902(?)-1963....... **CLC 40**
  See also CA 141; 93-96

Hildesheimer, Wolfgang
  1916-1991 .... **CLC 49**
  See also CA 101; 135; DLB 69, 124

Hill, Geoffrey (William)
  1932-................**CLC 5, 8, 18, 45**
  See also CA 81-84; CANR 21;
  CDBLB 1960 to Present; DLB 40;
  MTCW

Hill, George Roy 1921-........... **CLC 26**
  See also CA 110; 122

Hill, John
  See Koontz, Dean R(ay)

Hill, Susan (Elizabeth) 1942- .... **CLC 4**
  See also CA 33-36R; CANR 29; DLB 14,
  139; MTCW

Hillerman, Tony 1925-............ **CLC 62**
  See also AAYA 6; BEST 89:1; CA 29-32R;
  CANR 21, 42; SATA-Obit 6

Hilliard, Noel (Harvey) 1929-...... **CLC 15**
  See also CA 9-12R; CANR 7

Hillis, Rick 1956-................ **CLC 66**
  See also CA 134

Himes, Chester (Bomar)
  1909-1984 .... **CLC 2, 4, 7, 18, 58; BLC**
  See also BW 2; CA 25-28R; 114; CANR 22;
  DLB 2, 76, 143; MTCW

Hinde, Thomas .... **CLC 6, 11**
  See also Chitty, Thomas Willes

Hindin, Nathan
  See Bloch, Robert (Albert)

Hine, (William) Daryl 1936-....... **CLC 15**
  See also CA 1-4R; CAAS 15; CANR 1, 20;
  DLB 60

Hinkson, Katharine Tynan
  See Tynan, Katharine

Hinton, S(usan) E(loise)
  1950- .... **CLC 30; DA**
  See also AAYA 2; CA 81-84; CANR 32;
  CLR 3, 23; JRDA; MAICYA; MTCW;
  SATA-Obit 19, 58

Hiraoka, Kimitake 1925-1970
  See Mishima, Yukio
  See also CA 97-100; 29-32R; MTCW

Hirsch, E(ric) D(onald), Jr. 1928-... **CLC 79**
  See also CA 25-28R; CANR 27; DLB 67;
  MTCW

Hirsch, Edward 1950- .... **CLC 31, 50**
  See also CA 104; CANR 20, 42; DLB 120

Hitchcock, Alfred (Joseph)
  1899-1980 .... **CLC 16**
  See also CA 97-100; SATA-Obit 24, 27

Hoagland, Edward 1932-.......... **CLC 28**
  See also CA 1-4R; CANR 2, 31; DLB 6;
  SATA-Obit 51

Hoban, Russell (Conwell) 1925- .. **CLC 7, 25**
  See also CA 5-8R; CANR 23, 37; CLR 3;
  DLB 52; MAICYA; MTCW;
  SATA-Obit 1, 40, 78

Hobbs, Perry
  See Blackmur, R(ichard) P(almer)

Hobson, Laura Z(ametkin)
  1900-1986 .... **CLC 7, 25**
  See also CA 17-20R; 118; DLB 28;
  SATA-Obit 52

Hochhuth, Rolf 1931-........ **CLC 4, 11, 18**
  See also CA 5-8R; CANR 33; DLB 124;
  MTCW

Hochman, Sandra 1936-.......... **CLC 3, 8**
  See also CA 5-8R; DLB 5

Hochwaelder, Fritz 1911-1986...... **CLC 36**
  See also CA 29-32R; 120; CANR 42;
  MTCW

Hochwalder, Fritz
  See Hochwaelder, Fritz

Hocking, Mary (Eunice) 1921-..... **CLC 13**
  See also CA 101; CANR 18, 40

Hodgins, Jack 1938-.............. **CLC 23**
  See also CA 93-96; DLB 60

Hoffman, Alice 1952-............. **CLC 51**
  See also CA 77-80; CANR 34; MTCW

Hoffman, Daniel (Gerard)
  1923-.................. **CLC 6, 13, 23**
  See also CA 1-4R; CANR 4; DLB 5

Hoffman, Stanley 1944-............ **CLC 5**
  See also CA 77-80

Hoffman, William M(oses) 1939- ... **CLC 40**
  See also CA 57-60; CANR 11

Hoffmann, E(rnst) T(heodor) A(madeus)
  1776-1822 .... **TCLC 13**
  See also DLB 90; NCLC 2; SATA-Obit 27

Hofmann, Gert 1931-............. **CLC 54**
  See also CA 128

Hofmannsthal, Hugo von 1874-1929... **DC 4**
  See also CA 106; DLB 81, 118; WLC 11

Hogan, Linda 1947-.............. **CLC 73**
  See also CA 120; CANR 45

Hogarth, Charles
  See Creasey, John

Joyce, James (Augustine Aloysius)
1882-1941 ..... **TCLC 3; DA; WLC 3, 8, 16, 35**
See also CA 104; 126; CDBLB 1914-1945; DLB 10, 19, 36; MTCW; YABC

Juana Ines de la Cruz 1651(?)-1695 ... **LC 5**

Judd, Cyril
See Kornbluth, C(yril) M.; Pohl, Frederik

Julian of Norwich 1342(?)-1416(?) .... **LC 6**

Just, Ward (Swift) 1935- .... **CLC 4, 27**
See also CA 25-28R; CANR 32

Justice, Donald (Rodney) 1925- .. **CLC 6, 19**
See also CA 5-8R; CANR 26; DLBY 83

Juvenal c. 55-c. 127 .... **CMLC 8**

Juvenis
See Bourne, Randolph S(illiman)

Kacew, Romain 1914-1980
See Gary, Romain
See also CA 108; 102

Kadare, Ismail 1936- .... **CLC 52**

Kadohata, Cynthia .... **CLC 59**
See also CA 140

Kafka, Franz
1883-1924 ..... **TCLC 5; DA; WLC 2, 6, 13, 29, 47, 53**
See also CA 105; 126; DLB 81; MTCW; YABC

Kahn, Roger 1927- .... **CLC 30**
See also CA 25-28R; CANR 44; SATA-Obit 37

Kain, Saul
See Sassoon, Siegfried (Lorraine)

Kaletski, Alexander 1946- .... **CLC 39**
See also CA 118; 143

Kalidasa fl. c. 400- .... **CMLC 9**

Kallman, Chester (Simon)
1921-1975 .... **CLC 2**
See also CA 45-48; 53-56; CANR 3

Kaminsky, Melvin 1926-
See Brooks, Mel
See also CA 65-68; CANR 16

Kaminsky, Stuart M(elvin) 1934- ... **CLC 59**
See also CA 73-76; CANR 29

Kane, Paul
See Simon, Paul

Kane, Wilson
See Bloch, Robert (Albert)

Kanin, Garson 1912- .... **CLC 22**
See also AITN 1; CA 5-8R; CANR 7; DLB 7

Kaniuk, Yoram 1930- .... **CLC 19**
See also CA 134

Kant, Immanuel 1724-1804 ...... **NCLC 27**
See also DLB 94

Kantor, MacKinlay 1904-1977 ...... **CLC 7**
See also CA 61-64; 73-76; DLB 9, 102

Kaplan, David Michael 1946- ...... **CLC 50**

Kaplan, James 1951- .... **CLC 59**
See also CA 135

Karageorge, Michael
See Anderson, Poul (William)

Karamzin, Nikolai Mikhailovich
1766-1826 .... **NCLC 3**

Karapanou, Margarita 1946- .... **CLC 13**
See also CA 101

Karl, Frederick R(obert) 1927- ..... **CLC 34**
See also CA 5-8R; CANR 3, 44

Kastel, Warren
See Silverberg, Robert

Kataev, Evgeny Petrovich 1903-1942
See Petrov, Evgeny
See also CA 120

Kataphusin
See Ruskin, John

Katz, Steve 1935- .... **CLC 47**
See also CA 25-28R; CAAS 14; CANR 12; DLBY 83

Kauffman, Janet 1945- .... **CLC 42**
See also CA 117; CANR 43; DLBY 86

Kaufman, Bob (Garnell)
1925-1986 .... **CLC 49**
See also BW 1; CA 41-44R; 118; CANR 22; DLB 16, 41

Kaufman, George S. 1889-1961 ..... **CLC 38**
See also CA 108; 93-96; DLB 7

Kaufman, Sue .... **CLC 3, 8**
See also Barondess, Sue K(aufman)

Kavafis, Konstantinos Petrou 1863-1933
See Cavafy, C(onstantine) P(eter)
See also CA 104

Kavan, Anna 1901-1968 ...... **CLC 5, 13, 82**
See also CA 5-8R; CANR 6; MTCW

Kavanagh, Dan
See Barnes, Julian

Kavanagh, Patrick (Joseph)
1904-1967 .... **CLC 22**
See also CA 123; 25-28R; DLB 15, 20; MTCW

Kawabata, Yasunari
1899-1972 .... **CLC 2, 5, 9, 18**
See also CA 93-96; 33-36R

Kaye, M(ary) M(argaret) 1909- ..... **CLC 28**
See also CA 89-92; CANR 24; MTCW; SATA-Obit 62

Kaye, Mollie
See Kaye, M(ary) M(argaret)

Kaymor, Patrice Maguilene
See Senghor, Leopold Sedar

Kazan, Elia 1909- .... **CLC 6, 16, 63**
See also CA 21-24R; CANR 32

Kazin, Alfred 1915- .... **CLC 34, 38**
See also CA 1-4R; CAAS 7; CANR 1, 45; DLB 67

Keane, Mary Nesta (Skrine) 1904-
See Keane, Molly
See also CA 108; 114

Keane, Molly .... **CLC 31**
See also Keane, Mary Nesta (Skrine)

Keates, Jonathan 19(?)- .... **CLC 34**

Keaton, Buster 1895-1966 .... **CLC 20**

Keats, John 1795-1821 ...... **NCLC 8; DA**
See also CDBLB 1789-1832; DLB 96, 110; SAAS 1; YABC

Keene, Donald 1922- .... **CLC 34**
See also CA 1-4R; CANR 5

Keillor, Garrison .... **CLC 40**
See also Keillor, Gary (Edward)
See also AAYA 2; BEST 89:3; DLBY 87; SATA-Obit 58

Keillor, Gary (Edward) 1942-
See Keillor, Garrison
See also CA 111; 117; CANR 36; MTCW

Keith, Michael
See Hubbard, L(afayette) Ron(ald)

Keller, Gottfried 1819-1890 ...... **NCLC 2**
See also DLB 129

Kellerman, Jonathan 1949- .... **CLC 44**
See also BEST 90:1; CA 106; CANR 29

Kelley, William Melvin 1937- ...... **CLC 22**
See also BW 1; CA 77-80; CANR 27; DLB 33

Kellogg, Marjorie 1922- .... **CLC 2**
See also CA 81-84

Kellow, Kathleen
See Hibbert, Eleanor Alice Burford

Kelly, M(ilton) T(erry) 1947- ...... **CLC 55**
See also CA 97-100; CANR 19, 43

Kelman, James 1946- .... **CLC 58**

Kemal, Yashar 1923- .... **CLC 14, 29**
See also CA 89-92; CANR 44

Kemble, Fanny 1809-1893 .... **NCLC 18**
See also DLB 32

Kemelman, Harry 1908- .... **CLC 2**
See also AITN 1; CA 9-12R; CANR 6; DLB 28

Kempe, Margery 1373(?)-1440(?) ..... **LC 6**

Kempis, Thomas a 1380-1471 .... **LC 11**

Kendall, Henry 1839-1882 .... **NCLC 12**

Keneally, Thomas (Michael)
1935- ...... **CLC 5, 8, 10, 14, 19, 27, 43**
See also CA 85-88; CANR 10; MTCW

Kennedy, Adrienne (Lita)
1931- .... **CLC 66; BLC**
See also BW 2; CA 103; CABS 3; CANR 26; DLB 38

Kennedy, John Pendleton
1795-1870 .... **NCLC 2**
See also DLB 3

Kennedy, Joseph Charles 1929- ...... **CLC 8**
See also Kennedy, X. J.
See also CA 1-4R; CANR 4, 30, 40; SATA-Obit 14

Kennedy, William 1928- ... **CLC 6, 28, 34, 53**
See also AAYA 1; CA 85-88; CANR 14, 31; DLB 143; DLBY 85; MTCW; SATA-Obit 57

Kennedy, X. J. .... **CLC 42**
See also Kennedy, Joseph Charles
See also CAAS 9; CLR 27; DLB 5

Kenny, Maurice 1929- .... **PC X**

Kent, Kelvin
See Kuttner, Henry

Kenton, Maxwell
See Southern, Terry

Kenyon, Robert O.
See Kuttner, Henry

Langland, William
1330(?)-1400(?) . . . . **LC 19; DA**

Langstaff, Launcelot
See Irving, Washington

Lanier, Sidney 1842-1881 . . . . **NCLC 6**
See also DLB 64; MAICYA; SATA-Obit 18

Lanyer, Aemilia 1569-1645 . . . . **LC 10**

Lao Tzu . . . . **CMLC 7**

Lapine, James (Elliot) 1949- . . . . **CLC 39**
See also CA 123; 130

Lardner, Ring
See Lardner, Ring(gold) W(ilmer)

Lardner, Ring W., Jr.
See Lardner, Ring(gold) W(ilmer)

Laredo, Betty
See Codrescu, Andrei

Larkin, Maia
See Wojciechowska, Maia (Teresa)

Larkin, Philip (Arthur)
1922-1985 . . . . **CLC 3, 5, 8, 9, 13, 18, 33,**
39, 64
See also CA 5-8R; 117; CANR 24;
CDBLB 1960 to Present; DLB 27;
MTCW

Larra (y Sanchez de Castro), Mariano Jose de
1809-1837 . . . . **NCLC 17**

Larsen, Eric 1941- . . . . **CLC 55**
See also CA 132

Larsen, Nella 1891-1964 . . . . . **CLC 37; BLC**
See also BW 1; CA 125; DLB 51

Larson, Charles R(aymond) 1938-. . . **CLC 31**
See also CA 53-56; CANR 4

Latham, Jean Lee 1902-. . . . . **CLC 12**
See also AITN 1; CA 5-8R; CANR 7;
MAICYA; SATA-Obit 2, 68

Latham, Mavis
See Clark, Mavis Thorpe

Lathen, Emma . . . . **CLC 2**
See also Hennissart, Martha; Latsis, Mary
J(ane)

Lathrop, Francis
See Leiber, Fritz (Reuter, Jr.)

Latsis, Mary J(ane)
See Lathen, Emma
See also CA 85-88

Lattimore, Richmond (Alexander)
1906-1984 . . . . **CLC 3**
See also CA 1-4R; 112; CANR 1

Laughlin, James 1914- . . . . **CLC 49**
See also CA 21-24R; CANR 9; DLB 48

Laurence, (Jean) Margaret (Wemyss)
1926-1987 . . . . **CLC 3, 6, 13, 50, 62**
See also CA 5-8R; 121; CANR 33; DLB 53;
MTCW; SATA-Obit 50; TCLC 7

Laurent, Antoine 1952- . . . . **CLC 50**

Lauscher, Hermann
See Hesse, Hermann

Lautreamont, Comte de
1846-1870 . . . . **TCLC 14**
See also NCLC 12

Laverty, Donald
See Blish, James (Benjamin)

Lavin, Mary 1912- . . . . **CLC 4, 18**
See also CA 9-12R; CANR 33; DLB 15;
MTCW; TCLC 4

Lavond, Paul Dennis
See Kornbluth, C(yril) M.; Pohl, Frederik

Lawler, Raymond Evenor 1922- . . . . **CLC 58**
See also CA 103

Lawrence, D(avid) H(erbert Richards)
1885-1930 . . . . . **TCLC 4; DA; WLC 2, 9,**
16, 33, 48
See also CA 104; 121; CDBLB 1914-1945;
DLB 10, 19, 36, 98; MTCW; YABC

Lawrence, T(homas) E(dward) 1888-1935
See Dale, Colin
See also CA 115; WLC 18

Lawrence of Arabia
See Lawrence, T(homas) E(dward)

Lawton, Dennis
See Faust, Frederick (Schiller)

Laxness, Halldor . . . . **CLC 25**
See also Gudjonsson, Halldor Kiljan

Layamon fl. c. 1200- . . . . **CMLC 10**

Laye, Camara 1928-1980 . . . **CLC 4, 38; BLC**
See also BW 1; CA 85-88; 97-100;
CANR 25; MTCW

Layton, Irving (Peter) 1912- . . . . . **CLC 2, 15**
See also CA 1-4R; CANR 2, 33, 43;
DLB 88; MTCW

Lazarus, Emma 1849-1887. . . . . . . **NCLC 8**

Lazarus, Felix
See Cable, George Washington

Lazarus, Henry
See Slavitt, David R(ytman)

Lea, Joan
See Neufeld, John (Arthur)

Lear, Edward 1812-1888 . . . . **NCLC 3**
See also CLR 1; DLB 32; MAICYA;
SATA-Obit 18

Lear, Norman (Milton) 1922- . . . . . . **CLC 12**
See also CA 73-76

Leavis, F(rank) R(aymond)
1895-1978 . . . . **CLC 24**
See also CA 21-24R; 77-80; CANR 44;
MTCW

Leavitt, David 1961- . . . . **CLC 34**
See also CA 116; 122; DLB 130

Lebowitz, Fran(ces Ann)
1951(?)- . . . . **CLC 11, 36**
See also CA 81-84; CANR 14; MTCW

le Carre, John . . . . **CLC 3, 5, 9, 15, 28**
See also Cornwell, David (John Moore)
See also BEST 89:4; CDBLB 1960 to
Present; DLB 87

Le Clezio, J(ean) M(arie) G(ustave)
1940- . . . . **CLC 31**
See also CA 116; 128; DLB 83

Leconte de Lisle, Charles-Marie-Rene
1818-1894 . . . . **NCLC 29**

Le Coq, Monsieur
See Simenon, Georges (Jacques Christian)

Leduc, Violette 1907-1972. . . . . **CLC 22**
See also CA 13-14; 33-36R; CAP 1

Lee, Andrea 1953- . . . . **CLC 36; BLC**
See also BW 1; CA 125

Lee, Andrew
See Auchincloss, Louis (Stanton)

Lee, Don L. . . . . **CLC 2**
See also Madhubuti, Haki R.

Lee, George W(ashington)
1894-1976 . . . . **CLC 52; BLC**
See also BW 1; CA 125; DLB 51

Lee, (Nelle) Harper
1926- . . . . **CLC 12, 60; DA**
See also CA 13-16R; CDALB 1941-1968;
DLB 6; MTCW; SATA-Obit 11; YABC

Lee, Julian
See Latham, Jean Lee

Lee, Larry
See Lee, Lawrence

Lee, Lawrence 1941-1990. . . . . **CLC 34**
See also CA 131; CANR 43

Lee, Manfred B(ennington)
1905-1971 . . . . **CLC 11**
See also Queen, Ellery
See also CA 1-4R; 29-32R; CANR 2;
DLB 137

Lee, Stan 1922-. . . . . **CLC 17**
See also AAYA 5; CA 108; 111

Lee, Tanith 1947- . . . . **CLC 46**
See also CA 37-40R; SATA-Obit 8

Lee, William
See Burroughs, William S(eward)

Lee, Willy
See Burroughs, William S(eward)

Leet, Judith 1935- . . . . **CLC 11**

Le Fanu, Joseph Sheridan
1814-1873 . . . . **TCLC 14**
See also DLB 21, 70; NCLC 9

Leffland, Ella 1931- . . . . **CLC 19**
See also CA 29-32R; CANR 35; DLBY 84;
SATA-Obit 65

Leger, Alexis
See Leger, (Marie-Rene Auguste) Alexis
Saint-Leger

Leger, (Marie-Rene Auguste) Alexis
Saint-Leger 1887-1975. . . . . **CLC 11**
See also Perse, St.-John
See also CA 13-16R; 61-64; CANR 43;
MTCW

Leger, Saintleger
See Leger, (Marie-Rene Auguste) Alexis
Saint-Leger

Le Guin, Ursula K(roeber)
1929- . . . . **CLC 8, 13, 22, 45, 71**
See also AAYA 9; AITN 1; CA 21-24R;
CANR 9, 32; CDALB 1968-1988; CLR 3,
28; DLB 8, 52; JRDA; MAICYA;
MTCW; SATA-Obit 4, 52; TCLC 12

Lehmann, Rosamond (Nina)
1901-1990 . . . . **CLC 5**
See also CA 77-80; 131; CANR 8; DLB 15

Leiber, Fritz (Reuter, Jr.)
1910-1992 . . . . **CLC 25**
See also CA 45-48; 139; CANR 2, 40;
DLB 8; MTCW; SATA-Obit 45; SC 73

Leimbach, Martha 1963-
See Leimbach, Marti
See also CA 130

Leimbach, Marti .... **CLC 65**
  See also Leimbach, Martha

Leiris, Michel (Julien) 1901-1990 ... **CLC 61**
  See also CA 119; 128; 132

Leithauser, Brad 1953- .... **CLC 27**
  See also CA 107; CANR 27; DLB 120

Lelchuk, Alan 1938- .... **CLC 5**
  See also CA 45-48; CANR 1

Lem, Stanislaw 1921- .... **CLC 8, 15, 40**
  See also CA 105; CAAS 1; CANR 32;
    MTCW

Lemann, Nancy 1956- .... **CLC 39**
  See also CA 118; 136

Lenau, Nikolaus 1802-1850 ...... **NCLC 16**

L'Engle, Madeleine (Camp Franklin)
  1918- .... **CLC 12**
  See also AAYA 1; AITN 2; CA 1-4R;
    CANR 3, 21, 39; CLR 1, 14; DLB 52;
    JRDA; MAICYA; MTCW; SATA 15;
    SATA-Obit 1, 27, 75

Lengyel, Jozsef 1896-1975 .... **CLC 7**
  See also CA 85-88; 57-60

Lennon, John (Ono)
  1940-1980 .... **CLC 12, 35**
  See also CA 102

Lennox, Charlotte Ramsay
  1729(?)-1804 .... **NCLC 23**
  See also DLB 39

Lentricchia, Frank (Jr.) 1940- ...... **CLC 34**
  See also CA 25-28R; CANR 19

Lenz, Siegfried 1926- .... **CLC 27**
  See also CA 89-92; DLB 75

Leonard, Elmore (John, Jr.)
  1925- .... **CLC 28, 34, 71**
  See also AITN 1; BEST 89:1, 90:4;
    CA 81-84; CANR 12, 28; MTCW

Leonard, Hugh
  See Byrne, John Keyes
  See also DLB 13

Leopardi, (Conte) Giacomo (Talegardo
    Francesco di Sales Save
  1798-1837 .... **NCLC 22**

Le Reveler
  See Artaud, Antonin

Lerman, Eleanor 1952- .... **CLC 9**
  See also CA 85-88

Lerman, Rhoda 1936- .... **CLC 56**
  See also CA 49-52

Lermontov, Mikhail Yuryevich
  1814-1841 .... **NCLC 5**

Lesage, Alain-Rene 1668-1747........ **LC 2**

Leskov, Nikolai (Semyonovich)
  1831-1895 .... **NCLC 25**

Lessing, Doris (May)
  1919- ..... **CLC 1, 2, 3, 6, 10, 15, 22, 40;**
    DA
  See also CA 9-12R; CAAS 14; CANR 33;
    CDBLB 1960 to Present; DLB 15, 139;
    DLBY 85; MTCW; TCLC 6

Lessing, Gotthold Ephraim
  1729-1781 .... **LC 8**
  See also DLB 97

Lester, Richard 1932- .... **CLC 20**

Lever, Charles (James)
  1806-1872 .... **NCLC 23**
  See also DLB 21

Leverson, Ada 1865(?)-1936(?)
  See Elaine
  See also CA 117; WLC 18

Levertov, Denise
  1923- ...... **CLC 1, 2, 3, 5, 8, 15, 28, 66**
  See also CA 1-4R; CAAS 19; CANR 3, 29;
    DLB 5; MTCW

Levi, Jonathan .... **CLC 76**

Levi, Peter (Chad Tigar) 1931- ..... **CLC 41**
  See also CA 5-8R; CANR 34; DLB 40

Levi, Primo 1919-1987 .... **CLC 37, 50**
  See also CA 13-16R; 122; CANR 12, 33;
    MTCW; TCLC 12

Levin, Ira 1929- .... **CLC 3, 6**
  See also CA 21-24R; CANR 17, 44;
    MTCW; SATA-Obit 66

Levin, Meyer 1905-1981 .... **CLC 7**
  See also AITN 1; CA 9-12R; 104;
    CANR 15; DLB 9, 28; DLBY 81;
    SATA-Obit 21, 27

Levine, Norman 1924- .... **CLC 54**
  See also CA 73-76; CANR 14; DLB 88

Levine, Philip 1928-.. **CLC 2, 4, 5, 9, 14, 33**
  See also CA 9-12R; CANR 9, 37; DLB 5

Levinson, Deirdre 1931- .... **CLC 49**
  See also CA 73-76

Levi-Strauss, Claude 1908- .... **CLC 38**
  See also CA 1-4R; CANR 6, 32; MTCW

Levitin, Sonia (Wolff) 1934- .... **CLC 17**
  See also CA 29-32R; CANR 14, 32; JRDA;
    MAICYA; SATA 2; SATA-Obit 4, 68

Levon, O. U.
  See Kesey, Ken (Elton)

Lewes, George Henry
  1817-1878 .... **NCLC 25**
  See also DLB 55, 144

Lewis, C. Day
  See Day Lewis, C(ecil)

Lewis, C(live) S(taples)
  1898-1963 ..... **CLC 1, 3, 6, 14, 27; DA**
  See also AAYA 3; CA 81-84; CANR 33;
    CDBLB 1945-1960; CLR 3, 27; DLB 15,
    100; JRDA; MAICYA; MTCW;
    SATA-Obit 13; YABC

Lewis, Janet 1899- .... **CLC 41**
  See also Winters, Janet Lewis
  See also CA 9-12R; CANR 29; CAP 1;
    DLBY 87

Lewis, Matthew Gregory
  1775-1818 .... **NCLC 11**
  See also DLB 39

Lezama Lima, Jose 1910-1976 ... **CLC 4, 10**
  See also CA 77-80; DLB 113; HW

L'Heureux, John (Clarke) 1934-.... **CLC 52**
  See also CA 13-16R; CANR 23, 45

Liddell, C. H.
  See Kuttner, Henry

Lieber, Joel 1937-1971............. **CLC 6**
  See also CA 73-76; 29-32R

Lieber, Stanley Martin
  See Lee, Stan

Lieberman, Laurence (James)
  1935- .... **CLC 4, 36**
  See also CA 17-20R; CANR 8, 36

Lieksman, Anders
  See Haavikko, Paavo Juhani

Li Fei-kan 1904- .... **CLC 18**
  See also CA 105

Lifton, Robert Jay 1926- .... **CLC 67**
  See also CA 17-20R; CANR 27;
    SATA-Obit 66

Lightfoot, Gordon 1938- .... **CLC 26**
  See also CA 109

Lightman, Alan P. 1948- .... **CLC 81**
  See also CA 141

Ligotti, Thomas 1953- .... **CLC 44**
  See also CA 123; TCLC 16

Lima, Jose Lezama
  See Lezama Lima, Jose

Limonov, Eduard .... **CLC 67**

Lin, Frank
  See Atherton, Gertrude (Franklin Horn)

Lincoln, Abraham 1809-1865..... **NCLC 18**

Lind, Jakov .... **CLC 1, 2, 4, 27, 82**
  See also Landwirth, Heinz
  See also CAAS 4

Lindbergh, Anne (Spencer) Morrow
  1906- .... **CLC 82**
  See also CA 17-20R; CANR 16; MTCW;
    SATA-Obit 33

Linke-Poot
  See Doeblin, Alfred

Linney, Romulus 1930- .... **CLC 51**
  See also CA 1-4R; CANR 40, 44

Linton, Eliza Lynn 1822-1898.... **NCLC 41**
  See also DLB 18

Li Po 701-763 .... **CMLC 2**

Lipsius, Justus 1547-1606 .... **LC 16**

Lipsyte, Robert (Michael)
  1938- .... **CLC 21; DA**
  See also AAYA 7; CA 17-20R; CANR 8;
    CLR 23; JRDA; MAICYA;
    SATA-Obit 5, 68

Lish, Gordon (Jay) 1934- .... **CLC 45**
  See also CA 113; 117; DLB 130

Lispector, Clarice 1925-1977....... **CLC 43**
  See also CA 139; 116; DLB 113

Littell, Robert 1935(?)- .... **CLC 42**
  See also CA 109; 112

Little, Malcolm 1925-1965
  See Malcolm X
  See also BW 1; CA 125; 111; DA; MTCW

Littlewit, Humphrey Gent.
  See Lovecraft, H(oward) P(hillips)

Litwos
  See Sienkiewicz, Henryk (Adam Alexander
    Pius)

Lively, Penelope (Margaret)
  1933- .... **CLC 32, 50**
  See also CA 41-44R; CANR 29; CLR 7;
    DLB 14; JRDA; MAICYA; MTCW;
    SATA-Obit 7, 60

MacBeth, George (Mann)
1932-1992 . . . . CLC **2, 5, 9**
See also CA 25-28R; 136; DLB 40; MTCW;
SATA-Obit 4; SC 70

MacCaig, Norman (Alexander)
1910- . . . . CLC **36**
See also CA 9-12R; CANR 3, 34; DLB 27

MacDiarmid, Hugh . . . . . CLC **2, 4, 11, 19, 63**
See also Grieve, C(hristopher) M(urray)
See also CDBLB 1945-1960; DLB 20;
SAAS 9

MacDonald, Anson
See Heinlein, Robert A(nson)

Macdonald, Cynthia 1928- . . . . . . CLC **13, 19**
See also CA 49-52; CANR 4, 44; DLB 105

Macdonald, John
See Millar, Kenneth

MacDonald, John D(ann)
1916-1986 . . . . CLC **3, 27, 44**
See also CA 1-4R; 121; CANR 1, 19;
DLB 8; DLBY 86; MTCW

Macdonald, John Ross
See Millar, Kenneth

Macdonald, Ross . . . . . CLC **1, 2, 3, 14, 34, 41**
See also Millar, Kenneth
See also DLBD 6

MacDougal, John
See Blish, James (Benjamin)

MacEwen, Gwendolyn (Margaret)
1941-1987 . . . . CLC **13, 55**
See also CA 9-12R; 124; CANR 7, 22;
DLB 53; SATA-Obit 50, 55

Machiavelli, Niccolo 1469-1527 . . LC **8; DA**

MacInnes, Colin 1914-1976 . . . . . . CLC **4, 23**
See also CA 69-72; 65-68; CANR 21;
DLB 14; MTCW

MacInnes, Helen (Clark)
1907-1985 . . . . CLC **27, 39**
See also CA 1-4R; 117; CANR 1, 28;
DLB 87; MTCW; SATA-Obit 22, 44

Mackay, Mary 1855-1924
See Corelli, Marie
See also CA 118

Mackenzie, Compton (Edward Montague)
1883-1972 . . . . CLC **18**
See also CA 21-22; 37-40R; CAP 2;
DLB 34, 100

Mackenzie, Henry 1745-1831 . . . . NCLC **41**
See also DLB 39

Mackintosh, Elizabeth 1896(?)-1952
See Tey, Josephine
See also CA 110

MacLaren, James
See Grieve, C(hristopher) M(urray)

Mac Laverty, Bernard 1942- . . . . CLC **31**
See also CA 116; 118; CANR 43

MacLean, Alistair (Stuart)
1922-1987 . . . . CLC **3, 13, 50, 63**
See also CA 57-60; 121; CANR 28; MTCW;
SATA-Obit 23, 50

Maclean, Norman (Fitzroy)
1902-1990 . . . . CLC **78**
See also CA 102; 132; TCLC 13

MacLeish, Archibald
1892-1982 . . . . CLC **3, 8, 14, 68**
See also CA 9-12R; 106; CANR 33; DLB 4,
7, 45; DLBY 82; MTCW

MacLennan, (John) Hugh
1907-1990 . . . . CLC **2, 14**
See also CA 5-8R; 142; CANR 33; DLB 68;
MTCW

MacLeod, Alistair 1936- . . . . CLC **56**
See also CA 123; DLB 60

MacNeice, (Frederick) Louis
1907-1963 . . . . CLC **1, 4, 10, 53**
See also CA 85-88; DLB 10, 20; MTCW

MacNeill, Dand
See Fraser, George MacDonald

Macpherson, (Jean) Jay 1931- . . . . . . CLC **14**
See also CA 5-8R; DLB 53

MacShane, Frank 1927- . . . . CLC **39**
See also CA 9-12R; CANR 3, 33; DLB 111

Macumber, Mari
See Sandoz, Mari(e Susette)

Madach, Imre 1823-1864 . . . . NCLC **19**

Madden, (Jerry) David 1933- . . . . CLC **5, 15**
See also CA 1-4R; CAAS 3; CANR 4, 45;
DLB 6; MTCW

Maddern, Al(an)
See Ellison, Harlan

Madhubuti, Haki R.
1942- . . . . CLC **6, 73; BLC**
See also Lee, Don L.
See also BW 2; CA 73-76; CANR 24;
DLB 5, 41; DLBD 8; SAAS 5

Madow, Pauline (Reichberg) . . . . CLC **1**
See also CA 9-12R

Maepenn, Hugh
See Kuttner, Henry

Maepenn, K. H.
See Kuttner, Henry

Maginn, William 1794-1842 . . . . . . NCLC **8**
See also DLB 110

Mahapatra, Jayanta 1928- . . . . CLC **33**
See also CA 73-76; CAAS 9; CANR 15, 33

Mahfouz, Naguib (Abdel Aziz Al-Sabilgi)
1911(?)-
See Mahfuz, Najib
See also BEST 89:2; CA 128; MTCW

Mahfuz, Najib . . . . CLC **52, 55**
See also Mahfouz, Naguib (Abdel Aziz
Al-Sabilgi)
See also DLBY 88

Mahon, Derek 1941- . . . . CLC **27**
See also CA 113; 128; DLB 40

Mailer, Norman
1923- . . . . . . CLC **1, 2, 3, 4, 5, 8, 11, 14,
28, 39, 74; DA**
See also AITN 2; CA 9-12R; CABS 1;
CANR 28; CDALB 1968-1988; DLB 2,
16, 28; DLBD 3; DLBY 80, 83; MTCW

Maillet, Antonine 1929- . . . . CLC **54**
See also CA 115; 120; DLB 60

Maistre, Joseph de 1753-1821 . . . . NCLC **37**

Maitland, Sara (Louise) 1950- . . . . . . CLC **49**
See also CA 69-72; CANR 13

Major, Clarence
1936- . . . . CLC **3, 19, 48; BLC**
See also BW 2; CA 21-24R; CAAS 6;
CANR 13, 25; DLB 33

Major, Kevin (Gerald) 1949- . . . . CLC **26**
See also CA 97-100; CANR 21, 38;
CLR 11; DLB 60; JRDA; MAICYA;
SATA-Obit 32

Maki, James
See Ozu, Yasujiro

Malabaila, Damiano
See Levi, Primo

Malamud, Bernard
1914-1986 . . . . . . CLC **1, 2, 3, 5, 8, 9, 11,
18, 27, 44, 78; DA**
See also CA 5-8R; 118; CABS 1; CANR 28;
CDALB 1941-1968; DLB 2, 28;
DLBY 80, 86; MTCW; TCLC 15; YABC

Malcolm, Dan
See Silverberg, Robert

Malcolm X . . . . CLC **82; BLC**
See also Little, Malcolm

Malherbe, Francois de 1555-1628 . . . . . LC **5**

Mallarme, Stephane
1842-1898 . . . . NCLC **4, 41**
See also SAAS 4

Mallet-Joris, Francoise 1930- . . . . . . CLC **11**
See also CA 65-68; CANR 17; DLB 83

Malley, Ern
See McAuley, James Phillip

Mallowan, Agatha Christie
See Christie, Agatha (Mary Clarissa)

Maloff, Saul 1922- . . . . CLC **5**
See also CA 33-36R

Malone, Louis
See MacNeice, (Frederick) Louis

Malone, Michael (Christopher)
1942- . . . . CLC **43**
See also CA 77-80; CANR 14, 32

Malory, (Sir) Thomas
1410(?)-1471(?) . . . . LC **11; DA**
See also CDBLB Before 1660;
SATA-Obit 33, 59

Malouf, (George Joseph) David
1934- . . . . CLC **28**
See also CA 124

Malraux, (Georges-)Andre
1901-1976 . . . . . . CLC **1, 4, 9, 13, 15, 57**
See also CA 21-22; 69-72; CANR 34;
CAP 2; DLB 72; MTCW

Malzberg, Barry N(athaniel) 1939- . . . CLC **7**
See also CA 61-64; CAAS 4; CANR 16;
DLB 8

Mamet, David (Alan)
1947- . . . . CLC **9, 15, 34, 46; DC 4**
See also AAYA 3; CA 81-84; CABS 3;
CANR 15, 41; DLB 7; MTCW

Mamoulian, Rouben (Zachary)
1897-1987 . . . . CLC **16**
See also CA 25-28R; 124

Mandiargues, Andre Pieyre de . . . . . . CLC **41**
See also Pieyre de Mandiargues, Andre
See also DLB 83

Mandrake, Ethel Belle
See Thurman, Wallace (Henry)

Mangan, James Clarence
1803-1849 . . . . NCLC 27

Maniere, J.-E.
See Giraudoux, (Hippolyte) Jean

Manley, (Mary) Delariviere
1672(?)-1724 . . . . LC 1
See also DLB 39, 80

Mann, Abel
See Creasey, John

Mann, (Paul) Thomas
1875-1955 . . . . . TCLC 5; DA; WLC 2, 8,
14, 21, 35, 44
See also CA 104; 128; DLB 66; MTCW;
YABC

Manning, David
See Faust, Frederick (Schiller)

Manning, Olivia 1915-1980 . . . . . . CLC 5, 19
See also CA 5-8R; 101; CANR 29; MTCW

Mano, D. Keith 1942- . . . . CLC 2, 10
See also CA 25-28R; CAAS 6; CANR 26;
DLB 6

Mansfield, Katherine
. . . . TCLC 9; WLC 2, 8, 39
See also Beauchamp, Kathleen Mansfield
See also YABC

Manso, Peter 1940- . . . . CLC 39
See also CA 29-32R; CANR 44

Mantecon, Juan Jimenez
See Jimenez (Mantecon), Juan Ramon

Manton, Peter
See Creasey, John

Man Without a Spleen, A
See Chekhov, Anton (Pavlovich)

Manzoni, Alessandro 1785-1873 . . NCLC 29

Mapu, Abraham (ben Jekutiel)
1808-1867 . . . . NCLC 18

Mara, Sally
See Queneau, Raymond

Maracle, Lee 1950- . . . . PC X

Marat, Jean Paul 1743-1793 . . . . LC 10

Marcel, Gabriel Honore
1889-1973 . . . . CLC 15
See also CA 102; 45-48; MTCW

Marchbanks, Samuel
See Davies, (William) Robertson

Marchi, Giacomo
See Bassani, Giorgio

Margulies, Donald . . . . CLC 76

Marie de France c. 12th cent. - . . . . CMLC 8

Marie de l'Incarnation 1599-1672 . . . . LC 10

Mariner, Scott
See Pohl, Frederik

Marivaux, Pierre Carlet de Chamblain de
1688-1763 . . . . LC 4

Markandaya, Kamala . . . . CLC 8, 38
See also Taylor, Kamala (Purnaiya)

Markfield, Wallace 1926- . . . . CLC 8
See also CA 69-72; CAAS 3; DLB 2, 28

Markham, Robert
See Amis, Kingsley (William)

Marks, J
See Highwater, Jamake (Mamake)

Marks-Highwater, J
See Highwater, Jamake (Mamake)

Markson, David M(errill) 1927- . . . . CLC 67
See also CA 49-52; CANR 1

Marley, Bob . . . . CLC 17
See also Marley, Robert Nesta

Marley, Robert Nesta 1945-1981
See Marley, Bob
See also CA 107; 103

Marlowe, Christopher
1564-1593 . . . . LC 22; DA; DC 1
See also CDBLB Before 1660; DLB 62;
YABC

Marmontel, Jean-Francois
1723-1799 . . . . LC 2

Marquand, John P(hillips)
1893-1960 . . . . CLC 2, 10
See also CA 85-88; DLB 9, 102

Marquez, Gabriel (Jose) Garcia . . . . . CLC 68
See also Garcia Marquez, Gabriel (Jose)

Marric, J. J.
See Creasey, John

Marrow, Bernard
See Moore, Brian

Marryat, Frederick 1792-1848 . . . . NCLC 3
See also DLB 21

Marsden, James
See Creasey, John

Marsh, (Edith) Ngaio
1899-1982 . . . . CLC 7, 53
See also CA 9-12R; CANR 6; DLB 77;
MTCW

Marshall, Garry 1934- . . . . CLC 17
See also AAYA 3; CA 111; SATA-Obit 60

Marshall, Paule 1929- . . . . CLC 27, 72; BLC
See also BW 2; CA 77-80; CANR 25;
DLB 33; MTCW; TCLC 3

Marsten, Richard
See Hunter, Evan

Martha, Henry
See Harris, Mark

Martin, Ken
See Hubbard, L(afayette) Ron(ald)

Martin, Richard
See Creasey, John

Martin, Steve 1945- . . . . CLC 30
See also CA 97-100; CANR 30; MTCW

Martin, Webber
See Silverberg, Robert

Martindale, Patrick Victor
See White, Patrick (Victor Martindale)

Martineau, Harriet 1802-1876 . . . . NCLC 26
See also DLB 21, 55; 2

Martines, Julia
See O'Faolain, Julia

Martinez, Jacinto Benavente y
See Benavente (y Martinez), Jacinto

Martinez Ruiz, Jose 1873-1967
See Azorin; Ruiz, Jose Martinez
See also CA 93-96; HW

Martinsen, Martin
See Follett, Ken(neth Martin)

Martinson, Harry (Edmund)
1904-1978 . . . . CLC 14
See also CA 77-80; CANR 34

Marut, Ret
See Traven, B.

Marut, Robert
See Traven, B.

Marvell, Andrew 1621-1678 . . . . . . LC 4; DA
See also CDBLB 1660-1789; DLB 131;
SAAS 10; YABC

Marx, Karl (Heinrich)
1818-1883 . . . . NCLC 17
See also DLB 129

Masaoka Tsunenori 1867-1902
See Masaoka Shiki
See also CA 117

Masefield, John (Edward)
1878-1967 . . . . CLC 11, 47
See also CA 19-20; 25-28R; CANR 33;
CAP 2; CDBLB 1890-1914; DLB 10;
MTCW; SATA-Obit 19

Maso, Carole 19(?)- . . . . CLC 44

Mason, Bobbie Ann 1940- . . . CLC 28, 43, 82
See also AAYA 5; CA 53-56; CANR 11,
31; DLBY 87; MTCW; TCLC 4

Mason, Ernst
See Pohl, Frederik

Mason, Lee W.
See Malzberg, Barry N(athaniel)

Mason, Nick 1945- . . . . CLC 35
See also Pink Floyd

Mason, Tally
See Derleth, August (William)

Mass, William
See Gibson, William

Masters, Hilary 1928- . . . . CLC 48
See also CA 25-28R; CANR 13

Mastrosimone, William 19(?)- . . . . . . CLC 36

Mathe, Albert
See Camus, Albert

Matheson, Richard Burton 1926- . . . CLC 37
See also CA 97-100; DLB 8, 44

Mathews, Harry 1930- . . . . CLC 6, 52
See also CA 21-24R; CAAS 6; CANR 18,
40

Mathews, John Joseph 1894-1979 . . . CLC 84
See also CA 19-20; 142; CANR 45; CAP 2

Mathias, Roland (Glyn) 1915- . . . . . . CLC 45
See also CA 97-100; CANR 19, 41; DLB 27

Mattheson, Rodney
See Creasey, John

Matthews, Greg 1949- . . . . CLC 45
See also CA 135

Matthews, William 1942- . . . . CLC 40
See also CA 29-32R; CAAS 18; CANR 12;
DLB 5

Matthias, John (Edward) 1941- . . . . . . CLC 9
See also CA 33-36R

Matthiessen, Peter
1927- . . . . CLC 5, 7, 11, 32, 64
See also AAYA 6; BEST 90:4; CA 9-12R;
CANR 21; DLB 6; MTCW;
SATA-Obit 27

Maturin, Charles Robert
1780(?)-1824 . . . . NCLC **6**

Matute (Ausejo), Ana Maria
1925- . . . . CLC **11**
See also CA 89-92; MTCW

Maugham, W. S.
See Maugham, W(illiam) Somerset

Maugham, W(illiam) Somerset
1874-1965 . . . . . . CLC **1, 11, 15, 67; DA**
See also CA 5-8R; 25-28R; CANR 40;
CDBLB 1914-1945; DLB 10, 36, 77, 100;
MTCW; SATA-Obit 54; TCLC 8; YABC

Maugham, William Somerset
See Maugham, W(illiam) Somerset

Maupassant, (Henri Rene Albert) Guy de
1850-1893 . . . . TCLC **1; DA**
See also DLB 123; NCLC 1, 42; YABC

Maurhut, Richard
See Traven, B.

Mauriac, Claude 1914- . . . . CLC **9**
See also CA 89-92; DLB 83

Mauriac, Francois (Charles)
1885-1970 . . . . CLC **4, 9, 56**
See also CA 25-28; CAP 2; DLB 65;
MTCW

Mavor, Osborne Henry 1888-1951
See Bridie, James
See also CA 104

Maxwell, William (Keepers, Jr.)
1908- . . . . CLC **19**
See also CA 93-96; DLBY 80

May, Elaine 1932- . . . . CLC **16**
See also CA 124; 142; DLB 44

Mayhew, Henry 1812-1887 . . . . . . NCLC **31**
See also DLB 18, 55

Maynard, Joyce 1953- . . . . CLC **23**
See also CA 111; 129

Mayne, William (James Carter)
1928- . . . . CLC **12**
See also CA 9-12R; CANR 37; CLR 25;
JRDA; MAICYA; SATA 11;
SATA-Obit 6, 68

Mayo, Jim
See L'Amour, Louis (Dearborn)

Maysles, Albert 1926- . . . . CLC **16**
See also CA 29-32R

Maysles, David 1932- . . . . CLC **16**

Mazer, Norma Fox 1931- . . . . CLC **26**
See also AAYA 5; CA 69-72; CANR 12,
32; CLR 23; JRDA; MAICYA; SATA 1;
SATA-Obit 24, 67

Mazzini, Guiseppe 1805-1872 . . . . NCLC **34**

McAuley, James Phillip
1917-1976 . . . . CLC **45**
See also CA 97-100

McBain, Ed
See Hunter, Evan

McBrien, William Augustine
1930- . . . . CLC **44**
See also CA 107

McCaffrey, Anne (Inez) 1926- . . . . . . CLC **17**
See also AAYA 6; AITN 2; BEST 89:2;
CA 25-28R; CANR 15, 35; DLB 8;
JRDA; MAICYA; MTCW; SATA 11;
SATA-Obit 8, 70

McCann, Arthur
See Campbell, John W(ood, Jr.)

McCann, Edson
See Pohl, Frederik

McCarthy, Charles, Jr. 1933-
See McCarthy, Cormac
See also CANR 42

McCarthy, Cormac 1933- . . . . CLC **4, 57**
See also McCarthy, Charles, Jr.
See also DLB 6, 143

McCarthy, Mary (Therese)
1912-1989 . . . CLC **1, 3, 5, 14, 24, 39, 59**
See also CA 5-8R; 129; CANR 16; DLB 2;
DLBY 81; MTCW

McCartney, (James) Paul
1942- . . . . CLC **12, 35**

McCauley, Stephen (D.) 1955- . . . . . CLC **50**
See also CA 141

McClure, Michael (Thomas)
1932- . . . . CLC **6, 10**
See also CA 21-24R; CANR 17; DLB 16

McCorkle, Jill (Collins) 1958- . . . . . . CLC **51**
See also CA 121; DLBY 87

McCourt, James 1941- . . . . CLC **5**
See also CA 57-60

McCreigh, James
See Pohl, Frederik

McCullers, (Lula) Carson (Smith)
1917-1967 . . . . CLC **1, 4, 10, 12, 48; DA**
See also CA 5-8R; 25-28R; CABS 1, 3;
CANR 18; CDALB 1941-1968; DLB 2, 7;
MTCW; SATA-Obit 27; TCLC 9; YABC

McCulloch, John Tyler
See Burroughs, Edgar Rice

McCullough, Colleen 1938(?)- . . . . . . CLC **27**
See also CA 81-84; CANR 17; MTCW

McElroy, Joseph 1930- . . . . CLC **5, 47**
See also CA 17-20R

McEwan, Ian (Russell) 1948- . . . CLC **13, 66**
See also BEST 90:4; CA 61-64; CANR 14,
41; DLB 14; MTCW

McFadden, David 1940- . . . . CLC **48**
See also CA 104; DLB 60

McFarland, Dennis 1950- . . . . CLC **65**

McGahern, John 1934- . . . . CLC **5, 9, 48**
See also CA 17-20R; CANR 29; DLB 14;
MTCW

McGinley, Patrick (Anthony)
1937- . . . . CLC **41**
See also CA 120; 127

McGinley, Phyllis 1905-1978 . . . . . . CLC **14**
See also CA 9-12R; 77-80; CANR 19;
DLB 11, 48; SATA-Obit 2, 24, 44

McGinniss, Joe 1942- . . . . CLC **32**
See also AITN 2; BEST 89:2; CA 25-28R;
CANR 26

McGivern, Maureen Daly
See Daly, Maureen

McGrath, Patrick 1950- . . . . CLC **55**
See also CA 136

McGrath, Thomas (Matthew)
1916-1990 . . . . CLC **28, 59**
See also CA 9-12R; 132; CANR 6, 33;
MTCW; SATA-Obit 41; SC 66

McGuane, Thomas (Francis III)
1939- . . . . CLC **3, 7, 18, 45**
See also AITN 2; CA 49-52; CANR 5, 24;
DLB 2; DLBY 80; MTCW

McGuckian, Medbh 1950- . . . . CLC **48**
See also CA 143; DLB 40

McHale, Tom 1942(?)-1982 . . . . CLC **3, 5**
See also AITN 1; CA 77-80; 106

McIlvanney, William 1936- . . . . CLC **42**
See also CA 25-28R; DLB 14

McIlwraith, Maureen Mollie Hunter
See Hunter, Mollie
See also SATA-Obit 2

McInerney, Jay 1955- . . . . CLC **34**
See also CA 116; 123

McIntyre, Vonda N(eel) 1948- . . . . . CLC **18**
See also CA 81-84; CANR 17, 34; MTCW

McKay, Festus Claudius 1889-1948
See McKay, Claude
See also BW 1; CA 104; 124; DA; MTCW;
YABC

McKuen, Rod 1933- . . . . CLC **1, 3**
See also AITN 1; CA 41-44R; CANR 40

McLoughlin, R. B.
See Mencken, H(enry) L(ouis)

McLuhan, (Herbert) Marshall
1911-1980 . . . . CLC **37, 83**
See also CA 9-12R; 102; CANR 12, 34;
DLB 88; MTCW

McMillan, Terry (L.) 1951- . . . . . CLC **50, 61**
See also BW 2; CA 140

McMurtry, Larry (Jeff)
1936- . . . . CLC **2, 3, 7, 11, 27, 44**
See also AITN 2; BEST 89:2; CA 5-8R;
CANR 19, 43; CDALB 1968-1988;
DLB 2, 143; DLBY 80, 87; MTCW

McNally, T. M. 1961- . . . . CLC **82**

McNally, Terrence 1939- . . . . . . CLC **4, 7, 41**
See also CA 45-48; CANR 2; DLB 7

McNamer, Deirdre 1950- . . . . CLC **70**

McNeile, Herman Cyril 1888-1937
See Sapper
See also DLB 77

McPhee, John (Angus) 1931- . . . . . . CLC **36**
See also BEST 90:1; CA 65-68; CANR 20;
MTCW

McPherson, James Alan
1943- . . . . CLC **19, 77**
See also BW 1; CA 25-28R; CAAS 17;
CANR 24; DLB 38; MTCW

McPherson, William (Alexander)
1933- . . . . CLC **34**
See also CA 69-72; CANR 28

McSweeney, Kerry . . . . CLC **34**

Mead, Margaret 1901-1978 . . . . CLC **37**
See also AITN 1; CA 1-4R; 81-84;
CANR 4; MTCW; SATA-Obit 20

Meaker, Marijane (Agnes) 1927-
See Kerr, M. E.
See also CA 107; CANR 37; JRDA;
MAICYA; MTCW; SATA-Obit 20, 61

Medoff, Mark (Howard) 1940- . . . CLC **6, 23**
See also AITN 1; CA 53-56; CANR 5;
DLB 7

Medvedev, P. N.
See Bakhtin, Mikhail Mikhailovich

Meged, Aharon
See Megged, Aharon

Meged, Aron
See Megged, Aharon

Megged, Aharon 1920-............. **CLC 9**
See also CA 49-52; CAAS 13; CANR 1

Mehta, Ved (Parkash) 1934-....... **CLC 37**
See also CA 1-4R; CANR 2, 23; MTCW

Melanter
See Blackmore, R(ichard) D(oddridge)

Melikow, Loris
See Hofmannsthal, Hugo von

Melmoth, Sebastian
See Wilde, Oscar (Fingal O'Flahertie Wills)

Meltzer, Milton 1915-............. **CLC 26**
See also AAYA 8; CA 13-16R; CANR 38;
CLR 13; DLB 61; JRDA; MAICYA;
SATA 1; SATA-Obit 1, 50

Melville, Herman 1819-1891... **TCLC 1; DA**
See also CDALB 1640-1865; DLB 3, 74;
NCLC 3, 12, 29, 45; SATA-Obit 59;
YABC

Menander
c. 342B.C.-c. 292B.C.... **CMLC 9; DC 3**

Mercer, David 1928-1980.......... **CLC 5**
See also CA 9-12R; 102; CANR 23;
DLB 13; MTCW

Merchant, Paul
See Ellison, Harlan

Meredith, William (Morris)
1919-.............. **CLC 4, 13, 22, 55**
See also CA 9-12R; CAAS 14; CANR 6, 40;
DLB 5

Merimee, Prosper 1803-1870....... **TCLC 7**
See also DLB 119; NCLC 6

Merkin, Daphne 1954-............. **CLC 44**
See also CA 123

Merlin, Arthur
See Blish, James (Benjamin)

Merrill, James (Ingram)
1926-........ **CLC 2, 3, 6, 8, 13, 18, 34**
See also CA 13-16R; CANR 10; DLB 5;
DLBY 85; MTCW

Merriman, Alex
See Silverberg, Robert

Merritt, E. B.
See Waddington, Miriam

Merton, Thomas
1915-1968 .... **CLC 1, 3, 11, 34, 83**
See also CA 5-8R; 25-28R; CANR 22;
DLB 48; DLBY 81; MTCW; SAAS 10

Merwin, W(illiam) S(tanley)
1927-...... **CLC 1, 2, 3, 5, 8, 13, 18, 45**
See also CA 13-16R; CANR 15; DLB 5;
MTCW

Metcalf, John 1938-............. **CLC 37**
See also CA 113; DLB 60

Metcalf, Suzanne
See Baum, L(yman) Frank

Mewshaw, Michael 1943-.......... **CLC 9**
See also CA 53-56; CANR 7; DLBY 80

Meyer, June
See Jordan, June

Meyer, Lynn
See Slavitt, David R(ytman)

Meyer-Meyrink, Gustav 1868-1932
See Meyrink, Gustav
See also CA 117

Meyers, Jeffrey 1939-............ **CLC 39**
See also CA 73-76; DLB 111

Michaels, Leonard 1933-........ **CLC 6, 25**
See also CA 61-64; CANR 21; DLB 130;
MTCW; TCLC 16

Michaux, Henri 1899-1984 ...... **CLC 8, 19**
See also CA 85-88; 114

Michelangelo 1475-1564............ **LC 12**

Michelet, Jules 1798-1874....... **NCLC 31**

Michener, James A(lbert)
1907(?)-......... **CLC 1, 5, 11, 29, 60**
See also AITN 1; BEST 90:1; CA 5-8R;
CANR 21, 45; DLB 6; MTCW

Mickiewicz, Adam 1798-1855..... **NCLC 3**

Middleton, Christopher 1926-...... **CLC 13**
See also CA 13-16R; CANR 29; DLB 40

Middleton, Stanley 1919-........ **CLC 7, 38**
See also CA 25-28R; CANR 21; DLB 14

Migueis, Jose Rodrigues 1901-..... **CLC 10**

Miles, Josephine
1911-1985 .... **CLC 1, 2, 14, 34, 39**
See also CA 1-4R; 116; CANR 2; DLB 48

Militant
See Sandburg, Carl (August)

Mill, John Stuart 1806-1873..... **NCLC 11**
See also CDBLB 1832-1890; DLB 55

Millar, Kenneth 1915-1983 .... **CLC 14**
See also Macdonald, Ross
See also CA 9-12R; 110; CANR 16; DLB 2;
DLBD 6; DLBY 83; MTCW

Millay, E. Vincent
See Millay, Edna St. Vincent

Miller, Arthur
1915-.... **CLC 1, 2, 6, 10, 15, 26, 47, 78;
DA; DC 1**
See also AITN 1; CA 1-4R; CABS 3;
CANR 2, 30; CDALB 1941-1968; DLB 7;
MTCW; YABC

Miller, Henry (Valentine)
1891-1980 .... **CLC 1, 2, 4, 9, 14, 43, 84;
DA**
See also CA 9-12R; 97-100; CANR 33;
CDALB 1929-1941; DLB 4, 9; DLBY 80;
MTCW; YABC

Miller, Jason 1939(?)-............. **CLC 2**
See also AITN 1; CA 73-76; DLB 7

Miller, Sue 1943-................ **CLC 44**
See also BEST 90:3; CA 139; DLB 143

Miller, Walter M(ichael, Jr.)
1923-..................... **CLC 4, 30**
See also CA 85-88; DLB 8

Millett, Kate 1934-............... **CLC 67**
See also AITN 1; CA 73-76; CANR 32;
MTCW

Millhauser, Steven 1943-....... **CLC 21, 54**
See also CA 110; 111; DLB 2

Millin, Sarah Gertrude 1889-1968 .. **CLC 49**
See also CA 102; 93-96

Milner, Ron(ald) 1938-...... **CLC 56; BLC**
See also AITN 1; BW 1; CA 73-76;
CANR 24; DLB 38; MTCW

Milosz, Czeslaw
1911-........ **CLC 5, 11, 22, 31, 56, 82**
See also CA 81-84; CANR 23; MTCW;
SAAS 8

Milton, John 1608-1674......... **LC 9; DA**
See also CDBLB 1660-1789; DLB 131;
YABC

Minehaha, Cornelius
See Wedekind, (Benjamin) Frank(lin)

Miner, Valerie 1947-............. **CLC 40**
See also CA 97-100

Minimo, Duca
See D'Annunzio, Gabriele

Minot, Susan 1956-............. **CLC 44**
See also CA 134

Minus, Ed 1938-................. **CLC 39**

Miranda, Javier
See Bioy Casares, Adolfo

Mishima, Yukio..... CLC 2, 4, 6, 9, 27; DC 1
See also Hiraoka, Kimitake
See also TCLC 4

Mistry, Rohinton 1952-........... **CLC 71**
See also CA 141

Mitchell, Clyde
See Ellison, Harlan; Silverberg, Robert

Mitchell, James Leslie 1901-1935
See Gibbon, Lewis Grassic
See also CA 104; DLB 15

Mitchell, Joni 1943-.............. **CLC 12**
See also CA 112

Mitchell, Peggy
See Mitchell, Margaret (Munnerlyn)

Mitchell, W(illiam) O(rmond)
1914-...................... **CLC 25**
See also CA 77-80; CANR 15, 43; DLB 88

Mitford, Mary Russell 1787-1855.. **NCLC 4**
See also DLB 110, 116

Mitford, Nancy 1904-1973........ **CLC 44**
See also CA 9-12R

Mo, Timothy (Peter) 1950(?)-...... **CLC 46**
See also CA 117; MTCW

Modarressi, Taghi (M.) 1931-...... **CLC 44**
See also CA 121; 134

Modiano, Patrick (Jean) 1945-..... **CLC 18**
See also CA 85-88; CANR 17, 40; DLB 83

Moerck, Paal
See Roelvaag, O(le) E(dvart)

Mohr, Nicholasa 1935-...... **CLC 12; HLC**
See also AAYA 8; CA 49-52; CANR 1, 32;
CLR 22; HW; JRDA; SATA 8;
SATA-Obit 8

Mojtabai, A(nn) G(race)
1938-............... **CLC 5, 9, 15, 29**
See also CA 85-88

Moliere 1622-1673............ **LC 10; DA**
See also YABC

Molin, Charles
See Mayne, William (James Carter)

Momaday, N(avarre) Scott
1934- . . . . **CLC 2, 19; DA; PC**
See also AAYA 11; CA 25-28R; CANR 14,
34; DLB 143; MTCW; SATA-Obit 30, 48

Monette, Paul 1945- . . . . **CLC 82**
See also CA 139

Monroe, Lyle
See Heinlein, Robert A(nson)

Montagu, Elizabeth 1917- . . . . **NCLC 7**
See also CA 9-12R

Montagu, Mary (Pierrepont) Wortley
1689-1762 . . . . **LC 9**
See also DLB 95, 101

Montagu, W. H.
See Coleridge, Samuel Taylor

Montague, John (Patrick)
1929- . . . . **CLC 13, 46**
See also CA 9-12R; CANR 9; DLB 40;
MTCW

Montaigne, Michel (Eyquem) de
1533-1592 . . . . **LC 8; DA**
See also YABC

Montale, Eugenio 1896-1981 . . . **CLC 7, 9, 18**
See also CA 17-20R; 104; CANR 30;
DLB 114; MTCW

Montesquieu, Charles-Louis de Secondat
1689-1755 . . . . **LC 7**

Montgomery, (Robert) Bruce 1921-1978
See Crispin, Edmund
See also CA 104

Montgomery, Marion H., Jr. 1925- . . **CLC 7**
See also AITN 1; CA 1-4R; CANR 3;
DLB 6

Montgomery, Max
See Davenport, Guy (Mattison, Jr.)

Montherlant, Henry (Milon) de
1896-1972 . . . . **CLC 8, 19**
See also CA 85-88; 37-40R; DLB 72;
MTCW

Monty Python . . . . **CLC 21**
See also Chapman, Graham; Cleese, John
(Marwood); Gilliam, Terry (Vance); Idle,
Eric; Jones, Terence Graham Parry; Palin,
Michael (Edward)
See also AAYA 7

Moodie, Susanna (Strickland)
1803-1885 . . . . **NCLC 14**
See also DLB 99

Mooney, Edward 1951- . . . . **CLC 25**
See also CA 130

Mooney, Ted
See Mooney, Edward

Moorcock, Michael (John)
1939- . . . . **CLC 5, 27, 58**
See also CA 45-48; CAAS 5; CANR 2, 17,
38; DLB 14; MTCW

Moore, Brian
1921- . . . . **CLC 1, 3, 5, 7, 8, 19, 32**
See also CA 1-4R; CANR 1, 25, 42; MTCW

Moore, Edward
See Muir, Edwin

Moore, Lorrie . . . . **CLC 39, 45, 68**
See also Moore, Marie Lorena

Moore, Marianne (Craig)
1887-1972 . . . . **CLC 1, 2, 4, 8, 10, 13, 19,
47; DA**
See also CA 1-4R; 33-36R; CANR 3;
CDALB 1929-1941; DLB 45; DLBD 7;
MTCW; SAAS 4; SATA-Obit 20

Moore, Marie Lorena 1957-
See Moore, Lorrie
See also CA 116; CANR 39

Moore, Thomas 1779-1852 . . . . **NCLC 6**
See also DLB 96, 144

Morand, Paul 1888-1976 . . . . **CLC 41**
See also CA 69-72; DLB 65

Morante, Elsa 1918-1985 . . . . **CLC 8, 47**
See also CA 85-88; 117; CANR 35; MTCW

Moravia, Alberto . . . . . . **CLC 2, 7, 11, 27, 46**
See also Pincherle, Alberto

More, Hannah 1745-1833 . . . . **NCLC 27**
See also DLB 107, 109, 116

More, Henry 1614-1687 . . . . **LC 9**
See also DLB 126

More, Sir Thomas 1478-1535 . . . . **LC 10**

Morgan, Berry 1919- . . . . **CLC 6**
See also CA 49-52; DLB 6

Morgan, Claire
See Highsmith, (Mary) Patricia

Morgan, Edwin (George) 1920- . . . . . **CLC 31**
See also CA 5-8R; CANR 3, 43; DLB 27

Morgan, (George) Frederick
1922- . . . . **CLC 23**
See also CA 17-20R; CANR 21

Morgan, Harriet
See Mencken, H(enry) L(ouis)

Morgan, Jane
See Cooper, James Fenimore

Morgan, Janet 1945- . . . . **CLC 39**
See also CA 65-68

Morgan, Lady 1776(?)-1859 . . . . . . **NCLC 29**
See also DLB 116

Morgan, Robin 1941- . . . . **CLC 2**
See also CA 69-72; CANR 29; MTCW

Morgan, Scott
See Kuttner, Henry

Morgan, Seth 1949(?)-1990 . . . . **CLC 65**
See also CA 132

Morgenstern, S.
See Goldman, William (W.)

Morike, Eduard (Friedrich)
1804-1875 . . . . **NCLC 10**
See also DLB 133

Mori Rintaro 1862-1922
See Mori Ogai
See also CA 110

Moritz, Karl Philipp 1756-1793 . . . . . . **LC 2**
See also DLB 94

Morland, Peter Henry
See Faust, Frederick (Schiller)

Morren, Theophil
See Hofmannsthal, Hugo von

Morris, Bill 1952- . . . . **CLC 76**

Morris, Julian
See West, Morris L(anglo)

Morris, Steveland Judkins 1950(?)-
See Wonder, Stevie
See also CA 111

Morris, William 1834-1896 . . . . **NCLC 4**
See also CDBLB 1832-1890; DLB 18, 35, 57

Morris, Wright 1910- . . . **CLC 1, 3, 7, 18, 37**
See also CA 9-12R; CANR 21; DLB 2;
DLBY 81; MTCW

Morrison, Chloe Anthony Wofford
See Morrison, Toni

Morrison, James Douglas 1943-1971
See Morrison, Jim
See also CA 73-76; CANR 40

Morrison, Jim . . . . **CLC 17**
See also Morrison, James Douglas

Morrison, Toni
1931- . . **CLC 4, 10, 22, 55, 81; BLC; DA**
See also AAYA 1; BW 2; CA 29-32R;
CANR 27, 42; CDALB 1968-1988;
DLB 6, 33, 143; DLBY 81; MTCW;
SATA-Obit 57

Morrison, Van 1945- . . . . **CLC 21**
See also CA 116

Mortimer, John (Clifford)
1923- . . . . **CLC 28, 43**
See also CA 13-16R; CANR 21;
CDBLB 1960 to Present; DLB 13;
MTCW

Mortimer, Penelope (Ruth) 1918- . . . . **CLC 5**
See also CA 57-60; CANR 45

Morton, Anthony
See Creasey, John

Moses, Daniel David 1952- . . . . **PC X**

Mosher, Howard Frank 1943- . . . . . . **CLC 62**
See also CA 139

Mosley, Nicholas 1923- . . . . **CLC 43, 70**
See also CA 69-72; CANR 41; DLB 14

Moss, Howard
1922-1987 . . . . **CLC 7, 14, 45, 50**
See also CA 1-4R; 123; CANR 1, 44;
DLB 5

Mossgiel, Rab
See Burns, Robert

Motion, Andrew 1952- . . . . **CLC 47**
See also DLB 40

Motley, Willard (Francis)
1909-1965 . . . . **CLC 18**
See also BW 1; CA 117; 106; DLB 76, 143

Motoori, Norinaga 1730-1801 . . . . **NCLC 45**

Mott, Michael (Charles Alston)
1930- . . . . **CLC 15, 34**
See also CA 5-8R; CAAS 7; CANR 7, 29

Mountain Wolf Woman 1884-1960 . . . . **PC X**

Mourning Dove 1888-1936 . . . . **PC X**

Mowat, Farley (McGill) 1921- . . . . . **CLC 26**
See also AAYA 1; CA 1-4R; CANR 4, 24,
42; CLR 20; DLB 68; JRDA; MAICYA;
MTCW; SATA-Obit 3, 55

Moyers, Bill 1934- . . . . **CLC 74**
See also AITN 2; CA 61-64; CANR 31

Mphahlele, Es'kia
See Mphahlele, Ezekiel
See also DLB 125

Oliphant, Margaret (Oliphant Wilson)
    1828-1897 .... **NCLC 11**
    See also DLB 18

Oliver, Mary 1935-........... **CLC 19, 34**
    See also CA 21-24R; CANR 9, 43; DLB 5

Olivier, Laurence (Kerr)
    1907-1989 .... **CLC 20**
    See also CA 111; 129

Olsen, Tillie 1913- .... **CLC 4, 13; DA**
    See also CA 1-4R; CANR 1, 43; DLB 28;
    DLBY 80; MTCW; TCLC 11

Olson, Charles (John)
    1910-1970 ..... **CLC 1, 2, 5, 6, 9, 11, 29**
    See also CA 13-16; 25-28R; CABS 2;
    CANR 35; CAP 1; DLB 5, 16; MTCW

Olson, Toby 1937- .... **CLC 28**
    See also CA 65-68; CANR 9, 31

Olyesha, Yuri
    See Olesha, Yuri (Karlovich)

Ondaatje, (Philip) Michael
    1943- .... **CLC 14, 29, 51, 76**
    See also CA 77-80; CANR 42; DLB 60

Oneal, Elizabeth 1934-
    See Oneal, Zibby
    See also CA 106; CANR 28; MAICYA;
    SATA-Obit 30

Oneal, Zibby .... **CLC 30**
    See also Oneal, Elizabeth
    See also AAYA 5; CLR 13; JRDA

Onetti, Juan Carlos 1909- .... **CLC 7, 10**
    See also CA 85-88; CANR 32; DLB 113;
    HW; MTCW

O Nuallain, Brian 1911-1966
    See O'Brien, Flann
    See also CA 21-22; 25-28R; CAP 2

Oppen, George 1908-1984 .... **CLC 7, 13, 34**
    See also CA 13-16R; 113; CANR 8; DLB 5

Orlovitz, Gil 1918-1973 .... **CLC 22**
    See also CA 77-80; 45-48; DLB 2, 5

Orris
    See Ingelow, Jean

Ortiz, Simon J(oseph) 1941- .... **CLC 45**
    See also CA 134; DLB 120

Orton, Joe .... **CLC 4, 13, 43; DC 3**
    See also Orton, John Kingsley
    See also CDBLB 1960 to Present; DLB 13

Orton, John Kingsley 1933-1967
    See Orton, Joe
    See also CA 85-88; CANR 35; MTCW

Osborne, David
    See Silverberg, Robert

Osborne, George
    See Silverberg, Robert

Osborne, John (James)
    1929- .... **CLC 1, 2, 5, 11, 45; DA**
    See also CA 13-16R; CANR 21;
    CDBLB 1945-1960; DLB 13; MTCW;
    YABC

Osborne, Lawrence 1958- .... **CLC 50**

Oshima, Nagisa 1932- .... **CLC 20**
    See also CA 116; 121

Ossoli, Sarah Margaret (Fuller marchesa d')
    1810-1850
    See Fuller, Margaret
    See also SATA-Obit 25

Ostrovsky, Alexander
    1823-1886 .... **NCLC 30**

Otero, Blas de 1916-1979......... **CLC 11**
    See also CA 89-92; DLB 134

Otto, Whitney 1955-............. **CLC 70**
    See also CA 140

Ousmane, Sembene 1923- .... **CLC 66; BLC**
    See also BW 1; CA 117; 125; MTCW

Ovid 43B.C.-18th cent. (?)....... **CMLC 7**
    See also SAAS 2

Owen, Hugh
    See Faust, Frederick (Schiller)

Owens, Rochelle 1936-............. **CLC 8**
    See also CA 17-20R; CAAS 2; CANR 39

Oz, Amos 1939- ... **CLC 5, 8, 11, 27, 33, 54**
    See also CA 53-56; CANR 27; MTCW

Ozick, Cynthia 1928-...... **CLC 3, 7, 28, 62**
    See also BEST 90:1; CA 17-20R; CANR 23;
    DLB 28; DLBY 82; MTCW; TCLC 15

Ozu, Yasujiro 1903-1963 .... **CLC 16**
    See also CA 112

Pacheco, C.
    See Pessoa, Fernando (Antonio Nogueira)

Pa Chin
    See Li Fei-kan

Pack, Robert 1929-............... **CLC 13**
    See also CA 1-4R; CANR 3, 44; DLB 5

Padgett, Lewis
    See Kuttner, Henry

Padilla (Lorenzo), Heberto 1932-... **CLC 38**
    See also AITN 1; CA 123; 131; HW

Page, Jimmy 1944-............... **CLC 12**

Page, Louise 1955-............... **CLC 40**
    See also CA 140

Page, P(atricia) K(athleen)
    1916- .... **CLC 7, 18**
    See also CA 53-56; CANR 4, 22; DLB 68;
    MTCW

Paget, Violet 1856-1935
    See Lee, Vernon
    See also CA 104

Paget-Lowe, Henry
    See Lovecraft, H(oward) P(hillips)

Paglia, Camille (Anna) 1947-....... **CLC 68**
    See also CA 140

Paige, Richard
    See Koontz, Dean R(ay)

Pakenham, Antonia
    See Fraser, (Lady) Antonia (Pakenham)

Palazzeschi, Aldo 1885-1974...... **CLC 11**
    See also CA 89-92; 53-56; DLB 114

Paley, Grace 1922-........... **CLC 4, 6, 37**
    See also CA 25-28R; CANR 13; DLB 28;
    MTCW; TCLC 8

Palin, Michael (Edward) 1943-..... **CLC 21**
    See also Monty Python
    See also CA 107; CANR 35; SATA-Obit 67

Palliser, Charles 1947-............ **CLC 65**
    See also CA 136

Pancake, Breece Dexter 1952-1979
    See Pancake, Breece D'J
    See also CA 123; 109

Pancake, Breece D'J............... **CLC 29**
    See also Pancake, Breece Dexter
    See also DLB 130

Panko, Rudy
    See Gogol, Nikolai (Vasilyevich)

Papadiamantopoulos, Johannes 1856-1910
    See Moreas, Jean
    See also CA 117

Paracelsus 1493-1541.............. **LC 14**

Parasol, Peter
    See Stevens, Wallace

Parfenie, Maria
    See Codrescu, Andrei

Parini, Jay (Lee) 1948- .... **CLC 54**
    See also CA 97-100; CAAS 16; CANR 32

Park, Jordan
    See Kornbluth, C(yril) M.; Pohl, Frederik

Parker, Bert
    See Ellison, Harlan

Parker, Dorothy (Rothschild)
    1893-1967 .... **CLC 15, 68**
    See also CA 19-20; 25-28R; CAP 2;
    DLB 11, 45, 86; MTCW; TCLC 2

Parker, Robert B(rown) 1932-...... **CLC 27**
    See also BEST 89:4; CA 49-52; CANR 1,
    26; MTCW

Parkes, Lucas
    See Harris, John (Wyndham Parkes Lucas)
    Beynon

Parkin, Frank 1940-.............. **CLC 43**

Parkman, Francis, Jr.
    1823-1893 .... **NCLC 12**
    See also DLB 1, 30

Parks, Gordon (Alexander Buchanan)
    1912- .... **CLC 1, 16; BLC**
    See also AITN 2; BW 2; CA 41-44R;
    CANR 26; DLB 33; SATA-Obit 8

Parnell, Thomas 1679-1718 .... **LC 3**
    See also DLB 94

Parra, Nicanor 1914- .... **CLC 2; HLC**
    See also CA 85-88; CANR 32; HW; MTCW

Parrish, Mary Frances
    See Fisher, M(ary) F(rances) K(ennedy)

Parson
    See Coleridge, Samuel Taylor

Parson Lot
    See Kingsley, Charles

Partridge, Anthony
    See Oppenheim, E(dward) Phillips

Pasolini, Pier Paolo
    1922-1975 .... **CLC 20, 37**
    See also CA 93-96; 61-64; DLB 128;
    MTCW

Pasquini
    See Silone, Ignazio

Pastan, Linda (Olenik) 1932- ...... **CLC 27**
    See also CA 61-64; CANR 18, 40; DLB 5

Pasternak, Boris (Leonidovich)
    1890-1960 ...... **CLC 7, 10, 18, 63; DA**
    See also CA 127; 116; MTCW; SAAS 6;
    YABC

Patchen, Kenneth 1911-1972 ... **CLC 1, 2, 18**
    See also CA 1-4R; 33-36R; CANR 3, 35;
    DLB 16, 48; MTCW

Pater, Walter (Horatio)
1839-1894 . . . . **NCLC 7**
See also CDBLB 1832-1890; DLB 57

Paterson, Katherine (Womeldorf)
1932- . . . . **CLC 12, 30**
See also AAYA 1; CA 21-24R; CANR 28;
CLR 7; DLB 52; JRDA; MAICYA;
MTCW; SATA-Obit 13, 53

Patmore, Coventry Kersey Dighton
1823-1896 . . . . **NCLC 9**
See also DLB 35, 98

Paton, Alan (Stewart)
1903-1988 . . . . . . **CLC 4, 10, 25, 55; DA**
See also CA 13-16; 125; CANR 22; CAP 1;
MTCW; SATA-Obit 11, 56; YABC

Paton Walsh, Gillian 1937-
See Walsh, Jill Paton
See also CANR 38; JRDA; MAICYA;
SATA 3; SATA-Obit 4, 72

Paulding, James Kirke 1778-1860 . . **NCLC 2**
See also DLB 3, 59, 74

Paulin, Thomas Neilson 1949-
See Paulin, Tom
See also CA 123; 128

Paulin, Tom . . . . **CLC 37**
See also Paulin, Thomas Neilson
See also DLB 40

Paustovsky, Konstantin (Georgievich)
1892-1968 . . . . **CLC 40**
See also CA 93-96; 25-28R

Pavic, Milorad 1929- . . . . **CLC 60**
See also CA 136

Payne, Alan
See Jakes, John (William)

Paz, Gil
See Lugones, Leopoldo

Paz, Octavio
1914- . . . . **CLC 3, 4, 6, 10, 19, 51, 65;**
DA; HLC
See also CA 73-76; CANR 32; DLBY 90;
HW; MTCW; SAAS 1; YABC

Peacock, Molly 1947- . . . . **CLC 60**
See also CA 103; DLB 120

Peacock, Thomas Love
1785-1866 . . . . **NCLC 22**
See also DLB 96, 116

Peake, Mervyn 1911-1968 . . . . . . **CLC 7, 54**
See also CA 5-8R; 25-28R; CANR 3;
DLB 15; MTCW; SATA-Obit 23

Pearce, Philippa . . . . **CLC 21**
See also Christie, (Ann) Philippa
See also CLR 9; MAICYA; SATA-Obit 1,
67

Pearl, Eric
See Elman, Richard

Pearson, T(homas) R(eid) 1956- . . . . **CLC 39**
See also CA 120; 130

Peck, Dale 1968(?)- . . . . **CLC 81**

Peck, John 1941- . . . . **CLC 3**
See also CA 49-52; CANR 3

Peck, Richard (Wayne) 1934- . . . . . . **CLC 21**
See also AAYA 1; CA 85-88; CANR 19,
38; JRDA; MAICYA; SATA 2;
SATA-Obit 18, 55

Peck, Robert Newton 1928- . . . . **CLC 17; DA**
See also AAYA 3; CA 81-84; CANR 31;
JRDA; MAICYA; SATA 1;
SATA-Obit 21, 62

Peckinpah, (David) Sam(uel)
1925-1984 . . . . **CLC 20**
See also CA 109; 114

Pedersen, Knut 1859-1952
See Hamsun, Knut
See also CA 104; 119; MTCW

Peeslake, Gaffer
See Durrell, Lawrence (George)

Pena, Ramon del Valle y
See Valle-Inclan, Ramon (Maria) del

Pendennis, Arthur Esquir
See Thackeray, William Makepeace

Penn, William 1644-1718 . . . . **LC 25**
See also DLB 24

Pepys, Samuel 1633-1703 . . . . . . **LC 11; DA**
See also CDBLB 1660-1789; DLB 101;
YABC

Percy, Walker
1916-1990 . . . . **CLC 2, 3, 6, 8, 14, 18, 47,**
65
See also CA 1-4R; 131; CANR 1, 23;
DLB 2; DLBY 80, 90; MTCW

Perec, Georges 1936-1982 . . . . **CLC 56**
See also CA 141; DLB 83

Pereda y Porrua, Jose Maria de
See Pereda (y Sanchez de Porrua), Jose
Maria de

Peregoy, George Weems
See Mencken, H(enry) L(ouis)

Perelman, S(idney) J(oseph)
1904-1979 . . . **CLC 3, 5, 9, 15, 23, 44, 49**
See also AITN 1, 2; CA 73-76; 89-92;
CANR 18; DLB 11, 44; MTCW

Peretz, Yitzhok Leibush
See Peretz, Isaac Loeb

Perrault, Charles 1628-1703 . . . . **LC 2**
See also MAICYA; SATA-Obit 25

Perry, Brighton
See Sherwood, Robert E(mmet)

Perse, St.-John . . . . **CLC 4, 11, 46**
See also Leger, (Marie-Rene Auguste) Alexis
Saint-Leger

Peseenz, Tulio F.
See Lopez y Fuentes, Gregorio

Pesetsky, Bette 1932- . . . . **CLC 28**
See also CA 133; DLB 130

Peshkov, Alexei Maximovich 1868-1936
See Gorky, Maxim
See also CA 105; 141; DA

Peterkin, Julia Mood 1880-1961 . . . . **CLC 31**
See also CA 102; DLB 9

Peters, Joan K. 1945- . . . . **CLC 39**

Peters, Robert L(ouis) 1924- . . . . **CLC 7**
See also CA 13-16R; CAAS 8; DLB 105

Petofi, Sandor 1823-1849 . . . . **NCLC 21**

Petrakis, Harry Mark 1923- . . . . **CLC 3**
See also CA 9-12R; CANR 4, 30

Petry, Ann (Lane) 1908- . . . . . . **CLC 1, 7, 18**
See also BW 1; CA 5-8R; CAAS 6;
CANR 4; CLR 12; DLB 76; JRDA;
MAICYA; MTCW; SATA-Obit 5

Petursson, Halligrimur 1614-1674 . . . . **LC 8**

Philipson, Morris H. 1926- . . . . **CLC 53**
See also CA 1-4R; CANR 4

Phillips, Jack
See Sandburg, Carl (August)

Phillips, Jayne Anne 1952- . . . . . **CLC 15, 33**
See also CA 101; CANR 24; DLBY 80;
MTCW; TCLC 16

Phillips, Richard
See Dick, Philip K(indred)

Phillips, Robert (Schaeffer) 1938- . . . **CLC 28**
See also CA 17-20R; CAAS 13; CANR 8;
DLB 105

Phillips, Ward
See Lovecraft, H(oward) P(hillips)

Piccolo, Lucio 1901-1969 . . . . **CLC 13**
See also CA 97-100; DLB 114

Pico della Mirandola, Giovanni
1463-1494 . . . . **LC 15**

Piercy, Marge
1936- . . . . **CLC 3, 6, 14, 18, 27, 62**
See also CA 21-24R; CAAS 1; CANR 13,
43; DLB 120; MTCW

Piers, Robert
See Anthony, Piers

Pieyre de Mandiargues, Andre 1909-1991
See Mandiargues, Andre Pieyre de
See also CA 103; 136; CANR 22

Pincherle, Alberto 1907-1990 . . . **CLC 11, 18**
See also Moravia, Alberto
See also CA 25-28R; 132; CANR 33;
MTCW

Pinckney, Darryl 1953- . . . . **CLC 76**
See also BW 2; CA 143

Pindar 518B.C.-446B.C. . . . . **CMLC 12**

Pineda, Cecile 1942- . . . . **CLC 39**
See also CA 118

Pinero, Miguel (Antonio Gomez)
1946-1988 . . . . **CLC 4, 55**
See also CA 61-64; 125; CANR 29; HW

Pinget, Robert 1919- . . . . **CLC 7, 13, 37**
See also CA 85-88; DLB 83

Pink Floyd . . . . **CLC 35**
See also Barrett, (Roger) Syd; Gilmour,
David; Mason, Nick; Waters, Roger;
Wright, Rick

Pinkney, Edward 1802-1828 . . . . . **NCLC 31**

Pinkwater, Daniel Manus 1941- . . . . **CLC 35**
See also Pinkwater, Manus
See also AAYA 1; CA 29-32R; CANR 12,
38; CLR 4; JRDA; MAICYA; SATA 3;
SATA-Obit 46, 76

Pinkwater, Manus
See Pinkwater, Daniel Manus
See also SATA-Obit 8

Pinsky, Robert 1940- . . . . **CLC 9, 19, 38**
See also CA 29-32R; CAAS 4; DLBY 82

Pinta, Harold
See Pinter, Harold

Prophet, The
 See Dreiser, Theodore (Herman Albert)

Prose, Francine 1947-............ **CLC 45**
 See also CA 109; 112

Proudhon
 See Cunha, Euclides (Rodrigues Pimenta) da

Proulx, E. Annie 1935- .... **CLC 81**

Prowler, Harley
 See Masters, Edgar Lee

Pryor, Richard (Franklin Lenox Thomas)
 1940-...................... **CLC 26**
 See also CA 122

Pteleon
 See Grieve, C(hristopher) M(urray)

Puckett, Lute
 See Masters, Edgar Lee

Puig, Manuel
 1932-1990 ... **CLC 3, 5, 10, 28, 65; HLC**
 See also CA 45-48; CANR 2, 32; DLB 113;
 HW; MTCW

Purdy, Al(fred Wellington)
 1918-................ **CLC 3, 6, 14, 50**
 See also CA 81-84; CAAS 17; CANR 42;
 DLB 88

Purdy, James (Amos)
 1923-........... **CLC 2, 4, 10, 28, 52**
 See also CA 33-36R; CAAS 1; CANR 19;
 DLB 2; MTCW

Pure, Simon
 See Swinnerton, Frank Arthur

Pushkin, Alexander (Sergeyevich)
 1799-1837 .... **NCLC 3, 27; DA**
 See also SAAS 10; SATA-Obit 61; YABC

P'u Sung-ling 1640-1715 .... **LC 3**

Putnam, Arthur Lee
 See Alger, Horatio, Jr.

Puzo, Mario 1920-......... **CLC 1, 2, 6, 36**
 See also CA 65-68; CANR 4, 42; DLB 6;
 MTCW

Pym, Barbara (Mary Crampton)
 1913-1980 .... **CLC 13, 19, 37**
 See also CA 13-14; 97-100; CANR 13, 34;
 CAP 1; DLB 14; DLBY 87; MTCW

Pynchon, Thomas (Ruggles, Jr.)
 1937- ..... **CLC 2, 3, 6, 9, 11, 18, 33, 62,**
                                        72; DA
 See also BEST 90:2; CA 17-20R; CANR 22;
 DLB 2; MTCW; TCLC 14; YABC

Q
 See Quiller-Couch, Arthur Thomas

Qian Zhongshu
 See Ch'ien Chung-shu

Qroll
 See Dagerman, Stig (Halvard)

Quarrington, Paul (Lewis) 1953-.... **CLC 65**
 See also CA 129

Quasimodo, Salvatore 1901-1968 ... **CLC 10**
 See also CA 13-16; 25-28R; CAP 1;
 DLB 114; MTCW

Queen, Ellery.............. **CLC 3, 11**
 See also Dannay, Frederic; Davidson,
 Avram; Lee, Manfred B(ennington);
 Sturgeon, Theodore (Hamilton); Vance,
 John Holbrook

Queen, Ellery, Jr.
 See Dannay, Frederic; Lee, Manfred
 B(ennington)

Queneau, Raymond
 1903-1976 .... **CLC 2, 5, 10, 42**
 See also CA 77-80; 69-72; CANR 32;
 DLB 72; MTCW

Quevedo, Francisco de 1580-1645.... **LC 23**

Quin, Ann (Marie) 1936-1973 .... **CLC 6**
 See also CA 9-12R; 45-48; DLB 14

Quinn, Martin
 See Smith, Martin Cruz

Quinn, Simon
 See Smith, Martin Cruz

Quoirez, Francoise 1935-........... **CLC 9**
 See also Sagan, Francoise
 See also CA 49-52; CANR 6, 39; MTCW

Rabe, David (William) 1940-... **CLC 4, 8, 33**
 See also CA 85-88; CABS 3; DLB 7

Rabelais, Francois 1483-1553 .... **LC 5; DA**
 See also YABC

Rabinovitch, Sholem 1859-1916
 See Aleichem, Sholom
 See also CA 104

Radcliffe, Ann (Ward) 1764-1823 .. **NCLC 6**
 See also DLB 39

Rado, James 1939-.............. **CLC 17**
 See also CA 105

Radvanyi, Netty 1900-1983
 See Seghers, Anna
 See also CA 85-88; 110

Rae, Ben
 See Griffiths, Trevor

Raeburn, John (Hay) 1941-........ **CLC 34**
 See also CA 57-60

Ragni, Gerome 1942-1991 .... **CLC 17**
 See also CA 105; 134

Rahv, Philip 1908-1973 .... **CLC 24**
 See also Greenberg, Ivan
 See also DLB 137

Raine, Craig 1944-.............. **CLC 32**
 See also CA 108; CANR 29; DLB 40

Raine, Kathleen (Jessie) 1908- ... **CLC 7, 45**
 See also CA 85-88; DLB 20; MTCW

Rakosi, Carl..................... **CLC 47**
 See also Rawley, Callman
 See also CAAS 5

Raleigh, Richard
 See Lovecraft, H(oward) P(hillips)

Rallentando, H. P.
 See Sayers, Dorothy L(eigh)

Ramal, Walter
 See de la Mare, Walter (John)

Ramon, Juan
 See Jimenez (Mantecon), Juan Ramon

Rampersad, Arnold 1941-.......... **CLC 44**
 See also BW 2; CA 127; 133; DLB 111

Rampling, Anne
 See Rice, Anne

Rand, Ayn
 1905-1982 ...... **CLC 3, 30, 44, 79; DA**
 See also AAYA 10; CA 13-16R; 105;
 CANR 27; MTCW; YABC

Randall, Dudley (Felker)
 1914- .... **CLC 1; BLC**
 See also BW 1; CA 25-28R; CANR 23;
 DLB 41

Randall, Robert
 See Silverberg, Robert

Ranger, Ken
 See Creasey, John

Ransom, John Crowe
 1888-1974 .... **CLC 2, 4, 5, 11, 24**
 See also CA 5-8R; 49-52; CANR 6, 34;
 DLB 45, 63; MTCW

Rao, Raja 1909-.............. **CLC 25, 56**
 See also CA 73-76; MTCW

Raphael, Frederic (Michael)
 1931-.................... **CLC 2, 14**
 See also CA 1-4R; CANR 1; DLB 14

Ratcliffe, James P.
 See Mencken, H(enry) L(ouis)

Rathbone, Julian 1935-.......... **CLC 41**
 See also CA 101; CANR 34

Rattigan, Terence (Mervyn)
 1911-1977 .... **CLC 7**
 See also CA 85-88; 73-76;
 CDBLB 1945-1960; DLB 13; MTCW

Ratushinskaya, Irina 1954-........ **CLC 54**
 See also CA 129

Raven, Simon (Arthur Noel)
 1927-.................... **CLC 14**
 See also CA 81-84

Rawley, Callman 1903-
 See Rakosi, Carl
 See also CA 21-24R; CANR 12, 32

Ray, Satyajit 1921-1992....... **CLC 16, 76**
 See also CA 114; 137

Read, Herbert Edward 1893-1968.... **CLC 4**
 See also CA 85-88; 25-28R; DLB 20

Read, Piers Paul 1941- ...... **CLC 4, 10, 25**
 See also CA 21-24R; CANR 38; DLB 14;
 SATA-Obit 21

Reade, Charles 1814-1884 .... **NCLC 2**
 See also DLB 21

Reade, Hamish
 See Gray, Simon (James Holliday)

Reading, Peter 1946-............. **CLC 47**
 See also CA 103; DLB 40

Reaney, James 1926-............. **CLC 13**
 See also CA 41-44R; CAAS 15; CANR 42;
 DLB 68; SATA-Obit 43

Rechy, John (Francisco)
 1934-........ **CLC 1, 7, 14, 18; HLC**
 See also CA 5-8R; CAAS 4; CANR 6, 32;
 DLB 122; DLBY 82; HW

Reddin, Keith.................... **CLC 67**

Redgrove, Peter (William)
 1932-.................... **CLC 6, 41**
 See also CA 1-4R; CANR 3, 39; DLB 40

Redmon, Anne..................... **CLC 22**
 See also Nightingale, Anne Redmon
 See also DLBY 86

Reed, Eliot
 See Ambler, Eric

Robinson, Jill 1936-............... **CLC 10**
See also CA 102

Robinson, Kim Stanley 1952-...... **CLC 34**
See also CA 126

Robinson, Lloyd
See Silverberg, Robert

Robinson, Marilynne 1944-........ **CLC 25**
See also CA 116

Robinson, Smokey................. **CLC 21**
See also Robinson, William, Jr.

Robinson, William, Jr. 1940-
See Robinson, Smokey
See also CA 116

Robison, Mary 1949-............. **CLC 42**
See also CA 113; 116; DLB 130

Roddenberry, Eugene Wesley 1921-1991
See Roddenberry, Gene
See also CA 110; 135; CANR 37;
SATA-Obit 45

Roddenberry, Gene................ **CLC 17**
See also Roddenberry, Eugene Wesley
See also AAYA 5; SC 69

Rodgers, Mary 1931-............. **CLC 12**
See also CA 49-52; CANR 8; CLR 20;
JRDA; MAICYA; SATA-Obit 8

Rodgers, W(illiam) R(obert)
1909-1969 .... **CLC 7**
See also CA 85-88; DLB 20

Rodman, Eric
See Silverberg, Robert

Rodman, Howard 1920(?)-1985..... **CLC 65**
See also CA 118

Rodman, Maia
See Wojciechowska, Maia (Teresa)

Rodriguez, Claudio 1934-......... **CLC 10**
See also DLB 134

Roethke, Theodore (Huebner)
1908-1963 ...... **CLC 1, 3, 8, 11, 19, 46**
See also CA 81-84; CABS 2;
CDALB 1941-1968; DLB 5; MTCW

Rogers, Thomas Hunton 1927-..... **CLC 57**
See also CA 89-92

Rogin, Gilbert 1929-............. **CLC 18**
See also CA 65-68; CANR 15

Rohmer, Eric.................... **CLC 16**
See also Scherer, Jean-Marie Maurice

Roiphe, Anne (Richardson)
1935-.................... **CLC 3, 9**
See also CA 89-92; CANR 45; DLBY 80

Rojas, Fernando de 1465-1541 ...... **LC 23**

Rolvaag, O(le) E(dvart)
See Roelvaag, O(le) E(dvart)

Romain Arnaud, Saint
See Aragon, Louis

Romains, Jules 1885-1972.......... **CLC 7**
See also CA 85-88; CANR 34; DLB 65;
MTCW

Ronsard, Pierre de 1524-1585........ **LC 6**

Rooke, Leon 1934-............ **CLC 25, 34**
See also CA 25-28R; CANR 23

Roper, William 1498-1578......... **LC 10**

Roquelaure, A. N.
See Rice, Anne

Rosa, Joao Guimaraes 1908-1967... **CLC 23**
See also CA 89-92; DLB 113

Rosen, Richard (Dean) 1949-....... **CLC 39**
See also CA 77-80

Rosenblatt, Joe.................. **CLC 15**
See also Rosenblatt, Joseph

Rosenblatt, Joseph 1933-
See Rosenblatt, Joe
See also CA 89-92

Rosenfeld, Samuel 1896-1963
See Tzara, Tristan
See also CA 89-92

Rosenthal, M(acha) L(ouis) 1917-... **CLC 28**
See also CA 1-4R; CAAS 6; CANR 4;
DLB 5; SATA-Obit 59

Ross, Barnaby
See Dannay, Frederic

Ross, Bernard L.
See Follett, Ken(neth Martin)

Ross, J. H.
See Lawrence, T(homas) E(dward)

Ross, Martin
See Martin, Violet Florence
See also DLB 135

Ross, (James) Sinclair 1908-....... **CLC 13**
See also CA 73-76; DLB 88

Rossetti, Christina (Georgina)
1830-1894 .... **NCLC 2; DA**
See also DLB 35; MAICYA; SAAS 7;
SATA-Obit 20; YABC

Rossetti, Dante Gabriel
1828-1882 .... **NCLC 4; DA**
See also CDBLB 1832-1890; DLB 35;
YABC

Rossner, Judith (Perelman)
1935-.................. **CLC 6, 9, 29**
See also AITN 2; BEST 90:3; CA 17-20R;
CANR 18; DLB 6; MTCW

Roth, Henry 1906-........... **CLC 2, 6, 11**
See also CA 11-12; CANR 38; CAP 1;
DLB 28; MTCW

Roth, Philip (Milton)
1933-...... **CLC 1, 2, 3, 4, 6, 9, 15, 22,
31, 47, 66; DA**
See also BEST 90:3; CA 1-4R; CANR 1, 22,
36; CDALB 1968-1988; DLB 2, 28;
DLBY 82; MTCW; YABC

Rothenberg, Jerome 1931-....... **CLC 6, 57**
See also CA 45-48; CANR 1; DLB 5

Rousseau, Jean-Baptiste 1671-1741 ... **LC 9**

Rousseau, Jean-Jacques
1712-1778 .... **LC 14; DA**
See also YABC

Rovit, Earl (Herbert) 1927-........ **CLC 7**
See also CA 5-8R; CANR 12

Rowe, Nicholas 1674-1718.......... **LC 8**
See also DLB 84

Rowley, Ames Dorrance
See Lovecraft, H(oward) P(hillips)

Rowson, Susanna Haswell
1762(?)-1824 .... **NCLC 5**
See also DLB 37

Roy, Gabrielle 1909-1983...... **CLC 10, 14**
See also CA 53-56; 110; CANR 5; DLB 68;
MTCW

Rozewicz, Tadeusz 1921-........ **CLC 9, 23**
See also CA 108; CANR 36; MTCW

Ruark, Gibbons 1941-............. **CLC 3**
See also CA 33-36R; CANR 14, 31;
DLB 120

Rubens, Bernice (Ruth) 1923-... **CLC 19, 31**
See also CA 25-28R; CANR 33; DLB 14;
MTCW

Rudkin, (James) David 1936-...... **CLC 14**
See also CA 89-92; DLB 13

Rudnik, Raphael 1933-............. **CLC 7**
See also CA 29-32R

Ruffian, M.
See Hasek, Jaroslav (Matej Frantisek)

Ruiz, Jose Martinez............... **CLC 11**
See also Martinez Ruiz, Jose

Rukeyser, Muriel
1913-1980 .... **CLC 6, 10, 15, 27**
See also CA 5-8R; 93-96; CANR 26;
DLB 48; MTCW; SATA-Obit 22

Rule, Jane (Vance) 1931-.......... **CLC 27**
See also CA 25-28R; CAAS 18; CANR 12;
DLB 60

Rulfo, Juan 1918-1986.... **CLC 8, 80; HLC**
See also CA 85-88; 118; CANR 26;
DLB 113; HW; MTCW

Runeberg, Johan 1804-1877...... **NCLC 41**

Rush, Norman 1933-............. **CLC 44**
See also CA 121; 126

Rushdie, (Ahmed) Salman
1947-.............. **CLC 23, 31, 55**
See also BEST 89:3; CA 108; 111;
CANR 33; MTCW

Rushforth, Peter (Scott) 1945-..... **CLC 19**
See also CA 101

Russ, Joanna 1937-.............. **CLC 15**
See also CA 25-28R; CANR 11, 31; DLB 8;
MTCW

Russell, George William 1867-1935
See A. E.
See also CA 104; CDBLB 1890-1914

Russell, (Henry) Ken(neth Alfred)
1927-...................... **CLC 16**
See also CA 105

Russell, Willy 1947-.............. **CLC 60**

Ruyslinck, Ward
See Belser, Reimond Karel Maria de

Ryan, Cornelius (John) 1920-1974 ... **CLC 7**
See also CA 69-72; 53-56; CANR 38

Ryan, Michael 1946-............. **CLC 65**
See also CA 49-52; DLBY 82

Rybakov, Anatoli (Naumovich)
1911-................... **CLC 23, 53**
See also CA 126; 135

Ryder, Jonathan
See Ludlum, Robert

Ryga, George 1932-1987 .... **CLC 14**
See also CA 101; 124; CANR 43; DLB 60

S. S.
See Sassoon, Siegfried (Lorraine)

Sabato, Ernesto (R.)
1911-.............. **CLC 10, 23; HLC**
See also CA 97-100; CANR 32; HW;
MTCW

Snyder, Gary (Sherman)
1930- . . . . **CLC 1, 2, 5, 9, 32**
See also CA 17-20R; CANR 30; DLB 5, 16

Snyder, Zilpha Keatley 1927- . . . . . . **CLC 17**
See also CA 9-12R; CANR 38; CLR 31;
JRDA; MAICYA; SATA 2;
SATA-Obit 1, 28, 75

Soares, Bernardo
See Pessoa, Fernando (Antonio Nogueira)

Sobh, A.
See Shamlu, Ahmad

Sobol, Joshua. . . . . **CLC 60**

Sodergran, Edith (Irene)
See Soedergran, Edith (Irene)

Softly, Edgar
See Lovecraft, H(oward) P(hillips)

Softly, Edward
See Lovecraft, H(oward) P(hillips)

Sokolov, Raymond 1941- . . . . **CLC 7**
See also CA 85-88

Solo, Jay
See Ellison, Harlan

Solomons, Ikey Esquir
See Thackeray, William Makepeace

Solomos, Dionysios 1798-1857 . . . **NCLC 15**

Solwoska, Mara
See French, Marilyn

Solzhenitsyn, Aleksandr I(sayevich)
1918- . . . . . . **CLC 1, 2, 4, 7, 9, 10, 18, 26,**
34, 78; DA
See also AITN 1; CA 69-72; CANR 40;
MTCW; YABC

Somers, Jane
See Lessing, Doris (May)

Somerville & Ross
See Martin, Violet Florence; Somerville,
Edith

Sommer, Scott 1951- . . . . **CLC 25**
See also CA 106

Sondheim, Stephen (Joshua)
1930- . . . . **CLC 30, 39**
See also AAYA 11; CA 103

Sontag, Susan 1933- . . . **CLC 1, 2, 10, 13, 31**
See also CA 17-20R; CANR 25; DLB 2, 67;
MTCW

Sophocles
496(?)B.C.-406(?)B.C. . . . . . **CMLC 2; DA;**
DC 1

Sorel, Julia
See Drexler, Rosalyn

Sorrentino, Gilbert
1929- . . . . **CLC 3, 7, 14, 22, 40**
See also CA 77-80; CANR 14, 33; DLB 5;
DLBY 80

Soto, Gary 1952- . . . . **CLC 32, 80; HLC**
See also AAYA 10; CA 119; 125; DLB 82;
HW; JRDA

Soupault, Philippe 1897-1990 . . . . . . **CLC 68**
See also CA 116; 131

Souster, (Holmes) Raymond
1921- . . . . **CLC 5, 14**
See also CA 13-16R; CAAS 14; CANR 13,
29; DLB 88; SATA-Obit 63

Southern, Terry 1926- . . . . **CLC 7**
See also CA 1-4R; CANR 1; DLB 2

Southey, Robert 1774-1843 . . . . **NCLC 8**
See also DLB 93, 107, 142; SATA-Obit 54

Southworth, Emma Dorothy Eliza Nevitte
1819-1899 . . . . **NCLC 26**

Souza, Ernest
See Scott, Evelyn

Soyinka, Wole
1934- . . . . **CLC 3, 5, 14, 36, 44; BLC;**
DA; DC 2
See also BW 2; CA 13-16R; CANR 27, 39;
DLB 125; MTCW; YABC

Spackman, W(illiam) M(ode)
1905-1990 . . . . **CLC 46**
See also CA 81-84; 132

Spacks, Barry 1931- . . . . **CLC 14**
See also CA 29-32R; CANR 33; DLB 105

Spanidou, Irini 1946- . . . . **CLC 44**

Spark, Muriel (Sarah)
1918- . . . . **CLC 2, 3, 5, 8, 13, 18, 40**
See also CA 5-8R; CANR 12, 36;
CDBLB 1945-1960; DLB 15, 139;
MTCW; TCLC 10

Spaulding, Douglas
See Bradbury, Ray (Douglas)

Spaulding, Leonard
See Bradbury, Ray (Douglas)

Spence, J. A. D.
See Eliot, T(homas) S(tearns)

Spencer, Elizabeth 1921- . . . . **CLC 22**
See also CA 13-16R; CANR 32; DLB 6;
MTCW; SATA-Obit 14

Spencer, Leonard G.
See Silverberg, Robert

Spencer, Scott 1945- . . . . **CLC 30**
See also CA 113; DLBY 86

Spender, Stephen (Harold)
1909- . . . . **CLC 1, 2, 5, 10, 41**
See also CA 9-12R; CANR 31;
CDBLB 1945-1960; DLB 20; MTCW

Spenser, Edmund 1552(?)-1599 . . . **LC 5; DA**
See also CDBLB Before 1660; SAAS 8;
YABC

Spicer, Jack 1925-1965 . . . . . . **CLC 8, 18, 72**
See also CA 85-88; DLB 5, 16

Spiegelman, Art 1948- . . . . **CLC 76**
See also AAYA 10; CA 125; CANR 41

Spielberg, Peter 1929- . . . . **CLC 6**
See also CA 5-8R; CANR 4; DLBY 81

Spielberg, Steven 1947- . . . . **CLC 20**
See also AAYA 8; CA 77-80; CANR 32;
SATA-Obit 32

Spillane, Frank Morrison 1918-
See Spillane, Mickey
See also CA 25-28R; CANR 28; MTCW;
SATA-Obit 66

Spillane, Mickey . . . . **CLC 3, 13**
See also Spillane, Frank Morrison

Spinoza, Benedictus de 1632-1677 . . . . **LC 9**

Spinrad, Norman (Richard) 1940- . . . **CLC 46**
See also CA 37-40R; CAAS 19; CANR 20;
DLB 8

Spivack, Kathleen (Romola Drucker)
1938- . . . . **CLC 6**
See also CA 49-52

Spoto, Donald 1941- . . . . **CLC 39**
See also CA 65-68; CANR 11

Springsteen, Bruce (F.) 1949- . . . . . . **CLC 17**
See also CA 111

Spurling, Hilary 1940- . . . . **CLC 34**
See also CA 104; CANR 25

Squires, (James) Radcliffe
1917-1993 . . . . **CLC 51**
See also CA 1-4R; 140; CANR 6, 21

Srivastava, Dhanpat Rai 1880(?)-1936
See Premchand
See also CA 118

Stacy, Donald
See Pohl, Frederik

Stael, Germaine de
See Stael-Holstein, Anne Louise Germaine
Necker Baronn
See also DLB 119

Stael-Holstein, Anne Louise Germaine Necker
Baronn 1766-1817 . . . . **NCLC 3**
See also Stael, Germaine de

Stafford, Jean 1915-1979 . . . **CLC 4, 7, 19, 68**
See also CA 1-4R; 85-88; CANR 3; DLB 2;
MTCW; SATA-Obit 22

Stafford, William (Edgar)
1914-1993 . . . . **CLC 4, 7, 29**
See also CA 5-8R; 142; CAAS 3; CANR 5,
22; DLB 5

Staines, Trevor
See Brunner, John (Kilian Houston)

Stairs, Gordon
See Austin, Mary (Hunter)

Stannard, Martin 1947- . . . . **CLC 44**
See also CA 142

Stanton, Maura 1946- . . . . **CLC 9**
See also CA 89-92; CANR 15; DLB 120

Stanton, Schuyler
See Baum, L(yman) Frank

Starbuck, George (Edwin) 1931- . . . . **CLC 53**
See also CA 21-24R; CANR 23

Stark, Richard
See Westlake, Donald E(dwin)

Staunton, Schuyler
See Baum, L(yman) Frank

Stead, Christina (Ellen)
1902-1983 . . . . **CLC 2, 5, 8, 32, 80**
See also CA 13-16R; 109; CANR 33, 40;
MTCW

Steele, Richard 1672-1729 . . . . **LC 18**
See also CDBLB 1660-1789; DLB 84, 101

Steele, Timothy (Reid) 1948- . . . . **CLC 45**
See also CA 93-96; CANR 16; DLB 120

Stegner, Wallace (Earle)
1909-1993 . . . . **CLC 9, 49, 81**
See also AITN 1; BEST 90:3; CA 1-4R;
141; CAAS 9; CANR 1, 21; DLB 9;
DLBY 93; MTCW

Steinbeck, John (Ernst)
1902-1968 . . . . . . **CLC 1, 5, 9, 13, 21, 34,**
45, 75; DA
See also AAYA 12; CA 1-4R; 25-28R;
CANR 1, 35; CDALB 1929-1941; DLB 7,
9; DLBD 2; MTCW; SATA-Obit 9;
TCLC 11; YABC

Steinem, Gloria 1934-. . . . . **CLC 63**
See also CA 53-56; CANR 28; MTCW

Steiner, George 1929-. . . . . **CLC 24**
See also CA 73-76; CANR 31; DLB 67;
MTCW; SATA-Obit 62

Steiner, K. Leslie
See Delany, Samuel R(ay, Jr.)

Stendhal 1783-1842. . . . . . **NCLC 23, 46; DA**
See also DLB 119; YABC

Stephen, Sir Leslie
See Stephen, Leslie

Stephen, Virginia
See Woolf, (Adeline) Virginia

Stephens, Reed
See Donaldson, Stephen R.

Steptoe, Lydia
See Barnes, Djuna

Sterchi, Beat 1949-. . . . . **CLC 65**

Sterling, Brett
See Bradbury, Ray (Douglas); Hamilton,
Edmond

Sterling, Bruce 1954-. . . . . **CLC 72**
See also CA 119; CANR 44

Stern, Gerald 1925- . . . . **CLC 40**
See also CA 81-84; CANR 28; DLB 105

Stern, Richard (Gustave) 1928-. . . **CLC 4, 39**
See also CA 1-4R; CANR 1, 25; DLBY 87

Sternberg, Josef von 1894-1969. . . . . **CLC 20**
See also CA 81-84

Sterne, Laurence 1713-1768. . . . . . **LC 2; DA**
See also CDBLB 1660-1789; DLB 39;
YABC

Stevens, Mark 1951- . . . . **CLC 34**
See also CA .122

Stevenson, Anne (Katharine)
1933-. . . . . **CLC 7, 33**
See also CA 17-20R; CAAS 9; CANR 9, 33;
DLB 40; MTCW

Stevenson, Robert Louis (Balfour)
1850-1894 . . . . **TCLC 11; DA**
See also CDBLB 1890-1914; CLR 10, 11;
DLB 18, 57, 141; JRDA; MAICYA;
NCLC 5, 14; YABC; 2

Stewart, J(ohn) I(nnes) M(ackintosh)
1906-. . . . . **CLC 7, 14, 32**
See also CA 85-88; CAAS 3; MTCW

Stewart, Mary (Florence Elinor)
1916-. . . . . **CLC 7, 35**
See also CA 1-4R; CANR 1; SATA-Obit 12

Stewart, Mary Rainbow
See Stewart, Mary (Florence Elinor)

Stifter, Adalbert 1805-1868. . . . . . **NCLC 41**
See also DLB 133

Still, James 1906-. . . . . **CLC 49**
See also CA 65-68; CAAS 17; CANR 10,
26; DLB 9; SATA-Obit 29

Sting
See Sumner, Gordon Matthew

Stirling, Arthur
See Sinclair, Upton (Beall)

Stitt, Milan 1941-. . . . . **CLC 29**
See also CA 69-72

Stockton, Francis Richard 1834-1902
See Stockton, Frank R.
See also CA 108; 137; MAICYA;
SATA-Obit 44

Stoddard, Charles
See Kuttner, Henry

Stoker, Abraham 1847-1912
See Stoker, Bram
See also CA 105; DA; SATA-Obit 29

Stolz, Mary (Slattery) 1920-. . . . . . . **CLC 12**
See also AAYA 8; AITN 1; CA 5-8R;
CANR 13, 41; JRDA; MAICYA;
SATA 3; SATA-Obit 10, 71

Stone, Irving 1903-1989. . . . . **CLC 7**
See also AITN 1; CA 1-4R; 129; CAAS 3;
CANR 1, 23; MTCW; SATA-Obit 3;
SC 64

Stone, Oliver 1946-. . . . . **CLC 73**
See also CA 110

Stone, Robert (Anthony)
1937-. . . . . **CLC 5, 23, 42**
See also CA 85-88; CANR 23; MTCW

Stone, Zachary
See Follett, Ken(neth Martin)

Stoppard, Tom
1937-. . . . . . **CLC 1, 3, 4, 5, 8, 15, 29, 34,**
63; DA
See also CA 81-84; CANR 39;
CDBLB 1960 to Present; DLB 13;
DLBY 85; MTCW; YABC

Storey, David (Malcolm)
1933-. . . . . **CLC 2, 4, 5, 8**
See also CA 81-84; CANR 36; DLB 13, 14;
MTCW

Storm, Hyemeyohsts 1935-. . . . . **CLC 3**
See also CA 81-84; CANR 45

Storm, (Hans) Theodor (Woldsen)
1817-1888 . . . . **NCLC 1**

Stout, Rex (Todhunter) 1886-1975 . . . **CLC 3**
See also AITN 2; CA 61-64

Stow, (Julian) Randolph 1935-. . **CLC 23, 48**
See also CA 13-16R; CANR 33; MTCW

Stowe, Harriet (Elizabeth) Beecher
1811-1896 . . . . **NCLC 3; DA**
See also CDALB 1865-1917; DLB 1, 12, 42,
74; JRDA; MAICYA; YABC; 1

Strand, Mark 1934-. . . . . . **CLC 6, 18, 41, 71**
See also CA 21-24R; CANR 40; DLB 5;
SATA-Obit 41

Straub, Peter (Francis) 1943- . . . . . . **CLC 28**
See also BEST 89:1; CA 85-88; CANR 28;
DLBY 84; MTCW

Strauss, Botho 1944-. . . . . **CLC 22**
See also DLB 124

Streatfeild, (Mary) Noel
1895(?)-1986 . . . . **CLC 21**
See also CA 81-84; 120; CANR 31;
CLR 17; MAICYA; SATA-Obit 20, 48

Stribling, T(homas) S(igismund)
1881-1965 . . . . **CLC 23**
See also CA 107; DLB 9

Stringer, David
See Roberts, Keith (John Kingston)

Strugatskii, Arkadii (Natanovich)
1925-1991 . . . . **CLC 27**
See also CA 106; 135

Strugatskii, Boris (Natanovich)
1933-. . . . . **CLC 27**
See also CA 106

Strummer, Joe 1953(?)-. . . . . **CLC 30**
See also Clash, The

Stuart, Don A.
See Campbell, John W(ood, Jr.)

Stuart, Ian
See MacLean, Alistair (Stuart)

Stuart, Jesse (Hilton)
1906-1984 . . . . **CLC 1, 8, 11, 14, 34**
See also CA 5-8R; 112; CANR 31; DLB 9,
48, 102; DLBY 84; SATA-Obit 2, 36

Sturgeon, Theodore (Hamilton)
1918-1985 . . . . **CLC 22, 39**
See also Queen, Ellery
See also CA 81-84; 116; CANR 32; DLB 8;
DLBY 85; MTCW

Styron, William
1925-. . . . . **CLC 1, 3, 5, 11, 15, 60**
See also BEST 90:4; CA 5-8R; CANR 6, 33;
CDALB 1968-1988; DLB 2, 143;
DLBY 80; MTCW

Suarez Lynch, B.
See Bioy Casares, Adolfo; Borges, Jorge
Luis

Su Chien 1884-1918
See Su Man-shu
See also CA 123

Sue, Eugene 1804-1857 . . . . **NCLC 1**
See also DLB 119

Sueskind, Patrick 1949-. . . . . **CLC 44**

Sukenick, Ronald 1932-. . . . . **CLC 3, 4, 6, 48**
See also CA 25-28R; CAAS 8; CANR 32;
DLBY 81

Suknaski, Andrew 1942- . . . . **CLC 19**
See also CA 101; DLB 53

Sullivan, Vernon
See Vian, Boris

Summerforest, Ivy B.
See Kirkup, James

Summers, Andrew James 1942-. . . . . **CLC 26**
See also Police, The

Summers, Andy
See Summers, Andrew James

Summers, Hollis (Spurgeon, Jr.)
1916-. . . . . **CLC 10**
See also CA 5-8R; CANR 3; DLB 6

Sumner, Gordon Matthew 1951-. . . . **CLC 26**
See also Police, The

Surtees, Robert Smith
1803-1864 . . . . **NCLC 14**
See also DLB 21

Susann, Jacqueline 1921-1974. . . . . . . **CLC 3**
See also AITN 1; CA 65-68; 53-56; MTCW

Theroux, Paul (Edward)
1941- .... **CLC 5, 8, 11, 15, 28, 46**
See also BEST 89:4; CA 33-36R; CANR 20,
45; DLB 2; MTCW; SATA-Obit 44

Thesen, Sharon 1946- .... **CLC 56**

Thevenin, Denis
See Duhamel, Georges

Thibault, Jacques Anatole Francois
1844-1924
See France, Anatole
See also CA 106; 127; MTCW

Thiele, Colin (Milton) 1920- .... **CLC 17**
See also CA 29-32R; CANR 12, 28;
CLR 27; MAICYA; SATA 2;
SATA-Obit 14, 72

Thomas, Audrey (Callahan)
1935- .... **CLC 7, 13, 37**
See also AITN 2; CA 21-24R; CAAS 19;
CANR 36; DLB 60; MTCW

Thomas, D(onald) M(ichael)
1935- .... **CLC 13, 22, 31**
See also CA 61-64; CAAS 11; CANR 17,
45; CDBLB 1960 to Present; DLB 40;
MTCW

Thomas, Dylan (Marlais)
1914-1953 .. **TCLC 3; DA; WLC 1, 8, 45**
See also CA 104; 120; CDBLB 1945-1960;
DLB 13, 20, 139; MTCW; SAAS 2;
SATA-Obit 60; YABC

Thomas, Joyce Carol 1938- .... **CLC 35**
See also AAYA 12; BW 2; CA 113; 116;
CLR 19; DLB 33; JRDA; MAICYA;
MTCW; SATA 7; SATA-Obit 40, 78

Thomas, Lewis 1913-1993 .... **CLC 35**
See also CA 85-88; 143; CANR 38; MTCW

Thomas, Paul
See Mann, (Paul) Thomas

Thomas, Piri 1928- .... **CLC 17**
See also CA 73-76; HW

Thomas, R(onald) S(tuart)
1913- .... **CLC 6, 13, 48**
See also CA 89-92; CAAS 4; CANR 30;
CDBLB 1960 to Present; DLB 27;
MTCW

Thomas, Ross (Elmore) 1926- ...... **CLC 39**
See also CA 33-36R; CANR 22

Thompson, Francis Clegg
See Mencken, H(enry) L(ouis)

Thompson, Hunter S(tockton)
1939- .... **CLC 9, 17, 40**
See also BEST 89:1; CA 17-20R; CANR 23;
MTCW

Thompson, James Myers
See Thompson, Jim (Myers)

Thompson, Jim (Myers)
1906-1977(?) .... **CLC 69**
See also CA 140

Thompson, Judith .... **CLC 39**

Thomson, James 1700-1748 .... **LC 16**

Thomson, James 1834-1882 ...... **NCLC 18**

Thoreau, Henry David
1817-1862 .... **NCLC 7, 21; DA**
See also CDALB 1640-1865; DLB 1; YABC

Thornton, Hall
See Silverberg, Robert

Thurber, James (Grover)
1894-1961 .... **CLC 5, 11, 25; DA**
See also CA 73-76; CANR 17, 39;
CDALB 1929-1941; DLB 4, 11, 22, 102;
MAICYA; MTCW; SATA-Obit 13;
TCLC 1

Ticheburn, Cheviot
See Ainsworth, William Harrison

Tieck, (Johann) Ludwig
1773-1853 .... **NCLC 5, 46**
See also DLB 90

Tiger, Derry
See Ellison, Harlan

Tilghman, Christopher 1948(?)- ..... **CLC 65**

Tillinghast, Richard (Williford)
1940- .... **CLC 29**
See also CA 29-32R; CANR 26

Timrod, Henry 1828-1867 .... **NCLC 25**
See also DLB 3

Tindall, Gillian 1938- .... **CLC 7**
See also CA 21-24R; CANR 11

Tiptree, James, Jr. .... **CLC 48, 50**
See also Sheldon, Alice Hastings Bradley
See also DLB 8

Titmarsh, Michael Angelo
See Thackeray, William Makepeace

**Tocqueville, Alexis (Charles Henri Maurice
Clerel Comte)** 1805-1859 ..... **NCLC 7**

Tolkien, J(ohn) R(onald) R(euel)
1892-1973 ... **CLC 1, 2, 3, 8, 12, 38; DA**
See also AAYA 10; AITN 1; CA 17-18;
45-48; CANR 36; CAP 2;
CDBLB 1914-1945; DLB 15; JRDA;
MAICYA; MTCW; SATA-Obit 2, 24, 32;
YABC

Tolson, M. B.
See Tolson, Melvin B(eaunorus)

Tolson, Melvin B(eaunorus)
1898(?)-1966 .... **CLC 36; BLC**
See also BW 1; CA 124; 89-92; DLB 48, 76

Tolstoi, Aleksei Nikolaevich
See Tolstoy, Alexey Nikolaevich

Tolstoy, Count Leo
See Tolstoy, Leo (Nikolaevich)

Tolstoy, Leo (Nikolaevich)
1828-1910 .... **TCLC 9; DA; WLC 4, 11,
17, 28, 44**
See also CA 104; 123; SATA-Obit 26;
YABC

Tomasi di Lampedusa, Giuseppe 1896-1957
See Lampedusa, Giuseppe (Tomasi) di
See also CA 111

Tomlin, Lily .... **CLC 17**
See also Tomlin, Mary Jean

Tomlin, Mary Jean 1939(?)-
See Tomlin, Lily
See also CA 117

Tomlinson, (Alfred) Charles
1927- .... **CLC 2, 4, 6, 13, 45**
See also CA 5-8R; CANR 33; DLB 40

Tonson, Jacob
See Bennett, (Enoch) Arnold

Toole, John Kennedy
1937-1969 .... **CLC 19, 64**
See also CA 104; DLBY 81

Toomer, Jean
1894-1967 ...... **CLC 1, 4, 13, 22; BLC**
See also BW 1; CA 85-88;
CDALB 1917-1929; DLB 45, 51; MTCW;
SAAS 7; TCLC 1

Torley, Luke
See Blish, James (Benjamin)

Tornimparte, Alessandra
See Ginzburg, Natalia

Torre, Raoul della
See Mencken, H(enry) L(ouis)

Torrey, E(dwin) Fuller 1937- .... **CLC 34**
See also CA 119

Torsvan, Ben Traven
See Traven, B.

Torsvan, Benno Traven
See Traven, B.

Torsvan, Berick Traven
See Traven, B.

Torsvan, Berwick Traven
See Traven, B.

Torsvan, Bruno Traven
See Traven, B.

Torsvan, Traven
See Traven, B.

Tournier, Michel (Edouard)
1924- .... **CLC 6, 23, 36**
See also CA 49-52; CANR 3, 36; DLB 83;
MTCW; SATA-Obit 23

Tournimparte, Alessandra
See Ginzburg, Natalia

Towers, Ivar
See Kornbluth, C(yril) M.

Townsend, Sue 1946- .... **CLC 61**
See also CA 119; 127; MTCW;
SATA-Obit 48, 55

Townshend, Peter (Dennis Blandford)
1945- .... **CLC 17, 42**
See also CA 107

Traill, Catharine Parr
1802-1899 .... **NCLC 31**
See also DLB 99

Transtroemer, Tomas (Goesta)
1931- .... **CLC 52, 65**
See also CA 117; 129; CAAS 17

Transtromer, Tomas Gosta
See Transtroemer, Tomas (Goesta)

Traven, B. (?)-1969 .... **CLC 8, 11**
See also CA 19-20; 25-28R; CAP 2; DLB 9,
56; MTCW

Treitel, Jonathan 1959- .... **CLC 70**

Tremain, Rose 1943- .... **CLC 42**
See also CA 97-100; CANR 44; DLB 14

Tremblay, Michel 1942- .... **CLC 29**
See also CA 116; 128; DLB 60; MTCW

Trevor, Glen
See Hilton, James

Trevor, William
1928- .... **CLC 7, 9, 14, 25, 71**
See also Cox, William Trevor
See also DLB 14, 139

Trifonov, Yuri (Valentinovich)
1925-1981 .... **CLC 45**
See also CA 126; 103; MTCW

Trilling, Lionel   1905-1975 . . . . **CLC 9, 11, 24**
  See also CA 9-12R; 61-64; CANR 10;
    DLB 28, 63; MTCW

Trimball, W. H.
  See Mencken, H(enry) L(ouis)

Tristan
  See Gomez de la Serna, Ramon

Tristram
  See Housman, A(lfred) E(dward)

Trogdon, William (Lewis)   1939-
  See Heat-Moon, William Least
  See also CA 115; 119

Trollope, Anthony
  1815-1882 . . . . **NCLC 6, 33; DA**
  See also CDBLB 1832-1890; DLB 21, 57;
    SATA-Obit 22; YABC

Trollope, Frances   1779-1863 . . . . . **NCLC 30**
  See also DLB 21

Trotter (Cockburn), Catharine
  1679-1749 . . . . **LC 8**
  See also DLB 84

Trout, Kilgore
  See Farmer, Philip Jose

Trow, George W. S.   1943- . . . . **CLC 52**
  See also CA 126

Troyat, Henri   1911- . . . . **CLC 23**
  See also CA 45-48; CANR 2, 33; MTCW

Trudeau, G(arretson) B(eekman)   1948-
  See Trudeau, Garry B.
  See also CA 81-84; CANR 31;
    SATA-Obit 35

Trudeau, Garry B. . . . . **CLC 12**
  See also Trudeau, G(arretson) B(eekman)
  See also AAYA 10; AITN 2

Truffaut, Francois   1932-1984 . . . . **CLC 20**
  See also CA 81-84; 113; CANR 34

Trumbo, Dalton   1905-1976 . . . . **CLC 19**
  See also CA 21-24R; 69-72; CANR 10;
    DLB 26

Trumbull, John   1750-1831 . . . . **NCLC 30**
  See also DLB 31

Trundlett, Helen B.
  See Eliot, T(homas) S(tearns)

Tryon, Thomas   1926-1991 . . . . **CLC 3, 11**
  See also AITN 1; CA 29-32R; 135;
    CANR 32; MTCW

Tryon, Tom
  See Tryon, Thomas

Ts'ao Hsueh-ch'in   1715(?)-1763 . . . . **LC 1**

Tsushima, Shuji   1909-1948
  See Dazai, Osamu
  See also CA 107

Tuck, Lily   1938- . . . . **CLC 70**
  See also CA 139

Tunis, John R(oberts)   1889-1975 . . . **CLC 12**
  See also CA 61-64; DLB 22; JRDA;
    MAICYA; SATA-Obit 30, 37

Tuohy, Frank . . . . **CLC 37**
  See also Tuohy, John Francis
  See also DLB 14, 139

Tuohy, John Francis   1925-
  See Tuohy, Frank
  See also CA 5-8R; CANR 3

Turco, Lewis (Putnam)   1934- . . . **CLC 11, 63**
  See also CA 13-16R; CANR 24; DLBY 84

Turgenev, Ivan   1818-1883 . . . . . **TCLC 7; DA**
  See also NCLC 21; YABC

Turner, Frederick   1943- . . . . **CLC 48**
  See also CA 73-76; CAAS 10; CANR 12,
    30; DLB 40

Tusan, Stan   1936- . . . . **CLC 22**
  See also CA 105

Tutu, Desmond M(pilo)
  1931- . . . . **CLC 80; BLC**
  See also BW 1; CA 125

Tutuola, Amos   1920- . . . **CLC 5, 14, 29; BLC**
  See also BW 2; CA 9-12R; CANR 27;
    DLB 125; MTCW

Twain, Mark
  . . . . **TCLC 6; WLC 6, 12, 19, 36, 48**
  See also Clemens, Samuel Langhorne
  See also DLB 11, 12, 23, 64, 74; YABC

Tyler, Anne
  1941- . . . . **CLC 7, 11, 18, 28, 44, 59**
  See also BEST 89:1; CA 9-12R; CANR 11,
    33; DLB 6, 143; DLBY 82; MTCW;
    SATA-Obit 7

Tyler, Royall   1757-1826 . . . . **NCLC 3**
  See also DLB 37

Tytell, John   1939- . . . . **CLC 50**
  See also CA 29-32R

Tyutchev, Fyodor   1803-1873 . . . . . **NCLC 34**

Tzara, Tristan . . . . **CLC 47**
  See also Rosenfeld, Samuel

Uhry, Alfred   1936- . . . . **CLC 55**
  See also CA 127; 133

Ulf, Haerved
  See Strindberg, (Johan) August

Ulf, Harved
  See Strindberg, (Johan) August

Ulibarri, Sabine R(eyes)   1919- . . . . . **CLC 83**
  See also CA 131; DLB 82; HW

Unamuno (y Jugo), Miguel de
  1864-1936 . . . **TCLC 11; HLC; WLC 2, 9**
  See also CA 104; 131; DLB 108; HW;
    MTCW

Undercliffe, Errol
  See Campbell, (John) Ramsey

Underwood, Miles
  See Glassco, John

Ungaretti, Giuseppe
  1888-1970 . . . . **CLC 7, 11, 15**
  See also CA 19-20; 25-28R; CAP 2;
    DLB 114

Unger, Douglas   1952- . . . . **CLC 34**
  See also CA 130

Unsworth, Barry (Forster)   1930- . . . . **CLC 76**
  See also CA 25-28R; CANR 30

Updike, John (Hoyer)
  1932- . . . . . . **CLC 1, 2, 3, 5, 7, 9, 13, 15,**
                  23, 34, 43, 70; DA
  See also CA 1-4R; CABS 1; CANR 4, 33;
    CDALB 1968-1988; DLB 2, 5, 143;
    DLBD 3; DLBY 80, 82; MTCW;
    TCLC 13; YABC

Upshaw, Margaret Mitchell
  See Mitchell, Margaret (Munnerlyn)

Upton, Mark
  See Sanders, Lawrence

Urdang, Constance (Henriette)
  1922- . . . . **CLC 47**
  See also CA 21-24R; CANR 9, 24

Uriel, Henry
  See Faust, Frederick (Schiller)

Uris, Leon (Marcus)   1924- . . . . **CLC 7, 32**
  See also AITN 1, 2; BEST 89:2; CA 1-4R;
    CANR 1, 40; MTCW; SATA-Obit 49

Urmuz
  See Codrescu, Andrei

Ustinov, Peter (Alexander)   1921- . . . . . **CLC 1**
  See also AITN 1; CA 13-16R; CANR 25;
    DLB 13

V
  See Chekhov, Anton (Pavlovich)

Vaculik, Ludvik   1926- . . . . **CLC 7**
  See also CA 53-56

Valdez, Luis (Miguel)
  1940- . . . . **CLC 84; HLC**
  See also CA 101; CANR 32; DLB 122; HW

Valenzuela, Luisa   1938- . . . . **CLC 31**
  See also CA 101; CANR 32; DLB 113;
    HW; TCLC 14

Vallejo, Antonio Buero
  See Buero Vallejo, Antonio

Valle Y Pena, Ramon del
  See Valle-Inclan, Ramon (Maria) del

Van Ash, Cay   1918- . . . . **CLC 34**

Vanbrugh, Sir John   1664-1726 . . . . . . **LC 21**
  See also DLB 80

Van Campen, Karl
  See Campbell, John W(ood, Jr.)

Vance, Gerald
  See Silverberg, Robert

Vance, Jack . . . . **CLC 35**
  See also Vance, John Holbrook
  See also DLB 8

Vance, John Holbrook   1916-
  See Queen, Ellery; Vance, Jack
  See also CA 29-32R; CANR 17; MTCW

Van Den Bogarde, Derek Jules Gaspard Ulric
  Niven   1921-
  See Bogarde, Dirk
  See also CA 77-80

Vandenburgh, Jane . . . . **CLC 59**

Vanderhaeghe, Guy   1951- . . . . **CLC 41**
  See also CA 113

van der Post, Laurens (Jan)   1906- . . . **CLC 5**
  See also CA 5-8R; CANR 35

van de Wetering, Janwillem   1931- . . **CLC 47**
  See also CA 49-52; CANR 4

Van Doren, Mark   1894-1972 . . . . . **CLC 6, 10**
  See also CA 1-4R; 37-40R; CANR 3;
    DLB 45; MTCW

Van Duyn, Mona (Jane)
  1921- . . . . **CLC 3, 7, 63**
  See also CA 9-12R; CANR 7, 38; DLB 5

Van Dyne, Edith
  See Baum, L(yman) Frank

van Itallie, Jean-Claude   1936- . . . . **CLC 3**
  See also CA 45-48; CAAS 2; CANR 1;
    DLB 7

Wells, Rosemary 1943-. . . . . **CLC 12**
See also CA 85-88; CLR 16; MAICYA;
SATA 1; SATA-Obit 18, 69

Welty, Eudora
1909- . . . . . . **CLC 1, 2, 5, 14, 22, 33; DA**
See also CA 9-12R; CABS 1; CANR 32;
CDALB 1941-1968; DLB 2, 102, 143;
DLBY 87; MTCW; TCLC 1; YABC

Wentworth, Robert
See Hamilton, Edmond

Wergeland, Henrik Arnold
1808-1845 . . . . **NCLC 5**

Wersba, Barbara 1932-. . . . . **CLC 30**
See also AAYA 2; CA 29-32R; CANR 16,
38; CLR 3; DLB 52; JRDA; MAICYA;
SATA 2; SATA-Obit 1, 58

Wertmueller, Lina 1928- . . . . **CLC 16**
See also CA 97-100; CANR 39

Wescott, Glenway 1901-1987. . . . . . . **CLC 13**
See also CA 13-16R; 121; CANR 23;
DLB 4, 9, 102

Wesker, Arnold 1932- . . . . **CLC 3, 5, 42**
See also CA 1-4R; CAAS 7; CANR 1, 33;
CDBLB 1960 to Present; DLB 13;
MTCW

Wesley, Richard (Errol) 1945-. . . . . . . **CLC 7**
See also BW 1; CA 57-60; CANR 27;
DLB 38

Wessel, Johan Herman 1742-1785 . . . . **LC 7**

West, Anthony (Panther)
1914-1987 . . . . **CLC 50**
See also CA 45-48; 124; CANR 3, 19;
DLB 15

West, C. P.
See Wodehouse, P(elham) G(renville)

West, (Mary) Jessamyn
1902-1984 . . . . **CLC 7, 17**
See also CA 9-12R; 112; CANR 27; DLB 6;
DLBY 84; MTCW; SATA-Obit 37

West, Morris L(anglo) 1916-. . . . . **CLC 6, 33**
See also CA 5-8R; CANR 24; MTCW

West, Nathanael
1903-1940 . . . . **TCLC 16; WLC 1, 14, 44**
See also CA 104; 125; CDALB 1929-1941;
DLB 4, 9, 28; MTCW

West, Owen
See Koontz, Dean R(ay)

West, Paul 1930- . . . . **CLC 7, 14**
See also CA 13-16R; CAAS 7; CANR 22;
DLB 14

West, Rebecca 1892-1983 . . **CLC 7, 9, 31, 50**
See also CA 5-8R; 109; CANR 19; DLB 36;
DLBY 83; MTCW

Westall, Robert (Atkinson)
1929-1993 . . . . **CLC 17**
See also AAYA 12; CA 69-72; 141;
CANR 18; CLR 13; JRDA; MAICYA;
SATA 2; SATA-Obit 23, 69; SC 75

Westlake, Donald E(dwin)
1933- . . . . **CLC 7, 33**
See also CA 17-20R; CAAS 13; CANR 16,
44

Westmacott, Mary
See Christie, Agatha (Mary Clarissa)

Weston, Allen
See Norton, Andre

Wetcheek, J. L.
See Feuchtwanger, Lion

Wetering, Janwillem van de
See van de Wetering, Janwillem

Wetherell, Elizabeth
See Warner, Susan (Bogert)

Whalen, Philip 1923-. . . . . **CLC 6, 29**
See also CA 9-12R; CANR 5, 39; DLB 16

Wharton, Edith (Newbold Jones)
1862-1937 . . . . . **TCLC 6; DA; WLC 3, 9,
27, 53**
See also CA 104; 132; CDALB 1865-1917;
DLB 4, 9, 12, 78; MTCW; YABC

Wharton, James
See Mencken, H(enry) L(ouis)

Wharton, William (a pseudonym)
. . . . **CLC 18, 37**
See also CA 93-96; DLBY 80

Wheatley (Peters), Phillis
1754(?)-1784 . . . . **LC 3; BLC; DA**
See also CDALB 1640-1865; DLB 31, 50;
SAAS 3; YABC

Wheelock, John Hall 1886-1978. . . . **CLC 14**
See also CA 13-16R; 77-80; CANR 14;
DLB 45

White, E(lwyn) B(rooks)
1899-1985 . . . . **CLC 10, 34, 39**
See also AITN 2; CA 13-16R; 116;
CANR 16, 37; CLR 1, 21; DLB 11, 22;
MAICYA; MTCW; SATA-Obit 2, 29, 44

White, Edmund (Valentine III)
1940- . . . . **CLC 27**
See also AAYA 7; CA 45-48; CANR 3, 19,
36; MTCW

White, Patrick (Victor Martindale)
1912-1990 . . **CLC 3, 4, 5, 7, 9, 18, 65, 69**
See also CA 81-84; 132; CANR 43; MTCW

White, Phyllis Dorothy James 1920-
See James, P. D.
See also CA 21-24R; CANR 17, 43; MTCW

White, T(erence) H(anbury)
1906-1964 . . . . **CLC 30**
See also CA 73-76; CANR 37; JRDA;
MAICYA; SATA-Obit 12

White, Terence de Vere 1912-. . . . . . **CLC 49**
See also CA 49-52; CANR 3

White, William Hale 1831-1913
See Rutherford, Mark
See also CA 121

Whitehead, E(dward) A(nthony)
1933- . . . . **CLC 5**
See also CA 65-68

Whiteman, Roberta Hill 1947- . . . . **PC X**

Whitemore, Hugh (John) 1936-. . . . . **CLC 37**
See also CA 132

Whitman, Sarah Helen (Power)
1803-1878 . . . . **NCLC 19**
See also DLB 1

Whitman, Walt(er)
1819-1892 . . . . **NCLC 4, 31; DA**
See also CDALB 1640-1865; DLB 3, 64;
SAAS 3; SATA-Obit 20; YABC

Whitney, Phyllis A(yame) 1903-. . . . **CLC 42**
See also AITN 2; BEST 90:3; CA 1-4R;
CANR 3, 25, 38; JRDA; MAICYA;
SATA-Obit 1, 30

Whittemore, (Edward) Reed (Jr.)
1919- . . . . **CLC 4**
See also CA 9-12R; CAAS 8; CANR 4;
DLB 5

Whittier, John Greenleaf
1807-1892 . . . . **NCLC 8**
See also CDALB 1640-1865; DLB 1

Whittlebot, Hernia
See Coward, Noel (Peirce)

Wicker, Thomas Grey 1926-
See Wicker, Tom
See also CA 65-68; CANR 21

Wicker, Tom . . . . **CLC 7**
See also Wicker, Thomas Grey

Wideman, John Edgar
1941- . . . . **CLC 5, 34, 36, 67; BLC**
See also BW 2; CA 85-88; CANR 14, 42;
DLB 33, 143

Wiebe, Rudy (Henry) 1934-. . . **CLC 6, 11, 14**
See also CA 37-40R; CANR 42; DLB 60

Wieland, Christoph Martin
1733-1813 . . . . **NCLC 17**
See also DLB 97

Wieners, John 1934-. . . . . **CLC 7**
See also CA 13-16R; DLB 16

Wiesel, Elie(zer)
1928- . . . . **CLC 3, 5, 11, 37; DA**
See also AAYA 7; AITN 1; CA 5-8R;
CAAS 4; CANR 8, 40; DLB 83;
DLBY 87; MTCW; SATA-Obit 56

Wiggins, Marianne 1947-. . . . . **CLC 57**
See also BEST 89:3; CA 130

Wight, James Alfred 1916-
See Herriot, James
See also CA 77-80; SATA-Obit 44, 55

Wilbur, Richard (Purdy)
1921- . . . . **CLC 3, 6, 9, 14, 53; DA**
See also CA 1-4R; CABS 2; CANR 2, 29;
DLB 5; MTCW; SATA-Obit 9

Wild, Peter 1940-. . . . . **CLC 14**
See also CA 37-40R; DLB 5

Wilde, Oscar (Fingal O'Flahertie Wills)
1854(?)-1900 . . . . **TCLC 11; DA; WLC 1,
8, 23, 41**
See also CA 104; 119; CDBLB 1890-1914;
DLB 10, 19, 34, 57, 141; SATA-Obit 24;
YABC

Wilder, Billy . . . . **CLC 20**
See also Wilder, Samuel
See also DLB 26

Wilder, Samuel 1906-
See Wilder, Billy
See also CA 89-92

Wilder, Thornton (Niven)
1897-1975 . . . . . . **CLC 1, 5, 6, 10, 15, 35,
82; DA; DC 1**
See also AITN 2; CA 13-16R; 61-64;
CANR 40; DLB 4, 7, 9; MTCW; YABC

Wilding, Michael 1942-. . . . . **CLC 73**
See also CA 104; CANR 24

Wiley, Richard 1944-. . . . . **CLC 44**
See also CA 121; 129

Woolf, (Adeline) Virginia
1882-1941 . . . . . **TCLC 7; DA; WLC 1, 5, 20, 43, 56**
See also CA 104; 130; CDBLB 1914-1945; DLB 36, 100; DLBD 10; MTCW; YABC

Woolrich, Cornell 1903-1968 . . . . . . **CLC 77**
See also Hopley-Woolrich, Cornell George

Wordsworth, Dorothy
1771-1855 . . . . **NCLC 25**
See also DLB 107

Wordsworth, William
1770-1850 . . . . **NCLC 12, 38; DA**
See also CDBLB 1789-1832; DLB 93, 107; SAAS 4; YABC

Wouk, Herman 1915- . . . . **CLC 1, 9, 38**
See also CA 5-8R; CANR 6, 33; DLBY 82; MTCW

Wright, Charles (Penzel, Jr.)
1935- . . . . **CLC 6, 13, 28**
See also CA 29-32R; CAAS 7; CANR 23, 36; DLBY 82; MTCW

Wright, Charles Stevenson
1932- . . . . **CLC 49; BLC 3**
See also BW 1; CA 9-12R; CANR 26; DLB 33

Wright, Jack R.
See Harris, Mark

Wright, James (Arlington)
1927-1980 . . . . **CLC 3, 5, 10, 28**
See also AITN 2; CA 49-52; 97-100; CANR 4, 34; DLB 5; MTCW

Wright, Judith (Arandell)
1915- . . . . **CLC 11, 53**
See also CA 13-16R; CANR 31; MTCW; SATA-Obit 14

Wright, L(aurali) R. 1939- . . . . **CLC 44**
See also CA 138

Wright, Richard (Nathaniel)
1908-1960 . . . . **CLC 1, 3, 4, 9, 14, 21, 48, 74; BLC; DA**
See also AAYA 5; BW 1; CA 108; CDALB 1929-1941; DLB 76, 102; DLBD 2; MTCW; TCLC 2; YABC

Wright, Richard B(ruce) 1937- . . . . . . **CLC 6**
See also CA 85-88; DLB 53

Wright, Rick 1945- . . . . **CLC 35**
See also Pink Floyd

Wright, Rowland
See Wells, Carolyn

Wright, Stephen Caldwell 1946- . . . . **CLC 33**
See also BW 2

Wright, Willard Huntington 1888-1939
See Van Dine, S. S.
See also CA 115

Wright, William 1930- . . . . **CLC 44**
See also CA 53-56; CANR 7, 23

Wu Ch'eng-en 1500(?)-1582(?) . . . . **LC 7**

Wu Ching-tzu 1701-1754 . . . . **LC 2**

Wurlitzer, Rudolph 1938(?)- . . . **CLC 2, 4, 15**
See also CA 85-88

Wycherley, William 1641-1715 . . . . **LC 8, 21**
See also CDBLB 1660-1789; DLB 80

Wylie, Philip (Gordon) 1902-1971 . . . **CLC 43**
See also CA 21-22; 33-36R; CAP 2; DLB 9

Wyndham, John
See Harris, John (Wyndham Parkes Lucas) Beynon

Wyss, Johann David Von
1743-1818 . . . . **NCLC 10**
See also JRDA; MAICYA; SATA-Obit 27, 29

Yakumo Koizumi
See Hearn, (Patricio) Lafcadio (Tessima Carlos)

Yanez, Jose Donoso
See Donoso (Yanez), Jose

Yanovsky, Basile S.
See Yanovsky, V(assily) S(emenovich)

Yanovsky, V(assily) S(emenovich)
1906-1989 . . . . **CLC 2, 18**
See also CA 97-100; 129

Yates, Richard 1926-1992 . . . . . **CLC 7, 8, 23**
See also CA 5-8R; 139; CANR 10, 43; DLB 2; DLBY 81, 92

Yeats, W. B.
See Yeats, William Butler

Yehoshua, A(braham) B.
1936- . . . . **CLC 13, 31**
See also CA 33-36R; CANR 43

Yep, Laurence Michael 1948- . . . . . . **CLC 35**
See also AAYA 5; CA 49-52; CANR 1; CLR 3, 17; DLB 52; JRDA; MAICYA; SATA-Obit 7, 69

Yerby, Frank G(arvin)
1916-1991 . . . . **CLC 1, 7, 22; BLC**
See also BW 1; CA 9-12R; 136; CANR 16; DLB 76; MTCW

Yesenin, Sergei Alexandrovich
See Esenin, Sergei (Alexandrovich)

Yevtushenko, Yevgeny (Alexandrovich)
1933- . . . . **CLC 1, 3, 13, 26, 51**
See also CA 81-84; CANR 33; MTCW

Yezierska, Anzia 1885(?)-1970 . . . . . **CLC 46**
See also CA 126; 89-92; DLB 28; MTCW

Yglesias, Helen 1915- . . . . **CLC 7, 22**
See also CA 37-40R; CANR 15; MTCW

York, Jeremy
See Creasey, John

York, Simon
See Heinlein, Robert A(nson)

Yorke, Henry Vincent 1905-1974 . . . **CLC 13**
See also Green, Henry
See also CA 85-88; 49-52

Yoshimoto, Banana . . . . **CLC 84**
See also Yoshimoto, Mahoko

Yoshimoto, Mahoko 1964-
See Yoshimoto, Banana
See also CA 144

Young, Al(bert James)
1939- . . . . **CLC 19; BLC**
See also BW 2; CA 29-32R; CANR 26; DLB 33

Young, Andrew (John) 1885-1971 . . . . **CLC 5**
See also CA 5-8R; CANR 7, 29

Young, Collier
See Bloch, Robert (Albert)

Young, Edward 1683-1765 . . . . **LC 3**
See also DLB 95

Young, Marguerite 1909- . . . . **CLC 82**
See also CA 13-16; CAP 1

Young, Neil 1945- . . . . **CLC 17**
See also CA 110

Young Bear, Ray A. (?)- . . . . **PC X**

Yourcenar, Marguerite
1903-1987 . . . . **CLC 19, 38, 50**
See also CA 69-72; CANR 23; DLB 72; DLBY 88; MTCW

Yurick, Sol 1925- . . . . **CLC 6**
See also CA 13-16R; CANR 25

Zamiatin, Yevgenii
See Zamyatin, Evgeny Ivanovich

Zappa, Francis Vincent, Jr. 1940-1993
See Zappa, Frank
See also CA 108; 143

Zappa, Frank . . . . **CLC 17**
See also Zappa, Francis Vincent, Jr.

Zaturenska, Marya 1902-1982 . . . . **CLC 6, 11**
See also CA 13-16R; 105; CANR 22

Zelazny, Roger (Joseph) 1937- . . . . . **CLC 21**
See also AAYA 7; CA 21-24R; CANR 26; DLB 8; MTCW; SATA-Obit 39, 57

Zhukovsky, Vasily 1783-1852 . . . . **NCLC 35**

Ziegenhagen, Eric . . . . **CLC 55**

Zimmer, Jill Schary
See Robinson, Jill

Zimmerman, Robert
See Dylan, Bob

Zindel, Paul 1936- . . . . **CLC 6, 26; DA**
See also AAYA 2; CA 73-76; CANR 31; CLR 3; DLB 7, 52; JRDA; MAICYA; MTCW; SATA-Obit 16, 58

Zinov'Ev, A. A.
See Zinoviev, Alexander (Aleksandrovich)

Zinoviev, Alexander (Aleksandrovich)
1922- . . . . **CLC 19**
See also CA 116; 133; CAAS 10

Zoilus
See Lovecraft, H(oward) P(hillips)

Zoline, Pamela 1941- . . . . **CLC 62**

Zorrilla y Moral, Jose 1817-1893 . . **NCLC 6**

Zoshchenko, Mikhail (Mikhailovich)
1895-1958 . . . . **TCLC 15; WLC 15**
See also CA 115

Zuckmayer, Carl 1896-1977 . . . . **CLC 18**
See also CA 69-72; DLB 56, 124

Zuk, Georges
See Skelton, Robin

Zukofsky, Louis
1904-1978 . . . . **CLC 1, 2, 4, 7, 11, 18**
See also CA 9-12R; 77-80; CANR 39; DLB 5; MTCW

Zweig, Paul 1935-1984 . . . . **CLC 34, 42**
See also CA 85-88; 113

Literary Criticism Series
Cumulative Topic Index

This index lists all topic entries in the Gale Literary Criticism Series *Classical and Medieval Literature Criticism, Contemporary Literary Criticism, Literature Criticism from 1400 to 1800, Nineteenth-Century Literature Criticism,* and *Twentieth-Century Literary Criticism.*

Topic Index

Irish fiction, 256-86

Irish Nationalism and Literature NCLC 44: 203-273
the Celtic element in literature, 203-19
anti-Irish sentiment and the Celtic response, 219-34
literary ideals in Ireland, 234-45
literary expressions, 245-73

Italian Futurism
See **Futurism, Italian**

Italian Humanism LC 12: 205-77
origins and early development, 206-18
revival of classical letters, 218-23
humanism and other philosophies, 224-39
humanisms and humanists, 239-46
the plastic arts, 246-57
achievement and significance, 258-76

Larkin, Philip, Controversy CLC 81: 417-64

Madness in Twentieth-Century Literature TCLC-50: 160-225
overviews, 161-71
madness and the creative process, 171-86
suicide, 186-91
madness in American literature, 191-207
madness in German literature, 207-13
madness and feminist artists, 213-24

Metaphysical Poets LC 24: 356-439
early definitions, 358-67
surveys and overviews, 367-92
cultural and social influences, 392-406
stylistic and thematic variations, 407-38

Muckraking Movement in American Journalism TCLC 34: 161-242
development, principles, and major figures, 162-70
publications, 170-79
social and political ideas, 179-86
targets, 186-208
fiction, 208-19

decline, 219-29
impact and accomplishments, 229-40

Multiculturalism in Literature and Education CLC 70: 361-413

Native American Literature CLC 76: 440-76

Natural School, Russian NCLC 24: 205-40
history and characteristics, 205-25
contemporary criticism, 225-40

Naturalism NCLC 36: 285-382
definitions and theories, 286-305
critical debates on Naturalism, 305-16
Naturalism in theater, 316-32
European Naturalism, 332-61
American Naturalism, 361-72
the legacy of Naturalism, 372-81

Negritude TCLC 50: 226-361
origins and evolution, 227-56
definitions, 256-91
Negritude in literature, 291-343
Negritude reconsidered, 343-58

New Criticism TCLC 34: 243-318
development and ideas, 244-70
debate and defense, 270-99
influence and legacy, 299-315

New York Intellectuals and *Partisan Review* TCLC 30: 117-98
development and major figures, 118-28
influence of Judaism, 128-39
Partisan Review, 139-57
literary philosophy and practice, 157-75
political philosophy, 175-87
achievement and significance, 187-97

Newgate Novel NCLC 24: 166-204
development of Newgate literature, 166-73
Newgate Calendar, 173-77
Newgate fiction, 177-95
Newgate drama, 195-204

Nigerian Literature of the Twentieth Century TCLC 30: 199-265
surveys of, 199-227
English language and African life, 227-45
politics and the Nigerian writer, 245-54

Nigerian writers and society, 255-62

Northern Humanism LC 16: 281-356
background, 282-305
precursor of the Reformation, 305-14
the Brethren of the Common Life, the Devotio Moderna, and education, 314-40
the impact of printing, 340-56

Nuclear Literature: Writings and Criticism in the Nuclear Age TCLC 46: 288-390
overviews, 290-301
fiction, 301-35
poetry, 335-38
nuclear war in Russo-Japanese literature, 338-55
nuclear war and women writers, 355-67
the nuclear referent and literary criticism, 367-88

Occultism in Modern Literature TCLC 50: 362-406
influence of occultism on modern literature, 363-72
occultism, literature, and society, 372-87
fiction, 387-96
drama, 396-405

Opium and the Nineteenth-Century Literary Imagination NCLC 20: 250-301
original sources, 250-62
historical background, 262-71
and literary society, 271-79
and literary creativity, 279-300

Periodicals, Nineteenth-Century British NCLC 24: 100-65
overviews, 100-30
in the Romantic Age, 130-41
in the Victorian era, 142-54
and the reviewer, 154-64

Pre-Raphaelite Movement NCLC 20: 302-401
overview, 302-04
genesis, 304-12
Germ and *Oxford and Cambridge Magazine,* 312-20
Robert Buchanan and the "Fleshly School of Poetry," 320-31
satires and parodies, 331-34
surveys, 334-51
aesthetics, 351-75
sister arts of poetry and painting, 375-

Topic Index

TCLC Cumulative Nationality Index

WELSH

Nationality Index